Aslib Directory

VOLUME TWO

Aslib Directory
Volume 2

*Information Sources in
Medicine, the Social Sciences and
the Humanities*

Edited by
BRIAN J. WILSON
M.A., M.I.Inf.Sc.

Aslib

LONDON

1970

1970 © Aslib and Brian J. Wilson

First edition 1928
Second edition 1957
Third edition 1970

SBN 85142 022 2

Published by Aslib
3 Belgrave Square, London S.W.1.

Distributed in Canada, the U.S.A. and
the Philippines by
Chicorel Library Publishing Co.,
330 West 58th Street, New York,
N.Y. 10019

Set in Bembo
Printed by Butler & Tanner Ltd, Frome and London

CONTENTS

INFORMATION SOURCES IN MEDICINE, THE SOCIAL SCIENCES AND THE HUMANITIES   1

NATIONAL, REGIONAL AND LOCAL SCHEMES OF LIBRARY CO-OPERATION   645

NAME INDEX   670

SUBJECT INDEX   707

INTRODUCTION

THE last edition of the *Aslib Directory*, published in 1957, covered all disciplines and concentrated mainly on fairly well-developed library and information services. In the two volumes of the present edition the emphasis is very much more on organizations as sources of information and some explanation of how these have been selected may be helpful.

The specification for the subject coverage of volume one of the new edition was 'sources of information in science, technology and commerce' and this was interpreted broadly to include information on the fringes of these subjects which might be of value to users in commerce and industry. Thus, sources of information on trade unionism were included, although this subject might more properly perhaps appear in a volume devoted to social sciences. This second volume of the *Aslib Directory* includes sources of information on medicine, the social sciences and the humanities, including law, history, geography, theology, sport and the arts generally. The fact that a source of information appeared in the first volume does not mean that it is not included in this volume also, and there is some deliberate duplication in overlapping areas (for example, industrial medicine and pharmacy and, indeed, trade unionism).

The arrangement of the individual entries remains geographical. To avoid confusion, however, they have been arranged in strict alphabetical order of postal towns (that is those towns listed in capital letters in the April 1968 edition of *Post Offices in the United Kingdom*). This has meant that a few towns, for example those with the postal address WIRRAL, appear rather oddly placed. However, cross references have been used fairly lavishly. Within each postal town the entries are arranged alphabetically by the first word of the title, ignoring 'The'. Telephone numbers have been quoted in either the old or the new (STD) form, depending on which was in use when the entries were checked in November 1969.

The layout of each entry is self-evident. The details given are intended to emphasize the importance of the particular organization as a source of information. The stock of libraries is therefore given only approximately, and administrative details, such as opening times of libraries and the type of classification used, have been omitted. It should be noted, however, that inclusion in the *Aslib Directory* does not necessarily mean that an information service will be provided to all and sundry and that, if information is provided, it will not have to be paid for. A list of publications has been added to many entries, as it is felt that this helps to give some indication of the 'authority' of the organization concerned in its subject fields. In fact, although quite a lot of editing has been done to ensure general consistency, much of the original wording from the questionnaires has been used in a deliberate attempt to give to each entry a 'flavour' of the organization which it represents. Even so, very little actual evaluation of the sources can be carried out by the editor when the material has been collected by questionnaire, since he lacks the detailed knowledge of each organization which would be needed for this. As Miriam Alman said in the introduction to the first edition, 'The librarian of a small library will rightly report a special collection which might pass unnoticed on the shelves of a large one.'

The name index (pages 670 to 706) includes not only the names of the organizations in the book, these forming the 'first lines' of each entry, but also the names of any organizations mentioned in the texts of the entries themselves and those of any named special collections of library or other material noted. The numbers in both this and the subject index refer to entries and *not* to pages.

The alphabetical subject index (pages 707 to 849) is extensive, but makes no pretence to being a subject classification scheme on any logical basis. For the convenience of users, entries have been repeated in many cases where this is not strictly necessary; for example, the entries under *History, Africa* are included also under *Africa, history*. Explanatory notes are given under some of the main headings. In general both the primary and secondary interests of organizations have been entered, although the latter have been ignored in certain cases where there are much better collections close by geographically. Subjects right outside the scope of this volume which occur in entries (for example, chemistry, engineering) have also been ignored in indexing unless the organization concerned did not have an entry in volume one. It must be remembered that some large general libraries may contain collections on certain specialized subjects which do not appear in their entries in detail, and may not, therefore, have been indexed. Indeed, it may well be that one of these large libraries may contain a more comprehensive collection on a particular subject than a small library devoted entirely to that subject! As in all books of reference, commonsense must be used when consulting it.

Finally, it should be remembered by the user of this Directory, that many public libraries which are not included here do contain quite considerable general collections although these are not large enough or specialized enough to warrant inclusion. However, these libraries usually have access to local or national co-operative schemes, and in this sense any public library can be considered, and used, as a source of information in these fields.

Many completed and returned questionnaires have not had their contents included in this Directory, either because their subject-matter appeared not to be relevant to this volume or because the organization concerned was willing to provide nothing in the way of an information or loans service, or because all the answers on the form were negative.

The chapter on National, Regional and Local Schemes of Library Co-operation in this volume is based on that prepared for volume one by Mr H. A. Chesshyre which has been revised and extended. I would like to express my thanks to all those busy people who took the trouble to fill in yet another questionnaire; and particularly to Mr A. E. Woodbridge and Mrs E. C. M. Bradford, successively my editorial assistants, and to my own family.

BRIAN J. WILSON
November 1969

INFORMATION SOURCES IN MEDICINE, THE SOCIAL SCIENCES AND THE HUMANITIES

ABERAERON
Cardiganshire

1

CARDIGANSHIRE ANTIQUARIAN SOCIETY   *Tel.:* Aberaeron 331
26 Alban Square
Aberaeron
Cardiganshire

Aims to bring together persons interested in the study of the history, antiquities and folk-lore of Cardiganshire; to encourage public interest in local history; and to encourage the preservation of local records, antiquities and objects of historical interest

Enquiries: To Secretary, by letter only

Scope: Information supplied on the history of Cardiganshire
No library

Publications: Ceredigion (Society's annual journal)
Reading lists

ABERDARE
Glam

2

ABERDARE CENTRAL PUBLIC LIBRARY   *Tel.:* Aberdare 2441 ext. 45
Greenfach
Aberdare
Glamorgan

Enquiries: To Librarian

Scope: Subject specialization: Transport, theatre, photography

Stock: 300 books; 200 pamphlets; 2 current periodicals

ABERDEEN

3

ABERDEEN COLLEGE OF EDUCATION   *Tel.:* Aberdeen 42341
Hilton Place
Aberdeen AB9 1FA

Enquiries: To Librarian

Scope: The subject coverage reflects the subjects taught in the College and in schools: the humanities (including philosophy and religion), the social sciences (particularly psychology and education) and the natural sciences. The level reflects the teaching commitment of the College and, at the top end, is determined by the need to provide courses leading to the degree of B.Ed. In a number of subjects this means up to second-year university level

Stock: 21,000 books; 1,000 pamphlets; 150 current periodicals

ABERDEEN

4

ABERDEEN COUNTY LIBRARY   *Tel.:* Aberdeen 23444
14 Crown Terrace
Aberdeen AB9 2BH

Enquiries: To Librarian

Scope: *Education Section:* 2,500 books on all aspects of education, provided for teachers and students
Visual Aids Library: 2,300 films, filmstrips, film loops, art slides, for use by schools and organizations in the county
Local History Collection: 2,000 volumes about Aberdeenshire
George MacDonald Collection: 200 volumes of the works of G. MacDonald and critical material

Stock: 210,000 volumes (total stock)

ABERDEEN	ABERDEEN PUBLIC LIBRARY Rosemount Viaduct	*Tel.:* Aberdeen 28991
5	Aberdeen	

Enquiries: To Librarian

Scope: Includes a special collection of statistical information on economics, in addition to a general collection covering the social sciences and the humanities. Local history library

Stock: 316,800 books; 23,600 pamphlets; 100 current periodicals (total stock)

ABERDEEN	FORESTERHILL COLLEGE Westburn Road	*Tel.:* Aberdeen 23423 ext. 2544
6	Aberdeen AB9 2XS	
	Nurse Training College	

Enquiries: To Librarian

Scope: Nursing

Secondary: Biology, surgical and medical texts, nutrition, bacteriology, environmental health, hospital administration and management, psychiatry, welfare services, psychology and sociology

Stock: 4,000 books; 100 pamphlets; 50 reports; 46 current periodicals. Stock available on loan locally only

ABERDEEN	THE GORDON HIGHLANDERS Regimental Headquarters	*Tel.:* Aberdeen 38174
7	Viewfield Road	
	Aberdeen AB1 7XH	
	Regimental Headquarters and Museum	

Enquiries: To Curator

Scope: Regimental history. Medal collection

Stock: 200 books; 50 pamphlets. Stock not available on loan

Publications: Regimental Magazine
Regimental History: Life of a Regiment (5 volumes)
Recruiting Literature

ABERDEEN	GREAT NORTH OF SCOTLAND RAILWAY ASSOCIATION	*Tel.:* Aberdeen 42298
8	Auchlochan	
	14 Gordon Road	
	Bridge of Don	
	Aberdeen AB2 8PT	

Enquiries: To Secretary

Scope: All aspects of the Great North of Scotland Railway and its constituents up to the present day. Selection of working timetables, photographs, financial reports, diagrams and other documents

No library

Publications: Great North Review (quarterly journal)
Abstracts on particular topics, for example Tablet Exchanger, Station locations
Time Table Reprints: 1860, 1863, 1922

ABERDEEN 9	ROBERT GORDON'S INSTITUTE OF TECHNOLOGY Schoolhill Aberdeen AB9 1FR	*Tel.:* Aberdeen 29384

Enquiries: To Librarian

Scope: Electronics, electrical and mechanical engineering, chemistry, physics, mathematics; pharmacy, business management, paper technology, domestic science, dietetics, architecture, building, art and librarianship

Stock: 35,000 books; 1,000 pamphlets; 800 current periodicals

Departmental libraries include: Aberdeen School of Domestic Science, Queens Road, Aberdeen; Gray's School of Art, Garthdee, Aberdeen; Scott Sutherland School of Architecture, Garthdee, Aberdeen

Specific enquiries on these subjects should be sent direct to the Librarians at these addresses

Robert Gordon's Institute of Technology Library is to be the Headquarters of the Aberdeen and North of Scotland Inter-library Scheme and Service to Industry (ANSLICS)—proposed date of operation Autumn 1970. *See also* no. 2355

ABERDEEN 10	SCOTTISH CANOE ASSOCIATION 2 Kildrumm Road Aberdeen

Enquiries: To Secretary

Scope: All aspects of canoeing in Scotland

No library

Publications: Various pamphlets on, for example, tides, knots, which refer to canoeing teaching certificates

Safety Recommendations

List of Clubs

ABERDEEN 11	SOCIETY FOR AFRICAN CHURCH HISTORY Department of Church History University of Aberdeen King's College Aberdeen AB9 2UB	*Tel.:* Aberdeen 40241 ext. OA 295

Aims to promote the study of Christian history in Africa; to encourage awareness of Christian origins and development in Africa within the Church; to facilitate fellowship, mutual assistance and exchange of information between those engaged in the study of African Christian history; and to encourage discovery, preservation and use of the relevant materials

Enquiries: To Editor, by letter only

Scope: Christian history in Africa; published and unpublished materials for its study; work in progress in this field

No library, but able to draw upon the resources of institutions in Europe and Africa for its information service

Publications: The Bulletin of the Society for African Church History (annually)

Bibliography of the Society for African Church History (part 1, Leiden, 1967; part 2 in preparation)

ABERDEEN 12	UNIVERSITY OF ABERDEEN CENTRE FOR SOCIAL STUDIES Westburn Road Aberdeen AB9 2ZE	*Tel.:* 0224 23423 ext. 2420

ABERDEEN, UNIVERSITY OF ABERDEEN, CENTRE FOR SOCIAL STUDIES, *cont.*
Teaching and research in medical sociology and social work
Enquiries: To Director, by letter only
Scope: Medical sociology, including child development
Stock: 1,000 books; 500 pamphlets; 30 current periodicals
Publications: Research papers in professional journals

ABERDEEN

13

UNIVERSITY OF ABERDEEN LIBRARY *Tel.:* Aberdeen 40241
King's College
Aberdeen

Enquiries: To Librarian
Scope: All subjects covered by the Faculties of Arts, Science, Medicine, Law and Divinity with special emphasis on the history, topography and antiquities of the North-East of Scotland in particular and of the Scottish Highlands in general and on the fields covered by the following special collections:
Primary: Macbean (Jacobites)
Taylor (Psalmody)
Gregory (History of science and medicine)
O'Dell (Railways)
Secondary: Celtic literature. English literature of the British Commonwealth
Stock: 500,000 books; 30,000 pamphlets; 5,000 current periodicals
Publications: Aberdeen University Studies
Aberdeen University Review

ABERDEEN

14

UNIVERSITY OF ABERDEEN *Tel.:* Aberdeen 40241
SCOTTISH INSTITUTE OF MISSIONARY STUDIES ext. OA 295
Department of Church History
King's College
Aberdeen AB9 2UB

Aims to encourage and provide means for the study of Christian missions; to locate and encourage preservation of the materials for such study, particularly in Scotland; and to facilitate co-operation among institutions and individuals interested in such study
Enquiries: To Secretary
Scope: Christian missions, Christianity in Africa, Asia and Central and South America; collection of literature, including periodical and fugitive literature, on these subjects; missionary archives and unpublished papers particularly in Scotland
Publications: Bulletin of the Scottish Institute of Missionary Studies (three issues each year, two of them bibliographical)
Theses on Missionary subjects in British Universities. A. C. Ross, ed.
500 Basic Books on Missions. G. H. Anderson and A. F. Walls, eds.
Union Catalogue of Periodicals on Missions in Scottish Libraries

ABERYSTWYTH
Cardiganshire

15

COLLEGE OF LIBRARIANSHIP, WALES *Tel.:* Aberystwyth 3842
Llanbadarn Fawr
Aberystwyth
Cardiganshire

Education and research in librarianship
Enquiries: To Librarian

Scope: Librarianship, including history of libraries, bibliography, print technology, library management, data processing, information retrieval, communication media, library reports and publications, book trade literature, library equipment literature
Secondary: Education
Special teaching collections: Welsh books; Children's literature; Fine printing; Sample reference books and bibliographies

Stock: 21,000 books; 300 current periodicals

Publications: C.L.W. Reprint Series
Library Bulletin and Accessions List

ABERYSTWYTH NATIONAL LIBRARY OF WALES *Tel.:* Aberystwyth 3816
Cardiganshire Aberystwyth *Telex:* 35165
  Cardiganshire

16 *Enquiries:* To Librarian

Scope: Copyright library, making also large purchases of foreign books. *Special collections include:* Celtic; Arthurian; Bell (papyrology); Euclid; Hartland (folklore, anthropology and ethnology); English grammars and dictionaries; Robert Owen; and incunabula
Department of Manuscripts and Records houses an extensive collection of manuscripts and records relating to Wales, including literary manuscripts (mainly in Welsh, but also Latin and English); ecclesiastical, industrial and estate records
Department of Prints, Drawings and Maps collects graphic material of Welsh interest, including topographical prints and engravings, water colour and other drawings, portraits, atlases and maps (both printed and manuscript)

Stock: About two million volumes; large collection of pamphlets; 4,000 current periodicals; 95,000 maps; 25,000 manuscripts; 2,000 microfilms; 1,000 slides; $3\frac{1}{2}$ million archives

Publications: Journal of the National Library of Wales (twice each year)
Handlist of MSS
Bibliotheca Celtica

ABERYSTWYTH UNIVERSITY COLLEGE OF WALES LIBRARY *Tel.:* Aberystwyth 2711
Cardiganshire Aberystwyth *Telex:* 35181
  Cardiganshire

17 *Enquiries:* To Librarian

Scope: The Library service is as follows: The two main libraries in humanities and the social sciences are *The General Library* which houses the main arts collection and *The Llandinam Library* which serves the social sciences
Humanities:
The General Library has comprehensive collections on English Literature, History, Philosophy, Welsh Language and Literature, and rich collections on American History and Literature and the French Revolution. A subject specialist is provided for English and History and this service is being extended to cover other fields. The Modern Languages Library and the Classics Library (a strong collection) are branches of the General Library. The Classics Library also contains the collections of Palaeography and Archaeology
The Library of the Education Department includes also the collection on Fine Art. The Music Department has a separate library
Social Sciences:
The Llandinam Library contains the collections of Economics, Political Science, International Politics, Law, Geography and Geology. A considerable collection of Command Papers and House of Commons Papers are housed here. A subject specialist is also available
The *Agricultural Economics Library* is housed in the library of the *Institute of Rural Science*

ABERYSTWYTH, UNIVERSITY COLLEGE OF WALES LIBRARY, *cont.*
Stock: 150,000 books and pamphlets; 1,200 current periodicals
Publications: Accessions Lists
Periodicals List
Handlist series giving details of specialized holdings

ABINGDON CULHAM COLLEGE OF EDUCATION *Tel.:* Abingdon 458
Berks Abingdon
  Berkshire
18 *Enquiries:* To Librarian
  Scope: General coverage with particular emphasis on education and including a collection on Special Education (E.S.N. and S.S.N.)
  Stock: 28,000 books and pamphlets; 100 current periodicals

ABINGDON NORTH BERKSHIRE COLLEGE OF FURTHER *Tel.:* Abingdon 1585
Berks   EDUCATION
  North Court Road
19 Abingdon
  Berkshire
  Enquiries: To Librarian
  Scope: Motor engineering (handbooks, workshop manuals and service data)
  Secondary: Engineering science, workshop engineering, electrical installation, commerce, office practice, economics and economic history
  Stock: 14,000 books; 600 pamphlets; 120 current periodicals

ACCRINGTON ACCRINGTON PUBLIC LIBRARY *Tel.:* Accrington 32411
Lancs Public Library
  St James Street
20 Accrington
  Lancashire
  Enquiries: To Librarian
  Scope: Regional specialization includes: World War I. National specialization includes: History of technology; circulatory systems, respiration, digestion, and glandular systems
  Stock: 85,000 books and pamphlets; 140 current periodicals (total stock)

AIRDRIE AIRDRIE PUBLIC LIBRARY *Tel.:* Airdrie 3221
Lanarkshire Wellwynd
  Airdrie
21 Lanarkshire
  Enquiries: To Librarian
  Scope: Special collections: Scottish history; Local history of North Lanarkshire; Dogs, particularly sheep dogs; Mountaineering
  Stock: 65,000 books and pamphlets; 104 current periodicals (total stock)

ALDENHAM *See under* **WATFORD** *for*
Watford WALL HALL COLLEGE OF EDUCATION (no. 2257)
Herts

ALDERLEY PARK   *See under* **MACCLESFIELD** for
Macclesfield   IMPERIAL CHEMICAL INDUSTRIES LTD., INDUSTRIAL
Cheshire   HYGIENE RESEARCH LABORATORIES (no. 1723)
     IMPERIAL CHEMICAL INDUSTRIES LTD., PHARMACEUTICALS
        DIVISION (no. 1724)

ALDERNEY   THE ALDERNEY SOCIETY AND MUSEUM   *Tel:* 0481-82 2246
Channel Islands   Royal Connaught Square
     Alderney
22   Channel Islands

Enquiries: To Hon. Secretary, by letter only

Scope: Aims to promote interest in the natural history, history and geology of the Island, to collect information from visiting professionals and good amateurs and make check-lists available to subsequent visitors (there is no complete history of the Island as yet, and references are being traced) and to use the information to compile non-specialist information for ordinary museum visitors and the local school children

Publications: It is hoped to produce a paperback of the authoritative history of the evacuation of Alderney 1940 to the resettlement in 1945–46. This was published in the Bulletin of the Society (quarterly)
Check-list of birds
The Alderney Library is separate though in the same building. Books are not usually lent to other libraries

ALDERSHOT   ALDERSHOT PUBLIC LIBRARY   *Tel.:* Aldershot 22456
Hants   High Street
     Aldershot
23   Hampshire

Enquiries: To Borough Librarian

Scope: General stock including music. Aldershot local collection. Military science and military engineering. Old Testament material (Genesis—Song of Solomon)

Stock: 58,903 books; 1,000 pamphlets; 100 current periodicals. Old Testament material: 500 books; Military Science collection: 2,000 books, 270 pamphlets, 10 current periodicals

ALDERSHOT   PRINCE CONSORT'S LIBRARY   *Tel.:* Aldershot 24431 ext.
Hants   Knollys Road   3340
     Aldershot
24   Hampshire

Enquiries: To Librarian

Scope: Military section comprises military science and organization; military history including that of the Royal Navy and Royal Air Force; Army and regimental history; services and political biography

Stock: 40,000 books (including 11,200 in military section); 30 current periodicals

Publications: Prince Consort's Library 1860–1960. Centenary booklet and catalogues

ALLOA   THE SCOTTISH POLICE COLLEGE   *Tel.:* Kincardine 333
Clackmannanshire   Tulliallan Castle
     Kincardine
25   Alloa
     Clackmannanshire

ALLOA, THE SCOTTISH POLICE COLLEGE, *cont.*

Central training of all police officers in Scotland, with courses ranging from recruit training to the higher training of senior police officers

Enquiries: To Librarian

Scope: Law, particularly criminal law with an emphasis on Scottish criminal law; criminology, criminal investigation; police science and administration
Secondary: Road traffic control and organization; road safety. Central and local government, particularly those aspects of public administration which concern the police. Wide range of background information on subjects included in the syllabus of police training

Stock: 7,950 books; 3,225 pamphlets; complete set of current Chief Constables', Scotland, annual reports; 125 current periodicals

ALTRINCHAM
Cheshire

26

THE VEGETARIAN SOCIETY OF THE UNITED KINGDOM LTD
Parkdale
Dunham Road
Altrincham
Cheshire

Tel.: 061-928 0793

Aims to propagate the advantages of vegetarianism

Enquiries: To Secretary

Scope: All aspects of vegetarianism: athletic, economic, medical, scientific, nutritional, cookery, ethical. Amenities in Great Britain and abroad

Stock: 10,000 books; 20,000 pamphlets. Stock not available on loan, but open for reference

Publications: The British Vegetarian (bi-monthly)

Vegetarian Nutritional Research Centre, Science Council of the International Vegetarian Union has team which makes extracts on scientific and medical nutrition from journals published all over the world. Information considered relevant is published in *Plant Foods for Human Nutrition* (Pergamon Press) and *The British Vegetarian*

See also no. 1670

AMERSHAM
Bucks

27

MASTER MUSIC PRINTERS' AND ENGRAVERS' ASSOCIATION
Plantation Road
Amersham
Buckinghamshire

Tel.: Amersham 5525

Enquiries: To Secretary, by letter only

Scope: Very little information can be given to the general public and to specialist enquiries normally only sources of information are recommended. Very few enquiries are dealt with, but among those few are questions on music notation and layout, the history of music printing and requests for technical information on papers and bindings

No library

ANDOVER
Hants

28

THE BLADON SOCIETY OF ARTS AND CRAFTS
Hurstbourne Tarrant
Andover
Hampshire

Tel.: Hurstbourne Tarrant 278

Aims to stimulate interest among the public in the Arts and Crafts and to help artists and craftsmen in the exhibition and sale of their work

Enquiries: To Hon. Curator

Scope: A comprehensive reference library exists from which information can be given regarding all the leading societies and organizations dealing with paintings, sculpture and crafts. Information and advice is offered to artists and craftsmen regarding opportunities for exhibitions and sale of their work. Information can be supplied as to craftsmen and artists who in their own field will take individual commissions

Stock: 50 books; numerous pamphlets including notice board information on all matters of interest to the artist and craftsman. Stock not available on loan

ARMAGH

29

ARMAGH COUNTY MUSEUM *Tel.:* Armagh 2404
The Mall
Armagh

A museum dealing with the pre-history, history, natural history and other aspects of life in County Armagh

Enquiries: To Curator

Scope: One of the functions of the museum is to answer enquiries about the subjects of the museum collections but owing to the small number of staff employed it is usual to give references to sources for the enquirers' own use. The reference library is normally open to students for consultation and a number of the specimens in the museum collection constitute documentary evidence on historical matters

Stock not normally available on loan

ARMAGH

30

ROYAL IRISH FUSILIERS REGIMENTAL *Tel.:* Armagh 2911
   MUSEUM
Sovereigns House
The Mall
Armagh

Enquiries: To Curator

Scope: Details of the history of the Regiment from 1793, its uniforms and badges, but not of individual soldiers who served. The library includes histories of the campaigns in which the Regiment took part. These books are all published works

Stock: 600 books; 3 current periodicals

ASHFORD
Kent

31

WYE COLLEGE AGRICULTURAL MUSEUM *Tel.:* Wye 401
Wye
Ashford
Kent

Collection of old implements and machinery

Enquiries: To Hon. Curator of Museum, by letter only

Scope: No Information Service as such, but the Museum would be prepared to deal with enquiries in the specialized field of hop production

ASHINGTON
Northumberland

32

NORTHUMBERLAND COUNTY TECHNICAL *Tel.:* Ashington 3248
   COLLEGE
College Road
Ashington
Northumberland

Enquiries: To Tutor Librarian

ASHINGTON, NORTHUMBERLAND COUNTY TECHNICAL COLLEGE, *cont.*
- *Scope:* Mining (including geology and surveying). Building. Engineering (motor vehicle, workshop, electrical and mechanical)
  Secondary: Commerce and business; art, music and literature; housecraft and biological sciences. J. F. Kennedy Collection
- *Stock:* 16,000 books and pamphlets; complete set from mid-1965 of United States Bureau of Mines reports; 350 current periodicals; complete set of British Standards
- *Publications:* Occasional bibliographies in the building field

ASHRIDGE
Berkhamsted
Herts

See under **BERKHAMSTED** *for*
ASHRIDGE MANAGEMENT COLLEGE (no. 114)

ASHTON-IN-MAKERFIELD
Wigan
Lancs

See under **WIGAN** *for*
ASHTON-IN-MAKERFIELD PUBLIC LIBRARY (no. 2285)

ASHTON-UNDER-LYNE
Lancs

33

ASHTON-UNDER-LYNE COLLEGE OF FURTHER EDUCATION
Beaufort Road
Ashton-under-Lyne
Lancashire

Tel.: 061-330 6911

- *Enquiries:* To Librarian
- *Scope:* Textbooks on all subjects studied at the College: Secretarial, commerce, public administration, engineering, craft, automobile engineering, electronics, radio and television, electrical installation, metalwork, building, catering, bakery, art, fashion, hairdressing, beauty culture, display, photography, graphic design and education
- *Stock:* 11,000 books and pamphlets; 100 current periodicals

ASHTON-UNDER-LYNE
Lancs

34

ASHTON-UNDER-LYNE PUBLIC LIBRARIES
Central Library
Ashton-under-Lyne
Lancashire

Tel.: 061-330 2151

- *Enquiries:* To Librarian
- *Scope:* Ashton-under-Lyne local history reference collection
  Secondary: Printed material on Lancashire, Cheshire, parts of Yorkshire and Derbyshire. Subject specialization includes: Islam; Non-Christian religions arranged geographically; Medicine—mechanical remedies; General books on diseases at special developmental periods
- *Stock:* 3,000 books, pamphlets and reports; 6 current periodicals

ATHERTON
Manchester

See under **MANCHESTER** *for*
ATHERTON PUBLIC LIBRARY (no. 1739)

AYLESBURY
Bucks

35

AYLESBURY COLLEGE OF FURTHER EDUCATION
Oxford Road
Aylesbury
Buckinghamshire

Tel.: Aylesbury 4571

- *Enquiries:* To Librarian

Scope: Law, economics, technical education, criminology. Elementary books on history, geography, literature, fine arts

Stock: 5,000 books; 60 current periodicals

AYLESBURY
Bucks

36

BUCKINGHAMSHIRE COUNTY LIBRARY
County Library Headquarters
County Offices
Walton Street
Aylesbury
Buckinghamshire

Tel.: Aylesbury 4671
Telex: Administration
83101; County
Reference Library
83262

Enquiries: To Librarian

Scope: L.A.S.E.R. subject specialization includes: Metapsychology; character analysis; general psychology; slavery; accidents of natural origin; first aid; pediatrics; India and farther India. Buckinghamshire collection
Secondary: Times 1908 and onwards (microfilm). Major periodical indexing services. H.M.S.O. Selected Subscription Service

Stock: 850,000 books and pamphlets; 250 current periodicals (total stock)

Publications: Union List of Periodicals (County Library and College Library holdings)
Union List of Directories

Regional Reference Libraries at Amersham, Bletchley, Slough

AYLESBURY
Bucks

37

BUCKINGHAMSHIRE COUNTY MUSEUM
Church Street
Aylesbury
Buckinghamshire

Tel.: Aylesbury 2158

The Museum collects material relating to the geology, natural history, archaeology, history, folk life, costume of Buckinghamshire, and paintings and prints connected with the County

Enquiries: To Curator

Scope: The information service is related to the subjects covered by the Museum

AYLESBURY
Bucks

38

BUCKS ARCHAEOLOGICAL SOCIETY
Church Street
Aylesbury
Buckinghamshire

Tel.: Aylesbury 2158

Enquiries: To Secretary, by letter only

Scope: History of Buckinghamshire, including village histories, family histories, natural history, manorial and general histories. Archive Collection, mainly Manorial Rolls, Estate papers and Parish registers

Stock: 2,000 books; 200 pamphlets. Stock not available on loan

Publications: Records of Bucks (annually)

AYLESBURY
Bucks

39

INTERNATIONAL MEDICAL SOCIETY OF
 PARAPLEGIA
Stoke Mandeville Hospital
Aylesbury
Buckinghamshire

Tel.: Aylesbury 5050

Society to correlate and encourage further development in the knowledge and treatment of spinal cord injuries

AYLESBURY, INTERNATIONAL MEDICAL SOCIETY OF PARAPLEGIA, *cont.*
    Enquiries: To Secretary
    Scope: All subjects relevant to the treatment and long term care, including rehabilitation, of spinal cord injuries and certain other spinal cord lesions
    No library
    Publications: Paraplegia (quarterly, published by E. & S. Livingston Ltd)

AYLESBURY   ST JOHN'S HOSPITAL   *Tel.:* Stone 383
Bucks   Stone
    Aylesbury
40   Buckinghamshire
    Enquiries: To Medical Librarian
    Scope: Psychiatry and psychology
    Stock: 600 books; 21 current periodicals

AYR   AYR CARNEGIE LIBRARY   *Tel.:* Ayr 64505
    12 Main Street
41   Ayr
    Enquiries: To Librarian
    Scope: The Ayrshire Collection (books about the region and books by local authors). Robert Burns Collection (editions of the poems and books about the poet and his work)
    Stock: 5,000 books and pamphlets

AYR   AYR COUNTY LIBRARY   *Tel.:* Ayr 66922 ext. 16
    County Buildings
42   Ayr
    Enquiries: To Librarian
    Scope: Subject specialization: General education
    Stock: 84,000 books (total stock)

AYR   AYRSHIRE ARCHAEOLOGICAL AND NATURAL HISTORY SOCIETY   *Tel.:* Ayr 64505
43   Carnegie Library
    12 Main Street
    Ayr
    Enquiries: To Secretary, by letter only
    Scope: Information supplied (if available) on archaeological sites and finds within the County
    No library
    Publications: The 'Collections' of the Society contain articles on the history and natural history of Ayrshire and include papers on field work and surveys carried out in the study of prehistoric, medieval and industrial archaeology
    Bibliography for Ayrshire

AYR   CRAIGIE COLLEGE OF EDUCATION   *Tel.:* Ayr 67981
    Ayr
44   *Enquiries:* To Principal Librarian

Scope: Education (particularly, but not exclusively, primary). Educational psychology. Children's books and libraries, including School Libraries
Secondary: Coverage of subjects wide-ranging including many major bibliographical and reference works. Picture collection

Stock: 30,000 books, including 10,000 children's books; 500 pamphlets. Government publications on education and allied subjects; 220 current periodicals; 800 gramophone records; 800 visual aids (filmstrips, slides, cassettes)

Publications: Occasional bibliographies for limited use and circulation
Recent additions lists for internal use
Current awareness service for periodical contents (internal)

BABRAHAM
Cambridge

See under **CAMBRIDGE** for
AGRICULTURAL RESEARCH COUNCIL,
  INSTITUTE OF ANIMAL PHYSIOLOGY (no. 274)

BACUP
Lancs

45

BACUP PUBLIC LIBRARY
St James Square
Bacup
Lancashire

Tel.: Bacup 3324

Enquiries: To Librarian

Scope: General enquiries dealt with and any relating to Bacup in particular and Rossendale in general. Subject specialization includes: Environmental hygiene, food and drug control; sanitation; cemetery planning. Comprehensive 'local history' envisaged for 1970–72 (in effect updating Newbigging's 'History of Rossendale' and also correlating under one head local information not easily obtainable elsewhere)

Stock: 1,000 books and pamphlets; 5 current periodicals on subject specialization

Publications: Occasional bibliographies

BACUP
Lancs

46

NATURAL HISTORY SOCIETY, BACUP
24 Yorkshire Street
Bacup
Lancashire

Enquiries: To Secretary, by letter only

Scope: Natural history of Bacup

Stock: 200 books. Stock not available on loan

BAGSHOT
Surrey

47

ROYAL ARMY CHAPLAINS' DEPARTMENT
  CENTRE
Bagshot Park
Bagshot
Surrey

Tel.: Bagshot 3172

Chaplaincy Services in the British Army. Christian Leadership and Information Courses for all ranks. Reception of newly appointed Chaplains

Enquiries: To Warden or Secretary, by letter only

Scope: Theological and historical works in connection with the Chaplaincy Services in the British Army. The role of the military chaplain in peace and war. General works on Church denominations other than the Roman Catholic Church

Stock: 5,750 books; various pamphlets; majority of theological and inter-denominational current periodicals

BAGSHOT, ROYAL ARMY CHAPLAINS' DEPARTMENT CENTRE, *cont.*
Publications: The Journal of the R.A.Ch.D. (May and December each year)
The Bagshot Bulletin (deals mainly with religious education in the Army)

BALLYNAHINCH   DOWN COUNTY LIBRARY   *Tel.:* Ballynahinch 639
Co. Down
Ballynahinch
Co. Down

48   *Enquiries:* To Librarian
Scope: County Down local collection

BAMBURGH   GRACE DARLING MUSEUM
Northumberland   ROYAL NATIONAL LIFE-BOAT INSTITUTION
Bamburgh
49   Northumberland

Enquiries: To Hon. Curator, Wynding Lea, Bamburgh, Northumberland, by letter only
Scope: Information is available concerning the heroine Grace Darling, her immediate family and the circumstances attending the loss of s.s. *Forfarshire* including the aftermath. Information can be supplied about books relating to Grace Darling that have been published
No library

BANBURY   BANBURY HISTORICAL SOCIETY   *Tel.:* Banbury 2282
Oxon
c/o Borough Library
Banbury
50   Oxfordshire

Aims to encourage interest in the history of the town and borough of Banbury and of neighbouring parts of Oxfordshire, Northamptonshire and Warwickshire

Enquiries: To Hon. Secretary, Humber House, Bloxham, Banbury, Oxfordshire, by letter only
Scope: The Society's library is maintained within the Public Reference Library in Banbury, and is designed to complement that Library's already extremely comprehensive local history collection. Transcripts of local parish registers, a run of the North Oxon. Archaeological Society Transactions, and a copy of a photoprint of an index to Oxfordshire Marriage Licenses are the most notable parts of the small collection
Stock: 100 books
Publications: Cake and Cockhorse (quarterly)
Index to Wills Proved in the Peculiar Court of Banbury, 1542–1858
Marriage Register of Banbury, parts 2 and 3, 1724–1790, 1790–1837
Baptism and Burial Registers of Banbury, part 1, 1558–1653; part 2, 1653–1723
South Newington Churchwardens Accounts, 1560–1684
A Victorian M.P. and his Constituents: The correspondence of H. W. Tancred, 1841–1859

BANGOR   BANGOR CITY LIBRARY   *Tel.:* Bangor 3479
Caernarvonshire
Ffordd Gwynedd
Bangor
51   Caernarvonshire

Enquiries: To Librarian
Scope: All aspects of Welsh life, history, archaeology and in co-operation with Bangor University Library (no. 54) many other subjects
Stock: 8,000 books; 500 pamphlets; most Welsh periodicals, religious and secular

BANGOR
Caernarvonshire

52

CAERNARVONSHIRE AND ANGLESEY
   MANAGEMENT COMMITTEE MEDICAL
   LIBRARY
c/o Science Library
University College of North Wales
Bangor
Caernarvonshire

Tel.: Bangor 2501 ext. 434 and 435
Telex: 61100

Serves medical staff attached to hospitals, and members of the medical profession in Caernarvonshire and Anglesey

Enquiries: To Librarian
Scope: The information resources of the Science Library are available; there is no special medical information service. The library is housed partly in U.C.N.W. and partly in a library in the main hospital—the latter containing reference works and recent issues of the periodicals
Publications: 5,000 books; 60 current periodicals

BANGOR
Caernarvonshire

53

NORMAL COLLEGE OF EDUCATION
Bangor
Caernarvonshire

Tel.: Bangor 2122

Enquiries: To Librarian
Scope: Education and related subjects
Stock: 10,000 books and pamphlets; 200 current periodicals. Books only available on loan

BANGOR
Caernarvonshire

54

UNIVERSITY COLLEGE OF NORTH WALES
   LIBRARY
Bangor
Caernarvonshire

Tel.: Bangor 2501
Telex: 61100

Enquiries: To Librarian, preferably by letter
Scope: All subjects. *Special subjects:* Welsh literature and history
Stock: 300,000 books and pamphlets; 850 current periodicals

BANSTEAD
Surrey

55

MUSICAL EDUCATION OF THE
   UNDER-TWELVES ASSOCIATION
100 Hillside
Banstead
Surrey

Tel.: Burgh Heath 53823

Enquiries: To Secretary, by letter only
Scope: Music in the Primary School
Publications: Bulletin (twice yearly)

BARNET
Herts

56

BARNET COLLEGE OF FURTHER EDUCATION
Wood Street
Barnet
Hertfordshire

Tel.: 01-449 9191

Enquiries: To Senior Tutor Librarian
Scope: Engineering, art, science, commerce and general topics
Stock: 15,000 books; 200 current periodicals

BARNSLEY Yorkshire **57**	BARNSLEY PUBLIC LIBRARY Eldon Street Barnsley Yorkshire	*Tel.:* Barnsley 3170

Enquiries: To Librarian

Scope: General stock including music.
Special collections: Local Collection (Barnsley and district coverage); Yorkshire Collection (all Yorkshire)
National subject specialization: Judicial branch of government

Stock: 70,000 books plus 5,500 (local collection), 3,000 (Yorkshire collection) and 300 (Judicial collection); 230 current periodicals; 850 maps

Publications: Monthly book lists
Subject book lists
List of filmstrips available
List of Local Societies, Clubs and Organisations
Bibliographical List of books, pamphlets and articles connected with Barnsley and the immediate district. 1916

BARNSTAPLE Devon **58**	NORTH DEVON ATHENAEUM The Square Barnstaple Devon Library and museum	*Tel.:* Barnstaple 2174

Enquiries: To Head Librarian, by letter only

Scope: Library: Established by William Frederick Rock in 1888. Special collection of books on local history, geography, geology, biology, classical literature, topography and travel. Provides a meeting place for the Devonshire Association and other local societies devoted to local and general cultural activities, and offers facilities for students engaged in historical research
Museum: Collection of local antiques and North Devon earthenware, ceremonial spoons, geological and fossil collection, Roman pottery excavated at Martinhoe, butterfly and coin collections and maps

Stock: 30,000 books; pamphlets; 10 current periodicals

BARNSTAPLE Devon **59**	NORTH DEVON TECHNICAL COLLEGE AND COLLEGE OF FURTHER EDUCATION Old Sticklepath Hill Barnstaple Devon	*Tel.:* Barnstaple 5291

Enquiries: To Librarian

Scope: Subject fields include: Mechanical and electrical engineering, catering, commercial practice and secretarial work, building, art and general school subjects. A section of local interest is being developed

Stock: 11,000 books; 150 current periodicals

College Library serves Bideford School of Art and several Further Education Centres, at which small libraries are maintained, as well as main college

BARRY
Glam

60

BARRY PUBLIC LIBRARY
King Square
Barry
Glamorgan

Tel.: Barry 5722

Enquiries: To Librarian
Scope: Subject specialization includes: Economic organization; criminology
Stock: 1,119 books; 6 current periodicals

BARRY
Glam

61

COLEG Y FRO
Y.M.C.A. Training College
Rhoose
Barry
Glamorgan

Tel.: Rhoose 255

Courses in liberal studies for young workers, in general studies for foreign students, in youth leadership and activities for Y.M.C.A. members

Enquiries: To Principal, by letter only
Scope: Liberal studies (including industry, local history and youth leadership, Y.M.C.A. history and activities)
Stock: 6,000 books; 1,000 pamphlets; 500 reports; 45 current periodicals; 100 films and film strips

BARRY
Glam

62

GLAMORGAN COLLEGE OF EDUCATION
Buttrills Road
Barry
Glamorgan CF6 8E

Tel.: Barry 3101

Enquiries: To Librarian
Scope: Education. General stock for college courses. Teaching practice collection, including children's literature. Small collections of music scores, filmstrips, slides and illustrations
Stock: 32,000 books; 3,000 pamphlets; 235 current periodicals

BASINGSTOKE
Hants

63

BASINGSTOKE TECHNICAL COLLEGE
Worting Road
Basingstoke
Hampshire

Tel.: Basingstoke 5551

Enquiries: To Principal, by letter only
Scope: Engineering, building, business studies, languages and art; general stock covering all subjects including medicine and sociology
Stock: 10,000 books; 5,000 pamphlets; 150 current periodicals. Complete set of British Standards

BASINGSTOKE
Hants

64

ELI LILLY AND COMPANY LIMITED
Kingsclere Road
Basingstoke
Hampshire
Pharmaceutical Company

Tel.: Basingstoke 3241
Telex: 85247

Enquiries: To Head of Medical Information Services
Scope: Prepared to answer questions on the Company's products to members of the medical and related professions
Stock: 500 books (general reference and texts on the subjects covered by products); 3,500 reports (mostly in the form of published clinical and pharmacological work); 100 current periodicals

BASINGSTOKE Hants **65**	ILEOSTOMY ASSOCIATION OF GT BRITAIN & IRELAND Drove Cottage Fuzzy Drove Kempshott Basingstoke Hampshire	*Tel.:* Basingstoke 21288

Enquiries: To Secretary

Scope: The organization provides information on appliances, adhesives and personal problems, arranges meetings and exhibitions of appliances and dressings, organizes visits to patients about to undergo an ileostomy, advises on matters of employment, marriage, pregnancy, life insurance and pensions, and gathers statistical data from members for medical, surgical and other studies

Publications: Quarterly journal
Film, film strips, slides
A New Life (2nd edition)
Welcoming the art of living a full life with an Ileostomy
Weight gain after Ileostomy. D. A. Seaton
Skin problems of Ileostomies. I. Martin-Scott

BASINGSTOKE Hants **66**	PARK PREWETT HOSPITAL Basingstoke Hampshire Psychiatric hospital	*Tel.:* Basingstoke 3202

Enquiries: To Librarian

Scope: Main emphasis of the library is on psychiatric textbooks but there are a number of books on general medicine and the library is being extended to form a comprehensive medical library
Secondary: Small collection of early writings on psychiatric subjects

Stock: 1,400 books and bound periodicals; 53 current periodicals

BASINGSTOKE Hants **67**	THE POLICE COLLEGE Bramshill House Basingstoke Hampshire	*Tel.:* Hartley Wintney 2931

As the central police library, the library of the College provides a loans and information service to the staff and students of the College, and to the police forces throughout the United Kingdom

Enquiries: To Librarian

Scope: Police science
Secondary: Law; criminology; penology; road traffic

Stock: 2,500 books; 1,000 pamphlets; 125 current periodicals; complete set of current Chief Constables' annual reports; 1,600 College theses and research papers
Special collections: 634 truncheons and tipstaves (including the Acworth, Dixon and Langton collections); 8 boards of police badges (Kent Sim collection); 23 rattles; 15 swords; 42 police films

Publications: Police College Magazine (twice each year)
Additions to the Library (monthly)

BASINGSTOKE Hants **68**	TWYFORD PHARMACEUTICAL SERVICES LTD Telford Road Houndmills Estate Basingstoke Hampshire	*Tel.:* Basingstoke 3212 *Telex:* 85131

Enquiries: To Librarian
Scope: Medical, pharmaceutical and veterinary information
Stock: Includes 120 current periodicals

BATH Somerset **69**	THE AMERICAN MUSEUM IN BRITAIN Claverton Manor Bath Somerset	*Tel.:* Bath 60503

Illustrates the development of American decorative arts from the 17th to the 19th century and interprets the history and arts of the United States to schoolchildren and students through as many different media as possible

Enquiries: To Director, by letter only
Scope: American history and the American arts as they relate to the Museum collection
Stock: 2,000 books. Stock not available on loan
Publications: Guide book to the Museum

BATH Somerset **70**	BATH COLLEGE OF EDUCATION (HOME ECONOMICS) Sion Hill Place Bath Somerset	*Tel.:* Bath 24691

Enquiries: To Librarian, by letter only
Scope: Education and social studies; dress, needlework and design; cookery and nutrition. General library stock
Stock: 1,500 books and pamphlets; 120 current periodicals

BATH Somerset **71**	BATH MUNICIPAL LIBRARIES AND VICTORIA ART GALLERY Reference Library 18 Queen Square Bath BA1 2HP Somerset	*Tel.:* Bath 24747

Enquiries: To Director
Scope: All subjects; *Special collections* on Bath; bibliography; naval and military history; fine arts; English history; English literature; Napoleon; French Revolution newspapers; early children's books
Stock: 70,276 books; 10,122 pamphlets; 320 current periodicals
Publications: Printed Books 1476–1640. 1968
Catalogue of Incunabula. 1966
Select List of Books on Bath. 1967
Bath Guides, Directories and Newspapers. 1967
Philately: A catalogue of the library of the Bath Philatelic Society and books in Bath Reference Library. 1967
Bath: Architecture and Planning. 1969

BATH
Somerset

72

BATH UNIVERSITY OF TECHNOLOGY   *Tel.*: Bath 6941
Claverton Down
Bath BA2 7AY
Somerset

Technological University

Enquiries: To Librarian

Scope: Architecture and building technology, biological sciences, chemistry and chemical engineering, education, electrical engineering, aeronautical engineering, mechanical engineering, management, materials science, mathematics, modern languages and modern European studies, pharmacy, physics, social sciences (sociology and economics) and nuclear studies

Stock: 50,000 books, pamphlets and reports; 1,860 current periodicals

BATH
Somerset

73

CITY OF BATH TECHNICAL COLLEGE   *Tel.*: Bath 64191
James Street West
Bath BA1 1UP
Somerset

Enquiries: To Principal

Scope: Education, sociology, English literature and modern history

Stock: 7,500 books; 25 current periodicals

BATH
Somerset

74

THE MUSEUM OF COSTUME   *Tel.*: Bath 21278
Assembly Rooms
Alfred Street
Bath
Somerset

Enquiries: Director, or Chief Costume Assistant, by letter only

Scope: Costume and accessories, 17th century to present day
Limited library only

Publications: Guidebook

BATH
Somerset

75

NEWTON PARK COLLEGE OF EDUCATION   *Tel.*: Newton St Loe 255
Newton St Loe
Bath BA2 9BN
Somerset

Enquiries: To Librarian

Scope: Education: theory, history, comparative; educational techniques; educational psychology, developmental psychology; educational sociology. Special techniques in the teaching of English, French, mathematics, religion, history, geography, art, craft and design, music, biology, rural science. Veterinary science, soil science, animal husbandry
Secondary: Library resources in other subject fields (those in which prospective teachers will choose to specialize) include relatively little material not available from the largest Public Libraries. These fields are: English language and literature; mathematics; religion; history; geography; art and design; music

Stock: 26,000 books; 4,000 pamphlets; few reports; 200 current periodicals

BATH
Somerset

76

ROMAN BATHS AND MUSEUM   *Tel.*: Bath 5481
Pump Rooms
Bath
Somerset

Enquiries: To Curator
Scope: Archaeology of Bath and surrounding area
No library
Publications: Guidebook

BATHGATE West Lothian **77**	WEST LOTHIAN COUNTY LIBRARY Wellpark Marjoribanks Street Bathgate West Lothian	*Tel.:* Bathgate 2866 (Headquarters)

Enquiries: To Librarian
Scope: Local collection. Subject specialization: State education
Stock: Local collection: 200 books

BATLEY Yorkshire **78**	BATLEY MUSEUMS AND ART GALLERY Bagshaw Museum Batley Yorkshire	*Tel.:* Batley 2514

Art Gallery: Collections of 19th and 20th century contemporary works. Bagshaw Museum: General collections. Oakwell Hall: 16th century Manor House, furniture

Enquiries: To Curator
Scope: Arts, fine and applied. General museum subjects
Stock: Some hundreds of books and pamphlets in arts, science and museology. Stock not available on loan
Publications: Guides to Oakwell Hall and Bagshaw Museum
Ephemera on nature and local history

BATLEY Yorkshire **79**	BATLEY PUBLIC LIBRARY Market Place Batley Yorkshire	*Tel.:* Batley 3141

Enquiries: To Librarian
Scope: National subject specialization includes: Economic planning
Stock: 400 books; 250 pamphlets; 50 current periodicals

BATLEY Yorkshire **80**	HOWARD LLOYD & CO. LIMITED Clerk Green Batley Yorkshire	*Tel.:* Batley 2331 *Telex:* 55223

Manufacturers of pharmaceuticals and fine chemicals

Enquiries: To Information Officer
Scope: Pharmacy, pharmacology, medicine, organic chemistry, analytical chemistry
Stock: 500 books; 200 pamphlets; 100 reports; 60 current periodicals. Stock available on loan through BRASTACS
Publications: Information Bulletin (weekly)

BEACONSFIELD   ARMY SCHOOL OF EDUCATION   *Tel.:* Beaconsfield 5501
Bucks   Wilton Park   ext. 42
   Beaconsfield
81   Buckinghamshire

     Enquiries: To Librarian

     Scope: Military science; military history
         Secondary: Limited Russian fiction, reference works, encyclopaedias, textbooks and periodicals. A few Arabic text books and dictionaries. Recreational material

     Stock: 20,000 books (largely recreational); 50 current periodicals (mainly recreational, but some technical, and excludes Russian periodicals)

         The library is a 'Command Library' of the Army Library Service, administered by The Institute of Army Education, Eltham Palace, Court Road, Eltham, London S.E. (no. 1242)

BEACONSFIELD   THE INSTITUTION OF TRAINING OFFICERS   *Tel.:* Beaconsfield 3994
Bucks   55 Station Road
   Beaconsfield
82   Buckinghamshire

     Enquiries: To Information Officer

     Scope: All aspects of training in industry and commerce

     Stock: 100 books. Stock not available on loan

     Publications: The Training Officer (monthly)

BEBINGTON   *See under* **WIRRAL** *for*
Wirral   BEBINGTON PUBLIC LIBRARIES (no. 2297)
Cheshire

BECKENHAM   ASSOCIATION OF VOLUNTARY AIDED   *Tel.:* 01-778 7270
Kent   SECONDARY SCHOOLS
   20 Reddons Road
83   Beckenham
   Kent

     Enquiries: To Secretary

     Scope: The Secretary is prepared to supply information about various aspects of Voluntary Aided Secondary Schools and their work

         No library

     Publications: Pamphlets
         Termly Bulletin

BECKENHAM   C.B.D. RESEARCH LTD   *Tel.:* 01-650 7745
Kent   154 High Street
   Beckenham
84   Kent BR3 1EA

     Enquiries: To Director

     Scope: Publishers of guides to information sources, particularly in the fields of business information, directories, associations, market research and statistics. Research and compilation of custom-built lists, bibliographies and reports in the same fields

     Stock: Small reference collection of specimen material—United Kingdom and overseas directories, documentation on associations

Publications: Current British Directories. 6th edition 1969 (biennially)
Directory of British Associations. 3rd edition 1970 (biennially)
European Companies: A Guide to Sources of Information. 2nd edition 1966
Current European Directories. 1st edition 1969
Statistics—Europe: Sources for Market Research. 1st edition 1968
Marketing & Management: A World Register of Organisations. 1st edition 1969

BECKENHAM   WELLCOME RESEARCH LABORATORIES   *Tel.:* 01-650 3422
Kent   Langley Court   *Telex:* 23937
   Beckenham
85   Kent BR3 3BS

Research under two headings: chemical and pharmacological work in the search for new drugs of both synthetic and natural origins; and biological investigations, in the field of immunology

Enquiries: To the Librarian for books and journals
To Research Information Centre for other research enquiries
To Medical Information Centre, Wellcome Building, Euston Road, London, for information on marketed products

Scope: Tropical medicine; chemistry; pharmacology; chemotherapy; virology; immunology; bacteriology; biochemistry; veterinary science

Stock: 4,000 books; 300 pamphlets; 700 current periodicals

Publications: Foot and Mouth Disease Bulletin

BEDFORD   ASSOCIATION OF PRINCIPALS OF WOMEN'S   *Tel.:* 0234-51966
     COLLEGES OF PHYSICAL EDUCATION
86   Bedford College of Physical Education
   Lansdowne Road
   Bedford

Enquiries: To Hon. Secretary

Scope: Teachers' training in the field of physical education

No library

BEDFORD   BEDFORD COLLEGE OF PHYSICAL EDUCATION   *Tel.:* Bedford 51966
   Lansdowne Road
87   Bedford

The education of specialist teachers of physical education

Enquiries: To Librarian

Scope: Physical education, dance, movement education, kinesiology, games, outdoor activities
Secondary: Physiology, anatomy, youth leadership

Stock: 13,000 books; 84 current periodicals

BEDFORD   BEDFORD MEDICAL INSTITUTE   *Tel.:* Bedford 55122
   Bedford General Hospital South Wing
88   Kempston Road
   Bedford

Library provided for the use of hospital medical staff, local medical practitioners and dental practitioners

Enquiries: To Organizer

Scope: All medical subjects

BEDFORD, BEDFORD MEDICAL INSTITUTE, *cont.*
Stock: 4,000 books; 35 current periodicals
Stock lent to, and enquiries dealt with from, other medical libraries only

BEDFORD

89

BEDFORD PUBLIC LIBRARY *Tel.:* Bedford 50931
Harpur Street *Telex:* 82233
Bedford

Enquiries: To Librarian

Scope: Special collections: John Bunyan Library (Mott Harrison Collection): Early editions, biography, bibliography, prints, illustrations devoted to life and works of John Bunyan.
Old Bedford Library (founded 1700): 17th-century literature; chief in importance the 17th-century pamphlets; Commonwealth and Restoration periods (catalogued in Wing)

Stock: John Bunyan Library 1,260 books and pamphlets; Old Bedford Library 680 books; 600 pamphlets

Publications: Catalogue of the John Bunyan Library

BEDFORD

90

BEDFORDSHIRE COUNTY LIBRARY *Tel.:* Bedford 56181
County Hall *Telex:* 82244
Bedford

Enquiries: To Reference Librarian

Scope: Subject specialization includes: Literary methods; pastoral theology; organic chemistry and aeronautics. Local History collection for Bedfordshire. Fowler Collection of printed sources relating to mediaeval English history. Bagshawe Collection of Local History

Stock: 331,406 items

BEDFORD

91

BUNYAN MUSEUM LIBRARY
c/o 55 Mill Street
Bedford

Provides a collection of early editions of Bunyan's works, a unique collection of *The Pilgrim's Progress* in 160 languages, and the surviving personal relics of Bunyan

Enquiries: To Honorary Advisor, Bunyan Museum Library, 12 Birchdale Avenue, Kempston, Bedford. *Tel.:* Kempston 2160

Scope: Bunyan bibliography and biography

Stock: 1,500 books and pamphlets including 15 Bunyan First English editions and 360 volumes of Bunyan's works in 160 languages. Stock not available on loan

Publications: Catalogue of the library and museum

BELFAST

92

BELFAST CITY LIBRARIES *Tel.:* Belfast 43233
Central Library
Royal Avenue
Belfast BT1 1EA

Enquiries: To City Librarian

Scope: Humanities and Social Sciences Library: 72,346 books; 260 current periodicals. Special collections include those on law, costume, heraldry, foreign encyclopaedias; United Nations, UNESCO, British Government Publications
Local History Library: 40,470 books; 118 current periodicals; 72 current newspapers. Stock includes many volumes on whole of Ireland. Special collections include: F. J. Bigger Collection of Irish history and archaeology and antiquarian material; J. S. Crone Collection of Irish

books, pamphlets and periodicals. Other important collections include those of Grainger, Horner, Riddell, Doyle and Moore. Large collection of Irish and Belfast newspapers from 1761, and of periodicals, directories, maps, plans, letters, manuscripts, cuttings and microfilms. Early Belfast printed books

Fine Arts and Literature Library: 53,056 books; 100 current periodicals; 3,000 colour reproductions of paintings; slides; special collection on architecture

Music and Gramophone Records Library: 19,000 books; 45 current periodicals; 8,500 records. Lending and reference service with special attention to all aspects of Irish music. Gramophone records stock covers whole of standard repertory with sections devoted to folk music, jazz, drama, poetry, languages and speeches. Houses the library of the Society of Professional Musicians in Ulster

Staff Library: 4,167 books; 36 current periodicals; covers all aspects of librarianship. Houses the library of the Northern Ireland Branch of the Library Association

Children's Library: Special collections on bibliography of children's literature, and illustrations collection for teachers

Stock: 635,628 books; 1,970 periodicals (total stock including that noted above)

BELFAST

93

BELFAST COLLEGE OF DOMESTIC SCIENCE   *Tel.:* Belfast 63431
Garnerville Road
Belfast 4

Enquiries: To Principal, by letter only

Scope: Food science, cookery and catering; nutrition; household management; needlecraft and dress subjects; chemistry and general science; English; educational psychology
Secondary: Related art and sociology

Stock: 5,400 books; 20 pamphlets; 54 current periodicals. Stock available on loan locally only

BELFAST

94

BELFAST TRANSPORT MUSEUM   *Tel.:* Belfast 51519
Witham Street
Belfast BT4 1HP

Preservation of a representative collection of items having associations with the development of transport in Ireland

Enquiries: To Curator

Scope: Documentation of historical material is in its early stages, but information and sources are given within limitations of staffing and facilities

Stock: 300 books; 200 pamphlets; 2 current periodicals. Stock not available on loan

Publications: Transport Handbooks:
   No. 1: Tramways and Light Railways of Ulster
   No. 2: Coastal Passenger Services and Inland Navigations in the North of Ireland
   No. 4: Cross-channel Services in the North of Ireland
   No. 5: Standard-gauge Railways in the North of Ireland
   No. 6: Coastal Passenger Services and Inland Navigations in the South of Ireland

BELFAST

95

EDGEHILL THEOLOGICAL COLLEGE   *Tel.:* Belfast 665870
Lennoxvale
Malone Road
Belfast BT9 5BY

Training college for the Methodist ministry

Enquiries: To Librarian

BELFAST, EDGEHILL THEOLOGICAL COLLEGE, *cont.*

Scope: Biblical and theological books, church history, comparative religion, philosophy and psychology of religion, homoletics, liturgiology
Special emphasis on Methodist theology, history and hymnology. Some general history and biography

Stock: 7,000 books

BELFAST

96

GENERAL REGISTER OFFICE *Tel.:* Belfast 27311
Fermanagh House
Ormeau Avenue
Belfast BT2 8HX

Enquiries: To Registrar General

Scope: Vital statistics in Northern Ireland since 1922 (annually); census of population 1841, 1851, 1861, 1871, 1881, 1891, 1901, 1911, 1926, 1937, 1951, 1961 and 1966

BELFAST

97

GOVERNMENT INFORMATION SERVICE *Tel.:* Belfast 63011
Stormont Castle *Telex:* 74578
Belfast BT4 3ST

Enquiries: To Director and to the Ulster Office, 11 Berkeley Street, London W.1.

Scope: The primary role of the Information Service is to pass on to the communication media information about Government activities
Secondary: The Information Service will endeavour to answer or have answered questions about Northern Ireland or to direct enquiries to relevant sources of information

Publications: Ulster Year Book
Ulster Annual (a popular compilation of stories and articles)
Ulster Commentary (monthly, popular magazine)
Northern Ireland (dealing with history, resources and people)
Introduction to Northern Ireland (a folder providing easy reference to important aspects of life in Ulster)
Notes on Northern Ireland (a looseleaf compilation of notes on history, geography and industry)
Facts and Figures (a treatment in greater depth of different subjects relating to Northern Ireland, for example, industry, forestry)

BELFAST

98

JAMES MUNCE PARTNERSHIP *Tel.:* Belfast 32966
133 University Street *Telex:* 74655
Belfast BT7 1HQ

Enquiries: To Information Officer

Scope: All specialist aspects of hospital design

Stock: 75 books; 1,000 pamphlets; 250 reports; 2 current periodicals

BELFAST

99

MINISTRY OF AGRICULTURE *Tel.:* Belfast 63038
VETERINARY RESEARCH LABORATORIES
Stormont
Belfast BT4 3SD

Veterinary research, veterinary advisory service and poultry diagnostic service

Enquiries: To Librarian, by letter only

Scope: Veterinary medicine, including veterinary pathology, parasitology, bacteriology and biochemistry, virology

Secondary: Medical and agricultural subjects

Stock: 500 books; 10 reports; 90 current periodicals

The laboratory has a link with the Queen's University of Belfast. The professional staff of the laboratory provide the teaching staff for the Faculty of Agriculture in the subject of Veterinary Science; books and periodicals are obtained through the University library (no. 107)

BELFAST

100

NATIONAL POISONS INFORMATION SERVICE *Tel.:* 0232 30503
Royal Victoria Hospital
Belfast 12

Enquiries: To Director

Scope: Service exists to inform doctors only of the constituents and toxicity of substances which patients may take accidentally or in self-poisoning. Much of the information has been given in confidence by industry and is only for use in situations of importance to life of patients

BELFAST

101

NORTHERN IRELAND ASSOCIATION OF *Tel.:* Belfast 26556 and
   YOUTH CLUBS 26875
26 Wellington Place
Belfast 1

Aims to help young people through their leisure-time activities so to develop their physical, mental and spiritual capacities that they may grow to full maturity as individuals and as members of society and that their conditions of life may be improved

Enquiries: To Youth Officer

Scope: General field of youth work

Stock: Small library

BELFAST

102

NORTHERN IRELAND COUNCIL OF SOCIAL *Tel.:* Belfast 20791 and
   SERVICE 23134
Bryson House
28 Bedford Street
Belfast BT2 7FL

Central Community organization in Northern Ireland

Enquiries: To Secretary, preferably by letter

Scope: Information on community organization and community care generally in Northern Ireland

Stock: 300 books; 400 pamphlets; 100 current periodicals. Stock not available on loan

Publications: Developing Communities
The Child in the Community
Drug Dependence in Northern Ireland
Developing the New Ulster
Adult Vocational Guidance
The Story of the Northern Ireland Council of Social Service

BELFAST

103

NORTHERN IRELAND HOSPITALS AUTHORITY *Tel.:* Belfast 27871 and
25 Adelaide Street 40321
Belfast BT2 8FG

Enquiries: To Secretary

Scope: Information can be provided on any aspect of the hospital and specialists' services in Northern Ireland for which the Authority is responsible. This covers general and psychiatric hospitals, and Special Care, Laboratory, Ambulance, Mass Radiography and Blood Transfusion Services

BELFAST	NORTHERN IRELAND TOURIST BOARD	*Tel.:* Belfast 41222
104	6 Royal Avenue Belfast BT1 1DQ	

Enquiries: To Information Officer

Scope: Tourist leaflets about Northern Ireland, that is the six counties of Antrim, Down, Armagh, Fermanagh, Londonderry and Tyrone

No library

Publications: Northern Ireland Tourist Guide Book
Hotel Accommodation Lists for Northern Ireland
Angler's Eden (fishing book)
Various booklets dealing with tourism, for example, angling, shooting, motoring, golf

BELFAST	THE PRESBYTERIAN CHURCH IN IRELAND	*Tel.:* Belfast 22284
105	Church House Belfast BT1 6DW	

Enquiries: To Information Officer

Scope: Presbyterian historical reference library

Publications: The Information Office produces miscellaneous publicity material, a monthly general magazine and two children's monthly magazines
Two other periodicals are issued by missionary departments
Volume of Reports of Committees and Boards for presentation to the annual General Assembly

BELFAST	PUBLIC RECORD OFFICE NORTHERN IRELAND	*Tel.:* Belfast 35111
106	Law Courts Building Belfast BT1 3JJ	

Care and organization of Records produced by Northern Ireland Government Departments and Law Courts. Depositing of official Northern Ireland and private papers relating to Northern Ireland families

Enquiries: To Deputy Keeper of the Records, by letter only

Scope: The Records contain material for historical study of the political, social and economic development of Northern Ireland, roughly from the post-1650 period. Because of the destruction of much of the pre-1900 Irish Records in 1922, surviving papers are the basic source

Stock: 8,000 books. Stock not available on loan

Publications: Annual Reports (abstracts of manuscript materials acquired during the year)
Educational Facsimiles
Local History Studies

BELFAST	THE QUEEN'S UNIVERSITY OF BELFAST	*Tel.:* Belfast 45133
	LIBRARY	*Telex:* 74487
107	Belfast BT7 1NN	

Enquiries: To Librarian

Scope: Caters for teaching staff and students in humanities, law, social sciences and education
Special collections: McDouall (Sanskrit and Indo-European); Hamilton-Harty (music); Rosenzweig (Hebrew); Henry (Hibernica); Percy (Early English and Romance literature); Savory (Huguenot); Simms (early material of Irish interest published abroad)
Manuscripts: Bunting (Irish music); Somerville and Ross papers

Stock: 480,000 books (total stock for main and branch libraries); current periodicals: general 1,400, humanities 700, law 120, social sciences 150, education 25

BELFAST

108

THE QUEEN'S UNIVERSITY OF BELFAST
  MEDICAL LIBRARY
Institute of Clinical Science
Grosvenor Road
Belfast BT12 6BJ

Tel.: 0232-22043
Telex: 74487

Serves staff and students of the Faculty of Medicine, the staffs of the Northern Ireland Hospitals Authority, members of the Ulster Medical Society, members of Post-graduate Medical Centres, without charge. Any other medical and dental practitioners not covered by the foregoing may use the library's facilities on payment of a deposit

Enquiries: To Librarian

Scope: Clinical medicine
Collections: Works by Northern Ireland Doctors.
Historical works, which include the Samuel Simms Collection on the history of medicine
Current awareness service
Bibliographies
Reference checking

Stock: 30,000 books; 650 current periodicals

Medical Library is responsible for library provision in Postgraduate Medical Centres being established at the five teaching hospitals in the Province

BELFAST

109

THE QUEEN'S UNIVERSITY OF BELFAST
  SCIENCE LIBRARY
ARCHITECTURE AND PLANNING
  INFORMATION SERVICE
Belfast BT9 5EQ

Tel.: Belfast 45133 ext. 679
Telex: 74487

Enquiries: To Librarian

Scope: Architecture and planning including theory, design and history of architecture, buildings and environmental design, building construction and materials, history and theory of planning, regional development, urban sociology, land use and conservation, landscape architecture

Stock: 5,000 books, pamphlets and reports; 140 current periodicals. Trade and Technical collection, classified by CI/SfB. 16,000 items, mainly manufacturers' catalogues

Publications: Bibliographies and Reading Lists compiled for use of readers
Weekly Information Bulletin

BELFAST

110

ST JOSEPH'S COLLEGE OF EDUCATION
Stewarts Town Road
Belfast BT11 9GA

Tel.: Belfast 612144

Enquiries: To Librarian, by letter only

Scope: No formalized information service exists but the library deals with enquiries in the educational field from college lecturers and students and from members of the teaching profession and research workers

Stock: 10,000 books; 300 pamphlets; 180 current periodicals

BELFAST	THE STANDING CONFERENCE OF YOUTH ORGANISATIONS IN N. IRELAND	*Tel.:* Belfast 29211
111	Education Offices 40 Academy Street Belfast BT1 2NQ	

Enquiries: To Hon. Secretary

Scope: Matters of concern to the Youth Service and constituent organizations in Northern Ireland
No library

BELFAST	STRANMILLIS COLLEGE	*Tel.:* Belfast 665271 ext. 309, 310, 312
112	Stranmillis Road Belfast BT9 5DY College of Education	

Enquiries: To Librarian

Scope: General library stock with particular emphasis on education. A collection of illustrations, filmstrips and slides, textbooks and children's books is available in the Teaching Practice section of the library

Stock: 45,000 books, pamphlets and non-book materials; 250 current periodicals

BELFAST	ULSTER MUSEUM	*Tel.:* Belfast 668251
113	Stranmillis Road Belfast BT9 5AB	

Enquiries: To Director

Scope: Painting and sculpture—British, Irish and contemporary international schools; British and (particularly) Irish ceramics, silver and glassware; Irish archaeology; History of Ulster; Industrial history of Ulster, particularly of the linen industry; British and Irish numismatics
Secondary: British and Irish furniture; British and Irish costume; British archaeology; History of Ireland; Numismatic literature generally

Stock: Books: Art (fine and applied) 1,000; Archaeology and history 2,500; Numismatics 750; large number of pamphlets; 500 reports.
Current periodicals: Art 16; Archaeology and history 27; Numismatics 8

Publications: Irish Williamite Glass. W. A. Seaby
Spinning Wheels (The John Horner Collection)
Ulster, Prehistoric Antiquities
Ulster, Celtic Antiquities
The Changing Face of Belfast (Photographic record). J. N. H. Nesbitt
Reprints from Ulster Journal of Archaeology, including Archaeological Acquisitions of Irish Origin
Irish Portraits, 1660–1860
Jonathan Swift, 1667–1745

BERKHAMSTED	ASHRIDGE MANAGEMENT COLLEGE	*Tel.:* Lt. Gaddesden 3491
Herts	Berkhamsted Hertfordshire	
114		

Enquiries: To Librarian/Information Officer

Scope: Management studies—principles, services, processes, managerial economics, industrial psychology, personnel, industrial relations, office practices, finance and management, marketing

Stock: 5,600 books; 1,000 pamphlets and reports; 90 current periodicals. Stock not normally available on loan
Publications: Leadership Style, Confidence in Management and Job Satisfaction. P. J. Sadler. 1966
Budgetary Control. A. P. Robson. 1966
The Exporters: A Study of Organisation, Staffing and Training. D. A. Tookey *et al.* 1967

BERWICK-UPON-TWEED

115

BERWICK-UPON-TWEED PUBLIC LIBRARY, MUSEUM AND ART GALLERY
Marygate
Berwick-upon-Tweed

Tel.: Berwick 7320

Enquiries: To Librarian
Scope: General Public Library, Art Gallery consisting of 42 pictures from the Burrell collection, and small museum including ceramics, glass, silver and local history. No special collections except local history

BERWICK-UPON-TWEED

116

REGIMENTAL MUSEUM K.O.S.B.
The Barracks
Berwick-upon-Tweed

Tel.: Berwick-upon-Tweed 7426

Enquiries: To Regimental Secretary, The K.O.S.B. by letter only
Scope: K.O.S.B. Regimental history
Stock: 300 books

BETCHWORTH
Surrey

117

BEECHAM RESEARCH LABORATORIES
Brockham Park
Betchworth
Surrey
Pharmaceutical research

Tel.: Betchworth 3202

Enquiries: To Information Officer
Scope: Organic chemistry; medicine; pharmacy; pharmacology; biology; biochemistry
Secondary: Physical chemistry; chemical engineering
Special collection: Allergy and antibiotics
Stock: 3,500 books; 1,000 pamphlets; 400 current periodicals

BEVERLEY
Yorkshire

118

EAST RIDING COUNTY LIBRARY
County Hall
Beverley
Yorkshire

Tel.: Beverley 881281

Enquiries: To Librarian
Scope: National subject specialization: Industrial economics and production economics; agricultural industries (excluding periodicals)
Stock: 1,778 books and pamphlets

BEXLEY
Kent

119

LONDON BOROUGH OF BEXLEY
Libraries and Museums Department
Central Administrative Offices
Hall Place
Bourne Road
Bexley
Kent

Tel.: Crayford 26574

Enquiries: To Librarian

BEXLEY, LONDON BOROUGH OF BEXLEY, *cont.*

Scope: L.A.S.E.R. subject specialization: Mental physiology and mental derangements; Bible: history, exegesis, commentary; general church history, Saints, matryrs; primitive and oriental churches; suffrage, elections; legislation; constitution; mental hospitals; mental and nervous physiology and hygiene, pathology and treatment, institutions, psychiatry, analysis; hygiene of the nervous system; diseases of the body as a whole
Complete set of All England Law Reports, 1555–date
Special collections: Local history of Bexley, and County of Kent

Stock: 366,000 books (total stock)

Member South East Area Libraries Information Service (SEAL) operating in areas of Boroughs of Bexley, Greenwich and Dartford

BEXLEYHEATH THE ENGLISH LACROSSE UNION *Tel.:* Erith 36067
Kent 3 Chessington Avenue
  Bexleyheath
120 Kent

Promotes and controls men's Lacrosse within the United Kingdom

Enquiries: To Hon. Secretary
No library

Publications: Laws of Lacrosse
Coaching Manual   Northern Lacrosse (quarterly magazine)
Lacrosse News (monthly magazine)   Training films and loops

BIBURY See under **CIRENCESTER** for
Cirencester ARLINGTON MILL MUSEUM (no. 404)
Glos

BIGGLESWADE THE SHUTTLEWORTH COLLECTION *Tel.:* Northill 288
Beds Old Warden Aerodrome
  Biggleswade
121 Bedfordshire

Enquiries: To Information Officer or Librarian

Scope: Fairly extensive library covering the history of aviation and including complete bound volumes of principal periodicals for the period 1909 to 1937, supplemented by a selection of biographical and descriptive literature on the subject and a variety of textbooks, manufacturers' manuals, drawings and photographs. Similar material is held for the subsequent period, but not of uninterrupted continuity. A complementary series is available in respect of the motor car, but for the period 1895 to 1937 and in rather less completeness. Other items embrace motor cycles and cycles

Stock: 1,200 books and pamphlets; 7 current periodicals

Publications: Shuttleworth Collection Guide
Shuttleworth Collection Catalogue
Fire Engines of the Shuttleworth Collection
Pilots' Notes for World War I Warplanes and their Rotary Engines
Memories of Early Flying Days
Motor Cars of the Shuttleworth Collection
Cycles of the Shuttleworth Collection

Horse Drawn Carriages of the Shuttleworth Collection
How it works leaflets (series of 7)
Colour booklet

BILSTON
Staffs

122

BILSTON COLLEGE OF FURTHER EDUCATION   *Tel.:* Bilston 42871
Westfield Road
Bilston
Staffordshire

Enquiries: To Librarian

Scope: Stock includes: Business and general studies; mechanical and general engineering; woodwork; domestic science, catering, needlework; hairdressing; dressmaking; general science subjects; languages as current college prospectus

Stock: 22,000 books and pamphlets; 200 current periodicals; 800 filmstrips; 500 wallcharts and maps; many hundreds of past examination papers

Publications: Accessions List (fortnightly)
Reading Lists

Member of SOSCOL (South Staffordshire College Librarians) and W.M.R.L.S.

BINGLEY
Yorkshire

123

THE YORKSHIRE DIALECT SOCIETY   *Tel.:* Bingley 3736
East View
Warren Lane
Eldwick
Bingley
Yorkshire

Enquiries: To Hon. Secretary

Scope: Library holds complete volumes of the Society's 'Transactions' going back to 1897—the year of foundation. Articles in 'Transactions' and other books collected and donated refer principally to English dialects and English language and comparative linguistics where the study of dialects is concerned in English and European languages. Also included in library stock and in the information available is a vast quantity of material relating to folk-lore studies and social customs in Yorkshire and elsewhere, including the most comprehensive stock of writings in dialect and about it. The officers of Council also have considerable knowledge of source material and speakers of dialect throughout England as many of them have done research as field-workers into English dialects for the Linguistic Atlas published by the Department of Dialectology and Folk-lore at Leeds University

Stock: 1,000 books; 4 current periodicals

Publications: Yorkshire Dialect Poems. 1943
Yorkshire Dialect Prose. 1944
Yorkshire Dialect Prose. 1945
The York Minster Screen 1833. Yorkshire reprint I, 1967
A Yorkshire Dialogue by George Meriton, 1683 edited by A. C. Cawley. Yorkshire reprint II, 1959
A New Yorkshire Dialect Anthology. 1954
A Study of the Yorkshire Dialect of Meriton's 'A Yorkshire Dialogue'. C. Dean. Yorkshire reprint III, 1962
An Anthology of Cleveland Poetry. W. Cowley, ed. 1963
An Anthology of West Riding Dialect Verse. G. Wade, ed. 1964
An Anthology of East Yorkshire Dialect Verse. B. Cowley, ed. 1965
The White Rose Garland. W. J. Halliday and A. S. Umpleby, eds.

BINGLEY, THE YORKSHIRE DIALECT SOCIETY, *cont.*
Transactions of the Yorkshire Dialect Society (annually)
Summer Bulletin (annually)

The Library is in the Department of English, Leeds University, but the Brotherton Library, Leeds University, also houses much of the stock and has been donated many publications relating to English dialects and folk-lore

BIRKENHEAD
Cheshire

124

BIRKENHEAD PUBLIC LIBRARIES   *Tel.:* 051-652 6106
Central Library
Borough Road
Birkenhead
Cheshire

Enquiries: To Librarian

Scope: N.W.R.L.S. subject specialization includes: Orthopaedics, surgical operations, thorax and respiratory system, abdominal and pelvic cavities, upper extremities.
Oil painting—British, American, French; criticism and history of English drama. Psychology, excluding industrial and child psychology but covering most other aspects

Stock: 500 books

BIRKENHEAD
Cheshire

125

HISTORIC SOCIETY OF LANCASHIRE AND
   CHESHIRE
Hon. Secretary
c/o Liverpool Central Libraries
William Brown Street
Liverpool L3 8EW

Enquiries: To Hon. Secretary

Scope: Library is on permanent loan to the Liverpool Public Libraries, and is housed in the Record Office and Local History Library of the Central Public Libraries, William Brown Street, Liverpool 3. It is available for reference by the general public but only members may borrow books from it. Together with the books owned by the Public Library there is an excellent coverage of books and articles relating to the two counties' history. The City Archivist answers questions on local history in the normal course of his duties. The Society does not have an information service as such

Stock: 1,500 books

Publications: Transactions of the Historic Society of Lancashire and Cheshire
William Yates's Map of Lancashire 1786, with introduction by J. B. Harley
Pamphlet in co-operation with the Lancashire and Cheshire Antiquarian Society on Museums and Historic Buildings in Lancashire and Cheshire. M. Craft, with an introduction to industrial archaeology in the two counties by O. Ashmore and J. H. Norris

BIRMINGHAM

126

AFRICAN STUDIES ASSOCIATION OF THE   *Tel.:* 021-472 1301 ext. 239
   UNITED KINGDOM
c/o Centre of West African Studies
University of Birmingham
P.O. Box 363
Birmingham 15

Aims to advance academic studies relating to Africa by providing facilities for the interchange of information and ideas

Enquiries: To Secretary, by letter only

Scope: Members are drawn from a wide variety of disciplines, and on the staff there are historians, economists, geographers, agriculturalists, sociologists and politicians with African experience

Publications: Bulletin (three times each year)
African Affairs special issue: Report of First Conference, 1964. Spring 1965
Soil Resources of Tropical Africa. R. P. Moss, ed. 1968
Directory of African Studies in U.K. Universities. R. E. Bradbury, ed. 1969
Education on Africa: research and action, ed. R. Jolly. Report of Third Conference, 1968. 1969

BIRMINGHAM ASLIB *Tel.:* 021-643 1914
127 The Engineering and Building Centre
Broad Street
Birmingham 1
See no. 909

BIRMINGHAM AVERY HISTORICAL MUSEUM *Tel.:* 021-558 1112
128 Soho Foundry and 2161
Birmingham 40
Records of history of weighing

Enquiries: To Curator, by letter only

Scope: Prepared to answer questions and give information to anyone genuinely interested in the history of weighing, provided such information is available in the records of the Company
No library

BIRMINGHAM BIRMINGHAM COLLEGE OF ART & DESIGN *Tel.:* 021-359 3611 ext. 442
129 New Corporation Street
Birmingham 4 (Gosta Green Library)
and
Margaret Street *Tel.:* 021-235 2207
Birmingham 3

Enquiries: To Librarian

Scope: Architecture, town and country planning, landscape architecture, dress design, printed and woven textiles design, embroidery, industrial design, furniture design, interior design, printing (Gosta Green Library)
Fine arts, history of art, graphic design, ceramics (Margaret Street Library)
Photography, silversmithing and jewellery, theatrical design, art education, are each located in separate buildings

Stock: 26,000 books and pamphlets; 200 current periodicals; 18,500 slides

BIRMINGHAM BIRMINGHAM JEWISH REFERENCE LIBRARY *Tel.:* 021-643 6155 and 0884
130 Birmingham Hebrew Congregation
Singers Hill
Ellis Street
Birmingham 1
Reference library and Department of Jewish Education

Enquiries: To Director of Education and Librarian

Scope: Mainly concerned with Hebraica and Judaica. Advice and help is given also to those preparing for GCE and University examinations. There is a most comprehensive press cutting file

BIRMINGHAM, BIRMINGHAM JEWISH REFERENCE LIBRARY, *cont.*
system available on Jewish subjects only. Students preparing theses on Jewish subjects are given every help
Secondary: The late Rev. Dr. A. Cohen collection of books on Judaica is housed in the Library

Stock: 4,000 books; 5,000 pamphlets; 4 current periodicals. Stock not available on loan

Publications: Sects in Judaism
Main Events and Personalities in Jewish History
Guide to Jewish Names
Festival Guides
Spanish Jewry
Guide to Jewish Knowledge
Dictionary of Judaism

BIRMINGHAM BIRMINGHAM LAW SOCIETY *Tel.:* 021-643 9116
The Law Library
131 8 Temple Street
Birmingham 2

Enquiries: To Librarian, by letter only

Scope: Law
Secondary: Historical legal collection

Stock: 30,000 books and pamphlets; 40 current periodicals. Stock not normally available on loan

BIRMINGHAM BIRMINGHAM LIBRARY *Tel.:* 021-236 3591
Margaret Street
132 Birmingham 3

Private subscription library of books and gramophone records

Enquiries: To Librarian

Scope: History, literature and fine arts
Secondary: Social sciences, theology. No information service. Stock available on loan only through Regional Library Bureaux

BIRMINGHAM BIRMINGHAM PUBLIC LIBRARIES *Tel.:* 021-643 2948, 5153,
Central Library 7670 and 7677
133 Ratcliff Place *Telex:* 33455
Birmingham 1

Enquiries: To City Librarian

Scope: *Local Studies Library:* 88,000 printed and 100,000 manuscript items relating to Birmingham and Staffordshire, Warwickshire and Worcestershire. Includes Baskerville and Priestley Collections
Shakespeare Library: 40,000 volumes in 86 languages
Social Sciences Library: including British and U.S. Patents
Visual Aids Department: 280,000 mounted illustrations, and lantern slides and transparencies, available for loan
Gramophone Record Library: 5,000 records available for loan
Other Special Collections: Byron; Cervantes; Civil War tracts; Samuel Johnson; Kings Norton and Sheldon Parish libraries; Milton; Parker Collection of children's books; William Shenstone; Sir Benjamin Stone Collection of photographs; Warwickshire Photographic Survey; World War I poetry
United Nations Depository Library
Diocesan Record Office for Birmingham and approved manorial depository

Stock: Total stock of Reference Library 800,000 books of which 90,000 are technical and 11,000 commercial, some of these falling within the category of 'social sciences'; 2,600 current periodicals including 1,000 technical and 600 commercial (including some in social sciences); 120 incunabula

Publications: Catalogue of the Birmingham Collection, 1918–1931. 2 volumes
Periodicals in the Commercial Library. 1966
Birmingham Shakespeare Library: brief description. 1968
Shakespeare Exhibition Catalogue. 1964
List of play sets in the Central Lending Library. 1967
Birmingham before 1800: six maps. 1968
Miscellaneous duplicated booklists

BIRMINGHAM 134 BIRMINGHAM REGIONAL HOSPITAL BOARD   *Tel.:* 021-454 4828
146 Hagley Road
Birmingham 16

Enquiries: To Medical Officer, Publications, by letter only

Scope: Capital programme in Birmingham Region (Hereford, Shropshire, Stafford, Warwickshire, Worcester). Details of building projects, policies in development of services, and of work completed in Birmingham Region. Details of hospital activity analysis, populations, bed-states, computer projects. Details of medical research supported financially by the Board. Details of some organizational investigations into hospital management carried out by the Board

Stock: 200 books (on various aspects of medical administration and planning); 500 pamphlets; 15 current periodicals. Stock not available on loan

BIRMINGHAM 135 BRITISH POSTAL CHESS FEDERATION   *Tel.:* 021-440 3352
75 Bristol Road
Edgbaston
Birmingham 15
Aims to harmonize the activities of Correspondence Chess organizations

Enquiries: To Hon. Secretary

Scope: Information can be given on correspondence chess matters (not tuition)
No library

BIRMINGHAM 136 THE BUDGERIGAR SOCIETY   *Tel.:* 021-554 0897
6 Grove Lane
Handsworth
Birmingham 21

Enquiries: To General Secretary

Scope: Information on all matters appertaining to the Budgerigar, its breeding, exhibiting, new colours and expectations from varied matings
No library

Publications: Four bulletins per year of general interest to all who keep budgerigars
Year Book and Members List (every three years)

BIRMINGHAM 137 CITY OF BIRMINGHAM COLLEGE OF EDUCATION   *Tel.:* 021-454 5106
Westbourne Road
Edgbaston
Birmingham 15

Enquiries: To Librarian

BIRMINGHAM, CITY OF BIRMINGHAM COLLEGE OF EDUCATION, *cont.*

Scope: Education; children's literature

Stock: 42,000 books and pamphlets; 200 current periodicals

BIRMINGHAM	CITY OF BIRMINGHAM MUSEUM AND ART GALLERY *Tel.:* 021-235 2835
138	Congreve Street Birmingham 3

Enquiries: To Director

Scope: Literature is published and enquiries answered on items in the permanent collections, particularly in the field of art. Opinions on paintings, ceramics, coins and other material are given to members of the public who bring these in for inspection

No library

Publications: Various guidebooks and catalogues

BIRMINGHAM	ERGONOMICS INFORMATION ANALYSIS CENTRE *Tel.:* 021-472 1301 ext. 1066 and 516
139	Department of Engineering Production University of Birmingham Edgbaston Birmingham 15

Collects and disseminates information in the field of ergonomics; investigates the optimum method of storage, retrieval and dissemination to meet the current needs of research and industry in this field

Enquiries: To Director

Scope: The information service provides information in aspects of psychology, physiology, anatomy and engineering which are concerned with the scientific study of human performance and human factors in work, which, in turn, can be applied to machine control and equipment design and environment for optimum man–machine efficiency. The Centre provides the service in the following ways: a quarterly abstract journal, Ergonomics Abstracts; preparation of special bibliographies in particular areas; detailed answering service to enquiries by telephone or post; consultancy by a member of the Centre's staff to deal with applied problems which cannot be dealt with by factual information only

Stock: Reports and 500 current periodicals

Publications: Ergonomics Abstracts (quarterly, published by Taylor & Francis Ltd)

BIRMINGHAM	FIRCROFT COLLEGE *Tel.:* 021-472 0116
140	1018 Bristol Road Selly Oak Birmingham 29

Liberal adult education for men over 20, with experience of working life

Enquiries: To Principal

Scope: Economics, politics, government, history, sociology, English literature

Secondary: Psychology, social sciences, philosophy, international affairs, education, particularly adult education

Stock: 8,000 books; 7 current periodicals. Stock not available on loan

Publications: Will Harvey Memorial Lectures (on topics concerning adult education)

BIRMINGHAM	GARRETTS GREEN TECHNICAL COLLEGE	*Tel.:* 021-743 4471
141	Garretts Green Lane Birmingham 33	

Enquiries: To Librarian

Scope: Stock covers the subjects offered at the College, including English language and literature, French, German, geography, history, principles of accounts and commerce
Human biology, general studies, calculations, English and physics, for Cadet Nurses
Commercial and secretarial subjects

Stock: 12,000 items, including information folders of newspaper and periodical cuttings

Publications: Accessions Lists

Member of the Birmingham Public Libraries Works Libraries Loan Scheme

BIRMINGHAM	HANDSWORTH AND ERDINGTON TECHNICAL COLLEGE	*Tel.:* 021-554 5614
142	Golds Hill Road Handsworth Birmingham 21	

Enquiries: To Librarian

Scope: Social sciences, law, economics (including economic history), education, language, literature, history of costume
Secondary: History, geography, fine arts

Stock: 3,500 books; 150 pamphlets; 30 current periodicals

Member of the Birmingham Public Libraries Works Libraries Loan Scheme

BIRMINGHAM	HOLLYMOOR HOSPITAL
	Northfield
143	Birmingham 31

Enquiries: To Medical Librarian, by letter only

Scope: Psychiatry, psychology and neurology
Secondary: Collections of papers and books relating to the Focal Sepsis era in psychiatry, and to the work of Sir F. Mott

Stock: 650 books; 50 pamphlets; 30 reports; 23 current periodicals. Stock not available on loan but photocopies may be supplied

There are libraries of much smaller scope at Rubery Hill Hospital and John Conolly Hospital (adjacent to this hospital) which share common facilities

BIRMINGHAM	INSTITUTE OF ACCIDENT SURGERY	*Tel.:* 021-643 7041
	Birmingham Accident Hospital	
144	Bath Row Birmingham 15	

Promotion of knowledge and skill in the care of injured persons

Enquiries: To Secretary

Scope: The Institute has no library of its own but advises the hospital management committee on the selection and purchase of books. The service is that of teaching rather than providing information

Stock: 140 books on orthopaedic, plastic and other surgery related to the care of the injured; physiology, pathology and general medical subjects; 19 current periodicals

Publications: Injury (quarterly, published by John Wright & Sons Ltd)

BIRMINGHAM	MATTHEW BOULTON TECHNICAL COLLEGE	*Tel.:* 021-440 2681
145	Sherlock Street Birmingham 5	

Enquiries: To Librarian

Scope: Accountancy; animal nursing; audiology; banking; chiropody; dentistry; government; law; management; marketing; medical laboratory technology; pharmacy; public cleansing; public health inspection; retail and wholesale distribution; sociology and social welfare

Stock: 7,000 books; 500 pamphlets; 75 current periodicals

BIRMINGHAM	MEDICAL RESEARCH COUNCIL EXPERIMENTAL PATHOLOGY OF SKIN UNIT	*Tel.:* 021-472 2103
146	The Medical School University of Birmingham Birmingham 15	

Enquiries: To Director, by letter only

Scope: Research into the experimental pathology of both normal and abnormal skin

Stock: 500 books; 100 pamphlets; 25 current periodicals. Stock not available on loan

BIRMINGHAM	MEDICAL RESEARCH COUNCIL NEUROPHARMACOLOGY UNIT	*Tel.:* 021-472 1642
147	Department of Experimental Neuropharmacology The Medical School University of Birmingham Birmingham 15	

Study of the actions of drugs on the central nervous system, with particular reference to the correlation between electrophysiological and behavioural effects and to interactions with sensory stimuli; also the sites of action of drugs in the brain, particularly in relation to synaptic transmission

Enquiries: To Director, by letter only

Scope: Pharmacology, physiology, biochemistry
Secondary: Neuro-anatomy, psychology, laboratory animal books

Stock: 220 books; 50 pamphlets; 20 current periodicals

BIRMINGHAM	ST ANDREW'S HALL	*Tel.:* 021-472 0143
148	Weoley Park Road Selly Oak Birmingham 29	

Missionary training college. A community (one of the Selly Oak Colleges) of those engaged in this training for service in their homeland or away from it, from many nationalities

Enquiries: To Librarian

Scope: Training in mission, with particular reference to missionary work of the Baptist Missionary Society, the Congregational Council for World Mission (formerly the London Missionary Society) and the Presbyterian Church of England Overseas Committee with countries and churches involved

Stock: 9,000 books; 10 current periodicals

Main Library is the Central Library of the Selly Oak Colleges (no. 149), to whom reference should first be made

BIRMINGHAM	SELLY OAK COLLEGES LIBRARY	*Tel.:* 021-472 4231
	Birmingham 29	
149	Provides for staff and students of colleges engaged in adult education and in training for social, educational and Christian evangelistic work, in this country and overseas	

Enquiries: To Librarian

Scope: Theology; comparative religion (particularly Islamic studies); Christian missionary movement
Secondary: Sociology, social work, social anthropology
Special collections: Mingana Collection of Oriental Manuscripts (600 Syriac, 2,000 Arabic, a few Persian, Ethiopic and Armenian)
20 Western Manuscripts (Greek and Latin)
9 Incunabula
Rendel Harris Collection of papyri

Stock: 60,000 books and pamphlets; 214 current periodicals

Publications: Catalogue of the Mingana Collection of manuscripts. Volumes 1–4, 1933–1963. A. Mingana and D. Hopwood, eds.

BIRMINGHAM	SOUTH BIRMINGHAM TECHNICAL COLLEGE	*Tel.:* 021-476 1131
	Bristol Road South	
150	Birmingham 31	

Enquiries: To Librarian

Scope: Electrical, mechanical and production engineering, civil engineering, building, architecture, management, general studies, physics, chemistry, mathematics, metallurgy, economics, law and sociology

Stock: 7,500 books; 2,500 pamphlets; 100 current periodicals

BIRMINGHAM	SWIMMING TEACHER'S ASSOCIATION OF GREAT	*Tel.:* 021-357 4040
	BRITAIN AND THE COMMONWEALTH	
151	29 Scott Road	
	Great Barr	
	Birmingham 22a	
	Professional Association for teachers of swimming and diving	

Enquiries: To Secretary, by letter only

Scope: Swimming and diving and all forms of the aquatic arts
Secondary: Underwater swimming

Stock: 200 books; 3,000 pamphlets; 3 current periodicals

Publications: Incorporated Swimming Teacher

BIRMINGHAM	UNIVERSITY OF ASTON IN BIRMINGHAM	*Tel.:* 021-359 3611
	LIBRARY	
152	Gosta Green	
	Birmingham 4	

Enquiries: To Librarian

Scope: Physics, chemistry, mathematics, biological sciences, chemical, mechanical, civil and production engineering, metallurgy, pharmacy, building, physiology
Secondary: Law, history, education, languages (French, German, Russian), philosophy, psychology, librarianship

BIRMINGHAM, UNIVERSITY OF ASTON IN BIRMINGHAM LIBRARY, *cont.*

Stock: 80,000 books including 5,000 humanities and 1,500 medicine; 400 pamphlets; 1,500 current periodicals including 140 humanities and 115 medicine

See also no. 153

BIRMINGHAM

153

UNIVERSITY OF ASTON IN BIRMINGHAM
SOCIAL SCIENCES LIBRARY
Maple House
158 Corporation Street
Birmingham 4

Tel.: 021-359 3611 ext. 532

Enquiries: To Librarian

Scope: Psychology, sociology, statistics, politics, economics, industrial/commercial law, administration, welfare, trade, business management

Stock: 15,000 books; 150 current periodicals

See also no. 152

BIRMINGHAM

154

UNIVERSITY OF BIRMINGHAM LIBRARY
P.O. Box 363
Edgbaston
Birmingham 15

Tel.: 021-472 1301
Telex: 338160

Enquiries: To Librarian

Scope: Those subjects covered by the Faculties of the University which fall within the scope of this volume are arts (including education); commerce and social science; law; medicine (including dentistry). Main subjects represented in the bookstock are:

Arts: Ancient history and archaeology; drama and theatre arts; fine arts; education; English, French, German, Italian, Spanish and Portuguese languages and literatures; geography; linguistics; Latin and Greek language and literature; history (including American history); philosophy; music; theology

Commerce and Social Sciences: Accounting; economics, econometrics, mathematical economics, economic and social history, industrial economics and business studies; political science; social administration; sociology; Russian and East European studies

Law (all in the Harding Law Library)

Medicine (all in the Barnes Medical Library): Anaesthetics, anatomy, bacteriology, biochemistry, medicine, neurosurgery, obstetrics and gynaecology, paediatrics and child health, mental subnormality, pathological studies, pharmacology, physiology, psychiatry, social medicine, surgery; dentistry (dental prosthetics, oral pathology, conservative dentistry, dental health)

Secondary: Less common subjects taught in the University (and therefore represented in the bookstock) are physical education (including collections on history of physical education and on athletics); modern Greek language and literature; drama (including large collection of theatre programmes and criticism); programmed learning; local government administration; American history

Special Collections: Manuscripts: Papers of Joseph and Austen Chamberlain; of John Galsworthy; of Francis Brett Young

Books: Hely Hutchinson (Baskerville books); Wedgwood (philology); Thos. Wigan library (17th century literature and theology); Parish libraries: St Mary's Warwick and Bengeworth; Library of the Birmingham Medical Institute; Alma-Tadema Collection (mainly photographs of archaeological interest)

Institutes and Centres within the University (whose interests are strongly represented in the

bookstock of the Main Library or of Institute or Department libraries): Centre of West Africa Studies; Centre for Russian and East European Studies; Institute of Local Government Studies; Centre for Urban and Regional Studies; National Centre for Programmed Learning (no. 155); Institute for the Study of Worship and Religious Architecture; Institute of Judicial Administration; Shakespeare Institute; Institute of Child Health; Centre for Child Study
Other Libraries in the University:
School of Education (no. 156); Barber Fine Art library; Shakespeare Institute (mainly microfilm and microprint editions of early printed books)

Stock: 500,000 books and pamphlets (in subjects mentioned above); 6,500 current periodicals (in all subjects)

Publications: University Research Committee: Research and Publications (annually)

BIRMINGHAM

155

UNIVERSITY OF BIRMINGHAM
NATIONAL CENTRE FOR PROGRAMMED
    LEARNING
50 Wellington Road
Edgbaston
Birmingham 15

Tel.: 021-440 2332

Aims to collect and disseminate information about the development and use of programmed learning in the U.K. and abroad; to conduct research into fundamental problems in the area of programmed learning and of learning theory in general; and to act as an advisory centre and maintain an exhibition of programmed texts and other techniques

Enquiries: To Information Officer

Scope: Programmed learning and structured instruction in general, presented by the teacher, the printed word, audio-visual aids, computers, self-instructional kits. Details of materials available and of research in progress

Stock: 520 programmed texts; 150 reports; 18 current periodicals. Stock not available on loan

Publications: Research Reports, 1–29
Research Memoranda
Programmed instruction and teaching machines: an annotated bibliography. W. E. Dodd and A. England. 2nd edition 1965
Programmed learning and foreign language teaching: a bibliography of programmes and reports. M. J. Tobin and H. St. Matthew-Daniel. 1967
Programmes in the health sciences: a bibliography of self-instructional materials for dental, medical and nursing students. L. A. Biran and R. E. Wakeford. 1970
Programmes in print which are suitable for use in the primary school. J. A. F. Waller. 1968
Exhibition open to all. Anyone interested should write or telephone to arrange a visit

BIRMINGHAM

156

UNIVERSITY OF BIRMINGHAM
SCHOOL OF EDUCATION
P.O. Box 363
Birmingham 15

Tel.: 021-472 1301 ext. 663

Enquiries: To Librarian

Scope: Education
Secondary: Psychology; sociology

Stock: 46,000 books, pamphlets and reports; 300 current periodicals

Publications: Educational Review
Educational Monographs

BIRMINGHAM, UNIVERSITY OF BIRMINGHAM, SCHOOL OF EDUCATION, *cont.*

The Library provides a service of education literature and information both within the University and to teachers and others in the West Midlands. It houses the Union Catalogue of books in Institutes and Schools of Education libraries

BIRMINGHAM

157

WESTHILL COLLEGE OF EDUCATION *Tel.:* 021-472 1563
Selly Oak
Birmingham 29

Training of teachers and youth leaders. Courses for community wardens and workers in Church education

Enquiries: To Deputy Principal or Principal, by letter only

Scope: Library stock falling within the scope of the Directory is as follows: Philosophy, economics, education, psychology, all aspects of the social sciences, theology, history, geography, literature, fine arts and physical education. No Information Service or special collections

Stock: 20,000 books and pamphlets; 140 current periodicals

Publications: Experience and Worship
Living and Praising
Eighty Thousand Adolescents; a study of young people in the City of Birmingham

BIRMINGHAM

158

WOODBROOKE COLLEGE *Tel.:* 021-472 0072 and 4516
1046 Bristol Road
Selly Oak
Birmingham 29

Established in 1903 by the Society of Friends this college offers preparation for various forms of Christian service to men and women of 18 years and upwards, whether or not connected with the Society of Friends

Enquiries: To Librarian, by letter only

Scope: The Quaker Library formed of collections belonging to John Wilhelm Rowntree, Thomas Hodgkin, William Charles Braithwaite, William Littleboy and Edward Grubb. A group of books used by the late F. J. Powicke in writing his volumes on the life of Richard Baxter and the Cambridge Platonists. The Bevan-Naish collections of Quaker thought and history in tracts and broadsides of the 17th and 18th centuries
Secondary: The foundations of the Christian faith; modern religious thought; the Bible; education, social studies and international relations

Stock: 20,000 books and pamphlets; 21 current periodicals

Publications: Swarthmore Lectures
Woodbrooke Occasional Papers

BISHOP AUCKLAND
Co. Durham

159

BISHOP AUCKLAND TECHNICAL COLLEGE *Tel.:* Bishop Auckland 3052
Woodhouse Lane
Bishop Auckland
Co. Durham

Enquiries: To Librarian

Scope: Books, mostly general, in social sciences and medicine

Stock: 1,000 books in all classes; 250 pamphlets; 9 current periodicals in social sciences and humanities; filmstrips; wallcharts

Publications: Monthly Bulletin of Recent Additions
Catalogue of Wallcharts

BISHOP'S STORTFORD Herts **160**	HOCKERILL COLLEGE OF EDUCATION Dunmow Road Bishop's Stortford Hertfordshire	*Tel.:* Bishop's Stortford 3475

Enquiries: To Librarian

Scope: Education. Religion and theology, English literature, fine arts, music, French and German languages, British history, social science

Stock: 25,000 books; 1,000 pamphlets; 125 current periodicals

BLACKBURN Lancs **161**	BLACKBURN COLLEGE OF TECHNOLOGY AND DESIGN Feilden Street Blackburn BB2 1LH Lancashire	*Tel.:* Blackburn 54111

Enquiries: To Librarian

Scope: Stock related to the courses offered by the College covering: economics, education, fine arts, geography, history, law, languages and literature, nursing and sociology

Stock: 13,000 books; 620 pamphlets; 230 current periodicals (total stock). Complete set of British Standards

BLACKBURN Lancs **162**	BLACKBURN PUBLIC LIBRARIES Library Street Blackburn BB1 7AJ Lancashire	*Tel.:* Blackburn 59511

Enquiries: To Director

Scope: Subject specialization: Diseases of the glandular system; Numismatics; Artistic metalwork; European paintings; Engraving and lithography; General geography of Great Britain
Special Collections: Hart Collection—incunabula, early printed books, illuminated manuscripts, bibliography, numismatics, fine bindings
James Dunn Collection—18th and 19th century illustrations and illustrated books, incunabula, fine bindings and first editions

Stock: 187,500 books and pamphlets; 100 current periodicals (total stock)

Publications: Hart Catalogue
Select catalogue

Linguaphone language courses available
Joint administration of Law Library with Blackburn Law Association

BLACKBURN Lancs **163**	CHORLEY COLLEGE OF EDUCATION (BLACKBURN DIVISION) 103 Preston New Road Blackburn Lancashire	*Tel.:* Blackburn 60877

Enquiries: To Librarian

Scope: Education, drama, English, environmental studies, French, human biology, sociology
Secondary: Music, physical education, social statistics

Stock: 4,500 books; 75 current periodicals

BLACKBURN Lancs **164**	COUNTY BOROUGH OF BLACKBURN MUSEUM AND ART GALLERY Library Street Blackburn Lancashire	*Tel.:* Blackburn 59511

Enquiries: To Director
Scope: English Watercolours. T. B. Lewis Collection of Japanese Prints
Secondary: 19th and 20th century British Oil Paintings
Publications: Catalogue of Japanese Prints

BLACKBURN Lancs **165**	NATIONAL FEDERATION OF OLD AGE PENSIONS ASSOCIATIONS Pensioner House 91 Preston New Road Blackburn Lancashire	*Tel.:* Blackburn 52606

Enquiries: To General Secretary
Scope: Old age pensions
No library
Publications: The Pensioners' Voice (monthly)

BLACKPOOL Lancs **166**	ASSOCIATION OF BRITISH DENTAL SURGERY ASSISTANTS LTD. Bank Chambers 3 Market Place Poulton Blackpool Lancashire	*Tel.:* 0391-2 4223

Enquiries: To Secretary
Scope: All information regarding education, training, qualification and employment of dental surgery assistants
Publications: Dental Surgery Assisting as a Career (booklet)

BLACKPOOL Lancs **167**	BLACKPOOL CENTRAL PUBLIC LIBRARY Queen Street Blackpool Lancashire	*Tel.:* Blackpool 23977

Enquiries: To Librarian
Scope: N.W.R.L.S. subject specialization includes: Medicine of the digestive system; domestic science; fine arts; Russia, history and travel (1,800 volumes)
Fiction Reserve scheme: Authors BRI–BRO (400 volumes)
Blackpool and District Law Society Library (2,000 volumes)
Local history (560 books, 747 pamphlets and 520 illustrations)
Music sets of vocal scores and miscellaneous sheet music
Stock: As noted above, plus 117 current periodicals (total stock)

BLACKPOOL Lancs **168**	BLACKPOOL COLLEGE OF TECHNOLOGY AND ART Palatine Road Blackpool Lancashire	*Tel.:* Blackpool 29071

Enquiries: To Librarian

Scope: Hotel management, food technology, art, graphic design, photography, mechanical and electrical engineering, building
Secondary: Economics, accountancy, language, law, general science

Stock: 15,000 books; 500 pamphlets; 300 current periodicals

BLETCHLEY Bucks **169**	NORTH BUCKS COLLEGE OF EDUCATION Bletchley Park Bletchley Buckinghamshire	*Tel.:* Bletchley 2416

Enquiries: To Principal

Scope: Subjects which bear a relation to the training of teachers, including child psychology, sociology and In-Service training

Stock: 16,500 books; 54 current periodicals. Stock not normally available on loan, but photocopies of periodical articles supplied

BLETCHLEY Bucks **170**	WOLVERTON COLLEGE OF FURTHER EDUCATION BUSINESS STUDIES DEPARTMENT Westfield Road Bletchley Buckinghamshire	*Tel.:* Bletchley 2199

See no. 2308

BODMIN Cornwall **171**	BODMIN BOROUGH MUSEUM Guildhall Fore Street Bodmin Cornwall

Enquiries: To Curator, Bodmin Borough Museum, 13 Rock Lane, Bodmin, Cornwall

Scope: Local history of Bodmin area
No library

BODMIN Cornwall **172**	BODMIN MEDICAL LIBRARY St Lawrence's Hospital Bodmin Cornwall	*Tel.:* Bodmin 3281

Enquiries: To Hon. Librarian, by letter only

Scope: Psychiatric, neurological, physiological and psychological studies at Postgraduate level
Stock not available on loan

BOGNOR REGIS Sussex 173	BOGNOR REGIS COLLEGE OF EDUCATION Bognor Regis Sussex	*Tel.:* Bognor Regis 5581

Enquiries: To Librarian, by letter only
Scope: General subjects; education
Stock: 21,700 books; 150 current periodicals

BOLTON Lancs 174	BOLTON COLLEGE OF EDUCATION (TECHNICAL) Chadwick Street Bolton Lancashire	*Tel.:* Bolton 22132

Enquiries: To Librarian
Scope: Education (particularly further education) and including educational psychology, educational technology (programmed learning and audiovisual aids, which form a special collection), industrial training and nursing education
Stock: 31,000 books and pamphlets; 300 current periodicals; 1,400 visual aids
Publications: Monthly library Bulletin (indexes periodicals for subjects in education and training)
College shares publication of *Vocational Aspect* with three other Colleges of Education (Technical): Huddersfield, Wolverhampton, Garnett.

Learning Resources Centre of all types of visual aids and programmed instruction materials, which it is hoped, will develop into a regional centre for study of Educational Technology. At present administered by the library

BOLTON Lancs 175	BOLTON INSTITUTE OF TECHNOLOGY Deane Road Bolton Lancashire	*Tel.:* Bolton 28851

Enquiries: To Librarian
Scope: The scope of the stock covers a wide range of scientific, technical and managerial fields, the subjects corresponding primarily to the subjects of the teaching departments. The stock in arts, social sciences and humanities is being developed and strengthened to meet the needs of an expanding curriculum. N.W.R.L.S. subject specialization: Man-made textiles; industrial safety
Stock: 26,000 books; 5,000 pamphlets and reports; 380 current periodicals. Complete set of British Standards
Publications: Fortnightly lists of contents of periodical articles received
Occasional bibliographies, for example Nodular Iron
Accessions lists

BOLTON Lancs 176	BOLTON MEDICAL INSTITUTE LIBRARY The Royal Infirmary Bolton Lancashire Postgraduate Medical Library

Enquiries: To Librarian
Scope: Books and periodicals on all aspects of medicine, surgery, gynaecology, ophthalmology,

orthopaedics, paediatrics, geriatrics, laryngology and otology, anaesthetics, pathology, obstetrics, oralogy

Stock: 250 books; 44 current periodicals. Stock available on loan to Members of The Bolton Medical Society and the Bolton Medical Institute including Doctors, Pharmacists and Dentists in the area

BOLTON   BOLTON MUSEUM AND ART GALLERY   *Tel.:* Bolton 22311
Lancs   Civic Centre
  Bolton
177   Lancashire

Enquiries: To Director

Scope: Natural history including vertebrate and invertebrate zoology and geology
Secondary: Egyptology. Fine and applied art; archaeology

Stock: Several thousand books

Publications: Guides to Collections

BOLTON   BOLTON PUBLIC LIBRARIES   *Tel.:* Bolton 22311
Lancs   Central Library   (evenings and Satur-
  Bolton   days 23543)
178   Lancashire

Enquiries: To Librarian

Scope: *Special collections* include: Architecture of public buildings, churches and educational and scientific buildings; diseases of the cardiovascular system
Whitman Collection: many inscribed copies and association items, some personal relics, numerous letters from Whitman's literary executors

Stock: 117,000 non-fiction books; 348 current periodicals (total stock)

BOLTON   FARNWORTH PUBLIC LIBRARY   *Tel.:* Farnworth 72101 or
Lancs   Farnworth   Farnworth 72790
  Bolton BL4 7PG   (after 5.30 pm and
179   Lancashire   Saturdays)

Enquiries: To Librarian

Scope: N.W.R.L.S. subject specialization includes: American literature; Australasia

Stock: 44,000 books; 60 current periodicals (total stock)

BOLTON   ST ANNE'S CHURCH TURTON   *Tel.:* Turton 222
Lancs   High Street
  Turton
180   Bolton
  Lancashire

Enquiries: To Vicar, Turton Vicarage, Bolton, Lancashire

Scope: This chained library was given to the Church in 1651 by the will of Humphrey Chetham of Manchester and contains Scripture commentaries of the late 16th and early 17th century

BOLTON   TILLOTSONS NEWSPAPERS LTD   *Tel.:* Bolton 22345
Lancs   Mealhouse Lane
  Bolton
181   Lancashire

Enquiries: To Librarian, by letter only

BOLTON, TILLOTSONS NEWSPAPERS LTD, *cont.*
    Scope: Information on Bolton and circulation area of the Bolton Evening News
    Stock: Principally cuttings. Stock not available on loan
  Publications: Evening News, Bolton
       Bolton Journal and Guardian
       Six other local journals

BOOTLE BOOTLE COLLEGE OF FURTHER EDUCATION *Tel.:* 051-922 4040
Lancs   Balliol Road
      Bootle 20
182   Lancashire
  Enquiries: To Librarian, by letter only
    Scope: Mechanical engineering, electrical engineering, building, commerce and general studies, art and liberal studies
    Stock: 4,000 books; 30 current periodicals

BOOTLE COUNTY BOROUGH OF BOOTLE LIBRARIES, *Tel.:* 051-922 4040 ext. 245
Lancs   MUSEUM AND ART GALLERY
    Central Library
183   Oriel Road
      Bootle L20 7AG
      Lancashire
  Enquiries: To Director
    Scope: N.W.R.L.S. subject specialization includes: Economics of manufacturing industries; criminology; penology; personal hygiene—effects of stimulants and narcotics
      Fiction: Authors BAL–BAN
      Local history of Bootle and Merseyside
    Stock: 2,000 books; 60 current periodicals
  Publications: Subject guides periodically, for example Canals; Motor Vehicles; Education
       The museum has a small local collection and a collection of English pottery, with 300 books

BOREHAM ATV NETWORK LTD *Tel.:* 01-953 6100
WOOD   Elstree Studios
Herts   Eldon Avenue
      Boreham Wood
184   Hertfordshire
  Enquiries: To Librarian
    Scope: Art, architecture, design, graphic design, television, theatre
    Stock: 2,700 books; 75 current periodicals; 20,000 photographs (mainly architectural)

BOREHAM BOREHAM WOOD COLLEGE OF FURTHER *Tel.:* 01-953 6024
WOOD   EDUCATION
Herts   Elstree Way
      Boreham Wood
185   Hertfordshire
  Enquiries: To Tutor Librarian
    Scope: Technical and further education. Modern methods of language teaching. Home economics
    Stock: 2,000 books; 30 current periodicals

BOSTON Lincs 186	BOSTON PARISH LIBRARY St Botolph's Church Boston Lincolnshire	

Enquiries: To Librarian

Scope: A number of 16th and 17th century Latin, Greek and Hebrew grammars and texts. A very few scientific and botanical books of the 17th century which have a little herbal medical material. A few cosmographies. Two or three books on 16th and 17th century education

Stock: Books: 12 (medical information), 3 (educational), 100 (humanities). Stock not available on loan, and for reference by appointment only

BOSTON Lincs 187	BOSTON PUBLIC LIBRARY Municipal Buildings West Street Boston Lincolnshire	*Tel.:* Boston 4601

Enquiries: To Librarian

Scope: The local collection contains the 19th century W. H. Wheeler Collection relating to Boston and the Fens with particular reference to Fen drainage and has some original maps of the area. It also contains papers relating to the building of Boston Dock in 1880

Stock: 500 books (local collection; total stock 23,000); 50 pamphlets

BOSTON SPA Yorkshire 188	NATIONAL LENDING LIBRARY FOR SCIENCE AND TECHNOLOGY Boston Spa Yorkshire	*Tel.:* Boston Spa 2031 *Telex:* 55442

Collects the literature of the world in science and technology, including agriculture and medicine and the periodical literature of the world in all aspects of the social sciences, and provides a rapid postal loan and photocopying service

Enquiries: To Director

Scope: The National Lending Library aims to supplement the internal library resources of existing organizations by providing a rapid postal loan service to organizations on its list of registered borrowers. A photocopying service is available to any organizations or individual in the United Kingdom and overseas
Secondary: The U.K. MEDLARS service is a computer information retrieval service in the broad field of medical science. Its data base is the 1,000,000 references included in *Index Medicus* since January 1964. Enquiries should be addressed to the U.K. MEDLARS Service, at the Library. Unpublished German war-time industrial documents—available in photocopy form only—and the English summaries of these as the CIOS, BIOS and FIAT Reports

Stock: 750,000 book and periodical volumes in all languages; U.S. Government agencies research reports: intake approximately 50,000 per year. Microfiche: more than 200,000 reports. Microfilm of translations and reports: 160 miles, equivalent to about 100,000 volumes; 34,000 current periodicals (total stock)

Publications: List of Current Serials Received from Asia. August 1967
Index of Conference Proceedings received by the N.L.L. (monthly)
List of Books Received from the U.S.S.R. and Translated Books (monthly)
British Research and Development Reports (monthly)
U.K. MEDLARS Information Retrieval Service: A Handbook for Users. October 1968

BOSTON SPA, NATIONAL LENDING LIBRARY FOR SCIENCE AND TECHNOLOGY, *cont.*
    A KWIC Index to the English Language Abstracting and Indexing Publications currently being received by the National Lending Library, 3rd edition. January 1969
    NLL Translations Bulletin (monthly, available from H.M.S.O.)
    Current Serials received by the N.L.L. March, 1967 (available from H.M.S.O.)

BOURNEMOUTH BOURNEMOUTH & POOLE COLLEGE OF ART   *Tel.:* Bournemouth 20772
Hants   Royal London House
     Lansdowne
189   Bournemouth
     Hampshire

    Enquiries: To Librarian
    Scope: Architecture; interior design; environment art and design; dress design; photography; cine film; sculpture; printing; ceramics; graphic design
    Stock: 18,000 books; 500 pamphlets; 190 current periodicals; 20,000 slides. Stock available on loan to local libraries only, but photocopies offered to others
    Publications: Guides to the published work of Art Historians:
         No. 1. Sir Kenneth Clark
         No. 2. Sir Herbert Read
         Architecture: History and Social Studies: Bibliography

BOURNEMOUTH BOURNEMOUTH AND POOLE MEDICAL   *Tel.:* Bournemouth 35201
Hants   SOCIETY
     Post Graduate Medical Centre
190   Royal Victoria Hospital
     Bournemouth
     Hampshire

    Enquiries: To Secretary, by letter only
    Scope: Advances in medical specialities and clinical medicine
         Secondary: Provision of knowledge from standard medical textbooks
    Stock: 696 books; 36 current periodicals

BOURNEMOUTH BOURNEMOUTH COLLEGE OF TECHNOLOGY   *Tel.:* Bournemouth 20844
Hants   Lansdowne
     Bournemouth BH1 3JJ
191   Hampshire

    Enquiries: To Librarian
    Scope: Science; mechanical and electrical engineering; building; economics; politics; languages, literature, law; hotel and catering subjects; tourism; domestic subjects
    Stock: 45,000 books and pamphlets; 500 reports; 650 current periodicals; 300 filmstrips
    Publications: Occasional bibliographies on special subjects

BOURNEMOUTH BOURNEMOUTH MUNICIPAL LIBRARIES   *Tel.:* Bournemouth 26603
Hants   Central Library   *Telex:* 41271
     Lansdowne
192   Bournemouth BH1 3DJ
     Hampshire

    Enquiries: To Librarian
    Scope: Subject specialization: Musical literature; Epistles; Apocalypse; Apocryphal books; Judaism

Special collection of music and musical literature in John B. M. Camm Music Library at the Central Library
H.M.S.O. Selective Subscription Service

Stock: 106,000 books; 1,500 pamphlets; 80 current periodicals (total stock, including 11,000 items in the John B. M. Camm Music Library)

Publications: Local Government Information Sheet (monthly)

BOURNEMOUTH BRITISH MIGRAINE ASSOCIATION *Tel.:* Bournemouth 59379
Hants
6 Bryanstone Road
Bournemouth
193 Hampshire

Enquiries: To Secretary, by letter only

Scope: Mainly devoted to explaining known facts about migraine and its treatment and appropriate medical papers dealing with various aspects of treatment and research

Stock: 4 current periodicals. All National and International References to Migraine

Publications: Migraine—The Facts
Migraine News-Letter

BOURNEMOUTH RUSSELL-COTES ART GALLERY AND MUSEUM *Tel.:* Bournemouth 21009
Hants
East Cliff
Bournemouth BH1 3AA
194 Hampshire

Enquiries: To Curator, by letter only

Scope: Large reference collection of 19th and 20th century theatrical history material, mostly relating to Sir Henry Irving

Stock: 1,000 books; 3,000 pamphlets; 500 reports; 12 current periodicals

Publications: List of Publications
Schools Museum Service Loan and Reference Collection Catalogue

---

BRACKNELL R.A.F. STAFF COLLEGE *Tel.:* Bracknell 4593 ext.
Berks
Bracknell
241
Berkshire
195 *Enquiries:* To Librarian

Scope: Defence subjects, campaign and war histories, strategic studies, aviation, political subjects, history, geography, racial problems and economics

Stock: 10,000 books; 500 pamphlets; 100 current periodicals

BRACKNELL SOUTH EAST BERKS COLLEGE OF FURTHER *Tel.:* Bracknell 20411
Berks
EDUCATION
Church Road
196 Bracknell
Berkshire

Enquiries: To Principal

Scope: Electrical and mechanical engineering, commerce and languages (elementary and intermediate)

Stock: 10,000 books; 1,000 pamphlets; 100 current periodicals

BRADFORD BOLLING HALL MUSEUM *Tel.:* Bradford 25974
Yorkshire Bradford 4
 Yorkshire
197 *Enquiries:* To Keeper
 Scope: Enquiries about local and Bradford history, furniture, costume, ceramics and numismatics. The Museum has collections of material relating to these

BRADFORD BRADFORD CENTRAL PUBLIC LIBRARY *Tel.:* Bradford 33081
Yorkshire Prince's Way *Telex:* 51480
 Bradford 5
198 Yorkshire
 Enquiries: To City Librarian
 Scope: General, divided among separate Departments of Art; Commerce, Science and Technology, including medicine and economics; Local History, covering Bradford and immediate neighbourhood; Music; Social Sciences, including education, language and literature, history, geography and theology. Lending and reference material in all Departments
 Secondary: Special collections: Sociology; local archives; Federer Collection of Yorkshire books and pamphlets
 Stock: 209,000 books and pamphlets; 300 current periodicals; 17,500 musical scores; 4,500 gramophone records

BRADFORD BRADFORD CITY ART GALLERY AND *Tel.:* Bradford 48247
Yorkshire   MUSEUMS
 Cartwright Hall
199 Lister Park
 Bradford 9
 Yorkshire
 Enquiries: To Director
 Scope: Specialist departments in fine art, ceramics; local collections of natural history, archaeology, geology and industry. Specialist staff and reference books are available in these subjects
 Stock not available on loan

BRADFORD BRADFORD TECHNICAL COLLEGE *Tel.:* Bradford 28837
Yorkshire Great Horton Road
 Bradford 7
200 Yorkshire
 Enquiries: To Librarian
 Scope: Textiles, building, civil engineering, metallurgy, banking, accountancy, marketing, food technology, hairdressing, social sciences, languages
 Stock: 18,000 books; 300 current periodicals. Barbour Index. British Standards. Halsbury's Laws

BRADFORD UNIVERSITY OF BRADFORD LIBRARY *Tel.:* Bradford 33466
Yorkshire Bradford 7 *Telex:* 51309
 Yorkshire
201 *Enquiries:* To Librarian
 Scope: Pharmacy; ophthalmic optics. Philosophy; geography; history; psychology; sociology; social services; politics; government and public administration; education; economics; modern languages and literature (French, German, Russian, Spanish)

Secondary: Religion; law; medicine; town and country planning; architecture; fine arts; photography

Stock: 45,000 books and pamphlets; 700 current periodicals

Publications: Periodicals in Stock (annually)

BRADFORD WOOL, JUTE AND FLAX INDUSTRY *Tel.:* Bradford 26493
Yorkshire   TRAINING BOARD
             55 Well Street
202   Bradford 1

Enquiries: To Secretary

Scope: All aspects of training, including management training, relating to activities in the industries within the scope of the Board, namely the wool, jute, flax and cordage industries. Limited number of films on job opportunities in the textile industry

Stock: 500 books and pamphlets; 18 current periodicals

Publications: Training Recommendations
Regular bulletins and newsheets on the Board's activities
Systematic Training Schemes for selected operative tasks

BRECHIN   GLENESK FOLK MUSEUM   *Tel.:* Tarfside 236
Angus   The Retreat
              Glenesk
203   Brechin
              Angus

Enquiries: To Hon. Curator

Scope: Information on local social history can be provided from a collection of documentary evidence and from the Museum exhibits themselves

Stock: 8,000 exhibits, including documents collected in book form. Stock not available on loan

Publications: A Guide to Glenesk Folk Museum
A Glen Anthology

BRECON   THE BRECKNOCK COUNTY MUSEUM   *Tel.:* Brecon 2218
              Glamorgan Street
204   Brecon

Enquiries: To Hon. Curator, by letter only

Scope: Natural history collections, archaeology, folk material, documents, papers and books relating to Breconshire history

Publications: Include booklets on local families, local roads and bridges, railways, organizations, ornithology, which usually appear first as articles in the local journal

BRECON   BRECONSHIRE COUNTY LIBRARY   *Tel.:* Brecon 3346
              County Library Headquarters
205   32 High Street
              Brecon

Enquiries: To Librarian

Scope: Local history of Breconshire
Books on Wales and most Welsh books now published

Stock: 500 books

BRECON 206	THE SOUTH WALES BORDERERS REGIMENTAL MUSEUM The Barracks Brecon	*Tel.:* Brecon 3111 ext. 263

Enquiries: To Museum Curator, by letter only
Scope: History of the South Wales Borderers and Monmouthshire Regiment
No library
Publications: Short History of the South Wales Borderers and Monmouthshire Regiment

BRENTFORD Middx 207	BEECHAM PRODUCTS U.K. Lucozade Annexe Great West Road Brentford Middlesex	*Tel.:* 01-560 5151 *Telex:* 22743

Enquiries: To Librarian
Scope: This unit serves the Research and Development Product Laboratories of the Beecham Group and its subject fields include proprietary medicines, pharmaceuticals, food and drink, toiletries and cosmetics. Scope includes: medicine, pharmacy, biology, biochemistry, microbiology, dental science, physical chemistry
Stock: 2,500 books; 300 current periodicals

BRENTFORD Middx 208	BRITISH BROADCASTING CORPORATION TV FILM LIBRARY South Block Reynard Mills Industrial Estate Windmill Road Brentford Middlesex	*Tel.:* 01-567 6655 *Telex:* 22182

Storage and exploitation of all BBC programme material recorded on film
Enquiries: To Assistant in Charge, Film Library Sales for 'footage' requests only
Enquiries about complete programmes (sale or hire) should be put to BBC Television Enterprises, Villiers House, Ealing Broadway, London, W.5. *Tel.:* 01-743 8000
Scope: The entire range of subjects covered by BBC television
Stock: 150,000 film cans

BRENTFORD Middx 209	THE BRITISH PIANO MUSEUM 368 High Street Brentford Middlesex	*Tel.:* 01-560 8108

Enquiries: To Director
Scope: A collection registered as a charitable trust for the preservation of automatic, old and odd musical instruments, including reproducing pianos and organs, orchestrions, nickelodeons, street organs and pianos, automatic violins with piano accompaniment, musical boxes, barrel pianos, square pianos, piano with two vertical key-boards, phonographs, dulcimer, scale model piano and orchestrelle. Technical enquiries and all correspondence must be accompanied by a stamped, addressed envelope, and donations are expected in exchange for extended information supplied
Stock: 20 books; many pamphlets; 6 current periodicals. Stock not available on loan
Publications: Player Piano Group News Letter

BRENTWOOD BRENTWOOD COLLEGE OF EDUCATION *Tel.:* Brentwood 6306
Essex Sawyers' Hall Lane
  Brentwood
210 Essex
  Enquiries: To Tutor Librarian
  Scope: Education: history, methods and psychology. Teaching practice collection. Children's collection. General stock for college courses
  Stock: 30,000 books; 2,000 pamphlets and reports; 200 current periodicals

BRENTWOOD ESPERANTO TEACHERS ASSOCIATION *Tel.:* Brentwood 4574
Essex 87 Sebastian Avenue
  Shenfield
211 Brentwood
  Essex
  Enquiries: To Secretary
  Scope: Education for international understanding through the teaching of Esperanto
  Publications: Esperanto Teacher (3 issues each year, in English about the teaching of Esperanto in Schools)
  Provides exchanges for pupils of Esperanto with almost any country in the world

BRIDGE OF DON *See under* **ABERDEEN** *for*
Aberdeen GREAT NORTH OF SCOTLAND RAILWAY
    ASSOCIATION (no. 8)

BRIDGEND GLAMORGAN COUNTY LIBRARY *Tel.:* Bridgend 55889 and
Glam Coed Parc 4210
  Park Street
212 Bridgend
  Glamorgan
  Enquiries: To Librarian
  Scope: Welsh R.L.S. subject specialization includes: History of philosophy; psychiatry; law; travel; geography
  Stock: 7,300 titles

BRIDGWATER ADMIRAL BLAKE MUSEUM *Tel.:* Bridgwater 2597
Somerset Blake Street
  Bridgwater
213 Somerset
  Enquiries: To Curator
  Scope: History and archaeology of Bridgwater. Life and career of Admiral Robert Blake (1598–1657)
    Secondary: The Monmouth Rebellion and Battle of Sedgemoor, 1685
  Publications: Brief Guide to the Museum (contains extensive reading lists)

BRIDGWATER BRIDGWATER PUBLIC LIBRARY *Tel.:* Bridgwater 2597
Somerset Binford Place
  Bridgwater
214 Somerset
  Enquiries: To Librarian

BRIDGWATER, BRIDGWATER PUBLIC LIBRARY, *cont.*

Scope: Bridgwater History; Battle of Sedgemoor, 1685; Life of Admiral Robert Blake (1598–1657). Subject specialization includes: God; Decorative art and design; Hunting sports—hunting, shooting and fishing

Stock: 2,100 books; 100 pamphlets; 10 current periodicals

BRIDGWATER BRIDGWATER TECHNICAL COLLEGE *Tel.:* Bridgwater 2585
Somerset Broadway
  Bridgwater
215 Somerset

Enquiries: To Tutor Librarian

Scope: Chemistry, engineering and economics, trade unionism and industrial relations

Stock: 6,000 books; 600 pamphlets; 95 current periodicals

The college library forms part of the Somerset County Technical Library Service

BRIDGWATER THE JOHANN STRAUSS SOCIETY OF
Somerset   GREAT BRITAIN
  17 Taunton Road
216 Bridgwater
  Somerset

Aims to promote the performance and recording and further the study and deeper appreciation of the music of the Strauss family and their Viennese contemporaries

Enquiries: To Secretary, by letter only

Scope: All subjects concerning the lives and music of the Strauss family. The Society's Library contains most of the important books dealing with these subjects in English and (mainly) German, and the results of much original research

Stock: 30 books; all publications of Svenska Strauss-Sällskapet and the Association française Johann Strauss et des Maîtres du Divertissement

Publications: Tritsch-Tratsch (magazine, three issues each year)

BRIDGWATER SOMERSET COUNTY LIBRARY *Tel.:* Bridgwater 3494
Somerset Mount Street
  Bridgwater
217 Somerset

Enquiries: To Librarian

Scope: Subject specialization includes: Ancient and oriental philosophers; New Testament; Gospels and Acts; Roman Catholic Church; education; physiology and personal hygiene; China; Japan; Far Eastern Islands; Polar Regions; Somerset; collection of early children's books

Stock: 14,000 books in these subjects

BRIDLINGTON BRIDLINGTON PUBLIC LIBRARY *Tel.:* Bridlington 2917
Yorkshire King Street
  Bridlington
218 Yorkshire

Enquiries: To Librarian

Scope: Small collection of manuscripts of Winifred Holtby. Good collection of books, maps and photographs of Bridlington and East Riding

Stock: 3,000 books and 250 pamphlets in local collection

BRIERLEY HILL Staffs **219**	DUDLEY PUBLIC LIBRARIES BRIERLEY HILL BRANCH LIBRARY Moor Street Brierley Hill Staffordshire *See no. 465*	
BRIGHTON **220**	BRIGHTON COLLEGE OF ART Grand Parade Brighton BN2 2JY Part of Brighton Polytechnic designate	*Tel.:* Brighton 64141

Enquiries: To Librarian

Scope: Fine art, graphic design, interior design, architecture and print making
Secondary: Printing; dress and textiles; decorating; art education

Stock: 16,000 books; 300 pamphlets; 175 current periodicals

BRIGHTON **221**	BRIGHTON COLLEGE OF EDUCATION Falmer Brighton BN1 9PH	*Tel.:* Brighton 66622

Enquiries: To Librarian

Scope: Emphasis on education and related subjects

Stock: 55,000 books; 240 current periodicals

BRIGHTON **222**	BRIGHTON COLLEGE OF TECHNOLOGY Moulsecoomb Brighton BN2 4GJ	*Tel.:* Brighton 67304

Enquiries: To Librarian

Scope: Provision for subjects in College degree or diploma courses as follows: Pharmacy, business studies, social studies, health visiting, management studies, librarianship
Secondary: History, English and foreign literature and fine arts as 'background' studies (small collection)

Stock: 25,000 books; 10,000 pamphlets and reports; 750 current periodicals (total stock)

The business studies and management studies collections are at the College Annexe, 25 Preston Road, Brighton BN1 6SE

BRIGHTON **223**	BRIGHTON PUBLIC LIBRARIES Church Street Brighton	*Tel.:* Brighton 63005 *Telex:* 87167

Enquiries: To Chief Librarian

Scope: *Lewis Collection of foreign books and periodicals:* mainly French, German and Italian, particularly on art and architecture (3,000 volumes)
Matthews Collection of Oriental Books: 3,000 volumes, many early and rare (reference only except in special cases)
Elliot Collection of Religious Books: 3,000 volumes, many early Greek texts, many in French (reference only)
Cobden Pamphlets: rare and early pamphlets on politics and economics, part of *Richard Cobden's Library* (reference only).
Topography, particularly Ackerman fine illustrations 1780–1830 (reference only)

BRIGHTON, BRIGHTON PUBLIC LIBRARIES, *cont.*
>> Bibliography (reference only)
>> Printing and typography (reference and lending)
>> Early biography. Early Religious books. 300 volumes of early children's books (reference only)
>> Incunabula and early printed books (reference only)
>> *Long Collection of Classical Books,* many early Latin and Greek texts (reference only)
>> *Sussex collection,* including photographic survey
>> Houses Brighton and Hove Natural History Society Library (3,000 volumes)
>
> *Stock:* 110,000 reference, 90,000 lending books; 70,000 books in 8 branches; 25,000 pamphlets; 1,100 maps; several thousand illustrations; photographs; 4,000 Sussex postcards; 40 folio cuttings books on Sussex; 425 current periodicals

BRIGHTON

224

INSTITUTE OF DEVELOPMENT STUDIES
>> at the University of Sussex
>> Falmer
>> Brighton
>
> *Enquiries:* To Librarian
>
> *Scope:* Library is a deposit library for UN, FAO, UNESCO, GATT publications. Global subscribers to ILO and WHO publications. (All these are general distribution documents only.) Selective acquisition of other international organizations' publications. As complete a coverage of national government publications as possible within the fields of economic, social and political development, post-1960. Selective holdings of major social science serials and monographs. Library is prepared to answer *ad hoc* requests for information in these fields, either by preparing subject lists or providing addresses of institutions or individuals more competent to answer such requests. There is no formally organized Information Service
>
> *Stock:* 15,000 books, pamphlets and reports; 3,000 current periodicals
>
> *Publications:* Bulletin (termly)
>> Communications
>> Joint Reprint Series (with the School of African and Asian Studies of the University of Sussex)

BRIGHTON

225

UNIVERSITY OF SUSSEX LIBRARY   *Tel.:* Brighton 66755
>> Falmer
>> Brighton BN1 9QL
>
> *Enquiries:* To Librarian
>
> *Scope:* Library service to the Schools of African and Asian Studies; Cultural and Community Studies; English and American Studies; European Studies; and Social Sciences
>> *Secondary:* The library is also concerned in supporting the work of the following: Centre for Contemporary European Studies; Centre for Insurance Studies; Centre for Research in Collective Psychopathology; Institute of Manpower Studies; and Institute for the Study of International Organization
>
> *Stock:* 150,000 books, pamphlets and reports; 1,000 current periodicals (estimated proportions of total stock in the subjects covered by this volume of the Directory)
>> The library and the media services materials of the University have recently been amalgamated and there is a growing collection of non-book materials (sound and video tapes, films and slides) for use in connection with the teaching and research work of the University

BRIGHTON	UNIVERSITY OF SUSSEX	*Tel.:* Brighton 66755
	SCHOOL OF EDUCATION LIBRARY	
226	Falmer	
	Brighton BN1 9QL	

Enquiries: To Librarian

Scope: Curriculum development, including audio-visual materials. Teacher training. Enquiries in the wider field of education should be directed to the University Library (no. 225) where there are 6,000 books on education and related topics

Stock: 1,000 books and pamphlets; 8 current periodicals. Stock available on loan to teachers and student teachers in Sussex

BRIGHTON	UNIVERSITY OF SUSSEX	*Tel.:* Brighton 66755
	SCIENCE POLICY RESEARCH UNIT	
227	Falmer	
	Brighton	

Aims to contribute through its research to the advancement of knowledge of the complex social process of research, invention, development and innovation and thereby to a deeper understanding of policy for science and technology

Enquiries: To Librarian

Scope: The library itself does not offer an information service, but requests for specific information will be passed to the appropriate research worker. The stock covers: history of science; sociology of science, creativity; education, careers; manpower, brain drain; economics of science—R & D evaluation, patents and licensing, innovation and technical change; statistics of science; management of R & D. A collection of material on science in developing countries, particularly China, is being built up

Stock: 2,000 books; 1,000 pamphlets; 1,000 reports; 50 current periodicals

BRISTOL	BRISTOL CITY MUSEUM	*Tel.:* 0272-27256
	Queens Road	
228	Bristol BS8 1RL	

Collection, conservation, research and education in fields of archaeology, natural science, folk life, industrial history, substantially related to the Bristol area

Enquiries: To Director

Scope: Any enquiry relating to the collections of archaeology, natural history, folk life and technology. Any enquiry relating to the study of these subjects in the Bristol area. To this end the museum holds not only collections of objects but also classified collections of information, for example, Distribution of archaeological sites in the area; Photographs of ships which have visited Bristol

Publications: A Brief Numismatic History of Bristol
Guide Catalogue to the South Western Collections of British Archaeology

BRISTOL	BRISTOL MORAVIAN CHURCH	*Tel.:* Bristol 35545
	Upper Maudlin Street	
229	Bristol 2	

Enquiries: To Archivist

Scope: *The Moravian Collection* has now been given to the Library at Bristol Unversity. It contains theological books of the 18th century pertaining to the beginning of the Renewed Moravian Church, founded 1457, under Count Zinzendorf.

BRISTOL, BRISTOL MORAVIAN CHURCH, *cont.*
Other material has been deposited in the Archives of the Moravian Church, 5 Muswell Hill, London N.10

BRISTOL

230

BRISTOL POLYTECHNIC
Unity Street Branch
Bristol 1

Tel.: Bristol 23016

Enquiries: To Librarian

Scope: The Library's main holdings are in the fields of social sciences, modern languages, business management, office management and accountancy

Stock: 27,000 books and pamphlets; 150 reports; 270 current periodicals

BRISTOL

231

BRISTOL POLYTECHNIC
FACULTY OF ART AND DESIGN
Clanage Road
Bower Ashton
Bristol BS3 2JU

Tel.: Bristol 662454

Enquiries: To Librarian

Scope: Fine and applied arts

Stock: 8,500 books; 500 pamphlets; 120 current periodicals

BRISTOL

232

BRISTOL RECORD SOCIETY
Department of History
The University
Bristol

Tel.: Bristol 24161

Enquiries: To Secretary

Scope: The Society is a record publishing body, but it will where possible give information about records relating to the history of Bristol

No library

Publications: Bristol Record Society Publications

BRISTOL

233

BRISTOL REFERENCE LIBRARY
Central Library
College Green
Bristol BS1 5TL

Tel.: Bristol 26121
Telex: 44200

Enquiries: To Librarian

Scope: General information and library service in all subjects except music, fine arts, commerce and technology. *Special collections:* Folk-lore and proverbs (Stuckey Lean Collection); Somerset (Emanuel Green Collection); the private press. Particular attention paid to Bristol history, modern literature, doctrinal theology, caving and pot-holing

Stock: 190,000 books and pamphlets; 3,000 engravings and photographs of local interest; 450 current periodicals. Local history material, manuscripts and other valuable items not available on loan

BRISTOL

234

BRITISH BROADCASTING CORPORATION
Whiteladies Road
Bristol BS8 2LR

Tel.: Bristol 32211

Enquiries: To Information Officer or Assistant Reference Librarian

Scope: Enquiries on broadcasting dealt with. Library stock general

Stock: 2,000 books; 400 pamphlets; 100 reports; 90 current periodicals

BRISTOL	CLIFTON COLLEGE	
	THE PERCIVAL LIBRARY	
235	Bristol 8	

Enquiries: To Librarian, by letter only

Scope: Important collections in the following fields: English literature and criticism; history; biography; classics; modern languages
Secondary: Secondary collections in: art and architecture; music; theatre and cinema; religion and philosophy; social sciences. Collection of material relating to history of the School and the public school movement in the nineteenth century

Stock: 25,000 books

BRISTOL	COLLEGE OF ST MATTHIAS	*Tel.:* Bristol 655384
	Fishponds	
236	Bristol	
	Church of England College of Education	

Enquiries: To Librarian
Scope: General library with a strong education section
Stock: 35,000 books and pamphlets; 170 current periodicals

BRISTOL	MEDICAL RESEARCH COUNCIL	*Tel.:* Bristol 20473 and
	DENTAL UNIT	26884
237	The Dental School	
	Lower Maudlin Street	
	Bristol BS1 2LY	

The Unit is principally concerned with the pathology of dental caries. Present work aims at determining the histological, chemical and physical properties of normal enamel, and the changes occurring in these properties as caries develops

Enquiries: To Secretary, by letter only
Stock: 60 books; 15 pamphlets; 12 reports; 11 current periodicals

This small collection of books and publications forms part of the library of the Dental School of the University of Bristol to whom other enquiries should be addressed

BRISTOL	REDLAND COLLEGE OF EDUCATION	*Tel.:* Bristol 38245
	Redland Hill	
238	Bristol BS6 6UZ	

Enquiries: To Librarian
Scope: Education and child development are areas of specialization
Stock: 5,000 books and pamphlets; 60 current periodicals

BRISTOL	REGIONAL COUNCIL FOR FURTHER	*Tel.:* Bristol 25626
	EDUCATION FOR THE SOUTH WEST	
239	Kent House	
	31/35 Prince Street	
	Bristol BS1 4PH	

Enquiries: To Secretary
Scope: Information on further education in the region which includes Bath, Bristol, Exeter, Gloucester, Plymouth, Torbay, Cornwall, Devon, Dorset, Gloucestershire, Isles of Scilly, Somerset and Wiltshire

BRISTOL, REGIONAL COUNCIL FOR FURTHER EDUCATION FOR THE SOUTH WEST, *cont.*

Publications: Annual Directory of Further Education Courses in the Region (August)
Bulletin of Short Courses (September and January)
Compendium of Advanced Full-time and Sandwich Courses (joint publication of all Regional Councils for Further Education)

BRISTOL

240

SOUNDWELL TECHNICAL COLLEGE *Tel.:* Bristol 671427
St Stephen's Road
Soundwell
Bristol BS16 4RL

Enquiries: To Tutor Librarian

Scope: General collection of textbook material at a fairly low level academically, but education covered widely in connection with Teaching Certificate Courses. Economics, law and nursing have wide selection but emphasis mainly on technical subjects covered by the College

Stock: 10,000 books and pamphlets including 5,000 in the humanities; 100 current periodical including 37 in the humanities

BRISTOL

241

SOUTH WESTERN BLOOD TRANSFUSION SERVICE *Tel.:* Bristol 628021
Southmead Hospital
Southmead
Bristol

Enquiries: To Director, by letter only

Scope: Blood transfusion, medical and technical, including blood bank, blood groups, serology, blood products, Rh haemolytic disease, cross-matching and automation. Tissue typing
Secondary: Immunology

Stock: 50 books; 9 current periodicals. Stock not available on loan

BRISTOL

242

SOUTH WESTERN LARYNGOLOGICAL ASSOCIATION *Tel.:* Bristol 34904
7 Percival Road
Clifton
Bristol BS8 3LE

Enquiries: To Secretary

Scope: Information on all aspects of the otorhinolaryngological service in the South West of England, including teaching facilities for undergraduates and postgraduates, reference sources available in the South West, guidance for visiting overseas specialists
No library

BRISTOL

243

SOUTH WESTERN REGIONAL HOSPITAL BOARD *Tel.:* Bristol 38471
27 Tyndalls Park Road
Bristol BS8 1PJ
Hospital Administration

Enquiries: To Secretary

Scope: No library service, but willing to assist genuine enquirers in the field of hospital administration

| BRISTOL | SOUTHMEAD HOSPITAL | Tel.: Bristol 622821 ext. 243 |

BRISTOL
244

SOUTHMEAD HOSPITAL
Medical Library
Westbury-on-Trym
Bristol

Tel.: Bristol 622821 ext. 243

Enquiries: To Medical Librarian
Scope: General medicine and surgery
Stock: 500 books; 100 pamphlets; 68 current periodicals

BRISTOL
245

UNITED BRISTOL HOSPITALS
HOSPITAL LIBRARIES
Royal Infirmary
Bristol BS2 8HW

Tel.: Bristol 22041 ext. 209

Provide: A recreational service to all staff and patients in the group of 7 hospitals; an information service to all staff; a reference service to 'on the spot' medical staff; and a professional nursing library service to trained and untrained nurses

Enquiries: To Hospital Librarian
Scope: The scope of the information service is to provide patients, medical staff, nursing staff and hospital departmental staff with answers to enquiries from the working collection of general, medical, nursing and administrative material which is in the form of books, journals, reports, King Edwards Hospital Fund for London literature and clinical reprints. A *special collection* of use to those doing historical research is the volumes of Richard Smith's Memoirs containing original manuscripts concerned with early medical progress and history on and around Bristol. The Poisons Index is housed in the Casualty Department of the Royal Infirmary and can be drawn upon for information
Stock: 160 medical, 1,985 nursing, 13,358 general books; 436 pamphlets and reprints; 62 reports; 98 current periodicals

BRISTOL
246

UNIVERSITY OF BRISTOL
WILLS MEMORIAL LIBRARY
Queens Road
Bristol BS8 1RJ

Tel.: Bristol 24161 ext. 2

Enquiries: To Librarian
Scope: A Library service to Faculties of Arts, Law, Social Sciences, Science, Medicine and Engineering
Special Collections include: British philosophical writings, business history, early medicine, mineral waters and spas, historical chemistry, early mathematics, Wiglesworth ornithological library, historical works of famous engineers
Stock: 385,000 books; 100,000 pamphlets; 3,800 current periodicals (total stock)

The Medical Library houses 56,000 books and 600 current periodicals, and includes a considerable number of early medical books

BRISTOL
247

WESLEY COLLEGE, BRISTOL
Henbury Road
Bristol BS10 7QD

A theological college of the Ministerial Training Department of the Methodist Church of Great Britain

Enquiries: To Librarian, by letter only

BRISTOL, WESLEY COLLEGE, BRISTOL, *cont.*
Scope: Theology and philosophy.
Special collection: The Wesleys (John and Charles), Methodist history and theology
Secondary: History, sociology of religion, psychology
Stock: 20,000 books; 22 current periodicals

BROADSTAIRS
Kent
248

SIMPLIFIED SPELLING SOCIETY
48 Dumpton Park Drive
Broadstairs
Kent

Tel.: Thanet 62797 (after 5 pm)

Aims to encourage the study of English orthography and to promote reform
Enquiries: To Hon. Secretary
Scope: The Hon. Secretary replies personally to all letters and all requests for information
Publications: New Spelling, 6th edition. 1948
8 pamphlets

BROCKENHURST
Hants
249

BUCKLERS' HARD MARITIME MUSEUM
Beaulieu
Brockenhurst
Hampshire

Tel.: Bucklers' Hard 203

Maritime museum, mostly 18th century
Enquiries: To Curator, by letter only
Scope: Local history, shipbuilding and maritime affairs
Publications: Bucklers' Hard and the Beaulieu River

BROCKENHURST
Hants
250

MONTAGU MOTOR MUSEUM
Beaulieu
Brockenhurst
Hampshire

Tel.: Beaulieu 374

Enquiries: To Librarian
Scope: Public reference library, covering all aspects of motor transport, both historical and modern. Information and photocopying service. Photographic library
Stock: More than 3,000 books; 21,000 sales catalogues; 7,000 Instruction Manuals; The main British Motoring periodicals and main Veteran and Vintage Magazines of America; 50,000 photographs

BROMLEY
Kent
251

BROMLEY COLLEGE OF TECHNOLOGY
Rookery Lane
Bromley Common
Bromley BR2 8HE
Kent

Tel.: 01-462 6331

Enquiries: To Librarian
Scope: Science including biology; business studies; engineering; social studies
Stock: 10,000 books; 1,000 pamphlets; 200 current periodicals

BROMLEY Kent **252**	LONDON BOROUGH OF BROMLEY PUBLIC LIBRARIES Central Library Bromley BR1 1EX Kent	*Tel.:* 01-460 9955 *Telex:* 896712

Enquiries: To Borough Librarian

Scope: L.A.S.E.R. subject specialization: Art metalwork; commercial law; history and description of Central and Southern Africa.
Special collections: H. G. Wells; Walter de la Mare (in process of formation).

Beckenham Branch Library, 24 Beckenham Road, Beckenham BR3 4PE, Kent (*Tel.:* 01-650 4701). L.A.S.E.R. subject specialization: Child psychology, child and family welfare services; juvenile delinquency

Orpington Branch Library, The Priory, Church Hill, Orpington, BR6 0HH (*Tel.:* Orpington 31551). L.A.S.E.R. subject specialization: American poetry (texts)

Anerley Branch Library, 206D Anerley Road, London, S.E.20 (*Tel.:* 01-778 7457). L.A.S.E.R. subject specialization: English and American letters (text and criticism)
Special collection: Crystal Palace

Stock: 670,196 books, pamphlets and reports; 400 current periodicals (total stock)

Publications: A Bibliography of Printed Material relating to Bromley, Hayes and Keston, in the County of Kent. B. Burch. 1964.
Careers Booklist. 2nd edition. 1968 (published in conjunction with Borough Youth Employment Service)

BROMLEY Kent **253**	RAVENSBOURNE COLLEGE OF ART AND DESIGN Rookery Lane Bromley Common Bromley Kent	*Tel.:* 01-462 1233

Covers diploma courses in fine arts, graphic design, 3-dimensional design and fashion

Enquiries: To Librarian

Scope: Design including industrial and furniture design. Graphic design including advertising art and package design. Fine arts including history and techniques of painting, drawing and sculpture. Fashion
Secondary: Architecture; textiles

Stock: 11,000 books; 1,000 pamphlets (including exhibition catalogues); 120 current periodicals; 16,000 slides on history of art. A collection of slides covering the other subject areas will be built up during the next two years, doubling the size of the existing collection

BROMLEY Kent **254**	THE SCHOOLS MUSIC ASSOCIATION 4 Newman Road Bromley BR1 1RJ Kent	*Tel.:* 01-460 4043

Promotion of all aspects of music in schools

Enquiries: To Secretary

Scope: Covers a very wide field over the range of music in primary, secondary and special schools, and in colleges of education

BROMLEY, THE SCHOOLS MUSIC ASSOCIATION, *cont.*

Stock: 3,000 songs, books and orchestrations of songs; 10 reports; 7 current periodicals

Publications: Music (bi-monthly)
News Bulletin (three times each year)

BROMSGROVE Worcs **255**	BROMSGROVE COLLEGE OF FURTHER EDUCATION School Drive Stratford Road Bromsgrove Worcestershire	*Tel.:* Bromsgrove 3881 *Telex:* 338867

Enquiries: To Librarian

Scope: Engineering; motor vehicle engineering; garage management; business studies
Secondary: Child care; computer science; domestic science; hairdressing; science; woodwork

Stock: 9,000 books; 1,600 pamphlets; 200 current periodicals. Complete set of British Standards
Member of Worcestershire Association of Technical Libraries

BROMSGROVE Worcs **256**	SHENSTONE COLLEGE Burcot Lane Bromsgrove Worcestershire College of Education	*Tel.:* Bromsgrove 4151

Enquiries: To Librarian

Scope: General library with a special bias towards education and the teaching of all school subjects

Stock: 30,000 books and pamphlets; 200 current periodicals

BURGESS HILL Sussex **257**	SCHERING CHEMICALS LTD Victoria Way Burgess Hill Sussex Pharmaceutical manufacturers	*Tel.:* Burgess Hill 2736

Enquiries: To Medical Information Department

Scope: Medical, particularly in the fields of endocrinology, dermatology, radiography, biochemistry and pharmacology

Stock: 500 books; 11,000 reprints; 150 current periodicals. Stock not normally available on loan

BURNLEY Lancs **258**	BURNLEY PUBLIC LIBRARIES Central Library Burnley Lancashire	*Tel.:* Burnley 23313

Enquiries: To Librarian

Scope: N.W.R.L.S. subject specialization includes: Therapeutics; drawing; painting (general works); Arabia (geography and history); South East Asia (geography)
Secondary: Burnley Grammar School Library of 17th and 18th century books. Edward Stocks Massey Music Library

Stock: General lending stock (excluding science and technology) 60,100 books
General reference stock (excluding science and technology) 20,500 books
Medicine 2,800 books; Music 13,000 books and scores; Gramophone records 2,200

Publications: History of Burnley (4 volumes). W. Bennett
Pendle Witches. W. Bennett
Natural History of the Burnley Area. ed. R. Caul. 1968
Booklists, for example Antiques, Retirement, Local Government, Socialism

BURTON-ON-TRENT
Staffs
259

BURTON-ON-TRENT AND DISTRICT POST
    GRADUATE MEDICAL CENTRE
Medical Library
General Hospital
New Street
Burton-on-Trent
Staffordshire

Medical library in process of development under guidance from Public Library

Stock: 540 books; 50 current periodicals

BURTON-ON-TRENT
Staffs
260

BURTON-UPON-TRENT PUBLIC LIBRARY   *Tel.:* Burton-on-Trent 3042
Union Street
Burton-on-Trent
Staffordshire

Enquiries: To Librarian

Scope: Useful collection of Early English Text Society publications. Representative music collection—literature, scores and records

Stock: 42,000 books; 1,000 pamphlets; 57 current periodicals

BURTON-ON-TRENT
Staffs
261

BURTON-UPON-TRENT TECHNICAL COLLEGE   *Tel.:* Burton-on-Trent 61041
Abbey Street
Burton-on-Trent
Staffordshire

Enquiries: To Librarian or Principal

Scope: Economics
Secondary: Education, social sciences, history, geography, literature

Stock: 7,000 books and pamphlets; 95 current periodicals

BURY
Lancs
262

BURY PUBLIC LIBRARY   *Tel.:* 061-764 4110
Manchester Road
Bury
Lancashire

Enquiries: To Librarian

Scope: N.W.R.L.S. subject specialization includes: Leprosy; Scandinavian countries—history and travel; papermaking; office administration; lithography; bookbinding

Stock: 100,690 books; 120 current periodicals (total stock)

BURY ST EDMUNDS
Suffolk
263

BURY ST EDMUNDS PUBLIC LIBRARY   *Tel.:* Bury St Edmunds 5340
Cornhill
Bury St Edmunds
Suffolk

Enquiries: To Librarian

BURY ST EDMUNDS, BURY ST EDMUNDS PUBLIC LIBRARY, *cont.*

Scope: Cullum collection: A 'gentleman's' library mainly of 18th and 19th century books, particularly on genealogy and topography

Stock: 5,000 books

BURY ST EDMUNDS
Suffolk

264

THE SUFFOLK REGIMENT MUSEUM
The Keep
Gibraltar Barracks
Bury St Edmunds
Suffolk

Tel.: Bury St Edmunds 2394

Enquiries: To Secretary

Scope: Exhibits, books and papers connected with the Regiment and the army dating back to 1685

Stock: 500 books. Stock not available on loan

Publications: Regimental histories

BURY ST EDMUNDS
Suffolk

265

WEST SUFFOLK COUNTY LIBRARY
Shire Hall
Bury St Edmunds
Suffolk

Tel.: Bury St Edmunds 2281

Enquiries: To Librarian

Scope: Local Collection
National Subject specialization: English poetry 1800-1900

Stock: Local collection, 1,200 volumes; 19th century English poets, 850 volumes

BUXTON
Derbyshire

266

BUXTON DIVISIONAL LIBRARY AND MUSEUM
Terrace Road
Buxton
Derbyshire

Tel.: Buxton 4658

Enquiries: To Librarian

Scope: Special collections in archaeology, anthropology and local history

Stock: 45,000 books; 2,000 pamphlets; 20 current periodicals (total stock)

Publications: The Royal Forest of the Peak (a history of the Peak District). I. E. Burton

CAERNARVON

267

CAERNARVON PUBLIC LIBRARY
Pavilion Hill
Caernarvon

Tel.: Caernarvon 2253

Enquiries: To Librarian

Scope: Welsh reference collection; Books relating to Wales. *Special collection* of newspaper cuttings and postcards record of 1911 Investiture Ceremony held in Caernarvon

Stock: 2,000 books; 500 pamphlets; 90 current periodicals
Member of the North Wales Urban Libraries Group

CAERNARVON

268

CAERNARVONSHIRE COUNTY LIBRARY
Llanberis Road
Caernarvon

Tel.: Caernarvon 2061

Enquiries: To Librarian

Scope: Regional subject specialization: Sociology; general history
Stock: 2,300 books and pamphlets

CAMBERLEY NATIONAL ARMY MUSEUM *Tel.:* 0276-633
Surrey RMA Sandhurst
  Camberley
269 Surrey
Enquiries: To Director
Scope: History of the British Army 1570–1914
  Secondary: Study of uniforms, weapons and equipment of the Army
Stock: 20,000 books; 50 current periodicals including most military and Regimental journals; 250 ft run of manuscripts. Stock not available on loan
Publications: National Army Museum Historical Series:
  No. 1. Granadiers Exercise 1735
  No. 2. Sabretaches of the British Army

CAMBERLEY ROYAL MILITARY ACADEMY SANDHURST *Tel.:* Camberley 63344
Surrey Camberley
  Surrey
270 Officer Cadet Training for British Regular Army
Enquiries: To Librarian
Scope: *Central Library:* History; military history and science of war; special sections for Asia, Africa, Middle East; modern Britain; political and social sciences; economics; geography; sports; travel; European Languages
Stock: 80,000 books; 390 current periodicals (including Service and Military journals)

CAMBERLEY STAFF COLLEGE *Tel.:* Camberley 5411
Surrey Camberley
  Surrey
271 Training of officers in the armed forces for staff duties
Enquiries: To Librarian
Scope: British military history; war; study of strategy
  Secondary: Geo-politics; international affairs; management
Stock: 40,000 books and pamphlets; 100 current periodicals and Regimental journals. Stock not normally available on loan
Publications: Owl Pie (a review of the year edited by students, annually)
  Special Staff College Collection is being formed. This will contain material relating to the Staff College and books and articles by and about the Staff College graduates and students

CAMBORNE CAMBORNE–REDRUTH PUBLIC LIBRARIES *Tel.:* Camborne 3544
Cornwall Public Library
  The Cross
272 Camborne
  Cornwall
Enquiries: To Librarian
Scope: Small local history collection, but the major local collection is at the Redruth Library (*see* no. 2033)

CAMBRIDGE 273	ADVISORY CENTRE FOR EDUCATION (ACE) LTD 32 Trumpington Street Cambridge CB2 1QY Advisory Service on education	*Tel.:* 0223 51456

Enquiries: To Head of Advisory Service, by letter only

Scope: Advisory Service on education in all its aspects but with special emphasis on the problems and issues which are of interest to parents

Publications: Where (6 times each year) and supplements
Booklets: How to choose a School; Secretarial Courses with Languages; Industrial Scholarships and Training Schemes
Many leaflets and pamphlets

CAMBRIDGE 274	AGRICULTURAL RESEARCH COUNCIL INSTITUTE OF ANIMAL PHYSIOLOGY Babraham Cambridge CB2 4AT Fundamental research into the physiology, biochemistry and pathology of farm animals	*Tel.:* Sawston 2312

Enquiries: To the Institute, by letter only

Scope: Physiology, biochemistry, pathology, immunology, pharmacology, neurochemistry and veterinary science

Stock: 3,000 books; 500 pamphlets; 339 current periodicals

CAMBRIDGE 275	ASSOCIATION FOR LIBERAL EDUCATION Stuart House Mill Lane Cambridge CB2 1RY Aims to encourage the extension of liberal education in an industrial society that increasingly demands specialization	*Tel.:* Cambridge 56275

Enquiries: To Membership Secretary, by letter only

Scope: The small Library is situated at Barnet College of Further Education and is primarily concerned with liberal studies

Publications: Liberal Education (twice each year)
The Bulletin (nine times each year)

CAMBRIDGE 276	CAMBRIDGE AND COUNTY FOLK MUSEUM 2 Castle Street Cambridge CB3 0AQ Preservation of objects illustrating the history of life in the City and County of Cambridge from 1700, compilation of photograph record of City and County and collection of folklore of the county	*Tel.:* Cambridge 55159

Enquiries: To Curator

Scope: History of Cambridge. Folk Life and Folklore of Cambridgeshire
No library

Publications: A Brief Guide to the Museum
Museum Booklet No. 1: The Hearth and the Kitchen

CAMBRIDGE 277	CAMBRIDGE CITY LIBRARIES The Guildhall Cambridge CB2 3QD	*Tel.:* Cambridge 58977

Enquiries: To Librarian

Scope: Cambridge and Cambridgeshire
Subject specialization: Italian language and literature; literary composition (poetry, drama and fiction)
Stock: Local collection: 9,000 books and pamphlets; 1,250 prints and photographs; 800 maps and plans; 600 slides; 100 current periodicals. Subject specialization: 650 books
Publications: Monumental Brasses in Cambridgeshire

CAMBRIDGE

278

CAMBRIDGE INSTITUTE OF EDUCATION   *Tel.:* Cambridge 56207
Shaftesbury Road
Cambridge CB2 2BX

Provides a service for Institute staff and students, constituent colleges, and teachers and others concerned with education within the Institute area (East Anglia, Hertfordshire, part of Essex)

Enquiries: To Librarian
Scope: Education
Stock: 9,000 books; 2,500 pamphlets; 100 current periodicals
Publications: Cambridge Monographs on Teaching Methods
Research Papers
Accessions and Subject Lists

CAMBRIDGE

279

CAMBRIDGE UNIVERSITY APPOINTMENTS   *Tel.:* Cambridge 54242
  BOARD
6 Chaucer Road
Cambridge

Advice and information on careers

Enquiries: To Secretary
Scope: Information Room containing careers literature relating to fields of work, specific employers, postgraduate instruction and research both in the United Kingdom and overseas
Stock: 50 reference books; 750 ring binders of pamphlets; 6 current periodicals. Stock not available on loan

CAMBRIDGE

CAMBRIDGESHIRE AND ISLE OF ELY
  COUNTY LIBRARY
See under **MARCH,** Cambs (no. 1796)

CAMBRIDGE

280

CAREERS RESEARCH AND ADVISORY CENTRE   *Tel.:* Cambridge 54445
Bateman Street
Cambridge

Aims to act as a link between all those concerned with education and employment through specialized publications and courses, films, question service, careers library index card service and other aids

Enquiries: To Information Officer, by letter only
Scope: All information relating to choice of career, further education, higher education and employment. Material on the techniques of career advice; recent developments in vocational guidance, further and higher education, industrial training
Stock: 200 books; 2,500 pamphlets, surveys, reports; 40 current periodicals; relevant newspaper cuttings for past 12 months; prospectuses of universities, colleges of education, technical

CAMBRIDGE, CAREERS RESEARCH AND ADVISORY CENTRE, *cont.*
colleges, colleges of further education and technology, polytechnics, colleges of agriculture, art and commerce; past CRAC publications

Publications: Middle School Choice   Arts Degree Choice
Upper School Choice   Science Degree Choice
44 Degree Course Guides
CRAC/CBI Yearbook of Education and Training Opportunities Volume I and Volume III (Beyond a Degree)
Blue Book of Degree Course Prospectuses
Blue Book of Recruitment Literature
While You Wait (in conjunction with Barclay's Bank)
A Good Start in Life
Further Education (journal)

CAMBRIDGE

281

THE COMMUNITY COUNCIL FOR CAMBRIDGESHIRE AND ISLE OF ELY, HUNTINGDON AND PETERBOROUGH
7 Hills Road
Cambridge

Tel.: Cambridge 50666

Enquiries: To Secretary
Scope: Can give information on voluntary organizations and social welfare services in the area
No library

CAMBRIDGE

282

CORPUS CHRISTI COLLEGE
Cambridge

Tel.: Cambridge 59418

Enquiries: To Librarian, preferably by letter
Scope: Collections of manuscripts and printed books. The manuscripts include a large collection of Anglo-Saxon and medieval works, as well as numbers of reformation writings. The archives also contain much material relating to the early possessions of the college
Stock: 6,000 books
Publications: Occasional catalogues of exhibitions held in the library

CAMBRIDGE

283

EAST ANGLIAN REGIONAL HOSPITAL BOARD
Union Lane
Chesterton
Cambridge CB4 1PU

Tel.: Cambridge 61212

Responsible, under the general guidance of the Department of Health, for planning and co-ordinating the development of the hospital and specialist services in East Anglia

Enquiries: To Secretary
Scope: Working library for use in connection with health service administration
Stock: The library is distributed over different departments, and the stock includes a very large number of journals for use in the Medical (including Blood Transfusion and Mass Radiography), Nursing, Architect. Engineer, Secretariat, Work Study, Training and Supplies departments. Stock not available on loan

CAMBRIDGE

284

EMMANUEL COLLEGE
Cambridge CB2 3AP

Tel.: Cambridge 58356

Enquiries: To Librarian, by letter only

Scope: Western Manuscripts (catalogued in M. R. James, *Western Manuscripts in the Library of Emmanuel College*, 1904)
English books before 1641 (in P. W. Wood, *English Books in Emmanuel College Library before 1641*. 1915)
Foreign books to 1600 (in H. M. Adams, *Catalogue of Books printed on the Continent 1501–1600 in Cambridge Libraries*. 1967)
The Library is particularly rich in 17th century books, and includes the Library of Archbishop Wm. Sancroft (d. 1693), and the W. C. Bishop Liturgical collection. The modern books range over most academic subjects studied at undergraduate level. The Library does not operate an information service as such, but enquiries about the manuscript and other rare materials and the history of the College are dealt with

Stock: 18,000 books before 1800; 35,000 books since 1800; 100 incunabula; 300 manuscripts (of which a few oriental)

CAMBRIDGE

285

ENGLISH CROSS COUNTRY UNION
Woodlin
Stapleford
Cambridge

Tel.: Shelford 3166

The promotion of cross country running in England

Enquiries: To Secretary, by letter only
Scope: Prepared to answer all types of questions concerning cross country running
Stock: No library

CAMBRIDGE

286

W. HEFFER AND SONS LTD
3/4 Petty Cury
Cambridge

Tel.: Cambridge 58351
Telex: 81298

Publishers and Booksellers

Enquiries: To Manager, Secondhand and Rare Books Department
Scope: Reference books, bibliographies and all trade reference books, on the following subjects: English literature and history
Stock: 600 books. Stock not available on loan

CAMBRIDGE

287

INDUSTRIAL TRAINING RESEARCH UNIT
32 Trumpington Street
Cambridge

Tel.: Cambridge 51576

Enquiries: To Director, by letter only
Scope: Research into adult recruitment, selection, training and labour turnover in industry
Publications: Many papers in periodicals and books

CAMBRIDGE

288

KING'S COLLEGE
Cambridge CB2 1ST

Tel.: Cambridge 50411

Enquiries: To Librarian
Scope: General library for needs of staff and students, with much older research material, including:
Manuscripts
Mediaeval (40); Oriental (260); extensive 20th century literary collections, particularly papers of C. R. Ashbee (1863–1942), Roger Fry (1866–1934), Rupert Brooke (1887–1915), T. S. Eliot (1888–1965) and members of the 'Bloomsbury' group
Printed Books

CAMBRIDGE, KING'S COLLEGE, *cont.*

Incunabula (240); English books printed before 1701 (3,150); author collections of Aeschylus, Rochester and Saint-Évremond. The Keynes Library (6,000) mainly of authors important in the history of thought, particularly Bentham, Berkeley, Descartes, Galileo, Hobbes, Hume (manuscripts), Kant, Locke, Malebranche, Mandeville, J. S. Mill (manuscripts), Henry More, Newton (manuscripts), Pascal, Rousseau, Spinoza and Voltaire

Music

Rowe Music Library. Large general collection, particularly rich in 18th century music, especially Handel

Stock: 120,000 books; 10,000 pamphlets; 25 current periodicals. Stock not normally available on loan

CAMBRIDGE 289	MEDICAL RESEARCH COUNCIL APPLIED PSYCHOLOGY UNIT 15 Chaucer Road Cambridge CB2 2EF	*Tel.:* Cambridge 55294

Enquiries: To Information Officer and Librarian
Scope: Applied psychology
Stock: 1,450 books; 12,765 pamphlets; 770 reports; 50 current periodicals

CAMBRIDGE 290	PAPWORTH HOSPITAL The Medical Library Papworth Everard Cambridge	*Tel.:* Papworth St, Agnes 271

Enquiries: To Librarian, by letter only
Scope: Chest diseases
Stock: 230 books; 33 current periodicals

CAMBRIDGE 291	PEMBROKE COLLEGE Cambridge	*Tel.:* Cambridge 52241 ext. 35

Enquiries: To Librarian
Scope: English literature. Literature in other languages (European, Oriental); classics; theology; history; economics; fine arts; music; law; philosophy; medicine and veterinary medicine
Stock: 43,000 books; 32 current periodicals. Stock not available on loan

CAMBRIDGE 292	QUEEN'S COLLEGE Cambridge	*Tel.:* Cambridge 50425

Enquiries: To Librarian, by letter only
Scope: Manuscripts, books and pamphlets in the Old Library (chiefly theology, classics, law, medicine, but also scientific and literary works) from the 15th century onwards. Modern (Memorial) Library
Stock: 30,000 books and pamphlets. Stock not available on loan

CAMBRIDGE 293	REGIONAL TRANSFUSION AND IMMUNO-HAEMATOLOGY CENTRE Long Road Cambridge CB2 2PT	*Tel.:* Cambridge 45921

All aspects of a regional transfusion centre's routine work plus reference centre work on research

Enquiries: To Director, preferably by letter
Scope: Blood transfusion. Blood group serology
Secondary: Background literature for example, haematology, immunology, genetics
Stock not available on loan

CAMBRIDGE   ST JOHN'S COLLEGE   *Tel.:* Cambridge 61621
Cambridge

294
Enquiries: To Librarian, by letter only
Scope: All subjects
Special collections: Samuel Butler Collection; W. F. Smith Collection of Rabelais literature; Yule Collection of editions of A' Kempis, *Imitation of Christ*; Souldern Lawrence 18th century Law library
Stock: 60,000 books; 65 current periodicals. Stock not normally available on loan
Publications: A descriptive catalogue of the manuscripts in St John's College, Cambridge. M. R. James. 1913
Printed list of incunabula. C. Sayle. 1911
The Samuel Butler Collection at St John's College. A catalogue. J. F. Jones and A. T. Bartholomew. 1921

CAMBRIDGE   SCOTT POLAR RESEARCH INSTITUTE   *Tel.:* Cambridge 55601
Lensfield Road

295
Cambridge
Provision of information and promotion of research on all aspects of the Polar regions
Enquiries: To Librarian
Scope: All aspects pertinent to the Arctic (south to the tree-line), the Antarctic continent and sub-Antarctic islands. Snow and ice *everywhere*. Strong in glaciology (including permafrost), zoology, meteorology, oceanography, geophysics. Economic development of the Arctic. Current and historical expedition files. All Russian material relevant to the Arctic
Stock: 9,000 books; 14,000 pamphlets; 5,000 reports; 700 current periodicals. Manuscript collection, maps, photographs, picture collection
Publications: The Polar Record (3 times a year, and includes supplement bibliography Recent Polar Literature)

CAMBRIDGE   SELWYN COLLEGE
Cambridge

296
Enquiries: To Librarian, by letter only
Scope: Old Library contains 16th to 18th century books mostly in the field of biblical studies, patristics, liturgy and theology.
Collection of 19th century ecclesiastical pamphlets; papers left by Bishop Selwyn, Bishop Westcott and F. S. Marsh
Stock: 500 books. Stock not available on loan

CAMBRIDGE   TYNDALE HOUSE   *Tel.:* 0223 52159
36 Selwyn Gardens

297
Cambridge CB3 9BA
Residential library of the Inter-Varsity Fellowship of Evangelical Unions for those doing

CAMBRIDGE, TYNDALE HOUSE, *cont.*

research in biblical and theological studies at postgraduate level. Facilities are available to others resident in Cambridge

Enquiries: To Librarian

Stock: 11,000 volumes of books and periodicals; 90 current periodicals

A cumulative subject index is kept to articles in periodicals and volumes of essays received by the library

See also no. 1284

CAMBRIDGE

298

UNIVERSITY OF CAMBRIDGE
AFRICAN STUDIES CENTRE
Sidgwick Avenue
Cambridge

Tel.: Cambridge 58944 ext. 245

The Centre was founded in order to facilitate inter-disciplinary research in modern African studies. It has a small specialist library and an extensive bibliography of works on Africa and also runs seminars for interested people and special research projects

Enquiries: To Librarian, by letter only

Scope: Modern African studies including anthropology, sociology, history, geography, agriculture, economics, education, law, political science and demography

Stock: 5,000 books; 1,000 pamphlets; 500 reports; 100 current periodicals and serials. Stock not available on loan

Publications: Occasional papers
Cambridge African Studies series

CAMBRIDGE

299

UNIVERSITY OF CAMBRIDGE
CENTRE OF LATIN AMERICAN STUDIES
History Faculty Building
West Road
Cambridge CB3 9EF

Tel.: Cambridge 61661

Enquiries: To Director

Scope: The library of the Centre is being built up as a reference collection. It therefore includes mainly dictionaries, bibliographies, catalogues and inventories relating to Latin American history, politics, economics, anthropology and sociology

Stock: 600 books; 12 current periodicals. Stock not available on loan

Publications: The Cambridge Latin American Series (a series of monographs on Latin America, generally in the field of the social sciences and history)

CAMBRIDGE

300

UNIVERSITY OF CAMBRIDGE
CENTRE OF SOUTH ASIAN STUDIES
Faculty Rooms
Laundress Lane
Cambridge CB2 1SD

Tel.: Cambridge 57884

Enquiries: To Secretary/Librarian

Scope: Holdings are mostly obtained from the area of study and do not generally duplicate holdings of the University Library or other specialist libraries in Cambridge. Subjects on which most material is held are history (British period), economics (planning and development), social studies of South Asia. An archive is being collected but is not yet generally accessible

Stock: 5,000 books (including periodicals volumes and boxes of pamphlets); 96 current periodicals. Stock not available on loan

Publications: A guide to South Asian material in the Libraries of London, Oxford and Cambridge: November 1966 (compiled by R. Datta)
Union Catalogue of the Government of Pakistan publications held by Libraries in London, Oxford and Cambridge (compiled by R. Datta)
Union catalogue of Government of India publications (in progress)
Cambridge South Asian Studies
Modern Asian Studies

The library holds and maintains:
an index of modern South Asian material held in Faculty and College libraries in Cambridge; a record of such material received by the University Library (from 1965); a subject index of Pakistan and India Official Publications held in the University Library; and relevant press cuttings (mostly from *The Times*) since 1963

CAMBRIDGE

301

UNIVERSITY OF CAMBRIDGE
CLASSICAL FACULTY LIBRARY
Mill Lane Lecture Rooms
Mill Lane
Cambridge CB2 1RX

Tel.: Cambridge 56064

Enquiries: To Librarian, by letter only

Scope: Greek and Latin language and literature, ancient history, ancient philosophy, linguistics and Modern Greek
Secondary: Archaeology and numismatics, but these are covered more by the Museum of Classical Archaeology (no. 316)
The Library is willing to pass on subject enquiries to a senior member of the Faculty

Stock: 13,250 books; 1,550 pamphlets; 47 current periodicals

CAMBRIDGE

302

UNIVERSITY OF CAMBRIDGE
DEPARTMENT OF APPLIED ECONOMICS
Sidgwick Avenue
Cambridge

Tel.: Cambridge 58944

Enquiries: To Librarian

Scope: The library contains specialized books on economics, mainly relating to projects being done by research staff. Statistical material and British government publications

Stock: 19,000 books, pamphlets and British government publications; 190 current periodicals. Stock not available on loan

Publications: Departmental Reprint series
Departmental Occasional papers
Monograph series
Programme for Growth series
Cambridge Studies in Sociology
Cambridge Papers in Sociology

CAMBRIDGE

303

UNIVERSITY OF CAMBRIDGE
DEPARTMENT OF GEOGRAPHY
Downing Place
Cambridge

Tel.: Cambridge 53809

Enquiries: To Librarian

Scope: Teaching collection on geography for undergraduates and research students of the Department
Secondary: Clarke Collection of 18th and 19th century books; Steers Collection of pamphlets on physiography; Offprint Collection

CAMBRIDGE, UNIVERSITY OF CAMBRIDGE, DEPARTMENT OF GEOGRAPHY, *cont.*

Stock: 16,500 books; 5,500 pamphlets; 175 current periodicals; 30,000 maps. Stock not available on loan

CAMBRIDGE **304**	UNIVERSITY OF CAMBRIDGE DEPARTMENT OF MEDICINE LIBRARY Hills Road Cambridge CB2 1QT	*Tel.:* Cambridge 45171 (*Librarian's office:* Cambridge 53327)

Enquiries: To Librarian

Scope: Haematology; leukemia
Secondary: General medicine

Stock: Stock includes 35 current periodicals. Stock not available on loan

CAMBRIDGE **305**	UNIVERSITY OF CAMBRIDGE DEPARTMENT OF PATHOLOGY Tennis Court Road Cambridge	*Tel.:* Cambridge 58251

Enquiries: To Librarian

Scope: Pathology, bacteriology, virology, immunology, histology, haematology, cryobiology. Some general medicine and surgery

Stock: 5,167 books; 10,000 volumes of periodicals; 117 current periodicals. Periodicals only available on loan

CAMBRIDGE **306**	UNIVERSITY OF CAMBRIDGE DEPARTMENT OF PHARMACOLOGY New Addenbrookes Hospital Site (Medical School) Hills Road Cambridge

Enquiries: To Librarian, by letter only

Scope: The Library contains books and periodicals primarily pharmacological, but also biochemistry, medicine, therapeutics, physiology, molecular biology, immunology

Stock: 600 books including bound periodicals; 36 current periodicals. Stock not normally available on loan

CAMBRIDGE **307**	UNIVERSITY OF CAMBRIDGE DEPARTMENT OF RADIOTHERAPEUTICS Tennis Court Road Cambridge	*Tel.:* Cambridge 58341 (office) or 55612 (library)

Enquiries: To Secretary, by letter only

Scope: Medical research with special reference to radiotherapy, chemotherapy and the treatment of cancer generally
Secondary: Collected Papers of members of the Department

Stock: 2,000 books; 74 current periodicals

CAMBRIDGE **308**	UNIVERSITY OF CAMBRIDGE DEPARTMENT OF SURGERY Addenbrooke's Hospital Douglas House Trumpington Road Cambridge	*Tel.:* Cambridge 61467

Enquiries: To Secretary

Scope: Departmental library providing specialized information on all aspects of organ transplantation. Journals taken are those not subscribed to by other local libraries

Stock not available on loan

CAMBRIDGE

309

UNIVERSITY OF CAMBRIDGE
DIVINITY SCHOOL
St John's Street
Cambridge

Tel.: Cambridge 56034

Enquiries: To Librarian, by letter only

Scope: Biblical studies, church history, theology, philosophy, comparative religion. No formal information services are provided, but the Librarian, with the assistance of members of the Faculty, answers enquiries so far as this is possible

Stock: 10,700 books; 22 current periodicals

CAMBRIDGE

310

UNIVERSITY OF CAMBRIDGE
FACULTY OF ARCHAEOLOGY AND
    ANTHROPOLOGY
HADDON LIBRARY
Downing Street
Cambridge

Tel.: Cambridge 59714

Enquiries: To Librarian, by letter only

Scope: Archaeology, social anthropology, physical anthropology
Secondary: Religion, folklore, linguistics and allied subjects
Special collections: Cambridge Antiquarian Library (books, pamphlets and photographs on Cambridge, Cambridgeshire and adjoining areas); Haddon Collection of ethnological photographs

Stock: 26,000 books and periodicals; 7,000 pamphlets; 364 current periodicals. Photographs and periodicals not available on loan

Publications: Cambridge Papers in Social Anthropology
Cambridge Studies in Social Anthropology
Occasional Publications of Cambridge University

Museum of Archaeology and Ethnology

CAMBRIDGE

311

UNIVERSITY OF CAMBRIDGE
FACULTY OF MODERN AND MEDIEVAL
    LANGUAGES
DEPARTMENT OF SLAVONIC STUDIES
Sidgwick Avenue
Cambridge

Tel.: Cambridge 56411
ext. 33 and 34

Enquiries: To Librarian or Secretary, by letter only

Scope: Language, literature and history of Bulgaria, Czechoslovakia, Poland, Russia and Yugoslavia
Secondary: Folklore, philosophy and religion of Bulgaria, Czechoslovakia, Poland, Russia and Yugoslavia

Stock: 28,000 books; 50 current periodicals. Stock not available on loan

CAMBRIDGE

312

UNIVERSITY OF CAMBRIDGE
FITZWILLIAM MUSEUM LIBRARY
Trumpington Street
Cambridge

Art Museum

Tel.: Cambridge 50023

CAMBRIDGE, UNIVERSITY OF CAMBRIDGE, FITZWILLIAM MUSEUM LIBRARY, *cont.*

Enquiries: To Librarian

Scope: History of fine arts, including painting, sculpture, drawings, engravings, illuminated manuscripts, ceramics, textiles, ancient art, and numismatics
Secondary: Incunabula and illustrated books of 16th to 17th centuries. 18th century books (general library) in the Founder's collection. Fine bindings. Music Collection (mainly manuscripts)

Stock: 30,000 books and pamphlets; 68 current periodicals

Publications: The Fitzwilliam Museum: An illustrated survey. With an Introduction and Commentary by C. Winter. 1958
Handbook to the Museum
Catalogue of the Pictures. S. Colvin and F. R. Earp. 1902
Corpus Vasorum Antiquorum, Fitzwilliam Museum. Fascicules 1 and 2. W. Lamb. 1930 and 1936
Catalogue of the Greek Vases. E. A. Gardner. 1897
McClean Bequest, Catalogue of the Medieval Ivories, Enamels, Jewellery, Gems, and Miscellaneous Objects. O. M. Dalton. 1912
A Handlist of the Additional Manuscripts. F. Wormald and P. M. Giles. 1951–54. Parts I-V
Catalogue of the Music. J. A. Fuller-Maitland and A. H. Mann. 1893
Sylloge Nummorum Graecorum. Fitzwilliam Museum. Part IV, 1956; Part VI, 1965
Catalogue of the Greek and Roman Sculpture. L. Budde and R. V. Nicholls. 1964
Catalogue of the G. E. Beddington Collection of Colour-prints. 1959
Exhibition Catalogue: Illuminated Manuscripts in the Fitzwilliam Museum. F. Wormald and P. M. Giles. 1966
Exhibition Catalogue: Drawings by Rembrandt and his Circle, from the Fitzwilliam Museum. M. Cormack. 1966
Postcards

CAMBRIDGE
313

UNIVERSITY OF CAMBRIDGE
INSTITUTE OF CRIMINOLOGY
7 West Road
Cambridge CB3 9DT

Tel.: Cambridge 59196 and 59375
Telex: c/o Scientific Periodicals Library, 81240

Enquiries: To Librarian

Scope: Criminology, treatment of offenders
Secondary: Criminal law, administration of justice, social deviance, psychopathology and psychiatry (in so far as related to criminal behaviour). Foreign and historical materials are included

Stock: 13,000 books; 5,000 pamphlets; 150 current periodicals

Publications: Accessions Lists (quarterly)
Bibliographical series (in print: No. 3—Parole; No. 4—Soviet criminology)

CAMBRIDGE
314

UNIVERSITY OF CAMBRIDGE LIBRARY
Cambridge

Tel.: Cambridge 61441
Telex: 81395

Enquiries: To Librarian, by letter and telex only

Scope: All subjects

Stock: 3 million books and pamphlets; 10,000 current periodicals

Publications: Chronological List of the Graces, Documents, and other Papers in the University Registry which concern the University Library. 1870
Current Serials Available in the University Library and in other Libraries connected with the University (in preparation)
Library Classification Schemes
Readers' Guide. 1968
Catalogues of Manuscripts: Adversaria; Cholmondeley (Houghton) MSS; Darwin Papers; Ethiopean MSS; Georgian MSS; Hebrew MSS; Muhammadan MSS; Newton MSS; Ostraca; Sanskrit MSS; Syriac MSS
Catalogues of Books: Acton Collection; Adams Collection; Bradshaw Irish Collection; Clark Collection; Early English Printed Books; Fifteenth-Century Printed Books; Gibb Collection; Maccoll Collection; Venn Collection; Wade Collection
Catalogues of Exhibitions
Reproductions
Postcards

CAMBRIDGE　　UNIVERSITY OF CAMBRIDGE　　*Tel.:* Cambridge 56411
315　　MODERN LANGUAGES FACULTY LIBRARY　　ext. 32 and 59
Sidgwick Avenue
Cambridge

The Library caters for the needs of undergraduates reading modern European languages and is comprehensive enough to be of value to some researchers also. Together with the (at present separate) Slavonic Library (no. 311) at the same address, it is among the largest of specialist language and literature libraries in the United Kingdom

Enquiries: To Librarian

Scope: Language and literature as follows: French; Italian; Spanish; Catalan; Portuguese; Rumanian; Hungarian; German; Dutch; Danish; Norwegian; Swedish; Icelandic; Medieval Latin. Reference material; General literature (including literary theory); Linguistics; Romance philology
Secondary: Background material for example, history, philosophy, art
The Library incorporates the *Beit Library* of German research material

Stock: 43,000 books and pamphlets; 70 current periodicals
Reading lists for subjects covered by the University of Cambridge Modern Languages Tripos are distributed from this Library
Library closed to readers during vacations

CAMBRIDGE　　UNIVERSITY OF CAMBRIDGE　　*Tel.:* Cambridge 52410
316　　MUSEUM OF CLASSICAL ARCHAEOLOGY
Little St Mary's Lane
Cambridge CB2 1RR

Enquiries: To Curator
Scope: No special information service, but individual enquiries are dealt with. Library contains material on Greek and Roman archaeology
Stock: 11,775 books (including periodicals); 2,460 pamphlets; 50 current periodicals

CAMBRIDGE　　UNIVERSITY OF CAMBRIDGE　　*Tel.:* Cambridge 53322
317　　PENDLEBURY LIBRARY OF MUSIC
Music School
Downing Place
Cambridge

Enquiries: To Curator

83

CAMBRIDGE, UNIVERSITY OF CAMBRIDGE, PENDLEBURY LIBRARY OF MUSIC, *cont.*

Scope: Music (serious)
Secondary: Music in Cambridge, from historical aspect
Stock: 40,000 books, scores and pamphlets; 24 current periodicals. Stock not normally available on loan
Microfilm Archive of British Music

CAMBRIDGE

318

UNIVERSITY OF CAMBRIDGE
POSTGRADUATE MEDICAL SCHOOL LIBRARY
Addenbrooke's Hospital
Trumpington Street
Cambridge CB2 1QE

Tel.: Cambridge 53327

Enquiries: To Librarian
Scope: All branches of general medicine and surgery. Cambridge M.D. theses are kept in this library and can be lent subject to copyright conditions being observed. All sections of *Excerpta Medica; Index Medicus*
Stock: 2,500 books; 90 current periodicals. Stock not available on loan

CAMBRIDGE

319

UNIVERSITY OF CAMBRIDGE
SCHOOL OF VETERINARY MEDICINE
Madingley Road
Cambridge CB3 0ES

Tel.: Cambridge 55641

Enquiries: To Librarian
Scope: Veterinary medicine and animal husbandry. Sir John Hammond reprint collection on nutrition
Stock: 2,500 books; 260 current periodicals
Publications: Collected Papers (very limited distribution only)

CAMBRIDGE

320

UNIVERSITY OF CAMBRIDGE
SCIENTIFIC PERIODICALS LIBRARY
Bene't Street
Cambridge

Tel.: Cambridge 54724 and 54926
Telex: 81240

Scientific periodicals reference library for the University of Cambridge and scientific periodicals lending library for Fellows and Associates of the Cambridge Philosophical Society

Enquiries: To Librarian
Scope: Scientific periodicals in mathematics, physics, chemistry, biological sciences, earth sciences and electrical engineering. Bibliographical reference works and language dictionaries
Secondary: Scientific periodicals in medicine, experimental psychology, technology, geography and anthropology. Collection of 19th century scientific books
Stock: More than 1,400 current periodicals and serials

CAMBRIDGE

321

UNIVERSITY OF CAMBRIDGE
THE UNIVERSITY ARCHIVES
The Old Schools
Trinity Lane
Cambridge CB2 1TN

Tel.: Cambridge 58933 ext. 227

Enquiries: To the Keeper of the Archives

Scope: Manuscripts relating to the University and to its members, and dating from the 13th century, including charters of privilege, statutes, Grace books, minutes of the Council of the Senate, matriculation, supplicat, subscription (containing autograph signatures) and degree books, University accounts, muniments of title, records (including those of the Vice-Chancellor's testamentary jurisdiction) of the University Courts

Special collections: Letters and Mandates; records of the University Press (16th to early 20th century); some maps, local and otherwise; plans of University buildings; 'Guard-book' series (papers relating to University officers, endowments, buildings, faculties and departments); faculty and departmental minute books. Probate records (1449–1857) of the Consistory and Archidiaconal Courts of Ely and Cambridge on deposit

Stock: Accessions are recorded annually in National Register of Archives *List of Accessions to repositories*. Stock not available on loan, but microfilms and photocopies supplied

Publications: The Archives of the University of Cambridge: An Historical Introduction. H. E. Peek and C. P. Hall. 1962

CAMBRIDGE

322

UNIVERSITY OF CAMBRIDGE
WHIPPLE SCIENCE MUSEUM AND LIBRARY
Free School Lane
Cambridge

Tel.: Cambridge 50329

Enquiries: To Librarian

Scope: Primary source material on the history of science 1600 to 1900, including a large collection of books by Robert Boyle. Large collection of books on ancient scientific instruments (1500 to 1800). Collection of scientific instruments 17th to 19th centuries.
Secondary: Collection of books on the history of science and philosophy of science

Stock: 6,000 books; periodicals on the history of science, medicine, and the philosophy of science

CAMBRIDGE

323

UNIVERSITY OF CAMBRIDGE *and* MEDICAL RESEARCH COUNCIL
DUNN NUTRITIONAL LABORATORY
Milton Road
Cambridge

Tel.: Cambridge 63356

Research on vitamins and other nutrients

Enquiries: To Librarian, by letter only

Scope: Vitamins and other nutrients, including the elucidation of the biochemical and physiological processes underlying their mode of action, the effects of deficiency, and methods for their estimation in living tissues and in natural and processed products
Secondary: Food values

Stock: 800 books; 700 pamphlets; 50 reports; 88 current periodicals. The library includes the Chick Collection of reprints of early works on nutrition

CANNOCK
Staffs

324

CANNOCK CHASE TECHNICAL COLLEGE
Stafford Road
Cannock
Staffordshire

Tel.: Cannock 3137

Enquiries: To Librarian

Scope: Commerce, law, education and social sciences

Stock: 11,000 books; 140 current periodicals

CANTERBURY	CANTERBURY CATHEDRAL	
Kent	CHAPTER LIBRARY	
	Precincts	
325	Canterbury	
	Kent	

Enquiries: To Librarian, by letter only

Scope: The library is now primarily a repository for archives and contains those of the Dean and Chapter (8th century to present day); the Diocese (14th century to 19th century); City Corporation of Canterbury (14th century to 19th century) and a miscellaneous small library of history and theology; the latter subject is not up to date

Stock: More than half million manuscripts; 30,000 books; 6 current periodicals. Stock not available on loan

CANTERBURY	CANTERBURY COLLEGE OF ART	*Tel.:* Canterbury 66294
Kent	St Peter's Lane	
	Canterbury	
326	Kent	

Enquiries: To Librarian

Scope: History of the visual arts and design. History of architecture. Architectural practice and building construction

Stock: 8,000 books; 100 current periodicals; 100 exhibition catalogues; building trade literature

CANTERBURY	CANTERBURY PUBLIC LIBRARY	*Tel.:* Canterbury 63608
Kent	High Street	
	Canterbury	
327	Kent	

Enquiries: To City Librarian

Scope: L.A.S.E.R. subject specialization: Jews (550 books); Colonies; migration (600 books)
Local history and topography of Canterbury and East Kent (4,500 books and pamphlets; 600 prints; 400 maps; newscuttings from 1950)
Special collection of shorthand books (Philip Found Shorthand Collection), 750 items, including some early English and French systems and a large Pitman section. Some runs of shorthand periodicals. All items are available for loan. The Librarian is an expert on old shorthand systems and codes and ciphers
Enquiries are answered on local history and archaeology

CANTERBURY	CANTERBURY TECHNICAL COLLEGE	*Tel.:* Canterbury 66081
Kent	New Dover Road	
	Canterbury	
328	Kent	

Enquiries: To Librarian

Scope: Emphasis on economic history, law, education, sciences, engineering, coal mining, management and business studies, literature, building, secretarial topics

Stock: 8,000 books; 1,000 pamphlets; 100 current periodicals

CANTERBURY	CHRIST CHURCH COLLEGE	*Tel.:* Canterbury 65548
Kent	North Holmes Road	
	Canterbury	
329	College of Education	

Enquiries: To Librarian

Scope: Education, child psychology, teaching method; and books to support main courses in art, divinity, English, geography, music, physical education, mathematics, science and contemporary studies
Special collection: Historical collection of text and children's books (650 volumes)

Stock: 30,000 books and pamphlets; 150 current periodicals

CANTERBURY UNIVERSITY OF KENT AT CANTERBURY *Tel.:* Canterbury 66822
Kent LIBRARY
 The University
330 Canterbury
 Kent

Enquiries: To Librarian

Scope: All subjects covered by the Faculties. Social Sciences includes economics, economic history, politics, law, accounting, statistics and sociology. Humanities includes history, English, French, German, Italian, Classics, philosophy and theology. There is no medicine
Secondary: Russian, linguistics, music, fine arts, psychology, anthropology, human geography

Stock: Books and pamphlets—total stock 155,000 (omitting natural sciences, about 140,000); 1,460 current periodicals in all (omitting natural sciences, about 1,000)

CARDIFF CARDIFF COLLEGE OF EDUCATION *Tel.:* Cardiff 751345
 Cyncoed Road
331 Cardiff CF2 6XD

Enquiries: To Librarian

Scope: General
Special interests: Education, child psychology, physical education
Teaching methods at infant, primary and secondary level. Children's books

Stock: Books and pamphlets: 3,000 education, 1,500 physical education, 6,000 children's books; current periodicals: 52 education, 18 physical education, 5 children's books. Total stock: 35,000 books and pamphlets

CARDIFF CITY OF CARDIFF PUBLIC LIBRARIES *Tel.:* Cardiff 22116
 Central Library
332 The Hayes
 Cardiff CF1 2QU

Enquiries: To City Librarian

Scope: The stock includes extensive collections of: bound periodicals (50,000 volumes); government publications (including early items); and material relating to Wales (stock of 82,000 items attempts to preserve every book and pamphlet concerning Wales and border counties irrespective of language). Other collections include fine bindings, private press publications, limited editions, some early music. Depository for United Nations publications in English. Recognized repository for manorial records, deeds and documents

Stock: 264,000 books; 56,000 pamphlets; 400 current periodicals

CARDIFF CIVIC TRUST FOR WALES *Tel.:* 0222-37146
 Treftadaeth Cymru
333 46 The Parade
 Cardiff CF2 3UE

See no. 1067

CARDIFF	GLAMORGAN COUNTY RECORD OFFICE	*Tel.:* Cardiff 28033 ext. 282
334	County Hall Cathays Park Cardiff CF1 3NE	

Enquiries: To County Archivist

Scope: Historical documents relating to the county of Glamorgan, including records of the County Council, Quarter Sessions, Petty Sessions, and former *ad hoc* bodies (Turnpikes, Boards of Guardians, Local Boards of Health); deposited family estate and industrial collections; maps; some newspapers. No ecclesiastical records. The following are of specific medical and social science interest:

Swansea Gaol. Journals of Governor, Surgeon and Chaplain, 1729–1878 (33 volumes)

Annual Returns of Medical Officers of Health of District Councils and Boroughs to County Medical Officer of Health, 1892–1910 (16 volumes)

Cardiff Medical Society. Minutes, 1870–1948 (6 volumes)

South Wales & Monmouthshire Branch of the British Medical Association. Minutes, 1871–1943 (6 volumes)

Stock: About 500 books and pamphlets of general archive interest and works of local history relating to Glamorgan subjects; 5 current periodicals and Transactions of local History Societies

Publications: Iron in the Making. Dowlais Iron Company Letters, 1782–1860. M. Elsas, ed. 1960
Handlists

CARDIFF	LLANDAFF TECHNICAL COLLEGE	*Tel.:* Cardiff 561241
335	Western Avenue Cardiff CF5 2YB	

Enquiries: To Librarian

Scope: Chiropody; medical laboratory technology; dental laboratory technology; technical education; industrial relations; applied biology; biochemistry; microbiology

CARDIFF	MEDICAL RESEARCH COUNCIL EPIDEMIOLOGY UNIT	*Tel.:* Cardiff 20376
336	4 Richmond Road Cardiff	

The unit is using epidemiological techniques to study the attack rate, prevalence and progression of many diseases, and to test hypotheses about aetiology and prevention

Enquiries: To Director, by letter only

Scope: Epidemiology

CARDIFF	THE NATIONAL MUSEUM OF WALES	*Tel.:* Cardiff 26241
337	Cathays Park Cardiff CF1 3NP	

The primary purpose of the institution is to picture the kind of place Wales is, and man's life and progress therein. This it does by illustrating the geology, botany and zoology of the country and the archaeology, folk-life, industries and art of the people. Folk-life is illustrated at the Welsh Folk Museum, St Fagans (no. 342)

Enquiries: To Director

Scope: Scope of library limited to the subjects represented in the Museum

Stock: 78,000 books and pamphlets; 620 current periodicals. The Museum library houses the Cardiff Naturalists Society's library, rich in natural history periodicals.

Special collections: Tomlin collection (books on molluscs). Willoughby Gardner collection (early books on natural history)

Publications: The Museum issues many publications on the geology, botany, zoology, archaeology, folklife, industry and art of Wales
Amgueddfa: Bulletin of the National Museum of Wales

CARDIFF

338

POISONS INFORMATION SERVICE—CARDIFF   *Tel.:* Cardiff 33101
Cardiff Royal Infirmary
Cardiff

Enquiries: Cardiff 33101 and ask for Poisons Information

Scope: Provides a service to medical profession only on nature, content and probable toxicity of substances listed alphabetically in the Index

CARDIFF

339

SCHOOL BROADCASTING COUNCIL FOR WALES   *Tel.:* Cardiff 564888
Broadcasting House
Llandaff
Cardiff

Set up to advise and direct BBC in its provision of broadcasts to schools in Wales

Enquiries: To Secretary

Scope: Information about all aspects of the BBC's school and Further Education output
No library

CARDIFF

340

THE UNIVERSITY OF WALES INSTITUTE OF SCIENCE AND TECHNOLOGY   *Tel.:* Cardiff 42522
Cathays Park
Cardiff CF1 3NU

Enquiries: To Librarian

Scope: Applied biology; applied physics; architecture; business and social studies; chemistry; civil engineering and building technology; electrical engineering; mechanical and production engineering; English and liberal studies; maritime studies; mathematics; pharmacy; town planning

Stock: 40,000 books; 6,000 pamphlets and reports; 1,200 current periodicals

CARDIFF

341

VIOLET HUGHES LIBRARY
TENOVUS LABORATORIES
VELINDRE MEMORIAL CENTRE FOR CANCER RESEARCH   *Tel.:* Cardiff 63325 ext. 31
Velindre Road
Whitchurch
Cardiff
CF4 7XL

Enquiries: To Librarian

Scope: Cancer research, radiotherapy, chemotherapy, biochemistry, radiobiology, radiology, radioactivity, physics applied to medicine, nuclear medicine, computer science, radiation hazards and protection, radioisotopes

Stock: 400 books; 103 current periodicals; 4,000 clinical and technical photographic slides

CARDIFF	WELSH FOLK MUSEUM	*Tel.:* Cardiff 561357
342	St Fagans Cardiff	

Illustrates Welsh culture and traditions

Enquiries: To Curator

Scope: Welsh Folk Life and ethnology—traditional architecture, domestic implements, costume, lighting, laundering, agriculture and life in the fields, crafts (including clock-making), social institutions, civil organization, law and order, weights and measures, religion, oral traditions, folk tales, folk music and dance, dialects in Wales (all spoken Welsh is being recorded)

Stock: 12,000 books; numerous current periodicals

Publications: Questionnaire on Welsh Folk Culture (in English and Welsh). 1937
Monmouthshire Houses. C. Fox and Lord Raglan: Part 1, 1951; Part 2, 1953; Part 3, 1954
Clock and Watch Makers in Wales. 2nd edition. I. C. Peate. 1960
Hendre'r-ywydd Uchaf, Llangynhafal, Denbighshire: a late 15th century house. I. C. Peate. 1962
Agricultural Transport in Wales. J. G. Jenkins. 1962
Edward Lhuyd ac Iolo Morganwg. G. J. Williams. 1964
Welsh Peasant Costume. F. G. Payne. 1969
The Esgair Moel Woollen Mill. J. G. Jenkins. 1965
Farmhouses and Cottages in Wales: a Picture Book. 1967
Welsh Folk Museum, St Fagans, Handbook. 1968
Welsh Folk Customs. T. M. Owen. 2nd edition. 1968
The Welsh Woollen Industry. J. G. Jenkins. 1969
Postcards
Transparencies

CARDIFF	WELSH HOCKEY ASSOCIATION	*Tel.:* Cardiff 36750
343	9 Cathedral Road Cardiff CF1 9UR	

Enquiries: To Secretary

Scope: International hockey

No library

Publications: Welsh Hockey Times

CARDIFF	THE WELSH NATIONAL SCHOOL OF MEDICINE	*Tel.:* Cardiff 30629
344	Medical School House Howard Place Cardiff CF2 1XE	

Provides central library and information services in all fields of medicine, other than veterinary, for medical practitioners, teachers and research workers in Wales

Enquiries: To Librarian

Scope: Clinical medicine; social and psychological medicine; pathology; metabolism; oral medicine and dentistry; surgery
Secondary: Pharmacology and toxicology; bacteriology; pediatrics; haematology; tuberculosis; cancer; radiology

Stock: 22,000 books and bound periodicals; 1,000 pamphlets; 400 current periodicals
Translation service
In 1971 the Library, with the School of Medicine, will move to a new University Teaching

Hospital at The Heath, Cardiff. Existing departmental collections at Sully Hospital and the Cardiff Royal Infirmary will be enlarged and maintained

CARDIFF

345

WELSH NATIONAL SCHOOL OF MEDICINE *Tel.:* Cardiff 753288 ext. 323
DENTAL SCHOOL
The Heath
Cardiff

Enquiries: To Librarian

Scope: Dentistry in general

Stock: 1,250 books; 250 pamphlets; 135 current periodicals

CARLISLE
Cumberland

346

CARLISLE CATHEDRAL LIBRARY *Tel.:* Carlisle 21614
Carlisle
Cumberland

Enquiries: To Librarian

Scope: Dean and Chapter Records from 1660 (some earlier manuscripts). 17th and 18th century theology (nucleus presented by Bishop Thomas Smith)
Secondary: 19th century volumes of local history. (The 500 volumes of the Record Office Publications are now deposited with the County Record Office, The Castle, Carlisle, no. 354)

Stock: 4,070 books including 105 volumes of 17th century tracts and sermons. Stock not available on loan, but microfilming arranged

CARLISLE
Cumberland

347

CARLISLE CITY ART GALLERY *Tel.:* Carlisle 24166
Tullie House
Castle Street
Carlisle
Cumberland

Enquiries: To Curator

Scope: Permanent collection is mainly modern (that is, painters from about 1930 onwards) plus the Dr Gordon Bottomley Bequest of 19th century paintings, drawings and prints

CARLISLE
Cumberland

348

CARLISLE CITY MUSEUM *Tel.:* Carlisle 24166
Tullie House
Castle Street
Carlisle
Cumberland

Enquiries: To Curator

Scope: Collection covers geological area of Cumberland, Westmorland, Lake District and North Lancashire, in particular antiquities of Pre-historic, Roman, Medieval and later periods, and natural history and geology
Williamson collection of English porcelain

CARLISLE
Cumberland

349

CARLISLE COLLEGE OF ART AND DESIGN *Tel.:* Carlisle 25333
Brampton Road
Carlisle
Cumberland

Enquiries: To Tutor Librarian

Scope: Fine art (painting, sculpture, architecture); graphic design (including typography); textiles (including fashion and dress); design (including industrial design)

CARLISLE, CARLISLE COLLEGE OF ART AND DESIGN, *cont.*

Secondary: Interior design, ceramics, letterpress printing, lithography

Stock: 8,000 books; 100 current periodicals; 8,000 slides

CARLISLE CARLISLE PUBLIC LIBRARIES *Tel.:* Carlisle 24166
Cumberland Tullie House
  Castle Street
350 Carlisle
  Cumberland

Enquiries: To Librarian

Scope: General, with *Special Collection* (Jackson Library) of printed material on all aspects of Cumberland, Westmorland and the Lake District, including early engravings and maps, and special Wordsworth collection

Stock: 140,000 books and pamphlets; 118 current periodicals (total stock)

Library houses exchange transactions received by Cumberland and Westmorland Antiquarian and Archaeological Society (no. 351)

CARLISLE CUMBERLAND & WESTMORLAND *Tel.:* Grange-over-Sands 2407
Cumberland ANTIQUARIAN & ARCHAEOLOGICAL SOCIETY
  Tullie House
351 Carlisle
  Cumberland

Enquiries: To Hon. Secretary, Affetside, Kilmidyke Road, Grange-over-Sands, Lancashire, by letter only

Scope: Antiquities, archaeology and historical records of Cumberland, Westmorland and Lancashire north of the Sands

Publications: Transactions (annually)

CARLISLE CUMBERLAND COUNCIL OF SOCIAL SERVICE *Tel.:* Carlisle 25159
Cumberland 6 West Walls
  Carlisle
352 Cumberland

Enquiries: To Secretary

Scope: Generally concerned with assisting and advising individuals and community groups in the following fields: Old people's welfare, care of the handicapped, voluntary service by young people, pre-retirement courses, citizens advice bureaux, training of voluntary workers, village halls, parish councils, best kept village competition, countryside development and conservation, any kind of voluntary action in meeting social needs or providing community care

No library

CARLISLE CUMBERLAND COUNTY LIBRARY *Tel.:* Carlisle 23456
Cumberland 1 Portland Square
  Carlisle
353 Cumberland

Enquiries: To Librarian

Scope: General stock strong in agriculture and education and including music. Local history and drama collections. Joint Fiction Reserve Scheme FAU-FEZ

Stock: 330,000 books and pamphlets; 150 current periodicals (total stock)

Publications: Printed Catalogue of Drama Collection

Houses library of the Lakeland Dialect Society

CARLISLE Cumberland 354	JOINT ARCHIVES COMMITTEE FOR CUMBERLAND, WESTMORLAND AND CARLISLE The Record Office The Castle Carlisle *and* The Record Office County Hall Kendal Westmorland	*Tel.:* Carlisle 24248 *Tel.:* Kendal 1000

Enquiries: To Archivist at the Record Office at Carlisle or Kendal

Scope: The usual range of records of County and City Record offices, including ample primary sources for study of medicine (as practised), social sciences, and humanities: for example, Quarter Sessions (particularly petitions), Parish and Poor Law Union records, extensive private deposits (including some literary manuscripts)
Secondary: The Carlisle Law Library (supplemented by privately deposited manuscripts or printed lawbooks). Public Record Office publications up to 1909. Publication in the Rolls Series (these two on loan from Dean and Chapter Library, Carlisle)
Hansard Parliamentary History of England 1066–1803 and Parliamentary Debates 1803–1832
Lords and Commons Journals
The Carlisle and Moorhouse Quaker Libraries

Stock not available on loan

Publications: Bibliography of the History and Topography of Cumberland and Westmorland. H. W. Hodgson. 1969
Fleming-Senhouse Papers. E. Hughes. 1961

Records and books in the library of the Dean and Chapter, Carlisle, are available at the Record Office, The Castle, Carlisle, upon application to the Chapter Librarian

CARLTON Nottingham	*See under* **NOTTINGHAM** for CARLTON PUBLIC LIBRARY (no. 1887)

CARMARTHEN 355	CARMARTHENSHIRE COUNTY MUSEUM 5 Quay Street Carmarthen	*Tel.:* Carmarthen 6641 ext. 81

Museum of local history and folk culture (including archaeology)

Enquiries: To Curator

Scope: Carmarthenshire Local History particularly the 19th century, and the Roman Period
Secondary: Natural history; botany, geology and animal life
Some knowledge of surrounding counties (Pembrokeshire and Cardiganshire)

CARMARTHEN 356	CARMARTHENSHIRE COUNTY RECORD OFFICE County Hall Carmarthen	*Tel.:* Carmarthen 6641

Collection and preservation of records, documents, and manuscripts concerned with the county of Carmarthenshire

Enquiries: The County Archivist, preferably by letter

Scope: All the material held is primary, for example, records, documents, deeds, maps and plans

Publications: Typewritten schedules of the manuscript collections

CARMARTHEN	THE HISTORICAL SOCIETY OF THE CHURCH IN WALES	*Tel.*: Carmarthen 7971
357	Trinity College Carmarthen	

Enquiries: To Secretary or Hon. Editor, Llangibby Rectory, Usk, Monmouthshire, by letter only
Scope: History of the Church in Wales
No library
Publications: Annual journal and occasional collections of documents

CARMARTHEN	TRINITY COLLEGE	*Tel.*: Carmarthen 7971
358	Carmarthen College of Education	

Enquiries: To Librarian
Scope: Education
Stock: Special runs of periodicals include:
Archaeologia Cambrensis 1846– ; British Academy Proceedings 1903– ; Bulletin of the John Rylands Library 1913– ; Dublin Review 1906– ; Edinburgh Review 1802–1929; Expository Times 1875– ; Hibbert Journal 1902– ; Journal of Theological Studies 1900– ; Lumen Vitae 1946– ; Quarterly Review 1809–1960

CARSHALTON Surrey	CARSHALTON COLLEGE OF FURTHER EDUCATION	*Tel.*: 01-669 0202
359	Nightingale Road Carshalton Surrey	

Enquiries: To Librarian, by letter only
Scope: Law, economics, social science, history, geography and literature (to GCE 'A' level)
Stock: 7,500 books; 75 current periodicals

CARSHALTON Surrey	LONDON BOROUGH OF SUTTON PUBLIC LIBRARIES CARSHALTON PUBLIC LIBRARY	*Tel.*: 01-647 1151
360	The Square Carshalton Surrey	

See no. 2196

CARSHALTON Surrey	MEDICAL RESEARCH COUNCIL MEDICAL RESEARCH COUNCIL LABORATORIES	*Tel.*: 01-643 4461
361	Woodmansterne Road Carshalton Surrey	

Toxicology Unit. Neuropsychiatry Unit. Laboratory Animals Centre
Enquiries: To Director of Unit concerned, by letter only
Scope: Toxicology; neuropsychiatry; biochemistry; chemistry; laboratory animal science
Stock: 9,000 books; 750 pamphlets; 290 current periodicals

CARSHALTON Surrey **362**	POSTGRADUATE MEDICAL CENTRE St Helier Hospital Wrythe Lane Carshalton Surrey	*Tel.:* 01-644 4343 ext. 419

Enquiries: To Administrative Organizer
Scope: Small medical library
Stock: 230 books; 20 pamphlets; 35 current periodicals. Stock not available on loan

---

CASTLEFORD CASTLEFORD PUBLIC LIBRARIES *Tel.:* Castleford 3553
Yorkshire Central Library and Museum
    Castleford
363 Yorkshire

Enquiries: To Librarian
Scope: Collection of 600 books and pamphlets on Yorkshire
Subject specialization: Industrial training, trade unions, labour disputes, coal mining
Stock: 68,500 books; 600 pamphlets; 80 current periodicals (total stock)
Publications: Catalogue of Yorkshire Collection

CATERHAM ST LAWRENCE'S HOSPITAL *Tel.:* Caterham 42377
Surrey Caterham
    Surrey
364 Hospital for the care of the mentally subnormal

Enquiries: To Librarian, by letter only
Scope: Mental subnormality and allied subjects
Stock: 700 books; 2,500 pamphlets; 35 current periodicals. Stock not available on loan
Publications: Proceedings of the First Congress of the International Association for the Scientific Study of Mental Deficiency, 1967. 1968

CHADDERTON See under **OLDHAM** for
Oldham CHADDERTON PUBLIC LIBRARY (no. 1908)
Lancs

CHALFONT ST MILTON'S COTTAGE *Tel.:* Chalfont St Giles 2313
GILES Chalfont St Giles
Bucks Buckinghamshire

Milton's Cottage is maintained for the benefit of the public, and particularly of all interested
365 in the life and works of John Milton, as a museum for objects connected with John Milton
and other objects of historic interest in the parish of Chalfont St Giles and the neighbourhood

Enquiries: To Curator
Scope: John Milton, his life and works. A collection of first and early editions of John Milton's works is in the library. Historical and biographical literature and criticism in connection with John Milton and his works
Secondary: Local history
Stock: 500 books. Stock available for study on premises by students and scholars

CHATHAM Kent 366	CHATHAM PUBLIC LIBRARY New Road Chatham Kent	*Tel.:* Medway 43589 and 44083

Enquiries: To Borough Librarian

Scope: General stock in medicine, the social sciences and the humanities
Secondary: Collection of works by and about Dickens: 330 works about, plus the works by (including runs of *Household Words* and *All the Year Round*) and a complete run of *The Dickensian*
Navy collection: 340 volumes, including Naval Chronicle 1799–1814, short runs of the *Navy List*, and the Navy Records Society's publications (111 volumes to date)

Stock: 90,000 books in the specified fields; 2,000 pamphlets in these fields; 150 current periodicals taken in the specified fields

CHATHAM Kent 367	MEDWAY AND MAIDSTONE COLLEGE OF TECHNOLOGY Horsted Chatham Kent *See* no. 1734

CHELMSFORD Essex 368	CHELMSFORD AND ESSEX MUSEUM Oaklands Park Moulsham Street Chelmsford Essex	*Tel.:* Chelmsford 53066

Enquiries: To Borough Librarian and Curator

Scope: Collections deal with birds (mostly British), Roman and prehistoric Britain, local industries, geology, conchology, coins, butterflies and beetles, foreign mammals, Essex bygones, dress and uniform, pottery, glass. An identification service is given on a general level

Stock: 250 books; 10 current periodicals

Publications: Guide to local industries and coins rooms
A Twenty Minute Guide to the Museum
A Programme of Forthcoming Exhibitions (issued annually)
26 postcards, fourteen of which are views of Chelmsford in former times

CHELMSFORD Essex 369	CHELMSFORD CATHEDRAL LIBRARY The Cathedral Chelmsford Essex	*Tel.:* Chelmsford 52702

Enquiries: To Librarian, by letter only

Scope: Contemporary works in Biblical, missionary and ecumenical, and socio-psychological fields. Official reports of the Church of England and of the Diocese of Chelmsford
Secondary: The Knightbridge collection of 16th and 17th century theological works (500 volumes)

Stock: 3,500 books; 1,000 pamphlets; 500 reports; 6 current periodicals

Publications: Occasional booklists

CHELMSFORD	CHELMSFORD PUBLIC LIBRARY	*Tel.:* Chelmsford 61733
Essex	Civic Centre	(59292 evenings and
	Duke Street	Saturdays)
370	Chelmsford	
	Essex	

Enquiries: To Librarian

Scope: General stock including music. Chelmsford and Essex local collection. L.A.S.E.R. subject specialization includes: English central and local government, including departments, except public health, national health service and national insurance; welfare of paupers and aged; postal service excluding postage stamps

Stock: 46,000 books; 8,750 pamphlets; 250 current periodicals; 4,750 maps, illustrations, slides, microfilms

CHELMSFORD	ESSEX COUNTY LIBRARY	*Tel.:* Chelmsford 51141
Essex	Goldlay Gardens	*Telex:* 99223
	Chelmsford	
371	Essex	

Enquiries: To Librarian

Scope: Special collections: Political parties; certain aspects of medicine; painting; archaeology; statistics

Stock: 2,000,000 books; many pamphlets; 500 current periodicals including 70 abstracts journals (total stock)

Publications: Monthly List of Additions   Bibliographies
List of Abstracts   Union List of Periodicals
Technical and Commercial Library Service is Headquarters for Co-operative Information Service for firms and medical centres

CHELMSFORD	ESSEX RECORD OFFICE	*Tel.:* Chelmsford 53233
Essex	County Hall	
	Chelmsford	
372	Essex	

Enquiries: To County Archivist

Scope: The Essex Record Office endeavours to answer any enquiry of a geneaological, topographical or subject nature to the extent of checking its comprehensive indexes and typescript catalogues, but cannot undertake research into the original records themselves or into printed sources in its extensive library of Essex books and general works of reference

Stock: 5,000 books; 6,000 pamphlets; printed reports of other county record offices and similar archive repositories. Most important historical journals and all local historical publications and periodicals are held

Publications: Essex Parish Records, 1240–1894. 1966
Second and Third Supplements to Catalogue of Maps in Essex Record Office 1964, 1968
Guide to Essex Record Office. 1969
Reproductions of Maps
Examples of English Handwriting, 1150–1750. H. Grieve. 3rd edition. 1966
Ingatestone Hall in 1600. F. G. Emmison. 1954
Petre Family Portraits, from 1565. D. Piper. 1956
Thaxted in the Fourteenth Century. K. C. Newton. 1960
Royal Progress: Report on the Essex Record Office, 1956–1961. 1962
Record Retrospect: The Essex Record Office, 1938–1963. 1964
The Fields of Saffron Walden in 1400. D. Cromarty. 1966

CHELMSFORD, ESSEX RECORD OFFICE, *cont.*
Audley End, The Restoration of 1762–1797. J. D. Williams. 1966
Essex at Work, 1700–1815. A. F. J. Brown. 1969
Picture Booklets
Essex Historic Buildings (Subject booklets)

The Essex Record Office also has a large exhibition and teaching centre during the summer months at Ingatestone Hall, about 8 miles from Chelmsford

CHELMSFORD GRAND NATIONAL ARCHERY SOCIETY *Tel.:* Chelmsford 57982
Essex 20 Broomfield Road
  Chelmsford
373 Essex

Enquiries: To Secretary

Scope: Placing of individuals in archery clubs. Formation of new clubs
Secondary: Coaching and instruction, and advice on equipment

No library

Publications: Leaflet: Introduction to Archery
Periodical News Letter

CHELMSFORD MEDICAL RECORDING SERVICE *Tel.:* Writtle 316
Essex Kitts Croft
  Writtle
374 Chelmsford
  Essex

Enquiries: To Secretary

Scope: Audiotapes with slides (no special equipment required except tape recorder and slide viewer) for continuing education primarily of general medical practitioners but also nearly all fields of medicine including some health education; also small collection of slides for illustrating for teachers. Tapes also include tapes acquired from other similar services and medical schools. Enquiries about techniques of medical sound recording

Stock: 600 audiotape titles—copies are supplied from master tape so that almost unlimited stock available on loan on 24 hour demand by post

Publications: Duplicated loose-leaf Catalogue

CHELMSFORD MID ESSEX TECHNICAL COLLEGE AND SCHOOL *Tel.:* Chelmsford 54491
Essex   OF ART
  Victoria Road South
375 Chelmsford
  Essex

Enquiries: To Librarian

Scope: Large collection of law books and periodicals. Human relations, with particular reference to management. Chemistry and biology

Stock: 5,000 books; 200 pamphlets; 47 current periodicals

CHELTENHAM CHELTENHAM ART GALLERY AND MUSEUM *Tel.:* Cheltenham 22476
Glos Clarence Street
  Cheltenham
376 Gloucestershire GL50 3JT

Enquiries: To Curator

Scope: Baron de Ferrieres Gallery of Dutch paintings and permanent collection of oils, water-colours, etchings and local prints. The Museum contains a large collection of English pottery and porcelain and there are rooms devoted to local geology, natural history, archaeology, Cotswold bygones, Edward Wilson personalia, Georgian room, Victorian kitchen, Cotswold furniture and Chinese Porcelain room

No library

CHELTENHAM Glos 377	CHELTENHAM PUBLIC LIBRARY Clarence Street Cheltenham Gloucestershire GL50 3JT	*Tel.:* Cheltenham 22476

Enquiries: To Librarian

Scope: Regional subject specialization includes: Christian sacraments; planning cemeteries and natural landscape reserves; glassware; painting (art)—except history of; prints and print-making; English fiction: critical works
Special collections: Day Library of Natural History, 700 rare books, 19th century and earlier, on natural history mainly on fishes; Local—Cheltenham and Cotswolds

Stock: 175,000 books; 180 current periodicals (total stock)

CHELTENHAM Glos 378	GLOUCESTERSHIRE COLLEGE OF ART AND DESIGN Albert Road Pittville Cheltenham Gloucestershire	*Tel.:* Cheltenham 21612

Enquiries: To Librarian

Scope: Fine art, painting, sculpture, fashion, history of costume, architecture, town planning and landscape architecture

Stock: 12,000 books; 170 current periodicals

CHELTENHAM Glos 379	ST MARY'S COLLEGE OF EDUCATION The Park Cheltenham GL50 2RH Gloucestershire Church of England College of Education for women	*Tel.:* Cheltenham 53836

Enquiries: To Tutor Librarian

Scope: Education, psychology, religion

Stock: 23,470 books; 181 current periodicals

CHELTENHAM Glos 380	ST PAUL'S COLLEGE OF EDUCATION Swindon Road Cheltenham Gloucestershire GL50 4AZ Church of England College for men	*Tel.:* Cheltenham 28111

Enquiries: To Librarian

Scope: General stock with specialist emphasis in education, psychology, science, physical education and design. The Children's library used for teaching practice has a wide selection of fiction

CHELTENHAM, ST PAUL'S COLLEGE OF EDUCATION, *cont.*
and non-fiction ranging from books for very young children to school leavers. Textbooks and teachers' manuals are also included

Stock: 35,000 books; including 8,000 Children's books in the Teaching Practice Library; 2,000 pamphlets; 1,000 reports; 230 current periodicals

CHERTSEY
Surrey

381

CHERTSEY LIBRARY
Guildford Street
Chertsey
Surrey

Tel.: Chertsey 3747 and 4101

Enquiries: To Reference Librarian

Scope: Regional specialization: Road accidents, road safety and road signs; French literature (including some 18th and 19th century texts in French); biographical material in these two subject fields

Stock: 36,000 books and pamphlets (Lending Department), 5,000 books and pamphlets (Reference Department); complete set of Road Research Laboratory RRL Reports; 170 current periodicals including permanent files of *Apollo* from 1967 and *Daily Telegraph and supplements* from 1964; 532 (1,475 sheets) maps

Publications: Directory of Trades and Professions for Chertsey Urban District
Directory of Schools and Colleges in Chertsey Urban District
List of additions to stock in all subject fields
List of periodical holdings
List of maps and atlases in stock

Founder member of the Surrey Reference and Information Group

CHESHUNT
Waltham Cross
Herts

See under **WALTHAM CROSS** for
CHESHUNT PUBLIC LIBRARY (no. 2246)

CHESTER

382

CHESHIRE COUNTY COUNCIL LIBRARY &
MUSEUM SERVICES
County Library Headquarters
91 Hoole Road
Chester CH2 3NG

Tel.: Chester 20055

Enquiries: To Director

Scope: All subjects with particular emphasis on Cheshire topography

Stock: 800,000 books, pamphlets and reports, 100 current periodicals (total stock)

CHESTER

383

CHESHIRE RECORD OFFICE
The Castle
Chester

Tel.: Chester 24678

Enquiries: To County Archivist

Scope: The collections include records of local authorities and courts, the diocese, parishes, private estates and business, antiquarian collections within the county. Enquirers are expected to make their own searches, searches by staff being strictly limited to specific enquiries and information about sources available. The small reference library seeks to provide information about sources for the history of the county, and for interpreting the records in its care

Stock: 1,600 books; 400 pamphlets. Stock not available on loan

CHESTER

384

THE CHESHIRE REGIMENT MUSEUM
The Castle
Chester

Enquiries: To RHQ The Cheshire Regiment, The Castle, Chester

Scope: The history of The Cheshire Regiment from its foundation in 1689
Secondary: The Army as a whole

Stock: 300 books: large collection of photographs and miscellania

Publications: The Oak Tree (Regimental journal)

CHESTER

385

CHESTER ARCHAEOLOGICAL SOCIETY   *Tel.:* OCH 4 21938 and
c/o Chester Public Library   43427
St John Street
Chester CH1 1DH

Enquiries: To Hon. Librarian

Scope: Archaeology, history and architecture of Chester, Cheshire and North Wales
Secondary: Archaeology in general

Stock: 6,500 books, pamphlets and reports; 29 current periodicals; 2,000 manuscripts and original papers housed at Chester Record Office, Town Hall, Chester

Publications: Journal of the Chester Archaeological Society (annually)

CHESTER

386

CHESTER COLLEGE OF FURTHER EDUCATION   *Tel.:* Chester 26321
Eaton Road
Chester

Enquiries: To Librarian

Scope: Engineering (mechanical and electrical); industrial engineering; building; business, general and liberal studies; art

Stock: 12,000 books; many pamphlets and reports; 120 current periodicals

CHESTER

387

CHESTER PUBLIC LIBRARY   *Tel.:* OCH 4 21938 and
St John Street   43427
Chester CH1 1DH

Enquiries: To City Librarian

Scope: N.W.R.L.S. subject specialization includes: Martial law

Stock: 157,000 books, pamphlets, maps and manuscripts; 310 current periodicals (total stock). Chester Photographic Survey on 35mm slides with contact prints on record cards (not available on loan)

Publications: Chester Newspaper Index (every five years—first volume covers the years 1955–59)

Chester Archaeological Society Library housed in Public Library

CHESTER

388

DEVA HOSPITAL MEDICAL LIBRARY   *Tel.:* Chester 22282
Deva Hospital
Liverpool Road
Chester

Enquiries: To Librarian, by letter only

Scope: Library of psychiatric subjects, including, as well as general psychiatry, drug addiction, adolescent problems, alcoholics, and problems of the young mother and child
Secondary: General medical periodicals

CHESTER, DEVA HOSPITAL MEDICAL LIBRARY, *cont.*

Stock: 650 books; most reports published by governmental sources related to hospital organization. Stock not normally available on loan

---

CHESTER

389

THE GROSVENOR MUSEUM *Tel.:* 0244-21616
27 Grosvenor Street
Chester CH1 2DD

Enquiries: To Curator

Scope: Archaeology, local history (including numismatics), natural history and topographical art relating to Chester, Cheshire and North Wales

Stock: 200 books; 500 pamphlets; 50 current periodicals; 2,000 slides; 3,000 photographic negatives. Stock not available on loan

Publications: Short Guide to the Inscribed and Sculptured Stones in the Grosvenor Museum. G. Webster
The Roman Army. G. Webster
Deva—Roman Chester. F. H. Thompson
Catalogue of the Roman Inscribed and Sculptured Stones in the Grosvenor Museum. R. P. Wright and I. A. Richmond

---

CHESTERFIELD
Derbyshire

390

CHESTERFIELD COLLEGE OF TECHNOLOGY *Tel.:* Chesterfield 76761
Infirmary Road
Chesterfield
Derbyshire

Enquiries: To Librarian

Scope: Politics, government, economics, education, industrial training, accountancy, management, literature, language, history, geography

Stock: 16,000 books; 5,000 pamphlets; 100 reports; 330 current periodicals

Publications: Booklists (for example, Education, Bank Reviews Index)
Library Bulletin (contains reviews of newly acquired books and pamphlets)
Subject List of Periodical Articles (weekly or fortnightly)
Periodicals Holdings List

CHESTERFIELD
Derbyshire

391

CHESTERFIELD PUBLIC LIBRARY AND *Tel.:* Chesterfield 2661 and
   INFORMATION BUREAU 2047
Corporation Street
Chesterfield
Derbyshire

Enquiries: To Borough Librarian

Scope: Local history collection includes material on Derbyshire industries particularly lead-mining and coal-mining
Special collection: The George Stephenson Collection of more than 700 items on early railway history

Stock: 7,000 books (General reference stock of Reference Library and Information Service); 1,500 pamphlets; 180 current periodicals

Publications: List of Periodical Holdings

CHESTERFIELD
Derbyshire

392

SURGICAL DRESSINGS MANUFACTURERS' ASSOCIATION
Wheat Bridge Mills
Chesterfield
Derbyshire
Trade Association

Tel.: Chesterfield 2105

Enquiries: To Secretary
Scope: Any information on surgical dressings and the surgical dressings industry
No library

CHICHESTER
Sussex

393

AEROMEDICAL INTERNATIONAL
6 Cawley Road
Chichester
Sussex
Co-ordination of research into the behavioural problems of aviation

Tel.: Chichester 86045

Enquiries: To Director of Research
Scope: Aviation psychology: selection proceedings and techniques applied to flight crew and other personnel; pilot skills, assessment and limitations; effects of stress, electrophysiological recording techniques; mental health; clinical psychology
Stock: 10 books; (Members Libraries forming part of information service: 2,000 books); 200 reports; 16 current periodicals
Publications: Flight Safety (quarterly, official journal of the Society)
Lector Medicus Book Review Index (in association with the Society of Honorary Medical Librarians)

CHICHESTER
Sussex

394

CHICHESTER CATHEDRAL LIBRARY
Chichester
Sussex

Enquiries: To Librarian, by letter only, at 63 Orchard Street, Chichester, Sussex. (*Tel.:* Chichester 83490)
Scope: Library of works principally on theology, general, ecclesiastical and local history, and biography, 17th to 20th centuries
Stock: 3,500 books; 600 pamphlets. Stock not available on loan
Publications: Chichester Cathedral Library. F. W. Steer. 1964

CHICHESTER
Sussex

395

CHICHESTER CITY MUSEUM
29 Little London
Chichester
Sussex

Tel.: Chichester 84683

Enquiries: To Curator
Scope: The history, archaeology, trade and pastimes of the City and surrounding area in West Sussex. The collections are small as the Museum was only opened in 1964
See also no. 399 for Sussex collection
Stock: Limited reference library, mostly archaeology and folk life; 6 current periodicals
Publications: 51 'Chichester Papers' (booklets on important people and buildings of the City)
Guide to the City Museum
Guide and history of Greyfriars Church, Priory Park

CHICHESTER	CHICHESTER POSTGRADUATE MEDICAL	*Tel.:* Chichester 82671
Sussex	LIBRARY	
	St Richards Hospital	
396	Chichester	
	Sussex	

Enquiries: To Secretary

Scope: All branches of medical interest
Secondary: Some dental and veterinary books and periodicals

Stock: 1,070 books; 47 current periodicals. Stock not available on loan

CHICHESTER	CHICHESTER THEOLOGICAL COLLEGE	*Tel.:* Chichester 83369
Sussex	Chichester	
	Sussex	
397	College training men for the Ministry in the Church of England	

Enquiries: To Librarian

Scope: The Library covers all branches of theology (the Bible, doctrine, liturgy, church history) with some philosophy and ethics; and more specialist collections of Tractarian literature

Stock: 15,000 books; 25 current periodicals (all theological)

CHICHESTER	THE ROYAL SUSSEX REGIMENT MUSEUM	*Tel.:* Chichester 86311
Sussex	Roussillon Barracks	ext. 28
	Chichester	
398	Sussex	

Enquiries: To Curator, by letter only

Scope: Museum and small library concerned with the history and relics of The Royal Sussex Regiment

Stock: 50 books

CHICHESTER	WEST SUSSEX COUNTY LIBRARY	*Tel.:* Chichester 86563
Sussex	Tower Street	*Telex:* 86279
	Chichester	
399	Sussex	

Enquiries: To County Librarian

Scope: L.A.S.E.R. subject specialization: Birds; comparative and historical law; growth and physical development; gynaecology and obstetrics; diseases at special development periods; religion of primitive peoples; Egypt. Local history of East and West Sussex

Stock: 624,000 books and pamphlets, including 3,000 on subject specialization, and 5,000 on local history; 700 current periodicals

CHIGWELL	CHIGWELL SCHOOL	*Tel.:* 01-500 2014
Essex	SWALLOW LIBRARY	
	High Road	
400	Chigwell	
	Essex	

Enquiries: To Librarian

Scope: Library stock is based on principal school subjects, but any enquiries related to humanities will be answered

Stock: 4,000 books. Stock not available on loan

CHIPPING NORTON Oxon **401**	HEYTHROP COLLEGE Chipping Norton Oxfordshire OX7 5UE	*Tel.:* 0608-72 336

Ecclesiastical college conducted by the Society of Jesus, with power to confer Roman degrees in philosophy and theology

Enquiries: To Librarian

Scope: Biblical literature, theology, philosophy, church history, canon law, ascetical and devotional literature, liturgy

Special collections: Patristic and scholastic theology; 17th century religious controversial literature; Roman Catholic recusant history

Secondary: General literature, history

Stock: 160,000 books; 7,000 pamphlets; 300 current periodicals

Publications: The Heythrop Journal

CHIPPING NORTON Oxon **402**	MASTERS' OF FOXHOUNDS ASSOCIATION The Elm Chipping Norton Oxfordshire OX7 5NS	*Tel.:* Chipping Norton 2309

Governing body of foxhunting

Enquiries: To Secretary

Scope: Any information on foxhunting

Publications: Foxhound Kennel Stud Book (annually)
Members Handbook

CHORLEY Lancs **403**	CHORLEY COLLEGE OF EDUCATION Union Street Chorley Lancashire	*Tel.:* Chorley 4981

Enquiries: To Senior Tutor Librarian

Scope: Theory and practice of education. Art and design, biology, chemistry, dance, drama, economics, English, French, geography, history, human biology, international relations, mathematics, music, philosophy, physical education, physics, psychology, rural studies, sociology, educational technology, linguistics, religious education

Stock: 36,000 books; 225 current periodicals

CIRENCESTER Glos **404**	ARLINGTON MILL MUSEUM Bibury Cirencester Gloucestershire	*Tel.:* Bibury 368

Enquiries: To Director, by letter only

Scope: In the Mill there is the working machinery of an 18th century Corn Mill, altered in the 19th century, and a collection of old farm implements, carpenters tools, Victorian furniture and costume, Victorian Staffordshire pottery named figures and furniture by Ernest Gimson

No library

CLAYGATE Esher Surrey	*See under* **ESHER** *for* GENERAL AND MUNICIPAL WORKERS' UNION (no. 580)

CLYDEBANK	CLYDEBANK PUBLIC LIBRARIES	*Tel.:* 041-952 1416
Dunbartonshire	Central Library	
	Dunbarton Road	
405	Clydebank	
	Dunbartonshire	

Enquiries: To Burgh Librarian

Scope: General stock including music and gramophone record library. Small local collection relating to Clydebank and Dunbartonshire

Stock: 79,000 books and pamphlets; 250 maps; 1,000 music scores; 2,000 stereo records (total stock) 128 current periodicals

Publications: A View of Clydebank 1870–1900: a brochure of local history photographs

Displays of local historical and archaeological interest, fine printing, bookbinding and early printed books. Local and other art exhibitions

COATBRIDGE	COATBRIDGE TECHNICAL COLLEGE	*Tel.:* Coatbridge 22316
Lancashire	Kildonan Street	
	Coatbridge	
406	Lanarkshire	

Enquiries: To Principal

Scope: Economics, mathematics, physics, chemistry, mechanical engineering, electrical engineering, electronics, civil engineering, building, metallurgy, commerce, literature and social studies

Stock: 9,000 books; 100 current periodicals; 3,000 British Standards

COLCHESTER	COLCHESTER AND ESSEX MUSEUM	*Tel.:* Colchester 77475 and
Essex	The Castle	76071
	Colchester	
407	Essex	

The collection, preservation and display of historical material relating to Colchester and Essex

Enquiries: To Curator

Scope: The Museum welcomes enquiries for the identification of objects and relating to the history of the area. The reserve collections are available for specialized research. There is a Schools Officer who deals with school visits. The library is maintained for the convenience of the staff, but is available for students

Stock: 600 books; 200 pamphlets; 12 current periodicals

Publications: Guides to the town, Castle, Roman Colchester, The Hollytrees and related subjects

The Hollytrees, High Street, Colchester is a Branch Museum for the display of later antiquities, and houses the Library of the Essex Archaeological Society on the history of Essex
The natural history collection is housed at the Natural History Museum, All Saint's Church, High Street, Colchester (*Tel.:* Colchester 76071 and 73669) where there is a library of 250 books, 100 pamphlets and 6 current periodicals

COLCHESTER	COLCHESTER PUBLIC LIBRARY	*Tel.:* Colchester 70378
Essex	Shewell Road	
	Colchester	
408	Essex	

Enquiries: To Librarian

Scope: Essex Collection: Books, pamphlets, maps and illustrations relating to Colchester and Essex

Archbishop Harsnett's Library (bequeathed to town 1631)—mainly theology (850 volumes)
Castle Library (begun as private collection, later Castle Society Subscription Library)—general 17th to early 19th century (2,500 volumes)
Music
L.A.S.E.R. subject specialization includes: Drawing (technique, collections) including cartoons and book illustration. Iceland; Netherlands; Belgium; Luxemburg; Switzerland; Greece; Albania; Yugoslavia; Bulgaria; Rumania; Crete; Aegean Islands
Gramophone Record Library

Stock: 17,000 (reference), 59,000 (lending) books; 1,500 (reference) pamphlets; 50 current periodicals (total stock); 2,500 records

Publications: Subject lists (particularly local and music)

COLCHESTER   UNIVERSITY OF ESSEX LIBRARY   *Tel.:* Colchester (0206) 5114
Essex   Wivenhoe Park   *Telex:* 98440
   Colchester
409   Essex

Enquiries: To Librarian

Scope: Subjects covered by Schools of Social Studies and Comparative Studies (Departments of Art, Economics, Government, Literature, and Sociology). Strong holdings in North American, Latin American and Russian literature, government and history

Stock: 100,000 books; 1,400 current periodicals

Publications: List of holdings of serials
Comparative and Social Studies, a guide of reference material held in the Library
Reference Leaflet No. 1. British Government publications. 1968

COLERAINE   LONDONDERRY COUNTY LIBRARY   *Tel.:* Coleraine 4111
Co. Londonderry   County Hall
   Coleraine
410   Co. Londonderry

Enquiries: To Librarian

Scope: Library of Irish books; Londonderry County (including paintings and prints)

Stock: Total stock includes 200 current periodicals

Publications: List of periodicals taken, including back files of local firms housed under co-operative storage scheme

COLERAINE   NEW UNIVERSITY OF ULSTER LIBRARY   *Tel.:* Coleraine 4141
Co. Londonderry   Coleraine
   Co. Londonderry
411

Enquiries: To Librarian

Scope: Covered on a rapidly growing scale are economics, social administration, social organization, all aspects of education, history (modern only), literature, Russian and East European studies, geography and regional studies

Stock: 50,000 books; 1,600 current periodicals

COLNE   COLNE PUBLIC LIBRARY   *Tel.:* Colne 298
Lancs   Albert Road
   Colne
412   Lancashire

COLNE, COLNE PUBLIC LIBRARY, *cont.*
Enquiries: To Borough Librarian
Scope: Subject specialization includes: Obstetrics (diseases) and labour; Asia
Stock: 29 books on obstetrics; 279 books on Asia

COLWYN BAY BOROUGH OF COLWYN BAY PUBLIC LIBRARY *Tel.:* Colwyn Bay 2358
Denbighshire Woodland Road West
  Colwyn Bay
413 Denbighshire
Enquiries: To Librarian
Scope: Welsh Reference Collection (8,000 volumes)
Plays (sets and singles)
Hilaire Belloc Collection
Secondary: Strong in biography, economics, religion and humanities generally
Subject specialization: Oriental and ancient philosophy; modern philosophy; non-Christian religions
Stock: 89,000 books; 100 current periodicals (total stock)

COLWYN BAY LLANDRILLO TECHNICAL COLLEGE *Tel.:* Colwyn Bay 44216
Denbighshire Llandudno Road
  Colwyn Bay
414 Denbighshire
Enquiries: To Librarian
Scope: Hotel-keeping and catering, hairdressing, commercial subjects, engineering and construction, pre-health service
Secondary: Domestic science, general science and food subjects
Stock: 8,000 books; 75 current periodicals

COMPTON *See under* **GUILDFORD** *for*
Guildford WATTS GALLERY (no. 662)
Surrey

CONNAH'S QUAY *See under* **DEESIDE** *for*
Deeside FLINTSHIRE COLLEGE OF TECHNOLOGY (no. 446)
Flintshire

CONSETT ADVERSE DRUG REACTION BULLETIN *Tel.:* Consett 2341
Co. Durham EDITORIAL OFFICE
  Postgraduate Education Centre
415 Shotley Bridge Hospital
  Consett
  Co. Durham
Postgraduate medical education. Information on adverse drug reactions
Enquiries: To Editor, Adverse Drug Reaction Bulletin
Scope: Information on published work concerned with adverse reactions to drugs used in medicine
Stock: Comprehensive collection of reference works, case abstracts and reprints concerned with adverse drug reactions. Stock not available on loan

Publications: Adverse Drug Reaction Bulletin (published for the Organization of Postgraduate Medical Education, Newcastle Region)

COSHAM
Portsmouth
Hants

See under **PORTSMOUTH** for
HIGHBURY TECHNICAL COLLEGE (no. 2003)

COULSDON
Surrey

416

NETHERNE AND FAIRDENE HOSPITALS
P.O. Box 150
Coulsdon
Surrey CR3 1YE
Psychiatric Hospital and Rehabilitation Unit

Tel.: Downland 52285

Enquiries: To Librarian, by letter only

Scope: Psychiatry; psychology; geriatrics; rehabilitation; group therapy; social psychiatry
Secondary: Neurology

Stock: 1,200 books; 40 current periodicals. Stock not available on loan

Publications: Netherne Monographs (one only so far)

COVENTRY

417

CITY OF COVENTRY COLLEGE OF ART AND
DESIGN
Gosford Street
Coventry CV1 5RZ

Tel.: 0203-21166 ext. 46
(Librarian) or 38
(Enquiry Desk)

Enquiries: To Tutor Librarian

Scope: All aspects of art, architecture and design, including printing, engineering design, industrial archaeology, music, theatre, cinema. Particular emphasis on fine art and graphic design
Secondary: Background reading to the study of art: literature, philosophy, psychology, science and technology, history

Stock: 6,000 books; 200 current periodicals; visual and information material: 50,000 items (exhibition catalogues, illustrations, pamphlets, cuttings, posters, maps, theses, prospectuses, trade literature, British Standard Specifications, library compiled information)

COVENTRY

418

COVENTRY REFERENCE LIBRARY
Bayley Lane
Coventry CV1 5RG

Tel.: Coventry 25555 ext.
2115, 2116 and 2165
Telex: 31469

Enquiries: To Director

Scope: Coventry and Warwickshire collection dealing with all aspects of the area and including the George Eliot collection
Good collection of government publications and of legal textbooks

Stock: 5,000 books and pamphlets; 100 current periodicals

Publications: CADIG (*see* below and no. 2365) produces a series of bibliographies, which although at present covering only technical subjects are expected to deal with humanities when demand is indicated
Booklets on local history topics

The Reference Library is the Headquarters of CADIG (Coventry and District Information Group, entry no. 2365) which has 56 members many of whom have humanities literature in their stock

COVENTRY

419

COVENTRY TECHNICAL COLLEGE *Tel.:* Coventry 57221
The Butts
Coventry CV1 3GD

Enquiries: To Tutor Librarian

Scope: Commerce, electrical engineering, building, mechanical engineering, mathematics, science, homecrafts, physical education, liberal studies

Stock: More than 38,000 books, pamphlets and reports; 380 current periodicals

COVENTRY

420

THE GENERAL STUDIES ASSOCIATION *Tel.:* Coventry 4-66606
Coventry College of Education
Kirby Corner Road
Canley
Coventry CV4 8EE

Aims to promote general studies in schools, colleges and universities

Enquiries: To Secretary, by letter only

Scope: Information on general studies in schools, colleges and universities, including relevant articles, reviews and editorial comment

Publications: Bulletin
   Special pamphlets:
      Economics in General Studies
      Screen Education
      Aims and Approaches to Non-specialist English Studies in the Sixth Form—a collection of papers by the General Studies English Study Group
      The Social Sciences in Secondary and Further Education—four papers given at a Conference held at York University by the Association for the Teaching of the Social Sciences and the General Studies Association. August 1967
      Moral Education in Sixth Forms—Three lectures given at the Annual Conference of the G.S.A. at Coventry Cathedral in 1967
      History for the Non-specialists. M. G. Bruce and I. Lister
   Offprints
   Occasional Publications

COVENTRY

421

LANCHESTER COLLEGE OF TECHNOLOGY *Tel.:* Coventry 23522
Priory Street
Coventry

Enquiries: To Librarian

Scope: Accountancy, biological sciences, building, business, chemistry, economics, engineering (civil, electrical, mechanical and production), languages, law, management, mathematics, metallurgy, physics, politics, social science, town planning, geography, marketing, public administration, international relations
Special collection: F. W. Lanchester

Stock: 46,000 books, pamphlets and reports; 1,200 current periodicals

COVENTRY

422

UNIVERSITY OF WARWICK LIBRARY *Tel.:* Coventry 24011
Coventry CV4 7AL *Telex:* 31406

Enquiries: To Librarian

Scope: Stock and Information Service to staff and students (provided by subject specialists) in the fields of: Economics and Business studies (with special interest in economic statistics); Politics

and Law (with special interest in official national and international publications); Philosophy; History (particularly Labour History); Literatures (English, French, German, Italian)
Secondary: Stock is being built up in the following fields but with no specific information services: Psychology, music, fine art
Special collections: Howard League Library for Penal Reform—pre-1948 material
Maitland/Sara collection of socialist pamphlets and journals

Stock: 110,000 books and pamphlets; deposit arrangements for reports with GATT, ILO, UNCTAD and European Communities; 550 (humanities), 800 (social sciences) current periodicals; 3,500 statistical series titles

Publications: List of periodical holdings and subscriptions

CRANWELL
Sleaford
Lincs

See under **SLEAFORD** *for*
ROYAL AIR FORCE COLLEGE (no. 2129)

CRAWLEY
Sussex

423

CRAWLEY COLLEGE OF FURTHER EDUCATION   *Tel.:* Crawley 25686
College Road
Crawley
Sussex

Enquiries: To Librarian, by letter or in person only
Scope: Management and business, economics, accounting
Secondary: Sociology, government, trade, finance
Stock: 7,000 books; 1,000 pamphlets; 150 current periodicals

CRAWLEY
Sussex

424

WORTH ABBEY   *Tel.:* Turner's Hill 340
Turner's Hill
Crawley
Sussex

Enquiries: To Librarian, by letter only
Scope: Roman Catholic theology; monastic history; liturgy; church history; philosophy (particularly scholastic)
Secondary: Local history; biblical studies
Stock: 25,000 books; 300 pamphlets; 20 current periodicals. Stock not available on loan
Publications: Worth Record (twice each year)

CREWE
Cheshire

425

CHESHIRE COLLEGE OF EDUCATION   *Tel.:* Crewe 4231
Crewe Road
Crewe
Cheshire

Enquiries: To Librarian
Scope: General collection with strong sections on education and children's books
Stock: 40,000 books, pamphlets and reports; 260 current periodicals

CREWE
Cheshire

426

CREWE PUBLIC LIBRARY   *Tel.:* Crewe 2156
Prince Albert Street
Crewe
Cheshire

Enquiries: To Librarian

CREWE, CREWE PUBLIC LIBRARY, *cont.*
Scope: Subject specialization: General operative surgery—anaesthetics, plastic surgery
Stock: 180 books

CREWE
Cheshire

427

MADELEY COLLEGE OF EDUCATION   *Tel.:* Madeley 356
Madeley
Crewe
Cheshire

Enquiries: To Librarian
Scope: General stock supporting courses in the following subjects, many to the level of B.Ed. degree: English, French, geography, history, mathematics, religious studies, biological sciences, science, German, economics, art and craft, dance, drama, film, music, physical education and home economics. Largest sections are education, history and geography. Large Junior section (fiction and non-fiction)
Stock: 55,000 books; 270 current periodicals

CRICH
Matlock
Derbyshire

See under **MATLOCK** *for*
TRAMWAY MUSEUM SOCIETY (no. 1802)

CRIEFF
Perthshire

428

INNERPEFFRAY LIBRARY   *Tel.:* Crieff 2819
Crieff
Perthshire

Museum of early printed books, founded about 1691 by David Drummond, 3rd Lord Madertie. Oldest lending library in Scotland

Enquiries: To Librarian
Scope: Examples of early printed volumes—some very rare—from the early 16th century. Many works published in 17th and 18th centuries are also of considerable interest.
Secondary: Early editions of Bible from 1530, religious commentaries and sermons
Local histories
The Library continued to purchase books until the beginning of 20th century
Stock: 3,000 books

CROMPTON
Oldham
Lancs

See under **OLDHAM** *for*
CROMPTON PUBLIC LIBRARY (no. 1909)

CROSBY
Liverpool

See under **LIVERPOOL** *for*
CROSBY PUBLIC LIBRARIES (no. 862)

CROSSKEYS
Newport
Mon

See under **NEWPORT** *for*
THE TECHNICAL COLLEGE OF MONMOUTHSHIRE (no. 1860)

CROYDON

429

CROYDON NATURAL HISTORY AND SCIENTIFIC SOCIETY LIMITED
96A Brighton Road
Croydon CR2 6AD

Study of the geology, geography, archaeology, history, industry, present state, planning and natural history of Croydon and the surrounding 200 square miles of North West Kent and North East Surrey

Enquiries: To Secretary, preferably by letter

Scope: Croydon area and North West Kent and North East Surrey—topography, geographical studies, local history, archaeology, industrial archaeology, industries, planning
Secondary: Surrey, Kent and South East England as a whole

Stock: 500 books; 500 pamphlets; 23 local current periodicals; 400 maps and plans; ground and vertical aerial photographs

Publications: Atlas of Croydon and District (new sheets issued occasionally)
Proceedings (issued at least annually)
Bulletin (every two months)
Croydon Bibliographies (about three each year)
General Excursion Notes (detailed accounts of specific areas, 4 or 5 each year)
Papers for Schools (local information)

Card index to locally relevant literature, including a very full coverage of periodicals articles, of about 12,000 author, subject and location cards

CROYDON

430

CROYDON TECHNICAL COLLEGE & CROYDON COLLEGE OF ART
Fairfield
Croydon CR9 1DX

Tel.: 01-688 9271

Enquiries: To Librarian

Scope: Building; business studies; domestic subjects; electrical engineering; food trades; mechanical engineering; science; arts and languages; social studies; fine arts; graphic design; printing and bookbinding; theatre design; dress; textiles; ceramics; art history and liberal studies

Stock: 18,000 books; 6,000 pamphlets; 400 current periodicals

CROYDON

431

LONDON BOROUGH OF CROYDON PUBLIC LIBRARIES
Katharine Street
Croydon CR9 1ET

Tel.: 01-688 3627

Enquiries: To Librarian

Scope: Surrey Local Collection
Regional subject specialization includes: Political theory; internal relations with individuals. Economic theory; Production and distribution of resources and wealth. Sculpture and woodcarving. U.S.A. in general—history, geography and topography; Australasia—history, geography and topography. Biographies relating to above subjects

CROYDON

432

THE NATIONAL ANTI-VACCINATION LEAGUE
2A Lebanon Road
Croydon CR0 6UR

Tel.: 01-654 5817

Aims to expose the failures and dangers of vaccination and inoculation

Enquiries: To Secretary

Scope: Information for travellers not wishing to be vaccinated, concerned with their rights under Article 83 of the International Sanitary Regulations

Stock: Textbooks, periodicals and tape talks. Books and periodicals not available on loan

Publications: The Vaccination Inquirer & Health Review (quarterly)
Many brochures and pamphlets

CROYDON	ROYAL SCHOOL OF CHURCH MUSIC	*Tel.:* 01-654 7676
433	Addington Palace Croydon CR9 5AD	

Aims to improve the standard of music in worship in all Churches which are members of the World Council of Churches and the Roman Catholic Church. There is a training college for church musicians, and a world-wide membership of affiliated churches, chapels and schools

Enquiries: To Secretary

Scope: Church music in all its aspects. The accent is on practical application rather than depth of scholarship. Stock includes music, the liturgy, hymn books and psalters

Stock: 4,000 books; 5 current periodicals. Stock not available on loan

Publications: Sheet choral music
Service Books of Music
Lists of Recommended Church Music
Booklets of practical help to church musicians
English Church Music (annually)
Magazine (quarterly)

The books in the Colles Library, Addington Palace, are retained within the building for use by the students of the college, for those attending courses and visiting members only. Members of the public may visit the Library by arrangement with the Warden

CUFFLEY
Potters Bar
Herts

See under **POTTERS BAR** for
THE SOCIETY OF ORNAMENTAL TURNERS (no. 2009)

CULHAM
Abingdon
Berks

See under **ABINGDON** for
CULHAM COLLEGE OF EDUCATION (no. 18)

CURRIE Midlothian **434**	SCOTTISH ORIENTEERING ASSOCIATION 47 Corslet Road Currie Midlothian	*Tel.:* 031-449 2969

Control and development of the sport of orienteering throughout Scotland

Enquiries: To Secretary, by letter only

Scope: General information on the sport of orienteering; rules; promotion of events; contacts throughout Scotland; equipment; books

No library

Publications: S.O.A. Newsletter (bi-monthly)   Know the Game Orienteering
Short Guide to Orienteering   Stop Press (monthly)

DAGENHAM Essex **435**	BARKING REGIONAL COLLEGE OF TECHNOLOGY Longbridge Road Dagenham Essex	*Tel.:* 01-599 5141 ext. 59

Enquiries: To Librarian, by letter or in person only (or, for purely industrial questions, Industrial Liaison Officer)

Scope: Philosophy and psychology, religion, social sciences (including health visiting and social welfare), education, languages (French and German principally), mathematics, physics, geology, biology (botany and zoology), pharmacology, anatomy and physiology, engineering, business management, art (painting and sculpture), photography, music, sports, literature (English, French and German mainly), biography, geography, economics, law, accountancy

Stock: 40,000 books; 3,500 pamphlets; 705 current periodicals

Business Management Studies Department is housed separately at Asta House, 156-164 High Road, Chadwell Heath, Essex (*Tel.:* 01-590 5652) and has its own library stock of 5,000 books, 500 pamphlets and 180 current periodicals included in the above totals

DAGENHAM
Essex
436

LONDON BOROUGH OF BARKING PUBLIC LIBRARIES
Valence House
Becontree Avenue
Dagenham RM8 3HS
Essex

Tel.: 01-592 2211

Enquiries: To Librarian

Scope: Population (including vital statistics)
International law
Biographies of children
History and topography of Germany, Austria, Czechoslovakia, Poland and Hungary
Barking, Dagenham and Essex collection
Fanshawe portraits and collection

Stock: 332,000 books; 1,000 pamphlets; 230 current periodicals (total stock)

Publications: Book of Dagenham. J. G. O'Leary. 1964
Dagenham place names. J. G. O'Leary. 1958
Essex and Dagenham catalogue. J. G. O'Leary. 2nd edition. 1961
Valence House: A Guide. W. C. Pugsley. 1966
Dagenham and Fanshawe portraits: Exhibition catalogue. J. G. O'Leary. 1963
Catalogue of Gramophone Records. W. C. Pugsley and C. H. Tripp. 1962-1963
Catalogue of Music. W. C. Pugsley and C. H. Tripp. Revised edition. 1964

DAGENHAM
Essex
437

MAY & BAKER LTD
Dagenham
Essex

Tel.: 01-592 3060
Telex: 28691

Manufacturers of pharmaceutical, veterinary, agricultural, industrial, laboratory and photographic chemicals and aromatic products

Enquiries: To Librarian

Scope: *Research Library:* chemistry, mainly organic; biology; biochemistry; physiology; pharmacy and pharmacology; toxicology; agriculture; photographic chemistry
Medical Information Library: medicine, pharmacy, veterinary medicine
Agricultural Research Library: agriculture; horticulture; veterinary science

Stock: 7,750 books; 4,800 pamphlets; 725 current periodicals

Publications: Abstracts (informative style, restricted distribution): Medical—85,000; Veterinary—2,500; Pest Control—16,000
Medical Bulletin (available only to medical profession)
Laboratory Bulletin
Pharmaceutical Bulletin
Veterinary Bulletin
Poultry Review

DAGENHAM, MAY & BAKER LTD, *cont.*
Poisoning—symptoms and treatment
Weeds of the West Indies and Mauritius
M & B Medical films and filmstrips
May & Baker Published Scientific Papers 1958–1967 with 1968 Supplement

DARLINGTON   DARLINGTON COLLEGE OF TECHNOLOGY   *Tel.:* Darlington 67651 ext. 50
Co. Durham   Cleveland Avenue
   Darlington
438   Co. Durham

Enquiries: To Librarian

Scope: Accountancy, business management, economics, education, geography, journalism
Secondary: Biography, law, government, history, sociology, political science

Stock: 7,000 books; 350 pamphlets; 100 current periodicals

DARLINGTON   EDWARD PEASE PUBLIC LIBRARY, MUSEUM   *Tel.:* Darlington 2034 and
Co. Durham   ART GALLERY   69858 (Reference
   Crown Street   Library only)
439   Darlington
   Co. Durham

Enquiries: To Librarian

Scope: General stock
Secondary: Local history collection; Quaker collection; tourist information; railway history

Stock: 162,644 books and pamphlets; 300 current periodicals (total stock)

Publications: Darlington: What's on this Month

DARLINGTON   MIDDLETON ST GEORGE COLLEGE OF   *Tel.:* Dinsdale 661
Co. Durham   EDUCATION
   Middleton St George
440   Darlington
   Co. Durham

Enquiries: To Librarian

Scope: General collection, particular interest all aspects of education

Stock: 20,000 books; 250 pamphlets; 200 current periodicals. Stock not normally available on loan

DARTFORD   DARTFORD BOROUGH MUSEUM   *Tel.:* Dartford 21133
Kent   Market Street
   Dartford
441   Kent

Enquiries: To Borough Curator

Scope: Specializing in local history, history, archaeology, geology and natural history of Borough of Dartford and the Darent Valley as far south as Sevenoaks
Secondary: Research collections of museum material for student use (geology, archaeology, local history and natural history). A small loan collection of museum specimens is available for teaching and study purposes in local schools

DARTFORD Kent **442**	DARTFORD HOSPITAL MANAGEMENT COMMITTEE Medical Library Joyce Green Hospital Dartford Kent	*Tel.:* Dartford 23231

Enquiries: To Librarian
Scope: Medical only
Stock: 200 books; 39 current periodicals. Periodicals only available on loan

DARTFORD Kent **443**	DARTFORD PUBLIC LIBRARIES Central Park Dartford Kent	*Tel.:* Dartford 21133

Enquiries: To Librarian
Scope: Subject specialization includes: Sexual ethics, reproductive system, sex in general, diseases of genito-urinary system. History and criticism of Teutonic literature. Dartford local history collection, including Dartford and District Historical Society Library
Stock: 3,000 books; small number of pamphlets; 2 current periodicals (total stock 130,000 books, 200 current periodicals)

DARTMOUTH Devon **444**	BRITANNIA ROYAL NAVAL COLLEGE Dartmouth Devonshire General education of naval officers under training	*Tel.:* Dartmouth 2141

Enquiries: To Librarian
Scope: General stock, specializing in science and naval history
Stock: 24,000 books (3,000 scientific and technical); 150 current periodicals (60 scientific and technical); file of 1,000 scientific and technical papers, with subject index

DARWEN Lancs **445**	DARWEN PUBLIC LIBRARY Knott Street Darwen Lancashire	*Tel.:* Darwen 72131

Enquiries: To Librarian
Scope: Subject specialization includes: Modern European history (post-war); kinesiology
Stock: 1,000 books; 200 pamphlets

DEESIDE Flintshire **446**	FLINTSHIRE COLLEGE OF TECHNOLOGY Connah's Quay Deeside Flintshire CH5 4BR	*Tel.:* Connah's Quay 3491 ext. 25

Enquiries: To Librarian
Scope: Chemistry and physics, engineering and metallurgy, commerce and management studies
Secondary: Fine arts, law, economics, education, history, geography, computer and mathematical studies, domestic science subjects
Stock: 9,000 books; 150 current periodicals

DEESIDE
Flintshire

447

FLINTSHIRE RECORD OFFICE *Tel.:* Hawarden 2364
The Old Rectory
Hawarden
Deeside
Flintshire CH5 3NR

Enquiries: To County Archivist

Scope: Official Records: Quarter Sessions, County Council, Education, Poor Law Union and Turnpike Trusts
Secondary: Deposited records of businesses and county families. Collections of prints and photographs of Flintshire

Stock: 1,500 books; 500 pamphlets; All North Wales Historical and Archaeological Societies: and Welsh Historical journals. Stock not available on loan

Publications: Hand List of the County Records. 1955
Farmhouses and Cottages. 1964
Early Industry in Flintshire. 1966

DEESIDE
Flintshire

448

SAINT DEINIOL'S LIBRARY *Tel.:* Hawarden 2350
Hawarden
Deeside
Flintshire

St Deiniol's, the Gladstone Memorial Library, is the only residential academic library in the United Kingdom, and has room for full board residence for 30 guests

Enquiries: To Warden

Scope: Theology, history, philosophy and literature
Manuscript material: 50,000 letters of Gladstone and his family; Personal papers of Archbishop Green of Wales

Stock: 100,000 books. Stock not available on loan

DERBY

449

BISHOP LONSDALE COLLEGE OF EDUCATION *Tel.:* Derby 54911
Western Road
Mickleover
Derby DE3 5GX

Teacher training courses for men and women: Nursery, Infant, Junior and specialist Physical Education for women

Enquiries: To Librarian

Scope: General subject coverage for college courses including art and craft, divinity, English, French, geography, history, mathematics, music, physical education, science (biology and physics)
Education including philosophy, psychology, sociology
Teaching Practice collection (children's books for use in schools)
General Reference collection

Stock: 44,500 books and pamphlets; 200 current periodicals

Publications: Family Treasures in a college library. C. E. Saunders. 1968
Catalogue of the Collection of Early Children's Books, together with other books of special educational interest, in the library of Bishop Lonsdale College of Education. C. E. Saunders. 1968

DERBY

450

DERBY AND DISTRICT COLLEGES OF ART *Tel.:* Derby 47181 (College
AND TECHNOLOGY of Technology);
Kedleston Road Derby 31681 (College
Derby DE3 1GB of Art)

Enquiries: To Librarian

Scope: Arts, including art, architecture, sculpture, ceramics, metalwork, printing, graphic design, lettering, design, furniture, cabinet making, painting, photography, print-making, dress, needlework subjects and fashion
Mechanical engineering, electrical engineering, civil engineering and building, mathematics, chemistry, physics, textiles, management and business studies, domestic science, catering and bakery, liberal studies. Particularly strong in engineering, chemistry, economics and commerce

Stock: 47,000 books and pamphlets; 600 current periodicals

Publications: Accessions lists

DERBY
451

DERBY BOROUGH LIBRARY *Tel.:* Derby 31111 ext. 306
The Wardwick
Derby DE1 1HS

Enquiries: To Librarian

Scope: Local history collections of Derby and Derbyshire, strong in Derbyshire manuscripts and maps, and including Wilmot Horton collection of over 10,000 items concerning 18th century parish affairs, colonial affairs, early 19th century economic and political affairs generally. Other family collections including the Devonshire and Bemrose families. English literary criticism, particularly the history of fiction

Stock: 350,000 books; 460 current periodicals (total stock)

DERBY
452

DERBY CATHEDRAL LIBRARY *Tel.:* Derby 41201
2 College Place
Derby

Enquiries: To Provost

Scope: General theology and some sociology

Stock: 4,000 books

DEVIZES
Wilts
453

WILTSHIRE ARCHAEOLOGICAL AND *Tel.:* Devizes 2765
NATURAL HISTORY SOCIETY
41 Long Street
Devizes
Wiltshire

Enquiries: To Librarian

Scope: Anything to do with the history and pre-history of Wiltshire including books on Wiltshire or by Wiltshire authors. Natural history, industrial archaeology, genealogy, local history, topography and economic history are all covered

Stock: 6,000 books; 4,000 pamphlets; 61 current periodicals. Stock not available on loan

Publications: Wiltshire Archaeological and Natural History Magazine (annually)
Guide Catalogue to the Neolithic and Bronze Age Collections

DEVIZES
Wilts
454

WILTSHIRE REGIMENT MUSEUM *Tel.:* Devizes 2241 ext. 339
Le Marchant Barracks
Devizes
Wiltshire

Enquiries: To Curator

Scope: A small Regimental collection of papers, documents, medals, weapons and photographs

DEVONPORT
Plymouth
Devon

See under **PLYMOUTH** for
COLLEGE OF S. MARK & S. JOHN (no. 1992)

DIDCOT
Berks

455

MEDICAL RESEARCH COUNCIL
RADIOBIOLOGY UNIT
Harwell
Didcot
Berkshire

Tel.: Rowstock 393 ext. 42

Research on action of ionizing radiations on living cells. Particular attention is paid to fast neutrons and to x- and γ-radiations

Enquiries: To Librarian, by letter only

Scope: Effects of radiation in the following fields: Biochemistry; biophysics; cytogenetics; genetics; cell biology; experimental pathology; physiology; radiochemistry; molecular ecology; low temperature work; tissue transplantation; laboratory animal breeding. Statistical analysis; laboratory techniques

Stock: 3,000 books; 5,000 pamphlets; 3,000 reports; 210 current periodicals

DIDSBURY
Manchester

See under **MANCHESTER** for
DIDSBURY COLLEGE OF EDUCATION (no. 1746)

DINGWALL
Ross-shire

456

ROSS AND CROMARTY COUNTY LIBRARY
The Old Academy
Tulloch Street
Dingwall
Ross-shire

Tel.: Dingwall 3163
Telex: 7562

Enquiries: To Librarian

Scope: Gaelic collection held at Lewis District Library, Stornoway Public Library

Stock: 250 books

DONCASTER
Yorkshire

457

SCAWSBY COLLEGE OF EDUCATION
Barnsley Road
Scawsby
Doncaster
Yorkshire

Tel.: Doncaster 67421

Enquiries: To Librarian

Scope: Education, English language and literature, drama, history, music, geography, mathematics, religious studies, physical education, art and crafts, chemistry, physics, biology
Secondary: Psychology and sociology

Stock: 26,500 books and pamphlets; 150 current periodicals

Publications: Occasional reading lists and bibliographies

DONCASTER
Yorkshire

458

SOUTH YORKSHIRE INDUSTRIAL MUSEUM
Cusworth Hall
Doncaster
Yorkshire

Tel.: Doncaster 61842

Museum and large research collection appertaining to the industrial and social history of the southern half of the West Riding

Enquiries: To Curator, by letter only

Scope: Manuscripts and printed books appertaining to the following subjects almost entirely within South Yorkshire
Industries: Coal, agriculture, inclosure, markets and malting, lime quarrying, glass, pottery, iron, textiles, peat, corn milling, soap, steam power, use and introduction in industry
Transport: Waterways, roads and bridges, railways, street tramways and colliery waggonways
Social: The poor, local government, public health and medical, education, entertainment, housing (of rich and poor) politics, religion, pubs and brewing, friendly societies, water supply, banking, South Yorkshire maps and plans, gas supply

Stock: 2,000 books and pamphlets; 10,000 manuscripts; photographs, prints and maps

Publications: South Yorkshire Journal of Industrial and Social History (twice each year)
Pamphlets on local historical subjects

DORCHESTER
Dorset
459

DORSET COUNTY LIBRARY
Colliton Park
Dorchester
Dorset

Tel.: Dorchester 3131 (night extensions and Saturdays, Lending Library Dorchester 3723; Reference Library Dorchester 2734)

Enquiries: To County Librarian

Scope: Dorset history and description. The Literature of Dorset (T. Hardy, W. Barnes, J. C. Powys, J. F. Powys, Ll. Powys, T. E. Lawrence)
Secondary: General coverage with subject specialization including psychology of groups; Ethics; Protestant churches; Law of Persons and property; Family welfare services; Juvenile delinquency; Central and Southern Africa including Islands of the South Indian Ocean

Publications: Thomas Hardy Catalogue

DORCHESTER
Dorset
460

DORSET NATURAL HISTORY AND
    ARCHAEOLOGICAL SOCIETY
Dorset County Museum
High West Street
Dorchester
Dorset

Tel.: Dorchester 2735

Enquiries: To Curator and Secretary

Scope: Dorset archaeology, natural history, geology and local history.
Special collections: Thomas Hardy; William Barnes, Dorset poet, Vicar and schoolmaster; Alfred Stevens; and other Dorset worthies
Limited information on Dorset rural life and bygones, and on Dorset artists
Photographic record

Stock: 10,000 books; large number of pamphlets; 50 current periodicals. Stock not available on loan, but may be used by appointment

Publications: Annual Proceedings

DORKING
Surrey
461

THE PEOPLE'S DISPENSARY FOR SICK ANIMALS
Head Office P.D.S.A. House
South Street
Dorking
Surrey

Tel.: Dorking 81691

Enquiries: To Information Officer

DORKING, THE PEOPLE'S DISPENSARY FOR SICK ANIMALS, *cont.*

Scope: Pet care and animal welfare
No library

Publications: Films
Pet Care leaflets and posters
Busy Bees News (monthly)
Guild News (bi-monthly)
Animals Magazine (monthly)

DOUGLAS
Isle of Man

462

THE MANX MUSEUM LIBRARY
Kingswood Grove
Douglas
Isle of Man

Tel.: Douglas 5522

Enquiries: To Librarian or Director

Scope: Manx public records, manuscript maps and plans, newspapers, printed books relating to the Isle of Man, particularly its political, social and economic history, geography, archaeology, folk-lore and folk life, natural history and Manx language
Secondary: Small general archaeology and folk life sections of printed books

Stock: 15,000 books and pamphlets; 6,000 deposits of manuscripts; Manx government reports; 50 current periodicals

Publications: Journal of the Manx Museum (annually)
Bibliography of Literature relating to the Isle of Man
Manx Archaeological Survey, parts I-V
Manx Archaeological Survey, part VI
Ancient Monuments Handbook
Early Maps of the Isle of Man
Birds of the Isle of Man
Coin Collection: a check-list
Guides to the Museum and Branch Folk-museums

DOVER
Kent

463

DOVER PUBLIC LIBRARY
Maison Dieu House
Dover
Kent

Tel.: Dover 46

Enquiries: To Borough Librarian
Scope: L.A.S.E.R. subject specialization includes: Fire protection
Stock: 69,000 books; 75 current periodicals (total stock)
Publications: Select List of Additions (monthly)

DUDLEY
Worcs

464

DUDLEY COLLEGE OF EDUCATION
Castle View
Dudley
Worcestershire

Tel.: Dudley 53451

Enquiries: To Librarian
Scope: Specialist collection in education and associated social sciences. Books on teaching method (some of historical interest). Textbook collection
Stock: 37,500 books; 2,500 pamphlets; 250 current periodicals
Publications: Information bulletin and new books list

DUDLEY Worcs **465**	DUDLEY PUBLIC LIBRARIES, MUSEUM AND ART GALLERY Central Library St James's Road Dudley Worcestershire	*Tel.:* Dudley 56321

Enquiries: To Librarian

Scope: Large local history collection particularly strong on industrial history of the Black Country. The Archives Department includes records of local Manor Courts, the Earl of Dudley's Collection dealing mainly with the Himley Estates, and diocesan archives for the Deanery of Dudley. A special collection of material on art glass and glass-making, with a selection of material on stained and painted glass, is housed with the Glass Collection at the Brierley Hill Branch Library, Moor Street, Brierley Hill, Staffordshire

Stock: Local collection: 4,700 books; 550 pamphlets; 3,000 maps; 7,000 photographs; 700 posters
Glass collection: 500 books and pamphlets; 6 current periodicals

Publications: Transcript series, 1–15
The Collections of Glass at the Brierley Hill Public Library. W. A. Thorpe. 1949
Check List of the Special Collection of Material on Glass and Glass-making

DUMFRIES **466**	DUMFRIES BURGH MUSEUM The Observatory Corberry Hill Dumfries	*Tel.:* Dumfries 3374

An active regional museum covering south-west Scottish counties in natural history, history, archaeology, dress, bygones and folk material

Enquiries: To Curator

Scope: Local Parish histories; local Antiquarian Society Transactions; local natural history works, typescript transcripts of local archives from 1506 onwards; duplicated leaflets on local archaeology, history and natural history
Slides of local and non-local archaeology
Large collection of archaeological, natural history, folk and museological periodicals and reports, British and world-wide
Tape recording collection of local tales

Stock: 2,500 books; 200 pamphlets; 22 current periodicals

Publications:
The Coastal Mesolithic in S.W. Scotland	Sawrie Bane
Inland Mesolithic in S.W. Scotland	The Rerrick Ghost
Dates of Founding of Burghs of S.W. Scotland	The Bogle o' the Todshawhill
	Malachy's Curse and the Annan Vampire
The Mesolithic in S.W. Scotland	History of Dumfries
The Bronze Age in S.W. Scotland	A Solway Compendium
Iron Age in S.W. Scotland	The Heidless Horseman o' Tynron Doon
The Romans in S.W. Scotland	16th Century Dumfries Property Lists
After the Romans	The Contents of Torthorwald Castle in 1546
Northumbria in S.W. Scotland	The Contents of Comlongan Castle 1628
The Lost Centuries	The Contents of Caerlaverock Castle 1640
Not Men but Brute Beasts (the Galwegians)	The Camera Obscura at Dumfries

DUMFRIES **467**	DUMFRIES TECHNICAL COLLEGE George Street Dumfries	*Tel.:* Dumfries 4351

123

DUMFRIES, DUMFRIES TECHNICAL COLLEGE, *cont.*
Enquiries: To Librarian
Scope: Nursing subjects: Anatomy, physiology, hygiene, ward administration, nursing psychology. Home economics. Consumer education
Stock: 1,000 books; 100 pamphlets; 10 current periodicals

DUNBLANE   ASSOCIATION OF SCOTTISH CLIMBING CLUBS   *Tel.:* Dunblane 2288
Perthshire   Queen Victoria School
    Dunblane
468   Perthshire
Enquiries: To Hon. Secretary, by letter only
Scope: List of club secretaries, climbing huts, and guide books to various areas of interest to climbers. Courses being held on mountaineering at the various training centres, and courses and expeditions abroad
No library
Publications: Exposure on the Mountains (pamphlet)

DUNDEE   DUNCAN OF JORDANSTONE COLLEGE OF ART   *Tel.:* Dundee 21182
469   Perth Road
    Dundee
Enquiries: To Librarian
Scope: Architecture, building, town planning, fine arts, landscape, architecture, sculpture, pottery, graphic design, painting and drawing, illustration, printing, interior design
Secondary: Sociology, economics as backing material. Medical and social, for health visitors course for nurses
Stock: 12,500 books; 2,500 pamphlets; 170 current periodicals; 25,000 35 mm slides, mainly in colour. Complete set of British Standards

DUNDEE   DUNDEE COLLEGE OF EDUCATION   *Tel.:* Dundee 25484
    Park Place
470   Dundee DD1 4HP
Enquiries: To Librarian
Scope: English, history, geography, mathematics, needlework, handwork, science
Secondary: Art, education, home economics, psychology, modern languages, music, technical education, physical education, religion, speech and drama
Stock: 44,250 books and pamphlets; 250 current periodicals
Publications: Glen Fincastle 1841–1901. W. Taylor. 1967
Activity Methods in Infant Classes. I. Logan. 1967
Careers Guidance: A Symposium. J. Halliday, ed. 1968
Modern Studies: A Teacher's Handbook. R. M. Petrie. 1968

DUNDEE   DUNDEE COLLEGE OF TECHNOLOGY   *Tel.:* Dundee 27225
    Bell Street
471   Dundee
Enquiries: To Librarian
Scope: Economics, mathematics, physics, chemistry, mechanical, electrical, production and civil

engineering, business management (particularly accountancy), metallurgy, textiles (particularly jute) and building

Stock: 27,000 books; 3,000 pamphlets; 750 current periodicals

Publications: Library Guide
Bulletin of Accessions
List of Journal Holdings

DUNDEE

472

DUNDEE PUBLIC LIBRARIES *Tel.:* Dundee 24938
Albert Square
Dundee DD1 1DB

Enquiries: To Librarian

Scope: Special collections include: The A. C. Lamb Collection of books and pamphlets on Old Dundee; The Wighton Music Collection (500 volumes of early music, including manuscripts); The Sturrock Collection of fine printing and private press books; The Charles Ower Collection of architectural books

Stock: 370,000 books; 5,000 pamphlets; 250 current periodicals (total stock)

DUNDEE

473

EASTERN REGIONAL HOSPITAL BOARD *Tel.:* Dundee 68296
Vernonholme
Riverside Drive
Dundee

Enquiries: To Information Officer

Scope: Information can be provided about the provision of hospital and specialist services in the Cities of Dundee and Perth and the Counties of Angus and Perthshire. Limited morbidity statistics for this area are available from time to time

No library

Publications: Eastern Regional Hospital Board's Quarterly Magazine

DUNDEE

474

UNIVERSITY OF DUNDEE LIBRARY *Tel.:* Dundee 23181
Dundee DD1 4HN *Telex:* 76293

Enquiries: To Librarian

Scope: Faculties of Medicine, Social Sciences and Letters, Science, Law and Engineering
Special collections: Brechin Diocesan Library; Nicoll Collection (Fine arts); Lang Collection (Scottish philosophy); History of medicine and dentistry

Stock: 210,000 books and pamphlets; 3,250 current periodicals

DUNFERMLINE
Fife

475

CARNEGIE DUNFERMLINE TRUST *Tel.:* Dunfermline 23638
Abbey Park House
Abbey Park Place
Dunfermline
Fife

Aims to improve social, cultural and recreational facilities in Carnegie's native town of Dunfermline

Enquiries: To Secretary

Scope: There is no library but the Trust is willing to assist in research on Andrew Carnegie and his various institutions and in particular on the work of the Trust itself

DUNFERMLINE Fife **476**	THE CARNEGIE HERO FUND TRUST Abbey Park House Abbey Park Place Dunfermline Fife	*Tel.:* Dunfermline 23638

Gives financial assistance to persons who in heroically rescuing others suffer injury or financial loss, and to the families of those killed while performing heroic rescues

Enquiries: To Secretary

Scope: There is no library but the Trust is willing to assist in research on Andrew Carnegie and his various institutions and in particular on the work of the Trust itself

DUNFERMLINE Fife **477**	DUNFERMLINE MUSEUM Viewfield Terrace Dunfermline Fife	*Tel.:* Dunfermline 21814

Enquiries: To Librarian and Curator

Scope: Aspects of the local and natural history of Dunfermline and district

DUNFERMLINE Fife **478**	DUNFERMLINE PUBLIC LIBRARY 1 Abbot Street Dunfermline Fife	*Tel.:* Dunfermline 24404

Enquiries: To Librarian

Scope: Murison Burns Collection on Robert Burns (one of the best collections in Scotland). Fairly comprehensive local history collection on Dunfermline and West Fife. Andrew Carnegie Collection. George Reid Collection of early books

Publications: Catalogue of Murison Burns Collection

DUNOON Argyll **479**	ARGYLL COUNTY LIBRARY County Offices East Bay Dunoon Argyll	*Tel.:* Dunoon 981

Enquiries: To Librarian

Scope: Argyll Local Collection

Stock: 170,085 books (total stock)

DURHAM **480**	ARCHAEOLOGICAL AND ARCHITECTURAL SOCIETY OF DURHAM AND NORTHUMBERLAND c/o Neville's Cross College Durham

Enquiries: To Hon. Secretary, by letter only

No library

Scope: Willing to answer specific questions relating to the architectural and archaeological heritage of the North East

Publications: Transactions

DURHAM 481	CIVIC TRUST FOR THE NORTH-EAST 34/35 Saddler Street Durham *See* no. 1067	*Tel.:* Durham 61182

DURHAM 482	COLLEGE OF THE VENERABLE BEDE Durham *See* no. 488	

DURHAM   DURHAM COUNTY LIBRARY   *Tel.:* Durham 4411
483   County Hall   *Telex:* 53281
    Durham

Enquiries: To Librarian
Scope: Whole field of the Social Sciences and the Humanities. Reference works are housed at Durham City Branch Library in the Central Reference Library (*Tel.:* Durham 4003) Medical books are mainly housed in local hospitals, the joint resources being co-ordinated
Stock: 1,400,000 books and pamphlets; 850 current periodicals (total stock)
Publications: Periodicals. 1968

DURHAM   DURHAM POSTGRADUATE MEDICAL CENTRE   *Tel.:* Durham 2311 ext. 276
484   Dryburn Hospital
    Durham

Small medical library for the use of all grades of hospital medical and dental staff, general practitioners and Public Health Authority doctors

Enquiries: To Secretary/Librarian
Scope: Current medical literature in all general branches, and medical periodicals
Stock: 500 books; 50 reports; 40 current periodicals

DURHAM   DURHAM TECHNICAL COLLEGE   *Tel.:* Durham 62421
485   Framwelgate Moor
    Durham

Enquiries: To Librarian
Scope: Departments: Business Study; Construction; Engineering; Mining; Domestic Science and Art; General Vocational Studies. Subjects stocked in depth: Local Government; Management; Central Government; Education; Economics; Building; Highways; Surveying; Materials engineering; Electrical engineering; Mechanical engineering; Mental Retardation Studies; Mining engineering; Office practice; Politics
Secondary: Sociology, statistics, law, languages (basically German, French), literature (French, German, mostly English), science, geology, geography, cookery, welding, motor vehicle engineering, art, art needlework, structural engineering, drama
Stock: 17,500 books and pamphlets; 500 reports; 500 current periodicals. Complete set of British Standards
Publications: Accessions lists
Subject catalogues

DURHAM   LOWE MEMORIAL LIBRARY   *Tel.:* Durham 5481
    UNIVERSITY COLLEGE
486   Durham

DURHAM, LOWE MEMORIAL LIBRARY, UNIVERSITY COLLEGE, *cont.*

This is the library of one of the constituent Colleges of the University of Durham, and supplements the services of the University library by providing for members of the college a small collection of reference books and of books needed for the undergraduate courses

Enquiries: To Librarian, by letter only

Scope: General reference collection; books required for undergraduate courses in all faculties of the University, including social sciences, geography, history, philosophy, English language and literature, European language and literature, Greek and Latin language and literature, music, theology
Secondary: Small collection of works of local interest; small collection of books printed before 1850—mostly theology and Greek and Latin classics

Stock: 3,000 books on subjects covered by Directory; 5,000 total stock

DURHAM

487

NEVILLE'S CROSS COLLEGE
Durham

College of Education

Tel.: Durham 2325

Enquiries: To Principal

Scope: Books necessary for studies directed towards teachers' certificate. A range of books in education, English, French, geography, history, mathematics, science. Not a specialist collection

Stock: 24,000 books

DURHAM

488

ST HILD'S COLLEGE
Durham

Tel.: Durham 5393 (library)

College of Education. The Library is a Joint Library with the College of the Venerable Bede

Enquiries: To the Librarian, by letter only

Scope: The Joint Library is housed in two buildings and the stock is divided by subjects. In the Haworth Building, St Hild's College, the following subjects are housed: Physical education; education in all its branches, including psychology and sociology; history (including a growing collection of antiquarian books on local history); theology; social welfare. Small sections on economics and politics. A number of volumes of the Minutes of the Committee of Council on Education between 1844 and 1858, and 1896–1899

Stock: 14,000 books; pamphlets and reports; 125 current periodicals

DURHAM

489

ST JOHN'S COLLEGE
Durham

Tel.: Durham 2306

Church of England Theological College; constituent College of Durham University

Enquiries: To Librarian

Scope: Theology

Stock: 7,000 books; 100 pamphlets; 10 current periodicals

DURHAM

490

UNIVERSITY OF DURHAM
DEPARTMENT OF GEOGRAPHY
South Road
Durham

Tel.: Durham 4971

Enquiries: To Administrative Assistant

Scope: Standard geographical texts, physical, regional and human. Research material relating to the Middle East and North Africa (for reference only)

Stock: 3,000 books; 2,000 pamphlets; 500 reports; 199 current periodicals; 23,000 maps and air photographs

Publications: Occasional Paper Series—Geographical. 9 volumes to date
Research Paper Series—Geographical. 10 volumes to date
Special Reports—Land Use, Soil Surveys and Development Projects, mostly Middle East. 11 volumes to date

DURHAM

491

UNIVERSITY OF DURHAM *Tel.:* Durham 4466 ext. 309
INSTITUTE OF EDUCATION
Old Shire Hall
Old Elvet
Durham

To provide a library for students and staff of the Department and Institute of Education, staff of Colleges of Education, teachers and others employed in the field of education. Students of Colleges of Education (except for B.Ed candidates who may borrow), may consult but not borrow books direct

Enquiries: To Librarian

Scope: Education (history, theory, practice), psychology, sociology and other subjects of interest to educationists. Not school or university textbooks, or books on subjects of the curriculum

Stock: 12,000 books and pamphlets; 160 current periodicals

Publications: Durham Research Review

DURHAM

492

UNIVERSITY OF DURHAM LIBRARY *Tel.:* Durham 61262
Palace Green
Durham

Enquiries: To Librarian, preferably by letter

Scope: All subjects other than agriculture and medicine
Special collections:
Cosin's (the Episcopal) Library, founded 1669 (augmented up to 1830), entrusted to the University in 1936: chiefly 16th and 17th century scriptural, patristics, scholastic, Tridentine and Reformed theology; eastern and western liturgy; canon and common law; philosophy and politics; ancient, ecclesiastical and European history; geography; natural science; English and classical literature (16th to 18th century). Many items in French as well as English, Latin and Greek
Bamburgh Library, founded 1778, deposited by Lord Crewe's Trustees in 1958 (augmented up to 1860): similar scope to above, but stronger in natural science, atlases, political and religious controversy, runs of 17th–19th century periodicals
Routh collection, received 1854: similar scope to above, but stronger in bibliography, patristics, classical literature and philology, English history, archaeology, topography; little natural science and limited in belles lettres
Maltby collection, received 1856: chiefly classics, ancient history, philosophy and theology
Winterbottom collection, received 1859: strong in science, travel (particularly Africa and Asia), European languages and literatures
Oriental collections: Egyptology; ancient and modern Near and Middle East; Chinese

Stock: Books, periodicals and pamphlets:
Main Library: 220,000 (including 45,000 published before 1850); *Science Section:* 45,000; *Oriental Section:* 90,000.
2,500 current periodicals

Publications: Durham University Journal
Inaugural Lectures

DURHAM, UNIVERSITY OF DURHAM LIBRARY, *cont.*
A Union List of Periodicals in the Learned Libraries of Durham. G. S. Darlow. 1962
Summary List of the Additional Manuscripts. D. Ramage. 1963
Maps of Durham, 1576–1872, in the University Library, Durham. R. M. Turner. 1954; Supplement. A. I. Doyle. 1960
Durham Topographical Prints up to 1800; an Annotated Bibliography. P. M. Benedikz. 1968

DURHAM   USHAW COLLEGE   *Tel.:* Langley Park 226
Durham

493   Education of aspirants to the Roman Catholic Priesthood

Enquiries: To Librarian, by letter only

Scope: Theology (19,000 volumes)
Secondary: Medieval history; general 17th and 18th century literature
Leadbitter Law Library: Illustrated history of law particularly English (1,600 volumes)
Mann Library of Papal and medieval history (4,000 volumes)

Stock: 43,000 books and pamphlets; 59 current periodicals

EAST GRINSTEAD   MEDICAL LIBRARY, QUEEN VICTORIA HOSPITAL   *Tel.:* East Grinstead 24111 ext. 40
Sussex   East Grinstead
Sussex

494   Provides a medical library service for the medical staff at the hospital, mainly devoted to plastic and reconstructive surgery and oral surgery

Enquiries: To Medical Librarian, by letter only

Scope: Small library, but willing to provide information and references on plastic and reconstructive surgery and oral surgery, for other medical people or medical libraries, the main emphasis of the hospital and library being on plastic surgery. Index of literature on this subject

Stock: 180 books on reconstructive surgery; 1,500 reprints; 6 plastic surgery current periodicals; 33 other subjects current periodicals

EASTBOURNE   ARMOUR PHARMACEUTICAL COMPANY LIMITED   *Tel.:* Eastbourne 51111
Sussex   *Telex:* 87323
Hampden Park
495   Eastbourne
Sussex

Marketing of pharmaceutical and surgical preparations for the use of the medical profession

Enquiries: To Manager, Medical Department

Scope: On products marketed by the Company
Secondary: Hormones and enzymes (for medical use). Surgical sutures
Information supplied to members of the medical profession only

Stock includes all British and some American medical journals

EASTBOURNE   CHELSEA COLLEGE OF PHYSICAL EDUCATION   *Tel.:* Eastbourne 22571
Sussex   Denton Road
Eastbourne
496   Sussex

The education and professional training of women specialist teachers of physical education

Enquiries: To Librarian, by letter only

Scope: Education, physical education, sport, dance
Secondary: Drama, art, biology
Stock: 15,000 books and pamphlets; 150 current periodicals. Stock not normally available on loan

EASTBOURNE COUNTY BOROUGH OF EASTBOURNE   *Tel.:* Eastbourne 21333
Sussex   PUBLIC LIBRARIES
    Grove Road
497   Eastbourne
    Sussex

Enquiries: To Borough Librarian
Scope: Subject specialization includes: Dietetics; National Health Service; care of invalids and infirm. American Fiction: history and criticism; English Fiction: history and criticism; biographies of English and American novelists. Eastbourne local history. Dickens First Editions (may be consulted only by permission of the Librarian)
Secondary: Sussex Local Collection; collection of more than 700 play sets
Stock: 6,000 books; pamphlets; general medical and literary current periodicals
Publications: Catalogue of the Local Collection; Comprising Books on Eastbourne and Sussex. 1956
Play Sets. 1966

EASTBOURNE EASTBOURNE COLLEGE OF EDUCATION   *Tel.:* Eastbourne 27633
Sussex   Darley Road
    Eastbourne
498   Sussex

Enquiries: To Librarian, by letter or telephone
Scope: The Library is a general one supporting the College syllabus and courses, with a large section on education, including education of the handicapped. Subjects taken as main subjects are: Art, English, French, geography, history, mathematics, music, religious studies, science. There is also a library of children's books (Teaching Practice Library)
Stock: 30,000 books and pamphlets; 190 current periodicals. Stock available on loan only to local Colleges of Education

EASTCOTE *See under* **RUISLIP** for
Ruislip   BUSINESS STATISTICS OFFICE (no. 2060)
Middx

EASTHAM *See under* **WIRRAL** for
Wirral   WEST CHESHIRE CENTRAL COLLEGE OF
Cheshire   FURTHER EDUCATION (no. 2300)

EASTLEIGH EASTLEIGH TECHNICAL COLLEGE   *Tel.:* Eastleigh 3091
Hants   Cranbury Road
    Eastleigh
499   Hampshire SO5 5HT

Enquiries: To Tutor Librarian
Scope: General stock and particularly engineering, science, economics, and law
Stock: 11,000 books; 2,000 pamphlets; 100 current periodicals
Member of HATRICS

EASTLEIGH Hants **500**	WILLIAM R. WARNER & CO. LTD Chestnut Avenue Eastleigh Hampshire SO5 3ZQ	*Tel.:* Eastleigh 3131 ext. 128 *Telex:* 47266

Manufacturers of ethical and lay pharmaceuticals, toilet requisites and hairdressing preparations

Enquiries: To Librarian, preferably by telephone

Scope: Medicine; pharmacy; chemistry. Information on own products
Secondary: Management; packaging, hairdressing; engineering

Stock: 800 books; 250 current periodicals; films and slides. Stock not normally available on loan

Publications: Programmed learning booklets
Film synopsis catalogue

ECCLES
Manchester

See under **MANCHESTER** for
ECCLES PUBLIC LIBRARY (no. 1748)

EDGWARE Middx **501**	THE NORTH LONDON BLOOD TRANSFUSION CENTRE Deansbrook Road Edgware Middlesex	*Tel.:* 01-952 5511

Enquiries: To Director

Scope: Blood transfusion and blood group serology. Clotting disorders
Secondary: Blood group genetics

Stock: 250 books; 19 current periodicals. Stock not available on loan

EDINBURGH

502

ANIMAL DISEASES RESEARCH ASSOCIATION
Moredun Institute
408 Gilmerton Road
Edinburgh EH17 7JH

Researches into diseases of farm livestock

Enquiries: To Librarian

Scope: Bacteriology, biochemistry, immunology, pathology, veterinary parasitology, virology, small laboratory animals

Stock: 1,000 books; pamphlets and reports; 134 current periodicals

EDINBURGH **503**	THE BOARD FOR INFORMATION AND NATIONAL TESTS IN YOUTH AND COMMUNITY SERVICE 67 York Place Edinburgh EH1 3JB	*Tel.:* 031-556 8671

The Board operates the Scottish Youth and Community Service Information Centre which collects, sifts and disseminates information relevant to youth and community work

Enquiries: To Information Officer

Scope: Adolescence: physical, mental, emotional and social development; environmental influences, for example family relations, mass media, pop culture; transition from school to work, gangs, delinquency

Youth Service: youth leadership and training, 'detached' work, youth organizations, youth group activities
Education: Scottish educational system, social education, youth work in schools
Community Work: community development, community studies, new towns
Social Work: voluntary and statutory social services, social group work
Adventure playgrounds, recreation and planning for leisure. Files on national and local organizations concerned with youth and community work. Leaflets on training courses. Brochures on holiday and conference centres in Scotland for young people. Film catalogues. Plans of buildings

Stock: 530 books; 950 pamphlets; 36 current periodicals

Publications: Information Bulletin: an occasional publication giving news on the Centre's activities, topical information on the youth and community service, recent literature and details of forthcoming conferences and courses
Information Sheets: provide in concise form factual data on services, agencies and trends
Information Centre Papers: on subjects of special interest; may be texts of lectures, periodical articles
Select Bibliographies: Annotated lists

EDINBURGH

504

THE BRITISH LEGION SCOTLAND   *Tel.:* 031-225 7901
23 Drumsheugh Gardens
Edinburgh EH3 7RR

Enquiries: To General Secretary

Scope: War disablement pensions and welfare concerning ex-service men and women and their dependants in Scotland

No library

Publications: The Claymore (Official Journal, quarterly)
Pamphlets

EDINBURGH

505

BRITISH ORIENTEERING FEDERATION
National Office: 3 Glenfinlas Street
Edinburgh 3

Encourages, promotes and controls the sport of orienteering in the United Kingdom

Enquiries: Hon. Secretary, 2 Stanley Villas, Hoghton, Preston, Lancashire   *Tel.:* Hoghton 841

Scope: Orienteering

No library

Publications: The Orienteer (quarterly)
Stop Press (duplicated reading paper, monthly)

EDINBURGH

506

CENTRE FOR INFORMATION ON THE   *Tel.:* 031-556 4415 ext. 38
   TEACHING OF ENGLISH
Moray House College of Education
Holyrood Road
Edinburgh 8

Collects and distributes information on the teaching of English language and literature to pupils whose mother tongue is English, for the benefit particularly of local development centres—in English—in Scotland

Enquiries: To Director

EDINBURGH, CENTRE FOR INFORMATION ON THE TEACHING OF ENGLISH, *cont.*

Scope: Information service includes circulation of documents produced by local development centres in English and replies to individual enquiries from persons interested in the teaching of English as the mother tongue. Library stock includes selected works on principles of education, psychology of education and sociology of education, on current classroom practices in the teaching of English *throughout* the school. The latter category includes materials from United Kingdom, Eire, Canada, Australia, New Zealand and United States of America

Special collection: works on linguistics, including psycholinguistics and sociolinguistics as relevant today to the teaching of English

Periodicals on the teaching of English and microfiche copies of selected E.R.I.C. papers are stocked

Stock: 1,500 books; 100 pamphlets; 200 reports; 50 current periodicals. Stock not available on loan

Publications: Teaching English (C.I.T.E. Newsletter, 3 issues each year)
Bibliographies of textbooks, texts relevant to particular fields of English teaching, reviews of examination practices, summaries of research in relevant fields, reports of classroom work done in Scottish schools

See also no. 525

EDINBURGH

507

THE COCKBURN ASSOCIATION
(THE EDINBURGH CIVIC TRUST)
10 Albyn Place
Edinburgh EH2 4NG

Tel.: 031-225 3616

Preservation and improvement of the amenity of the City of Edinburgh and its environment

Enquiries: To Secretary, by letter only

Scope: Access can be given to records of the Association's activities since its foundation in 1874. An integral part of the Association today is its three panels of experts concerned with Town Planning, Open Spaces and Historic Buildings

No library

EDINBURGH

508

COMMONWEALTH INSTITUTE, SCOTLAND
8 Rutland Square
Edinburgh EH1 2AS

Tel.: 031-229 6668

See no. 1082

EDINBURGH

509

CONSTRUCTION TECHNOLOGY BUILDING
AND ARCHITECTURE IN SCOTLAND
45 Moray Place
Edinburgh 3

Tel.: 031-226 6461

Monthly magazine of architecture, public works and surveying in Scotland

Enquiries: To Director

Scope: Architecture, building, civil engineering and surveying in Scotland

No library

EDINBURGH

510

DUNFERMLINE COLLEGE OF PHYSICAL
EDUCATION
Cramond Road North
Edinburgh EH4 6JD

Tel.: 031-336 2147

Enquiries: To Librarian

Scope: Philosophy, psychology, sociology, education, biology, medicine, dance, sports, physical education

Stock: 8,000 books; 120 current periodicals

EDINBURGH	THE EDINBURGH CIVIC TRUST See **THE COCKBURN ASSOCIATION** (no. 507)	

EDINBURGH

511

EDINBURGH COLLEGE OF COMMERCE
Sighthill Court
Edinburgh

Enquiries: To Librarian

Scope: Library stock includes: Economics, statistics, management, business studies, accounting, banking, geography, psychology, sociology, law, data processing, transport, marketing, language, insurance

Stock: 10,000 books, pamphlets, and reports; 350 current periodicals. Stock not available on loan

EDINBURGH

512

EDINBURGH FOOT CLINIC AND SCHOOL OF CHIROPODY
81 Newington Road
Edinburgh EH9 1QW

Tel.: 031-667 3197

Provides training course in chiropody for State Registration and chiropody service within National Health Service for priority categories of patients, mainly those of medical/surgical significance

Enquiries: To Principal, by letter only

Scope: Careers in chiropody. Regulations and syllabus of training. Technical information on human locomotion, diagnosis and management of foot disabilities and related subjects
Secondary: Foot health education literature

Stock: 450 books; 20 pamphlets; 4 current periodicals. Stock not available on loan

Publications: School Prospectus
Technical Papers:
    The Mechanics of the Foot
    Care of the Feet in the Elderly
    Aims and Methods in Examination of Children's Feet
    Management of the Feet in Rheumatoid Disease

EDINBURGH

513

EDINBURGH PUBLIC LIBRARIES
George IV Bridge
Edinburgh EH1 1EG

Tel.: 031-225 5584

Enquiries: To Librarian

Scope: The following special departments are available: Edinburgh Room; Scottish Library; Music Room; Art Library. The first two include material relating to Edinburgh and Scotland. *Special collections* on Sir Walter Scott, R. L. Stevenson, R. M. Ballantyne and on Gaelic literature

Stock: 500,000 books and pamphlets; 432 current periodicals; 80,000 prints

Publications: Scottish Glass: a collector's notes. 1958
Museum of Childhood: a descriptive handbook. 1960
The Town Council of Edinburgh and The Reformation: extracts from the Records of the Town Council, 1556-1565. 1960

EDINBURGH, EDINBURGH PUBIC LIBRARIES, *cont.*
  The Buckstane: its history and romance. 1964
  Across the Cevennes in the footsteps of R. L. Stevenson and his donkey. 1965
  Edinburgh 1767-1967: a select list of books. 1967
  The Library of the Royal Cartographic Society is deposited in the Reference Library

EDINBURGH ENTERPRISE YOUTH *Tel.:* 031-226 3192
  29 Queen Street
514 Edinburgh EH2 1JX
  Co-ordinating and promoting voluntary service in Scotland
 Enquiries: To Director
 Scope: Information on voluntary service organizations, suggested activities and contact addresses
 Publications: Newsletter
  Information sheets
  Annual Report

EDINBURGH ETHICON LIMITED *Tel.:* 031-443 4050
  Bankhead Avenue
515 Edinburgh 11
  Manufacturers of surgical ligatures and sutures
 Enquiries: To Technical Director or Director of Surgical Research, by letter only
 Scope: Physical, chemical and biological properties of absorbable and non-absorbable surgical suture materials. Uses of surgical materials, including devices, for haemostasis and vascular replacement in all aspects of surgical practice including newer methods of wound closure and wound healing by devices other than sutures
 Stock: 16 current periodicals. Stock not available on loan
 Publications: Nursing Care of the Patient in Ophthalmic Surgery
  Nursing Care of the Patient in Orthopaedic Surgery
  Nursing Care of the Patient in Obs. Gyn. Surgery
  Digest of Basic Surgery
  Manual of Surgical Knots
  Anatomical Insights—The Abdomen
  Sutures and Ligatures

EDINBURGH THE FACULTY OF ACTUARIES *Tel.:* 031-556 6791
  23 St Andrew Square
516 Edinburgh EH2 1AQ
  Professional Society
 Enquiries: To Secretary, by letter or personal visit only
 Scope: Actuarial science. Demography
  Secondary: Mathematics; economics; financial and company law
 Stock: 3,000 books, pamphlets and reports; mainly actuarial and insurance periodicals; also selected periodicals on economics and law
 Publications: Transactions of the Faculty of Actuaries

EDINBURGH FREE CHURCH OF SCOTLAND COLLEGE *Tel.:* 031-226 4978
  The Mound
517 Edinburgh 1

Training College for aspirants to the Ministry of the Church

Enquiries: To Secretary

Scope: Theological literature, comprising: philosophy of religion; dogmatics; exegetics; church history; apologetics; homiletics; missions; biblical languages
Secondary: Gaelic literature

Stock: 30,000 books; 2,500 pamphlets; 20 current periodicals

EDINBURGH THE GALPIN SOCIETY
518 Hon. Curator/Archivist
46 Craigmount View
Edinburgh EH12 8BR

See no. 1169

EDINBURGH GENERAL REGISTER OFFICE FOR SCOTLAND *Tel.:* 031-556 3952
519 New Register House
Edinburgh EH1 3YT

Civil registration of births, deaths and marriages in Scotland. Maintenance of the registers of these events and issue of certified copies of entries in these registers. Preparation and analysis of statistics relating to population, fertility, births, marriages and deaths. Population censuses

Enquiries: To Registrar General (Branch dealing with specific subjects—Statistics Branch, Census Branch or Registration Branch)

Scope: The library, which is primarily for the use of genealogical searchers, contains population and vital statistics reports of the United Kingdom and a few British Commonwealth and foreign countries. Any enquiries relating to Scottish vital and census statistics will be dealt with

Stock: 2,000 books and pamphlets; 20 current periodicals. Stock not available on loan

Publications: Registrar General's Annual Reports, quarterly and weekly returns and Reports on Censuses of the Population in Scotland

EDINBURGH HERIOT-WATT UNIVERSITY LIBRARY *Tel.:* 031-225 8432
520 Chambers Street
Edinburgh EH1 1HX

Enquiries: To Librarian

Scope: Social sciences: Economics, accountancy and finance, industrial administration and commerce (including law, economic geography, moral and social philosophy, psychology, government and public administration, sociology, marketing)
Humanities: Languages (French, German, Russian, Spanish), pharmacy, biochemistry

Stock: 40,000 books and pamphlets; 750 current periodicals (total stock)

Divisional Library for social sciences and humanities is at Heriot-Watt University, Mountbatten Building, Grassmarket, Edinburgh, EH1 2HT
Ethicon Library (Pharmacy) is at Pharmacy Department, Heriot-Watt University, 79 Grassmarket, Edinburgh EH1 2HJ, but enquiries other than in person to Librarian at Chambers Street

EDINBURGH INSTITUTE OF OCCUPATIONAL MEDICINE *Tel.:* 031-667 5131
521 Roxburgh Place
Edinburgh EH8 9SU

Research into medical problems of working conditions in industry

Enquiries: To Librarian/Information Officer

EDINBURGH, INSTITUTE OF OCCUPATIONAL MEDICINE, *cont.*

Scope: Occupational medicine, primarily in the mining field (that is pneumoconiosis), but also applied to other industries
Secondary: Industrial hygiene, safety. Atmospheric pollution by dust. All aspects of particle counting, sampling. Noise hazards. Ergonomics
Stock: 200 books and pamphlets; 50 reports; 50 current periodicals

EDINBURGH

522

MANKIND QUARTERLY
1 Darnaway Street
Edinburgh 3

Tel.: 031-225 1896

Publication of researches and discussions

Enquiries: To Editor

Scope: Ethnology, ethno-psychology, anthropology, ethno-genetics, human geography, comparative linguistics and religion related to human evolution
Secondary: In addition, as an extension of genetics and social anthropology and history the library covers the whole fields of heraldry, genealogy, orders of chivalry, and nobiliary law

Publications: The Mankind Quarterly   The Armorial Who is Who
Mankind Monographs   Roll of Scottish Arms
The Armorial

EDINBURGH

523

MEDICAL RESEARCH COUNCIL
BRAIN METABOLISM UNIT
University Medical School
Teviot Place
Edinburgh EH1 2QZ

Tel.: 031-667 1011

Enquiries: To Director, by letter only

Scope: Studies of cerebral metabolism in animals and man with particular reference to those aspects which may have a relevance to aetiology or treatment of neurological disease
The development of techniques for the study of cerebral metabolism in animal experiments with the intention of obtaining information on the metabolism of the brain which may have relevance to the understanding of the relationship between function and metabolism and to the action of drugs on the brain; or of subsequent application of the techniques to the study of patients with neurological and psychiatric illness

EDINBURGH

524

MEDICAL RESEARCH COUNCIL
SPEECH AND COMMUNICATION UNIT
University of Edinburgh
31 Buccleuch Place
Edinburgh EH8 9JT

Tel.: 031-667 5265

Enquiries: To Secretary
Scope: Research in language behaviour, normal and pathological
Small (specialized) library
Publications: Papers in scientific journals, reports and Symposia

EDINBURGH

525

MORAY HOUSE COLLEGE OF EDUCATION
Holyrood Road
Edinburgh EH8 8AQ

Tel.: 031-556 4415

Enquiries: To Principal Librarian

Scope: Education and psychology
Secondary: All other subjects in the College curriculum
Stock: 50,000 books; 6,000 pamphlets; 350 current periodicals
Publications: Moray House College of Education Publications
See also Centre for Information on the Teaching of English (no. 506)

EDINBURGH

526

MUSEUM OF CHILDHOOD *Tel.:* 031-556 5447
'Opposite John Knox's House'
38 High Street
Edinburgh

Museum for the study of the historical background of childhood, primarily for adults. Includes toys, games, dolls, hobbies, education, health, costume, reading matter and upbringing. The first museum in the world to devote itself entirely to the study of childhood

Enquiries: To Curator
Scope: Information service covers entire field of the museum's subject and collections. The library stock includes all juvenile reading from Tiny Tots picture books to school and adventure stories. Fair collection of chap books, excellent collection of ephemera, Jack Harkaway, Chums, Rainbow, Magnet and Gem, Schoolgirl's Weekly. Very full collection of Victoriana in its dullest forms, from Kate Greenaway upwards; great stress being laid on the forgotten illustrators and one time popular authors. Pop-ups, rag books, albums of scraps. Very full coverage of educational books from *The English Schoolmaster* to *Kennedy and Fraser*. Writing pieces and strips, schoolroom varia, copybooks, cat on the mat readers. French without Tears. Very large reference section, with card index of children's books running into thousands of entries
Stock: 10,000 books; 2,000 pamphlets; trade journals of the toy world, and collector's journals

EDINBURGH

527

NAPIER COLLEGE OF SCIENCE AND *Tel.:* 031-447 1011
TECHNOLOGY
Colinton Road
Edinburgh EH10 5DT
Regional Polytechnic

Enquiries: To Librarian or Principal
Scope: Engineering. Printing and photography. Catering. Science. Building. Programmed learning (College is a research centre in Scotland for the Scottish Education Department). Good collections on industrial training and computer programming; industrial design, and ergonomics. Considerable audio-visual resources in these fields
Special collection: Edward Clark collection of books relating to printing and book production (a catalogue with annotations by Harry Carter is in the press)
Stock: 22,000 books; 2,000 pamphlets; 450 current periodicals; complete set of British Standards

EDINBURGH

528

NATIONAL GALLERY OF SCOTLAND *Tel.:* 031-225 6824
The Mound
Edinburgh EH2 2EL

Enquiries: To Secretary
Scope: Books, catalogues (dealers and exhibitions), photographic library on paintings, drawings (up to 1900) with special emphasis on Scottish artists and paintings and drawings in Scottish private collections
Stock not usually available on loan

EDINBURGH, NATIONAL GALLERY OF SCOTLAND, *cont.*

Publications: The Maitland Gift and related pictures. 1963
A short guide to the Gallery (annually)
Forty Scottish Paintings. 1958 (illustrations)
Fifty Master Drawings. 1961 (illustrations)
Selected Scottish Drawings. 1960 (illustrations)
A Shorter Catalogue of Paintings and Sculpture. 1970
National Gallery of Scotland Illustrations. 1965
Catalogue of Italian Drawings. 2 volumes. K. Andrews. 1968

EDINBURGH

529

NATIONAL LIBRARY OF SCOTLAND
George IV Bridge
Edinburgh EH1 1EW

Tel.: 031-225 4104
Telex: 72638

Enquiries: To Librarian

Scope: The library was founded in 1682 as the Library of the Faculty of Advocates, and was transferred, except for its law books, to the nation in 1925; the holdings of the Advocates' library are available for consultation in the National Library. It has been a Copyright Library since 1710. While its Scottish resources, both books and manuscripts, are particularly important, it is also rich in European and English books from the beginning of printing onwards. The Library has many *special collections*, mainly relating to the humanities. Included in the non-Scottish collections are:
Astorga: Hispanic
Bute: English plays from Elizabethan period onwards
Hopkinson-Berlioz: Musical and literary works of Berlioz, and works about him
Scandinavian: Older Scandinavian books, including Library of Thorkelin
Nichol Smith: Relations between English and French literature and criticism, 16th to 18th century
Most of the holdings in the Department of Manuscripts provide material for the study of the subjects with which this volume of the Directory is concerned

Stock: 3,000,000 books and pamphlets; 5,220 current periodicals (estimated total stock). Stock not available on loan

Publications: Catalogue of Manuscripts acquired since 1925, Vol. I. 1938
Catalogue of Manuscripts acquired since 1925, Vol. II. 1966
Catalogue of Manuscripts acquired since 1925, Vol. III, Blackwood Papers 1805-1900. 1968
Summary Catalogue of the Advocates' Manuscripts
Short-Title Catalogue of Books Published Abroad to 1600
Advocates' Library Notable Accessions to 1925. A book of illustrations. 1965
National Library of Scotland. Notable Accessions since 1925. A Book of Illustrations. 1965
The Taill of Rauf Coilyer. A facsimile of the only known copy. 1966
List of books printed in Scotland before 1700. Revised edition. H. G. Aldis
Catalogues of Exhibitions
Catalogues of National Exhibitions

EDINBURGH

530

NATIONAL MUSEUM OF ANTIQUITIES OF SCOTLAND
Edinburgh 2

Tel.: 031-556 5984

Aims to provide an adequate library service for those working in the archaeological and antiquarian fields, with the accent on Scotland

Enquiries: To Keeper

Scope: The archaeology of Western Europe. Agricultural history

Secondary: Scottish local and national history, family history, decorative arts and crafts, architecture, numismatics

Stock: 20,000 books and pamphlets; 287 current periodicals

The Library is the joint library of the Museum and of the Society of Antiquaries of Scotland and its accession lists (excluding periodicals) are published in the Society's annual Proceedings, which also contain the Museum's accession lists

Records and manuscripts of the Society of Antiquaries of Scotland are housed separately, as are manuscripts and abstract collections on subjects covered by the work of the various departments of the Museum

EDINBURGH

531

PHARMACEUTICAL SOCIETY (SCOTTISH DEPARTMENT)
36 York Place
Edinburgh EH1 3HU

Tel.: 031-556 4386

Enquiries: To Librarian

Scope: Subjects relating to the training of pharmacists and the practice of all branches of pharmacy, the main ones being pharmaceutics, pharmaceutical chemistry and pharmacology, law relating to pharmacy and the history of pharmacy and medicine
Secondary: Bacteriology, biology, chemistry and physics

Stock: 2,000 books; 20 current periodicals

EDINBURGH

532

THE ROYAL CALEDONIAN CURLING CLUB
2 Coates Crescent
Edinburgh 3

Tel.: 031-225 7083

Enquiries: To Secretary

Scope: Valuable collection of volumes on curling, ancient and modern

Stock: Wide collection of books; various curling periodicals from overseas. Stock not available on loan

Publications: The Royal Caledonian Curling Club Annual
Films, 16mm sound and colour

EDINBURGH

533

ROYAL COLLEGE OF NURSING AND NATIONAL COUNCIL OF NURSES OF THE UK SCOTTISH BOARD
43/44 Heriot Row
Edinburgh EH3 6EY

Tel.: 031-225 7231

The advancement of nursing as a profession and the running of courses for registered nurses in administration and clinical instruction

Enquiries: To Librarian, by letter only

Scope: General nursing; specialized nursing; nursing history; nursing ethics; nursing education and training. Hospital administration and planning. Sociology; psychology
Secondary: History of medicine. Clinical specialities. General education

Stock: 2,000 books and pamphlets; 42 current periodicals. Stock not available on loan

EDINBURGH

534

ROYAL COLLEGE OF PHYSICIANS OF EDINBURGH
9 Queen Street
Edinburgh EH2 1JQ

Tel.: 031-225 5968

EDINBURGH, ROYAL COLLEGE OF PHYSICIANS OF EDINBURGH, *cont.*

Enquiries: To Librarian

Scope: Medicine, particularly clinical, but excluding general surgery, and allied sciences. History of medicine

Stock: 200,000 books, pamphlets and reports; 460 current periodicals; 1,000 volumes of manuscripts, many relating to 18th century Edinburgh medical school

EDINBURGH

535

ROYAL COLLEGE OF SURGEONS OF EDINBURGH
18 Nicolson Street
Edinburgh EH8 9DW

Tel.: 031-556 6206

Enquiries: To Librarian

Scope: Surgery and the basic sciences

Stock: 26,000 books; 180 current periodicals

Publications: Journal of the Royal College of Surgeons of Edinburgh

EDINBURGH

536

THE ROYAL MEDICAL SOCIETY
3 Hill Square
Edinburgh 8

Tel.: 031-667 8159

Society with extensive library and museum

Enquiries: To Secretary

Scope: The Library, whose collection started in 1737, accumulated a remarkable collection of medical books, most of which have been, or are in the process of being sold by auction. Some of the most rare and those not present in Edinburgh are retained. From 1750 it was the rule that each member should compose a dissertation which was handwritten and signed by its author, and the Society's collection of these is complete. This provides a unique picture of the development of medical thought and practice during the last two hundred years. Society also has a comprehensive modern library and journal room

Publications: Res Medica (Society's Journal, 2 issues each year)

EDINBURGH

537

ROYAL SCOTTISH GEOGRAPHICAL SOCIETY
10 Randolph Crescent
Edinburgh 3

Tel.: 031-225 3330

Enquiries: To Secretary

Scope: Geography and cartography
Secondary: Topography of Scotland

Stock: 20,000 books; 1,000 pamphlets; 200 current periodicals; large map collection, both of modern maps and of old maps of Scotland

Publications: Scottish Geographical Magazine (annually since 1885, now 3 times a year)

EDINBURGH

538

ROYAL SCOTTISH SOCIETY FOR PREVENTION OF CRUELTY TO CHILDREN
16 Melville Street
Edinburgh 3

Tel.: 031-225 5377 and 2912

Enquiries: To Secretary-General

Scope: Information provided on law related to protection or welfare of children; and to parents who seek specific help on where to go or whom to approach

EDINBURGH **539**	ROYAL SOCIETY OF EDINBURGH 22/24 George Street Edinburgh EH2 2PQ	*Tel.:* 031-225 6057

Promotion of science and learning

Enquiries: To Assistant Secretary and Librarian

Stock: The library has a stock of 200,000 volumes, mainly scientific periodical literature with relatively few individual books (mainly pre-1940). Subject coverage: Science generally, particularly material emanating from scientific academies, societies and similar institutions. Limited coverage in social sciences, medicine, veterinary medicine, and geography. Substantial collection of pamphlets in various sciences; 2,000 current periodicals

Publications: Transactions of the Royal Society of Edinburgh
Proceedings of the Royal Society of Edinburgh—in two sections: 'A' Mathematical and Physical Sciences, including Chemistry, Astronomy. 'B'—Biological Sciences, including Geology, Medicine
Year Book of the Royal Society of Edinburgh
Billets of Meetings (include periodical Library Accession Lists)

EDINBURGH **540**	THE SCOTTISH ANGLERS' ASSOCIATION 117 Hanover Street Edinburgh 2	*Tel.:* 031-664 1740

Enquiries: To Secretary, by letter only

Scope: Information regarding Angling Clubs and Angling Waters in Scotland. Not an authority on how to fish

No library

EDINBURGH **541**	SCOTTISH ARTS COUNCIL 11 Rothesay Terrace Edinburgh EH3 7RY	*Tel.:* 031-225 2769

Subsidy and promotion of the Arts

Enquiries: To Director

Scope: The Arts in Scotland: in particular professional organizations concerned with the Arts and specifically those in receipt of grants from the Council

No library

EDINBURGH **542**	SCOTTISH ASSOCIATION OF BOYS CLUBS 12 Alva Street Edinburgh 2	*Tel.:* 031-225 7087

Enquiries: To Secretary

Scope: Any enquiry relating to work amongst boys can be dealt with. Specialists employed for advising on new buildings for boys' clubs, training of leaders and boys, industrial training, work with deprived boys

EDINBURGH **543**	SCOTTISH ASSOCIATION OF OCCUPATIONAL THERAPISTS 77 George Street Edinburgh 2	*Tel.:* 031-225 5740

Enquiries: To Secretary

EDINBURGH, SCOTTISH ASSOCIATION OF OCCUPATIONAL THERAPISTS, *cont.*

Scope: Pamphlets on occupational therapy as career and profession are available. Detailed information on specific aspects of occupational therapy is available through members

Stock: Stock includes many foreign occupational therapy journals

Publications: S.A.O.T. Journal (quarterly)

EDINBURGH

544

THE SCOTTISH ASSOCIATION OF VOLUNTARY *Tel.:* 031-556 3882
CHILD CARE ORGANISATIONS
19 Claremont Crescent
Edinburgh EH7 4HX

Enquiries: To Secretary

Scope: Source of information on questions pertaining to child care in voluntary organizations
No library

EDINBURGH

545

SCOTTISH CONGREGATIONAL COLLEGE *Tel.:* 031-447 1807
29 Hope Terrace
Edinburgh EH9 2AP

Enquiries: To Librarian

Scope: Various branches of theological studies (Old and New Testament, theology, church history). Considerable number of volumes on history of Congregationalism in Scotland, and collection of 19th century missionary literature

Stock: 12,000 books; 12 current periodicals

EDINBURGH

546

SCOTTISH CONSERVATIVE CENTRAL OFFICE *Tel.:* 031-229 1342
11 Atholl Crescent *Telex:* 72421
Edinburgh EH3 8HG

Enquiries: To Librarian

Scope: The Library holds stocks of publications relating mainly to the Government of Scotland, divided into four main sections:
Politics and Government; Social; Economic; and Overseas;
and further sub-divided into four main categories:
Government Publications; Non-Government Publications; General Information Files; and Press Cuttings
Set of Hansard (Commons and Lords) since 1951; set of Public Acts and Measures from 1880
The Press Cuttings Section provides a comprehensive coverage of Scottish Affairs since 1967
Stock not available on loan

Publications: The Year Book for Scotland 1967 (biographies of all Scottish Members of Parliament, election results and analysis—this item is available for the period 1945-1967)
Putting Scotland Right Ahead (statement of aims prior to 1966)
Action for Scotland (1966 General Election Manifesto)
Current Pamphlets:
Make Life Better in Scotland (May 1969 statement of Party aims)
The Grandest Thing in the World—Education. I. MacArthur
The Dead End People—Youth Amenities. V. MacColl
Scotland—The Political Choice (a report on nationalism by a Scottish Young Conservative Policy Group)
The Inventor (the story of a great inventor frustrated by our tax system)

EDINBURGH	THE SCOTTISH COUNCIL FOR RESEARCH IN EDUCATION	*Tel.:* 031-225 3578
547	46 Moray Place Edinburgh EH3 6BH	

Conducting research in education, publishing results of educational research carried out in Scotland, maintaining register of research, advising and making grants to those engaged in educational research

Enquiries: To Secretary

Scope: Statistical methods, reports on investigations in the subjects of the curriculum, and bibliographies of educational research, from pre-school to University. Theses presented for degrees in Scottish Universities in education and educational psychology

Stock: 1,250 books and pamphlets; 35 current periodicals

Publications: Reports 59
Newsletter (2 or 3 issues each year)

EDINBURGH	SCOTTISH COUNCIL FOR THE UNMARRIED MOTHER AND HER CHILD	*Tel.:* 031-556 3899
548	44 Albany Street Edinburgh EH1 3QR	

To bring together interested bodies concerned with the well-being of the unmarried mother and her child, to encourage provision of adequate accommodation for mothers bringing up their own children and to watch trend of laws which affect such children and organize conferences and study groups for social workers and others involved in this work

Enquiries: To Director and Senior Social Worker

Stock: Small library of informative booklets and pamphlets

Publications: Report of Day Conference held in Edinburgh in June, 1967: Unmarried Mothers—Their Medical and Social Needs
List of Mother and Baby Homes in Scotland
Report of Day Conference held in Edinburgh in June, 1968: Fatherless families—do we meet their needs?

EDINBURGH	THE SCOTTISH GENEALOGY SOCIETY	*Tel.:* 031-556 3844
549	21 Howard Place Edinburgh EH3 5JY	

Promotes research into Scottish family history and undertakes the collection, exchange, and publication of material relating to genealogy

Enquiries: To Hon. Secretary, by letter only

Scope: Scottish family history and genealogy. Scottish emigrants, particularly pre-1855

Stock: 500 books and pamphlets; 36 current periodicals

Publications: The Scottish Genealogist
Library Catalogue. 1964
Library Accessions 1964-66
Monumental Inscriptions (pre-1855) in Kinross-shire
Monumental Inscriptions (pre-1855) in Clackmannan
Monumental Inscriptions (pre-1855) in West Lothian

EDINBURGH	SCOTTISH HOSPITAL CENTRE	*Tel.:* 031-332 2335
550	Crewe Road South Edinburgh EH4 2LF	

EDINBURGH, SCOTTISH HOSPITAL CENTRE, *cont.*

Research in the fields of hospital planning, building and administration. Hospital operational research and work study

Enquiries: To Librarian

Scope: Hospital design, planning, function and administration. Social Welfare. National Health Service. Local Authority Welfare and Health Services. Planning hospital libraries
Secondary: Bio-engineering, computers in medicine, metrication, literature about audio-visual material

Stock: 4,000 books, pamphlets and reports; 107 current periodicals
Special collections: 2,000 architects' plans of new hospital buildings illustrating 400 projects. 1,000 35 mm slides illustrating aspects of hospital planning

Publications: Bulletin of Additions (monthly)
Periodicals List (annually)
Library Guide
Bibliographies (19 subjects to date)
An Introduction to Reading Architects' Drawings
The Functional Analysis of Ward Plans
Collected Conference Reports 1966
Changing Accommodation for Non-resident Staff in Hospitals
Upgrading of Wards
Collected Conference Reports 1967
Collected Conference Reports 1968
Libraries in Hospitals (bibliography)
Information Sheets:
  Domestic Service Room
  Surface-mounted Wardrobe Incorporating Bed-head Services
  Preparation Room
  Outpatient Consulting/Examination Room
  A Survey of Hospital Bedsteads, Cots and Bedside Lockers
  Residential Accommodation for Hospital Medical Staff
  Office Accommodation and Secretarial Services for Hospital Clinicians
  Central Sterile Supply in Scotland
  Centre News (a newsletter reviewing activities at the Centre published at two-monthly intervals)

EDINBURGH

551

SCOTTISH NATIONAL GALLERY OF MODERN ART
Royal Botanic Garden
Edinburgh EH3 5LR

Tel.: 031-332 3754

Collects and exhibits works characteristic of 20th century art and modern Scottish art

Enquiries: To Keeper

Scope: In the general field of modern art the Keeper will answer detailed questions on works in the collection
Secondary: Questions on modern Scottish art and artists will always be answered if possible

Publications: National Galleries of Scotland Poster Bulletin (4 issues each year)
Exhibition catalogues

EDINBURGH

552

SCOTTISH NATIONAL PORTRAIT GALLERY
1 Queen Street
Edinburgh EH2 1JD

Tel.: 031-556 7975

Enquiries: To Keeper

Scope: Preservation and recording of Scottish portraiture in all media

Publications: Illustrated Catalogue. 1951
               The Royal House of Stewart. 1967
               Scott and His Circle. 1964
               The Jacobite Rising of 1715. 1965
               Scottish History in Perspective. 1966
               Scots in Italy in the 18th Century. 1966
               Mr Boswell. 1967

EDINBURGH 553

SCOTTISH OFFICE LIBRARY
St Andrew's House
Edinburgh EH1 3DH
Tel.: 031-556 8404 ext. 380
Telex: 72202

Library serves the four Departments of the Secretary of State for Scotland (Department of Agriculture and Fisheries for Scotland, Scottish Development Department, Scottish Education Department, Scottish Home and Health Department)

Enquiries: To Librarian

Scope: Scottish administration and law. Agriculture and horticulture. Plant breeding, diseases and pests. Fisheries. Industrial development. Housing, Town and country planning. Transport. Road engineering. Local government. Public health. Hospitals. Welfare and social services. Police, prison and fire services. Education. (All subjects with special emphasis on their Scottish aspects)

Stock: 40,000 books; 80,000 pamphlets and reports; 1,000 current periodicals

Publications: Government reports on all aspects of Scottish administration
Scottish Agriculture (quarterly)

Separate branch libraries: Architecture, building, civil engineering. Plant breeding, diseases and pests. Scots Law

EDINBURGH 554

SCOTTISH POISONS INFORMATION BUREAU
The Royal Infirmary of Edinburgh
Edinburgh EH3 9YW
Tel.: 031-229 2477

Enquiries: To Director

Scope: Provides information to doctors as to whether substances, medicinal, agricultural, industrial and domestic are poisonous and advises on the treatment of poisoned patients **to doctors only**

EDINBURGH 555

THE SCOTTISH SCHOOLMASTERS ASSOCIATION
41 York Place
Edinburgh EH1 3HP
Tel.: 031-556 8825

Aims to improve educational services in Scotland and the conditions of teachers in Scotland

Enquiries: To Secretary

Scope: Primary, secondary and further education
Secondary: Conditions of service of teachers

Publications: The Scottish Schoolmaster (6 issues each year)

EDINBURGH 556

SCOTTISH SOCIETY FOR PREVENTION OF CRUELTY TO ANIMALS
19 Melville Street
Edinburgh EH3 7PL
Tel.: 031-225 6418

Enquiries: To Secretary

Scope: Animal welfare
No library

Publications: Leaflets on animal welfare

EDINBURGH	SCOTTISH SOCIETY FOR THE PREVENTION OF VIVISECTION	*Tel.:* 031-225 6039
557	10 Queensferry Street Edinburgh EH2 4PG	

Enquiries: To Secretary

Scope: Anti-vivisection literature and films

No library

Publications: Annual Pictorial Review (85 pages containing some 70 half-tone and colour photographs, free on request)

EDINBURGH	SCOTTISH SQUASH RACKETS ASSOCIATION	*Tel.:* 031-336 2309
558	5 Barnton Gardens Edinburgh EH4 6AF	

Enquiries: To Hon. Secretary

Scope: Squash rackets, including advice on building of courts

No library

EDINBURGH	THE SCOTTISH TOURIST BOARD	*Tel.:* 031-299 1561
559	2 Rutland Place Edinburgh EH1 2YU	

Promotion of tourism in Scotland

Enquiries: a. To Research and Development Officer (tourism development enquiries)
b. To Information Officer (general visitor enquiries)

Scope: a. Provision of advice and information to potential developers on possible sites in suitable locations
b. Servicing of all enquiries from potential and actual visitors on all aspects of holidays in Scotland—travel, touring, accommodation, recreation, places of interest, countryside

Stock: a. Limited stocks of research surveys on specific topics
b. Bulk stocks of general publications for sale and for free distribution

Publications: a. Upper Tay and Tummel Regional Study
Firth of Clyde Regional Study (Phase 1)
Galloway and South West Scotland Regional Study
Eastern Cairngorms Regional Study
Central Borders Regional Study
Summer Tourism Surveys 1967
Edinburgh Hotel Survey
Survey of Winter Sports Potential of Beinn A'Bhuird
Highlands and Islands Visitors Survey 1966
Coach Tour Survey
Hotel Economics Survey
Recreation and Tourism in the Loch Lomond Area
Caravan Survey 1969
Wester Ross Regional Study
Tourism in Scotland
b. Where to Stay in Scotland (Accommodation Register)
Scotland for Caravan Holidays
Scotland for Fishing   Map of Scotland (16 m/1 in)
Scotland for Sea Angling   Public Holidays in Scotland

                    Scotland for Coarse Fishing   Holidays in Scotland
                    Scotland, Home of Golf   Highland Holiday
                  Many free publications on specific regions, places of interest, motor routes, sports, birdwatching, events and festivities

EDINBURGH   SCOTTISH WOMEN'S RURAL INSTITUTES   *Tel.*: 031-225 6490
                  42 Heriot Row
560   Edinburgh EH3 6EU

                  Provides centres and educational, recreational and social activities for women in villages and small towns throughout Scotland. Programmes include drama, music, painting, talks on education, citizenship, local history, overseas countries, demonstrations and tuition in handicrafts and housewifery

       Enquiries: To General Secretary
           Scope: Drama, handicrafts, homecrafts, local history, decimal currency, crafts judging. Specimen Loan Boxes of many crafts
           Stock: 2,500 plays (Drama Library), 400 books (Handicrafts), 153 books (Homecrafts); magazines from overseas country women's organizations
    Publications: S.W.R.I. Cookery Book
                    Bed and Breakfast Booklet
                    Slides and Records of paintings and costumes
                    Scottish Home and Country (monthly magazine)

EDINBURGH   THE SIGNET LIBRARY   *Tel.*: 031-225 4923
                  Parliament Square
561   Edinburgh EH1 1RF

                  This private library serves the requirements of the Society of Writers to Her Majesty's Signet (solicitors). *Bona fide* enquiries, however, will be answered

       Enquiries: To Librarian
           Scope: Legal, in particular Scots Law; the library attempts to answer all legal queries by its members from its own resources, and usually does so where Scots Law is concerned
                    Special collection of Court of Sessions Papers, 1713 to date (2,500 volumes), with index 1713–1820
                    William Roughhead collection on criminal trials (500 volumes)
                    Secondary: The library has a large general stock and *all* types of enquiry are dealt with. In addition to serving the professional and recreational needs of the members of the W.S. Society, the library endeavours to assist scholars and research workers, particularly in the fields of Scottish history, topography and genealogy
           Stock: 25,000 legal books; 85,000 general books; 2,500 legal pamphlets; 2,500 general pamphlets; 30 legal current periodicals; 35 general current periodicals. Stock not available on loan except to members

EDINBURGH   SOCIETY FOR FOLK LIFE STUDIES   *Tel.*: 031-556 5984
                  c/o National Museum of Antiquities
562   Queen Street
                  Edinburgh
                  Society for the study of the changing and traditional ways of life in Great Britain and Ireland
       Enquiries: To Society
           Scope: Folk life

EDINBURGH, SOCIETY FOR FOLK LIFE STUDIES, *cont.*
    Stock: No library
    Publications: Folk Life (Vol. 1, 1963, and annually to date)
    Studies in Folk Life. J. G. Jenkins, ed.

EDINBURGH

563

SOCIETY OF SOLICITORS IN THE SUPREME COURTS OF SCOTLAND
Parliament House
Parliament Square
Edinburgh

    Enquiries: To Librarian, by letter only
    Scope: Law library
    Stock: 10,000 books; 7 current periodicals. Stock not available on loan

EDINBURGH

564

THE THEOSOPHICAL SOCIETY IN SCOTLAND   *Tel.:* 031-556 5385
28 Great King Street
Edinburgh EH3 6QH

Society which forms a nucleus of the universal brotherhood of humanity without distinction of race, creed, sex or colour, encourages the study of comparative religion, philosophy and science, and investigates unexplained laws of nature and the powers latent in man

    Enquiries: To General Secretary, by letter only
    Scope: Works of Madame H. B. Blavatsky and of writers in the field of theosophy, including Krishnamurti, Jinarajadasa, Sri Ram, G. S. Arundale. Books on occult science, Kabala, astrology, sociology, symbolism, initiation and meditation, yoga, applied art, psychology, philosophy, medical healing, comparative religion, anthropology, archaeology and education
    Secondary: Psychic, legends and mythology, palmistry and occult arts, animal welfare, plays, poetry, belles lettres including Rabindranath Tagore, mathematics and fiction
    Stock: 7,000 books
    Publications: Theosophical Journal

EDINBURGH

565

UNIVERSITY OF EDINBURGH   *Tel.:* 031-667 1011 ext. 2258
CENTRAL MEDICAL LIBRARY
Medical School
Teviot Place
Edinburgh EH8 9AG

Provides a reference and limited lending service for the teaching staff of the medical school, clinical teaching staff of local hospitals, and certain postgraduate research workers

    Enquiries: To Sub-Librarian, Medical Libraries, by letter only
    Scope: All branches of medicine and medical sciences; limited resources in dentistry, psychiatry and social medicine, for which there are special departmental libraries. Enquiries accepted when routed through other medical libraries
    Stock: 46,000 books; 5,000 pamphlets; 600 current periodicals. Recent periodicals not normally available on loan, but photocopies can be supplied
    MEDLARS Liaison Officer
    See also no. 568

EDINBURGH	UNIVERSITY OF EDINBURGH	*Tel.:* 031-667 1011 ext. 4292
	CENTRE OF EUROPEAN GOVERNMENTAL	
566	STUDIES	
	Old College	
	South Bridge	
	Edinburgh EH8 9YL	

Enquiries: To Librarian

Scope: The scope of the information service and library is limited. The material is available to answer enquiries on all aspects of the affairs of the European Communities and background information on Europe in general, particularly in the fields of law, politics, and economics. A good range of official journals and law reports from European countries is held. The librarian will help readers to find the material they require, but is unable to undertake extensive searches

Stock: 2,000 books; 300 pamphlets; 77 current periodicals, excluding those of the European Communities

The library is a depository library for the publications of the European Communities, and receives everything they publish. Council of Europe publications are also received

See also no. 568

EDINBURGH	UNIVERSITY OF EDINBURGH	*Tel.:* 031-667 1011 ext. 4279
	THE LAW LIBRARY	
567	Old College	
	South Bridge	
	Edinburgh EH8 9YL	

Enquiries: To Librarian

Scope: Comprehensive law library

Stock: 21,000 books; 950 pamphlets; 175 current periodicals. Stock available on loan through Edinburgh University main library (no. 568)

EDINBURGH	UNIVERSITY OF EDINBURGH LIBRARY	*Tel.:* 031-667 1011
	George Square	
568	Edinburgh EH8 9LJ	

Enquiries: To Librarian

Scope: A general collection of modern works covering all fields. The following *special collection* is of interest:

Murray Collection: About 1,000 volumes chiefly on zoology, geography and geology from the library of Sir John Murray, presented in 1921

The library has also many older works, British and foreign, of interest from the viewpoint of the history of science and medicine in particular. These include the Thomson-Walker Collection of 2,700 engraved portraits of British and foreign medical men. The library also holds copies of theses submitted to the University. These include a collection of 18th and 19th century printed medical theses as well as modern theses in all fields. There is also a collection of printed theses of foreign Universities, 19th century to date

The following libraries, all fully staffed, but part of the University Library, have separate entries:

Central Medical Library (no. 565)
Centre of European Governmental Studies (no. 566)
Law Library (no. 567)
New College Library (no. 569)
Reid Music Library (no. 570)
Royal (Dick) School of Veterinary Studies (no. 571)

EDINBURGH, UNIVERSITY OF EDINBURGH LIBRARY, *cont.*

The following departmental libraries do not duplicate material held in the main library or in those noted in other entries:

Centre of African Studies; Dentistry; Psychiatry; and Social Medicine

Publications: Catalogue of the printed books in the Library of the University of Edinburgh. 3 volumes. Edinburgh, 1918–23 (covers a large proportion of the older material in the Main Library)

EDINBURGH

569

UNIVERSITY OF EDINBURGH
NEW COLLEGE LIBRARY
Mound Place
Edinburgh EH1 2LU

Tel.: 031-225 8400

Theological Section of Edinburgh University Library (no. 568)

Enquiries: To Librarian

Scope: Theology, philosophy, patristics, biblical study, church history, liturgiology, hymnology, homiletics, missions

Secondary: Bibliography (large stock of rare books, particularly 16th and 17th centuries)

Stock: 175,000 books; 20,000 pamphlets; 300 current periodicals

Publications: New College Bulletin (3 issues each year, with an important theological article in each issue)
Abridged Catalogue of Books in New College Library, Edinburgh

Department Libraries: Christian Ethics Library
Divinity (Baillie) Library
Dogmatics (Mackintosh) Library
Ecclesiastical History Library
New Testament Library
Old Testament and Semitic Library

EDINBURGH

570

UNIVERSITY OF EDINBURGH
REID MUSIC LIBRARY
Alison House
Nicolson Square
Edinburgh EH8 9BH

Tel.: 031-667 1011 ext. 2471

The library of the Faculty of Music in Edinburgh University

Enquiries: To Librarian

Scope: Music

Stock: 7,650 books; 23 current periodicals; 32,850 music scores. Periodicals not available on loan, but photocopying provided

Publications: Catalogue of manuscripts, printed music and books on music up to 1850 in the Library of the Music Department at the University of Edinburgh (Reid Library). 1941. H. Gal

See also The Galpin Society, no. 518 and 1169, and no. 568

EDINBURGH

571

UNIVERSITY OF EDINBURGH
ROYAL (DICK) SCHOOL OF VETERINARY
STUDIES
Summerhall
Edinburgh EH9 1QH

Tel.: 01-667 6801

Veterinary Faculty of Edinburgh University

Enquiries: To Librarian, by letter only

Scope: Since veterinary science is to a great extent a duplication of human medicine, but applied to domestic animals, stock includes in addition to books on veterinary science, books on various branches of the medical sciences and some on agriculture. Enquiries dealt with only if received through other libraries

Stock: 5,000 books; 6,000 pamphlets; 360 current periodicals

Publications: Bound volumes of collected papers by members of staff are distributed to 28 veterinary schools and colleges all over the world every two or three years

See also no. 568

EDINBURGH

572

UNIVERSITY OF EDINBURGH
SCHOOL OF SCOTTISH STUDIES
27 George Square
Edinburgh EH8 9LD

Tel.: 031-667 1011 ext. 6676

Enquiries: To Director, or Archivist

Scope: Scottish folklore, including Scots and Gaelic folktale and folksong; Scottish folk life, local history, sociology and archaeology; place-names of Scotland; Gaelic literature; Scottish pipe and fiddle music
Secondary: Folklore, folk life, folk music and place-names of other countries

Stock: 4,000 books; 1,000 pamphlets; 20 series reports; 125 current periodicals
Sound Archive: Tape-recordings: more than 3,000 reels of original Scottish material (folksong, folktale, folk music, information on custom and belief and folk life) together with 900 direct-recorded discs and 100 Ediphone cylinders of similar material
Small manuscript collection of Scottish folktales, folksongs, information on folk life, fiddle music and Gaelic literature
Photographic archive illustrating traditional buildings, techniques and tools
Printed books available on loan through Edinburgh University Library (no. 568)

Publications: Scottish Studies (twice each year, including an annual bibliography)

Limited listening facilities are available for material from the Sound Archive, and there are transcriptions of words and music of about 10 per cent of the material

EGHAM
Surrey

573

BRITISH WATER SKI FEDERATION
Egham
Surrey

Tel.: Wentworth 3711 and Egham 3804

Enquiries: To Secretary

Scope: The Secretariat is pleased to answer any general enquiries about water ski-ing

Publications: Water Skier Magazine (monthly during summer, bi-monthly in winter)
Water Skier Year Book

EGHAM
Surrey

574

UNIVERSITY OF LONDON
ROYAL HOLLOWAY COLLEGE
Englefield Green
Surrey

Tel.: Egham 4455

Enquiries: To Librarian

Scope: English, French, German, Italian, classics, history, statistics, mathematics, music, art and sciences

Stock: 100,000 books and pamphlets; 750 current periodicals (total stock)

ELDWICK
Bingley
Yorkshire

See under **BINGLEY** for
THE YORKSHIRE DIALECT SOCIETY (no. 123)

ELGIN
Morayshire

575

MORAY AND NAIRN LIBRARY
    HEADQUARTERS
Grant Lodge
Cooper Park
Elgin
Morayshire

Tel.: Elgin 2746

Enquiries: To Librarian
Scope: Local collection
Stock: 100,000 books and pamphlets; 24 current periodicals (total stock)

ELLESMERE PORT
Wirral
Cheshire

See under **WIRRAL** for
ELLESMERE PORT CORPORATION CENTRAL
    LIBRARY (no. 2298)

ENFIELD
Middx

576

ENFIELD COLLEGE OF TECHNOLOGY
Queensway
Enfield
Middlesex

Tel.: 01-804 8131

Enquiries: To Senior Library Tutor
Scope: Civil, electrical and mechanical engineering; sociology; business mathematics; economics; business management. Microwaves and computers at postgraduate level
    Secondary: Gas engineering; chemistry; history; English literature; philosophy; German; French; programmed instruction; education; geography
Stock: 45,000 books and pamphlets; 800 current periodicals

ENFIELD
Middx

577

FORTY HALL MUSEUM AND ART GALLERY
Forty Hall
Forty Hill
Enfield
Middlesex

Tel.: 01-363 8196

Enquiries: To Curator
Scope: A furnished country-house Museum of the early 17th century, exhibiting pictures, furniture, ceramics, glass, and local antiquities, chiefly of the 17th and 18th centuries. Temporary exhibitions
Publications: Forty Hall (four-page leaflet)

EPSOM
Surrey

578

EPSOM AND EWELL PUBLIC LIBRARIES
Administrative Offices
Bourne Hall
Ewell
Epsom
Surrey

Tel.: 01-394 0088
Telex: 262298

Enquiries: To Borough Librarian
Scope: General stock, with some specialization in local history (including documents) and art
Stock: 168,100 books and pamphlets; 206 current periodicals (total stock)

EPSOM Surrey 579	EPSOM COLLEGE Surrey	

Enquiries: To Librarian

Scope: Textbooks on school subjects
Separate Physics, Chemistry and Biology Department Libraries
Bernard Wallis collection: mainly English literature and Church architecture

Stock: 9,000 books; 200 pamphlets; 8 current periodicals, including *The Epsomian* from 1870 (total stock)

ESHER Surrey 580	GENERAL AND MUNICIPAL WORKERS' UNION Ruxley Towers Claygate Esher Surrey Trade Union	*Tel.:* Esher 62081

Enquiries: To Research Officer

Scope: The Research Department Library contains Union records and minutes of meetings from the date of formation (1889) to the present day
Secondary: Books, periodicals and newspapers on industrial relations and sociology, economics, politics, trade union law and industrial training

Stock: 1,800 books; all national daily newspapers and many periodicals

Publications: Monthly Journal
Ad hoc publications and broadsheets
Small number of films

ESHER Surrey 581	SURREY COUNTY LIBRARY Headquarters 140 High Street Esher Surrey	*Tel.:* Esher 63585 *Telex:* 262061

Enquiries: To County Librarian

Scope: General stock including music and drama. Surrey local collection. L.A.S.E.R. subject specialization includes: Genetic psychology excluding child psychology. Evolution. Heredity. Ancient and Oriental philosophers. Non-Christian religions excluding Judaism. Martial law. Eye diseases and surgery. Mechanical remedies. Ceramic art and industry. Design. Lettering. Illumination. Transfer pictures. Technique of painting. English and American drama texts. History of World War II. History and topography of China and Japan

Stock: Total adult non-fiction stock 666,321 volumes

ETON Windsor Berks	*See under* **WINDSOR** for ETON COLLEGE (no. 2295)

EVESHAM Worcs 582	VALE OF EVESHAM HISTORICAL SOCIETY The Almonry Museum Evesham Worcestershire

Enquiries: To Secretary, by letter only

EVESHAM, VALE OF EVESHAM HISTORICAL SOCIETY, *cont.*

Scope: Information on matters concerning the life, culture and industry of Evesham and District and Evesham Abbey in particular

Publications: First English Translation of the Chronicle of Evesham Abbey. D. C. Cox
Research Papers
The Battle of Evesham. D. C. Cox
Abbey Guide Book
History of Offenham
Romano-British Sites in the Vale of Evesham

EWELL
Epsom
Surrey

See under **EPSOM** for
EPSOM AND EWELL PUBLIC LIBRARIES (no. 578)

EXETER
Devon

583

DEVON COUNTY LIBRARY
Barley House
St Thomas
Exeter
Devon

Tel.: Exeter 74142
Telex: 42933

Enquiries: To Librarian

Scope: Bibliographies (2,000 volumes); philosophy (1,000 volumes); naval history (500 volumes); veterinary medicine (250 volumes); American literature (1,000 volumes); English poetry (6,000 volumes); English drama (3,000 sets); American history, including a large number of books on the American Civil War (2,000 volumes); Devon history (4,000 volumes); Doctrinal theology (1,000 volumes); Ecclesiastical polity (500 volumes); Music (2,000 books, 5,000 scores, many sets)

Stock: See under *Scope* above; 40 current periodicals

Publications: Playsets (Printed Catalogue of 3,000 sets of plays)
Choral music in sets
Songs in sets
Orchestral music in sets

EXETER
Devon

584

EXETER CATHEDRAL LIBRARY
Bishop's Palace
Exeter
Devon

Tel.: Exeter 72894

Enquiries: To Assistant Librarian

Scope: The Cathedral Library contains a useful collection of books on theological subjects: Bibles (many early printed), Biblical commentaries, sermons (many 17th century), church history, liturgy. These form half the book stock. There are also a number of books on history, including local history. Apart from these there are small sections of books on other subjects for example, literature, law, travel, many of them 17th century
There is also an interesting collection of books, dating from the 16th to the 19th century, on medicine and science (*see also* no. 586)
Another section contains a collection of pamphlets and sermons, part of which was formerly the property of John Bradshaw, the regicide

Stock: 25,000 books; 6 current periodicals; 100 volumes of tracts, mostly of the 17th century

Publications: The Library of Exeter Cathedral. L. J. Lloyd, with description of the archives by A. M. Erskine

In addition to the items mentioned above there is a small group of manuscript books dating from 10th to 16th century from the ancient Cathedral Library. The Archives Department contains a large collection of the archives and papers of the Dean and Chapter, dating from the 10th century to the present day

EXETER
Devon
585

EXETER COLLEGE OF ART
Gandy Street
Exeter
Devon

Tel.: Exeter 55316 and 77104

Enquiries: To Librarian, by letter only

Scope: All aspects of art, including painting, sculpture, architecture, graphics, film, printmaking and photography. Small collection on literature, mainly poetry

Stock: 6,000 books; 38 current periodicals; 10,000 slides

EXETER
Devon
586

EXETER MEDICAL LIBRARY
Royal Devon & Exeter Hospital
Exeter
Devon

Tel.: Exeter 72261

Enquiries: To Librarian/Secretary, by letter only

Scope: General medicine and surgery

Stock: 320 books; 65 current periodicals

Large collection of ancient medical books housed in Exeter Cathedral Library (no. 584)

EXETER
Devon
587

EXETER TECHNICAL COLLEGE
Hele Road
Exeter
Devon

Tel.: Exeter 76381

Enquiries: To Librarian

Scope: Social sciences, political sciences, economics, law, banking, public administration, education, economic history, language, mathematics, physics, chemistry, biology, botany, zoology, mechanical and electrical engineering, literature, history, technical drawing, geography, building construction, business (particularly accountancy and management), domestic sciences. Child care, food education and catering, pre-nursing and nursing management, art, computer programming

Stock: 10,000 books; 500 pamphlets; 100 reports; 300 current periodicals. Complete set of British Standards. Barbour Index

Publications: Accession lists

EXETER
Devon
588

UNIVERSITY OF EXETER
INSTITUTE OF EDUCATION LIBRARY
The University
Gandy Street
Exeter
Devon

Tel.: Exeter 77911
Telex: 42894

Enquiries: To Librarian

Scope: Education (not including school textbooks)
Secondary: Psychology, sociology

Stock: 17,000 books, pamphlets and reports; 160 current periodicals

EXETER, UNIVERSITY OF EXETER, INSTITUTE OF EDUCATION LIBRARY, *cont.*
    Publications: Themes in Education (pamphlet series of reports of conferences and experimental work)
                       Educational Directory for the South West

EXETER UNIVERSITY OF EXETER LIBRARY *Tel.:* Exeter 77911
Devon Prince of Wales Road *Telex:* 42894
                Exeter
589 Devon
    Enquiries: To Sub-Librarian, Readers' Service
        Scope: Subjects covered by the University's faculties namely, arts, law, science, social studies
        Stock: 230,000 books and pamphlets; 2,000 current periodicals. Departmental libraries are included in the Main Library Catalogue
    Publications: New Accessions lists (monthly)
                     Index to theses submitted to Exeter University since 1955
                See also no. 588

FAILSWORTH *See under* **MANCHESTER** for
Manchester FAILSWORTH PUBLIC LIBRARY (no. 1749)

FALKIRK CALLENDAR PARK COLLEGE OF EDUCATION *Tel.:* OFA 4-22982
Stirlingshire Falkirk
                Stirlingshire
590 *Enquiries:* To Librarian, by letter only
        Scope: Education; educational psychology
                Secondary: General academic and school subjects at student and Primary School levels
        Stock: 30,500 books and pamphlets including children's books and Primary School textbooks; 200 current periodicals; 3,500 Audio-visual collection (tapes, filmstrips, illustrations, charts)

FALMER *See under* **BRIGHTON** for
Brighton BRIGHTON COLLEGE OF EDUCATION (no. 221)
                INSTITUTE OF DEVELOPMENT STUDIES (no. 224)
                UNIVERSITY OF SUSSEX LIBRARY (no. 225)
                UNIVERSITY OF SUSSEX, SCHOOL OF
                    EDUCATION LIBRARY (no. 226)
                UNIVERSITY OF SUSSEX, SCIENCE POLICY
                    RESEARCH UNIT (no. 227)

FALMOUTH FALMOUTH SCHOOL OF ART *Tel.:* Falmouth 313269
Cornwall Woodlane
                Falmouth
591 Cornwall
    Enquiries: To Librarian
        Scope: Painting and sculpture; philosophy, theory, and aesthetics of art
                Secondary: Photography, ceramics, graphic art, textiles. Also a number of works of psychology, philosophy, folklore and magic
                Locally published books on Cornwall, local antiquities, folklore, personages, architecture, and shipping
        Stock: 4,500 books; pamphlets; 25 current art periodicals

FARNHAM Surrey **592**	WILLMER HOUSE MUSEUM 38 West Street Farnham Surrey Local history museum	*Tel.:* Farnham 5094

Enquiries: To Curator, by letter only
Scope: Local history and archaeology, transport, agriculture and arts and crafts
Secondary: English and French glass paper weights
A collection of 19th Century English Costume and of the crafts of the blacksmith and wheelwright are in store awaiting the construction of a new gallery
Publications: La Medmulle—the Story of Weydon Mill. F. W. Simmonds. 1968
Willmer House (description and history of the house). H. G. A. Booth. 1967

FARNHAM ROYAL *See under* **SLOUGH** *for*
Slough BRITISH ASSOCIATION OF SPORT AND
Bucks MEDICINE (no. 2130)

FARNLEY *See under* **LEEDS** *for*
Leeds JAMES GRAHAM COLLEGE OF EDUCATION (no. 799)

FARNWORTH *See under* **BOLTON** *for*
Bolton FARNWORTH PUBLIC LIBRARY (no. 179)
Lancs

FLINT **593**	FLINT PUBLIC LIBRARIES Central Library Church Street Flint CH6 5AP	*Tel.:* Flint 3168

Enquiries: To Borough Librarian
Scope: Local history of Borough of Flint
Secondary: Local history of Flintshire; Welsh studies
Stock: 6,000 books; 1,500 pamphlets; 23 current periodicals (total stock 72,000)
Publications: Reading lists
Fflint (bilingual magazine)
A Translations Advisory Service is available

FOLKESTONE Kent **594**	ARMY BRANCH LIBRARY Sir John Moore Hall Shorncliffe Folkestone Kent See no. 906

FOLKESTONE Kent **595**	FOLKESTONE PUBLIC LIBRARY Grace Hill Folkestone Kent	*Tel.:* Folkestone 55221 (55228 after 5.30 pm and on Saturdays)

Enquiries: To Librarian

FOLKESTONE, FOLKESTONE PUBLIC LIBRARY, *cont.*

Scope: Local collection: Folkestone in particular, other parts of Kent to limited extent. L.A.S.E.R. subject specialization: Theatre excluding ballet; history and travel in Palestine

Stock: Local collection: 3,000 books and pamphlets; cuttings, photographs, prints and maps
Theatre: 1,400 books and pamphlets; 5 current periodicals
Palestine: 600 books and pamphlets

FORFAR
Angus

596

FORFAR PUBLIC LIBRARY
20 West High Street
Forfar
Angus

Tel.: Forfar 3468

Enquiries: To Librarian, by letter only

Scope: Scottish social history
Secondary: Collection of photographs and pamphlets

Stock: 150 books; 50 pamphlets

FORT GEORGE
Inverness

See under **INVERNESS** for
REGIMENTAL MUSEUM OF SEAFORTH HIGHLANDERS (no. 752)

GAINSBOROUGH
Lincs

597

GAINSBOROUGH PUBLIC LIBRARY
Cobden Street
Gainsborough
Lincolnshire

Tel.: Gainsborough 2381

Enquiries: To Librarian

Scope: General stock; *Special collection:* local history of Lincolnshire and particularly Gainsborough, including Brace collection of Lincolnshire material and university and college theses on Gainsborough and district

Stock: 14,000 books and pamphlets; 40 current periodicals (total stock)

Publications: Local Catalogue 1965 (2nd edition in preparation)
Local History Pamphlets

GALASHIELS
Selkirkshire

598

SCOTTISH COLLEGE OF TEXTILES
Netherdale
Galashiels
Selkirkshire

Tel.: Galashiels 3351

Enquiries: To Librarian

Scope: Library stock includes economics, mathematics, statistics, physics, chemistry, engineering, chemical technology, textile industries, business and industrial organization, management, art and design. An information service can be provided in the subjects of textile technology, textile design and management studies

Stock: 4,500 books; many pamphlets and reports; 160 current periodicals

GATESHEAD
Co Durham

599

GATESHEAD PUBLIC LIBRARIES
Prince Consort Road
Gateshead NE8 4LN
Co Durham

Tel.: Gateshead 73478

Enquiries: To Librarian

Scope: General stock, strong in law and the arts
Special collections: Music and Gramophone Record Library (3,300 records)
Local History and Archives Collection. The Central Library is also the Borough Record Office, and is approved by the Master of the Rolls and the Office of the Lord Chancellor as a repository for manorial and legal documents. There is a stock of about 2,000 books and pamphlets on the history of the area, and a large and growing collection of local photographs, prints and maps. The Archives Section contains records of local government departments, statutory authorities, local churches, and local industry. There are two important collections of 18th century family papers, the Cotesworth Manuscripts and the Ellison Manuscripts, which have special relevance to the early history of the coal trade

Stock: *Reference Library stock:* 18,000 books and pamphlets (excluding science, technology and commerce)
Lending and Branch Library stocks: 25,000 non-fiction books and pamphlets (excluding science, technology and commerce)
250 current periodicals

Publications: Historic Gateshead: a select bibliography. 1967
Gateshead Archives. 1968
Religion and Religions: a select booklist. 1969
Local Government Literature (monthly abstracting publication)

GILLINGHAM GILLINGHAM PUBLIC LIBRARY *Tel.:* Medway 51066
Kent Central Library
High Street
600 Gillingham
Kent

Enquiries: To Librarian

Scope: *Special collection:* Local history of Kent, particularly the Medway Towns

GLASGOW ARCHDIOCESE OF GLASGOW *Tel.:* 041-332 6103
CATHOLIC YOUTH COUNCIL
601 Catholic Youth Office
14 Newton Place
Glasgow C.3

Aims to form and develop the Christian character essential to the noblest citizenship, by means of spiritual, cultural and physical training provided in a network of youth organizations

Enquiries: To Secretary

Scope: Spiritual, cultural and physical training within Youth Organizations

GLASGOW ASSOCIATION OF UNIVERSITY TEACHERS *Tel.:* 041-339 8855 ext. 448
(SCOTLAND)
602 c/o Department of Botany
The University
Glasgow W.2

Enquiries: To Secretary, by letter only

Scope: The Universities of Scotland and relevant matters concerning their staffs
No library

GLASGOW BAILLIE'S LIBRARY *Tel.:* 041-339 9627
69 Oakfield Avenue
603 Glasgow W.2

Library founded and endowed in 1863 by George Baillie, then Senior Member of the Royal

GLASGOW, BAILLIE'S LIBRARY, cont.
Faculty of Procurators in Glasgow, and maintained in accordance with the terms of the endowment
Enquiries: To Librarian
Scope: Scottish Life and Letters. Holdings are strongest in the fields of Scottish history, Scottish literature and Glasgow studies. A Glasgow Collection of some 3,000 volumes is maintained
Stock: 16,000 books; 26 current periodicals

GLASGOW
604
BAPTIST UNION OF SCOTLAND
113 West Regent Street
Glasgow C.2
Tel.: 041-248 5438

Enquiries: To Secretary
Scope: Through College a limited theological library
Stock: Records, Year Books and certain copies of Scottish Baptist Publications
Publications: Christian Baptism   Why Communion?
The Church You Join   Where Baptists Meet
History of Baptists in Scotland. 1926
The First 100 Years (Centenary Publication). 1969

GLASGOW
605
BRITISH NEUROPATHOLOGICAL SOCIETY
Department of Neuropathology
Western Infirmary
Glasgow W.1
Tel.: 041-339 8822 ext. 170

Enquiries: To Secretary
Scope: Information about neuropathology in the United Kingdom
No library

GLASGOW
606
CENTRAL COLLEGE OF COMMERCE AND DISTRIBUTION
300 Cathedral Street
Glasgow C.1
Tel.: 041-552 3941

Enquiries: To Librarian
Scope: Economics, economic history, taxation, banking, commerce, accountancy, management, marketing, retailing, foreign languages
Secondary: General literature in other fields
Stock: 13,500 books; 1,000 pamphlets; 120 current periodicals. Stock not normally available on loan

GLASGOW
607
CLYDE YACHT CLUBS ASSOCIATION
St Andrew House
141 West Nile Street
Glasgow C.1
Tel.: 041-332 7662

Enquiries: To Secretary
Scope: General information on yachting (motor and sail), including yacht racing events
No library
Publications: Year Book (including fixture list and list of clubs and classes)

GLASGOW	GARDINER INSTITUTE LIBRARY	*Tel.:* 041-339 8822
	Department of Medicine	
608	Western Infirmary	
	Glasgow W.1	

Enquiries: To Librarian

Scope: Provides a comprehensive selection of medical and surgical periodicals and surgical textbooks and reference books for use of hospital staff, medical students and ancillary workers

Stock: 500 books; 60 pamphlets. Stock not available on loan

GLASGOW	GLASGOW ARCHAEOLOGICAL SOCIETY	*Tel.:* 041-339 8855
	c/o Hunterian Museum	
609	The University	
	Glasgow W.2	

Enquiries: To Secretary

Scope: Prehistoric, Roman, medieval and historic archaeology

Publications: Glasgow Archaeological Journal
The Antonine Wall (a guide and handbook)

GLASGOW	GLASGOW CORPORATION PUBLIC LIBRARIES	*Tel.:* 041-248 7121
	The Mitchell Library	
610	North Street	
	Glasgow C.3	

Enquiries: To City Librarian

Scope: The Mitchell Library has a large general reference stock covering all subjects, but particularly strong in Scottish history, genealogy and literature. *Special collections* include Scottish poetry and Robert Burns. Depository collections of United Nations, UNESCO and FAO publications are held, and all H.M.S.O. publications taken

The Glasgow Collection includes 20,000 books, and directories from 1783, parochial records from the 17th century on microfilm, maps from the early 18th century, registers of voters from 1858, valuation rolls from 1913, 5,000 prints and photographs, programmes and playbills of theatrical productions from 1850, and family papers including those of the Campbells of Shawfield, Bogles, Dunlops of Tollcross and Garnkirk

The Music Library includes 9,000 books, 25 current periodicals, 24,000 vocal and instrumental scores and the Kidson (5,000 books) and Moody Manners (2,900 scores) special collections

Stock: Reference stock (less science, technology and commerce) 700,000 books and pamphlets; 800 current periodicals

Publications: The Mitchell Library Catalogue of Additions 1915–1949. 2 volumes. 1959
The Mitchell Library Catalogue of Periodicals. 1962
Catalogue of Robert Burns Collection in the Mitchell Library. 1959
Catalogue of Incunables and STC books in the Mitchell Library. 1964

Collection of 13,000 volumes of foreign literature in 26 languages available for lending from Gorbals District Library
Collection of 3,700 volumes in Braille available for lending from Elder Park and Townhead Libraries

GLASGOW	GLASGOW MUSEUM OF TRANSPORT	*Tel.:* 041-423 8000
	25 Albert Drive	
611	Glasgow S.1	

GLASGOW, GLASGOW MUSEUM OF TRANSPORT, *cont.*

Preservation and display of full-size vehicles, and models illustrating the history of transport, particularly in Glasgow and the West of Scotland

Enquiries: To Curator

Scope: Scottish motor industry; public transport in Glasgow; Scottish aircraft industry; shipbuilding on the Clyde
Secondary: All aspects of the history of transport technology

Publications: Scottish Cars
Scottish Railway Locomotives
Glasgow Trams
Engineering
Horse-Drawn Carriages
Shipmodels (parts 1 and 2)

Shipbuilding Section at Art Gallery and Museum, Kelvingrove

GLASGOW

612

NOTRE DAME COLLEGE OF EDUCATION *Tel.:* 041-942 2363
Bearsden
Glasgow

Enquiries: To Librarian, by letter only

Scope: Education (including health and physical education)
Secondary: Biblical history and theology, Roman Catholic Church history, Catholic theology, philosophy and apologetics, Catholic social doctrine, catechetics, psychology, modern studies, English literary history and criticism, theory of linguistics, modern languages and literature, history, Scottish history and Glasgow, geography, mathematics, biology, physics, chemistry, art, music, speech and drama, children's literature and non-fiction

Stock: 23,500 books; 500 pamphlets; 250 reports; 155 current periodicals

GLASGOW

613

THE ROYAL HIGHLAND FUSILIERS *Tel.:* 041-332 0961
REGIMENTAL HEADQUARTERS AND MUSEUM
518 Sauchiehall Street
Glasgow C.2

Enquiries: To Museum Curator, by letter only

Scope: Regimental Museum in which are exhibits pertaining to The Royal Scots Fusiliers, The Highland Light Infantry and The Royal Highland Fusiliers. Historical enquiries concerning the Royal Highland Fusiliers can be dealt with

GLASGOW

614

ROYAL SCOTTISH ACADEMY OF MUSIC AND *Tel.:* 041-332 4101
DRAMA
58 St George's Place
Glasgow C.2

Enquiries: To Librarian

Scope: Music and theatre arts

Stock: 35,000 books; 50 current periodicals. Stock available on loan only through S.C.L.

GLASGOW

615

RUTHERGLEN PUBLIC LIBRARY *Tel.:* 041-647 6453
Main Street
Rutherglen
Glasgow

Enquiries: To Librarian

Scope: Local collection

Stock: 5,000 books; 16 current periodicals

GLASGOW	ST ANDREW'S AMBULANCE ASSOCIATION	*Tel.:* 041-332 4031
616	Milton Street Glasgow C.4	

Enquiries: To Secretary

Scope: First aid, home nursing and allied subjects

Publications: First Aid Manual   ABC of Nursing
Nursing Manual   First Aid Questions and Answers
Junior First Aid   Nursing Questions and Answers
Jurning Nursing   Note: for First Aid Students
ABC of First Aid   Junior Mothercraft

GLASGOW	SCOTTISH ANTI-VIVISECTION SOCIETY	*Tel.:* 041-221 2300
617	121 West Regent Street Glasgow C.2	

Enquiries: To Secretary

Scope: Anti-vivisection. Alternative research methods
Secondary: General animal welfare

No library

Publications: Various leaflets containing facts about animal experimentation; and material outlining the case against vivisection

GLASGOW	SCOTTISH ASSOCIATION FOR NATIONAL CERTIFICATES AND DIPLOMAS	*Tel.:* 041-221 0901
618	38 Queen Street Glasgow C.1	

Administers National Certificate and Diploma courses

Enquiries: To Secretary, by letter only

Scope: Syllabuses of National Certificate and Diploma courses administered by the Association, copies of past examination papers. Copies of Annual Reports with statistical analysis of examination results

No library

GLASGOW	SCOTTISH CIVIC TRUST	*Tel.:* 041-221 1466
619	24 George Square Glasgow C.2	

See no. 1067

GLASGOW	SCOTTISH DAILY RECORD AND SUNDAY MAIL LTD	*Tel.:* 041-248 7000
620	Record House Glasgow C.2	

Newspaper publishers

Enquiries: To Librarian

Scope: Information service consists of press clippings, arranged and filed under 80,000 subject headings, primarily for future use by the editorial department. The picture library is only for use of members of staff. Readers' and other enquiries are dealt with

Stock: 600 books. Stock not available on loan

GLASGOW	SCOTTISH EPILEPSY ASSOCIATION	*Tel.:* 041-248 3543

621

24 St Vincent Place
Glasgow C.1

Enquiries: To Chief Executive Officer

Scope: Social problems of epileptics. Location of medical and other facilities for epileptics. Liaison with local authorities, government departments and other authorities and services concerned with epileptics

Small library

GLASGOW	SCOTTISH LIBRARY ASSOCIATION	*Tel.:* 041-552 4400
		ext. 674

622

Hon. Secretary, Department of Librarianship
University of Strathclyde
Livingstone Tower
Richmond Street
Glasgow C.1

Enquiries: To Secretary

Scope: Library and bibliographical matters in Scotland

No library

Publications: S.L.A. News (6 issues each year)
Proceedings of the Annual Conference
Scottish Libraries: a triennial review
Library Resources in Scotland (triennially)
Memorandum on Public Library Standards. 1968

Holds an annual Summer School of Librarianship at Newbattle Abbey College

GLASGOW	SCOTTISH NATIONAL PARTY	*Tel.:* 041-332 2287

623

59 Elmbank Street
Glasgow W.2

Political party seeking Dominion status self-government for Scotland

Enquiries: To Information Officer, preferably by letter

Scope: Political situation, particularly electorally, in Scotland
Secondary: Scottish social and economic affairs

Publications: Pamphlets, for example:
SNP and You. Aims & Policy of the Scottish National Party
Independence and Your Job
Agriculture and Land Use

Publications and Research Departments at 100 Main Street, West Calder, Midlothian

GLASGOW	SCOTTISH NATIONAL SKI COUNCIL	*Tel.:* Balmore 496

624

The Barn
Balmore
Torrance
Glasgow

National Amateur Body for ski-ing in Scotland

Enquiries: To the Secretary and Treasurer

Scope: Registration and Qualification of Ski Party Leaders with the approval of the British Ski Instruction Council; Guidance of Local Education Authorities in technical ski-ing matters, erection of artificial slopes, conduct of School and Youth Organization led ski parties;

Competition at National level for Schools and Junior skiers; provision of grants for Junior Race Training, and continental and home based National Junior Race Training programmes
Library for reference only
Register of Ski Films

GLASGOW

625

SCOTTISH TRADES UNION CONGRESS   *Tel.:* 041-332 4946
12 Woodlands Terrace
Glasgow C.3
Central body of the Trade Union movement in Scotland

Enquiries: To General Secretary, by letter only

Scope: Trade Unionism in economic, industrial, social and organizational settings

Stock: Library stock available to *bona fide* research workers and students for reference by permission in writing. Microfilm copies of Minutes in National Library of Scotland (no. 529)

Publications: Bulletin (bi-monthly)
Congress Annual Report
Industrial Newsletter

GLASGOW

626

STOW COLLEGE OF ENGINEERING   *Tel.:* 041-332 1786
43 Shamrock Street
Glasgow C.4

Enquiries: To Principal

Scope: Optics, ophthalmic and dispensing. Limited social sciences stock

Stock: Books: optics 650, general studies 700; current periodicals: optics 20, general studies 6

GLASGOW

627

TRINITY COLLEGE   *Tel.:* 041-332 2080
Lynedoch Place
Glasgow C.3
Theological college

Enquiries: To Librarian, by letter only

Scope: Theology with some books in related areas, for example church history and philosophy.
Secondary: Mearns Hymnological Collection

Stock: 100,000 books. Stock not normally available on loan

GLASGOW

628

UNIVERSITY OF GLASGOW   *Tel.:* 041-334 2269
BUILDING SERVICES RESEARCH UNIT
3 Lilybank Gardens
Glasgow W.2
Research in building services and engineering, with emphasis on hospitals

Enquiries: To Leader of Unit

Scope: Air conditioning, heating and ventilating. Electrical services. Piped services. Waste disposal. Hospital design. No formal organization for dealing with enquiries. These are routed to staff best qualified to answer

Stock: 50 books; 100 pamphlets and reports; 20 current periodicals

Publications: Research reports
Classified list of publications

GLASGOW	UNIVERSITY OF GLASGOW	*Tel.:* 041-339 8855
	HUNTERIAN MUSEUM	
629	The University	
	Glasgow W.2	

Enquiries: To Keeper

Scope: Fine art collections   Geological collections
Hunter Coin Cabinet   Books and manuscripts
Roman collections   Prehistoric collections
Mediterranean collections   Ethnographical collections

Stock: Working library only

Publications: Catalogue of Roman Imperial Coins in the Hunter Coin Cabinet
Sylloge of Coins of the British Isles
Excavation Reports (Prehistoric and Roman)

GLASGOW	UNIVERSITY OF GLASGOW LIBRARY	*Tel.:* 041-334 2122
	University of Glasgow	*Telex:* 778421
630	Glasgow W.2	

Enquiries: To Librarian, by letter only

Scope: General, covering the whole range of studies pursued in the University, which has Faculties of Arts (including Social Science), Divinity, Medicine, Law, Science, Engineering and Veterinary Medicine
Particular features: collections on Soviet economic and social institutions and on Latin American studies
Special collections: Hunterian books and manuscripts (10,000 volumes, rich in early printing, mediaeval illuminated manuscripts, and history of medicine); Ferguson (8,000 volumes, mainly on history of chemistry); Euing music library; David Murray (bibliography and local history); Stirling-Maxwell (emblem literature, perhaps the greatest collection known in this field); and many others

Stock: 850,000 books including holdings of departmental libraries; many pamphlets and reports; 7,500 current periodicals

Publications: Summaries of theses approved for higher degrees in the Faculty of Science
Collected Papers from the Department of Geology
Collected Papers from the Department of Physiology
Fleck Lectures
David Murray Lectures
W. P. Ker Memorial Lectures   Macewen Memorial Lectures
Maurice Bloch Lectures   Edwards Lectures

Holdings in Chemistry, Dentistry, Veterinary Medicine, and Soviet Institutions are located in separate branch libraries in the Schools or Institutes concerned. There are also strong Faculty or Departmental libraries (reinforcing and to a large extent duplicating the University Library's holdings) in Social Sciences, Law and Engineering

GLASGOW	UNIVERSITY OF STRATHCLYDE	*Tel.:* 041-552 4400
	THE ANDERSONIAN LIBRARY	*Telex:* 77472
631	McCance Building	
	Richmond Street	
	Glasgow C.1	

Enquiries: To Librarian

Scope: Two schools of study—Business and Administration, and Arts and Social Studies—are of primary concern in the subjects covered by this Directory. In addition, although there is no medical school, there is a school of Pharmaceutical Sciences and a sub-department of Bio-engineering. The Library stock covers these fields, supplementing them with a wide range of bibliographies and abstract journals. In addition a separate Government publications section collects a wide range of British government publications and also those of international agencies. The Scottish College library, separately housed, serves the Business and Administration School, and also covers law. A Readers' Adviser service is part of the library staff structure

Special collections: The Young Collection (alchemical, chemical and pharmaceutical books)
The Anderson Collection (library of John Anderson, founder—history of science)

Stock: 120,000 books; 2,700 current periodicals

GLASGOW
632

WESTERN REGIONAL HOSPITAL BOARD (SCOTLAND)
351 Sauchiehall Street
Glasgow C.2

Enquiries: To Librarian, by letter only

Scope: Library and Information Service to the staff of the Regional Board and to the Boards of Management on all subjects relating to hospital planning and management. Departments catered for are work study, O and M, planning, personnel, administration and management

Stock: 200 books; 600 pamphlets; 200 reports; 60 current periodicals

GLASTONBURY
Somerset
633

GLASTONBURY ANTIQUARIAN SOCIETY
Hon. Secretary
2 Albert Buildings
Glastonbury
Somerset

Enquiries: To Hon. Secretary, by letter only

Scope: History and archaeology of Glastonbury district
Secondary: Library includes material on history and archaeology of Somerset and general historical works. Library housed at Glastonbury Branch, Somerset County Library

Stock: 40 books and 60 pamphlets on Glastonbury area; 6 current periodicals. Large collection of newspapers, cuttings and illustrations

Publications: Lake villages of Somerset. A. Bulleid

GLOUCESTER
634

BRISTOL AND GLOUCESTER ARCHAEOLOGICAL SOCIETY
c/o The City Library
Brunswick Road
Gloucester GL1 1HT

Tel.: Gloucester 20020 and 20684

Enquiries: To Hon. Librarian

Scope: Local history and archaeology

Stock: 6,521 books. Stock not available on loan

Publications: Transactions (annually)
Records Section Publications

GLOUCESTER
635

GLOUCESTER CITY LIBRARIES
Brunswick Road
Gloucester GL1 1HT

Tel.: Gloucester 20020 and 20684

Enquiries: To Librarian

GLOUCESTER, GLOUCESTER CITY LIBRARIES, *cont.*

Scope: Local history—Gloucestershire (all aspects)
Secondary: Genealogy—Gloucestershire

Stock: 7,000 books; 40,000 pamphlets; 200,000 manuscripts; all relevant current periodicals. Stock not normally available on loan

Publications: Local History Pamphlets
Catalogue of Records of Diocese of Gloucester
Gloucestershire Collection Catalogue

Official repository for: Manorial, Diocesan, Probate, Hospital, and Quarter Sessions records

GLOUCESTER

636

GLOUCESTERSHIRE COLLEGE OF EDUCATION
Oxstalls Lane
Gloucester GL2 9HW

Tel.: Gloucester 26321

Enquiries: To Librarian, by letter only

Scope: Education, and in particular the history of education and early children's books
Secondary: Gloucestershire local history. Limited collections of books in history, geography, sociology, English Literature and the visual arts

Stock: 36,000 books; 202 current periodicals. Books only available on loan

Member of the Gloucestershire Technical Information Service

GLOUCESTER

637

GLOUCESTERSHIRE RECORD OFFICE
Shire Hall
Westgate Street
Gloucester

Tel.: Gloucester 21444
ext. 229

Enquiries: To County Archivist

Scope: Small but good local history library. General scope unlimited: Local records for students and to the ordinary public interested in general historical matters; genealogical records for family historians. Lecture and exhibition service for schools and societies
Main collections: Quarter Sessions records from 1660 to date relating to crime and punishment as well as administrative matters
Parish records: registers, churchwardens, poor law records
Family and private records: a vast source of diversified record classes from the 12th century

Stock not available on loan. Photocopying service

Publications: Gloucestershire Quarter Sessions Archives 1660–1889. A Guide. 1958
A Short Handlist of the Contents of The Gloucestershire Record Office. 1968
Gloucestershire—A Local History Handbook. 1968
Dean and Chapter of Gloucester. A Catalogue of the Records. 1967
Bristol and Gloucestershire Parish Records. A Guide. 1963

GODALMING
Surrey

638

DISABLEMENT INCOME GROUP (DIG)
Godalming
Surrey

Tel.: Godalming 5181

Enquiries: To Secretary

Scope: The economic and social welfare of disabled people

Publications: DIG papers: for example, Towards a National Disability Income
Progress (quarterly)

GOOLE
Yorkshire

639

GOOLE PUBLIC LIBRARY
Carlisle Street
Goole
Yorkshire

Tel.: Goole 3784

Enquiries: To Librarian

Scope: The Garside Collection of local history material, including large collection of photographs illustrating the history of the town, deeds, documents, pamphlets, paintings and ship models. Small loan collection of Rockingham china

Stock: 36,442 books; 34 current periodicals (total stock)

GOSFORTH
Newcastle upon Tyne

See under **NEWCASTLE UPON TYNE** for
GOSFORTH PUBLIC LIBRARY (no. 1832)
NORTHUMBERLAND LOCAL HISTORY SOCIETY (no. 1847)
NORTHUMBERLAND RURAL COMMUNITY COUNCIL (no. 1848)

GOSPORT
Hants

640

GOSPORT PUBLIC LIBRARIES
Walpole Road
Gosport
Hampshire

Tel.: Gosport 80432 and 84242

Enquiries: To Librarian

Scope: Subject specialization includes: English Language; Arabia; minor prophets

Stock: 80,000 books; 75 current periodicals (total stock)

GRANTHAM
Lincs

641

GRANTHAM PUBLIC LIBRARY & MUSEUM
St Peter's Hill
Grantham
Lincolnshire

Tel.: Grantham 3926

Enquiries: To Librarian

Scope: Normal public library service plus detailed information on the history of the town and its area, and a small museum with a good collection of local material covering the history of Grantham and its immediate vicinity from Stone Age to present day. Good collection of Bronze Age pottery
Special collection includes the Newcome Library of 17th century and early 18th century books on religion, philosophy and history, comprising 720 volumes

Stock: 28,500 non-fiction books and pamphlets; 50 current periodicals of a general nature including titles covering subjects within the field of sociology
880 books and pamphlets in local collection covering the same subject range as the museum exhibits

GRANTHAM
Lincs

642

KESTEVEN COLLEGE OF EDUCATION
Stoke Rochford
Grantham
Lincolnshire

Tel.: Great Ponton 337

Enquiries: To Librarian, by letter only

Scope: Education

Stock: 31,000 books, pamphlets and reports; 190 current periodicals. Stock normally available on loan only to other Colleges of Education

GRANTHAM Lincs **643**	WILLOUGHBY MEMORIAL TRUST WILLOUGHBY MEMORIAL ART GALLERY AND LIBRARY Corby Glen Grantham Lincolnshire Educational library and art gallery	

Enquiries: To Treasurer, Estate Office, Grimsthorpe, Bourne, Lincolnshire, by letter only

Scope: The theme of the collection is 'A library in the countryside' and the stock includes natural science, natural history, local history and rural crafts

GRAVESEND Kent **644**	GRAVESEND CENTRAL LIBRARY Windmill Street Gravesend Kent	*Tel.:* Gravesend 2758

Enquiries: To Librarian

Scope: Subject specialization scheme includes: Africa—history and travel (excluding Egypt, Sudan, Lower Guinea, Gabon, Congo, Angola, Chad, Ruanda-Urundi, Uganda, Kenya, Somaliland, Tanzania, Mozambique, South Africa, Rhodesia, Zambia, Malawi)

Stock: 1,200 books. Total stock: 72,396 books; 200 current periodicals; 500 pamphlets

GRAYS Essex **645**	THURROCK PUBLIC LIBRARIES Central Library Orsett Road Grays RM17 5DX Essex	*Tel.:* Grays Thurrock 76827

Enquiries: To Librarian

Scope: L.A.S.E.R. subject specialization: Welfare service for blind and deaf. Educational psychology; teaching, school organization, administration; primary education; secondary education; education curriculum

Local history collection covers Essex in general and Thurrock in particular, and includes books, pamphlets, archive material (originals, photocopies, microfilms), illustrations and slides

Stock: Local Collection: 2,000 books; 1,000 pamphlets; 24 current periodicals

Subject specialization: 3,500 books; 450 pamphlets; 10 current periodicals (total stock 240,000 volumes)

GRAYS Essex **646**	THURROCK TECHNICAL COLLEGE Woodview Grays Essex	*Tel.:* Grays Thurrock 3073 ext. 16

Enquiries: To Librarian

Scope: Engineering, marketing, management, domestic science, general education, science, shipping, art, languages, sociology, geography, economics

Stock: 16,000 books; 2,000 pamphlets; 252 current periodicals

Publications: Bibliographies

GREAT **YARMOUTH** Norfolk **647**	GREAT YARMOUTH PUBLIC LIBRARIES Central Library Great Yarmouth Norfolk	*Tel.:* Great Yarmouth 4551

Enquiries: To Librarian

Scope: Special Collections: Great Yarmouth and surrounding area. Careers library. Elizabethan drama other than Shakespeare. Textbook library (mainly history, geography, English literature, economics)

Stock: 110,000 books and pamphlets (total stock, including 220 books on Elizabethan drama other than Shakespeare); 25 current periodicals

GREENFORD
Middx
648

GLAXO LABORATORIES LTD *and*
    GLAXO RESEARCH LTD
Greenford
Middlesex

Tel.: 01-422 3434
Telex: 22134

Manufacturers of medical and pharmaceutical preparations, infant and invalid foods, and veterinary preparations

Enquiries: To Librarian (Medical enquiries: To Medical Information Department)
Scope: Chemistry. Medicine, particularly the use of antibiotics, corticosteroids and immunologicals. Veterinary science. Biological sciences. Nutrition
Secondary: Industrial and laboratory hazards
Stock: 5,000 books; many pamphlets; 550 current periodicals; 3,000 patent specifications

GRIMSBY
Lincs
649

THE DOUGHTY MUSEUM
Town Hall Square
Grimsby
Lincolnshire

Tel.: Grimsby 56012

Enquiries: To Borough Librarian and Curator
Scope: Small museum with emphasis on ship models with special reference to the history of the fishing industry
No library
Publications: Catalogue of Ship Models in the Doughty Museum

GRIMSBY
Lincs
650

GRIMSBY COLLEGE OF TECHNOLOGY
Nuns Corner
Grimsby
Lincolnshire

Tel.: Grimsby 79292

Enquiries: To Librarian
Scope: General coverage of the social sciences and humanities
Stock: 11,500 books and pamphlets; 210 current periodicals (total stock)

GRIMSBY
Lincs
651

GRIMSBY PUBLIC LIBRARY
Town Hall Square
Grimsby
Lincolnshire

Tel.: Grimsby 56012

Enquiries: To Librarian
Scope: E.M.R.L.S. subject specialization: Danish, Swedish, Norwegian, Lapp, Icelandic, Estonian, Lettish and Hungarian language and literature, representative collections of adult and junior fiction, dictionaries and language textbooks being maintained. A collection of about 6,000 volumes, pamphlets, prints, illustrations, maps and plans, newscuttings, and files of newspapers (original copies and microfilm) relating to all aspects of Lincolnshire history and literature is maintained in the Lincolnshire Library, a special collection within the orbit of the

GRIMSBY, GRIMSBY PUBLIC LIBRARY, *cont.*
Reference Library. The Borough archives, commencing with Court Books of the 14th century, are stored in the Central Library. The gramophone record library has 6,000 mono and stereo L.P. records with supporting scores and a reference and lending collection of musical literature. A world-wide range of gramophone record catalogues is maintained

Stock: 7,000 books and pamphlets; 1,250 photographs and other illustrations; 130 current periodicals

Publications: The Enclosures of Scartho and Great Grimsby. E. Gillett, R. Russell and E. H. Trevitt. 1964
The Fishing Log of Edwin Green Smith. D. Boswell, ed. 1966
Loss List of Grimsby Vessels, 1800–1960. D. Boswell. 1969

GRIMSBY
Lincs

652

NATIONAL ASSOCIATION OF YOUTH ORCHESTRAS
30 Park Drive
Grimsby
Lincolnshire

Tel.: Grimsby 78002

Enquiries: To Secretary

Scope: Information Service on most Youth Orchestras in the British Isles, world-wide exchange facilities for orchestras and musicians, World Youth Symphony Orchestra, the formation of Youth Orchestras, advice on professional fees, deputizing players in emergencies, courses and summer schools, and promising young soloists available for concert performance

Stock: A library of full orchestral scores of newly published music available on loan to members only

Publications: A Register of Youth Orchestras
A list of sets of orchestral parts a member is willing to loan to other members
A catalogue of scores of newly published music available for perusal by conductors of Member orchestras—the library being built up through the good offices of the Music Publishers Association
An annual survey of Youth Orchestral repertoire

GUERNSEY
Channel Islands

653

PRIAULX LIBRARY
St Peter Port
Guernsey
Channel Islands

Tel.: Guernsey 21998

Enquiries: To Librarian

Scope: Art, history, biography, specializing in local history and genealogy

Stock: 25,000 books and pamphlets (total stock)

GUILDFORD
Surrey

654

FEDERATION OF PLAYGOER'S SOCIETIES
Public Library
North Street
Guildford
Surrey

Tel.: Guildford 68496

Aims to link together those who serve the Repertory Movement, to keep the provincial repertory theatre alive and solvent through the efforts of the audience support organizations and to influence and promote legislation in the interests of the theatre

Enquiries: To Hon. Secretary

Scope: Information and advice on the running and constitution of clubs and organizations; advice on constitutions; theatre building and appeals for money for large and small enterprises; information on theatre trusts and management organization in relation to audience representation and participation

No library, but books and plays are traced in the Public Library system for enquirers
Publications: Annual Secretary's Report
Annual Conference Report
Synthesis of Reports and Questionnaires

GUILDFORD   GUILDFORD COUNTY TECHNICAL COLLEGE   *Tel.:* Guildford 73201
Surrey   Stoke Park
   Guildford
655   Surrey
   Enquiries: To Librarian
   Scope: Law, economics, education, social sciences, history, geography, literature
   Stock: 17,000 books and pamphlets; 150 current periodicals (total stock)

GUILDFORD   GUILDFORD MUSEUM AND MUNIMENT ROOM   *Tel.:* Guildford 66551
Surrey   Castle Arch
   Guildford
656   Surrey
   Enquiries: To Curator, preferably by letter
   Scope: Archaeology, history and records of Surrey, particularly West Surrey
   No library

GUILDFORD   GUILDFORD PUBLIC LIBRARY   *Tel.:* Guildford 68496
Surrey   North Street
   Guildford
657   Surrey
   Enquiries: To Librarian
   Scope: L.A.S.E.R. subject specialization includes: Glass. This collection is supported by subject periodicals and covers all aspects from modern methods of producing glass containers to art books on stained glass
   Stock: 12,000 books in Reference Library (200 on glass); 8,000 pamphlets in Reference Library; 180 current periodicals (5 on glass)

GUILDFORD   MINISTRY OF AGRICULTURE, FISHERIES AND
Surrey   FOOD
   Tangley Place
658   Worplesdon
   Guildford
   Surrey
   See no. 2190

GUILDFORD   NATIONAL FEDERATION OF SPIRITUAL   *Tel.:* Shere 2054
Surrey   HEALERS
   Burrows Lea
659   Shere
   Guildford
   Surrey
   Aims to co-ordinate Spiritual Healing; to provide study courses and education to its members; and to conduct research into spiritual healing and the treatment of the sick

GUILDFORD, NATIONAL FEDERATION OF SPIRITUAL HEALERS, *cont.*

Enquiries: To Administrator

Scope: Directory of Healers—names and addresses are supplied on request to those in need

Stock: 600 books; 3 study courses: 16 mm films; tape recordings; gramophone recordings; periodicals. Use of library restricted to Members

Publications: Spiritual Healer (monthly)
    Books: The Power of Spirit Healing   The Evidence for Spirit Healing
            Spirit Healing   The Mediumship of Jack Webber
            The Healing Intelligence   Born to Heal
            A Guide to Spirit Healing   Spirit Stories for Children
            Thirty Years a Spiritual Healer   The Way to Absent Healing

---

GUILDFORD
Surrey

660

SURREY ARCHAEOLOGICAL SOCIETY
Castle Arch
Guildford
Surrey

Enquiries: To Secretary, by letter only

Scope: Archaeology and antiquities of Surrey. Maps, illustrations, pamphlets and other graphic material relating to Surrey. General archaeological works and transactions of other archaeological societies. Books on allied subjects

Stock: 6,000 books; 400 pamphlets; 8 current periodicals. Stock not available on loan

Publications: Surrey Archaeological Collections (annually)
Bulletin (monthly)

GUILDFORD
Surrey

661

UNIVERSITY OF SURREY LIBRARY
Guildford
Surrey

Tel.: Guildford 71281
Telex: 85331

Enquiries: To Librarian

Scope: Chemical, electrical, control, mechanical and civil engineering and materials technology. Biochemistry, chemical physics and spectroscopy. Chemistry, mathematics, physics. Biological and health studies. Hotel and catering management. Humanities and social sciences. Linguistic and regional studies. International economics. Assists in the provision of technical information to industry in the County of Surrey

Stock: 80,000 books; minor collections of pamphlets in many subjects; 2,500 current periodicals

Publications: Library Newsletter
Index to Periodicals
Library Guide

GUILDFORD
Surrey

662

WATTS GALLERY
Compton
Guildford
Surrey

Tel.: Puttenham 235

Collection of paintings and drawings by George Frederic Watts, O.M., R.A.

Enquiries: To Curator, by letter only
No library

GUILDFORD Surrey 663	WOMEN'S ROYAL ARMY CORPS REGIMENTAL MUSEUM Queen Elizabeth Barracks Guildford Surrey	*Tel.:* Guildford 60681 ext. 256

Enquiries: To Curator, Corps Headquarters, Block 'E', Duke of York's Headquarters, King's Road, London S.W.3

Scope: Records of WAAC, QMAAC, ATS and WRAC (Women in the Army apart from nurses)

HADDINGTON East Lothian 664	EAST LOTHIAN COUNTY LIBRARY Victoria Road Haddington East Lothian	*Tel.:* Haddington 2370

Enquiries: To Librarian

Scope: Local history. Education of special classes

Stock: *Local History:* 400 books and pamphlets; *Education of special classes:* 270 books and pamphlets

HALESOWEN Worcs 665	HALESOWEN COLLEGE OF FURTHER EDUCATION Whittingham Road Halesowen Worcestershire	*Tel.:* 021-550 1451 and 2477

Enquiries: To Tutor Librarian

Scope: Business studies; catering; engineering; management; science; general studies; literature and the arts; social sciences
Secondary: Small law collection. Local collection

Stock: 6,000 books and pamphlets; 95 current periodicals

HALIFAX Yorkshire 666	HALIFAX PUBLIC LIBRARY Central Library Belle Vue Lister Lane Halifax Yorkshire	*Tel.:* Halifax 65105, 60425 and 65701

Enquiries: To Librarian

Scope: General stock, including music
Horsfall Turner collection of Halifax and Yorkshire literature
National subject specialization: Political science
Archives Collection. William Milner Collection. Rare bindings by Edwards

Stock: 239,123 books and pamphlets; 170 current periodicals; 379 maps; 38 manuscripts; 102 prints (total stock)
Member of HALDIS

HALIFAX Yorkshire 667	PERCIVAL WHITLEY COLLEGE OF FURTHER EDUCATION Francis Street Halifax Yorkshire	*Tel.:* Halifax 54764 ext. 15

Enquiries: To Librarian

HALIFAX, PERCIVAL WHITLEY COLLEGE OF FURTHER EDUCATION, *cont.*

Scope: Further education; vocational training; business; management; economics; English literature and language; modern history; geography; fine and commercial art
Secondary: Sociology; local government; education welfare; nursery nursing; modern European language and literature; history of industry; domestic subjects; hairdressing

Stock: 21,000 books; 6,000 pamphlets; 400 current periodicals; 2,000 art slides; 450 gramophone records; 100 teaching machine programmes; 20 tapes; 10 reels of microfilm

Publications: HALDIS Directory
List of local translators and interpreters
HALDIS Progress (bulletin, 5 issues each year)
College staff bulletin
College reading lists
HALDIS Industrial and Management Training Bulletin

Centre for Halifax and District Information Service for Business and Industry (HALDIS). See also no. 2371

HALIFAX　　MEDICAL LIBRARY　　*Tel.:* Halifax 60234 ext. 207
Yorkshire　　ROYAL HALIFAX INFIRMARY
　　　　　　Halifax
668　　　Yorkshire

Provides a source of reference and information in association with the Post Graduate Medical Centre for all medical graduates (and science graduates concerned with medicine) in the Halifax Hospitals Area

Enquiries: To Librarian, by letter only
Scope: All aspects of medicine
Stock: 350 books; 46 current periodicals

HAMILTON　　HAMILTON COLLEGE OF EDUCATION　　*Tel.:* Hamilton 23241
Lanarkshire　　Bothwell Road
　　　　　　　Hamilton
669　　　　Lancashire

Enquiries: To Librarian
Scope: Books and periodicals on education and psychology. General collection on most subjects. Children's books. Illustrations, filmstrips, gramophone records
Stock: 17,000 books and pamphlets; 230 current periodicals

HAMILTON　　HAMILTON PUBLIC LIBRARIES AND MUSEUM　　*Tel.:* Hamilton 24651
Lanarkshire　　98 Cadzow Street　　　　　　　　　　　　　　　　　　ext. 53
　　　　　　　Hamilton
670　　　　Lanarkshire

Enquiries: To Director
Scope: Sources of history in Hamilton
Stock: 40,640 books; 15 current periodicals (total stock)

HARLECH　　COLEG HARLECH　　*Tel.:* Harlech 363
Merioneth　　Harlech
　　　　　　Merioneth
671　　　Residential College for adult education

Enquiries: To Librarian

Scope: Social Sciences and Humanities: Main collection includes basic liberal studies subjects: Economics, economic history, literature (extensive in English), philosophy, political science, religion
Adult Education: Being developed into an extensive, comprehensive coverage
Welsh Library: Coverage of liberal study subjects in Welsh language. Long runs of Welsh periodicals
Greeynol, Private P., Collection
Special Collection: T. J. Jeffries Jones Youth Memorial Library (collection of works related to youth work, and available on postal loan to full and part time youth workers in England and Wales)

Stock: 27,000 books; 147 current periodicals

Publications: Y Bont (Student Union magazine, annually)

HARLOW
Essex
672

HARLOW INDUSTRIAL HEALTH SERVICE
Edinburgh House
Edinburgh Way
Harlow
Essex

Tel.: Harlow 22377

Occupational health service for industry, shops and offices in Harlow

Enquiries: To Director

Scope: Industrial health problems; physical and chemical hazards; first aid training for industry; occupational health nursing training; safety engineering problems

Publications: Duplicated information sheets

HARLOW
Essex
673

HARLOW TECHNICAL COLLEGE
College Gate
The High
Harlow
Essex

Tel.: Harlow 20131 ext. 47

Enquiries: To Librarian

Scope: Strong in journalism, sociology, liberal studies
Secondary: Languages, art, literature, music

Stock: 19,000 books; 2,000 pamphlets; 250 current periodicals

Publications: Booklists on domestic science, journalism

HARLOW
Essex
674

SMITH & NEPHEW RESEARCH LTD
Gilston Park
Harlow
Essex

Tel.: Harlow 26751
Telex: 81327

Research organization of Smith & Nephew Associated Companies. Main studies are in chemotherapy, surgical dressings and plastics

Enquiries: To Librarian, by letter only

Scope: Organic and analytical chemistry. Biochemistry; pharmacology; pharmacy; medicine. Plastics; surgical dressings; pressure-sensitive adhesive tapes; microbiology; textiles
Secondary: Cosmetics

Stock: 6,000 books; 20,000 pamphlets; 200 current periodicals; 5,000 patent specifications

Member of Essex Special Libraries Group and HASL

HARPENDEN Herts **675**	ADDITIONAL CURATES SOCIETY 14 Rothamsted Avenue Harpenden Hertfordshire	*Tel.:* Harpenden 3512

Primarily to maintain assistant curates in poor parishes

Enquiries: To Secretary

Scope: Fairly comprehensive record of most town parishes since 1837, on population, number of churches, services and payments of clergy

No library

Publications: Home Mission News (quarterly)

HARROGATE Yorkshire **676**	HARROGATE COLLEGE OF FURTHER EDUCATION Haywra Crescent Harrogate Yorkshire	*Tel.:* Harrogate 69052

Enquiries: To Tutor Librarian

Scope: Commerce and business studies including office practice. Art, including painting, sculpture, graphic design
Secondary: Law, banking, retail trades, languages and local government

Stock: 12,000 books; 500 pamphlets; 60 current periodicals

HARROGATE Yorkshire **677**	HARROGATE PUBLIC LIBRARY Victoria Avenue Harrogate Yorkshire	*Tel.:* Harrogate 2744

Enquiries: To Librarian

Scope: General stock including music
Secondary: Harrogate and Yorkshire local collection. Illustrated 19th and 20th century English books. Books on mineral waters from 1572 with particular reference to Harrogate from 1626

Stock: Total stock 100,600 books, including 3,000 local history

HARROW Middx **678**	CERAMICS GLASS AND MINERAL PRODUCTS INDUSTRY TRAINING BOARD Bovis House Northolt Road Harrow HA2 0EF Middlesex	*Tel.:* 01-422 7101

Aims to ensure an adequate supply of properly trained men and women at all levels in the industry; to secure an improvement in the quality and efficiency of industrial training; and to share the cost of training more evenly between firms

Enquiries: To Information and Public Relations Officer

Scope: An extensive index is maintained of training courses currently available in the United Kingdom, with special emphasis on training for industries within the Board's scope
Secondary: Small stock of literature on industrial training (and related fields) and material relevant to the Board's industries

Stock: 500 books and pamphlets; 250 reports; 60 current periodicals

Publications: *Recommendations for Training:*
General; safety; craftsmen; management; supervisors; operatives; office staff
Information Papers:
Selection of external courses; how to assess your training needs; guide to job analysis for the preparation of job training; qualified to instruct?; designing training programmes; induction training
Training Guidelines:
Specimen syllabuses for training in occupations common in industries within the Board's scope

HARROW
Middx

679

HARROW COLLEGE OF TECHNOLOGY AND ART   *Tel.:* 01-422 5535
Northwick Park
Watford Road
Harrow
Middlesex

Enquiries: To Librarian
Scope: Engineering, science, photography, business studies and art
Stock: 12,000 books and pamphlets; 335 current periodicals; 400 slides
Publications: Monthly Accessions List
List of Periodicals

HARROW
Middx

680

LONDON BOROUGH OF HARROW PUBLIC   *Tel.:* 01-427 9030 and
    LIBRARIES   01-427 1956 (direct
Central Reference Library   lines)
Gayton Road
Harrow
Middlesex (enquiries) *and*

2 Courtfield Avenue   *Tel.:* 01-427 4247
Harrow
Middlesex (administrative)

Enquiries: To Librarian
Scope: General reference library which is agent of the National Lending Library and holds appropriate abstracts and indexes. About 200 technical journals amongst general periodicals list, all filed. Complete set of British Standards. Technical translating dictionaries. British trade directories (CICRIS special subject). All Kompass series. Postal code directories. British 1" Ordnance and geological maps; larger scales locally; many foreign sheet maps. H.M.S.O. collection, not complete but most important material stocked, including 1951, 1961 and 1966 Censuses and Census of Production. Statutes and Statutory Instruments
Stock: 28,000 books; 200 current periodicals
Member of CICRIS

HARROW
Middx

681

MEDICAL RESEARCH COUNCIL
CLINICAL RESEARCH CENTRE LIBRARY
Northwick Park
Watford Road
Harrow
Middlesex

Enquiries: To Librarian

HARROW, MEDICAL RESEARCH COUNCIL, CLINICAL RESEARCH CENTRE LIBRARY, *cont.*

Scope: All aspects of clinical medicine, and complementary basic sciences to provide literature for research staff of Medical Research Council and clinicians of the hospital. The following represent the major fields concerned: anaesthetics, bacteriology, bioengineering, cardiology, cell pathology, clinical chemistry, communicable diseases, dietetics, electron microscopy, endocrinology, engineering services, epidemiology, E.N.T., genetics, geriatrics, haematology, immunology, isotopes, laboratory animals, low temperature biology, mathematics and statistics, medicine, metabolism, morbid anatomy, neurology, nursing, nutrition, obstetrics and gynaecology, ophthalmology, paediatrics, pharmacology, physiology, physiotherapy, psychiatry, radiology, surgery, veterinary medicine. Dentistry is specifically excluded

Stock: 5,000 books; 500 current periodicals

HARTLEPOOL HARTLEPOOL PUBLIC LIBRARIES *Tel.:* Hartlepool 2905
Co Durham Central Library
 Clarence Road
682 Hartlepool
 Co Durham

Enquiries: To Borough Librarian

Scope: Local history collection including maps, photographs and microfilms of early local newspapers

Stock: 38,000 books; 65 current periodicals (total stock)

HARWELL *See under* **DIDCOT** *for*
Didcot MEDICAL RESEARCH COUNCIL,
Berks RADIOBIOLOGY UNIT (no. 455)

HASLINGDEN *See under* **ROSSENDALE** *for*
Rossendale HASLINGDEN PUBLIC LIBRARY (no. 2051)
Lancs

HASTINGS HASTINGS PUBLIC LIBRARY *Tel.:* Hastings 501
Sussex Brassey Institute
 Claremont
683 Hastings
 Sussex

Enquiries: To Librarian

Scope: L.A.S.E.R. subject specialization: Judicial systems; history and criticism of American drama; history and criticism of English drama. Extensive local collection on Hastings and St Leonards, Sussex and Kent. The correspondence of Oscar Browning (1837–1923). The printed publications of the first Earl Brassey (1836–1918) and of his wife (1839–1887)
Secondary: The Reference Library has a general stock of 10,000 volumes including medicine, social sciences and humanities including P.G.A. 1870 to date and Annual Register 1758 to date

Stock: 13,721 books; 10,800 pamphlets; 1,874 periodicals

Publications: Shakespeare: a quatercentenary booklet
The Norman Conquest: a book list (with addenda). 1966

HASTINGS Sussex **684**	HASTINGS PUBLIC MUSEUM AND ART GALLERY John's Place Cambridge Road Hastings Sussex	*Tel.:* Hastings 1952

    Enquiries: To Director
        Scope: Local social history

HASTINGS Sussex **685**	SOCIETY OF METAPHYSICIANS LTD Archers Court Stonestile Lane The Ridge Hastings Sussex	*Tel.:* Hastings 51577

    Enquiries: To Secretary
        Scope: Development and application of infinitely based general system and derivation of policies for ourselves and groups with respect to human welfare both in transcendental and physical fields
                Secondary: Parapsychology; paraphysics; borderline sciences, including: psychics, occult, esoteric, spiritual science, systems engineering, and computers
        Stock: 2,000 books; many and varied pamphlets; many reports and current periodicals
  Publications: The Metaphysician (journal, annually)
                Borderline Science booklet series:
                    Handbook of the Aura Biometer. Benham
                    Biometric Analysis of the Flying Saucer Photographs (with photographic plates)
                    Seeing the Aura
                    The Amplifying Pendulum. Pasquini
                    The Cameron Aurameter. 2nd edition
                    Researches on the Aura Phenomena, Parts 1 and 2. Mahoud K. Muftic
                    Introduction to the Science of Biorhythmic Periods. L. Turcke
                    Theoretical & Philosophical Aspects of Psychical Research. A. J. Mayne
                The New Metaphysics Series
                Esoteric Series

HATFIELD Herts **686**	ASSOCIATION FOR SCIENCE EDUCATION College Lane Hatfield Hertfordshire	*Tel.:* Hatfield 67411

    Enquiries: To Secretary
        Scope: Reports from specialist committees of own members on most topics concerned with the teaching of science
  Publications: School Science Review (4 issues each year)
                Education in Science (5 issues each year)

HATFIELD Herts **687**	HATFIELD POLYTECHNIC Roe Green Hatfield Hertfordshire *and* Bayfordbury House Bayfordbury Hertford	*Tel.:* Hatfield 66771 *Telex:* 262413

HATFIELD, HATFIELD POLYTECHNIC, *cont.*

Enquiries: To Chief Information Officer or Librarian

Scope: Science (biology, chemistry, physics and mathematics)
Technology (production engineering, management sciences and applied psychology)
Engineering (aeronautical, civil, electrical (light current) and mechanical)
Social sciences (economics, law, sociology, accountancy, industrial relations) at Bayfordbury House annexe

Stock: 60,000 books and pamphlets; many series of reports; 1,400 current periodicals; comprehensive collections of abstracts, directories and patent specifications

Publications: Library Bulletin (monthly)
Bibliographies on special subjects
Current awareness service (on cards) to local industry (weekly)

Headquarters of HERTIS (Hertfordshire Technical Library and Information Service)
Advisory centre for microforms and documentary reproduction (National Reprographic Centre for documentation)

HAVANT
Hants

688

NATIONAL SOCIETY FOR ART EDUCATION
37a East Street
Havant
Hampshire

Enquiries: To Secretary, by letter only

Scope: General matters of art education

Publications: Conference Journal (annually)
Bulletin (quarterly)

HAVERFORD-WEST
Pembs

689

PEMBROKESHIRE COMMUNITY COUNCIL
4 Victoria Place
Haverfordwest
Pembrokeshire

Tel.: Haverfordwest 2341

Enquiries: To General Secretary

Scope: Information on matters relating to Old People's Welfare and general enquiries (through its Citizen's Advice Bureau)

HAVERFORD-WEST
Pembs

690

PEMBROKESHIRE COUNTY LIBRARY
Dew Street
Haverfordwest
Pembrokeshire

Tel.: Haverfordwest 2070

Enquiries: To Librarian

Scope: West Wales genealogy (papers made available to researchers, but staff are unable to undertake research). Local collection relating to Pembrokeshire

Stock: 750 pamphlets in local collection

HAVERFORD-WEST
Pembs

691

PEMBROKESHIRE RECORD OFFICE
The Castle
Haverfordwest
Pembrokeshire

Tel.: Haverfordwest 3707

Enquiries: To Archivist

Scope: Official archive of the County Council, and Quarter Sessions, and such privately owned documents relating to Pembrokeshire as have been deposited

Stock not available on loan

HAWARDEN
Deeside
Flintshire

See under **DEESIDE** for
FLINTSHIRE RECORD OFFICE (no. 447)
ST DEINIOL'S LIBRARY (no. 448)

HAWICK
Roxburghshire

692

HAWICK ARCHAEOLOGICAL SOCIETY *Tel.:* Hawick 2660
c/o 3 Rinkvale Cottages
Hawick
Roxburghshire

Enquiries: To Secretary or Librarian, Public Library, Hawick, by letter only

Scope: Reference Section of library contains large collection of Scottish Border books and manuscripts. The Wilton Lodge Museum (no. 694) deals mainly with Border relics and natural history

Publications: Hawick Archaeological Society Transactions

HAWICK
Roxburghshire

693

HAWICK PUBLIC LIBRARY *Tel.:* Hawick 2637
Bridge Street
Hawick
Roxburghshire

Enquiries: To Librarian

Scope: A local Borders collection

Stock: 3,000 books; 150 pamphlets

HAWICK
Roxburghshire

694

WILTON LODGE MUSEUM *Tel.:* Hawick 3457
Hawick
Roxburghshire

Museum of local and Scottish Border history

Enquiries: To Curator

Scope: Books and manuscripts relating to Scottish Border History are housed in the Reference Room, Hawick Public Library (no. 693)

Publications: Hawick Archaeological Society Transactions (annually)

HAWORTH
Keighley
Yorkshire

See under **KEIGHLEY** for
THE BRONTË SOCIETY (no. 760)

HECKMONDWIKE
Yorkshire

695

HECKMONDWIKE PUBLIC LIBRARY *Tel.:* Heckmondwike 3764
Walkley Lane
Heckmondwike
Yorkshire

Enquiries: To Librarian, by letter only

Scope: Subject specialization: Prices, costs, business cycles; forms of industrial enterprise

Stock: 220 books

HELSTON Cornwall **696**	WESLEY HISTORICAL SOCIETY The Manse St Keverne Helston Cornwall	*Tel.:* St. Keverne 399

Enquiries: To Secretary

Scope: Large manuscript and printed collections relating to all periods of Methodist history, particularly the 19th century

Publications: Wesley Historical Society Proceedings (3 issues each year)
How to Write a Local Methodist History
Index to Volumes I to XXX of Proceedings

Branches of the Wesley Historical Society exist in many parts of the country, some with small libraries and archives relating to their localities

HEMEL HEMPSTEAD Herts **697**	DACORUM COLLEGE OF FURTHER EDUCATION Marlowes Hemel Hempstead Hertfordshire	*Tel.:* Hemel Hempstead 2461

Enquiries: To Librarian

Scope: General collection suitable for 'A' Level sociology

Member of HERTIS

HEMEL HEMPSTEAD Herts **698**	NATIONAL FEDERATION OF PROFESSIONAL WORKERS Lord Alexander House Hemel Hempstead Hertfordshire	*Tel.:* Hemel Hempstead 55421

Federation of non-manual, clerical and professional unions. Information and research for member unions and representation of collective viewpoints at government level

Enquiries: To Secretary

Scope: Salaries and conditions of white-collar workers. Education and training of white-collars workers. Pension policy affecting white-collar workers. Legislation affecting trade union

Publications: Pamphlets and reports on issues of current interest

HEMEL HEMPSTEAD Herts **699**	THE SOCIETY FOR THE AID OF THALIDOMIDE CHILDREN (LIMITED) 28 Fouracres Walk Hemel Hempstead Hertfordshire	*Tel.:* Hemel Hempstead 51878

The parents' association for families where there is a child handicapped by thalidomide or similarly handicapped

Enquiries: To Secretary

No library

Publications: Leaflet (on aims)
Newsletter (monthly)
Film: One of Them is Brett

HENLEY-ON-THAMES Oxon	THE ADMINISTRATIVE STAFF COLLEGE Greenlands Henley-on-Thames Oxfordshire RG9 3AU	*Tel.:* Hambleden (Bucks) 454

700 The College provides short, intensive and specialized courses designed for men and women drawn from industry, commerce, trade unions and the public service who already hold positions of authority and are likely to qualify for greater responsibilities. The studies examine the principle and practice of management and administration

Enquiries: To Librarian

Scope: Management (general, office, production and personnel management; marketing and selling). Administrative units (public administration, national and local, both British and Foreign; some histories of non-public organizations). Social sciences (sociology; political theory and party politics; economics; money and banking; law; education; public relations; industrial relations; psychology). Statistical method and operational research
Secondary: Biography. History

Stock: 2,000 books; 5,000 pamphlets; 250 current periodicals

Publications: Books and Monographs:
The Administrative Staff Colleges at Home and Overseas. H. J. B. Taylor. 1968
British Coal: A Review of the Industry, its Organisation and Management. John Platt. 1968
Data Processing Managers. R. J. Harper. 1967
Fayol on Administration. M. B. Brodie. 1967
Accountability in Government Departments, Public Corporations and Public Companies. R. W. Ennis, ed. 1967
Management and the Social Sciences. T. Lupton. 1966; 2nd imp. 1967
New Thinking in Management. F. de P. Hanika. 1965; 3rd imp. 1968
Writers on Organizations. D. S. Pugh, D. J. Hickson and C. R. Hinings. 1964; 3rd imp. 1969
Biography in Management Studies. Humphrey Lloyd. 1964
On Thinking Statistically. M. B. Brodie. 1963; 3rd imp. 1969
Occasional Papers:
Management Services Techniques and Departments. B. R. Aston. 1969
Behaviour in the Working Environment. E. Andrew Life. 1968
Management Education in Spain. G. F. Evans-Vaughan. 1968
An Approach to Short-Term Business Forecasting. James Morrell. 1968
Management Information: a Systematic Approach. P. L. Cloot. 1968
Management Consultancy. B. R. Aston. 1967
Management Education in West Germany. J. Adler and P. Cherrington. 1966
Management Education in the Netherlands. G. F. Evans-Vaughan. rev. 1968
Management Information. C. W. Smith. 1966
Management Education in Belgium. G. A. G. Ormsby. 1965; rev. 1969
The Committee Concept and Business. M. B. Brodie. 1963
Course of Studies Papers:
Trade Union Law. 4th rev. edition 1966
The Organisation of Trade Unions. 4th rev. edition 1966
The State and Collective Bargaining. 4th rev. edition 1966
Industrial and Commercial Associations. 3rd rev. edition 1966
College Papers:
Notes on Financial and Costing Statements. H. J. B. Taylor. 196
The Financial Mechanism of the United Kingdom. 1969
Research and Development. G. F. Evans-Vaughan. 1969
Others:
Basic Economic Data (an annual compendium). May 1969

HENLEY-ON-THAMES, THE ADMINISTRATIVE STAFF COLLEGE, *cont.*

Henley Book Notes. A guide to a selection of recent management books. First issued April 1966. Issued 3 times a year. Annual index

HEREFORD

701

CHURCHILL GARDENS MUSEUM *Tel.:* Hereford 67409
3 Venn's Lane
Hereford

Collection and display of English costume

Enquiries: To City Librarian and Curator, Broad Street, Hereford, by letter only

Scope: Specimens of costume and accessories
Secondary: Books, fashion plates, prints, and other documents

HEREFORD

702

HEREFORD CATHEDRAL LIBRARY *Tel.:* Hereford 66193 and
The Cathedral 3537
Hereford

Enquiries: To Librarian

Scope: Mainly books on religion and ecclesiastical history from very early times to present day
Archives of the Dean and Chapter of Hereford Cathedral from Anglo-Saxon times
Sacred music including manuscripts of 18th and early 19th century

Stock: 227 manuscript volumes from 8th to 15th century (chained); 10,000 printed books of which more than 1,200 chained, and including 56 incunabula, majority 16th to 18th century; 30,000 archives of the Dean and Chapter; 800 negatives and 700 lantern slides of cathedral and its treasures; 2 current periodicals. Modern books only available on loan

Publications: A Short Account of the Chained Library
Hereford Cathedral Library (including the chained library) its History and Contents. F. C. Morgan
A Concise List of Seals Belonging to the Dean and Chapter of Hereford Cathedral. F. C. and P. E. Morgan
Illustrated pamphlets on: Mappa Mundi; Bosses; Misericords; Glass; Brasses; the Cathedral
Manuscript volumes have been microfilmed and copies can be supplied on request

HEREFORD

703

HEREFORD CITY LIBRARY *Tel.:* Hereford 2456
Broad Street
Hereford

Enquiries: To Librarian

Scope: Local history, including the Pilley Collection which is strong in books published during the late nineteenth century over a wide subject area as well as local history
Agricultural history, particularly agricultural manuals and textbooks of the seventeenth to early twentieth centuries

Stock: 8,000 books and pamphlets; 10 current periodicals; 10,000 manuscripts; 11,000 negatives; 2,000 slides; many prints. Local history stock not normally available on loan

Depository Library for Herefordshire parish registers. Holds the records and minute books of Hereford City Council (generally those pre-1915). Houses the Woolhope Naturalists' Field Club Library (no. 706)

HEREFORD

704

HEREFORD COLLEGE OF EDUCATION *Tel.:* Hereford 5725
College Road
Hereford

Enquiries: To Librarian

Scope: Education, English, history, geography, art, music, drama, children's books
Stock: 30,000 books; 240 current periodicals. Books on education not available on loan

HEREFORD

705

HEREFORDSHIRE COUNTY RECORD OFFICE   *Tel.:* Hereford 5441
Old Barracks
Harold Street
Hereford

Enquiries: To Archivist
Scope: Manuscript material on the diocesan, political, social and economic history of Herefordshire
16th to 18th century iron industry (Midlands iron works)
16th to 20th century agriculture (particularly High Farming in the 19th century)
Publications: Calendars available for consultation

HEREFORD

706

WOOLHOPE NATURALISTS' FIELD CLUB   *Tel.:* Hereford 2456
c/o City Library
Broad Street
Hereford

Study of the natural history, archaeology, history and geography of Herefordshire

Enquiries: To Librarian
Scope: Natural history and archaeology of Herefordshire
Secondary: General archaeology, architecture, and antiquities
Stock: 5,000 books; 200 pamphlets; 25 current periodicals; 100 maps
Publications: Off-prints of articles in Transactions (annually), and special publications within the Herefordshire subject field

HERTFORD

707

HATFIELD POLYTECHNIC
Bayfordbury House
Bayfordbury
Hertford
See no. 687

HERTFORD

708

HERTFORD MUSEUM   *Tel.:* Hertford 2686
18 Bull Plain
Hertford

Records and illustrates the history of Hertford and its surrounding area through objects

Enquiries: To Curator
Scope: The Museum collections. Local History Library. General Library (uncatalogued and mainly 19th century)
Secondary: Photographs, maps, prints, drawings, paintings and archives
Stock: 180 feet of books; 10 current periodicals. Stock not normally available on loan

HERTFORD

709

HERTFORDSHIRE COUNTY LIBRARY   *Tel.:* Hertford 4242 ext.
County Hall   5485
Hertford   *Telex:* 81272

Enquiries: To Librarian

HERTFORD, HERTFORDSHIRE COUNTY LIBRARY, *cont.*
Scope: General stock. Hertfordshire local history collection
Secondary: Music. Drama
Surgery at Queen Elizabeth II Hospital, Welwyn Garden City, Hertfordshire

HERTFORD	MIMRAM BOOKS	*Tel..:* Hertford 5700
	STEPHEN AUSTIN & SONS LTD	
710	Caxton Hill	
	Hertford	

Printers and publishers

Enquiries: To Manager

Scope: No information service as such, but enquiries on subjects relating to the journals published will be passed to the relevant Editors
No library

Publications: The Geological Magazine
Journal of African Languages

HERTFORD	PONSBOURNE COLLEGE	*Tel.:* Cuffley 3630
	Newgate St Village	
711	Hertford	

Men's Church of England pre-theological college

Enquiries: To Warden, by letter only

Scope: General theology, sociology, British constitution, New Testament Greek, Biblical Hebrew
Ordination requirements for Church of England

Stock: 1,400 books; 12 current periodicals. Stock not available on loan

HEYWOOD	HEYWOOD PUBLIC LIBRARIES	*Tel.:* Heywood 60947
Lancs	Central Library	
	Church Street	
712	Heywood	
	Lancashire	

Enquiries: To Librarian

Scope: N.W.R.L.S. subject specialization includes: Tuberculosis, scrofula and rickets
Secondary: Local history of Heywood

Stock: Books: 50 (tuberculosis, scrofula, rickets); 1,600 (local history); pamphlets: 200 (local history)

HIGH WYCOMBE	THE DISRAELI MUSEUM	*Tel.:* High Wycombe 32580
Bucks	Hughenden Manor	and 28051
	High Wycombe	
713	Buckinghamshire	

Hughenden Manor was the country home of Benjamin Disraeli, Earl of Beaconsfield, and is preserved by the National Trust, with his books, papers, some of his furniture and personal possessions

Enquiries: To Area Agent, by letter only

Scope: The Disraeli Papers are held in the Archives at Hughenden. They are available to *bona fide* students and historians and permission to view them may be obtained by prior application

HIGH WYCOMBE
Bucks

714

HIGH WYCOMBE PUBLIC LIBRARY
Queen Victoria Road
High Wycombe
Buckinghamshire

Tel.: High Wycombe 23981

Enquiries: To Librarian
Scope: Subject specialization: Criminology
Stock: 1,000 books; 50 pamphlets

HIGH WYCOMBE
Bucks

715

G. D. SEARLE AND CO. LTD
Lane End Road
High Wycombe
Buckinghamshire
Manufacturers of pharmaceuticals

Tel.: High Wycombe 21124
Telex: 83205

Enquiries: To Medical Information Officer
Scope: Use of progestational agents in gynaecology and contraception. Treatment of infertility with gonadotrophins. Clinical application of aldosterone antagonists. Diseases of the gastro-intestinal and genito-urinary tracts. The use of neuroleptic drugs in the treatment of psychiatric disorders. Biochemical assay techniques and health screening procedures
Stock: 17,000 reports; 80 current periodicals. Stock not available on loan
Publications: Technical manuals on medical aspects of the drugs produced by the Company
Publication of proceedings of symposia and other scientific meetings
Medical films on oral contraception

HILLINGDON
Middx

See under **WEST DRAYTON** for
LONDON BOROUGH OF HILLINGDON
LIBRARY HEADQUARTERS (no. 2271)

HINCKLEY
Leics

716

HINCKLEY PUBLIC LIBRARIES
Central Library
Station Road
Hinckley
Leicestershire

Tel.: Hinckley 5106

Enquiries: To Librarian
Scope: Subject specialization: Language
Stock: 100 books; 7 current periodicals

HITCHIN
Herts

717

HITCHIN COLLEGE
Cambridge Road
Hitchin
Hertfordshire

Tel.: Hitchin 2351

Enquiries: To Senior Tutor Librarian
Scope: Economics and business studies (particularly accountancy, marketing and retail distribution
General subjects to G.C.E. 'A' level
Stock: 13,200 books and pamphlets; 170 current periodicals (total stock)
Member of HERTIS

HITCHIN Herts **718**	HITCHIN MUSEUM AND ART GALLERY Paynes Park Hitchin Hertfordshire	*Tel.:* Hitchin 4476

Enquiries: To Curator

Scope: The Museum has the manuscripts of books by Reginald L. Hine, FSA, and his collection of papers relating to Hertfordshire villages and Hitchin, the diary of William Lucas, 1804–1861, published as a Quaker Journal by E. G. Bryant and G. P. Baker in 1933, and letters of Matilda and Anne Lucas, also published by Hitchinson & Co 1938, *Two Englishwomen in Rome 1871–1900*. There are diaries of other members of the Lucas family and minute books of various societies and organizations in the town in the 19th and early 20th century together with a collection of photographs and scrap books of the same period. The Library contains a good collection of local history books and works of local authors

Stock: 900 books; 5 current periodicals. Stock not normally available on loan

Publications: The Flora of Hertfordshire. J. G. Dony

HITCHIN Herts **719**	RURAL MUSIC SCHOOLS ASSOCIATION Little Benslow Hills Hitchin Hertfordshire	*Tel.:* Hitchin 3446

Aims to further the study of good music by people of all ages through the establishment of music centres in country areas by county music schools, which provide teachers, instruments and music, and work to encourage amateur music-making. Special interest: amateur music, particularly instrumental class teaching

Enquiries: To Director

Scope: Music: books and sheet music, including orchestral works, chamber music, choral works, solos for instruments and voices, records. Reference Library of music included in published lists of graded music for teaching: Graded Music for String Class Teaching; A List of Chamber Music (for strings, and strings with piano, intended to serve as an introduction to the standard works of the ensemble repertory); A List of Orchestral Music for school and amateur orchestras. Large selection of chamber music for strings

Stock: 500 books and pamphlets; 10 current periodicals; 5,000 items of music

Publications: Graded Music for String Class Teaching (and Supplement)
A List of Chamber Music
A List of Orchestral Music (and Supplement)
An Introduction to String Class Teaching
An Informal Introduction to Bass Beginnings (hints for the beginner on the double bass)
Making Music (three issues each year)

HORLEY Surrey **720**	FELINE ADVISORY BUREAU 92 Church Road Horley Surrey

See no. 2324

HORNCHURCH Essex **721**	HAVERING TECHNICAL COLLEGE Ardleigh Green Road Hornchurch Essex RM11 2LL	*Tel.:* Hornchurch 52263

Enquiries: To Librarian

Scope: General scope including the social sciences and humanities but main specializations are in mechanical engineering, electrical engineering, commerce, nursing and hairdressing

Stock: 11,000 books; 1,100 pamphlets; 130 current periodicals

HORSFORTH
Leeds

See *under* **LEEDS** for
HORSFORTH URBAN DISTRICT COUNCIL
   PUBLIC LIBRARY (no. 798)
TRINITY AND ALL SAINTS COLLEGES (no. 812)

HOUNSLOW
Middx

722

LONDON BOROUGH OF HOUNSLOW
   LIBRARY SERVICES
Hounslow House
724/734 London Road
Hounslow
Middlesex

Tel.: 01-570 7728 ext. 296
Reference Libraries:
01-994 5295, 01-570 6082

Enquiries: To Librarian

Scope: Subject specialization includes: Foreign relations; UNO (excluding official publications); international organizations and treaties; diplomacy and consular service; adult and higher education

Stock: 2,390 books and pamphlets

HOUNSLOW
Middx

723

PARKE, DAVIS & COMPANY
Staines Road
Hounslow
Middlesex

Tel.: 01-570 2361
Telex: 22419

Manufacturers of ethical pharmaceuticals

Enquiries: To Librarian

Scope: Chemistry (for research into the medical field)
Secondary: Medicine

Stock: 2,000 books; 1,000 pamphlets; 240 current periodicals

Publications: Therapeutic Notes (medical journal usually distributed to qualified practitioners only)

HOVE
Sussex

724

HOVE PUBLIC LIBRARY
Church Road
Hove BN3 2DJ
Sussex

Tel.: Hove 70472

Enquiries: To Librarian

Scope: Special emphasis on painting, ceramics, furniture, art metalwork and glass
Field Marshal Lord Wolseley and Viscountess Wolseley collection: correspondence of the Wolseley family and miscellaneous material, throwing light on the military history of Britain in the late 19th century, and on the social scene
Manuscript topographical notes on Sussex villages with emphasis on the smaller manor houses
Miéville family: pedigree notes and newspaper cuttings, throwing light on Anglo-Egyptian relations in Victoria's reign
Secondary: General collection of film strips; transparencies of art reproductions, and local photographs with particular emphasis on Hove history. Local documents, original records relating to Brighton, Hove and Portslade and parish registers of Hove

HOVE, HOVE PUBLIC LIBRARY, *cont.*

Collections of old children's books and books of fine printing and binding
Music and Record Library: scores, books on the history and theory of music, records

Stock: 67,000 books total non-fiction stock (Reference Library 16,000 including about 5,000 on fine arts); 940 film strips; 900 transparencies; 2,500 Sussex photographs; 150 current periodicals; 3,000 gramophone records

Publications: Catalogues: Rare Books, Gramophone Records, and Film Strips

Tourist Information Bureau

HOYLAKE
Wirral
Cheshire

See under **WIRRAL** for
HOYLAKE HISTORICAL SOCIETY (no. 2299)

HUDDERSFIELD
Yorkshire

725

HUDDERSFIELD COLLEGE OF EDUCATION (TECHNICAL)
Holly Bank Road
Lindley
Huddersfield HD3 3BP
Yorkshire

Tel.: Huddersfield 25611

Enquiries: To Librarian

Scope: Education, particularly vocational education, industrial training, programmed learning, teaching method, curriculum development, comparative education. Psychology, particularly social/educational, learning, testing, psychology of adolescence, vocational guidance
Secondary: Social sciences, law, economics, and a wide range of technologies

Stock: 10,500 books; 8,700 pamphlets; 400 current periodicals including 220 in humanities

Publications: General Course in Science Teaching Project: Teachers Guides for Chemistry, Biology, Physics, Mathematics
Occasional Publications
Industrial Training Booklist
Report on General and Technical Education in Sweden

HUDDERSFIELD
Yorkshire

726

HUDDERSFIELD COLLEGE OF TECHNOLOGY
Huddersfield HD1 3DH
Yorkshire

Tel.: Huddersfield 30501

Enquiries: To Librarian

Scope: Architecture, building; catering; chemistry; civil, electrical and mechanical engineering; business and management; geography, history, modern languages; mathematics; physics; textile industries; commercial and applied arts including typography, design, decorating

Stock: 25,000 books; 2,000 pamphlets; 200 reports; 300 current periodicals
Special collection: The G. H. Wood collection of nineteenth-century books and pamphlets on sociology and economics

Member of HADIS

HUDDERSFIELD
Yorkshire

727

HUDDERSFIELD PUBLIC LIBRARIES
Central Library
Huddersfield HD1 2SU
Yorkshire

Tel.: Huddersfield 21356

Enquiries: To Librarian

Scope: Local history material including family and municipal archives, microfilm copies of all local papers and a wide range of census returns and parish registers. The area covered is Huddersfield and surrounding districts. Good collection of illustrated art books. Subject specialization: Income and wealth, general treatises on law

Stock: 50,000 books; 300 current periodicals; gramophone records; illustrations; local films; local archives

HUDDERSFIELD NARROW GAUGE RAILWAY SOCIETY *Tel.:* Elland 4526
Yorkshire 47 Birchington Avenue
  Birchencliffe
728 Huddersfield HD3 3RD
  Yorkshire

Aims to encourage an interest in all forms of narrow gauge rail transport

Enquiries: To Secretary

Scope: *Library:* Contains 200 files of information, photographs, drawings and maps giving detailed information on narrow gauge railways in all parts of the world; 300 books and bound volumes
Information Service: Provides up to date information on industrial and passenger railways in the British Isles, and is currently being expanded to include overseas countries
Modelling Service: Provides information and advice for railway modellers

Stock: 300 books and pamphlets; 8 current periodicals

Publications: Narrow Gauge News (bi-monthly)
The Narrow Gauge (quarterly)
Occasional booklets dealing with narrow gauge railways in the United Kingdom

HUDDERSFIELD THORNTON & ROSS LTD *Tel.:* 084-84 2218
Yorkshire Linthwaite Laboratories
  Huddersfield
729 Yorkshire

Manufacturers of pharmaceutical and cosmetic products, detergents and disinfectants

Enquiries: To The Company

Stock: 150 books; 20 current periodicals. Comprehensive collection of British Pharmacopoeias and Codexes over last 50 years. Perfumery formularies. Reference books on analytical chemistry and punched card references to analytical methods for pharmaceuticals, perfumes and detergents

HULL ENDSLEIGH COLLEGE OF EDUCATION *Tel.:* Hull 42157
Yorkshire Beverley Road
  Hull
730 Yorkshire

Enquiries: To Librarian, by letter only

Scope: Education
Special collection: Recusant history material (the Postgate collection)

Stock: 35,000 books, pamphlets, and reports; 283 current periodicals

HULL HULL REGIONAL COLLEGE OF ART *Tel.:* Hull 28153
Yorkshire Anlaby Road
  Hull
731 Yorkshire

Enquiries: To Librarian

HULL, HULL REGIONAL COLLEGE OF ART, *cont.*

Scope: Architecture and building, history of art, design
Secondary: Printing, photography, textiles
Stock: 9,000 books (total; 8,000 in subjects referred to above) 300 pamphlets including exhibition catalogues; 170 current periodicals

HULL
Yorkshire

732

THE INSTITUTE OF CRAFT EDUCATION
Hillside
Little Weighton
Hull HU20 3XH
Yorkshire

Professional organization devoted solely to the interests and problems of craft education

Enquiries: To General Secretary
Scope: Craft education
Publications: Practical Education (monthly)
Special Reports:
   Metrication in Craft Education
   Craftwork in the Junior High School
   The C.S.E. Reports: 1, 2 and 3

The College of Craft Education founded by the Institute conducts courses of study and training and pursues the general educational aims of the Institute, including examinations and Summer Schools

HULL
Yorkshire

733

KINGSTON UPON HULL CITY LIBRARIES
Central Library
Albion Street
Hull
Yorkshire

Tel.: Hull 36680
Telex: 52211

Enquiries: To Chief Librarian
Scope: *Reference Library:* All subjects except science, technology and commerce. *Special collections:* Napoleon, background material 1740–1759
Local History Library: Including special collections on Andrew Marvell; William Wilberforce and slavery; whaling; local playbills; Civil War tracts; Winifred Holtby
Music Library: Books about music, scores and gramophone records and Illustrations Collection
Medical Library: Specifically for medical profession
City Information Service: A general information bureau answering 240 enquiries a day. Maintains many indexes and uses the stock of the Hull City Libraries as background
Stock: *Reference Library:* 102,000 volumes; 170 current periodicals
Local History Library: 15,000 volumes, plus pamphlets, maps, plans, films and manuscripts
Music Library: 14,000 books; 11,000 scores; 9,000 gramophone records
Medical Library: 6,000 volumes; 72 current periodicals
Publications: Hull Reference Library Review (monthly)
Civic Index: a monthly guide to local government literature
Music Library Notes (quarterly)
Diary of Events (monthly)
Books on Hull and district (a bibliography)
Local History Quarterly

HULL
Yorkshire

734

    KINGSTON UPON HULL COLLEGE OF
        EDUCATION
    Cottingham Road
    Hull
    Yorkshire

        Tel.: Hull 41451

Enquiries: To Librarian

Scope: All aspects of education
Secondary: Academic subjects covered: Economics, English literature, geography, history, mathematics, biology, commerce, drama and telecommunication, evolution and prehistory, music, fine and applied art, physical education, physical science, religion, sociology
Local collection of books on Hull and district
Special collection of books on all aspects of filming and the cinema

Stock: 40,000 books and pamphlets; 250 current periodicals

HULL
Yorkshire

735

    KINGSTON UPON HULL MUSEUMS
    23/24 High Street
    Hull
    Yorkshire

        Tel.: Hull 27625

Archaeology, local history, slavery, transport, shipping, whaling, in three museums

Enquiries: To Director

Stock: Books: Slavery 200; local history 500; transport 100; shipping and whaling 500; archaeology 300. Stock not available on loan

HULL
Yorkshire

736

    KINGSTON UPON HULL NAUTICAL COLLEGE
    Boulevard
    Hull
    Yorkshire

        Tel.: Hull 35590

Enquiries: To Librarian

Scope: Technical information on nautical subjects
Secondary: Maritime law, history of nautical sciences, nautical applications of sociology and medicine, oceanography, nautical education

Stock: 3,000 books (about 200 on secondary topics listed); 100 pamphlets

HULL
Yorkshire

737

    THE NATIONAL BASEBALL LEAGUE (U.K.)
    88 Westerdale Grove
    Southcoates Lane
    Hull
    Yorkshire

        Tel.: 0482-72181

Enquiries: To Secretary
Scope: Baseball

HULL
Yorkshire

738

    RECKITT AND COLMAN LTD
    Dansom Lane
    Hull
    Yorkshire

        Tel.: Hull 26151
        Telex: 52166

Manufacture of household products, toiletries, disinfectants and pharmaceuticals

Enquiries: To Information Officer

HULL, RECKITT AND COLMAN LTD, *cont.*

Scope: Bacteriology, medicinal chemistry, pharmacology and physiology in support of company's interests in pharmaceutical and disinfectant manufactures
Secondary: Pathology

Publications: 2,000 books; 1,000 pamphlets; 100 current periodicals
Subscriber to RINGDOC and FARMDOC

HULL
Yorkshire

739

UNIVERSITY OF HULL
THE BRYNMOR JONES LIBRARY
Hull
Yorkshire

Tel.: 0482-408960

Enquiries: To Librarian

Scope: Holdings to assist in study, teaching and research in the subjects in which courses and degrees are offered, the arts, pure sciences, social sciences and law, and a small amount of applied science
South East Asia (for Centre for South East Asian studies). Labour history

Stock: 318,000 books and pamphlets; 4,750 current periodicals

Publications: The University publishes books through Oxford University Press. On its own account it publishes: Inaugural Lectures; Occasional Papers in Geography; Occasional Papers in Modern Languages; Occasional Papers in Economic and Social History; and St John's College Cambridge Lectures

HUNTINGDON

740

HUNTINGDON TECHNICAL COLLEGE
California Road
Huntingdon

Tel.: Huntingdon 2346

Enquiries: To Librarian

Scope: General subjects in fields of science, engineering (including all aspects of motor vehicle engineering, sales and industry), commerce and arts
Secondary: Education and industrial training

Stock: 6,000 books; 100 pamphlets; 100 current periodicals

HUNTINGDON

741

HUNTINGDONSHIRE COUNTY RECORD OFFICE
County Buildings
Huntingdon

Tel.: Huntingdon 2181

Enquiries: To County Archivist

Scope: Official Archives; Records of Clerk of the Peace, public utilities, statutory authorities, education, ecclesiastical, probate, manorial, parochial, estate and family; maps and photographs
Stock not available on loan but photocopies may be provided

HURSTBOURNE TARRANT
Andover
Hants

See under **ANDOVER** for
THE BLADON SOCIETY OF ARTS AND CRAFTS
(no. 28)

HUYTON-WITH-ROBY
Liverpool

See under **LIVERPOOL** for
HUYTON-WITH-ROBY HISTORIC SOCIETY
(no. 865)

HYDE	HYDE PUBLIC LIBRARY	*Tel.:* 061-368 2447
Cheshire	Union Street	
	Hyde	
742	Cheshire	

    Enquiries: To Librarian

        Scope: Subject specialization includes: Various aspects of employment, labour, trade unions, strikes. Diseases of the musculo-skeletal system
Secondary: Small local collection on Hyde, and on Cheshire and neighbouring counties of Lancashire, Derbyshire and Yorkshire

        Stock: 45,732 books; 48 current periodicals; 15 newspapers (total stock)

ILCHESTER	See under **YEOVIL** for
Yeovil	FLEET AIR ARM MUSEUM (no. 2325)
Somerset	

ILFORD	ALBANIAN SOCIETY
Essex	26 Cambridge Road
	Ilford
743	Essex

Aims to spread information about the People's Republic of Albania and to foster friendship and cultural relations between the British and Albanian peoples

    Enquiries: To Secretary, by letter only

        Scope: All aspects of life in the People's Republic of Albania

        Stock: 85 books; 450 pamphlets

Publications: Albanian Life
Albanian News
Albanian Statistics
A Short Guide to the People's Republic of Albania
A Short Albanian Phrase Book
The Ghost at the Wedding: A Play in Three Acts. W. B. Bland
John Newport: An Englishman with Skanderbeg. W. B. Bland

ILFORD	DR BARNARDO'S	*Tel.:* 01-550 8822
Essex	Tanners Lane	
	Barkingside	
744	Ilford	
	Essex	

The largest voluntary child care organization caring for 8,000 children in residential or non-residential setting, including those physically, mentally, or emotionally handicapped or educationally sub-normal. There are 110 homes and special schools in Britain, 12 in Australia, one in Kenya, and one is planned for New Zealand

    Enquiries: To Librarian or for general and public relations enquiries to Information Officer

        Scope: Child care and allied topics
Secondary: Charity administration, social legislation, taxation and other legal matters

        Stock: 1,500 books; 600 pamphlets; 300 reports; 35 current periodicals

Publications: Occasional booklets and reports on child care

ILFORD
Essex

745

LAPORTE INDUSTRIES LTD
Howards Works
Uphall Road
Ilford
Essex

Tel.: 01-478 3333
Telex: 262735

Manufacturers of chemicals and pharmaceuticals

Enquiries: To Information Officer, by letter only
Scope: Limited information on pharmaceutical chemicals including aspirin and quinine
Stock: Small library. Stock not available on loan

ILFORD
Essex

746

LONDON BOROUGH OF REDBRIDGE PUBLIC
    LIBRARIES
Central Library
Oakfield Road
Ilford
Essex

Tel.: 01-478 0017

Enquiries: To Librarian
Scope: Large general stock covering all aspects of medicine, the social sciences, and the humanities, with *special collections* in public health, sanitary inspection and food adulteration, smoke, disinfection and immunology, disposal of the dead and cemeteries (together with the biography of these subjects); infectious diseases, tuberculosis, scrofula, rickets, leprosy; and photography, general and applied (together with biography but excluding cinematography and photomechanical printing processes)
Stock: 319,805 books; 317 current periodicals (total stock)
Publications: Bibliographies as requested

ILKESTON
Derbyshire

747

ILKESTON PUBLIC LIBRARY
Market Place
Ilkeston
Derbyshire DE7 5RN

Tel.: Ilkeston 3361 (Evenings and Saturdays 3363)

Enquiries: To Borough Librarian
Scope: General stock specializing in local industries, such as hosiery and iron founding. Local collection. D. H. Lawrence collection
Stock: 50,000 books, pamphlets and reports; 90 current periodicals (total stock); 2,000 illustrations, including transparencies

Member of NANTIS
Member of Achilles Scheme
Member of Tamworth Scheme

ILKESTON
Derbyshire

748

SOUTH EAST DERBYSHIRE COLLEGE OF
    FURTHER EDUCATION (ILKESTON BRANCH)
Field Road
Ilkeston
Derbyshire DE7 5RS

Tel.: Ilkeston 2301

Enquiries: To Librarian
Scope: Basic texts and background material in: Human biology, law, economics, education, sociology, scripture, economic, social and political history, fine arts, literature and geography
Stock: 5,000 books (social sciences and humanities); 312 pamphlets; 46 current periodicals

ILKLEY
Yorkshire

749

HIGH ROYDS HOSPITAL   *Tel.:* Menston 2491
Menston
Ilkley
Yorkshire
Psychiatric hospital

Enquiries: To Librarian
Scope: Psychiatry
   Secondary: General medicine
Stock: 500 books; 30 current periodicals. Stock not normally available on loan outside the hospital
Branch of Aireborough Public Libraries giving normal public library services to patients and staff

ILKLEY
Yorkshire

750

ILKLEY COLLEGE OF EDUCATION   *Tel.:* Ilkley 2892
Wells Road
Ilkley
Yorkshire
Constituent member of the University of Leeds Institute of Education

Enquiries: To Librarian
Scope: Good collection of books on home economics (cookery, dress, needlework); all aspects of the social sciences and English. Other subjects covered in detail are drama, geography, biology and art. Music section is beginning to expand. School Practice Library provides a representative selection of books a student may expect to find in current use in schools
Scope: 23,860 books and pamphlets; 163 current periodicals

INVERNESS

751

AN COMUNN GAIDHEALACH   *Tel.:* 0463-21226
Abertarff House
Church Street
Inverness
The organization is a social and cultural one and its aims are to encourage and support the learning, teaching and use of the Gaelic language

Enquiries: Information Officer
Scope: Gaelic books and records, historical information, place names, genealogy
   Secondary: Pamphlets and social and economic matter on the Highlands
Stock: Library of books that are now out of print
Publications: Who are The Highlanders?   Gaelic Proverbs
               The Highland Way of Life   Highland Whisky
               Modern Gaelic Verse   Early Churches
               Close-Up on Peat   Highland Homes
               Aluminium in the Highlands   The Highlands Prehistory
               A Key to Highland Place Names   Harris Tweed
               The Story of Tartan   Highland Communications
               The Clarsach   Pictish Art
               The Industrial Highlands   Gaelic Is.
               Crofting   Highland Plant Badges

INVERNESS **752**	REGIMENTAL MUSEUM OF SEAFORTH HIGHLANDERS, THE QUEEN'S OWN CAMERON HIGHLANDERS AND QUEEN'S OWN HIGHLANDERS (SEAFORTH AND CAMERONS) Fort George Inverness	*Tel.:* Ardersier 274 ext. 47

To record for all time the history of the Regiment in peace and war, to house the collection of regimental trophies and to open this valuable collection of regimental records to the public

Enquiries: To Curator, by letter only

Scope: The library includes the documental histories of the Regiments; records of personnel who took part in campaigns and were awarded medals; and records of regimental music. The history of the Regiments and their dress is well illustrated by means of uniforms, paintings, prints, photographs and statuettes. An armoury, medal rooms and a silver room complete the museum

Stock: 500 books. Stock not available on loan, but extracts and information may be requested

Publications: The Queen's Own Highlander (Regimental journal)
History of the Seaforth Highlanders
Short History of Queen's Own Highlanders (Seaforth & Camerons)

Pointer exhibits in the Burgh Museum, Inverness and in The West Highland Museum, Fort William

IPSWICH Suffolk **753**	EAST SUFFOLK COUNTY LIBRARY County Library County Hall St Helen's Street Ipswich Suffolk	*Tel.:* Ipswich 55801

Enquiries: To Librarian

Scope: Material relating to the County of East Suffolk
Secondary: Peripheral material relating to Ipswich, Lowestoft, and contiguous counties

Stock: 259,000 books; 60 current periodicals (total stock)

Publications: Gramophone record catalogue

IPSWICH Suffolk **754**	IPSWICH CIVIC COLLEGE Rope Walk Ipswich Suffolk	*Tel.:* Ipswich 55981

Enquiries: To Librarian

Scope: Art, management, sociology and social work, education, English literature, history, geography, economics

Stock: 20,000 books and pamphlets; 200 current periodicals

IPSWICH Suffolk **755**	IPSWICH MEDICAL LIBRARY Ipswich and East Suffolk Hospital Anglesea Road Wing Ipswich Suffolk	*Tel.:* Ipswich 51021 ext. 217

Enquiries: To Medical Librarian

Scope: Literature searches undertaken and bibliographies prepared. Information service for medical and ancillary staff based on the fields of medicine, general surgery, orthopaedic surgery, ophthalmology, ear, nose and throat; extensive use of *Index Medicus*. Small historical section chiefly of local interest

Stock: 300 books; 97 current periodicals

IPSWICH
Suffolk

756

IPSWICH MUSEUMS AND ART GALLERIES   *Tel.:* Ipswich 53504
High Street
Ipswich
Suffolk

Public Museum with the following departments: Archaeology, Ethnology, Geology, Natural History. Fine and Applied Arts at Christchurch Mansion, Christchurch Park, Ipswich—a period house museum furnished from late Tudor to mid-Victorian Times, and picture gallery

Enquiries: To Curator

Stock: 30 current periodicals

Publications: Offprints of the Proceedings of the Suffolk Institute of Archaeology

IRONBRIDGE
Telford
Salop

See under **TELFORD** for
IRONBRIDGE GORGE MUSEUM TRUST
   LIMITED (no. 2211)

ISLEWORTH
Middx

757

BOEHRINGER INGELHEIM LIMITED   *Tel.:* 01-568 9911
Isleworth House   *Telex:* 24452
Great West Road
Isleworth
Middlesex

Manufacturers of pharmaceuticals

Enquiries: To Librarian, by letter only

Scope: Medicine, pharmacology and toxicology of drugs, and methodology of drug evaluation

Stock: 940 books; 3,000 pamphlets; 75 current periodicals. Stock not available on loan

ISLEWORTH
Middx

758

BOROUGH ROAD COLLEGE   *Tel.:* 01-560 5991
Isleworth
Middlesex

College of Education

Enquiries: To Librarian

Scope: Education. Curriculum Subjects: Social science, humanities
Secondary: General coverage of other subjects
Special collection: Salmon Collection of Books on Joseph Lancaster and the British and Foreign School Society

Stock: 30,000 books; 1,000 pamphlets; 200 current periodicals (including 60 on education)

IVER
Bucks

759

THE BRITISH ASSOCIATION OF THE HARD
   OF HEARING
Briarfield
Syke Ings
Iver
Buckinghamshire

Aims to assist and advise in every way possible those people who have lost part or all of their hearing after being normally educated and possessing normal speech

IVER, THE BRITISH ASSOCIATION OF THE HARD OF HEARING, *cont.*

Enquiries: To Hon. Secretary, by letter only

Scope: Information and help on problems arising from hearing loss and on hearing aids, lip reading tuition facilities, employment problems, provision of social life, holidays and week-end educational courses run by the Association
Secondary: Co-operation with Government Departments and Local Authorities in the provision and improvement of services for the hard of hearing. Study of the effects of hearing loss on individuals. Causes and cures of deafness

Publications: Hark (quarterly journal)
Leaflets on various aspects and problems of hearing loss
Occasional specialized papers; for example: Mental Health and the Hard of Hearing
Enquiry into the Servicing of National Health Hearing Aids
Directory of over 200 social clubs for the hard of hearing in Great Britain

---

KEIGHLEY
Yorkshire

760

THE BRONTË SOCIETY
Haworth Parsonage Museum
Haworth
Keighley
Yorkshire

Tel.: Haworth 2323

Enquiries: To Hon. Secretary, by letter only

Scope: Information in respect of the lives, associations and writings of the Brontë Family
Bronteana and the Bonnell collection of manuscripts

Stock: 800 books

Publications: Transactions (annually, contain well-informed articles, details of manuscripts, documents and Bronteana acquired, to stimulate a wider knowledge of the Brontë family)
Guide to Museum
Catalogue of Museum Exhibits

KEIGHLEY
Yorkshire

761

KEIGHLEY PUBLIC LIBRARY
North Street
Keighley
Yorkshire

Tel.: Keighley 2309 and 61453

Enquiries: To Librarian

Scope: Special collections: Local history
The Brontës. Snowden collection—political and social history of the late 19th and early 20th centuries
National subject specialization: Forms of State
Brigg manuscripts (mainly local history)

Stock: 128,000 books and pamphlets; 120 current periodicals

Publications: Select list of books on marriage and family planning. 1968
Law Library of Keighley and Craven Law Society deposited at Central Library

---

KEIGHLEY
Yorkshire

762

KEIGHLEY TECHNICAL COLLEGE
Cavendish Street
Keighley
Yorkshire

Tel.: Keighley 4248

Enquiries: To Librarian

Scope: Small collections of books on hospitals, nursing, law, sociology, economics, education, geography, history (social and economic), literature and the fine arts

Stock: 10,000 books; 2,000 pamphlets; 170 current periodicals

KEITH
Banffshire

763

BANFFSHIRE COUNTY LIBRARY
70 Mid Street
Keith
Banffshire AB5 3AF

Tel.: Keith 2221

Enquiries: To Librarian

Scope: Local history collection (all about Banffshire); Government

Stock: 270 books and pamphlets on local history, 170 on government

KEMPSHOTT
Basingstoke
Hants

See under **BASINGSTOKE** for
ILEOSTOMY ASSOCIATION OF
   GT BRITAIN & IRELAND (no. 65)

KENDAL
Westmorland

764

ABBOT HALL ART GALLERY
Kendal
Westmorland

Tel.: Kendal 2464

Enquiries: To Director

Scope: Permanent Collection; local artists, such as George Romney, Julius Caesar Ibbetson, Daniel Gardner and John Ruskin. Furniture by Gillow of Lancaster. Willing to help with any enquiries relating to cultural heritage of the Lake District. Temporary exhibitions covering wide range of decorative arts, old and new, from Roman pottery to modern sculpture and embroidery

Stock not available on loan

Publications: Quarto (quarterly magazine)
Exhibition catalogues
Historical Guide to Abbot Hall Art Gallery

KENDAL
Westmorland

765

JOINT ARCHIVES COMMITTEE FOR
   CUMBERLAND, WESTMORLAND AND
   CARLISLE
The Record Office
County Hall
Kendal
Westmorland

See no. 354

KENDAL
Westmorland

766

MUSEUM OF LAKELAND LIFE AND INDUSTRY
Abbot Hall
Kendal
Westmorland

Enquiries: To Director

Scope: Exhibition of local life through the ages

KENILWORTH Warwickshire **767**	THE BRITISH HORSE SOCIETY NATIONAL EQUESTRIAN CENTRE Kenilworth Warwickshire CV8 2LR	*Tel.*: Coventry 27192

The objects of the British Horse Society are to promote the interests of horse and pony breeding, to further the art of riding and to encourage horsemastership and the welfare of horses and ponies

Enquiries: To Secretary

Scope: All matters relating to the breeding, upkeep and training of horses and ponies, instruction of riders, general information on riding schools, riding clubs, the Pony Club, show jumping, combined training and dressage competitions and records, instructors', horsemasters', horse knowledge and riding examinations

No library

Publications: Books and pamphlets
Films (instructional and entertaining) and filmstrip lectures for hire

KENLEY Surrey **768**	THE ASSOCIATION OF CRICKET UMPIRES 4 The Towers Hayes Lane Kenley Surrey	*Tel.*: 01-660 6967

Training and education of cricket umpires in their craft and study of the laws of cricket and measures for the good of the game in general

Enquiries: To Hon. General Secretary

Scope: Cricket umpiring in general. Laws of the game including latest experimental laws and modern interpretations. Efforts are directed towards keeping umpires and players up to date and enquiries are dealt with. Information on the history of cricket law

Stock: 350 books and film 'A Look at Umpiring' available for sale or hire. All current cricket periodicals

Publications: Textbook: Cricket Umpiring and Scoring. R. S. Rait Kerr, revised by T. E. Smith
Monthly News Letter: Hows That?
Pamphlet: LBW and Forward Playing Batsman. T. E. Smith

KESWICK Norwich	*See under* **NORWICH** for KESWICK HALL (no. 1877)

KETTERING Northants **769**	KETTERING PUBLIC LIBRARY Sheep Street Kettering Northamptonshire	*Tel.*: 0536-2315

Enquiries: To Librarian

Scope: Special collection of books and material on Kettering and Northamptonshire

Stock: 93,000 books; 200 current periodicals (total stock)

Museum and Art Gallery

KETTERING Northants **770**	KETTERING TECHNICAL COLLEGE St Mary's Road Kettering Northamptonshire	*Tel.*: Kettering 5353

Enquiries: To Librarian

Scope: Management studies; medical laboratory technology; human biology
Stock: 7,200 books (total stock all subjects); 15 pamphlets; 35 current periodicals

KIDDERMINSTER KIDDERMINSTER PUBLIC LIBRARY, ART *Tel.:* Kidderminster 2478
Worcs   GALLERY AND MUSEUM
      Market Street
771   Kidderminster
      Worcestershire

Enquiries: To Borough Librarian and Curator

Scope: General stock, including music and gramophone records. Local studies appertaining to Worcestershire, Kidderminster and Richard Baxter. The Kidderminster collection contains a number of books relating to Sir Rowland Hill and to Cuthbert Bede. Textile design (part of the Carpet Collection). Fine arts (painting, drawing, prints)
Museum material relates to Kidderminster and areas within the immediate vicinity and includes: folk; costume; broadsheets; playbills; coins; tokens; medals; firearms and swords; pottery; other archaeological items; oriental ivories; and street furniture
This museum is also the official depository of the Kidderminster and District Archaeological Society excavation finds

Stock: 83,500 books; 200 current periodicals (total stock); 12,000 local manuscripts; 1,000 local photographs; 50 local microfilms; 1,400 gramophone records
Art Gallery: Exhibits, loan collections (Victoria and Albert Museum; Arts Council; Art Exhibitions Bureau) and works by individual artists and groups of artists. Local Art Clubs. Small permanent collection of paintings, water-colours, prints and drawings, including prints by Sir Frank Brangwyn

KIDDERMINSTER WORCESTERSHIRE COUNTY MUSEUM *Tel.:* Hartlebury 416
Worcs   Hartlebury Castle
      Kidderminster
772   Worcestershire

Enquiries: To Keeper

Scope: The library contains books dealing with subjects covered in the Museum and particularly with costume, crafts, industries and professions, social and domestic life of the 19th century and earlier; collections of Worcestershire books; and specialist files of cuttings relating to specific objects. Library formed part of the Tickenhill Collection

Stock: 4,000 books, pamphlets and reports; 4 current periodicals

Publications: Various catalogues and booklets on specific groups of material in the collection, for example, Costume Catalogue
Annual report contains articles on items in collection

KILMARNOCK KILMARNOCK TECHNICAL COLLEGE *Tel.:* Kilmarnock 0563-
Ayrshire   1 Holehouse Road   23501
      Kilmarnock
773   Ayrshire

Enquiries: To Principal, by letter and personal visit only

Scope: Heavily biassed towards engineering. About 60 books on medicine—mostly anatomy and physiology, for physical education and pediatric nursing studies—and a few on human biology. A section on animal anatomy and basic veterinary science is provided for agriculture students. Provision of material on social sciences and humanities is broad, although there are few

KILMARNOCK, KILMARNOCK TECHNICAL COLLEGE, *cont.*
specialized books, and amounts to about 580 volumes. This includes a rapidly-growing history section and a fairly large economics section. Information service on all subjects mentioned above

Stock: 5,800 books, pamphlets and reports

KINCARDINE
Alloa
Clackmannanshire

See under **ALLOA** for
THE SCOTTISH POLICE COLLEGE (no. 25)

KING'S LYNN
Norfolk

774

KING'S LYNN MUSEUM AND ART GALLERY *Tel.:* King's Lynn 3596
Market Street
King's Lynn
Norfolk

Enquiries: To Curator

Scope: History, archaeology (including industrial), geology, natural history, and topography, of King's Lynn and district

KING'S LYNN
Norfolk

775

KING'S LYNN PUBLIC LIBRARY
London Road
King's Lynn
Norfolk

Enquiries: To Borough Librarian

Scope: St Nicholas' Library Collection (founded 1617)
St Margaret's Library Collection (founded 1631)
Stanley Library Collection (founded 1854)
Local History Library (covering King's Lynn in detail, and the surrounding county district in general)

Stock: St Nicholas' Library and St Margaret's Library: 2,000 books; Stanley Library: 2,000 books; Local History Library: 2,000 books; 12,000 items filed

Publications: Stanley Library 1854–1964, a selection from the Stanley Library Collection now housed in the Central Library, King's Lynn (revised edition in preparation)

The St Nicholas and St Margaret collections include numerous donations and bequests made between the period 1617–1835, with items of incunabula and 16th century works
The Stanley Library, endowed by Lord Stanley, MP in 1854, includes books covering the 18th and 19th centuries

KINGSTON UPON HULL
Yorkshire

See **HULL,** Yorkshire

KINGSTON UPON THAMES
Surrey

776

GIPSY HILL COLLEGE *Tel.:* 01-549 1141
Kenry House
Kingston Hill
Kingston upon Thames
Surrey

Teacher training college

Enquiries: To Librarian

Scope: Education

Stock: 40,000 books (including School Practice Library); 126 current periodicals

KINGSTON	KINGSTON COLLEGE OF ART	*Tel.:* 01-549 0063 ext. 11
UPON THAMES	Knights Park	
Surrey	Kingston upon Thames	
	Surrey	
777	*Enquiries:* To Librarian	

Scope: Architecture; fine art; three-dimensional design
Secondary: Fashion; graphic design

Stock: 11,000 books; 4,000 pamphlets; 150 current periodicals. Stock not available on loan

KINGSTON	KINGSTON COLLEGE OF TECHNOLOGY	*Tel.:* 01-546 1126
UPON THAMES	Penrhyn Road	
Surrey	Kingston upon Thames	
	Surrey	
778	*Enquiries:* To Librarian	

Scope: Social sciences (sociology, politics, economics, management); language and literature (English, French, German, Spanish, Russian); law, education, history, geography
Secondary: Fine arts

Stock: 30,000 books; 6,000 pamphlets; 600 current periodicals

Publications: College Research report

Member of INESKA

KINGSTON	KINGSTON UPON THAMES PUBLIC LIBRARIES	*Tel.:* 01-546 8905
UPON THAMES	Central Library and Administrative Headquarters	
Surrey	Fairfield Road	
	Kingston upon Thames	
779	Surrey	

Enquiries: To Librarian

Scope: General medicine, the social services and the humanities
L.A.S.E.R. subject specialization includes: Microbiology; law (real and personal property; family law and inheritance); history and geography of the Near East (except Eastern Mediterranean), Siberia and Central Asia

KINGUSSIE	ASSOCIATION OF SKI SCHOOLS IN	*Tel.:* Kingussie 228
Inverness-shire	GT BRITAIN	
	c/o Badenoch Ski & Sports	
780	Kingussie	
	Inverness-shire	

Enquiries: To Chairman, by letter only

Scope: Ski instruction requirements by the general public, organized groups, and specific techniques or proficiency testing
Secondary: General ski-ing advisory service with particular emphasis on Scottish ski-ing and development

No library

KIRKCALDY	FIFE COUNTY LIBRARY	*Tel.:* Kirkcaldy 62351
Fife	East Fergus Place	
	Kirkcaldy	
781	Fife	

Enquiries: To County Librarian

KIRKCALDY, FIFE COUNTY LIBRARY, *cont.*

Scope: Agriculture; criminology

Stock: 355,000 items (total stock)

Publications: Bibliographies and booklets

KIRKWALL
Orkney

782

ORKNEY COUNTY LIBRARY
Laing Street
Kirkwall
Orkney

Tel.: Kirkwall 341

Enquiries: To Librarian

Scope: Large local collection of books, pamphlets and maps and a collection of over 200,000 documents and manuscripts of local historical interest from 1400 to 1850. Collection of books in the Norwegian language. Hugh Marwick Collection (Norse philology and history). Icelandic saga collection

Stock: 10,000 books; 2,000 pamphlets; 50 current periodicals (total stock)

Reports exchange arrangement with many Scandinavian universities and learned societies

LAMPETER
Cardiganshire

783

ST DAVID'S UNIVERSITY COLLEGE LIBRARY
Lampeter
Cardiganshire

Tel.: Lampeter 351

Enquiries: To Librarian

Scope: Subjects taught at College: Classics, English, French, German, history, philosophy, theology, Welsh, geography
Special collections: Tracts—political, religious, literary, chiefly 17th century (6,000 items)
Small manuscript collection including 15th century Books of Hours and Service books
Incunabula: more than 60 items representing most of the important centres of early printing
Early Welsh periodicals
Welsh Bibles, Hymnals, Catechisms, Ballads
Early printed books—some 500 STC items
No formal information service but the College and library does everything possible to answer all questions related to its history and to material in the library and in the archives

Stock: 63,000 books and pamphlets; 190 current periodicals

Publications: Trivium (annual learned journal covering wide range of arts subjects, with some bias towards Celtic studies)
Typescript hand-list of STC items

LANCASTER

784

THE KING'S OWN REGIMENT MUSEUM
Lancaster City Museum
Old Town Hall
Market Square
Lancaster

Tel.: Lancaster 64637

Enquiries: To Curator, by letter only

Scope: History of the King's Own Royal Lancaster Regiment

LANCASTER

785

LANCASTER & MORECAMBE COLLEGE OF
FURTHER EDUCATION
Torrisholme Road
Lancaster

Tel.: Lancaster 66215

Enquiries: To Principal

Scope: Science, engineering, commerce, catering, hairdressing, building and social sciences
Stock: 12,000 books; 155 current periodicals

LANCASTER	LANCASTER CITY MUSEUM	*Tel.:* Lancaster 64637
786	Old Town Hall Market Square Lancaster	

Enquiries: To Curator, by letter or appointment
Scope: The history and development of Lancaster and the decorative arts
No library

LANCASTER	LANCASTER PUBLIC LIBRARIES	*Tel.:* Lancaster 2800
787	Central Library Market Square Lancaster	

Enquiries: To Librarian
Scope: Extensive Lancaster local records collection. Cumberland, Westmorland and North Lancashire. Subject specialization includes: History of art; Free Church history
Fuller Maitland Music Collection of several thousand items
Stock: 7,500 books; 28,000 miscellaneous documents including 8,000 manuscripts
Repository for Manorial Records

LANCASTER	THE ROYAL GRAMMAR SCHOOL MEMORIAL LIBRARY	*Tel.:* Lancaster 2109
788	Lancaster	

Enquiries: To Librarian, by letter only
Scope: Texts and works of criticism in Classics, French and Spanish Literature, history, geography, economics, English; works of general interest in natural sciences, mathematics; standard reference works
Secondary: General readings suitable for 6th form, particularly modern novels, plays, poems in English, and some Hachette Livres de Poche
Stock: 13,000 books
Publications: The Lancastrian (School magazine)

LANCASTER	ST MARTIN'S COLLEGE OF EDUCATION	*Tel.:* Lancaster 3446
789	Bowerham Road Lancaster	

Enquiries: To Librarian
Scope: Education. Child psychology
Secondary: General psychology (not abnormal or clinical); sociology, welfare services, particularly in connection with children
Stock: 7,000 books and pamphlets; 50 current periodicals

LANCASTER	UNIVERSITY OF LANCASTER LIBRARY	*Tel.:* Lancaster 65201
790	Bailrigg Lancaster	*Telex:* 6511

Enquiries: To Librarian

LANCASTER, UNIVERSITY OF LANCASTER LIBRARY, *cont.*

Scope: Usual fields of university study, excluding medicine and law, but including business studies and operational research

Stock: 180,000 books; 2,250 current periodicals

LASSWADE
Midlothian

791

MINISTRY OF AGRICULTURE, FISHERIES AND FOOD
Veterinary Laboratory
Lasswade
Midlothian

Tel.: Lasswade 2025

Investigation and control of diseases of farm animals

Enquiries: To Director, by letter only

Scope: Diseases of farm animals, particularly poultry

Stock: 1,200 books; 40 current periodicals

Branch of no. 2276

LEAMINGTON SPA
Warwickshire

792

BOROUGH OF ROYAL LEAMINGTON SPA PUBLIC LIBRARY, ART GALLERY AND MUSEUM
Avenue Road
Leamington Spa
Warwickshire

Tel.: Leamington Spa 25873
Telex: O WA 6 25873

Enquiries: To Librarian

Scope: Good general collections in all fields of the social sciences and humanities
Special collections: Large local collection of books, manuscripts and illustrations (all varieties) for Leamington and Warwickshire. Fowler Collection of 20th century books relating to the theatre

Stock: 97,376 books and pamphlets; 68 current periodicals

Publications: Catalogue of Pottery and Porcelain Collection
Catalogue of an Exhibition of Ecclesiastical Heraldry

LEAMINGTON SPA
Warwickshire

793

MID-WARWICKSHIRE COLLEGE OF FURTHER EDUCATION
Warwick New Road
Leamington Spa
Warwickshire

Tel.: Leamington Spa 23144

Enquiries: To Librarian

Scope: Law, economics, education, social sciences, child care, geography, history, fine arts including history of 20th century art and embroidery

Stock: 7,000 books; 1,000 pamphlets; 50 current periodicals

Publications: Books on Social subjects (annually)
Index to Articles of Current Interest in Periodicals (monthly)

LECHLADE
Glos

794

KELMSCOTT MANOR
Lechlade
Gloucestershire

See no. 1598

LEEDS

795

THE AMATEUR BASKET BALL ASSOCIATION   *Tel.:* Leeds 31751 ext. 282
Physical Education Department
The University
Leeds 2

Enquiries: To General Secretary
Scope: Basketball
No library
Publications: Rules of the Game (F.I.B.A.)
Official Scorepads

LEEDS

796

BRITISH SOCIETY FOR RESEARCH ON AGEING   *Tel.:* Leeds 32799 ext. 475
Department of Medicine
'F' Floor Martin Wing
The General Infirmary
Leeds LS1 3EX

Enquiries: To Secretary
Scope: Biological and clinical ageing research
No library

LEEDS

797

CITY OF LEEDS AND CARNEGIE COLLEGE   *Tel.:* Leeds 59061
Beckett Park
Leeds LS6 3QS
College of Education

Enquiries: To Librarian
Scope: Education; child psychology; physical education, including medical gymnastics. General academic subjects
Secondary: Carnegie historical collection of physical education books published before 1946 (about 750 titles)
Stock: 50,000 books and pamphlets; 280 current periodicals
Publications: Catalogue of the Carnegie Historical Collection

LEEDS

798

HORSFORTH URBAN DISTRICT COUNCIL   *Tel.:* Horsforth 2807
Public Library
Town Street
Horsforth
Leeds LS18 5BL

Enquiries: To Librarian
Scope: Subject specialization: Monopolies and restrictive trade practices
Stock: 29,000 books; 24 current periodicals (total stock)

LEEDS

799

JAMES GRAHAM COLLEGE OF EDUCATION   *Tel.:* Leeds 636691 ext. 34
Lawns House
Chapel Lane
Farnley
Leeds 12

Enquiries: To Librarian, by letter only

LEEDS, JAMES GRAHAM COLLEGE OF EDUCATION, *cont.*

Scope: The Library collection is biased towards education, philosophy, theory, and practical application, and the education aspect of specific subjects
Secondary: Teaching practice library

Stock: 20,000 books (including 6,000 on education); 160 current periodicals

LEEDS

800

LANGUAGE TEACHING INFORMATION CENTRE   *Tel.:* Leeds 629361
31 Harrogate Road
Leeds 7

Enquiries: To Information Officer

Scope: Information to anyone interested (usually teachers, students, and administrators) on language teaching materials in French, German, Spanish and Russian
Linguistics and Language Teaching
Linguistics (general, grammar, vocabulary, general phonetics and phonology, psychology and language, semantics). Language Teaching (general, primary, audio-visual techniques and equipment, the language laboratory, programmed learning, hearing and speaking, reading and writing, psychology, testing, teacher training)
Bibliographies and source lists. Periodicals
Teaching Materials
Reference and practice materials (dictionaries and vocabularies, grammars, phonetics and pronunciation practice, oral and written exercises and tests, conversation and oral and written composition). Textbook Courses (primary, secondary, post-secondary). Audio-visual and audio-lingual materials (primary, primary-secondary, secondary and adult). Visual and audio aids (wallcharts, posters and flashcards, filmstrips, slides and films, gramophone records and tapes). Activities (songs and dances, games and other activities). Readers (early stages—prose, early stages—verse and drama, later stages—prose, later stages—verse and drama). Background and cultural information (general, social sciences, the arts, science and technology)
Mother tongue materials (language course textbooks, grammar course textbooks, geography textbooks, history textbooks, miscellaneous textbooks, general readers and anthologies, children's reference)

Stock: 2,000 books (excluding those belonging with audio-visual/audio-lingual courses); 15 current periodicals; 130 audio-visual and audio-lingual courses; 150 supplementary sets of wall-pictures, film-strips, sets of slides, gramophone records, tapes

Publications: The Library Catalogue, 1967, is available with up-dating supplements from Publications Section, Micklegate House, Micklegate, York

LEEDS

801

THE LEEDS CITY ART GALLERIES   *Tel.:* Leeds 647321 and
(incorporating Temple Newsam House, Leeds City Art   641358
    Gallery, Lotherton Hall)
Temple Newsam House
Leeds LS15 0AE

Enquiries: To Director

Scope: Collections of pictures, furniture, silver, English and Chinese pottery and porcelain (including a fine collection of Leeds cream coloured earthenware); expanding collection of 19th and 20th century decorative arts. The Print Room at the City Art Gallery houses the Agnes and Norman Lupton Bequest of English watercolours, their collection of Rembrandt etchings and the Sidney D. Kitson Bequest of Cotman watercolours and drawings

Publications: Leeds Arts Calendar (published twice each year)
Catalogue of Paintings, Artists born before 1800

Booklets: Temple Newsam House
Lotherton Hall
English Watercolours
Chinese Pottery and Porcelain
Exhibition Catalogues (back numbers of some are available)

LEEDS
802

LEEDS CITY LIBRARIES *Tel.:* Leeds 31301
Central Library
Municipal Buildings
Leeds LS1 3AB

Enquiries: To Librarian

Scope: *Reference Library:* All subjects not covered by Library of Commerce, Science and Technology, Art Library and Music Library. *Special collections:* Local history; Gott Bequest (early gardening books); Yorkshire Ramblers' Club Library (mountaineering, speleology); Leeds Philatelic Society Library; Porton Collection (Judaica); Gascoigne Collection (military and naval history); National Background Collection Scheme 1640–1649; National Subject Specialization Scheme: International law, constitutional law

Art Library: Fine arts. *Special collections:* Leeds pottery; Sanderson Collection (19th century fashion plates and periodicals). Jointly with City Art Gallery: Extensive collection of English watercolours and drawings; Kitson Collection of Cotman drawings; Rembrandt etchings.

Music Library: Includes Taphouse Collection (17th and 18th century music and books on music)

Archives Collection (see no. 803)

Stock: Reference Library: 234,000 books and pamphlets; 660 current periodicals
Art Library: 20,000 books and pamphlets; 70 current periodicals
Music Library: 31,800 books and pamphlets; 35 current periodicals; 13,000 gramophone records
All H.M.S.O. publications. UN Official Records. Depository Library for UNESCO publications

Publications: Print Room and Art Library Bulletin (quarterly)

LEEDS
803

LEEDS CITY LIBRARIES *Tel.:* Leeds 628339
ARCHIVES DEPARTMENT
Sheepscar Library
Chapeltown Road
Leeds LS7 3AP

Enquiries: To Archivist

Scope: Older official records of the City of Leeds and certain other classes of records concerning the Northern Section of the West Riding including diocesan, probate, parish, family, estate and business archives. For the contents of this department and arrangements for local archives in the area, reference may be made to *A Brief Guide to Yorkshire Record Offices* 1968 (published by the Borthwick Institute of Historical Research) (no. 2311)

LEEDS
804

LEEDS (OLD) LIBRARY *Tel.:* Leeds 23071
18 Commercial Street
Leeds LS1 6AL

Proprietary Library

Enquiries: To Librarian

215

LEEDS, LEEDS (OLD) LIBRARY, *cont.*

Scope: The Library has a general arts bias. As it has been in existence for 200 years the stock is particularly strong in 18th and 19th century material. There is a fine collection of rare fiction and complete runs of early periodicals

Stock: 106,000 books; 61 current periodicals. Stock not available on loan

LEEDS

805

LEEDS POLYTECHNIC *Tel.:* Leeds 36191
Calverley Street
Leeds LS1 3HE

Enquiries: To Librarian

Scope: Art (drawing, painting, sculpture, design, graphics); architecture; landscape architecture; town planning; education; home economics; law; languages; literature in German, French, Spanish, Italian and Russian; social studies; psychology; politics; economics

Stock: 43,000 books and pamphlets; 366 current periodicals; 31,000 slides (art and architecture)

LEEDS

806

MEDICAL RESEARCH COUNCIL *Tel.:* Leeds 32799 ext. 487
ENVIRONMENTAL RADIATION UNIT
Department of Medical Physics
The General Infirmary
Leeds 1

The study of ionizing radiation in man and his environment

Enquiries: To Director

Scope: Measurement of natural and acquired radioactivity in man, biological samples and soils. Measurement of levels of ionizing radiation in the natural environment. Calculation of absorbed dose to bone marrow and other distinctive tissues in man from natural and acquired radioactive materials. Assessment of the biological hazards of ionizing radiation, especially leukaemogenic, carcinogenic and ageing effects. Study of the metabolism of elements in man using radioactive tracers and whole-body counting

Secondary: Development of ionization chambers, scintillation counters and thermoluminescent dosimeters to achieve the above objectives. Development of computer techniques for the analysis of complex γ-ray spectra and the kinetics of metabolites

Stock: 50 books; 100 pamphlets; 4 current periodicals. Stock not available on loan

LEEDS

807

MEDICAL RESEARCH COUNCIL *Tel.:* Leeds 32799 ext. 481
MINERAL METABOLISM UNIT
Wellcome Wing
The General Infirmary
Leeds 1

Research into osteoporosis and renal stone disease

Enquiries: To Director

Scope: Calcium metabolism and bone

Publications: Calcified Tissue Research (published by Springer)
Calcified Tissue Abstracts (published by Information Retrieval Limited)

LEEDS

808

MORLEY PUBLIC LIBRARY *Tel.:* Morley 2780
Commercial Street
Morley
Leeds LS27 8HZ

Enquiries: To Librarian

Scope: National subject specialization: Secondary manufacturing industries: economics

LEEDS　　ROTHWELL PUBLIC LIBRARY　　*Tel.:* Rothwell 2225
　　　　　　Public Library
809　　　Rothwell
　　　　　　Leeds LS26 0AE

Enquiries: To Librarian
Scope: Subject specialization: Industrial working and living conditions
Stock: 55,000 books; 2,000 pamphlets; 80 current periodicals (total stock)

LEEDS　　RUGBY FOOTBALL LEAGUE　　*Tel.:* Leeds 624637
　　　　　　180 Chapeltown Road
810　　　Leeds LS7 4HT

　　　　　　Control and development of Rugby League football

Enquiries: To Secretary
Scope: Rugby League football
　　　　No library

LEEDS　　THE THORESBY SOCIETY
　　　　　　Claremont
811　　　23 Clarendon Road
　　　　　　Leeds LS2 9NZ

　　　　　　Private Society to encourage an interest in the history of Leeds and district and for collection and publication of material relating to Leeds and district

Enquiries: To Librarian, by letter or in person only
Scope: History of Leeds and district. Genealogical enquiries not dealt with
Stock: 5,000 books and pamphlets; 17 current periodicals; pictures and maps
Publications: Thoresby Society Publications

LEEDS　　TRINITY AND ALL SAINTS COLLEGES　　*Tel.:* Horsforth 4341
　　　　　　Brownberrie Lane
812　　　Troy
　　　　　　Horsforth
　　　　　　Leeds LS18 5HD

　　　　　　Roman Catholic Colleges of Education

Enquiries: To Librarian
Scope: Divinity, social sciences (geography, economics, history, sociology, psychology, home economics), languages (linguistics, English, French, Spanish), science (mathematics, biology physics, chemistry), communications (instructional media, CCTV), creative arts (art and design, drama, human movement, physical education, music), education, local area studies
Stock: 30,000 books; 5,000 pamphlets; 300 current periodicals. Multi-media instructional teaching aids, filmstrips and slides, records, tapes, illustrations, study kits, models

LEEDS　　UNIVERSITY OF LEEDS　　*Tel.:* Leeds 31751 ext. 6556
　　　　　　THE BROTHERTON LIBRARY
813　　　The University
　　　　　　Leeds LS2 9JT

Enquiries: To the Librarian

LEEDS, UNIVERSITY OF LEEDS, THE BROTHERTON LIBRARY, *cont.*

Scope: Collections cover all subjects, other than those mentioned in separate entries (no. 814–817) in the social sciences and humanities which the teaching and research of the University involve including: bibliography, Chinese studies (modern), classics, economics, English, French, general language and literature, geography, German, history, Italian, linguistics, music, philosophy, politics, Portuguese, Semitics (including modern Arabic), Slavonic and Russian studies, sociology, Spanish and theology

No developed information service is provided, but enquiries are accepted

Special collections include: Anglo-French collection (French translations of English literature to 1805); Blanche Leigh and Preston collections of historical books on cookery and domestic management; Brotherton Collection (general rare-book collection with special interests in English literature of late 17th, early 18th, and late 19th centuries, and in Romany literature); Icelandic and Old Norse; Roth collection of Judaica; Whitaker collection of atlases

Stock: 470,000 volumes; 144,000 pamphlets; 4,800 current periodicals, all including sciences but excluding rare book collection (the Brotherton Collection)

LEEDS

814

UNIVERSITY OF LEEDS
THE DENTAL LIBRARY
The School of Dentistry
Blundell Street
Leeds LS1 3EU

Tel.: Leeds 32006

Enquiries: To Librarian-in-charge

Scope: Collections cover all aspects of dentistry. No developed information service is provided but enquiries are accepted

Stock: 3,800 volumes; 800 pamphlets; 76 current periodicals

See also no. 813

LEEDS

815

UNIVERSITY OF LEEDS
INSTITUTE OF EDUCATION LIBRARY
The University
Leeds LS2 9JT

Tel.: Leeds 31751 ext. 6102

Enquiries: To Librarian-in-charge

Scope: Collections cover all aspects of educational theory and practice, and related subjects, in which teaching and research by the Institute are carried out. *Special collections* include: a general textbook collection and collections of obsolescent textbooks for classics (Latin and Greek) and for biology

Stock: 35,000 volumes and pamphlets; 300 current periodicals

Publications: Select book lists of the library stock, on relevant topics, are produced. The library is the editorial centre for *British Education Index*

See also no. 813

LEEDS

816

UNIVERSITY OF LEEDS
THE LAW LIBRARY
The University
Leeds LS2 9JT

Tel.: Leeds 31751 ext. 6398

Enquiries: To Librarian

Scope: Collections cover all subjects in which the Faculty of Law carries out teaching and research, including: English law, international law and jurisprudence. There is an extensive collection of English, Scottish, Irish, Commonwealth and United States law reports. No developed information service is provided but enquiries are accepted

Stock: 15,000 volumes; 490 pamphlets; 140 current periodicals (including law reports)

See also no. 813

LEEDS

817

UNIVERSITY OF LEEDS
THE MEDICAL LIBRARY
The School of Medicine
Thoresby Place
Leeds LS2 9NL

Tel.: Leeds 36171

Enquiries: To Librarian-in-charge

Scope: Collections cover all subjects in which the University Medical School carries out teaching and research, including the medical sciences, clinical medicine and public health. No developed information service is provided but enquiries are accepted

Stock: 46,000 volumes; 4,600 pamphlets; 750 current periodicals

See also no. 813

LEEDS

818

UNIVERSITY OF LEEDS
MUSEUM OF THE HISTORY OF EDUCATION
The University
Leeds LS2 9JT

Tel.: Leeds 31751

Aims to document and illustrate the history of education in England, to provide facilities for record and to encourage publication in the history of education

Enquiries: To Curators

Scope: History of education in England and Wales

Stock: 2,000 books and pamphlets, mainly 19th century school text and exercise books; 3 current periodicals

Publications: Journal of Educational Administration and History (twice each year)

LEEDS

819

YORKSHIRE POST NEWSPAPERS LTD
Albion Street
Leeds

Newspaper

Tel.: Leeds 32701

Enquiries: To Librarian

Scope: Files of newspaper cuttings on general subjects. Compiled primarily for the use of journalists. Indexes to *The Yorkshire Post* from 1873

Stock: 3,000 books. Stock not available on loan

LEEK
Staffs

820

LEEK PUBLIC LIBRARY
Leek
Staffordshire ST13 6DW

Tel.: Leek 2615

Enquiries: To Librarian

Scope: General stock, including local collection

LEICESTER

821

BRITISH COLLEGE OF ACCORDIONISTS
5 University Road
Leicester

Tel.: Leicester 23345

Holds Grade Examinations in Accordion Playing, and Diploma Examinations for teachers

LEICESTER, BRITISH COLLEGE OF ACCORDIONISTS, *cont.*
and performers on the accordion at many centres all over Britain, Malta and New Zealand

Enquiries: To Secretary

Scope: All information relative to the accordion, accordion teachers, accordion music, interest of local Music Festivals and the establishment of accordion classes therein. Contact with accordionists in other countries

No library

Publications: Syllabus of Grade and Diploma Examinations both practical and written
Schedule of Studies and Pieces for use in conjunction with Syllabus
Leaflets relative to various facets of the organization: for example, Constitution of the College 1969; BCA Approved Teacher Scheme

LEICESTER

822

CHARLES KEENE COLLEGE OF FURTHER EDUCATION
Painter Street
Leicester LE1 3WA

Tel.: Leicester 56037

Enquiries: To Librarian

Scope: Library service covering general education, modern languages, science and mathematics to 'A' level, business studies, mechanical engineering, automobile engineering, electrical engineering, and electronics to C. and G. level

Stock: 15,000 books and pamphlets; 150 current periodicals

LEICESTER

823

CITY OF LEICESTER COLLEGE OF EDUCATION
Scraptoft
Leicester LE7 9SU

Tel.: Thurnby 4101

Enquiries: To Librarian

Scope: General stock with bias towards the history, psychology and methods of education, teaching methods and all school subjects; also child study. Strong collection on the physically and mentally handicapped. Separate teaching practice library consisting of children's non-fiction, fiction and picture books

Stock: 50,000 volumes including pamphlets and music scores; 234 current periodicals; 1,200 gramophone records; 10,650 illustrations; 597 filmstrips

LEICESTER

824

CITY OF LEICESTER POLYTECHNIC
P.O. Box 143
Leicester LE1 9BH

Tel.: Leicester 50181

Enquiries: To Librarian

Scope: Three libraries:
Architecture and Building Library: Architecture; building; art teacher training
Art Library: Fashion and textiles, shoe design; fine art; graphic design; typography; industrial design; pre-diploma studies
Technology Library: Biology; chemistry; pharmacy; physics; electrical and mechanical engineering; business and management studies; textiles; physical education; mathematics and computer science

Stock: 39,000 books; 10,000 pamphlets; 17,000 slides; 7,000 illustrations; 1,000 maps

LEICESTER	LEICESTER CITY LIBRARIES & PUBLICITY DEPARTMENT	*Tel.:* Leicester 20644
825	Information Centre Bishop Street Leicester LE1 6AA	

Enquiries: To Librarian

Scope: Local History Department covering Leicester and Leicestershire
Music Library contains a substantial stock of musical scores

Stock: 40,000 books; 550 current periodicals (total stock)

Publications: Various, on Leicestershire history and topography

Leicester City Information Centre houses the headquarters of the East Midlands Regional Library System (no. 2347)

LEICESTER	LEICESTERSHIRE COUNTY LIBRARY	*Tel.:* Leicester 22012
826	Clarence Street Lee Circle Leicester LG1 3RW	*Telex:* 34307

Enquiries: To Librarian

Scope: General stock in the humanities, music collection, including orchestral scores and parts; Leicestershire collection, growing stock of current general titles in French, German, Italian, Polish, Spanish, Scandinavian languages and Russian
Secondary: Film and filmstrip library for educational use. Gramophone record library for educational use, including drama and speech recordings

Stock: 614,000 books and pamphlets including books on hire to Rutland County Library; 250 current periodicals (total stock)

Publications: Monthly booklists on a subject basis

LEICESTER	LEICESTERSHIRE RURAL COMMUNITY COUNCIL	*Tel.:* Leicester 62905
827	133 Loughborough Road Leicester LE4 5LX	

Enquiries: To Secretary

Scope: Village halls, erection, improvement and usage; playing fields, technical advice on provision, Parish councils, legal and administrative advice
Secondary: Preservation of rural England, local history and rural industries, technical advice and information

No library

Publications: Local History—The Leicestershire Historian

LEICESTER	LONDON RECORD SOCIETY
828	c/o Leicester University Library University Road Leicester LE1 7RH

Enquiries: To Secretary, by letter only

Scope: No library or information service, but enquiries relating to London history, particularly concerning source materials, will be answered

No library

Publications: Annual series of hitherto unpublished material relating to London history (4 volumes to date)

LEICESTER **829**	MEDICAL RESEARCH COUNCIL MICROBIAL SYSTEMATICS UNIT University of Leicester University Road Leicester LE1 7RH	*Tel.:* Leicester 50000

Enquiries: To Director, by letter only

Scope: Main information service on computer programs in numerical taxonomy
Secondary: Specific technical questions on systematics of microorganisms, mainly bacteria
No library

Publications: The Classification Programs Newsletter (listing computer programs for numerical taxonomy, issued irregularly)

LEICESTER **830**	MOUNT SAINT BERNARD ABBEY Coalville Leicester LE6 3UL Monastery of the Cistercian Order	*Tel.:* Coalville 2298

Enquiries: To Librarian, by letter only

Scope: Scholastic theology. Cistercian history
Secondary: Scripture and ascetic theology

Stock: 7,700 books; 25 current periodicals

LEICESTER **831**	UNIVERSITY OF LEICESTER LIBRARY University Road Leicester	*Tel.:* Leicester 50000

Enquiries: To Librarian

Scope: There are three Faculties in the University—Arts, Science (including engineering) and Social Science, and a School of Education with a separate branch library. The library stock reflects the faculty and departmental structure. The reference collection now numbers over 1,000 titles. *Special collections* include Transport History, English Local History and French Memoirs. New developments in the University include a Department of Museum Studies, a Victorian Studies Centre and a Department of the History of Art, and these are reflected in the library stock. The Library of the Mathematical Association is housed. Reference service mainly confined to own readers, but occasional bibliographical enquiries received by post are dealt with

Stock: 267,000 books; 16,200 pamphlets; 3,200 current periodicals

Publications: The University Press publishes monographs by members of staff and others, including three journals

LEICESTER **832**	YOUTH SERVICE INFORMATION CENTRE NATIONAL COLLEGE FOR THE TRAINING OF YOUTH LEADERS Humberstone Drive Leicester LE5 0RG	*Tel.:* Leicester 67855

Collects, indexes and disseminates by means of Digests and other publications, information on the Youth Service in England and Wales, with particular emphasis on development and experiment

Enquiries: To Head

Scope: Youth work in England and Wales
Adolescence (attitudes, behaviour, learning)
Leisure and recreational provision for young people
Out of school education
Training materials (youth work training)
Youth work overseas (particularly in Europe)

Stock: 5,000 documents; the periodicals of all national youth organizations in England and Wales, and those of professional associations in allied social work and educational fields

Publications: Youth Service Information Digest (abstracts, 10 issues each year)
Annotated Youth Work Book List (900 titles)
Annotated Youth Work Training Films (800 titles)
Research, Surveys and Theses in Youth Work, Adolescence and Allied Educational and Social Work Fields (950 titles)
Youth Work Project Summaries (1st edition of 25 studies complete, 2nd edition running)
Experiments and Development Projects in Work with Young People (1st set of 150 complete, 2nd set of 100 in preparation)
Conference Centres and Holidays for Youth (list of 650 centres)
Holidays and Work Camps for Youth (list of 150 organizations)
Teaching Materials in Youth Work Training
Counselling Services for Young People

LEIGH-ON-SEA
Essex

833

CONFEDERATE HISTORICAL SOCIETY
19 Montague Avenue
Leigh-on-Sea
Essex

Tel.: Southend-on-Sea 78075

Society to dispense information and encourage research on the American Civil War 1861–65

Enquiries: To Secretary

Scope: Will provide information on the American Civil War, either from own resources, or through contacts in this field. Library covers all aspects of this subject

Stock: 500 books and pamphlets

Publications: Quarterly Journal and Newsletter

LETCHWORTH
Herts

834

LETCHWORTH COLLEGE OF TECHNOLOGY
Broadway
Letchworth
Hertfordshire

Tel.: Letchworth 3911
Telex: 82139

Courses include training for technical teachers and instructors

Enquiries: To Librarian

Scope: Education, particularly technical

Stock: 1,000 books and pamphlets; 25 current periodicals. Stock not available on loan
Member of HERTIS

LETCHWORTH
Herts

835

LETCHWORTH PUBLIC LIBRARY
Broadway
Letchworth
Hertfordshire

Tel.: Letchworth 5646

Enquiries: To Librarian

LETCHWORTH, LETCHWORTH PUBLIC LIBRARY, *cont.*

Scope: L.A.S.E.R. subject specialization includes: Clothing and the clothing trades; chiropody
Local specialization: Town planning; the Garden City movement

Stock: 473 books (special collections only); 114 current periodicals
Member of Hertfordshire Association of Special Libraries (HASL)

LEWES   EAST SUSSEX COUNTY LIBRARY   *Tel.:* Lewes 5400
Sussex   Southdown House
    44 St Anne's Crescent
836   Lewes
    Sussex

Enquiries: To Librarian

Scope: Economics of agricultural production; economics of food manufacture. Esoteric associations and societies; social clubs; youth associations and societies; service clubs. Human anatomy; human physiology. Home economics; household utilities; housekeeping, laundering; and biographies of people engaged in the above fields. Sussex collection. Biology; pure science

LICHFIELD   THE JOHNSON SOCIETY, LICHFIELD
Staffs   c/o Guildhall
    Lichfield
837   Staffordshire

Enquiries: To Hon. Secretary, by letter only

Scope: Dr Samuel Johnson and his circle; their lives, works and times
Secondary: 18th century history and literature. Lichfield in the 18th century

Stock: 3,000 books; 200 pamphlets. Stock not available on loan

Publications: Annual Transactions

The Library is housed in the Johnson Birthplace Museum which is under the management and control of the Lichfield City Council

LICHFIELD   LICHFIELD CATHEDRAL LIBRARY   *Tel.:* Lichfield 2802
Staffs   1 Vicars Close
    Lichfield
838   Staffordshire

Enquiries: To Librarian

Stock: 10,000 books; pamphlets. Stock not available on loan

Publications: Catalogue. 1911

LICHFIELD   LICHFIELD JOINT RECORD OFFICE   *Tel.:* Lichfield 2177
Staffs   Public Library
    Bird Street
839   Lichfield
    Staffordshire

Enquiries: To Archivist

Scope: Information can be provided as to the scope of the records preserved in this office, and specific enquiries on matters relating to the history of the diocese, and aspects of parochial history and genealogy within the area can be answered. For lengthy enquiries, the enquirer must visit the office and use the records himself. The City Library is developing rapidly in local history, archives and ecclesiastical history, and this part of its stock is in the Record Office Search

Room, as is its collection (not strictly relevant to the record office) of books on Dr Samuel Johnson

Stock: 1,000 books; 50 pamphlets; 4 current periodicals

Publications: A Guide to Diocesan Records

The area covered by the diocesan records is Staffordshire, Derbyshire, parts of Warwickshire and Shropshire and (pre-1541) Cheshire and south Lancashire

LICHFIELD LICHFIELD PUBLIC LIBRARY *Tel.:* Lichfield 2177
Staffs Bird Street
  Lichfield
840 Staffordshire

Enquiries: To Librarian

Scope: Lichfield Joint Record Office. Contains the ancient Probate Records of the Diocese of Lichfield amounting to 250,000 documents dating from 1472–1858 and the historical records of the Diocese, dating from 1298 (*see* no. 839)
Johnson Birthplace and Museum. Collection of books and documents relating to Samuel Johnson (*see* no. 837)

LICHFIELD THE STAFFORDSHIRE REGIMENT REGIMENTAL *Tel.:* Lichfield 2971 ext.
Staffs   MUSEUM 64 and 44
  RHQ, The Staffordshire Regiment
841 Whittington Barracks
  Lichfield
  Staffordshire

Recounts the history of the Staffordshire Regiment and its predecessors

Enquiries: To Curator

Scope: War diaries and records of Battalions of the Regiment; some private diaries and a fair number of original documents
Secondary: A number of books, including some long out of print, dealing with campaigns in which the Regiment has fought. Army Lists from 1845

Stock: 800 books and pamphlets; 2 current periodicals

LINCOLN BISHOP GROSSETESTE COLLEGE *Tel.:* Lincoln 27347
  Lincoln
842 College of Education

Enquiries: To Librarian

Scope: Education and other subjects taught in the college. Teaching Practice collection of children's books

Stock: 35,000 books and pamphlets; 230 current periodicals

LINCOLN LINCOLN ARCHAEOLOGICAL RESEARCH *Tel.:* Lincoln 30401
    COMMITTEE
843 City and County Museum
  Lincoln

Enquiries: To Director

Scope: Lincolnshire archaeology: record and discoveries. Index of all archaeological sites in Lincolnshire available

LINCOLN, LINCOLN ARCHAEOLOGICAL RESEARCH COMMITTEE, *cont.*

Stock: Library shared with Lincoln City Libraries (no. 847) and City and County Museum (no. 846)

Publications: Occasional publications only

LINCOLN

844

LINCOLN CATHEDRAL LIBRARY   *Tel.:* Lincoln 21089
3 Vicars' Court
Lincoln

Enquiries: To Librarian

Scope: Valuable collections of theological manuscripts, early printed books, 17th century pamphlets, broadsides, and foreign literature. Some local topographical drawings and manuscript material
Secondary: Working library of 19th and 20th century theology, history, biography and local topography
There are three libraries, all administered by the Dean and Chapter—Honywood (Wren): Rare Books and Manuscripts; Canons' Library: Reference; and Wickham Library: Lending and Reference

Stock: 25,000 books; 2,500 pamphlets (mostly 17th and 19th century); 9 current periodicals

Publications: Catalogue of Chapter Manuscripts. R. M. Wooley. O.U.P. 1927
Catalogue of Foreign Books. W. H. Kynaston. O.U.P. 1937
Minster Pamphlets (series published by Friends of Lincoln Minster)

Enquiries relating to Archive material should be addressed to the Archivist, Lincoln Castle

LINCOLN

845

LINCOLN CATHEDRAL TREASURY   *Tel.:* 052-227 637
Lincoln

Enquiries: To Custos Thesauri, by letter only

Scope: Church Plate in the Diocese and County of Lincoln
Secondary: Plate in general. Magna Carta (the Lincoln Exemplar)

Publications: A booklet on Treasury

LINCOLN

846

LINCOLN CITY AND COUNTY MUSEUM   *Tel.:* Lincoln 30401
Broadgate
Lincoln

Mainly local collections illustrating the archaeology, natural history and local history of the city and county

Enquiries: To Keeper

Scope: Archaeology, natural history and local history of the city and county (new Natural History Gallery opened 1969)
Special collections: Prehistoric, Roman, Anglo-Saxon, medieval and post-medieval antiquities relating to the city and county
Secondary: John H. Smith collection of arms and armour
Lincolnshire Naturalists' Union Collection of natural history and related subjects

Stock: See under Lincoln City Libraries (no. 847)

Publications: Guide to the Greyfriars
The City and County Museum, Lincoln: a brief outline of the Collections
Postcards

LINCOLN

847

LINCOLN CITY LIBRARIES   *Tel.:* Lincoln 28621 and 27491
Free School Lane
Lincoln

Enquiries: To Director

Scope: In addition to the usual Public Library services, the library has two special departments: the Lincoln Medical Library (see entry no. 848) and the Tennyson Research Centre (see entry no. 854)

The Lincolnshire Local History Collection includes a large collection of books and pamphlets, maps, photographs, slides, manuscripts, illustrations and newspapers relating both to Lincoln and Lincolnshire

National subject specialization includes: Germanic languages; history of literature; American fiction; Germanic literatures. E.M.R.L.S. subject specialization includes: Books in Dutch

Stock: 190,000 books; 430 current periodicals, including about 50 in the Lincoln Medical Library

Publications: *See* under Lincoln Medical Library (no. 848), Usher Gallery (no. 855) and Tennyson Research Centre (no. 854)

Member of NANTIS

LINCOLN

848

LINCOLN MEDICAL LIBRARY
County Hospital
Sewell Road
Lincoln

Tel.: Lincoln 29921 ext. 404 and 379

Aims to provide a book, journal and information service on all aspects of medicine to doctors and nurses working in the Lincoln Hospitals, and to General Practitioners in the area

Enquiries: To Librarian

Scope: All aspects of medicine and allied subjects. Lengthy literature searches can be undertaken only for the staff of the hospitals

Stock: 800 books; 54 current periodicals

Publications: Monthly list of new books on medicine and allied subjects

The Lincoln Medical Library is administered as a department of the Hospital Library, which in its turn is a branch of the Lincoln City Libraries (no. 847). It is the medical library of the Lincoln No. 1 Hospital Group

LINCOLN

849

LINCOLN THEOLOGICAL COLLEGE
Lincoln

Tel.: Lincoln 25896
(Warden: 25879)

The college trains men for the Ministry in the Church of England

Enquiries: To Warden

Scope: Apart from a few books of antiquarian interest the Library is a general theological library

LINCOLN

850

LINCOLNSHIRE LOCAL HISTORY SOCIETY
(incorporating the Lincolnshire Architectural and
   Archaeological Society)
86 Newland
Lincoln

Tel.: Lincoln 24020 and 20956

Aims to promote within the area the study of history, topography, architecture, archaeology, dialect, manners and customs and other subjects of local interest

Enquiries: To Secretary

Scope: A small library of works on architecture, archaeology, ecclesiology, and local history. Apart from current periodicals, most of the works belong to the period 1850–1920. About three-quarters of the stock consists of periodicals on local history and archaeology, mainly received in exchange. Catalogues available in Lincolnshire Archives Office. It is the library of the

LINCOLN, LINCOLNSHIRE LOCAL HISTORY SOCIETY, *cont.*
former Lincolnshire Architectural and Archaeological Society. No information service in connection with library. No books may be borrowed or lent

Stock: 2,000 books, pamphlets and bound periodicals; 25 current periodicals

Publications: Lincolnshire History and Archaeology (annual journal of the Lincolnshire Local History Society, and successor to Reports and Papers of the Lincolnshire Architectural and Archaeological Society, and to *The Lincolnshire Historian*)

LINCOLN

851

LINDSEY AND HOLLAND COUNTY LIBRARY *Tel.:* Lincoln 26445
45 Newland
Lincoln

Enquiries: To Librarian

Scope: County Reference Library. Lincolnshire Local History collection including the Goulding collection on Louth and maps, pamphlets, illustrations and cuttings

Publications: Index to Lincolnshire Life (local history)
Agricultural Index

LINCOLN

852

MUSEUM OF LINCOLNSHIRE LIFE *Tel.:* Lincoln 28448,
LINCOLNSHIRE ASSOCIATION 26866 and 29864
Old Barracks
Burton Road
Lincoln

Records, conserves and displays material illustrating Lincolnshire life from Elizabeth I to present day

Enquiries: To Curator

Scope: Classified museum stores and display, including agricultural, industrial, commercial, social and domestic sections
Classified records, photographs and catalogues
Small reference library only

Publications: Exhibition catalogues

LINCOLN

853

ROYAL LINCOLNSHIRE REGIMENT *Tel.:* Lincoln 25444
   MUSEUM
Sobraon Barracks
Burton Road
Lincoln

Enquiries: To Curator, by letter only

Scope: Enquiries in connection with the Royal Lincolnshire Regiment and its history
No library

LINCOLN

854

TENNYSON RESEARCH CENTRE *Tel.:* Lincoln 28621
Lincoln City Libraries
Free School Lane
Lincoln

The Research Centre, at the City Libraries, consists of 4,700 books, letters and manuscripts relating to Alfred Lord Tennyson, deposited by the Tennyson family, and the City Library's own Tennyson collection. There is also much illustrative material, tapes, records, proofs and family papers. Written application should be made to work in the Centre

Publications: A catalogue is to be published in three parts. This will consist of:
Part 1. Libraries of members of the Tennyson family
Part 2. Books written by and about Alfred Lord Tennyson
Part 3. Manuscript material including letters

Associated with the Research Centre is a Tennyson Exhibition Room at the Usher Gallery (no. 855), where exhibits illustrate the poet's personality, his life and family background, the range and sources of his poetic output and his methods of work

The Tennyson Research Centre is supported in its work by the Tennyson Society and the Tennyson Trust which is a charitable trust receiving grants for the work of cataloguing the material in the Centre. The Society publishes annually the Tennyson Research Bulletin

See also no. 847

LINCOLN

855

USHER GALLERY   *Tel.:* Lincoln 27980
Lindum Road
Lincoln

General fine art collection

Enquiries: To Keeper

Scope: All fine arts
Special collections: Peter de Wint oils and watercolours, and personalia (local artist); Pictures of Lincoln and the County; Usher Collection of watches, miniatures, silver and porcelain; Collection of manuscripts, proofs, books and personalia associated with Alfred Lord Tennyson

Stock: See under Lincoln City Libraries (no. 847)

Publications: Catalogue of the Tennyson Collection with foreword and annotations by Sir Charles Tennyson, CMG
Catalogue of Watches in the Usher Collection
De Wint Picture Book
Postcards

See also no. 854

LISBURN
Co. Antrim

856

ARMY BRANCH LIBRARY   *Tel.:* Lisburn 5111 ext. 498
Thiepval Barracks, HQ
N.I.
Lisburn
Co. Antrim

This is a small general lending library for the use of Army personnel in Northern Ireland and the Garrison, civilian employees of the Ministry of Defence and army families

Enquiries: To Librarian

Scope: Stock includes a *special collection* on military science and history

Stock: 31,000 books (total stock). Stock not normally available on loan to outsiders, but information will be given by letter or telephone

LITTLE
WEIGHTON
Hull
Yorkshire

See under **HULL** for
THE INSTITUTE OF CRAFT EDUCATION (no. 732)

LIVERPOOL	THE ATHENAEUM	*Tel.:* 051-709 7770
	Church Alley	
857	Liverpool 1	
	Literary and Scientific Institution	

Enquiries: To Librarian

Scope: The information service and the resources of the Library are primarily for the use of Proprietors (Members). Other enquiries will be answered but are not solicited. There are *special collections* in the field of local history, particularly the City of Liverpool. Otherwise the scope of the Library is general

Stock: 70,000 books; 5,000 pamphlets; 20 current periodicals

Publications: Printed Catalogues:
Catalogue of the Athenaeum Library 1864
Supplement to the Catalogue of the Athenaeum Library 1864–1892
Athenaeum, Liverpool, Author-List 1892–1905

LIVERPOOL	BRITISH HOSPITALS CONTRIBUTORY SCHEMES	*Tel.:* 051-236 7051
	ASSOCIATION (1948)	
858	87 Lord Street	
	Liverpool L2 6PQ	

Encouragement and development of Hospital Contributory Schemes in England and Wales

Enquiries: To Secretary, by letter only

Scope: Information about Hospital Contributory Schemes in England and Wales
Secondary: Information about Convalescent Homes in England and Wales

Publications: Directory of Hospital Contributory Scheme Benefits
Directory of Convalescent Homes in the Provinces

LIVERPOOL	CHRIST'S COLLEGE OF EDUCATION
	Woolton Road
859	Liverpool L16 8ND

Enquiries: To Librarian, by letter only

Scope: Education, divinity, sociology of religion, new methods in primary school mathematics teaching
Secondary: Sociology, local history, drama, children's books

Stock: 28,200 books; 2,300 pamphlets; 212 current periodicals

LIVERPOOL	CITY OF LIVERPOOL MUSEUMS	*Tel.:* 051-207 0001
	William Brown Street	
860	Liverpool L3 8EN	

Local authority museum recognized as a teaching museum by Department of Education and Science

Enquiries: To Director

Scope: All activities of the Museum's departments: Archaeology, astronomy, botany, geology, ceramics and applied art, ethnology, invertebrate zoology, vertebrate zoology, shipping
Secondary: Conservation, design and photography, and Museum Education Service. Technical services

Publications: Liverpool Pottery
Coptic Textiles
Guide to Shipping Gallery
Earth before Man Gallery
List of Ship Models
Railway locomotive drawings
Egyptian Mummies in the Liverpool Museum
Lovelace Clock

LIVERPOOL CITY OF LIVERPOOL PUBLIC RELATIONS OFFICE *Tel.:* 051-227 3911
861 Municipal Buildings
Dale Street
Liverpool L69 2DH

Enquiries: To Public Relations Officer, by letter or telephone only
Scope: Public relations and publicity material relating to the City of Liverpool generally and to the work of the City Council and its Committees
No library
Publications: Liverpool '69 (Liverpool's international magazine)
Liverpool Industrial Handbook
Liverpool Official Handbook
What's on in Liverpool

LIVERPOOL CROSBY PUBLIC LIBRARIES *Tel.:* 051-928 6487
862 Central Library
Crosby Road North
Crosby
Liverpool L22 0LQ

Enquiries: To Borough Librarian
Scope: Subject specialization includes: Urology and renal diseases
Stock: 145,000 books; 3,000 pamphlets; 180 current periodicals (total stock)

LIVERPOOL EVANS MEDICAL LTD *Tel.:* 051-486 1881
 Speke *Telex:* 62673
863 Liverpool L24 9JD

Development and manufacture of vaccines, pharmaceuticals, biologicals, fine chemicals and veterinary supplies

Enquiries: To Librarian
Scope: Virology, immunology, pharmacy, microbiology, medicine, chemistry and veterinary science
Stock: 1,300 books; 52 current periodicals

LIVERPOOL F. L. CALDER COLLEGE OF EDUCATION FOR *Tel.:* 051-428 4041
 DOMESTIC SCIENCE
864 Dowsefield Lane
Liverpool 18

Training college for domestic science teachers

Enquiries: To Librarian
Scope: Domestic science; needlecrafts and textiles; education
Secondary: Science in relation to domestic subjects, with particular emphasis on nutrition; social science

LIVERPOOL, F. L. CALDER COLLEGE OF EDUCATION FOR DOMESTIC SCIENCE, *cont.*

Stock: 9,500 books; 950 pamphlets; 100 current periodicals

Publications: The History of F. L. Calder College of Domestic Science, 1875–1965. M. E. Scott

LIVERPOOL

865

HUYTON-WITH-ROBY HISTORIC SOCIETY
238 Kingsway
Huyton-with-Roby
Liverpool L36 9UF

The collection, arrangement and preservation of information and objects of interest, relating to the past and present history of the town, research into records and history of the locality and the encouragement of interest in the same, by meetings, lectures and other suitable means

Enquiries: To Hon. Secretary, by letter only

Scope: Information of all kinds, dealing mainly with the history of the area, including Churches, schools, transport, buildings, families, watch making. This service is provided for students (including postgraduate), Duke of Edinburgh Award Scheme, local schools and other similar organizations

Stock: 100 books; 40 pamphlets; 200 photographs

Publications: A Brief History of Church School Education in Huyton 1523–1969
A History of Huyton Village
Huyton Church Register Transcripts 1578–1759
The Huyton and Roby Turnpikes

LIVERPOOL

866

LIVERPOOL CENTRAL LIBRARIES
William Brown Street
Liverpool L3 8EW

Tel.: 051-207 2147
Telex: 62500

Enquiries: To City Librarian

Scope: More than 2 million books and several million items are in the stock of the Liverpool City Libraries, which are fully departmentalized by subject, each with a specialist librarian in charge. The departments most used for the humanities, social sciences and medicine include:
Picton Reference Library: The Reference Librarian is responsible for the Bibliographical Unit and the Philosophy and Religion Library
Hornby Library: The Librarian controls a magnificent collection of rare books; incunabula; first editions; illustrated and fine bindings; prints and autographs
Commercial and Social Sciences Library: The Commercial and Social Sciences Librarian has responsibility for literature on business training, commerce, law and government, and social sciences. The stock includes current government publications, directories, codes, customs, tariffs, trade catalogues, official statistics, and commercial newspapers
Special indexes are maintained of company statistics, trade names, commodities, manufacturers, geographical names, cable addresses, and law cases. An information bulletin is produced
Arts and Recreations Library contains on open shelves 20,000 volumes, many available for home reading. The Art Librarian has responsibility for literature on architecture, painting, drawing, sculpture, design, costume, photography, the theatre and recreations, and a bookplate collection by prominent artists
Music and Records Library has an open access collection of over 45,000 volumes comprising classical and modern scores and books on the history and theory of music. Orchestral parts and multiple copies of vocal works may be borrowed by societies and corporate bodies for an annual subscription of 21s. (£1·05) if located in Liverpool; 42s. (£2·10) per annum if non-resident

Records are available to societies and individuals for group listening. The annual subscription is 42s. (£2·10) if located in Liverpool; 63s. (£3·15) if non-resident

Commonwealth Library covers the literatures (including fiction) and histories and topographies of the British Commonwealth (including the United Kingdom) arranged by country. There are special sections for Wales, Scotland, Ireland, Canada, Africa, India, Australia and other countries

International Library is a reference and lending library of 100,000 books covering languages, literature, history and topography of the world except the British Commonwealth and United States of America. A translations advisory service is operated and a wide selection of dictionaries and other aids maintained

American Library covers the literature (including fiction) and history and topography of the United States of America

Record Office: The Archivist and Local History Librarian has responsibility for the Liverpool Corporation Archives and archives of firms, corporate bodies, societies and individuals, manuscripts, documents and deeds of local and national importance

Local History Library contains printed material for reference and home reading on all aspects, of Liverpool's history, with books on Lancashire and Cheshire

Stock: 2,135,000 books; 10,000 current serials

Publications: Liverpool, 1207–1957
Liverpool Under James I
Liverpool Under Charles I
New Books and Announcements (monthly)
Liverpool Bulletin
Some Fine Bindings Specially Commissioned
Engravings by Stephen Gooden, CBE, RA, RE
Music Catalogue
Catalogues of Non-fiction, 1952–55, 1956–59, 1960–63, 1964–66
Catalogues of Fiction added to the Lending Libraries, 1951–57, 1958–66, 1967
Children's Books, 1958, 1959–66
Ladsirlac Technical Bulletin (monthly)
Ladsirlac Commercial Bulletin (monthly)
Municipal Research Library Service

Municipal Research Library Service helps members of the City Council and staffs of Corporation Departments to trace relevant information by research into the holdings of the City Libraries and by contacts with national and regional libraries and information centres

Ladsirlac Industrial Library Services. Special extra-mural library services are available to LADSIRLAC subscribers. These services include literature searches, postal borrowing service and information bulletins (*See also* no. 2385)

LIVERPOOL

867

LIVERPOOL COLLEGE OF BUILDING
Clarence Street
Liverpool L3 5TP

Tel.: 051-709 0571

Enquiries: To Principal, by letter only

Scope: Technical information concerned with the Construction industry, including building, civil, structural and municipal engineering, public health engineering, building supervision, all branches of surveying, estate management, architecture, town and country planning

Secondary: Aspects of liberal education in the above fields and educational problems generally

Stock: 15,000 books; 3,000 pamphlets; 300 reports; 175 current periodicals. Stock not available on loan

LIVERPOOL 868	LIVERPOOL COLLEGE OF COMMERCE Tithebarn Street Liverpool 2	*Tel.:* 051-227 1781

Enquiries: To Librarian

Scope: Business management, commerce, languages and liberal studies, law, accountancy and economics, librarianship, printing, sociology, transport, company secretaryship, estate management, insurance and hospital administration. Houses the library of the Chartered Institute of Secretaries (Liverpool and District Branch)

Stock: 17,000 books and pamphlets; 300 current periodicals

LIVERPOOL 869	LIVERPOOL COUNCIL OF SOCIAL SERVICE 14 Castle Street Liverpool L2 0NJ	*Tel.:* 051-236 7728

The promotion and assistance of voluntary action and social welfare on Merseyside

Enquiries: To Secretary, by letter only

Scope: Voluntary organizations in Liverpool since 1909. Coverage varies a good deal and is chiefly in the form of files, minutes, annual reports and similar material. Specific enquiries dealt with from postgraduates only

Stock: Library very limited. Archival material can be lent in suitable circumstances, but best selected *in situ* by the researcher

Publications: Report on charitable effort in Liverpool. F. G. D'Aeth. 1910
Miscellaneous articles 1904–1923. F. G. D'Aeth
Liverpool Council of Voluntary Aid and Liverpool Council of Social Service Annual Reports 1910–1968
Liverpool Council of Voluntary Aid Quarterly Papers 1914–1930
Liverpool Quarterly 1932–1936
The Flowing Tide 1938–1939
Liverpool Council of Social Service Monthly Bulletin 1939–1965
Castle Street Circular. 1966 continuing
History of Liverpool Council of Social Service 1909–1959. H. R. Poole
Special but not Separate (Report on Liverpool Coloured). 1968

LIVERPOOL 870	LIVERPOOL MEDICAL INSTITUTION 114 Mount Pleasant Liverpool L3 5SR	*Tel.:* 051-709 9125

Enquiries: To Librarian, by letter only

Scope: The scope of the library covers all aspects of medicine and surgery. There is a representative historical collection, and special collections on orthopaedics and cancer

Stock: 35,000 books; journals and pamphlets; 380 current periodicals

Publications: Catalogue of the Historical Collection (to the end of the nineteenth century). Contains some 11,000 entries. 1968

LIVERPOOL 871	LIVERPOOL REGIONAL COLLEGE OF ART AND DESIGN Hope Street Liverpool L1 9EB	*Tel.:* 051-709 9711

Enquiries: To Librarian, by letter only

Scope: Fine art, graphic art, fashion and textiles, painting, sculpture, architecture, photography
Secondary: Printing (history and various processes), painting and decorating

Stock: 10,000 books; 110 current periodicals. Stock not available on loan

LIVERPOOL

872

LIVERPOOL REGIONAL COLLEGE OF TECHNOLOGY *Tel.:* 051-207 3581
Byrom Street
Liverpool 3

Enquiries: To Librarian

Scope: In addition to the main stock in science and technology, the library has small collections of material on pharmacy, medical laboratory technology, management studies, economics, social history, literature, the humanities, art and maritime law, national and international

LIVERPOOL

873

LIVERPOOL SCHOOL OF TROPICAL MEDICINE *Tel.:* 051-709 7611
Pembroke Place
Liverpool L3 5QA

Enquiries: To Librarian

Scope: Tropical medicine; tropical hygiene; entomology; parasitology, helminthology, protozoology

Stock: 12,000 books; 20,000 pamphlets; 1,000 reports; 300 current periodicals. Stock available on loan through the Inter-Library Loan service of the University Library, University of Liverpool (no. 878)

Publications: The Annals of Tropical Medicine and Parasitology (quarterly journal)

LIVERPOOL

874

MABEL FLETCHER TECHNICAL COLLEGE *Tel.:* 051-733 3314
Sandown Road
Liverpool 15

Enquiries: To Librarian

Scope: Nursing and childcare, anatomy and physiology, laboratory techniques, physics, chemistry, botany, zoology. Retail trade distribution. Costume clothing manufacture and textiles, dressmaking, millinery, ladies tailoring. Catering, cookery, waiting and nutrition

Stock: 5,500 books; 200 pamphlets; 90 current periodicals

LIVERPOOL

875

MERSEYSIDE CANCER EDUCATION COMMITTEE *Tel.:* 051-227 1429
9 Produce Exchange Building
8 Victoria Street
Liverpool L2 6QC
Public education about cancer

Enquiries: To Administrator

Scope: Provides speakers (mainly Doctors) to give talks, show films, and lead discussions on cancer, to any organized groups, free of charge. Provides leaflets, visual aids, filmstrips, posters and teaching kits for use in public education about cancer and arranges small exhibitions. Specific and general information provided as and when requested

Stock: 30 books (on cancer related to public education); 3 current periodicals

Publications: Pamphlets on cervical cytology, breast self-examination, smokers' self-test kits and cancer in general
Public Opinion on Cancer in Merseyside (Social Survey)

LIVERPOOL

876

MERSEYSIDE COUNCIL ON ALCOHOLISM
14B The Temple
Dale Street
Liverpool L2 5RU

Tel.: 051-236 0300 and 1372

Aims to combat the ever-increasing community problem presented by alcoholism through education, research and the provision of community service in the shape of Information and Advisory Centres on Alcoholism

Enquiries: To Executive Director

Scope: Literature aimed at the alcoholic in lay form to help towards the recognition of the illness and to be of assistance to those closely connected with the alcoholic. Annual Report gives statistics: medical and social services used; number of cases seen; whether male or female, married or single, children involved, classification of employment, town of origin. As the first Council to set up an Information Service many other cities and towns where Regional Councils are contemplated contact the Centre for advice. Educational service offered and used by Trainee Social Workers, Probation Officers, Students taking degrees or diplomas in Social Science and Student Nurses

No library

Publications: About Alcoholism. W. H. Kenyon

LIVERPOOL

877

NOTRE DAME COLLEGE OF EDUCATION
Mount Pleasant
Liverpool L3 5SP

Tel.: 051-709 7454

Enquiries: To Librarian

Scope: Education and psychology; divinity
Secondary: Standard works on general subjects including history, literature, music, art and social sciences
Special collection of children's books

Stock: 25,000 books; 500 pamphlets; 132 current periodicals

LIVERPOOL

878

UNIVERSITY OF LIVERPOOL
HAROLD COHEN LIBRARY
P.O. Box 123
Ashton Street
Liverpool

Tel.: 051-709 6022 ext. 136
(Librarian)

Enquiries: To Librarian, preferably by letter

Scope: Library has no separate information service as such, but through Faculty Sub-librarians (for Medicine, Veterinary Science and Dental Studies; Arts and Social Sciences; Law; Education) will provide information in these fields. Medical Librarian undertakes MEDLARS searches. Rare book collections consist of manuscripts, early printed books, fine press books, pamphlets published in England 1685–1727, a collection on gypsy folklore and literature and several manuscript archival collections such as the Rathbone papers

Stock: Total stock 688,000 books, pamphlets, bound periodicals and reports, of which 400,000 relate to medicine, the social sciences and the humanities; 5,500 current periodicals, of which 2,000 relate to medicine, the social sciences and the humanities

Publications: Guide to the Manuscript Collections in Liverpool University Library. 1963
Finding List of Scientific, Medical and Technical Periodicals. 1st edition 1966

LIVERPOOL	UNIVERSITY OF LIVERPOOL	*Tel.:* 051-709 7312
	SCHOOL OF EDUCATION LIBRARY	
879	Abercromby House P.O. Box 147	
	22 Abercromby Square	
	Liverpool L69 3BX	

Enquiries: To Tutor-Librarian

Scope: Education
Secondary: Collection of pre-1914 children's books

Stock: 40,000 books and pamphlets; 170 current periodicals

Publications: British government publications concerning education. J. E. Vaughan and M. Argles. 3rd edition 1969
A Guide to the Literature of Special Education. D. J. Thomas. 1968

LIVERPOOL	WALKER ART GALLERY	*Tel.:* 051-207 1371
	William Brown Street	
880	Liverpool 3	

Permanent collection of old master and modern paintings, drawings, prints and sculpture

Enquiries: To Director

Scope: Opinions are given to any person on paintings, drawings, prints and sculpture brought to the Gallery. General information on the history of art can also be given. The Library consists of catalogues, bulletins, annual reports related to the fine arts

Stock: 5,000 catalogues and bulletins; 1,000 reports. Stock not available on loan

Publications: *Permanent Collection:*
    Foreign Schools Catalogue—Text. 1963
    Foreign Schools Catalogue—Plates. 1966
    The Emma Holt Bequest, Sudley, Liverpool—Catalogue. 1964
    Some Watercolours & Drawings of the W.A.G. 1960
    Victorian Watercolours & Drawings in the W.A.G. 1966
    Old Master Drawings and Prints in the W.A.G. 1967
    Early English Drawings & Watercolours in the W.A.G. 1968
    Cleaned Pictures, 1955, with technical information by J. C. Witherop
    20th Century British Drawings & Watercolours in the W.A.G. 1969
Monographs:
    Alfred Stevens. 1951
    George Stubbs. 1951
Bulletins, 1951–1967
Loan Collection:
    Heywood-Lonsdale, 1959
    A Selection from the Ince Blundell Marble. 1961
    Masterpieces from Christ Church—The Paintings. 1964
    Masterpieces from Christ Church—The Drawings. 1964
Exhibition Catalogues   Postcards
Slides   Christmas Cards

LIVERPOOL	WILLIAM RATHBONE STAFF COLLEGE	*Tel.:* 051-709 1642
	1 Princes Road	
881	Liverpool L8 1TG	

College for the training of senior members of the National Health Service in management, and the running of refresher courses for other grades of nursing staff

LIVERPOOL, WILLIAM RATHBONE STAFF COLLEGE, *cont.*

Enquiries: To Principal

Scope: Library service covers hospital management and administration, nursing and medicine. Anbar Documentation service
Special Collection: Historical collection, uncatalogued, of books and papers relating to the foundation of district nursing in Liverpool, including letters between Florence Nightingale and William Rathbone (property of Liverpool Queen Victoria District Nursing Association)

Stock: 1,000 books; 24 current periodicals

LLANELLI
Carms

882

LLANELLI PUBLIC LIBRARY
Vaughan Street
Llanelli
Carmarthenshire

Tel.: Llanelli 3538

Enquiries: To Librarian

Scope: Subject specialization includes: Social welfare; careers; metaphysics
Secondary: Medical library of books and periodicals established in 1962 in conjunction with committee of local hospital medical staff and general practitioners

Stock: 120,000 books; 25,000 pamphlets; 270 current periodicals (total stock)

LLANGEFNI
Anglesey

883

ANGLESEY COUNTY LIBRARY
Shire Hall
Llangefni
Anglesey

Tel.: Llangefni 3262

Enquiries: To Librarian

Scope: Specializes in books of maritime interest. The County archives are administered by the County Library staff which enables the library to have at its disposal original sources of information on the local history of Anglesey

Stock: 150,000 books (total stock)

LONDON

884

ADVERTISING ASSOCIATION
1 Bell Yard
London W.C.2

Tel.: 01-405 3922

Enquiries: To Librarian (any careers enquiries answered by Education and Examinations Officer)

Scope: Advertising, copywriting, English, design and reproduction, marketing, economics, law, media and psychology, including related American, European and English journals

Stock: 3,000 books; various pamphlets and press cuttings; 100 current periodicals. Reference collection of historical advertisements

Publications: Many publications on all aspects of advertising
Advertising Quarterly
Advertising Activities (monthly)

LONDON

885

ADVISORY COUNCIL FOR THE CHURCH'S MINISTRY
Church House
Dean's Yard
London S.W.1

Tel.: 01-222 9011

Responsible to the Bishops and to the Church Assembly for the recruitment, selection and training of Ministers and for keeping under review all forms of accredited Lay Ministry, all in an advisory capacity

Enquiries: To Administration Secretary

Scope: All aspects of selection and training for the Ordained Ministry (Church of England). Details of reports on the ordained ministry before the Church Assembly. Advice to men interested in ordination

No library

Publications: Ministry—Spring 1969 Ordained Ministry Today
Women in Ministry: A Study A Supporting Ministry
Doing Theology Today
No Time to Waste (Mainly for Young People)
Prayer Material
Where Does the Money Come From?
Posters
Church's Ministry Series:
The Ordained Ministry. J. Townroe (An introductory pamphlet discussing the work of the ordained minister as such, within the context of the work of the Church today. This pamphlet is the key to the whole series)
New Area Ministry. T. Beeson The Hospital Ministry. N. Autton
The Overseas Ministry. B. Till A City Ministry. E. Saxon
The Rural Ministry. S. Hopkinson Urban Life and Ministry. T. Bridge
The Team Ministry. P. Croft Women's Ministry. A. Hopkinson
Ministry in Community. J. Young and B. Jeffrey
Group Ministry in an Urban Area. J. Hammersley
A Priest-Worker Ministry. D. Wilson

LONDON

886

THE AFRICA BUREAU *Tel.:* 01-836 4585
2 Arundel Street
London W.C.2

The Bureau aims to influence British public opinion in regard to African questions, and is concerned to strengthen good relations between the peoples of Britain and Africa and to promote policies which further the economic, social and political development of all communities in Africa

Enquiries: To Secretary

Scope: General information on African affairs and advice as to alternative sources of such information

Stock: 1,500 books; 25 current periodicals plus foreign and British newspapers

Publications: Africa Digest (bi-monthly journal)
Broadsheet (quarterly)
Justice in South Africa. A. Reeves. 1955
Tomorrow in Africa. The Africa Bureau Anniversary Address for 1957. Lord Hailey
Collaboration in Development in the New Africa. The Africa Bureau Anniversary Address for 1958. S. Caine
Facing 1960 in Central Africa. The Africa Bureau Anniversary Address for 1959. G. C. Brock
Land in Southern Rhodesia. K. Brown. 1959
Central Africa. Background to the Argument. F. Raven. 1960
This New Africa. Pride and Prejudice: Sense and Sensibility. The Africa Bureau Anniversary Address for 1962. J. Campbell
Conflict and Nationhood. The Essentials of Freedom in Africa. The Africa Bureau Anniversary Address for 1963. T. Mboya

LONDON, THE AFRICA BUREAU, *cont.*
Sanctions Against Rhodesia. The Economic Background. R. B. Sutcliffe. 1966
Economic Development and Poverty. The Africa Bureau Anniversary Address for 1966. E. F. Schumacher
The Character and Legislation of the Rhodesian Front since UDI. R. Austin. 1968
The State of Anglo-Tanzanian Relations. T. Huddleston. 1968
Zambia. The Moulding of a Nation. M. Faber. 1968
Rhodesia: The 'Fearless' Proposals and the Six Principles. J. Christie. 1969
Some Educational Problems of Africa. The Africa Bureau Anniversary Address for 1968. R. Birley
Bibliography of recent pamphlets on South Africa and Rhodesia

LONDON

887

AGENT-GENERAL FOR VICTORIA
Victoria House
Melbourne Place
Strand
London W.C.2

Tel.: 01-836 2656
Telex: 21813

Enquiries: Office of the Agent-General

Scope: General information on Victoria

LONDON

888

ALBANY TRUST
32 Shaftesbury Avenue
London W1V 8EP

Tel.: 01-734 5588 and 0960,

Aims to promote psychological health by collecting data and conducting research; to take suitable steps based thereon for the public benefit and to improve the social and general conditions necessary for such healthy psychological development

Enquiries: To Director

Scope: Information is supplied upon request to the Press and research workers. Personal advice and counselling services are operated for those seeking the Trust's assistance. Apart from available publications of the Trust, books are not available to outside enquirers, but the Trust's press cuttings files can be consulted upon request by *bona fide* research workers

Publications: Man and Society (Journal of the Albany Trust, twice each year)
Spectrum (AT/HLRS Newsletter)
The Albany Trust and its Work. New edition, 1969
Some Questions and Answers about Homosexuality. Third edition, 1969
Winter Talks 1962–63 (Lectures by C. H. Rolph, Dr W. Lindesay Neustatter, Kenneth Robinson, MP, Gordon Westwood, Anne Allen, JP, and Antony Grey)
Christian Society and the Homosexual. A. Grey
Talking points:
Homosexuality and the Sickness theory. L. Crompton
The Citizen in the Street. A. Grey

See also no. 1207

LONDON

889

ALPINE CLUB
74 South Audley Street
London W.1.

Tel.: 01-499 1542

Enquiries: To Secretary, by letter only

Scope: Mountaineering and mountaineering history. No information service

Stock: The largest mountaineering library in the United Kingdom, and possibly in the world. Stock not available on loan

LONDON **890**	AMATEUR ROWING ASSOCIATION 160 Great Portland Street London W1N 5TB	*Tel.:* 01-580 0854

Enquiries: To the Association, by letter only

Scope: History, technical aspects, future fixtures and past results of boat races. (Not boat construction)

Publications: The British Rowing Almanack (annually)
Technical pamphlets

LONDON **891**	THE AMATEUR SWIMMING ASSOCIATION 64 Cannon Street London E.C.4	*Tel.:* 01-236 4868 and 4750

Promotes the teaching of swimming in all its aspects, and organizes competitions under uniform Laws

Enquiries: To Hon. Secretary

Scope: The library contains a collection of historic documents relating to the Association

Publications: Many books

LONDON **892**	AMERICAN EMBASSY Grosvenor Square London W1A 1AE	*Tel.:* 01-499 9000 *Telex:* 22407 and 21718

Enquiries: To Office of Counselor for Commercial Affairs (letters) or Librarian (telephone)

Scope: The Commercial Library contains business publications, trade and economic statistics, commodity and product directories, United States Government and non-official publications, trade periodicals, and economic and financial journals

Stock: 5,000 books; 14,000 pamphlets; 80 current periodicals. Stock not available on loan

LONDON **893**	ANCIENT MONUMENTS SOCIETY 12 Edwardes Square London W.8	*Tel.:* 01-937 1414

Study and conservation of ancient monuments, historic buildings and fine old craftsmanship

Enquiries: To Secretary

Scope: Preservation of buildings of architectural or historic interest
Secondary: Ancient Monuments legislation, Town and Country Planning legislation, ecclesiastical legislation relating to the care of churches, organizations concerned with the preservation of buildings of architectural or historic interest

No library

Publications: Transactions, issued annually
Newsletter (occasionally)

LONDON **894**	THE ANGLO-CHILEAN SOCIETY 3 Hamilton Place London W.1	*Tel.:* 01-629 0178

The aim of the Society is to advance the education of the people of Great Britain about Chile by maintaining libraries, organizing film shows, art exhibitions, conferences, classes, lectures and similar functions and supplying information to schools, colleges, teacher training colleges and universities

Enquiries: To Secretary, by letter only

LONDON, THE ANGLO-CHILEAN SOCIETY, *cont.*

Scope: Chile, its people, history, language and literature, its institutions, folklore and culture, and its intellectual, artistic and economic life

Stock: 400 books mainly in Spanish; long playing records of Chilean music and Chilean folklore; films, filmstrips and coloured transparencies. A few Chilean newspapers in Spanish

Publications: Chilean News (quarterly bulletin)
Chile (booklet of general information)

LONDON

895

ANGLO-DANISH STUDENTS' BUREAU   *Tel.:* 01-493 1862
Berkeley Square House
8 Berkeley Square
London W1X 6HJ

Enquiries: To Secretary

Scope: Information on Denmark to English students (or those of any other nationality if they apply) on study, student transport and lodgings and to others on any general cultural information concerning Denmark. Most enquiries concern Danish architecture and sociology, including social welfare, prison reform and adult education. Information on English and other courses in England for visiting Danish students

No library

Club for young Danes and English

LONDON

896

THE ANGLO-JAPANESE ECONOMIC INSTITUTE   *Tel.:* 01-930 5567
342 Grand Buildings
Trafalgar Square
London W.C.2

Enquiries: To Director

Scope: Economic information unit, covering general questions on Japan

LONDON

897

ANGLO-JEWISH ARCHIVES   *Private tel. number of*
Mocatta Library   *Director:* 01-286 9002
University College
Gower Street
London W.C.1

Lists and/or collects documents of Anglo-Jewish historical interest, and prevents their destruction

Enquiries: To Director, by letter only

Scope: This organization is only in its infancy, but is actively collecting and/or listing historic material, received both from public bodies and from private individuals. It is hoped to compile a comprehensive Index to serve as a guide to the future historian. Anglo-Jewish Archives works under the auspices of the Jewish Historical Society of England, and of University College, London

See also no. 1383

LONDON

898

THE ANGLO-NORSE SOCIETY IN LONDON   *Tel.:* 01-235 7151
c/o Royal Norwegian Embassy
25 Belgrave Square
London S.W.1

Aims to further understanding, friendship and contacts between British people interested in Norway, and Norwegian people, and to assist in the learning of the Norwegian language

Enquiries: To Secretary
Scope: Advice on learning the Norwegian language
Stock: 500 books (travel 1800–1900); lantern slides (Norwegian scenes 1890–1914). Stock available on loan to universities only

LONDON   THE ANTI-COMMON MARKET LEAGUE   *Tel.:* 01-937 7686
899   79B Inverna Court
         London W.8.

Campaign against Britain ever signing the Treaty of Rome

Enquiries: To Secretary
Scope: The League has issued a number of leaflets and booklets dealing with general and detailed problems arising from membership of EEC

LONDON   APOSTOLIC DELEGATION   *Tel.:* 01-946 1410
900   54 Parkside
         Wimbledon
         London S.W.19

The representation of the Holy See in Great Britain

Enquiries: To Secretary
Scope: Documents of the Holy See, including papal addresses and encyclicals
Secondary: Information about Vatican City
Stock: 100 books. Stock not available on loan

LONDON   THE ARCHITECTURAL ASSOCIATION   *Tel.:* 01-636 0974
901   34/36 Bedford Square
         London W.C.1

Enquiries: To Librarian, from Members only
Scope: Architecture; building; urban and regional planning; tropical architecture and building
Stock: 20,000 books and pamphlets; 255 current periodicals; 20,000 classified periodical articles; 4,500 trade catalogues; 40,000 slides
Publications: Architectural Association Quarterly
Architectural Association Notes
A.A. Papers
New Additions to the A.A. Library Lists (three each year)
Guides to the A.A. Library and A.A. Technical Library (annually)
Periodical and serial holdings
Bibliographies (irregularly)

LONDON   ARCHIVES OF THE MORAVIAN CHURCH
902   5 Muswell Hill
         London N.10

See no. 229

LONDON   THE ARMOURIES   *Tel.:* 01-709 0765
903   H.M. Tower of London
         London E.C.3

National museum of arms and armour. The primary collection is of European arms and

LONDON, THE ARMOURIES, *cont.*

armour from the end of the Iron Age to 1914, but there is also a comparative collection of Oriental armour and weapons and an important study collection of firearms

Enquiries: To Master of the Armouries

Scope: European arms and armour, including firearms and ordnance. Oriental arms and armour. Large collections of arms and armour sale catalogues and of catalogues of other collections, both public and private
Secondary: The Tower of London. Military history. Fortification. Costume and military dress

Stock: 4,000 books and pamphlets; 20 current periodicals. Stock not available on loan

Publications: Arms and Armour in England. J. G. Mann (revised A. R. Dufty)
Short History of Japanese Armour. H. R. Robinson
European Armour in the Tower of London. A. R. Dufty, ed.
Royal Sporting Guns from Windsor. H. L. Blackmore (Exhibition catalogue)

LONDON

904

ARMS AND ARMOUR SOCIETY
40 Great James Street
Holborn
London W.C.1

Tel.: 01-405 7933

The study, preservation and collection of antique arms and armour

Enquiries: To Secretary, by letter only

Scope: Information service only on the subject of arms and armour; able to call on members for information in fields in which they are qualified, but all officers are voluntary

No library

Publications: Quarterly Journal

LONDON

905

THE ARMY CADET FORCE ASSOCIATION
58 Buckingham Gate
London S.W.1

Tel.: 01-834 1727

Administration of The Army Cadet Force

Enquiries: To Secretary, by letter only

Scope: Enquiries on the Army Cadet Force

No library

Publications: Cadet Journal and Gazette (monthly)

LONDON

906

ARMY CENTRAL LIBRARY
Institute of Army Education
433 Holloway Road
London N.7

Tel.: 01-272 4381

Enquiries: To Librarian

Scope: Military science; military history; education (particularly for adults)
Secondary: Drama (particularly play sets); educational psychology; foreign languages; history

Stock: 48,000 books; 2,300 pamphlets; 26 current periodicals

Publications: Drama Library Catalogue
Catalogue of Regimental Histories

Army Branch Library, Shorncliffe, Sir John Moore Hall, Shorncliffe, Kent: *Special collection* on Sir John Moore

LONDON   THE ARTHRITIS & RHEUMATISM COUNCIL   *Tel.:* 01-240 0871
907   FOR RESEARCH IN GT BRITAIN AND THE
                 COMMONWEALTH
                 8/10 Charing Cross Road
                 London W.C.2

                 Organizes research into the causes and treatment of rheumatic disease

Enquiries: To Secretary

Scope: Arthritis and other rheumatic diseases, incidence, research activities, treatment facilities (but not names of consultants)

No library

Publications: Handbooks for patients on Rheumatoid Arthritis, Osteo-Arthritis, Gout, Lumbar Disc Disorders, Ankylosing Spondylitis, Rheumatic Fever
Reports on Rheumatic Diseases (all supplied only to doctors)
ARC Magazine

LONDON   THE ARTS COUNCIL OF GREAT BRITAIN   *Tel.:* 01-629 9495
908   105 Piccadilly
                 London W1V 0AU

The Council's objects, as defined by the 1967 Charter, are to develop and improve the knowledge, understanding and practice of the arts; to increase the accessibility of the arts to the public throughout Great Britain; and to advise and co-operate with Government Departments, local authorities and other bodies on any matters concerned whether directly or indirectly with these objects

Enquiries: To Secretary-General, by letter only

Scope: The Arts Council Poetry Library is a library of books of modern verse in English published since 1930. The books are available to the general public for reference or loan

Publications: The Council's publications include catalogues of many exhibitions of the visual arts

LONDON   ASLIB   *Tel.:* 01-235 5050
909   3 Belgrave Square   *Telex:* 23667
                 London S.W.1

Aims to promote the development and systematic use of sources of information through research, training, consultancy and publication, and to provide information services for member organizations

Enquiries: To Librarian (for enquiries on information science and documentation) or Information Officer (for enquiries on any other subject)

Scope: *Library:* All aspects of library and information science and documentation including library planning, equipment, furnishing, mechanization and information systems planning
Secondary: Library: Editing and writing, rapid reading techniques, document reproduction, copyright
Information Department: Provides referral and enquiry services on any subject, in any depth. Enquiries are answered by referring to literature sources where these exist or to specialized organizational sources when appropriate

Stock: 10,000 books; 8,000 pamphlets and reports; 350 current periodicals; collection of trade literature on furniture and equipment designed for, or with relevance to, special library and information units

Publications: Aslib Proceedings (monthly)
Aslib Booklist (monthly)

LONDON, ASLIB, *cont.*
Journal of Documentation (quarterly)
Program: news of computers in libraries (quarterly)
Index to theses accepted for higher degrees in the Universities of Great Britain and Ireland (annually)
Aslib Directory, 3rd edition:
  Vol. 1, Information Sources in Science, Technology and Commerce. B. J. Wilson, ed. 1968
  Vol. 2, Information Sources in Medicine, the Social Sciences and the Humanities. B. J Wilson, ed. 1970
Handbook of Special Librarianship and Information Work. W. Ashworth, ed. 3rd edition 1967
Faceted Classification. B. C. Vickery. 1968
Periodicals and Serials, Their Treatment in Special Libraries. D. Grenfell. 2nd edition 196
Use of Mechanized Methods in Documentation Work. H. Coblans. 1966
Guide to Foreign-language Printed Patents and Applications. I. F. Finlay. 1969

Occasional publications (Research reports)
An Evaluation of British Scientific Journals. J. Martyn and A. Gilchrist. 1968
Use Made of Technical Libraries. M. Slater and P. Fisher. 1969
The Use of Bibliographic Records in Libraries. P. A. Thomas and H. East. 1969

Research and Training: Aslib also carries out a comprehensive research programme and offer advisory and consultancy courses, and training courses in information systems and operation
Subject Groups: There are at present 11 Aslib Groups, each representing a subject area o special function; they include audio-visual, biological, economics, social sciences, technica translations and transport
Abstracting and current awareness services: The Aslib library provides about 50% of the entrie for *Library and Information Science Abstracts* and will lend or provide copies of articles an reports abstracted. A current awareness service of recently published articles and reports in th field of information science and documentation is provided in *Aslib Proceedings*

See also no. 127

LONDON	ASSOCIATED NEWS SERVICE	*Tel.:* 01-353 6280
	30 Fleet Street	
910	London E.C.4	

Dissemination of news, features, and photographs, to all parts of the world

Enquiries: To Librarian, preferably by letter

Scope: Information can be provided on any subject on which cuttings are held. The list is comprehen sive and widely varied

Library of newspaper cuttings only, not available on loan

LONDON	ASSOCIATES OF THE LATE DR BRAY	*Tel.:* 01-387 5282
	SOCIETY FOR PROMOTING CHRISTIAN	
911	KNOWLEDGE	
	Holy Trinity Church	
	Marylebone Road	
	London N.W.1	

Forty-one libraries functioning in Great Britain and 26 overseas founded or aided by th Associates

See also no. 1592

LONDON 912	ASSOCIATION FOR JEWISH YOUTH 33 Henriques Street Commercial Road London E.1	*Tel.:* 01-481 1654

A central organization providing a variety of services for Jewish youth clubs and organizations, including sporting and cultural activities, advice and publications on observance of religious festivals, training courses, an advisory service, and an extensive library of Jewish and general books of interest to youth workers

Enquiries: To Deputy General Secretary, by letter only

Scope: Collection of books on all aspects of Judaism; for example, liturgy, sociology, history, religious observance. The intention is to provide resources in Jewish culture for members, senior members, managers, professional and voluntary leaders and members of committees. There is also a growing collection of pamphlets and books specifically on the subject of youth work, training, adolescence, general psychology and sociology, including books on arts, crafts and other programme activities

The library was founded in memory of the late Sir Basil Henriques and contains copies of material by and concerning him

Stock: 1,000 books; many pamphlets; reports; 17 current periodicals; all publications of the Youth Service Information Centre; film strips; records of Jewish music

Publications: Judaism in the Club

A.J.Y. Practical Papers: Celebrating the Festivals; the Problem member; Voluntary Service by Young People; Subscriptions and new Members; Parents and Youth Clubs; The Role of the Club Manager Today; Training and the Part-time Club Worker; The Club Assembly; Discipline in the Club; Finding and Keeping the Voluntary Club Worker; Self-Governing Groups in Youth Clubs; Synagogue Youth Clubs; It's Fun to be a Girl; The Club Notice Board; Organizing a Club Holiday; Democracy in the Club

Practical Papers: Collected edition

Illustrated booklets on the Jewish Festivals:

    The Chanukah Companion; The Club Companion (Holiday Edition); The Haggadah Companion; Tishri Companion; Exodus; The Pesach Companion; The Purim Companion; The Shabbat Companion

LONDON 913	ASSOCIATION FOR PROGRAMMED LEARNING AND EDUCATIONAL TECHNOLOGY 27 Torrington Square London W.C.1

Enquiries: To Secretary, by letter only

Scope: Specialist secretaries are in touch with most workers in the field, and enquiries can normally be referred to the appropriate expert

No library

Publications: The Journal of Programmed Learning and Educational Technology (quarterly, research papers and abstracts)

The Yearbook of Educational and Instructional Technology, incorporating Programmes in Print

Programmed Learning News

LONDON 914	ASSOCIATION FOR THE STUDY OF MEDICAL EDUCATION (TELEVISION SECTION) 80 Torridon Road Catford London S.E.6	*Tel.:* 01-698 3485

LONDON, ASSOCIATION FOR THE STUDY OF MEDICAL EDUCATION (TELEVISION SECTION), *cont.*

Studies the uses of television in medical education and provides advice on programme content, and evaluation

Enquiries: To Secretary, by letter only

Scope: Small specialist library, the main purpose of which is to indicate where further information can be found, on the subjects of television programme content and programme evaluation, and the specific use of television in medical education. Some material is available also on the use of other media and the general subject of personal and mass communication

Stock: 20 books; 200 pamphlets; 20 reports. Stock not available on loan

Publications: Postscript/Prescript. Monthly notes to accompany BBC programmes
Television in Postgraduate and Continuing Medical Education. 1969
Effectiveness of Broadcast Television in Medical Education. 1967
Small scale investigation of Responses of G.P.s to Broadcast T.V. 1968/69

The Television Section is one section of the Parent Organization which concerns itself with wider aspects of medical education in both the undergraduate and postgraduate fields. There is a small library maintained at 53 Philpot Street, London E.1

LONDON

915

ASSOCIATION OF BRITISH CORRESPONDENCE COLLEGES   *Tel.:* 01-606 0255

4/7 Chiswell Street
London E.C.1

Professional association of leading correspondence colleges, aimed at improving standards of postal tuition and co-operating with examining bodies and education authorities, and advising students

Enquiries: To Secretary, by letter only

Scope: Brochures of all Member Colleges and many non-members, listing subjects and examinations covered by correspondence courses. Association Handbook (revised annually) available to enquirers. Regulations of professional, academic and other examining bodies. Liaison with Department of Education and Science
Secondary: Information on suitable sources of postal tuition is given free to older students (all ages from 15 upwards)
No library

Publications: Annual handbook

LONDON

916

ASSOCIATION OF BRITISH THEATRE TECHNICIANS   *Tel.:* 01-387 2666

9 Fitzroy Square
London W1P 6AE

Enquiries: To Secretary

Scope: The Association provides information on matters relating to the technical aspects of the theatre through publications and offers a technical advisory service to prospective theatre builders, for which there is a fee
No library

Publications: Adaptable Theatres. 1962
Theatre Planning 2. 1967
Information Sheet 1 (Stage lighting recommendations for a small unenclosed end stage). 1968
Information Sheet 2 (Stage sound recommendations). 1969
Newsletter

LONDON	THE ASSOCIATION OF COMMONWEALTH UNIVERSITIES	*Tel.:* 01-387 8572
917	36 Gordon Square London W.C.1	

The Association works in a variety of practical ways to implement its aim of serving the interests of the universities of the Commonwealth, and, in particular, of promoting contact and co-operation between them

Enquiries: To Secretary-General

Scope: The Association will try to answer any reasonable enquiry about universities in Britain and the other countries of the Commonwealth, and about access to them. It is able to refer enquirers to standard sources of information in such fields as scholarships and entrance requirements. The library contains a good collection of such official publications of Commonwealth universities as Calendars, Annual Reports, Gazettes and Bulletins

Stock: 5,000 books, pamphlets and reports; 250 current periodicals

Publications: Commonwealth Universities Yearbook (annually)
Higher Education in the United Kingdom: a handbook for students from overseas and their advisers (every two years in conjunction with the British Council)
United Kingdom Postgraduate Awards (every two years)
List of University Institutions in the Commonwealth (annually)
A Compendium of University Entrance Requirements for First Degree Courses in the United Kingdom (annually)
Reports of Quinquennial Commonwealth Universities Congresses

LONDON	THE ASSOCIATION OF DISPENSING OPTICIANS	*Tel.:* 01-935 7411
918	22 Nottingham Place London W1M 4AT	

Association to protect and further the interests of dispensing opticians and to provide training schemes and examination

Enquiries: To Secretary

Scope: Most technical and semi-technical books dealing with optical dispensing
Enquiries about most aspects of ophthalmic instruments can also be dealt with

Stock: 100 books; 50 pamphlets; 10 current periodicals. Stock not normally available on loan except to members

Publications: The Optics of Contact Lenses. Bennett   Bifocals Without Tears. Swift
The Principles of Ophthalmic Lenses. Jalie   Ocular Prostheses. Warren

LONDON	THE ASSOCIATION OF OPTICAL PRACTITIONERS	*Tel.:* 01-629 1091
919	65 Brook Street London W1Y 2DT	

Aims to inform the public of the importance of eye care; to protect and promote the interests of members of the ophthalmic optical profession, in particular, their clinical and political independence and to encourage high standards of professional practice

Enquiries: To Secretary

Scope: Public information service on eye care includes press work, leaflets and films
No library

Publications: The Ophthalmic Optician (jointly with the British Optical Association, fortnightly)
Film: The Gift of Sight

LONDON   THE ASSOCIATION OF PUBLIC ANALYSTS   *Tel.:* 01-407 2067
               16 Southwark Street
920   London S.E.1
      Enquiries: To Secretary, by letter only
          Scope: Food legislation and food standards in the United Kingdom, United States of America and Canada
          Stock: 50 books; 50 pamphlets
   Publications: Journal of the Association of Public Analysts

LONDON   ASSOCIATION OF PUBLIC HEALTH   *Tel.:* 01-235 5158
               INSPECTORS
921   19 Grosvenor Place
               London S.W.1
               Professional and educational body
      Enquiries: To Secretary
          Scope: The Association is concerned with the subject of environmental health (which may be roughly described as the non-medical aspects of public health). It exists primarily to assist members by the provision of information and advice, but is also willing to give what assistance it can to members of the public
          Stock: Small library. Stock not normally available on loan
   Publications: Environmental Health (monthly journal)
               Annual Report on Environmental Health

LONDON   ASSOCIATION OF TEACHERS IN COLLEGES   *Tel.:* 01-387 1437
               AND DEPARTMENTS OF EDUCATION
922   151 Gower Street
               London W.C.1
               Aims to improve the education and training of teachers
      Enquiries: To Secretary
          Scope: Teacher training in England and Wales
               No library
   Publications: Education for Teaching (three times each year)

LONDON   ASSOCIATION OF TEACHERS IN TECHNICAL   *Tel.:* 01-387 2442, library
               INSTITUTIONS   ext. 107
923   4th Floor Hamilton House
               Mabledon Place
               London W.C.1
               Professional Association
      Enquiries: To Librarian
          Scope: Technical and vocational education and training; further education; higher education; teachers' salaries and conditions of service
          Stock: 1,000 books; 2,000 pamphlets and reports; 120 current periodicals; DES circulars, administrative memoranda, college and LEA letters; Statutory Instruments; industrial training boards' literature; courses bulletin of City and Guilds, Regional Advisory Councils and professional examining bodies
   Publications: Publications received at ATTI library (monthly)

LONDON 924	ASSOCIATION OF WORKERS FOR MALADJUSTED CHILDREN 13 Addison Park Mansions Richmond Way London W.14	*Tel.*: 01-603 0801

To bring together all people and organizations connected with working for maladjusted children

Enquiries: To Secretary, by letter only

Scope: Very small information service but the Secretary is prepared to answer any questions concerning working with maladjusted children if these are sent to him by letter

No library

Publications: Journal (twice a year)
Bibliography on maladjusted children

LONDON 925	ASTHMA RESEARCH COUNCIL 28 Norfolk Place London W.2	*Tel.*: 01-723 1252

Aims to seek to discover the causes and cure of asthma and to alleviate the sufferings from the disease

Enquiries: To Hon. Secretary, preferably by letter

Scope: It is not the function of the Council to advise individual enquirers, but in some cases the Hon. Secretary replies briefly to patients, and tries to help Press and scientific surveys. The daily pollen count issued to Press and radio comes under the auspices of the Council

No library

Publications: Exercises for Asthma and Emphysema (illustrated booklet)
Brochures

LONDON 926	THE ATHENAEUM Pall Mall London S.W.1	*Tel.*: 01-839 5004

Enquiries: To Librarian, by letter only

Scope: Holdings in all subjects covered in this volume of the Directory except nursing and veterinary medicine. Particular emphasis on history, literature, fine arts and theology

Stock: 70,000 books. Large collection of 19th century pamphlets. Stock not available on loan

This is a private library for the use of members of the Club, but the Committee will consider individual enquiries from students and researchers to view unique material in the Club's collection

LONDON 927	ATLANTIC EDUCATION TRUST ATLANTIC INFORMATION CENTRE FOR TEACHERS 23/25 Abbey House 8 Victoria Street London S.W.1	*Tel.*: 01-799 4471

Enquiries: To Information Officer

Scope: International relations and allied subjects, contemporary history and geography

LONDON	AUSTRALIAN HIGH COMMISSION	*Tel.:* 01-836 2435
928	The Strand London W.C.2	

Australian diplomatic and trade post in the United Kingdom

Enquiries: To Librarian

Scope: The Australian Reference Library provides a reference service on all aspects of Australian life and culture. The library has particular strengths in the fields of history, literature, and the social sciences, and holds a comprehensive range of Australian federal government publications and statistics, and of Australian bibliographical material. The Australian News and Information Bureau provides general information on Australia for the public and Press

Stock: 11,000 books; 6,000 pamphlets; 1,300 Australian current periodicals

Publications: The Australian News and Information Bureau distributes a wide range of news sheets, booklets and other informative material on Australia

The Librarian of the Australian Reference Library is also Liaison Officer in London for the National Library of Australia, Canberra

LONDON	AUSTRIAN INSTITUTE	*Tel.:* 01-584 8653
929	28 Rutland Gate London S.W.7	

Fosters cultural exchange between the United Kingdom and Austria

Enquiries: To Librarian

Scope: Austrian history, music, literature, art, folklore and theatre

Stock: 8,000 books mostly in German; 50 current periodicals; films, slides, records, photographs

LONDON	THE AUTOMOBILE ASSOCIATION	*Tel.:* 01-930 1200
930	Fanum House Leicester Square London W.C.2	*Telex:* 22185

Originally formed to protect motorists from the harsh and indiscriminate speed traps of the police, the Association provides today a comprehensive motoring service and continues to act as a guardian of the interests of motorists

Enquiries: To Central Reference Librarian, by letter only

Scope: All aspects of motoring, except commercial and sporting; safety. Archives of the Association
Secondary: Travel

LONDON	AVERY HILL COLLEGE OF EDUCATION	*Tel.:* 01-850 0081
931	Bexley Road Eltham London S.E.9	

Enquiries: To Librarian, by letter only

Scope: Education—theory and practice. Psychology—particularly child study and development
Secondary: General subjects of the school curriculum and methods of teaching

Stock: 43,000 books and pamphlets (including school practice books); 320 current periodicals. Stock available on loan only to the Inner London Education Authority Colleges and Schools

LONDON	BAKER & McKENZIE	*Tel.:* 01-242 6531
932	Crompton House Aldwych London W.C.2	*Telex:* 25660

Solicitors in International Law, specializing in Company Law and Taxation

Enquiries: To Librarian

Scope: Most United Kingdom law text books. Reports of tax cases and patent reports. Extensive tax library. Large United States section covering taxation, company law, balance of payments, antitrust. EEC section including CCH reporter. European section including European Taxation. International section including United Nations double taxation conventions, OECD restrictive practices

Stock: 800 books; 1,000 pamphlets; 30 current periodicals

LONDON

933

BAPTIST HISTORICAL SOCIETY   *Tel.:* 01-405 2045
4 Southampton Row
London W.C.1

Enquiries: To Librarian

Scope: The Library consists for the most part of works relating specifically to Baptist thought, work and history, including a number of manuscripts (mostly church books of certain local Baptist churches), some of which date from the 17th century

Stock not available on loan

Publications: The Baptist Quarterly

LONDON

934

BAPTIST MISSIONARY SOCIETY   *Tel.:* 01-935 1482
97 Gloucester Place
London W1H 4AA

Enquiries: To Secretary

Scope: Correspondence, reports, and other material relating to the establishment of Christian Missions in India, Pakistan, Burma, Ceylon, West and Central Africa, West Indies, North China and Brazil

Secondary: Films, film strips, tapes and books relating to the above

Publications: The Missionary Herald (monthly)

LONDON

935

THE BAPTIST UNION OF GREAT BRITAIN   *Tel.:* 01-405 2045
    AND IRELAND
4 Southampton Row
London W.C.1

Enquiries: To Secretary

Scope: Unique stock of books on Baptist history and principles

Stock not available on loan

Publications: Printed Catalogue

LONDON

936

BASIC IDEOLOGY RESEARCH UNIT   *Tel.:* 01-427 4243
12 Soho Square
London W.1

Enquiries: To Information Officer

Scope: The scientific investigation of basic ideologies and how they are produced. (A basic ideology comprises the more or less organized system of ideas and habits which determine a human being's general attitude and behaviour to life, to other human beings and to his environment)

Secondary: Sexual behaviour and censorship

LONDON, BASIC IDEOLOGY RESEARCH UNIT, *cont.*

Stock: Several hundreds of books. Stock not available on loan

Publications: The Conflict of Ideas. 1967
Christianity, Freethinking and Sex. 1968

LONDON

937

BATTERSEA COLLEGE OF EDUCATION *Tel.:* 01-228 2015
Manor House
58 North Side
Clapham Common
London S.W.4 *and*

Manresa House *Tel.:* 01-788 7771
Holybourne Avenue
Roehampton
London S.W.15

Teacher training college for home economics (secondary level) at Manor House and for primary schools, infant and junior (primary level) at Manresa House

Enquiries: To Librarian

Scope: Both parts of the Library are general in coverage, with special emphasis on education. In addition, that at Manor House specializes in home economics and that at Manresa House in all aspects of primary education

Stock: Books: 19,000 Manor House, 22,000 Manresa House; current periodicals: 121 Manor House, 202 Manresa House

LONDON

938

BAX SOCIETY
26 Rutland Court
Queen's Drive
London W.3

Promotes performance, recording and study of the music of Sir Arnold Bax (1883-1953)

Enquiries: To Hon. Secretary, by letter only

Scope: Modern British music (1880-1960). Music generally

Stock: 30 books specifically relating to Bax, 500 general; 10 current periodicals; 50 music scores of Bax, 250 others; many recordings; file of periodical articles

Publications: Bax Society Bulletin (quarterly)

The Bax Society itself has no library, but the Hon. Secretary is willing to answer any enquiries from his personal library, of which the details are given above

LONDON

939

BETH DIN AND BETH HAMMIDRASH LIBRARY *Tel.:* 01-387 5772 and 1066
Adler House
Tavistock Square
London W.C.1

A reference library for the internal use of the members of the Court of the Chief Rabbi

Enquiries: To Librarian, by letter only

Scope: All matters of Jewish religious law and jurisprudence. Library is entirely in the Hebrew language

Stock: 5,000 books; 150 manuscripts

LONDON

940

BIBLIOGRAPHICAL SOCIETY
c/o The British Academy
Burlington House
Piccadilly
London W1V 0NS

Society to promote study and research in the fields of historical, analytical, descriptive and textual bibliography, and the history of printing, publishing, bookselling, collecting and bookbinding

Scope: No information service. Library deposited at University College, London

Stock: 12,000 books and pamphlets

Publications: The Library (quarterly)
Annual monographs on bibliographical subjects

LONDON

941

BIOLOGICAL ENGINEERING SOCIETY   *Tel.:* 01-959 3666
c/o National Institute for Medical
Research
London N.W.7

The Society was founded to further the co-operation of workers in the fields spanning the physical and life sciences, and the members include biologists, medical scientists, engineers, physicists and mathematicians

Enquiries: To Hon. Secretary

Scope: Biological engineering. The Society is assisting in the development of an information retrieval system on this subject
No library

LONDON

942

BIRKBECK COLLEGE (UNIVERSITY OF LONDON)   *Tel.:* 01-580 6622
Malet Street
London W.C.1

Enquiries: To Librarian

Scope: Anthropology, classics, English, French, geography (including a small collection of historical geography and cartography), German, history, history of art, Italian, mathematics, philosophy, psychology (including occupational psychology and some management), sociology, Spanish, as well as the normal range of sciences (excluding technology and engineering)

Stock: 117,000 books; 800 current periodicals

LONDON

943

BISHOPSGATE INSTITUTE LIBRARY   *Tel.:* 01-247 2254
230 Bishopsgate
London E.C.2
Public General Reference library

Enquiries: To Librarian

Scope: London Collection: History and topography of London (10,000 books and pamphlets); collection of 300 London maps; 2,000 framed pictures, prints and drawings
George Howell Library: Books and pamphlets on economics, early history of trade unionism and labour movement (3,500 books; 6,000 pamphlets); large quantity of manuscript material, including Howell's Diaries, correspondence and autobiography; Reform League papers 1866–1869; International Working Men's Association minutes 1866–1869; notes on Trades Union Congresses. Period covered 1860–1890 in the main, with *no* material later than

LONDON, BISHOPSGATE INSTITUTE LIBRARY, *cont.*

1914. Biography and personal diaries of Ernest Jones, Chartist. Most manuscripts now on microfilm

George Jacob Holyoake Collection: Books and pamphlets on early co-operative movement (350 books; 440 pamphlets); manuscript material, including muster roll of Garibaldi's British Legion, with minute book of committee 1860–1861, diaries, correspondence, logbooks, proofs of early books and lecture notes. Period covered is 1830–1905, with emphasis on 1840–1870. Originals and microfilm

Stock: See above. Stock of general reference library is 3,200 books and 1,250 directories; 140 current periodicals and a total of another 250 in the Howell and Holyoake Collections

Publications: Catalogue of the London Collection (in preparation)

LONDON

944

BOARD FOR SOCIAL RESPONSIBILITY OF THE CHURCH OF ENGLAND *Tel.:* 01-222 9011
Church House
Dean's Yard
Westminster
London S.W.1

Informs and advises the Church of England on social, industrial and political questions

Enquiries: To Secretary

Scope: The Church of England's work:
Social work and social services; industry; international affairs, migration and race relations; drug addiction and alcoholism; recidivism (crime); medical and legal practices (abortion, euthanasia, fatherless families); police and community; housing; current legislation on social questions; and use and conservation of natural resources

Reference library only

Publications:
Police—A Social Study
Work in Britain Today
International Morality—an Agenda for the Churches
Abortion—An Ethical Discussion
Fatherless by Law?
Decisions about Life and Death
Sterilization
Punishment
Housing and Community
Threshold of Marriage
Church and Social Services
Law, Morality and Gospel. E. Rogers
Police and Community. L. Tyler
The Drug Subculture
Crucible (six issues each year)

LONDON

945

THE BOARD OF DEPUTIES OF BRITISH JEWS *Tel.:* 01-387 3952
Woburn House
Upper Woburn Place
London W.C.1

Watches over the interests and welfare of Jews in the British Commonwealth of Nations and, where necessary, intervenes on behalf of Jewish communities or individuals abroad

Enquiries: To Secretary

Scope: The office of the Board is always ready to answer enquiries or provide information in regard to matters relating to the Jewish community in this country

No library

Publications: Fate and Future of Soviet Jewry. J. Cang
Judaism and Inter-Group Relations. M. Domnitz
Shehita. B. Homa
Studies in Anglo-Jewish Statistics. M. Schmool

LONDON	BOARD OF INLAND REVENUE LIBRARY	*Tel.:* 01-836 2407 ext. 325
946	New Wing Somerset House Strand London W.C.2	

Enquiries: To Librarian, preferably by letter

Scope: Direct taxation, economics, law, financial statistics and foreign and commonwealth direct taxation laws and commentaries. *Special Collection:* Translations of foreign direct tax legislation

Stock: 25,000 books; 4,000 pamphlets; 20 reports; 250 current periodicals

Publications: Monthly Accessions Lists
Income Taxes Outside the United Kingdom (annual edition of 8 volumes, H.M.S.O.)
Double Taxation Agreements of the United Kingdom (1,000 pp. in 2 volumes, H.M.S.O.)
Overseas Tax Development Circulars (about 14 each year)

LONDON	BOARD OF TRADE	*Tel.:* 01-222 7877
947	1 Victoria Street London S.W.1	*Telex:* 27366

Government Department, responsible for trade and commerce, civil aviation, and merchant shipping

Enquiries: To Librarian

Scope: Mainly current material on the social sciences, with emphasis on trade, economics, political science and government, and home and overseas economic affairs. *Special collections* on merchant shipping and civil aviation (*see also* Statistics and Market Intelligence Library, no. 948)

Stock: 250,000 books and pamphlets; 3,000 current periodicals; 7,000 annuals. Nearly complete set from 1801 of House of Commons and House of Lords Sessional Papers, available for loan through the N.C.L.; 3,000 foreign language dictionaries (reference only)

Publications: Board of Trade Journal (weekly)
For others, see H.M.S.O. Sectional List 51 and 'Commerce, Industry and H.M.S.O.'

LONDON	BOARD OF TRADE STATISTICS AND MARKET INTELLIGENCE	*Tel.:* 01-248 5757 ext. 368 *Telex:* 886143
948	LIBRARY Hillgate House 35 Old Bailey London E.C.4	

Enquiries: To Librarian

Scope: Foreign economic statistics. Comprehensive in the field of trade statistics, selective elsewhere. British economic statistics. Foreign market information
Secondary: Population and other general statistics

Stock: 85,000 volumes of statistics, mainly serials; 12,000 catalogues of foreign manufacturers; 2,000 foreign trade directories (reference only); 4,000 current periodicals and annuals

Publications: Board of Trade Statistics and Market Intelligence Library

LONDON	BOOK DEVELOPMENT COUNCIL	*Tel.:* 01-459 7221
949	New Building North Circular Road Neasden London N.W.10	*Telex:* 261721

Aims to promote the increased use of British books overseas

LONDON, BOOK DEVELOPMENT COUNCIL, *cont.*

Enquiries: To Head of Research

Scope: Computerized lists of libraries and academics throughout the Commonwealth, Western Europe, Asia, Latin America, Africa (1,200 subject fields). Book trade periodicals, university calendars, education reports, library directories, educational syllabuses, and other information of use to the book trade

Stock: 1,000 books; 1,000 pamphlets; 25 current periodicals. Stock not normally available on loan

Publications: Area market reports
Select book lists

LONDON
950

BOOKS ACROSS THE SEA OF ENGLISH SPEAKING UNION
37 Charles Street
London W.1

Tel.: 01-629 7400

Receives, maintains and makes available books from the United States of America, (and some from Canada, Australia, New Zealand) and supplies in exchange books about England and English affairs to these countries

Enquiries: To Librarian

Scope: Americana: social studies, history, biography, literature and large regional collection. Some books not otherwise obtainable in Britain. American children's books, fiction and non-fiction
Secondary: Smaller similar collections of Canadian, Australian and New Zealand books

Stock: 17,000 books

Publications: Annotated quarterly lists of books received from America and of English books (supplied on request)
Periodic lists of Commonwealth books

LONDON
951

THE BOROUGH POLYTECHNIC
Borough Road
London S.E.1

Tel.: 01-928 8989

Enquiries: To Librarian

Scope: Sociology and Humanities Library for B.Sc. Sociology, Health Visitors, Sister Tutors and Teacher Training

Stock: 6,000 books; 2,000 pamphlets; 60 current periodicals; Collection of photocopies from out of print Sociology Journals, considered classic contributions to the Literature. History and philosophy of science, biochemistry and molecular biology in Main Library

LONDON
952

BOTSWANA HIGH COMMISSION
3 Buckingham Gate
London S.W.1

Tel.: 01-828 0445

Enquiries: To High Commissioner

Scope: Botswana
No library

LONDON
953

THE BRITISH ACADEMY
Burlington House
Piccadilly
London W.1

Tel.: 01-734 0457

The promotion of historical, philosophical and philological studies

Enquiries: To Secretary

Scope: The Academy, from an early date, decided not to form a library covering the fields of its interests. Instead, it has confined itself to retaining, for record purposes, a complete set of its publications and the publications it has supported

Publications: Proceedings of the British Academy
Presidential Addresses
Foundation Lectures:
   Albert Reckitt Archaeological lectures
   Aspects of Art Lectures (Henriette Hertz Trust)
   Chatterton Lectures on an English Poet
   Dawes Hicks Lectures on Philosophy
   Italian Lectures
   Maccabaean Lectures in Jurisprudence
   Master-Mind Lectures (Henriette Hertz Trust)
   Philosophical Lectures (Henriette Hertz Trust)
   Raleigh Lectures on History
   Sarah Tryphena Phillips Lectures in American Literature and History
   Shakespeare Lectures
   Sir Israel Gollancz Memorial Lectures
   Sir John Rhŷs Memorial Lectures
   'Thank-Offering to Britain Fund' Lectures
   Warton Lectures on English Poetry
Records of the Social and Economic History of England and Wales
Schweich Lectures on Biblical Archaeology
Sylloge Nummorum Graecorum
Sylloge of Coins of the British Isles
Corpus Vasorum Antiquorum
Early English Church Music
Auctores Britannici Medii Aevi
Lectures, papers, monographs and miscellanea

LONDON

54

BRITISH ALLERGY SOCIETY
Brompton Hospital
London S.W.3

Aims to advance the study of allergy, both clinical and experimental

Enquiries: To Hon. Secretary, by letter only

Scope: Enquiries from the medical profession dealt with
No library

Publications: Clinical Allergy (quarterly from 1971)

LONDON

55

BRITISH AMATEUR PRESS ASSOCIATION *Tel.:* 01-946 2122
9 Glendale Drive
Wimbledon
London S.W.19

Enquiries: To Hon. Publicity Officer, by letter only

Scope: Advice about private press printing and publishing, particularly in respect of member's publications

Stock: 120 books. Stock not available on loan except to members

Publications: British Amateur Journalist (quarterly)

LONDON	BRITISH AMATEUR WRESTLING ASSOCIATION	*Tel.:* 01-226 3931
956	60 Calabria Road London N.5	

Enquiries: To Secretary
Scope: Amateur wrestling
No library
Publications: Know the Game Wrestling

LONDON	BRITISH ANTARCTIC SURVEY	*Tel.:* 01-834 3687
957	30 Gillingham Street London S.W.1	

Mapping and scientific investigation of British Antarctic territory

Enquiries: Information Officer
Scope: British activities in Antarctic
Secondary: General polar exploration. Advice on sources of information
Publications: British Antarctic Survey Scientific Reports (monographs published intermittently)
British Antarctic Bulletin (collections of shorter papers on a variety of subjects, chiefly scientific, published 3 times each year)

LONDON	BRITISH ASSOCIATION FOR COMMERCIAL AND INDUSTRIAL EDUCATION (BACIE)	*Tel.:* 01-636 5351
958	16 Park Crescent London W1N 4AP	

To promote the better education of employees at all levels in industry and commerce

Enquiries: To Information Officer
Scope: Vocational training, further and higher education
Stock: 1,000 books; 1,000 pamphlets; 400 reports; 100 current periodicals. Items lent to members
Publications: BACIE Journal (quarterly) *and* BACIE Memoranda (7 each year), available to Association members only
Occasional handbooks

LONDON	BRITISH ASSOCIATION OF MANIPULATIVE MEDICINE	*Tel.:* 01-486 1471
959	32 Wimpole Street London W1M 7AE	

Enquiries: To Hon. Secretary, 3 Arundel Terrace, Brighton BN2 1GA, by letter only
Scope: Medical enquiries, British and foreign, including arrangement of demonstrations and tuition
Scope of manipulative treatment, indications and contra-indications, books and films on the subject
Secondary: Enquiries on such subjects as locomotor medicine, the treatment of minor joint injuries, spondylosis, the effects of posture, osteopathy, chiropractice, manipulation orthopaedic medicine, manipulative surgery, the manipulative treatment of rheumatism (including fibrositis)
No library

| LONDON | BRITISH BROADCASTING CORPORATION | Tel.: 01-580 4468 |
| 960 | MUSIC LIBRARY | |

Yalding House
156 Great Portland Street
London W.1

Provides a library and information service adequate for all the requirements of music-making (as distinct from commercially recorded music). The bulk of the effort goes, therefore, in service to orchestras, choirs, artists, and producers throughout the United Kingdom

Enquiries: To Music-Librarian

Scope: Data about availability and background of published and manuscript music used in BBC transmissions of live or pre-recorded music. Popular Music and Television each have their own music libraries and special librarians who give appropriate information. Enquiries from the public are filtered through the Programme Correspondence Section

Stock: 250,000 music sets; 4,000 books and pamphlets; 12 current periodicals

Publications: Music catalogues

The six regions all have local music libraries

| LONDON | BRITISH BROADCASTING CORPORATION | Tel.: 01-580 4468 |
| 961 | REFERENCE LIBRARY | |

Broadcasting House
London W1A 1AA

Enquiries: To Librarian

Scope: General Library including the technical and non-technical aspects of broadcasting. The non-technical material covers history, biography, surveys and statistics of broadcasting, mainly British. Other *special collections* include books on drama, film and music. Branch in Television Centre holds collection of over 300,000 illustrations on all subjects. Book stock is supplemented by various card indexes and files compiled by staff. These include indexes to articles in music, film and drama periodicals, reviews of plays and films, music programme notes, short story index and poetry index

Stock: 110,000 books and pamphlets; 1,300 current periodicals. Stock not available on loan except for material relating to broadcasting

Publications: Books about Broadcasting. Revised edition 1958, with supplement 1961

| LONDON | THE BRITISH CANCER COUNCIL | Tel.: 01-636 3291 |
| 962 | 2 Harley Street | |

London W1N 1AA

Promotes education on the subject of cancer and its prevention, treatment and after-care

Enquiries: To Information Officer, by letter only

Scope: To provide a better flow of information between workers in the medical, scientific and social areas at the professional level
To distribute information from the International sphere of cancer work. To provide authoritative information for the mass media on the subject of cancer
Facilities are not yet available for answering general enquiries from the public, but these will be developed

No library

LONDON, THE BRITISH CANCER COUNCIL, *cont.*

Publications: Monographs of Symposia on broad themes concerned with cancer will be published from time to time

It is intended to develop current-awareness bulletins as a future activity of the Council's information service

LONDON

963

THE BRITISH CANOE UNION *Tel.:* 01-580 4710
26/29 Park Crescent
London W1N 4DT

Governing body of the sport of canoeing

Enquiries: To General Secretary

Scope: Canoeing

No library

Publications: Choosing your Canoe and its Equipment
Canoe Handling and Management
Canoe Camping
The Eskimo Roll
Canadian Canoeing
Long Distance Racing
Canoe Building, Soft Skin and Moulded Veneer Canoes
Canoe Building, Glass Fibre
Guide to Waterways of the British Isles

LONDON

964

BRITISH CARIBBEAN ASSOCIATION *Tel.:* 01-248 8051
Bucklersbury House
Cannon Street
London E.C.4

Aims to strengthen the ties of friendship between the peoples of the Commonwealth Caribbean and Britain

Enquiries: To Hon. Secretary, preferably by letter

Scope: Information about race relations in the West Indies and Britain so far as Caribbean and British people are concerned

No library

Publications: Newsletter (twice each year)

LONDON

965

BRITISH CENTRE OF THE INTERNATIONAL THEATRE INSTITUTE *Tel.:* 01-928 2033
The Archway
10a Aquinas Street
London S.E.1

Non-governmental organization, set up by UNESCO. Primarily a liaison and advisory body, it acts as a clearing house for theatrical information and facilitates international exchange of professional theatre personnel

Enquiries: To Director, by letter only

Scope: General information on the British theatre, for example, State aid, the repertory movement, theatre for young people

No library

LONDON	BRITISH COMMITTEE FOR STANDARDS IN HAEMATOLOGY	*Tel.*: 01-743 2030 ext. 511
966	c/o Dr S. M. Lewis
Royal Postgraduate Medical School
London W.12	

Aims to ensure accuracy and interlaboratory comparability of data from diagnostic haematological procedures

Enquiries: To Secretary

Scope: Provides information to haematologists on specifications of instruments and materials used in Britain. Acts as information and liaison service for the International Committee for Standardization in Haematology, keeping on file all reports and reviews published by that Committee

No library

Publications: Papers in haematological journals

LONDON	THE BRITISH COUNCIL	*Tel.*: 01-499 8011
967	65 Davies Street
London W1Y 2AA	

To promote a wider knowledge of Britain and the English language abroad, and to develop closer cultural relations between Britain and other countries. In recent years the Council has concentrated on educational work particularly in developing countries in Asia and Africa; it advises and assists in English language teaching; runs or supplies about 200 libraries overseas; promotes educational and other exchanges; presents overseas the best in the arts in Britain. It is represented in 75 countries overseas, and has in Britain some 25 centres organizing welfare of overseas students and programming visits by recommended overseas visitors

Enquiries: To Director, Information

Publications: British Book News (a monthly guide to books published in Britain and other Commonwealth countries)
British Medical Bulletin (three times each year)
Higher Education in the United Kingdom (every two years)
Writers and their Work (every two months)
Pamphlets and pamphlet bibliographies: for example, Libraries in Britain; How to Live in Britain: a handbook for Students; English Literature from the 16th Century to the Present: a select list of editions; Public Administration: a select list of books and periodicals; The Novel Today

See also no. 968–973

LONDON	THE BRITISH COUNCIL
DRAMA LIBRARY	*Tel.*: 01-499 8011
968	97/99 Park Street,
London W1Y 4HQ	

Enquiries: To Librarian

Scope: The library has sections dealing with British plays, with dramatic biography, costume, stage design and architecture, theatre history, ballet, criticisms, essays, and technical and reference books. British Council staff, students, and visitors can borrow plays and consult reference books. Enquiries for information by foreign embassies in London are also dealt with either direct or by suggesting other possible sources

Stock: 4,000 items; 12 current periodicals

LONDON, THE BRITISH COUNCIL, DRAMA LIBRARY, *cont.*

Publications: Play Bulletin (a selective collection of press reviews of plays and productions in Britain)

See also no. 967

LONDON **969**	BRITISH COUNCIL ENGLISH-TEACHING INFORMATION CENTRE THE LANGUAGE-TEACHING LIBRARY 63 High Holborn London W.C.1	*Tel.:* 01-242 9020

See no. 967 and 1307

LONDON **970**	THE BRITISH COUNCIL HOME LIBRARY 59 New Oxford Street London W.C.1	*Tel.:* 01-240 2468

Enquiries: To Librarian, by letter only

Scope: Bibliographical enquiries on the humanities and social sciences and on British civilization and institutions
Secondary: Collections on British civilization and institutions, cultural relations, librarianship and of books on and bibliographies of countries in which the Council works overseas

Stock: 21,000 books and pamphlets; 230 current periodicals

The Library acts as a clearing-house for requests for international loans from certain overseas countries, and deals with bibliographical enquiries forwarded by British Council Representatives and Embassies overseas

See also no. 967

LONDON **971**	BRITISH COUNCIL MEDICAL LIBRARY 65 Davies Street London W1Y 2AA	*Tel.:* 01-499 8011

Enquiries: To Librarian

Scope: The information and library activities cover the whole field of medicine and the medical-social services and are directed to international agency fellows and British Council scholars studying in Britain, and to overseas consultants, research workers and public health administrators. The library specializes in literature relating to government and voluntary social services

Stock: 6,000 books and pamphlets; 400 current periodicals

Publications: British Medical Book List
British Medical Index
Select List of British Medical Periodicals

Periodical articles indexed

See also no. 967

LONDON **972**	THE BRITISH COUNCIL MUSIC LIBRARY 97/99 Park Street London W.1	*Tel.:* 01-499 8011 ext. 414

Enquiries: To Librarian

Scope: Lending Library: Gramophone records of works by **British** composers and of works by foreign composers in performances by British artists. Scores and sheet music of works by British composers. Books on music: biographical, folk, history, reference, technical, with particular emphasis on British music and musicians

Archives Section: Copies of all recordings made in association with the British Council and other rare early recordings of British music. Information service on British music and musicians

Stock: 3,000 gramophone records; 1,300 books; 1,300 music scores and sheet music (works, not items); 30 current periodicals

LONDON

973

THE BRITISH COUNCIL
PERIODICALS SPECIMEN LIBRARY
59 New Oxford Street
London W.C.1

Tel.: 01-240 2468

Enquiries: To Librarian

Scope: Specimen copies of current British periodicals, for reference only

Stock: 6,000 specimens

See also no. 967

LONDON

974

BRITISH COUNCIL FOR REHABILITATION
OF THE DISABLED
Tavistock House South
Tavistock Square
London W.C.1

Tel.: 01-387 4037

Rehabilitation of the disabled, medically, socially, psychological and economic

Enquiries: To Secretary-General

Scope: All matters dealing with resettlement of the disabled in the community. Further education (for the disabled). Postgraduate and post registration education for medical and allied professions in the field of rehabilitation medicine

Stock: 400 books; hundreds of pamphlets; many current periodicals

Publications: Rehabilitation (quarterly journal)
Working Party Reports

LONDON

975

THE BRITISH COUNCIL OF CHURCHES
10 Eaton Gate
London S.W.1

Tel.: 01-730 9611

Enquiries: To General Secretary

Scope: The British Council of Churches has the following Departments: Mission and Unity; Christian aid; Education; International affairs; Social responsibility (including the British Churches Housing Trust); and Youth, which are willing to answer enquiries

No library

Publications: Voyage (bulletin of the Council, six issues each year)

LONDON

976

BRITISH COUNCIL OF THE EUROPEAN
MOVEMENT
Chandos House
Buckingham Gate
London S.W.1

Tel.: 01-799 2922

Furtherance of full participation of the United Kingdom in a European Economic and Political Community and promotion of European consciousness in the United Kingdom and

LONDON, BRITISH COUNCIL OF THE EUROPEAN MOVEMENT, *cont.*
representation of the British viewpoint on the Continent through Conferences, Seminars, publications and lectures

Enquiries: To Director
Scope: European integration
Stock: 200 books; 300 pamphlets; reports, including OECD and EEC publications
Publications: Into Europe (monthly journal)
Occasional pamphlets on European topics

LONDON

977

BRITISH CYCLING FEDERATION *Tel.:* 01-636 4602
26/29 Park Crescent
London W.1

Encouragement, promotion, development and control of the sport and pastime of cycling

Enquiries: To Secretary
Scope: Within limits any enquiry concerned with the sport and pastime of cycling
Publications: Racing Handbook (annually)
Touring Handbook (bi-annually)

LONDON

978

BRITISH DENTAL ASSOCIATION *Tel.:* 01-935 0875
64 Wimpole Street
London W1M 8AL

The advancement of dental science and the promotion of the status and well-being of practitioners in the dental profession

Enquiries: To Librarian
Scope: All aspects of dentistry are covered in books and periodicals. Rare Book Collection which includes almost every historical dental book, early periodicals, and minute books and manufacturers catalogues
Secondary: Works on anaesthesia, plastic and general surgery, and some general medicine, particularly history and biography
Stock: 8,000 books; 2,000 pamphlets; 250 reports; 200 current periodicals. Periodicals only available on loan
Publications: Catalogue of Dental and Allied Works since 1950
Catalogue of Rare Book Room
British Dental Journal
Occasional Association publications on, for example, fluoridation, ethics

LONDON

979

BRITISH DIABETIC ASSOCIATION *Tel.:* 01-636 7355
3/6 Alfred Place
London W.C.1
Research and welfare

Enquiries: To Secretary-General
Scope: The Association will try to answer any enquiries in connection with lay diabetic problems, but does not give medical advice
No library
Publications: Quarterly journal
Leaflets on various aspects of diabetes
Books on diabetes, including a Cookery Book
Two films: Diagnosis Diabetes   Balance is Life

LONDON	THE BRITISH DIETETIC ASSOCIATION	*Tel.*: 01-589 9173
980	251 Brompton Road London S.W.3	

Aims to advance the science and practice of dietetics and associated subjects

Enquiries: To Secretary, preferably by letter

Scope: Information on training and work of dietitians. Guidance on sources of information on dietetics and nutrition

Stock: 9 current periodicals

Publications: Nutrition (quarterly)
Leaflet: Good Food for Better Health—Easy Eating for the Over-Sixties
Basic Exchange List for Diabetics ⎫ published jointly
Exchange List for Diabetics ⎬ with the British
Carbohydrate Values of Proprietary Foods ⎭ Diabetic Association

LONDON	BRITISH DRAMA LEAGUE	*Tel.*: 01-387 2666
981	9/10 Fitzroy Square London W1P 6AE	

Aims to assist the development of the art of the theatre and to promote a right relation between Drama and the life of the community

Enquiries: To Librarian

Scope: The library contains books, sets of plays, and a unique collection of press-cuttings and play programmes, which provide an invaluable source for information, reference and research
The Information and Advisory Service is available to all library subscribers and covers choice of plays, rights and royalties, artistic and technical aspects of play production, and history and criticism of the theatre. There is also an Information Bureau attached to the Training Department. This deals with non-library enquiries and its services are available to all members of the League. Services to playwrights include written criticisms of members' scripts
The Dialect Survey provides examples of the main forms of British and American speech on gramophone records

Stock: 200,000 books including 5,000 sets of plays. Majority of current periodicals relating to the Theatre at home and abroad

Publications: Drama (quarterly Theatre Review)
Services available only to members of the League

LONDON	BRITISH EPILEPSY ASSOCIATION	*Tel.*: 01-580 2704
982	3/6 Alfred Place London W.C.1	

Seeks to improve public understanding about epilepsy. A comprehensive lecture and educational programme is available; a free advice service is available to those with epilepsy and their families and friends, or to anyone concerned with the many associated problems. The Association supports and encourages research through the Epilepsy Research Fund

Enquiries: To General Secretary
Reference library only

LONDON	BRITISH ESPERANTO ASSOCIATION INCORPORATED	*Tel.*: 01-727 7821
983	140 Holland Park Avenue London W.11	

Enquiries: To Librarian or Secretary, preferably by letter or in person

LONDON, BRITISH ESPERANTO ASSOCIATION INCORPORATED, *cont.*

Scope: Aims to collect and preserve for students and historians everything of value relating to Esperanto and the international language movement in general and related subjects

Stock: Books and pamphlets: 100 current periodicals; reports and summaries from many sources, including the Centre for Esperantist Documentation; photographs. All items are indexed

Publications: Many books, including textbooks in English and Esperanto, dictionaries, books on Esperanto language and history, original and translated literature in Esperanto

LONDON

984

BRITISH FILM INSTITUTE
81 Dean Street
London W.1

Tel.: 01-437 4355
Telex: 27624

To encourage the development of the art of the film, and to foster public appreciation and study of it, and since 1961 to foster study and appreciation of films for television and television programmes generally, to encourage the best use of television

Enquiries: To Information Officer or Librarian (book enquiries)

Scope: The whole range of the history (including economic aspects) and art of the cinema, with some material on technical aspects. Periodical indexes are maintained on individual films, personalities and general film topics. The library aims to be comprehensive with regard to English language material and also has large collections of French and Italian literature and material in other languages
Secondary: Television (all aspects except engineering). Mass media

Stock: 18,000 books and pamphlets; half a million newscuttings; 200 current periodicals; film scripts; 700,000 stills. Books and pamphlets available on loan only when duplicate copies are held

Publications: Sight and Sound (quarterly)
Monthly Film Bulletin (monthly)
National Film Archive catalogues
Many other books and pamphlets about the cinema and film industry

LONDON

985

BRITISH GERIATRICS SOCIETY
c/o Institute of Biology
41 Queen's Gate
London S.W.7

Aims to improve standards of medical care for elderly patients and encourage research in the problems of old age

Enquiries: To Secretary, by letter only

Scope: Information about the meetings of the Society, the subjects discussed, memoranda produced and recommendations made
Secondary: Information about other matters related to geriatrics which can be obtained from the personal knowledge of the Society's Officers or members of the Executive Committee

No library

Publications: Gerontologia Clinica (official journal)

LONDON

986

BRITISH HOMOEOPATHIC ASSOCIATION
27A Devonshire Street
London W1N 1RJ

Tel.: 01-935 2163

Enquiries: To Secretary

Scope: Dissemination of information on the homoeopathic branch of medicine, its philosophy, principles and practice. Sources of treatment

Stock: 750 books; 50 pamphlets. Stock not normally available on loan

Publications: A Guide to Homoeopathy
Elements of Homoeopathy. Gibson
First Aid Homoeopathy in Accidents and Ailments. Gibson
Children's Types. Borland
Influenzas. Borland
Homoeopathy for Mother and Infant. Borland
Pneumonias. Borland
Digestive Drugs. Borland
Acute Conditions. Tyler
Science and Art of Homoeopathy. Weir
Pointers to the common remedies. Tyler
Homoeopathy (monthly)

LONDON

987

BRITISH HOUSEWIVES LEAGUE LTD   *Tel.:* 01-790 3878
2 Stepney Green
London E.1

Aims to provide British housewives with an effective voice in matters concerning their welfare

Enquiries: To Secretary

Scope: Advice and information so that housewives may take action in matters which affect their interests. Concerned with the political aspects of domestic affairs, on a non-party basis

No library

Publications: Housewives Today (monthly bulletin)

LONDON

988

BRITISH HUNGARIAN FRIENDSHIP SOCIETY   *Tel.:* 01-828 2915
84A Claverton Street
London S.W.1

Aims to promote friendship and the extension of good relations between the people of Britain and the people of Hungary

Enquiries: To Secretary

Scope: Material on the history and geography of Hungary; the visual arts, the theatre, music (particularly on Bartok and Kodaly) and on folk art and folk music

Publications: Various publications on statistics of education, the arts, and economics in Hungary
Small exhibitions on various aspects of Hungarian life
Film Library

LONDON

989

BRITISH INDUSTRIAL AND SCIENTIFIC   *Tel.:* 01-734 4536
FILM ASSOCIATION
193/197 Regent Street
London W.1

Promotes the use of film in industry and science, supports film research and organizes the British Industrial Film Festival

Enquiries: To Information Officer

Scope: Information on films, film programmes, visual aids. Guidance for those who wish to sponsor or make a film
Secondary: Limited help with technical problems allied to making and showing films

Stock: 300 books; 200 pamphlets

Publications: Guide to Films on the Construction Industry. Appraisals of 120 films. 1968
Guide to Films on Psychology and Psychiatry. Appraisals of 290 films. 1968

LONDON, BRITISH INDUSTRIAL AND SCIENTIFIC FILM ASSOCIATION, *cont.*

Guide to Films on Education. Appraisals of 270 films. 1969
Communication Media in Medicine. 1967

LONDON

990

BRITISH INSTITUTE OF RADIOLOGY   *Tel.:* 01-935 6237 and 6867
32 Welbeck Street
London W1M 7PG

Aims to encourage liaison of persons interested in radiology and allied subjects

Enquiries: To Secretary

Scope: Diagnostic and therapeutic radiological textbooks and periodicals, national and international
Secondary: Textbooks and some periodicals on allied subjects, for example, medical physics, radiobiology, nuclear medicine, industrial radiology and radiation hazards and protection

Stock: 1,200 books; 65 current periodicals. Stock not available on loan but photocopies supplied

Publications: The British Journal of Radiology (monthly)

LONDON

991

BRITISH INSTITUTE OF RECORDED SOUND   *Tel.:* 01-589 6603
29 Exhibition Road
London S.W.7

National archive of sound recordings and information and documentation centre

Enquiries: To Director

Scope: The Institute aims to acquire all books and periodicals in any language on aspects of recorded sound other than the purely technical, record manufacturers' catalogues from many countries, catalogues of other recorded libraries, and details of important recorded broadcasts

Stock: 100 current periodicals (in many languages); 170,000 discs (monthly intake 1,000); 5,000 hours of tapes (average monthly intake 100 hours). Stock not available on loan

Publications: Recorded Sound (quarterly journal)
Occasional publications

LONDON

992

BRITISH JUDO ASSOCIATION   *Tel.:* 01-580 7585
26 Park Crescent
London W.1

Fosters and develops the sport of judo in Great Britain, nationally and internationally

Enquiries: To Secretary

Scope: Mainly information on registered clubs in particular districts for people interested in taking up the sport of judo
Secondary: Specialized information on past champions and history of the Association
No library

Publications: No. 3 booklet—Promotion and Coaching Syllabi for Men
No. 4 booklet—Promotion and Coaching Syllabi for Women
Contest Rules
Pamphlet of general information

LONDON

993

BRITISH LEPROSY RELIEF ASSOCIATION (LEPRA)   *Tel.:* 01-387 7283
50 Fitzroy Street
London W.1

Anti-Leprosy campaign in countries of the Commonwealth

Enquiries: To General Secretary (organization) or Medical Secretary (medical aspects)
Scope: Enquirers can be put in touch with experts in all branches of leprosy, in Britain and abroad
No library
Publications: Leprosy Review (quarterly)

LONDON BRITISH LIBRARY OF POLITICAL AND *Tel.:* 01-405 7686
994 ECONOMIC SCIENCE
Houghton Street
London W.C.2

Reference library of the social sciences which is also the working library of the London School of Economics

Enquiries: To Librarian by letter; to Enquiry Desk by telephone or in person
Scope: The social sciences in the widest sense of the term. Economics; commerce; commerce and business administration; transport; statistics; political science; public administration; law; international law; social, economic, political and international history. Strong collection of world-wide government publications. Depository collections of United States Federal documents and publications of United Nations and its specialized agencies. Collections (probably unique) of reports of local authorities, banks and railways. Passfield collection contains manuscript diaries and correspondence of the Webbs and all their publications. Particularly strong collections on the history of socialist movements. Manuscript collections contain papers of Ramsay MacDonald, Dalton and others. *Special collection* on the history of the book trade
Secondary: History, philosophy, psychology, linguistics, mathematics
Stock: 540,000 bound volumes, estimated to contain more than $1\frac{3}{4}$ million items, of which 450,000 are pamphlets; 10,000 current periodicals, of which 5,800 are governmental; 20,000 total serials, including non-current; several large manuscript collections; microfilms
Publications: Library: Subject catalogue published as *A London Bibliography of the Social Sciences*
Classified Catalogue of a collection of works on publishing and bookselling
London School of Economics:
British Journal of Industrial Relations   Journal of Transport Economics
Economica   British Journal of Sociology

Other libraries for the use of members of the London School of Economics are: the Teaching Library, consisting of 25,000 extra copies, for lending, of works in great student demand; the Shaw Library, containing 5,000 volumes of general literature not duplicated in the British Library; small, highly specialized collections in teaching departments
The stock of these is represented in the author catalogue of the British Library

LONDON BRITISH MEDICAL ASSOCIATION *Tel.:* 01-387 4499
995 B.M.A. House
Tavistock Square
London W.C.1

Promotes the medical and allied sciences, and maintains the honour and interests of the medical profession

Enquiries: To Secretary
Scope: The Nuffield Library of the B.M.A. contains literature on medicine and its allied sciences. It possesses special collections of the medical theses of Paris (1892 to date) and of Lyons (1894–1919)

LONDON, BRITISH MEDICAL ASSOCIATION, *cont.*

Stock: 80,000 books, pamphlets and reports; 2,000 current periodicals. Stock not available on loan but photocopying service is operated

Publications: British Medical Journal (weekly)
Abstracts of World Medicine (monthly)
British Journal of Ophthalmology (monthly)
Ophthalmic Literature (abstracts, six issues each year)
Gut (monthly)
Journal of Clinical Pathology (nine issues each year)
British Heart Journal (six issues each year)
Journal of Neurology, Neurosurgery and Psychiatry (six issues each year)
Archives of Disease in Childhood (six issues each year)
Thorax (six issues each year)
British Journal of Venereal Diseases (six issues each year)
Annals of the Rheumatic Diseases (six issues each year)
British Journal of Industrial Medicine (quarterly)
British Journal of Preventive and Social Medicine (quarterly)
Medical and Biological Illustration (quarterly)
Journal of Medical Genetics (quarterly)
British Journal of Medical Education (quarterly)
Cardiovascular Research (quarterly)
World Medical Periodicals. Reprinted 1968
Supplement to World Medical Periodicals. 1968
The New General Practice. 1968
Porphyria—A Royal Malady. 1968
Is there an Alternative? 1967
Aids for the Disabled. B.M.A. Planning Unit Report no. 2. 1968
Research Funds Guide. 1968
Intensive Care. 1967
Becoming a Doctor. Revised 1967
Medical Examination of Immigrants. 1966
Summary of Regulations for Postgraduate Diplomas and of Courses of Instruction in Postgraduate Medicine. Revised 1968
Medical Evidence in Courts of Law. A Joint Report by the General Council of the Bar of England and Wales, The Law Society and the British Medical Association. 1965
The Drinking Driver. Report of a Special Committee of the British Medical Association. 1965
Diseases of the Digestive System. 1969
The Hospital Gazetteer: a Guide to Hospitals in the United Kingdom. 1969
Computers in Medicine. B.M.A. Planning Unit Report no. 3. 1969
British National Formulary. 1968

LONDON

996

BRITISH MUSEUM
DEPARTMENT OF PRINTED BOOKS
London W.C.1

Tel.: 01-636 1555
Telex: 21462

Copyright and general research library

Enquiries: To Principal Keeper

Scope: The Library receives and keeps all United Kingdom publications, although some medical and veterinary science material is transferred to the National Reference Library of Science and Invention (no. 1432–1434). Foreign acquisitions cover a wide field, mainly in the humanities and social sciences. The Library has special collections of maps and music. There is a general information service, not specializing in a particular subject field, able to deal with enquiries which do not involve considerable research.

Stock: 7,000,000 books; 25,000 current periodicals (total stock). The library is a recognized repository for UNO and UNESCO publications and those of the European Community. It has deposit or exchange agreements for official publications with most Commonwealth and Foreign governments. Stock not available on loan

Publications: The British Museum: a guide to its public services (in preparation)
The General Catalogue of Printed Books, Photolithographic Edition, to 1955 (263 volumes, 1960–1966); Ten-year supplement, 1956–1965 (50 volumes, 1968)

See also no. 997 and 1432–1434

LONDON

997

BRITISH MUSEUM
NEWSPAPER LIBRARY
130 Colindale Avenue
London N.W.9

Tel.: 01-205 6039 and 4788

Provides research and reference facilities in the field of newspapers

Enquiries: To Superintendent

Scope: The collection comprises all the newspapers received under the Copyright Act and most of the weekly periodicals, together with a wide selection of Commonwealth and Foreign newspapers. The United Kingdom collection includes a considerable number of periodicals dealing with trade and business activities

Stock: 500,000 volumes

LONDON

998

BRITISH MUSIC HALL SOCIETY
1 King Henry Street
London N.16

Tel.: 01-254 4209

Aims to preserve the variety theatre by actively opposing demolition, to collect and exhibit programmes, posters, photographs, and personal effects connected with the Music Hall, and to bring together for social reasons devotees of the Music Hall

Enquiries: To Information Officer

Scope: Enquiries about any music hall matters

Publications: The Call Boy (quarterly)

LONDON

999

BRITISH MUSIC INFORMATION CENTRE
10 Stratford Place
London W.1

Tel.: 01-499 8567

Enquiries: To Librarian

Scope: Established as a showroom for 20th century British music, published and unpublished; particularly the music of living British composers: scores, tapes, records. Facilities for score reading are provided to visitors, also listening facilities for tapes and records. Also provided: publishers' catalogues and composers' brochures (where available); biographical information for concert notes; information on performing right. Special section kept for music suitable for schools; operas, musical dramas, orchestral, choral, solo and duo instrumental and piano works

Stock: 8,500 music scores (including manuscripts); 200 hours of tape recording; 150 long-playing records. Stock not available on loan

LONDON, BRITISH MUSIC INFORMATION CENTRE, *cont.*

Publications: Catalogue of Chamber Music for Three or More Instruments by Living British Composers, including unpublished works
Catalogue of Orchestral Music by Living British Composers, including unpublished works

LONDON

1000

BRITISH NATIONAL FILM CATALOGUE *Tel.:* 01-734 4536
193/197 Regent Street
London W.1

Catalogues films and provides a classified list of all films released in the United Kingdom since 1963

Enquiries: To Information Officer

Scope: Classified and title information on non-fiction and short feature films held in this country and available for non-theatrical distribution
Secondary: Files of certain periodicals, British and foreign, on documentary and sponsored films. Information on the problems of cataloguing, classifying and allied problems to do with films and liaison with organizations abroad on these subjects

Stock: 300 books; 200 pamphlets; 10 current periodicals

Publications: The British National Film Catalogue 1963–
Bi-monthly with annual cumulated volume 1963–1968
Quarterly with annual cumulated volume 1969

LONDON

1001

BRITISH OPTICAL ASSOCIATION *Tel.:* 01-629 3382
65 Brook Street
London W1Y 2DT

Aims to encourage the science of optics and its application to the improvement of human vision. Professional association

Enquiries: To Librarian, by letter only

Scope: Books and periodicals relating to ophthalmic and physiological optics and to ophthalmology

Stock: 10,000 books; 50 current periodicals

Publications: The British Journal of Physiological Optics
The Ophthalmic Optician

LONDON

1002

THE BRITISH POLIO FELLOWSHIP *Tel.:* 01-387 5851
Clifton House
83/117 Euston Road
London N.W.1

Enquiries: To General Secretary, by letter only

Scope: Aims to keep the polio-disabled informed of beneficial legislation and developments in aids and equipment for the disabled
Secondary: Aims to associate in fellowship sufferers from polio; to find means of training members to be self-supporting; to alleviate the loneliness of friendless sufferers; and to bring those who need advice or assistance into contact with available sources of help

Publications: Fellowship Bulletin   16 mm film

LONDON

1003

THE BRITISH PSYCHOLOGICAL SOCIETY *Tel.:* 01-499 4719
18/19 Albermarle Street
London W1X 4DN

Aims to promote the advancement and diffusion of a knowledge of psychology, pure and applied

Enquiries: To Secretary, by letter only

Scope: Details of psychology as a career to sixth formers and undergraduates
Secondary: Information on postgraduate professional training in psychology and reports on matters in which psychologists are concerned

Stock: 125 current psychological periodicals

Publications: The Psychological Study of Deafness and Hearing Impairment. M. Rodda, ed.
Careers in Psychology (and supplement Careers in Clinical Psychology)
List of Clinical Psychologists in the National Health Service
Teaching Educational Psychology in Training Colleges
Children in Hospitals for the Subnormal
Technical Recommendations for Psychological and Educational Tests
The Nature and Consequences of Brain Lesions in Children and Adults
Aspects of Autism. P. J. Mittler, ed.

LONDON

1004

THE BRITISH SCHOOL OF OSTEOPATHY LTD
16 Buckingham Gate
London S.W.1

Tel.: 01-828 9479, 01-834 5085 and 0385

Enquiries: To Principal

Scope: Requirements for osteopathic training. General information about osteopathic treatment and distribution of osteopaths. Liaison with press concerning nature and scope of osteopathic treatment and particular applications

Stock not available on loan

Publications: Prospectus
Leaflet: Osteopathy as a Career

From Summer 1969 there will be thirteen Regional Osteopathic Careers Officers who will deal with local careers advisers and allied services

LONDON

1005

BRITISH SOCIETY FOR INTERNATIONAL HEALTH EDUCATION
24 Southwark Street
London S.E.1

Tel.: 01-407 1815

Enquiries: To General Secretary, by letter only

Scope: Social and behavioural sciences in their application to health and medical care

Stock: 300 books; 200 pamphlets. Stock not normally available on loan

LONDON

1006

THE BRITISH SOCIETY FOR THE STUDY OF ORTHODONTICS
Manson House
26 Portland Place
London W.1

Enquiries: To Hon. Secretary, by letter only

Scope: General matters relating to orthodontics
No library

Publications: Transactions of the British Society for the Study of Orthodontics (annually)

LONDON

1007

BRITISH SOCIETY OF MASTER GLASS
  PAINTERS
6 Queen Square
London W.C.1

Enquiries: To Hon. Secretary, 18 Gordon Place, Kensington, London W.8

Publications: The Journal of the Society is usually published annually; recently a brochure on *The Extended Uses of Glass* was published to encourage the greater use of decorative glass in secular buildings. This provides architects for the first time with clear illustrated descriptions of all modern techniques, together with an indication of their cost, and list of craftsmen competent to work in them. Further brochures are being planned
A Directory of members work and where it may be found is published from time to time; the last in 1967

LONDON

1008

BRITISH SOCIETY OF MEDICAL AND
  DENTAL HYPNOSIS
Manson House
26 Portland Place
London W.1

This Society was instituted for the study, advancement and practice of hypnosis in connection with medicine and dentistry

Enquiries: To Secretary, 91 Booth Road, London N.W.9 (*Tel.:* 01-205 2287)

Scope: Medical and dental hypnosis

LONDON

1009

BRITISH SOVIET FRIENDSHIP SOCIETY   *Tel.:* 01-253 4161
36 St John's Square
London E.C.1

Enquiries: To Information Officer, by letter only

Scope: Soviet Union. British Soviet relations

Stock: 800 books and pamphlets. Stock not available on loan

Publications: British Soviet Friendship (monthly)

LONDON

1010

THE BRITISH SURGICAL EXPORT GROUP   *Tel.:* 01-930 6711
21 Tothill Street
London S.W.1
Trade Association

Enquiries: To Secretary

Scope: Surgical instruments and equipment
No library

LONDON

1011

THE BRITISH THEATRE MUSEUM ASSOCIATION   *Tel.:* 01-937 3052
Leighton House
12 Holland Park Road
London W.14

Aims to promote the creation by the Government of a National Museum of the Theatre, and to prevent as far as possible valuable theatre material from being sold abroad

Enquiries: To Curator

Scope: Information and assistance can be given in connection with enquiries on the general history of the British theatre

Stock: 3,000 books. The Library is at present on deposit at the University of London Library, Senate House, Malet Street, London, W.C.1. (no. 1662). The books may be studied by students and scholars in the Library by arrangement

Publications: Catalogues of current exhibitions

LONDON

1012

THE BRITISH THORACIC AND TUBERCULOSIS ASSOCIATION
59 Portland Place
London W.1

Tel.: 01-636 3810

Enquiries: To Secretary, by letter only

Scope: Research in chest medicine and thoracic nursing

Publications: Tubercle (journal of the Association)

LONDON

1013

BRITISH VOLUNTEER PROGRAMME
26 Bedford Square
London W.C.1

Tel.: 01-636 4066

Co-ordinates the activities of voluntary societies sending graduate and qualified volunteers to serve in developing countries overseas

Enquiries: To Secretary, preferably by letter

Scope: Advice on the structure and operation of voluntary service overseas stemming from the United Kingdom. Also provides information on international aspects of voluntary service
No library

Publications: Pamphlets, booklets, photographs and films about voluntary service in developing countries

LONDON

1014

BRITISH YOUTH COUNCIL
57 Chalton Street
London N.W.1

Tel.: 01-387 7559

Main consultative body in Great Britain for international youth work, providing information for Youth Leaders at home and abroad. Free advisory service for young people visiting or staying in London

Enquiries: To Secretary General

Scope: Help and guidance to young people (15–30 years) on accommodation and employment problems, personal difficulties or problems (particularly in the case of young visitors to Britain). Help with programming for overseas youth workers visiting Britain and provision of contacts for British youth workers with their counterparts overseas
Secondary: Provision of inexpensive travel facilities for young people and arrangements for Conferences and Seminars dealing with, for example, youth, politics and social change
No library

Publications: W.A.Y. Forum (monthly magazine dealing with all aspects of international youth work)

LONDON

1015

BRIXTON SCHOOL OF BUILDING
Ferndale Road
London S.W.4

Tel.: 01-274 0944

Enquiries: To Librarian

LONDON, BRIXTON SCHOOL OF BUILDING, *cont.*

Scope: Architecture and Town Planning; economics
Secondary: Education, law, sociology

Stock: 18,000 books; 11,000 pamphlets and reports; 330 current periodicals

Publications: Accession list (bi-monthly)
Subject bibliographies (mainly internal use)

LONDON

1016

BUREAU OF HYGIENE AND TROPICAL DISEASES
Keppel Street
London W.C.1

Tel.: 01-636 8636

Publication of two medical abstracting journals

Enquiries: To Director

Scope: Information service through abstracts, in *Tropical Diseases Bulletin* and *Abstracts on Hygiene*
Subjects covered are generally those shown in the entry for the London School of Hygiene and Tropical Medicine (no. 1344)

Stock: Eventually, all literature received by the Bureau is incorporated in the Library of the London School of Hygiene and Tropical Medicine

Publications: Tropical Diseases Bulletin (monthly)
Abstracts on Hygiene (formerly Bulletin of Hygiene, monthly)

Although an independent organization, the Bureau works closely with the Library of the London School of Hygiene and Tropical Medicine and, for external library purposes, the Librarian of the School acts on its behalf

LONDON

1017

BUSINESS ARCHIVES COUNCIL
Ormond House
63 Queen Victoria Street
London E.C.4

Tel.: 01-248 5521

To encourage businessmen to preserve their records; to provide skilled advice for the owner of business records; to provide advice for historians as to the whereabouts and accessibility of collections of business records; and to promote interest in business history generally

Enquiries: To the Secretary

Scope: Business Histories; archive administration and records management; historical surveys of individual industries

Stock: Some 3,000 items of business histories published privately and publicly. The whereabouts of business records over the past century are noted in the Council's register of business archives. Small collection of historical industrial films

Publications: Business Archives (bi-annually, June and December)
Occasional Newsletters
Letters of a West African Trader: Edward Grace 1767-70, with an introduction by the late Professor T. S. Ashton. 1950
The Walker Family: Iron Founders & Lead Manufacturers 1741-1893. Professor A. H. John ed. 1951
The First Five Hundred: a duplicated list of chronicles and house histories of companies and organizations in the B.A.C. Library. 1959
The Management and Control of Business Records. 1966
A Survey of the Records of the Shipping Industry (shortly to be published)

LONDON

1018

CAMBERWELL SCHOOL OF ART AND CRAFTS   *Tel.:* 01-703 7485
Peckham Road
London S.E.5

Enquiries: To Librarian

Scope: Fine art (painting and sculpture), ceramics, graphic design, textiles. Printing, typographic design and bookbinding

Stock: 13,000 books; 2,000 pamphlets; 90 current periodicals

LONDON

1019

CAMDEN SCHOOL FOR GIRLS   *Tel.:* 01-485 3414
Sandall Road
Kentish Town
London N.W.5

Enquiries: To Librarian, during school terms

Scope: The only items of particular interest are a very small number of unusual books illustrating the growth and development of women's education in the 19th century

Stock not available on loan

LONDON

1020

CAMPAIGN FOR NUCLEAR DISARMAMENT   *Tel.:* 01-242 3872
14 Grays Inn Road
London W.C.1

Aims to secure nuclear and general disarmament and to strengthen the peace movement in general

Enquiries: To Information Officer or Secretary

Scope: Nuclear and general disarmament (particularly nuclear disarmament). Biological and chemical warfare
Secondary: Extensive newspaper cuttings library on foreign affairs, armament developments, student protests, Vietnam war

Stock: Daily newspapers. Pictures, but not books or periodicals, available on loan

Publications: Sanity (monthly paper)
Briefing (information service on international affairs in relation to peace and disarmament)
Pamphlets on disarmament and foreign affairs

LONDON

1021

THE CARAVAN CLUB   *Tel.:* 01-629 6441
65 South Molton Street
London W1Y 2AB

Enquiries: To Information Officer

Scope: All aspects of caravan touring at home and abroad including the law relating to land use, casual caravanning, and legal and technical matters

Publications: Sites Directory and Handbook } Both for members only
En Route (monthly magazine) }
Foreign Touring Handbook

LONDON

1022

CATHOLIC CENTRAL LIBRARY   *Tel.:* 01-834 6128
47 Francis Street
London S.W.1

Makes available (to members for home reading; to students on the premises) up-to-date books and periodicals mainly, but not exclusively, of Roman Catholic interest

LONDON, CATHOLIC CENTRAL LIBRARY, *cont.*

Enquiries: To Librarian

Scope: Theology, scripture, Church history, mysticism, ecumenism, religious life, philosophy, sociology, liturgy, hagiology, catechetics. Many acquisitions in recent years reflect the developing ecumenical relations between the Churches

Stock: 50,000 books; 3,000 pamphlets; 100 current periodicals. Periodicals not available on loan

LONDON

1023

CATHOLIC EDUCATION COUNCIL *Tel.:* 01-584 7491
41 Cromwell Road
London S.W.7

Official national body representing Catholic education and giving advice and information to schools and other interested persons

Enquiries: To Secretary

Scope: Information where available or advice about sources of information on matters relating to Catholic education and educational institutions in England and Wales

Publications: Biennial handbook of reference to Catholic education in England and Wales, listing all schools

LONDON

1024

THE CATHOLIC MARRIAGE ADVISORY COUNCIL *Tel.:* 01-727 0141
15 Lansdowne Road
London W.11

Enquiries: To Secretary

Scope: General information on the work of the Council. The principles on which it is based, and methods used to select and train personnel for marriage counselling, education work and for the medical advisory service. Literature and statistics are most readily available for medical work

Publications: Book List on Marriage and Family Life
Books on sex education for boys and on running courses for engaged couples
Medical supplies leaflets, charts and case sheets

LONDON

1025

THE CATHOLIC RECORD SOCIETY
c/o 114 Mount Street
London W.1

Study of post-Reformation Catholic history in England and Wales and publication of sources within this field

Enquiries: To Hon. Secretary, 48 Lowndes Square, London S.W.1, by letter only

Scope: Enquirers can be put in touch with specialists. No library as such, but a collection of about 2,000 16th to 19th century books, the Gillow Collection, which is mainly Catholic devotional and controversial books and pamphlets, may be consulted by appointment in writing at the Jesuit Library, 114 Mount Street, London W.1. In the archives there are two specialist collections: The County Files, which are collections of notes arranged under Counties, giving details of Catholic communities, Missions and families or Houses in the various counties from 1559 to 1829; and the priest card index of 2,000 cards listing the Catholic priests working in England from 1559 to 1829. These collections may be consulted only by appointment

Publications: Annual volumes in Record series
Occasional volumes in Monograph series
Recusant History (journal, three issues each year)

LONDON	CATHOLIC TEACHERS FEDERATION	*Tel.:* 01-202 6494
1026	12 Queens Road Hendon London N.W.4	

Aims to unite Catholic teachers for the furtherance of Catholic education

Enquiries: To Secretary, preferably by letter

Scope: Most aspects of Catholic teaching including primary and secondary

No library

Publications: Catholic Teacher (annually)
Catholic Education Today (in conjunction with Principals of Colleges, bi-monthly)

LONDON	CATHOLIC YOUTH SERVICE COUNCIL	*Tel.:* 01-589 7550
1027	41 Cromwell Road London S.W.7	

The servicing of Catholic youth organizations throughout England and Wales

Enquiries: General Secretary

Scope: Information on all aspects of Catholic youth work, including the training of leaders and senior members and the provision of premises

No library

LONDON	CENTRAL ASIAN RESEARCH CENTRE	*Tel.:* 01-589 1934
1028	66A King's Road London S.W.3	

Research on Soviet Central Asia and Soviet relations with Asian and African countries

Enquiries: To Director

Scope: Soviet Central Asia: Russian-language books and periodicals. Soviet books and publications on Asian and African countries
Secondary: Non-Soviet writing on these subjects

Stock: 4,000 books; 50 Soviet periodicals, and many Western journals

Publications: Mizan (incorporating Central Asian Review, six issues each year)
Monographs (eight)
Bibliographies
Map of Central Asia

LONDON	CENTRAL BUREAU FOR EDUCATIONAL VISITS AND EXCHANGES	*Tel.:* 01-799 3941
1029	91 Victoria Street London S.W.1	

Enquiries: To Secretary

Scope: Whole field of educational (and youth) visits, travel and exchange, with exception of academic and scientific exchange

Publications: Young Visitors to Britain (English, French, German and Spanish editions, annually)
Youth Visits Abroad (annually)
Vacation courses abroad (annually)
Working holidays abroad (annually)
Educational Exchange (termly)

LONDON 1030	CENTRAL COUNCIL FOR THE DISABLED 34 Eccleston Square London S.W.1	*Tel.:* 01-834 0747

The Council is a national co-ordinating body for organizations working for the welfare of the physically handicapped

Enquiries: To Administrator

Scope: Rehabilitation of the physically disabled
Secondary: General information on the welfare of the disabled—aids, education, holidays, residential accommodation, including a number of biographies on disabled people who have overcome their handicaps

Publications: Many books, pamphlets, leaflets and drawings

LONDON 1031	CENTRAL COUNCIL OF PHYSICAL RECREATION 26 Park Crescent London W1N 4AJ	*Tel.:* 01-580 6822

A servicing organization for sport representative of over 200 National organizations and with a professional staff deployed throughout England and Wales and in Northern Ireland. Part of the servicing role of the Council is to provide technical, administrative and research services to the Sports Council which advises the Government on amateur sport and physical recreation

Enquiries: To General Secretary

Scope: Comprehensive collection of publications on sport and physical recreation

Stock: Many books, pamphlets and reports; 200 current periodicals. Stock not available on loan

Publications: Sport and Recreation (quarterly journal)
Sports Development Bulletin (quarterly)
Special reports dealing with specific topics

LONDON 1032	CENTRAL JEWISH LECTURE COMMITTEE OF THE BOARD OF DEPUTIES OF BRITISH JEWS Woburn House (4th Floor) Upper Woburn Place London W.C.1	*Tel.:* 01-387 3952

Enquiries: To Secretary

Scope: Information service includes material on Judaism, Jewish life and Inter-group Relations

Publications: Learning to Live with our Neighbours
Judaism and Inter-group Relations
Immigration and Integration—Experiences of the Anglo-Jewish Community (published by The Council of Christians and Jews)

LONDON 1033	CENTRAL MIDDLESEX HOSPITAL MEDICAL LIBRARY Acton Lane Park Royal London N.W.10	*Tel.:* 01-965 5733 ext. 578

Enquiries: To Medical Librarian

Scope: Textbooks are mainly standard works in medicine, surgery, obstetrics, gynaecology and pathology with a coverage of other specialities including anaesthetics, pharmacology, orthopaedics and chest and heart diseases

Stock: 180 books; 50 current periodicals; National Health Service Circulars from 1963

LONDON CENTRAL MIDWIVES BOARD *Tel.:* 01-373 4801
1034 39 Harrington Gardens
  South Kensington
  London S.W.7

  Enquiries: To Secretary
  Scope: The training of midwives; regulating and restricting within due limits the practice of midwives in the hospital and domiciliary services and in private practice
  No library

LONDON CENTRAL OFFICE OF INFORMATION *Tel.:* 01-928 2345
1035 Hercules Road *Telex:* 21773, 22737 and
  London S.E.1 24460

  Enquiries: To Librarian
  Scope: Britain, Commonwealth, other countries in that order. Illustration collection, especially old engravings and woodcuts, primarily concerned with Britain and the Commonwealth but covers other fields as well
  Stock: 40,000 books; pamphlets and reports; 400 current periodicals
  Publications: Reference pamphlets on various topics
  Britain: an Official handbook (annually)
  Survey (fortnightly)
  See also no. 1036

LONDON CENTRAL OFFICE OF INFORMATION *Tel.:* 01-928 2345
  PHOTOGRAPHS LIBRARY
1036 Hercules Road
  London S.E.1

  An agency department of the Government providing material for the British Information Services; the library also provides a sales outlet for official photographs
  Enquiries: To Librarian
  Scope: Britain with special emphasis on social welfare and economic conditions (not historical)
  Portraits
  Stock: 300,000 photographs; 40,000 colour transparencies
  See also no. 1035

LONDON CENTRAL PUBLIC HEALTH LABORATORY *Tel.:* 01-205 7041
  Colindale Avenue
1037 London N.W.9

  Diagnostic and reference laboratories in the field of medical microbiology and hygiene
  Enquiries: To Librarian
  Scope: Medical microbiology. Hygiene of air, water and food. Disinfection
  Stock: 15,000 volumes; large collection of pamphlets and reports; 450 current periodicals
  Publications: Library Bulletin of selected current periodical literature (weekly with indexes)
  Bibliographies

LONDON CENTRAL REGISTER OF CHARITIES
  57/60 Haymarket
1038 London S.W.1

  See no. 1044

| LONDON | CENTRAL SCHOOL OF ART AND DESIGN | *Tel.:* 01-405 1825 |

LONDON

1039

CENTRAL SCHOOL OF ART AND DESIGN   *Tel.:* 01-405 1825
Southampton Row
London W.C.1

Enquiries: To Librarian

Scope: Fine arts, graphic design, industrial design, jewellery design, ceramics, textile design, theatre design, furniture, history of art

Stock: 16,000 books; 6,000 pamphlets; 150 current periodicals

LONDON

1040

CENTRAL STATISTICAL OFFICE   *Tel.:* 01-930 5422
Cabinet Office
Whitehall
London S.W.1

Publication of statistics on national income, finance, balance of payments and social statistics

Enquiries: To Information Officer, preferably by letter

Scope: Redistribution of income in relation to household budgets
Secondary: Enquiries of a general nature relating to social statistics

Library stock available on loan to Government librarians only

Publications: Annual Abstract of Statistics
Abstract of Regional Statistics (annually)
National Income and Expenditure (annually)
United Kingdom Balance of Payments (annually)
Statistical News (quarterly)
Monthly Digest of Statistics
Economic Trends (monthly)
Social Trends (twice each year)

LONDON

1041

CENTRAL YOUTH EMPLOYMENT EXECUTIVE   *Tel.:* 01-636 8022
97 Tottenham Court Road
London W1P 0ER

Responsible for the organization and operation of the Youth Employment Service

Enquiries: To Local Careers Offices of the Youth Employment Service or the Librarian, Central Youth Employment Executive

Scope: Library stock consist of books on occupations, education and training and vocational guidance; and an extensive collection of employers' recruitment literature and information on careers from professional bodies
The Information Service provides occupational information relevant to pupils in schools, and covering the nature of occupations, the qualifications and personal qualities required, education and training and, where possible, the availability of openings and future prospects

Stock: 700 books, excluding College and University Prospectuses; 2,000 pamphlets; 100 reports; 18 current periodicals

Publications: Careers Bulletin (issued free to schools and other bodies concerned with careers guidance)
Careers Bulletin Supplement (annually, summary of awards for Higher Education)
Careers Films and Filmstrips (annual catalogue)
Careers Library Classification Index (prepared in conjunction with the Careers Research and Advisory Centre, no. 280)

Items obtainable from H.M.S.O.: Careers Guide
Careers Leaflets
Careers Wallsheets
Choice of Careers booklets
'Signposts' Careers Index Cards (issued free to schools and Careers offices)

LONDON

1042

CENTRE FOR INFORMATION ON LANGUAGE TEACHING *Tel.:* 01-242 9020
State House
High Holborn
London W.C.1

Collects and coordinates information about all aspects of modern languages and their teaching and makes this information available to individuals and organizations professionally concerned in Britain

Enquiries: To Director

Scope: The Centre shares library resources with the English-Teaching Information Centre of the British Council. The Language-Teaching library is described in entry no. 1307

Publications: Language Teaching Abstracts (quarterly)
A Language-Teaching Bibliography
Select Lists (short introductory bibliographies for language teachers)
Teaching Materials (lists of available audio-visual and recorded courses)
Information Guides:
  English for the Children of Immigrants. 1969
  Manufacturers and Suppliers of Language Laboratory Equipment. 1968
  Foreign periodicals on non-literary topics (French, German, Italian, Russian, Spanish). 1969
Information Papers:
  CILT Research Register. 1969
  The Language-Teaching Library. 1968
  Specialised Bibliography: Language testing. 1969
  CILT Reports and Papers: no. 1. Languages for Special Purposes. 1969
  CILT Reports and Papers: no. 2. Aims and Techniques: Language-Teaching Methods and their comparative assessment. 1969

LONDON

1043

CHARING CROSS HOSPITAL MEDICAL SCHOOL *Tel.:* 01-836 7788
Adelphi
John Adam Street
London W.C.2

Enquiries: To Librarian

Scope: Medicine and ancillary subjects
Small collection of historical texts (900 volumes)

Stock: 20,000 books; 1,800 pamphlets and reports; 395 current periodicals

Publications: Charing Cross Hospital Gazette (3 issues each year)

Branch libraries: Fulham Hospital, St Dunstan's Road, London W.6 and West London Hospital, Hammersmith Road, London W.6

LONDON

1044

CHARITY COMMISSION *Tel.:* 01-930 7621
14 Ryder Street
St James's
London S.W.1

Promotes the effective use of charitable resources and keeps a register of charities for England

LONDON, CHARITY COMMISSION, *cont.*

and Wales. The official Custodian for Charities holds investments for charities and remits the income, free of income tax, to trustees

Enquiries: To Secretary

Scope: The Charity Commission as a repository for public records has considerable historical records open to the public, covering charities and their origin. The *Central Register of Charities*, 57/60 Haymarket, London S.W.1, is also open to public inspection and contains information about all registered charities in England and Wales (except educational charities)

LONDON

1045

CHARTERED INSURANCE INSTITUTE *Tel.:* 01-606 3835
20 Aldermanbury
London E.C.2

Enquiries: To Librarian

Scope: Insurance
Secondary: Law; finance and economics, management, shipping and aviation (small section only), manufacturing processes and industrial fire hazards

Stock: 20,000 books and pamphlets; 600 current periodicals (including annuals and reports)

Publications: C.I.I. Journal (annually)
Occasional papers
Contact (Bulletin of the C.I.I.)
Study courses on all branches of insurance

LONDON

1046

CHARTERED SOCIETY OF PHYSIOTHERAPY *Tel.:* 01-242 1941
14 Bedford Row
London W.C.1

Enquiries: To Secretary

Scope: Information service on physiotherapy using press hand-outs and supplying information on request to newspapers, magazines (both lay and medical) and to members and the general public
No library

Publications: Physiotherapy (The Journal of the Chartered Society of Physiotherapy)
Physiotherapy as a Career
Syllabus and Regulations for Training
Lifting Patients in the Home
Lifting Patients in Hospitals
Lifting Patients in Industry

LONDON

1047

CHELSEA SCHOOL OF ART *Tel.:* 01-352 4846
Manresa Road
London S.W.3

Enquiries: To Librarian

Scope: Painting and sculpture in the nineteenth and twentieth centuries
Secondary: History of European painting and sculpture in general. A small amount of material on applied arts, design and graphic design

Stock: 11,000 books and pamphlets; 40 current periodicals

LONDON   CHELSEA SCHOOL OF CHIROPODY   *Tel.:* 01-402 5621
1048
18 Samford Street
London N.W.8

School of chiropody and research into aspects of foot disorders

Enquiries: To Principal
Scope: Chiropody; feet, all aspects including anatomy, physiology and pathology; history
Stock: 2,000 books; 500 pamphlets; 4 current periodicals

LONDON   THE CHEST AND HEART ASSOCIATION   *Tel.:* 01-387 3012
1049
Tavistock House North
Tavistock Square
London W.C.1

Research into chest, heart and 'stroke' illnesses and health education and rehabilitation by books, leaflets, magazines, conferences, personal welfare service

Enquiries: To Information Officer, by letter only
Scope: Library service is on limited scale at present, but practical advice and information are always available by personal letter or free specimen leaflets on chest, heart and 'stroke' illnesses
Stock: 1,000 books; 300 pamphlets; 400 reports; 50 current periodicals
Publications: Leaflets and posters
Health (six issues each year)
Hope (quarterly)
Books:
New ideas in Asthma and its Management. 1969
Modern Drug Treatment in Tuberculosis. J. D. Ross and N. W. Horne. Fourth edition 1969
Helen's Victory—The Story of a Chest Illness. J. Mead. 1969
My Brother's Keeper? M. Stewart. 1968
Transactions of the International Chest and Heart Conference, 4–7 April 1967
The Will to Health. H. Williams. 1967
Intensive Care and Resuscitation in Heart Disease. 1966
British Pioneers in the Study of Heart Disease. H. Williams. 1966
Holiday Addresses for Cardiac and 'Stroke' Patients. 1970 edition
Chest Clinic Handbook. 1965
Some Nursing Homes (England and Wales). 1970
The 'Chesty' Child. 1965
The Social Effects of Chronic Bronchitis. M. G. C. Neilson and E. Crofton. 1965
Need I Ever Retire? W. Evans. 1965
Return to Independence—Exercises for 'Stroke' Patients. T. Wareham. 1965
Chest Fibrosis. 1964
Cystic Bronchitis in Great Britain. L. H. Capel and M. Caplin. 1964
New Ideas on Rehabilitation. 1963
Chronic Bronchitis—Prevention and Management. 1963
Tuberculosis—Prevention and Control. 1962
Modern Views on 'Stroke' Illness. 1962
'Stroke' Illness—Help for Patient and Family. N. P. R. Clyde. 1961
Pneumoconiosis—Modern Trends. 1961
Cardiac Problems. 1961
BCG and Vole Vaccination. Dr K. N. Irvine. 1957
A Psychiatrist Looks at Tuberculosis. E. Wittkower. 1955

LONDON, THE CHEST AND HEART ASSOCIATION, *cont.*

In preparation:
Asthma—a Patient's Guide
The Human Kidney—What Everyone Should Know
Heart Trouble in the Family

LONDON

1050

CHESTER BEATTY RESEARCH INSTITUTE *Tel.:* 01-352 5946
Fulham Road
London S.W.3

See no. 1245

LONDON

1051

CHILEAN IODINE EDUCATIONAL BUREAU *Tel.:* 01-606 7744
Chile House
20/24 Ropemaker Street
London E.C.2

To disseminate information on the uses of iodine and its compounds in medicine, industry and agriculture

Enquiries: To Director

Scope: Iodine, and its uses in medicine, industry, agriculture and veterinary medicine. Literature on thyroid gland and world prevalence of endemic goitre

Stock: 3,000 books; 40,500 pamphlets, patents and photocopies; 100 current periodicals. Stock not available on loan

Publications: Occasional bibliographies and technical booklets

LONDON

1052

THE CHINA ASSOCIATION *Tel.:* 01-588 1160
Broad Street House
54 Old Broad Street
London E.C.2

The promotion of trade between the United Kingdom and China

Enquiries: To Secretary

Scope: Commercial enquiries in respect of trade with China
Library of China literature, recent volumes mainly on economic and political subjects. For internal reference only. Archives available for research purposes

Publications: Monthly Bulletin published on behalf of the Association by the Sino-British Trade Council (includes economic, industrial and agricultural developments in China, and trade statistics)

LONDON

1053

CHISWICK POLYTECHNIC *Tel.:* 01-994 6602
Bath Road
Bedford Park
London W.4

Enquiries: To Librarian

Scope: General education. Fashion (including trade dress and hairdressing), health and social studies (including social work), business studies and public administration

Stock: 16,000 books; 2,000 pamphlets; 170 current periodicals

LONDON	CHRISTIAN ECONOMIC AND SOCIAL RESEARCH FOUNDATION	*Tel.:* 01-222 4001
1054	12 Caxton Street London S.W.1	

Objective research into the social and economic conditions affecting the individual and society in Britain, having regard to moral and spiritual values as well as material factors

Enquiries: To Liaison Officer

Scope: Alcohol-caused problems

Publications: Annual Report of Drink Offences

LONDON	CHRISTIAN SCIENCE COMMITTEE ON PUBLICATIONS FOR GREAT BRITAIN AND IRELAND	*Tel.:* 01-836 2808
1055	Ingersoll House 9 Kingsway London W.C.2	

Enquiries: To District Manager

Scope: Acts as a source of information concerning Christian Science and its Discoverer and Founder, Mary Baker Eddy

Publications: The Christian Science textbook: Science and Health with Key to the Scriptures. Mary Baker Eddy
The Christian Science Journal (monthly)
The Christian Science Sentinel (weekly)
The Christian Science Monitor (international daily newspaper). *See no.* 1056
Christian Science and its Discoverer. E. M. Ramsay
Historical Sketches. C. P. Smith
Mary Baker Eddy and Her Books. W. D. Orcutt
A Century of Christian Science Healing
The Story of Christian Science Wartime Activities, 1939-1946
Commitment to Freedom: The Story of The Christian Science Monitor. E. D. Canham
Mary Baker Eddy: The Years of Discovery. R. Peel (New York: Holt, Rinehart and Winston, 1966)

LONDON	THE CHRISTIAN SCIENCE MONITOR Africa House	*Tel.:* 01-405 0442
1056	Kingsway London W.C.2	

International daily newspaper

Enquiries: To Librarian

Scope: Small research library adapted to needs of the London Bureau of the newspaper. Includes a press cutting file based on national British papers, books, and periodicals

LONDON	CHRISTIAN SOCIALIST MOVEMENT Kingsway Hall	*Tel.:* 01-405 3246
1057	Kingsway London W.C.2	

Aims to show that Christianity and Socialism are bound up together and that each ought to influence the other

Enquiries: To Secretary

Scope: Christian Socialism

LONDON, CHRISTIAN SOCIALIST MOVEMENT, *cont.*

No library

Publications: Christian Socialist (6 issues each year)
Occasional pamphlets and booklets, usually on social and economic matters, written from the Christian standpoint

LONDON

1058

CHURCH MISSIONARY SOCIETY *Tel.:* 01-928 8681
157 Waterloo Road
London S.E.1

Voluntary Society (founded 1799) within the Church of England

Enquiries: To Librarian or Information Officer

Scope: Books on the history and theology of mission, and the growth of the Church overseas, and other religions. Audio-visual aids, and information sheets on the church overseas, are available through the Information Officer
Secondary: Books on the ecumenical movement, race relations, and those giving information on the social and economic life of those countries where the Society works

Stock: 20,000 books and pamphlets; current Annual Reports of most British Missionary Societies; 172 current periodicals

LONDON

1059

THE CHURCH OF ENGLAND CHILDREN'S *Tel.:* 01-735 2441
SOCIETY
Old Town Hall
Kennington
London S.E.11

Helps children in England and Wales who are homeless, unwanted, neglected or physically or emotionally handicapped

Enquiries: To Information Officer

Scope: Child care, adoption, fostering

No library

Publications: Gateway (quarterly magazine)
Pamphlets, colour film and slides

LONDON

1060

CHURCH OF ENGLAND YOUTH COUNCIL *Tel.:* 01-222 9011
Church House
Dean's Yard
London S.W.1

Enquiries: To Secretary

Scope: All matters relating to: training of leaders and young people; schools, further education and youth service; ecumenical work; and experimental research and investigation

No library

Publications: Various on training

LONDON

1061

THE CHURCHES' FELLOWSHIP FOR PSYCHICAL *Tel.:* 01-834 4329
AND SPIRITUAL STUDIES
5 Denison House
296 Vauxhall Bridge Road
London S.W.1

The study of paranormal and extra-sensory perception in their relation to the Christian faith

Enquiries: To Secretary
Scope: Library covers all aspects of psychical phenomena
Stock: 1,000 books; 50 pamphlets. Stock available to members only
Publications: Many booklets and pamphlets

There are committees covering psychic phenomena, healing, mental illness, scientific research and mysticism and a Regional and Branch organization

LONDON 1062

THE CHURCH'S MINISTRY AMONG THE JEWS *Tel.:* 01-242 2149 and
16 Lincoln's Inn Fields 01-405 0354
London W.C.2

Aims to promote a knowledge of Christianity among the Jews, to combat anti-semitism and to give Christians information about Jews and Judaism

Enquiries: To Secretary or Librarian
Scope: Works connected with the relationship of Judaism to Christianity in English and Hebrew
Secondary: Historical and general theological works with some bearing on this subject
Stock: 1,000 books; 50 pamphlets; 5 current periodicals
Publications: C.M.J. Quarterly
Books and pamphlets: for example, Sons of the Law
Go tell my Brethren (history of the Society)

LONDON 1063

THE CIBA FOUNDATION *Tel.:* 01-636 9456
41 Portland Place
London W1N 4BN

Charitable Trust for the promotion of international co-operation in medical and chemical research

Enquiries: To Librarian
Scope: Endocrinology
Secondary: General medicine; biochemistry; medical biographies
Stock: 2,000 books; collection of reprints; 220 current periodicals. Stock not available on loan
Publications: Ciba Foundation Symposia; Ciba Foundation Colloquia on Endocrinology; Ciba Foundation Study Groups (all published by J. & A. Churchill, London)

LONDON 1064

CITY OF LONDON COLLEGE *Tel.:* 01-606 8112
Moorgate
London E.C.2

Enquiries: To Librarian
Scope: General stock for college courses; strongest sections are commerce, law, economics, foreign languages, transport and economic history
Stock: 26,000 books; 5,000 pamphlets; 300 current periodicals
Publications: Printed subject book lists

LONDON 1065

CITY OF WESTMINSTER COLLEGE *Tel.:* 01-828 0801
Francis Street
London S.W.1

Enquiries: To Librarian
Scope: Business studies, accountancy, public administration, languages

LONDON, CITY OF WESTMINSTER COLLEGE, *cont.*

Secondary: Hospital administration, business law, office administration, organization and methods, data processing

Stock: 15,000 books; 240 current periodicals

LONDON

1066

THE CITY UNIVERSITY
SKINNERS' LIBRARY
St John Street
London E.C.1

Tel.: 01-253 4399
Telex: 263896

Enquiries: To Librarian

Scope: Science and technology, with special emphasis on engineering
Secondary: Management; social science
Special collection: Ophthalmic optics

Stock: 45,000 books and pamphlets; 900 current periodicals

LONDON

1067

CIVIC TRUST
18 Carlton House Terrace
London S.W.1

Tel.: 01-930 0914

Trust for the preservation and enhancement of the appearance of Town and Country

Enquiries: To Librarian

Scope: All aspects of dealing with the environment, specifically by visual aids, backed up with relevant books, pamphlets, periodicals and government publications, to provide information on planning problems, colour layout, traffic management, preservation and architecture. Details of Civic Trust awards

Stock: 300 books; 500 pamphlets; 90 current periodicals; 3,000 slides; 10,000 photographs; 16 films; 3 exhibitions. Slides, photographs, films and exhibitions only available on loan

Publications: Civic Trust
Green and Pleasant Land
The Civic Societies Movement
Register of local Civic and Amenity Societies
National Organizations affecting Amenity
Civic Trust Awards
The List of Civic Trust Awards, 1959–66
Operation Eyesores
Magdalen Street, Norwich
Street Improvement Schemes
Shop Front
The Civic Trust Trees Campaign
Moving Big Trees
Tree Planting
The Preservation and Planting of Trees
The Trust in Planning
Civic Amenities Act
Disposal of Unwanted Vehicles and Bulky Rubbish
A Lea Valley Regional Park
The Challenge of Leisure
Regent's Canal: A Policy for its Future
Conservation Areas
Protection of Areas of Architectural Importance

Derelict Land
Rhondda
Humber
Reshaping our Physical Environment
The Function of Open Country in Industrial Britain
Land Planning and Building Resources
Regional Planning and Urban Development in Western Europe
The Effect of Public Utility Works upon the Environment
Suiting Street Lighting to the Setting
London 1990
The Problems of Historic Towns in a period of population growth and technological change
The Appearance of Farm Buildings
Conservation and the Role of the Local Society
The Organization of an Amenity Society
Local Amenity Societies and Local Government
The Democratic Voice
York Conference of Amenity Societies: Report of Proceedings and Background Papers
Planning for Leisure in Britain
Historic Buildings in Greater London
Catalogue of slides available from the library

Associate Trusts:
Civic Trust for the North-West, Century House, St Peter's Square, Manchester 2 (*Tel.:* 061-236 0333)
Civic Trust for the North East, 34/35 Saddler Street, Durham (*Tel.:* Durham 61182)
Civic Trust for Wales, Treftadaeth Cymru, 46 The Parade, Cardiff CF2 3UE (*Tel.:* 0222-37146)
Scottish Civic Trust, 24 George Square, Glasgow C2 (*Tel.:* 041-221 1466)

LONDON

1068

CIVIL AND PUBLIC SERVICES ASSOCIATION   *Tel.:* 01-672 1299
215 Balham High Road
London S.W.17
Trade union

Enquiries: To Research Officer
Scope: Industrial relations in the Civil and Public Services
Secondary: Industrial relations in general and managerial techniques
Stock: 500 books; 1,000 pamphlets; 11 current periodicals and all journals published by Civil Service unions
Publications: Red Tape (journal)

LONDON

1069

CLAPHAM ANTIQUARIAN SOCIETY   *Tel.:* 01-673 2925
49 Mayford Road
London S.W.12

Enquiries: To Secretary
Scope: Anything connected with the local history, topography, genealogy, and archaeology of Clapham and the adjacent parts of Battersea
No library
Publications: Monthly duplicated news-sheet containing local history notes

LONDON	THE CLASSICAL ASSOCIATION	
	Institute of Classical Studies	
1070	31/34 Gordon Square	
	London W.C.1	

Enquiries: To Joint Hon. Secretaries, by letter only

Scope: The Association receives enquiries on any aspect of classical studies. If it cannot answer the enquiry itself, it will pass it on to an organization that can, for example to one of the classical bodies with which it has links such as the Joint Association of Classical Teachers, the Association for the Reform of Latin Teaching, the Orbilean Society

No library

Publications: The Classical Quarterly
Classical Review
Greece and Rome
New Surveys in the Classics (in conjunction with JACT)

The Association has 31 local branches in England, Scotland and Wales and a number of overseas branches

LONDON	COLLEGE OF ALL SAINTS	*Tel.:* 01-808 2842
	White Hart Lane	
1071	Tottenham	
	London N.17	
	College of Education	

Enquiries: To Librarian

Scope: Education
Secondary: General primary subjects and home economics

Stock: 40,000 books; 1,000 pamphlets; 180 current periodicals. Stock available on loan only to other Colleges of Education

LONDON	THE COLLEGE OF ARMS	*Tel.:* 01-248 2762
	Queen Victoria Street	
1072	London E.C.4	

Enquiries: To The Officer in Waiting

Scope: Heraldry and genealogy

Stock: 30,000 records and printed books. Stock not available on loan

LONDON	COLLEGE OF ESTATE MANAGEMENT	*Tel.:* 01-937 1546
	St Albans Grove	
1073	Kensington	
	London W.8	

Courses for Reading University B.Sc. degree in Estate Management and Quantity Surveying

Enquiries: To Librarian

Scope: Estate management; economics; valuation of property; rural studies; town planning; building construction; quantity surveying and elementary engineering; law relating to real estate, town planning and forestry

Stock: 10,000 books; 150 current periodicals

LONDON   COLLEGE OF FASHION AND CLOTHING   *Tel.*: 01-493 8341
TECHNOLOGY

1074   20 John Prince's Street
London W.1

Technical College teaching clothing design, tailoring, dressmaking, millinery, furriery, embroidery, hairdressing and beauty culture

Enquiries: To Librarian

Scope: Clothing (history and manufacture). Hairdressing and beauty culture
Secondary: Fine arts; management

Stock: Stock includes: Reference collection of fashion photographs from 1948. Books only available on loan

LONDON   COLLEGE OF PATHOLOGISTS   *Tel.*: 01-580 0893
16 Park Crescent

1075   London W.1

Enquiries: To Librarian, by letter only

Scope: History of pathology in all its branches; morbid anatomy, bacteriology, virology, parasitology, haematology and chemical pathology

Stock: 600 books; numerous pamphlets

LONDON   THE COLLEGE OF PREACHERS   *Tel.*: 01-589 1597
All Saints Hall

1076   Ennismore Gardens
London S.W.7

Aims to assist ordained and lay people to preach more efficiently

Enquiries: To Librarian

Scope: Books on Preaching. Books of Sermons by well-known preachers
Secondary: Theology, Commentaries on the Scriptures, Biblical exposition

Stock: 800 books

LONDON   THE COLLEGE OF S. MARK AND S. JOHN   *Tel.*: 01-352 4821
King's Road

1077   London S.W.10

College of Education

Enquiries: To Principal, by letter only

Scope: General collection including books and manuscripts relating to the College, and books relating to English education in the nineteenth century

Stock: 40,000 books and pamphlets; 250 current periodicals. Stock not normally available on loan. Enquiries relating to the history of the College and to its members only dealt with

The College has an 'Advance Post' at Albert Road, Devonport, Plymouth (no. 1992), where a collection of educational publications is being developed which will be available to local teachers

LONDON   THE COLLEGE OF SPECIAL EDUCATION   *Tel.*: 01-636 9334
85 Newman Street

1078   London W1P 3LD

Aims to assist teachers and other professional workers in their work with children who have learning handicaps

Enquiries: To Registrar

Scope: Advisory and Information Service: Enquiries received daily from teachers, students and parents, tutors at Colleges of Education, staff at Training Centres, professional workers and colleagues working overseas and local education authorities. The College organizes one-day courses and evening lectures

No library

Publications: Guide Lines for Teachers:
- No. 1: Training to Teach the Backward Child
- No. 2: Vocational Guidance—Employment and After-Care
- No. 3: Introductory Handbook on the Severely Subnormal (mentally handicapped)
- No. 4: Backward Readers. M. D. Vernon
- No. 5: Teaching Autistic Children. Wing and Elgar
- No. 6: The Frostig Approach. Arkwright

Book List on the S.S.N.
Film List for Special Education
Education in Hospital Schools for the Mentally Handicapped. G. A. Bland
Understanding Phonics. K. Hadley
Research Relevant to the Education of Children with Learning Handicaps (Report of January 1968 One Day Course)

LONDON

1079

THE COMBINED CADET FORCE ASSOCIATION *Tel.:* 01-834 1727
58 Buckingham Gate
London S.W.1

Administration of the Combined Cadet Force

Enquiries: To Secretary, by letter only

Scope: Enquiries on the Combined Cadet Force

No library

LONDON

1080

COMMISSION ON INDUSTRIAL RELATIONS *Tel.:* 01-242 6828 ext. 313
22 Kingsway
London W.C.2

Voluntary persuasive organization which seeks to promote developments in industrial relations by reason and argument

Enquiries: To Librarian, by letter only

Scope: Theory and practice of industrial relations in the United Kingdom. Publications of major unions. Trade union and industrial training. Management

Stock: 1,000 books; 400 pamphlets; 50 current periodicals

LONDON

1081

COMMONWEALTH ASSOCIATION OF ARCHITECTS *Tel.:* 01-580 5533
66 Portland Place
London W1N 4AD

Collaboration between societies and institutes of architects in the Commonwealth, especially in education

Enquiries: To Secretary

Scope: Information about: requirements for membership of national societies; requirements for local statutory registration; courses and training in architecture in Commonwealth countries; Codes of Conduct, Professional Services, Conditions of Engagement and the general organization of the Architectural profession in Commonwealth countries

Stock: No library, but Yearbooks and Handbooks of societies of architects in the Commonwealth are held

Publications: The Handbook of the Commonwealth Association of Architects (published every two years)
List of Recognised Schools of Architecture

LONDON

1082

COMMONWEALTH INSTITUTE *Tel.:* 01-937 8252
Kensington High Street
London W.8

Enquiries: To Librarian

Scope: The aim of the library is to cover all aspects of the Commonwealth today and of its individual members. Its stock consists of general descriptions of the countries and their peoples, economic and political studies, introductory histories and a full range of geographical studies, as well as books on flora and fauna, religions, laws and fine arts and works of contemporary literature. A special feature of the library is that it includes many books and journals published in other Commonwealth countries which are not readily available in libraries in Britain. Another useful feature is the collection of recommended books for class use (up to GCE 'O' level standard)

Besides serving as a contemporary reference library on the Commonwealth for the use of the general public and the Institute staff, the Commonwealth Institute Library is intended to be of particular service to teachers, students in colleges of education and other students of sixth-form level and above, for whom a loan service is provided. In addition to normal loan facilities, small collections of books will be assembled at the request of those engaged on more intensive study, and issued on extended loan

Stock: 20,000 books and pamphlets; 200 current periodicals. Separate collection of teaching and learning aids for teachers consisting of several thousand pamphlets, charts and pictures

Publications: Selected Reading Lists for Advanced Study
Selected Reading Lists for Secondary Schools
Selected Reading Lists for Primary Schools
Leaflets describing services of Institute
Books added to the library (monthly)
Art Gallery catalogues (for example, Canadian Abstract Art)
The Commonwealth Institute Journal

The same information services are available to Scotland from the Commonwealth Institute, Scotland, 8 Rutland Square, Edinburgh EH1 2AS (*Tel.:* 031-229 6668)

LONDON

1083

COMMUNITY SERVICE VOLUNTEERS *Tel.:* 01-247 8113
Toynbee Hall
28 Commercial Street
London E.1

Helps young people to play a responsible role in the community and gain experience of social problems

Enquiries: To Deputy Director

Scope: Information on community service projects throughout the British Isles which are being undertaken or planned. This includes local initiatives, changes in the school curriculum, trends in professional social work related to the role of volunteers

No library

Publications: Broadsheets
Films
A provisional bibliography on community service in Great Britain

LONDON	CONFEDERATION OF BRITISH INDUSTRY	*Tel.:* 01-930 6711
1084	21 Tothill Street London S.W.1	

To promote the prosperity of industry. Deals with all matters affecting the interests of employers and acts as advisory and consultative body for members

Enquiries: To Information Officer (enquiries relating to C.B.I. and its policy) or Librarian (other enquiries)

Scope: All matters of concern to industry including legislation, industrial relations and economics

Stock: 15,000 books, pamphlets and reports; 400 current periodicals. Much material is kept by specializing departments, for example overseas, economic and legal, technical, to whom enquirers may be referred from library. Stock not normally available on loan

Publications: British Industry Week
Education and Training Bulletin (quarterly)
Fanfare for Britain (2 issues each year)
Home Bulletin (fortnightly)
Industrial Trends Survey (3 issues each year)
Books and pamphlets

LONDON	CONFERENCE OF MISSIONARY SOCIETIES IN GT BRITAIN AND IRELAND	*Tel.:* 01-730 9611
1085	Edinburgh House 2 Eaton Gate London S.W.1	

The Conference is an association of missionary societies

Enquiries: To Assistant for Information, preferably by letter

Scope: Matters concerned with the Christian missionary enterprise: in particular the work of British missionary organizations and that of the churches in Asia, Africa, the Pacific and Latin America to which they are related, including their work in the spheres of education, medical services, social development, and literature production in countries abroad
Secondary: The relationships between churches in their mission; the ecumenical movement

Stock: 500 books, pamphlets and reports. Publications of member missionary societies; World Council of Churches; related ecumenical bodies. Stock not available on loan

LONDON	CONGREGATIONAL COUNCIL FOR WORLD MISSION	*Tel.:* 01-930 0061
1086	Livingstone House 11 Carteret Street Westminster London S.W.1	

Enquiries: To Librarian (historical) or Secretary (current)

Scope: Correspondence from missionaries serving since 1797 in many parts of the world: South Seas, India, China, Africa, Papua, of historical and anthropological interest
Secondary: Books supporting the above

Stock: 10,000 books and pamphlets. Stock not available on loan

LONDON	CONSULATE GENERAL OF MONACO	*Tel.:* 01-629 0734
1087	4 Audley Square London W.1	

Enquiries: To Consul General, by letter only

Scope: Information on Monaco (if not available may be obtained from Monaco)
No library
Publications: Tourist material

LONDON

1088

CONSUMER'S ASSOCIATION *Tel.:* 01-930 9921
14 Buckingham Street
London W.C.2

Publication of reports based on comparative testing of consumer goods. Information for consumers in general

Enquiries: To Librarian

Scope: Consumer information and protection: United Kingdom and overseas. A small collection of books on consumer behaviour, education, and consumer protection. Collection of consumer periodicals from overseas. Standards: United Kingdom and overseas

Stock: 2,500 books; 4,000 pamphlets and reports; 250 current periodicals

Publications: Which? (monthly)   The Individual Consumer: a reading list
Money Which? (quarterly)   Daily consumer news sheet
Good Food Guide   The Law for Consumers

LONDON

1089

CORPORATION OF LONDON RECORDS OFFICE *Tel.:* 01-606 3030
P.O. Box 270
Guildhall
London E.C.2

Custody of the official archives of the Corporation

Enquiries: To The Deputy Keeper of Records

Scope: This is the most extensive collection of municipal archives in the country, ranging in date from the 11th to the 20th centuries. Because of London's special position as the capital city with its large and closely knit population and special relationship with the Crown, the archives include much that is of national as well as purely civic interest. It is, however, difficult to particularize their subject content since they reflect the manifold and changing interests and activities of the Corporation through the centuries which interests must touch upon medicine and the social sciences. In general terms they include: royal charters; medieval compilations of City law and custom; administrative records such as the proceedings of the Courts of Aldermen and Common Council and their numerous committees; judicial records arising from the civic courts and the Sessions of Gaol Delivery and Peace; financial records of many kinds including ledgers, accounts, assessments for the levying of taxes; and records such as rentals and deeds relating to property, some of which lay outside the City

LONDON

1090

COUNCIL FOR EDUCATION IN WORLD CITIZENSHIP *Tel.:* 01-735 0181
93 Albert Embankment
London S.E.1

Aims to encourage in schools and Colleges of Education in the United Kingdom the study of international affairs and of the United Nations

Enquiries: To Secretary

Scope: Film-strips and charts concerned with the work of the United Nations and its Specialized Agencies with specific emphasis on social and economic development, and with individual countries

Stock: 90 film-strips; 82 charts

LONDON, COUNCIL FOR EDUCATION IN WORLD CITIZENSHIP, *cont.*
- *Publications:* Duplicated catalogue
  Duplicated broadsheet and map (seven issues each year, devoted to topical international problems)

LONDON

1091

COUNCIL FOR NATIONAL ACADEMIC AWARDS   *Tel.:* 01-580 3141
3 Devonshire Street
London W1N 2BA

Established by Royal Charter with powers to award degrees and other academic awards to students who complete courses of study or carry out programmes of research at establishments other than Universities

- *Enquiries:* To Registrar and Secretary
- *Scope:* Can provide lists of courses of study which lead to the Council's degrees and details of colleges at which these courses are available, together with information about conditions for the award of its research degrees
  No library
- *Publications:* Lists of courses leading to the Council's degrees
  Statements of Policy

LONDON

1092

COUNCIL FOR SMALL INDUSTRIES IN   *Tel.:* 01-946 5101
   RURAL AREAS
ADVISORY SERVICES DIVISION
35 Camp Road
Wimbledon S.W.19

The main CoSIRA service is the provision of advice and help in improving the efficiency of small firms in the rural areas of England and Wales

- *Enquiries:* To Senior Information Officer, by letter only
- *Scope:* Management advice on specific problems connected with accountancy, work study, marketing and export
  Technical advice on a wide range of subjects including: workshop design and plant layout, structural designs, machine shop re-organization, plastics fabrication techniques, machinery and equipment evaluation, woodworking machinery instruction, electrical specifications, product value analysis and development, semi-automatic welding techniques
- *Stock:* Technical Library: 4,000 books; 5,000 pamphlets and extracts; 130 reports; 135 current periodicals
- *Publications:* Technical books and booklets, bibliographies and newsletter

LONDON

1093

COUNCIL FOR THE CARE OF CHURCHES   *Tel.:* 01-538 3843
83 London Wall
London E.C.2

Advises on all aspects of the care of church buildings and their furnishings and on the building of new churches (Church of England)

- *Enquiries:* To Librarian
- *Scope:* The library includes the following subjects as they relate to churches: topography, church furnishings, English art history, liturgy, hagiography, conservation of buildings, law as it relates to church buildings and architectural histories; may be consulted by appointment
- *Stock:* 4,000 books; local and national archaeological proceedings and related periodicals, and British and foreign periodicals on modern church building and architecture; Friends of Cathedrals

reports; files of living artists and craftsmen who produce work for churches, including sculpture and stained glass artists, may be inspected by appointment; files on about 15,000 individual cathedrals and churches in England with photographs and guide books; slide collection (2 inch, largely in colour)

Publications: A list of books helpful to those planning to build new churches
Church Planning and Arrangement. I. Problems from the Past; II. Planning for the Present
How to Look after your Church
Re-decorating the Church
Wall Surfaces
The Conservation of English Wall Paintings
Lighting and Wiring of Churches. Parts I and II
Sound Amplification in your Church
Church Timberwork: Damage and Repair
The Care of Monuments, Brasses and Ledger Slabs in Churches
Inspection of Churches Measure 1955
Parish Church Log Book
Faculty Jurisdiction Measure 1964
Faculty Jurisdiction Rules 1967
The Churchyards Handbook
The Disposal of Cremated Remains
Lettering for Churches
Altar Frontals: their History and Construction with Special Reference to the English Tradition. J. M. Petersen
How to Choose Stained Glass. E. Milner-White
It Won't Happen to Us (insurance, security and theft)
Church Organs
Wall Paintings: Questions and Answers
Economic Churchyard Maintenance
Lighting and Wiring of Churches
Church Roof Coverings
Repair and Maintenance of Stone Buildings
Heating your Church
Monumental Brasses and Brass Rubbing: Questions and Answers

The Cathedrals Advisory Committee shares the offices and staff of the Council for the Care of Churches, but it is quite independent of that Council. Its function is to advise on the fabric and furnishings of Church of England Cathedrals

LONDON

1094

COUNCIL OF INDUSTRIAL DESIGN *Tel.:* 01-839 8000
28 Haymarket
London S.W.1

Aims to promote the improvement of design of the products of British industry

Enquiries: To the Photographic Librarian or Book Librarian, as appropriate
Scope: Industrial design, product design, interior design, graphics and related subjects
Slide Library: All 35 mm colour or black and white slides which may be hired for lectures
Stock: 6,000 accessions, exclusive of loan copies. Total additions during past 12 months: 585
Photographic Library: Photographs or photocopy prints of most of the 8,000 products which are shown in Design Index in the Design Centre may be ordered from the Photo Library
Also all CoID copyright photographs used in DESIGN magazine as well as photographs of room settings and other exhibitions held in the Design Centre
Book Library: Small staff library, open to the public during normal office hours for reference only. No loans of either books or magazines can be made

LONDON, COUNCIL OF INDUSTRIAL DESIGN, *cont.*

Stock: Approximately 1,000 books and bound volumes of industrial design magazines

Publications: Comprehensive slide catalogue
Catalogue of recommended films and filmstrips
DESIGN (monthly)
Contract Catalogue from Design Index
Street Furniture Catalogue from Design Index
Reports on various activities: for example, hotel furniture and furnishings; prefabricated farm buildings

A detailed leaflet on the Slide and Photographic Libraries is available on request

LONDON

1095

THE COUNCIL OF THE BRITISH NATIONAL BIBLIOGRAPHY LTD
7 & 9 Rathbone Street
London W1P 2AL

Tel.: 01-580 3681

To compile, edit and publish in appropriate bibliographical form lists of books, pamphlets and other recorded material of whatever nature published in Great Britain, the Dominions and Colonies and foreign countries, together with such annotations or further information as may be desirable for the use of librarians, bibliographers and others

Enquiries: To General Editor

Scope: Enquiries of a special bibliographical nature which cannot be answered from the published volumes or by reference to other sources are accepted. The Editorial Staff of B.N.B. can be regarded as experts in the field of cataloguing, classification, subject indexing, application of automation to problems of bibliographical data handling, editorial and production processes

No library

Publications: British National Bibliography: Weekly Lists, Quarterly Cumulations, Annual Volumes and Five-Yearly Cumulations of Subject Catalogues and Indexes

LONDON

1096

COUNTRYSIDE COMMISSION
1 Cambridge Gate
Regent's Park
London N.W.1

Tel.: 01-935 5533 and 0366

Statutory body charged with keeping under review all matters relating to the provision and improvement of facilities for the enjoyment of the countryside in England and Wales, the conservation and enhancement of its natural beauty and amenity, and the need to secure public access for open air recreation. Special responsibilities for National Parks, Areas of Outstanding Natural Beauty, Long Distance Paths and Bridle-ways, Country Parks, camping and picnic sites, research and experimental projects and information services

Enquiries: To Information section

Scope: All aspects of the Commission's interests. United Kingdom focal point for countryside information, and national agency for the Council of Europe's Information Centre for Nature Conservation. A register of countryside organizations, public and voluntary, is maintained and enquiries about most countryside matters can be directed to the sources providing the information required including research projects on recreational use completed or in progress. The Commission are preparing a Source Directory of organizations concerned with conservation or with producing information about the countryside in all its aspects. The scope of the service extends to information about Nature Conservation publications, visual aids and films. There will be a source bank of data relating to the countryside including summaries of articles, books, booklets, leaflets and papers mainly for the research worker

Stock: 500 books; 1,500 pamphlets; 500 reports; 100 current periodicals

Publications: Recreation News Posters and wall charts
National Park Guide Books Advisory booklets
Photographic library

LONDON

1097

THE CUMING MUSEUM *Tel.:* 01-703 3324
Walworth Road
London S.E.17

The preservation of information of the archaeological source material for the history of the region immediately south of London Bridge and for London superstitions and their educational use in the widest sense. This is implemented by: collecting, including participation in archaeological excavation; processing, including conservation and cataloguing; and exposition, including answering enquiries, publications, displays and lectures

Enquiries: To Keeper

Scope: Technical books, offprints, and journals relevant to the museum's interests listed above. Information leaflets and children's worksheets. Provisional reports of local archaeological excavations are reprinted by the museum and made available to the general public
Public enquiries are answered relating to local archaeology and London charms

LONDON

1098

DAILY MIRROR LIBRARY *Tel.:* 01-353 0246
Daily Mirror Newspapers Ltd *Telex:* 27286
(International Publishing Corporation Ltd)
33 Holborn
London E.C.1

Comprehensive information and illustration service for the Daily Mirror and Sunday Mirror

Enquiries: To Library Manager, by letter only

Scope: Information in all fields with the exception of specialized technical information. Primary interests are biographical, sociological and political. Period of time covered varies according to subject; the majority of cuttings and photographs cover the past fifteen years. Earlier items are reduced to essentials, some classifications being merged or discarded completely

Stock: 8,000 books; 2,000 pamphlets; 800 reports; 45 current periodicals; 6,000,000 cuttings; 804,000 photographs; 600,000 negatives. Stock not available on loan. Copies of staff photographs and cuttings can be made for purchase

Publications: The Daily Mirror
The Sunday Mirror

LONDON

1099

THE DALCROZE SOCIETY INCORPORATED *Tel.:* 01-455 1268
16 Heathcroft
Hampstead Way
London N.W.11

See no. 2302

LONDON

1100

THE DANISH TOURIST BOARD *Tel.:* 01-734 2637
Sceptre House
169/173 Regent Street
London W1R 8PY

Scope: Tourist information on Denmark
No library

| LONDON | THE DAVID DAVIES MEMORIAL INSTITUTE OF INTERNATIONAL STUDIES | *Tel.:* 01-222 7331 |

1101
Thorney House
34 Smith Square
London S.W.1

Enquiries: To Secretary General and Editor

Scope: Work of the Institute on the peaceful settlement of international disputes and the role and function of a United Nations force
Secondary: Environmental conservation study from the point of view of prevention of further deterioration of the environment

No library

Publications: United Nations Forces: A Legal Study of United Nations Practice
International Relations
Report of a Study Group on the Peaceful Settlement of International Disputes
Annual Memorial Lectures (for example, Britain and the I.L.O.)
Draft Rules Concerning Changes in the Environment of the Earth
Draft Treaty on Outer Space, the Moon and other Celestial Bodies
Principles Governing certain Changes in the Environment of Man
Oceanic Pollution: a Survey and some Suggestions for Control
Two Nations and Kashmir

| LONDON | DEPARTMENT OF EDUCATION AND SCIENCE | *Tel.:* 01-493 7070 |
| | Curzon Street | *Telex:* 264329 |

1102
London W.1

Enquiries: To Librarian

Scope: Education in all its aspects, including the principles, philosophy and psychology of education; child study and health, including handicapped children; adult education; youth services; technical and vocational training; school buildings and libraries; educational administration, both in this country and abroad; university and higher education
Secondary: Administration of the arts

Stock: 180,000 books and pamphlets; 600 current periodicals

Publications: Monthly Accessions List   Science Bulletins
Education Developments Abroad (abstracts)   Education information leaflets
Trends in Education (quarterly)   On Course Journal
Reports on Education   On Course Bulletins
Other publications listed in H.M.S.O. Sectional List no. 2

The Department's Information Division runs a further education information service

For Architect's and Building Branch Library *see* no. 1103

| LONDON | DEPARTMENT OF EDUCATION AND SCIENCE ARCHITECT'S AND BUILDING BRANCH | *Tel.:* 01-493 7070 *Telex:* 264329 |

1103
Curzon Street
London W.1

Responsible for the handling of building projects sponsored in England by the Schools and Further Education Branches and in England and Wales by the Teachers and Special Service Branches once they have been included in the building programme

Enquiries: To Librarian

Scope: Subject field of library covers educational buildings, technical report literature in the building field and trade literature of the construction industry. The library provides an information service, indexes articles, traces products, circulates periodicals and compiles bibliographies. Enquiries from outside the branch are dealt with when possible

Stock: Includes 34 current periodicals

Publications: Building Bulletins (periodically relating to development work undertaken by the Branch)
Design Notes

See also no. 1102

LONDON

1104

DEPARTMENT OF EMPLOYMENT AND PRODUCTIVITY LIBRARY
11/12 St James's Square
London S.W.1

Tel.: 01-930 6200

Enquiries: To Librarian

Scope: Industrial relations, manpower, productivity, employment and unemployment, communication in industry. All aspects of factory and shops inspection: legal, social, medical. Monopolies; Prices and incomes
Secondary: Public administration

Stock: 50,000 books and pamphlets; 400 current periodicals

Publications: H.M.S.O. Sectional List no. 21
Occupational Classification Guide
Family Expenditure Survey (annually, from 1960–61)
DEP Gazette (monthly)
Time Rates and Wages and Hours of Labour (serial)
Industrial Training Publications
Safety Health and Welfare Publications
Directory of Employers and Employers Associations
Manpower Studies (series)
Industrial Relations Handbook
Industrial Tribunals Reports
Industrial Court Awards
Careers Pamphlets (continually revised)

For Training Department see no. 1105

LONDON

1105

DEPARTMENT OF EMPLOYMENT AND PRODUCTIVITY
TRAINING DEPARTMENT (TD4)
168 Regent Street
London W.1

Tel.: 01-437 9088 ext. 5

Information on industrial training and on development of new techniques

Enquiries: To Information Officer TD4

Scope: The basis of the system is the Training Abstracts Service available on annual subscription. This provides about 80 abstracts a month printed on cards and offering a resumé of new publications, journal articles and research reports relevant to industrial training
Secondary: Some primary source material is available but most enquiries are dealt with by reference to the cumulative store of training abstracts which embrace both British and overseas material

Stock: Limited stock of books and pamphlets; 100 specialist British and overseas periodicals

Publications: Training Research Register
Glossary of Training Terms

LONDON, DEPARTMENT OF EMPLOYMENT AND PRODUCTIVITY, TRAINING DEPARTMENT (TD4), *cont.*

Training Information papers (a series of booklets written in everyday language describing research investigations relevant to practical training problems; 5 published to date)

See also no. 1104

LONDON

1106

DEPARTMENT OF HEALTH AND SOCIAL SECURITY *Tel.*: 01-407 5522
Alexander Fleming House
Elephant and Castle
London S.E.1

Government department dealing with health and medical services including hospitals, nursing, general medical practice, food hygiene, international health, welfare services including those for the elderly and handicapped; and social security

Enquiries: To Librarian

Scope: The Library and information services cover the whole of the Department's interests as listed above
The Main Library at Alexander Fleming House deals with all the subjects except social security. It is responsible for the Hospital Abstracting service which is the primary international source of information in this field
Special collection: 1,000 early pamphlets on the poor laws and related subjects

Stock: 115,000 books, pamphlets and reports; 1,000 current periodicals
Complete files of reports of Medical Officers of Health of local authorities in England and Wales. Depository library for the World Health Organization and receives all publications of the United States Public Health Service

Publications: Hospital Abstracts (monthly)
Library Bulletin (monthly)
Other Departmental (Health) publications listed in H.M.S.O. Sectional List no. 11
For Social Security Library, *see* no. 1107

LONDON

1107

DEPARTMENT OF HEALTH AND SOCIAL *Tel.*: 01-930 9066
SECURITY (SOCIAL SECURITY LIBRARY) *Telex*: 22843
10 John Adam Street
London W.C.2

This library provides for the Social Security side of the Department

Enquiries: To Librarian

Scope: Social security including national insurance, family allowances, war and industrial injury pensions and allowances; social welfare; supplementary benefits
Secondary: Management, computers

Stock: 37,000 books and pamphlets; 250 current periodicals; all publications of the International Social Security Association

Publications: Monthly list of additions to the library
Departmental (Social Security) publications listed in H.M.S.O. Sectional List no. 49

See also no. 1106

LONDON

1108

DESIGN & INDUSTRIES ASSOCIATION *Tel.*: 01-930 0540
Nash House
12 Carlton House Terrace
London S.W.1

An independent non-professional organization which campaigns for higher standards in the design of industrial products and the man-made environment

Enquiries: To Secretary, by letter only

Scope: The Association is one of the participating societies in the new national centre for design and the arts at Carlton House Terrace, Westminster, London, S.W.1. Library facilities are available to members managed jointly by all the participating societies (Institute of Contemporary Art, Society of Industrial Artists and Designers, Design & Industries Association, Design and Art Directors Association and Institute of Landscape Architects). Stock not available on loan

Publications: DIA Newsletter (twice each year)
DIA Yearbook (annually)

LONDON

1109

THE DICKENS HOUSE *Tel.:* 01-405 2127
48 Doughty Street
London W.C.1

Headquarters of the Dickens Fellowship

Enquiries: To Curator

Scope: The works of Dickens, criticism, illustrators, translations. The life of Dickens; the work of Dickens in other fields

Stock: 5,000 books; *The Dickensian* since 1906. Books may be consulted by appointment

Publications: The Dickensian (three issues each year)

LONDON

1110

DIGBY STUART COLLEGE OF EDUCATION *Tel.:* 01-876 8273
Roehampton Lane
London S.W.15

Enquiries: To Librarian, by letter only

Scope: An information service in relation to the courses provided in the college. The subject fields of the library bookstock and periodicals are closely connected with the subjects taught: Education, which is of primary interest, theology, sociology, history, science, geography, home economics, literature and fine arts

Stock: 31,400 books and pamphlets; 145 current periodicals

LONDON

1111

DIRECTORATE GENERAL OF MEDICAL *Tel.:* 01-387 5040
SERVICES (R.A.F.)
Ministry of Defence
1/6 Tavistock Square
London W.C.1

Administration and organization of Royal Air Force Medical Services

Enquiries: To Director General, by letter only

Scope: Advice and information to Medical Practitioners on the medical aspects of service in the Royal Air Force and information concerning their patients' past service medical history (subject to the patient's consent)

LONDON

1112

DIRECTORATE OF ARMY EDUCATION *Tel.:* 01-930 9400 ext. 221
Ministry of Defence (Army)
Old War Office
Whitehall
London S.W.1

Enquiries: To Director, by letter only

LONDON, DIRECTORATE OF ARMY EDUCATION, *cont.*

Scope: Education in the Army, including remedial education
Education of service children
Language training (including English as a foreign language)
Resettlement of soldiers into civilian life
Instructional technology
No library

LONDON

1113

DISABLED LIVING ACTIVITIES GROUP OF THE
CENTRAL COUNCIL FOR THE DISABLED
Vincent House
Vincent Square
London S.W.1

Tel.: 01-834 8016

The philosophy of the Group is that careful study will invariably ameliorate bad conditions; and that, in the case of the disabled, study of their environment in the widest sense can return some of the opportunities in life which have hitherto been lost to them

Enquiries: To Information Officer

Scope: The Information Service for the Disabled was started in 1964 and since 1966 has been running on a subscription basis. Enquiries regarding the physically handicapped may be made in the following subjects: Personal activities of daily living (large equipment which will help persons to move from one place to another or make more effective movement on the same spot; aids which will assist functions such as eating, drinking, washing, cooking, housework, leisure and communications). Design and construction (buildings generally, their fixtures and fittings). Facilities for education (accessibility for the disabled of Universities, Colleges and other education establishments; home tuition). Facilities for training (addresses of rehabilitation units and training centres). Employment (information and advice on whom to contact regarding sheltered workshops and home employment). Accommodation (information will be given as to where there are flats, bungalows, permanent residential homes and convalescent homes for the disabled). Extra facilities and services

Copies of information files may be borrowed through the Hospital Centre's Package library system (no. 1213)

LONDON

1114

DR WILLIAMS'S TRUST
14 Gordon Square
London W.C.1

Tel.: 01-387 3727

Charitable trust with various benefactions, including the Library, mainly for the benefit of Nonconformists

Enquiries: To Librarian

Scope: Theology; ecclesiastical history, particularly (early) Nonconformist history; philosophy
Secondary: Other humanities generally
Special Collections: Crabb Robinson manuscripts and transcripts. Norman Baynes Byzantine Collection

Stock: 112,500 books including 20,000 pamphlets; 80 current periodicals; numerous manuscripts, mainly but not exclusively of Nonconformist interest; 150 microfilms of printed and manuscript material; 100 photographic and other reproductions

Publications: Fifty-year Catalogue (1900–1950)
Ten-year Catalogue (1951–1960)
Annual Bulletin of Accessions
Friends of Dr Williams's Library Annual Lectures, 1947–

Guide to the Manuscripts in the Library
Bibliography of early Nonconformity (slips)

LONDON   THE DUCHY OF CORNWALL OFFICE   *Tel.:* 01-834 7346
1115
10 Buckingham Gate
London S.W.1
Administration of the estates of Duke of Cornwall

Enquiries: To Secretary

Scope: The papers of a great landed estate, mostly agricultural, dating from 1337 with significant gaps. They include Council minutes; Minister's accounts; Havenor's accounts; surveys of manors; papers relating to the Stannaries of Devon and Cornwall; some Household accounts of Princes of Wales and other Royal persons

Stock: 5,000 books. The archives and library are available for inspection by students on request. Stock not available on loan

LONDON   THE DUKE OF EDINBURGH'S AWARD SCHEME   *Tel.:* 01-930 7681
1116
2 Old Queen Street
London S.W.1

The Award Scheme provides a programme of leisure time activities for young people of 14 to 21 years old

Enquiries: To General Secretary

Scope: Information on subjects within the sections of the scheme: Service, expeditions, interests, physical activity, design for living
No library

Publications: Gauntlet (3 issues each year)

LONDON   EALING TECHNICAL COLLEGE   *Tel.:* 01-579 4111
1117
St Mary's Road
London W.5

Enquiries: To Librarian

Scope: Language library (Chinese, French, German, Italian, Spanish, Russian); business studies; hotel and catering studies; librarianship; law
Secondary: Linguistics; bibliography; economics; accounting; management; economic geography; industrial psychology; printing; art. Bibliographical enquiries only dealt with

Stock: 32,500 books; 5,000 pamphlets; 700 current periodicals

Publications: Occasional bibliographies

LONDON   EAST HAM TECHNICAL COLLEGE   *Tel.:* 01-472 1430 ext. 157
1118
High Street South
London E.6

Enquiries: To Librarian

Scope: Art, business and general studies, languages, music, building, electrical engineering, mechanical engineering, science

Stock: 20,000 books and pamphlets; 200 current periodicals. Complete set of British Standards

| LONDON

1119 | THE ECONOMIST INTELLIGENCE UNIT LIMITED
Spencer House
27 St James's Place
London S.W.1 | *Tel.:* 01-493 6711
Telex: 266353 |

International business research and consultancy organization

Enquiries: To Business Promotion Manager

Scope: Market research; studies on economic and social development; transport and planning; marketing; financial, statistical and management consultancy

Library not available for reference purposes

Publications: 62 Quarterly Economic Reviews (covering business, political and economic conditions in over 130 countries)
European Trends (puts the EEC and EFTA in perspective)
Retail Business (monthly, covers United Kingdom market for consumer goods)
Marketing in Europe (monthly, covers European consumer goods market)
Motor Business (quarterly, for the automotive and allied industries)
Paper Bulletin (quarterly)
Rubber Trends (quarterly)

| LONDON

1120 | THE ECONOMIST NEWSPAPER LTD
25 St James's Street
London S.W.1 | *Tel.:* 01-930 5155
Telex: 24344 |

Weekly newspaper

Enquiries: To Librarian

Scope: Wide general subject coverage

Stock: 1,750 books; pamphlets; 1,000 current periodicals

Publications: The Economist (weekly)
Foreign Report (confidential weekly bulletin)
Brief Booklets (series of illustrated 28-page booklets on a variety of subjects)
Industrial Profits and Assets (analysis of profits of companies)

LONDON

1121

EDUCATIONAL PUPPETRY ASSOCIATION
23A Southampton Place
London W.C.1

Aims to present and develop the full educational possibilities of puppetry as a creative and dramatic activity, including experimental work with retarded, subnormal and maladjusted children and in adult rehabilitation

Enquiries: To Secretary, by letter only

Scope: General advice and information, for example on choice of literature, courses, forthcoming events, is available to all; specific advice on techniques necessarily restricted to members. Enquiries dealt with by appropriate Council members

Stock: 350 books (all new books on the subject are reviewed and added to library; members receive library list)

Publications: Puppet Post (official journal, twice each year)
Spotlight (newsletter, 8 times each year)
List of Instructional Leaflets and Books
The Puppet Book. 3rd edition (published by Faber, covers all educational aspects)
Eight Plays for Hand Puppets. G. Miller

Regional Representatives in Scotland, Midlands, Wales and Southern England

| LONDON | THE EEG SOCIETY | *Tel.:* 01-856 5555 ext. 310 |

1122 EEG Department
Brook General Hospital
Shooters Hill Road
London S.E.18

Promotes the science and practice and facilitates the exchange of information on matters affecting electroencephalography and allied subjects

Enquiries: To Hon. Secretary, by letter only
Publications: Electroencephalography and clinical neurophysiology

| LONDON | ELECTRICITY SUPPLY INDUSTRY TRAINING BOARD | *Tel.:* 01-834 2333 *Telex:* London 23385 |

1123 30 Millbank
London S.W.1

Further development of training throughout the electricity supply industry in England, Wales and Scotland

Enquiries: To Secretary
Scope: Training recommendations covering the various major occupations found in the electricity supply industry
Publications: Bulletins
Occasional reports

| LONDON | ELGAR BIRTHPLACE TRUST | *Tel.:* 01-834 2858 |

1124 91A Grosvenor Road
London S.W.1

Maintenance and administration of the Elgar Birthplace Museum at Broadheath, Worcester

Enquiries: To Curator (*Tel.:* Cotheridge 224)
Scope: Information on Elgar's life and work
Stock: Few books on Elgar. Stock not available on loan
Publications: Booklets and miniature music scores

| LONDON | EMBASSY OF AUSTRIA | *Tel.:* 01-235 3731 |

1125 18 Belgrave Mews West
London S.W.1

Enquiries: To Information Officer, by letter only
Scope: Information on Austria generally

| LONDON | EMBASSY OF IRELAND | *Tel.:* 01-235 2171 |

1126 17 Grosvenor Place
London S.W.1

Enquiries: To Secretary
Scope: Information on Ireland
Stock: 500 books; Irish national daily newspapers and periodicals; Irish official publications, statutes, parliamentary debates. Stock not available on loan

| LONDON | EMBASSY OF THE REPUBLIC OF VIETNAM | *Tel.:* 01-937 3765 |

1127 12 Victoria Road
London W.8

Enquiries: To Press and Information Office

LONDON, EMBASSY OF THE REPUBLIC OF VIETNAM, *cont.*

Scope: Dissemination of news from Vietnam. General information on other aspects (for example, cultural and historical) of the Republic of Vietnam (South Vietnam)

No library

Publications: Vietnam, Yesterday and Today (monthly magazine)
News from Vietnam (weekly news bulletin)
Pamphlets
Films

LONDON

1128

THE EMBROIDERERS' GUILD *Tel.:* 01-935 3281
73 Wimpole Street
London W1M 8AX

To promote the art of embroidery and related crafts

Enquiries: To Secretary

Scope: Embroidery

Stock: Library contains many historical and foreign books on embroidery, and all new books published are added. Books are lent only to members of the Guild. New books are sold to the public. Collection of embroideries: Historical and contemporary, includes work from overseas

Publications: Embroidery (quarterly journal of the Guild)
Church Needlework Booklets
Designs and leaflets
Transfer designs
Charts
General leaflets
Colour slides

LONDON

1129

THE ENGLISH ASSOCIATION *Tel.:* 01-589 8480
8 Cromwell Place
London S.W.7

Aims to promote knowledge and appreciation of English language and literature, and to uphold the standards of English writing and speech

Enquiries: To Secretary, by letter only

No library

Publications: English (journal)
A Guide to English Courses in the Universities
Presidential Addresses and Pamphlets
The Year's Work in English Studies. G. Harlow and J. Redmond, ed.
Poems of Today
English Essays of Today
English Short Stories of Today
English One Act Plays of Today
Essays and Studies
Commonwealth Poems of Today
The Teaching of English in Schools
Shakespeare—a Reading Guide

LONDON

1130

THE ENGLISH PLACE-NAME SOCIETY *Tel.:* 01-387 3930
University College London
Gower Street
London W.C.1

Aims to carry out the Survey of English Place-Names, and to promote such activities as may assist this work

Enquiries: To Hon. Secretary, by letter only

Scope: English place-names

Stock: 5 current periodicals. Published and unpublished surveys and monographs. Card and Slip Index collections of spellings for various counties in Society's Series: Oxfordshire, Yorkshire West Riding, Gloucestershire, Norfolk, Westmorland. Stock not available on loan

Publications: The Survey of English Place-Names (Volume 1 onwards, 43 volumes to date)
The Journal of The English Place-Name Society (annually)
The Preparation of County Place-Name Surveys. 1956

LONDON

1131

ERGONOMICS RESEARCH SOCIETY *Tel.*: 01-764 5060
c/o Construction Industry Training Board
Radnor House
London Road
Norbury
London S.W.16

To provide a common meeting ground for those interested in the study of anatomy, physiology and psychology as applied to practical problems

Enquiries: To R. G. Sell, Secretary, by letter only

Scope: The Secretary will direct any written enquiry to the person he considers most competent to deal with it

No library

Publications: Ergonomics

LONDON

1132

THE EUGENICS SOCIETY *Tel.*: 01-834 2091
69 Eccleston Square
London S.W.1

To study hereditary and environmental aspects of human qualities, to formulate and support policies for improving these qualities and enabling them to develop to their full potential in the individual, to foster a responsible attitude to parenthood, to promote relevant research and to facilitate communication between those interested

Enquiries: To Librarian

Scope: Eugenics. Genetics: general, human; plural births, abnormalities. Pathology; psychopathology. Psychology: measurement of intelligence. Population: vital statistics, migration, world food resources. Sex: marriage, prostitution, contraception, abortion, sterilization, infertility, differential fertility. Sociology: general. Biology: human biology; evolution
Secondary: Anthropology: race crossing. Biography

Stock: 4,700 books; 3,000 pamphlets; 45 current periodicals

Publications: Journal of Biosocial Science (official journal, published for the Galton Foundation by Blackwell Scientific Publications, Oxford)
Eugenics Society Bulletin (quarterly)
The Eugenics Society Symposia Proceedings: Vol. 1, 1965, Biological Aspects of Social Problems; Vol. 2, 1966, Genetic and Environmental Factors in Human Ability; Vol. 3, 1967, Social and Genetic Influences on Life and Death; Vol. 4, 1968, Genetic and Environmental Influences on Behaviour; 1969, Biosocial Aspects of Race

LONDON

1133

EUROPEAN COMMUNITIES PRESS AND *Tel.*: 01-235 4904
  INFORMATION OFFICE *Telex:* 23266
23 Chesham Street
London S.W.1

The Press and Information Office of the European Commission in London exists to provide

LONDON, EUROPEAN COMMUNITIES PRESS AND INFORMATION OFFICE, *cont.*

enquirers with information about the European Communities and, more widely, about European integration in general. It has contacts with the press, radio and television; it lends travelling exhibitions; it produces a monthly magazine 'European Community' and a range of booklets and leaflets; has available for hire or sale films, a filmstrip, a series of photographs telling the story of the Community, and assists schools and universities who provide courses or organize conferences on European studies; it has a speakers panel

Enquiries: To Director

Scope: The European Communities (European Economic Community, European Coal and Steel Community, Euratom)
Secondary: All aspects of European integration and of European unity in general
The library contains, with few exceptions, a complete set of the public documents produced by the three European Communities (European Economic Community, Euratom and European Coal and Steel Community), since their inception. It also contains a much wider selection of books, pamphlets and periodicals dealing with all aspects of European economic integration and of European unity in general

Stock: 1,000 books; 1,000 pamphlets. Wide range of journals dealing with current affairs, and particularly with European integration, in English, French and German

Publications: Catalogue: Publications of the European Communities (lists all official publications of the three Communities)
European Community (monthly)
The Facts. 1967
Uniting Europe: the European Community 1950–67. 1967
The Common Market and the Common Man. 1969
Survey of the Nuclear Policy of the European Community. 1968
Guide to the Study of the European Communities. 1967
The Common Market: the Basic Facts about the European Community. 1968
Farming in the Common Market. 1968
Q & A on the EEC. 1968
Agriculture 1980. 1969
The Nuclear Industry (wall map)
The European Community in maps
European Studies (series of fact sheets)
How the European Economic Community's Institutions Work. E. Noël. 1969
Tax harmonization in the European Community. 1968
Harmonizing taxes—a Step to European Integration. H. von der Groeben. 1968
Economic Union: the Second Phase of European Integration. J. Rey. 1969
Regional Development in an Integrated Europe. H. von der Groeben. 1969

The office can provide standard bibliographies on many aspects of European integration and special bibliographies can be prepared on request

LONDON

1134

THE EUTHANASIA SOCIETY　　　　　　　　　　*Tel.:* 01-937 7770
13 Prince of Wales Terrace
London W.8

Aims to obtain the legalization of voluntary euthanasia

Enquiries: To Secretary

Scope: Literature covering the aims of the Society and explanations of any aspects raised by enquirers

Publications: Newsletters
Bibliography

| LONDON | EVANGELICAL ALLIANCE | *Tel.:* 01-580 9361 |

1135

30 Bedford Place
London W.C.1

Aims to promote the cause of evangelical Christianity

Enquiries: To Secretary

Scope: History of evangelical movement in the United Kingdom and Western Europe. Present position of Evangelicals in the British Churches. Evangelical involvement in ethical, social and church reform

Stock: The Alliance's own reports and periodicals going back to foundation in 1846 are available for inspection on the premises. Bound copies of *Evangelical Christendom* from 1846–1955; and of *Crusade* from 1955 onwards

| LONDON | THE EVANGELICAL LIBRARY | *Tel.:* 01-935 6997 |

1136

78A Chiltern Street
London W1M 2HB

Propagation and promotion of evangelical writings particularly those of the Reformers and Puritans, and books on Revivals and Evangelical Hymnody

Enquiries: To Secretary and Librarian

Scope: The world-wide circulation of literature concerning Evangelical and Reformed religion, particularly Puritan literature and works on revival; Preservation of Evangelical works of rare character; Reference section

Stock: 100,000 books; pamphlets; all current evangelical periodicals including The Evangelical Quarterly, Bibliotheca Sacra and Evangelical Times

Publications: Bi-annual Bulletin (containing articles by Reformed Scholars and articles of Huguenot interest)
Bibliographies

| LONDON | EVENING STANDARD | *Tel.:* 01-353 3000 |
| | | *Telex:* 21909 |

1137

47 Shoe Lane
London E.C.4

National daily newspaper

Enquiries: To Librarian

Stock: Newspaper cuttings and microfilm from each national newspaper, filed under 200,000 subject and 500,000 personal headings. Who's Who for various industries and countries

| LONDON | FABIAN SOCIETY | *Tel.:* 01-930 3077 |

1138

11 Dartmouth Street
London S.W.1

Socialist education and research

Enquiries: To General Secretary

Scope: Enquirers wishing to consult Fabian printed documents may do so but should telephone Administrative Assistant in advance. All other records at Nuffield College, Oxford (no. 1932)

Stock: All Fabian publications from 1884 to date

| LONDON | FACULTY OF ANAESTHETISTS | *Tel.:* 01-405 3474 |

1139

Royal College of Surgeons of England
Lincolns Inn Fields
London W.C.2

The advancement of the art and science of anaesthesia by education, examination and research

LONDON, FACULTY OF ANAESTHETISTS, *cont.*

Enquiries: To Secretary, by letter only

Scope: Although not primarily an information service, attempts to help responsible enquirers whenever possible

No library

LONDON

1140

THE FACULTY OF ARCHITECTS AND SURVEYORS *Tel.:* 01-935 9966
68 Gloucester Place
London W1H 3HL

Central organization for architects and surveyors

Enquiries: To Secretary

Scope: Architecture and surveying

Stock: 400 books

Publications: Portico (quarterly journal)
Scales of Professional Charges for Architects and Surveyors

LONDON

1141

FACULTY OF ROYAL DESIGNERS FOR INDUSTRY *Tel.:* 01-839 2366
Royal Society of Arts
John Adam Street
Adelphi
London W.C.2

To further the development of design and in particular its application to industrial purposes

Enquiries: To Secretary

The Faculty has no library of its own but uses that of its parent organization, The Royal Society of Arts (no. 1553)

LONDON

1142

FAMILY PLANNING ASSOCIATION *Tel.:* 01-636 9135
27/35 Mortimer Street
London W1N 8BQ

Aims to preserve and protect the mental and physical health of parents, young people and children and to prevent the poverty, hardship and distress caused by unwanted conception; to educate the public in the field of procreation, contraception and health with particular reference to personal responsibility in sexual relationships; and to provide medical advice and assistance in the fields of contraception, sterility and marriage and sex problems

Enquiries: To Information Officer

Scope: Books, films and periodicals on contraception, both medical and sociological aspects, historical and current material, reports on clinical trials, lay and professional reading matter. Library is concerned with all aspects of birth control, from population problems to communication problems, and maintains files of press clippings (predominantly English press) from popular journals and periodicals

Secondary: Related fields such as subfertility, marriage counselling, maternal and child health, sex and health education, population and demography, poverty and social issues

Stock: 1,000 books; 300 pamphlets; 9 current periodicals

Publications: FPA Reading List
All About Family Planning Clinics
Cervical Smears

Sterilisation
The Pill
To Every Mother of a New Baby

Domiciliary Family Planning Services
Family Planning and the Nurse
IUDs—Some Questions and Answers
Methods of Family Planning
Family Planning Services—A Guide to Social Workers
Family Planning (quarterly journal)

Growing Up
Rhythm Method
Sex in Married Life
Wanted—A Baby

LONDON

143

FAMILY WELFARE ASSOCIATION
Denison House
296 Vauxhall Bridge Road
London S.W.1

Tel.: 01-834 7334

Independent social work organization

Enquiries: To Information Officer, by letter only

Scope: Within Inner London boroughs provides family social work service for those in personal and social distress, and Citizens' Advice Bureaux. Also provides Charities Information Service Library on permanent loan to Goldsmith's Library, University of London (no. 1662)

Publications: Guide to the Social Services (annually)
Annual Charities Digest

LONDON

144

FEDERAL TRUST FOR EDUCATION AND
 RESEARCH
12A Maddox Street
London W1R 9PL

Tel.: 01-493 5311

Education and research through conferences, study groups, seminars and publications on subjects of international relations and particularly those relating to international organization, for example trade, finance, law and economic and political integration

Enquiries: To Secretary

Scope: No library or information service as such but willing to answer enquiries within the above field and to provide information on alternative sources

Publications: Conference reports and occasional papers or monographs on special study areas, for example:
   The European Capital Market
   Sterling-European Monetary Co-operation and World Monetary Reform
   Ten Years of EEC Lessons and Prospects for Industry

LONDON

145

FÉDÉRATION DENTAIRE INTERNATIONALE
64 Wimpole Street
London W.1

Tel.: 01-935 7852

Represents the profession of dentistry on a voluntary international basis

Enquiries: To Secretary General, by letter only

Scope: The Federation is able to provide data from all over the world on subjects relating to dental manpower, dental research, dental education, public dental health services, dental care services in the armed forces, the utilization of auxiliary dental personnel, fluoridation of drinking water supplies

Stock: Includes dental journals from all over the world. Stock not available on loan

Publications: International Dental Journal
   A Dental Lexicon (English, French, German, Spanish, Italian)
   The Story of the F.D.I.
   General Principles concerning the International Standardization of Dental Caries Statistics

LONDON, FÉDÉRATION DENTAIRE INTERNATIONALE, *cont.*
Principal Requirements for Controlled Clinical Trials
Rules for Dental Radiation Hygiene
Transactions of an International Conference on Oral Epidemiology
Nine Specifications of Dental Materials

LONDON

1146

THE FEDERATION OF BRITISH ARTISTS *Tel.*: 01-930 6844
6½ Suffolk Street
Pall Mall East
London S.W.1

The following Societies, all of which work from the above address arrange annual exhibitions of work and in some cases are prepared to answer any questions by letter:

The Royal Society of British Artists
The Royal Society of Portrait Painters
The Royal Institute of Painters in Watercolour
The Royal Institute of Oil Painters
The Royal Society of Marine Artists
The Royal Society of Miniature Painters, Sculptors and Gravers
The Royal British Colonial Society of Artists (temporarily known as The Commonwealth Society of Artists)

The Royal Drawing Society	The United Society of Artists
The New English Art Club	The Senefelder Group
The National Society	The Society of Mural Painters
The Society of Portrait Sculptors	The Society of Wildlife Artists
The Society of Aviation Artists	The Society of Graphic Artists
The Artists of Chelsea	The Art Exhibitions Bureau
The Pastel Society	

Enquiries: To Administrator

No libraries

Publications: Catalogues of annual exhibitions

LONDON

1147

FEDERATION OF SPECIALISED FILM *Tel.*: 01-499 0631
ASSOCIATIONS
25 Green Street
London W.1

Trade Association

Enquiries: To Executive Secretary

Scope: The Federation, in addition to its normal work as a trade association, acts as an information centre for certain film festivals other than those which are dealt with by the National Selection Panel

Stock: 200 books; 100 pamphlets; 5 current periodicals. Stock not available on loan

LONDON

1148

FELLOWSHIP OF POSTGRADUATE MEDICINE *Tel.*: 01-242 6900
9 Great James Street
London W.C.1.

Enquiries: To Secretary

Scope: Information on postgraduate medical courses run by the Fellowship
Secondary: Information on postgraduate medical facilities generally

No library

Publications: Monthly Postgraduate Medical Journal (with occasional supplements)

LONDON 1149	THE FELLOWSHIP OF ST ALBAN AND ST SERGIUS 52 Ladbroke Grove London W.11	*Tel.*: 01-727 7713

An unofficial fellowship of Christians, mainly Anglican and Orthodox, to promote contact and mutual understanding between Christians of East and West

Enquiries: To Secretary

Scope: Library is primarily theological and devotional in scope, with emphasis on ecumenism and information about different Christian traditions

Stock: 3,000 books; 50 current theological and ecumenical reviews. The library contains quantities of periodical material, largely unsorted and uncatalogued. Gramophone records; slides of Orthodox services

Publications: Sobornost (journal of the Fellowship, twice each year)
Books and pamphlets

LONDON 1150	FIELD STUDIES COUNCIL 9 Devereux Court Strand London W.C.2	*Tel.*: 01-583 7471

The Council aims to encourage the pursuit of fieldwork and research in every branch of knowledge whose essential subject matter is out of doors. For this purpose nine residential centres have so far been established in England and Wales, in localities which afford opportunities for studying both general and specialized aspects of botany, zoology, geology, geography, natural history, local history, archaeology, and the landscape

Enquiries: To Secretary, preferably by letter

No central library. Each Field Centre has a library for the use of resident students only

Publications: Field Studies (annually; reprints of papers available)
Programme of Courses (annually)

The Council hopes increasingly to act in an advisory capacity to all other bodies, both private and public, who provide facilities for field work

LONDON 1151	FILM CENTRE (INTERNATIONAL) LTD 24 Conduit Street London W.1	*Tel.*: 01-629 8661

Advisers in audio-visual communication, mainly film and television. Consultancy service on all aspects of film production and distribution

Enquiries: To the Secretary

See also entry no. 1152, below

LONDON 1152	FILM CENTRE PRODUCTION LIBRARY 37 Warren Street London W.1	*Tel.*: 01-387 4052

Enquiries: To the Librarian

Scope: The aim of the library is to place at the disposal of film and television producers material resulting from high quality documentary film-making at home and abroad. The diversity of topographical, scientific and industrial subject matter makes the library unique; it ranges from geographical coverage on a world-wide scale to agriculture, transportation, engineering, manufacture, scientific research, medicine, history and the arts

LONDON, FILM CENTRE PRODUCTION LIBRARY, *cont.*
  Stock: 6 million feet of film
  See also entry no. 1151, above

LONDON

1153

THE FILM PRODUCTION ASSOCIATION OF GREAT BRITAIN
25 Green Street
London W1Y 3FD
Trade Association

Tel.: 01-499 0631

 Enquiries: To General Secretary
  Scope: British first feature film production, including production records, legislation, export and television series
  Stock: 200 books; 50 pamphlets; 300 reports; 30 current periodicals. Stock lent only to members

LONDON

1154

THE FINANCIAL TIMES
Bracken House
Cannon Street
London E.C.4
Daily newspaper

Tel.: 01-248 8000
Telex: 21213

 Enquiries: To Librarian
  Scope: Economics, finance, industry, politics
  Stock: 6,000 books; 500 current periodicals
  Special collection: Dossiers of public companies

LONDON

1155

FINNISH EMBASSY
66 Chester Square
London S.W.1

Tel.: 01-730 0771
Telex: 24786

 Enquiries: To Finnish Embassy
  Scope: Informative material about Finland (books, leaflets, maps). Films available on loan

LONDON

1156

FINNISH TOURIST BOARD UNITED KINGDOM OFFICE
Finland House
56 Haymarket
London S.W.1

Tel.: 01-839 4048

 Enquiries: To Secretary
  Scope: Information on all aspects of travel in Finland
  Stock: Photograph library (travel). Travel brochures

LONDON

1157

THE FOLKLORE SOCIETY
c/o University College London
Gower Street
London W.C.1

Tel.: 01-387 5894

Aims to promote research into and record folklore in all parts of the world and to make available academically and culturally the results of its studies to all persons whether members of the Society or not

 Enquiries: To Secretary
  Scope: Folklore under the following headings: Locality (British Countries, other countries); mankind and its activities and customs; animal, vegetable, mineral and natural folklore; calendar

customs, religion and the supernatural; narrative, including ballads and folk and ritual drama
Secondary: Sociology, archaeology, anthropology where these are approached through folklore

Stock: 10,000 books including periodicals; 1,000 pamphlets; 100 current periodicals

Publications: Folklore (the Society's journal, quarterly)
Monographs on subjects in the field of Folklore including series of County Folklore and Calendar Customs of the British Isles
Most recent publications: Somerset Folklore; English Ritual Drama

The Society's library is housed in one section of University College London and is generally available to the public in College hours. The Society is a learned (voluntary) Society and this fact restricts the external services it can offer, although not the value of the Library itself

LONDON

1158

FOOD EDUCATION SOCIETY
160 Piccadilly
London W.1

Tel.: 01-734 5351 and
01-727 8406

Enquiries: To Hon. Secretary

Scope: Publishes and disseminates scientific and medical information and educational material on food and nutrition

Publications: Monthly Bulletin (members and associates only)
Booklets and reports on Feeding Children, Obesity, Feeding in Pregnancy and Lactation, Reports on Malnutrition in Elderly and Old, Research into Vitamin C in the Diet of Children and Factory Workers, Food Values at a Glance

LONDON

1159

FOREIGN AND COMMONWEALTH OFFICE
Library and Records Department
Sanctuary Buildings
Great Smith Street
London S.W.1

Tel.: 01-839 7010 ext. 269

Following the merger in October 1968 of the Foreign Office and the Commonwealth Office, a unified Library and Records Department has been set up. The library of the Ministry of Overseas Development is also administered jointly with that of the Foreign and Commonwealth Office

The joint library system operates in four locations:

Main Library, Sanctuary Buildings, Great Smith Street, London S.W.1. (*Tel.:* 01-839 7010 ext. 261)
Book, pamphlet and periodical material relating to foreign and Commonwealth countries

Downing Street, London S.W.1. (*Tel.:* 01-930 2323 ext. 1018)
Legal, economic and statistical publications relating to Commonwealth countries

Cornwall House, Stamford Street, London S.E.1. (*Tel.:* 01-928 7511 ext. 10)
Material on foreign affairs. Maps

Ministry of Overseas Development, Eland House, Stag Place, London S.W.1. (*Tel.:* 01-834 2377 ext. 507)
Material on aid to developing countries

Enquiries: To Librarian at the appropriate address

Scope: The general scope of the joint library service includes: Political, economic and legal aspects of foreign states. International affairs. International law. All aspects of Commonwealth

LONDON, FOREIGN AND COMMONWEALTH OFFICE, *cont.*
countries and dependent territories. Aid to developing countries. Comprehensive collections of Commonwealth official publications
Libraries open to the public for reference purposes only

Stock: 750,000 books and pamphlets; 2,500 current periodicals; 150,000 maps

Publications: Selective list of accessions (monthly)
Technical Co-operation (monthly bibliography of Commonwealth official publications)
Public Administration—a Select Bibliography (with annual supplements)

See also no. 1229 and 1230

LONDON

1160

FOREST MEDICAL SOCIETY *Tel.:* 01-539 5522 ext. 310
Medical Education Centre
Whipps Cross Hospital
London E.11

Enquiries: To Secretary

Scope: Most sections of medicine (including surgery, pathology and certain allied subjects)

Stock: 1,000 books; 90 current periodicals. Stock not available on loan

LONDON

1161

FREE CHURCH FEDERAL COUNCIL *Tel.:* 01-387 8413
26 Tavistock Square
London W.C.1

Co-ordinates the activities and interests of the Free Churches of England and Wales

Enquiries: To General Secretary

Scope: Any matters concerned with the work, witness, interests and opinions of the Free Churches (Methodist, Baptist, Congregational, Presbyterian and others)

Publications: Free Church Chronicle (monthly)

LONDON

1162

FREEDOM FROM HUNGER CAMPAIGN *Tel.:* 01-930 8248
17 Northumberland Avenue
London W.C.2

Enquiries: To Secretary, Information Service

Scope: Long term overseas aid and promotion of agricultural development in poor countries

Publications: World Hunger (bimonthly)

LONDON

1163

FRENCH INSTITUTE *Tel.:* 01-589 6211
Queensberry Place
London S.W.7

Aims to maintain and develop cultural relations between Great Britain and France. Includes a school, theatre, ciné club and library; holds lectures and confers university degrees

Enquiries: To Librarian

Scope: French literature. France: history, life and art. Stock mostly in French

Stock: 58,000 books; 150 current periodicals

LONDON

1164

FRIENDS HISTORICAL SOCIETY *Tel.:* 01-387 3601
Friends House
Euston Road
London N.W.1

Promotion of Quaker historical studies

Enquiries: To Secretary
Publications: Journal of the Friends Historical Society (annually, supplements issued occasionally)
All enquiries dealt with by the Religious Society of Friends Library, no. 1502

LONDON

1165

FROEBEL INSTITUTE COLLEGE OF EDUCATION   *Tel.:* 01-876 2242
Roehampton Lane
London S.W.15

Enquiries: Books to Librarian; General to Principal
Scope: General library for students and staff. Courses include: Art (printing, graphic art, ceramics, sculpture, textiles); art of movement; biology; divinity; drama; English literature; French language and literature; geography; history; mathematics; music; natural science; principles, practice and history of education; psychology; health education. Small collection of books on Froebel and the Froebelian movement
Stock: 34,000 books and pamphlets; 200 current periodicals

LONDON

1166

FULHAM HOSPITAL LIBRARY
St Dunstans Road
London W.6

See no. 1043

LONDON

1167

FURZEDOWN COLLEGE OF EDUCATION   *Tel.:* 01-672 0131
Welham Road
London S.W.17

Enquiries: To Chief Librarian
Scope: Education, history, geography, literature, French, art, language method, divinity, music, mathematics, sociology, psychology, teaching practice library
Secondary: Physical education
Stock: 50,000 books and pamphlets; 240 current periodicals; 2,300 gramophone records; 24,000 illustrations
Publications: Bibliographies (about 40 each year)

LONDON

1168

THE GALLUP POLL   *Tel.:* 01-734 3671
211 Regent Street   *Telex:* 261712
London W1A 3AU

Opinion, social and market research of all types including continuous trend information
Enquiries: To Director
Scope: No library as such, only a collection of books and journals for internal use. However, a large collection of public opinion survey results on a wide variety of topics dating back for over 30 years is available, and the information in them can be supplied, in some cases free of charge, and in others on payment. Examples of recent surveys are:
Medicine: Survey on women's attitudes and knowledge in relation to cancer, 1969; bronchitis, 1967; fluoridation of water, 1967; sleep-learning, 1968; animal treatments, 1968
Law, economics: Public opinion survey results on topical subjects related to the law and the economic situation; survey on savings banks, 1969; series of special surveys on savings and investment, 1969; labour wastage in the shipping industry, 1969; qualified staff recruitment survey: accountants and other financial staff, 1969
Education: Survey on student power, 1968

LONDON, THE GALLUP POLL, *cont.*

Social sciences: Survey among Roman Catholics on topical religious and moral issues, 1967; survey on ideal holiday, 1967, repeat of 1961 survey; visitor profile survey—Strathspey, 1968–69; Irish newspapers readership survey, 1968; Diet in the home: regular survey, quarterly reports 1969–70

Publications: Gallup Political Index (monthly report giving voting figures; the standing of the Government and the Opposition; public opinion on topical matters)

GEFF (Gallup Economic Facts and Forecasting, monthly reports on consumer buying intentions and consumer expectations about employment, prices, productivity, incomes and hire purchase commitments)

Gallup News

Occasional special reports

LONDON

1169

THE GALPIN SOCIETY *Tel.:* 01-274 8104
Hon. Sec.: 7 Pickwick Road
Dulwich Village
London S.E.21

Society for serious research on musical instruments of all kinds and from all parts of the world

Enquiries: To Hon. Curator/Archivist, 46 Craigmount View, Edinburgh EH12 8BR, by letter only

Scope: Information of all kinds on musical instruments of all types. A permanent Collection and Archive has been set up in the Reid School of Music, University of Edinburgh (no. 570). This includes instruments of all kinds and an archive of scholars' notes, makers' working notes, drawings and research documents, as well as books

Publications: The Galpin Society Journal (annually) and index volumes I–V

European Musical Instruments—the catalogue of the Society's 21st Anniversary Exhibition, Edinburgh 1968 (ed. G. Melville-Mason)

LONDON

1170

GARNETT COLLEGE *Tel.:* 01-788 2586
Downshire House
Roehampton Lane
London S.W.15

College of Education (Technical) for teachers in further education

Enquiries: To Librarian

Scope: Education generally, omitting primary education but specializing in further education and educational sociology and psychology

Secondary: General library to serve needs of students of engineering, business studies, catering, clothing subjects, nautical subjects, printing, science and mathematics and liberal and general studies

Stock: 23,000 books and pamphlets; 200 current periodicals

LONDON

1171

GAS INDUSTRY TRAINING BOARD *Tel.:* 01-245 9811
17 Grosvenor Crescent
London S.W.1

Enquiries: To Secretary

Scope: Information on industrial training within the gas industry

Stock: No library

Publications: Training Recommendations and Levy Grant Scheme Research Information Papers

LONDON	GEFFRYE MUSEUM	*Tel.:* 01-739 8368
	Kingsland Road	
1172	London E.2	

Enquiries: To Curator

Scope: The Geffrye Museum shows a series of period rooms dating from 1600 to the present day. Each room contains furniture and domestic equipment of a middle-class English home, with a photographic enlargement of a figure showing the costume of each period. In addition, there are 18th century shop-fronts and other features arranged as part of a street, and an 18th century woodworker's shop with an open-hearth kitchen behind

Publications: Handbook to the Geffrye Museum
Introducing the Geffrye Museum
Supplements to Introducing the Geffrye Museum
Introducing the Educational Work of the Geffrye Museum
Children's Visits to the Geffrye Museum (leaflet for teachers)
My Visit to the Geffrye Museum (booklet planned for children's use in recording their observations in the Museum)
Outline Picture Books   Children at Home
English Homes   Study Notebooks
Postcards
Study Folders on 16th, 17th, 18th and 19th centuries (in preparation)

LONDON	THE GENERAL CONFERENCE OF THE NEW	*Tel.:* 01-242 8574
	CHURCH	
1173	20 Bloomsbury Way	
	London W.C.1	

Religious organization based on the teachings of Emanuel Swedenborg (1688–1772)

Enquiries: To Secretary, 36 Warminster Road, London S.E.25. *Tel.:* 01-653 2854

Scope: The religious teachings of the New Church and its history both in Great Britain and elsewhere

Stock: Includes a full range of books on Swedenborgiana and historical records of the New Church

Publications: Printed catalogues
New Church Herald (fortnightly)
New Church Magazine (quarterly)

Libraries also in Manchester and Glasgow, less fully stocked than in London
College Library at Woodford Green, Essex

LONDON	GENERAL DENTAL COUNCIL	*Tel.:* 01-486 2171
	37 Wimpole Street	
1174	London W1M 8DQ	

Control of dental practice in the United Kingdom

Enquiries: To Registrar

Scope: Names of dentists entitled to practise in the United Kingdom; conditions governing dental practice in the United Kingdom; eligibility of overseas dentists to practise in the United Kingdom; dental ethics and professional conduct; dental postgraduate education in the United Kingdom; undergraduate education (courses of study and qualifications for entry); dentistry as a career; dental health education; work and training of dental hygienists and dental auxiliaries

No library

LONDON, GENERAL DENTAL COUNCIL, *cont.*

Publications: Dentists Register (annually)
Careers in Dentistry
Dental Postgraduate Study in the United Kingdom and the Republic of Ireland
Dental Health Education material including models, posters, charts and films
Dental recruitment material including exhibits, films, leaflets

LONDON

1175

GENERAL REGISTER OFFICE *Tel.:* 01-836 2407
Somerset House
Strand
London W.C.2

Civil registration of births, deaths and marriages in England and Wales. Maintenance of central records of these events and issue of certified copies of entries in these records. Preparation and analysis of statistics relating to population, fertility, births, marriages, deaths and diseases. Population censuses

Enquiries: To Registrar General (correspondence), Librarian (telephone enquiries on published figures), or Section dealing with the specific subject

Scope: Library stock contains population census and vital statistics reports of the United Kingdom, British Commonwealth and foreign countries and books relating to the law and administration of births, deaths and marriage registration
Secondary: Demography, mathematics, statistical methods, and specific subjects in the social sciences

Stock: 16,000 books; 150 current periodicals. Stock available on loan to other Government Departments only

Publications: Listed in H.M.S.O. Sectional List no. 56

LONDON

1176

GERMAN EMBASSY *Tel.:* 01-235 5033
23 Belgrave Square
London S.W.1

Enquiries: To Press or Cultural Department
Scope: Information on all aspects of life, science and culture in Germany
Stock: Films, available on loan through Curzon Publicity Ltd, 31 St James's Place, London S.W.1

LONDON

1177

GERMAN INSTITUTE (Goethe Institut) *Tel.:* 01-589 3648
51 Princes Gate
Exhibition Road
London S.W.7

Aims to promote knowledge of the German language and culture

Enquiries: To Librarian
Scope: Library: Collection of German books, with some English books on Germany. The main emphasis is on modern German literature, history, art and language
Secondary: Works on sociology, philosophy, music, folklore
Teachers' Centre: Lending service for teachers of German including tapes, records, slides, background material and books

Stock: 18,000 books; 156 current periodicals

Publications: Programme of Events (two-monthly)   Accession List (irregularly)
Programme of Language Courses   Catalogue of Teachers' Collection
List of periodicals taken
Postal service for readers outside London   German interlending services

LONDON 1178	THE GIRL GUIDES ASSOCIATION 17/19 Buckingham Palace Road London S.W.1	*Tel.:* 01-834 6242

Enquiries: To Public Relations Officer or Archivist

Scope: Information leaflets and display material available on all aspects of the Movement

Publications: Many books on all aspects of training and work of the Association
 The Guider (monthly)   Today's Guide (weekly)
 The Ranger (monthly)   The Brownie (weekly)

LONDON 1179	GLYN, MILLS & CO 67 Lombard Street London E.C.3 Bankers	*Tel.:* 01-626 5400

Enquiries: To Archivist, by letter only

Scope: Banking History including: Ledgers of Child & Co. from 1663–1731; Ledgers of Edward Backwell 1663–1672; Banking business of Glyn, Mills & Co. from 1753. There are many gaps but records may be useful for certain enquiries for example, early railways from 1837; Canada 1837–1892. Also subsidiary records on a miscellany of non-banking subjects such as estate papers of the 16th to 18th centuries

Stock: 300 banking histories. Stock not available on loan

Publications: The Three Banks Review

Museum of Banking History—open 10 am to 3 pm Monday to Friday on application

LONDON	GOETHE INSTITUT *see* **GERMAN INSTITUTE** (no. 1177)

LONDON 1180	GOVERNMENT SOCIAL SURVEY DEPARTMENT Atlantic House Holborn Viaduct London E.C.1	*Tel.:* 01-583 8931

Specialist Government research organization covering aspects of departmental economics and social research

Enquiries: To Librarian, preferably by letter

Scope: Economic, sociological and psychological journals. Books on survey methods, sociology and psychology. Relevant publications to studies carried out by the Social Survey. Enquiries answered about reports published by the Social Survey and about survey methods

Stock: 4,000 books, pamphlets and reports; 150 current periodicals

Publications: Published Reports on surveys carried out by the Social Survey

LONDON 1181	GREATER LONDON COUNCIL (MEMBERS') LIBRARY Room 114 The County Hall London S.E.1	*Tel.:* 01-633 5000 ext. 6759 and 7132

Enquiries: To Librarian

LONDON, GREATER LONDON COUNCIL (MEMBERS') LIBRARY, *cont.*

Scope: History and topography of Greater London, local government and subjects connected with the work of the Greater London Council and Inner London Education Authority such as architecture, planning, education and transportation

Special collection: John Burns (books on London)

Stock: 78,000 books and pamphlets; 260 current periodicals; 7,000 maps; 20,000 prints and drawings; 150,000 photographs

Publications: Guide to the Records in the London County Record Office, Part 1
Records of the Predecessors of the London County Council except the Boards of Guardians. 1962
A Survey of the Parish Records of the Diocese of London, Inner London Area. 1968
Court Rolls of Tooting Beck Manor, 1394–1422. 1909
Members' Library Catalogue: London History and Topography. 1939
A series of fine-line lithographic reproductions of historical maps and prints of the London area
The Greater London Council publishes extensively on matters connected with its work, including statistics, planning projects, transportation, parks and open spaces

The Greater London Record Office houses the archives of the Greater London Council and its predecessors and many records of estates, charities and businesses in Greater London. It is also recognized as a repository for manorial records and for public records under the Public Records Act, 1958, and as a diocesan record office for the dioceses of London and Southwark

See also no. 1182 and 1184

LONDON

1182

GREATER LONDON COUNCIL *Tel.:* 01-928 0303
PUBLIC INFORMATION BRANCH
Information Centre
The County Hall
London S.E.1

Enquiries: To Greater London Information telephone service on 01-928 0303; to Information Officer by letter; or to Information Centre, The County Hall, London S.E.1, by letter or personal call (particularly for publications enquiries)

Scope: Information about the Greater London Council and Greater London. Organized parties of visitors wishing to know more about the work of the Greater London Council are welcomed

Publications: Free literature on many Greater London Council services is always available, together with publications lists of the priced books; 300 to 400 are likely to be of current interest at any one time and they cover administration, education, housing, parks, planning, public health, transportation and other services. Postcards and reproductions of old prints and maps and a whole range of by-laws and statutory planning maps are also on sale

LONDON

1183

GREATER LONDON RECORD OFFICE
The County Hall
London S.E.1

See no. 1181

LONDON

1184

GREATER LONDON RECORD OFFICE *Tel.:* 01-839 7799
(MIDDLESEX SECTION)
1 Queen Anne's Gate Buildings
Dartmouth Street
London S.W.1

Repository for manuscripts, archives, and records relating to the former County of Middlesex. Its holdings include official, ecclesiastical, and private records

Enquiries: To Deputy Head Archivist

Scope: Middlesex history; London history

Secondary: Apart from their Middlesex interest, the records are a source for many non-local subjects, for example, poor law administration, the administration of justice, and the urbanization of rural areas. The private collections deposited touch upon a wide range of topics

Stock: Reference library: 2,500 books; 200 pamphlets; Annual reports from almost all other manuscript repositories in Great Britain; bulletins from Middlesex local history Societies; 5 current periodicals

Publications: Guide to the Middlesex Sessions Records, 1549–1889. 1965

Middlesex County Records, 1549–1688 (old series), Vols. I–IV. J. Cordy Jeaffreson, ed. 1886–1892

Middlesex County Records: Calendar of the Sessions Books, 1689–1709. W. J. Hardy, ed. 1905

Middlesex County Records, Reports, 1902–1928 (being reports by W. J. and W. Le Hardy on the contents of unpublished Calendars of the Sessions Records). 1928

Middlesex Sessions Records, 1612–1617 (new series), Vols. I–IV. W. Le Hardy, ed. 1935–1941

See also no. 1181

LONDON

1185

GUILD OF PUBLIC PHARMACISTS
Premier House
150 Southampton Row
London W.C.1

Tel.: 01-278 2737

Enquiries: To Secretary

Scope: Design and planning of hospital pharmacies. Equipment suitable for use in hospital pharmacy

No library

Publications: Journal of Hospital Pharmacy (monthly)
Hospital Pharmacy Planning (booklet)
Current Abstracts of Pharmacy and Therapeutics

LONDON

1186

GUILDHALL ART GALLERY
Guildhall
London E.C.2

Tel.: 01-606 3030

London paintings. The gallery has some other notable paintings mainly of the 19th century. Loan exhibitions held

Enquiries: To Director

Publications: Illustrated Booklets:
London Pictures in the Guildhall Art Gallery
Ceremonial Pictures in the Guildhall Art Gallery
English Landscapes in the Guildhall Art Gallery
English Portraits in the Guildhall Art Gallery
Narrative Pictures in the Guildhall Art Gallery
Catalogue of Selected Prints and Drawings in Guildhall Library
Selected Prints and Drawings Part II, Metropolitan Boroughs

Postcards	Catalogues of Prints and Drawings
Colour Slides	Greetings Cards
Exhibition Catalogues	Large Reproduction

LONDON	GUILDHALL LIBRARY	*Tel.:* 01-606 3030 (General
1187	London E.C.2	enquiries ext. 277 and
	General reference library	279)

Enquiries: To Librarian, preferably by letter

Scope: London (all aspects). English topography, including unique collections of provincial directories and poll books. English law reports from 17th century. British official publications, past and current (for example, Parliamentary papers complete from 1835 and many earlier; complete Lords and Commons debates and journals; Public Record Office publications; public, private and local Acts). Long, usually complete, files of historical, bibliographical, commercial periodicals and annuals including proceedings of local societies. Historical horology. Sir Thomas More collection. Publications of international organizations. Historical technology

Stock: 100,000 books and pamphlets; 40,000 manuscripts; 35,000 prints, drawings (total stock)
Stock available on loan through Regional Schemes. Photocopies of articles in periodicals provided

Publications: Guildhall Miscellany. A journal of original contributions, mainly in the field of London history (issued twice each year)
Parish Registers. A handlist. Part I: Registers of Church of England parishes within the City of London. 2nd edition, revised and enlarged, 1966
Parish Registers. A handlist. Part II: Containing i. Register of Church of England parishes outside the City of London; ii. Non-parochial Registers and Registers of foreign denominations; iii. Burial Ground Records. 1964
Parish Registers. A handlist. Part III: Provisional guide to 'Foreign Registers', i.e. registers and register transcripts of Anglican communities abroad, forming part of the archives of the Diocese of London. 1967
Vestry Minutes of Parishes within the City of London. A handlist. 2nd edition. 1964
London Rate Assessments and Inhabitants Lists in Guildhall Library and in the Corporation of London Records Office. A handlist. 2nd edition, revised and enlarged, 1968
London Business House Histories. A handlist. 1964
Gresham Music Library. A catalogue of printed books and manuscripts deposited in the Guildhall Library. 1965
A List of Books Printed in the British Isles and of English Books printed Abroad before 1701, in Guildhall Library. Part I. A–K. 1966; Part II. L–Z. With Addenda and Concordance. 1967
Selected Prints and Drawings in Guildhall Library
    Part 1. The City. 1964
    Part 2. Metropolitan Boroughs. 1965
    Part 3. The Environs of London

LONDON	GUILDHALL MUSEUM	*Tel.:* 01-606 3030 ext. 744
1188	Gillett House	
	55 Basinghall Street	
	London E.C.2	

History and archaeology of the City of London

Enquiries: To Director

Scope: Roman and mediaeval archaeological material including the finds from the Temple of Mithras (1954). Particularly strong in Roman pottery and objects of everyday use. Large and famous collection of mediaeval pottery

Publications: Finds from the Temple of Mithras   Postcards
Small Finds from Walbrook (Roman)   Slides
CASTS—Reproductions of Museum objects

| LONDON

1189 | GUILDHALL SCHOOL OF MUSIC AND DRAMA   *Tel.*: 01-353 7774
John Carpenter Street
London E.C.4

Trains teachers and performers in music and in drama |

Enquiries: To Librarian

Scope: Information on most aspects of music and drama; as there is a large academic staff, information not necessarily easily accessible can sometimes be obtained. Any material on music-making within the City of London both past and present is being obtained and a collection of orchestral music and chamber music in separate parts for performance purposes is being built up

Stock: 6,000 books; 8,000 music scores (including orchestral and choral sets); 16 current periodicals; 2,000 records (including samples of music from 800 AD to present day)

| LONDON

1190 | GUNNERSBURY PARK MUSEUM   *Tel.*: 01-992 2247
London W.3

The Museum aims to collect, conserve and display all types of exhibits illustrating the history and topography of the Greater London Boroughs of Ealing and Hounslow |

Enquiries: To Curator, by letter only

Scope: The history, in its widest sense, and topography of West Middlesex and peripheral places. Some items from the Chiswick Press (and two presses). Sadler collection of literature by famous local residents for example Richard Baxter and Bulwer Lytton
Secondary: Museum reference books for staff use. Collection of children's books of the 19th and early 20th century, including some works by Mrs Trimmer of Brentford

Stock: 650 books (of which 150 are children's 19th century). Numerous maps, photographs and slides of local history and topography

Publications: A History of Gunnersbury

| LONDON

1191 | GUY'S HOSPITAL MEDICAL SCHOOL   *Tel.*: 01-407 0378
DEPARTMENT OF FORENSIC MEDICINE
London S.E.1 |

Enquiries: To Director

Scope: Forensic medicine and pathology, toxicology, aspects of public health and industrial disease related to these

Stock: 4,000 books and pamphlets; all current periodicals in these fields

National Poisons Information and Reference Service available on demand (*see* no. 1430)

| LONDON

1192 | GYPSY COUNCIL   *Tel.*: 01-349 9427
14 Princes Avenue
London N.3

Movement for civil rights of the Gypsy people affiliated to Comité International Tzigane |

Enquiries: To Secretary

Scope: Information on the world Romani movement, the Romani communities in different countries, and their history, culture, and present problems including education

No library

Publications: Romano Drom

| LONDON

1193 | HACKNEY HOSPITAL MEDICAL LIBRARY   *Tel.:* 01-985 5555
Homerton High Street
London E.9 |

Service, including emergency reference, for hospital staff (primarily medical), general practitioners and students (resident and in district)

Enquiries: To Hon. Librarian, by letter only

Scope: Medical only, with Departmental sections in pathology, obstetrics and psychiatry
Secondary: Nursing library and pharmacological reference section

Stock: 200 books; 45 current periodicals

| LONDON

1194 | HAMMERSMITH COLLEGE OF ART & BUILDING   *Tel.:* 01-743 3321
Lime Grove
London W.12 |

Enquiries: To Librarian

Scope: Art, architecture, building, structural engineering, surveying, building trades

Stock: 20,000 books and pamphlets; 250 current periodicals

Publications: Bibliographies (mostly in the field of building)
Accession lists
Periodical lists

| LONDON

1195 | THE HANSARD SOCIETY FOR PARLIAMENTARY   *Tel.:* 01-730 2281
GOVERNMENT
162 Buckingham Palace Road
London S.W.1 |

Promotes knowledge of, and interest in, Parliamentary Government all over the world

Enquiries: To Information Officer, by letter only

Scope: Small reference library about government, constitution, Parliaments and political science

Stock: 3,500 books; 500 pamphlets. Principal journals of political science, British, American and French. Complete set of 5th series of *Hansard*. Stock not available on loan

Publications: Our Parliament. S. Gordon. 1964
Parliamentary Reform—A Survey of Recent Proposals for the Commons. D. Pring and D. Menhennet. 1968
Parliament and Public Ownership. A. H. Hanson. 1961
Parliament through Seven Centuries: Reading and Its MPs. A. Aspinall. 1962
Federalism in the Commonwealth: A Bibliographical Commentary. W. S. Livingston. 1963
The Parliament of Switzerland. C. Hughes. 1962
Emergency Powers and the Parliamentary Watchdog: Parliament and the Executive in Great Britain, 1939–1951. J. Eaves. 1957
The Future of The House of Lords. S. D. Bailey. 1954
Problems of Parliamentary Government in the Colonies. 1953
What are the Problems of Parliamentary Government in West Africa? 1958
German Parliaments. S. King-Hall and R. K. Ullman. 1954
The Parliament of The Kingdom of the Netherlands. E. van Raalte. 1959
Present Trends in American National Government. J. Junz. 1960
Government and Parliament in Britain: A Bibliography. J. Palmer. 1964
A Visit to Parliament. 1960
Constitutional Relations Between the Labour and Co-operative Parties: An Historical Review. B. Smith and G. Ostergaard. 1960

The Case for Televising Parliament. R. Day. 1963
The Legislature of Lower Austria. W. Crane. 1961
The Organization and Procedure of the National Assembly of the Fifth French Republic. A. Mavrinac. 1960
The North Atlantic Treaty Organization Parliamentarians' Conference 1955–1959. 1960 (also a French language edition)
Atlantic Assembly: Proposals and Prospects. J. Harned and G. Mally. 1965 (also a French language edition)
Britain and European Unity. G. Mally. 1966
The Great Liberal Revival. 1903–1906. M. Craton and H. W. McCready. 1966
Parliamentary Affairs (quarterly journal)

LONDON

1196

THE HEALTH EDUCATION COUNCIL *Tel.:* 01-387 0581
Lynton House
7/12 Tavistock Square
London W.C.1

The objects for which the Council is established are to promote and encourage in England, Wales and Northern Ireland education and research in the science and art of healthy living and the principles of hygiene and the teaching thereof, and to assist Government Departments, local authorities and other statutory and voluntary bodies in so far as their work comprises health education and propaganda directed to the promotion or safeguard of public health or to the prevention and cure of disease

Enquiries: To Director General

Scope: Health education and its associated fields

Stock: 1,500 books; 90 pamphlets and leaflets; 163 current periodicals

Publications: Health Education Journal
Health Information Digest

LONDON

1197

HENDON COLLEGE OF TECHNOLOGY *Tel.:* 01-202 0083
The Burroughs
Hendon
London N.W.4

Enquiries: To Librarian

Scope: General stock particularly strong in science, engineering, economics, management and business studies, hotel and catering subjects, social studies, English and geography

Stock: 30,000 books; 1,500 pamphlets; 460 current periodicals

LONDON

1198

HENRY GEORGE SCHOOL OF SOCIAL SCIENCE *Tel.:* 01-834 4266
177 Vauxhall Bridge Road
London S.W.1

Educational work in economics and the philosophy of Henry George

Enquiries: To Director

Scope: Economics, land use, planning, land taxation

Stock: 1,000 books; 500 pamphlets; 300 reports

Publications: Land and Liberty (monthly journal)
Conference Papers (every 3 to 4 years, latest 1968)

LONDON

1199

H.M. TREASURY AND CABINET OFFICE LIBRARY
Treasury Chambers
Great George Street
London S.W.1

Tel.: 01-930 1234

Primarily to provide library and information service for members of H.M. Treasury and Cabinet Office

Enquiries: To Librarian

Scope: Economics, both general and relating to major countries of the world. Public and private finance. Statistics. Management
Secondary: Trade and industry. Social services. History of World War II. Biographies of statesmen
Special collection: Lister collection of prints illustrating the history of Whitehall

Stock: 65,000 books and pamphlets; 170 current periodicals; Parliamentary Papers from 1881

LONDON

1200

HIGH COMMISSION FOR CEYLON IN BRITAIN
13 Hyde Park Gardens
London W.2

Tel.: 01-262 1841
Telex: 25844

Enquiries: To Information Officer

Scope: Information regarding all matters concerning Ceylon

LONDON

1201

HIGH COMMISSION FOR MALAYSIA
45 Belgrave Square
London S.W.1

Tel.: 01-245 9221

Enquiries: To Information Attaché

Scope: Reference (non-lending) Library on all aspects of Malaysia
Film Library (lending)

LONDON

1202

HIGHER EDUCATION RESEARCH UNIT
London School of Economics
Houghton Street
Aldwych
London W.C.2

Tel.: 01-405 7686

Research into educational planning and the economics of education

Enquiries: To Secretary

Scope: Educational system: schools, universities, further education, teachers in the United Kingdom
Educational system: other countries
Education and the economy: educational finance
Manpower planning: United Kingdom and abroad
Economic analysis of education: Educational models
Administration of education, educational research, statistical methods
Economic growth and development, foreign aid and underdeveloped areas
Production functions, industrial productivity and management
Science policy, research and development
Statistical sources: educational system United Kingdom and abroad
Population statistics, United Kingdom and abroad
Economic statistics, United Kingdom and abroad
General Reference works: bibliographies, University prospectuses, Career Handbooks, Government publication lists, Yearbooks, annual reports

Stock: 1,500 books and pamphlets; 68 current periodicals. Stock not available on loan
Publications: Many reprints. 9 books

LONDON

1203

THE HISTORICAL ASSOCIATION *Tel.:* 01-735 3901
59A Kennington Park Road
London S.E.11

Association to advance the study and teaching of history at all levels, to increase public interest in all aspects of the subject, and to develop it as an essential element in the education of all

Enquiries: To Secretary

Scope: Study and teaching of history. Membership open to all. The library covers history generally. Permanent exhibition of textbooks

Stock: 6,000 books, pamphlets and reports; 12 current periodicals

Publications: History (journal of the Association, three issues each year)
Annual Bulletin of Historical Literature
General series of pamphlets
Helps for Students of History
Teaching of History Pamphlets
Aids for Teachers
History at the Universities
Library Catalogue
History in the Sixth Form and in Higher Education
Beginning Local History
Teaching History (Bulletin, twice each year)

Tours, courses, conferences, branch activities

LONDON

1204

HISTORICAL MANUSCRIPTS COMMISSION *Tel.:* 01-242 2981 and 3205
Quality House
Quality Court
Chancery Lane
London W.C.2

The location, registration, publication, care and use of privately owned manuscripts and records of historical importance

Enquiries: To Assistant Secretary, preferably by letter or in person

Scope: Advice to researchers in history and the social sciences about the nature and location of the primary sources for their studies

Stock: Includes lists of private archives made for the National Register of Archives maintained by the Commission (14,000) and being added to; Subject and Personal indexes to these reports; and Location Register of Manorial Records

Publications: Printed reports of the Commission, mainly lists, calendars and edited texts

Quinquennial Reports to the Crown by the Commission ⎫ Both these publications contain
Annual Reports of the Secretary to the Commissioners ⎬ details of collections recently dealt
⎭ with

Lists of Accessions to Repositories
Record Repositories in Great Britain. 3rd edition. 1968
(All these publications are ordered direct from H.M.S.O. For List *see* H.M.S.O. Sectional List no. 17)

LONDON	THE HOCKEY ASSOCIATION	*Tel.:* 01-580 4840
1205	26 Park Crescent London W.1	

Governing body of sport for men's hockey in England

Enquiries: To Secretary

Scope: Hockey

Publications: Official Manual—Hockey Coaching (Hodder and Stoughton)
Teach Yourself Hockey (English Universities Press)

LONDON	HOME OFFICE	*Tel.:* 01-930 8100
	Whitehall	*Telex:* 24986
1206	London S.W.1	

Enquiries: To Librarian

Scope: Social sciences, with special emphasis on law
Secondary: Public safety

LONDON	THE HOMOSEXUAL LAW REFORM SOCIETY	*Tel.:* 01-734 5588 and 0960
	32 Shaftesbury Avenue	
1207	London W1V 8EP	

Aims to secure reform of the law relating to homosexual behaviour; to promote, through research, publication and discussion, greater understanding of the problems connected with homosexuality and their effects upon the individual and society; and to further those objects by all necessary means of political and social action and publicity

Enquiries: To Secretary

Scope: An information and advisory service is operated; there is not an extensive library and apart from available publications issued by the Society and the Albany Trust (no. 888) books are not available to outside enquirers. The Society's press cutting files are made available for use by *bona fide* research workers by individual arrangement

Publications: Summary of Sexual Offences Act, 1967

See also list of Albany Trust publications (no. 888)

LONDON	HONG KONG GOVERNMENT OFFICE	*Tel.:* 01-930 7951
	54 Pall Mall	
1208	London S.W.1	

Enquiries: To Information Officer or Librarian

Scope: Information on all aspects of Hong Kong

Stock: 1,000 books; 1,500 pamphlets; official reports; Hong Kong general, trade, technical and academic periodicals; all Hong Kong English language newspapers; classified subject files; 16 mm documentary films; very large collection of photographs depicting every aspect of life and development in Hong Kong

LONDON	THE HONOURABLE SOCIETY OF LINCOLNS INN	*Tel.:* 01-242 4371
	Holborn	
1209	London W.C.2	

Enquiries: To Librarian, by letter only

Scope: Information on law books, manuscript material, biographical details of Members, and the Inns of Court generally

Stock: 100,000 books; large collection of pamphlets; 65 current periodicals. Stock not available on loan

Publications: Catalogue of Library, 1859. 1890
Catalogue of Pamphlets. 1506–1700
Records of the Society. 1422–1914
Guide to Commonwealth Law Reports and Legislation in Lincolns Inn. 1967

LONDON HONOURABLE SOCIETY OF THE INNER TEMPLE *Tel.:* 01-353 2959
1210 The Temple
London E.C.4

Enquiries: To Librarian

Scope: English Law: legal bibliography, legal history (Inns of Court: lawyers and the Bar, all social aspects, courts of justice and the judiciary including costume of and education of)
Commonwealth Law: all territories; Common Market Law; International Law; Foreign Law
Secondary: Biographical (particularly legal figures); Heraldry and genealogy; London (topographical only); County History; French and English Literature and History; Ecclesiastical Law and History; Records of Parliament; Calendars of State Papers; Rolls Series; Learned Society Publications
In no circumstances is legal advice given

Stock: 90,000 books and pamphlets

LONDON HORNIMAN MUSEUM AND LIBRARY *Tel.:* 01-699 2339 and 1872
1211 Forest Hill
London S.E.23

Enquiries: To Librarian

Scope: Anthropology; art; archaeology; musical instruments; comparative religion; ethnography (including travel); natural history (particularly zoology)

Stock: 36,000 books and pamphlets; 100 current periodicals; reference collection of 23,000 to 24,000 illustrations

Publications: Handbooks to Museum's departments

LONDON HORSERACE TOTALISATOR BOARD *Tel.:* 01-353 1066
1212 Tote House *Telex:* 22284
8/12 New Bridge Street
London E.C.4

Operation of Totalisator cash betting facilities on British racecourses and credit and cash betting facilities off course

Enquiries: To Press Officer

Scope: Reference books on a wide range of horse racing subjects, appertaining to both British and foreign racing
Secondary: Cuttings library on horse racing, British and foreign

Stock: 300 books; 4 current periodicals. Stock not available on loan

Publications: Tote Racing Annual

LONDON THE HOSPITAL CENTRE (KING'S FUND) *Tel.:* 01-262 2641
1213 24 Nutford Place
London W1H 6AN

Aims to provide a meeting place and a source of information for all who are interested in hospitals and health services

LONDON, THE HOSPITAL CENTRE (KING'S FUND), *cont.*
- *Enquiries:* To Information Officer
- *Scope:* Hospital planning, organization, equipment and practice. Hospital catering advisory service
  Secondary: Health services planning and organization
- *Stock:* 8,000 books, pamphlets and reports; 200 current periodicals. Very large collection of tear sheets and reports filed in a classified sequence. Books not available on loan, but information folders covering a wide variety of topics are made up to suit individual requests and are lent to enquirers
- *Publications:* Many publications in the fields noted above

LONDON

1214

HOSPITAL PHYSICISTS' ASSOCIATION   *Tel.:* 01-235 6111
47 Belgrave Square
London S.W.1

Promotes the advancement of physics applied to medicine and the biological sciences

- *Enquiries:* To Secretary or Scientific Secretary
- *Scope:* Information by personal contact
  No library
- *Publications:* Physics in Medicine and Biology (quarterly)
  Scope of Physics Applied to Medicine (booklet)
  Careers in Medical Physics (booklet)

LONDON

1215

HOUSE OF COMMONS LIBRARY   *Tel.:* 01-930 6240
London S.W.1

- *Enquiries:* To Librarian, by letter only
- *Scope:* Parliamentary publications, H.M. Stationery Office publications, social sciences, history and politics, general reference works and publications of the United Nations and other inter-governmental organizations
- *Stock:* More than 100,000 volumes; 2,000 current periodicals
- *Publications:* A series of House of Commons Library Documents including:
  A Bibliography of Parliamentary Debates. 1956
  Acts of Parliament. 1955

LONDON

1216

HOUSE OF LORDS LIBRARY   *Tel.:* 01-930 6240 ext. 138
Westminster
London S.W.1

- *Enquiries:* To Librarian, preferably by letter
- *Stock:* 85,000 books and pamphlets; 200 current periodicals. Stock not available on loan

LONDON

1217

HOUSING CENTRE TRUST   *Tel.:* 01-930 2881
13 Suffolk Street
Pall Mall East
London S.W.1

A centre for information, publicity and research on housing and urban renewal

- *Enquiries:* To Director
- *Scope:* Housing, town and country planning and closely related subjects
- *Stock:* 2,000 books; 2,000 pamphlets and cuttings filed under subject; 20 current periodicals
- *Publications:* Housing Review (six times each year)

LONDON 1218	HOWARD LEAGUE FOR PENAL REFORM 125 Kennington Park Road London S.E.11	*Tel.:* 01-735 3773

Education and treatment of offenders and prevention of crime

Enquiries: To Secretary

Scope: Penology and criminology
Secondary: Sociology, psychology, psychoanalysis, group therapy, criminal law, criminal statistics

Stock: 1,000 books; 1,000 pamphlets; 150 reports; 20 current periodicals

Publications: Howard Journal of Penology
Occasional pamphlets

LONDON 1219	THE HUGUENOT LIBRARY University College Gower Street London W.C.1	*Tel.:* 01-387 7050 ext. 245

Joint library of the Huguenot Society of London and the French Protestant Hospital 'La Providence', deposited at University College, London

Enquiries: Academic enquiries to the Hon. Librarian (C. F. A. Marmoy, FLA); genealogical information is available through the Society's Research Assistant (Miss V. M. Carruthers, BA, FLA, 42 Regent's Park Road, London N.W.1) on payment of a fee

Scope: The Huguenots and their dispersion, particularly in Great Britain and Ireland. Stock consists of French history, French Protestant history, theology, biography; Protestant liturgies, psalters; biographies of Huguenot refugees and of their descendants, histories of their families (includes the Wagner collection of pedigrees of about 800 families); records of the 'Royal Bounty' funds; archives of the French Hospital 'La Providence'

Stock: 4,000 books; 400 pamphlets; 12 current periodicals. Stock available on loan only to libraries subscribing to the Society's publications

Publications: Proceedings and Publications

LONDON 1220	ICELANDIC EMBASSY 1 Eaton Terrace London S.W.1	*Tel.:* 01-730 5131

Enquiries: To Embassy Secretary, by letter only

Scope: A reference library containing a modest number of books on Icelandic history, law and general information

LONDON 1221	IMPERIAL CANCER RESEARCH FUND Lincoln's Inn Fields London W.C.2	*Tel.:* 01-242 9901

Enquiries: To Librarian

Scope: Cancer research

Stock: 1,000 books; 147 current periodicals; 52 serials

LONDON 1222	IMPERIAL COLLEGE DEPARTMENT OF BIOCHEMISTRY LIBRARY Imperial Institute Road London S.W.7

See no. 1366

LONDON

1223

IMPERIAL WAR MUSEUM
LIBRARIES AND ARCHIVES
Lambeth Road
London S.E.1

Tel.: 01-735 8922

The museum illustrates and records all aspects of the two World Wars and other operations involving Britain and the Commonwealth since 1914

Enquiries: To Director

FILM SECTION

Enquiries: To Film Librarian

Scope: The section holds and provides information on cinematograph film records covering the naval, military and air services in two world wars, together with propaganda, industrial, captured German, Japanese and Italian film records

Stock: 30 million feet of film

DEPARTMENT OF EXHIBITS

Preserves, conserves and displays all three-dimensional objects relating to the two world wars and other operations in which British or Commonwealth Forces have been involved since 1914. The collections administered by the department include badges and insignia, uniforms, medals and decorations, weapons, models, personal relics, aircraft, naval vessels and armoured and other vehicles

Enquiries: To Keeper of Exhibits

Scope: The department provides information on all the objects in its collections by giving information on its exhibitions and displays; by answering public enquiries; and by organizing and providing reserve and study collections which may be used for research by students. The department is also prepared to provide information about objects and artefacts which are related to its terms of reference but which are not necessarily represented in its own collections. This service may take the form of identification of objects brought in by members of the public, advice about conservation and treatment of objects in other institutions or in private hands, and guidance on modelling techniques

REFERENCE LIBRARY

Enquiries: To Librarian

Scope: All aspects of war in which the forces of Britain and the Commonwealth have been involved since 1914

Stock: 80,000 books; 23,000 pamphlets; 323 current periodicals; 10,000 trench maps, situation and order of battle maps 1914-18; 3,000 miscellaneous campaign maps 1939-45. Stock not available on loan

Publications: Bibliographies on campaigns and other selected subjects
Shorter booklists for school project enquiries

ART DEPARTMENT

Enquiries: To Keeper of Art

Scope: British War Artists schemes in the 1914-18 and 1939-45 wars. War art in the 20th century

Stock: The department's archive is the national collection of documents relating to the British War Artists schemes

Publications: A Concise Catalogue of Paintings, Drawings and Sculpture of the First World War 1914-1918. 2nd edition 1963
A Concise Catalogue of Paintings, Drawings and Sculpture of the Second World War 1939-1945. 2nd edition 1964

DOCUMENT SECTION

Enquiries: To Head of Document Section

Scope: The section provides information and research facilities for its own holdings and information about the holdings of archives in the United Kingdom, Europe and North America, in the field of contemporary European history

Stock: Documents—2,000 shelf feet, covering the following groups:
1. Captured German Army, Luftwaffe and ministerial records 1933–45
2. Captured German scientific and technological records 1920–45
3. German industrial records 1920–45
4. Records of the International, American and British war crimes trials 1946–49
5. Private papers of British service personnel of the 20th century

Publications: Provisional Reports on archives:
1. Repositories in the United Kingdom
2. Repositories in the German Federal Republic
3. Repositories in Italy
4. Repositories in the German Democratic Republic
5. Repositories in Austria
6. Repositories in Poland

PHOTOGRAPHIC SECTION

Enquiries: To Head of the Photographic Section

Scope: This section administers and makes available the national photographic collection covering war in the 20th century

Stock: 4 million prints and negatives

LONDON

1224

INCORPORATED ASSOCIATION OF ASSISTANT MASTERS IN SECONDARY SCHOOLS (THE A.M.A.)
Gordon House
29 Gordon Square
London W.C.1

Tel.: 01-387 5238

Teachers' professional organization

Enquiries: To Secretary, by letter only

Scope: The Secretariat will answer any enquiry directly related to the work of teachers, but the services of its Information Bureau, about conditions of service in schools, are confidential to its members

Publications: The A.M.A. (journal, 8 times each year)
The Teaching of Geography. Revised edition 1968
The Teaching of Science. J. Murray. 1958
The Teaching of History. Revised edition 1965
The Teaching of Modern Languages. Revised edition 1967
The Teaching of English. Revised edition 1966
The Teaching of Classics. Revised edition 1961
The Teaching of Mathematics. 1957
Teaching in Comprehensive Schools. First report, 1960; Second report, 1967
General Education in Grammar Schools. 1962

LONDON

1225

THE INCORPORATED ASSOCIATION OF PREPARATORY SCHOOLS
138 Church Street
Kensington
London W.8

Tel.: 01-727 2316

Association of Headmasters of Independent Preparatory Schools recognized as efficient by the Department of Education and Science

341

LONDON, THE INCORPORATED ASSOCIATION OF PREPARATORY SCHOOLS, *cont.*

Enquiries: To Secretary, preferably by letter

Scope: All matters connected with preparatory schools in Great Britain and overseas

No library

Publications: The Preparatory Schools Review
Preparatory Schools Today
Education for your Son
Prospect
Preparing for Decimal Coinage

LONDON

1226

INCORPORATED SOCIETY OF MUSICIANS *Tel.:* 01-935 9791
48 Gloucester Place
London W1A 4LN

Representative Society for professional musicians of all categories

Enquiries: To General Secretary, by letter only

Scope: Information to members (and sometimes non-members who are musicians) on all professional matters, including fees, contractual terms and professional etiquette. Information to members of the public on suitable music teachers, training for the musical profession, and other items

No library

Publications: Handbook and Register of Members (biennially)
Musical Journal (twice each year to members only)
Various leaflets on matters of professional interest

LONDON

1227

INDEPENDENT TELEVISION AUTHORITY *Tel.:* 01-584 7011
70 Brompton Road
London S.W.3

Government-appointed authority responsible for providing television programmes additional to those of the BBC. The Authority builds and maintains transmitters in the United Kingdom and appoints programme companies to provide its programmes

Enquiries: To Librarian

Scope: World television services in all aspects including financial and administrative

Stock: 3,000 books; 4,000 pamphlets; 160 current periodicals

Publications: ITV 19.. (a handbook produced annually as a guide to Independent Television for the general public and as a reference book for use in the industry)

LONDON

1228

INDIA HOUSE LIBRARY *Tel.:* 01-836 8484
High Commission of India
India House
Aldwych
London W.C.2

To provide information about India

Enquiries: To Information Officer and Librarian

Scope: Indian official scientific publications (for example, the important geological and meteorological series) are available, and the journals issued by the Council of Scientific and Industrial Research, but little other scientific material. Technology is not well served, but comprehensive information on finance, production and trade is available for those needing commercial data, both official and commercially published material being kept. Collection of post-independence Indian Government publications is probably the best in Europe

Stock: 118,650 books, pamphlets, reports and current periodicals

Publications: Library Catalogue, 1933 (supplemented by accession lists)
India News (weekly)
India (general booklet for children)

LONDON

229

INDIA OFFICE LIBRARY *Tel.:* 01-928 9531
FOREIGN AND COMMONWEALTH OFFICE
197 Blackfriars Road
London S.E.1

Reference and research library for all aspects of South Asia particularly the Indian sub-continent

Enquiries: To Librarian

Scope: Every aspect of South Asian studies

Stock: 350,000 volumes (100,000 in European languages, 250,000 in oriental languages); 40,000 manuscripts (of which 20,000 in oriental languages); 23,500 drawings (11,000 British, 5,000 Indian, 2,000 Persian, 5,000 Indian natural history); many thousands of photographs; much micro-film and photocopy material, particularly of manuscripts; 450 current periodicals in European languages; 60 current periodicals in oriental languages

Publications: Guide to the India Office Library. S. C. Sutton. 2nd edition revised 1969
About 60 published catalogues of books, manuscripts and drawings

See also no. 1159 and 1230

LONDON

230

INDIA OFFICE RECORDS *Tel.:* 01-928 9531
FOREIGN AND COMMONWEALTH OFFICE
197 Blackfriars Road
London S.E.1

Record office, preserving, listing and making available to readers the archival sources in London for studies relating to the Indian sub-continent and other parts of Asia during the British period

Enquiries: To Keeper

Scope: History and administration of the East India Company (1600–1858), the Board of Control (1784–1858), the India Office (1858–1947) and the Burma Office (1937–1948) in London, and historical studies relating to undivided India and other territories in Asia which had diplomatic or commercial relations with India, or were administered by the Government of India

Stock: 170,000 volumes and files of archival materials; 20,000 sheets of maps; 100,000 volumes of Official Publications. Stock not available on loan

Publications: Guide to the India Office Records 1600–1858. W. Foster. 1919 reprinted 1966
Catalogue of the Home Miscellaneous Series. S. C. Hill. 1927
Fifteen printed lists
Guide to lists and catalogues. J. C. Lancaster. 1966
Two series of Calendars of Minutes of the Court of Directors, 1635–1679, and of Factory records, 1600–1684
Guides to Departmental Records (in preparation)

See also no. 1159 and 1229

LONDON 1231	THE INDUSTRIAL CHRISTIAN FELLOWSHIP St Katharine Cree Church Leadenhall Street London E.C.3	*Tel.:* 01-283 5733

Aims to help people understand the convictions which they hold about God and Man, and to relate these to the world of everyday work

Enquiries: To Secretary

Scope: Information relating to the industrial work of the Churches in the United Kingdom, particularly of the Church of England. Information on work being done from the side of the churches on matters of current concern such as redundancy and redeployment, regional planning and automation

Secondary: Services for research in the field of the social witness of the churches

Stock: 3,000 books (basic theological works, and standard works on economic history and industrial relations); 20 current periodicals

Publications: ICF Quarterly
Occasional Papers

LONDON 1232	INDUSTRIAL CO-PARTNERSHIP ASSOCIATION 60 Buckingham Gate London S.W.1	*Tel.:* 01-828 8754

Association to extend and disseminate knowledge of, and to exchange information in relation to, the practice of co-partnership in industry

Enquiries: To Secretary

Scope: Co-partnership; profit-sharing; employee-shareholding; joint consultation; participation and involvement in industry; co-determination
Secondary: Human relations in industry; industrial democracy in practice

Publications: Co-Partnership (quarterly since 1894)

LONDON 1233	INDUSTRIAL HEALTH & SAFETY CENTRE 97 Horseferry Road London S.W.1	*Tel.:* 01-828 9255

Enquiries: To Director

Scope: Supplies advice on the requirements of the Factories Act and Regulations for the promotion of safety and health in industry. The Centre is a permanent exhibition of methods, arrangements and appliances for ensuring the safety and safeguarding the health of industrial workers against the risks that arise from their work

No library

LONDON 1234	INNER LONDON EDUCATION AUTHORITY LIBRARY Room 453 County Hall London S.E.1	*Tel.:* 01-928 5000 ext. 6990

Library service to lecturers, teachers, schools and colleges of the I.L.E.A.

Enquiries: To Librarian

Scope: General, with special emphasis on education, child study, psychology

Stock: 250,000 books; 125 current periodicals (total stock)

LONDON	INNS OF COURT SCHOOL OF LAW	*Tel.*: 01-405 4665
1235	4 Gray's Inn Place London W.C.1	

Enquiries: To Sub-Dean

Scope: Education and training for the Bar

LONDON	INSTITUT FRANÇAIS *see* **FRENCH INSTITUTE** (no. 1163)	

LONDON	INSTITUTE FOR RESEARCH INTO MENTAL RETARDATION LTD	*Tel.*: 01-636 0408
1236	85 Newman Street London W1P 3LD	

Promotes and co-ordinates research into mental retardation in all its disciplines: medical, biological, psychological, educational and sociological

Enquiries: To Secretary/Librarian, by letter only

Scope: Research into mental retardation:
Clinical aspects, for example, Mongolism
Education for the subnormal
Social and environmental development of the subnormal
Scientific research into biochemical, metabolic, pathological, genetic and other related sciences
Secondary: Mental health; psychiatry; psychology; general medicine; hospitals and nursing; anatomy; physiology; biology; anthropology; sociology; education; child development

Stock: 1,500 books and reports; 550 pamphlets; 75 current periodicals. Stock not normally available on loan

Publications: Monograph series   Study Group series
Occasional Paper series   Symposia series
Research Information series

Information is available only to professional workers at post-graduate level

LONDON	INSTITUTE FOR STRATEGIC STUDIES	*Tel.*: 01-930 3757
	18 Adam Street London W.C.2	
1237	Aims to create an international centre in Europe for continuous study, discussion and research on the problems of defence and disarmament in the nuclear-missile age	

Enquiries: To Information Officer

Scope: National defence problems, strategic planning and weapon development

Stock: 1,600 books; 180 current periodicals. Press files. Books only available on loan

Publications: Survival (monthly journal)   Adelphi Papers (monographs, monthly)
Military Balance (annually)   Studies in International Security
Strategic Survey (annually)

LONDON	INSTITUTE FOR THE STUDY AND TREATMENT OF DELINQUENCY	*Tel.*: 01-629 0622
1238	8 Bourdon Street London W.1	

Educational activities, research and publications, in the field of criminology and allied social sciences

LONDON, INSTITUTE FOR THE STUDY AND TREATMENT OF DELINQUENCY, *cont.*

Enquiries: To Secretary, by letter only

Scope: Criminology and penology; sociology; medico-psychology
    Secondary: Criminal law, juvenile delinquency, education, psychiatry, psycho-analysis

Stock: 2,400 books; 200 pamphlets; 50 current periodicals

Publications: British Journal of Criminology (quarterly)
Occasional pamphlets (on results of research, reports of conferences and study tours)

LONDON

1239

THE INSTITUTE FOR THE STUDY OF DRUG DEPENDENCE   *Tel.:* 01-580 2518
Chandos House
2 Queen Anne Street
London W1M 0BR

Provides a centre for the study of drug dependence and advances public understanding of the subject

Enquiries: To Information Officer

Scope: All aspects of drug dependence

Stock: 1,500 books and reprints from learned journals; 100 pamphlets; 60 reports; 6 current periodicals. Stock not available on loan

Publications: News Bulletin

LONDON

1240

INSTITUTE OF ACTUARIES   *Tel.:* 01-242 0106
Staple Inn Hall
High Holborn
London W.C.1

Enquiries: To Secretary

Scope: Actuarial science, life assurance, superannuation and pension funds, statistics, demography, economics

Stock: 10,000 books

Publications: Journal of the Institute of Actuaries (3 times each year)

LONDON

1241

INSTITUTE OF ADVANCED MOTORISTS   *Tel.:* 01-944 4403
4th Floor Empire House
Chiswick
London W.4

Promotion of road safety and a higher driving standard through the medium of an Advanced Driving Test

Enquiries: To Secretary

Scope: Raising of driving standards
No library

Publications: Milestones (quarterly)
16 mm films

LONDON

1242

INSTITUTE OF ARMY EDUCATION   *Tel.:* 01-850 3861
Court Road
Eltham
London S.E.9

Inspection, research and administration in connection with the Army Education Scheme

Enquiries: To Commandant, by letter only

Scope: Problems of adults' and children's education as they affect the Army, particularly those dealing with examinations, correspondence courses, Army Library Service (provided through Books Section, 433 Holloway Road, London N.7, no. 906), children's records, handicapped children, and appointment of teachers to service children's schools overseas

Stock: 3,000 books; 500 pamphlets; 74 current periodicals

Publications: RAEC Gazette
Torch
Forces Correspondence Course Bulletin
Services Resettlement Bulletin
Pamphlet: The Education of Service Children

LONDON

1243

THE INSTITUTE OF BANKERS LIBRARY   *Tel.:* 01-623 3531
10 Lombard Street
London E.C.3

Reference and Lending Library facilities and Information Service available primarily for the use of the Institute's members

Enquiries: To Librarian

Scope: Banking and finance—theory and practice; institutional, legal and comparative aspects; history of banks and banking. Strong in bound sets of economic and banking periodicals
Secondary: Economics; law, including comprehensive collection of law reports; accountancy
The Institute of Bankers Collection of Paper Money

Stock: 30,000 books and pamphlets; 300 reports; 350 current periodicals

Publications: List of Publications
Journal of The Institute of Bankers (published in alternate months)
Questions on Banking Practice (standard work of reference)
Legal Decisions Affecting Bankers (series of volumes 1879 onwards)

LONDON

1244

INSTITUTE OF BRITISH GEOGRAPHERS   *Tel.:* 01-584 6371
1 Kensington Gore
London S.W.7

Research oriented society for professional geographers

Enquiries: To Administrative Assistant

Scope: Simple enquiries for factual or bibliographical information not dealt with, but more advanced questions passed to an appropriate member

No library

Publications: Transactions (three each year)
Area (quarterly)
Special Publications

LONDON

1245

INSTITUTE OF CANCER RESEARCH   *Tel.:* 01-352 8133
Royal Cancer Hospital
Fulham Road
London S.W.3

Cancer research in its widest aspects, experimental and clinical

Enquiries: To Librarian, Chester Beatty Research Institute, Fulham Road, London S.W.3. (*Tel.:* 01-352 5946)

LONDON, INSTITUTE OF CANCER RESEARCH, *cont.*

Scope: All aspects of experimental and clinical cancer research and clinical treatment of cancer
Secondary: Thurstan Holland Collection of early radiological literature

Stock: 10,000 books and pamphlets; 800 current periodicals

Publications: Catalogue of periodicals
Selected Papers of the Institute of Cancer Research and Royal Marsden Hospital (discontinued, last issue volume 22, 1967, published 1969)
Classified list of current literature
Quarterly list of publications
Special Publications from time to time

Branch library at Belmont (Surrey Branch) which serves the Institute personnel on that site and the staff of the Royal Marsden Hospital Surrey Branch. This library is particularly strong in physics applied to medicine

The Institute library also serves the Royal Marsden Hospital itself

LONDON

1246

INSTITUTE OF CARDIOLOGY   *Tel.:* 01-486 3043
35 Wimpole Street
London W.1

Teaching and research in cardiology

Enquiries: To Secretary or Librarian

Scope: Books and periodicals on cardiology, cardiovascular diseases, anaesthetics, thoracic and cardiovascular surgery (including transplants)

Stock: 1,000 books; 65 current periodicals. An international reprint collection is being built up

LONDON

1247

THE INSTITUTE OF CHILD PSYCHOLOGY   *Tel.:* 01-229 4759
6 Pembridge Villas
London W.11

Enquiries: To Secretary

Scope: No official information service but enquiries passed to the appropriate place. Library on psychological and psychotherapy subjects

Stock: 500 books; 150 pamphlets; 6 current periodicals. Stock not available on loan

Publications: The Non-Verbal 'Thinking' of Children and its Place in Psychotherapy. M. Lowerfeld, P M. Traill and F. Rowles

LONDON

1248

INSTITUTE OF CHOREOLOGY   *Tel.:* 01-748 7121
4 Margravine Gardens
London W.6

Institute for the development of and research in choreology (the scientific and aesthetic study of movement made possible by movement notation)

Enquiries: To General Secretary

Scope: Choreographic scores, including ballets, collections of folk and ethnic dances, and other movement studies and research. Educational use and application of choreology. Analysis of scores and study of techniques of composition. Research in all aspects of movement
Secondary: Drama; medical (neurological research, physiotherapy, kinesiology); sport work study; scientific research involving analysis of movement of human and other primate

LONDON

249

| | THE INSTITUTE OF CIVIL DEFENCE | *Tel.:* 01-828 8784 |

316 Vauxhall Bridge Road
London S.W.1

Enquiries: To Secretary, by letter only

Scope: All aspects of Civil Defence and similar services in many parts of world

Stock: 1,200 books; 3,500 pamphlets

Publications: Journal of Institute of Civil Defence (quarterly)

LONDON

250

INSTITUTE OF CLASSICAL STUDIES *and* JOINT   *Tel.:* 01-387 7697
    LIBRARY OF THE HELLENIC AND ROMAN
    STUDIES
31/34 Gordon Square
London W.C.1

Enquiries: To Librarian

Scope: Greek and Roman antiquity: Literature, language, philosophy, history, epigraphy, papyrology, art and archaeology

Stock: 40,000 books and pamphlets; 350 current periodicals

Publications: Bulletin of the Institute of Classical Studies, and Supplements
Journal of Hellenic Studies
Journal of Roman Studies
Union Catalogue of Periodicals Relevant to Classical Studies in certain British Libraries. 1962
Survey of Periodicals Relevant to Byzantine Studies in several London Libraries. 1968

LONDON

251

INSTITUTE OF CONTEMPORARY HISTORY   *Tel.:* 01-636 7247
    AND WIENER LIBRARY
4 Devonshire Street
London W1N 2BH

Provides source material for research in contemporary history

Enquiries: To Librarian

Scope: History of Germany since 1870 and particularly since 1914. History of European Jewry since 1800, particularly German Jewry; and Antisemitism. History of Fascism and World War II. History of Middle East in 20th century, particularly Israel
Secondary: History of Europe (outside Germany) in the 20th century, particularly France, Italy, U.S.S.R. and Czechoslovakia

Stock: 60,000 books and pamphlets; 175 current periodicals; Documents: Nuremberg Trials collection and additional miscellaneous collections; Press Archives: eight series; Photo Archive

Publications: Wiener Library Catalogue Series. 5 volumes 1949-1964 (including revised editions of 1, 2). I. R. Wolff, ed.
Catalogue of Nuremberg Documents. 1961; Supplements 1-3, 1962-1963
Wiener Library Bulletin (quarterly)
Journal of Contemporary History (quarterly)

LONDON

252

THE INSTITUTE OF DERMATOLOGY   *Tel.:* 01-437 8383
St John's Hospital for Diseases of the Skin
Lisle Street
Leicester Square
London W.C.2

University of London, British Postgraduate Medical Federation

LONDON, THE INSTITUTE OF DERMATOLOGY, *cont.*

Enquiries: To Librarian

Scope: The library contains about 1,500 books on dermatology and related subjects such as immunology, photobiology, medical mycology and biochemistry. Of the 126 current journals 37 are dermatological in English and several foreign languages; 89 are devoted to other subjects. Reference works include the old and new editions of *Jadassohn's Handbuch fur Haut und Geschlechtskrankheiten*

Stock: 1,500 books; 126 current periodicals; Reprint collection on subjects of special interest to the dermatologist

Publications: A monthly bulletin of articles on dermatology and related subjects compiled from the literature and circulated to interested readers in Britain and abroad

LONDON

1253

INSTITUTE OF DIRECTORS
10 Belgrave Square
London S.W.1

Tel.: 01-235 3601

Enquiries: To Librarian and Information Officer, or Secretary

Scope: Books in the library cover: Company law, taxation, estate duty, directors and managers duties and responsibilities of management, management education, structure of British industry, Stock Exchange and the City, trade unions, monopolies and mergers, restrictive practices, cybernetics, ergonomics, automation, marketing and distribution, computers nationalized industries and public services, exports, scientific and industrial research, autobiographies and biographies of public and industrial figures, politics, Russia and China European Economic Community, European Free Trade Area, America and the Common wealth, broadcasting and television, and advertising, with special sections on Company Histories and Art in Industry

Stock: Books; wide range of industrial journals; extensive file of press cuttings on industrial topics bound copies of all the Institute's publications, including *The Director* (monthly journal)

LONDON

1254

INSTITUTE OF DISEASES OF THE CHEST
Brompton
London S.W.3

Tel.: 01-352 8144 ext. 329

Postgraduate teaching and research in chest medicine and surgery

Enquiries: To Librarian

Scope: Chest medicine and surgery (including tuberculosis). Historical collection of classics of chest medicine and surgery (including tuberculosis). Works by past members of the Brompton Hospital staff. Thomas Bevill Peacock Collection (19th century medicine). Marcus Paterson Collection of letters relating to the early history of Frimley Sanatorium
Secondary: General medicine and allied subjects (selected coverage)

Stock: 10,000 books and bound volumes of periodicals; 10,000 reprints, unbound pamphlets and reports; 370 current periodicals

Publications: Institute Handbook (irregularly)
Bulletin of the Library of the Institute of Diseases of the Chest (irregularly, listing additions to the library and news of the library's activities)

Library undertakes documentation in its special subject field: chest medicine and surgery–tuberculosis (from 1954 onwards) based on periodicals received in the library

LONDON	THE INSTITUTE OF HOSPITAL ADMINISTRATORS	*Tel.:* 01-580 5041
1255	75 Portland Place London W1N 4AN	

Aims to promote the professional education and training of hospital administrators

Enquiries: To Secretary

Scope: Hospital organization and administration in Great Britain
Secondary: Health Service organization in Great Britain

Stock: 1,000 books; 1,200 pamphlets and reports; 50 current periodicals. Stock not available on loan

Publications: The Hospitals Year Book
The Hospital (monthly)
Modern Hospital Management. 1969 (textbook)

LONDON	INSTITUTE OF INFORMATION SCIENTISTS	*Tel.:* 01-606 7662
1256	5/7 Russia Row Cheapside London E.C.2	

Professional qualifying body for information scientists

Enquiries: To Hon. Secretary, by letter only, or by telephone on Tuesdays and Thursdays

Scope: Standards of and training for information work
No library

Publications: The Information Scientist (Journal of the Institute)
Conference Proceedings
Handbook for Members

LONDON	INSTITUTE OF JEWISH AFFAIRS	*Tel.:* 01-935 1436
	(In Association with the World Jewish Congress)	
1257	13/16 Jacob's Well Mews George Street London W.1	

The objects of the Institute are to advance education in the field of human relationships, with particular reference to the history and social conditions of the Jewish people both past and present and of the communities of which they have formed or form part and to the causes of racial and religious stress

Enquiries: To Director

Scope: Current Affairs: Problems of antisemitism, racial and religious stresses, neo-Nazi and radical right movements. The position of Jews in the U.S.S.R. and Eastern Europe. The changing attitudes of the Christian Churches to Jews and Judaism. Middle East problems: Arab-Jewish relations. Anti-Israel and anti-Zionist attitudes of the New Left. International Legal Problems: Human Rights. War Crimes, Statute of Limitations. Indemnification to victims of Nazi persecution.
Cultural Issues
Sociology of Jews and Jewish Communities, with the following projects in progress: study of Jewish identity conducted on a comparative basis in several countries; a world-wide study of the organizational and institutional structure of Jewish communities; an annual survey of Jewish demographic data in the Diaspora; a study of poverty among Jews and of Jewish social services

Stock: 5,000 books; 3,000 pamphlets; 2,000 reports; 150 current periodicals; newspaper clippings

LONDON	THE INSTITUTE OF LARYNGOLOGY AND OTOLOGY	*Tel.*: 01-837 8855
1258	330/336 and 261/265 Gray's Inn Road London W.C.1	

Postgraduate medical school

Enquiries: Secretary-Administrator

Scope: Otorhinolaryngology
Secondary: Allied subjects

Stock: 830 books; many reprints of Institute publications; 63 current periodicals

LONDON	THE INSTITUTE OF LINGUISTS	*Tel.*: 01-407 4755
1259	91 Newington Causeway London S.E.1	

Professional body for practising linguists

Enquiries: To Secretary

Scope: Provision of information to employers of linguists as translators, interpreters and teachers, about the languages, special skills and location of members of the Institute. The *Index of Members of the Translators' Guild* gives names and other particulars of members of Translators' Guild, a specialist body of translators within the membership
Secondary: Information to public on professional training, careers, linguistic matters in general. Library concentrates on dictionaries with emphasis on technical dictionaries, glossaries and vocabularies, and reference grammars

Stock: 2,500 books; 35 current periodicals. Dictionaries and periodicals not available on loan

Publications: The Incorporated Linguist (quarterly)
Preparations for an International Conference. A. G. Readett
Working with Languages. I. F. Finlay
Earning your Living with Languages

LONDON	INSTITUTE OF MEDICAL LABORATORY TECHNOLOGY	*Tel.*: 01-636 8192
1260	12 Queen Anne Street London W.1	

Professional society

Enquiries: To Librarian or Secretary

Scope: Bacteriology, chemical pathology, haematology, histopathology, histochemistry, parasitology, virology. Laboratory management, practice and administration. Microscopy, including electron microscopy.

Stock: 300 books; 70 current periodicals. Theses submitted for Fellowship of the Institute available on restricted loan

Publications: Journal of Medical Laboratory Technology
Gazette of the Institute of Medical Laboratory Technology

LONDON	INSTITUTE OF NEUROLOGY ROCKEFELLER MEDICAL LIBRARY	*Tel.*: 01-837 3611
1261	The National Hospital Queen Square London W.C.1	

Enquiries: To Librarian

Scope: Neurology: all branches including clinical neurology, neurosurgery, neuroanatomy, neurophysiology. Early works on neurology
Secondary: Psychiatry, psychology, general medicine, biochemistry, physiology, anatomy
Stock: 10,000 books (including bound periodicals); several thousand reprints; 140 current periodicals. Almost complete in works from National Hospital

LONDON
1262

INSTITUTE OF OPERATING THEATRE TECHNICIANS
c/o B.R.M.A., B.M.A. House
Tavistock Square
London W.C.1

Tel.: 01-387 1602

Aims to improve the training and status of operating theatre technicians

Enquiries: To Secretary
Scope: Provision of syllabus of training; prospectus; lecture notes for guidance of trainees
No library
Publications: Technic (Journal of the Institute, 6 times each year)
Booklets

LONDON
1263

INSTITUTE OF OPHTHALMOLOGY
Judd Street
London W.C.1
Research Institute

Tel.: 01-387 9621

Enquiries: To Librarian
Scope: Anything related to ophthalmology and cognate subjects
Stock: 10,800 text-books and bound periodicals; 180 current periodicals. Stock not available on loan

LONDON
1264

INSTITUTE OF ORTHOPAEDICS
Royal National Orthopaedic Hospital
234 Great Portland Street
London W.1

Tel.: 01-387 5070

Postgraduate training and research in orthopaedics. (The Institute is a federated institute of the British Postgraduate Medical Federation, University of London)

Enquiries: To Librarian or Secretary
Scope: Orthopaedics
Stock: 2,000 books; 500 pamphlets; 50 current periodicals

LONDON
1265

THE INSTITUTE OF PROFESSIONAL DESIGNERS
1/5 Rosslyn Mews
Hampstead
London N.W.3

Tel.: 01-794 3233

The Institute, previously the Institute of Practising Designers, was founded in 1963, to represent an international multi-discipline composition of designers in the following fields: architecture, interior design, industrial design, town planning, and including all those concerned with environmental design

Enquiries: To Secretary
Scope: The Institute provides information for its members on all aspects of design
Stock: 400 books; 5,000 pamphlets. Stock not available on loan

LONDON, THE INSTITUTE OF PROFESSIONAL DESIGNERS, *cont.*
Publications: Annual Calendar listing all members
Regular newsletter
Brochure

LONDON

1266

THE INSTITUTE OF PSYCHIATRY   *Tel.:* 01-703 5411
De Crespigny Park
Denmark Hill
London S.E.5

Teaching and research in psychiatry and related disciplines

Enquiries: To Librarian

Scope: Psychiatry; psychoanalysis; psychology; psychosomatic medicine; the neurosciences (neuroanatomy, neurochemistry, neuroendocrinology, neurophysiology, neuropsychopharmacology)
Secondary: Neurology, medicine, biochemistry, sociology, social psychology, statistics and art, in-so-far as they apply to psychiatry
Special Collections: Guttman-Maclay Collection of Psychopathological Art; Mayer-Gross Collection; Historical Collection

Stock: 12,500 books; 16,000 pamphlets; 350 current periodicals. Guttman-Maclay Collection of Psychopathological Art: 110 pictures. Theses and dissertations: 300

Publications: Maudsley Monographs (report work carried out at the Institute of Psychiatry and at the associated joint hospital, The Bethlem Royal Hospital and the Maudsley Hospital)

LONDON

1267

THE INSTITUTE OF PSYCHO-ANALYSIS   *Tel.:* 01-580 4952
Mansfield House
63 New Cavendish Street
London W.1

Aims to facilitate communications between psycho-analysts, train psycho-analysts, research work, meetings and lectures, publications, running a psycho-analytic clinic

Enquiries: To Public Relations Officer or Library Secretary, by letter only

Scope: Psychoanalysis (particularly Freud's works); psychiatry; psychology
Secondary: Psychotherapy; anthropology; psychosomatic medicine

Stock: 7,600 books; 100 pamphlets; 150 reports; 62 current periodicals

Publications: International Journal of Psychoanalysis
Booklets on specific items
Winter Lecture series
The International Psychoanalytic Library with the the Hogarth Press

This information applies also to the British Psychoanalytical Society and the London Clinic of Psychoanalysis

LONDON

1268

INSTITUTE OF REGISTERED ARCHITECTS   *Tel.:* 01-486 1945
68 Gloucester Place
London W.1

Society of private practising architects primarily concerned with the problems arising out of, and in the course of, the practice of architecture

Enquiries: To Secretary

Scope: The Institute offers a consultative service, mainly to practising architects, on matters of professional practice

Small reference library only

Publications: Scale of Professional Fees The Architect and the Law-body
Guide to the Scale of Fees Fees Account Form
Form of Building Contract

LONDON

1269

THE INSTITUTE OF SHOPS ACTS *Tel.:* 01-606 3030 ext. 262
ADMINISTRATION
SHOPS AND OTHER ACTS DEPARTMENT
Guildhall
London E.C.2

Enquiries: To Secretary

Scope: To answer enquiries on the application of the Shops Acts, 1950–1965, the Offices, Shops and Railway Premises Act, 1963, and contiguous legislation administered by the members of the Institute and to give advice

Stock: Small library, including books on the law relating to shops, and equipment manufacturers' literature

Publications: The Inspector (monthly journal)
Annual Conference Verbatim Report of Papers and Proceedings

LONDON

1270

THE INSTITUTE OF SPORTS MEDICINE *Tel.:* 01-486 1303
Ling House
10 Nottingham Place
London W1M 4AX

Short-term objectives include the establishment of: post-graduate research fellowships into medical problems of fitness and sports injuries; specialist treatment centres; medical advisory service (including advice on selection and training); and regular teaching courses

Enquiries: To Hon. Secretary, by letter only

Scope: Enquiries dealt with only from qualified medical practitioners

Joint library with the Physical Education Association of Great Britain and Northern Ireland (no. 1475)

LONDON

1271

INSTITUTE OF UROLOGY *Tel.:* 01-836 5361
10 Henrietta Street
London W.C.2

Enquiries: To Librarian

Scope: All aspects of urology

Stock: 500 books; 400 pamphlets; 26 current periodicals

Publications: British Journal of Urology

LONDON

1272

THE INSTITUTION OF PROFESSIONAL CIVIL *Tel.:* 01-930 9161
SERVANTS
3/9 Northumberland Street
London W.C.2
Trade Union

Enquiries: To Research Officer

Scope: Civil Service conditions and salary scales. History of the Civil Service, Whitleyism and staff associations. Scientists, technologists and other specialist staffs in the Civil Service

Stock: 500 books; 1,000 pamphlets; 180 current periodicals. Stock not available on loan

LONDON	INTERNATIONAL AFRICAN INSTITUTE	*Tel.*: 01-353 4751
1273	St Dunstan's Chambers 10/11 Fetter Lane Fleet Street London E.C.4	

Aims to promote the serious study of the African peoples, their languages, cultures and social life, including the traditional patterns of tribal organization with their associated beliefs and values, and the new social forms and cultural developments which are emerging

Enquiries: To Librarian or Secretary

Scope: The main emphasis of the Institute's small, international, reference library is on African social, cultural and linguistic studies. Short runs of all relevant periodicals and longer runs or complete sets of the main journals specializing in African studies are kept

The Information and Liaison Service of the Institute provides information and aid of all kinds to researchers in the subject field of African studies, including: recommendations on conference programmes in the field of social sciences in Africa, and specialists who could be invited; advice on research projects in Africa undertaken by organizations or individuals, including personal introductions; information on the facilities for instruction and research for the study of African social sciences in Europe, the United States of America and Africa; details of current research; assistance in the preparation of studies for publication; advice and information on the problems of African linguistics, and on the facilities for study of African languages; suggestions of scholars for lectures; specialized bibliographies on particular African peoples and languages, and on other questions; verification of bibliographical references; and library techniques and co-operation in the field of African studies

Stock: 6,000 books; 5,000 pamphlets; 200 current periodicals

Publications: Africa (quarterly journal of the Institute which includes a current bibliography also available as an offprint)
African Abstracts (quarterly)
Africa Bibliography Series A: Ethnology, Sociology and Linguistics
Africa Bibliography Series B: Special Subjects
Many books, and some memoranda, on African ethnography, sociology, history, languages and linguistics
Ethnographic Survey of Africa
Handbook of African Languages

The Library maintains a card index, now containing about 50,000 book and article references of current Africanist social and cultural publications. The index is in two sections, one classified geographically with subject subdivision and an ethnic and linguistic index, and the other by author

LONDON	INTERNATIONAL ASSOCIATION OF MMM LTD	*Tel.*: 01-486 0791
1274	MARGARET MORRIS MOVEMENT 2 Manchester Square London S.E.22	

Enquiries: To the Secretary, by letter only

Scope: Physical education and creative dance combining the medical and aesthetic values of movement
No library

Publications: Margaret Morris Dancing. Routledge and Kegan Paul, 1925
Notation of Movement. Margaret Morris. Routledge and Kegan Paul, 1928
Skiing Exercises. Margaret Morris and H. Falkner. Heinemann, 1934

Maternity and Post-operative Exercises. Margaret Morris and Sister Randell. Heinemann 1936
Basic Physical Training. Margaret Morris. Heinemann, 1937
Tennis by Simple Exercises. Margaret Morris and S. Lenglen. Heinemann, 1937
My Galsworthy Story. Margaret Morris. Peter Owen, 1967
My Life in Movement. Margaret Morris. Peter Owen, 1969

LONDON

1275

INTERNATIONAL BUREAU FOR EPILEPSY   *Tel.:* 01-580 2704
3/6 Alfred Place
London W.C.1

Acts as the Bureau for social affairs for the International League against Epilepsy, brings together and makes available information about social and medical care for people with epilepsy, organises meetings and seminars, stimulates and assists in the formation of epilepsy associations

Enquiries: To Secretary General

Scope: Enquiries concerning social aspects of epilepsy on an international scale

Stock: Journals of member organisations and other periodicals

Publications: Newsletter (three times each year)
Conference Reports
Leaflets
Film Catalogue (of films on epilepsy)

LONDON

1276

INTERNATIONAL CO-OPERATIVE ALLIANCE   *Tel.:* 01-499 5991
11 Upper Grosvenor Street
London W1X 9PA

International confederation of co-operative organizations of all types, dedicated to the promotion of co-operation in all parts of the world

Enquiries: To Director

Scope: Co-operative movements of all countries. Socio-economic matters such as consumer affairs, education, management and organization

Stock: 12,000 books; 565 current periodicals. Library stock not available on loan. Films available on loan

Publications: Reports of Congresses of the Alliance
Review of International Cooperation (bi-monthly in English, French, German and Spanish)
Cooperative News Service (monthly)
Agricultural Cooperative Bulletin (monthly)
Consumer Affairs Bulletin (monthly in English and French)
International Cooperation—Reports of Activities of National Cooperative Organisations
Statistics of Affiliated National Organizations
Annual Statements
Film Bulletin. 1968
Cooperative Principles (English, French and German)
Three lectures on International Cooperative Insurance (English)
International Directory of the Cooperative Press
Directory of Cooperative Travel Facilities and Accommodation offered by Member Organisations
Directory of Cooperative Banks and Finance Institutions
Directory of Cooperative Colleges, Schools, Training Centres and University Institutes

LONDON, INTERNATIONAL CO-OPERATIVE ALLIANCE, *cont.*
Calendar of Technical Assistance for Cooperatives (annually)
Reports of ICA Congresses
Miscellaneous Publications
Trading of Cooperatives—South East Asia
Cooperatives and Monopolies in Contemporary Economic Systems
International Cooperation
Structural changes in Cooperatives
Manual for Cooperative Libraries and Documentation Services (English, French and German)

LONDON

1277

THE INTERNATIONAL INSTITUTE FOR   *Tel.:* 01-373 5975
   CONSERVATION OF HISTORIC AND ARTISTIC
      WORKS
176 Old Brompton Road
London S.W.5

Aims to co-ordinate and improve the knowledge, methods and working standards needed to protect and preserve works of historic and artistic merit

Enquiries: To Secretary General

Scope: Advice on restorers, equipment and materials for restoration and conservation

No library

Publications: Studies in Conservation (quarterly)
Art and Archaeology Technical Abstracts (twice each year)
IIC News (twice each year)

LONDON

1278

INTERNATIONAL PHONETIC ASSOCIATION   *Tel.:* 01-387 7050
University College London
Gower Street
London W.C.1

Promotion of the study of phonetics and its applications

Enquiries: To Secretary, by letter only

Scope: Phonetics and its applications, including information about the International Phonetic Alphabet

No library

Publications: Le Maître Phonétique (twice each year, journal of the Association)
Principles of the International Phonetic Association
Chart of the International Phonetic Alphabet
Various other booklets and pamphlets

LONDON

1279

INTERNATIONAL PLANNED PARENTHOOD   *Tel.:* 01-839 2911
   FEDERATION
18/20 Lower Regent Street
London S.W.1

Aims to advance the education of the countries of the world in family planning and responsible parenthood in the interest of family welfare, community well-being and international goodwill and to stimulate appropriate scientific research in the following subjects: the biological, demographic, social, economic, eugenic and psychological implications of human fertility and its regulation; methods of contraception; fertility, subfertility and sterility; sex education and marriage counselling

Enquiries: To Information Officer or Librarian

Scope: Contraception, family planning, programmes, population, demography, sex education, the family, and social and economic aspects of these above subjects. Fertility and sterility; abortion; family planning movements
Secondary: Background materials to support the work of the Federation. Materials on the situation in various countries; obstetrics and gynaecology. Communications and use of mass media; education; genetics

Stock: 2,000 books; 9,000 pamphlets; 7,000 reports; 215 current periodicals. Large collection of films, slides, educational materials, audio-visual aids and programmed learning texts

Publications: Library Bulletin
Calendar of International Meetings
Various handbooks and periodicals on medical, scientific and general aspects
Directories of Training Facilities and of Planned Parenthood Organizations

LONDON

1280

INTERNATIONAL SOCIETY FOR CLINICAL AND EXPERIMENTAL HYPNOSIS, BRITISH NATIONAL DIVISION
152 Harley Street
London W.1.

Tel.: 01-935 8868

Enquiries: To Hon. Secretary, by letter only

Scope: The Hon. Secretary is available to answer enquiries in the field of clinical and experimental hypnosis

LONDON

1281

INTERNATIONAL SOCIETY FOR THE PROTECTION OF ANIMALS (ISPA)
106 Jermyn Street
London S.W.1

Tel.: 01-839 3066

Enquiries: To Executive Director

Scope: International animal welfare
Secondary: Conservation

LONDON

1282

INTERNATIONAL TRANSPORT WORKERS' FEDERATION
Maritime House
Old Town
Clapham
London S.W.4

Tel.: 01-622 5501
Telex: 25604

International Trade Union Federation

Enquiries: To Research and Information Department (or Publications Department)

Scope: Transport industry; transport trade unionism and working conditions
Secondary: Trade unionism in general; industrial relations

Stock: Several thousand books, pamphlets and reports; 200 current periodicals

Publications: Journal (in English, German, Spanish and Japanese)
Newsletter (in English, French, German, Swedish, Japanese and Arabic)

In 1959 the Federation published a report entitled 'Transport Policy Problems at National and International Level' (English, German, French and Swedish) and in 1968 a report on the social and economic consequences of container traffic, entitled 'Containerization' (English, German, French, Spanish and Swedish). A limited number of copies of both these reports are still available

| LONDON | INTERNATIONAL VOLUNTARY SERVICE | *Tel.:* 01-965 1446 |

LONDON

1283

INTERNATIONAL VOLUNTARY SERVICE   *Tel.:* 01-965 1446
91 High Street
Harlesden
London N.W.10

Provides opportunities for volunteers to carry out social service jobs in an international context

Enquiries: To Secretary

Scope: As the British branch of an international organization (Service Civil International), IVS can pass on applications from volunteers wishing to work abroad to the relevant agency. Similarly, as one of the member organizations of the British Volunteer Programme, IVS helps co-ordinate applications from trained volunteers wishing to do longterm service in a developing country

No library

Publications: Service (journal)

LONDON

1284

INTER-VARSITY FELLOWSHIP OF EVANGELICAL   *Tel.:* 01-636 5113
UNIONS
39 Bedford Square
London W.C.1

Evangelism and pastoral work among students; promotion of biblical research and systematic and applied biblical theology; publication of books and periodicals; maintaining a research library at Tyndale House, Cambridge

Enquiries: To the General Secretary, IVF, 39 Bedford Square, London W.C.1, *or* The Librarian, Tyndale House, 36 Selwyn Gardens, Cambridge

Scope: Affiliated to the Inter-Varsity Fellowship is the Graduates' Fellowship. Among the professional sections of the Graduates' Fellowship are the Christian Medical Fellowship, with its own journal, and the Christian Education Fellowship which produces a Religious Education Book Review Service (duplicated) and, in conjunction with two other societies, *Spectrum*, a journal for Christians in Education

Publications: Tyndale Bulletin (annually, journal of the Tyndale Fellowship for Biblical and Theological Research and of Tyndale House)
Christian Graduate (quarterly)
Inter-Varsity (termly)
Theological Students' Fellowship Bulletin (termly)

Inter-Varsity Press and Tyndale Press, subsidiary organizations, have a combined catalogue of more than 300 titles, all on Christian themes, and ranging from the New Bible Dictionary to small booklets and Bible Study Outlines

LONDON

1285

THE ISLAMIC CULTURAL CENTRE   *Tel.:* 01-723 7611
Regent's Lodge
146 Park Road
London N.W.8

Looks after the Muslim Community in the United Kingdom and gives explanations to those wanting to know about Islam

Enquiries: To Director

Scope: Islamic and Arabic literature. Muslim and Arabic research including religion, history, literature and law

Publications: The Islamic Quarterly
Various pamphlets about Islam
The Centre runs Arabic classes and classes for Muslim children to receive Islamic teaching and arranges lectures on Islam

LONDON

1286

ITALIAN EMBASSY
14 Three Kings Yard
Davies Street
London W.1

Tel.: 01-629 8200

Enquiries: To Italian Embassy, by letter only
Scope: Italy in general

LONDON

1287

ITALIAN STATE TOURIST
DEPARTMENT (ENIT)
201 Regent Street
London W.1

Tel.: 01-734 4631

Enquiries: To Italian State Tourist Department
Scope: Italy: tourist information including art cities, historical cities, events and festivals
Publications: Tourist literature
Film list of 16 mm hire library

LONDON

1288

THE IVEAGH BEQUEST, KENWOOD
Hampstead Lane
London N.W.3

Tel.: 01-348 1286

English 18th-century painting and furniture. Dutch 17th-century painting (Rembrandt/Vermeer); neo-classical architecture (Robert Adam)

Enquiries: To Curator, by letter only
Scope: Art Library on subject fields, including complete runs of bound periodicals such as *Country Life*. Sale catalogues. Exhibition and permanent catalogues of other institutions
Secondary: Lord Iveagh's Irish History Library
Stock: 5,000 books; 1,500 pamphlets (excluding sales catalogues); 9 current periodicals. Stock not available on loan
Publications: Iveagh Bequest, Kenwood. A short account by Sir John Summerson
Catalogue of Paintings. Introduction by Sir Anthony Blunt
Exhibition Catalogues in English 18th century paintings and furniture 1951–

LONDON

1289

JAPAN INFORMATION CENTRE
EMBASSY OF JAPAN
9 Grosvenor Square
London W1X 9LB

Tel.: 01-493 6030

Enquiries: To Information Officer
Scope: General information on Japan. Library stock includes education, fine arts, literature and history, in both Japanese and English
Stock: 1,500 books; 30 current periodicals. Slides and films
Publications: Japan Information Bulletin (monthly)

LONDON

1290

JESUIT LIBRARY
114 Mount Street
London W.1

See no. 1025

LONDON **1291**	JEWISH HISTORICAL SOCIETY OF ENGLAND 33 Seymour Place London W.1	*Tel.:* 01-723 4404

Promotes the study of the history of the Jews of the Commonwealth

Enquiries: To Hon. Secretary, by letter only

Publications: Transactions
Miscellanies
Exchequer of the Jews. J. M. Rigg and H. Jenkinson
Anglo-Jewish Notabilities
The Western Synagogue Through Two Centuries. Barnett
The British Consulate in Jerusalem: Vols. I & II. Hyamson
Leeds Jewry. Krausz
Three Centuries of Anglo-Jewish History. Lipman
Magna Bibliotheca Anglo-Judaica. Revised by C. Roth
Nova Bibliotheca Anglo-Judaica. R. P. Lehmann
English Jewry under the Angevin Kings. Richardson
Mediaeval Lincoln Jewry. Roth
Sepher Hashoham (The Onyx Book)
Starrs and Jewish Charters: Vols. I, II & III
Weizmann and England. Stein
Diplomatic History of the Jewish Question. Wolf
Writings of Rabbi Elijah of London
Jews in the Canary Isles
Remember the Days: Essays in Honour of Cecil Roth
Jews of Medieval Norwich. U. P. Lipman
Israel and Elath. E. Elath
Lucien Wolf Memorial Lectures
Arthur Davis Memorial Lectures
Presidential Addresses

See also Mocatta Library (no. 1383)

LONDON **1292**	JEWS' COLLEGE 11 Montagu Place Montagu Square London W.1	*Tel.:* 01-723 2041 (College); 01-723 9974 (Library)

College for the education and training of Rabbis, Ministers, Preachers, Readers and teachers of religion for Jewish communities and the provision of higher Jewish learning for the laity

Enquiries: To Librarian or Principal

Scope: Library contains standard works on Bible and Biblical Studies, Talmudic and Rabbinic literature, Jewish history, literature, language, music, homiletics, antisemitism, Israel and Palestine and information can be given based on this type of material

Stock: 60,000 books; 110 current periodicals; 700 manuscripts

Publications: Jews' College Publications: new series

LONDON **1293**	JOINT ASSOCIATION OF CLASSICAL TEACHERS 31/34 Gordon Square London W.C.1

In the belief that classical studies have something of irreplaceable value to contribute to education, the Association aims to help classics teachers maintain and improve the standard of classics teaching.

Enquiries: To Executive Secretary, by letter only

Scope: Any enquiry relating to Greek, Latin and Ancient History for both pupils and teachers (although the service and information bureau is normally only for members)

No library

Publications: Didaskalos (published annually by Blackwell)
Bulletin (termly, for members only)

LONDON

1294

THE JOINT FOUR: JOINT EXECUTIVE COMMITTEE OF THE ASSOCIATIONS OF HEAD MASTERS, HEAD MISTRESSES, ASSISTANT MASTERS AND ASSISTANT MISTRESSES
Gordon House
29 Gordon Square
London W.C.1

Tel.: 01-387 7512

Enquiries: To Secretary, by letter only

Scope: Information limited to the policy of the Joint Four and of its constituent Associations on educational matters

No library

LONDON

1295

JOINT LIBRARY OF THE HELLENIC AND ROMAN STUDIES
31/34 Gordon Square
London W.C.1

Tel.: 01-387 7697

See no. 1250

LONDON

1296

THE JORDAN EMBASSY
6 Upper Phillimore Gardens
London W.8

Tel.: 01-937 3685

Enquiries: To Attaché for Information

Scope: All aspects of Jordan

No library

LONDON

1297

JOSEPHINE BUTLER EDUCATIONAL TRUST
82 Denison House
296 Vauxhall Bridge Road
London S.W.1

Tel.: 01-824 5193

Trust for the study of the problems of prostitution and legislation bearing on these

Enquiries: To Secretary

Scope: Probably the best collection of books and periodicals dealing with the problem of prostitution for the last century
Secondary: Books on women's rights

Stock: 1,200 books; 250 pamphlets

Publications: The Shield (annual publication of the Trust)

LONDON

1298

KAY SONS & DAUGHTER LTD
Artillery Mansions
Victoria Street
London S.W.1

Tel.: 01-799 1864
Telex: 23417

Publishers of biographical reference books

LONDON, KAY SONS & DAUGHTER LTD, *cont.*

Enquiries: To Director

Scope: Biographical reference (in all some 40,000 biographies)

Stock: 1,500 books; hundreds of pamphlets; 2 current periodicals

Publications: Dictionary of International Biography   Dictionary of Black American Biography
Dictionary of African Biography   International Who's Who in Poetry
Dictionary of Caribbean Biography   The Two Thousand Men of Achievement
The Two Thousand Women of Achievement

LONDON

1299

KEATS MEMORIAL HOUSE
Keats Grove
Hampstead
London N.W.3

Tel.: 01-435 2062

Preservation of relics of John Keats (poet) and maintenance of his home and a library devoted to Keats and his circle

Enquiries: To Borough Librarian and Curator

Scope: John Keats, the poet, 1795–1821: preservation and maintenance of relics associated with him and his family and books and periodicals by and about him
Secondary: Byron, Shelley, Leigh Hunt and Charles Lamb and their circles

Stock: 5,000 books; 1,000 pamphlets; 5 current periodicals

Publications: Guide to Keats House and Museum

LONDON

1300

THE KEATS–SHELLEY MEMORIAL ASSOCIATION
Longfield Cottage
Longfield Drive
Sheen Common
London S.W.14

Tel.: 01-876 8136

Aims to support the house at Rome where John Keats died and to celebrate the fame of Keats together with Shelley, Byron and Leigh Hunt

Enquiries: To Secretary

Scope: The Library consists of 8,000 books and a number of manuscripts dealing with Keats, Shelley, Byron, Leigh Hunt and their circle. Enquiries can be directed either to the Secretary at the above address or to the Curator, Keats House, 26 Piazza di Spagna, Rome

Stock: 8,000 books

Publications: The Keats–Shelley Memorial Bulletin (annually, contains works of original scholarship on subjects connected with Keats, Shelley, Byron, Leigh Hunt and their contemporaries)

LONDON

1301

KEEP BRITAIN TIDY GROUP
Cecil Chambers
76/86 Strand
London W.C.2

Tel.: 01-836 6463

Enquiries: To Director General

Scope: To create an awareness of the problem of litter and to organize a campaign against it

Publications: Litter Report and publicity material

LONDON 302

KENNINGTON COLLEGE
West Square
St George's Road
London S.E.11

Tel.: 01-735 9636

The college provides instruction in general and commercial subjects for adults of 18 and over, up to and including G.C.E. 'O' levels

Enquiries: To Librarian

Scope: Art, British constitution, dressmaking, economics, economic history, history, history of art, geography, music, nutrition and cookery, religious knowledge, sociology, social economics, general principles of English law, structure of commerce, principles of accounts, English language and literature, French, German, Latin, Spanish, biology, botany

Stock: 5,000 books; 350 pamphlets; 73 current periodicals

LONDON 303

KING'S COLLEGE LONDON
Strand
London W.C.2

Tel.: 01-836 5454

Enquiries: To Librarian, by letter or in person

Scope: The College library serves all subjects taught in the College in its eight faculties of arts, education, music, theology, laws, natural science, medical science (pre-clinical only), and engineering. It is particularly strong in certain subjects in which the College specializes within the University of London, including Ecclesiastical history, Imperial history, modern Greek, Portuguese, Spanish (including Latin-American literature), theology and war studies. It includes the Centre for Military Archives, which serves as a depository for papers bearing on Britain's defence policy since 1900 and her strategy in the two world wars which are still in private hands. *Special collections* include: Marsden Collection (philology, early Bibles, travel); Box Library (Hebrew and Old Testament studies); Enk Library (classics)

Stock: 192,250 books; 12,750 pamphlets; 1,150 current periodicals; (total stock: 275,000 volumes)

A considerable proportion of older and less used material is temporarily housed at the University of London Library Depository at Egham

LONDON 304

KOREAN EMBASSY
36 Cadogan Square
London S.W.1

Tel.: 01-581 0247

Enquiries: To Secretary

Scope: Any information on Korea

Publications: Pamphlets

LONDON 305

THE LABOUR PARTY LIBRARY
Transport House
Smith Square
London S.W.1

Tel.: 01-834 9434

Enquiries: To Librarian

Scope: Socialism at home and abroad. Economics and industry
Secondary: Social sciences, history and biography

Stock: 6,000 books; 30,000 pamphlets; 300 current periodicals; about ½ million press cuttings from 1945; 8,000 photographs. Stock not normally available on loan

Publications: Policy statements, leaflets, a bibliography of all Party and associated organizations' publications

LONDON		LAMBETH PALACE LIBRARY London S.E.1	*Tel.:* 01-928 6222
1306	*Enquiries:*	To Librarian	
	Scope:	Ecclesiastical history	
	Stock:	100,000 books; 2,500 manuscripts; archives of Vicar General of Canterbury, Faculty Office, Court of Arches, Papers of Archbishops of Canterbury, temporalities of the see of Canterbury; 100 current periodicals	
	Publications:	Catalogue of manuscripts, 1812. H. J. Todd Catalogue of Mediaeval Manuscripts in Lambeth Palace Library. M. R. James. 1932 Lambeth Palace. C. R. Dodwell. 1958 Calendar of Fulham Papers (American Section). W. W. Manross. 1966 Catalogue of estate documents. J. E. Sayers. 1965 Calendar of the Shrewsbury Papers. C. Jamison and E. G. W. Bill. 1966 Catalogue of the Selborne Papers. E. G. W. Bill. 1967 Original Papal documents in the Lambeth Palace Library. J. E. Sayers. 1967 Catalogue of ecclesiastical records, Commonwealth period, 1650–60. J. Houston. 1968 Charters in Lambeth Palace Library. D. M. Owen. 1968	

LONDON		THE LANGUAGE-TEACHING LIBRARY 63 High Holborn	*Tel.:* 01-242 9020
1307		London W.C.1	
		Jointly maintained by the English-Teaching Information Centre, British Council, and the Centre for Information on Language Teaching (no. 1042)	
	Enquiries:	To Director, English-Teaching Information Centre	
	Scope:	Linguistics, language-teaching principles and methods with special reference to English as a foreign or second language, French, German, Italian, Russian, Spanish. Includes linguistic studies and a teaching materials collection for each language *Secondary:* British and overseas education, mainly in relation to language teaching	
	Stock:	21,100 books; 355 current periodicals; 325 filmstrips; 1,000 speech records; 1,550 tape recordings; 100 microfiches; 10 cineloops	
	Publications:	Language Teaching Abstracts *and* A Language-Teaching Bibliography (both compiled jointly with the Centre for Information on Language Teaching) Academic Courses in Great Britain Relevant to the Teaching of English as a Second Language (annually) Occasional papers on matters relating to the teaching of English as a second or foreign language	

LONDON		LANGUAGE TUITION CENTRE 26/32 Oxford Street	*Tel.:* 01-580 1005
1308		London W1A 4DY	
		English language tuition to foreign students. Foreign language tuition, secretarial college for training of bilingual secretaries and interpreter/translators, commerce and industry's language laboratory	
	Enquiries:	To Principal, by letter or in person only	
	Scope:	Advice on aspects of language learning can be given	

LONDON		LAW COMMISSION Lacon House	*Tel.:* 01-405 8700 ext. 128
1309		Theobalds Road London W.C.1	
		Established by Law Commissions Act 1965 to keep under review the whole of the law of	

England with a view to its development and reform and generally to simplify and modernise the law

Enquiries: To Librarian (bibliographical) or Secretary (concerning work of Commission)

Scope: Law (especially English law), comparative and international law and law of other countries especially common law jurisdictions, France, Germany, and Scandinavia. Law reform materials from diverse sources
Secondary: Related and background material in social sciences, criminology, politics and public administration and parliamentary procedure

Stock: 6,600 books; 1,700 pamphlets; 121 current periodicals

Publications: H.M.S.O. Sectional List no. 51 includes Law Commission
Monthly bulletin of recent additions

LONDON

1310

THE LAW SOCIETY
The Law Society's Hall
113 Chancery Lane
London W.C.2

Tel.: 01-242 1222
Telex: 261203

The Law Society controls the education and examination of articled clerks, the admission of solicitors in England and Wales, and their professional regulation after admission

Enquiries: To Librarian, preferably by letter or telex

Scope: General law library for members of the Law Society. Current and earlier editions of legal treatises, English, Scottish and Irish Acts of Parliament, law reports and professional journals

Stock: 80,000 books; 25 current *legal* periodicals. Stock not available on loan

Publications: Memoranda of the Council of the Law Society to Government and public bodies, usually on matters of reform of the law
Law Society's Gazette (monthly)
Obiter (the Society's newspaper)

LONDON

1311

THE LEAGUE OF SAFE DRIVERS
Apex House
Grand Arcade
London N.12

Tel.: 01-445 1000

Aims to improve the standard of general driving, thus reducing accidents, by means of graded and repetitive advanced driving tests

Enquiries: To Secretary

Scope: Advanced driving techniques; courses for both private and professional drivers; courses for driving instructors on the techniques of teaching advanced driving; special instructions for accident-prone drivers

No library

LONDON

1312

THE LEPROSY MISSION
50 Portland Place
London W1N 3DG

Tel.: 01-637 2611

Enquiries: To Editorial Secretary

Scope: The work of the Mission since 1874
Secondary: Library of books on leprosy and leprosy workers to which serious students may have access on request

Stock: 250 books; 500 pamphlets

LONDON, THE LEPROSY MISSION, *cont.*

Publications: Booklist of current literature, annual report and quarterly magazines
Many books and pamphlets

LONDON

1313

H. K. LEWIS & CO. LTD
136 Gower Street
London W.C.1

Tel.: 01-387 4282

Supplies books on loan, on a subscription basis, from a comprehensive collection of the latest editions of British and American medical and scientific works of reference, textbooks and specialized monographs, together with foreign works which have been translated into English

Enquiries: To the library

Scope: Medicine. Surgery. General science and technology. The library does not undertake any form of research

Stock: 150,000 books; no periodicals

Publications: Library Catalogue, revised to 31st December 1963
Pt. 1. Authors and Titles
Pt. 2. Classified Index of Subjects with the names of Authors who have written upon them
Supplement to the Library Catalogue 1964–66
Quarterly List of acquisitions

LONDON

1314

THE LIBERAL PARTY ORGANISATION
7 Exchange Court
Strand
London W.C.2

Tel.: 01-240 0701

Enquiries: To Information Officer

Scope: Information on the current policies and activities of the Liberal Party

Publications: Liberal News Commentary (weekly newspaper)
Pamphlets and leaflets on all aspects of Liberal Policy

LONDON

1315

LIBRARY ASSOCIATION
7 Ridgmount Street
Store Street
London W.C.1

Tel.: 01-636 7543
Telex: 21897

Professional Association

Enquiries: To Librarian and Information Officer

Scope: Librarianship: library methods, information on particular libraries current and historical, British and overseas; library equipment and services; library education and conditions of service (handled by separate departments). Librarianship is taken to include documentation
Secondary: Historical bibliography, censorship, copyright, bookselling, publishing, subject bibliography (methods, not subject enquiries), reading habits

Stock: 25,000 books, pamphlets and reports; several thousand annual reports; 800 current periodicals. Stock available on loan through N.C.L.

Publications: British Technology Index (monthly) Monographs on library subjects
British Humanities Index (quarterly) British Education Index (4-monthly)
Catalogue of the Library. 1958 Subject Bibliographies
Public Library Conference Proceedings Library Association Record (monthly)
Library and Information Science Abstracts (2-monthly)
Library and Information Bulletin (occasionally)

LONDON

1316

THE LIBRARY OF THE GRAND PRIORY IN THE BRITISH REALM OF THE MOST VENERABLE ORDER OF THE HOSPITAL OF ST JOHN OF JERUSALEM
Tel.: 01-253 6644
St John's Gate
Clerkenwell
London E.C.1

The Order has two Foundations: Ophthalmic Hospital in Jerusalem and St John Ambulance Association and Brigade, which operates in most countries of the Commonwealth

Enquiries: To Librarian

Scope: Books, pamphlets and other documents, concerning all aspects of the order of St John, past and present in Great Britain, the Commonwealth, Europe and the Near East. (Malta is particularly well covered)

Stock: 6,000 books; 1,000 pamphlets. Stock not available on loan

Publications: The Order of St John: A Short History. E. D. Renwick
The Knights of St John in the British Realm. Sir Edwin King and Sir Harry Luke
Training Manuals and teaching aids of the St John Ambulance Association

LONDON

1317

LISTER INSTITUTE OF PREVENTIVE MEDICINE
Tel.: 01-730 2181
Chelsea Bridge Road
London S.W.1

Enquiries: To Librarian

Scope: Chemistry, immunology and biology
Secondary: Medicine and veterinary science

Stock: 675 books; 265 current periodicals

LONDON

1318

LITHUANIAN ASSOCIATION IN GREAT BRITAIN
Tel.: 01-727 2470
Lithuanian House
1 Ladbroke Gardens
London W.11

Enquiries: To Secretary

Scope: Lithuania

Stock: 600 books; 4 current periodicals

Publications: Europos Lietuvis (weekly paper)
4 to 6 books each year in the Lithuanian language

LONDON

1319

LOCAL GOVERNMENT INFORMATION OFFICE
Tel.: 01-930 8214
36 Old Queen Street
Westminster
London S.W.1

To create a better understanding of local government, its structure and its functions

Enquiries: To Head of Information Services
No library

Publications: Digests, posters and booklets

LONDON

1320

LOCATION OF OFFICES BUREAU
Tel.: 01-405 2921
27 Chancery Lane
London W.C.2

The Bureau was established with the purpose of encouraging the decentralization of office

LONDON, LOCATION OF OFFICES BUREAU, *cont.*

employment from congested central London to suitable centres elsewhere. Its functions include the promotion of publicity and research, and the provision of information

Enquiries: To Information Officer (publicity), Secretary or Chairman (policy) or Research Officer (research)

Scope: Data on the Bureau's activities 1964 to 1969. Information provided wherever available on all enquiries related to offices and office employment, including the provision of references and other material to persons engaged in relevant research

No library

Publications: Annual Report (contains statistical tables of interest to office movement research)
Research papers

LONDON

1321

LONDON ASSOCIATION FOR THE BLIND *Tel.:* 01-703 6153
88/92 Peckham Road
London S.E.15

Charity for the employment, training and general welfare of the blind

Enquiries: To General Secretary, preferably by letter

Scope: No information service, but would be willing to answer enquiries in connection with the welfare of the blind, or suggest to enquirers other sources of information

No library

LONDON

1322

LONDON BOROUGH OF BARNET PUBLIC LIBRARIES *Tel.:* 01-202 5625
Telex: 25665
Administrative Offices
Ravensfield House
The Burroughs
London N.W.4

Enquiries: To Borough Librarian

Scope: L.A.S.E.R. subject specialization includes: Book rarities; Christian Church; the Church; Sabbath; Anglican churches; general social science; Church and state; contract and tort; accident law; libel; Church law; ballet; folk and classical dancing; history and criticism of Italian, Roumanian, Spanish and Portuguese literatures; biography related to any of the above

Stock: 700,000 books, pamphlets and reports; 392 current periodicals (total stock)
Member of CICRIS

LONDON

1323

LONDON BOROUGH OF BRENT LIBRARIES DEPARTMENT *Tel.:* 01-459 5242
Central Library
High Road
Willesden Green
London N.W.10

Enquiries: To Borough Librarian

Scope: L.A.S.E.R. subject specialization includes: Etiquette; gypsies; folk-lore; war customs; skin; diseases of skin; bacterial blood diseases; venereal diseases; parasitic diseases

Stock: 603,000 books and pamphlets; 390 current periodicals, of which 150 are concerned, wholly or in part, with medicine, the social sciences and the humanities
Member of CICRIS

LONDON	LONDON BOROUGH OF CAMDEN	*Tel.*: 01-586 0061
	HAMPSTEAD CENTRAL LIBRARY	
1324	Swiss Cottage	
	London N.W.3	

Enquiries: To Librarian

Scope: Local history of Hampstead and St Pancras areas
John Keats and his circle *housed at* Keats Memorial Library, Heath Branch Library, Keats Grove, London N.W.3.
Kate Greenaway. Eleanor Farjeon. Philosophy and psychology

Stock: Local history: 5,000 books; 5,000 pamphlets and illustrations; 10 current periodicals; Keats: 5,000 books; 1,000 pamphlets; 5 current periodicals; Greenaway: 40 books; 90 original drawings; 1,000 proofs; Farjeon: 117 books

Publications: Guide to Keats House and Museum. 6th edition 1966; 2nd imp. with minor corrections 1968
Sound Verdict: An index to Audio Articles and Equipment Reviews ... 1969 (annually)

See also no. 1325

LONDON	LONDON BOROUGH OF CAMDEN	*Tel.*: 01-405 2705
	HOLBORN CENTRAL LIBRARY	
1325	32/38 Theobalds Road	
	London W.C.1	

Enquiries: To Librarian

Scope: Local history of Holborn area

Stock: 650 books; 1,000 pamphlets; 4,000 illustrations; 5,660 volumes of archive material; 6 current periodicals

See also no. 1324

LONDON	LONDON BOROUGH OF EALING	*Tel.*: 01-567 3456
	Central Library	*Telex:* 262289
1326	Walpole Park	
	London W.5	

Enquiries: To Librarian

Scope: Social sciences and humanities in general; limited coverage on medicine
L.A.S.E.R. subject specialization: Texts: American and English essays, oratory and satire, humour and miscellany and related biography (some of this material is at branch libraries). German, French, Italian and Spanish languages, and minor derivations, and related biography (all this material is at a branch library). Scotland, and related biography.
Special collections: G. D. H. Cole; Austin Dobson; Librarianship and allied subjects (2,000 items not normally available on loan); London Natural History Society's Library (not normally available on loan); Selborne Society's Library (not normally available on loan); Peal Collection on natural history (1,500 items).
Special interests: A collection of state papers and related material is being established. It contains a selection from British National Archives, Historical Manuscripts Commission and British Parliamentary Papers (Irish Universities Press). There is a complete collection of the List and Index Society.

Stock: 79,000 books; 4,500 pamphlets; 334 current periodicals

See also no. 1327 and 2137

LONDON	LONDON BOROUGH OF EALING	*Tel.:* 01-992 3295
	ACTON DISTRICT LIBRARY	*Telex:* 24363
1327	High Street	
	London W.3	

Enquiries: To Librarian

Scope: General coverage of medicine, social sciences and humanities

Stock: 28,007 books; 2,800 gramophone records

Publications: H. G. Wells 1866–1946: a centenary booklist. J. W. Thirsk, *compiler*. 1966
Thomas Hardy 1840–1928: a list of books by and about Thomas Hardy available at Ealing Public Libraries. J. W. Thirsk, *compiler*. 1968

See also no. 1326 and 2137

LONDON	LONDON BOROUGH OF GREENWICH	*Tel.:* 01-858 6656
	Greenwich Library	
1328	Woolwich Road	
	London S.E.10	

Enquiries: To Librarian

Scope: Metropolitan special collection: Recreation, including history: indoor and outdoor games and sports; dancing; mountaineering and camping; automobile sports; rowing, yachting and motor-boating; equestrian sports; fishing, hunting and shooting, but excluding radio, television, cinema, theatre and ballet

Secondary: The Kent collection at the Local History Centre, Woodlands, Mycenae Road, London S.E.3 is mainly of an historical, topographical and archaeological character.

Stock: 7,000 books and pamphlets; 15 current periodicals; official year books of most sports associations, for reference use only at Greenwich Library. Older material in the Metropolitan Special Collection is housed at the Plumstead Library, Plumstead High Street, London S.E.18. Current material is housed at all branches. All location records of specific items held at Greenwich Library

LONDON	LONDON BOROUGH OF HACKNEY	*Tel.:* 01-985 8262
	Central Library	
1329	Mare Street	
	Hackney	
	London E.8	

Enquiries: To Librarian

Scope: Special collections include: History and geography of Africa at the Stoke Newington District Library, Stoke Newington Church Street, London N.16; history and geography of the Americas and Polar Regions, and automobile engineering at Homerton Branch Library, Brooksby's Walk, London E.9; and furniture at the Shoreditch District Library, Pitfield Street, London N.1

Stock: 676,661 books; 372 current periodicals

LONDON	LONDON BOROUGH OF HAMMERSMITH	*Tel.:* 01-748 6032
	PUBLIC LIBRARIES	
1330	Central Library	
	Shepherds Bush Road	
	Hammersmith	
	London W.6	

Enquiries: To Librarian

Scope: Special Collections: Natural theology; Christianity; sociology; statistics and politics; law and civil administration; literature in Hungarian, Russian and Serbian languages

Stock: 50,000 books; 140 current periodicals

LONDON

1331

LONDON BOROUGH OF HARINGEY LIBRARIES, MUSEUM & ARTS DEPARTMENT
Central Offices
Bruce Castle
Lordship Lane
Tottenham
London N.17

Tel.: 01-808 8772
Telex: 263257

Enquiries: To Director

Scope: L.A.S.E.R. subject specialization includes: Geography; journalism; comparative religion

Stock: 497,248 books; 382 current periodicals (total stock)

Museum of Postal History and Local History and archives

LONDON

1332

LONDON BOROUGH OF ISLINGTON LIBRARIES
Central Library
68 Holloway Road
London N.7

Tel.: 01-607 4038
Telex: 263674

Enquiries: To Librarian

Scope: The Central Library has a special collection devoted to Walter Richard Sickert, R.A. (1860–1942)
The Finsbury Library, St John Street, London E.C.1 has a special collection devoted to the Sadler's Wells Theatre
The Central Reference Library has a collection of works on the social sciences and the humanities, with representation in London topography, bibliographies and encyclopaedias on the humanities and social sciences

Stock: 507,662 books; 447 current periodicals (total stock at 31 March 1969)

Publications: Walter Richard Sickert, 1860–1942: a handbook to the Drawings, Paintings, Etchings, Engravings and other material in the possession of Islington Public Libraries. 1964

LONDON

1333

LONDON BOROUGH OF LAMBETH
Tate Central Library
Brixton Oval
London S.W.2

Tel.: 01-274 7451
Telex: 25821

Enquiries: To Borough Librarian

Scope: Extensive general stock in social sciences and humanities but only basic books on medicine. *Special collections* on Bacon–Shakespeare controversy, William Blake and Alexandre Dumas. All government publications taken since 1950. L.A.S.E.R. subject specialization: Polish literature; fiction and play sets of authors KEM-L (housed at North Lambeth Library, 114 Lower Marsh, London S.E.1)

Stock: 825,000 books; pamphlets; 550 current periodicals

Publications: Short Guide to the Surrey Collection. M. Y. Williams. 1965

The Surrey Collection of archives of Lambeth and the old County of Surrey is based at the Minet Library, Knatchbull Road, London S.E.5 and is an official repository in the care of a qualified archivist

LONDON	LONDON BOROUGH OF LEWISHAM LIBRARY SERVICE	*Tel.:* 01-690 1247
1334	Lewisham Library Lewisham High Street London S.E.13	*Telex:* 25830

Enquiries: To Borough Librarian

Scope: General reference and information service in the arts, humanities and social sciences, concentrating on aids to the study of literature, history, religion and philosophy. Comprehensive set of Government publications in subject fields

Stock: Books: 14,000 in Reference Library; 30,000 in Bookstore (London Special Collection); 2,000 in Teachers' Library.
Pamphlets: 6,500 in Reference Library; 650 in Teachers' Library; 225 (general), 28 (education) current periodicals

Publications: Education Library Catalogue. 1967
Lists of local schools and churches
Subject bibliographies produced on request

Library Service Bookstore, 305/315 Hither Green Lane, London S.E.13 (*Tel.:* 01-698 5286) contains the London Special Collection: Bible, theology, British geography and history
Downham Library, Moorside Road, Downham, Kent (*Tel.* 01-698 1475): Teachers' Library —Works on education for working teachers, students of education, university entrants; Careers Library—Information on careers for school leavers and graduates

LONDON	LONDON BOROUGH OF LEWISHAM LIBRARY SERVICE	*Tel.:* 01-690 4311
1335	MEDICAL AND PATIENTS' LIBRARIES LEWISHAM HOSPITAL GROUP Lewisham Hospital High Street London S.E.13	

The Medical Library is part of the integrated Medical and Patients' Library and provides a reference, loan and information service to the medical, nursing and ancillary staff of the Hospital Group, and to the general practitioners and health and welfare staff in the Borough

Enquiries: To Librarian

Scope: General medicine; hospital administration

Stock: 500 books; 700 reports; 1,800 bound volumes of periodicals; 80 current periodicals (covering pathology, surgery, obstetrics and gynaecology, general medicine, paediatrics, hospital administration, general practice)

Publications: Bulletin (listing contents of current medical journals as received, for current awareness)

LONDON	LONDON BOROUGH OF MERTON PUBLIC LIBRARIES	*Tel.:* 01-542 6211
1336	Administrative Offices Merton Cottage Church Path London S.W.19	

Enquiries: To Librarian

Scope: For all subjects noted below, inter-library loans are handled at the Administrative Offices, but bookstocks are held, and reference enquiries dealt with, at the libraries named.
Mitcham Library, London Road, Mitcham, Surrey (*Tel.:* 01-648 4070 and 6516)—Cricket

(1,000 books and 4 current periodicals); L.A.S.E.R. subject specialization: World history (800 books and 5 current periodicals)

Morden Library, Morden Road, London S.W.19 (*Tel.*: 01-542 2842 and 1701)—L.A.S.E.R. subject specialization: English language (500 books and 10 current periodicals); Nelson (50 books); William Morris (30 books and 2 current periodicals)

Wimbledon Library, Wimbledon Hill Road, London S.W.19 (*Tel.*: 01-946 7979 and 7432)—L.A.S.E.R. subject specialization: Ear, nose and throat medicine (200 books and 2 current periodicals); nursing (600 books and 8 current periodicals); tennis (300 books and 2 current periodicals)

Stock: 420,000 books and pamphlets; 700 current periodicals (total stock)

LONDON
1337

LONDON BOROUGH OF NEWHAM PUBLIC LIBRARIES
Stratford Reference Library
Water Lane
London E.15

Tel.: 01-534 4545 ext. 334

Enquiries: To Librarian

Scope: L.A.S.E.R. subject specialization: Therapeutics and pharmacology (excluding anaesthetics and physical medicine); allergies and diseases due to physical and climatic conditions; tumours and cancer. Prehistoric archaeology and anthropology
Local collections on East Ham and West Ham, Essex and London, and a special collection on historic commercial vehicles
Standing subscription to Parliamentary papers, Statutory Instruments
All England Law Reports, 1958 to date
Times Index 1790 to date
Annual Register 1758 to date
Notes and Queries 1849 to date
The Times 1900–1926 (on microfilm, progressing at five-year intervals)

Stock: Subject specialization, 3,000 books; Local collections, 5,500 books and 3,200 pamphlets; 650 current periodicals

LONDON
1338

LONDON BOROUGH OF SOUTHWARK
Dulwich District Library
Lordship Lane
London S.E.22

Tel.: 01-693 5171

Enquiries: To Librarian

Scope: Latin literature; bibliography (including librarianship); Greek literature; ancient history and antiquities of ancient countries; Dante
Secondary: Journalism; Norwegian literature; Finnish literature

Stock: 12,000 books and pamphlets; 55 current periodicals (mostly on bibliography and librarianship)

The special collections are housed at Newington District Library, Walworth Road, London S.E.17 with the exception of bibliography, librarianship and journalism which are housed at Bermondsey District Library, Spa Road, London S.E.16

LONDON
1339

LONDON BOROUGH OF TOWER HAMLETS LIBRARIES DEPARTMENT
Central Library
Bancroft Road
London E.1

Tel.: 01-980 4366

Enquiries: To Librarian

LONDON, LONDON BOROUGH OF TOWER HAMLETS LIBRARIES DEPARTMENT, *cont.*

Scope: *Local History Library:* relating to Tower Hamlets—books, pamphlets, documents, maps, photographs, illustrations, slides and Shipping Collection including the Bolt collection of shipping company house flags, photographs and illustrations of ships, mainly sail and early steam, primarily to the year 1912 (all at Central Library)
Art Library: painting, sculpture, drawing, graphic arts, including commercial and industrial art (at Whitechapel Area Library, 77 High Street, London E.1)
Music Library: (Cambridge Heath Road, London E.2) 4,000 volumes; foreign language records
General and American Literature: Inner London Special collection—7,000 volumes (at Central Library)
French, German and Portuguese Literature: Inner London Special collection—16,000 volumes (at Bethnal Green Area Library, Cambridge Heath Road, London E.2)
Hebrew: 1,000 volumes (at Whitechapel Area Library)
Yiddish: 1,800 volumes (at Whitechapel Area Library)
Judaica Collection: all aspects of Jewish history, religion, social life and literature (at Whitechapel Area Library)
Play-Reading Sets: 150 sets (at Central Library)
Joint Fiction Reserve: Authors BEM-BOR, OP-PIC and SO-THI, 14,000 volumes (at Limehouse Area Library, 638, Commercial Road, London E.14)

Stock: 380,000 books; 1,000 pamphlets; 250 current periodicals
Gramophone Records held at Music Library, Central Library and Whitechapel, Limehouse and Poplar, Brunswick Road, London E.14, Area Libraries, total 13,000

LONDON

1340

LONDON BOROUGH OF WALTHAM FOREST PUBLIC LIBRARIES
Central Library
High Street
Walthamstow
London E.17

Tel.: 01-520 3031 and 4733

Enquiries: To Librarian

Scope: L.A.S.E.R. subject specialization includes: Town Planning; land, natural resources and land utilization; furniture and furnishings; tapestries; interior decoration; artistic furniture; William Morris Collection; Russian history and description; Arctic and Antarctica

Stock: 428,000 books and pamphlets; 415 current periodicals (total stock)

LONDON

1341

LONDON BOROUGH OF WANDSWORTH PUBLIC LIBRARIES
Administrative Offices
West Hill District Library
London S.W.18

Tel.: 01-874 1143
Telex: 25632

Enquiries: To Librarian

Scope: Subject specialization: European history, geography, travel and archaeology. General world history, geography, travel and archaeology. Architecture, building, town planning. Occult sciences. Metropolitan Joint Fiction Reserve A-BAI and TRE-WEB. Early children's books. Education

Stock: 817,478 books and pamphlets, including 2,194 early children's books; 560 current periodicals

Publications: Focus (monthly abstract of local government periodical literature)

LONDON	THE LONDON HOSPITAL MEDICAL COLLEGE	*Tel.*: 01-247 0644 ext. 17
1342	LIBRARY (University of London)	
	Turner Street	
	London E.1	

Enquiries: To Librarian

Scope: In addition to a wide range of books and journals concerned with the medical sciences and clinical medicine, surgery and dentistry, the basic biological and physical sciences are well represented and there is a comprehensive section on the history of medicine
A card index system includes the books and journals held in the main library and the eighteen departmental libraries of the Hospital and Medical College
Secondary: Portraits of past members of staff. Non-medical Reference Section

Stock: 18,000 books (including bound periodicals); various pamphlets; 300 current periodicals. Stock available on loan only to other medical and scientific institutions

Publications: The London Hospital Gazette (5 times each year) includes a clinical supplement

LONDON	THE LONDON LIBRARY	*Tel.*: 01-930 7705
1343	14 St James's Square	
	London S.W.1	
	Private subscription library	

Enquiries: To Librarian

Scope: Serious and scholarly works in all non-technical subjects particularly archaeology, arts, history, humanities, literature, politics, theology, in all European languages

Stock: 750,000 books; 4,000 volumes of pamphlets; 380 current periodicals. Enquiries accepted from and stock lent to members only

Publications: Author Catalogue, to 1950, in 5 volumes
Subject Index, to 1953, in 4 volumes

LONDON	LONDON SCHOOL OF ECONOMICS AND POLITICAL SCIENCE (UNIVERSITY OF LONDON)
	See **BRITISH LIBRARY OF POLITICAL AND ECONOMIC SCIENCE**, no. 994

LONDON	LONDON SCHOOL OF HYGIENE AND	*Tel.*: 01-636 8636
1344	TROPICAL MEDICINE	
	Keppel Street	
	Gower Street	
	London W.C.1	

Postgraduate teaching and research in all fields of environmental and community health. Constituent school of the University of London

Enquiries: To Librarian, by letter only

Scope: Public health, including social medicine and occupational health. Tropical medicine and hygiene. Parasitology; vital statistics; bacteriology; nutrition
Secondary: Reece collection on vaccination against smallpox
Brownlee collection on epidemiology

Stock: 20,000 books; 27,000 pamphlets; 970 current series of reports; 956 current periodicals

Publications: Memoir series
Journal of Helminthology
Ross Institute Industrial Advisory Committee Bulletins

LONDON, LONDON SCHOOL OF HYGIENE AND TROPICAL MEDICINE, *cont.*

T.U.C. Centenary Institute of Occupational Health offers advisory service to industry, trade unions and government. Ross Institute of Tropical Hygiene offers advisory service to industry, government and individuals in the tropics

LONDON

1345

LONDON TOPOGRAPHICAL SOCIETY *Tel.:* 01-703 2719
50 Grove Lane
London S.E.5

Publication of facsimiles of old maps, plans and views of London and of research on London topography

Enquiries: To Hon. Secretary

Scope: Simple enquiries answered, others referred to specialists or institutions
No library

Publications: Facsimiles of old maps and views of London
Research on London topography contained in occasional journal and in monographs
Printed list of publications

LONDON

1346

LONDON TOURIST BOARD *Tel.:* 01-629 8964
170 Piccadilly
London W1V 9DD

Enquiries: To Information and Accommodation Service

Scope: Information on all aspects of London which tourists may require, including hotel accommodation. Brochures and booklets available on request
No library

Publications: London, Capital for Conferences and Conventions

LONDON

1347

D. F. LONG & CO (TRANSLATIONS) LTD *Tel.:* 01-407 3385
68 Newington Causeway *Telex:* 262108
London S.E.1

Translators and language consultants (emphasis on engineering)

Enquiries: To Director

Stock: 2,000 special dictionaries and glossaries that may be consulted by *bona fide* enquirers

Publications: Newsletter
General booklet describing linguistic services

LONDON

1348

THE LORD'S DAY OBSERVANCE SOCIETY *Tel.:* 01-353 3157
INCORPORATED
55 Fleet Street
London E.C.4

Aims to preserve Sunday as the national day of rest and to promote its observance as the Lord's Day

Enquiries: To General Secretary

Scope: Books relating to the specific subject of Lord's Day Observance
Secondary: Some statistical information relating to general spiritual and moral conditions

Stock: 200 books; various pamphlets. Stock not available on loan

Publications: General publications on the subject for which the Society stands

LONDON	LUXEMBOURG EMBASSY	*Tel.:* 01-235 6961
1349	27 Wilton Crescent London S.W.1	

Enquiries: To Information Officer

Scope: Information about the Grand Duchy of Luxembourg, general, political, commercial, financial and economic

LONDON	LUXEMBOURG NATIONAL TOURIST OFFICE	*Tel.:* 01-930 8906
1350	66 Haymarket London S.W.1	

Enquiries: To Director, by letter only

Scope: Tourist and trade literature
Film library
Photographic library

LONDON	THE MAGISTRATES' ASSOCIATION	*Tel.:* 01-387 2302
1351	28 Fitzroy Square London W1P 6DD	

Enquiries: To Librarian

Scope: Reference library for Members of the Association (but available for reference purposes to others concerned in the administration of justice). Subjects covered by the stock include law, administration of justice, treatment of offenders and best methods of preventing crime

Stock: 250 books; 150 pamphlets; 170 reports; 20 current periodicals. Stock not available on loan

Publications: The Magistrate (monthly journal)   Questions and Answers for Justices
Notes for New Magistrates   The Work of the Juvenile Courts
Six Lectures for Justices

LONDON	MARIA ASSUMPTA COLLEGE OF EDUCATION	*Tel.:* 01-937 6434
1352	23 Kensington Square London W.8	

Enquiries: To Librarian

Scope: Roman Catholic and educational
Secondary: Ronald Knox collection, mainly first editions (220 items)
Early children's books, school books and educational works (280 items)

Stock: 2,000 educational, 2,000 Roman Catholic books; 1,400 pamphlets (of which 1,000 specifically of Roman Catholic interest); 104 current periodicals. Stock only exceptionally available on loan

LONDON	MARIE STOPES MEMORIAL CENTRE	*Tel.:* 01-387 4628
1353	106/108 Whitfield Street London W.1	

The Centre is open every day to give advice on birth control, marriage problems, pregnancy tests, help with the problem of unwanted pregnancies and training courses

Enquiries: To Secretary

Scope: Birth control. Population matters

Stock: 700 books

| LONDON | MARLOWE SOCIETY | *Tel.*: 01-653 2275 |

1354

45 Waldegrave Road
London S.E.19

Organization at popular level which aims to extend appreciation of Christopher Marlowe, both as a poet and a dramatist, by the production of his plays and those of his contemporaries and near contemporaries

Enquiries: To Secretary, by letter only

Scope: Literature on life and works of Marlowe. Elizabethan history, literature and criticism.

Stock: 200 books. Applications to borrow to 193 White Horse Hill, Chislehurst, Kent

| LONDON | MARX MEMORIAL LIBRARY | *Tel.*: 01-253 1485 |

1355

37A Clerkenwell Green
London E.C.1

Enquiries: To Librarian, by letter only

Scope: Social sciences; Marxist theory; political economy; labour history

Stock: 15,000 books; 18,000 pamphlets

Publications: Quarterly Bulletin

| LONDON | MARYLEBONE CRICKET CLUB | *Tel.*: 01-289 1611 |

1356

Lord's Cricket Ground
London N.W.8

Enquiries: To Curator, preferably by letter

Scope: The M.C.C. Library and the adjacent Imperial Cricket Memorial Gallery possess the largest collection of books, pictures and objets d'art connected with cricket in existence
Secondary: Small collection of books relating to other sports

Stock: 10,000 books and pamphlets; many reports; almost all cricket periodicals, including some in foreign languages. Thousands of prints, films, photographs and documents

Publications: M.C.C. Guide to Better Cricket   Postcards
Know the Game—Cricket   Photographs
Cricket—How to Play   Prints
Coaching Charts
The M.C.C. Coaching Book
The Laws of Cricket—Official 1947 Code. 4th edition 1968
Cricket Umpiring & Scoring. R. S. Rait Kerr
The Pitkin Illustrated History of Lord's & M.C.C.
The Heart of Cricket
Lord's Pamphlets—(A) The Story of the Ashes (B) History of Lord's & M.C.C.

| LONDON | MASTER PHOTOGRAPHERS ASSOCIATION OF GREAT BRITAIN | *Tel.*: 01-828 9174 |

1357

80 Rochester Row
London S.W.1

Enquiries: To Secretary, by letter only

Scope: Professional photography in all its aspects

Stock: 50 books; 2 current periodicals

Publications: The Master Photographer (quarterly journal)

LONDON	THE MEDICAL ACUPUNCTURE SOCIETY	*Tel.:* 01-935 7575
1358	15 Devonshire Place London W1N 1PB	

Aims to advance the teaching and exchange of information on acupuncture amongst doctors

Enquiries: To Secretary

Scope: Nearly anything concerning acupuncture

LONDON	MEDICAL COUNCIL ON ALCOHOLISM	*Tel.:* 01-636 5669
1359	74 New Oxford Street London W.C.1	

Acquires and disseminates information on alcoholism and promotes research

Enquiries: To Secretary, by letter only

Scope: Library not yet organized but suitable literature recommended

Publications: Journal on Alcoholism (quarterly)
Film strip with commentary available on loan

LONDON	THE MEDICAL OFFICERS OF SCHOOLS ASSOCIATION	*Tel.:* 01-526 1043
1360	11 Chandos Street Cavendish Square London W.1	

Enquiries: To Hon. Secretary, by letter only

Scope: The Association is willing to answer questions relating to the whole field of the health of the school child in the widest possible context. Results of surveys of morbidity are available for study

Secondary: Conditions of service and salary scales of the School Medical Officer in the Independent School

No Library

Publications: Handbook of guidance for School Medical Officers
Proceedings and Report (about every three years)

LONDON	MEDICAL RESEARCH COUNCIL AIR POLLUTION RESEARCH UNIT	*Tel.:* 01-253 1537
1361	St Bartholomew's Hospital Medical College Charterhouse Square London E.C.1	

Research into the effects of air pollution on human health

Enquiries: To Director, by letter only

Scope: The nature, chemical and physical, of air pollution from domestic sources and industries and from smoking, and its effect on human health, with particular reference to chronic bronchitis and lung cancer

Secondary: Other problems in environmental medicine, and techniques (for example, epidemiological, physiological and microscopical methods)

Stock: 250 books; 550 pamphlets; 36 current periodicals. Stock not available on loan, but available for personal reference

LONDON	MEDICAL RESEARCH COUNCIL	*Tel.:* 01-242 9789
	CLINICAL GENETICS UNIT	
1362	Institute of Child Health	
	30 Guilford Street	
	London W.C.1	

Enquiries: To Director

Scope: Genetic and other factors in the causation of developmental abnormalities in man; and the role of inheritance in the causation of common diseases

LONDON	MEDICAL RESEARCH COUNCIL	*Tel.:* 01-837 7842
	COMPUTER UNIT (LONDON)	
1363	242 Pentonville Road	
	London N.1	

Enquiries: To Director

Scope: Small library of books and journals relating to computers and computing in medicine

Stock: 135 books; 23 current periodicals

LONDON	MEDICAL RESEARCH COUNCIL	*Tel.:* 01-387 4692
	DEVELOPMENTAL PSYCHOLOGY UNIT	
1364	Drayton House	
	Gordon Street	
	London W.C.1	

Study of abnormalities of cognitive development in children

Enquiries: To Director, by letter only

Scope: Developmental psychology

No Library

LONDON	MEDICAL RESEARCH COUNCIL	*Tel.:* 01-743 4594
	EXPERIMENTAL RADIOPATHOLOGY UNIT	
1365	Hammersmith Hospital	
	Ducane Road	
	London W.12	

Investigations on the effects of radiation on living organisms aimed at elucidating basic mechanisms of action of ionizing radiation, particularly with reference to the bearing of such studies on radiotherapy

Enquiries: To Librarian

Scope: The library is a small and specialized one, used by two Medical Research Council units, and managed by a part-time librarian. Information other than bibliographical would have to be provided by members of the scientific staffs and would concern two main topics: Effects of ionizing and ultraviolet radiation on biological systems; and design and construction of specialized equipment for producing high-energy radiation. The scientific basis of clinical radiotherapy is a main interest

Stock: 2,000 books including bound volumes of journals; 25 reports; 34 current periodicals

LONDON	MEDICAL RESEARCH COUNCIL	*Tel.:* 01-589 5111 ext. 1108
	METABOLIC REACTIONS RESEARCH UNIT	*Telex:* 261503
1366	Department of Biochemistry	
	Imperial College	
	Imperial Institute Road	
	London S.W.7	

Studies on brain biochemistry (neurochemistry), diabetes, action of insulin and glucagon cardiac metabolism, intestinal biochemistry and physiology, instrumentation to automate and speed the acquisition of results in the above fields

Enquiries: To Librarian

Scope: The library is the library of the Biochemistry Department of Imperial College, London S.W.7, and is definitely biochemistry, and not medically biased

Stock: 1,000 books; 170 current periodicals

LONDON

1367

MEDICAL RESEARCH COUNCIL LIBRARY   *Tel.:* 01-959 3666
NATIONAL INSTITUTE FOR MEDICAL RESEARCH
The Ridgeway
Mill Hill
London N.W.7

Enquiries: To Librarian

Scope: Biochemistry, biology, biophysics, chemistry, endocrinology, genetics, immunology, microbiology, parasitology, pharmacology, physiology, protozoology, and veterinary science

Stock: 5,500 books; 35,000 pamphlets; 650 current periodicals

See also entries for separate units of the Medical Research Council (nos. 146–147, 237, 289, 323, 336, 361, 455, 523–524, 681, 806–807, 829, 1361–1366, 1368–1373, 1929–1931, 1980 and 2109)

LONDON

1368

MEDICAL RESEARCH COUNCIL   *Tel.:* 01-435 2232
PROJECT FAIR, DIVISION OF BIOMEDICAL
    ENGINEERING
National Institute for Medical Research (Hampstead Laboratories)
Holly Hill
London N.W.3

Collection, organization, storage and dissemination of biomedical engineering information

Enquiries: To the Project

Scope: The application of engineering, particularly electronic, electrical and mechanical engineering, to problems in biology and medicine

Stock: 20 books; 50 pamphlets; 100 reports; 120 current periodicals; 4,000 Xerox copies of journal articles, 4,000 microfiche copies of journal articles (both increasing at 1,500 each year)

Publications: Indexed References to Biomedical Engineering Literature (with conventional author, and feature card subject index)
FAIR Newsletter (quarterly)

'Who is doing what, where?' type files to enable interested parties to be put in touch with others with similar biomedical engineering specialities

LONDON

1369

MEDICAL RESEARCH COUNCIL   *Tel.:* 01-636 8636
SOCIAL MEDICINE UNIT
London School of Hygiene and Tropical Medicine
Keppel Street
Gower Street
London W.C.1

Enquiries: To Assistant Director

Scope: Social medicine research. Books and periodicals on social medicine and public health
Secondary: Books and periodicals on statistics, nutrition and juvenile delinquency

Stock: 250 books; 39 current periodicals

LONDON	MEDICAL RESEARCH COUNCIL	*Tel.:* 01-703 5411
	SOCIAL PSYCHIATRY RESEARCH UNIT	
1370	Institute of Psychiatry	
	De Crespigny Park	
	London S.E.5	

Enquiries: To Director, by letter only

Scope: The influence of social factors on the course of chronic psychiatric illness

No library

Publications: Scientific papers concerned with the work of the Unit

LONDON	MEDICAL RESEARCH COUNCIL	*Tel.:* 01-730 2181
	TRACHOMA UNIT	
1371	The Lister Institute of Preventive Medicine	
	Chelsea Bridge Road	
	London S.W.1	

Enquiries: To Director

Scope: Research on trachoma and allied diseases with special reference to diagnosis, pathogenesis and immunology

LONDON	MEDICAL RESEARCH COUNCIL	*Tel.:* 01-405 7686 ext. 683
	UNIT FOR THE STUDY OF	
1372	ENVIRONMENTAL FACTORS IN	
	MENTAL AND PHYSICAL ILLNESS	
	London School of Economics	
	Houghton Street	
	London W.C.2	

Enquiries: To Director

Scope: Cohort Studies
The factors connected with educational success or failure
Methods of assessing maternal care
Early social and intellectual development of children

LONDON	MEDICAL RESEARCH COUNCIL	*Tel.:* 01-743 2030 ext. 428
	UNIT ON DRUG SENSITIVITY IN	
1373	TUBERCULOSIS	
	Department of Bacteriology	
	Royal Postgraduate Medical School	
	Ducane Road	
	London W.12	

Enquiries: To Director

Scope: Bacteriology and chemotherapy of tuberculosis

No library

Publications: Research papers

LONDON	METHODIST CHURCH ARCHIVES CENTRE
	23/35 City Road
1374	London E.C.1
	See no. 1375

LONDON   METHODIST CHURCH (CONFERENCE OFFICE)   *Tel.:* 01-930 7608
                 1 Central Buildings
1375   Westminster
                 London S.W.1
        Enquiries: To Secretary of the Conference
           Scope: All matters relating to the work of the Methodist Church in Great Britain, including records
                 from the beginning of Methodism in the eighteenth century
     Publications: Minutes (and associated documents) of the Methodist Conference
                 Records are available for consultation in the Archives Centre, 23/35 City Road, London E.C.1

LONDON   METHODIST MISSIONARY SOCIETY   *Tel.:* 01-935 2541
                 25 Marylebone Road
1376   London N.W.1
        Enquiries: To Archivist and Librarian
           Scope: The history of Methodist churches and missions in Ceylon, India, Burma, China, Hong
                 Kong, The Gambia, Ghana, Ivory Coast, Dahomey, Togo, Nigeria, Rhodesia, Kenya,
                 Zambia, South Africa and the Caribbean (including Bahamas, Panama, Honduras and
                 Guyana)
                 Secondary: The history of Methodist churches and missions in Europe, South East Asia,
                 United States of America and Canada
                 General missionary literature
           Stock: 5,000 books; 1,000 pamphlets; 400 reports; 50 current periodicals. Stock not available on loan

LONDON   THE METROPOLITAN POLICE OFFICE   *Tel.:* 01-230 1212
                 10 Broadway
1377   London S.W.1
                 A reference library mainly for the department's architects, surveyors and engineers
        Enquiries: To Librarian
           Scope: Architecture; building; surveying; engineering; and public health
                 Secondary: Police history
           Stock: 2,500 books; 1,000 pamphlets; 100 reports; 100 current periodicals. Stock not normally
                 available on loan

LONDON   MEXICAN EMBASSY   *Tel.:* 01-235 6393
                 8 Halkin Street
1378   London S.W.1
        Enquiries: To Mexican Embassy
           Scope: Basic information on all aspects of Mexico, and help in suggesting alternative sources
                 No library

LONDON   MIDDLE TEMPLE LIBRARY   *Tel.:* 01-353 4303
                 Middle Temple Lane
1379   London E.C.4
        Enquiries: To The Librarian and Keeper of the Records
           Scope: Mainly legal material covering all parts of the world but with particular emphasis on the law
                 of Great Britain, the Commonwealth and U.S.A. Smaller collections on history, genealogy,
                 heraldry, medicine and literature

LONDON, MIDDLE TEMPLE LIBRARY, *cont.*
Special Collections: Books belonging to John Donne, poet and Dean of St Paul's, and to Robert Ashley, Founder of the Library
Stock: 93,100 items
Publications: Middle Temple Library Catalogue 1914–25. 4 volumes
List of all other publications available on request

LONDON

1380

MIDDLESEX HOSPITAL MEDICAL SCHOOL *Tel.:* 01-636 8333
London W1P 7PN
Medical education and research
Enquiries: To Librarian
Scope: Medical sciences
Secondary: Biological sciences, chemistry, physics. Nuffield Collection (psychiatry)
Local collection: books by Middlesex Hospital and Medical School authors
Stock: 4,000 books; 3,000 pamphlets; 230 current periodicals

LONDON

1381

MINISTRY OF HOUSING AND LOCAL *Tel.:* 01-930 4300
  GOVERNMENT *Telex:* 22801
Whitehall
London S.W.1

Government department dealing with housing, local government, regional planning, town and country planning, land use and natural resources, water supply, sewage disposal, countryside, clean air and other aspects of environmental health
Enquiries: To Librarian
Scope: Housing, in all its aspects, including design, economics and industrialized building. Local government, including finance. Town and country planning. New towns. Environmental health, including water supply, sewage disposal, clean air, river pollution, refuse disposal and alkali works. Urban development. Countryside. Land use. Natural resources, including mineral workings such as sand and gravel. Scientific and technical staff employed on all these subjects in the Ministry and its agencies are served by the library and the contents of the library and its services reflect their needs and interests
Stock: 120,000 books and pamphlets; 800 current periodicals
Publications: Index to Periodical Articles (monthly abstracts)
Classified Accessions List
Subject Bibliographies:

No. 65—New Towns	No. 107—Derelict Land
No. 70—Town and Country Planning	No. 148—Environmental Pollution

Her Majesty's Stationery Office Sectional List no. 5
3 sub-libraries
6 Regional office libraries
4 Information rooms
Separate map library and aerial photographs library as part of the Ministry's Map Office

LONDON

1382

MINISTRY OF OVERSEAS DEVELOPMENT *Tel.:* 01-834 2377 ext. 507
Eland House
Stag Place
London S.W.1

See no. 1159

LONDON **1383**	MOCATTA LIBRARY AND MUSEUM University College Gower Street London W.C.1	*Tel.:* 01-387 7050

Official library of the Jewish Historical Society of England (no. 1291), incorporated with the library of University College London

Enquiries: To Assistant Librarian in charge of the Mocatta Library, preferably by letter

Scope: Anglo-Jewish history. Collections include the Anglo-Jewish Archives (*see* no. 897) and the Gaster Archives (papers of Moses Gaster, on deposit). Some illustrative material of interest (portraits, cartoons)
Secondary: The whole range of Jewish history, including Palestiniana; Hebrew literature and Rabbinica. Since in these fields the library is dependent mainly on bequests, gifts and deposits, the coverage is very uneven

Stock: 9,000 books; 11,000 pamphlets. The main periodicals in the field of Jewish history, sociology and learning, in English, French, German and Hebrew. Official reports of Anglo-Jewish institutes and religious and social bodies. Bound series of the Jewish Chronicle

Publications: Magna bibliotheca Anglo-Judaica. C. Roth. 1937
Nova bibliotheca Anglo-Judaica. R. P. Lehmann. 1961

The Mocatta Museum consists of objects of Anglo-Jewish interest, mainly of synagogue ritual-ware. At present this is not on exhibition and is not available to the public

LONDON **1384**	THE MONTESSORI SOCIETY IN ENGLAND BCM/Montessori London W.C.1	*Tel.:* 01-242 2320

Enquiries: To Secretary, by letter only

Scope: All Montessori reference books and publications are available. Enquiries on Montessori ideas or courses dealt with. Films and recordings available for hire

Publications: The Montessori Journal (3 issues each year)

LONDON **1385**	MORLEY COLLEGE 61 Westminster Bridge Road London S.E.1	*Tel.:* 01-928 6863

Literary Institute providing non-vocational adult education in liberal studies, including music, art and languages

Enquiries: To Librarian

Scope: Book-stock covers the subjects in the syllabus and is particularly strong in music, art and languages
Secondary: Recorded music library

Stock: 18,000 books; 40 current periodicals

LONDON **1386**	MORNING STAR 75 Farringdon Road London E.C.1	*Tel.:* 01-405 9242

Daily newspaper promoting communist and left views

Enquiries: To Librarian

Scope: Press cuttings of political, cultural and general interest. Marxist books
Stock not available on loan

LONDON	THE MOTHER'S UNION	*Tel.:* 01-222 5533
1387	The Mary Sumner House 24 Tufton Street London S.W.1	

The Society's aims are concerned with the permanence and stability of marriage, the welfare of the family, parental responsibility, and Christian education; its activities, religious, social and educational, are not confined to its own members

Enquiries: To Librarian

Scope: The Christian religion; marriage; the family. Material in the field of Christian spirituality, including some out-of-print books, Anglican, Roman Catholic and Orthodox
Secondary: Education, social sciences (with special reference to marriage and the family), history, geography, literature, fine arts, useful arts, fiction, children's books

Stock: 10,000 books; Church of England and ecumenical reports; reports concerned with *marriage*; 8 current periodicals

Publications: Books, booklets, pamphlets, leaflets, on the Christian religion, religious education in the home, the family and social problems, and other subjects of special interest to parents
Home and Family (quarterly)
Mothers' Union News (monthly)

LONDON	MUSCULAR DYSTROPHY GROUP OF GREAT BRITAIN	*Tel.:* 01-407 5116
1388	26 Borough High Street London S.E.1	

Raising funds for and supporting an international research programme into a cure and treatment for muscular dystrophy and allied muscular and neuromuscular diseases

Enquiries: To Information Officer

Scope: Information on all aspects of the disease and on the Group's work particularly on research progress and details of carrier detection tests and where these can be carried out
Secondary: The Group's Medical Social Worker will answer welfare enquiries, and offer advice on, for example, equipment

Stock: Proceedings of 1968, 1965 and 1963 Symposia. Various reprints from medical journals. 2 current periodicals

Publications: Muscular Dystrophy Journal (quarterly)

LONDON	MUSEUM OF ARTILLERY (THE ROTUNDA)	*Tel.:* 01-854 2424 ext. 385
1389	c/o R.A. Institution Woolwich London S.E.18	

Museum of artillery equipment (international)

Enquiries: To Historical Assistant Secretary, by letter only

Scope: Artillery equipment
Secondary: Ammunition; small arms

LONDON	MUSEUM OF BRITISH TRANSPORT	*Tel.:* 01-622 3241
1390	Triangle Place Clapham High Street London S.W.4	

Collection and display of railway and road relics connected with British Railways and London Transport

    Enquiries: To Curator
        Scope: The history and growth of railways in Great Britain and of public road transport in London from 1800 to the present day
        Stock: Postcards, booklets. Stock not available on loan
  Publications: London on Wheels   Transport Treasures
               Popular Carriage   Transport Preserved
               Steam Locomotive   Royal Journey

LONDON   THE MUSEUM OF LEATHERCRAFT
1391   9 St Thomas Street
    London S.E.1

    The collection, conservation and display to the public of objects relating to the history of leather use in all ages and from all parts of the world
    Enquiries: To Secretary, by letter only
        Scope: Books, pamphlets and manuscripts relating to the making and use of leather

LONDON   MUSEUMS ASSOCIATION   *Tel.:* 01-636 4600
1392   87 Charlotte Street
    London W1P 2BX
    Enquiries: To Secretary
        Scope: Very small library with stock consisting mainly of publications by or about museums and museum subjects, and what is becoming increasingly widely termed 'museology', including annual reports, exhibition catalogues, detailed catalogues of permanent collections and miscellaneous and occasional publications of many museums in the United Kingdom and overseas
  Publications: Museums Journal (quarterly)
               Bulletin (monthly)
               Museums Calendar (a directory, annually)
               Handbooks and information sheets on various subjects of museum interest
               Handbooks for Museum Curators:
                    Administration. D. A. Allan, D. E. Owen and F. S. Wallis. 1960
                    Archaeological Fieldwork. R. Rainbird Clarke. 1958
                    Ethnography. B. A. L. Cranstone. 1957
                    Folk Life Collection and Classification. J. W. Y. Higgs. 1963
                    Personalia. M. Holmes. 1957
                    Pictures. T. Cox. 1956
                    Costume. A. Buck. 1958
                    A Guide to Herbarium Practice. J. W. Franks. 1965
                    Applied Science and Technology before the Industrial Revolution. C. M. Mitchell. 1961
                    Circulating Exhibitions. H. Wakefield and G. White. 1959
                    Special Exhibitions. S. M. K. Henderson and H. Kapp. 1959
                    Lectures, Filmshows and Concerts. D. E. Owen. 1957
                    Museum School Services, compiled by The Group for Educational Services in Museums. 1967
                    The Conservation of Antiquities and Works of Art. H. J. Plenderleith. 1957 (through Oxford University Press)
               Local Museums: Notes on their Building and Conduct. H. A. Kennedy. 1938

LONDON **1393**	MUSIC USERS COUNCIL 7 Buckingham Gate London S.W.1	*Tel.:* 01-834 1645

Aims to look after the interests of all who use copyright music in public, for example in hotels, ballrooms, theatres, cinemas and holiday camps

Enquiries: To Secretary

Scope: Occasional summaries are published of the tariffs charged by the Performing Rights Society for the public use of copyright music in various places

LONDON **1394**	NATIONAL ANTIVIVISECTION SOCIETY LTD 51 Harley Street London W.1	*Tel.:* 01-580 4034

Aims for the total prohibition of all experiments on animals calculated to cause suffering or distress

Enquiries: To Secretary

Scope: Library consists of medical and scientific books and publications that contain information relating to the history of, or present prosecution of, the aims of the Society

Stock: 1,000 books; 15 current periodicals; daily newspapers

Publications: The Animals' Defender (bi-monthly journal)
Propaganda pamphlets (about 30)
Books (4 on sale)

LONDON **1395**	NATIONAL ASSOCIATION FOR THE CARE AND RESETTLEMENT OF OFFENDERS 125 Kennington Park Road London S.E.11	*Tel.:* 01-735 1151

Aims to stimulate and co-ordinate voluntary effort in the field of delinquency and after-care and to foster closer co-operation between the voluntary and statutory services

Enquiries: To Information Officer

Scope: All matters relating to crime prevention and the after-care of offenders whether they have been committed to an institution or not. Particularly concerned with the work of voluntary organizations in providing support and aid for offenders and their families

No library

Publications: Manual and Directory (giving detailed information about projects relating to crime prevention and after-care throughout the British Isles, and guidance on the procedures and regulations of relevant government departments and other bodies)
Papers and Reprints (series)
Information Bulletins (for members)

LONDON **1396**	NATIONAL ASSOCIATION OF BOYS' CLUBS 17 Bedford Square London W.C.1	*Tel.:* 01-636 5357

Responsible for development and co-ordination of Boys' Club work throughout the country

Enquiries: To General Secretary

Scope: Complete information about the work of Boys' Clubs throughout the country through liaison with Clubs and County Organizers

Stock: Very small reference library

Publications: Charles Russell Memorial Lectures
Basil Henriques Memorial Lectures

LONDON	NATIONAL ASSOCIATION OF LEAGUES OF HOSPITAL FRIENDS	*Tel.:* 01-799 6353
1397	Hope House 45 Great Peter Street London S.W.1	

Enquiries: To General Secretary

Scope: The National Association was formed to provide common user services to the (now) 767 local Leagues of Hospital Friends, which support hospitals throughout the country. These services include: Liaison with the Department of Health, the Charity Commissioners and similar bodies; Advice on legal, financial and similar problems; supply of publicity material
Secondary: Dealing with enquiries from individuals who wish to undertake voluntary work with local Leagues of Hospital Friends. Fund Raising and Publicity on behalf of the organization as a whole

Publications: Young Volunteers in Hospitals

LONDON	NATIONAL ASSOCIATION OF PARISH COUNCILS	*Tel.:* 01-636 4066
1398	99 Great Russell Street London W.C.1	

Protection, advice and encouragement for parish councils

Enquiries: To Secretary

Scope: Legal and technical material concerned with the administration and government of rural parishes in England and Wales, and of other small communities
Secondary: Other local government and central bodies which affect the above

No library

Publications: Handbooks on various aspects of parish administration
Parish Councils Review (quarterly)
Variety of leaflets on specialized matters

LONDON	NATIONAL ASSOCIATION OF PROBATION OFFICERS	*Tel.:* 01-387 3883
1399	6 Endsleigh Street, London W.C.1	

Enquiries: To Secretary, by letter only

Scope: The history and activities of the Association and the views of the Association on certain current issues

No library

Publications: Probation (journal, 3 issues each year)
Occasional Probation Papers

LONDON	THE NATIONAL ASSOCIATION OF STATE ENROLLED NURSES	*Tel.:* 01-629 0870
1400	1 Vere Street London W1M 9HQ	

Enquiries: To General Secretary

Scope: Training and employment of the State Enrolled Nurse

LONDON, THE NATIONAL ASSOCIATION OF STATE ENROLLED NURSES, *cont.*
No library
Publications: Courses for State Enrolled Nurses
The State Enrolled Nurse in Public Health Nursing Services (Report of a Survey)

LONDON

1401

NATIONAL ASSOCIATION OF TENANTS AND RESIDENTS
219 Blackfriars Road
London S.E.1

Tel.: 01-928 2884

Co-ordination and organization of tenants' and residents' associations. Improvement of housing conditions, resistance to rent increases

Enquiries: To General Secretary
Publications: People and Homes (twice each year)
Memoranda for deputations

LONDON

1402

NATIONAL AUDIO-VISUAL AIDS CENTRE
254/256 Belsize Road
London N.W.6

Tel.: 01-624 8812

See no. 1407

LONDON

1403

NATIONAL AUDIO-VISUAL AIDS LIBRARY
Paxton Place
Gipsy Road
London S.E.27

See no. 1407

LONDON

1404

THE NATIONAL BOOK LEAGUE
7 Albemarle Street
London W1X 4BB

Tel.: 01-493 9001

Encouragement of the wider and wiser use of books by means of information, exhibitions, research, and through various publications

Enquiries: To Book Information Bureau or Education Department as relevant
Scope: The Book Information Bureau accepts any questions about books from Members. The Education Department gives advice to educational institutions only on expenditure and selection processes
The Morrison Library has a comprehensive collection of books about books, including the *Winterbottom Production Library*, dealing with all aspects of book manufacture, and contains an extensive collection on the history and practice of publishing, bookselling and authorship, and the *May Lamberton Becker Library* dealing with reading habits
Stock: 8,000 books, pamphlets and reports; all literary, technical and general periodicals relating to books. Stock available on loan through N.C.L. only
Publications: Annotated Subject lists (60 each year)
Exhibition Catalogues (50 each year)

LONDON

1405

NATIONAL BUREAU FOR CO-OPERATION IN CHILD CARE
Adam House
1 Fitzroy Square
London W.1

Tel.: 01-387 4263

Enquiries: To Librarian

Scope: Psychology, sociology, education and other subjects in so far as they relate to children. The acquisitions are linked to the needs of current research projects. Thus the stock is comprehensive in the literature on handicapped children, children in care, adoption, fostercare and gifted children

Stock: 1,500 books; 1,300 pamphlets; 63 current periodicals; 79 newsletters

Publications: Quarterly List of Additions to the Library
First Four Years
Concern (newsletter)
Studies in Child Development (Longmans):
 Four Years On. S. Gooch and M. L. Kellmer Pringle. 1966
 11,000 Seven-Year-Olds. M. L. Kellmer Pringle, N. R. Butler and R. Davie. 1966
 Adoption—Facts and Fallacies. M. L. Kellmer Pringle. 1967
 Family Advice Services. A. Leissner. 1967
 Residential Child Care—Facts and Fallacies. R. Dinnage and M. L. Kellmer Pringle. 1967
 Foster Home Care—Facts and Fallacies. R. Dinnage and M. L. Kellmer Pringle. 1967
 The Community's Children. J. Parfit, ed. 1967
 Caring for Children. M. L. Kellmer Pringle, ed. 1968
 A Directory of National Voluntary Children's Organisations. M. L. Kellmer Pringle, R. Davie and L. E. Hancock, eds. 1969
 The Hostage Seekers. M. Humphrey. 1969
 Street Club Work in Tel Aviv and New York. A. Leissner. 1969
Other Books:
Investment in Children. M. L. Kellmer Pringle, ed. Longmans. 1965
The Emotional and Social Adjustment of Blind Children. M. L. Kellmer Pringle. National Foundation for Educational Research. 1965
The Emotional and Social Adjustment of Physically Handicapped Children. M. L. Kellmer Pringle. National Foundation for Educational Research. 1965

LONDON

1406

NATIONAL CITIZENS' ADVICE BUREAUX COUNCIL
26 Bedford Square
London W.C.1

Tel.: 01-636 4066

Scope: Makes available to the individual accurate information and skilled advice on many of the personal problems that arise in daily life; explains legislation; and helps the citizen to benefit from and to use the services provided for him by the State

Publications: Advising the Citizen
The Story of the Citizens' Advice Bureaux
Training in the Citizens' Advice Bureau Service

LONDON

1407

NATIONAL COMMITTEE FOR AUDIO-VISUAL AIDS IN EDUCATION
33 Queen Anne Street
London W1M 0AL

Tel.: 01-636 5742 and 5791

Responsible for determining audio-visual aids policy at a national level, promotion of the use of audio-visual methods and an information service on audio-visual matters

The Educational Foundation for Visual Aids has special responsibilities for the distribution, production and cataloguing of classroom films and filmstrips, the supply of equipment and the provision of technical advisory and maintenance services

The National Audio-visual Aids Library, Paxton Place, Gipsy Road, London S.E.27, is the national library of educational film material for England and Wales. It holds for distribution

LONDON, NATIONAL COMMITTEE FOR AUDIO-VISUAL AIDS IN EDUCATION, *cont.*

about 1,700 films (16 mm, 15,000 prints) and 4,000 filmstrips (30,000 copies). A supplementary section contains films of a more general or background nature. The eight parts of the E.F.V.A. National Catalogue give brief descriptions of all films and filmstrips held in the library

The National Audio-visual Aids Centre, 254–256 Belsize Road, London N.W.6 (*Tel.:* 01-624 8812), was established to provide educationalists with a centralized and authoritative source of information and advice on all practical problems associated with audio-visual methods in education. The Centre provides a wide range of equipment which may be examined and evaluated by appointment, including cine projectors, filmstrip projectors, episcopes, overhead projectors, micro-projectors, television receivers, radios, record players, tape recorders, language laboratories and teaching machines. There is also a reference library of books and journals covering all aspects of audio-visual aids, and catalogues of films, filmstrips, wallcharts and recordings. The Centre runs courses on the application of audio-visual techniques in education and training and houses an experimental development unit

The Visual Education National Information Service for Schools (VENISS) is operated jointly by the National Committee and the E.F.V.A. for the benefit of teachers and educationalists. It keeps its members up to date with all aspects of audio-visual equipment and education, and supplies them automatically with publications of the national organization for visual aids

Publications: National Catalogue of Films, Filmstrips, Slides and Overhead Projector Transparencies (in eight parts by subject)
Films and Filmstrips for use in Colleges and Institutes of Education
Catalogue of 8 mm cassette loop films
Catalogue of wallcharts
Supplementary catalogues and lists
Information leaflets
Visual Education (monthly)
Catalogue of Recorded Sound for Education
Visual Education Yearbook
The Audio-visual Approach to Modern Language Teaching (a symposium)
Classroom Display Material. A. Vincent
Film Projecting, without Tears or Technicalities. M. Simpson
The Overhead Projector in Education (a symposium)
Programmed Learning (a symposium)
The Tape Recorder in the Classroom. J. Weston
Television at the University of Leeds (a symposium)
Wall Sheets: their Design, Production and Use. H. Coppen

LONDON

1408

NATIONAL COUNCIL FOR EDUCATIONAL TECHNOLOGY
160 Great Portland Street
London W1N 5TB

Tel.: 01-580 7553

Encourages the development, application and evaluation of systems, techniques and aids to improve the processes of education and training

Enquiries: To Director

Scope: The Council does not provide a direct information service, but can often put enquirers in touch with specialist organizations and agencies able to handle particular problems in respect of such matters as audio-visual devices, methods and materials; educational processes and techniques; evaluation techniques; design and construction of learning resources and environments; organization and management. A detailed research study on the question of information in relation to educational technology has been initiated, which will help in dealing with enquiries

No library

Publications: Towards More Effective Learning
Learning and Teaching Tomorrow. E. W. H. Briault
Second Thoughts on Programmed Learning. G. O. M. Leith
Computers for Education (Report of Working Party)
Continuing Mathematics. A. G. Howson and M. R. Eraut
NCET and the Rights of Producers and Authors in New Media; and Rights in Recorded Material

LONDON

1409

NATIONAL COUNCIL OF SOCIAL SERVICE (INCORPORATED)
26 Bedford Square
London W.C.1

Tel.: 01-636 4066

The National Council of Social Service is the central agency for co-ordination of voluntary social welfare. It is a non-governmental body, representative of its 20 associated specialist groups and committees and many other voluntary agencies and public authorities throughout the country, and carries out research, initiates experiments and undertakes promotional work in the United Kingdom and abroad. It services its associated groups with up-to-date information and advice, seeks fullest co-operation with central and local government, and plays an active part in discussion and negotiation relating to legislation affecting the voluntary societies as a whole

Enquiries: To Information Officer

Scope: General information service on the voluntary and statutory social services, including synopses of relevant major government reports and committees of enquiry. General enquiries from the public and press on the social services and particularly the voluntary sector are answered

Small library for internal use only

Publications: NCSS Newsletter (6 times each year)
Community News (for community associations)
Matters Arising (for local Councils of Social Service)
The Village (for Rural Community Councils)
Citizens' Advice Notes
Very many books, pamphlets and reports

LONDON

1410

NATIONAL COUNCIL OF Y.M.C.A.s
112 Great Russell Street
London W.C.1

Tel.: 01-636 8954

The Young Men's Christian Association seeks to unite young men and boys in the service of Jesus Christ and in fellowship through activities designed to help them in the development and training of their powers of body, mind and spirit to enable them to take their share in the service of God and man

Enquiries: To Secretary

Scope: About the movement itself, and work with young people generally

Publications: Y.M.C.A. World (quarterly)

LONDON		NATIONAL COUNCIL ON ALCOHOLISM	*Tel.:* 01-222 9011
1411		Room 359 Church House Dean's Yard Westminster London S.W.1	

Enquiries: To Secretary

Scope: Alcoholism

Publications: About Alcoholism. W. H. Kenyon
About Your Drinking. L. Williams
Alcoholism Explained. L. Williams
Alcoholism Information Centres. G. Edwards
Alcoholism in Industry. L. Williams
Chart of Alcohol Addiction and Recovery. M. M. Glatt
Chronic Alcoholics. Steering Group on Alcoholism, Joseph Rowntree Social Service Trust
Drinking and Alcoholism. R. Kemp
Recurrent Driving 'Under the Influence'. M. M. Glatt
The Alcoholic in Employment. P. Perfect
The Alcoholism Complex (Synopsis of 'The Disease Concept of Alcoholism')
The Facts about Alcohol. D. S. Elliott
The Sober Truth. L. Williams
Treatment Aspects of Alcoholism. L. Williams
What YOU should know about ALCOHOLISM
Your Alcoholism Information Centre

LONDON		NATIONAL FARMERS' UNION	*Tel.:* 01-235 5077
1412		Agriculture House 25/31 Knightsbridge London S.W.1	

Trade Union

Enquiries: To Librarian

Scope: Agriculture and horticulture; their policies, politics, economics and marketing; their general and technical aspects; their history
Secondary collection: Land use; trade in agricultural products

Stock: 6,000 books; 6,000 pamphlets; 280 current periodicals

Publications: British Farmer
N.F.U. Information Service
N.F.U. Guide to Prices and Services

LONDON		NATIONAL FEDERATION OF CONSUMER GROUPS	*Tel.:* 01-930 0258
1413		Kipling House 43 Villiers Street London W.C.2	

Headquarters of about 75 local voluntary Groups which aim to improve, by constructive criticism, the standards of goods and services locally, and to educate the consumer

Enquiries: To Secretary

Scope: Reports and results of surveys carried out by member Consumer Groups into prices and services within their area, including prices of, for example, grocery, consumer durables, pharmaceuticals, and services, for example, health and welfare, facilities for elderly consumers, public and local authority services, and commercial services (hairdressers, builders, coal merchants)

Articles on consumer legislation and protection, wise buying, and all matters of interest to consumers

Stock: 500 Group magazines and booklets

Publications: Index of Group Reports (quarterly)

LONDON

1414

NATIONAL FROEBEL FOUNDATION *Tel.:* 01-935 4555
2 Manchester Square
London W1M 5RF

Enquiries: To Secretary

Scope: Education up to the age of twelve, and training of teachers
No library

Publications: Catalogue
Journal (termly)

LONDON

1415

THE NATIONAL GALLERY
Trafalgar Square
London W.C.2

Enquiries: To Director

Scope: Information on pictures in the Gallery
Secondary: Information concerning some other pictures not in the Gallery, but related to those that are

Stock: Library for use of the staff only

Publications: List available from National Gallery Publications

See also no. 1416

LONDON

1416

THE NATIONAL GALLERY *Tel.:* 01-930 7618
SCIENTIFIC DEPARTMENT
London W.C.2

Research on the conservation of easel paintings, including analysis of painting materials, examination of painting techniques, control of museum environment, development and application of new materials for restoration

Enquiries: To Librarian (Technical Library)

Scope: Books on painting materials and techniques, both early and modern. The Library includes rare books on painting materials and techniques from the Eastlake Library (compiled in the first half of the 19th century by a former Director of the National Gallery, Sir Charles Eastlake). Some treatises date from the 16th century
Secondary: Modern scientific and technical books; scientific journals and national and international journals and periodicals relating to museology and conservation of works of art and archaeology

Stock: 500 books; 1,000 pamphlets; 100 reports; 15 current periodicals

See also no. 1415

LONDON

1417

NATIONAL GREYHOUND RACING SOCIETY *Tel.:* 01-387 0705
St Martin's House
140 Tottenham Court Road
London W.1

Enquiries: To Secretary

LONDON, NATIONAL GREYHOUND RACING SOCIETY, *cont.*

Scope: Statistical data and general information concerning greyhound racing in Great Britain
Publications: Booklets and pamphlets

LONDON

1418

NATIONAL INSTITUTE FOR SOCIAL WORK TRAINING *Tel.:* 01-387 9681
5 Tavistock Place
London W.C.1

Enquiries: To Librarian, by letter only

Scope: Literature on social work, social services and social work education, with supporting literature on sociological theory, psychology, education and government administration, particularly local government
Secondary: Small collection on permanent loan from the Family Welfare Association, mainly of historical interest to research students. Includes a file of the journal *Social Work* formerly *Charity Organisation Reporter* from 1872

Stock: 6,000 books; 5,000 pamphlets; 200 reports; 60 current periodicals. Periodicals not available on loan

Publications: Supervision in Social Work. A Method of Student Training and Staff Development. D. E. Pettes
Social Work and Social Change. E. Younghusband
Introduction to a Social Worker
Social Policy and Administration. D. V. Donnison, V. Chapman and others
Social Work with Families. Compiled by E. Younghusband
Professional Education for Social Work in Britain. M. Smith
New Developments in Casework
The Field Training of Social Workers. A Survey. S. C. Brown and E. R. Gloyne
Decision in Child Care: A Study of Prediction in Fostering Children. R. Parker
Adoption Policy and Practice. I. Goodacre
Child Care: Needs and Numbers. J. Packman
Social Work and Social Values. Compiled by E. Younghusband
Education for Social Work. Compiled by E. Younghusband
Explorations in Social Casework. E. M. Goldberg
Interviewing in the Social Services
Research in the Personal Social Services: Proposals for a Code of Practice
Welfare in the Community. E. M. Goldberg
Fieldwork in Social Administration Courses
Use of Predictive Methods in Social Work

LONDON

1419

THE NATIONAL INSTITUTE OF ADULT EDUCATION (ENGLAND AND WALES) *Tel.:* 01-580 3155
35 Queen Anne Street
London W.1

Aims to promote co-operation between the various agencies providing adult education and to serve as a centre of information

Enquiries: To Secretary

Scope: All aspects of adult education, that is education for people in mature life who have completed continuous attendance at school, college or university

Stock: 2,000 books and pamphlets; 20 current periodicals

Publications: Adult Education (bi-monthly journal)   Year Book of Adult Education
Teaching Adults (quarterly)   Calendar of Residential short courses
Accommodation and Staffing; Recruitment and Training
A Select Bibliography of Adult Education in Great Britain. T. Kelly, ed.
Teaching Literature. R. Hoggart
Craft Exhibitions (with the National Union of Townswomen's Guilds). H. M. W. Newton
Television and Social Work. A. Hancock and J. Robinson
Adult Education and Television (with UNESCO). B. Groombridge, ed.
International and Inter-Racial Understanding. F. W. Jessup and E. K. Townsend Coles
Teaching at a Distance. E. G. Wedell and H. D. Perraton
Planning Industrial Training. E. Evans and others
Emergent Patterns in L.E.A. Adult Education. D. J. Buchanan and K. Percy
Adult Education and Industrial Workers. M. Barratt-Brown (with the Society of Industrial Tutors)

LONDON

1420

NATIONAL INSTITUTE OF ECONOMIC AND SOCIAL RESEARCH   *Tel.:* 01-222 7665
2 Dean Trench Street
Smith Square
London S.W.1

Propagation of knowledge of economic conditions of contemporary society

Enquiries: To Librarian

Scope: Economics, statistics, econometrics, income and wealth

Stock: 28,000 books and pamphlets; 400 current periodicals

Publications: National Institute Economic Review (quarterly)
Economic & Social Studies
Occasional Papers
Library additions list (3 issues each year)

LONDON

1421

NATIONAL INSTITUTE OF INDUSTRIAL PSYCHOLOGY   *Tel.:* 01-935 1144
14 Welbeck Street
London W1M 8DR

The development of occupational psychology, including research into problems bearing on the adjustment of people to their working life, advice to organizations and individuals, and dissemination of information through publications and short training courses

Enquiries: To Information Officer or Librarian

Scope: All aspects of occupational psychology, including vocational guidance, selection, training, conditions of work (hours, physical environment, safety, wages), motivation, attitudes and behaviour at work. Management and administration
Secondary: Limited material on social and general psychology and on psychometrics

Stock: 6,000 books; 10,000 pamphlets; 130 current periodicals. U.S.A. Office of Naval Research reports which are of relevance to occupational psychology; U.S.A. Educational Testing Service bulletins

Publications: Occupational Psychology   Papers
Research Reports   Handbooks

LONDON	THE NATIONAL INSTITUTE OF MEDICAL HERBALISTS	*Tel.*: 01-594 5892
1422	673 Barking Road Plaistow London E.13	
	See no. 2110	

LONDON	NATIONAL LIBERAL CLUB GLADSTONE LIBRARY	*Tel.*: 01-930 9871
1423	Whitehall Place London S.W.1	

Enquiries: To Librarian

Scope: Political and historical, mainly 19th century, with emphasis on Liberal side, and on later years of century. Election addresses of candidates in general elections 1892 to present day. Unique collection, items not available on loan

Stock: 30,000 books; 10,000 pamphlets. A large mass of pamphlets formerly held, is now on permanent loan to St Deiniols Library, Hawarden, Deeside, Flintshire (no. 448)

LONDON	NATIONAL LIBRARY FOR THE BLIND	*Tel.*: 01-222 2725
1424	35 Great Smith Street London S.W.1 *and*	
	5 St John Street Manchester M3 4DL	*Tel.*: 061-834 0432

Library service for the blind and partially sighted

Enquiries: To Secretary

Scope: General information and library service to blind readers

Stock: 350,000 books and pamphlets; 2 current periodicals

Publications: Printed catalogue of books in Moon type. 1960
Printed catalogue of books in Braille type
In course of publication: Biography. 1965; History and Travel. 1966; Fiction. 1967; Language, Literature and Fine Arts. 1969
Moon catalogue also in Moon and Braille catalogue in Braille

LONDON	NATIONAL MARITIME MUSEUM	*Tel.*: 01-858 4422
1425	Romney Road Greenwich London S.E.10	

This museum illustrates and preserves the maritime history of Great Britain, and covers the Royal Navy, merchant shipping, commercial fishing and pleasure sailing. As well as models, photographs, tools, ships' gear and relics, it has extensive archives, a library and a large department concerned with the history of navigation at sea

Enquiries: To Secretary

Scope: *Library:* About 50,000 books covering the maritime history of Great Britain in war and peace, including such subjects as trade and exploration, navigation and nautical astronomy, fisheries, yachting, piracy, cartography, safety and danger at sea, topography of maritime countries, and signals and communications. The collections of atlases and sailing pilots, signal books and navigational works in particular contain many rare and some unique items. The scope is not confined to British maritime activities. Material from and about other countries appears in all sections, particularly those on cartography, navigation, naval architecture, naval history,

exploration and merchant shipping
Important collections acquired by the library include:
A. G. H. Macpherson collection of atlases and other works
Sir James Caird's collection, including the Henry Stevens set of de Bry's 'Grands et Petits Voyages' 1590–1634
The Philip Gosse Pirate library
The Reynolds Polar library
Collections of books, pamphlets and other material on merchant shipping formed by Lord Leathers, Marischal Murray, H. H. Brindley, Basil Lubbock, Alfred Dingley and others
The Anderson collection of books on maritime subjects generally
The Styring collection of illustrated data on the flags and funnels of British and foreign ship-owners, past and present
The Bowen collection of nautical press cuttings
Books transferred from the Board of Trade library, Admiralty library and Royal Naval College
Extensive collection of pamphlets and press cuttings, bound and unbound periodicals, *The Times* on microfilm, Lloyds Register of Shipping from 1768 and an extensive collection of Lloyds Weekly Lists
A reading room is available for students, and staff will advise readers on their studies and answer enquiries

Information Index: A central card index of information is being built up, classified under ships' names, persons, places, events in date order, and miscellaneous. This both contains information not available elsewhere and acts as a guide to the information which can be found in the library and other departments of the museum

Stock: 50,000 books, plus many thousands of volumes of bound periodicals; 125,000 pamphlets; 80 current periodicals

Publications: Many guides, picture booklets, books, colour reproductions, models, medals and colour transparencies
Analytical Printed Catalogue of the Library, arranged by Subjects (Voyages and Travel; Biography; Atlases and Cartography)

LONDON

1426

NATIONAL MONUMENTS RECORD
Fielden House
10 Great College Street
London S.W.1

Tel.: 01-930 6554

Enquiries: To Secretary

Scope: The aims of the Record are: To compile a complete record of architecture in England by means of photographs and measured drawings. This survey includes ecclesiastical, domestic and civic buildings of every class, as well as architectural detail, sculpture, woodwork, glass and fittings. It is assisted, by the acquisition of collections by purchase and gift, to maintain a library in which these records are available to the public for consultation and study; to supply to applicants copies of photographs where the negatives are available; and to maintain an index of architectural records in public and private possession; and to assist and encourage the study of English architecture of all periods and the collection of historical information useful to students of the subject
Provision is being made for inclusion of archaeological material in the Record. This will comprise air photographs, excavation reports, and photographs of earthworks, structures and finds

Stock: 650,000 records, arranged topographically; 500,000 photographic negatives

LONDON **1427**	NATIONAL NURSERY EXAMINATION BOARD 90 Buckingham Palace Road London S.W.1	*Tel.:* 01-730 5134

Enquiries: To Secretary

Scope: Enquiries relating to the training for and entry to the examination are dealt with

No library

Publications: Pamphlet containing examination regulations and syllabus
Brochure relating to the career of a nursery nurse

LONDON **1428**	NATIONAL OLD PEOPLE'S WELFARE COUNCIL 26 Bedford Square London W.C.1	*Tel.:* 01-636 4066

Independent, non-political, interdenominational charity

Enquiries: To Information Officer

Scope: National focal point for information and advice on all aspects of care of the elderly, with the exception of medical and architectural matters of a technical nature. Aims to provide an information service to students, research workers and statutory and voluntary organizations working for the elderly; enquiries from individuals about particular services are referred to the appropriate local source

Stock: 600 books; 100 pamphlets; numerous papers and research reports; 100 current periodicals. Stock not normally available on loan

Publications: The Elderly (handbook on care and services)
Quarterly Bulletin
Handbooks on various aspects of care of the elderly (list on request)

LONDON **1429**	NATIONAL PHARMACEUTICAL UNION 321 Chase Road Southgate London N.14	*Tel.:* 01-886 6544

Trade Association for Retail Proprietor Pharmacists

Enquiries: To Secretary

Scope: Medical and pharmaceutical enquiries accepted from members and medical or hospital sources
Secondary: Technical enquiries, mainly associated with day-to-day questions from the public to members of the union

Stock: 400 books; 350 pamphlets; 40 current periodicals. Stock not available on loan

Publications: Supplement
NHS Newsletters

LONDON **1430**	NATIONAL POISONS REFERENCE SERVICE Guy's Hospital London S.E.1	*Tel.:* 01-407 7600

Enquiries: To Director

Scope: To advise, as a matter of urgency, on the diagnosis, investigation and management of cases of acute poisoning (in humans, *not* in animals) to members of the medical profession only. A 24-hour telephone service is provided. Generally to provide information on poisoning, acute and chronic, to members of the medical profession only

No library

LONDON **1431**	NATIONAL POSTAL MUSEUM King Edward Building King Edward Street London E.C.1	*Tel.*: 01-432 3851

The history and development of the British postal stamp from 1840 onwards

Enquiries: To Curator

Scope: Philatelic literature with special reference to British postage stamps
Secondary: Philately generally

Stock: 500 books; 350 pamphlets; 9 current periodicals and many foreign publications

Publications: The British Postage Stamps of the 19th century. R. Lowe
A short account of the Reginald M. Phillips Collection of 19th century British Postage Stamps. F. M. Arman
The Postage Stamps of Queen Elizabeth II

Extensive photographic library, mainly of British stamps, including the 'Imprimatur' sheets of almost every stamp issued since 1840

LONDON

1432

NATIONAL REFERENCE LIBRARY OF SCIENCE
AND INVENTION

The National Reference Library of Science and Invention is a part of the British Museum (*see* no. 996). It is being formed from the former Patent Office Library, from the scientific literature held by the British Museum, and by the acquisition of literature held by neither body. It exists at present in two parts. The Holborn Division is the former Patent Office Library, which has been in existence on its present site since 1855. The Bayswater Division has been engaged since 1963 on building up and organizing the rest of the future collection. This Division is still in the middle of a period of intensive preparatory work but is now open to the public. In these circumstances, it was thought more helpful to present the two divisions of National Reference Library of Science and Invention separately, as follows:

1433	NATIONAL REFERENCE LIBRARY OF SCIENCE AND INVENTION (HOLBORN DIVISION) (formerly the Patent Office Library) 25 Southampton Buildings Chancery Lane London W.C.2	*Tel.*: 01-405 8721

The provision of a very extensive, open-access public reference library, for graduates and other professional scientists and technologists, covering the physical sciences, engineering and related industrial technologies. No formal membership or ticket is required to use this library

Enquiries: To Keeper

Scope: The primary stock of the library comprises the literature of the physical sciences (physics, chemistry, mathematics, metallurgy), all branches of engineering and all manufacturing technologies. Holdings of periodicals are particularly strong. In human and veterinary medicine and related fields, including dentistry, it covers instruments and instrumentation, prosthetics, the manufacture of drugs and pharmacology, biochemistry and biophysics
The library is unique in the United Kingdom in also having comprehensive holdings of British and overseas patent specifications, together with official patents and trade mark journals, and other associated literature
Secondary holdings include a very wide range of dictionaries and glossaries. Trade literature of technical interest is also held

LONDON, NATIONAL REFERENCE LIBRARY OF SCIENCE AND INVENTION, *cont.*

Great emphasis is placed on the speedy provision of photocopies to both postal and personal applicants. A while-you-wait service is available to the latter

Stock: 100,000 books and pamphlets (reports series are included in the figures for periodicals); 100,000 current periodicals and 7,000 closed sets of periodicals, dating from 1910 onwards. A comprehensive collection of British and foreign patent specifications and other patent, trademark and design literature. About 110,000 volumes in all. Stock not available on loan. Earlier literature is passed to the British Museum (no. 996)

Publications: Periodical publications in the Patent Office Library: list of current titles. 3rd edition 1965.

Aids to Readers (an irregular series of stencilled bibliographies and guides to special aspects of the collection)

Guide to the National Reference Library of Science and Invention

Translations held by the Library are indexed and their existence noted in the journal containing the original, foreign language article

See also no. 1434, below

1434

NATIONAL REFERENCE LIBRARY OF SCIENCE AND INVENTION (BAYSWATER DIVISION)
10 Porchester Gardens
Queensway
London W.2

Tel.: 01-727 3022
Telex: 22717

This part of the National Reference Library of Science and Invention is being built up as a supplement to the Holborn Division (*see above*) so that the two parts together give a complete coverage of the natural sciences and technology

Enquiries: To Keeper

Scope: The Library covers all the natural sciences, pure and applied, engineering and associated industrial technologies. This part of the N.R.L.S.I. is being built up to hold the literature of the life sciences in depth, and the holdings in the other sciences will cover the literature not held by the Holborn Division (*see above*). The holdings of the Bayswater Division will be particularly strong in the biological sciences, including medical and veterinary sciences. The only exception is purely clinical medicine, of which subject British literature is comprehensively held by the parent organization, the British Museum. A reading room is now open daily, Mondays to Fridays, but most of the literature is stored in closed-access stacks. Therefore a full service will not be feasible until the two separate collections are brought together in one building. Orders for photocopies from the Bayswater stock can be accepted

Stock: 20,000 books and pamphlets; 10,000 current periodicals including report series. The holdings are of current scientific and technical literature, mainly post-1950, but some earlier material is held. When the need to refer to older literature arises, the library has access to the holdings of the British Museum at Bloomsbury (no. 996). Stock not available on loan

Publications: Periodical Publications in the National Reference Library of Science and Invention. Bayswater Division. Part 1. List of non-Slavonic Titles. 1st edition 1969

LONDON

1435

NATIONAL ROLLER HOCKEY ASSOCIATION OF GT BRITAIN
c/o Radio Conversions Ltd
Clarendon Road
London N.8

Tel.: 01-888 3043

Enquiries: To Public Relations Officer

Scope: Any matter appertaining to roller hockey at all levels

No library

Publications: Official Handbook
Rules of the Game
Know your Sport (pamphlet)

LONDON

1436

NATIONAL SAVINGS COMMITTEE *Tel.:* 01-836 1599
Alexandra House
Kingsway
London W.C.2

Enquiries: Refer to local telephone directory

Scope: General information about all matters relating to the National Savings Movement

No library service

Publications: Monthly Bulletin of Statistics and Economic Information
Newsletter
Group Secretary
Money Management Booklets
Various other publications in connection with the work of The National Savings Movement and money management in general

LONDON

1437

NATIONAL SECULAR SOCIETY *Tel.:* 01-407 2717
103 Borough High Street
London S.E.1

Promotion of freethought, rational ethics, and civil liberties

Enquiries: To Secretary

Scope: Books on freethought, humanism, and secularism

Stock: 2,000 books; 1,000 pamphlets; 2 current periodicals

Publications: Religion and Ethics in Schools. D. Tribe
The Necessity for Atheism. P. B. Shelley
RI and Surveys. M. Hill

LONDON

1438

THE NATIONAL SOCIETY FOR AUTISTIC *Tel.:* 01-458 4375
CHILDREN
1A Golders Green Road
London N.W.11

Charity providing day and weekly residential centres for the care and education of autistic children

Enquiries: To Secretary

Scope: Information and Advisory Service for both parents of autistic children and for those who are professionally interested, including information on special schools for autistic children, the latest research into the problem, the implications of a child being assessed as 'ineducable' and statistics and advice on management problems

No library

Publications: Bibliography
Diagnosis of Early Childhood Autism. L. Wing and J. K. Wing
Services Memorandum
Memorandum on Assessment and Placement of Autistic Children
Teaching Aphasic Children. M. A. McGinnis, F. R. Kleffner and R. Goldstein

LONDON, THE NATIONAL SOCIETY FOR AUTISTIC CHILDREN, *cont.*

List of Toys and Equipment
Training Aphasic Children. H. R. Myklebust
Breakthrough in the Treatment of Mentally Ill Children. B. Rimland
Family Services in Childhood Autism. J. K. Wing and L. Wing
A Short Guide to Careers which might lead to Work with Autistic Children
Early Childhood Autism—Clinical, Educational and Social Aspects. J. K. Wing, ed.
Autistic Children. L. Wing
Collection of Papers deriving from the course of lectures on the education of autistic children held at the Society School for Autistic Children in Autumn 1967
Forgotten Teenagers
Innocents at Risk
What is operant conditioning? L. Wing
Beginnings. M. Baron
A Survey taken from the Parent Questionnaire
Teaching Autistic Children. S. Elgar and L. Wing (published by the Association for Special Education)
Misplaced Children
Communication (quarterly journal)
Newsletter

LONDON

1439

NATIONAL SOCIETY FOR CLEAN AIR   *Tel.:* 01-242 5038
Field House
Breams Buildings
London E.C.4

Voluntary association to secure throughout the United Kingdom the maximum of natural light and air free from every form of pollution

Enquiries: To Information Officer and Librarian

Scope: All matters concerning air pollution, its control and prevention; smoke control progress; clean air regulations. Library stock covers smoke and its effects; effects of air pollution on health, amenities, economics, vegetation and materials; prevention of pollution; legislation including overseas; and domestic heating, industrial problems, sources of energy and fuels

Stock: 2,000 books; 50 pamphlets; 70 reports; 35 current periodicals; air pollution photographs

Publications: Smokeless Air (quarterly journal which includes air pollution abstracts)
Clean Air Year Book
Annual conference proceedings
Various leaflets

LONDON

1440

NATIONAL SOCIETY FOR THE PREVENTION OF   *Tel.:* 01-580 8812
CRUELTY TO CHILDREN
1 Riding House Street
London W.1

Enquiries: To Librarian or Information Officer

Scope: Child Welfare

Stock: Small library only

Publications: Child's Guardian
Blue Bird
Pamphlets dealing with various aspects of the Society's work
Film: This is your child

LONDON	NATIONAL UNEMPLOYED WORKERS ASSOCIATION	*Tel.:* 01-435 1773
1441	Sixteen The Pryors East Heath Road London N.W.3	

Enquiries: To Secretary

Scope: Information service to unemployed senior executives. Statistical details from Department of Employment and Productivity
Secondary: News-cutting service on unemployment with specific reference to unemployed senior executives

Stock: 50 books; 100 pamphlets; 10 reports
Industrial Training Research Unit Library to be developed

LONDON	NATIONAL UNION OF SEAMEN	*Tel.:* 01-622 5581
1442	Maritime House Old Town Clapham London S.W.4	

Aims to further the interests of British seamen

Enquiries: To Research Officer, by letter only

Scope: The primary function of the library is to provide information relative to the British shipping industry. Considerable amount of historical material concerning the National Union of Seamen and its predecessors
Secondary: Labour and social statistics

Publications: Monthly journal

LONDON	NATIONAL UNION OF TEACHERS	*Tel.:* 01-387 2442 ext. 133
1443	Hamilton House Mabledon Place London W.C.1	

Enquiries: To General-Secretary, endorsed Library

Scope: Education (particularly primary and secondary, tertiary to a lesser degree)
Secondary: Child psychology and sociology in relation to education

Stock: 10,000 books; 15,000 pamphlets; 200 current periodicals. Union records, reports and journals back to 1870

Publications: Printed catalogue of the library
The N.U.T. View On:
    Higher Education and the Future of Teacher Training. 1967
    Ancillaries and Auxiliaries. 1967
    Sixth Form Curriculum. 1967
    National Standards and Monitoring Procedures for the C.S.E. 1967
Challenge of Change. E. Davies. 1967
The Social Sciences and Education. J. Vaizey. 1967
Science Education and the Future. Chuter Ede Lecture 1967. C. F. Powell
The Financing of Education—A Study Document. 1964
Popular Culture and Personal Responsibility—A Study Outline. B. Groombridge
Schools Television—A Discussion Document. 1961
Some Aspects of Religious Education in Secondary Schools. An Inquiry by the British Council of Churches and the N.U.T. 1965

LONDON, NATIONAL UNION OF TEACHERS, *cont.*
What Chance has your Child? A study of the Effects of Overcrowded Classes in our Schools. K. Gibberd. 1965
School of the Future. The Verbatim report of a two-day conference organised by the N.U.T. to discuss teaching methods and equipment trends in schools organisation and design and developments in all these fields in the next twenty years and the position of the teacher in regard to them. 1966
The First Year of Teaching. E. L. Edmonds. 1967
Teachers and National Insurance. 1967
Annual Guide to Careers for Young People
Member's Handbook (annually)
First Class: The Guide to your new Profession (annually)
The Teacher (weekly)
Youth Review (three times each year)
Higher Education Journal (three times each year)
Various recruitment leaflets

LONDON

1444

NEW FREEDOM GROUP
87 George Street
London W.1

Tel.: 01-935 8913

Upholds the freedom of the individual. Anti-socialist and advocating trade union reform

Enquiries: To Secretary

Scope: Information about trade union activities, particularly their abuses of power
Secondary: Information about the folly and waste of bureaucracy

Stock: 500 books; 200 pamphlets; all weekly and monthly reviews

Publications: The Recorder

LONDON

1445

NEW SOUTH WALES GOVERNMENT OFFICES
56 Strand
London W.C.2

Tel.: 01-839 6651
Telex: 915858

Enquiries: To Official Secretary

Scope: All aspects of New South Wales

Stock: Includes films, photographs and slides

LONDON

1446

NEW ZEALAND FILM LIBRARY
New Zealand House
Haymarket
London S.W.1

Tel.: 01-930 8422
Telex: 24368

Distributors of 16 mm and 35 mm prints of New Zealand Government films

Enquiries: To Films Officer

Scope: Nature, life, industries and leisure of New Zealand

Publications: Film catalogues and supplements

LONDON

1447

NEW ZEALAND HIGH COMMISSION
Haymarket
London S.W.1

Tel.: 01-930 8422
Telex: 24368

Provides an information and library service to the public on any aspect of New Zealand

Enquiries: To High Commissioner

Scope: The library contains books, pamphlets and periodicals on or about New Zealand, including official publications such as Parliamentary Papers, Parliamentary Debates, Statutes, Law Reports, Official Yearbooks and Statistics and a wide range of books on New Zealand, the South Pacific and the Antarctic, including history, geography, biography, anthropology, flora, fauna, agriculture, sport and novels, poems and other works by New Zealand authors

Stock: 11,000 books, pamphlets and reports; 123 New Zealand current periodicals

LONDON 1448

NIGERIA HIGH COMMISSION
9 Northumberland Avenue
London W.C.2

Tel.: 01-839 1244

Enquiries: To Information Officer

Scope: General information on and concerning Nigeria

LONDON 1449

NORTHERN IRELAND GOVERNMENT OFFICE
11 Berkeley Street
London W.1

Tel.: 01-493 0601
Telex: 21839

Enquiries: To Information Officer

Scope: General information service about Northern Ireland

LONDON 1450

NORTHERN POLYTECHNIC
Holloway Road
London N.7

Tel.: 01-607 6767 ext. 265

Enquiries: To Librarian

Scope: Chemistry, physics, mathematics, geology, biology, botany, zoology, electronics and telecommunications, home economics, architecture, building and interior decoration, surveying, estate management and town planning. Polymer science and technology. Dietetics and nutrition

Stock: 36,000 books and pamphlets; 800 current periodicals

LONDON 1451

NORTH-WESTERN POLYTECHNIC
Prince of Wales Road
London N.W.5

Tel.: 01-485 0101

Enquiries: To Librarian

Scope: Librarianship, sociology, social work, child care, teacher training, transport, management studies, business studies, accountancy, English studies, French studies, German studies, Spanish studies, geography, history, philosophy, Greek and Latin

Stock: 68,000 books (distributed between four libraries); 5,000 pamphlets; 1,000 reports; 1,145 current periodicals

LONDON 1452

NORWEGIAN EMBASSY
25 Belgrave Square
London S.W.1

Tel.: 01-235 7151
Telex: 22321

Enquiries: To Press Office and/or Cultural Office

Scope: Any aspect of Norway (but the library is rather poorly stocked in science). If the information is not available, indication will be given of where it can be obtained

Stock: 7,000 books

Publications: Weekly press bulletin giving current news of Norway

LONDON **1453**	NORWOOD TECHNICAL COLLEGE Tower Bridge Centre Tooley Street London S.E.1	*Tel.:* 01-407 1831

Enquiries: To Librarian
Scope: Dental technology; food technology; medical laboratory science
Stock: 3,000 books; 60 current periodicals

LONDON **1454**	THE OBSERVER 160 Queen Victoria Street London E.C.4 Sunday newspaper	*Tel.:* 01-236 0202 *Telex:* 22206

Enquiries: To Librarian
Scope: Information on articles appearing in the *Observer*. Compilation of index—both subject and author—of the *Observer* newspaper and colour magazine

LONDON **1455**	THE OFFICE OF HEALTH ECONOMICS 162 Regent Street London W.1	*Tel.:* 01-734 0757

Undertakes research to evaluate the economic aspects of medical care; investigates, from time to time, other health and social problems; collects data on experience in other countries and publishes results, data and conclusions

Enquiries: To Librarian
Scope: All published material on the subjects noted above
Stock: 200 current periodicals
Publications: Technical booklets

LONDON **1456**	OFFICE OF THE AGENT GENERAL FOR QUEBEC 12 Upper Grosvenor Street London W.1	*Tel.:* 01-629 4155 *Telex:* 261618

Enquiries: To Director of Information
Scope: Information on all aspects of Quebec Province including investment and industrial development possibilities
Publications: Publications on industrial development opportunities, on tourism and on Quebec in general

LONDON **1457**	OFFICE OF THE AGENT GENERAL FOR TASMANIA 458/459 Strand London W.C.2	*Tel.:* 01-839 2291

Enquiries: To Secretary
Scope: Information and advice concerning Tasmania. Reasonable collection of reference books, tourist leaflets and trade reports, and would obtain for a genuine enquirer any specific books published in Tasmania. Films on different aspects of life in Tasmania are available on free loan
Publications: Lists of 16 mm films
List of transparencies
Monthly newsletter

LONDON	OFFICE OF THE CHIEF RABBI	*Tel.*: 01-387 1066
1458	Adler House Tavistock Square London W.C.1	

Administration of the Chief Rabbinate of Great Britain. The Chief Rabbi is the religious head of the United Hebrew Congregations of the British Commonwealth and, as such, is the spokesman for British Jewry on religious issues

Enquiries: To Executive Director

Scope: General questions on Anglo-Jewry, on attitude of religious leadership to specific situations and on the Jewish view of matters of general concern

Publications: Publications of the Office of the Chief Rabbi which include speeches and sermons by the Chief Rabbi and proceedings of the Conference of European Rabbis and a booklet on Jewish religious issues involved in the adoption of children

LONDON	OFFICE OF THE HIGH COMMISSIONER FOR SINGAPORE IN THE UNITED KINGDOM	*Tel.*: 01-235 8315
1459	2 Wilton Crescent London S.W.1	

Enquiries: To:
Director, Students Department, on information relating to education;
First Secretary (Trade), on information relating to trade and economic development;
Information Officer, on general information relating to Singapore;
Consular Officer, information relating to visas and passports, visits to Singapore

LONDON	OFFICE OF THE HIGH COMMISSIONER FOR UGANDA	*Tel.*: 01-839 1963 *Telex*: 262241
1460	P.O. Box 257 Uganda House Trafalgar Square London W.C.2	

Enquiries: To Third Secretary (Information) or Counsellor

Scope: The information service provided by the Mission covers all the general aspects of Uganda. There are essentially three sections: general information; economic, commercial and financial information; and tourism. Most of the information required can be provided by the Mission but if it is not available, the Office of the High Commission seeks it from Uganda and passes it on to the enquirer

Library stock not available on loan

Publication: Uganda Trade Directory
Commercial, economic and trade bulletins

LONDON	THE OLD WATER COLOUR SOCIETY'S CLUB	*Tel.*: 01-629 8300
1461	R.W.S. Galleries 26 Conduit Street London W.1	

Enquiries: To Secretary

Scope: Water-colour painting. Club for those interested in any aspect

Publications: Annual volumes (44 to date) containing articles on old and present masters of the medium

LONDON	OPEN DOOR COUNCIL (BRITISH BRANCH OF OPEN DOOR INTERNATIONAL)	*Tel.:* 01-946 8844
1462	43 Seymour Road Wimbledon London S.W.19	

Aims to secure that a woman shall be free to work, and protected as a worker on the same terms as a man, and that legislation and regulations dealing with conditions and hours, payment, entry and training shall be based upon the nature of the work and not upon the sex of the worker. And to secure for a woman, irrespective of marriage or childbirth, the right at all times to decide whether or not she shall engage in paid work, and to ensure that no legislation or regulation shall deprive her of this right

Enquiries: To Secretary, by letter only

Stock: Pamphlets dealing with legislative and trade union restrictions based on sex

Publications: Pamphlets on protective legislation based on the sex of the worker

LONDON	OPTICAL INFORMATION COUNCIL	*Tel.:* 01-242 5146
1463	Aldwych House London W.C.2	

To promote the concept of eye care and the products of the ophthalmic optical industry in Britain

Enquiries: To Information Officer

Scope: The use of powered lenses for correcting vision; the promotion of visual screening processes; new spectacle styles

No library

LONDON	OVE ARUP AND PARTNERS, CONSULTING ENGINEERS	*Tel.:* 01-636 1531
1464	13 Fitzroy Street London W.1	

Consulting structural engineers

Enquiries: To Librarian

Scope: All aspects of building
Secondary: Architecture

Stock: 2,500 books; 40,000 pamphlets; 135 current periodicals; 8,500 slides; 8,700 photographs

Publications: Arups Journal (quarterly)
Newsletter (monthly)

LONDON	OVERSEA VISUAL AID CENTRE	*Tel.:* 01-387 8455
1465	Tavistock House South Tavistock Square London, W.C.1	

Enquiries: To Director

Scope: Sources of supply for audio-visual materials in all school subjects
Secondary: Sources of supply of audio-visual materials for adults with particular reference to overseas (mainly developing countries) requirements

Stock: Reference library only

Publications: Bulletin (twice a year including articles and reports on audio-visual methods and equipment for overseas situations)

Leaflets on audio-visual material, according to subject and/or equipment
Booklets: Flannelgraph; Care and use of projectors
Research: A Study of Understanding of Visual Symbols in Kenya
Problems and Communication in Extension and Community Development Campaigns

Permanent display of materials and equipment at the Centre

LONDON

1466

OVERSEAS DEVELOPMENT INSTITUTE   *Tel.:* 01-493 2654
160 Piccadilly
London W1V 0JS

The Overseas Development Institute is an independent, non-government body aiming to promote wise action in the field of overseas development. It was set up in 1960 and is financed by donations from British business and by grants from British and American foundations

Enquiries: To Librarian

Scope: Foreign aid, economics of development
Secondary: Foreign trade, population problems, rural development, education

Stock: 3,000 books; 3,500 pamphlets; 100 current periodicals. Stock not available on loan

Publications: Periodical Review (monthly list of articles on aid and development)
The Business of Development. 1968
The Aid Relationship. A. Krassowski. 1968
Consultancy in Overseas Development. C. Young. 1968
ODI Review 2. British Development Policies, Needs and Prospects. 1968
The Less Developed Countries in World Trade. M. Z. Cutajar and A. Franks. 1967
Aid in Uganda—Agriculture. H. Mettrick. 1967
Pledged to Development. J. White. 1967
Rich World/Poor World (Arrow book of the ABC Television series). J. Lambe, ed. 1967
Aid Management Overseas. T. Soper. 1967
Effective Aid. T. Hayter. 1967
The Soviet Middle East. A. Nove and J. A. Newth (published Allen and Unwin)
Food Aid and Britain. H. Mettrick. 1969
ODI Review 3. British Development Policies, Needs and Prospects. 1969
Opting for Development: a Guide to Opportunities for Development Studies in British Higher Education. N. A. Sims. 1968
Many earlier publications

LONDON

1467

OXFORD UNIVERSITY PRESS   *Tel.:* 01-629 8494
Ely House
37 Dover Street
London W1X 4AH

The library, which is open to the public as a reference library, contains all the books at present in print published by the Oxford University Press and the Clarendon Press and a wide selection of books published by American University Presses

Enquiries: To Librarian

Scope: On any subject connected with Oxford University Press books or on the University of Oxford

Stock: 10,000 books; 100 pamphlets; 20 reports; those current periodicals published by Oxford University Press

LONDON

1468

PADDINGTON TECHNICAL COLLEGE
25 Paddington Green
London W.2

Enquiries: To Librarian

LONDON, PADDINGTON TECHNICAL COLLEGE, *cont.*

Scope: Engineering (production, electronic, electrical, mechanical, radio and television, gas and motor vehicle). Heating and ventilating. Welding. Medical laboratory technology, science laboratory technology, photographic technology. Mathematics, physics, chemistry, botany, biology and zoology. Clinical chemistry, haematology, histopathology, medical bacteriology, immunology. Animal technology

Stock: 14,000 books; 1,500 pamphlets; 300 current periodicals

LONDON

1469

PALI TEXT SOCIETY *Tel.:* 01-229 1037
30 Dawson Place
London W.2

Publishes in roman characters such Pali works as conduce to the study of Buddhism, translations of these and ancillary material, for example, dictionaries, grammars

Enquiries: To President, by letter only

Scope: Restricted to Buddhist texts in Pali and Sanskrit in various oriental characters and romanized editions together with various translations

Stock: 750 books

LONDON

1470

PASSMORE EDWARDS MUSEUM *Tel.:* 01-534 4545 ext. 376
(LONDON BOROUGH OF NEWHAM)
Romford Road
Stratford
London E.15

A centre for information and study of the archaeology, history, geology and biology of Essex

Enquiries: To Curator, by letter only

Stock: 10,000 books; 5,000 pamphlets; 110 current periodicals; large photographic collection of Essex subjects. Stock not available on loan

Publications: Reproduction in British Deer. R. E. Chaplin

LONDON

1471

PATIENTS' ASSOCIATION *Tel.:* 01-837 7241
335, Gray's Inn Road
London W.C.1

Aims to represent and further the interest of patients, to provide assistance and advice, to acquire and disseminate information and to promote understanding and goodwill between patients and all persons engaged in medical practice and related activities

Enquiries: To Secretary, by letter only

Scope: The Association will give information on all questions concerning the health services and advice on personal problems and complaints related to this field

Publications: Organizations concerned with Particular Diseases or Handicaps
A Guide to the Rights of a Patient
Changing your Doctor under the National Health Service
Information and Advice on Going into Hospital
Some lesser known services and concessions available under the National Health Service
The Compulsory Admission and Detention of Mental Patients
The Constitution, Appointment and General Functions of Regional Hospital Boards, Boards of Governors, Hospital Management Committees and Executive Councils in England and Wales under the National Health Service
Miscellaneous Queries on the N.H.S., mainly concerning Patients' Rights

LONDON	PHARMACEUTICAL SOCIETY OF GREAT BRITAIN	*Tel.:* 01-405 8967
1472	17 Bloomsbury Square London W.C.1	

Representative body of pharmacists in Great Britain; responsible under the Pharmacy Acts for the registration and discipline of pharmacists, and for the enforcement of its main provisions. The Society is also concerned with the education of pharmacists

Enquiries: To Librarian

Scope: Pharmaceutical subjects, materia medica, pharmacology, toxicology, chemistry, botany

Stock: 38,880 books; 10,900 pamphlets; 400 current periodicals
Special collections: Historical collection includes many herbals; London, Edinburgh and Dublin pharmacopoeias from 1618
Hanbury library of about 500 volumes including many rare illustrated botanical works
Books, literature and cards on proprietary medicines (both English and foreign)

Publications: The publications of the society are published by the Pharmaceutical Press, and include:
British National Formulary (published jointly with British Medical Association)
British Pharmaceutical Codex
British Pharmacopoeia
British Veterinary Codex
Dental Practitioners' Formulary
Drug Identification
Drugs: Actions, Uses and Dosage
The Extra Pharmacopoeia (Martindale)
Identification of Drugs and Poisons
Mathematics and Statistics for use in Pharmacy, Biology and Chemistry. L. Saunders and R. Fleming
The Pharmaceutical Pocket Book
Poisons and T.S.A. Guide
A Short History of Surgical Dressings
Isolation and Identification of Drugs
Bibliography of Pharmaceutical Reference Literature

LONDON	PHILIPPA FAWCETT COLLEGE	*Tel.:* 01-677 9641
1473	94/100 Leigham Court Road Streatham London S.W.16	

College of Education for primary and secondary teachers. Affiliated to Institute of Education, London University

Enquiries: To Librarian

Scope: Law, economics, education (history, theory and method), social sciences, theology, history, geography, literature, fine arts

Stock: 30,000 books and pamphlets; 130 current periodicals. Periodicals not available on loan, but photocopies supplied

LONDON	PHILOLOGICAL SOCIETY University College
1474	Gower Street London W.C.1

Aims to promote the study and knowledge of the structure and the history of language

LONDON, PHILOLOGICAL SOCIETY, *cont.*

Enquiries: To Secretary, by letter only

Scope: Enquiries on linguistic topics can be referred to the Council of the Society, which endeavours to pass them to those able to help

No library

Publications: Transactions of the Philological Society (annually)
Special publications (irregularly)

LONDON

1475

THE PHYSICAL EDUCATION ASSOCIATION OF GREAT BRITAIN AND NORTHERN IRELAND
Ling House
10 Nottingham Place
London W1M 4AX

Tel.: 01-486 1301

Aims to educate and instruct specialist teachers in physical and health education and recreation in current theory and practice both in the United Kingdom and overseas and the best methods of improving the physical health of the community

Enquiries: To Librarian

Scope: Physical education, sport, leisure and allied medical subjects including general anatomy, physiology, medical gymnastics, physiotherapy and remedial work. Gymnastics, dance and movement, athletics, swimming, all major and minor indoor and outdoor games and sports. Health education
Secondary: Sports medicine including injuries, fitness and drugs

Stock: 7,000 books, pamphlets and reports; 418 current periodicals

Publications: The British Journal of Physical Education (6 issues each year, including abstracts and book reviews)
Bibliography of Books: Physical and health education, sport and allied subjects (quarterly)
Bibliography of Articles: Physical and health education, sport and allied subjects (quarterly)
Other occasional publications, for example. Some aspects of the law relating to physical education teachers

See also no. 1270

LONDON

1476

PLUNKETT FOUNDATION FOR CO-OPERATIVE STUDIES
10 Doughty Street
London W.C.1

Tel.: 01-405 9304

To further the study of agricultural and industrial co-operation. Offers a library and information service and runs a correspondence Business Training course with emphasis on co-operation. Makes continual research into co-operative matters

Enquiries: To Librarian

Scope: All aspects of co-operation, especially agricultural

Stock: 20,000 books and pamphlets; a large collection of annual reports from co-operative organizations in many countries; 30 current periodicals
Special collection: Sir Horace Plunkett's diaries and the Plunkett letters

Publications: Year Book of Agricultural Co-operation
Bibliography and occasional papers on co-operative subjects

LONDON **1477**	THE POETRY SOCIETY 21 Earls Court Square London S.W.5	*Tel.:* 01-373 3556

Knowledge and appreciation of poetry, particularly as a living art form

Enquiries: To Librarian or Secretary
Scope: Poetry: British, American, Foreign (some in translation, some in original language), of all periods
Secondary: Critical and comparative studies; anthologies; appreciation; children's section
Stock: 15,000 books. Library for reference, on the premises only
Publications: The Poetry Review (quarterly)

LONDON **1478**	POLISH CULTURAL INSTITUTE 16 Devonshire Street London W.1	*Tel.:* 01-636 6032

Documentation and information centre on science and culture in Poland

Enquiries: To Librarian
Scope: Any information on Poland of scientific and cultural nature
Stock: 5,000 books; 10,000 pamphlets; 200 current periodicals. All publications of the Polish Academy of Sciences
Publications: Programme of Events (quarterly)

LONDON **1479**	POLISH INSTITUTE AND SIKORSKI MUSEUM 26/28 Pont Street London S.W.1 (*Library*) 20 Princes Gate London S.W.7 (*Records*)

Enquiries: To Librarian, by letter or in person
Scope: *Library:* Large collections of books (Polish and English) on all aspects of Polish past and contemporary history, economy, politics, law, literature (except sciences and technology)
Records: Diplomatic documents relating to the events preceding the outbreak of the Second World War; materials dealing with September Campaign 1939; documents illustrating the reconstruction of Polish National Life in exile and the activities of Polish Government, both in the political and military fields
Stock: 70,000 books and pamphlets; 96 current periodicals

LONDON **1480**	THE POLISH LIBRARY 9 Princes Gardens London S.W.7	*Tel.:* 01-589 2154

Provides the Polish community in London and Great Britain with books and periodicals in Polish published both in Poland and outside that country and makes available to all scholars and students of Polish affairs publications on Poland or relating to Poland

Enquiries: To Librarian
Scope: Bibliographical information on Poland and Polish affairs, particularly in the field of humanities and to a lesser extent in the field of natural sciences, pure science and technology
Special collections: Polish émigré publications
Books by Joseph Conrad and Conradiana in general
Lanckoronski Collection (old Polish books and prints)

LONDON, THE POLISH LIBRARY, *cont.*
Elseviers (more than 200 titles)
Book-plates (Polish, English)
Old maps of Poland
Polish music scores
Polish manuscripts
Photographs of Polish interest

Stock: 70,000 books; 10,000 pamphlets; 250 current periodicals; 4,000 bookplates; 10,000 photographs

Publications: Quarterly books in Polish or relating to Poland (list of new acquisitions)
Bibliography of books in Polish or relating to Poland, volumes 1–3

LONDON

1481

POLITICAL STUDIES ASSOCIATION OF THE UNITED KINGDOM
c/o London School of Economics and Political Science
Houghton Street
London W.C.2

Tel.: 01-405 7686

Aims to promote the development of political studies in universities and other institutes of higher education and to promote and assist research in politics and allied subjects

Enquiries: To Secretary, by letter only
No library

Publications: Political Studies (journal, 4 times each year)

LONDON

1482

THE POLYTECHNIC OF CENTRAL LONDON (DESIGNATE)
309 Regent Street
London W1R 8AL

Tel.: 01-580 2020

Enquiries: To Chief Librarian

Scope: Economics, sociology and management; architecture; modern foreign languages; law

Stock: 10,000 books; 2,000 pamphlets; 200 current periodicals. Total stock: 71,000 books and reports; 3,700 pamphlets; 600 current periodicals

Publications: Quarterly Digest of periodicals taken in the School of Commerce and Social Studies and the Department of Management Studies
Select bibliographies on: Sociology; Economics; Management Studies and Industrial Administration

LONDON

1483

POST OFFICE
Headquarters Building
St Martin's-le-Grand
London E.C.1

Tel.: 01-432 4046 (Library);
01-432 4521 (Records)

Reference library for staff of the headquarters departments of the Post Office; Records room

Enquiries: To Librarian (for current information) or Departmental Record Officer (for historical information)

Scope: Library: General reference books on subjects relating to administration, management and organization and on specialized subjects including postal and telecommunications subjects
Records: Postal, personnel, telecommunications and broadcasting archives
Secondary: Record library covering these subjects and philately

Stock: 6,000 books; 1,500 pamphlets; foreign reports on postal and telecommunication matters; 280 current periodicals

Publications: Post Office Courier (staff newspaper)
Telecommunications Journal

LONDON	POST OFFICE ENGINEERING UNION	*Tel.:* 01-998 1612
1484	Greystoke House Hanger Lane Ealing London W.5	

Trade Union

Enquiries: To Research Officer (letters and personal enquiries only)

Scope: Schedules of wage rates and earnings. Periodicals dealing with the telecommunications industry. Relevant Government White Papers. Economics

Stock: 750 books; 2,000 pamphlets; 90 current periodicals. Stock not available on loan

Publications: The Telephone Ring—Time to Investigate
Evidence to the Royal Commission on Trade Unions and Employers' Associations
Notes on Telephone Development—July 1967–June 1968
Memorandum to the National Board for Prices and Incomes in Connection with its Examination of Proposals to increase Post Office Charges—January 1968
Freedom to Manufacture

LONDON	THE PRE-RETIREMENT ASSOCIATION	*Tel.:* 01-580 3155
1485	35 Queen Anne Street London W1M 9FB	

Aims to stimulate all working men and women to prepare for retirement as a positive phase of life, as they have prepared for all its other phases

Enquiries: To Secretary, by letter only

Scope: Advisory service on organizing conferences, running pre-retirement advisory courses/counselling services and promoting research into post and pre-retirement attitudes

Publications: Solving the Problems of Retirement, Symposium. H. B. Wright, ed. 1968
Living Arrangements and £.s.d. L. M. Hubbard. 1966
The Years Still Unexplored: Thoughts on being Retired from Work. F. Le Gros Clark and F. S. Milligan. 1964
Preparation for Retirement—Whose Responsibility? Report of the first national conference 1963
Aspects of Health in Preparation for Retirement—Promoting Health in Middle Life—Report of a Conference held on 26th July 1967 at Royal College of General Practitioners
Pensioners in Search of a Job. F. Le Gros Clark. 1969
The Personal Problems of Retirement. L. M. Hubbard. 1961
Pre-Retirement Budgeting, Purchasing, Saving and Planning

LONDON	THE PREHISTORIC SOCIETY	*Tel.:* 01-636 1555 ext. 292
1486	c/o Hon. Secretary Department of Prehistoric and Romano-British Antiquities British Museum London W.C.1	

Aims to promote interest in prehistoric archaeology, to encourage and engage in research, and to disseminate information on prehistory

Enquiries: To Secretary

Scope: Prehistory
No library

Publications: Proceedings of the Prehistoric Society

LONDON 1487	PRESBYTERIAN CHURCH OF ENGLAND OFFICES Presbyterian Church House 86 Tavistock Place London W.C.1	*Tel.:* 01-837 0862 (Tavistock Bookshop: 01-837 9116)	

Enquiries: To Secretary (for general information). To Hon. Librarian (for historical information)

Scope: All matters directly concerned with the Presbyterian Church of England and its congregations, ministers and history

Secondary: Some information about the Presbyterian Churches elsewhere in the world

Stock: 10,000 books and pamphlets

Publications: Outlook (monthly)
Presbyterian Historical Society Journal (annually)

See also no. 1488

LONDON

1488

PRESBYTERIAN HISTORICAL SOCIETY OF ENGLAND
86 Tavistock Place
London W.C.1

Aims to promote study of the history of Presbyterianism in England, and to collect and preserve manuscripts and books relating thereto

Enquiries: To Hon. Librarian, by letter only

For scope, stock and publications, *see* entry no. 1487

LONDON

1489

PRINCE OF WALES AND ST ANN'S MEDICAL LIBRARIES
The Green
Tottenham
London N.15

Tel.: 01-808 0303

Service to medical staff and postgraduate students

Enquiries: To Librarian, by letter only

Scope: General medicine

Stock: 200 books; 18 current periodicals. Stock not available on loan

---

LONDON

1490

PRINT COLLECTORS' CLUB
R.W.S. Galleries
28 Conduit Street
London W.1.

Tel.: 01-493 5436

Enquiries: To Secretary

Scope: Prints and print-makers, but mainly restricted to members' enquiries. Lectures and free presentation print annually

---

LONDON

1491

PRINTING HISTORICAL SOCIETY
St Bride Institute
Bride Lane
Fleet Street
London E.C.4

The Society was founded in 1964 to encourage the study of and foster interest in the history of printing, to encourage the preservation of historical equipment and printed matter, to promote meetings and exhibitions, and to produce publications in connection with these aims

Enquiries: To Secretary, by letter only

Scope: Enquiries are referred to specialists on the committee or among the membership

No library

Publications: Charles Earl Stanhope and the Oxford University Press. H. Hart. 1896
The Working Man's Way in the World, being the Autobiography of a Journeyman Printer. C. M. Smith. 1853
Vincent Figgins, Type Specimens, 1801 and 1815. Bertholde Wolpe, ed.
A Dictionary of London Printers, 1800-1840, compiled with an introduction by W. B. Todd (in preparation)
Patents for Inventions Relating to Printing. Abridgements of Specifications 1617-1857. J. Harrison
Journal

LONDON

1492

PROFESSIONAL CLASSES AID COUNCIL (INC)   *Tel.:* 01-935 0641
10 St Christopher's Place
London W1M 6HY

Enquiries: To Secretary

Scope: Information concerning appropriate sources of financial aid for professional people in financial difficulty

LONDON

1493

PUBLIC HEALTH INSPECTORS EDUCATION   *Tel.:* 01-730 5134
BOARD
90 Buckingham Palace Road
London S.W.1

Enquiries: To Secretary

Scope: Enquiries relating to the training for and entry to the Board's examination are dealt with

No library

Publications: Pamphlet containing examination regulations and brief syllabus
Pamphlet containing the Board's full syllabuses

LONDON

1494

PUBLIC RECORD OFFICE   *Tel.:* 01-405 0741
Chancery Lane
London W.C.2

The Public Record Office houses the national archives of the United Kingdom and makes them available for inspection in accordance with the provisions of the Public Records Acts 1958 and 1967

Enquiries: To Keeper

Scope: The many millions of documents preserved in the Public Record Office occupy at present more than 300,000 ft of shelves, and fall into two main categories:
Records from the Norman Conquest onwards of the King's Court and the divergent branches and offshoots through which it discharges its administrative, financial and judicial functions—the Chancery, the Exchequer and the various courts of common law and equity—together with those of Palatinate and other special jurisdictions and certain analogous groups of documents
State Papers from the accession of Henry VIII onwards, together with records of the Admiralty and all central government departments of later origin
Records are normally open to inspection when they are 30 years old

Stock: Small library. Stock not available on loan

LONDON, PUBLIC RECORD OFFICE, *cont.*

Publications: The publications of the Office are described in the booklet *British National Archives* (H.M.S.O. Sectional List no. 24)

The Public Record Office provides a service to the public for the making of copies by microfilm, Xerox, photostat, photographic and offset-litho processes

LONDON

1495

PULTENEY COLLEGE *Tel.:* 01-437 8381
Peter Street
Wardour Street
London W.1

General and commercial college

Enquiries: Principal or Librarian, as appropriate

Scope: English for students from abroad, English language and literature, French, German, history, geography, economics and economic history, British Constitution, mathematics, biology, chemistry, physics, book-keeping, shorthand and typewriting, and general 'background' books on other subjects

Stock: 3,500 books; 300 pamphlets; 70 current periodicals. Stock available on loan only through I.L.E.A. Education Library Service

LONDON

1496

QUEEN'S INSTITUTE OF DISTRICT NURSING *Tel.:* 01-730 0355
57 Lower Belgrave Street
London S.W.1

An organization supported by voluntary subscription and health authority membership for the promotion and development of services for the betterment of domiciliary nursing and community care

Enquiries: To Information Officer

Scope: The Institute's information service is largely concentrated on nursing in the community, as opposed to nursing in hospital. The subjects are, therefore, concerned with such matters as the role of the district nurse in respect of: the organization and administration of community nursing services under the National Health Service; postgraduate education and training; relations with hospital, medical, para-medical and voluntary services; nursing equipment as well as technical equipment for the use of the district nurse or the patient at home; pre-symptomatic detection, early diagnosis and treatment (screening); and public health services abroad

A monthly sheet of extracts from the medical and nursing press is compiled and distributed to membership authorities' medical and nursing officers. These bulletins are compiled from material under the heads referred to above

Publications: District Nursing (monthly)
Research reports such as *Feeling the Pulse* and *Care in the Balance*

LONDON

1497

RACE RELATIONS BOARD *Tel.:* 01-930 6322
St Stephens House
Victoria Embankment
London S.W.1

Statutory body which exists to secure compliance with the Race Relations Act

Enquiries: To Information Officer

Scope: The Board will furnish information about the Race Relations Act and the Board's functions in securing compliance with it. The Board will also consider requests for speakers to speak about the legislation. The Board do not reply to general questions on Community and Race Relations which are more properly the responsibility of the Runnymede Trust, the Institute of Race Relations and the Community Relations Commission. Immigration questions are the responsibility of the Home Office and complaints of 'incitement to racial hatred' are for the Police and the Attorney General

Stock: Books and pamphlets on race relations matters. Reports from Institute of Race Relations, Government Departments and other bodies working in the race relations field. Daily and weekly, regional and national newspapers and periodicals from Institutes and Societies dealing with race relations matters. All immigrant publications

Publications: The Board's Quarterly Bulletin and guides, leaflets, posters and display material in English, Urdu, Bengali, Punjabi, Hindi and Gujerati. The Board also has available limited film material in 16 mm and 35 mm about the Act

LONDON

1498

RACHEL McMILLAN COLLEGE OF EDUCATION *Tel.:* 01-692 7574
Creek Road
London S.E.8

Enquiries: To Librarian

Scope: Books on education, art, music, English, history, science, geography, Divinity and psychology. Rachel McMillan was a pioneer of nursery education and information about her and her work is available

Stock: 24,000 books; 3,000 pamphlets; 120 current periodicals

LONDON

1499

RADIO TIMES HULTON PICTURE LIBRARY *Tel.:* 01-580 5577 ext. 4735
35 Marylebone High Street and 4737
London W1M 1AA *Telex:* 22182

Commercial picture-lending library which exists to supply illustrations to *bona fide* users of pictures in return for appropriate fees

Enquiries: To Librarian

Scope: Illustrations range in time from cave-paintings of 20,000 B.C. to stroboscopic photographs of the 1950s. The collection comes to an end in 1957, with the demise of *Picture Post*; but before that date, it may include virtually anything. The bias is Western European and coverage is particularly rich from the beginning of photography in the 1850s onwards. Contents include: the Gordon Anthony Collection (portraits and theatrical, 1930s); the Baron Collection (portraits and ballet 1930s–1950s); the W. & D. Downey Collection (portraits, particularly Royalty, 1860s–1930s); the Rischgitz Collection (1,000,000 historical prints and photographs); the Sasha London Theatre Collection (1920s–1940); the Studio Lisa Royal Portraits (1936–1954)

Stock: 6,000,000 pictures, the great majority on negative

LONDON

1500

RATIONALIST PRESS ASSOCIATION LTD *Tel.:* 01-226 7251
88 Islington High Street
London N.1

Aims to promote rational thinking and conduct in human affairs; to fight irrationality and superstition; to defend freedom of thought and enquiry; and to advance secular education

Enquiries: To Librarian, by letter only

Scope: Rationalism, humanism and freethought; biblical and theological criticism; philosophy; ethics; evolution; religion

Secondary: Science, social issues

LONDON, RATIONALIST PRESS ASSOCIATION LTD, *cont.*

Stock: 2,000 books; world-wide selection of humanist, rationalist and freethought journals. Complete run of publications of C. A. Watts & Co up to 1960

Publications: Humanist (monthly)   Pamphlets
Question (annually)   Library catalogue
Books published by subsidiary, Pemberton Publishing Co. Ltd.

LONDON REFORM CLUB   *Tel.:* 01-930 9374 ext. 14
104 Pall Mall
1501 London S.W.1

Formerly political now social rendezvous

Enquiries: General: To Secretary; Library: To Librarian, by Members or sponsored persons

Scope: The Reform Club: foundation and history; general cultural interest; political and economic works; the humanities

Stock: Club records. Stock not available on loan to outside bodies

LONDON RELIGIOUS SOCIETY OF FRIENDS (QUAKERS)   *Tel.:* 01-387 3601
Friends House
1502 Euston Road
London N.W.1

Enquiries: To Librarian

Scope: Quaker beliefs, history and activities
Secondary: Subjects in which Quakers have traditionally been interested, for example peace, anti-slavery movement, race relations

Stock: 15,000 books; 30,000 pamphlets; 150 current periodicals. Library holds central archives of Society of Friends and catalogue of local archives; substantial collection of other manuscripts; collection of drawings, prints and photographs of Quaker personalities and meeting houses

LONDON REMPLOY LIMITED   *Tel.:* 01-452 8020
Remploy House   *Telex:* 23178
1503 415 Edgware Road
Cricklewood
London N.W.2

General manufacturers. The Company provide sheltered employment for severely disabled persons who would otherwise be unable to obtain work

Enquiries: To Librarian or Public Relations Officer

Scope: The Library includes, in addition to information normally found in industrial libraries, a collection of literature on the employment of and services for the disabled

Stock: 1,750 books; 70 current periodicals (total stock, of which 300 books and 3 periodicals are concerned with the disabled); series of Final Reports of the Vocational Rehabilitation Administration, Division of Research and Demonstration, Washington, U.S.A.

LONDON RESEARCH INSTITUTE FOR CONSUMER AFFAIRS   *Tel.:* 01-930 3360
43 Villiers Street
1504 London W.C.2

Research into how far goods and services meet the needs and wants of those who use them, particularly under-privileged consumers

Enquiries: To Secretary

Scope: Consumer information and protection

LONDON	REUTERS LTD	*Tel.:* 01-353 6060
	85 Fleet Street	*Telex:* 24145
1505	London E.C.4	

World news agency

Enquiries: To Chief Librarian, by letter only

Scope: Library is based on the Reuters news report which is classified and filed daily

Publications: Background information about Reuters

LONDON	RICHARD III SOCIETY	*Tel.:* 01-733 5874
	84 Stockwell Park Road	
1506	London S.W.9	

Aims to discover as much as possible of Richard III and his period

Enquiries: To Secretary

Scope: Life and character of Richard III
Secondary: Social and political history of late 15th century England

Stock: 120 books; 410 pamphlets. Stock not normally available on loan

Publications: The Ricardian: journal of the Richard III Society (quarterly)
Ricardian Britain: a guide to places connected with Richard III
Catalogue of the Library of the Richard III Society
The College of King Richard III, Middleham. J. M. Melhuish

LONDON	ROAD TIME TRIALS COUNCIL	*Tel.:* 01-888 8691
	210 Devonshire Hill Lane	
1507	London N.17	

Controlling authority for cycling time trials in England and Wales

Enquiries: To Secretary at above address, or to Information Officer, 57 Fox Lane, London N.13 (*Tel.:* 01-882 0943)

Scope: Any information on the sport of cycling time trials
No library

Publications: Handbook (annually)
Timetrial (journal quarterly)

LONDON	RoSPA	*Tel.:* 01-730 2246
	Terminal House	
1508	52 Grosvenor Gardens	
	London S.W.1	

Enquiries: To Librarian

Scope: Safety and accident prevention in the home, on the road, in industry and agriculture

Stock: 1,400 books; 8,000 pamphlets; 340 current periodicals

Publications: Safety Education (termly)
Home Safety Journal (quarterly)
Occupational Safety Bulletin (monthly)
British Journal of Occupational Safety (quarterly)
Driver's Digest (monthly)
Agricultural Safety Bulletin (quarterly)
Safety News (monthly)
Road Accident Statistics (annually)

LONDON, RoSPA, *cont.*

  Road Accident Statistical Review (monthly)
  Driving Safely Bulletin (monthly)
  RoSPA is the National Centre for the International Occupational Safety and Health Information service covering world literature on all aspects of Occupational Safety and Health

LONDON

1509

ROSS INSTITUTE OF TROPICAL HYGIENE
London School of Hygiene and Tropical Medicine
Keppel Street
Gower Street
London W.C.1

See no. 1344

LONDON

1510

ROTARY INTERNATIONAL IN GREAT BRITAIN AND IRELAND   *Tel.:* 01-878 0931
Sheen Lane House
Sheen Lane
London S.W.14

Enquiries: To Secretary, preferably by letter

Scope: The voluntary work of Rotarians in the business and professional, community and international fields

LONDON

1511

ROYAL ACADEMY OF ARTS   *Tel.:* 01-734 9052
Burlington House
Piccadilly
London W1V 0DS

Founded in 1768, the Royal Academy is the oldest institution in Great Britain that is solely devoted to the fine arts. Its main activities are 'to promote the Arts of Design' including the maintenance of a School of Art and by holding Art Exhibitions

Enquiries: To Librarian, by letter only

Scope: Information about the Royal Academy and its history, members, exhibitors and exhibitions. The Library consists of books on the fine arts, many of them extremely rare, and collections of drawings and engravings available for scholarly research on material not easily obtainable elsewhere

Stock: 15,000 books and pamphlets; 5 current periodicals. Stock not available on loan

Publications: Catalogues and illustrated publications on exhibitions held at the Royal Academy

LONDON

1512

ROYAL ACADEMY OF DRAMATIC ART   *Tel.:* 01-636 7076
62/64 Gower Street
London W.C.1

Aims to advance the art of drama by means of instruction and promoting the study, practice and knowledge of dramatic literature and acting in all or any of its branches

Enquiries: To Registrar

Scope: Dramatic art and literature

LONDON

1513

ROYAL ACADEMY OF MUSIC   *Tel.:* 01-935 5680
Marylebone Road
London N.W.1

Enquiries: To Librarian

Scope: Music

Stock: 10,000 books and pamphlets; 40 current periodicals; 80,000 music scores; 550 gramophone records. Stock not normally available on loan

LONDON	THE ROYAL AFRICAN SOCIETY	*Tel.:* 01-930 6733
1514	18 Northumberland Avenue	
	London W.C.2	

Aims to develop public interest in African problems and conditions and to serve as a link between the peoples of the United Kingdom and Africa

Enquiries: To Secretary

Stock: Library is shared with that of the Royal Commonwealth Society

Publications: African Affairs (quarterly journal covering all aspects of African life and conditions)

LONDON	ROYAL AIR FORCE MUSEUM	
	R.A.F. Hendon	
1515	London N.W.9	

Enquiries: To Director

Scope: The history of the RAF, the RFC, the RNAS, and other flying services; the history of British aviation. Materials include books, plans, archives, films, photographs and recordings

Stock: Library—Archive stock: 100,000 items; 30 current periodicals. Stock not available on loan

Publications: Occasional Publications

LONDON	ROYAL ANTHROPOLOGICAL INSTITUTE OF	*Tel.:* 01-636 2980 and 9129
	GREAT BRITAIN AND IRELAND	
1516	21 Bedford Square	
	London W.C.1	

Promotion of the study of the science of man

Enquiries: To Secretary, by letter only

Scope: The library is one of the finest anthropological libraries in the world with comprehensive coverage. It does not, however, generally provide an information service, but non-members are permitted to use it for reference purposes
Library of Sir Richard Burton

Stock: 53,300 books and pamphlets; 550 current periodicals

Publications: Man, the journal of the Royal Anthropological Institute (quarterly)
Proceedings of the Royal Anthropological Institute (annually)
Anthropological index to current periodicals in the library of the Royal Anthropological Institute (quarterly index by regions and subjects)
Occasional papers

LONDON	ROYAL ARTILLERY REGIMENTAL MUSEUM	*Tel.:* 01-854 2424 ext. 384
	c/o R.A. Institution	
1517	Woolwich	
	London S.E.18	

Enquiries: To Historical Assistant Secretary, by letter only

Scope: Royal Artillery history

Stock: 20,000 books and pamphlets. Books not available on loan

LONDON	ROYAL ASIATIC SOCIETY OF GREAT BRITAIN AND IRELAND	*Tel.:* 01-935 8944
1518	56 Queen Anne Street London W1M 9LA	

Society for the investigation of subjects connected with and for the encouragement of science, literature, and the arts in relation to Asia

Enquiries: To Secretary

Stock: 100,000 books; many current periodicals; 1,000 manuscripts

Publications: Journal of the Royal Asiatic Society
Translations, monographs and other publications

LONDON	THE ROYAL ASSOCIATION IN AID OF THE DEAF AND DUMB	*Tel.:* 01-743 6187
1519	7 Armstrong Road Acton London W.3	

Enquiries: To Secretary

Scope: Spiritual and social welfare of the adult profoundly deaf, and the visually handicapped deaf in London and the Home Counties. Problems of the deaf in psychiatric hospitals

No library

LONDON	THE ROYAL AUTOMOBILE CLUB	*Tel.:* 01-930 4343
1520	83/85 Pall Mall London S.W.1	*Telex:* 23340

Aims to further the interests of motoring and motorists in the United Kingdom and the British Commonwealth

Enquiries: To Public Relations Officer

Scope: Information can be provided on matters apertaining to motoring, including the law, legislative and Parliamentary affairs, the roads system, road safety, driver and motor cycle rider training, insurance, the technical aspect, touring in Britain and overseas and motor sport

Reference library only

Publications: RAC Guide and Handbook
RAC Continental Handbooks and Guides to Europe (Western and Eastern editions)
RAC Guide to Touring in Ireland
RAC Camping and Caravanning Guide and Atlas of Europe
Sunday Times/RAC Road Atlas and Gazetteer of the British Isles
RAC Motor Sport Yearbook and Fixture List
RAC Maps, Guides, Publications and Touring Aids price list
Booklets

LONDON	THE ROYAL BALLET SCHOOL
1521	155 Talgarth Road London W.14

School for the teaching of classical, character and national dance, music and kindred arts essential for students of ballet. Part of the Royal Ballet Organization

Enquiries: To Librarian, by letter only

Scope: Fairly comprehensive selection of modern books on ballet in English, French and some Russian, published since 1910. Material from a private collection of original notebooks not available in any other organization. Able to call on the assistance of other specialists, including the main English choreographers and on a small collection of films belonging and exclusive to the Royal Ballet Organization. Enquiries on history and technique of ballet dealt with

Stock: 2,000 books; 2 current periodicals. Stock not available on loan

LONDON

1522

ROYAL BOROUGH OF KENSINGTON AND CHELSEA PUBLIC LIBRARIES
Phillimore Walk
London W.8

Tel.: 01-937 2542

Enquiries: To Librarian

Scope: All subject fields. The Metropolitan Special Collection on biography has a stock of over 40,000 volumes arranged alphabetically by biographee with analytical indexes, and 11,000 illustrations

Stock: 70,000 books (Central Reference Library general stock); 700 current periodicals; (total stock of these libraries is 407,000 volumes)

LONDON

1523

ROYAL CENTRAL ASIAN SOCIETY
42 Devonshire Street
London W1N 1LN

Tel.: 01-580 5728

Aims to promote greater knowledge and understanding of the whole of Asia, from the Mediterranean to Japan

Enquiries: To Secretary

Scope: Books on territories of Asia (including Transcaucasia and Asiatic Russia) as well as sections on religion, biography, language, and bibliography, related to the area
Secondary: Journals on Asia

Stock: 4,000 books; 45 current periodicals

Publications: Journal of the Royal Central Asian Society (3 issues each year)

LONDON

1524

THE ROYAL COLLEGE OF ART
Kensington Gore
London S.W.7

Tel.: 01-584 5020

Enquiries: To Librarian

Scope: History and criticism of the visual arts including painting, sculpture, textiles, jewellery, fashion, industrial design, typography, furniture, glass, ceramics, interior design and film. General subjects

Stock: 16,000 books; 100 current periodicals

LONDON

1525

THE ROYAL COLLEGE OF GENERAL PRACTITIONERS
14 Princes Gate
London S.W.7

Tel.: 01-584 6262

Enquiries: To Librarian

Scope: The library is primarily a reference library for members and associates of the Royal Colleges. It collects information and material on general practice and answers enquiries from members and associates, undertakes bibliographical searches, and checks references
Secondary: Papers written by members and associates, whether on general practice or not

Stock: 1,000 books; 500 pamphlets; 100 current periodicals. Stock not available on loan

Publications: Journal of the Royal College of General Practitioners

LONDON		THE ROYAL COLLEGE OF MIDWIVES	*Tel.:* 01-580 6523
1526		15 Mansfield Street London W1M 0BE	

Educational and professional organization for midwives, founded in 1881

Enquiries: To General Secretary

Scope: Information service on all aspects of the midwifery profession in the United Kingdom, and on obstetrics, paediatrics and social services
Secondary: Information on maternity services overseas

Library stock available to Members only

Publications: Midwives Chronicle (official journal)
Preparation for Parenthood
Report of a symposium on preparation for parenthood
The Midwife's Role in Public Health
Human Relationships in the Care of Mother and Baby
Episiotomy   Postnatal Exercises
Congenital Diseases of the Hip   Mechanisms of Labour

LONDON		ROYAL COLLEGE OF MUSIC	*Tel.:* 01-589 3643
1527		Prince Consort Road London S.W.7	

Enquiries: To Reference Librarian

Scope: Entirely concerned with music and includes collections of manuscripts, printed music, books, portraits, instruments and concert programmes

Stock not available on loan

LONDON		ROYAL COLLEGE OF NURSING AND NATIONAL COUNCIL OF NURSES OF THE UNITED KINGDOM	*Tel.:* 01-580 2646
1528		Henrietta Place Cavendish Square London W1M 0AB	

Aims to promote the advancement of nursing as a profession and to provide post-graduate courses for nurses

Enquiries: To Librarian

Scope: All branches of nursing, nursing history and nursing education
Secondary: Medicine and allied subjects; public health, sociology, psychology

Stock: 20,000 books, pamphlets and reports; 200 current periodicals; 400 lantern slides. Books only available on loan, but photocopies of periodical articles may be supplied

Publications: A Library Guide for Schools of Nursing

LONDON		ROYAL COLLEGE OF OBSTETRICIANS AND GYNAECOLOGISTS	*Tel.:* 01-262 5425
1529		27 Sussex Place Regent's Park London, N.W.1	

Enquiries: To Secretary

Scope: Obstetrics and gynaecology

Stock: 6,000 books; 2,000 pamphlets and reports; 80 current periodicals

Publications: Journal of Obstetrics and Gynaecology of the British Commonwealth
Special Reports
Short Title Catalogue of Books printed before 1851 in the Library. 2nd edition 1968

LONDON 1530 THE ROYAL COLLEGE OF ORGANISTS *Tel.:* 01-589 1765
Kensington Gore
London S.W.7

Enquiries: To Librarian
Scope: All aspects of the organ and organ music
Stock: 500 books and pamphlets; 5,000 items of music; 7 current periodicals

LONDON 1531 ROYAL COLLEGE OF PHYSICIANS OF LONDON *Tel.:* 01-935 1174
11 St Andrew's Place
Regent's Park
London N.W.1

Enquiries: To Librarian
Scope: Medical history and biography, particularly portraiture. Original material and primary sources available
Stock: 32,000 books; 11,000 pamphlets; 90 current periodicals; 6,000 engraved and other portraits of medical men; lantern slides
Publications: Catalogues of exhibitions mainly on the history of medicine and its specialities (duplicated typescript)
Catalogue of Engraved Portraits. A. H. Driver. 1952
Roll of the Royal College of Physicians of London (lives of Fellows), 1518–1965. 5 volumes, 1878–1968. W. Munk
The Gold-headed Cane. Facsimile of author's annotated copy, 1827. W. MacMichael. 1968
Royal College of Physicians, Portraits. G. Wolstenholme, ed. J. & A. Churchill, 1964

LONDON 1532 ROYAL COLLEGE OF SURGEONS OF ENGLAND *Tel.:* 01-405 3474
Lincoln's Inn Fields
London W.C.2

Promotion of surgery and the specialities of surgery, and the maintenance of the national Hunterian Museum (*see* no. 1533). Research carried on by Departments of Anaesthetics, Anatomy, Biochemistry, Dental Science, Ophthalmology, Pharmacology, Physiology, Surgical Sciences. The teaching facilities of the Departments of Anatomy, Biochemistry, Pathology, Pharmacology and Physiology comprise the Institute of Basic Medical Sciences of the University of London

Enquiries: To Librarian
Scope: Surgery and the surgical sciences, particularly anatomy, applied physiology, surgical pathology and the specialities of anaesthesia, dental, ophthalmic and orthopaedic surgery. Historical collections in all these fields, particularly in anatomy and surgery. The Library's holdings of current literature in biochemistry and pharmacology are less extensive than its holdings in the fields mentioned above
Secondary: General medicine
Stock: 130,000 books; 50,000 pamphlets; 650 current periodicals; 3,000 engraved portraits; 3,000 portfolios of college archives since 1754; 57 incunabula
Publications: Annals of the Royal College of Surgeons of England (monthly)
History of the College. Sir Zachary Cope. 1959
Catalogue of Portraits. 1960

LONDON, ROYAL COLLEGE OF SURGEONS OF ENGLAND, *cont.*
Catalogue of English Books printed before 1701 in the Library of R.C.S. 1963
Artistic Possessions of the College. 1967
Catalogue of the Hunterian Museum, pathological series, part 1, 1966 (other catalogues in preparation)
Lives of the Fellows of the Royal College of Surgeons, Vol. 4 (1952–65). In preparation

LONDON

1533

THE ROYAL COLLEGE OF SURGEONS OF ENGLAND *Tel.:* 01-405 3474
HUNTERIAN MUSEUM
Lincoln's Inn Fields
London W.C.2

Conservation and display of John Hunter's collection of specimens of human and comparative anatomy and physiology and pathology

Enquiries: To Curator

Scope: Information about John Hunter (1728–1793), his life and achievements, publications, research work. Information about the contents of the museum
Secondary: Surgery and surgeons of the eighteenth century

Publications: Guide to the Physiological Series of the Hunterian Museum
An Account of the Conservators of the Hunterian Museum
Catalogue of the Pathological Series of the Hunterian Museum. Part I (Part II is in course of preparation)
Catalogue of the Physiological Series (Parts I and II)—in course of preparation

LONDON

1534

ROYAL COLLEGE OF VETERINARY SURGEONS *Tel.:* 01-235 6568
WELLCOME LIBRARY
32 Belgrave Square
London S.W.1

The Royal College is the registration and disciplinary body of the veterinary profession

Enquiries: To Librarian

Scope: Veterinary science
Special collection: Early works on veterinary medicine, agriculture and medicine
Secondary: Animal nutrition, husbandry, comparative medicine. Henry Gray special collection on ornithology (mainly late 19th century and early 20th century)
Bibliographies compiled on request

Stock: 25,000 books (Historical collection 1,500); 12,000 pamphlets; 250 reports; 250 current periodicals. College archives. College theses. Continental theses

Publications: R.C.V.S. Registers and Directory (annually)
R.C.V.S. Annual Reports
R.C.V.S. Guide to Professional Conduct
R.C.V.S. Recommendations as to the Veterinary Curriculum
R.C.V.S. Veterinary Education
R.C.V.S. Animal Nursing Auxiliaries Scheme
R.C.V.S. Animal Nursing Auxiliaries—a Guide
R.C.V.S. Report on the Preparation of a System of Description of Colours and Markings of Horses
Published catalogues: Modern works 1900–1954. 1955 plus supplements; Historical Collection (printed works before 1850). 1953 plus supplement

LONDON	ROYAL COMMISSION ON HISTORICAL MONUMENTS (ENGLAND)	*Tel.:* 01-930 9652
1535	10 Great College Street Westminster London S.W.1	

Records, by survey, description and photography, those monuments dating from earliest times to 1850 surviving in England, with a view to producing published illustrated inventories and to building up a national photographic archive

Enquiries: To Secretary

Scope: Information about field monuments and buildings in England (dating from earliest times to A.D. 1850) in those areas surveyed in detail for purposes of the inventories. The National Monuments Record, administered by the Royal Commission on Historical Monuments (England), makes available to scrutiny as full a photographic record as possible of monuments throughout England, the Record Library being open to the public on six days a week

Stock: 750,000 photographs; 50,000 record cards. Prints from photographs may be purchased

Publications: Twenty-two illustrated inventories of monuments in different English counties and cities
Four occasional publications devoted to special subjects

LONDON	ROYAL DANISH EMBASSY	
1536	Press and Cultural Department 29 Pont Street London S.W.1	

Enquiries: To Press and Cultural Counsellor, by letter only

Scope: General information on Denmark, including medicine, the social sciences and the humanities
No library

Publications: Danish Journal (6 issues each year)

LONDON	ROYAL FREE HOSPITAL SCHOOL OF MEDICINE	*Tel.:* 01-837 5385
1537	8 Hunter Street London W.C.1	

Library service for academic staff, research workers, postgraduate students and medical students, within the medical school

Enquiries: To Librarian

Scope: Bookstock comprises material on biology, physics, chemistry, biochemistry, anatomy, physiology, pharmacology and clinical medicine. Periodicals cover biology, physics, chemistry, biochemistry and preclinical medicine

Stock: 20,000 books; 1,000 pamphlets; 190 current periodicals

LONDON	ROYAL GEOGRAPHICAL SOCIETY	*Tel.:* 01-589 5466
1538	Kensington Gore London S.W.7	

Advancement of geographical knowledge including assistance by advice, grants and instruments to expeditions and research

Enquiries: To Librarian (if on maps or cartography, to Keeper of the Map Room)

Scope: Geography, including exploration and travel, and related subjects. Cartography and surveying

LONDON, ROYAL GEOGRAPHICAL SOCIETY, *cont.*

Special collections:
Brown Collection on Morocco
Fielden Collection on Polar regions
Fordham Collection of Road-books
Collection of maps and atlases in the Map Room

Stock: 90,000 books; 25,000 pamphlets; 600 current periodicals

Publications: Geographical Journal (quarterly)
New Geographical Literature and Maps (twice each year)
R.G.S. Research Series (occasional)

LONDON

1539

ROYAL GREEK EMBASSY
PRESS AND INFORMATION OFFICE
49 Upper Brook Street
London W.1

Tel.: 01-499 1354

Enquiries: To Director, by letter only

Scope: Information on politics, science, literature, history, social sciences, humanities and statistics of Greece

Publications: News From Greece (weekly bulletin)
Sheets on several subjects concerning Greece (archaeology, geography, agriculture, history, tourism)

LONDON

1540

ROYAL INSTITUTE OF BRITISH
ARCHITECTS
66 Portland Place
London W1N 4AD

Tel.: 01-580 5533

Professional and examining body and learned society

Enquiries: To Librarian

Scope: Primary subject fields of library: World architecture past and present; architectural practice; theory and design; building types; building materials and methods
Secondary: Planning and environment; landscape; interior design; decorative arts

Stock: 80,000 books and reports; 7,000 pamphlets; 500 current periodicals; 250,000 architectural drawings from 16th century to present

Publications: Wide range of technical and management publications for the construction industry
RIBA Journal (monthly)   RIBA Book List (annually)
RIBA Library Bulletin (quarterly)   Catalogue of RIBA Drawings Collection
RIBA Annual Review of Periodical Articles

LONDON

1541

THE ROYAL INSTITUTE OF INTERNATIONAL
AFFAIRS
10 St James's Square
London S.W.1

Tel.: 01-930 2233

Aims to advance the scientific study of international politics, economics and jurisprudence

Enquiries: To Librarian or Press Librarian

Scope: Books, pamphlets, periodicals and documents in European languages including Russian on international affairs since 1918

Stock: 126,000 books and pamphlets; 645 current periodicals. Periodicals not available on loan, but photocopies supplied. Collections of cuttings on international affairs since 1924

Publications: International Affairs (quarterly)
Report on World Affairs (quarterly)
World Today (monthly)
British Yearbook of International Law (annually)
Survey of international affairs (annually)
Documents on international affairs (annually)
Monographs on aspects of international affairs

LONDON ROYAL INSTITUTE OF PUBLIC   *Tel.:* 01-636 2722
  ADMINISTRATION
1542 24 Park Crescent
  London W.1

To advance the study of public administration and promote the exchange of information and ideas on all aspects of the subject

Enquiries: To Librarian

Scope: British public administration: the administration of all branches of the public service, including central and local government, the nationalized industries and the National Health Service. Some comparative material

Stock: 4,500 books; 5,000 pamphlets; 6,000 reports; 50 current periodicals

Publications: Public Administration (quarterly journal)
British Public Administration: A Select Bibliography. 1963
Many books on general administration, central government, nationalized industries, local government and administrative methods

LONDON THE ROYAL INSTITUTION OF GREAT BRITAIN   *Tel.:* 01-493 0669 and 5716
  21 Albemarle Street
1543 London W.1

Promotion of science and the dissemination and extension of useful knowledge. Original scientific research is carried out at the Davy Faraday Research Laboratory, attached to the Institution

Enquiries: To Librarian

Scope: All branches of science, and particularly the physical sciences, scientific biography, popular science and the history of science
Secondary: The old library of books before 1857 covers all subjects, and more modern books on many non-scientific subjects are held

Stock: 60,000 books, pamphlets, manuscripts and archives; 300 current periodicals
Special collections: Manuscripts of Davy, Faraday, Tyndall, of other scientists who have worked at the Institution, and of their correspondents

Publications: Proceedings (three times each year)

LONDON ROYAL NATIONAL INSTITUTE FOR THE BLIND   *Tel.:* 01-387 5251 and 5571
  224/228 Great Portland Street
1544 London W.1

Enquiries: To Reference Librarian

Scope: Blind welfare
Secondary: Allied subjects, such as welfare of the handicapped

Stock: 600 books; 2,600 pamphlets; 650 reports; 100 current periodicals

LONDON, ROYAL NATIONAL INSTITUTE FOR THE BLIND, *cont.*

Publications: Catalogue of Apparatus and Games
Braille Music Catalogues (for sale and for loan)
Catalogue of Books for the Blind in Moon Type
Students Library Catalogue of Braille Books for Loan
Catalogue of Braille Books (for sale)
Catalogue of Talking Books for the Blind
Catalogue of the Reference Library
List of letterpress publications
Student Tape Library: Catalogue of Books Available

LONDON

1545

THE ROYAL NATIONAL INSTITUTE FOR THE DEAF
105 Gower Street
London W.C.1

Tel.: 01-387 8033

Protective association for deaf, deaf-blind and hard of hearing people in the United Kingdom

Enquiries: To Chief Librarian and Information Officer

Scope: The library covers speech and language disorders as well as hearing disorders, and their physical, psychological, clinical, educational and sociological aspects. Briefly it is concerned with human communication and communication disorders, of which deafness is one aspect. The Information Service is a comparatively new development, and its main concern has been compiling and recording information about speech and hearing facilities within the United Kingdom and Eire, including audiology units and clinics; schools for deaf and partially-hearing children with or without additional handicaps and units for partially-hearing children in ordinary schools; further education centres for people with hearing impairment; training centres for teachers of deaf children and training schools for speech therapists; clubs for deaf people and for those who are hard of hearing; and residential homes for deaf people and hostels for young deaf people. Some of this information has been prepared for distribution in the form of stencilled leaflets, and it is hoped gradually to extend the records to include similar facilities abroad

Stock: 6,500 books; 9,000 pamphlets, including photocopies of periodical articles for loan; 300 current periodicals

Publications: Hearing (monthly)
Sound (quarterly technical journal)
Clinical Aspects of Hearing
Conversation with the Deaf
Lipreading, a handbook of visible speech. J. H. Burchett
Many other leaflets on various topics

Hearing Aids
The Highway Code for Deaf Children
A list of current hearing aids
Special aids to hearing

LONDON

1546

ROYAL NATIONAL LIFE-BOAT INSTITUTION
42 Grosvenor Gardens
London S.W.1

Tel.: 01-730 0031

Provides a life-boat service around the coasts of Great Britain and Ireland

Enquiries: To Public Relations Officer

Scope: Books, records, photographs and films covering the Royal National Life-boat Institution from its foundation in 1824 up to the present day. The Institution acts as the central secretariat of the International Life-Boat Conference which meets in a different country every four years to discuss world life-boat problems

Publications: The Life-boat (quarterly)

LONDON	ROYAL NAVAL COLLEGE	*Tel.:* 01-858 2154
1547	Greenwich	
	London S.E.10	

Education (mostly scientific) of Naval Officers

Enquiries: To Secretary

Scope: Naval history
Secondary: International affairs

Stock: 4,000 books; 500 pamphlets; 100 current periodicals

LONDON	ROYAL NETHERLANDS EMBASSY	*Tel.:* 01-584 5040
1548	38 Hyde Park Gate	
	London S.W.7	

Enquiries: To Information Officer, by letter only

Scope: All aspects of the Netherlands. Enquiries which cannot be answered are passed to relevant sources in the Netherlands

No library

LONDON	THE ROYAL PHILHARMONIC SOCIETY	*Tel.:* 01-584 5751
1549	29 Exhibition Road	
	London S.W.7	

Enquiries: To Hon. Librarian

Scope: Chiefly confined to giving information about the history of the Society (founded in 1813) and the manuscripts and printed music in its possession. Most of the leading composers and executants, British and foreign, have been associated with the Society's activities and the Society possesses an extensive collection of letters from them. These letters as well as the most important of the Society's musical manuscripts may be consulted in the Department of Manuscripts at the British Museum, where they have been placed on permanent loan

Stock: *On loan to the British Museum:* 50 musical manuscripts mainly autograph. 6,000 autograph letters from composers, performers and conductors
On loan to the Royal Academy of Music: 700 musical scores, mainly printed

LONDON	ROYAL PHOTOGRAPHIC SOCIETY
1550	14 South Audley Street
	London W.1

Promotion of the general advancement of photographic science and its applications

Enquiries: To Librarian or Secretary

Scope: Library covers all aspects of photography, but has a particularly good collection of older works of historical interest. Books consisting entirely of photographs are not included unless the work of leading photographers. Du Mont collection of books illustrated by early photographs. Permanent collection of prints and equipment mainly historical

Stock: 6,800 books; 150 current periodicals

Publications: The Photographic Journal (monthly)
The Journal of Photographic Science (bi-monthly)
Photographic Abstracts (6 times each year)
Library Catalogues:
Subject Catalogue, to 1949; Supplement 1950–52
Author Catalogue, to 1939; Supplement 1939–49; Supplement 1950–52
Periodicals Catalogue, to 1956

LONDON, ROYAL PHOTOGRAPHIC SOCIETY, *cont.*
Pictorial Group Publications:
Tyng Portfolio (six large reproductions from the Society's Permanent Collection). 1931
Alex. Keighley Memorial Book. 1947
Pictorial Photography of J. Dudley Johnston. 1952
Illustrated Monographs of Work by Distinguished Photographers: Bertram Cox, George Halford, J. Ortiz Echagüe, Will Till, M. O. Dell, H. A. Murch, S. D. Jouhar, W. Marynowicz and Leo Herbert Felton
Monograph 1965—Selection from the Stephen Tyng Collection

LONDON

1551

ROYAL POSTGRADUATE MEDICAL SCHOOL *Tel.:* 01-743 2030 ext. 97
(UNIVERSITY OF LONDON)
WELLCOME LIBRARY
Hammersmith Hospital
Ducane Road
London W.12

Postgraduate medical education and research

Enquiries: To Librarian

Scope: Medicine, including biochemistry, physiology, clinical medicine, biophysics, bio-engineering and pathology

Stock: 1,000 books; 550 current periodicals. Periodicals not available on loan, but photocopies supplied if item not available elsewhere

Publications: Library Bulletin (weekly, listing contents of periodicals received)

LONDON

1552

ROYAL SOCIETY FOR THE PREVENTION OF *Tel.:* 01-930 0971
CRUELTY TO ANIMALS
105 Jermyn Street
London S.W.1

The promotion of kindness to animals

Enquiries: To Secretary

Scope: Information on the activities of the Society from its foundation in 1824

Publications: List of publications
Leaflets and pamphlets on care of domestic animals, and leaflets giving R.S.P.C.A. views on controversial topics related to animal welfare

LONDON

1553

ROYAL SOCIETY OF ARTS *Tel.:* 01-839 2366
6/8 John Adam Street
London W.C.2

Encouragement of arts, commerce and manufactures, and the application of art and science in industry

Enquiries: To Curator-Librarian

Scope: Publications relating to the history of the Society, including fine arts, applied arts, history of science, history of agriculture and history of design

Stock: 6,000 books; 106 current periodicals; 10,000 manuscripts
Special collections: Industrial design. Catalogues of major international exhibitions
Stock available on loan through N.C.L.

Publications: Journal (monthly)
Published catalogues, 1790, 1828 and 1953

LONDON	ROYAL SOCIETY OF BRITISH SCULPTORS	Tel.: 01-235 1467
1554	8 Chesham Place London S.W.1	

Aims to promote the interest of sculpture and sculptors in the United Kingdom

Enquiries: To Secretary

Scope: Sculpture

Publications: Rules for Guidance for Open Air Exhibitions
Contract Forms   Paper on Heavyweight
Rules for Competitions   Business Guidance for Sculptors
Copyright Digest   Certificate of Authenticity

LONDON	ROYAL SOCIETY OF MEDICINE	Tel.: 01-580 2070
1555	1 Wimpole Street London W1M 8AE	

Advancement of medicine in all its aspects

Enquiries: To Librarian

Scope: Lists of references, or selections of books and journals, made in response to specific requests from readers. Abstracts and summaries traced, and where necessary, translated. Both within any field in the broad scope of medicine. Books and journals lent freely throughout United Kingdom to members. Photocopy service for overseas members

Stock: 400,000 books; 30,000 pamphlets; 2,300 current periodicals

Publications: Proceedings of the Royal Society of Medicine (monthly)
Special symposia

Persons not members of the Society may be admitted for a limited period, on introduction by a Fellow, to consult material in the library not readily available in public collections
S.E. Region Medlars Liaison Officer is based on the Library and is available to all enquirers

LONDON	THE ROYAL SOCIETY OF MUSICIANS OF GREAT BRITAIN	Tel.: 01-629 6137
1556	10 Stratford Place London W.1	

The oldest charity for the relief of aged and infirm musicians and widows and children of musicians

Enquiries: To Secretary

Scope: Early Members of the Society (from 1738)
The Society's manuscripts
The Society's portraits, pictures and other treasures

LONDON	ROYAL SOCIETY OF PAINTER-ETCHERS AND ENGRAVERS	Tel.: 01-493 5436
1557	26 Conduit Street London W.1	

Enquiries: To Secretary

Scope: An Exhibiting Society devoted to the art of engraving in all its forms and willing to answer enquiries

LONDON	ROYAL SOCIETY OF PAINTERS IN WATER COLOURS	*Tel.:* 01-629 8300
1558	26 Conduit Street London W.1	

Enquiries: To Secretary

Scope: Professional Exhibiting Society, willing to answer enquiries on water colours

LONDON	ROYAL SWEDISH EMBASSY	
	23 North Row	
1559	London W.1	

Enquiries: To the Embassy

Scope: All aspects of Sweden

No library

Publications: Leaflets, pamphlets and booklets on Sweden

LONDON	ROYAL UNITED SERVICE INSTITUTION	*Tel.:* 01-930 5854
	Whitehall	
1560	London S.W.1	

The intensive study of military science, ranging from military history to modern defence studies

Enquiries: To Librarian, preferably by letter

Scope: History of the British armed services (particularly strong in 19th century material)
Special collections on India during the period of British rule. Modern military strategy and defence studies; Regimental histories
Secondary: Current international affairs; management; military fiction

Stock: 100,000 books; 25,000 pamphlets; 250 current periodicals; Long runs of the Army, Navy and Air Force Lists and the London Gazette from 1689

Publications: List of periodical holdings
Royal United Service Institution Journal (quarterly)
Seminar Reports and Defence Studies (irregularly)

LONDON	THE ROYAL VETERINARY COLLEGE (UNIVERSITY OF LONDON)	*Tel.:* 01-387 2898
1561	Royal College Street London N.W.1	

Teaching and research in veterinary science

Enquiries: To Librarian

Scope: Veterinary science

Stock: 22,000 books (including bound volumes of periodicals); 390 current periodicals

LONDON	RUGBY FIVES ASSOCIATION	*Tel.:* 01-584 1256
	7 Ennismore Mews	
1562	London S.W.7	

Enquiries: To Secretary, by letter only

Scope: Rugby Fives

Publications: Rules of the Game and Yearly Handbook

LONDON	ST BARTHOLOMEW'S HOSPITAL MEDICAL COLLEGE	*Tel.:* 01-606 7777 ext. 315
1563	West Smithfield London E.C.1	

Enquiries: To Librarian

Scope: The field of medicine, and pre-medical subjects studied for 2nd MB
Special collection devoted to the history of the Hospital and to writings by Barts' Men
Basic historical collection, with texts on history and biography of medicine
The Hospital possesses extensive archives, with an archivist as custodian

Stock: 32,000 books; 5,000 pamphlets; 245 current periodicals

The Main Library is in the Hospital but the Charterhouse Branch Library, devoted to pre-clinical subjects, is in Charterhouse Square, London E.C.1

LONDON	ST DUNSTAN'S	*Tel.:* 01-723 5021
1564	191 Old Marylebone Road (P.O. Box 58) London N.W.1	

Rehabilitation, settlement and life-long after-care of men and women blinded on war service

Enquiries: To Public Relations Officer

No library

Publications: Proceedings of the International Conference on Sensory Devices for the Blind. 1966
Special Aids for the War Blinded. 1969

LONDON	ST GEORGE'S HOSPITAL MEDICAL SCHOOL	*Tel.:* 01-235 4343
1565	Hyde Park Corner London S.W.1	

Provides a Library and Information Service in clinical medicine and supporting subjects to Medical Students, academic, research and hospital clinical staff

Enquiries: To Librarian

Scope: Clinical medicine
Secondary: Material on 'St George's Men' including John Hunter and Edward Jenner. Manuscript collection of Sir Benjamin Brodie

Stock: 12,000 books and bound volumes of periodicals; 220 current periodicals

Publications: St George's Hospital Gazette (3 times each year)

LONDON	ST MARTIN'S SCHOOL OF ART	*Tel.:* 01-437 0058
1566	109 Charing Cross Road London W.C.2	

Enquiries: To Librarian

Scope: Painting, sculpture, graphic design. Dress design and textiles. History of art, photography
Secondary: Social history, philosophy, psychology, music, theatre, cinema, biography, travel

Stock: 10,000 books; 500 pamphlets (including exhibition catalogues); 120 current periodicals. Large collection of classified photographs on all subjects

LONDON	ST MARY'S HOSPITAL MEDICAL SCHOOL	*Tel.:* 01-723 1252
1567	Paddington London, W.2	

Enquiries: To Librarian

LONDON, ST MARY'S HOSPITAL MEDICAL SCHOOL, *cont.*

Scope: Medical subjects. Collection of writings by the staff of the Medical School

Stock: 7,000 books; 300 pamphlets; 265 current periodicals

LONDON

1568

SAINT PAUL'S CATHEDRAL LIBRARY
London E.C.4

Typical 17th century cathedral library for learning and scholarship

Enquiries: To Librarian, by letter only

Scope: Theology; The Fathers; Canon Law

Stock: 13,500 books; 80,000 pamphlets. Stock not available on loan

---

LONDON

1569

ST THOMAS'S HOSPITAL MEDICAL SCHOOL *Tel.:* 01-928 9292 ext. 2367
London S.E.1

Enquiries: To Librarian

Scope: Medicine and surgery

Stock: 19,310 books (including periodicals); 107 current periodicals (Main Library) plus 232 in forty departmental libraries

Publications: St Thomas's Hospital Gazette

LONDON

1570

THE SALVATION ARMY *Tel.:* 01-236 5222
101 Queen Victoria Street
London E.C.4

An international, multi-racial community which combines a fervent, joyous religious faith with a practical, efficient and world-wide social service

Enquiries: To Salvation Army Information Services

Scope: Through literature, booklets, pamphlets, and films, information is provided about Salvation Army evangelism, social service, teaching and medical missionary work. Social service in Britain includes: Care of unmarried mothers and babies, children's homes, approved schools and homes, probation homes and hostels, guidance to neglectful mothers and their families, hostels for homeless men and women, eventide homes for the elderly, alcoholics homes and clinics, missing persons bureaux

Stock: A comparatively small reference library of Salvation Army history books is available to student visitors

See also no. 1571

LONDON

1571

THE SALVATION ARMY *Tel.:* 01-733 1191
INTERNATIONAL TRAINING COLLEGE
Denmark Hill
London S.E.5

Training of Salvation Army Officers

Enquiries: To Education Officer

Scope: Salvation Army history, doctrine, practice, biographies and organization. Theology, Bible studies, history of Christianity

Stock: 7,000 books; 25 current periodicals

See also no. 1570

LONDON	SANDOZ PRODUCTS LTD	*Tel.:* 01-629 5011
1572	23 Great Castle Street London W1N 8AE	

Manufacturers of ethical pharmaceuticals

Enquiries: To Librarian

Scope: Textbooks and journals relating to the practice of medicine and pharmacy, particularly with relationship to the Company's product fields
Secondary: Index system of references to the Company's and competitors' products in the treatment of disease, including side-effects

Stock: 500 books; 70 current periodicals. Periodicals only available on loan

Publications: Triangle   Sandoz News Bulletin
Sandorama   Bibliographia
Index Clinicus   Reviews
Monographs on specific medical subjects and various booklets

LONDON	SAUDI ARABIAN EMBASSY	*Tel.:* 01-235 8431
1573	27 Eaton Place London S.W.1	

Enquiries: To Information Officer, by letter only

Scope: General information on Saudi Arabia

No library

LONDON	THE SAVE THE CHILDREN FUND	*Tel.:* 01-930 2461
1574	29 Queen Anne's Gate London S.W.1	

An independent voluntary organization, professionally staffed, now 50 years old, whose purpose is the welfare of needy children, irrespective of nationality or religion

Enquiries: To Public Relations Officer, by letter only

Scope: All aspects of child care, including nutrition, medical and health education; vocational training; pre-school playgroups; and junior clubs and residential homes
Secondary: Guidance for those wishing to work in the field overseas

No library

Publications: Suggestions for Play Activities for Young Children (details of how to organize a playgroup). D. E. May
The World's Children (quarterly magazine of the Fund, includes articles on child care both in the United Kingdom and overseas)

LONDON	THE SCHOOL BROADCASTING COUNCIL FOR THE UNITED KINGDOM	*Tel.:* 01-935 2801
1575	The Langham Portland Place London W1A 1AA	

Set up by the BBC to guide it in the provision of broadcast programmes to schools in radio and television

Enquiries: To Secretary

Scope: BBC School Broadcasting Services in Radio and Television: Information about programmes and publications and about the use of broadcasts in schools

LONDON, THE SCHOOL BROADCASTING COUNCIL FOR THE UNITED KINGDOM, *cont.*

Publications: BBC radio and television broadcasts to schools. Selective Bibliography of Titles:
1. Radio and television broadcasts to schools, in particular the BBC School Broadcasting Service
2. General Broadcasting. (This contains information about BBC and School Broadcasting Council publications on the BBC's services to schools as well as titles likely to be of interest to students of education and broadcasting)

A Background Note on BBC School Broadcasting

Occasional Bulletins on the response of schools to school broadcast series

BBC School Broadcasts Catalogue of recordings available for loan (see below)

The Council operates a Loan Scheme to provide lecturers in colleges, departments and institutes of education, and others concerned with the in-service training of teachers, with material to enable them to study with teachers-in-training and with practising teachers the classroom use of BBC school radio and television broadcasts. The material includes tape-recordings of radio broadcasts, 16 mm film of television programmes and in some cases tape-recordings of children's work, where appropriate illustrated on filmstrip. The recordings can be used solely for the purpose of studying school broadcasting with teachers-in-training, and for in-service training of practising teachers

LONDON

1576

THE SCHOOL OF MEDITATION *Tel.:* 01-493 6296
45 South Molton Street
London W.1

Aims to pass on the technique of meditation to all those who want it, meditation being a means of self-realization, bringing about full development of man's latent faculties

Enquiries: Direct to office above

Scope: The School finds its fulfilment in teaching the simple technique of meditation. This invariably produces fundamental questions and the school passes on guidance given by the tradition from which meditation comes. Those who are not members of the School are, however, free to contact the School and put their questions. The answers they get, of course, depend entirely upon who is asking what, and why. Types of question asked usually relate to meditation and man's inner and outer nature; self knowledge and the insight it brings; the unified nature of mankind as a whole; purpose of life, meaning to creation; source of energy, life within; happiness, confidence, peace

No library

LONDON

1577

SCHOOLS COUNCIL FOR CURRICULUM AND *Tel.:* 01-580 0352
EXAMINATIONS
160 Great Portland Street
London W1N 6LL

An independent body representing all sections of the education service, with practising teachers making up an overall majority of its membership. Set up in 1964 to review and to undertake research and development in curricula, teaching methods and examinations in primary and secondary schools, including aspects of school organization so far as they affect the curriculum

Enquiries: To Senior Information Officer, by letter only

Scope: Information on national curriculum development projects sponsored by the Schools Council can be obtained for enquirers. Information on aspects of examinations (CSE and GCE)

Stock: Small reference library including 42 current periodicals, but no regular loan service

Publications: Examinations Bulletins 1–18 (HMSO); 19 (Evans/Methuen Educational)

Curriculum Bulletins 1 and 2 (HMSO)
Working Papers 1 (Schools Council); 2–23 (HMSO); 24 (Evans/Methuen Educational)
Field Reports 1–6 (Schools Council)
The new curriculum (A selection from Schools Council publications 1964–7). 1967 (HMSO)
Humanities for the Young School Leaver:
   An Approach through Classics. 1967 (HMSO)
   An Approach through English. 1968 (HMSO)
   An Approach through History. 1969 (Evans/Methuen Educational)
   An Approach through Religious Education. 1969 (Evans/Methuen Educational)
Curriculum innovation in practice: Canada, England and Wales, United States. (A report of the Third International Curriculum Conference.) 1968 (HMSO)
Enquiry 1. Young School Leavers. 1968 (HMSO)
Change for a Pound. A teaching guide for the introduction of decimal currency and the adoption of metric measures. 1968 (HMSO)
The First Three Years: 1964/7. 1968 (HMSO)
School Council Report 1968/69. 1969 (Evans/Methuen Educational)

A full list of all publications is available from the Publications Section, Schools Council. (Please note that from 1969 new publications in the above series have been published for Schools Council by Evans/Methuen Educational)

LONDON

1578

SCIENCE MUSEUM LIBRARY
South Kensington
London S.W.7

Tel.: 01-589 6371
Telex: 21200

National library of pure and applied science

Enquiries: To Keeper

Scope: Whole field of science and technology (excluding clinical medicine, nursing and veterinary science), photography, biography, the history of science and technology, and certain specialist aspects of geography
Secondary: Lists of references and bibliographies on sufficiently specific subjects can be supplied on request

Stock: 90,000 books; British, United States and other atomic energy reports; NACA and NASA reports; 5,000 current periodicals (14,000 closed sets)

Publications: Science Library Bibliographical Series
List of accessions to the Science Museum Library (monthly)
Hand List of Short Titles of Current Periodicals in the Science Museum Library: 9th edition 1965
Books on Engineering: a subject catalogue of books in the Science Library, published 1930 and onwards 1957
Science Library Bibliographical Series No. 745: a list of books on engineering subjects received in the Science Library from July 1st 1955 to September 30th 1956. 1957
Books on the Chemical and Allied Industries: a subject catalogue of books in the Science Library published 1930 and onwards. 1961
Science Library Bibliographical Series No. 781: a list of books on the Chemical and Allied Industries received in the Science Library in 1960. 1961

The Library is particularly rich in the literature of the history of science and technology including its relationships with the humanities and social sciences, and is maintaining special indexes to published and unpublished work in this field, including an index to portraits of scientists and engineers

LONDON	THE SCOUT ASSOCIATION	*Tel.:* 01-834 6005
	25 Buckingham Palace Road	
1579	London S.W.1	

Enquiries: To Secretary

Scope: Full information service on all aspects of the Scout Movement, and in particular The Scout Association (formerly The Boy Scouts Association). Information sheets, pamphlets and sources of reference given on a wide range of topics including: history, development and training programme of Scout Movement
Secondary: Photographic reference library and Scout Film Library

Publications: Handbooks and training manuals dealing with Scout training, policy and organization
The Scouter (monthly)

LONDON	SEAFARERS EDUCATION SERVICE	*Tel.:* 01-673 8866
	207 Balham High Road	
1580	London S.W.17	

Supplies libraries to the British Merchant Navy and general educational facilities to British merchant seafarers

Enquiries: To Secretary

Scope: Willing to answer questions from anybody about entry into the Merchant Navy; to lend to other libraries books on Merchant Navy history and organization; to answer any educational question from a merchant seaman; and to supply such seamen with any book on loan

Stock: Books on the Merchant Navy: 5,000
Books for loan to merchant seamen: 200,000

Publications: Annual annotated list of new books about the Merchant Navy and impinging on a seafarer's professional training

LONDON	SELDEN SOCIETY	*Tel.:* 01-980 4811 ext. 584
	Faculty of Laws	
1581	Queen Mary College	
	Mile End Road	
	London E.1	

Promotes research into and publication of translations of original source materials on the history of English Law and institutions

Enquiries: To Secretary

Scope: Enquiries concerned with the contents of the Society's publications and related matters in the field of English Legal History; and with reference to manuscripts and materials of legal interest
No library

Publications: *Main Series:* Annual Volumes (86 up to 1969, Court Rolls, Reports, Treatises)
Supplementary Series: Occasional Volumes (Letters, Treatises, Bibliographies)
General Guide to Publications. 1960
List of Publications (booklet)

LONDON	THE SHAW SOCIETY	*Tel.:* 01-340 8331
	3 Chestnut Court	
1582	Middle Lane	
	London N.8	

Enquiries: To Hon. Secretary

Scope: George Bernard Shaw
Publications: The Shavian (3 issues each year)

LONDON
1583
THE SHERLOCK HOLMES SOCIETY OF LONDON *Tel.:* 01-589 6688
39 Clabon Mews
London S.W.1
Enquiries: To Hon. Secretary
Scope: Sherlock Holmes
No library
Publications: Sherlock Holmes Journal (bi-annually)

LONDON
1584
SIDNEY WEBB COLLEGE OF EDUCATION *Tel.:* 01-486 4771
9/12 Barrett Street
London W1M 6DE
Enquiries: To Librarian
Scope: To meet the needs of mature students and of the teaching staff concerned with the training of primary school teachers and secondary school home economics teachers
Stock: 28,600 books and pamphlets; 150 current periodicals

LONDON
1585
SION COLLEGE *Tel.:* 01-353 7983
Victoria Embankment
London E.C.4
Society of Anglican clergymen. Library open to other clergy and lay men and women
Enquiries: To Librarian
Scope: Library stock: Current—Theology, church history (particularly Anglican) and allied subjects; Past—As above, plus the humanities in general
Special collections: The Port Royal Library (collection of about 400 volumes relating to, or by, members of the Abbey of Port Royal, originally collected by Mrs Schimmel Penninck), with separate printed catalogue, Aberdeen University Press, 1898; Bishop Edmund Gibson's pamphlet collection, nearly 4,000 pamphlets (late 17th and early 18th century general); Rev. J. Russell's pamphlet collection, about 4,000 pamphlets (early 19th with a few late 18th century general); Rev. W. Scott's pamphlet collection, approximately 6,000 pamphlets (mid-19th century—theological and historical); Dr William Goode's pamphlet collection, 1,670 pamphlets (17th and 18th century and 19th century up to 1860)
Information Service is related to library stock
Stock: 100,000 books and pamphlets; 45 current periodicals

LONDON
1586
SIR JOHN CASS COLLEGE LIBRARY *Tel.:* 01-481 8321
Jewry Street
London E.C.3
Enquiries: To Librarian
Scope: Mathematics; physics; chemistry; botany; zoology; navigation; geology; geography and metallurgy at undergraduate and post-graduate levels. Heads of Departments are willing to assist enquirers
Stock: 11,000 books; 1,500 pamphlets; 660 current periodicals
Special collection: London Collection
Branch Library at Central House, Whitechapel High Street, London E.1, serving the Departments of Mathematics, Metallurgy and the School of Art and Crafts

LONDON, SIR JOHN CASS COLLEGE LIBRARY, *cont.*

Branch Library at Nautical College, Tower Hill, London E.C.3, serving Nautical College and The Merchant Navy College

LONDON

1587

SIR JOHN SOANE'S MUSEUM   *Tel.:* 01-405 2107
13 Lincoln's Inn Fields
London W.C.2
Public museum

Enquiries: To Curator

Scope: The library is exclusively the library of Sir John Soane, nothing having been added since his death in January 1837. It is divided into two parts: General library, containing books of reference and general literature; Art and architecture

Stock: 7,780 books; 680 pamphlets; 30,000 architectural drawings. Owing to its special character the Soane Library is not suitable for general use but facilities are always given to research students on prior application

Publications: A New Description of Sir John Soane's Museum. 2nd edition. 1966

LONDON

1588

SKI CLUB OF GREAT BRITAIN   *Tel.:* 01-235 4711
118 Eaton Square
London S.W.1

Enquiries: To Secretary

Scope: All aspects of the sport of ski-ing. Prestige clubhouse with restaurant and bar. Winter Sports Offices above. Lending and reference library and a map library and film library open to members

Stock: 800 books in lending library and more in the reference library; all ski periodicals and some on alps and travel generally. Brochures from travel agents and tourist offices. Film Library—27 films on winter sports. Stock available on loan to members only

Publications: Ski Notes and Queries (club magazine. 3 issues each year)
British Ski Year Book

Representatives in the Alps as official guests of 35 top resorts (Ski Leaders)

Regional representatives in Birmingham, East Midlands, Dorset and Hampshire, Gloucestershire and Somerset, North East, North West, Sussex, Yorkshire, North Wales, South Wales areas

LONDON

1589

SOCIAL SCIENCE RESEARCH COUNCIL   *Tel.:* 01-405 6491
State House
High Holborn
London W.C.1

Scope: Social science research—support, training and policy. The Library forms a small part of the Science Research Council's Library (vol 1, no. 1760)

Publications: SSRC Newsletter (three times each year)
Postgraduate Training in the Social Sciences (annually)
Research Reviews (published by Heinemann Educational Books Limited) on Automation, Comparability in Social Research, International Organization, Political Science, Population Census, Poverty, and Social Anthropology
Forecasting and the Social Sciences (published by Heinemann Educational Books Limited)
Annual Report (includes Research supported by the SSRC, published by HMSO)

LONDON	SOCIALIST EDUCATIONAL ASSOCIATION	*Tel.:* 01-828 0951
1590	26 Bessborough Gardens London S.W.1	

Aims to promote a socialist educational system in Britain

Enquiries: To Secretary, by letter only

Scope: Membership is of Labour Party members particularly interested in or qualified in a wide variety of educational spheres. Enquiries dealt with by the General Secretary himself or in collaboration with a member who has personal knowledge of a specialized field of education

No library

Publications: Guide to Comprehensive Education
The Public Schools
Examining at 16 +, a Threat to Comprehensive Education
Socialism and Education (journal of the Association, three times each year)

LONDON	SOCIETY FOR CULTURAL RELATIONS WITH U.S.S.R.	*Tel.:* 01-274 2282
1591	320 Brixton Road London S.W.9	

Aims to inform the U.S.S.R. about scientific and literary matters in Britain and Britain about the U.S.S.R.

Enquiries: To Information Officer and Librarian

Scope: Science, technology, Russian and Soviet history, the arts (graphic, plastic, sculpture), architecture and housing, education, theatre and cinema, Russian and Soviet literature, social sciences, geography. Film strips, photographs

Stock: Including 160 current Soviet periodicals (in Russian and English); filmstrips; photographs

Publications: Anglo-Soviet Journal (quarterly)

LONDON	SOCIETY FOR PROMOTING CHRISTIAN KNOWLEDGE	*Tel.:* 01-387 5282
1592	Holy Trinity Church Marylebone Road London N.W.1	

Enquiries: To Public Relations Officer and Librarian

Scope: Information service is provided from the Society's own comprehensive archives dating from 1698; from file-room collection of the Society's publications (19th century to date); from small reference library; and from specialized staff experience. Annual Reports from early 18th century contain much valuable source material. Archives notable also for richness in special subject areas, for example, South India 1710–1825, the Salzburger emigration and settlement of Georgia, the Scilly Islands, early libraries and charity schools

Publications: Theology (monthly)   S.P.C.K. Classified Book Catalogue
View Review (quarterly)   Various special catalogues
The Church Quarterly

See also no. 911. The Society provides headquarters and Secretary for the Associates of the late Dr Bray, the principal founder of the Society

LONDON		THE SOCIETY FOR RESEARCH INTO HIGHER EDUCATION LTD	*Tel.*: 01-636 7322
1593		20 Gower Street
London W.C.1	

Society to encourage and co-ordinate research into all forms of higher education, to seek to make research findings more generally available and to promote their more effective use

Enquiries: To Organizing Secretary

Scope: Information Service and Library Service concerned with all aspects of research into higher education

Stock: Several hundred books, pamphlets, reports and periodicals

Publications: Quarterly Research into Higher Education Abstracts
Biennial Register of Research into Higher Education, with half-yearly supplements
Research into Higher Education Monographs
Occasional Publications on Research into Higher Education
News Bulletin (monthly)

LONDON		SOCIETY FOR THE PROTECTION OF UNBORN CHILDREN	*Tel.*: 01-235 5268
1594		47 Eaton Place
London S.W.1	

Enquiries: To Secretary

Scope: Abortion Law reform in Britain and its consequences
No library

Publications: Bulletin (two or three times each year)

LONDON		SOCIETY FOR THE STUDY OF ADDICTION TO ALCOHOL AND OTHER DRUGS	*Tel.*: 01-672 6655
1595		Tooting Bec Hospital
London S.W.17	

Enquiries: To Secretary

Scope: Alcoholism and drug dependence and their history

Stock: 400 books. Library is housed in the Wellcome Library (no. 1678)

Publications: British Journal of Addiction

LONDON		THE SOCIETY FOR THEATRE RESEARCH
103 Ralph Court	*Tel.*: 01-229 5150
1596		Queensway
London W.2	

Enquiries: To Librarian or Secretary

Scope: British theatre history

Stock: 3,000 books; 50 current periodicals

Publications: Annual Publications
Occasional pamphlets
Theatre Notebook (quarterly periodical)

LONDON		SOCIETY OF ANALYTICAL PSYCHOLOGY LTD
30 Devonshire Place	*Tel.*: 01-486 2321
1597		London W.1	

Enquiries: To Hon. Secretary, by letter only

Scope: Analytical psychology; the psychology of C. G. Jung
Secondary: Psychiatry, psychoanalysis, child psychology, comparative religion
Publications: Journal of Analytical Psychology

LONDON

1598

SOCIETY OF ANTIQUARIES OF LONDON
Burlington House
Piccadilly
London W1V 0HS

Tel.: 01-734 0193,
01-437 9954

Society for the study of history and archaeology and allied subjects

Enquiries: To Librarian

Scope: British and foreign archaeology and history, heraldry, genealogy and numismatics
Special collections: Manuscripts, broadsides and proclamations; prints and drawings; early printed books; brass rubbings; seal casts; transactions of British and foreign archaeological societies; photographs and slides. Extensive card catalogues to all collections

Stock: 130,000 books; 15,000 pamphlets; 550 current periodicals

Publications: Archaeologia
Antiquaries Journal
Research Reports (on various excavations)
(List of Publications, including offprints available from *Archaeologia* and *Antiquaries Journal*, obtainable free from the Society)

There is an extensive collection of works by and about William Morris and his influence in the library of Kelmscott Manor, Lechlade, Gloucestershire, owned by the Society of Antiquaries (access only by prior arrangement)

LONDON

1599

THE SOCIETY OF ARCHER-ANTIQUARIES
14 Grove Road
Barnes
London S.W.13

Tel.: 01-878 0573

Promotes the study of the history of archery in all its aspects

Enquiries: To Hon. Secretary

Scope: The Society's information service covers all aspects of archery, both ancient and modern. Specialized enquiries are placed with specialists whenever possible

No library

Publications: Annual Journal
Occasional Newsletter (for members only)

LONDON

1600

SOCIETY OF AUTHORS
84 Drayton Gardens
London S.W.10

Tel.: 01-373 6642

The Society was founded in 1884 by Sir Walter Besant with the object of representing, assisting and protecting authors. Since then its scope has been continuously extended until today within the framework of the Society separate associations have been created for playwrights, translators and writers for radio. There is also a Children's Writers Group and an Educational Writers Group

Enquiries: To Secretary

Scope: The Society exists primarily to assist and advise its own members. It is, however, prepared to answer any serious request for information on matters connected with the profession of authorship

LONDON, SOCIETY OF AUTHORS, *cont.*

No library

Publications: The Author (quarterly)
Quick Guides (series of pamphlets on Copyright, Protection of Titles, Photocopying, Income Tax, Libel, Copyrights after Death)
Bulletins (series of pamphlets on Teachers as Authors, Translators as Authors, Public Lending Right)
The Book Writers—Who are They? Richard Findlater
Your Pocket Brief to PLR

LONDON

1601

SOCIETY OF CARDIOLOGICAL TECHNICIANS LIMITED
80 Bishopsgate
London E.C.2

Enquiries: To Secretary, Cardiac Unit, Brook General Hospital, London S.E.18, by letter only
Scope: Anatomy and physiology; cardiology; physics and chemistry; electrocardiography
Stock: 100 books; 2 current periodicals. Stock not normally available on loan
Publications: Pacemaker (quarterly journal)

LONDON

1602

THE SOCIETY OF CHIROPODISTS *Tel.:* 01-570 3227
8 Wimpole Street
London W1M 8BX

Enquiries: To Secretary
Scope: Chiropody; foot health; chiropody as a career. Library of chiropodial literature
Stock: 500 books, including Seelig collection of historical books
Publications: The Chiropodist (monthly)
Directory of Members, last edition 1968
The Profession of Chiropody
Sundry foot health leaflets
Lending library (members only) catalogue

LONDON

1603

THE SOCIETY OF FILM AND TELEVISION ARTS, *Tel.:* 01-636 2357
LTD
80 Great Portland Street
London W1N 6JJ

Professional Association, formed in 1959 by an amalgamation of the British Film Academy and the Guild of Television Producers and Directors

Enquiries: To Secretary
Scope: Film and Television Awards. Details of careers of British film and television technicians. Information about current creative aspects of British film and television in general (Enquiries other than British should be addressed to the British Film Institute, no. 984)
Stock: 100 books; 800 feature film scripts; small number of periodicals. Library stock available for reference only
Publications: Journal of the Society of Film and Television Arts (4 issues each year)

LONDON

1604

THE SOCIETY OF GENEALOGISTS *Tel.:* 01-373 7054
37 Harrington Gardens
London S.W.7

Enquiries: To Secretary

Scope: Genealogy. British topography
Special collection: 560 microfilm reels of Chancery proceedings index
Stock: 37,000 books and pamphlets; 90 current periodicals; 20,000 manuscripts
Publications: Genealogists' Handbook. 6th edition 1969
National Index of Parish Registers, Vols. I and V published of projected series of 12 volumes
A Catalogue of Parish Register Copies in the Possession of the Society of Genealogists. Revised enlarged edition 1968
A Catalogue of Directories and Poll Books in the Possession of the Society of Genealogists. 1964
A Key to Boyd's Marriage Index. 2nd revised edition 1963
Genealogist's Magazine (quarterly; issues Library Accessions lists)
Card index of over 3 million genealogical references

LONDON

1605

THE SOCIETY OF HERBALISTS *Tel.:* 01-629 3157
21 Bruton Street
London W.1

A Society for the furtherance of botanic medicine, herbal study and the use of herbs

Enquiries: To Secretary
Scope: Books dealing with perfumes, cosmetics, soaps, medicinal plants; botany; medical botany; plant physiology; herbals; food; materia medica; homoeopathic books; general works on botany, herbs, medicines, medicinal products; herb cookery
Stock: 250 books; 3 current periodicals. Stock not available on loan

LONDON

1606

SOCIETY OF INDEXERS
c/o Barclays Bank
1 Pall Mall East
London S.W.1

Promotion of profession of indexing

Enquiries: To Secretary, by letter only
Scope: Will deal with: publishers and authors who want name and address of indexer; enquiries about rates of pay for indexing; advice on a particular problem in indexing normally referred to a Council Member for person-to-person discussion
Stock: Library held by Library Association (no. 1315)
Publications: The Indexer (twice each year)

LONDON

1607

SOCIETY OF INDUSTRIAL ARTISTS AND *Tel.:* 01-930 1911
DESIGNERS
12 Carlton House Terrace
London S.W.1

Professional Society for Designers in Britain

Enquiries: To Secretary
Scope: Industrial design
No library
Publications: The Designer (official journal of the Society)
SIAD Year Book
Information sheets, codes of conduct, fee schedules and regulations
Computers in Visual Communication (Proceedings of 1968 SIAD/ATD Symposium)

LONDON **1608**	SOCIETY OF LITHOGRAPH ARTISTS, DESIGNERS, ENGRAVERS AND PROCESS WORKERS 54 Doughty Street London W.C.1	*Tel.*: 01-405 0591

Trade union

Enquiries: To Secretary, by letter only

Scope: Brief account of process supplied in response to enquiries

No library

Publications: Slade Journal (quarterly magazine)
Camera and Process Work
Photo-Litho Offset

LONDON **1609**	SOCIETY OF MEDICAL OFFICERS OF HEALTH DENTAL GROUP c/o Tavistock House South Tavistock Square London W.C.1

Aims to promote interest in preventive dentistry and the public health dental service

Enquiries: To Secretary, preferably by letter

Scope: The Group's members are dental surgeons both administrative and practising, in the fields of dental public health, preventive dentistry, and children's dentistry, and are therefore qualified to give information on any aspect of these topics. From time to time the Group produces documents on topical subjects for example, radiation hazards in dentistry, the dental treatment of handicapped persons, the future of the local authority dental services, sale of foods in school tuck shops. The Group can also give information on the fluoridation of public water supplies

No library

LONDON **1610**	SOCIETY OF MINIATURISTS R.W.S. Galleries 26 Conduit Street London W.1	*Tel.*: 01-629 8300

Enquiries: To Secretary

Scope: An Exhibiting Society willing to answer enquiries in its own field

LONDON **1611**	SOCIETY OF OCCUPATIONAL MEDICINE c/o Royal College of Physicians 11 St Andrews Place London N.W.1	*Tel.*: 01-486 2641

Aims to improve the health of people at work by promoting and stimulating research and education in the field of occupational health

Enquiries: To the Secretariat, by letter only, who will forward them to the appropriate quarters, except for enquiries about work published by the Society, which should be addressed to the Hon. Editor, Nuffield House, Bury Road, Rochdale, Lancashire. *Tel.*: 0706 48855

Scope: Apart from the Transactions, the Society may be able to answer enquiries of a general nature in the occupational health field, or to refer enquirers to members with specialist knowledge

No library
Publications: Transactions of the Society of Occupational Medicine (quarterly)

LONDON	SOCIETY OF ST VINCENT DE PAUL	*Tel.:* 01-799 1342
1612	2 Iddesleigh House Caxton Street London S.W.1	

International voluntary Catholic Society attempting to help anyone in need

Enquiries: To Admin. Secretary

Scope: The history and development of the Society in England and Wales, its aims and structure

Publications: A variety of booklets and pamphlets about the work of the Society and its founder, Frederic Ozanam
Film: Charity means Love (16 mm)

LONDON	SOUTH AFRICAN EMBASSY	*Tel.:* 01-930 4488
1613	Trafalgar Square London W.C.2	

Enquiries: To Librarian

Scope: Information on all aspects of South African affairs

Stock: 3,000 books; all official South African Government Reports; 70 current periodicals. Stock not available on loan

LONDON	SOUTH LONDON ART GALLERY	*Tel.:* 01-703 6120
1614	Peckham Road London S.E.5	

Original prints of the 20th century

Enquiries: Curator, South London Art Gallery, Administration Department, Dulwich Library, Lordship Lane, London S.E.22

Scope: General information on print making. Transparencies of prints in stock available on loan. Collection of local views of historical interest may be seen by appointment
Secondary: Research or advice on history or source of paintings. Reference collection of books on art

Stock: 400 books; 4 current periodicals

Publications: Catalogues of current exhibitions

LONDON	SOUTHGATE TECHNICAL COLLEGE	*Tel.:* 01-886 6893
1615	High Street Southgate London N.14	

Enquiries: To Librarian, by letter only

Scope: Art, biography, biology, zoology, botany, chemistry, geography, history, languages and literature, physics, science, social sciences, technology
Secondary: Drama, music, photography and cinematography, and physical education

Stock: 19,476 books; 490 pamphlets; 370 current periodicals; 435 filmstrips, loops and slides; 446 gramophone records; 1,183 radio and television data sheets
Annexe stock: 4,650 books; 77 current periodicals

LONDON **1616**	SOUTHLANDS COLLEGE OF EDUCATION 65 Wimbledon Parkside London S.W.19	*Tel.:* 01-946 2234

Enquiries: To Librarian

Scope: Emphasis on education: history, theory, teaching, child psychology and backing material for general college courses. A school services collection is available to provide material to use on teaching practice. Of the general subjects represented, divinity is the most well represented forming a basis for students studying for external London BA in Divinity

Stock: 37,800 books; 500 pamphlets; 180 current periodicals

LONDON **1617**	SOUTH-WEST LONDON COLLEGE Tooting Broadway London S.W.17 College of advanced business studies	*Tel.:* 01-672 2441

Enquiries: To Librarian

Scope: Subjects particularly well represented include accountancy, banking, business management, company secretaryship, economics, geography, government, history, industrial relations, law, marketing, office administration, statistics, supervisory management and training

Stock: 8,500 books; 2,500 pamphlets; 205 current periodicals. Cuttings collection maintained of articles on economic and financial affairs

Member of WANDPETLS

LONDON **1618**	THE SPOTLIGHT 42 Cranbourn Street London W.C.2 Publishers	*Tel.:* 01-437 7631

Enquiries: To Enquiry and Records Department

Scope: Answers enquiries from casting directors and theatre managers, on the availability of actors and actresses
Secondary: Answers enquiries on 'What's going on' generally in the entertainment world

Publications: The Spotlight Casting Directory
Contacts (containing comprehensive lists of everything to do with the entertainment world)

LONDON **1619**	THE STANDING CONFERENCE FOR AMATEUR MUSIC 26 Bedford Square London W.C.1	*Tel.:* 01-636 4066

Co-ordinates the work of organizations concerned with amateur music at all ages, considers problems of musical education and collects information, studies problems, advises, produces new ideas, and spreads the results through publications and conferences

Enquiries: To Secretary

Scope: General information provided in connection with organizations concerned with amateur or school music

No library

Publications: Music and the Amateur. 1951
The Training of Music Teachers. 1954
Youth Makes Music. 1957

Music Centres and the Training of Specially Talented Children. 1966
Music and the Newsom Report. 1966
Leaflet on the Care and Maintenance of the Pianoforte
A Policy for Pianos
Specimen Planning Notes on Musical Requirements in School Buildings
Specimen Planning Notes on Musical Requirements in Further Education Colleges
List of Contemporary Choral Music suitable for Schools
List of Modern Choral Music for Adults
List of Charitable Trusts
Making Music (in conjunction with Rural Music Schools Association, no. 719)

LONDON

1620

STANDING CONFERENCE OF NATIONAL VOLUNTARY YOUTH ORGANISATIONS
26 Bedford Square
London W.C.1

Tel.: 01-636 4066

The Standing Conference is a co-ordinating and advisory body which has as members the major voluntary youth organizations in the country. It is recognized as the spokesman for the voluntary youth organizations as a whole and as a focal point for making contact with them

Enquiries: To Secretary

Scope: Informs enquirers from the United Kingdom and overseas of all matters relating to the Youth Service in general and voluntary organizations in particular, and disseminates reports drawn up by working parties on current youth problems
Secondary: Offers contacts with voluntary service organizations, local youth activities and Youth Service projects

No library

Publications: Young People To-day. D. Hawes. ed.
The Work of a Local Standing Conference

Aims and Activities of Members
SCNVYO Bulletin (quarterly)

LONDON

1621

STUDENT HUMANIST FEDERATION
13 Prince of Wales Terrace
London W.8

Tel.: 01-937 2341

Enquiries: To Chairman

Scope: Humanism, particularly in universities

LONDON

1622

THE SWEDENBORG SOCIETY
20 Bloomsbury Way
London W.C.1

Tel.: 01-405 7986

Publication and distribution of the works of Emanuel Swedenborg

Enquiries: To Secretary

Scope: Theological, philosophical, and scientific writings of Emanuel Swedenborg (1668–1772) and the related subject of the growth of the New Church

Stock: 12,300 books and pamphlets, including 3,000 items of archive material; New Church periodicals in English, Swedish and Sotho

Publications: Printed catalogue

See also no. 1173

LONDON

1623

THE SWEDISH INSTITUTE
23 North Row
London W1R 2DN

Tel.: 01-499 9500

Aims to foster Sweden's cultural relations with other countries

LONDON, THE SWEDISH INSTITUTE, *cont.*

Enquiries: To Secretary

Scope: Library concentrates on books in English dealing with Sweden and Swedish fiction translated into English. Information services relate to all subject areas, particularly education, arts and cultural life generally

Stock: 1,500 books; 200 pamphlets; 18 current periodicals

LONDON

1624

SWISS BANK CORPORATION
P.O. Box No. 114
99 Gresham Street
London E.C.2

Tel.: 01-606 4000
Telex: 887434

International bankers

Enquiries: To Statistical Department

Scope: Information relating to Switzerland. Foreign exchange rates, securities

Stock: 400 books; most banking and other economic and market reports

Publications: British Exports and Exchange Restrictions Abroad
Foreign Exchange   Bulletin (French and German)
Values and Measures of the World   Prospects and other items

LONDON

1625

THE TAIL-WAGGERS' CLUB (G.B.) LIMITED
356/360 Grays Inn Road
London W.C.1

Tel.: 01-837 1603

Enquiries: To Secretary

Scope: Engraved dog medallion supplied on enrolment. Expert free advice given on feeding or training dog (or other pet)
Secondary: List of kennels which board pets while owners on holiday and list of hotels and boarding houses where pets are welcome with their owners

No library

Publications: Tail Wagger and Family Magazine (monthly)
The Tail Waggers' Club Handbook (Guide to Dog Management)
The Tail Waggers' Club Handbook for Domestic Pets (other than dogs)

LONDON

1626

TATE GALLERY
Millbank
London S.W.1

Tel.: 01-828 4444

National collection of British painting and modern art. The Modern collection consists of works by artists of all nationalities, including British artists, born in or after 1850. The British collection consists of works by artists born before 1850 working in Britain

Enquiries: To Director, preferably by letter

Scope: Enquiries about works in the Tate Gallery are answered, but a general information service on art is not provided. The Library is mainly for the use of the staff but original material contained in it (there is some source material on 20th Century British art) may be consulted by appointment

Publications: William Blake (1757–1827). M. Butlin   Official Guide to the Tate Gallery
Victor Pasmore. R. Alley   The Collections of the Tate Gallery
Roy Lichtenstein. R. Morphet   Reproductions of Works in the Tate Gallery
Barbara Hepworth. R. Alley   Auguste Rodin: the Kiss
Watercolours from the Turner Bequest 1819–1845. M. Butlin

Little Book Series:
    William Blake. M. Butlin   British Painting since 1945. R. Alley
    The Pre-Raphaelites. L. Parris   British Sculpture since 1945. D. Farr
    Turner: Early Works. M. Chamot   Optical and Kinetic Art. M. Compton
    Turner: Later Works. M. Butlin   Recent American Art. R. Alley
    British Painting 1910–1945. R. Morphet   John Constable. C. Shields and L. Parris
Postcards

LONDON 1627

TAVISTOCK INSTITUTE OF HUMAN RELATIONS   *Tel.:* 01-435 7111
AND THE TAVISTOCK CLINIC
TAVISTOCK JOINT LIBRARY
Tavistock Centre
Belsize Lane
London N.W.3

The Tavistock Institute was incorporated to study human relations in conditions of well-being, conflict or breakdown, in the family, the work group and the larger organization. The Tavistock Clinic is an outpatient psychiatric clinic within the National Health Service

Enquiries: To Librarian

Scope: Psychology, psychiatry, psychoanalysis, sociology, organizational studies
Secondary: Anthropology, ethology

Stock: 7,000 books; 7,000 pamphlets; 200 current periodicals

Publications: Tavistock Institute and Tavistock Clinic: An Annotated List of Publications, 1946–1965
Supplement to the Annotated List: 1965–1968
Human Relations (journal 6 times each year)

LONDON 1628

THE TEXTILE COUNCIL
DESIGN AND EXPORT CENTRE
12 Gt Marborough Street
London W1V 2BH

Enquiries: To Librarian

Scope: The Library houses an unique and valuable collection of books dealing with textiles, fashion, design in general, and various other related subjects, for example, painting, architecture, needlework, interior design, colour, foreign textiles, decorative arts. It also possesses an unique collection of Macclesfield silks and other fabric samples from the last century, and a wide selection of fashion and design magazines

Stock: 1,300 books; British Colour Council pamphlets; 120 current periodicals. Stock not available on loan

Publications: Library Catalogues

LONDON 1629

THAMES CONSERVANCY   *Tel.:* 01-839 2441
Burdett House
15 Buckingham Street
London W.C.2

Navigation Authority for River Thames between Teddington and Cricklade; Land Drainage and Pollution Prevention Authority for Thames Catchment Area; Water Resources Authority

Enquiries: To Secretary

Scope: Leaflets concerning the Conservators' history, constitution, and functions are sent to enquirers

Stock: Small private library

Publications: Annual Report
Leaflets

LONDON	THAMES TELEVISION LIMITED	*Tel.:* 01-405 7888
1630	Television House Kingsway London W.C.2	

Television programme production

Enquiries: To Reference Library

Stock: 300,000 pictures and engravings incorporating The Weaver Smith collection of 17th, 18th and 19th century pictures, particularly of London. Stock may be hired

LONDON	THANE LIBRARY OF MEDICAL SCIENCES	*Tel.:* 01-387 7050 ext. 245
1631	University College Gower Street London W.C.1	

Teaching and research library in the pre-clinical medical sciences, and part of University College Library

Enquiries: To Librarian in charge, preferably by letter

Scope: Anatomy, biochemistry, biophysics, pharmacology, physiology
Secondary: History of the pre-clinical medical sciences

Stock: 30,000 books; 90,000 pamphlets; 350 current periodicals. Stock available on loan through N.C.L. only

LONDON	THEATRES' ADVISORY COUNCIL	*Tel.:* 01-387 2666
1632	9 Fitzroy Square London W1P 6AE	

Enquiries: To Secretary

Scope: Information and advice to those concerned in the preservation of existing theatre buildings and in the planning of new theatre buildings

No library

Publications: Planning the Multi-purpose Hall—some Theatrical Considerations
Civic Theatres—their Housing and Administration (Conference Report)
Annual surveys of theatre building developments

LONDON	TOBACCO RESEARCH COUNCIL	*Tel.:* 01-828 2041
1633	Glen House Stag Place London S.W.1	

To investigate the possible relationship between smoking and health

Enquiries: To Librarian

Scope: Smoking and health with particular emphasis on lung cancer and heart disease

Stock: 400 books; 160 current periodicals; 8,000 reprints

LONDON	THE TOBACCO WORKERS' UNION	*Tel.:* 01-226 2251
1634	218 Upper Street London N.1	

Trade union

Enquiries: To General Secretary

Scope: The tobacco industry and the trade union movement

Stock: 20 books; 5 current periodicals
Publications: The Tobacco Worker (bi-monthly)

LONDON

1635

TOC H
15 Trinity Square
London E.C.3

Tel.: 01-709 0472

Enquiries: To Public Relations Secretary, 41 Trinity Square, London E.C.3

Scope: Toc H is not equipped to deal with enquiries other than those concerned with the Movement itself and its activities. Such literary works as are in stock are concerned with the movement or with its Founder Padre, The Revd. Dr P. B. Clayton, CH, MC, DD

No library

LONDON

1636

TOWN PLANNING INSTITUTE
26 Portland Place
London W.1

Tel.: 01-636 9107

Enquiries: To Librarian

Scope: Planning; Urban Development; Environmental Studies; Ekistics; Development Plans for Cities and Counties; Transportation
Secondary: Social Surveys, methodology

Stock: 10,000 books, pamphlets and reports; 142 current periodicals

Publications: T.P.I. Journal (10 times each year)
Summer School Report (annually)

LONDON

1637

THE TRAINING COUNCIL FOR TEACHERS OF THE MENTALLY HANDICAPPED
Alexander Fleming House
Elephant and Castle
London S.E.1

Tel.: 01-407 5522

Promotes the provision of training for the staff (including hospital staff) of training centres for the mentally subnormal, and approves courses of training

Enquiries: To Secretary

Scope: Information and advice on courses available to people who wish to make a career in teaching the mentally handicapped

No library

Publications: Two booklets: Teaching Mentally Handicapped Children
The Training and Further Education of Mentally Handicapped adults

LONDON

1638

TRANSLATORS ASSOCIATION
84 Drayton Gardens
London S.W.10

Tel.: 01-373 6642

A self-governing unit within the network of the Society of Authors (no. 1600) exclusively concerned with the interests and special problems of writers who translate foreign literary, dramatic or technical work into English for publication or performance in Great Britain or English-speaking countries overseas

Enquiries: To Secretary

Scope: Members receive general and legal advice on all questions connected with the marketing of their work, such as rates of remuneration, contractual arrangements with publishers, editors,

LONDON, TRANSLATORS ASSOCIATION, *cont.*

broadcasting organizations; information on developments relating to translation work, including information about improvements in fees; consultation with all organizations and individuals, British and foreign, professionally concerned with the translation of literary, dramatic and technical work

No library

LONDON

1639

T.U.C. CENTENARY INSTITUTE OF OCCUPATIONAL HEALTH
London School of Hygiene and Tropical Medicine
Keppel Street
Gower Street
London W.C.1

See no. 1344

LONDON

1640

U.K. COMMITTEE FOR THE WORLD HEALTH ORGANIZATION *Tel.:* 01-636 8636
c/o London School of Hygiene and Tropical Medicine
Keppel Street
Gower Street
London W.C.1

Enquiries: To Secretary

Scope: Publicity and information about the work of the World Health Organization

Reference Library only

LONDON

ULSTER OFFICE *see* **NORTHERN IRELAND GOVERNMENT OFFICE** (no. 1449)

LONDON

1641

UNION INTERNATIONALE DE LA MARIONETTE (BRITISH SECTION) BRITISH UNIMA
23A Southampton Place
London W.C.1

Aims to further the art of puppetry and puppet theatre

Enquiries: To Secretary, by letter only

Scope: All aspects of puppetry, at home or abroad particularly about theatres, festivals and books dealing with puppetry

Publications: Catalogue of puppet films
International Directory of Puppet Theatres

LONDON

1642

UNION OF POST OFFICE WORKERS *Tel.:* 01-622 2291
UPW House
Crescent Lane
London S.W.4

Trade union

Enquiries: To General Secretary

Scope: Post Office history; Post Office trades union history; conditions of post office workers and civil service staffs
Secondary: Industrial relations; general industrial conditions; economic situation and effect on workers

    Stock: 1,350 books; 3,000 pamphlets; 350 current periodicals. Abstracts from Hansard on relevant subjects including complete set 1926 to date; 10,000 newspaper cuttings, from 1920
  Publications: The Post
        PTTI News

LONDON

1643

UNITED GRAND LODGE OF ENGLAND
LIBRARY AND MUSEUM
Freemasons' Hall
Great Queen Street
London W.C.2

 Enquiries: To Librarian, by letter only
   Scope: History of Freemasonry
   Stock: 30,000 books (23,000 Masonic, 7,000 non-Masonic). Stock not available on loan
      Admission restricted to members

LONDON

1644

UNITED KINGDOM ALLIANCE   *Tel.:* 01-222 4001
12 Caxton Street
London S.W.1

Aims to eliminate the drink evil from the life of the nation

 Enquiries: To Secretary
   Scope: The contemporary role of the temperance movement
      Secondary: The history and achievements of the temperance movement in the social life of England
   Stock: Books and other publications which are lent to personal researchers. Records are available to *bona fide* students
 Publications: Alliance News (6 issues each year)

LONDON

1645

UNITED LODGE OF THEOSOPHISTS   *Tel.:* 01-723 0688
62 Queen's Gardens
London W.C.2

A voluntary association of students of theosophy which aims to make known and practicable the teachings of theosophy (as recorded by H. P. Blavatsky and W. Q. Judge)

 Enquiries: To United Lodge of Theosophists
   Scope: Literature on theosophy
      Secondary: Comparative religions and philosophies
   Stock: 1,550 books; 3 current periodicals. Stock not available on loan

LONDON

1646

UNITED NATIONS INFORMATION CENTRE *Tel.:* 01-629 3816
14/15 Stratford Place
London W.1

This is one of 50 centres established by the United Nations throughout the world. It offers information services to organizations and individuals in the United Kingdom, Ireland and the Netherlands. In addition to a Press Office and Visual Information Section, it maintains a reference library of official publications and documentation published by the United Nations and certain specialized agencies such as Food and Agriculture Organization (FAO), U.N. Educational, Scientific & Cultural Organization (UNESCO), World Health Organization (WHO)

 Enquiries: To Librarian

LONDON, UNITED NATIONS INFORMATION CENTRE, *cont.*

Scope: The activities of the United Nations and its agencies cover a very wide field. In addition to regular published surveys and international statistics on economic and social subjects (including agriculture, education, culture, social and health conditions), there are special studies on such matters as international law, public health, preventive medicine, social sciences, art and literature, forestry and fisheries, nutrition and food supply. Furthermore, the Official Records of the United Nations contain information on subjects raised within the various bodies ranging from disarmament and the peaceful uses of outer space and the seabed, to population control, human rights, decolonization, land reform, juvenile delinquency and control of narcotic drugs

Stock: Only United Nations and specialized agency material

Publications: The Press Section issues weekly summaries and *ad hoc* press releases relating to United Nations activities

A network of depository libraries in England, Scotland, Wales and Northern Ireland (as well as Ireland and the Netherlands) has been established. These carry United Nations and agency material to a lesser or greater extent. A list will be supplied by the Centre on request

LONDON

1647

UNITED SOCIETY FOR THE PROPAGATION OF THE GOSPEL
15 Tufton Street
London S.W.1

Tel.: 01-799 1701

Anglican Missionary Society

Enquiries: To Librarian

Scope: Anglican missionary work and all Christian evangelization. Early travel and anthropological works and biography, particularly African
Secondary: Church history, liturgy and theology

Stock: 25,000 books and pamphlets

LONDON

1648

UNITED STATES INFORMATION SERVICE REFERENCE LIBRARY
American Embassy
P.O. Box 2LH
Grosvenor Square
London W.1

Tel.: 01-499 9000

Enquiries: To Librarian

Scope: United States reference service for media representatives and Government officials. The library of the United States Information Service has now been deposited at the University of London (no. 1662) where books are available for loan to those who apply through the inter-library loan scheme

LONDON

1649

UNIVERSITY COLLEGE HOSPITAL MEDICAL SCHOOL
University Street
London W.C.1

Tel.: 01-387 5861 ext. 62

Medical teaching and research

Enquiries: To Librarian

Scope: Within its limits the library covers medicine in the wider sense, including dentistry

Stock: 11,000 books; 250 current periodicals. Books not normally available on loan

LONDON	UNIVERSITY OF LONDON	*Tel.:* 01-486 4400
	BEDFORD COLLEGE	
1650	Regent's Park	
	London N.W.1	

Enquiries: To Librarian

Scope: A general collection covering the humanities (English and American literature, linguistics, French, German, Italian, Latin, Greek, history, philosophy), the social sciences (sociology, economics, anthropology, psychology, geography) and the pure sciences. In addition, the library of the Board of Dutch Studies of the University of London is housed in the College Library. A special collection on the Sociology of Medicine is being formed (to be housed initially in the Bedford College Annexe in Peto Place, London N.W.1). Background material published in the years 1847–1849 is collected on a modest scale

Stock: 150,000 books; 6,000 pamphlets; 1,000 current periodicals

LONDON	UNIVERSITY OF LONDON	*Tel.:* 01-352 6421
	CHELSEA COLLEGE	
1651	OF SCIENCE AND TECHNOLOGY	
	Manresa Road	
	London S.W.3	

Teaching and research in science

Enquiries: To Librarian

Scope: Botany; zoology; geology; mathematics; computing; physics; electronics; chemistry; pharmacy; pharmacology; physiology; pharmacognosy; history and philosophy of science; human biology; and Science Education Centre

Stock: 80,000 books; 4,000 pamphlets; 1,000 current periodicals

LONDON	UNIVERSITY OF LONDON	*Tel.:* 01-935 9292
	COURTAULD INSTITUTE OF ART	
1652	20 Portman Square	
	London W1H 0BE	

Enquiries: To Librarian, by letter only

Scope: History of European art

Stock: 31,000 books; 30,000 pamphlets and reports. Chief periodicals dealing with art historical subjects, museum bulletins and societies' publications

LONDON	UNIVERSITY OF LONDON	*Tel.:* 01-692 7171
	GOLDSMITHS' COLLEGE	
1653	Lewisham Way	
	New Cross	
	London S.E.14	

Enquiries: To Librarian

Scope: This is a general library, with a limited range of books and periodicals on most subjects except medicine, agriculture and industry. Slightly more emphasis on social sciences (including education) and on art and music, but relatively good also on psychology, history and English, French and German languages and literature

Stock: 70,000 books and pamphlets; 550 current periodicals

Publications: Publications of the Goldsmiths College
   Curriculum Laboratory:
     Ideas (periodical, somewhat irregular)
     Reports of pilot courses for experienced teachers

LONDON	UNIVERSITY OF LONDON	*Tel.:* 01-580 4868
	INSTITUTE OF ADVANCED LEGAL STUDIES	
1654	25 Russell Square	
	London W.C.1	

                Centre for legal research including post-graduate work

Enquiries: To Secretary and Librarian

Scope: The Law of the British Isles; the law of the British and former British Dominions and other territories (excluding the law of Burma, India and Pakistan and Islamic and primitive law); the law of the European Communities and of the countries of Western Europe; the law of the United States of America and of Latin America; Comparative law; Public and private international law
Bibliographical enquiries only dealt with

Stock: 96,400 books including volumes of serials; 1,567 current serials

Publications: Union List of Legal Periodicals: A Location Guide to Holdings of Legal Periodicals in Libraries in the United Kingdom. 3rd edition 1968
Union List of Commonwealth and South African Law. 1963 edition. A Location Guide to Commonwealth and South African Legislation, Law Reports and Digests held by Libraries in the United Kingdom at May 1963
Union List of United States Law Literature in Libraries in Oxford, Cambridge and London. New edition in preparation
Union List of West European Legal Literature: Publications held by libraries in Oxford, Cambridge and London. 1966
A Manual of Legal Citations. Part I: The British Isles. 1959. Part II: The Commonwealth. 1960
A Bibliographical Guide to the Law of the United Kingdom, the Channel Islands and the Isle of Man (published jointly with the United Kingdom National Committee of Comparative Law and the British Institute of International and Comparative Law). New edition in preparation
Index to Foreign Legal Periodicals (quarterly, published in co-operation with the American Association of Law Libraries)
University of London Legal Series (published by the Athlone Press under the auspices of the Institute of Advanced Legal Studies)

LONDON	UNIVERSITY OF LONDON	*Tel.:* 01-387 6052
	INSTITUTE OF ARCHAEOLOGY	
1655	31/34 Gordon Square	
	London W.C.1	

Enquiries: To Librarian

Scope: No information service, but will answer reasonable enquiries in the field of European, Near Eastern, and Latin American archaeology

Stock: 12,000 books; 9,000 pamphlets; 250 current periodicals

Publications: Bulletin

LONDON	UNIVERSITY OF LONDON	*Tel.:* 01-405 3474
	INSTITUTE OF BASIC MEDICAL SCIENCES	
1656	ROYAL COLLEGE OF SURGEONS OF ENGLAND	
	Lincoln's Inn Fields	
	London W.C.2	

                Comprises the teaching facilities of the Departments of Anatomy, Biochemistry, Pathology,

Pharmacology and Physiology of the Royal College of Surgeons of England. Staff and students use the library of the College (no. 1532)

LONDON
1657

UNIVERSITY OF LONDON *Tel.:* 01-637 0846
INSTITUTE OF EDUCATION LIBRARY
11/13 Ridgmount Street
London W.C.1

Enquiries: To Librarian
Scope: All aspects of education
Stock: 85,000 books; 15,000 pamphlets; 1,300 current periodicals
Publications: Education Libraries Bulletin and Supplements
Catalogue of Periodicals

LONDON
1658

UNIVERSITY OF LONDON *Tel.:* 01-580 2711
INSTITUTE OF GERMANIC STUDIES
29 Russell Square
London W.C.1

Provides a library and bibliographical facilities in German language and literature for graduate students and senior members of University teaching staffs

Enquiries: To Librarian
Scope: German language and literature
Special collections: Priebsch-Closs collection of about 2,500 17th and 18th century editions, mainly of German literature but including German translations from English literature and English translations from German
German translations and adaptations of Shakespeare from the 16th century onwards
German dialect dictionaries
Festschriften (including bibliographies of Festschriften in all fields)
Gundolf collection of manuscripts of Friedrich Gundolf, including literary works and correspondence with many writers and scholars of the late 19th and early 20th centuries
Goethe collection, including library of English Goethe Society
20th century collection, including many first editions of Expressionist and Exile literature
Secondary: Dictionaries and representative literary texts in Dutch and Scandinavian language
Stock: 25,000 books; 2,500 pamphlets; 200 current periodicals. Stock not available on loan
Publications: Schiller Bicentenary Lectures. F. Norman, ed. 1960
Schiller in England 1787–1960: a Bibliography. R. Pick, ed. 1961
Theses in Germanic Studies 1903–1961. 1962
Hoffmannstal Studies in Commemoration. F. Norman, ed. 1963
Hauptmann Centenary Lectures. K. G. Knight and F. Norman, eds. 1964
Essays in German Literature—1. F. Norman, ed. 1965
German Language and Literature: Select Bibliography. Compiled by L. M. Newman. 1966
Theses in German Studies 1962–1967. 1968
Probleme Mittelalterlicher Überlieferung Und Textkritik. Hrsg. von P. F. Ganz and W. Schroder. 1968
Essays in German Language, Culture and Society. S. S. Prawer, R. Hinton and L. W. Forster, eds. 1969
Hugo Von Hofmannsthal-Ausstellung Katalog. 1961
Gerhart Hauptmann Exhibition. Catalogue prepared by H. F. Garten. 1962
Hugo Von Hofmannsthal in England and America: a Bibliography. R. Pick and A. C. Weaver. 1963
Theses in Progress at British Universities, as known on 31.12.67. 1968

LONDON, UNIVERSITY OF LONDON, INSTITUTE OF GERMANIC STUDIES, *cont.*
Theses in Progress at British Universities, as known on 1.1.69. 1969
Theses in Progress at British Universities, as known on 1.1.70. 1970
Periodical Holdings 1970. 1970

LONDON

1659

UNIVERSITY OF LONDON   *Tel.:* 01-636 0272
INSTITUTE OF HISTORICAL RESEARCH
Senate House
London W.C.1

The Institute is the University of London's centre for postgraduate work in history

Enquiries: To Secretary and Librarian

Scope: 20 seminar libraries with books containing or discussing the main sources of the history of Great Britain, Europe, United States of America, and Latin America; Imperial and Colonial history, military and naval history, and the relations of the West with Asia

Stock: 100,000 books and pamphlets; 650 current periodicals

Publications: Bulletin of the Institute of Historical Research (twice each year)
Historical Research for University Degrees in the United Kingdom (annually in May in two parts)
Teachers of History in the Universities of the United Kingdom (annually in January)
Union List of American Historical Publications in United Kingdom Libraries. H. H. Bellot. 1959
Historical, Archaeological and Kindred Societies in the British Isles: a List. S. E. Harcup. Revised edition 1968
Registers of the Universities, Colleges and Schools of Great Britain and Ireland: a List. (Reprinted from *Bulletin*, November 1964.) P. M. Jacobs
Bibliography of Historical Works issued in the United Kingdom, 1961-5. W. Kellaway. 1967
Victoria History of the Counties of England
New edition of J. Le Neve: *Fasti Ecclesiae Anglicanae.* (in progress)

LONDON

1660

UNIVERSITY OF LONDON   *Tel.:* 01-387 5671
INSTITUTE OF LATIN AMERICAN STUDIES
31 Tavistock Square
London W.C.1

Enquiries: To Librarian

Scope: Recent subject bibliography of Latin America, in most fields (including some science). Other recent reference works on the area such as biographical dictionaries, gazetteers and directories in various fields (but not telephone directories). Union catalogue of books and periodicals on Latin America in major British research libraries
Secondary: Some recent news sources on Latin America (but not daily newspapers)

Stock: 1,000 books and pamphlets; 25 current periodicals. Stock not available on loan

Publications: Latin American Studies in the Universities of the United Kingdom (annual list of courses and teachers)
Theses in Progress and Completed in Latin American Studies in the Universities of the United Kingdom (annual list of students' research theses titles)
Staff Research in Progress in L.A. Studies in the Universities of the United Kingdom (annually)
Institute Monographs (extended essays on Latin American subjects)

LONDON	UNIVERSITY OF LONDON	*Tel.:* 01-387 5534
1661	INSTITUTE OF UNITED STATES STUDIES	
	31 Tavistock Square	
	London W.C.1	

Promotes and co-ordinates American Studies in the University of London; collects and distributes information about American Studies in British Universities; and aids the bibliographical work of scholars by assisting co-operation between libraries with American interests

Enquiries: To Secretary (about the University of London MA degree in Area Studies (U.S.) and in general about American Studies in British Universities)
Bibliographical enquiries about American Studies materials in British libraries may be addressed to the Librarian

Scope: Every aspect of the study of the United States except science, technology, medicine, law and geology. The library is a very small collection of bibliographies and reference works. It also includes several microcard projects such as all available items from T. W. Clark's *Travels in the Old South* and *Travels in the New South* and selected items from Sabin's *Dictionary of books relating to America*. A Union Catalogue of American Studies Materials is maintained

Stock: 600 books; 30 current periodicals; 8,000 items on microcard. Stock not available on loan

Publications: American Studies in Britain, a list of courses in and teachers of subjects relating to the study of the U.S.A. in British universities (appears occasionally)
A List of theses in progress or recently completed at universities throughout the British Isles (annually)
Report on a proposed Union Catalogue in the field of American Studies in Britain. S. A. McCarthy
Materials for the study of the United States in libraries of the University of London

LONDON	UNIVERSITY OF LONDON LIBRARY	*Tel.:* 01-636 4514
	Senate House	
1662	Malet Street	
	London W.C.1	

Enquiries: To Director and Goldsmiths' Librarian

Scope: All subjects. Particularly strong collections in bibliography, early economics (Goldsmiths' Library), English literature, history and archaeology, linguistics, music, palaeography, United States studies. Collection of manuscripts, maps, parliamentary Papers, gramophone records, slides (fine arts), seals (Fuller Collection). Other named collections: British Psychological Society (periodicals); Bromhead (London); Durning H. Lawrence (Shakespeare, Bacon, Defoe, Emblem books); Family Welfare Association (social work, charities); Harry Price (magic, psychical phenomena). Malcolm Morley (theatre); Porteus (late 18th century); Quick (early education); Sterling (English literature)

Stock: 1,000,000 books and pamphlets (total stock including Extra-Mural Library); 4,300 current periodicals (in relevant fields)

Publications: Catalogue of the Palaeography Collection. Publ. by G. K. Hall. 1969
Union list of periodicals in the Romance languages and literature. 1964
List of current periodicals in the Library
Union list of music periodicals
Catalogue of the Goldsmiths' Library (in preparation)
Depository library for all London University libraries at Egham, Surrey

LONDON **1663**	UNIVERSITY OF LONDON NEW COLLEGE, LONDON 527 Finchley Road Hampstead London N.W.3	*Tel.:* 01-435 3719

Divinity School, primarily for the training of men and women for the Congregational Ministry

Enquiries: To Librarian, by letter only

Scope: Books relating to theology. The library has an important collection of works formerly in the libraries of Dissenting academies, and also of works on Puritan and Dissenting history and theology. Among its manuscript collections are eleven volumes of the correspondence of Philip Doddridge (1702–1751)

Stock: 32,000 books; 10 current periodicals

LONDON **1664**	UNIVERSITY OF LONDON QUEEN ELIZABETH COLLEGE LIBRARY Campden Hill Road London W.8	*Tel.:* 01-937 5411

Enquiries: To Librarian

Scope: Subject fields are biochemistry, biology (including botany and zoology), chemistry, food and management science, mathematics, microbiology, nutrition, physics, physiology, social studies and community development

Stock: 22,000 books; 1,000 pamphlets; 360 current periodicals

LONDON **1665**	UNIVERSITY OF LONDON QUEEN MARY COLLEGE LIBRARY Mile End Road London E.1	*Tel.:* 01-980 4811

School in the Faculties of Arts, Laws, Science and Engineering

Enquiries: To Librarian

Scope: Library stock covers needs of departments of classics, English, French, geography, German history, Russian, economics, laws, botany, chemistry, geology, mathematics, physics, zoology, aeronautical, civil, electrical, mechanical and nuclear engineering

Stock: 115,000 books; 10,000 pamphlets; 2,000 current periodicals (total stock)

Publications: Accessions List (weekly)

LONDON **1666**	UNIVERSITY OF LONDON SCHOOL OF ORIENTAL AND AFRICAN STUDIES LIBRARY Malet Street London W.C.1	*Tel.:* 01-580 9021

Enquiries: To Librarian

Scope: Oriental and African studies in the humanities and social sciences

Stock: 320,000 books, pamphlets and other items; 1,600 current periodicals

Publications: Library catalogue, 1963, and supplement, 1969
Library guide, 1969
Monthly list of titles added to the catalogue

Cumulated list of periodical articles on the Far East and South East Asia, 1956–57, 1959; 1957–58. 1959

A list of the School's publications is available separately

LONDON
1667

UNIVERSITY OF LONDON
THE SCHOOL OF PHARMACY
29/39 Brunswick Square
London W.C.1

Tel.: 01-837 7651

A college of the University of London preparing students for B.Pharm. degree. Original research leading to higher degrees undertaken in departments of Pharmaceutics, Pharmacology, Pharmaceutical Chemistry and Pharmacognosy

Enquiries: To Librarian

Scope: Pharmaceutics; pharmaceutical chemistry; pharmaceutical engineering science; pharmacognosy; pharmacology

Stock: 8,000 books and bound periodicals; 600 pamphlets; 165 current periodicals

Publications: Library Guide, with notes for preparing dissertations
Library Bulletin (quarterly)

LONDON
1668

UNIVERSITY OF LONDON
SCHOOL OF SLAVONIC AND EAST
    EUROPEAN STUDIES
Senate House
London W.C.1

Tel.: 01-636 9782

Enquiries: To Librarian

Scope: Slavonic and East European studies in the field of the humanities (mainly history, language and literature, but also philosophy, religion, economic life, law, and the fine arts)

Stock: 125,000 books and pamphlets, including bound volumes of periodicals, 1,000 current periodicals

Publications: Slavonic and East European Review
The Habsburg Monarchy, 1804–1918: books and pamphlets published in the United Kingdom between 1818 and 1967. A critical bibliography. F. R. Bridge. 1967

LONDON
1669

UPPER NORWOOD PUBLIC LIBRARY
Westow Hill
London S.E.19

Tel.: 01-670 2551
  and 5468

Enquiries: To Librarian

Scope: General stock, including music. Limited amount of material on the Crystal Palace. Fair selection of workshop motor manuals

Stock: 98,000 books; 1,300 pamphlets; 93 current periodicals

LONDON
1670

THE VEGETARIAN SOCIETY OF THE UNITED
    KINGDOM
53 Marloes Road
London W.8

Tel.: 01-937 7739

Enquiries: To Secretary

Scope: All aspects of vegetarianism—ethical and moral, nutritional (including recipes), economic
Secondary: Food reform

No library

LONDON, THE VEGETARIAN SOCIETY OF THE UNITED KINGDOM, *cont.*

Publications: The British Vegetarian (bi-monthly)
The Vegetarian Handbook (triennially)
Pamphlets

Administrative Headquarters: Parkdale, Dunham Road, Altrincham, Cheshire (no. 26)

LONDON

1671

VETERAN CAR CLUB OF GREAT BRITAIN *Tel.:* 01-935 1661
14 Fitzhardinge Street
London W.1

Aims to preserve, restore and run veteran cars (pre-1919)

Enquiries: To Secretary

Scope: Enquiries regarding manufacture and makes of pre-1919 motor cars, and of some between 1919 and up to present day
Secondary: Comprehensive library on personalities of the early motoring era, and large collection of technical data

Stock: 5,000 books; numerous pamphlets; all motoring publications. Stock not available on loan

Publications: Quarterly Gazette
Annual Handbook

LONDON

1672

THE VICTORIAN SOCIETY *Tel.:* 01-994 1510
12 Magnolia Wharf
Strand-on-the-Green
London W.4

National preservation Society for 19th century buildings. Organizes lectures and tours of study of 19th century and case work on the preservation of buildings

Enquiries: To Secretary

Reference books only for Society's use

Publications: Many publications, including Reports of Historical and Architectural interest, and Architectural Notes for Walks and Visits in all parts of the United Kingdom (list available from Publications Secretary)

LONDON

1673

THE WALLACE COLLECTION *Tel.:* 01-935 0687
Manchester Square
London W.1

Enquiries: To Director

Scope: The Museum contains the Collection of three great 19th century connoisseurs, the 3rd and 4th Marquesses of Hertford and Sir Richard Wallace, and was bequeathed to the nation by Sir Richard's widow. The purpose of the Museum is to display this Collection and to provide information about the objects it contains.
The Library, which is solely for the use of the staff in answering enquiries and is not open to the public, consists primarily of books on painting, sculpture, ceramics, French furniture, and arms and armour of the Middle Ages and Renaissance in Europe. There is also a considerable collection of 18th and 19th century sales catalogues

LONDON	WALTHAM FOREST TECHNICAL COLLEGE AND SCHOOL OF ART, Constituent College of the Proposed North-East London Polytechnic Forest Road Walthamstow London E.17	*Tel.*: 01-527 2272 ext. 125
1674		

Enquiries: To Librarian

Scope: Land surveying, science and technology, humanities and fine arts
Special collections: Essex; London; William Morris

Stock: 38,000 books; 504 current periodicals

LONDON	WALTHAMSTOW ANTIQUARIAN SOCIETY Vestry House Museum Vestry Road London E.17
1675	

Promotion and study of local history with special reference to Walthamstow. Research, visits, outings, lectures, publications, recording. Amateur Society founded 1914 (oldest in Essex)

Enquiries: To Hon. Secretary, by letter only

Scope: Local history of Walthamstow
Secondary: Local history in Epping Forest area

No library

Publications: Many monographs and occasional publications
The Record (illustrated news sheet of the Society)

LONDON	WANDSWORTH TECHNICAL COLLEGE Wandsworth High Street London S.W.18 *and* Annexe: Plough Road St Johns Hill London S.W.11	*Tel.*: 01-874 2355 *Tel.*: 01-228 2600
1676		

Enquiries: To Principal, for the attention of Librarian

Scope: Electrical and mechanical engineering subjects and theoretical subjects which are supplementary such as physics and chemistry; Heating, ventilating and air conditioning; Metallurgy; Visual Aids in education; Motor vehicle technology
Secondary: Business studies; Economics, commerce and geography. Computer technology, programming and applications. Photography, cine-photography and television production. Sociology

Stock: 18,900 books; 1,000 pamphlets; 230 current periodicals; 2,800 British Standards
Publications: Bibliographies on: Metallurgy; Computers; Heating and Ventilating

LONDON	THE WEDGWOOD SOCIETY Flat 3 75 Anson Road London N.7
1677	

Enquiries: To Chairman

LONDON, THE WEDGWOOD SOCIETY, *cont.*

Scope: Information relating to the history and production of the Wedgwood factory, but not valuations of specimens

Publications: Proceedings of the Wedgwood Society

LONDON
1678

WELLCOME INSTITUTE OF THE HISTORY OF MEDICINE
183 Euston Road
London N.W.1
Library and Museum

Tel.: 01-387 4688

Enquiries: To Librarian or Curator

Scope: History of medicine and allied sciences
Special Collections: Americana; Orientalia manuscripts; Western manuscripts and a large quantity of autograph letters on all aspects of medical history. Adjacent museum in which there is a strong ceramic collection

Stock: 290,000 books and pamphlets; 100 current periodicals

Publications: Current Work in the History of Medicine (quarterly)
Catalogue series (printed books, incunabula, Western mediaeval manuscripts, Arabic manuscripts, ceramics)
Historical monographs series
Lecture series
Exhibition catalogues
Medical History (quarterly)
Postcards

Deposited Libraries: Medical Society of London Library; Society for the Study of Addiction to Alcohol and other Drugs Library

LONDON
1679

WELLCOME MUSEUM OF MEDICAL SCIENCE
P.O. Box 129
183 Euston Road
London N.W.1

Tel.: 01-387 4477

Provides information on tropical medicine and medical biology to graduates, undergraduates and para-medical trainees. The facilities include a tutorial room for the use of teachers and small classes, and visual aids are provided on request. A limited amount of technological and demonstrative research is carried out by the staff

Enquiries: To Director

Scope: The primary source of information lies in the museum displays which include abstracts and extracts from recent published work on the subjects exhibited
Secondary: More detailed and specific information is given where possible, either by reference to the literature or by making available items from the collections of pathological and biological material which are not usually exhibited in the museum

No library

LONDON
1680

WELLINGTON MUSEUM
Apsley House
149 Piccadilly
London W.1

Tel.: 01-499 5676

Enquiries: To Officer-in-Charge

Scope: The library which is departmental and not for public use, contains books on the life of the Duke of Wellington and other books on the fine arts

Stock: 250 books; 150 pamphlets

Publications: Life of the Duke of Wellington—a pictorial biography. 1969
The Duke of Wellington in Caricature. 1965   The Wellington Plate. 1954
The Waterloo Despatch. 1965   Paintings at Apsley House. 1965
Guide to the Wellington Museum. 1965

LONDON 1681 WEST END STAGE MANAGEMENT ASSOCIATION *Tel.:* 01-994 5261
81 St Mary's Grove
London W.4

Enquiries: To Hon. Secretary

Scope: Stage management
No library

Publications: Notes for the Guidance of Company and Stage Managers. D. Cornelissen (for members only)

LONDON 1682 WEST HAM COLLEGE OF TECHNOLOGY *Tel.:* 01-534 4545 ext. 561
Romford Road
Stratford
London E.15

Enquiries: To Tutor Librarian

Scope: Engineering (civil, chemical, electrical and mechanical); physics, chemistry (with particular reference to analytical chemistry); mathematics and statistics; psychology and sociology

Stock: 27,000 books; 600 current periodicals. Good stock of abstracting and indexing journals

LONDON 1683 THE WEST INDIA COMMITTEE *Tel.:* 01-836 8922
40 Norfolk Street
London W.C.2

Aims to foster Commonwealth Caribbean/United Kingdom trade and investment and to strengthen the ties of friendship between their peoples

Enquiries: To Information Officer, Librarian or Secretary

Scope: The reference library is particularly strong on West Indian history and law, sugar, slavery (a unique collection of pamphlets) and travels and voyages in the Caribbean. Altogether there are 64 subject headings, all pertinent to the Caribbean, ranging from Administration to West India Committee publications. The collection numbers about 6,000 items and is the finest collection of its kind in Europe

Stock: 6,000 items; 21 current periodicals. Stock not available on loan

Publications: The West Indies Chronicle (monthly)

LONDON 1684 THE WEST KENT MEDICO-CHIRURGICAL SOCIETY *Tel.:* 01-698 3485
80 Torridon Road
Catford
London S.E.6

Learned Society for the furtherance of the art and practice of medicine and surgery in the area of South East London and West Kent

Enquiries: To Hon. Secretary, by letter only

Scope: Archive of limited value to those interested in the history of medicine in the area (founded 1856)

LONDON	WEST LONDON HOSPITAL LIBRARY	
	Hammersmith Road	
1685	London W.6	
	See no. 1043	

LONDON	WESTFIELD COLLEGE (UNIVERSITY OF LONDON)	*Tel.:* 01-435 7601
1686	Kidderpore Avenue	
	London N.W.3	

Enquiries: To Librarian

Scope: The Library has no information service, but endeavours to answer questions which are within the field of its stock: Modern languages (including English, French, German, Spanish, Portuguese, Italian and Rumanian); Romance philology, classics (Greek and Latin), ancient history, modern history, history of art. No material on medicine or the social sciences
Special collection: Lyttleton letters, 19th to early 20th century (manuscript collection)

Stock: 80,000 books; 2,400 pamphlets; 430 current periodicals, of which 260 are arts

Publications: Inaugural Lectures

LONDON	WESTMINSTER ABBEY	*Tel.:* 01-222 4233
	Muniment Room and Library	
1687	London S.W.1	

Enquiries: To Keeper of the Muniments, by letter only

Scope: History and buildings of Westminster Abbey and its estates

Stock: Archive collection which is not available on loan

LONDON	WESTMINSTER CITY LIBRARIES	*Tel.:* 01-935 7766
	Public Library	*Telex:* 263305
1688	Marylebone Road	
	London N.W.1	

Enquiries: To City Librarian

Scope: SOCIAL SCIENCES AND HUMANITIES:

Central Reference Library, St Martin's Street, London W.C.2 (*Tel.:* 01-930 3274; *Telex:* 261845)
General: Extensive range of author and subject bibliographies. General and special encyclopaedias in many languages. Extensive collection of foreign language dictionaries, biographical dictionaries and publications of learned societies and the Public Record Office. Abstracts, indexes, periodicals. All H.M.S.O. publications since 1947, with most of United Nations and Agency publications. Almost complete set of Parliamentary Papers from 1826.
Theatre, cinema and ballet: Substantial collection of books and serials on theatre, cinema and ballet and entertainment in general. The Pavlova Memorial Library of books relating to the dance. The Critics' Circle Collection of older books on the theatre
Non-Christian religions: Large collection of books held under the Special Collection (London Scheme)
Reference Library, Marylebone Road, London N.W.1 (*Tel.:* 01-935 7766; *Telex:* 263305)
Reference Library, Porchester Road, London W.2 (*Tel.:* 01-229 6611)
Both libraries have holdings of material of the same nature as above although on a less substantial scale

SPECIAL LIBRARIES:

Fine Arts Library, Central Reference Library, St Martin's Street, London W.C.2 (*Tel.:* 01-930 3274; *Telex:* 261845)

A special library consisting of an extensive collection of books, pamphlets, periodicals, art reproductions and transparencies. Range of subjects covered includes painting, drawing, sculpture, ceramics, glassware, coins, tapestry, carpets, furniture, jewellery, interior design, costume, goldsmiths' work and silverware, arms and armour. A large number of serials on permanent file. Also includes the Preston 'Blake' Library—a comprehensive collection of material by and about William Blake, including manuscript letters

Medical Library, Marylebone Road District Library, London N.W.1 (*Tel.:* 01-935 7766; *Telex:* 263305)
Aim is to provide a comprehensive general medical collection including nursing and dentistry. Most British and many American textbooks for medical students. Highly specialized books for the postgraduate worker. Good collection of works on ophthalmology and speech therapy, and most of the available literature on music therapy. French books donated by the Institut Français. Publications of the World Health Organization. Index Medicus

LOCAL HISTORY AND ARCHIVES:

The District Library, Buckingham Palace Road, London S.W.1 (*Tel:* 01-730 0446)
Local History collection and archives repository for the City of Westminster. Includes parish registers and Gillow archives

Public Library, Marylebone Road, London N.W.1 (*Tel.:* 01-935 7766; *Telex:* 263305)
Local history collection and archives repository for Paddington and St Marylebone; Ashridge Collection (local topography) and Sherlock Holmes Collection

Central Music Library Ltd., The District Library, Buckingham Palace Road, London S.W.1 (*Tel.:* 01-730 0446)
A collection formed by bringing together the library of the late Mrs Christie Moór and the large central library of the Westminster City Council's Music Division. The stock includes books about music, miniature scores, song collections, instrumental collections and tutors, orchestral parts and periodicals. A directory of amateur musicians is maintained

LENDING LIBRARIES: SPECIAL COLLECTIONS

The District Library, Sutherland Avenue, Maida Vale, London W.9 (*Tel.:* 01-286 5788) houses a substantial collection of books on all aspects of education, together with a special collection on military and naval science and history

The District Library, Buckingham Palace Road, London S.W.1 (*Tel.:* 01-730 0446) is a repository library holding large lending collections of works on the fine arts and English literature

The District Library, South Audley Street, London W.1 (*Tel.:* 01-499 2351) houses an extensive collection on foreign languages

The District Library, 20 Circus Road, St John's Wood, London N.W.1 (*Tel.:* 01-722 1960) houses the lending collection on non-Christian religions

Stock: Central Reference Library, St Martin's Street, London W.C.2: General: 70,000 books; 3,000 pamphlets; 500 current periodicals
Theatre, cinema and ballet: 5,000 books; 500 pamphlets; 50 current periodicals
Fine Art Library: 20,000 books; 2,500 pamphlets; 70 current periodicals; 32,500 illustrations; 9,500 Fine Art colour transparencies; 2,500 prints (reproductions specially selected by UNESCO)
District Library, Marylebone Road, London N.W.1: Medical Library: 17,000 books and pamphlets; 100 current periodicals. Local history and archives; 10,000 archives; 7,500 cuttings and dossiers; 8,500 prints
District Library, Buckingham Palace Road, London S.W.1: Central Music Library: 80,000 books and scores
Local History and Archives: 100,000 archives; 20,000 cuttings and dossiers; 10,000 prints; 18,000 theatre programmes

LONDON, WESTMINSTER CITY LIBRARIES, *cont.*

Publications: Printed catalogue of books and pamphlets added to the libraries of the former City of Westminster, 1952–1964
Union List of periodicals held by Westminster City Libraries
Catalogue of the Preston 'Blake' Library

LONDON

1689

WESTMINSTER MEDICAL SCHOOL
Horseferry Road
London S.W.1

Tel.: 01-828 9811 ext. 2318

Enquiries: To Librarian, by letter only

Scope: Medicine, surgery and some ancillary subjects. The information service is internal except in individual cases to identified qualified practitioners without resource to other libraries

LONDON

1690

WHITELANDS COLLEGE OF EDUCATION
West Hill
Putney
London S.W.15

Tel.: 01-788 8268

Enquiries: To Librarian

Scope: Education, though not exhaustively and with the proviso that this section is under heavy pressure from the Library's student readers
Secondary: John Ruskin: a collection of his works and some critical material
19th century Children's Books: a small collection (about 70 items)

Stock: 47,000 books; 195 current periodicals

LONDON

1691

WIENER LIBRARY
4 Devonshire Street
London W1N 2BH

Tel.: 01-636 7247

See no. 1251

LONDON

1692

WILLIAM MORRIS GALLERY
Water House
Lloyd Park
Forest Road
Walthamstow
London E.17

Tel.: 01-527 5544 ext. 390

Museum and art gallery covering the work of William Morris and associates. English Art and Crafts Movement; paintings by Frank Brangwyn and other late 19th and early 20th century artists

Enquiries: To Curator

Scope: Work by Morris and his associates—Chintzes, wallpapers, furniture. Original designs for work produced by the Morris firm. Furniture and fabrics from the Century Guild and other Arts and Crafts bodies. Paintings, watercolours and graphic work by the Pre-Raphaelites, Frank Brangwyn and other artists of the period. Pottery by W. de Morgan and the Martin Brothers. Sculpture by Rodin and Dalou. Private Press books including Kelmscott Press
Secondary: Manuscripts (Morris and others), contemporary news cuttings, pamphlets (Morris political), catalogues. Kelmscott Press books. Complete works of William Morris. Biographies of Morris. Books and exhibition catalogues on Art Nouveau and Arts and Crafts movement. General books on art history. Books on or relating to Pre-Raphaelites, including *The Germ* and *Oxford and Cambridge Magazine*

Stock: 800 books; 200 pamphlets; 4 current periodicals. Stock not normally available on loan
Publications: Catalogue of the Morris Collection
Catalogue of the A. H. Mackmurdo and Century Guild Collection
Quarterly Bulletin of the William Morris Gallery

LONDON
1693

WIMBLEDON SCHOOL OF ART *Tel.:* 01-542 6003
Merton Hall Road
London S.W.19

Enquiries: To Librarian
Scope: History of art, drawing, painting, sculpture (4,410 books). Drama, stage design, costume, plays (1,460 books)
Secondary: Literature, history, landscape art and architecture, philosophy and religion
Stock: 10,800 books including exhibition catalogues; 60 current periodicals

LONDON
1694

WOMEN'S EMPLOYMENT FEDERATION *Tel.:* 01-589 9237
251 Brompton Road
London S.W.3

National Federation of organizations concerned with the employment and training of women

Enquiries: To Secretary
Scope: Advice on training and employment for girls and women
No library
Publications: Bulletin (three times each year)
Various pamphlets and books on careers, employment and training
Careers (revised every two years)

LONDON
1695

WOMEN'S GROUP ON PUBLIC WELFARE *Tel.:* 01-636 4066
26 Bedford Square
London W.C.1

Aims to direct the experience of its 53 constituent organizations towards questions of public welfare, in particular those affecting women and children, to facilitate co-operation between women's organizations and to maintain contact with women's organizations overseas by exchange visits and help to their visitors here

Enquiries: To Secretary
Scope: *General Information on Women's Organizations:*
Addresses, date of foundation, membership figures, aims and activities of the various women's organizations in Great Britain including professional, religious and political bodies and British branches of international women's organizations. Some information on overseas women's organizations, including Iron Curtain countries
Information on Social and Welfare Work:
Information on work done in this field by women's organizations. Information on various aspects of social problems of women and their families
Index of Resolutions passed by women's Organizations:
Index, catalogued by subject, of resolutions passed since 1962
Household Management:
Enquiries dealing with all aspects of domestic management are referred to a specialist committee: The Council of Scientific Management in the Home
No library
Publications: Women's Organizations in Great Britain: a classified directory

LONDON, WOMEN'S GROUP ON PUBLIC WELFARE, *cont.*

Loneliness: An enquiry into its causes and possible remedies (published by National Council of Social Service)

Newsletter (quarterly, an examination of a different social topic in each issue)

LONDON

1696

WOMEN'S INTERNATIONAL LEAGUE FOR PEACE AND FREEDOM (BRITISH SECTION) *Tel.:* 01-242 4817
29 Great James Street
London W.C.1

Non-party political work for peace and goodwill between nations

Enquiries: To Secretary

Scope: Archives of the League; history of various famous personalities; women's suffrage

Stock: 100 books; 150 pamphlets. Stock not available on loan

LONDON

1697

WOOLWICH HOSPITAL GROUP POSTGRADUATE MEDICAL LIBRARY *Tel.:* 01-856 5555 ext. 292
Brook Hospital
Woolwich
London S.E.18

Postgraduate medical library service to Consultants, Hospital Doctors and General Practitioners in South East London and North West Kent

Enquiries: To Librarian

Scope: Limited stock in the medical and surgical fields

Stock: 800 books; 200 pamphlets; 90 current periodicals. Books not available on loan

LONDON

1698

WOOLWICH POLYTECHNIC *Tel.:* 01-854 9624
Wellington Street
Woolwich
London S.E.18

Enquiries: To Librarian

Scope: Chemistry, physics, mathematics, engineering (civil, electrical and electronic, mechanical and production), biology, zoology, botany, economics, languages, management, business studies, humanities, history of science and technology

Stock: 25,000 books; 1,000 pamphlets; 700 current periodicals

LONDON

1699

WORKERS' EDUCATIONAL ASSOCIATION *Tel.:* 01-402 5608
Temple House
9 Upper Berkeley Street
London W1H 8BY

Aims to stimulate and satisfy the demand of workers for education, and to further the advancement of education

Enquiries: To Librarian, by letter only

Scope: Existing library is confined to adult education, but a library is being built up dealing with the social sciences

Stock not available on loan

Publications: Background Notes on Industrial Relations (monthly bulletin)

LONDON	WORKING MEN'S COLLEGE	*Tel.:* 01-387 2037
1700	Crowndale Road London N.W.1	

Liberal education for men and women by evening study

Enquiries: To Warden

Scope: Certain books and papers dealing with Christian Socialists and Founders of Working Men's College
Secondary: Social history of the 19th century

Stock: 25,000 books

Publications: Journal of W.M.C. (one issue each term)

LONDON	THE WORLD ASSOCIATION FOR CHRISTIAN COMMUNICATION	*Tel.:* 01-730 2162
1701	Edinburgh House 2 Eaton Gate London S.W.1	

Aims to assist persons and agencies engaged in various forms of Christian communication (broadcasting, print, audio-visual) to use the media in promoting human welfare and development

Enquiries: To Executive Director

Scope: Information on the use of communication media to achieve Christian goals. Communicating the Christian message. The effects of communication media for the world and implications for the work of the church
Secondary: Instruction in communications techniques, research. Information about the world church's use of the media. Information about the Association

No library

Publications: The WACC Quarterly Journal (previously called *The Christian Broadcaster*)
Radio Programming. R. Milton
FRAM, A Report on the Oslo Assembly, 1968. J. E. McEldowney, ed.

LONDON	WORLD CONFEDERATION FOR PHYSICAL THERAPY	*Tel.:* 01-930 2435
1702	Burdett House 15 Buckingham Street Strand London W.C.2	

Aims to encourage improved standards of physical therapy training and practice

Enquiries: To Secretary-General

Scope: Information on physical therapy training and patient services in the Confederation's 32 member organizations and in many other countries

No library

Publications: Proceedings of W.C.P.T.s international congresses
Pamphlets on the training of physical therapists
Physical Therapy in the Treatment of Leprosy
Physical Therapy Words and Phrases—in 19 languages

LONDON	WORLD CONGRESS OF FAITHS	*Tel.:* 01-723 9820
1703	23 Norfolk Square London W.2	

                Aims to extend genuine knowledge of all world religions and encourage friendly contacts amongst their adherents, but with no proselytizing or propaganda

Enquiries: To Hon. General Secretary

Scope: Information is disseminated mainly through lectures, visits to centres of religious interest, multi-faith services of worship and annual conferences

Publications: World Faiths (quarterly)

LONDON	WORLD'S WOMAN'S CHRISTIAN TEMPERANCE UNION	*Tel.:* 01-769 6649
1704	62 Becmead Avenue London S.W.16	

                Education of public, particularly youth, as to physical and moral harm resulting from use of alcohol and other drugs. Promotion of status of women, peace, literacy, anti-slavery, anti-gambling, child welfare, social and moral hygiene

Enquiries: To Corresponding Secretary

Scope: Temperance history, educational, alcohol and health

Publications: W.W.C.T.U. White Ribbon Bulletin (5 times each year)
Our Goodly Heritage (history of W.W.C.T.U.)
Clad with Zeal (story of founding of German W.C.T.U.)
African Horizons (account of pioneer temperance educational work in East and West Africa)
Properties with a Purpose (50 buildings owned by National Unions in various continents)

LONDON	THE WRITERS' GUILD OF GREAT BRITAIN	*Tel.:* 01-723 8074
1705	430 Edgware Road London W.2	

                Aims to maintain and improve the industrial conditions of writers in the media of radio, television, and film

Enquiries: To General Secretary

Scope: Books dealing with writing generally; with radio, television, and film in particular; and with the 'mechanical media' as an industry. A selection of film scripts over the period 1930 to present
Secondary: A small selection of trade union reference works. A selection of books intended as background reading for writers: varied subjects, fiction and non-fiction

Stock: 2,000 books and pamphlets; 7 current periodicals

Publications: The Writers Guide (annually)
Script Registration Service (a method of protecting copyright in written material)

LONDON	THE YOUTH SERVICE ASSOCIATION	*Tel.:* 01-808 4312
1706	628 High Road London N.17	

Enquiries: To Secretary

Scope: Knowledge of aspects of youth work for example, detached, experimental, immigrant, throughout the country. Small number of surveys for example, on teacher/youth leader statistics, drug taking

Publications: Youth Review

LONDON	THE ZAMBIA HIGH COMMISSION	*Tel.:* 01-580 0691
	Zambia House	*Telex:* 266360
1707	7/11 Cavendish Place	
	London W.1	

Enquiries: To Librarian
Scope: General information about Zambia, its people, government and industry, trade and commerce
Stock: 300 books; 10 pamphlets; 10 current periodicals

LONDONDERRY	LONDONDERRY POST GRADUATE MEDICAL CENTRE	*Tel.:* Londonderry 5171
1708	Altnagelvin Hospital	
	Londonderry	

Enquiries: To Clinical Tutor
Scope: General medicine and allied sciences
Stock: Several hundred books; 50 pamphlets; 50 current periodicals

LONDONDERRY	LONDONDERRY PUBLIC LIBRARIES	*Tel.:* Londonderry 3651
	Brooke Park	
1709	Londonderry	

Enquiries: To Librarian
Scope: Local history collection
Stock: 20,000 books; 9 current periodicals (total stock)

LONDONDERRY	MAGEE UNIVERSITY COLLEGE	*Tel.:* Londonderry 4353
	Londonderry	
1710	*Enquiries:* To Librarian	

Scope: General coverage of the humanities
Special Irish collection
Stock: 75,000 books; 7,000 pamphlets; 400 current periodicals

LONG EATON	*See under* **NOTTINGHAM** *for*
Nottingham	LONG EATON PUBLIC LIBRARY (no. 1889)

LOUGHBOROUGH	THE CO-OPERATIVE UNION LTD	*Tel.:* East Leake 333
Leics	THE CO-OPERATIVE COLLEGE	
	J. J. WORLEY MEMORIAL LIBRARY	
1711	Stanford Hall	
	Loughborough	
	Leicestershire	

Adult residential college which has three main tasks: education and training for the professional leaders of the Co-operative Movement and also for men and women who take voluntary responsibility in community service generally and Co-operative service in particular; presentation of British Co-operative experience for the help of Movements overseas and especially those in the developing countries; the promotion of research into problems of Co-operative development; and post-graduate courses in management studies

Enquiries: To Librarian, by letter only
Scope: General stock for College courses including co-operation at home and abroad, economics, accountancy, finance, banking, taxation, commerce, history, economic history, industrial

LOUGHBOROUGH, THE CO-OPERATIVE UNION LTD, THE CO-OPERATIVE COLLEGE, J. J. WORLEY MEMORIAL LIBRARY, *cont.*
history, central and local government, politics, law, sociology, philosophy. Histories of co-operative retail societies
Special collection: Robert Owen's publications

Stock: 12,000 books; 2,000 pamphlets; 60 current periodicals; Co-operative Congress Reports from 1869; Trade Union Congresses 1939; C.W.S. Almanack Annual 1881–1918

Publications: Co-operative College Occasional Paper
The Society for Co-operative Studies Bulletin
Co-operative Union, Education Department: various educational bulletins

---

LOUGHBOROUGH FISONS PHARMACEUTICALS LIMITED   *Tel.:* Loughborough 66361
Leics   Research and Development Laboratories   *Telex:* 34341
    Bakewell Road
1712   Loughborough
    Leicestershire

Research, manufacture and marketing of ethical and proprietary pharmaceuticals, toiletries and dietary foods

Enquiries: To Information Officer or Librarian

Scope: Medicine, organic chemistry, biochemistry, pharmacology, toxicology, cell biology, pharmacy
Secondary: Cosmetics and toiletries, chemical engineering

Stock: 7,000 books, pamphlets and reports; 400 current periodicals. Books only available on loan. Subscriber to FARMDOC and RINGDOC

Member of LETIS and NANTIS

LOUGHBOROUGH LOUGHBOROUGH COLLEGE OF ART   *Tel.:* Loughborough 2675
Leics   Ashby Road
    Loughborough
1713   Leicestershire

Enquiries: To Librarian

Scope: Fine art, textiles/fashion, furniture, silversmithing, ceramics, history of art

Stock: 5,500 books; 250 pamphlets; 65 current periodicals; 1,200 slides

Publications: Accessions lists
Bibliographies of subjects in stock

LOUGHBOROUGH LOUGHBOROUGH UNIVERSITY OF   *Tel.:* Loughborough 3171
Leics   TECHNOLOGY   *Telex:* 34319
    Loughborough
1714   Leicestershire

Enquiries: To Librarian

Scope: Ergonomics, economics, politics, education

Stock: 10,000 books; 2,000 pamphlets; 2,000 reports; 300 current periodicals

Publications: Bulletin (monthly accessions list)
Leicestershire Technical Information Service (LETIS, no. 2380) is based on this Library, and is primarily for industry or other libraries in the area

LOUGHBOROUGH	RIKER LABORATORIES	*Tel.:* Loughborough 3181
Leics	Morley Street	*Telex:* 34587
	Loughborough	
1715	Leicestershire	

Research on and manufacture of pharmaceutical preparations available on prescription

Enquiries: To Librarian

Scope: Medicine, pharmacy, pharmacology and chemistry
Secondary: Business management; packaging (including aerosols)

Stock: 1,000 books; 300 pamphlets; 220 current periodicals

Publications: Monthly Abstract Bulletin
Monthly List of Additions to the Library

LOUTH	LOUTH NATURALISTS', ANTIQUARIAN AND
Lincs	LITERARY SOCIETY
	The Museum
1716	4 Broadbank
	Louth
	Lincolnshire

Enquiries: To Secretary of the Museum

Scope: Mainly matters of antiquarian and naturalists' interest with some pamphlets and books on the history of Louth and places in the immediate neighbourhood

Stock: 900 books; 150 pamphlets. Stock available on loan only to members of the Society

LOWESTOFT	LOWESTOFT COLLEGE OF FURTHER	*Tel.:* Lowestoft 4177
Suffolk	EDUCATION	
	St Peter's Street	
1717	Lowestoft	
	Suffolk	

Enquiries: To Librarian

Scope: Sociology; education; child study. (Sociology is a comparatively new subject and coverage is mainly directed to 'A' level sociology and to courses for professional and voluntary social workers. The small educational collection serves mainly as an L.E.A. library for teachers within the area)

Stock: 500 books (sociology, education and child study); 50 pamphlets (mainly education); 15 current periodicals

Publications: Accession lists
Indexed collection of newspaper cuttings and magazine articles

LUTON	LUTON AND DUNSTABLE HOSPITAL
Beds	Medical Centre Library
1718	*See* no. 1721

LUTON	LUTON COLLEGE OF TECHNOLOGY	*Tel.:* Luton 29441
Beds	Park Square	
	Luton	
1719	Bedfordshire	

Enquiries: To Librarian

LUTON, LUTON COLLEGE OF TECHNOLOGY, *cont.*

Scope: Business studies including management, industrial relations, personnel management and secretarial. Mechanical, automotive, electrical and electronic engineering. Industrial design; metallurgy; mathematics; geology; geography; biology; biochemistry; mineralogy; and physics. Building, including wood treatment and construction; painting and decorating. Food and fashion, including hairdressing. Art (predominantly commercial art)

Stock: 23,000 books; 5,000 pamphlets; 256 current periodicals

---

LUTON
Beds

1720

LUTON MUSEUM AND ART GALLERY
Wardown Park
Luton
Bedfordshire

Tel.: Luton 21725

Regional museum of social and environmental history

Enquiries: To Director, by letter only

Scope: Industrial and agricultural history, particularly of South Bedfordshire. Rural trades and crafts. Industrial archaeology. 19th century social and educational studies. 19th century domestic life

Stock: 14,000 books and pamphlets; 2,000 archives; 2,000 historical slides; 3,000 photographs; abstracted newspaper cuttings (regional) from 1900. Stock not available on loan, but photocopies supplied

Publications: Pillow Lace of the East Midlands. Freeman
Luton and the Hat Industry. Freeman
Bedfordshire Vermin Payments. Steele-Elliot
Flora of Bedfordshire. Dony

LUTON
Beds

1721

LUTON PUBLIC LIBRARIES
Central Library
Bridge Street
Luton
Bedfordshire

Tel.: Luton 30161
Telex: 82347

Enquiries: To Librarian

Scope: Library on education for teachers (2,000 volumes). Luton and district local collection. Microfilm copy of 'Luton News'

Stock: 300,000 books (including 20,000 reference); 3,000 pamphlets; 300 current periodicals (total stock). British town guides and street maps

Medical library of 1,000 books and 100 current periodicals at Medical Centre, Luton and Dunstable Hospital

Headquarters of Luton and District Technical Information Service (no. 2386)

LUTON
Beds

1722

PUTTERIDGE BURY COLLEGE OF EDUCATION
Putteridge Bury
Luton
Bedfordshire

Tel.: Luton 26161

Enquiries: To Tutor Librarian

Scope: Education, child development, school practice textbooks. Mathematics, science, art, music, history, geography, English
Secondary: Local history (Bedfordshire, Buckinghamshire, Hertfordshire)

Stock: 12,000 books; 500 pamphlets; 200 reports; 40 current periodicals relating to education; 50 current periodicals relating to other subjects

Publications: Occasional recent additions lists

MACCLESFIELD
Cheshire

1723

IMPERIAL CHEMICAL INDUSTRIES LTD
INDUSTRIAL HYGIENE RESEARCH
   LABORATORIES
Alderley Park
Macclesfield
Cheshire SK10 4TJ

Tel.: Alderley Edge 2711
Telex: 66152

Investigation of the toxicological properties, metabolism and mechanism of action of industrial chemicals, including agricultural chemicals

Enquiries: To Information Officer

Scope: The Library specializes in books and periodicals in the fields of industrial toxicology, industrial hygiene, occupational health and food additives legislation but also includes small sections on biochemistry, pharmacology, physiology, pathology and medicine. The Information Service specializes in answering enquiries on the toxicology of industrial chemicals, including agricultural chemicals but can also deal with enquiries relating to industrial hygiene, occupational health and food additives legislation

Stock: 2,500 books and pamphlets; 175 current periodicals. Stock not available on loan, but photocopies may be supplied

Publications: Toxicological Abstracts Bulletin (monthly)

MACCLESFIELD
Cheshire

1724

IMPERIAL CHEMICAL INDUSTRIES LIMITED
PHARMACEUTICALS DIVISION
Mereside
Alderley Park
Macclesfield
Cheshire SK10 4TG

Tel.: Alderley Edge 2828
Telex: 669095

Research, development, manufacture and sale of pharmaceuticals

Enquiries: To Information Officer or Librarian (for loans)

Scope: Chemistry (particularly organic), biochemistry, applied chemistry, biology, pharmacology, physiology, pathology, human and veterinary medicine, pharmacy
Secondary: Economics, commerce, management, statistics, packaging, computer technology; economic information relating to the pharmaceutical industry in the United Kingdom and abroad

Stock: 18,000 books; 8,000 pamphlets; 800 current periodicals. Large collection of patent specifications, official journals and patent abstract publications primarily relating to pharmaceuticals and pesticides

MACCLESFIELD
Cheshire

1725

MACCLESFIELD PUBLIC LIBRARY
Park Green
Macclesfield
Cheshire SK11 6TW

Tel.: Macclesfield 2512

Enquiries: To Librarian

Scope: Regional specialization: Physiology of the nervous system (90 volumes). Travel and history; of Siberia and Central Asia (130 volumes). Local history

Stock: 47,500 books (total stock)

MACCLESFIELD	WEST PARK MUSEUM AND ART GALLERY	*Tel.:* Prestbury 89418
Cheshire	Prestbury Road	
	Macclesfield	
1726	Cheshire SK10 4PZ	

    Enquiries: To Hon. Curator, by letter only

    Scope: Egyptian antiquities and pictures, particularly topographical

MADELEY
Crewe
Cheshire

See under **CREWE** *for*
MADELEY COLLEGE OF EDUCATION (no. 427)

MAIDENHEAD
Berks

1727

BERKSHIRE COLLEGE OF ART
Marlow Road
Maidenhead
Berkshire

    Enquiries: To Librarian

    Scope: Fashion, design, aesthetics, painting, sculpture, architecture and town planning, ceramics
    Secondary: Printing

    Stock: 1,500 books, including fashion 100, design 100, painting 250, printing books 400; 8 current periodicals

MAIDENHEAD	EAST BERKS COLLEGE OF FURTHER EDUCATION	*Tel.:* Maidenhead 25221
Berks	Boyne Hill Avenue	
	Maidenhead	
1728	Berkshire	

    Enquiries: To Librarian

    Scope: All aspects of business studies, including law, economics and management (mainly to 'A' level and OND)

    Stock: 3,000 books and pamphlets; 40 current periodicals

MAIDENHEAD	JOHN WYETH & BROTHER LTD	*Tel.:* Slough 28311
Berks	Huntercombe Lane South	
	Taplow	
1729	Maidenhead	
	Berkshire	

    Enquiries: To Librarian

    Scope: Medicine, pharmacy, pharmacology, toxicology, microbiology, and organic chemistry

    Stock: 1,500 books; 480 pamphlets and reports; 185 current periodicals; 7,000 reprints and photographs

MAIDENHEAD	SYNTEX PHARMACEUTICALS	*Tel.:* Maidenhead 28424
Berks	St Ives House	*Telex:* 84387
	St Ives Road	
1730	Maidenhead	
	Berkshire	

    Research, clinical trial and marketing of ethical steroid products in the medical and veterinary field

    Enquiries: To Information Scientist

Scope: General: Research oriented reference library concerning steroid hormones, and the development of steroid drugs; biology, pharmacology, toxicology and clinical trial
Specific: Contraception, cancer, blood diseases, connective tissue disorders, anabolic steroids, veterinary applications, physiology of reproduction

Stock: Reference collection of books; 2,500 published articles incorporated into Information Retrieval System each year, stored as bound volume, reprint or microfilm; 50 current periodicals

Publications: Corporation and a Molecule
Series: Famous Dermatologists
Advances in Fertility Control
Fertility Control: a current appraisal. 1966
Cancer of the Breast. One year of international literature—1967. 1969
The Treatment of Carcinoma of the Breast. 1968
Chlormadinone Acetate: a New Departure in Oral Contraception. 1969

World literature scanned by the company in Mexico and United States of America for computerized storage and retrieval

MAIDSTONE
Kent

1731

KENT COUNTY LIBRARY
Springfield
Maidstone
Kent

Tel.: Maidstone 54371
(Students Library ext. 386)

Enquiries: To Librarian

Scope: L.A.S.E.R. subject specialization includes:
Sleep, dreams, somnambulism
Agricultural industries: economic questions
Medicine: general questions (excluding nursing and history)
Pathology: general questions (excluding microbiology, bacteriology, and aetiology)
Specific diseases not classified elsewhere
Diseases of the body as a whole; communicable and other diseases
Manufacture of musical instruments
Music and musicians
English poetry: texts
Latin and Greek literature: texts and criticism
'Other' literatures: history and criticism
Kent: topography
Biography of Kentish men and women, dreamers and somnambulists, agricultural economists, philologists, linguists, doctors, medical specialists, farmers, musical instrument makers, musicians, Latin and Greek authors, and authors of 'other' literatures
Kent: history

Stock: 100,000 books; 200 current periodicals

MAIDSTONE
Kent

1732

MAIDSTONE COLLEGE OF ART
Oakwood Park
Oakwood Road
Maidstone
Kent

Tel.: Maidstone 57286

Enquiries: To Tutor Librarian

Scope: General art history, specializing in 18th to 20th centuries, with particular interest in history of British Art
Secondary: Literature, design and photography, and 'visual reference' (comprising small collection of illustrations and miscellanea for use by graphic design students)

Stock: 4,000 books; 30 current periodicals; 6,000 slides

MAIDSTONE Kent **1733**	MAIDSTONE MUSEUMS AND ART GALLERY St Faith's Street Maidstone Kent	*Tel.:* Maidstone 54497

Enquiries: To Curator

Scope: Prehistory, history and natural history of Kent. Specialized sections on Japanese art, horse-drawn carriages (at Tyrwhitt-Drake Museum of Carriages, Mill Street, Maidstone) and regimental history of Volunteers and Q.O.R.W.K. Regiment)

Stock: 25,000 books and pamphlets; 10 current periodicals

MAIDSTONE Kent **1734**	MEDWAY AND MAIDSTONE COLLEGE OF 　TECHNOLOGY Oakwood Park Tonbridge Road Maidstone Kent	*Tel.:* Maidstone 56531

Branch library of the main College at Horsted, Chatham, Kent

Scope: Accountancy, management, law, social work

MALVERN Worcs **1735**	MALVERN PUBLIC LIBRARY Graham Road Malvern Worcestershire	*Tel.:* Malvern 61223

Enquiries: To Librarian

Scope: Local History Collection of books, pamphlets, newspapers, photographs, prints and paintings, relating to Malvern and district

Stock: 2,000 books; 1,000 pamphlets; 1 local newspaper

MALVERN Worcs **1736**	ST WULSTAN'S HOSPITAL Malvern Wells Worcestershire	*Tel.:* Malvern Wells 61874

Enquiries: To Director

Scope: Information on psychiatric rehabilitation

Stock: 100 books; 100 pamphlets; 20 current periodicals

MANCHESTER **1737**	THE AMALGAMATED ASSOCIATION OF 　OPERATIVE COTTON SPINNERS AND 　TWINERS General Offices 115 Newton Street Manchester M1 1EF	*Tel.:* 061-236 0959

Trade union

Enquiries: To Secretary

Scope: The cotton industry; trade union history

No library

MANCHESTER 1738	AMALGAMATED UNION OF ENGINEERING AND FOUNDRY WORKERS (FOUNDRY SECTION) 164 Chorlton Road Brooks's Bar Manchester M16 7NU	*Tel.:* 061-226 1151

Enquiries: To Secretary, by letter only
Scope: Mainly industrial health questions

MANCHESTER 1739	ATHERTON PUBLIC LIBRARY York Street Atherton Manchester M29 9JH	*Tel.:* Atherton 3602

Enquiries: To Librarian
Scope: N.W.R.L.S. subject specialization includes: Genetic psychology and evolution
Stock: 650 books

MANCHESTER 1740	BOOTH HALL CHILDREN'S HOSPITAL Blackley Manchester 9	*Tel.:* 061-740 2254

Enquiries: To Librarian
Scope: Medical and surgical paediatrics
Stock: 200 books; 40 current periodicals. Stock not available on loan

MANCHESTER 1741	CHETHAM'S LIBRARY Manchester 3 Public reference library	*Tel.:* 061-834 7961

Enquiries: To Librarian
Scope: General scholarly library specializing (since 1850) in topography and history, particularly of the north-west of England. Stock is of interest from the point of view of the history of science and technology. Stock not available on loan

MANCHESTER 1742	CHRISTIE HOSPITAL AND HOLT RADIUM INSTITUTE Wilmslow Road Withington Manchester M20 9BX	*Tel.:* 061-445 8123

Enquiries: To Medical Librarian, by letter only
Scope: Cancer, radiotherapy and radiological physics
Secondary: General cancer radiotherapy and research
Stock: 2,500 books; 80 current periodicals

MANCHESTER 1743	CIVIC TRUST FOR THE NORTH-WEST Century House St Peter's Square Manchester 2	*Tel.:* 061-236 0333

See no. 1067

| MANCHESTER | COMMUNITY COUNCIL OF LANCASHIRE | Tel.: 061-224 3366 |

1744
Selnec House
Wynnstay Grove
Manchester M14 6XG

Initiation, support and co-ordination of voluntary organizations

Enquiries: To Secretary

Publications: Guide to Social Work Courses in Lancashire
Bibliography of Lancashire History:
    Volume I. Lancashire Directories (1684–1957)
    Volume II. Lancashire Acts of Parliament (1266–1957)
Grassing and Bushing Spoil Tips for Recreational Use (Spoil Lands Reclamation Scheme Instruction Manual)
Red Rose Magazine for Over Sixties (half yearly)
Drama in Lancashire

| MANCHESTER | THE CO-OPERATIVE UNION LTD | Tel.: 061-834 0975 |

1745
Holyoake House
Hanover Street
Manchester M60 0AS

Central and apex organization of consumer co-operative societies in Britain and Irish Republic

Enquiries: To Librarian

Scope: All aspects of co-operation at home and abroad. Particularly strong on co-operative history and the library has valuable collections on Robert Owen and George Jacob Holyoake. It is also a centre for foreigners seeking information about the Co-operative Movement
Secondary collection: Trades and services in which co-operative societies are engaged, particularly distribution and consumer interests

Stock: 10,000 books; 5,000 pamphlets; 200 current periodicals

| MANCHESTER | DIDSBURY COLLEGE OF EDUCATION | Tel.: 061-445 7871 |

1746
Wilmslow Road
Didsbury
Manchester M20 8RR

Enquiries: To Librarian, by letter only

Scope: The library has a wide general stock covering all the subject fields of the curriculum, including American studies, art and design, drama, English, European studies, geography, history, mathematics, modern studies, music, physical education, religious studies, science, sociology and compensatory education but is particularly strong in all aspects of education. It has a large collection of modern children's books and school textbooks up to 'A' level, and an historical collection of older children's books, books on teaching method and textbooks. It is building up a small collection of books and pamphlets concerning the Brontë family

Stock: 55,000 books and pamphlets; 469 current periodicals. More than 5,000 items in a pictorial collection mainly used for school practice, and some tapes, records, slides, models and filmstrips

The college library shares in co-operative interlending with other colleges and the School of Education Library, Manchester University, with the aid of a Union list of periodical holdings and special collections

MANCHESTER	ECCLES AND DISTRICT HISTORY SOCIETY	*Tel.:* 061-794 1045
1747	Moorside County Secondary School East Lancashire Road Swinton Manchester	

Enquiries: To Secretary

Scope: All aspects of the history of Eccles, Swinton and Pendlebury, Worsley area and adjacent district

No library

Publications: Annual Lectures from 1966
Eccles and Swinton: the Past Speaks for Itself. F. R. Johnston
Eccles: the Growth of a Lancashire Town. F. R. Johnston
Eccles from Hamlet to Borough. F. R. Johnston
Portrait Gallery. J. R. Bleackley
The Member for Eccles. J. B. Watson

MANCHESTER	ECCLES PUBLIC LIBRARY	*Tel.:* 061-789 1430
1748	Church Street Eccles Manchester	

Enquiries: To Borough Librarian and Curator

Scope: N.W.R.L.S. subject specialization includes: Youth organizations; physiology; historical and descriptive architecture; history and criticism of the English novel; furniture and furnishings; tapestries; interior decoration. Substantial Local History Collection, including material relating to the life and work of James Nasmyth, engineer

Stock: 78,549 books; 130 current periodicals (total stock)

MANCHESTER	FAILSWORTH PUBLIC LIBRARY ROBERT SIDLOW LIBRARY	*Tel.:* 061-681 2405
1749	Main Street Failsworth Manchester	

Enquiries: To Librarian

Scope: N.W.R.L.S. subject specialization: History and geography of Abyssinia, Ethiopia, Morocco, Algeria (French), North Central Africa, European West Africa. Fiction authors BE-BEZ

Stock: 34,000 books; 50 pamphlets; 33 current periodicals (total stock)

MANCHESTER	THE GALLERY OF ENGLISH COSTUME	*Tel.:* 061-224 5217
1750	Platt Hall Rusholme Manchester M14 5LL	

Collection, display and study of English costume (branch of the Manchester City Art Galleries)

Enquiries: To Keeper

Scope: Costume history and techniques, mainly of English Costume. Series of fashion journals, 19th to 20th centuries. Trade catalogues 1880 onwards. 19th to 20th centuries photographs. 19th to 20th centuries fashion plates. Photographs of paintings and sculpture, mainly English of all periods

MANCHESTER, THE GALLERY OF ENGLISH COSTUME, *cont.*

Stock: 1,300 books and pamphlets, including bound volumes of periodicals; 3,000 unbound periodicals; 4 current periodicals. Stock not available on loan

Publications: Picture books, postcards, Christmas cards and colour transparencies

MANCHESTER

1751

GENERAL DENTAL PRACTITIONERS ASSOCIATION
49 Cromwell Grove
Levenshulme
Manchester M19 3QD

Tel.: 061-224 7442

Enquiries: To Secretary

Scope: Dental-political publications
Secondary: Dentistry

Stock: 50 books and pamphlets. Stock not available on loan

Publications: The Probe (journal of the Association)

MANCHESTER

1752

GRANADA TELEVISION FILM LIBRARY
Manchester 3

Tel.: 061-832 7211
Telex: 668859

Enquiries: To Librarian

Scope: 16 mm/35 mm stock shot film (black and white and colour) available for sale. Complete programmes available for sale or hire
Special collections: Zoological stock shot film; current affairs (medicine, social problems, political situations throughout the world; education)

Stock: Film only

MANCHESTER

1753

GRANADA TELEVISION LIMITED
Atherton Street
Manchester 3

Tel.: 061-832 7211
Telex: 668859

Provides information and illustrations for company and programme use and files programme scripts and company and programme files and information

Enquiries: To Librarian

Scope: The Book Library is a general library covering most subject fields; this applies also to the Cuttings library. The Picture Library is in two parts: Granada pictures, mostly of programmes and artistes; non-Granada pictures of personalities and general subjects

Stock: 4,500 books; 48 current periodicals; many thousands of photographs; many thousands of cuttings; all Granada TV's scripted programmes

MANCHESTER

1754

THE GUARDIAN
3 Cross Street
Manchester M60 2RR

Tel.: 061-832 7200
Telex: 66300

Publishers of The Guardian and The Guardian Weekly

Enquiries: To Librarian

Scope: Library stock reflects coverage of The Guardian: current social, economic and political developments, domestic and foreign

Stock: 12,000 books. Classified collection of press material. Stock not normally available on loan, but limited photocopying service for press cuttings

MANCHESTER	HALLÉ CONCERTS SOCIETY	*Tel.:* 061-834 8363
1755	30 Cross Street Manchester M2 7BA	

Maintenance of the Hallé Orchestra and presentation of Hallé Concerts

Enquiries: To Secretary

Scope: Hallé Concerts Society and Hallé Orchestra—their history since 1858 and matters relevant to symphonic music today and the maintenance of a symphony orchestra
Secondary: Music in Manchester since 1858 and concert programme details from 1858
No library

Publications: Hallé Magazine
Annual Prospectus

MANCHESTER	HARTLEY VICTORIA COLLEGE	
1756	Alexandra Road South Manchester M16	

Theological College

Enquiries: To Librarian, by letter only

Scope: Manuscripts of Primitive and other Methodists: notably Hugh Bourne, William Clowes, James Everett and Alexander Kilham
Secondary: All subjects within the field of religion and theological studies. Hobill Collection of 19th century Methodist pamphlets, biographies and periodicals (particularly Primitive Methodism and the United Methodist Free Churches)

Stock: 12,000 books and pamphlets; 22 current periodicals. Stock not available on loan

MANCHESTER	HENRY WATSON MUSIC LIBRARY	*Tel.:* 061-236 7401
1757	Central Library Manchester M2 5PD	

Enquiries: To Librarian

Scope: Primarily a lending library of music and books on music but will accept enquiries on general musical subjects such as can be answered from printed sources. Large holdings of bound volumes of periodicals

Stock: 11,000 books; 45 current periodicals

MANCHESTER	JOHN DALTON COLLEGE OF TECHNOLOGY	*Tel.:* 061-236 7784
1758	Chester Street Manchester M1 5GD	

Enquiries: To Librarian

Scope: Science and technology, with special reference to computer science, physics, chemistry, biology; mechanical, production, electrical and electronics engineering; metallurgy; plastics and rubber; education, including a teaching-practice collection of children's books; and management

Stock: 25,000 books; 1,000 pamphlets; 520 current periodicals

MANCHESTER	THE JOHN RYLANDS LIBRARY	*Tel.:* 061-834 5343
1759	Deansgate Manchester M3 3EH	

Enquiries: To Librarian

MANCHESTER, THE JOHN RYLANDS LIBRARY, *cont.*

Scope: Humanities

Stock: 14,000 manuscripts (Oriental and Western); 550,000 books and pamphlets; 600 current periodicals. Stock not available on loan but photographic facilities available

Publications: Bulletin of J.R.L. (twice each year)
Catalogues, exhibition catalogues, lectures

MANCHESTER

1760

LANCASHIRE AND CHESHIRE ANTIQUARIAN SOCIETY
22 Shawbrook Road
Manchester 19

Enquiries: To Hon. Secretary, by letter only

Scope: Archaeology, history, genealogy, customs and traditions with special reference to Lancashire and Cheshire

Stock: 1,917 books mainly relating to local history, now part of the stock of the Central Library, Manchester (no. 1771)

Publications: Transactions of the Lancashire and Cheshire Antiquarian Society

MANCHESTER

1761

THE LANCASHIRE PARISH REGISTER SOCIETY
c/o The John Rylands Library
Deansgate
Manchester M3 3EH

Enquiries: To Secretary

Scope: Information respecting Lancashire registers, their transcripts, and their preservation
No library

Publications: Each year one volume is published of an edited Lancashire register, fully indexed for names, places and occupations

MANCHESTER

1762

MANCHESTER ARTS LIBRARY
Central Library
St Peter's Square
Manchester M2 5PD

Tel.: 061-236 7401 ext. 37

Enquiries: To Librarian

Scope: Arts and recreation, plus costume. Most new English language books of acceptable standard and fair number of foreign books added. Holdings date back to 1850s
Secondary: Collection of local theatre material (estimated 10,000 plus playbills from 1760 onwards, programmes, photographs, clippings)

Stock: 50,000 books (42,000 reference, 8,000 lending); 92 current periodicals

MANCHESTER

1763

MANCHESTER CATHEDRAL
Manchester M3 1SX

Tel.: 061-834 0019

Enquiries: To Secretary

Scope: Enquiries may be made about the Church of England in the Diocese of Manchester
No library

| MANCHESTER | MANCHESTER CITY ART GALLERIES | Tel.: 061-236 2391 |
| 1764 | City Art Gallery
Mosley Street
Manchester M2 3JL | |

Enquiries: To Director
Scope: Paintings, costumes, ceramics, glass, silver, furniture, all mainly English
Stock: 6,000 books. Stock not available on loan
Publications: Catalogues of collections and exhibitions

| MANCHESTER | MANCHESTER COLLEGE OF ART AND DESIGN | Tel.: 061-273 2715 |
| 1765 | Cavendish Street
All Saints
Manchester 15 | |

Enquiries: To Librarian
Scope: Art, design, architecture (strong on source books), textiles, fashion, printing
Stock: 15,000 books; 250 current periodicals

| MANCHESTER | MANCHESTER COLLEGE OF COMMERCE | Tel.: 061-236 7702 |
| 1766 | Aytoun Street
Manchester M1 3GH | |

Enquiries: To Librarian
Scope: Sociology, economics, business administration, law, librarianship
Stock: 30,000 books and pamphlets; 400 current periodicals

| MANCHESTER | MANCHESTER EDUCATION COMMITTEE LIBRARY | Tel.: 061-834 8622 ext. 7213 |
| 1767 | Education Offices
Crown Square
Manchester 3 | |

Reference and lending services for the Education Committee and its teaching and administrative staffs, including bibliographical information

Enquiries: To Librarian
Scope: All aspects of education, current and past, including current school textbooks. Background books for teachers in all subjects of school curriculum
Secondary: Psychology, particularly child psychology. Handicapped children and their education
Stock: 25,000 books and pamphlets—Professional section; 13,500 books and pamphlets—School books; 60 current periodicals
Gramophone record library includes music, foreign languages and literature

| MANCHESTER | MANCHESTER LANGUAGE AND LITERATURE LIBRARY | Tel.: 061-236 7401
Telex: 66149 |
| 1768 | Central Library
St Peter's Square
Manchester M2 5PD | |

Enquiries: To Librarian
Scope: Language and literature
Special services: Foreign Library (10,000 lending books in modern European languages)

MANCHESTER, MANCHESTER LANGUAGE AND LITERATURE LIBRARY, *cont.*
Play Collection (2,600 sets)
Language courses on tape (for reference use)
The Spoken Word (plays and poetry on record for reference use)
Special collections: Brontë collection; Gaskell collection

Stock: 64,000 (reference), 46,000 (lending) books and pamphlets; 71 current periodicals. Books and pamphlets only available on loan

Publications: Handlist of Plays: sets available for loan
The Language Laboratory: a bibliography

MANCHESTER

1769

MANCHESTER LITERARY AND PHILOSOPHICAL SOCIETY *Tel.:* 061-236 6174
36 George Street
Manchester

Society Library

Enquiries: To Librarian, by letter only

Scope: Journals of the learned societies

Stock: 1,000 books; 600 current periodicals (kept for 2 years, then deposited at Manchester Central Library, no. 1768). Stock available on loan through Regional Library Bureau

Publications: Memoirs and Proceedings

The library was almost completely destroyed in 1940

MANCHESTER

1770

MANCHESTER LITERARY CLUB *Tel.:* 061-736 3596
The Manchester Club
King Street
Manchester 2

To encourage pursuit of literature and art

Enquiries: To Gen. Secretary, 26 Kingsway, Pendlebury, Swinton, Manchester M27 1JX

Scope: The publication every two years of the Transactions for nearly a century provides the most useful source of information for non-members. Literature has been reviewed over a wide field and in particular the literature and arts of the north-west of England

Stock: 600 books

Publications: Papers of the Manchester Literary Club

MANCHESTER

1771

MANCHESTER LOCAL HISTORY LIBRARY *Tel.:* 061-236 7401 ext. 38
Central Library
St Peter's Square
Manchester M2 5PD

Enquiries: To Librarian

Scope: Information is provided on the political, economic, religious, educational, historical development of Manchester and the region. A file of local trade directories is available, from 1772, local newspapers from early 18th century, parish registers in print, microfilm or manuscript transcript form, microfilm copies of the Enumerators' returns for the 1841, 1851 and 1861 Censuses for Manchester

Stock: Prints collection, which includes postcards, photographs, and prints, contains 68,000 items; 3,200 maps

Publications: Peterloo: a bibliography. 1969

Plans of Manchester, 1650–1848. 1969 (facsimile reproductions of six Manchester maps)
Peterloo 1819: a portfolio of contemporary documents with explanatory text. 1969
Facilities available for photographic reproduction, photocopying and microfilming of material

MANCHESTER

1772

MANCHESTER SOCIAL SCIENCES LIBRARY
Central Library
St Peter's Square
Manchester M2 5PD

Tel.: 061-236 7401 ext. 50 and 51

Enquiries: To Librarian

Scope: Philosophy, religion, social sciences, home economics, business, archaeology and history. Large holdings of Parliamentary Papers from 1800 onwards. United Nations printed material. 18th and 19th century pamphlets. Manchester newspapers of all dates. Parish registers and related genealogical material

Stock: 340,000 books and pamphlets; 500 current periodicals. Separate lending stock of 20,000 volumes in above subjects

Publications: Printed Catalogue of Reference Library—Private Press Books (2 parts). 1959–60
Printed Catalogue of Reference Library—Genealogy (3 parts). 1956–58
Printed Catalogue of Reference Library—Books on Printing (2 parts). 1961–63

MANCHESTER

1773

MATHER COLLEGE
Whitworth Street
Manchester M1 3HA
College of Education

Tel.: 061-236 5635

Enquiries: To Librarian

Scope: Education. Subjects of the curriculum. Children's books for use in Primary Schools

Stock: 23,000 books and pamphlets; 144 current periodicals

MANCHESTER

1774

MIDDLETON PUBLIC LIBRARIES
Central Library
Long Street
Middleton
Manchester M24 3DU

Tel.: 061-643 5228

Enquiries: To Librarian

Scope: N.W.R.L.S. subject specialization includes: Language in general, dictionaries, grammar, English language, dialects; drawing of specific subjects and perspective; diseases of the ear and their treatment

Stock: 2,661 books; 2 current periodicals

MANCHESTER

1775

NATIONAL LIBRARY FOR THE BLIND
5 St John Street
Manchester 3
See no. 1424

Tel.: 061-834 0432

MANCHESTER

1776

NATIONAL UNION OF VEHICLE BUILDERS
44 Hathersage Road
Manchester M13 0FH
Trade union

Tel.: 061-224 6231

MANCHESTER, NATIONAL UNION OF VEHICLE BUILDERS, *cont.*
Enquiries: To General Secretary
Scope: Trade union agreements for the vehicle building industry. The history of the union from 1834 to the present
No library

MANCHESTER

1777

NORTHERN SCHOOL OF MUSIC
99 Oxford Road
Manchester M1 7DS
Specialist college of music for full-time students

Tel.: 061-273 1844

Enquiries: To Secretary
Scope: Advice about lessons, training and examinations in music
No library

MANCHESTER

1778

PORTICO LIBRARY & NEWSROOM
57 Mosley Street
Manchester 2
Private proprietary library

Tel.: 061-236 6785

Enquiries: To Librarian, by letter only
Scope: General literature, mainly 18th and 19th century
Stock: 30,000 books

MANCHESTER

1779

RADCLIFFE PUBLIC LIBRARY
Stand Lane
Radcliffe
Manchester M26 9WR

Tel.: 061-723 2344

Enquiries: To Borough Librarian
Scope: Subject specialization includes: Evangelism; domestic architecture; plumbing; heating and ventilating engineering; metrology
Books, maps, plans and pamphlets on the history of Radcliffe and area
Stock: 54,000 books (of which 1,000 are on subject specialization); 1,000 pamphlets; 74 current periodicals

MANCHESTER

1780

RADCLIFFE TECHNICAL COLLEGE
Whittaker Street
Radcliffe
Manchester

Tel.: 061-723 2480

Enquiries: To Librarian
Scope: Mechanical and electrical engineering. Domestic subjects. Biography
Stock: 4,800 books

MANCHESTER

1781

ROYAL MANCHESTER COLLEGE OF MUSIC
Devas Street
Manchester M15 6FX

Tel.: 061-273 3735

Enquiries: To Librarian
Scope: Music: scores, books, gramophone records, instruments
Stock: 11,000 books and scores; 10 current periodicals

MANCHESTER	SEDGLEY PARK COLLEGE OF EDUCATION	*Tel.:* 061-773 4001
1782	Prestwich Manchester M25 8JT	

Enquiries: To Librarian

Scope: Literature in the following subjects: Art and design; drama; education; English literature; French; geography; history; mathematics; music; religion; science

Stock: 27,000 books and pamphlets; 125 current periodicals

MANCHESTER	THE SPIRITUALISTS NATIONAL UNION LTD BRITTEN MEMORIAL LIBRARY	*Tel.:* 061-834 2548
1783	Britten House 12 Tib House Cross Street Manchester M2 4JB	

Psychic science and religions

Enquiries: To Secretary, by letter only

Scope: The library consists mainly of 18th and 19th century books on spiritualism, psychic science and allied subjects and bound copies of early Spiritualist publications and pamphlets
Collections: Abraham Wallace, Blumenthal, Oaten, Alfred Kitson, and Curnow (latter presented by Conan Doyle)
Some 17th century books
Proceedings of Psychical Research Society
Proceedings of American Psychical Research Society

Stock: 6,000 books; 2,000 pamphlets. Duplicate copies only available on loan

Publications: Catalogue

Part of the Britten Library is housed at The Arthur Findlay College, Stansted Hall, Essex, which has in addition its own similar but smaller private Library. (The College is a branch of the Union)

MANCHESTER	STRETFORD PUBLIC LIBRARIES	*Tel.:* 061-865 2218
1784	Central Library King Street Stretford Manchester M32 8AP	

Enquiries: To Librarian

Scope: Medical dictionaries and encyclopaedias

Stock: 25 books

MANCHESTER	STRETFORD TECHNICAL COLLEGE	*Tel.:* 061-872 3731
1785	Talbot Road Stretford Manchester	

Enquiries: To Tutor Librarian

Scope: Chemistry, physics, biology and mathematics; electrical, mechanical, gas, production and automobile engineering. Economics, accountancy, management and nursing

Stock: 11,000 books; 3,000 pamphlets; 200 current periodicals

This is one of the few colleges in the country running advanced classes in gas technology for Gas Board employees and others and for this reason collects cuttings and any information available from any source on all aspects of the gas industry including the North Sea gas fields

MANCHESTER	SWINTON AND PENDLEBURY PUBLIC LIBRARIES	*Tel.:* 061-794 2236
1786	Central Library Swinton Manchester	

Enquiries: To Librarian

Scope: Slavery. American history and geography. American literary criticism (not texts). Local studies
Secondary: Esperanto

Stock: 3,000 books; 6 current periodicals

Publications: Occasional publications on local history (for example Pauper and Poorhouse, by G. E. Mullineux)

MANCHESTER	THE TEXTILE COUNCIL ECONOMICS AND STATISTICS DEPARTMENT	*Tel.:* 061-832 2402
1787	3 Alberton Street Manchester M3 2WA	

Enquiries: To Librarian

Scope: Economic and statistical data on the multi-fibre textile industry throughout the world and information on the general economic climate at home and overseas. A comprehensive specialized collection

Stock: 40,000 books, pamphlets and reports; 1,500 current periodicals

Publications: The Textile Council Quarterly Statistical Review

MANCHESTER	THOMSON WITHY GROVE LTD Thomson House	*Tel.:* 061-834 1234
1788	Withy Grove Manchester M60 4BJ	

Enquiries: To Librarian

Scope: Press cuttings and pictures. Bound newspaper files

Stock: Thousands of press photographs and cuttings. Stock not available on loan

MANCHESTER	UNITARIAN COLLEGE THE McLACHLAN LIBRARY	*Tel.:* 061-224 2849
1789	Victoria Park Manchester M14 5QL Theological College	

Enquiries: To Librarian and Principal

Scope: Large manuscript section of letters chiefly concerning Unitarian and Dissenting history
Secondary: Special interest of the Library is Unitarian and Dissenting history, and it has a large collection of 18th, 19th and 20th century journals. Theology, Bible, psychology, philosophy, comparative religion, classics, English literature and Judaism are all represented

Stock: 30,000 books; several thousand pamphlets

Publications: A Nonconformist Library. H. McLachlan. Manchester University Press, 1923
The Unitarian College Library: Its History, Contents and Character. 1939

MANCHESTER	UNITARIAN HISTORICAL SOCIETY	*Tel.:* 061-224 2849
1790	c/o Unitarian College Victoria Park Manchester M14 5QL	

Enquiries: To Secretary
Scope: Books on Unitarian history
Publications: Transactions of the Unitarian Historical Society (annually)

MANCHESTER	UNIVERSITY OF MANCHESTER LIBRARY	*Tel.:* 061-273 3333
1791	Oxford Road Manchester M13 9PL	

Enquiries: To Librarian, by letter only
Scope: Subjects pertaining to the Faculties of Arts, Law, Medicine, Music, Economics and Social Studies, Education and Theology
Special collections: Christie (French and Italian humanists), Bullock (16th century Italian books), Hartland (bibles), Arabic and Persian books, History and literature of the United States of America, History of medicine, Local medicine, Manchester Medical Society Library, Manchester Museum Library. Development Documentation Centre covers publications from African and other developing countries
Library for Deaf Education: Works on education of the deaf, including works on the anatomy and diseases of the ear, acoustics, and general education and psychology
Stock: 886,300 books, pamphlets and reports; 5,400 current periodicals (including science)

MANCHESTER	UNIVERSITY OF MANCHESTER WHITWORTH ART GALLERY	*Tel.:* 061-273 1880
1792	Whitworth Park Manchester M15 6ER	

Display and maintenance of permanent collections including English watercolours, Old Master prints and drawings, and textiles. Formation of a collection of contemporary works of art. Loan exhibitions. Art lectures

Enquiries: To Keeper, by letter only
Scope: British artists, 18th–20th centuries; European Schools, drawings; Contemporary British art; historical and modern textiles; prints; Museum and Gallery permanent collection catalogues; loan exhibition catalogues
Stock: 2,000 books; 6,000 Permanent Collection and Loan Exhibition catalogues; 4 current periodicals. Stock not available on loan
Publications: Brief Guide to Whitworth Art Gallery
Modern British Woodcuts and Wood-Engravings in the Collection of the Whitworth Art Gallery
Loan exhibition catalogues

MANSFIELD	HARLOW WOOD ORTHOPAEDIC HOSPITAL	*Tel.:* Mansfield 24855
Notts	Mansfield Nottinghamshire	
1793		

Enquiries: To Superintendent
Scope: Postgraduate orthopaedics
Stock: 224 books; 122 sets of periodicals. Stock not available on loan

MANSFIELD Notts **1794**	THE INTAKE TRUST MEDICAL LIBRARY Mansfield and District General Hospital West Hill Drive Mansfield Nottinghamshire	*Tel.:* Mansfield 22515

Enquiries: To Librarian

Scope: Medical literature covering all specialities at postgraduate level for medical staff and local General Practitioners
Secondary: Library facilities for senior nursing, technical and administrative staffs

Stock: 400 books; 100 pamphlets; 25 reports; 35 current periodicals. Stock not available on loan, but photocopies supplied

MANSFIELD Notts **1795**	MANSFIELD PUBLIC LIBRARY Leeming Street Mansfield Nottinghamshire	*Tel.:* Mansfield 23861

Enquiries: To Chief Librarian and Curator

Scope: Special collection: Mansfield Local History Museum collections: Buxton water-colours of Old Mansfield; Manners Collection of Lustre Ware

Stock: 45,000 non-fiction books and pamphlets, excluding science, technology and commerce; 77 current periodicals

MARCH Cambs **1796**	CAMBRIDGESHIRE AND ISLE OF ELY COUNTY LIBRARY Gordon Avenue March Cambridgeshire	*Tel.:* March 3349

Enquiries: To Librarian

Scope: Local Collection includes material on all aspects of the County of Cambridgeshire, the Isle of Ely and the Fens

Stock: 5,000 books, reports and maps

Publications: Catalogues of the Local Collection
The Fenland Story, from Prehistoric Times to the Present Day (an introduction to Fenland history)

MARKET **DRAYTON** Salop **1797**	NORTH STAFFORDSHIRE SOCIETY OF ARCHITECTS c/o Poynton House Market Drayton Shropshire	*Tel.:* Market Drayton 2918

Aims to advance the art and science of architecture and to safeguard the interests of the public in matters of professional practice and conduct

Enquiries: To Hon. Secretary, by letter only

Scope: The art and practice of architecture within the geographical area covered by the Organization
Secondary: All questions of Town Planning, Preservation and allied subjects

No library

Publications: The Molecular City: a proposal for the development and growth of the area between the Potteries and Crewe

Enquiries will be passed by the Secretary to the persons best able to deal with them

MARLBOROUGH MARLBOROUGH COLLEGE
Wilts Wiltshire

1798
Enquiries: To Librarian, by letter only

Scope: Boys' Working Library of 25,000 volumes
200 older and valuable books, mostly literary in interest
Marlburian poets, prose-writers and scholars, including Sassoon, MacNiece and Betjeman
Vicar's Library, housed and administered for the town

Stock not available on loan

MATLOCK DERBYSHIRE COUNTY LIBRARY *Tel.:* Matlock 3411
Derbyshire County Offices
  Matlock
1799 Derbyshire DE4 3AG

Enquiries: To Librarian

Scope: National subject specialization: Spanish language; English poetry, 1901- (E, L and T-V); Drama—Shakespeare; Latin literature. Sitwelliana

Stock: 1,600 books and pamphlets

See also no. 1800

MATLOCK DERBYSHIRE COUNTY LIBRARY *Tel.:* Matlock 2480
Derbyshire MATLOCK BRANCH LIBRARY
  Steep Turnpike
1800 Matlock
  Derbyshire DE4 3DP

Enquiries: To Librarian

Scope: History of Derbyshire

Stock: 3,000 books and pamphlets; 50 current periodicals

Publications: Printed catalogue of main holdings in preparation

MATLOCK MATLOCK COLLEGE OF EDUCATION *Tel.:* Matlock 2383
Derbyshire Rockside Hall
  Matlock
1801 Derbyshire DE4 3GT

Enquiries: To Tutor Librarian

Scope: The library provides books and information on subjects of the college courses, the largest departments and therefore the most comprehensive sections being Divinity, education, English, geography and mathematics
Secondary: Art, history, music, physical education and sciences

Stock: 35,000 books; 280 current periodicals

MATLOCK TRAMWAY MUSEUM SOCIETY *Tel.:* 077-385 2565
Derbyshire Crich
  Matlock
1802 Derbyshire DE4 5DP

Preserves and operates tramcars in the environment in which they were familiar

MATLOCK, TRAMWAY MUSEUM SOCIETY, *cont.*
Enquiries: To Secretary
Scope: Trams and tramways
No library
Publications: Museum Guide
Quarterly Journal

MEIFOD   CYMDEITHAS DIOGELU HARDWDWCH CYMRU   *Tel.:* Meifod 383
Montgomeryshire   (Council for the Protection of Rural Wales—CPRW)
Meifod
1803   Montgomeryshire
Enquiries: To General Secretary
Scope: The objects of the Council are to organize concerted action to secure the protection and improvement of rural scenery and of the amenities of the countryside and towns and villages in Wales and Monmouthshire; to act as a centre for furnishing or procuring advice and information upon any matters affecting such protection and improvement; and to arouse, form and educate opinion in order to ensure the promotion of the aforesaid objects
No library
Publications: News Letters (3 each year)

MERTHYR   MERTHYR TYDFIL PUBLIC LIBRARIES   *Tel.:* Merthyr Tydfil 3057
TYDFIL   Central Library
Glam   Merthyr Tydfil
Glamorgan
1804   *Enquiries:* To Chief Librarian
Scope: Subject specialization includes: Ceramics; etching and engraving

MEXBOROUGH   MEXBOROUGH SCHOFEILD TECHNICAL   *Tel.:* Mexborough 2306 and
Yorkshire   COLLEGE   3389
Park Road
1805   Mexborough
Yorkshire
Enquiries: To Librarian
Scope: Anatomy, physiology, hygiene, sociology, education
Stock: 1,500 books; 10 current periodicals

MIDDLESBROUGH   CLEVELAND SCIENTIFIC INSTITUTION   *Tel.:* Middlesbrough 2303
Teesside   Corporation Road
Middlesbrough
1806   Teesside
Enquiries: To Secretary
Scope: Manufacture of iron and steel, building, civil, structural, electrical, mechanical, chemical engineering and technology generally. Architecture, accountancy, commerce, ceramics, economics, management techniques, work study, law, insurance and pensions, nuclear physics, scientific instruments
Stock: 6,000 books; 160 pamphlets; 40 current periodicals
Member of LIST

MIDDLESBROUGH CONSTANTINE COLLEGE OF TECHNOLOGY *Tel.:* Middlesbrough 44176
Teesside   (POLYTECHNIC DESIGNATE)   ext. 39 and 40
                   Borough Road
1807   Middlesbrough
                   Teesside

Enquiries: To Tutor Librarian

Scope: Mechanical, civil, structural, electrical, instrument, control and chemical engineering, building, chemistry, sociology, mathematics, statistics and computing science, business and professional studies, economics, metallurgy, physics and management

Stock: 22,000 books, bound volumes of journals and pamphlets; 625 current journals

Publications: List of current journals
Your Library Service
Educational Television: a select reading list. April 1969

MIDDLESBROUGH TEESSIDE COLLEGE OF ART LIBRARY *Tel.:* Middlesbrough 89104
Teesside   Holmwood
                   Orchard Road
1808   Linthorpe
                   Middlesbrough
                   Teesside

Enquiries: To Librarian

Scope: Art and design, both historical and contemporary, including aesthetics, architecture, art history, sculpture, ceramics, design, painting, graphics, printing, interior design. Complementary studies, including philosophy, psychology (particularly visual perception), anthropology, sociology and folklore, natural history, basic sciences, technology, management, textiles, prints, theatre and dance, economic and social history and literature

Stock: 5,500 books; 300 pamphlets, with a bias towards education; 110 current periodicals; 12,000 slides on fine art and art history

Publications: Pamphlet of method study details for designers

Member of LIST

MIDDLESBROUGH TEESSIDE COLLEGE OF EDUCATION *Tel.:* Middlesbrough 47033
Teesside   154 Borough Road
                   Middlesbrough
1809   Teesside
                   Day College

Enquiries: To Tutor Librarian, by letter only

Scope: Education: general, particularly infant, junior and to 13-year-old age group; children's literature; text books for these age groups
Secondary: History, geography, English, biology, botany, mathematics, music, sociology, philosophy

Stock: 15,000 books and pamphlets; 149 current periodicals. Stock not normally available on loan

MIDDLESBROUGH TEESSIDE PUBLIC LIBRARIES *Tel.:* Middlesbrough 45294
Teesside   Central Library
                   Victoria Square
1810   Middlesbrough
                   Teesside

Enquiries: To Librarian

MIDDLESBROUGH, TEESSIDE PUBLIC LIBRARIES, *cont.*

Scope: Middlesbrough Reference Library contains extensive range of Government publications; large collection of theological works and Bibles (including many early and rare Greek texts and polyglots); houses the William Kelly Collection of theological and classical works

Stock: 600,000 books and pamphlets; 300 current periodicals (Central and Branch Libraries—total stock)

Headquarters for the Library Information Service for Teesside (LIST, no. 2383)

District Libraries at Stockton-on-Tees and Redcar

MIDDLETON
Manchester

See under **MANCHESTER** for
MIDDLETON PUBLIC LIBRARIES (no. 1774)

MIDDLETON ST GEORGE
Darlington
Co. Durham

See under **DARLINGTON** for
MIDDLETON ST GEORGE COLLEGE OF EDUCATION (no. 440)

MIRFIELD
Yorkshire

1811

COMMUNITY OF THE RESURRECTION
House of the Resurrection
Mirfield
Yorkshire

Tel.: Mirfield 4318

Evangelism, parochial missions, retreats, pastoral work, hostel for University students at Leeds, theological college at Mirfield (and at Alice, Cape Province), missionary work in South Africa, Rhodesia and Barbados

Enquiries: To Superior, Prior or Principal of College, by letter only

Scope: Theology—Biblical, historical, doctrinal, ecclesiastical, liturgical, pastoral and moral, including several hundred 16th, 17th and 18th century books, bound pamphlets and tracts
Secondary: History, biography, literature, art, music

Stock: 50,000 books; many pamphlets; 15 current periodicals. Stock not normally available on loan
Publications: C.R. Quarterly

MITCHAM
Surrey

1812

LONDON BOROUGH OF MERTON PUBLIC LIBRARIES
Mitcham Library
London Road
Mitcham
Surrey

Tel.: 01-648 4070 and 6516

See no. 1336

MOLD
Flintshire

1813

FLINTSHIRE COUNTY LIBRARY
County Library Headquarters
County Civic Centre
Mold
Flintshire

Enquiries: To Librarian

Scope: Local history of Flintshire. Arthurian Collection. Welsh Books
Secondary: Regional subject specialization includes: Psychology, genealogy

Stock: Total non-fiction stock 103,741 books (including Arthurian 1,459; local 2,684; and psychology 2,620); 216 current periodicals
Publications: Bibliography of County of Flint, Part 1, biographical sources. 1953

MONMOUTH NELSON MUSEUM *Tel.:* Monmouth 2122
  Monmouth
1814 *Enquiries:* To Curator, by letter only
  Scope: Letters to and from Nelson
  Monmouth Archives relating to the town, 1447–present day
  Secondary: Books about Nelson; books about Monmouth
  Stock: 300 books; 100 pamphlets. Stock not available on loan

MONTROSE ANGUS AND KINCARDINE COUNTY LIBRARY *Tel.:* Montrose 232
Angus County Library
  Montrose
1815 Angus
  Enquiries: To Librarian
  Scope: Special reserve stock: Postal service (all works on this subject published since 1959)
  Secondary: Local history
  Stock: 538 books

MONTROSE MONTROSE PUBLIC LIBRARY *Tel.:* Montrose 232
Angus Montrose
  Angus
1816 *Enquiries:* To Librarian
  Scope: Local history
  Stock: 500 books

MORDEN ORGANON LABORATORIES LTD *Tel.:* 01-542 6611
Surrey Crown House *Telex:* 25637
  London Road
1817 Morden
  Surrey
  Pharmaceutical manufacturer
  Enquiries: To Information Officer
  Scope: Endocrinology
  Secondary: Gynaecology; fertility and sterility; veterinary science
  Stock: 1,900 books; 9,000 pamphlets; 220 current periodicals. Stock not available on loan

MORLEY *See under* **LEEDS** *for*
Leeds MORLEY PUBLIC LIBRARY (no. 808)

MORPETH NORTHUMBERLAND COUNTY LIBRARY *Tel.:* Morpeth 2385
Northumberland The Willows
  Morpeth
1818 Northumberland
  Enquiries: To Librarian

MORPETH, NORTHUMBERLAND COUNTY LIBRARY, *cont.*

Scope: Drama collection. Central local history collection

Stock: 600,000 books (total stock)

MOTHERWELL MOTHERWELL AND WISHAW PUBLIC *Tel.:* Motherwell 62411
Lanarkshire LIBRARIES
  Motherwell Library
1819 Hamilton Road
  Motherwell
  Lanarkshire

Enquiries: To Librarian

Scope: Hamilton of Dalziel Collection (a family library, built up through the 1700s to present day. Contains biographies, histories and other general works on mathematics and literature) Regional subject specialization: Social welfare

Stock: 102,000 books and pamphlets; 99 current periodicals (total stock)

MUSSELBURGH MIDLOTHIAN COUNTY LIBRARY *Tel.:* 031-665 2931
Midlothian Fisherrow School
  South Street
1820 Musselburgh
  Midlothian

Enquiries: To Librarian

Scope: Local history within the County of Midlothian. Books by local authors
Subject specialization: Primary education

Stock: 119,159 books (total non-fiction stock)

NAIRN NAIRN LITERARY INSTITUTE
  Viewfield House
1821 Nairn

Enquiries: To Hon. Librarian

Scope: Macbean Collection of books of Scottish, mainly local, interest (catalogued at Scottish Central Library, no. 2340)

Stock: 900 books

NEATH NEATH PUBLIC LIBRARY *Tel.:* Neath 4604
Glam Victoria Gardens
  Neath
1822 Glamorgan

Enquiries: To Librarian

Scope: Collection of 28 books of American interest presented by the Rotary Club of East Hartford, Conn., U.S.A., mainly American history

NEATH NEATH TECHNICAL COLLEGE *Tel.:* Neath 3723
Glam Dwryfelin Road
  Neath
1823 Glamorgan

Enquiries: To Librarian

Scope: Commerce, engineering and science, including economics, law, welfare, education, mathematics, physics, chemistry, biology, biochemistry, electrical and mechanical engineering, building construction, business management, chemical engineering, metallurgy, welding, carpentry, plumbing, literature, geography, history, fuel technology, catering and bakery

Stock: 5,900 books; 50 pamphlets; 60 current periodicals

NELSON
Lancs

1824

NELSON PUBLIC LIBRARY　　　　　　　　　　　*Tel.:* Nelson 63341
Booth Street
Nelson
Lancashire

Enquiries: To Librarian

Scope: Local collection containing books on Nelson and District
Subject specialization: South America; skin

Stock: 48,000 books; 55 current periodicals (total stock)

NEW MALDEN
Surrey

1825

ENGLISH NEW EDUCATION FELLOWSHIP　　　　*Tel.:* 01-942 6821
(English Section of the World Education Fellowship)
2 Wilton Grove
New Malden
Surrey

Aims to promote reform in education in the light of child study and of the advances in the human and social sciences; to encourage experiment and innovation in education; and to link progressive educators throughout the world

Enquiries: To Hon. Secretary

Scope: Offers a limited and specialized service to those concerned with progressive education. The material available consists mainly of reports and copies of the *New Era* (monthly journal) which is a useful source of reference of educational pioneering work during the last fifty years

Publications: Advances in Understanding the Child
Advances in Understanding the Adolescent
Important Facts for All who Deal with Children
The Comprehensive School
Home and School Handbook
New Era (monthly)

NEWARK
Notts

1826

GILSTRAP PUBLIC LIBRARY　　　　　　　　　*Tel.:* Newark 3966
Castlegate
Newark
Nottinghamshire

Enquiries: To Librarian

Scope: General reference and information service from Central Reference Library. *Special collection* of local literature with particular interest in the Civil War period (in conjunction with Municipal Museum, no. 1827)

Stock: 50,000 books and pamphlets; 80 current periodicals (total stock)

NEWARK
Notts

1827

NEWARK ON TRENT MUSEUM & ART　　　　　*Tel.:* Newark 2358
　　GALLERY
Appleton Gate
Newark
Nottinghamshire

Enquiries: To Curator

511

NEWARK, NEWARK ON TRENT MUSEUM & ART GALLERY, *cont.*

Scope: Archaeology and local history of Newark and district with a collection of photographs and illustrations of the area

NEWBURN
Newcastle upon Tyne

See under **NEWCASTLE UPON TYNE** for NEWBURN URBAN DISTRICT COUNCIL LIBRARY (no. 1834)

NEWBURY
Berks

1828

AGRICULTURAL RESEARCH COUNCIL INSTITUTE FOR RESEARCH ON ANIMAL DISEASES
Compton
Newbury
Berkshire

Tel.: Compton (Berks) 343

Research to increase knowledge of and discover methods of prevention, treatment and cure of diseases of farm animals

Enquiries: To Director

Scope: Coverage in the fields of veterinary medicine and animal disease: animal husbandry; nutrition; anatomy; genetics; medicine; surgery; experimental biology; chemistry; histology; physiology; endocrinology; zoology; immunology; pathology; haematology; parasitology; virology; bacteriology; pharmacology; toxicology; electron microscopy

Stock: 762 books; 135 current periodicals

Publications: Reprints of scientific papers published by the staff of the Institute

The library is building up an information service for its users

NEWCASTLE
Staffs

1829

NEWCASTLE-UNDER-LYME PUBLIC LIBRARIES
Central Library
School Street
Newcastle
Staffordshire ST5 1AT

Tel.: 078-2-68125

Enquiries: To Librarian

Scope: General stock
Secondary: Local government; local history; gramophone records

Stock: 148,000 books; 1,400 pamphlets; 100 current periodicals; 3,300 LP gramophone records (total stock)

Publications: What's New (10 issues each year)

NEWCASTLE
Staffs

1830

UNIVERSITY OF KEELE LIBRARY
Keele
Newcastle
Staffordshire

Tel.: Keele Park 371
Telex: 36113

Enquiries: To Librarian

Scope: General

Stock: 150,000 books and pamphlets; 1,700 current periodicals

Publications: Sociological Review
North Staffordshire Journal of Field Studies

NEWCASTLE UPON TYNE **1831**	THE BRITISH OCCUPATIONAL HYGIENE SOCIETY Nuffield Department of Industrial Health Medical School, The University Newcastle upon Tyne	*Tel.:* Newcastle upon Tyne 28511 ext. 158

Enquiries: Hon. Secretary
Scope: Occupational hygiene
No library
Publications: The Annals of Occupational Hygiene (Pergamon Press)
Proceedings of International Symposia

NEWCASTLE UPON TYNE **1832**	GOSFORTH PUBLIC LIBRARY Regent Farm Road Gosforth Newcastle upon Tyne NE3 1JN	*Tel.:* 0632-54004

Enquiries: To Librarian
Scope: Local collection
Stock: 60,000 books; 1,000 pamphlets; 30 current periodicals (total stock)

NEWCASTLE UPON TYNE **1833**	THE LITERARY AND PHILOSOPHICAL SOCIETY OF NEWCASTLE UPON TYNE Newcastle upon Tyne NE1 1SE	*Tel.:* Newcastle upon Tyne 20192

Enquiries: To Librarian
Scope: The Society was founded in 1793 and it is an important repository of older material (including many early printed books) in these fields: Science, the social sciences and the humanities. It has many complete runs of periodicals in these fields. There is a local collection covering the City of Newcastle upon Tyne, and the counties of Northumberland and Durham. There is a Music Library—scores and books on music with a Gramophone Record Lending Library (available to members only)
Stock: 100,000 books; 150 current periodicals

NEWCASTLE UPON TYNE **1834**	NEWBURN URBAN DISTRICT COUNCIL LIBRARY Denton Park Centre West Denton Way Newcastle upon Tyne NE5 2LF	*Tel.:* Lemington 677922

Enquiries: To Librarian
Scope: General stock with Picture Loan Scheme and Gramophone Record Lending Service
Secondary: Local History Collection with special emphasis on the Roman Wall
Stock: 40,000 books; 100 pamphlets; 40 current periodicals (total stock)

NEWCASTLE UPON TYNE **1835**	NEWCASTLE CHRONICLE & JOURNAL LTD Thomson House Groat Market Newcastle upon Tyne NE99 1BO	*Tel.:* Newcastle upon Tyne 27500

Enquiries: To Librarian
Scope: Current events
Stock: Newspaper cuttings and photographs only. Stock not available on loan

NEWCASTLE UPON TYNE	NEWCASTLE UPON TYNE CITY LIBRARIES	*Tel.:* Newcastle upon Tyne
	Central Library	610691
1836	P.O. Box 1MC	*Telex:* 53373
	New Bridge Street	
	Newcastle upon Tyne	

Enquiries: To Librarian

Scope: Large general stock available for lending and reference and which provides a Regional reference service
Incorporates the City Information Service (Municipal and Tourist information); extensive collection on Local History (Northumberland Collection); other *special collections*: Complete Government Publications from 1957
Joseph Cowen Collection (19th century political, Northern Reform Union)
Thomas Bewick Collection, the engraver's books and blocks
Seymour Bell Collection of plans and charts of the area
Thomlinson Collection (16th–17th century books)

Stock: 399,450 books; 7,500 pamphlets; 950 current periodicals (total non-fiction stock, excluding deposit collections of patents and specifications)

Publications: Local Government Information Service (monthly index)
Various current information lists produced by City Information Service
Local History Printed Catalogue. 1932
Bewick Catalogue. 1904
Calendar of the Greenwell deeds. 1927

City Information Service staffs full time information desk at Civic Centre
Information services provided for staff of Corporation and council members
Post-graduate medical library, Newcastle General Hospital (no. 1840)
Nurses Library, Royal Victoria Infirmary, Newcastle

NEWCASTLE UPON TYNE	NEWCASTLE UPON TYNE COLLEGE OF EDUCATION	*Tel.:* Newcastle upon Tyne
	50 Northumberland Road	28834
1837	Newcastle upon Tyne NE1 8SR	

Enquiries: To Librarian

Scope: Education. Children's literature
Secondary: Child psychology, religion, mathematics, physics, chemistry, biology, art, music, history, English language and literature, geography

Stock: 23,000 books and pamphlets; 195 current periodicals

NEWCASTLE UPON TYNE	NEWCASTLE UPON TYNE COLLEGE OF FURTHER EDUCATION	*Tel.:* Newcastle upon Tyne
	Bath Lane	21876
1838	Newcastle upon Tyne NE4 5TQ	

Enquiries: To Librarian

Scope: Most GCE subjects and commerce, hairdressing, catering, bakery and English for overseas students

Stock: 6,500 books; 160 current periodicals

NEWCASTLE UPON TYNE 1839	NEWCASTLE UPON TYNE POLYTECHNIC LIBRARY Ellison Building Ellison Place Newcastle upon Tyne NE1 8ST	*Tel.:* Newcastle upon Tyne 26002

Enquiries: To Librarian

Scope: Librarianship and information science; economics; law; sociology; geography, language and literature (mainly English, French and German); commerce; business management; accountancy; fine art; history; advertising; marketing; chemistry; physics; mathematics; electrical, mechanical and civil engineering; industrial administration; chemical technology; materials science

Secondary: Philosophy, psychology, Russian language and literature, nursing, political science, estate management, surveying

Stock: 63,000 books and pamphlets; 880 current periodicals

NEWCASTLE UPON TYNE 1840	NEWCASTLE UPON TYNE POSTGRADUATE MEDICAL LIBRARY Newcastle General Hospital Westgate Road Newcastle upon Tyne NE4 6BE	*Tel.:* Newcastle upon Tyne 38811

Provision of library service for medical and nursing staff of the hospital and for General Practitioners in the area

Enquiries: To Librarian

Scope: Medicine

Stock: 650 books; 80 current periodicals. Stock not available on loan

NEWCASTLE UPON TYNE 1841	NORTH EAST DEVELOPMENT COUNCIL 20 Collingwood Street Newcastle upon Tyne NE1 1JT	*Tel.:* Newcastle upon Tyne 610026

To promote economic development in North East England

Enquiries: To Director

Scope: North East of England: statistics and reports. Regionalism

Stock: 200 books; 500 pamphlets; 150 reports; 10 current periodicals

Publications: North East News (a quarterly report on development in North East England)

NEWCASTLE UPON TYNE 1842	NORTH OF ENGLAND INDUSTRIAL HEALTH SERVICE 20 Claremont Place Newcastle upon Tyne NE2 4AA	*Tel.:* Newcastle upon Tyne 28511 ext 162

Investigates and advises on occupational health hazards and promotes occupational hygiene and health in industry

Enquiries: To Secretary

Publications: Bulletin (2 issues a year, each devoted to a special subject)

NEWCASTLE UPON TYNE 1843	THE NORTH OF ENGLAND INSTITUTE OF MINING AND MECHANICAL ENGINEERS Neville Hall Westgate Road Newcastle upon Tyne 1	*Tel.:* Newcastle upon Tyne 22201

Advancement and promotion of science and technology of mining engineering

NEWCASTLE UPON TYNE, THE NORTH OF ENGLAND INSTITUTE OF MINING AND MECHANICAL ENGINEERS, *cont.*

Enquiries: To Secretary, by letter only

Scope: Mining engineering and allied branches of engineering. Historical records and manuscript collections of early mining records, including John Buddle, Watson, Easton, Bell and The London Lead Company Court Minutes and Plans

Stock: 25,000 books; 10 current periodicals

Publications: Transactions of this Institute are included in the Mining Engineer, published by the Institution of Mining Engineers

The manuscript records of the Durham and Northumberland Coal Owners Association are housed at the Northumberland County Record Office, Gosforth, Newcastle upon Tyne 3

NEWCASTLE UPON TYNE

1844

NORTHERN ARTS ASSOCIATION
24 Northumberland Road
Newcastle upon Tyne NE1 8JY

Tel.: 0632 610446

Aims to improve the accessibility and appreciation of all the arts in Cumberland, Durham, Northumberland, Westmorland and the North of the North Riding of Yorkshire

Enquiries: To Director

Scope: Music, drama, visual arts, literature, film
Secondary: Northern Arts Poetry Library (consisting of all currently published English work)

Stock: 500 books; 100 pamphlets

Publications: Arts North
Notes of Guidance on formation of Regional Arts Association

NEWCASTLE UPON TYNE

1845

NORTHERN COUNTIES COLLEGE OF EDUCATION
Coach Lane
Newcastle upon Tyne NE7 7XA

Tel: Newcastle upon Tyne 666241

Enquiries: To Librarian

Scope: Education, psychology, sociology, religion, philosophy, English language and literature, geography, history, art, music, theatre, children's books
Special Interest: Home economics

Stock: 18,800 books and pamphlets; plus 2,300 home economics and 6,500 children's books; 140 current periodicals; plus 13 home economics periodicals

Publications: The Northern Counties Cookery Book. 4th edition, 1962

NEWCASTLE UPON TYNE

1846

NORTHUMBERLAND COLLEGE OF EDUCATION (PONTELAND)
Ponteland
Newcastle upon Tyne

Tel.: Ponteland 3391 ext. 213

Enquiries: To Librarian, preferably by letter

Scope: Education with strong bias towards Psychology; Sociology, English, French (literature and language), Music, History, Geography, Physical Education including Dance and Health Education, Mathematics, Environmental Studies, Divinity, Art. The stock covers the subjects at a variety of levels including 1st degree (B.Ed.) level, and reflects the approach through fieldwork and the use of primary source material

Stock: 50,000 books and pamphlets; 350 current periodicals

NEWCASTLE UPON TYNE	NORTHUMBERLAND LOCAL HISTORY SOCIETY 24 The Grove Gosforth	*Tel.:* Newcastle upon Tyne 55381
1847	Newcastle upon Tyne NE3 1NE	

Enquiries: To Secretary, Lewie Cottage, Kielder, Hexham, Northumberland (*Tel.:* Kielder 275) by letter only

Scope: County history, industrial history, dialect, tombstones, village history

Publications: Quarterly News Letter

NEWCASTLE UPON TYNE	NORTHUMBERLAND RURAL COMMUNITY COUNCIL 24 The Grove Gosforth	*Tel.:* 0632-55381
1848	Newcastle upon Tyne NE3 1NE	

Social and economic development in rural Northumberland

Enquiries: To Secretary

Scope: Social and economic conditions in rural Northumberland. Opportunities for industrial development
Secondary: Demographic information

NEWCASTLE UPON TYNE	SOCIETY OF ANTIQUARIES OF NEWCASTLE UPON TYNE The Black Gate Castle Garth	*Tel.:* Newcastle upon Tyne 27938
1849	Newcastle upon Tyne	

The research, recording and excavation of antiquities, particularly in Northumberland and Durham

Enquiries: To Curator

Scope: Local history of Northumberland and Durham from Bronze Age to Industrial Archaeology, with particular reference to the Roman Wall and occupation
Secondary: Mediaeval Archaeology

Stock: 20,000 books; 30 current periodicals

Publications: Archologia Aeliana (annually, original papers on archaeology, excavations and social history and other subjects within the scope of the Society's aims)

Collection of manuscripts lodged with the Northumberland County Record Office
The Roman Collection of Antiquities was used to found the Joint Museum of Antiquities of the Society of Antiquaries and the University of Newcastle at Newcastle University

NEWCASTLE UPON TYNE	UNIVERSITY OF NEWCASTLE UPON TYNE LIBRARY Newcastle upon Tyne NE1 7RU	*Tel.:* Newcastle upon Tyne 28511 ext. 245 (Enquiry Desk)
1850		*Telex:* 53654

Enquiries: To Librarian

Scope: Arts, architecture, pure science, applied science, economic and social studies, law, education, agriculture, medicine, dentistry
Secondary: Special Collections: Pybus Collection (Medical History): Gertrude Bell (Archaeology of Middle East); Robert White (English Literature, Border History and Antiquities)

Stock: 325,000 books; 50,000 pamphlets; 4,200 current periodicals

Publications: Library Publications

NEWPORT	COUNTY SEELY LIBRARY	*Tel.:* Newport 2324
Isle of Wight	Upper St James's Street	
	Newport	
1851	Isle of Wight	

Enquiries: To Librarian

Scope: National subject specialization: Divine service—liturgy (550 books)
Regional subject specialization: Social welfare; charitable and social aid; services for the sick (general); hospitals (600 books). Teutonic and Romance languages (800 books). Teutonic literature (1,700 books). French literature (4,000 books). France, travel (700 books); France, history (900 books). Isle of Wight

Stock: As noted above plus 10,000 items in the Isle of Wight collection and 50 current periodicals

Houses the library of the Isle of Wight Natural History and Archaeological Society

NEWPORT	ISLE OF WIGHT POSTGRADUATE MEDICAL CENTRE	*Tel.:* Newport 3081
Isle of Wight	St Mary's Hospital	
	Newport	
1852	Isle of Wight	

Enquiries: To Secretary, by letter only

Scope: General medical

Stock: 560 books; 37 current periodicals

NEWPORT	ISLE OF WIGHT TECHNICAL COLLEGE	*Tel.:* Newport 3511
Isle of Wight	Hunnyhill	
	Newport	
1853	Isle of Wight	

Enquiries: To Librarian

Scope: The college holds classes in child care, pre-nursing, banking, economics, central and local government and the usual subjects taught in a technical college and prepares candidates for the examinations of various professional institutions. Classes are also held in geography, mathematics, English, German, French and Italian for the General Certificate of Education 'O' and 'A' levels

Stock: 8,000 books; 15 current periodicals

NEWPORT	CAERLEON COLLEGE OF EDUCATION	*Tel.:* Caerleon Park 292
Mon	Caerleon	
	Newport	
1854	Monmouthshire NP6 1XJ	

Enquiries: To Librarian

Scope: Education, English literature, books and gramophone records. Because Welsh is often spoken within the college, the library has a fairly large stock of books written in the Welsh language
Secondary: 3-dimensional studies. Education of E.S.N. children. Non-musical records. Children's books and records

Stock: Books: 1,400 education, 200 drama, 2,000 literature; 100 current periodicals

NEWPORT	MONMOUTHSHIRE COUNTY LIBRARY	*Tel.:* Newport 65431
Mon	Cambria House	
	Caerleon	
1855	Newport	
	Monmouthshire NP6 1XG	

Enquiries: To Librarian

Scope: English Literature (except modern poetry), European history, education and child psychology. Small Monmouthshire collection
Secondary: Welsh R.L.S. subject specialization includes: Child psychology; English and American literature (except modern poetry); European history; physics since 1968
Stock: 450,000 books; 50 pamphlets (in local collection); 47 current periodicals

NEWPORT
Mon

1856

MONMOUTHSHIRE RECORD OFFICE
County Hall
Newport
Monmouthshire NPT 5XJ

Tel.: Newport 65431

Enquiries: To County Archivist
Scope: The records preserved relate to the judicial, local government, parochial and other forms of administration of the county of Monmouth. They also include records of family and estate, and of industry and cultural and other societies
Publications: Guide to Monmouthshire Record Office
Catalogues to individual collections of records may be seen in the record office and at the National Register of Archives

NEWPORT
Mon

1857

NEWPORT AND MONMOUTHSHIRE COLLEGE
OF TECHNOLOGY
Allt-yr-yn Avenue
Newport
Monmouthshire

Tel.: Newport 51525

Enquiries: To Librarian or Industrial Liaison Officer
Scope: Subject fields covered by the College and the Library are: Chemistry, mathematics, mechanical engineering, physics, biology, civil engineering, electrical engineering, metallurgy, business administration and management, education, instrumentation
Stock: 14,000 books; 250 current periodicals

NEWPORT
Mon

1858

NEWPORT COLLEGE OF ART AND DESIGN
Clarence Place
Newport
Monmouthshire NPT 0UW

Tel.: Newport 59984

Enquiries: To Librarian
Scope: Art (general), architecture, sculpture, drawing, painting, graphic arts, printing, photography, dressmaking, costume, literature, history, cinema, interior design, lettering
Secondary: Philosophy, social sciences, botany, zoology, transport
Collection of exhibition catalogues
Stock: 4,600 books; 270 pamphlets (mainly exhibition catalogues); 125 current periodicals
Publications: Recent Additions Catalogues (three times each year)

NEWPORT
Mon

1859

NEWPORT MUSEUM AND ART GALLERY
Newport
Monmouthshire

Tel.: Newport 65781

Enquiries: To Director
Scope: Geology, natural history, archaeology, history relating to Monmouthshire
Publications: Illustrated Handbook: The Roman Caerwent Collection
Illustrated Handbook: The Monmouthshire Chartists

NEWPORT, NEWPORT MUSEUM AND ART GALLERY, *cont.*
Birds of Monmouthshire
Screens, Lofts and Stalls in Monmouthshire
Picture book: Gwent as seen by the Artist
Illustrated Catalogue of Watercolour Drawings

NEWPORT Mon **1860**	THE TECHNICAL COLLEGE OF MONMOUTHSHIRE Cross Keys Newport Monmouthshire	*Tel.:* Crosskeys 295

Enquiries: To Librarian

Scope: Science, technology, commerce, economics, law, administration, English literature, general studies

Stock: 8,800 books; 500 pamphlets; 48 current periodicals

NEWTON ABBOT Devon **1861**	DARTMOOR PONY SOCIETY Lower Hisley Lustleigh Newton Abbot Devon	*Tel.:* Lustleigh 389

Aims to encourage and improve the breeding of Dartmoor ponies

Enquiries: To Secretary

No library

Publications: Booklet: The Dartmoor Pony
Information leaflet: The Dartmoor Pony (overseas edition published in English, French, German, Dutch and Danish)
Dartmoor Section of the National Pony Society's Stud Book
Supplementary Register
Register of Breeders
List of Stallions at Stud

NEWTON STEWART Wigtownshire **1862**	THE INDIVIDUAL POSTAL TUITION SERVICE Whithorn Newton Stewart Wigtownshire

Enquiries: To Principal, by letter only

Scope: The I.P.T.S. provides a full information service for all prospective students and for all other enquirers and, of course, for its own students living in most parts of the world. This information service covers most literary fields, particularly English language and literature, most aspects of education, and cultural and career guidance

No library

NORTH- **ALLERTON** Yorkshire **1863**	NORTH RIDING COUNTY LIBRARY County Library Headquarters Grammar School Lane Northallerton Yorkshire	*Tel.:* Northallerton 3071

Enquiries: To Librarian

Scope: Subject specialization: Foreign policy
Large North Riding local history and topography collection
Secondary: Drama—including sets of plays for loan to groups

Stock: Books: North Riding 9,000; Drama 8,000; (total non-fiction stock, including reference, 173,000); 2,500 pamphlets; 160 current periodicals

Publications: Around Richmond: a book list. 1967

NORTH-ALLERTON
Yorkshire

1864

NORTH RIDING RECORD OFFICE
County Hall
Northallerton
Yorkshire

Tel.: Northallerton 3123

Enquiries: To County Archivist

Scope: Local history and historical geography of the North Riding. The principal sources of information in the record office are: The archives of the North Riding Quarter Sessions, Parish Records and Family and Estate papers

Publications: Lists and catalogues of archives are available in the Record Office
Annual Reports list records deposited each year and describe some of the collections

---

NORTHAMPTON

1865

NORTHAMPTON CENTRAL PUBLIC LIBRARY
Abington Street
Northampton

Tel.: Northampton 35651
(and office hours 34881)

Enquiries: To Librarian

Scope: All aspects of Northamptonshire
John Clare Collection
Dryden Collection of archaeological drawings
Secondary: Charles Bradlaugh. Philip Doddridge

Stock: 20,000 books and 6,000 pamphlets in Local History Collection. Stock available on loan except for rare or unique copies

Publications: Catalogue of the John Clare Collection in the Northampton Public Library
Catalogue of the Dryden Collection of Drawings, Plans, Notes on Churches, Houses and various Archaeological matters

---

NORTHAMPTON

1866

NORTHAMPTON COLLEGE OF TECHNOLOGY
St George's Avenue
Northampton NN2 6JB

Tel.: Northampton 34286

Area College of Technology. The library also serves the Northampton School of Art, at the same address

Enquiries: To Librarian

Scope: Collection of books on leather technology and on the manufacture of boots and shoes, covering all aspects of the subjects, historical, artistic and commercial included. An important feature is the Osborne Robinson collection of posters containing about 1,250 items representing the best of poster art from all over the world. Small collection of books on Northampton and Northamptonshire and a centre for information on local studies. Collection of books illustrating the history of printing and the development of the private press movement. Good collection on art and related subjects

Stock: 15,000 books; 5,000 pamphlets; 70 current periodicals

Publications: Catalogue of the Leather & Footwear Collections in the Northampton Central Reference Library and the Library of the Northampton Central College of Further Education. 1968

NORTHAMPTON	NORTHAMPTONSHIRE COUNTY LIBRARY	*Tel.:* Northampton 34833
1867	Guildhall Road Northampton NN1 1EF	

Enquiries: To Librarian

Stock: 524,000 books and pamphlets; 520 current periodicals (total stock)

Publications: Printed Catalogue of Sets of Music
Printed Catalogue of Sets of Plays

NORTHAMPTON	NORTHAMPTONSHIRE RECORD OFFICE	*Tel.:* Northampton 62129
1868	Delapre Abbey Northampton	

Enquiries: To Chief Archivist

Scope: Historical information about places, persons, estates, businesses and organizations, both lay and ecclesiastical, in any way connected with Northamptonshire and the Soke of Peterborough, or any town within these
Secondary: Information about archives, manuscripts and documents, their meaning, conservation and repair

Stock: 500 books; 800 pamphlets; 10 current periodicals
Minutes, reports and publications of local authorities within the county

NORTHAMPTON	NORTHAMPTONSHIRE RECORD SOCIETY	*Tel.:* Northampton 62297
1869	Delapre Abbey Northampton NN4 9AW	

Publication of Northamptonshire historical records and encouragement of the study of local history

Enquiries: To Hon. Librarian, by letter only

Scope: English history and historical records, specializing in works relating to Northamptonshire

Stock: 4,000 books; 2,000 pamphlets; 12 current periodicals

Publications: Volumes of Records relating to the history of Northamptonshire (catalogue available)
Northamptonshire Past & Present (periodical published annually since 1948)

NORTHAMPTON	ROYAL PIONEER CORPS MUSEUM	*Tel.:* Northampton 62742
1870	Corps HQ, Royal Pioneer Corps Simpson Barracks Wootton Northampton	

Houses and displays items of the Corps Collection

Enquiries: To Curator, by letter only

Scope: Information on all matters concerning the Royal Pioneer Corps past and present
No library

Publications: The Royal Pioneer (Corps journal)

NORTHAMPTON	ST CRISPIN HOSPITAL	*Tel.:* Northampton 52323
1871	Duston Northampton	

Psychiatric hospital serving the county of Northamptonshire

Enquiries: To Librarian

Scope: The stock of the library covers psychiatry, psychology, child psychiatry and psychology, neurology, social work with mental illness and related subjects

Stock: 1,000 books; 24 current periodicals. Stock not available on loan

NORTHWICH BRUNNER PUBLIC LIBRARY *Tel.:* Northwich 2531
Cheshire Witton Street
  Northwich
1872 Cheshire

Enquiries: To Librarian

Scope: N.W.R.L.S. subject specialization: Ballet; history and topography of India

Stock: 25,000 books (total stock)

NORWICH CITY OF NORWICH MUSEUMS *Tel.:* Norwich 22233
  Castle Museum ext. 160
1873 Norwich NOR 65B

Enquiries: To Director

Scope: Museum staff will provide information in particular on the geology, natural history, archaeology, history and architecture of Norfolk; on the crafts and industries of Norwich and Norfolk, past and present; on English paintings, particularly Norwich School; English ceramics, particularly Lowestoft porcelain; Medieval English alabaster carvings; English silver especially Norwich made; English coinage; English costume particularly Norwich shawls; English embroidery; English dolls, toys, children's books, instructive playthings and teaching equipment; and on Norfolk clock and watchmakers, English domestic equipment, swords and guns

Publications: Catalogues of Museum collections:
  Bronze Age Metal work in Norwich Castle Museum
  Fossil Vertebrates of Cromer Forest Bed in Norwich Castle Museum
  Teaching Toys in Norwich Museums Collection
  History of St Peter Hungate Church Museum
  Catalogues of some of the loan exhibitions, for example, Norwich Silver 1565–1706. 1966

NORWICH EAST ANGLIAN REGIONAL ADVISORY COUNCIL *Tel.:* Norwich 22288
  FOR FURTHER EDUCATION
1874 County Hall
  Martineau Lane
  Norwich NOR 49A

Enquiries: To Secretary

Scope: General information on further education

No library

Publications: Directory of Institutions and Courses in Technology, Commerce, Art and Agriculture in the Region
  Bulletin of Special Short Courses

NORWICH EASTERN COUNTIES NEWSPAPERS LTD *Tel.:* Norwich 28311
  Prospect House
1875 Rouen Road
  Norwich NOR 87A

The library is primarily for the use and benefit of the Company's organization as newspaper publishers but deals with enquiries from the public

NORWICH, EASTERN COUNTIES NEWSPAPERS LTD, *cont.*
Enquiries: To Chief Librarian
Scope: Local history, archaeology, biography and reference books
Stock: 2,000 books; more than 250,000 newspaper cuttings

NORWICH	FEILDEN AND MAWSON	*Tel.:* Norwich 29571
1876	Ferry Road Norwich NOR 18S Architects and Diocesan Architects	

Enquiries: To Librarian, by letter and telephone only
Scope: Architecture and building construction. Stock includes trade literature and catalogues, books, pamphlets, government publications, photographs, slides of places of interest mainly in Norfolk but also in other counties and countries, samples of building materials, ordnance survey maps of Norfolk and Suffolk, newspaper cuttings dealing with buildings in Norfolk, York Minster and Norwich Cathedral
Stock: 450 books; 20 current periodicals; 300 files containing manufacturers literature. Stock not available on loan, but photocopies supplied

NORWICH	KESWICK HALL	*Tel.:* Norwich 52581
1877	Keswick Norwich NOR 93B College of Education	

Enquiries: To Librarian
Scope: Education and educational psychology
Stock: 7,000 books and pamphlets; 50 current periodicals. Stock not available on loan

NORWICH	NORFOLK AND NORWICH ARCHAEOLOGICAL SOCIETY
1878	Garsett House St Andrew's Hall Plain Norwich NOR 16J

Enquiries: To Secretary, by letter only
Scope: Matters relating to archaeology in Norfolk
Scope of Library: Printed books and pamphlets relating to archaeology in Britain
Manuscripts collection: chiefly Norfolk archaeology
Secondary: Parish Register Transcripts of many Norfolk Parishes. G. A. King collection of paintings and drawings of ancient stained glass—much of it local
The Frere and the Sir John Fenn Manuscripts, the property of the Society, are deposited with the Norfolk and Norwich Record Office
Stock: 3,000 books; 600 pamphlets; 20 current periodicals
Publications: Norfolk Archaeology; or Miscellaneous Tracts relating to the County of Norfolk (published annually in the autumn of each year)

NORWICH	NORFOLK AND NORWICH LIBRARY	*Tel.:* Norwich 21193
1879	Guildhall Hill Norwich	
	Non-profit making Subscription Library, founded in 1784	

Enquiries: To Librarian, by letter only

Scope: Long runs of 19th century periodicals and reviews. Comprehensive local collection on Norfolk, Suffolk and East Anglia

Stock: 5,000 books in local collection; numerous pamphlets; total stock 38,000

NORWICH

1880

NORFOLK COUNTY LIBRARY
County Hall
Norwich NOR 49A

Tel.: Norwich 22288 ext. 302

Enquiries: To Librarian

Scope: Thomas Paine Collection housed at the County Branch Library, Thetford. 300 items consisting of various editions of his works, pamphlets, tracts, newspaper cuttings, and biographical, critical and illustrative material. The collection includes complete issues of the *Thomas Paine Society Bulletin*

NORWICH

1881

NORWICH CITY COLLEGE
Ipswich Road
Norwich NOR 67D

Tel.: Norwich 24177

Enquiries: To Librarian

Scope: Business management. British constitution and government
Secondary: Economics, social welfare, accounting, British history from 1700

Stock: 10,000 books; 100 pamphlets; 110 current periodicals

NORWICH

1882

NORWICH PUBLIC LIBRARIES
Central Library
Bethel Street
Norwich NOR 57E

Tel.: Norwich 22233 (night and weekend:
Lending 26625
Reference 25038)

Enquiries: To Librarian

Scope: *Special collections* include: Colman and Rye Libraries of local history; City Library, 1608 (incunabula, theology and general literature); publications of the Public Record Office, Historical Manuscripts Commission and Early English Text Society; American Memorial Library (all aspects of United States life, particularly history); Bosworth Harcourt and Buck Bequests (literary and historical)
National subject specialization: Literature. Regional specialization (up to 1968): Philosophy; religion

Stock: 191,620 books and pamphlets; 290 current periodicals; 24,230 local prints and portraits; 17,760 local photographic survey; 78,550 cuttings (local press); 10,880 broadsides, posters; 5,400 slides, films and tape-recordings

Publications: Norwich Public Libraries. P. Hepworth and M. Alexander. Norfolk and Norwich Record Office, Norwich, Libraries Committee. 1965
Second Air Division Memorial Trust: Second Air Division Memorial, 8 USAAF Norwich. The Trust. 1963

Deposited libraries: Norfolk and Norwich Incorporated Law Society Library (3,170 volumes) Shipdham Parish Library (theological, historical and general literature, 500 volumes)

NORWICH

1883

NORWICH SCHOOL OF ART
St George Street
Norwich NOR 16J

Tel.: Norwich 29601

Enquiries: To Tutor Librarian

NORWICH, NORWICH SCHOOL OF ART, *cont.*

Scope: Books on fine art, graphic design and related subjects. Decimal index of the Art of the Low Countries (a collection of postcard-size reproductions of Netherlandish painting) and a collection of slides, mostly of painting, architecture and sculpture

Stock: 5,000 books; 7,000 slides; 75 current periodicals

NORWICH

1884

THE ROYAL NORFOLK REGIMENT MUSEUM   *Tel.:* Norwich 28455
Britannia Barracks
Norwich NOR 67A

To preserve the possessions and to perpetuate the traditions of the Regiment

Enquiries: To Curator

Scope: All aspects of the Regiment's 284 years history. Military records of officers 1685–1969 are maintained

Stock: 900 books; 150 pamphlets; 1 current periodical

NORWICH

1885

UNIVERSITY OF EAST ANGLIA LIBRARY   *Tel.:* Norwich 56161
University Plain   *Telex:* 97154
Norwich NOR 88C

Enquiries: To Librarian

Scope: General university library—coverage in the social sciences and the humanities but not medicine

Stock: 100,000 books; 8,000 pamphlets (total stock); 800 current periodicals (social sciences and humanities)

A bibliographical survey of East Anglia library resources (for Centre for East Anglian Studies at the University) is being carried out

NOTTINGHAM

1886

BOOTS PURE DRUG CO. LTD   *Tel.:* Nottingham 56255
Research Library
Nottingham NG2 3AA

Provides a library and information service for the employees of Boots Pure Drug Co. Ltd

Enquiries: To Librarian

Scope: Medicine, pharmacology, bacteriology, pharmacy, chemistry, biochemistry, veterinary medicine, food sciences, agriculture, horticulture
Secondary: Management, computer sciences

NOTTINGHAM

1887

CARLTON PUBLIC LIBRARY   *Tel.:* Nottingham 246319
Manor Road
Carlton
Nottingham NG4 3AZ

Enquiries: To Librarian

Scope: Local collection

Stock: 62,998 books; 200 pamphlets; 81 current periodicals (total stock)

NOTTINGHAM

1888

EAST MIDLANDS ECONOMIC PLANNING   *Tel.:* Nottingham 46121
    COUNCIL   *Telex:* 37143
Cranbrook House
Cranbrook Street
Nottingham NG1 1FB

Enquiries: To Secretary

Scope: Regional Economic Planning in the East Midlands Region. Information is restricted to that which is available within Government departments and which can be released
No library
Publications: East Midlands Study
Opportunity in the East Midlands
Reports of study groups or research projects
Regional Research Register (of studies related to economic planning conducted by Universities within the region). New edition due 1970

NOTTINGHAM

1889

LONG EATON PUBLIC LIBRARY
Tamworth Road
Long Eaton
Nottingham

Tel.: Long Eaton 5426

Enquiries: To Reference and Music Librarian
Scope: Lace. Modern British poets whose surnames begin with B. Fiction by authors whose surnames come within category JAN–JAZ
Stock: Lace, 20 books; poets, 50 books; fiction, 50 books

NOTTINGHAM

1890

MUSIC ADVISERS' NATIONAL ASSOCIATION
Education Office
Exchange Buildings
Nottingham

Enquiries: To Secretary, by letter only
Scope: Advice and information on the development of musical education

NOTTINGHAM

1891

NOTTINGHAM CITY LIBRARY
Central Library
South Sherwood Street
Nottingham

Tel.: Nottingham 43591
Telex: 37662

Enquiries: To City Librarian
Scope: Philosophy, religion, social sciences, law, economics, languages, literature, fine arts, geography, history
Special collections: Byron; D. H. Lawrence; Early children's books (pre-1900); genealogy; Robin Hood; Nottingham and Nottinghamshire local history; G. B. Shaw. Subject specialization: German literature
Stock: 160,000 books and pamphlets; 300 current periodicals
Publications: Architecture and Town Planning Index (monthly)

NOTTINGHAM

1892

NOTTINGHAM COLLEGE OF ART AND DESIGN
Waverley Street
Nottingham

Tel.: Nottingham 46555

Enquiries: To Librarian
Scope: Fine art; lace. Town planning. Fashion and textiles
Stock: 13,000 books; 1,000 pamphlets; 105 current periodicals

NOTTINGHAM

1893

NOTTINGHAM COLLEGE OF EDUCATION
Clifton
Nottingham NG11 8NS

Tel.: Nottingham 211181

Enquiries: To Librarian

NOTTINGHAM, NOTTINGHAM COLLEGE OF EDUCATION, *cont.*

Scope: Education, history, geography, English, mathematics, art and craft, physics, chemistry, biology, divinity, French, Russian, music, physical education

Stock: 40,000 books and pamphlets; 300 current periodicals

NOTTINGHAM

1894

NOTTINGHAM INDUSTRIAL MUSEUM *Tel.:* Nottingham 284602
Wollaton Park
Nottingham NG8 2AE

Preservation of local industrial artifacts and machinery especially those relating to the manufacture of machine lace

Enquiries: To Art Director, Castle Museum, Nottingham

NOTTINGHAM

1895

NOTTINGHAM REGIONAL COLLEGE OF TECHNOLOGY (PROPOSED TRENT POLYTECHNIC) *Tel.:* Nottingham 48248
Burton Street
Nottingham NG1 4BU

Enquiries: To Librarian

Scope: Law (complete sets Law Reports, All England Law Reports, Halsbury's Laws, Statutes and Statutory Instruments); economics; management; English, French and German language and literature; education (Teacher Training, including teaching of mentally handicapped children); social work; geography, history, biology; accountancy
Secondary: Psychology

Stock: 25,000 books and pamphlets; 400 current periodicals

NOTTINGHAM

1896

NOTTINGHAMSHIRE COUNTY LIBRARY *Tel.:* Nottingham 83366
County Hall
West Bridgford
Nottingham

Enquiries: To Librarian

Scope: Music; drama; D. H. Lawrence; Nottinghamshire history

Stock: 24,000 books and music scores; 30,000 sets of plays; 350 books D. H. Lawrence Collection

Publications: Sets of Choral Music
D. H. Lawrence 'Finding List'
Local History Catalogue

NOTTINGHAM

1897

NOTTINGHAMSHIRE RURAL COMMUNITY COUNCIL *Tel.:* Nottingham 53681
Shire Hall
High Pavement
Nottingham NG1 1HR

Enquiries: To Secretary

Scope: Information on rural life in Nottinghamshire
No library

Publications: The Nottinghamshire Countryside (Quarterly magazine)
News letters for members of most of the organizations served

NOTTINGHAM **1898**	PEOPLE'S COLLEGE OF FURTHER EDUCATION Castle Road Nottingham NG1 6AB Education up to 'A' level and O.N.C.	*Tel.:* Nottingham 47721

Enquiries: To Librarian

Scope: Electrical engineering, mechanical engineering, workshop practice, electronics, general science
Secondary: Teaching practice: audio-visual techniques, programmed learning

Stock: 8,000 books; 1,000 pamphlets; 90 current periodicals

Publications: Current Awareness Bulletin (fortnightly)   New Standards (monthly)
Introduction to Library Services   Introduction to Reference Books
Introduction to the Use of the Library (A Programmed Text)

Member of NANTIS

NOTTINGHAM
1899
	REGIONAL ADVISORY COUNCIL FOR THE
	  ORGANISATION OF FURTHER EDUCATION
	  IN THE EAST MIDLANDS
	Robins Wood House
	Robins Wood Road
	Aspley
	Nottingham
		Tel.: Nottingham 293291

Advises on all matters essential to the full development of Further Education in the Region, including the maintenance of contact with industry, the planning of new developments and the expansion of existing facilities, the review of courses and curricula

Enquiries: To Secretary

No library

Publications: Council publications giving details of where courses in the several technologies are available
Directory of Courses in Further Education (annually, regular course provision in all technologies)
Bulletin of Short Advanced and Special Courses (annually)
Lists of courses in individual technologies:
    Business Studies and Management   Sciences
    Building   Engineering
    Modern Language Course Facilities   Vocational Art Courses
    Catering and Bakery

NOTTINGHAM **1900**	THE SHERWOOD FORESTERS Regimental Headquarters Triumph Road Nottingham	*Tel.:* Nottingham 75516

Museum and Archives of The Sherwood Foresters (Nottingham and Derbyshire Regiment)

Enquiries: To Regimental Secretary, by letter only

Scope: The history of the regiment and relics relating to that history. The Regiment has existed under the titles 45th Regiment of Foot and 95th Regiment of Foot as well as The Sherwood Foresters
Secondary: The Militia Units, Volunteer Units and Territorial Units of Nottinghamshire and Derbyshire which do or have formed part of the Regiment

No library

NOTTINGHAM, THE SHERWOOD FORESTERS, *cont.*

Main Museum with an attendant in charge is housed in Nottingham Castle
Small displays in Corporation Museum in Newark (8th Territorial Battalion) and in Derby

NOTTINGHAM THOROTON SOCIETY OF NOTTINGHAMSHIRE
Bromley House
1901 Angel Row
Nottingham

Enquiries: To Librarian, by letter only
Scope: History and antiquities of Nottinghamshire
Stock: 2,000 books; 100 pamphlets
Publications: Transactions of the Thoroton Society (annually)
Thoroton Society Record Series (annually)

NOTTINGHAM UNIVERSITY OF NOTTINGHAM LIBRARY *Tel.:* ONO2-56101
Nottingham NG7 2RD
1902 *Enquiries:* To Librarian
Scope: Subjects covered by Faculties of Arts, Law and Social Sciences, Education, Pure Science, Applied Science, Agricultural Science, Board of Medical Studies
Special collections: D. H. Lawrence; Briggs Collection of early children's educational books; French Revolution; Coventry Patmore; Dante; Bacon-Shakespeare; Porter Collection of bird books; Mellish Collection on meteorology
Special Manuscript collections: Recognized repository for manorial records; Middleton, Clifton, Portland, Mellish, Newcastle and Archdeaconry of Nottingham manuscripts
E.M.R.L.S. Foreign Literature Specialization: Slavonic languages
Faculty and Departmental Libraries: Education, Medicine, Architecture, Fine Art, Law, Music, Chemistry, School of Agriculture (Sutton Bonington, Loughborough)
Stock: 320,000 books; 115,000 pamphlets; 4,200 current periodicals. Very large collection of manuscripts

NUNEATON NUNEATON LIBRARY *Tel.:* Nuneaton 4027
Warwickshire Church Street
Nuneaton
1903 Warwickshire

Enquiries: To Librarian
Scope: General stock including gramophone record library and picture lending library (framed colour prints, not originals). Local history collection. George Eliot collection. Small collections of works by and about Michael Drayton and Robert Burton
Stock: 132,000 books; 100 current periodicals (total stock)

NUNEATON NUNEATON MUSEUM AND ART GALLERY *Tel.:* Nuneaton 2683
Warwickshire Riversley Park
Nuneaton
1904 Warwickshire

Enquiries: To Curator
Scope: Local geology, prehistory and archaeology (Roman and Mediaeval). General ethnography and anthropology. Collections of local and mining relics; personalia with reference to Nuneaton notable people ... George Eliot, John Barber, Henry Beighton. Anatomy, physical anthropology, specialist in Arctic studies. Art Gallery, water colour, oil paintings and etchings from 18th to 20th century. Coins and medals

NUNEATON Warwickshire **1905**	NUNEATON TECHNICAL COLLEGE AND SCHOOL OF ART Hinckley Road Nuneaton Warwickshire	*Tel.:* Nuneaton 4186

    Enquiries: To Librarian

    Scope: Books and periodicals on mechanical and electrical engineering, building, commerce, mining, art (Art library is in a separate building)
Secondary: Small stock of books on general studies, history, languages, pure science and medicine

    Stock: 9,000 books and pamphlets; 80 current periodicals

OAKHAM Rutland **1906**	RUTLAND COUNTY LIBRARY County Library 56 High Street Oakham Rutland	*Tel.:* Oakham 2918

    Enquiries: To Librarian

    Scope: Local history collection on Rutland

OAKHAM Rutland **1907**	RUTLAND COUNTY MUSEUM Catmos Street Oakham Rutland	*Tel.:* Oakham 2544 ext. 42

    Enquiries: To Curator

    Scope: Archaeology, domestic and agricultural history of the county of Rutland. The collections are particularly strong in Romano-British and Anglo-Saxon remains, and in 19th century farming tools

OLDHAM Lancs **1908**	CHADDERTON PUBLIC LIBRARY Middleton Road Oldham Lancashire	*Tel.:* 061-633 2181 or 061-633 2187 (evenings, Saturdays)

    Enquiries: To Librarian

    Scope: N.W.R.L.S. subject specialization includes: Sculpture

    Stock: 300 books

OLDHAM Lancs **1909**	CROMPTON PUBLIC LIBRARY Beal Lane Shaw Oldham Lancashire	*Tel.:* Shaw 7292

    Enquiries: To Librarian

    Scope: Tropical medicine, fevers, bodyfluid abnormalities

OLDHAM Lancs **1910**	OLDHAM COLLEGE OF FURTHER EDUCATION Rochdale Road Oldham Lancashire	*Tel.:* 061-624 5214

    Enquiries: To Librarian

OLDHAM, OLDHAM COLLEGE OF FURTHER EDUCATION, *cont.*
Scope: Mechanical, electrical and production engineering, building, textiles, chemistry, physics and mathematics
Secondary: Language, literature, history and social sciences
Stock: 7,000 books; 120 current periodicals

OLDHAM
Lancs

1911

OLDHAM PUBLIC LIBRARY
Central Library
Union Street
Oldham
Lancashire

Tel.: 061-624 0371
Telex: 66779

Enquiries: To Director
Scope: General collections including Arts, Literature, History. N.W.R.L.S. subject specialization: Gynaecology; Technique of painting; French literature (vernacular texts published in Great Britain only, plus history and criticism); South-east and South Africa (history and geography) Local history library, including collection of published works by William Cobbett
Stock: Local history collection: 4,725 books; 3,200 pamphlets

OLNEY
Bucks

1912

COWPER AND NEWTON MUSEUM
Market Place
Olney
Buckinghamshire

Tel.: Olney 516

House in which poet William Cowper lived

Enquiries: To The Curator
Scope: Books, manuscripts, clothes, furniture, pictures, lace and numerous articles of Cowper and the Revd John Newton

ORMSKIRK
Lancs

1913

EDGE HILL COLLEGE OF EDUCATION
St Helens Road
Lancashire

Tel.: Ormskirk 3931

Enquiries: To Librarian
Scope: Education. Social Sciences in relation to education, counselling and guidance
Stock: 50,000 books *in total*—not just Education; 400 current periodicals (total stock)

ORMSKIRK
Lancs

1914

THE EVANGELICAL LIBRARY (MERSEYSIDE
   BRANCH)
St Mark's Vicarage
Scarisbrick
Ormskirk
Lancashire

Tel.: Scarisbrick 317

Library for use mainly of clergy and theological students

Enquiries: To Librarian
Scope: Puritan works, including recent reprints
Secondary: General theological works, commentaries and Church history
Stock: 2,500 books. Books may be borrowed on personal application only

ORPINGTON Kent **1915**	MEDICAL LIBRARY Farnborough Hospital Orpington Kent BR6 8ND	*Tel.*: Farnborough 53333

Enquiries: To Librarian

Scope: Small library covering main subjects in medical field and a separate library in the Nurses' Education Centre

Stock: 750 books; 55 current periodicals

General Library is part of London Borough of Bromley Library stock

ORPINGTON Kent **1916**	NATIONAL FEDERATION OF GRAMOPHONE SOCIETIES LTD 31 Lynwood Grove Orpington Kent BR6 0BD	*Tel.*: Orpington 21801

Furtherance of the interests of gramophone societies in Great Britain

Enquiries: To Secretary, 88 St George's Drive, London S.W.11 (*Tel.*: 01-828 1061)

Scope: Advice on the formation and organization of gramophone societies

No library

Publications: Bulletin (twice yearly)

OSWESTRY Salop **1917**	OSWESTRY COLLEGE OF FURTHER EDUCATION College Road Oswestry Shropshire	*Tel.*: Oswestry 3067

Enquiries: To Librarian

Scope: The library has a small but comprehensive stock of books and periodicals covering all subject fields, with a slight emphasis on English literature, British economic and social history 1700-1914 and the social sciences

Stock: 5,000 books; 65 current periodicals

OXFORD **1918**	BRASENOSE COLLEGE Oxford OX1 4AJ

Enquiries: To Librarian

Scope: History, economics, law, philosophy, theology, geography, language and literature (Classical, English, French, German, Italian and Spanish), art

Secondary: Small section of works in medicine and the social sciences; limited but expanding section of works in political science

Stock: 32,000 books; 500 pamphlets; 80 current periodicals. Stock not available on loan

Separate Libraries for law and history

OXFORD **1919**	CHRIST CHURCH Oxford	*Tel.*: Oxford 43957

Enquiries: To Librarian, preferably by letter

Scope: Collection of 16th and 17th century manuscript and printed music

Theology, particularly the Vulgate

Stock: Printed and manuscript music: 1,200 items

OXFORD	THE CHURCHILL HOSPITAL MEDICAL LIBRARY	*Tel.:* Oxford 64841 ext. 368
1920	Churchill Hospital Headington Oxford	

Enquiries: To Librarian

Scope: General medicine

Stock: 200 books; 21 current periodicals

OXFORD	CODRINGTON LIBRARY	*Tel.:* Oxford 49641
1921	All Souls College Oxford	

Enquiries: To Librarian, by letter only

Scope: History; law; economics; philosophy

Stock: 80,000 books; 82 current periodicals. Stock not available on loan

OXFORD	COMMONWEALTH BUREAU OF AGRICULTURAL ECONOMICS	*Tel.:* Oxford 59829
1922	31A St Giles Oxford	

One of the Commonwealth Agricultural Bureaux, this unit provides an information service, largely by abstracts journal, covering publications in agricultural economics and rural sociology

Enquiries: To Director

No library

Publications: World Agricultural Economics and Rural Sociology Abstracts (quarterly Journal, classified with quarterly and annual subject, author, and geographical indexes. 4,000 abstracts per annum, and review articles)

OXFORD	EXETER COLLEGE	*Tel.:* Oxford 44681
1923	Oxford	

Enquiries: To Librarian

Scope: Undergraduate working library, and historical and early printed collections and manuscripts

Stock: 60,000 books; 1,000 pamphlets; 38 current periodicals. Stock not normally available on loan

OXFORD	KEBLE COLLEGE	*Tel.:* Oxford 59201
1924	Oxford	

Enquiries: To Librarian

Scope: Undergraduate working library covering most Honours Schools subjects at Oxford University. Particularly good collection in classics, theology, and mediaeval history
Port Royale Collection of Jansenist Literature
Brooke Collection including mediaeval manuscripts
John Keble Library
Collection of 19th century liturgy and theology
Eighty mediaeval manuscripts (printed catalogue in preparation)
Large collection of 19th century correspondence associated with Keble and Liddon

Stock: 20,000 volumes on open shelves; 3,000 volumes in special collections; 6,000 volumes in bookstack; 100 current periodicals

OXFORD

1925

THE KILNER LIBRARY OF PLASTIC SURGERY   *Tel.:* Oxford 64841 ext. 368
Plastic Surgery Department
Churchill Hospital
Headington
Oxford

Enquiries: To Librarian

Scope: Plastic and reconstructive surgery. Reprints of plastic surgical literature since 1900

Stock: 700 books; 200 pamphlets; 22 current periodicals

OXFORD

1926

LATIMER HOUSE   *Tel.:* Oxford 59522
131 Banbury Road
Oxford

Theological research on current ecclesiastical problems

Enquiries: To Librarian

Scope: Theology

Stock: 4,000 books; 500 pamphlets; 25 current periodicals. Stock not available on loan

OXFORD

1927

MANCHESTER COLLEGE   *Tel.:* Oxford 41514
Mansfield Road
Oxford

A small residential college for general education in theology, sociology and the arts, and for research in these fields

Enquiries: To Librarian, preferably by letter

Scope: The library is particularly rich in theology, biblical studies, philosophy, Christian history (particularly the history of English Dissent). Since the college was founded in 1757, there is much material of historical interest and many valuable books

Stock: 65,000 books; about 9,000 pamphlets earlier than A.D. 1840; many theological and philosophical current periodicals

Publications: Faith and Freedom (three issues each year)

OXFORD

1928

MANSFIELD COLLEGE   *Tel.:* Oxford 43507
Oxford

Congregational Church College for training for Christian Ministry

Enquiries: To Librarian, by letter only

Scope: Theology, to research standard
Secondary: Undergraduate level in English, law, history, geography, natural sciences, French and German

Stock: 10,000 books; 2,000 pamphlets; 25 current periodicals

OXFORD

1929

MEDICAL RESEARCH COUNCIL
IMMUNOCHEMISTRY UNIT   *Tel.:* Oxford 59214
Department of Biochemistry
South Parks Road
Oxford

Enquiries: To Director, by letter only

Scope: Investigation of the structure of immunoglobulins and related immunological fields
No library

OXFORD 1930	MEDICAL RESEARCH COUNCIL NEUROENDOCRINOLOGY UNIT Department of Human Anatomy South Parks Road Oxford OX1 3QX	*Tel.:* Oxford 58686

Enquiries: To Director, by letter only

Scope: The Unit is concerned with investigations into the anatomical, physiological and behavioural relationships between the central nervous system and the endocrine glands

OXFORD 1931	MEDICAL RESEARCH COUNCIL POPULATION GENETICS UNIT Old Road Headington Oxford	*Tel.:* Oxford 62834

Enquiries: To Director, by letter only

Scope: Population genetics research

Stock: 500 books; 2,000 pamphlets; 50 current periodicals

OXFORD 1932	NUFFIELD COLLEGE Oxford OX1 1NF Graduate college specializing in the social sciences	*Tel.:* Oxford 48014

Enquiries: To Librarian, by letter only

Scope: Social Sciences
William Cobbett manuscripts collection; G. D. H. Cole collection; Fabian Society archives; British trade union material
No information service

Stock: 40,000 books; 65,000 pamphlets and official publications; 600 current periodicals

OXFORD 1933	ORDER OF FRIARS-SERVANTS OF MARY (SERVITES) St Philip's Priory Begbroke Oxford OX5 1RX Student House of Roman Catholic Religious Order	*Tel.:* Kidlington 2149

Enquiries: To Librarian, by letter only

Scope: Student library
Collection of works on the history of the Order of Friars-Servants. Collection of works from the 16th to 19th centuries will be housed within the next two years, drawn from other houses of the Order, and including works of interest to students of Florentine, Tuscan and Sienese life, where the Order originated in the 13th century
Collections of works by Fra Paolo Sarpi (Historian of the Council of Trent), Fra Giarni (Historian of the Order)
Acta (16th century); *Monumenta Ordinis Servorum Mariae* (19th century)

Stock: 7,000 books in Student library; 400 books on Servite history

Publications: Studi Storici
Marianum
Bibliographia Mariana

OXFORD ORIEL COLLEGE *Tel.:* Oxford 3135
Oxford

1934 *Enquiries:* To Librarian

Scope: General academic subjects
Special collections: Leigh library (a typical nobleman's library of the 18th century, 10,000 volumes including 187 volumes of music scores, mostly of the 18th century)
Books and pamphlets by members of the College

Stock: 33,000 books; thousands of pamphlets; 84 manuscripts; 33 incunabula

OXFORD OXFORD CITY LIBRARIES *Tel.:* Oxford 41717
Central Library
1935 St Aldate's
Oxford OX1 1DJ

Enquiries: To Librarian

Scope: National subject specialization: Brahmanism and religions deriving from it; Brahman and Hindu biography
SWRLS subject specialization: Genealogy, heraldry and family history; indoor games and amusements
Local history of Oxford and the surrounding region

Stock: 4,600 books; 2,100 pamphlets; 12,000 photographs; 33 current periodicals

OXFORD OXFORD MAIL AND TIMES (WESTMINSTER *Tel.:* Oxford 49841
PRESS) LTD
1936 New Inn Hall Street
Oxford

Publishers of newspapers

Enquiries: To Librarian

Scope: Information provided from extensive files of newspaper clippings, mainly for editorial purposes, supplemented with photographs. Oxford regional information is extensively covered

Stock: 1,000 books; 750 pamphlets; 400 reports; 750,000 newspaper cuttings; 80,000 photographs. Stock not available on loan

OXFORD OXFORD POLYTECHNIC *Tel.:* Oxford 63434
Headington
1937 Oxford

Enquiries: To Librarian

Scope: Science, engineering, architecture, building, art, business, languages, social science, economics. Strongest in architecture and planning

Stock: 35,000 books; 10,000 pamphlets; 650 current periodicals; 15,000 slides; 500 maps. Complete set of British Standards and Codes of Practice

Publications: Monthly accession list (subject classified)
Monthly selective index to periodicals mainly in architecture, planning, art, and economics

OXFORD OXFORD REGIONAL HOSPITAL BOARD *Tel.:* Oxford 64861
Old Road
1938 Headington
Oxford OX3 7LF

Enquiries: To Librarian

OXFORD, OXFORD REGIONAL HOSPITAL BOARD, *cont.*

Scope: All aspects of current health services administration with particular emphasis on hospitals and the planning and development of future services

Stock: 800 books; 1,300 pamphlets; 300 reports; 110 current periodicals

OXFORD

1939

OXFORDSHIRE COUNTY LIBRARY   *Tel.:* Wheatley 234
Holton Park
Oxford OX9 1QQ

Enquiries: To Librarian

Scope: Special collections: Logic; New Testament; international relations; international law; customs, costumes and folklore; India

Stock: 420,000 volumes including 3,600 in special collections; 90 current periodicals

OXFORD

1940

OXFORDSHIRE RURAL COMMUNITY COUNCIL   *Tel.:* Oxford 43105
Hadow House
20 Beaumont Street
Oxford OX1 2NQ

Aims to help dwellers in the rural areas to develop a social community and cultural life, based upon the best characteristics of traditional rural life while receiving the benefit of modern facilities

Enquiries: To Secretary

Scope: Informal education in villages, drama in the countryside, informal local history studies in the countryside, review of charities for the poor, best kept village competition, the work of parish councils, the provision of playing fields, the welfare of old people

No library

Publications: Bulletin of the Oxfordshire Association for the Care of Old People
Bulletin of the County Drama Committee

OXFORD

1941

PEMBROKE COLLEGE   *Tel.:* Oxford 42271
Oxford

Enquiries: To Librarian, by letter only

Scope: The library is mainly for the use of undergraduates of the College and is therefore geared to the Oxford degree courses in each subject
Secondary: Books bequeathed to the college over the years, notably the Chandler collection, which is mainly of Aristotelia. Manuscripts, including some letters and papers of Dr Samuel Johnson. These may be consulted, within the library only, by previous arrangement with the Librarian. Arrangements for photographing particular pages can be made at the cost of the enquirer

Stock: 27,000 books; 70 current periodicals

OXFORD

1942

PUSEY HOUSE
61 St Giles
Oxford

Enquiries: To Librarian

Scope: Theology, liturgy, Church history. The library is particularly strong in Patristic literature (complete set of Migne's Patrologia); and 19th century English Church History (a unique feature is the collection of about 18,000 19th century pamphlets, sermons and Bishop's charges relating to the controversies of the period). Large collection of manuscript material

including the Pusey Papers, Nugent Wade Papers, Ollard Papers and Mrs Humphrey Ward Papers
Secondary: Philosophy
Stock: 36,000 books; 18,000 pamphlets; 53 current periodicals

OXFORD THE QUEEN'S COLLEGE *Tel.:* Oxford 48411
Oxford

1943 *Enquiries:* To Librarian, by letter only
Scope: Early printed books on medicine
Stock: 5,000 books. Stock not available on loan

OXFORD REGENT'S PARK COLLEGE *Tel.:* Oxford 59887
Oxford

1944 Private Hall and Theological College in the University of Oxford
Enquiries: To Librarian, by letter only
Scope: Theology
Secondary: A fine collection of source material on Baptist history 17th to 19th centuries in the Angus Library (a separate collection from the main library)
Stock: 10,000 books; 13 current periodicals

OXFORD RIPON HALL *Tel.:* (Principal) Oxford 35579; (Librarian) 39387; (General) 35215
Boar's Hill
Oxford OX1 5ES

1945 Theological College
Enquiries: To Librarian
Scope: Theology (including ecclesiastical history)
Secondary: General history, philosophy, and social studies
Stock: 11,000 books; 400 pamphlets; 50 reports; 26 current periodicals. Stock not normally available on loan

OXFORD ST ANNE'S COLLEGE *Tel.:* Oxford 57417
Woodstock Road
Oxford OX2 6HS

1946 *Enquiries:* To Librarian, by letter only
Scope: No Information Service. Library is a lending library for the college. It covers: Medicine (700 books); philosophy (1,500 books); English literature and language (9,000 books); Modern languages (Large French section, also some German, Spanish, Italian, Russian, Norse, 6,000 books); Modern history (mostly English, General European and French, 12,000 books); Ancient history, archaeology and art (4,000 books); Classical literature (1,500 books); sociology, economics, politics (2,500 books); geography (1,000 books); Law (Geldart library for all women law students in Oxford, 3,000 books); theology and ecclesiastical history (5,000 books)
Stock: 46,000 books; 1,000 pamphlets; 88 current periodicals

OXFORD ST ANTONY'S COLLEGE *Tel.:* Oxford 59651
Oxford OX2 6JF

1947 Post-graduate College
Enquiries: To Librarian, by letter only

OXFORD, ST ANTONY'S COLLEGE, *cont.*

Scope: Modern history and politics and international affairs on a regional basis covering Latin America, Middle East, Far East, Russia and East Europe and Western Europe, particularly France, Germany and Italy
Secondary: Economics, philosophy

Stock: 60,000 books; 300 current periodicals; 1,000 reels of microfilm. Stock not available on loan

OXFORD

1948

ST EDMUND HALL *Tel.:* Oxford 43574
Oxford OX1 4AR

Library caters mainly for undergraduate use

Enquiries: To Librarian, by letter only

Scope: Philosophy, politics, economics, geography, education, psychology, law, theology, history, mathematics, engineering, physics, metallurgy, chemistry, geology, medicine, biology, English literature, French, German, Italian, Russian, Spanish, music
Special collection: works by old members of the Hall

Stock: 20,000 books and pamphlets (3,500 of these being books printed pre-1850); 40 current periodicals. Stock not available on loan

OXFORD

1949

ST HILDA'S COLLEGE *Tel.:* Oxford 41821
Cowley Place
Oxford OX4 1DY

College library catering for senior and junior members of the college

Enquiries: To Librarian

Scope: Caters for most subjects read for Final Honour Schools. *Special collections* of books on Marie Antoinette and Scotland

Stock: 23,000 books and pamphlets. Stock not normally available on loan

OXFORD

1950

ST HUGH'S COLLEGE *Tel.:* Oxford 57341
Oxford

Enquiries: To Librarian, preferably by letter

Scope: Small undergraduate library in medicine. Working undergraduate library in social sciences. Large undergraduate library in humanities with some rarer and more advanced material

Stock: 36,000 books

OXFORD

1951

UNIVERSITIES COUNCIL FOR ADULT
  EDUCATION
Rewley House
Wellington Square
Oxford

Enquiries: To Hon. Secretary, by letter only

Scope: Concerned with the provision of various forms of adult education by universities in Great Britain and the study, in universities, of adult education. Willing to deal with general enquiries about university policy and practice in the field of adult education, but not about the activities of individual universities

No library

Publications: Studies in Adult Education (twice each year)
Occasional papers

OXFORD UNIVERSITY OF OXFORD *Tel.:* Oxford 57522
         ASHMOLEAN MUSEUM OF ART AND
1952   ARCHAEOLOGY
         Beaumont Street
         Oxford

    Enquiries: To Librarian

    Scope: The Ashmolean Museum Library consists of a group of specialist libraries: the Library of the Department of Antiquities; the Heberden Coin Room Library; the Library of Classical Archaeology; the Library of Classical Literature; the Grenfell and Hunt Papyrological Library; the Haverfield Library of Ancient History; the Library of the Department of Western Art; the Library of the Department of Eastern Art; the Library of Medieval Archaeology; and the Library of the Griffith Institute. This last, a part of the Ashmolean, contains the Griffith Egyptological Library, collections dealing with Babylonian and Assyriological studies, and other sections dealing with the archaeology of the Near East

    Stock: 100,000 books; 40,000 pamphlets; 1,000 current periodicals. Library open to members of the university and to certain non-members on recommendation. With some restrictions books may be borrowed from all libraries, except those housed in the Departments of Western and Eastern Art

OXFORD UNIVERSITY OF OXFORD *Tel.:* Oxford 44675
         BODLEIAN LIBRARY
1953   Oxford OX1 3BG

         (Including dependent Libraries—Radcliffe Science Library, Law Library, Rhodes House Library)

         University and Copyright Library

    Enquiries: To Librarian

    Scope: All subjects. Science and medicine: Radcliffe Science Library (no. 1970). Law: Law Library. American and Commonwealth History: Rhodes House Library

    Stock: In excess of 2 million volumes; in excess of 50,000 manuscripts; in excess of 6,000 incunabula; numerous reports; numerous current periodicals

OXFORD UNIVERSITY OF OXFORD *Tel.:* Oxford 54121 ext. 38
         DEPARTMENT OF EDUCATIONAL STUDIES
1954   LIBRARY
         15 Norham Gardens
         Oxford OX2 6PY

    Enquiries: To Librarian

    Scope: Education and all relevant subjects

    Stock: 20,000 books and pamphlets; 200 current periodicals. Collection of 400 historical documents. Collection of school textbooks

    Publications: Miscellaneous monographs on various aspects of education

OXFORD UNIVERSITY OF OXFORD *Tel.:* Oxford 57062
         DEPARTMENT OF PHARMACOLOGY
1955   South Parks Road
         Oxford

    Enquiries: To Librarian, by letter only

OXFORD, UNIVERSITY OF OXFORD, DEPARTMENT OF PHARMACOLOGY, *cont.*

Scope: Pharmacology (mainly periodicals)
Secondary: Physiology and biochemistry (mainly periodicals)

Stock: 2,300 bound volumes; 45 current periodicals

OXFORD

1956

UNIVERSITY OF OXFORD
ENGLISH FACULTY LIBRARY
St Cross Building
Manor Road
Oxford

Tel.: Oxford 49631

Enquiries: To Librarian

Scope: Library primarily intended to serve members of the University reading for a degree in English or teaching English in the University, and covering English language and literature of all periods

The Old and Middle English sections of the library were based on Professor A. S. Napier's collections, which were acquired in 1916. The Napier pamphlets include many scarce academic dissertations of the late 19th and early 20th centuries on early English philology and allied subjects

Gifts and bequests from other scholars have done much to enrich the library. Special mention may be made of Professor Sir Walter Raleigh's books, and of the many early editions of 17th century authors (notably Milton and Burton), which have been bought from the Walter Raleigh Memorial Fund. The library possesses some 4,000 volumes printed before 1800 (including runs of early periodicals) acquired by gift, bequest, and purchase. It also possesses a collection of the printed works, letters, and other manuscripts of E. H. W. Meyerstein (1889-1952)

Among the ancillary subjects which are represented are bibliography, palaeography, and Germanic philology. The library also maintains a separate collection of Old Icelandic, and enjoys the use of the York–Powell collection, kindly lent by Christ Church

Stock: 43,800 books and pamphlets; 100 current periodicals. Stock not available on loan

OXFORD

1957

UNIVERSITY OF OXFORD
FACULTY OF MUSIC LIBRARY
32 Holywell
Oxford OX1 3SL

Tel.: Oxford 47069

Working library for the use of undergraduates and post-graduates in the Faculty of Music

Enquiries: To Librarian

Scope: Music textbooks, scores, collected editions and some early editions of the 16th, 17th and 18th centuries. The sections most fully covered are those of Byzantine and Mediaeval Music. The Music School manuscripts and Theses are all housed in the Bodleian Library (no. 1953)
Some microfilms are available for post-graduate use. Gramophone records are solely for the use of the academic staff

Stock: 15,500 volumes of books and music; 53 current periodicals

OXFORD

1958

UNIVERSITY OF OXFORD
FACULTY OF SOCIAL STUDIES
SOCIAL STUDIES LIBRARY
45 Wellington Square
Oxford OX1 2JF

Tel.: Oxford 55935

Lending library for undergraduates reading social studies

Enquiries: To Librarian

Scope: Economics, sociology, psychology, criminology, social welfare, history, politics and philosophy

Stock: 23,000 books; 3,000 pamphlets; 50 current periodicals. Stock not available on loan. Enquiries not dealt with

OXFORD UNIVERSITY OF OXFORD *Tel.:* Oxford 43395
1959 HISTORY FACULTY LIBRARY
Merton Street
Oxford

Enquiries: To Librarian

Scope: Modern history, A.D. 400–1960 (Books for undergraduates and graduates)

Stock: 25,000 books; 500 pamphlets; 50 current periodicals

OXFORD UNIVERSITY OF OXFORD *Tel.:* Oxford 57775
1960 INSTITUTE OF AGRICULTURAL ECONOMICS
Parks Road
Oxford OX1 3RJ

Enquiries: To Librarian

Scope: Agriculture—history and economics (mainly in the field of production economics including agricultural policy and commodity marketing). Land economics. Rural sociology. Population, with particular reference to food supply. Statistical theory with particular reference to economic problems. A substantial collection of reference statistics in the above fields

Stock: 12,000 books; 13,000 pamphlets and reports; 700 current periodicals

Publications: The Farm Economist (3 times each year)
The State of British Agriculture (2 yearly intervals)
The Agricultural Register (occasionally)

OXFORD UNIVERSITY OF OXFORD *Tel.:* Oxford 57541
1961 INSTITUTE OF COMMONWEALTH STUDIES
21 St Giles
Oxford OX1 3LA

Enquiries: To Librarian or Director

Scope: Library: Current economics, social and political material on and from the developing countries of Africa, Asia and Latin America including the West Indies
Secondary: Press cuttings files from 1946 onwards by region and country, and by subject (for example, Commodities, Education, Race Relations, Aid)

Stock: 6,000 books; 10,000 pamphlets and reports; 275 current periodicals

Publications: Occasional bibliographies
Quarterly list of select accessions
Quarterly index of periodical articles

OXFORD UNIVERSITY OF OXFORD *Tel.:* Oxford 49631
1962 INSTITUTE OF ECONOMICS AND STATISTICS
St Cross Building
Manor Road
Oxford

The application of statistical methods to economic and social problems. The study of the theory of statistics and of the methods of statistical analysis

OXFORD, UNIVERSITY OF OXFORD, INSTITUTE OF ECONOMICS AND STATISTICS, *cont.*

Enquiries: To Librarian

Scope: The economics of developing countries; prices and incomes policy; labour economics; national income and expenditure; statistical theory and method. Developing areas of special interest are Latin America and Africa south of the Sahara. Good collection of material on computers, operations research, and management science

Stock: 20,000 books; 20,000 pamphlets; 1,000 current periodicals. Stock not normally available on loan. Photocopying facilities available

Publications: Bulletin of the Oxford University Institute of Economics and Statistics (quarterly)
Oxford University Institute of Economics and Statistics Monographs (irregularly)

OXFORD

1963

UNIVERSITY OF OXFORD
INSTITUTE OF PSYCHIATRY
5 Walton Street
Oxford

Tel.: Oxford 54754

Postgraduate teaching in psychiatry; Academic instruction for the Diploma in Psychological Medicine; Psychiatric research and clinical work

Enquiries: To Director or Secretary

Scope: Psychological medicine

Limited library facilities

OXFORD

1964

UNIVERSITY OF OXFORD
INSTITUTE OF SOCIAL ANTHROPOLOGY
51 Banbury Road
Oxford

Tel.: Oxford 55971

Reference library for post-graduates and senior members of the university

Enquiries: To Professor of Social Anthropology, by letter only

Scope: Social anthropology; no formal information service is available

Stock: 7,600 books; several hundred pamphlets; 58 current periodicals

OXFORD

1965

UNIVERSITY OF OXFORD
MODERN LANGUAGES FACULTY LIBRARY
Taylor Institution
Oxford

Tel.: Oxford 56303
(Spanish Section:
Oxford 52739)

Enquiries: To Librarian

Scope: Modern European Languages and their literatures (medieval and modern): French, German, Italian and Rumanian. Owing to lack of space the sections for Spanish (including Portuguese and Latin American), Slavonic and Modern Greek, are housed and administered separately in the Taylorian Annexes. In general bookstock is composed of works commonly used by undergraduates. Small collection of scarce Rumanian books

Stock: 45,000 books (15,000 in the outlying sections); 39 current periodicals. Stock not available on loan except to members of the library

See also Taylor Institution (no. 1972)

OXFORD

1966

UNIVERSITY OF OXFORD
MUSEUM OF THE HISTORY OF SCIENCE
Broad Street
Oxford OX1 3AZ

Tel.: Oxford 43997

Collection of exhibits and research in the field of the history of science, with special reference to early scientific instruments

Enquiries: To Curator

Scope: Museum collection and library relates entirely to the history of science and more particularly to the history of scientific instruments. The staff of the Museum is prepared to answer enquiries from research workers in the specialized field of the Museum provided that this does not require protracted research

Stock: 8,000 books; 2,000 pamphlets; 12 current periodicals

Publications: Brief Guide, new edition in preparation
Catalogues of sections of the Museum's collection

OXFORD

1967

UNIVERSITY OF OXFORD *Tel.:* Oxford 64811
NUFFIELD DEPARTMENT OF ORTHOPAEDIC
     SURGERY
MEDICAL LIBRARY
Nuffield Orthopaedic Centre
Headington
Oxford OX3 7LD

Enquiries: To Librarian, by letter only

Scope: Orthopaedics; physical medicine
Subject enquiries cannot be dealt with, but library stock is available on loan

Stock: 800 books; 70 current periodicals

Publications: Orthopaedics: Oxford: the journal of the Nuffield Department of Orthopaedic Surgery

OXFORD

1968

UNIVERSITY OF OXFORD *Tel.:* Oxford 59272
ORIENTAL INSTITUTE LIBRARY
Pusey Lane
Oxford OX1 2LE

Enquiries: To Superintendent

Scope: The library maintains a large collection of works dealing with the languages, history, religion and literature of the countries of Asia and Africa. Its main interests lie within the Arab world, Hebrew and Semitic studies, Turkey, Persia, India, China and Japan

Stock: 40,000 books; 500 pamphlets; 226 current periodicals

OXFORD

1969

UNIVERSITY OF OXFORD *Tel.:* Oxford 54979
PITT RIVERS MUSEUM
Parks Road
Oxford

Enquiries: To Curator

Scope: Ethnology and prehistoric archaeology of the peoples of the world arranged typologically to demonstrate the origin, development and distribution of material culture. The Museum is a teaching and research department of the University of Oxford. The Balfour Library adjoins the Museum. Specific enquiries and requests for information and photographs are dealt with, but the collections are extensively labelled and to a large extent self-explanatory

OXFORD

1970

UNIVERSITY OF OXFORD *Tel.:* Oxford 54162
RADCLIFFE SCIENCE LIBRARY
South Parks Road
Oxford

The Science section of the Bodleian Library (no. 1953)

OXFORD, UNIVERSITY OF OXFORD, RADCLIFFE SCIENCE LIBRARY, *cont.*

Enquiries: To Loans Department

Scope: Science (including medicine). Subject enquiries not dealt with

Stock: 215,000 books; 7,000 current periodicals. Selected stock available on loan to other universities and non-industrial research establishments

OXFORD

1971

UNIVERSITY OF OXFORD
SCHOOL OF GEOGRAPHY
Mansfield Road
Oxford OX1 3TB

Tel.: Oxford 46134
(library only)

Enquiries: To Librarian

Scope: Geography and allied subjects. Map collection
Special collection: Radcliffe meteorological library

Stock: 30,000 books; 10,000 pamphlets; 15,000 government publications; 150 current periodicals; 46,000 maps; 900 atlases

OXFORD

1972

UNIVERSITY OF OXFORD
TAYLOR INSTITUTION
Oxford OX1 3NA

Tel.: Oxford 55059

The Taylor Institution is the centre of modern languages teaching in the University. The Library caters for undergraduates and senior members of the University in all interested faculties

Enquiries: To Librarian

Scope: Modern European languages and literatures, with the exception of English
Secondary: The Finch collection of literary and linguistic works printed in the 16th, 17th and 18th centuries (largely early editions of the chief European writers)
The Fiedler collection of German literary, philological, and historical works, presented by Miss H. E. Fiedler in memory of her late father, Professor H. G. Fiedler
The Rudler collection of French books, containing many rare Benjamin Constant items and many autographed works of 20th century French writers
The Martin collection of Spanish and Portuguese books, including early editions of Cervantes, Calderón and Lope de Vega, as well as many works on Spanish history
The Butler Clarke collection of Spanish books, dealing principally with Spanish language, literature and history
The Dante collection formed by the late Canon Edward Moore
The Nevill Forbes collection of Slavonic books bequeathed to the Institution by the late Professor Nevill Forbes
The Morfill collection of Slavonic books, formed by the late Professor W. R. Morfill, consisting of nearly 4,000 volumes on the language, literature and history of various Slavonic countries
The W. P. Ker collection of Icelandic and Scandinavian books, consisting of some 500 volumes of literary and philological works
The Dawkins Collection of Byzantine and Modern Greek books, formed by the late Professor R. M. Dawkins, and consisting of about 2,000 printed books, several manuscripts and a large number of pamphlets
Other *special collections* are the Portuguese Collection, the Dante and Goethe Collections, the Celtic Collection, the Afrikaans Collection, the Basque Collection, the Albanian Collection, the collection of works of 18th century French dramatists, and the collection of tracts and pamphlets by, or relating to, Luther. The Library also possesses considerable numbers of 16th, 17th and 18th century editions of foreign dictionaries and grammars, and many sets of 18th century French periodicals

Stock: Total number of volumes (which includes books, pamphlets and volumes of periodicals) is just under 250,000; 600 current periodicals. Stock not available on loan

Publications: Catalogue of the Fiedler Collection

In addition to this Library (the Main Library) there is a Modern Languages Faculty Library (no. 1965) containing books chiefly for undergraduate use

OXFORD

1973

WADHAM COLLEGE   *Tel.:* Oxford 42564
Oxford

Enquiries: To Librarian, by letter only

Scope: Special collections: 16th century theology. 16th–17th century Spanish books

Stock: Books—2,000 (theology) 1,000 (Spanish)

OXFORD

1974

WESTMINSTER COLLEGE OF EDUCATION   *Tel.:* Oxford 47644
North Hinksey
Oxford

Methodist Foundation College of Education

Enquiries: To Librarian

Scope: General Library including Education to post-graduate level and school curriculum subjects to teachers' certificate and Oxford B.Ed. degree level. Methodist history and methodism generally

OXFORD

1975

WORCESTER COLLEGE   *Tel.:* Oxford 47251
Oxford

Enquiries: To Librarian, preferably by letter

Scope: Literature, history, travel, architecture
Clarke Papers (English Civil War)
Clarke Collection of architectural drawings and of English poetry and drama, 16th to 18th centuries
Secondary: Classical archaeology

Stock: 75,000 books; 100,000 pamphlets. Stock not normally available on loan

PAIGNTON
Devon

1976

MARIST FATHERS' HOUSE OF STUDIES   *Tel.:* Paignton 59510
St Mary's Hill
Paignton
Devon

Education of young men for the Roman Catholic priesthood

Enquiries: To Librarian, by letter only

Scope: Small library of general works in philosophy, theology and canon law

Stock: 10,000 books; 20 current periodicals. Stock not available on loan

PAISLEY
Renfrewshire

1977

PAISLEY COLLEGE OF TECHNOLOGY   *Tel.:* 041-889 7881
High Street
Paisley
Renfrewshire

Enquiries: To Librarian or Industrial Liaison Officer

Scope: Mathematics; natural science; mechanical, electrical, civil and chemical engineering; textile technology; social sciences; land economics with special reference to Scotland

PAISLEY, PAISLEY COLLEGE OF TECHNOLOGY, *cont.*

Stock: 25,000 books, including bound volumes of periodicals; 2,000 pamphlets; 2,000 reports; 560 current periodicals; complete set of British Standards

Publications: List of Serial Holdings

PAISLEY PAISLEY PUBLIC LIBRARIES *Tel.:* 041-889 2360
Renfrewshire Central Library
  High Street
1978 Paisley
  Renfrewshire

Enquiries: To Librarian

Scope: Special collections: local collection; education; textiles

Stock: 150,000 books; 190 current periodicals (total stock)

PAPWORTH *See under* **CAMBRIDGE** for
EVERARD PAPWORTH HOSPITAL, THE MEDICAL LIBRARY
Cambridge   (no. 290)

PARKSTONE *See under* **POOLE** for
Poole POOLE TECHNICAL COLLEGE (no. 2000)
Dorset

PENARTH THE CHURCH IN WALES INFORMATION OFFICE *Tel.:* Penarth 708234
Glam Religious Education Centre
  8 Hickman Road
1979 Penarth
  Glamorgan CF6 2YQ

Enquiries: To Director, by letter only

Scope: Church history of Church in Wales, liturgical revision, religious education, publications and Church life and affairs

Publications: Church in Wales Publications Catalogue

PENARTH MEDICAL RESEARCH COUNCIL *Tel.:* Penarth 708761
Glam PNEUMOCONIOSIS RESEARCH UNIT
  Llandough Hospital
1980 Penarth
  Glamorgan CF6 1XW

Research into respiratory diseases, particularly the pneumoconioses

Enquiries: To Librarian

Scope: Respiratory diseases, particularly the pneumoconioses. Industrial medicine. Dust hazard sampling and control. Physiology of respiration. Pathology of the lung
Secondary: Physics, particularly applied to physiological measurement, small particle physics. Mineralogy as a background to dusts. Analytical chemistry as applied to respiration. Medical, biological, mathematical, physical and engineering sciences at general and student levels

Stock: 900 books; 6,000 pamphlets; many reports; 146 current periodicals

PENARTH PENARTH PUBLIC LIBRARY
Glam Stanwell Road
  Penarth
1981 Glamorgan

Enquiries: To Librarian

Scope: Regional subject specialization: Costume
Stock: 150 books

PENARTH
Glam

1982

WELSH SECONDARY SCHOOLS ASSOCIATION
Grammar School
Penarth
Glamorgan

Tel.: Penarth 707633

Professional Association of Headmasters and Headmistresses of Secondary Schools in Wales

Enquiries: To Secretary, by letter only
Scope: Advice on educational matters and careers
Publications: The Welsh Secondary Schools Review (twice each year)

PENTRE
Rhondda
Glam

1983

RHONDDA BOROUGH COUNCIL CENTRAL
  LIBRARY
Pleasant View
Pentre
Rhondda
Glamorgan

Tel.: Pentre 2204

Enquiries: To Librarian
Scope: Music; local history collection
Stock: 165,000 books; pamphlets; 65 current periodicals (total stock)

PENZANCE
Cornwall

1984

PENZANCE NATURAL HISTORY AND
  ANTIQUARIAN MUSEUM
Penlee House
Penlee Park
Penzance
Cornwall

Tel.: Penzance 3954

Enquiries: To Librarian and Curator
Scope: Information service and library is at Penzance Public Library (no. 1985). *Special collection* of books on Cornwall
Stock: 1,800 books; 200 pamphlets; 3 current periodicals

PENZANCE
Cornwall

1985

PENZANCE PUBLIC LIBRARY
Morrab Road
Penzance
Cornwall

Tel.: Penzance 3954 and
  2345

Enquiries: To Librarian
Scope: Collection of books on Cornwall
Stock: 55,000 books; 500 pamphlets (total stock)

PERTH

1986

THE BLACK WATCH (R.H.R.) MUSEUM
Balhousie Castle
Perth

Tel.: Perth 26287 ext. 1

Enquiries: To Curator, by letter only
Scope: Regimental trophies, prints, pictures, weapons and medals covering more than 240 years of Regimental history. Well stocked library covers primarily the regiment, but also the army in general

PERTH, THE BLACK WATCH (R.H.R.) MUSEUM, *cont.*

Publications: Brochure
Regimental histories
Prints

PERTH

1987

BOARD OF MANAGEMENT FOR THE COUNTY   *Tel.:* Perth 23311
AND CITY OF PERTH GENERAL HOSPITALS
Taymount Terrace
Perth

Enquiries dealt with from General Practitioners in the Counties of Perth and Kinross

Enquiries: To Librarian, Medical Library, Perth Royal Infirmary, Perth, preferably by letter

Scope: Medical books and journals only

Stock: Books—Perth Royal Infirmary 250, Bridge of Earn Hospital 150; current periodicals—Perth Royal Infirmary 42, Bridge of Earn Hospital 34; 30 reports

PERTH

1988

PERTH AND KINROSS COUNTY LIBRARY   *Tel.:* Perth 22318
7 Rose Terrace
Perth

Enquiries: To Librarian

Scope: Able to provide general information on most of the Social Sciences and Humanities, particularly with reference to Scotland and to Perthshire and Kinross-shire. Perthshire collection of local material includes Kinross-shire

Stock: Social Sciences 5,000 books; Humanities 5,000 books; Perthshire and Kinross-shire 3,500 books

PETERBOROUGH

1989

PETERBOROUGH CITY LIBRARIES   *Tel.:* Peterborough 69105
Central Library
Broadway
Peterborough

Enquiries: To Librarian

Scope: Local History Collection: Peterborough and district; Fenland
National subject specialization: German language

Stock: 112,283 books and pamphlets; 134 current periodicals (total stock)

PETERBOROUGH

1990

PETERBOROUGH TECHNICAL COLLEGE   *Tel.:* Peterborough 67366
Park Crescent
Peterborough

Enquiries: To Tutor Librarian

Scope: Electrical engineering, mechanical engineering, building construction, chemistry, physics, mathematics, biology, economics, geography, geology, education, government, economic history, art and architecture, domestic science, management

Stock: 17,000 books; 1,000 pamphlets; 275 current periodicals; complete set of British Standards

PINNER
Middx

1991

PRIVATE LIBRARIES ASSOCIATION
41 Cuckoo Hill Road
Pinner
Middlesex

Enquiries: To Secretary, by letter only

Scope: Enquiries relating to book collecting are referred to known specialists within the Society, or published in the News Letter (issued quarterly with the Exchange List)

No library

Publications: Private Press Books (an annual checklist of books printed by private presses)

John Buckland Wright, a personal memoir and a checklist of his illustrated books. A. Reid. 1968

Exchange List and News Letter (quarterly)

The Private Library (quarterly journal)

PIRBRIGHT *See under* **WOKING** for
Woking ANIMAL VIRUS RESEARCH INSTITUTE (no. 2301)
Surrey

PLYMOUTH COLLEGE OF S. MARK & S. JOHN *Tel.:* Plymouth 51591
Devon Albert Road
 Devonport
1992 Plymouth
 Devon
 College of Education

Enquiries: To Librarian

Scope: Education, including sociology and psychology of, teaching practice and special education. Mathematics, geography, English, art and craft. A collection of material of local interest is maintained including runs of the Transactions of The Devonshire Association and Devon & Cornwall Notes & Queries

Stock: 5,000 books; small collection of pamphlets mainly confined to education; 52 current periodicals. Stock available on loan and for reference to teachers, teachers in training and education research workers in the Plymouth area

An information index is maintained related specifically to the subjects covered by the library and containing references to periodical articles. Press cuttings and illustrations collections are also being built up

See also no. 1077

PLYMOUTH PLYMOUTH CITY ART GALLERY *Tel.:* Plymouth 68000 ext.
Devon Tavistock Road 3112
 Plymouth
1993 Devon

Enquiries: To Director

Scope: The Cottonian Collection of fine arts, manuscripts and early printed books is primarily devoted to the fine arts, drama and literature

Stock: 3,000 early printed books and 200 manuscripts

Publications: Catalogue of the Cottonian Paintings and Drawings

Card index catalogue (unpublished) of all the books and other material in the collection

PLYMOUTH PLYMOUTH COLLEGE OF TECHNOLOGY *Tel.:* Plymouth 68000 ext.
Devon Tavistock Road 3043
 Plymouth
1994 Devon

Enquiries: To Librarian, by letter only

PLYMOUTH, PLYMOUTH COLLEGE OF TECHNOLOGY, *cont.*

Scope: Engineering (civil, electrical, mechanical, marine and production). Construction. Nautical studies. Commerce (including social work, child care, health visitors, management and law). Science including physics, mathematics, chemistry, botany, biology and zoology

Stock: 26,000 books; 1,500 pamphlets; 560 current periodicals. Complete set of British Standards. The Geodex index

PLYMOUTH
Devon

1995

PLYMOUTH GENERAL HOSPITAL MEDICAL LIBRARY
North Friary House
Plymouth
Devon

Tel.: Plymouth 68080

Incorporates the Hospital Management Committee Library and the library of the Plymouth Medical Society founded in 1794

Enquiries: To Librarian

Scope: The library aims to provide a comprehensive coverage of information for all specialities of medicine, both in books and periodicals

Stock: 500 books; 64 current periodicals. Stock not available on loan

PLYMOUTH
Devon

1996

PLYMOUTH PUBLIC LIBRARIES
Central Public Library
Tavistock Road
Plymouth
Devon

Tel.: Plymouth 68000 ext. 3016
Telex: 45578

Enquiries: To Librarian

Scope: Mount Wise Naval History Library
Local History Library
Music and Drama Library
Archives Department

Stock: Special collections above contain 200,000 items (books, pamphlets, illustrations, orchestral and drama parts); 400 current periodicals (total stock)

Publications: Readers guides only, from time to time, for example Law, Accounting, Electronics
Plymouth City Charters
Guide to the Archives Department

PONTEFRACT
Yorkshire

1997

PONTEFRACT PUBLIC LIBRARY
Salter Row
Pontefract
Yorkshire

Tel.: Pontefract 3948

Enquiries: To Librarian

Scope: National subject specialization; Parliaments and legislatures; cuttings book of the First Secret Ballot election of 1872 (held in Pontefract). Various cuttings on history of liquorice growing generally and Pontefract confectionery industry

Stock: 47,000 books and pamphlets; 35 current periodicals (total stock)

PONTYPRIDD
Glam

1998

PONTYPRIDD PUBLIC LIBRARIES
Central Library
Library Road
Pontypridd
Glamorgan

Tel.: Pontypridd 2155

Enquiries: To Librarian

Scope: Regional subject specialization: Spiritualism. Christianity—personal experience; devotions, parochial work and preaching. General literature

Stock: 65,000 books and pamphlets; 140 current periodicals (total stock)

POOLE
Dorset

1999

POOLE PUBLIC LIBRARIES AND MUSEUMS
Poole Central Library
Arndale Centre
Poole
Dorset

Enquiries: To Librarian, by letter only

Scope: Commitments under subject specializations schemes: Christian sociology; Postal Service; Pottery; General literature; Humour; Asia: History, geography and description
Local collection. Teachers' library

Stock: 2,000 books and pamphlets; 12 current periodicals (on specialist topics)

POOLE
Dorset

2000

POOLE TECHNICAL COLLEGE
North Road
Parkstone
Poole
Dorset

Tel.: Parkstone 4202

Enquiries: To Librarian

Scope: Building; business studies; engineering; science; domestic science; art; social sciences; and general subjects

Stock: 10,000 books and pamphlets; 160 current periodicals

Publications: Booklists

PORT TALBOT
Glam

2001

BOROUGH OF PORT TALBOT PUBLIC
    LIBRARIES
Central Library
Commercial Road
Port Talbot
Glamorgan

Tel.: Port Talbot 3831

Enquiries: To Borough Librarian

Scope: Strong local collection, covering Port Talbot and Glamorgan

Stock: 1,000 books and 100 pamphlets (local collection); 120 current periodicals

Publications: Port Talbot: a bibliographical guide. C. Biscoe. 1968

PORTSMOUTH
Hants

2002

CITY OF PORTSMOUTH COLLEGE OF
    EDUCATION
Locksway Road
Portsmouth PO4 8JF
Hampshire

Tel.: Portsmouth 35241

Enquiries: To Librarian

Scope: All aspects of the English educational system and the training of teachers; educational theory and practice. Academic subjects at an undergraduate level: Theology, literature, history, sciences, fine arts, geography and sociology. Children's books collection of 10,000 volumes
Secondary: Local collection on Portsmouth, Hampshire and Isle of Wight (400 items)

Stock: 48,000 books; 2,000 pamphlets; 330 current periodicals

Publications: Guide to the Library

| PORTSMOUTH | HIGHBURY TECHNICAL COLLEGE | *Tel.:* Cosham 70351 |

PORTSMOUTH HIGHBURY TECHNICAL COLLEGE   *Tel.:* Cosham 70351
Hants   Cosham
               Portsmouth PO6 2SA
2003   Hampshire

Enquiries: To Librarian

Scope: Biology, botany, building, business studies, catering, chemistry, domestic science, electrical engineering, hotel keeping, mathematics, mechanical engineering, physics and zoology
Secondary: Audio-visual education, civil engineering, education, hairdressing, management, motor vehicle engineering, naval architecture, public health, social studies, surveying, timber technology, work study, yacht and boat building, geography, geology and history

Stock: 16,000 books and pamphlets; 300 current periodicals

PORTSMOUTH PORTSMOUTH CITY LIBRARIES   *Tel.:* Portsmouth 21441
Hants   Central Library
                Guildhall Square
2004   Portsmouth PO1 2DX
                Hampshire

Enquiries: To Librarian

Scope: Calendar of State Papers (printed volumes). Local history manuscript material
Secondary: Books and pamphlets covering humanities and social sciences, with special collections of local history material on Portsmouth and Hampshire. Naval history. Small genealogical collection

Stock: 80,000 books; 2,000 pamphlets; 200 current periodicals (total stock)

PORTSMOUTH PORTSMOUTH COLLEGE OF ART AND DESIGN   *Tel.:* Portsmouth 26435
Hants   Hyde Park Road
                Portsmouth
2005   Hampshire

Enquiries: To Librarian

Scope: European art; painting and sculpture

Stock: 10,000 books; 119 current periodicals

PORTSMOUTH THE PORTSMOUTH MEDICAL SOCIETY   *Tel.:* Portsmouth 22331
Hants   Postgraduate Medical Centre   ext. 346
                Saint Mary's General Hospital
2006   Milton
                Portsmouth
                Hampshire

To promote and provide postgraduate education for all hospital staff, general practitioners, dentists and veterinary surgeons in the area

Enquiries: To Librarian

Scope: The library is purely a medical library and covers all fields of medicine, surgery and dental surgery. It owns a number of valuable historical medical books

Stock: 900 books; 10 pamphlets; 90 current periodicals. Stock available on loan only within the Wessex Region

Small libraries at Royal Portsmouth Hospital, Queen Alexandra Hospital and Saint James' Hospital (Psychiatric)

PORTSMOUTH Hants **2007**	THE VICTORY MUSEUM H.M. Dockyard Portsmouth Hampshire	*Tel.:* Portsmouth 22351 ext. 23090

Enquiries: To Curator, by letter only

Scope: Naval history of the Napoleonic wars particularly as it affected Lord Nelson, his officers and men, and H.M.S. *Victory*

Stock: 250 books. Small reference library only

Publications: Museum Catalogue
Pamphlets on display of models on Trafalgar and on Figureheads in Museum

POTTERS BAR Herts **2008**	BARNET & DISTRICT LOCAL HISTORY SOCIETY 6 Mount Grace Road Potters Bar Hertfordshire	*Tel.:* Potters Bar 54150

Enquiries: To Secretary

Scope: Library consists in the main of books relating to history, archaeology, and like subjects, together with matters of local interest particularly historical and archaeological

Stock: 1,500 books; photographs; slides (belonging to the Museum, Wood Street, Barnet, Hertfordshire)

Publications: Bulletin

POTTERS BAR Herts **2009**	THE SOCIETY OF ORNAMENTAL TURNERS c/o 28 Hill Rise Cuffley Potters Bar Hertfordshire

Promotion and maintenance of knowledge concerning ornamental turning

Enquiries: To Secretary, by letter only

Scope: Specialist library, dealing with ornamental turning, with lathes, equipment and materials used, together with other relevant subjects. Stock not available on loan except to members resident in the United Kingdom

POTTERS BAR Herts **2010**	UFAW (UNIVERSITIES FEDERATION FOR ANIMAL WELFARE) 230 High Street Potters Bar Hertfordshire	*Tel.:* Potters Bar 9221

Enquiries: To Information Officer

Scope: Welfare of animals with particular reference to education in the care and management of animals in the wild, on farms, in laboratories, and those kept in schools

No library

Publications: The UFAW Handbook on the Care and Management of Laboratory Animals. 3rd edition (published by E. & S. Livingstone Ltd.)
Humane Killing of Animals
Information Leaflets on the care of various animals (sets of 5)
Sealing in U.K. and Canadian Waters
The Humane Control of Animals Living in the Wild

POTTERS BAR, UFAW (UNIVERSITIES FEDERATION FOR ANIMAL WELFARE), *cont.*
The Use of Animals in Toxicological Studies
The Otter Report (The Natural History of the Otter)
(Full publications list on request)

POULTON
Blackpool
Lancs

See under **BLACKPOOL** for
ASSOCIATION OF BRITISH DENTAL SURGERY
ASSISTANTS LTD (no. 166)

PRESCOT
Lancs

2011

C. F. MOTT COLLEGE OF EDUCATION *Tel.:* Huyton 6201
(Liverpool Education Committee)
Liverpool Road
Prescot
Lancashire

Enquiries: To Tutor Librarian, by letter only

Scope: Education is the subject field which is given priority in the library bookstock. All aspects are represented: Philosophy, history, comparative, primary, secondary, higher education, teaching method and psychology (including child psychology). In addition the more important educational journals are taken
Secondary: Books are also provided on the following subjects: Medicine (primarily for the use of physical education students), economics (mainly with respect to history and geography), theology, history, geography, fine arts, American literature, English literature, German language and literature, French language and literature

Stock: Books: education 2,000; psychology 1,000; sociology 400; economics 300; divinity 1,200; history 1,500; geography 800; fine arts 1,500; English literature 2,500; German 600; French 800; medicine 150; American literature 300; 170 current periodicals. Stock available on loan only to other colleges belonging to the Area Training Organization

PRESCOT
Lancs

2012

PRESCOT COLLEGE OF FURTHER EDUCATION *Tel.:* Prescot 4161
Warrington Road
Prescot
Lancashire

Enquiries: To Librarian

Scope: General background and specific books covering social sciences, economics, geography, history, literature and law to ONC and 'O' level

Stock: 4,500 books; 200 pamphlets; 40 current periodicals

PRESTON

2013

BRITISH ORIENTEERING FEDERATION
2 Stanley Villas
Hoghton
Preston

See no. 505

PRESTON

2014

THE HARRIS COLLEGE *Tel.:* Preston 51831 ext. 15
Corporation Street
Preston PR1 2TQ
College of Technology

Enquiries: To Librarian

Scope: The Library includes books and periodicals in the fields of sociology, social studies, politics, government economics (all to degree level), law, education and particularly special education,

(teaching of mentally handicapped) child care services, fine arts and design, linguistics.
Special collection: Work of book illustrators (mainly 19th century)
Secondary: Geography, history, philology

Stock: 8,000 books; 85 current periodicals

Publications: Books Lists
Periodical Holdings

PRESTON

2015

HARRIS PUBLIC LIBRARY
Market Square
Preston PR1 2PP

Tel.: Preston 53191
Telex: 67561

Enquiries: To Librarian

Scope: General stock including music
N.W.R.L.S. subject specialization includes: Pharmacy and therapeutics; types of painting. Private press books; Francis Thompson collection of books and manuscripts; Spencer collection of early children's books and manuscripts. The personal library of Richard Shepherd, MD (1694–1761) twice Mayor of Preston, bequeathed by him to the Corporation of Preston: a general collection, which includes many medical books of historical interest. A condition of the bequest is 'that no book or books be lent or removed out of the library'. The Borough Librarian is Librarian of Dr Shepherd's Library which is housed in the Reference Department, Harris Public Library and is available for suitably introduced readers for reference only. 10,000 volumes. Printed catalogue 1870. The collection is arranged in a press-mark system

Stock: 240,000 books; 450 current periodicals (total stock)

Publications: A Catalogue of the Spencer Collection of early children's books and chapbooks. 1967
Preston Commercial and Technical Service; list of periodicals held by members. 5th edition. 1969
Francis Thompson Centenary 1859–1959; catalogue of manuscripts, letters and books in the Harris Public Library, Preston. 1969
Harris Public Library, The Children's Library Magazine (published three times each year)

PRESTON

2016

LANCASHIRE COUNTY LIBRARY
County Hall
Preston PR1 8RH

Tel.: Preston 54868 ext. 385

Enquiries: To County Librarian

Scope: General library service with Headquarters Lending and Reference Library, Technical Information Centre, Music and Drama and Children's Departments

Stock: 2,500,000 books and pamphlets; 250 current periodicals

PRESTON

2017

LANCASHIRE RECORD OFFICE
Lancaster Road
Preston

Tel.: Preston 51905

Enquiries: To County Archivist

Scope: Parish registers and probate records; account books; mental hospital records

Publications: Guide to the Lancashire Records Office. 1962

PRESTON

2018

THE RIBCHESTER MUSEUM OF ROMAN ANTIQUITIES
Riverside
Ribchester
Preston

Tel.: Ribchester 261

Enquiries: To Curator

PRESTON, THE RIBCHESTER MUSEUM OF ROMAN ANTIQUITIES, *cont.*

Scope: Details of excavations and finds from Roman Ribchester. Details of present excavations being carried out by the Ribble Archaeological Society

Stock: Books and pamphlets on Roman Britain and Ribchester for reference only

PRESTWICH
Manchester

See under **MANCHESTER** for
SEDGLEY PARK COLLEGE OF EDUCATION (no. 1782)

RADCLIFFE
Manchester

See under **MANCHESTER** for
RADCLIFFE PUBLIC LIBRARY (no. 1779)
RADCLIFFE TECHNICAL COLLEGE (no. 1780)

READING
Berks

2019

THE ANGLO-MONGOLIAN SOCIETY
37 Kidmore End Road
Emmer Green
Reading RG4 8SN
Berkshire

Promotes on a non-political basis a closer understanding in the United Kingdom and Mongolia of the respective ways of life and cultural achievements of the other country and encourages contacts of all kinds between the peoples of the two countries

Enquiries: To Secretary, by letter only

Scope: No information service as such, but willing to help with all enquiries concerning Mongolia

Stock: The Society has no library, but many of its members have personal collections, and some of these include books of great rarity. The books cover all fields of Mongolian studies; many are not in English. Willingness to lend books would depend on the individuals concerned, who may be contacted through the Secretary. Part of the Viscount Furness's collection is now in the library of the Royal Central Asian Society (no. 1523)

Publications: Bulletin (irregularly)

READING
Berks

2020

BERKSHIRE COLLEGE OF EDUCATION *Tel.:* 0734-63387
Woodlands Avenue
Earley
Reading RG6 1HY
Berkshire

Enquiries: To Librarian

Scope: Education, educational psychology, sociology, children's literature
Secondary: Child psychology; physical education; religious education; history, geography, art, English literature, languages (French and German), music, mathematics, rural studies and biology
Special Collections: First World War; Film and television in education; Historical Manuscripts Commission material; urban and regional planning

Stock: 46,000 books and pamphlets; 342 current periodicals

Publications: Bulmershe Lecture (annually)
Library Occasional Papers

READING
Berks

2021

BERKSHIRE COUNTY LIBRARY *Tel.:* Reading 55981
Abbey Mill House
Abbey Square
Reading
Berkshire

Enquiries: To Librarian

Scope: L.A.S.E.R. subject specialization: Occult sciences; theology; welfare and charitable associations; history and criticism of general English and American literature; Anglo Saxon literature HQ Reference Library offers library service on local government topics including law, public administration, social services and education

Stock: 142,143 books; 1,800 pamphlets; 150 current periodicals (total non-fiction stock other than science and technology)
Parliamentary Papers from 1962
H.M.S.O. Selected Subscription Service, November 1969 onwards

READING   THE BRITISH AGRICULTURAL HISTORY SOCIETY   *Tel.:* Reading 85123 ext. 475
Berks   Museum of English Rural Life
                The University
2022   Reading RG6 2AG
                Berkshire

Enquiries: To Secretary, by letter only

Scope: History of agriculture and rural economy
No library

Publications: Agricultural History Review (twice each year)

READING   LOCAL GOVERNMENT OPERATIONAL RESEARCH   *Tel.:* 0734-580462
Berks   UNIT
                201 Kings Road
2023   Reading
                Berkshire

Enquiries: To Librarian

Scope: Mathematics, mathematical statistics, operational research, decision theory, cybernetics, computer theory, education, sociology, economics, local government statistics, roads, housing, refuse disposal, computer manuals

Stock: 770 books; 47 current periodicals

READING   READING COLLEGE OF TECHNOLOGY   *Tel.:* Reading 54451
Berks   Kings Road
                Reading RG1 4HJ
2024   Berkshire

Enquiries: To Librarian

Scope: Biology, building, catering, chemistry, cinema, economic history, economics, electronics, civil, electrical, mechanical and production engineering, graphic design, home economics, management, metal working, photography, physics and printing

Stock: 18,000 books; 200 current periodicals; British Standards

Member of Berkshire Libraries Group

READING   READING PATHOLOGICAL SOCIETY   *Tel.:* Reading 85111
Berks   Royal Berkshire Hospital
                Reading
2025   Berkshire

Maintains library service to all departments of the hospital, including postgraduate education, and to general practitioners for the surrounding area and gives library assistance to nearby institutions in medical subjects

READING, READING PATHOLOGICAL SOCIETY, *cont.*
Enquiries: To Hon. Librarian
Scope: Medicine and surgery
Secondary: Historical medical section includes a series of 18th century anatomical atlases
Stock: 5,000 books; 68 current periodicals
Long runs of medical and surgical journals with complete sets of Lancet, British Medical Journal and Quarterly Journal of Medicine
Publications: Quarterly book lists (acquisitions)

READING   SOUTHERN REGIONAL COUNCIL FOR FURTHER EDUCATION   *Tel.:* Reading 52120
Berks
9 Bath Road
2026   Reading
Berkshire
Enquiries: To Secretary
Scope: Location of technical courses in the region and in the British Isles
No library
Publications: Lists of courses provided in the Region
Books on teaching method in Technical Courses

READING   UNIVERSITY OF READING LIBRARY   *Tel.:* Reading 84331
Berks   Whiteknights
Reading RG6 2AG
2027   Berkshire
Enquiries: To Librarian
Scope: All aspects of the social sciences and the humanities studied in the University. There are separate Education, Music and Social Sciences Libraries
Special collections: Cole Library (including works on early medicine); Henley Parish Library (history, philosophy and literature); Overstone Library (economics, literature, history and topography); Turner Collection (French Revolution)
Stock: 325,000 books; 40,000 pamphlets; 3,500 current periodicals
Publications: Catalogue of the Cole Library. 1969

READING   UNIVERSITY OF READING MUSEUM OF ENGLISH RURAL LIFE   *Tel.:* Reading 85123 ext. 475
Berks   Whiteknights
Reading RG6 2AG
2028   Berkshire
National collection of material relating to the history of the English countryside, including agriculture, crafts, domestic utensils and village life
Enquiries: To Keeper, by letter only
Scope: Rural material culture (mainly English)
Agricultural history (mainly British)
Stock: 2,400 books; 600 pamphlets; 1,000 reports; 36 current periodicals; Photographic collection (prints and negatives) 120,000; Manuscripts and other documents, 500 items or groups; Classified information (tear sheets and cuttings) about 1,500 items
Publications: Commuters Village. R. Chrichton. 1964 (Publ. David & Charles)
West Country Friendly Societies. 1964 (Publ. The Oakwood Press for University of Reading)

Estate Villages: a study of the Berkshire Villages of Ardington and Lockinge. M. A. Havinden, 1966 (Publ. Lund Humphries)
The English Farm Wagon. J. G. Jenkins. 1961 (Publ. The Oakwood Press for University of Reading)
The English Plough. J. B. Passmore. 1930 (Publ. O.U.P.)
John Soulby, printer, Ulverston. M. Twyman. 1966
Fussell, G. E.: a bibliography of his writings on agricultural history. 1967
Catalogue of temporary exhibition of prints and paintings of British farm livestock, Portraits of Animals. 1964
Accession of Historical Farm Records up to Dec. 1967. 1967 (Publ. University of Reading)
Sickle to Combine. E. J. T. Collins. 1969

The resources of the Museum are closely linked with the specialized holdings of the University Library (no. 2027) on agriculture and, particularly, the collections of early farm records

READING UNIVERSITY OF READING *Tel.:* 0734-85123 ext. 269
Berks MUSEUM OF GREEK ARCHAEOLOGY
  Faculty of Letters
2029 The University
  Whiteknights
  Reading RG6 2AG
  Berkshire

  Teaching collection of Greek antiquities, mainly pottery, numbering about 700 pieces, plus a small Egyptian collection

Enquiries: To Curator, by letter or personal visit only

Scope: Prepared to try and deal with questions relating to Greek pottery generally. The museum is particularly well equipped with vases from Boeotia and South Italy
Secondary: Small Egyptian collection numbering nearly 200 objects about which some information can be supplied. No Egyptologist on staff

No library

Publications: Corpus Vasorum Antiquorum, Great Britain Fasc. 12 Reading Fasc. 1. (Published by Oxford University Press for the British Academy and the University of Reading)

REDDITCH REDDITCH COLLEGE OF FURTHER EDUCATION *Tel.:* Redditch 3607
Worcs Archer Road
  Redditch
2030 Worcestershire

Enquiries: To Tutor Librarian

Scope: Economics, management, engineering, law
Secondary: Education, mathematics, literature, sociology

Stock: 9,500 books; 1,000 pamphlets; 250 current periodicals

REDDITCH REDDITCH DEVELOPMENT CORPORATION *Tel.:* Redditch 64200
Worcs Holmwood
  Plymouth Road
2031 Redditch
  Worcestershire

Enquiries: To Librarian

Scope: New Towns, expanding towns, planning

Stock: 1,000 books; 10,000 pamphlets; 2,000 reports; 55 current periodicals

REDDITCH, REDDITCH DEVELOPMENT CORPORATION, *cont.*

Publications: Technical Library News (monthly classified by CI/SfB)
Master Plan. H. Wilson and L. Womersley
Various pamphlets on master plan, town centre and industrial estates

REDDITCH REDDITCH PUBLIC LIBRARY *Tel.:* Redditch 4252
Worcs Church Road
  Redditch
2032 Worcestershire

Enquiries: To Librarian

Scope: *Special collection* on needle-making, particularly its history. Includes many thousands of manuscripts relating to a needlemaking firm, 1750–1900. The collection is valuable as business archives, containing much correspondence with the United States of America, 1830–1880

REDRUTH CAMBORNE-REDRUTH PUBLIC LIBRARIES *Tel.:* Redruth 5243
Cornwall Public Library
  Clinton Road
2033 Redruth
  Cornwall

Enquiries: To Librarian

Scope: *Special collections* of local history material, including Hambly and Rowe and Hamilton Jenkin Collections

Stock: 55,000 books (total stock); 80 current periodicals (including Camborne holdings)
Local history collections: 5,000 books and 1,000 pamphlets
See also no. 272

REDRUTH CORNWALL TECHNICAL COLLEGE *Tel.:* Camborne 2911
Cornwall Pool
  Redruth
2034 Cornwall

Enquiries: To Librarian

Scope: Building, engineering, science, agriculture and horticulture, commerce and management, history, geography, hotel and catering, education, language teaching
Special Collections: Children's books for 3–10 year olds
County Language Laboratory Association Collection

Stock: 18,000 books; 2,500 pamphlets; 320 current periodicals

Publications: List of Additions (Subject classified)
Readers Guide to the Library

Largest collection of scientific literature in Cornwall; special service to schools
Headquarters of Cornwall Technical Information Service (no. 2364)

RETFORD EATON HALL COLLEGE OF EDUCATION *Tel.:* Retford 2544 ext. 11
Notts Retford
  Nottinghamshire
2035

Enquiries: To Tutor Librarian, by letter only

Scope: Education, educational psychology, child psychology, sociology, teaching methods
Secondary: Divinity, art and craft, music, English literature, linguistics, history, children's literature, school librarianship, geography, biology, rural studies

Stock: 35,000 books; 3,000 pamphlets; 200 current periodicals
Publications: Eaton Hall College of Education Monographs Series:
No. 1. The Enclosure of Norwell. W. Smith. 1968
No. 2. Looking at Old Retford. B. J. Biggs. 1968

RHONDDA
Glam

See under **PENTRE** for
RHONDDA BOROUGH COUNCIL CENTRAL LIBRARY (no. 1983)

RHOOSE
Barry
Glam

See under **BARRY** for
COLEG Y FRO (no. 61)

RHYL
Flintshire

2036

RHYL POST-GRADUATE MEDICAL CENTRE
Royal Alexandra Hospital
Rhyl
Flintshire

Tel.: Rhyl 4631

Enquiries: To Secretary
Scope: Medical Reference Library for the use of Hospital Staff and General Practitioners
Stock: 440 books; 50 current periodicals. Stock not available on loan

RIBCHESTER
Preston

See under **PRESTON** for
THE RIBCHESTER MUSEUM OF ROMAN
 ANTIQUITIES (no. 2018)

RICHMOND
Surrey

2037

CRUSE
The Charter House
Richmond
Surrey

Tel.: 01-940 2660

Organization for widows and their children

Enquiries: To Hon. Director
Scope: Includes a professional advisory service for widows
Publications: Cruse Chronicle (monthly)
Pamphlets and handbooks for both widows and counsellors and social workers
Caring for the Widow and her Family. 2nd edition
The Widow's Child. M. Torrie

RICHMOND
Surrey

2038

THE FOREIGN AFFAIRS CIRCLE
Church House
Petersham
Richmond
Surrey

Tel.: 01-940 2885

The relationship between Western foreign policy and the work of opposition movements in Communist countries

Enquiries: To Secretary
Scope: Library consists of books on Communism, foreign policy, international affairs, defence, East–West relations, trade, political and psychological warfare, defector reports, Marxist ideology, history of Soviet Union, China and Eastern European states, forced labour, refugee experience, guerilla warfare, espionage subversion, counter-intelligence and politics
Stock: 5,000 books; 400 pamphlets; 20 current periodicals

RICHMOND, THE FOREIGN AFFAIRS CIRCLE, *cont.*

Publications: East West Digest (monthly)
The following books are published by the Foreign Affairs Publishing Co.:
  The Defeat of Communism. D. G. Stewart-Smith
  No Vision Here: Non-Military Warfare in Britain. D. G. Stewart-Smith
  The Assault on the West. I. Greig
  Anno Humanitatis: The Soviet Invasion of Czechoslovakia and The Soviet Threat to Europe. Lord St Oswald

RICHMOND
Surrey

2039

LONDON BOROUGH OF RICHMOND UPON THAMES
CENTRAL REFERENCE LIBRARY
Richmond District Library
Little Green
Richmond
Surrey

Tel.: 01-940 0981

Enquiries: To Librarian

Scope: General stock. L.A.S.E.R. subject specialization includes: Dentistry; Labour economics, industrial relations, wages, industrial hygiene; cinema; public and industrial safety; George Vancouver, Alexander Pope and Sir Richard Burton Collections form part of Local Collection

Stock: 38,500 books (Reference Library only); 4,000 pamphlets; 120 current periodicals

Material from the L.A.S.E.R. subject specialization stock may be borrowed by application to the Inter-Library Loans Department, Parkshot Rooms, Richmond, Surrey. (*Tel.:* 01-940 3691)

RICHMOND
Surrey

2040

RIVER THAMES SOCIETY
2 Ruskin Avenue
Kew
Richmond
Surrey

Tel.: 01-876 1520

Aims to promote and preserve all aspects of the River Thames and its tributaries

Enquiries: To Information Officer, by letter only

Scope: Books on all aspects of River Thames; geography of area and region; planning and sociological subjects; river craft; waterways; pollution; natural history; conservation; tourism and holidays in Thames Valley
Secondary: Information Service on all kindred subjects associated with the Thames and tributaries, including boating, cruising, tourism

Stock: 160 books; 230 pamphlets; 12 current periodicals

Publications: Codes of Practice
News Bulletin (bi-monthly)

RICHMOND
Yorkshire

2041

THE GREEN HOWARDS MUSEUM
Gallowgate
Richmond
Yorkshire

Tel.: Richmond 2133

Enquiries: To Curator

Scope: The Museum is laid out to illustrate the history of the Regiment from 1688 to the present day, and includes relics, uniforms, medals, equipment, headdress and documents
Secondary: Illustrates the development of uniform worn by all units of The Green Howards

RIPON Yorkshire 2042	RIPON CATHEDRAL LIBRARY The Cathedral Ripon Yorkshire	*Tel.:* Ripon 2072 (Librarian: Ripon 2658)

The custodianship of manuscripts, incunabula, liturgical and theological and philosophical works of the 15th and 16th–18th centuries, sundry other publications of the subsequent centuries, mainly used by some clergy and a number of research students

Enquiries: To Canon Librarian

Scope: Manuscript fragments covering the mediaeval period, autograph letters, signatures. A limited field of reference to mediaeval music. Two volumes originally held by Fountains Abbey during its last 40–50 years of existence. Scriptural Commentary, 16th to the 20th century. Theological, liturgical, ecclesiastical-historical, philosophic authors. Works on such productions as the Lindisfarne Gospels, archaeology, Parish Registers, Cartularies, local history and topography, Surtees Society Publications, biographies, some hundreds of foreign octavos of the 16th century onward, many scores of foreign folios of the same period. Homiletics—some printed fragments: a limited number of pamphlets on ecclesiastical and ecclesiological subjects

Stock: 1,700 books of Dean Anthony Higgin's bequest (d. 1624)
Certain new volumes are added from time to time. Total now under 3,000; 100 pamphlets

Publications: Ripon Minster. E. L. Smith
Ripon Cathedral Organ. C. H. Moody
Guide to Ripon. J. R. Walbran
Guide to Ripon and Fountains Abbey. J. R. Walbran
Ripon Grammar School. Harrison
Wilfrid of Ripon. A. M. Wilkinson
The Fountains Story. A. M. Wilkinson
An Unrecorded Caxton at Ripon Cathedral. J. E. Mortimer
Guide to Ripon. A. M. Wilkinson
Ripon Cathedral Guide (Pitkin Publication). W. E. Wilkinson

RIPON Yorkshire 2043	RIPON COLLEGE OF EDUCATION Ripon Yorkshire	*Tel.:* Ripon 2691

Enquiries: To Librarian, by letter only

Scope: Education; art and craft (including costume and needlework); English literature; geography; history; mathematics; music; physical education; religion; science (mostly biology); agriculture; psychology; health. Collection of children's books for teaching practice purposes

Stock: Books and pamphlets: 22,000 in Main Library, 14,300 in School Practice Library; 200 current periodicals. Stock normally available on loan only to other Colleges of Education

ROCHDALE Lancs 2044	ROCHDALE PUBLIC LIBRARIES & ARTS SERVICES Central Library Rochdale Lancashire	*Tel.:* Rochdale 49116

Enquiries: To Director

Scope: Subject specialization includes: Dietetics and hygiene of body, habitation and employment. Art Galleries and Museums; types and techniques of engraving
Special collection: Books on co-operation

Stock: 82,000 books (total non-fiction stock); 300 current periodicals

ROCHESTER	EASTGATE HOUSE MUSEUM	*Tel.:* Medway 44176
Kent	High Street	
	Rochester	
2045	Kent	
	Rochester municipal museum	

Enquiries: To Curator

Scope: Includes the Fitzgerald Collection by and on Charles Dickens

Stock: 400 volumes

ROCHESTER	MEDWAY COLLEGE OF ART	*Tel.:* Rochester 44855
Kent	Eastgate	
	Rochester	
2046	Kent	
	(*After September 1970*): Fort Pitt, New Road, Rochester, Kent)	

Enquiries: To Librarian

Scope: General information service providing books, illustrations and magazines to cover subject enquiries from the different departments, which include pottery, dress, technical illustration, liberal studies. Close co-operation with Kent County Library and Medway and Maidstone College

Special items: Small collection of Vasan Reproductions; small collection of privately printed books on wooden dolls, essays, printing, poetry from the 1940s onwards printed by the Medway School of Art and Crafts, Rochester. Original bibliographies (unpublished) on Kent, costume and other indexes and details, compiled by the Librarian

Stock: 8,000 books; 120 current periodicals; 2,000 illustrations

ROCHESTER	ROCHESTER PUBLIC LIBRARIES	*Tel.:* Medway 43837 and
Kent	Central Library	42415
	Northgate	
2047	Rochester	
	Kent	

Enquiries: To Librarian

Scope: L.A.S.E.R. subject specialization includes: Veterinary science (to 1965)
Local collection on all aspects of Rochester and the Medway towns (Chatham, Gillingham)
Charles Dickens: biography and criticism (supplementing the Fitzgerald Collection at the Eastgate House Museum) (no. 2045)

Stock: 300 books and pamphlets; 10 current periodicals. Local collection 2,000 volumes

ROMFORD	BARKING REGIONAL COLLEGE OF TECHNOLOGY
Essex	BUSINESS MANAGEMENT STUDIES DEPARTMENT
	Asta House
2048	156/164 High Road
	Chadwell Heath
	Romford
	Essex

See no. 435

ROMFORD
Essex

2049

THE INTERNATIONAL AMATEUR RADIO UNION REGION I DIVISION
51 Pettits Lane
Romford
Essex

Tel.: Romford 46749

The co-ordination and regulation of communications activities throughout Region I of the ITU comprising Europe and Africa

Enquiries: To Secretary

Scope: Information can be provided on most aspects of radio communications (excluding broadcasting) in the countries of Europe and Africa

Stock: National amateur radio journals of about 50 different countries

Publications: The Region I News (quarterly)

ROMFORD
Essex

2050

LONDON BOROUGH OF HAVERING PUBLIC LIBRARIES
Central Library
Romford
Essex

Tel.: Romford 44297, 44298, 44299 and 44290

Enquiries: To Borough Librarian

Scope: Collection of books, pamphlets, prints, maps and other documents relating to the history of Havering and Essex (2,000 items). Teachers Reference Library (1,500 volumes on aspects of education and teaching practice)

Stock: 460,000 books; 3,000 pamphlets; 350 current periodicals (total stock)

Publications: LOGA—Local Government Annotations (monthly)
Biographies for Children. 1967

ROSSENDALE
Lancs

2051

HASLINGDEN PUBLIC LIBRARY
Deardengate
Haslingden
Rossendale
Lancashire

Tel.: Rossendale 5690

Enquiries: To Librarian

Scope: Subject specialization: Hygiene of recreation and sleep; hunting and trapping, and fish culture; other areas of Europe—Low countries, Switzerland, Rumania, Greece
David Halstead local history collection

Stock: Subject specialization: 865 books; local collection: 900 books

ROTHERHAM
Yorkshire

2052

LADY MABEL COLLEGE OF EDUCATION
Wentworth Woodhouse
Rotherham
Yorkshire

Tel.: Hoyland 2161

Enquiries: To Librarian

Scope: All aspects of physical education (including physiology and dance). Other main subjects covered: English, art, music, drama, biology, education

Stock: 12,500 books and pamphlets; 80 current periodicals

ROTHERHAM Yorkshire 2053	ROTHERHAM MUNICIPAL MUSEUM AND ART GALLERY Clifton Park Rotherham Yorkshire	*Tel.:* Rotherham 5481

Public museum specializing in South Yorkshire potteries and Roman antiquities from Templeborough (near Rotherham) but also having general collections and housing loan exhibitions

Enquiries: To Director

Scope: Identification of wares and general enquiries relating to South Yorkshire potteries, particularly Rockingham
Secondary: History of the Rotherham area, and in particular the Roman forts at Templeborough
Small but comprehensive library in these fields

Publications: Book: The Rockingham Pottery. A. A. Eaglestone and T. A. Lockett. 1964 (revised reprint 1967)

ROTHERHAM Yorkshire 2054	ROTHERHAM PUBLIC LIBRARY Howard Street Rotherham Yorkshire	*Tel.:* Rotherham 2121 and 5674

Enquiries: To Director

Scope: South Yorkshire Potteries, particularly Rockingham. Local history of the Rotherham area. National subject specialization: British law—treatises and law of property

Stock: South Yorkshire Potteries, 5 books; Law, 500 books; Local history collection, 1,500 books; 25 current periodicals in local history collection; 600 local prints, pictures and illustrations; collection of cuttings on local history; cuttings and articles on Rockingham Pottery

Publications: Occasional subject booklists

ROTHERHAM Yorkshire 2055	ROTHERHAM SCHOOL OF ART AND CRAFTS Howard Street Rotherham Yorkshire	*Tel.:* Rotherham 5015

Enquiries: To Principal

Scope: Visual arts, including drawing, painting, sculpture, fashion, textiles, metalwork, jewellery, silversmithing, photography, painting and decorating, graphic design, embroidery, soft furnishing, hairdressing
Secondary: Interior decoration, beauty culture

Stock: 3,000 books; 35 current periodicals. Stock not available on loan

ROTHESAY Bute 2056	BUTE COUNTY LIBRARY Norman Stewart Institute Rothesay Isle of Bute	*Tel.:* Rothesay 505

Enquiries: To Librarian

Scope: Local (Bute County) Collection, including River Clyde generally

Stock: 500 books; 100 pamphlets; 150 illustrations

Publications: Catalogue of local material

ROTHESAY Bute **2057**	THE BUTE MUSEUM Stuart Street Rothesay Isle of Bute	
Enquiries:	To Secretary	
Scope:	Natural history and archaeology of the Island of Bute	
Publications:	Occasional Transactions	

ROTHWELL *See under* **LEEDS** *for*
Leeds ROTHWELL PUBLIC LIBRARY (no. 809)

ROYAL *See* **LEAMINGTON SPA**, Warwickshire
LEAMINGTON SPA
Warwickshire

RUGBY BRITISH SOCIETY OF DOWSERS *Tel.:* Byfield 525
Warwickshire High Street
  Eydon
2058 Rugby
  Warwickshire

  To spread information among members, and others interested, on the uses of dowsing

Enquiries: To Librarian or Secretary, by letter only

Scope: Geophysical, medical, agricultural and other applications of dowsing. Register of competent dowsers. As the Society has members throughout the world, enquiries can usually be answered with knowledge of local conditions in the country concerned. Sources of dowsing equipment can be indicated

Stock: 600 books in English, French, German and Italian

Publications: Quarterly Journal
  Several books of instruction
  Symposium on Dowsing

RUGBY EAST WARWICKSHIRE COLLEGE OF FURTHER *Tel.:* Rugby 6161
Warwickshire   EDUCATION
  Clifton Road
2059 Rugby
  Warwickshire

Enquiries: To Librarian

Scope: Economics, law, technical education, languages, arts and crafts

Stock: 11,000 books and pamphlets; 175 current periodicals

Publications: Accessions list (monthly)

  Member of CADIG

RUISLIP BUSINESS STATISTICS OFFICE *Tel.:* 01-866 8771
Middx Lime Grove
  Eastcote
2060 Ruislip
  Middlesex HA4 8RS

  Formerly Board of Trade Census Office

RUISLIP, BUSINESS STATISTICS OFFICE, *cont.*

Enquiries: To Director

Scope: Censuses of production and distribution; annual and other periodic enquiries into various trades. In process of expansion to cover all Business Statistics. Library in process of expansion to cover all United Kingdom published statistics; statistical methodology; data processing

Publications: Censuses of Production and Distribution (see H.M.S.O. Sectional List 51)

Special analyses of data collected for censuses undertaken on payment of fee

RUNCORN
Cheshire

2061

RUNCORN PUBLIC LIBRARY
Egerton Street
Runcorn
Cheshire

Tel.: Runcorn 2068

Enquiries: To Librarian

Scope: Local information collection

Stock: 54,000 books and pamphlets; 60 current periodicals (total stock)

RUTHERGLEN
Glasgow

See under **GLASGOW** for
RUTHERGLEN PUBLIC LIBRARY (no. 615)

RUTHIN
Denbighshire

2062

DENBIGHSHIRE COUNTY LIBRARY
46 Clwyd Street
Ruthin
Denbighshire

Tel.: Ruthin 2451

Enquiries: To Librarian

Scope: Local history collection relating to Denbighshire

Stock: 390,000 books; 107 current periodicals, (including about 5,000 maps, microfilms, prints and manuscripts in the local history collection)

Publications: Bibliography of the County:
    Part 1, Biographical Sources. 1935
    Part 2, Historical & Topographical Sources. 2nd edition 1951
    Part 2, Supplement 1951–1957. 1959
    Part 3, Denbighshire Authors & Their Works. 1937

Member of the Denbighshire Libraries Group

SAFFRON WALDEN
Essex

2063

THE FELLOWSHIP OF FAITH FOR THE MUSLIMS
The Manse
Great Sampford
Saffron Walden
Essex

Tel.: Great Sampford 339

International, interdenominational and intermission prayer fellowship for regular and informed intercession for the evangelization of the Muslims

Enquiries: To Librarian, c/o All Nations Missionary College, Easneye, Ware, Hertfordshire for library material; to Secretary for other enquiries

Scope: Library covers all aspects of the Muslim religion, its origins, practices, founder and sects; Christian missions to Muslims; biographies of missionaries. Current work

Stock: 500 books; 100 pamphlets; 2 current periodicals and the publications of many missionary societies

Publications: Focus on Islam (series of six booklets)
Catalogue of Library

ST ALBANS Herts **2064**	ABORTION LAW REFORM ASSOCIATION 22 Brewhouse Hill Wheathampstead St Albans Hertfordshire	*Tel.:* 058-283 2347

Aims to obtain and publish information on the legal, social and medical aspects of abortion; to encourage research into these aspects and to secure such changes in relevant British law as may be considered necessary

Enquiries: To Secretary

Scope: Information available on all aspects (historical and current) of the British law on abortion. Details of the attitudes of various organizations and bodies to this subject, and of recent overseas legislation
Secondary: Information on 'pressure group' politics as exemplified by the campaign to change the abortion law

ST ALBANS Herts **2065**	AMBASSADOR COLLEGE St Albans Hertfordshire	*Tel.:* Garston 74151 *Telex:* 264114

Educational establishment in liberal arts based on three campuses and with a world-wide extension programme for home adult education

Enquiries: To Librarian, by letter only

Scope: General university level stock with special emphasis on works of historical interest in ancient, classical, mediaeval and church history. Unique collection of rare works. Stock not available on loan

Stock: 50,000 books; 210 current periodicals

Publications: Plain Truth   Educational books and booklets
Tomorrow's World   Correspondence course

ST ALBANS Herts **2066**	COMMONWEALTH BUREAU OF HELMINTHOLOGY The White House 103 St Peter's Street St Albans Hertfordshire	*Tel.:* St Albans 52126

One of the Commonwealth Agricultural Bureaux, its main activity is the provision of a world-wide information service on all aspects of animal helminthology, and plant nematology

Enquiries: To Director

Scope: The library contains most of the primary journals covering parasitology and helminthology. Medical, veterinary and fisheries helminthology, and plant nematology are all adequately covered. Enquiries on all these subjects and related topics are dealt with. There is also a laboratory identification service

Stock: 1,000 books; large reprint collection on helminthology; most Commonwealth agricultural and veterinary reports; 180 current periodicals

Publications: Helminthological Abstracts, Series A, Animal Helminthology
Helminthological Abstracts, Series B, Plant Nematology
Occasional publications including reviews and bibliographies

ST ALBANS	HARPERBURY HOSPITAL	*Tel.:* Radlett 4861
Herts	Harper Lane	
	Shenley	
2067	St Albans	
	Hertfordshire	
	Hospital for mentally subnormal	

Enquiries: To Librarian (Psychology Department)

Scope: Small library for use of professional staff covering: Subnormality, psychiatry, neurology, psychology, sociology, education, genetics, biochemistry, and allied subjects

Stock: 367 books and pamphlets; 20 current periodicals

Separate library for Nurses Training School

ST ALBANS	HUDSON MEMORIAL LIBRARY	*Tel.:* St Albans 61744
Herts	2 Sumpter Yard	
	St Albans	
2068	Hertfordshire	

A theological and historical library mainly for clergy but open to all *bona fide* students at Librarian's discretion

Enquiries: To Librarian

Scope: Theology, philosophy, psychology
Secondary: History, archaeology, sociology. Local history, particularly Parish Histories of Hertfordshire and Bedfordshire

Stock: 5,000 books; various pamphlets, mainly archaeological and historical; 7 current periodicals

ST ALBANS	ST ALBANS CITY LIBRARY	*Tel.:* St Albans 60000
Herts	Victoria Street	
	St Albans	
2069	Hertfordshire	

Enquiries: To City Librarian

Scope: Hertfordshire local history collection

Stock: 1,400 books; 1,600 pamphlets; 400 maps; 750 slides and illustrations (St Albans). Collection not available for loan

ST ALBANS	ST ALBANS COLLEGE OF FURTHER	*Tel.:* St Albans 60423
Herts	EDUCATION	*Telex:* 263208
	The Donald Newman Library	
2070	29 Hatfield Road	
	St Albans	
	Hertfordshire	

Enquiries: To Librarian

Scope: Art and craft, business studies, education, engineering, liberal studies and science. Special collection of books on education for St Albans Teachers Centre (600 volumes on primary, secondary and further education)

Stock: 10,000 books; 2,000 pamphlets; 215 current periodicals

Publications: Books for the Secretarial Student
The Teenage Reader in Further Education

ST ALBANS Herts **2071**	VERULAMIUM MUSEUM St Michael's St Albans Hertfordshire	*Tel.:* St Albans 54659

Houses, conserves and displays the objects from the Roman Site of Verulamium

Enquiries: To The Director

Scope: Archaeology of Roman Britain
Secondary: General aspects of archaeology

Library stock not available on loan, but may be consulted by appointment

Publications: Guidebooks   Postcards
Colour slides   Notes in many foreign languages

ST ALBANS Herts **2072**	YOUTH HOSTELS ASSOCIATION (ENGLAND AND WALES) Trevelyan House St Albans Hertfordshire	*Tel.:* St Albans 55215

Enquiries: To Public Relations Officer

Scope: Information about youth hostelling in England and Wales, and throughout the world
No library

Publications: Youth Hosteller (monthly magazine)
Short History of the YHA

ST ANDREWS Fife **2073**	UNIVERSITY OF ST ANDREWS LIBRARY St Andrews Fife	*Tel.:* St Andrews 4333 *Telex:* 76213

Enquiries: To Librarian

Scope: Subjects covered by the Faculties of Arts, Science, Medicine and Divinity. Was a copyright library from 1710 to 1836. Principal *special collections* include: Beveridge (bee culture and Norwegian literature and history), Forbes (science, including many early and rare works), Mackay (mathematics), Von Hugel (mainly philosophy), Bishop Low (theology), George Hay Forbes (liturgy, church history, patristics), Donaldson (classics and education) and McGillivray (Celtic history and literature)

Stock: 550,000 volumes including music scores; 30,000 pamphlets; 2,500 maps; 1,700 manuscripts; 150 incunabula; 2,400 current periodicals (total stock). Separate archives department

Publications: Illustrated Guide to the University Library
Notes for Readers
Henderson's Benefaction. 1942
Bibliography of St Andrews
An index to the correspondence and papers of James David Forbes (1809–1868) and also to some papers of his son, George Forbes. B. N. Smart

ST BOSWELLS Roxburghshire **2074**	ROXBURGHSHIRE COUNTY LIBRARY County Library Headquarters St Boswells Roxburghshire	*Tel.:* St Boswells 3260

Enquiries: To Librarian

Scope: National subject specialization: Air forces

Stock: 69 books

ST FAGANS Cardiff	*See under* **CARDIFF** for WELSH FOLK MUSEUM (no. 342)	
ST HELENS Lancs **2075**	PILKINGTON GLASS MUSEUM Prescot Road St Helens Lancashire	*Tel.:* St Helens 28882, ext. 2499

Enquiries: To Curator

Scope: The Museum tells the history of glassmaking by displaying models, diaramas and actual glass. A collection of 400 vessels illustrating the main techniques is being built up

Stock: 750 books; 50 pamphlets; 5 current periodicals. Stock not available on loan

Publicatons: Guides and catalogues

ST HELENS Lancs **2076**	ST HELENS CENTRAL PUBLIC LIBRARY Gamble Institute Victoria Square St Helens Lancashire	*Tel.:* St Helens 24061

Enquiries: To Librarian

Scope: N.W.R.L.S. subject specialization includes: Diseases of the nervous system. Geography and history of China and Japan

Stock: 200,000 books; 1,000 pamphlets; 225 current periodicals; 90 maps; 30 manuscripts (total stock)

ST HELENS Lancs **2077**	ST HELENS MUSEUM AND ART GALLERY Gamble Institute St Helens Lancashire	*Tel.:* St Helens 24061

Enquiries: To Director

Scope: Local history; glass containers; natural history
Secondary: Ceramics; antiques

ST IVES Cornwall **2078**	ST IVES PUBLIC LIBRARY Gabriel Street St Ives Cornwall	*Tel.:* St Ives 5377

Enquiries: To Librarian

Scope: Local history collection
S.W.R.L.S. subject specialization: Art

Stock: 20,000 books; 400 pamphlets in subject specialization and local collection; 53 current periodicals (total stock)

ST KEVERNE Helston Cornwall	*See under* **HELSTON** for WESLEY HISTORICAL SOCIETY (no. 696)	
ST LEONARDS- ON-SEA Sussex **2079**	HASTINGS COLLEGE OF FURTHER EDUCATION Archery Road St Leonards-on-Sea Sussex	*Tel.:* Hastings 3847

Enquiries: To Librarian

Scope: Social sciences, history

Stock: 9,000 books; 100 current periodicals

ST PETER PORT *See under* **GUERNSEY** for
Guernsey   PRIAULX LIBRARY (no. 653)
Channel Islands

SALE   FACULTY OF TEACHERS IN COMMERCE   *Tel.:* 061-973 5888
Cheshire   LIMITED
            13 Stamford Place
2080   Sale
            Cheshire M33 3BT
            National organization for teachers of commercial subjects

Enquiries: To Secretary, by letter only

Scope: Current textbooks on subject material and teaching method in all commercial subjects. Current syllabus booklets and past examination papers on all relevant bodies
Details of conditions of service, wage awards, and other related associations
Secondary: Organization was founded in 1872 and has some historical material though much relating to period 1872–1916 was destroyed in a fire

Stock: 1,000 volumes reference books for information service only; 8 current periodicals. Stock not available on loan

Publications: Teacher in Commerce (quarterly)
Supplements, published occasionally contain reports of research of the Visual Aids & Methods Sub-Committee on latest developments
A textbook or handbook on teaching method was recently published to replace an earlier edition now out of date and print

SALE   SALE PUBLIC LIBRARY   *Tel.:* 061-973 3142
Cheshire   Tatton Road
            Sale
2081   Cheshire M33 1YH

Enquiries: To Reader's Adviser

Scope: Subject specialization includes: Human biochemistry; English humour and satire; architectural design

Stock: 35 books on biochemistry; 340 on humour

SALFORD COLGATE–PALMOLIVE LTD   *Tel.:* 061-872 3321
Lancs   371 Ordsall Lane   *Telex:* 66540
             Salford 5
2802   Lancashire
             Manufacturers of soaps, detergents and toilet goods

Enquiries: To Information Officer

Scope: Dentistry and oral health. Soaps and detergents. Textiles and laundering. Cosmetics and pharmaceuticals. Perfumes—analytical chemistry methods
Secondary: Pesticides and toxicology; packaging

Stock: 900 books; 2,500 trade literature pamphlets; 105 current periodicals

SALFORD Lancs 2083	MANCHESTER CENTRAL BOARD OF HEBREW EDUCATION Emanuel Raffles House Upper Park Road Salford M7 0HL Lancashire	*Tel.:* 061-740 5445

Enquiries: To Director of Education
Scope: Modern and Classical Hebrew books on the State of Israel, Bible, Jewish education
Stock: 300 books; 500 pamphlets; current periodicals include *Hachinuch* (Israeli educational quarterly)
Publications: Children's textbooks

SALFORD Lancs 2084	SALFORD CENTRAL LIBRARY Peel Park Salford 5 Lancashire	*Tel.:* 061-736 3353 and 4246

Enquiries: To Librarian
Scope: History, topography, industries and social life of Salford and adjoining areas
Stock: General Reference Library stock 40,000 volumes. Local History Library includes more than 4,000 books and pamphlets, and back numbers of local newspapers are held from the early 19th century; 109 current periodicals

SALFORD Lancs 2085	SALFORD MUSEUMS AND ART GALLERY Peel Park Salford M5 4WU Lancashire	*Tel.:* 061-736 2649

Enquiries: To Director
Scope: Museum and Art Gallery with collections of local history (including Victorian Period Street exhibit), ceramics, art (large collection of L. S. Lowry paintings and drawings). The Branch Museum at Buile Hill Park, Salford, contains natural history collections and specializes in coal mining (replica coal mine exhibit)

SALFORD Lancs 2086	UNIVERSITY OF SALFORD LIBRARY Salford M5 4WT Lancashire	*Tel.:* 061-736 5843

Enquiries: To Librarian
Scope: Economics, geography, government, modern languages (French, German, Italian, Russian, Spanish), sociology
Secondary: Medicine, modern languages (Dutch, Polish, Portuguese, Swedish)
Stock: 60,000 books and pamphlets; 500 current periodicals
Publications: Occasional Special Subject lists

SALISBURY Wilts 2087	CATTERY INFORMATION SERVICE The Wing Orcheston House Orcheston Salisbury Wiltshire

See no. 2324

SALISBURY Wilts 2088	COLLEGE OF SARUM ST MICHAEL 65 The Close Salisbury Wiltshire College of Education	*Tel.*: Salisbury 3316

Enquiries: To Librarian
Scope: Education
Stock: 5,000 books and pamphlets; 120 current periodicals

SALISBURY Wilts 2089	THE SALISBURY AND SOUTH WILTSHIRE MUSEUM Ann Street Salisbury Wiltshire	*Tel.*: Salisbury 4465

Enquiries: To Curator
Scope: Archaeology; medieval and later antiquities; ceramics (English); numismatics
Stock: 2,000 books; 1,000 pamphlets; 8 current periodicals. Stock not available on loan

SALISBURY Wilts 2090	SALISBURY CITY LIBRARY Chipper Lane Salisbury Wiltshire	*Tel.*: Salisbury 4167

Enquiries: To Librarian
Scope: Salisbury and Wiltshire local collection of books, maps and newspapers
Stock: Salisbury and Wiltshire collection 1,500 books; total reference stock 8,000 books and pamphlets; 12 current periodicals (mainly archaeological)

SALISBURY Wilts 2091	THE SOWTER AND CLERICAL LIBRARY Church House Crane Street Salisbury Wiltshire	(May be contacted at the local Wiltshire Regional Library *Tel.*: Wilton 3230)

Aims to provide a collection of books on religious topics to clergy of the Salisbury diocese and to any person on payment of the annual subscription

Enquiries: To Librarian
Scope: Stock covers all aspects of religion, with a good deal of history and biography. Most was published in the years from 1870–1925, although expenditure on books recently has increased, so that the library includes much material published since 1960. A small reference collection, and a *special collection* of books and material on Salisbury, Wiltshire and the Diocese
Stock: 8,000 books; 6 current periodicals

SALTCOATS Ayrshire 2092	NORTH AYRSHIRE MUSEUM Kirkgate Saltcoats Ayrshire Regional Museum

Enquiries: To Curator, by letter only

SALTCOATS, NORTH AYRSHIRE MUSEUM, *cont.*

Scope: Local history. Cunninghame Collection (Documents, shipping, mining, property, personal, from 17th century)

Stock: 1,500 books; 100 pamphlets. Stock not available on loan

SANDOWN   SANDOWN–SHANKLIN PUBLIC LIBRARIES   *Tel.:* Sandown 2748
Isle of Wight   High Street
   Sandown
2093   Isle of Wight

Enquiries: To Librarian

Scope: Stock includes collection of books dealing with the Isle of Wight history and geology, in connection with the Museum of Isle of Wight Geology

Stock: 500 books

Publications: Conversations with an Island: being a short guide to the Museum of Isle of Wight Geology, Sandown, Isle of Wight

SANDWICH   PFIZER LIMITED   *Tel.:* Sandwich 3511
Kent   Ramsgate Road
   Sandwich
2094   Kent

   Pharmaceutical Research

Enquiries: To Librarian

Scope: Chemistry and technology of the pharmaceutical industry, medicine, biochemistry and pharmacology

Stock: 3,000 books; 400 current periodicals. Stock not available on loan

SCARBOROUGH   SCARBOROUGH MUSEUM   *Tel.:* Scarborough 64285
Yorkshire   Vernon Road
   Scarborough
2095   Yorkshire

Enquiries: To Curator

Scope: Local archaeology and history

Stock: 500 books; 250 pamphlets; 1,500 photographs and prints; 1,000 lantern slides. Stock available on loan through Scarborough Public Libraries (no. 2096)

SCARBOROUGH   SCARBOROUGH PUBLIC LIBRARIES   *Tel.:* Scarborough 64285
Yorkshire   Central Library
   Vernon Road
2096   Scarborough
   Yorkshire

Enquiries: To Director

Scope: General with local collection

Stock: 75,000 books and pamphlets including 4,000 in the local collection; 150 current periodicals

SCUNTHORPE   THE BRITISH SCIENCE FICTION ASSOCIATION
Lincs   LIMITED
   c/o 76 Old Brumby Street
2097   Scunthorpe
   Lincolnshire

   Association for the encouragement and furtherance of science fiction, for authors, publishers, booksellers and readers

Enquiries: To Executive Secretary, 25 Yewdale Crescent, Coventry CV2 2FF, by letter only

Scope: *Book library:* Large collection of science fiction works and books on the subject
Magazine library: Extensive, but incomplete, holdings of many periodicals in the field, including some published in, for example, Sweden, Germany, Japan
Reference library: Collection being built up—not at present available
Information service: A panel of experts on science fiction deals with postal enquiries. Any and every aspect of the field can be dealt with

Stock: 2,000 books; 120 periodicals

Publications: Vector (journal of the Association)
B.S.F.A. Bulletin (news and information)
List of Members
Book Catalogue (in progress)
Magazine Catalogue
Various checklists and bibliographies

SCUNTHORPE
Lincs
2098

NORTH LINDSEY TECHNICAL COLLEGE
Kingsway
Scunthorpe
Lincolnshire

Tel.: Scunthorpe 4738

Enquiries: To Librarian

Scope: Economics and sociology; engineering subjects; science and metallurgy subjects; building; general subjects including cookery, languages and literature

Stock: 10,000 books; 150 current periodicals

Headquarters of the County Technical Library Service

SCUNTHORPE
Lincs
2099

SCUNTHORPE MUSEUM AND ART GALLERY
Scunthorpe
Lincolnshire
and
Normanby Hall
Scunthorpe
Lincolnshire

Tel.: Scunthorpe 3533

Tel.: Burton Stather 215

Collection, conservation and display of material relating to the natural history and human history of the South Humberside region, including Art Galleries; Normanby Hall, 3 miles north, is a Regency Mansion furnished and decorated in period and open to the public

Enquiries: To Director or Secretary

Scope: Information can be supplied on most aspects of natural history and geology and human history and prehistory in North Lincolnshire. Sources include some documentary and pictorial material

Stock: 1,000 books; 600 pamphlets; various current periodicals in the fields of Natural History, Local History, museology, numismatics, fine arts, folk life and industrial archaeology. Stock not available on loan

Publications: Guide Books to Normanby Hall and (in preparation) Museum and Art Gallery
Bi-monthly Diary of Events published by Museum Society
Journals on archaeology and local history, natural history and other related subjects

SCUNTHORPE	SCUNTHORPE PUBLIC LIBRARY	*Tel.*: Scunthorpe 2724
Lincs	Central Library	*Telex*: 52369
	Market Hill	
2100	Scunthorpe	
	Lincolnshire	

Enquiries: To Chief Librarian

Scope: *Special collections:* Lincolnshire (700 items)
John Wesley (500 volumes)
Shakespeare (223 volumes)
Music Library (3091 records; 503 miniature scores; 773 scores; 761 music texts; 39 sets of scores)
Play sets (381)
Maps (746)
Collections of foreign literature: Urdu (422 volumes); French (93 volumes); German (41 volumes); Italian (21 volumes); Spanish (27 volumes); Polish; Russian (12 volumes)

Stock: 105,000 books; 350 pamphlets; 250 current periodicals (total stock)

Publications: Information Please (series), including:
Forthcoming Events
Where Can We Go
Local Societies

SEAFORD	SEAFORD COLLEGE OF EDUCATION	*Tel.*: Seaford 3556
Sussex	Cricketfield Road	
	Seaford	
2101	Sussex	
	Domestic Science teacher training	

Enquiries: To Librarian, by letter only

Scope: Domestic science (housecraft, cookery, nutrition)
Secondary: Education

Stock: Books—900 (Domestic science), 1,200 (Education); current periodicals—29 (Domestic science), 18 (Education)

SETTLE	BRITISH SPELEOLOGICAL ASSOCIATION
Yorkshire	Duke Street
	Settle
2102	Yorkshire

Enquiries: To Hon. Secretary, by letter only

Scope: All aspects of speleology and industrial history of mines, the United Kingdom in particular and overseas generally

Stock: 300 books; 1,000 periodicals and manuscripts; 50 current periodicals. Stock not available on loan

Publications: Cave Science (journal of the British Speleological Association)
Proceedings of the B.S.A.
Speleological Abstracts (annually)
Bulletin of the B.S.A.

SEVENOAKS Kent **2103**	INTERNATIONAL FEDERATION OF LIBRARY ASSOCIATIONS 13 Vine Court Road Sevenoaks Kent	*Tel.:* Sevenoaks 53011

Aims to promote co-operation in the field of librarianship and bibliography, and particularly to carry out investigations and make propositions on international relations between libraries, library associations and other organized groups

Enquiries: To General Secretary, by letter only

Scope: Professional associations of librarians in all countries. Libraries and library techniques and their standardization. The development of libraries. Unesco's work in the same field

Stock: 300 books; small selection current periodicals

Publications: Proceedings of the General Council (annually)
IFLA Communications FIAB (in *Libri*)
IFLA News/Nouvelles de la FIAB (quarterly)
Telecode and Telex address book, in 10 languages, for libraries and documentation centres (IFLA International Manuals no. 1)
Names of persons: national usages for entry in catalogues. Revised edition. 1967 (IFLA International Manuals no. 2). A. H. Chaplin
Bibliographie des répertoires nationaux de périodiques en cours. 1969 (IFLA International Manuals no. 3). G. Duprat, K. Liutova and M. L. Bossuat
International Standardization of Library Statistics; a progress report (IFLA International manuals no. 4). 1968

SEVENOAKS Kent **2104**	SEVENOAKS PUBLIC LIBRARY Central Library The Drive Sevenoaks Kent	*Tel.:* Sevenoaks 53118

Enquiries: To Librarian

Scope: Special collection on history of Sevenoaks and surrounding villages, including the Dr Gordon Ward Notebooks on Sevenoaks and District and the Farnaby-Austen Manuscripts on the Kippington Estate
Secondary: L.A.S.E.R. subject specialization: Modern philosophy; co-operation

Stock: 46,000 books; 40 current periodicals (total stock)

SHEFFIELD **2105**	BRITISH NATIONAL TEMPERANCE LEAGUE Livesey-Clegg House 44 Union Street Sheffield S1 2JP	*Tel.:* Sheffield 22770

Enquiries: To Secretary

Scope: The Joseph Livesey Library is a special collection of temperance biographies, autobiographies, social science and historical material, dealing with the temperance movement from 1832 to present day

Stock: 2,000 books; 500 pamphlets; 200 magazines and periodicals of temperance organizations; manuscript minutes of the British and National Temperance League

| SHEFFIELD 2106 | THE GEOGRAPHICAL ASSOCIATION | *Tel.:* Sheffield 61666 |

343 Fulwood Road
Sheffield S10 3BP

Aims to further the knowledge of geography and the teaching of geography in all categories of educational institutions

Enquiries: To Hon. Librarian

Scope: Books and pamphlets on geographical topics and regions, and on the teaching of geography in schools, colleges and universities. Current geographical journals from a wide range of countries, in English and other languages. Collection of school textbooks dealing with geography, both modern and historical

Stock: 12,000 books and pamphlets; 160 current periodicals. Stock not available on loan

Publications: British Landscapes through Maps (series)　　Geography in Secondary Schools
Teaching Geography (series)　　Teaching Geography in Junior Schools
Sample Studies　　The Geography Room and its Equipment
Asian Sample Studies
Library Catalogues—Africa, Asia, The Americas (and supplement), Australia and New Zealand

---

| SHEFFIELD 2107 | INSTITUTE OF HEALTH EDUCATION | *Tel.:* Sheffield 26921 (Day); Sheffield 60790 (Evening) |

35 Victoria Road
Sheffield S10 2DJ

Enquiries: To Secretary, by letter only

Scope: Information on organization and execution of health education, techniques, evaluation, content of subject matter of health education programme
Secondary: Sources of media, teaching aids, demonstration material, equipment
No library

Publications: Journal of the Institute of Health Education (quarterly)
Newsletters

| SHEFFIELD 2108 | INTESTINAL ABSORPTION INFORMATION CENTRE, BIOMEDICAL INFORMATION PROJECT | *Tel.:* Sheffield 78555 ext. 410 |

Department of Physiology
The University of Sheffield
Western Bank
Sheffield S10 2TN

Information service for research workers in the Department and subscribers elsewhere; and research and development in information retrieval techniques

Enquiries: To Information Officer

Scope: *In vitro* studies of mammalian absorption and digestion
Secondary: Absorption of water and ions, by other absorptive epithelia
Transport across membranes

Stock: 5,000 reprints or photocopies of periodical articles. Stock not available on loan

Publications: Intestinal Absorption and related topics (monthly bulletin of abstracts with indexes)

SHEFFIELD 2109	MEDICAL RESEARCH COUNCIL UNIT FOR METABOLIC STUDIES IN PSYCHIATRY University Department of Psychiatry Middlewood Hospital Sheffield S6 1TP	*Tel.:* Sheffield 349491

Enquiries: To Director, by letter only

Scope: Chemical and other changes in the subnormal and mentally ill
The Unit has a comparatively insignificant library of books on the subjects which are included within its field of research:
Chemical studies of subnormality
Psychopharmacology
Electroencephalography
Biochemistry of steroids and amines
Chemistry of hair
Bioassays, particularly for vasopressin
Animal activity (timing and amount of activity in rats)
Chromatographic methods

Publications: Research papers

SHEFFIELD 2110	THE NATIONAL INSTITUTE OF MEDICAL HERBALISTS *Registered address* 169 Norfolk Street Sheffield 1	*Secretary's address* 673 Barking Road Plaistow London E.13	*Tel.:* 01-594 5892

Enquiries: To Public Relations Officer, 25 Rosebery Avenue, Worthing, Sussex (*Tel.:* Worthing 43268)

Scope: Medical herbalism (through a supporting organization 'Friends of Herbalism')
No library

Publications: Health from Herbs (magazine)
Pamphlets, including: Herbal Medicine is Safe Medicine; History of Herbalism

SHEFFIELD

2111

SHEFFIELD CITY ART GALLERIES
Graves Art Gallery
Surrey Street
Sheffield 1
and
Mappin Art Gallery
Weston Park
Sheffield 10

Enquiries: To Director

Scope: Fine art in general. British, French, Dutch and Italian schools. Chinese, Japanese, Indian, Islamic and early Mediterranean art. Art and industry in the South Yorkshire area

Stock: Large collection of Gallery and Exhibition catalogues chiefly British, but with some coverage of American and European sources; 5 current periodicals

Publications: Exhibition catalogues, chiefly 19th and 20th century British artists, for example Victorian Paintings; Francis Danby; Edward Lear; J. J. Tissot; Henry Moore; Wright of Derby
Provisional catalogue of foreign schools paintings in Sheffield City Art Galleries
Catalogue of the Grice collection of Chinese ivories

SHEFFIELD

2112

SHEFFIELD CITY LIBRARIES
Central Library
Surrey Street
Sheffield S1 1XZ

Tel.: Sheffield 78771
Telex: 54243

Enquiries: To City Librarian and Information Officer

REFERENCE LIBRARIES

General Reference Library: Books printed in England between 1765 and 1779. National Subject Specialization Scheme: Law including torts, family law and inheritance, commercial and maritime law. Collection of private press books. Books on glass and silver

Stock: 121,000 books; 450 current periodicals

Department of Local History and Archives: Houses the Sheffield collection of printed material (16,000 volumes) and manuscript collections (500,000) including the Wentworth Woodhouse Muniments, Duke of Norfolk's Sheffield Estate Muniments, Fairbank Collection of local maps, and many other collections of local historical documents and business archives. Recognized respository for manorial records and parish records of Sheffield diocese. The Wentworth Woodhouse Muniments include: Edmund Burke's correspondence and the letters and papers of the great Earl of Strafford and the Marquis of Rockingham. *Other special collections:* Edward Carpenter's library, manuscripts and letters. Picture collection: 25,000. Collection of transparencies. Comprehensive collection of local newspapers from 18th century onwards, both in original form and microfilm copies. Local films of industrial and historical interest

Libraries of Commerce, Science and Technology: Cover all pure and applied sciences and commerce

Stock: 85,000 books and pamphlets; 1,000 current periodicals (including medical titles); directories collection (including Medical Register 1932 to date); Medical Directory 1958 to date; registers of professions supplementary to medicine such as chiropodists; *Index Medicus*

Assize Courts Library: A collection of standard legal texts and reports. Serves the needs of judges, barristers during Quarter Sessions and Assizes. At all other times the stock is available for reference use

Stock: Complete sets of All England Law Reports; Statutory Instruments, 1930 to date; complete sets of Statutes. All official law reports; selection of specialized reports

Music and Gramophone Record Library: 12,700 records
National Fiction Reserve: N–S (Yorkshire allocation)

Publications: 'Isms: a dictionary of words ending in -ism, -ology, and -phobia. 2nd edition 1968
Sheffield: England. Official brochure of the City of Sheffield
City Libraries of Sheffield, 1856–1956. 1956
Basic Books on Sheffield History. 5th edition 1966
Local history leaflets. (Duplicated). 1–13
Sheffield: its Story and its Achievements. M. Walton. 4th edition 1968 (jointly with S. R. Publishers Ltd)
Guide to the Manuscript Collection in the Sheffield City Libraries, 1956 and Supplements 1956–67
Catalogue of the Arundel Castle Manuscripts, 1965 (Duke of Norfolk's Sheffield and Worksop Estates)
Bibliography of Edward Carpenter. 1949
Guide to the Fairbank Collection of maps and plans. 1936
Catalogue of Business and Industrial Records. 1968
Letters from a Yorkshire Emigrant ... 1967
Research Bibliographies (3rd Series)
Catalogue of the Assize Courts Library (under revision)

SHEFFIELD 2113	SHEFFIELD CITY MUSEUMS Weston Park Sheffield S10 2TP	*Tel.:* 0742-27226

Regional museum collecting specimens and information relating to man and his environment in South Yorkshire and North Derbyshire

Enquiries: To Director

Scope: The museum collections and their documentation are available as a primary information source and cover the geology, botany, zoology, prehistory, social and industrial history and the applied art of the region. The Bateman collection of Antiquities from Derbyshire, North Staffordshire and Yorkshire includes the most important source material for the Bronze Age of the region. The Old Sheffield Plate and Cutlery collections are of international importance
Secondary: Identification (but not valuation) of public specimens undertaken freely
The staff library is available for public reference and includes most of the standard works relating to the area covered by the collections

Stock: 5,000 books; 1,000 pamphlets; 22 current periodicals

Publications: Booklets relating to the region and catalogues of special exhibitions and the permanent collection
Slides
Postcards

SHEFFIELD 2114	SHEFFIELD NATIONAL CENTRE FOR RADIOTHERAPY Weston Park Hospital Whitham Road Sheffield 10	*Tel.:* Sheffield 60072

Enquiries: To Librarian, by letter only

Scope: Clinical radiotherapy, cancer, radiobiology, radiological physics

Stock: 200 books; 10 pamphlets; 30 current periodicals

SHEFFIELD 2115	SHEFFIELD POLYTECHNIC Pond Street Sheffield S1 1WB	*Tel.:* Sheffield 29671

Enquiries: To Librarian

Scope: Art and design; building and civil engineering; business and economics; management studies; political and social studies; hotel and institutional management; chemistry and metallurgy; modern arts; engineering; applied mathematics and physics; Urban and Regional Studies. Library and lecturing staff willing to help with any enquiries in these subject fields

Stock: 39,000 books; 9,000 pamphlets; 200 reports; 750 current periodicals; 200 theses; abstracts

Publications: Monthly Bulletin and List of Accessions
Selected subject lists covering a wide range of subjects, and Abstracts Bulletin (fortnightly) are projected

SHEFFIELD 2116	SHEFFIELD POLYTECHNIC, SCHOOL OF ART AND DESIGN Brincliffe Psalter Lane Sheffield S11 8UZ	*Tel.:* Sheffield 56101

Enquiries: To Librarian

SHEFFIELD, SHEFFIELD POLYTECHNIC, SCHOOL OF ART AND DESIGN, *cont.*

Scope: History of art, painting and sculpture, architecture, graphics, photography and film, interior and industrial design, furniture, silver and jewellery, ceramics, costume and heraldry

Stock: 8,000 books and pamphlets (including 400 pre-1900); 60 current periodicals; 20,000 slides; illustrations and reproductions collection

Linked to SINTO

SHEFFIELD

2117

SHEFFIELD REGIONAL HOSPITAL BOARD *Tel.:* Sheffield 306511
Fulwood House
Old Fulwood Road
Sheffield S10 3TH

Enquiries: To Librarian

Scope: Management and administration of the Hospital Service in all its aspects, including building and architectural services, engineering, medical and supplies functions

Stock: Includes more than 100 current periodicals

SHEFFIELD

2118

THE SHEFFIELD SOCIETY OF ARCHITECTS *Tel.:* Sheffield 60069
12 Broomgrove Road
Sheffield S10 2LT

Enquiries: To Hon. Secretary

Scope: General enquiries regarding the appointment of Architects

No library

SHEFFIELD

2119

UNIVERSITY OF SHEFFIELD LIBRARY *Tel.:* Sheffield 78555
Western Bank *Telex:* 54348
Sheffield S10 2TN

Enquiries: To Librarian

Scope: The main university library covers books in the subject fields of the Faculties of Arts, Pure Science, Medicine, Law, Economic and Social Studies, Architectural Studies. The Applied Science Library covers those for the Faculties of Engineering and Metallurgy

Stock: 400,000 books; 41,000 pamphlets; 4,800 current periodicals

SHEFFIELD

2120

THE YORK AND LANCASTER REGIMENT *Tel.:* Sheffield 62734
Regimental Headquarters
Endcliffe Hall
Endcliffe Vale Road
Sheffield

Enquiries: To Curator of the Museum

Scope: Regimental history 1759 to 1968, including records of personnel who have served in the regiment and of campaigns and battles. Pictures, documents and exhibits such as medals, weapons and uniforms

SHENFIELD
Brentwood
Essex

See under **BRENTWOOD** for
ESPERANTO TEACHERS ASSOCIATION (no. 211)

SHERE
Guildford
Surrey

See under **GUILDFORD** for
NATIONAL FEDERATION OF SPIRITUAL
 HEALERS (no. 659)

SHREWSBURY Salop 2121	RADBROOK COLLEGE Shrewsbury Shropshire	*Tel.*: Shrewsbury 52686

Teacher Training College in Home Economics. Department of Institutional Management and Catering

Enquiries: To Librarian

Scope: Home economics, rural studies, theory and history of education, educational psychology, sociology, management, large scale catering, nutrition, public health and hygiene

Stock: 8,500 books and pamphlets; 94 current periodicals

SHREWSBURY Salop 2122	SALOP RECORD OFFICE Shirehall Abbey Foregate Shrewsbury Shropshire	*Tel.*: Shrewsbury 52211 ext. 407

Enquiries: To County Archivist, preferably by letter or in person

Scope: Sources of information on medicine primarily found in: Coroners' records from early 17th century for Ludlow Borough, from 18th century for County; references to individual doctors and surgeons in deeds; and references to treatment in correspondence and papers. Sources of information on social science: Quarter Sessions, Town Court, Manor court, records: Parish records, particularly Overseers of the poor; Union records, including the Unions' RSA records; police records for mid 19th century onward; school records, log books available to 1902 for closed schools; business records; manuscript medical notes of William Mason, St Thomas' Hospital, 18th century

Publications: Guide to the Shropshire Records. 1952
Shropshire Parish Documents. 1903
List of Inclosure Awards
List of Canal and Railway Plans deposited with the Clerk of the Peace
List and Partial Abstract of Contents of Quarter Sessions Rolls (2 parts)

SHREWSBURY Salop 2123	SHREWSBURY PUBLIC LIBRARY Castle Gates Shrewsbury Shropshire	*Tel.*: Shrewsbury 52255 (day); 54876 (outside office hours)

Enquiries: To Librarian and Curator

Scope: Shropshire history, and any subject approached from a Shropshire angle
Secondary: General, but strong in history and the arts

Stock: 109,000 books; 4,000 pamphlets; 6,000 manuscripts; 4,000 slides; 7,000 photographs and prints; 19,000 deeds; 300 maps; 103 current periodicals (total stock)

The museums at Clive House and Rowleys House display Roman, Prehistoric, geological, natural history, industrial archaeology and ceramic collections relating to Shropshire

SHREWSBURY Salop 2124	SHREWSBURY SCHOOL The Schools Shrewsbury Shropshire	*Tel.*: Shrewsbury 2926

School library with Ancient library of medieval manuscripts and 15th to 18th century printed books attached, belonging to the school since its foundation in 1552

SHREWSBURY, SHREWSBURY SCHOOL, *cont.*

Enquiries: To Librarian

Scope: Ancient library: Primarily of 15th century to middle of 18th century, with sections covering bibles and commentaries, theology, history, travel and geography, classical literature, classical grammars including Hebrew, science and medicine, and law
Special collections include a type series of English and Continental book-bindings 15th to 20th centuries which is particularly rich in 15th to 17th century blind-stamped bindings
Local History: Shrewsbury and Shropshire manuscripts and printed books

Stock: 7,000 (Ancient library) books. Stock not normally available on loan. Modern library of more than 20,000 books

Publications: Shrewsbury School Library Bindings—Catalogue Raisonné. J. B. Oldham
Shrewsbury School Library: its history and contents. J. B. Oldham (Transactions of the Salop Archaeological Society, vol. 51, 1943)

SHREWSBURY
Salop

2125

SHROPSHIRE ARCHAEOLOGICAL SOCIETY
Silverdale
Severn Bank
Shrewsbury
Shopshire

Tel.: Shrewsbury 3992

Enquiries: To Secretary

Scope: Archaeology and local history of Shropshire
No library

Publications: Transactions of The Shropshire Archaeological Society (annually)

SHREWSBURY
Salop

2126

SHROPSHIRE COUNTY LIBRARY
Column House
7 London Road
Shrewsbury
Shropshire

Tel.: Shrewsbury 52561
Telex: 35187

Enquiries: To Librarian

Scope: In addition to the general collection of books special attention is paid to education, local government and music
Secondary: Collection of Parochial Libraries numbering 8,000 volumes mainly of 16th–18th century works and bindings
Drama collection

Stock: 500,000 books; 3,000 pamphlets; 345 current periodicals (total stock)

Publications: Teenage Reading
The Coalbrookdale Coalfield: a catalogue of mines. I. J. Brown
Indexes to recent literature on Local Government, Education, Business Management, Farming, Horticulture
SULOP (Shropshire Union List of Periodicals)

Local history in branch libraries at Ludlow, Whitchurch, Madeley and Oswestry; the last has extensive coverage on the Welsh Marches
Shropshire Law Society Library housed at County Library Headquarters

SKIPTON
Yorkshire

2127

SKIPTON PUBLIC LIBRARY
High Street
Skipton
Yorkshire

Tel.: Skipton 3272
(Saturdays and evenings 3275)

Enquiries: To Librarian

    Scope: Special collection: The Petyt Library of 17th century history and theology
    Stock: 5,000 books and pamphlets (stock not available on loan)
  Publications: A Catalogue of the Petyt Library. 1964

SLEAFORD Lincs **2128**	KESTEVEN COUNTY LIBRARY Westholme Sleaford Lincolnshire	*Tel.:* Sleaford 2691

  Enquiries: To Librarian
    Scope: Local history collection
    National subject specialization: Anglo-Saxon language and literature (books in English only)
    Stock: 1,500 books and pamphlets on local history; 50 on Anglo-Saxon

SLEAFORD Lincs **2129**	ROYAL AIR FORCE COLLEGE Cranwell Sleaford Lincolnshire	*Tel.:* Cranwell 201

  Enquiries: To Librarian, by letter only
    Scope: Military history, particularly air power; economics, particularly economics of defence; management science and studies in leadership; history of aircraft and air warfare; history of the Royal Air Force
    Secondary: General history, geography, basic economics, political science and modern history, modern languages, basic science and mathematics, English literature
    Special Collection: Small but fairly comprehensive collection of works by or on T. E. Lawrence (Lawrence of Arabia)
    Stock: 80,000 books; 2,000 pamphlets; 250 current periodicals

SLOUGH Bucks **2130**	BRITISH ASSOCIATION OF SPORT AND MEDICINE Secretariat, Farnham Park Rehabilitation Centre Farnham Royal Slough Buckinghamshire	*Tel.:* Farnham Common 2271

    Aims to promote in all respects interest in and study of sports medicine in all its various disciplines and fields throughout Great Britain
  Enquiries: To Secretary, preferably by letter
    Scope: Sports medicine (direct contact made to specialists in the particular fields; lists of references in literature supplied)
    Stock: 50 books; 100 pamphlets; 4 current periodicals
  Publications: British Journal of Sports Medicine

SLOUGH Bucks **2131**	GLAXO RESEARCH LTD Sefton Park Stoke Poges Slough Buckinghamshire Pharmaceutical research	*Tel.:* Fulmer 2121

  Enquiries: To Librarian

SLOUGH, GLAXO RESEARCH LTD, *cont.*

Scope: Microbiology; virology; biochemistry
Secondary: Botany; chemical engineering
Stock: 1,500 books; 10,500 pamphlets; 180 current periodicals

SLOUGH Bucks **2132**	NATIONAL FOUNDATION FOR EDUCATIONAL RESEARCH IN ENGLAND AND WALES The Mere Upton Park Slough Buckinghamshire	*Tel.:* Slough 28161

Conducts and co-ordinates research relevant to the public education system in England and Wales and gives information on such research

Enquiries: To Research Officer—Information, preferably by letter

Scope: Information and consultative services, primarily for Member organizations, on educational research and testing. Library covers educational research and related subjects. It has a special collection of about 1,600 educational and psychological tests with cognitive, not clinical bias. Consultative services, by arrangement with the Research Officer—Information in the first instance. The Foundation may charge for enquiries other than those of a simple nature

Stock: 11,600 books and pamphlets; 1,600 Educational and Psychological Tests; 550 current periodicals. Admission to Library: to individuals connected with Member Organizations, by appointment and for reference only. Admission to Test Library: research workers, psychologists and others at discretion, for reference only and on written application

Publications: *Periodical and Serial Publications:*
Educational Research
Educational Research News (newsletter)
Current Researches in Education and Educational Psychology
Books and Pamphlets:
Research Reports (2nd series)
Occasional Publications (series)
Exploring Education (paperback series)
Research Pamphlets (series)
Test Catalogues:
Tests for Guidance and Assessment (N.F.E.R. Tests)
Test Agency catalogue
Information Service:
Bibliographies

SLOUGH Bucks **2133**	NICHOLAS RESEARCH INSTITUTE 225 Bath Road Slough Buckinghamshire Pharmaceutical research	*Tel.:* Slough 23971 *Telex:* 84388

Enquiries: To Information Officer, by letter and telex only

Scope: Chemistry; biochemistry; pharmacology; medicine; and pharmacy
Special collection: Material on aspirin salicylates in general

Stock: 400 pamphlets; 200 reports; 200 current periodicals; 40,000 patents; 4,000 bound volumes

SLOUGH Bucks **2134**	THE SAMARITANS 17 Uxbridge Road Slough Buckinghamshire	*Tel.:* Slough 32713

Organization to help the suicidal and despairing. Emergency listening plus referall with client's agreement and continued 'befriending' if desired

Enquiries: To General Secretary

Scope: The Samaritan service. Samaritan Branches (100 in United Kingdom). Suicide prevention service overseas. Suicide research

Publications: The Samaritans. Chad Varah, ed. (publ. Constable)

SLOUGH Bucks **2135**	SLOUGH COLLEGE OF TECHNOLOGY William Street Slough Buckinghamshire	*Tel.:* Slough 27511

Enquiries: To Librarian

Scope: Management (including marketing, purchasing, operational research). Professional and business studies (including law, banking, transport, accounting, secretarial). Catering, fashion and home economics (including hairdressing, pottery, art). General Studies (including education, languages, literature, music, physical education)

Stock: 14,000 books; 2,000 pamphlets; 200 current periodicals

SOUTH SHIELDS Co. Durham **2136**	SOUTH SHIELDS MARINE AND TECHNICAL COLLEGE Westoe South Shields Co. Durham	*Tel.:* South Shields 60403

Enquiries: To Tutor Librarian

Scope: Marine engineering; naval architecture and ship construction; navigation; seamanship; marine law; insurance and business practice; technical education
Secondary: Meteorology, oceanography, mechanical and electrical engineering

Stock: 16,500 books; 2,000 pamphlets; 200 current periodicals

SOUTHALL Middx **2137**	LONDON BOROUGH OF EALING SOUTHALL DISTRICT LIBRARY Osterley Park Road Southall Middlesex	*Tel.:* 01-574 3412 *Telex:* 262288

Enquiries: To Librarian

Scope: General coverage of medicine, social sciences and humanities
L.A.S.E.R. subject specialization: Hospital and Welfare services to special groups (300 items)
Special collection: Many examples of Martinware pottery and associated records

Stock: 25,000 books; 60 current periodicals; 3,000 gramophone records

See also no. 1326 and 1327

SOUTHAMPTON **2138**	LA SAINTE UNION COLLEGE OF EDUCATION The Avenue Southampton SO9 5HB Roman Catholic College of Education

SOUTHAMPTON, LA SAINTE UNION COLLEGE OF EDUCATION, *cont.*

Enquiries: To Librarian

Scope: Education (history; psychology; teaching methods)
General stock for college courses. Teaching practice library (books written for children and textbooks, 14,000 volumes). Catholic theology and education

Stock: 39,800 books, pamphlets and reports, including 14,000 in teaching practice library; 151 current periodicals

SOUTHAMPTON   THE PARKES LIBRARY   *Tel.:* Southampton 56331
University Library   *Telex:* 47661
2139   The University
Southampton

A library devoted to relations between Jews and non-Jews at all times and in all places

Enquiries: To Librarian

Scope: Printed books, pamphlets and ephemera dealing with: History of Jewish communities in exile; Zionism and Palestine; Middle Eastern history and Israel; Jewish society, religion and ethics; and anti-semitism

Stock: 7,000 books; 2,000 pamphlets; 85 current periodicals

Publications: Parkes Library Pamphlets (series)

Includes runs of rare periodicals and copies of ephemeral pamphlets

SOUTHAMPTON   SOCIETY FOR COMPARATIVE PHYSIOLOGY
Department of Physiology and Biochemistry
2140   Southampton University
Southampton SO9 5NH

Enquiries: To Secretary, by letter only

Scope: Comparative physiology, biochemistry and pharmacology
No library

SOUTHAMPTON   SOUTHAMPTON COLLEGE OF ART   *Tel.:* Southampton 23153
Marsh Lane
2141   Southampton SO9 4WU

Enquiries: To Librarian

Scope: Art (general): sculpture; ceramics; drawings; applied design; embroidery; clothing manufacture, textiles and dressmaking; history of fashion; interior design, furniture and cabinet making; painting; printmaking; illustration/graphic design; printing; bookbinding; private press illustrations; lettering and heraldry; painting and decorating. Illustrations collection
Secondary: Architecture, photography, film, theatre, radio, jewellery, art metalwork, window display, liberal studies

Stock: 6,000 books; 100 current periodicals; 10,000 slides. Stock not normally available on loan

SOUTHAMPTON   SOUTHAMPTON COLLEGE OF TECHNOLOGY   *Tel.:* Southampton 29381
East Park Terrace
2142   Southampton

Enquiries: To Librarian

Scope: Economics, law (particularly commercial), central and local government, further education, town planning

Secondary: Sociology, politics, librarianship
Stock: 2,500 books; 500 pamphlets; 85 current periodicals

SOUTHAMPTON

2143

SOUTHAMPTON PUBLIC LIBRARIES
Central Library
Civic Centre
Southampton SO9 4XP

Tel.: Southampton 23855
(outside normal
office hours 24014)

Enquiries: To Librarian

Scope: National subject specialization includes: Family prayers; Christian Church history
S.W.R.L.S. subject specialization includes: General economics; economic history; labour economics; economic co-operation and socialism; domestic and foreign trade; shipping economics; biographies including economists, socialists, Marxists, co-operativists, trade unionists and merchants
Special collections: Maritime collection
The Pitt collection of 1,400 volumes of 17th and 18th century scientific books
Local History collection
Containerization
Critical Path Methods

Stock: 254,000 books; 335 current periodicals (total stock)

Publications: Catalogue of the Pitt collection
HATRICS Quarterly Bulletin
Local Government Information Bulletin (quarterly)
Southampton's History: a guide to the printed resources
Select bibliographies published under the auspices of HATRICS, for example: Marketing in the Sixties

Headquarters of HATRICS (Hampshire Technical Research Industrial Commercial Service (no. 2372)

SOUTHAMPTON

2144

SOUTHAMPTON TECHNICAL COLLEGE
St Mary Street
Southampton SO9 4WX

Tel.: Southampton 26181

Enquiries: To Librarian

Scope: Education, British constitution and government, economics, languages (English, French, German), geography, history, sociology, and English literature

Stock: 3,000 books; 500 pamphlets; 55 current periodicals

SOUTHAMPTON

2145

UNIVERSITY OF SOUTHAMPTON LIBRARY
Highfield
Southampton SO9 5NH

Tel.: Southampton 56331
Telex: 47661

Enquiries: To Librarian

Scope: General collections in support of Faculty of Arts with Departments of Archaeology, Classics, English, French, Geography, German, History, Music, Philosophy, Spanish, Theology; Faculty of Social Sciences with Departments of Econometrics, Economics and Economic Theory, Economic and Social Statistics, Politics, Psychology, Sociology and Social Administration; Faculty of Law; Faculty of Medicine (*see* note below)
Special interests:
American studies, Latin American studies, Dante, history of anti-semitism, Middle East studies, criminology, international and strategic studies, demographic studies

SOUTHAMPTON, UNIVERSITY OF SOUTHAMPTON LIBRARY, *cont.*

Special collections:
The Ford Collection of Parliamentary Papers (including a bound set of Sessional Papers from 1801, statistical material and annual reports of various departments)
The Parkes Library (on relationship between Jews and non-Jews). *See* no. 2139
The Cope Collection on Hampshire and the Isle of Wight
The Perkins Agricultural Library (books on British and Irish agriculture published before 1901)

Stock: 300,000 books and pamphlets; 3,900 current periodicals (total stock)

Publications: Abstracts of Theses (annually)
Handlist of current periodicals
Library Leaflets (on various collections)

The new Faculty of Medicine is scheduled to receive its first students in October 1971. The Wessex Medical Library, a sub-library of the University Library, will also open on that date and, in co-operation with the Regional Library and Information Service of the Wessex Regional Hospital Board, offer a service to the whole region (*see also* no. 2147)

Member of HATRICS

SOUTHAMPTON

2146

UNIVERSITY OF SOUTHAMPTON
SCHOOL OF EDUCATION
The University
Southampton SO9 5NH

Tel.: Southampton 56331
ext. 483
Telex: 47661

Enquiries: To Librarian

Scope: Education and child psychology
Display collection of school textbooks
Historical collection of school textbooks in geography, history and social studies

Stock: 32,000 books, including 9,000 school textbooks; 340 current periodicals

Publications: Bibliographies on mathematics teaching and education in France

SOUTHAMPTON

2147

WESSEX REGIONAL HOSPITAL BOARD
Regional Library and Information Service
Southampton General Hospital
Tremona Road
Southampton

Tel.: Southampton 75522

Library and information service to all workers in the health sciences within the area of the Wessex Regional Hospital Board

Enquiries: To Librarian

Scope: Medicine; nursing; hospital management and design

Stock: 2,000 books; 300 pamphlets and reports; 300 current periodicals

Publications: Union List of periodicals taken by hospitals in the Wessex region

See also no. 2145

SOUTHEND-ON-SEA
Essex

2148

SOUTHEND-ON-SEA HISTORICAL SOCIETY
c/o Central Library
Victoria Avenue
Southend-on-Sea
Essex

Tel.: Southend-on-Sea
49451

Studies the history of the Rochford Hundred and examines and records all evidence of historic and prehistoric remains in the area

Enquiries: To Librarian, by letter only
Scope: History and topography of South-East Essex
Stock: 670 books; 2 current periodicals. Stock not available on loan
Publications: Transactions

SOUTHEND-ON-SEA
Essex
2149

SOUTHEND-ON-SEA PUBLIC LIBRARIES
Central Library
Victoria Avenue
Southend-on-Sea
Essex

Tel.: Southend-on-Sea 49451

Enquiries: To Librarian
Scope: Subject specialization collections include: General philosophy, cosmology and specific philosophical viewpoints; history and geography of South America; biographies of women not connected with any particular subject
Stock: 136,000 books and pamphlets; 90 current periodicals (total stock)
Publications: A History of Prittlewell
Prittlewell Priory
Guide to Prittlewell Priory and Museum
Some Literary Associations of Southend-on-Sea
Select Catalogue of the Thorpe Smith Collection illustrating the early days & development of Southend-on-Sea
Permanent Collections, Beecroft Art Gallery
Old Leigh
Southend Before the Norman Conquest
Illustrated Guide to Southchurch Hall

SOUTHPORT
Lancs
2150

SOUTHPORT PUBLIC LIBRARIES
Central Library
Lord Street
Southport
Lancashire

Tel.: Southport 5523

Enquiries: To Librarian
Scope: National Subject Specialization: Materia medica—therapeutics. N.W.R.L.S. Subject Specialization: Minor languages, and the history and criticism of their literature. Pure design. History and geography of Scotland, Iran, Iraq, Asia Minor and adjacent islands. Southport local history
Stock: 173,713 books; 100 current periodicals (total stock)
Publications: Select Bibliography of Southport Local History
A list of books on painting in the Central Reference Library

SOUTHWELL
Notts
2151

GUILD OF TEACHERS OF BACKWARD CHILDREN
Minster Chambers
Southwell
Nottinghamshire

Tel.: Southwell 3440

Enquiries: To Secretary, by letter only
Scope: Mental subnormality, educational subnormality, educational retardation
Stock: 100 books
Publications: Forward Trends (termly)

SOUTHWELL Notts 2152	SOUTHWELL MINSTER LIBRARY Southwell Nottinghamshire	

Enquiries: To Hon. Librarian, by letter and select personal enquiries only

Scope: Books mainly theology and history (particularly local history). Selected modern publications on ecclesiastical architecture and churches in local diocese and area. Chapter records and transcripts

Stock: 3,000 books; 400 pamphlets; Local diocesan and parish magazines. Stock not available on loan

SOWERBY BRIDGE Yorkshire 2153	SOWERBY BRIDGE PUBLIC LIBRARY Public Library Hollings Mill Lane Sowerby Bridge Yorkshire	*Tel.:* Halifax 31627

Enquiries: To Librarian

Scope: Local History of Halifax and district, including filmstrip and slides for loan, illustrations, prints, archives for reference
Subject specialization: Geographical statistics

Stock: 42,000 books; 1,000 pamphlets; 100 current periodicals
Member of HALDIS and Yorkshire Co-book Group

SPEKE Liverpool	*See under* **LIVERPOOL** for EVANS MEDICAL LTD (no. 863)

STAFFORD 2154	STAFFORDSHIRE COUNTY LIBRARY County Library Headquarters Friars Terrace Stafford	*Tel.:* Stafford 51733 and 52653 *Telex:* 36255

Enquiries: To Librarian

Scope: Special collections: Material on Staffordshire; Pottery and Ceramics
National Joint Fiction Reserve Scheme Responsibility: MAM–MAQ (housed at Rugeley Branch Library)

Stock: Total adult non-fiction stock in all subjects including science and technology 425,000 books and pamphlets; 150 current periodicals (not including scientific and technical)

STAFFORD 2155	WILLIAM SALT LIBRARY Eastgate Street Stafford	*Tel.:* Stafford 52276

Enquiries: To Librarian

Scope: Historical material relating to Staffordshire
Secondary: Similar material relating to other parts of England

Stock: Books, pamphlets, drawings, prints, photographs, antiquaries notes, original manuscripts and archives

The Library is run in close association with the Staffordshire Record Office and the Lichfield Joint Record Office (no. 839)

STALYBRIDGE Cheshire **2156**	ASTLEY CHEETHAM PUBLIC LIBRARY & ART GALLERY (STALYBRIDGE M.B.) Trinity Street Stalybridge Cheshire SK15 2BN	*Tel.:* 061-338 2708

Enquiries: To Librarian

Scope: General stock
Secondary: Special collection on Cheshire housed in Reference Library. N.W.R.L.S. subject specialization includes: Diseases of the body

Stock: 50,000 books (total stock; 9,000 in reference library)

STAMFORD Lincs **2157**	STAMFORD PUBLIC LIBRARY High Street Stamford Lincolnshire	*Tel.:* Stamford 3442

Enquiries: To Librarian

Scope: Local history collection. All known books and publications on Stamford are available to students on the premises
Secondary: Local archaeology; publications and a fine collection of local Stamford Ware on display

Stock: 400 books; 300 pamphlets; reports from Lincolnshire, Northamptonshire and Rutland; all archaeological periodicals

Publications: Library Story from Beginning of Service to Diamond Jubilee and Story of Stamford Pottery
The Mayor's Chain (collar of Ss and Regalia)—no. 1 in Stamford Story booklets
Archaeological report of 3 years of local digs and finds about to be published—no. 2 in above series
List of books (in date sequence) forming Local History Reference Collection

STAMFORD Lincs **2158**	STAMFORD SCHOOL BRAZENOSE LIBRARY Stamford Lincolnshire	*Tel.:* Stamford 2171

Enquiries: To Librarian

Scope: Books on topics covered by sixth form studies and works of a general nature
Special collections: Bound volumes of *Punch* from volume 1 to 1938; Local history of Stamford (Peck collection)

Stock: 6,000 books; 13 current periodicals

Publications: The Stamfordian (magazine of Stamford School, 3 issues each year)

STANSTED Essex **2159**	THE ARTHUR FINDLAY COLLEGE Stansted Hall Stansted Mountfitchet Essex	*Tel.:* Stansted 3636

College for the advancement of psychic science, and a centre for art and meditation and research work into spiritual healing under medical supervision

Enquiries: To Principal, by letter only

Scope: Spiritualism. Psychic science and research

Stock not available on loan

STAPLEFORD Cambridge	*See under* **CAMBRIDGE** for ENGLISH CROSS COUNTRY UNION (no. 285)	
STEVENAGE Herts **2160**	STEVENAGE COLLEGE OF FURTHER EDUCATION Monkswood Way Stevenage Hertfordshire	*Tel.:* Stevenage 2822

    Enquiries: To Senior Tutor Librarian

        Scope: Electrical engineering, sociology, art, mathematics, technical drawing, hairdressing, languages, workshop technology, commerce, management, education, and child care. The only specialist collection is in child care

        Stock: 11,000 books; 85 current periodicals
         Member of HERTIS

STIRLING **2161**	SCOTTISH TARTANS SOCIETY The Old Tolbooth Broad Street Stirling	

    Enquiries: To Secretary, by letter or in person

        Scope: Enquiries answered on tartans and highland dress. Extensive reference library: Books on clans, tartans, history and geography of Scotland, spinning, weaving, old and rare tartans, clan costumes, the Scottish nation, ancient Scottish weapons, piping and pipe music, Scottish songs, local history, heraldry. Relics of the Royal House of Stuart. Uniform and regimental histories. Scottish Woollens and District checks. Large selection of tartans available for inspection

        Stock: 200 books. Stock not available on loan

Publications: Proceedings (annually)   Make the Kilt your Delight
                Story of the Tartan   Highland Evening Fling

STIRLING **2162**	SCOTTISH YOUTH HOSTELS ASSOCIATION 7 Glebe Crescent Stirling	*Tel.:* OST6 2821

    Enquiries: To Secretary

        Scope: An Annual Handbook is published giving location, and matters of interest affecting all Youth Hostels in Scotland. This is supplemented by a specially printed map of Scotland showing not only these, but all areas with National Trust properties
        Secondary: Similar information is available for all countries throughout the world. Guides are produced economically and a travel service is available to members

STIRLING **2163**	SMITH ART GALLERY AND MUSEUM Albert Place Stirling	*Tel.:* Stirling 2849

    Enquiries: To Director

        Scope: Museum and Art Gallery covering art, history, archaeology, ethnology and geology
        Collections include:
        31 Stirling Heads (16th century wood carvings); Doune Pistols (18th century Scottish all metal); Stirling Jug (15th century measure); 19th century Stirling and South Perthshire domestic folk material; Local archaeology (mainly bronze age); Ethnological collection (South Africa, China, Oceania, Japan); Geology (local rocks, minerals and fossils); Water

colours (14 David Cox, 50 J. D. Harding, 1 Bonnington); Oils (studies by Sir George Harvey, 3 John Phillips, 1 Bonnington, 1 Diaz, 2 Bachuysen)

STIRLING

2164

STIRLING PUBLIC LIBRARY *Tel.*: Stirling 3969
Corn Exchange Road
Stirling

Enquiries: To Librarian

Scope: Theology (Thomson Collection)—2,650 volumes
Scottish History (including Spalding Club)—710 volumes
Local Collection
All publications of the Scottish History Society, Scottish Record Society and Scottish Text Society

Stock: 5,200 books; 175 pamphlets; 12 current periodicals

STIRLING

2165

STIRLINGSHIRE COUNTY LIBRARY *Tel.*: Stirling 3111 ext. 512, 513 and 531
Education Offices
Spittal Street
Stirling

Enquiries: To Reference Librarian

Scope: Special local collection. Inter-Regional Coverage Scheme collection on naval history

Stock: 375,261 books and pamphlets; 40 current periodicals (total stock)

Publications: Gramophone Record catalogues

STIRLING

2166

UNIVERSITY OF STIRLING LIBRARY *Tel.*: Stirling 3171
Stirling

Enquiries: To Librarian

Scope: Small collection of Napoleonic manuscripts
University microfilm project covering STC books
Secondary: Library stock covers economics, education, English studies, French, German, history, industrial science, philosophy, psychology, sociology. Special interest in developing collection of Scottish literature (100 chapbooks, set of 1st editions of Sir Walter Scott and Helen Cruickshank's library of contemporary poetry, including many autographed copies)

Stock: 65,000 books and pamphlets; 1,500 current periodicals

STOCKPORT
Cheshire

2167

STOCKPORT COLLEGE OF TECHNOLOGY *Tel.*: 061-480 7331
Wellington Road South
Stockport
Cheshire

Enquiries: To Librarian

Scope: Building, commerce, domestic studies, electrical, mechanical and production engineering, science, and art

Stock: 14,000 books; 270 current periodicals. Complete set of All-England Law Reports
Special collection: 300 folio volumes containing cloth pattern designs collected from the United States of America and European countries from 1945 to 1953

STOCKPORT
Cheshire

2168

STOCKPORT PUBLIC LIBRARIES *Tel.*: 061-480 2966 and 3038
Central Library
Wellington Road South *Telex:* 667184
Stockport
Cheshire

Enquiries: To Borough Librarian

STOCKPORT, STOCKPORT PUBLIC LIBRARIES, *cont.*

Scope: *Central Lending Library:* N.W.R.L.S. subject specialization includes: Paediatrics, child psychology and welfare
Reference Library: Stockport and Cheshire Collection
Local Government Information Service: Weekly list of selected periodical articles of technical and administrative interest

Stock: Books: 70,000 (Central Lending Library); 15,000 (Reference Library); 7,000 (local history); 1,500 pamphlets; 150 current periodicals

Publications: Handlists:
No. 1. Sets of Plays
No. 2. Stockport and Cheshire History
No. 3. Cheshire maps
No. 5. Novels in Spanish
No. 7. Children: Behaviour, Welfare and Health

STOCKPORT
Cheshire

2169

UNITED KINGDOM READING ASSOCIATION
69 Mile End Lane
Stockport
Cheshire

Association for all those interested in the teaching of reading skills at any level

Enquiries: To General Secretary, by letter only

Scope: All aspects of reading and reading problems
No library

Publications: Reading (three times each year)
Reading: Current Research and Practice. Vol. 1. 1966–67 (Proceedings of the Third Annual Conference of the Association)

STOKE
MANDEVILLE
Aylesbury
Bucks

See under **AYLESBURY** for
INTERNATIONAL MEDICAL SOCIETY OF
  PARAPLEGIA (no. 39)

STOKE-ON-TRENT
Staffs

2170

CITY OF STOKE-ON-TRENT MUSEUM & ART
  GALLERY
Broad Street
Hanley
Stoke-on-Trent
Staffordshire

Tel.: Stoke-on-Trent 22714

Enquiries: To Director

Scope: Specialist ceramic museum

Publications: Arnold Bennett's Five Towns Origins. T. Roberts
Museum Archaeological Society Reports
Guide to the Collection of English Lustre Ware
The N. Teulon-Porter Collection of Mocha Pottery
The Lightwood Hoard. A. R. Mountford and H. B. Mattingly

Two branch Museums: Ford Green Hall, Smallthorne—Folk Museum; Arnold Bennett House, Cobridge—house where Arnold Bennett lived as a young man

STOKE-ON-TRENT THE CONCOURSE LIBRARY   *Tel.:* Stoke-on-Trent 24651
Staffs   Stoke Road
     Shelton
2171   Stoke-on-Trent
     Staffordshire

     Provides college library services to the Elms Technical College and the College of Building and Commerce

Enquiries: To Librarian

Scope: General bookstock strong in law, management, accountancy and economic history

Stock: 10,000 books; 150 pamphlets; 93 current periodicals

STOKE-ON-TRENT THE NORTH STAFFORDSHIRE MEDICAL   *Tel.:* Stoke-on-Trent 44161
Staffs   INSTITUTE   ext. 4198
     (For Postgraduate Education and Research)
2172   Hartshill
     Stoke-on-Trent
     Staffordshire

Enquiries: To Librarian

Scope: General medicine, medical and surgical specialities, industrial medicine, hygiene, public health, pharmacy, dentistry, and veterinary science. Hospital management. Small section on medical history

Stock: 2,500 books; 800 pamphlets; Medical Research Council reports and special reports series; 180 current periodicals (3,000 bound volumes of periodicals)

Member of LINOSCO

STOKE-ON-TRENT NORTH STAFFORDSHIRE POLYTECHNIC   *Tel.:* Stoke-on-Trent 45531
Staffs   College Road   *Telex:* 36289
     Stoke-on-Trent
2173   Staffordshire

Enquiries: To Librarian or Director

Scope: Social sciences, including economics, law, geography, social anthropology, government, accounting, industry and trade, politics, psychology and philosophy, sociology and mathematics
Secondary: Bio-medical engineering

Stock: 4,000 books; 500 pamphlets; 150 current periodicals

STOKE-ON-TRENT NORTH STAFFORDSHIRE POLYTECHNIC   *Tel.:* Stoke-on-Trent 47159
Staffs   SCHOOL OF PRINTING AND GRAPHIC DESIGN
     College Road
2174   Stoke-on-Trent
     Staffordshire
     and
     SCHOOL OF FINE ART   *Tel.:* Stoke-on-Trent 87505
     Queen Street
     Burslem
     Stoke-on-Trent
     Staffordshire

Enquiries: To Librarian

STOKE-ON-TRENT, NORTH STAFFORDSHIRE POLYTECHNIC, SCHOOL OF PRINTING AND GRAPHIC DESIGN, *cont.*

Scope: Fine arts; graphics; industrial design; photography; cinema; printing; ceramics
Secondary: Liberal studies; philosophy; science; politics; literature

Stock: 3,500 books; 38 current periodicals

STOKE-ON-TRENT	ORNAMENTAL POTTERY ASSOCIATION	*Tel.:* 0782-48631
Staffs	Federation House	
	Station Road	
2175	Stoke-on-Trent	
	Staffordshire	
	Trade Association	

Enquiries: To Secretary

Scope: Information about ornamental pottery and sources of supply of particular types

No library

STOKE-ON-TRENT	STOKE-ON-TRENT CITY LIBRARIES	*Tel.:* Stoke-on-Trent 25108
Staffs	HORACE BARKS REFERENCE LIBRARY	and 23122
	Pall Mall	*Telex:* 36132
2176	Hanley	
	Stoke-on-Trent ST1 1HW	
	Staffordshire	

Enquiries: To Librarian

Scope: Special collections on ceramics and local history

Stock: 31,000 books; 11,000 pamphlets; 120 current periodicals (total stock)

Publications: Programmed Instruction and Teaching Machines: An Annotated Bibliography. W. E. Dodd and A. England. 2nd edition 1965 (now published by the National Centre for Programmed Learning, The University, Birmingham 15)
Staffordshire Directories: A Union List. N. Emery and D. R. Beard. 1966
Current Bibliography of Published Material relating to North Staffordshire & South Cheshire (quarterly)
William Henry Goss and Goss Heraldic China. N. Emery. 1969

STOKE POGES	*See under* **SLOUGH** for
Slough	GLAXO RESEARCH LTD (no. 2131)
Bucks	

STOKE ROCHFORD	*See under* **GRANTHAM** for
	KESTEVEN COLLEGE OF EDUCATION (no. 642)
Grantham	
Lincs	

STONE	*See under* **AYLESBURY** for
Aylesbury	ST JOHN'S HOSPITAL (no. 40)
Bucks	

STORNOWAY	STORNOWAY PUBLIC LIBRARY
Isle of Lewis	Lewis District Library
	Isle of Lewis
2177	*See* no. 456

STRATFORD- **UPON-AVON** Warwickshire	THE DUGDALE SOCIETY c/o Shakespeare's Birthplace Stratford-upon-Avon Warwickshire	*Tel.:* Stratford-upon-Avon 4016

2178

Undertakes publication of the historical records of Warwickshire

Enquiries: To Secretary and General Editor

Scope: Any subject connected with the history or historical records of Warwickshire
Secondary: Information concerning publications about the local history of the county or its sources
No library

Publications: Dugdale Society Main Records Series (from 1921, 26 volumes published to date)
Occasional Paper Series (19 published to date)

STRATFORD- **UPON-AVON** Warwickshire **2179**	SHAKESPEARE BIRTHPLACE TRUST The Shakespeare Centre Henley Street Stratford-upon-Avon Warwickshire	*Tel.:* Stratford-upon-Avon 4016

Preserves the Shakespeare properties for the benefit of the nation, promotes appreciation and study of the works of William Shakespeare and the general advancement of Shakespearian knowledge, and maintains a museum and library

Enquiries: To Director

Scope: The study of Shakespeare particularly in the theatre. English drama and English theatrical history and biography, with relevant pictorial collections. Local history, topography and genealogy
Special collections: Royal Shakespeare Theatre records including press cuttings, prompt books, photographs, music and programmes. Wheler and Saunders collections of Warwickshire documents and drawings. Bloom collection on local genealogy

Stock: 20,000 books and pamphlets; 30 current periodicals; 50,000 deeds and documents, including 6,000 manorial documents; 4,000 prints and drawings

Publications: Catalogue of the books, manuscripts, works of art, antiquities and relics exhibited in Shakespeare's Birthplace (out of print, last edition 1944; principal previous editions, 1868, 1910, 1925)
Shakespeare's Birthplace Library, English books 1529–1640 with STC references. 1955

The Shakespeare Centre library incorporates the Royal Shakespeare Theatre Library, established in 1880 as the Shakespeare Memorial Library, which amalgamated with the Shakespeare Birthplace Trust Library in 1964

STRATFORD- **UPON-AVON** Warwickshire **2180**	STRATFORD-UPON-AVON PUBLIC LIBRARY Henley Street Stratford-upon-Avon Warwickshire	*Tel.:* Stratford-upon-Avon 2209

Enquiries: To Librarian

Scope: Small local collection

Stock: 45,000 books; about 80 current periodicals (total stock)

STRETFORD Manchester	*See under* **MANCHESTER** for STRETFORD PUBLIC LIBRARIES (no. 1784) STRETFORD TECHNICAL COLLEGE (no. 1785)

STROUD Glos 2181	STROUD MUSEUM Lansdown Stroud Gloucestershire GL5 1BB	*Tel.:* Stroud 3394

Enquiries: To Curator, preferably in person

Scope: Important (though not extensive) geological and archaeological collections found locally

This museum has close ties with organizations such as Gloucestershire Society for Industrial Archaeology, Stroud Civic Society and other local societies

SUNDERLAND Co. Durham 2182	MONKWEARMOUTH COLLEGE OF FURTHER EDUCATION Swan Street Sunderland Co. Durham	*Tel.:* Sunderland 71193

Enquiries: To Librarian

Scope: Business Studies and Languages, including accountancy and secretarial. Food and Clothing Technology, including bakery, catering, clothing manufacture, demonstrating, home economics, nursery nursing, pre-nursing studies and sociology. General Studies, including English for overseas students and pre-teacher's training course. Science, including glass and plastics

Stock: 10,000 books, pamphlets and reports; 100 current periodicals

Publications: Accessions to the Library (monthly)

SUNDERLAND Co. Durham 2183	NATIONAL COUNCIL FOR CIVIC THEATRES Empire Civic Theatre High Street Sunderland Co. Durham	*Tel.:* Sunderland 73274 and 73766

Aims to promote, maintain, improve and advance Local Authorities' interest and participation in Civic Theatres and entertainment and to improve standards of theatrical performance and presentation in Civic Theatres and Halls by creating a Civic Touring Circuit

Enquiries: To General Secretary

Scope: Theatre building, administration, equipment and amenities, artistic policy and touring and creative theatre

No library

Publications: N.C.C.T. Survey 64/65
Theatre and Entertainment Facilities Directory

SUNDERLAND Co. Durham 2184	SUNDERLAND CENTRAL LIBRARY Borough Road Sunderland Co. Durham	*Tel.:* Sunderland 70417

Enquiries: To Director

Scope: General stock including medicine, social sciences and humanities

Secondary: Special collection (about 600 volumes) relating to all aspects of history and topography of Sunderland and Co. Durham

Small collection (about 70 volumes) of books (in English) on aspects of Jewish life, thought and history

Small collection (about 100 volumes) on medical subjects, for medical and nursing staff at hospitals

Stock: 70,000 books and pamphlets; 100 current periodicals (total stock)

SUNDERLAND Co. Durham **2185**	SUNDERLAND COLLEGE OF EDUCATION Langham Tower Ryhope Road Sunderland Co. Durham	*Tel.:* Sunderland 71217

Enquiries: To Librarian, by letter only

Scope: Coverage of general academic subjects to first degree level, particularly education in all its aspects. Small *special collections* on military and American history
Secondary: General collection of childrens' literature and textbooks

Stock: 26,000 books; 126 current periodicals

Member of Northern Circle of Librarians

SUNDERLAND Co. Durham **2186**	SUNDERLAND MUSEUM AND ART GALLERY Borough Road Sunderland Co. Durham	*Tel.:* Sunderland 70417

Enquiries: To Director

Scope: Information Service relating to the collections on local history, Sunderland pottery and glass, silver, coins, antiquities, natural history, oils, water colours, prints and engravings, maps and pamphlets

Publications: The Potteries of Sunderland and District. 1968
Old Sunderland Depicted in Exhibits from the Permanent Collection. 1954
Twenty-four Oil Paintings. 1954
Rhymes and Mottoes on Sunderland Pottery. 1960
Durham Cathedral: topographical prints from 16th to 20th centuries. 1969

SUNDERLAND Co. Durham **2187**	SUNDERLAND POLYTECHNIC SIR JOHN PRIESTMAN LIBRARY Green Terrace Sunderland Co. Durham	*Tel.:* Sunderland 71675 ext. 44

Enquiries: To Librarian

Scope: Psychology, sociology, politics, Company law, languages (German, French, Italian, Spanish and Russian grammars, texts and dictionaries), education (history of education, educational psychology, teaching methods, and the various subjects in the primary school curriculum, including French language and physical education), history and philosophy of science, pharmacy, business and industrial management, art, geography, history, town planning
Secondary: Communications, librarianship, public administration, social welfare, commerce, transportation, costume, archaeology, medicine, architecture, photography, music, theatre

Stock: 8,000 books; 330 pamphlets; 180 current periodicals

SUNDERLAND Co. Durham **2188**	SUNDERLAND POLYTECHNIC SCHOOL OF ART AND DESIGN Ryhope Road Sunderland Co. Durham	*Tel.:* Sunderland 5369

Enquiries: To Librarian, by letter only

SUNDERLAND, SUNDERLAND POLYTECHNIC SCHOOL OF ART AND DESIGN, *cont.*

Scope: Fine arts, history of art, photography, visual communications
Secondary: Psychology, sociology, philosophy

Stock: 7,500 books; 65 current periodicals

SUNDERLAND
Co. Durham

2189

SUNDERLAND POSTGRADUATE MEDICAL CENTRE
General Hospital
Sunderland
Co. Durham

Tel.: Sunderland 56256 ext. 344

Centre for both educational and social activities for general practitioners and hospital doctors

Enquiries: To Secretary
Scope: Small medical reference library
Stock: 250 books; 10 current periodicals

SURBITON
Surrey

2190

MINISTRY OF AGRICULTURE, FISHERIES AND FOOD
ANIMAL HEALTH DIVISION
Block B Government Buildings
Hook Rise South
Tolworth
Surbiton
Surrey

Tel.: 01-337 6611
Telex: 22203

The control of insect and rodent pests in stored products, and of injurious mammals and birds; the administration of veterinary services to farm livestock and the inspection of meat and slaughterhouses

Enquiries: To Librarian
Scope: Control of insects and rodents in stored products, and of injurious mammals and birds; and the effects of pesticides on wildlife. Veterinary science. Meat hygiene and slaughter-houses
Secondary: General biology, as related to the species covered
Stock: 4,000 books (of which 600 are held at Tangley Place, Worplesdon); pamphlets; 4,875 separates (of which 1,960 are at Worplesdon); reports; 450 current periodicals
Publications: Animal Health: a centenary, 1865–1965
State Veterinary Journal
Infestation Control: report of the Infestation Control Laboratory for 1965–67
M.A.F.F. Tech. Bull. no. 6: Common names of British insect and other pests
M.A.F.F. Tech. Bull. no. 12: Proofing of buildings against rats and mice

Forms part of the Ministry's main library. Books and periodicals are bought through the main library. They are catalogued at Tolworth and entered on a fortnightly accessions list, which also indexes relevant journal articles. There is a subsidiary library covering Land Pests and Birds at Tangley Place, Worplesdon

SURBITON
Surrey

2191

STERLING-WINTHROP GROUP LIMITED
Winthrop House
Surbiton
Surrey

Tel.: 01-546 7733
Telex: 264013

Pharmaceutical company manufacturing and selling ethical products and household medicines

Enquiries: To Technical Documentation Department

Scope: Provision of medical and pharmacological information on all aspects of the products marketed by the constituent companies. The library forms part of the Technical Documentation Department which issues periodically a full range of bibliographies and literature surveys on specific products. An extensive translation service is operated in support of the Company's operations throughout Europe. Reprint service covering selected journals is offered free to the medical profession and *bona fide* enquirers

Stock: 2,550 books; 375 current periodicals; comprehensive collection of European Pharmacopoeias

Publications: Standard medical product booklets (for the medical profession only)
Conference proceedings

SURBITON
Surrey

2192

SURREY PRODUCTION CENTRE R.E.
MAP RESEARCH AND LIBRARY GROUP
Block A Government Buildings
Hook Rise South
Tolworth
Surbiton
Surrey

Enquiries: To Chief Map Research Officer, by letter only

Scope: Libraries of maps and related material
Secondary: As the principal government collection of maps and related material, serves all official and authorized users in a wide range of map-oriented activities

Stock: 100,000 books, pamphlets and reports; 100 current periodicals; in excess of $1\frac{1}{2}$ million maps

SUTTON
Surrey

2193

THE ECONOMICS ASSOCIATION
110 Banstead Road South
Sutton
Surrey

Tel.: 01-642 4667

Enquiries: To Hon. Secretary

Scope: Economics education

Stock: 100 books; numerous pamphlets, mostly American. Stock not available on loan except to members

Publications: Teaching Economics. N. Lee, ed. 1967
Economics (journal of the Association, 3 issues each year)
Pamphlets on the teaching of economics, careers in economics and scholarships and courses
Film strips

SUTTON
Surrey

2194

INTERNATIONAL COMMISSION ON
    RADIOLOGICAL PROTECTION
Clifton Avenue
Sutton
Surrey

Tel.: 01-642 4680

Provides the fundamental principles upon which appropriate radiation protection measures can be based

Enquiries: To Secretary

No library

Publications: Recommendations of the International Commission on Radiological Protection, *Report of Committee II on Permissible Dose for Internal Radiation.* 1959
ICRP Publication 2, Pergamon Press. 1960

SUTTON, INTERNATIONAL COMMISSION ON RADIOLOGICAL PROTECTION, *cont.*

Recommendations of the International Commission on Radiological Protection, Report of Committee III on Protection Against X-rays up to Energies of 3 MeV and Beta- and Gamma-rays from Sealed Sources. 1960
ICRP Publication 3, Pergamon Press. 1960

Recommendations of the International Commission on Radiological Protection, Report of Committee IV (1953–1959) on Protection against Electromagnetic Radiation above 3 MeV and Electrons, Neutrons and Protons. Adopted 1962; with revisions adopted 1963
ICRP Publication 4, Pergamon Press. 1964

Recommendations of the International Commission on Radiological Protection, Report of Committee V on the Handling and Disposal of Radioactive Materials in Hospitals and Medical Research Establishments. 1964
ICRP Publication 5, Pergamon Press. 1965

Recommendations of the International Commission on Radiological Protection. As amended 1959 and revised 1962
ICRP Publication 6, Pergamon Press. 1964

Principles of Environmental Monitoring related to the Handling of Radioactive Materials. A Report by Committee 4 of the International Commission on Radiological Protection
ICRP Publication 7, Pergamon Press. 1966

The Evaluation of Risks from Radiation. A Report prepared for Committee 1 of the International Commission on Radiological Protection
ICRP Publication 8, Pergamon Press. 1966

Recommendations of the International Commission on Radiological Protection. Adopted September 17, 1965
ICRP Publication 9, Pergamon Press. 1966

Recommendations of the International Commission on Radiological Protection, Report of Committee 4 on Evaluation of Radiation Doses to Body Tissues from Internal Contamination due to Occupational Exposure
ICRP Publication 10, Pergamon Press. 1968

A Review of the Radiosensitivity of the Tissues in Bone. A report prepared for Committees 1 and 2 of the International Commission on Radiological Protection
ICRP Publication 11, Pergamon Press. 1968

General Principles of Monitoring for Radiation Protection of Workers. A Report by Committee 4 of the International Commission on Radiological Protection. Adopted by the Commission on May 24, 1968
ICRP Publication 12, Pergamon Press. 1969

Radiosensitivity and Spatial Distribution of Dose. Reports prepared by two Task Groups of Committee 1 of the International Commission on Radiological Protection
ICRP Publication 14, Pergamon Press. 1969

SUTTON
Surrey

2195

INTERNATIONAL LEPROSY ASSOCIATION   *Tel.:* 01-642 1656
16 Bridgefield Road
Sutton
Surrey

Aims to disseminate knowledge of leprosy and its control and to facilitate collaboration in leprosy work and research

Enquiries: To Secretary-Treasurer, by letter only

Scope: Most enquiries about any aspect of leprosy can be dealt with
No library

Publications: International Journal of Leprosy and other Mycobacterial Diseases

See also no. 993

SUTTON Surrey 2196	LONDON BOROUGH OF SUTTON PUBLIC LIBRARIES Central Library Manor Park Road Sutton Surrey	*Tel.:* 01-642 9536

Enquiries: To Librarian

Scope: Subject specialization includes:
At Wallington Public Library, Shotfield, Wallington, Surrey (*Tel.:* 01-647 4458)
Genealogy and heraldry
At Carshalton Public Library, The Square, Carshalton, Surrey (*Tel.:* 01-647 1151)
European geography and history (excluding World War II)

Stock: Wallington: 750 books and pamphlets; 9 current periodicals
Carshalton: 1,900 books and pamphlets; 3 current periodicals

SUTTON Surrey 2197	SOUTH LONDON REGIONAL BLOOD TRANSFUSION CENTRE 38 Stanley Road Sutton Surrey	*Tel.:* 01-642 8221

Enquiries: To Director, by letter only

Scope: Blood transfusion problems of any description

SUTTON COLDFIELD Warwickshire 2198	SUTTON COLDFIELD COLLEGE OF FURTHER EDUCATION Lichfield Road Sutton Coldfield Warwickshire	*Tel.:* 021-355 1081

Enquiries: To Librarian

Scope: Nursing, law, economics, education, social sciences, social studies, general and liberal studies, history, geography, literature, fine arts, fiction, current affairs, politics, government, social welfare, languages. Special emphasis is given to further education, adult education, technical colleges and social studies
Secondary: Theology, philosophy, psychology, recreation and sport
All stock at elementary levels

Stock: 6,000 books and pamphlets. Fine arts stock is in separate library and amounts to 1,000 books and pamphlets; 105 current periodicals

SWANSEA Glam 2199	GLYNN VIVIAN ART GALLERY Alexandra Road Swansea SA1 5DZ Glamorgan	*Tel.:* Swansea 55006

Collection, conservation, display, research and information in fine and applied arts, particularly the pottery and porcelain of South Wales

Enquiries: To Curator

Scope: Swansea pottery, Nantgarw porcelain, Swansea porcelain, small Welsh potteries including Llanelli; fine arts particularly South Wales artists
Secondary: British and Continental pottery and porcelain generally; English glass of all periods

Stock: 500 books; 500 pamphlets; 3 current periodicals. Stock not available on loan

SWANSEA, GLYNN VIVIAN ART GALLERY, *cont.*
Publications: Swansea and Nantgarw Porcelain from the Clyne Castle Collection
The Kildare S. Meager Bequest of Swansea Pottery
The Sir Leslie Joseph Collection of Swansea Porcelain
The British Empire Panels

SWANSEA　　　SWANSEA MEMORIAL COLLEGE　　　*Tel.:* Swansea 59260
Glam　　　　　　Swansea
　　　　　　　　Glamorgan
2200　　　　Associated Theological College of the University of Wales
　　Enquiries: To Librarian, by letter only
　　　　Scope: Theology; philosophy; church history. Special Welsh section in connection with these subjects
　　　　Stock: 10,000 books; 1,500 pamphlets; 35 current periodicals
　Publications: W. M. Llewelyn Lecture (trienially)
　　　　　　　　Periodical lectures published in booklet form

SWANSEA　　　SWANSEA PUBLIC LIBRARY　　　*Tel.:* Swansea 54065, 55521
Glam　　　　　　Alexandra Road　　　　　　　　　　　　(Reference and
　　　　　　　　Swansea　　　　　　　　　　　　　　　Information Dept)
2201　　　　Glamorgan
　　Enquiries: To Librarian
　　　　Scope: The Library and Information Service is a general one, and includes medicine, social sciences and the Humanities. *Special collections:* Welsh; Local; Dylan Thomas; Victorian fiction; Devonshire
　　　　　　　Regional subject specialization includes: Abnormal psychology; Political science; Economics
　　　　Stock: 186,000 books; 17,800 pamphlets; 540 current periodicals (total stock)

SWANSEA　　　UNIVERSITY COLLEGE OF SWANSEA LIBRARY　　　*Tel.:* Swansea 25678 ext.
Glam　　　　　　Singleton Park　　　　　　　　　　　　　　368
　　　　　　　　Swansea SA2 8PP
2202　　　　Glamorgan
　　Enquiries: To Librarian, by letter only
　　　　Scope: Humanities, economics and social sciences
　　　　Stock: 200,000 books and volumes of bound periodicals; 30,000 pamphlets; 3,000 reports; 1,550 current periodicals
　Publications: Inaugural lectures

SWINDON　　　THE COLLEGE　　　*Tel.:* Swindon 29141
Wilts　　　　　　Regent Circus
　　　　　　　　Swindon
2203　　　　Wiltshire
　　Enquiries: To Librarian
　　　　Scope: Electrical and mechanical engineering, production engineering, mathematics and science, sociology, languages and general studies, household arts, commerce, art and building. Strong on engineering subjects, management and computers
　　　　Stock: 10,000 books and pamphlets; 240 current periodicals

SWINDON
Wilts

2204

SWINDON PUBLIC LIBRARIES
Central Library
Regent Circus
Swindon
Wiltshire

Tel.: Swindon 27211

Enquiries: To Librarian

Scope: Special collections: Education (teaching techniques and history); Local collection (Swindon, North Wiltshire and adjacent county areas) S.W.R.L.S. subject specialization: Railways

Stock: 186,000 books and pamphlets; 250 current periodicals (total stock). Local collection: 5,000 books; 20 current periodicals. Education: 2,000 books, 5 current periodicals; Railways: 3,000 books, 20 current periodicals

Publications: List of yearbooks and periodicals currently taken
In Print (monthly)
Printed catalogue of Goddard Family (Swindon Manor) documents
Studies in the History of Swindon. Grinsell ed.

Headquarters of the Swindon Area Association of Libraries for Industry and Commerce (SAALIC)
Princess Margaret Hospital Medical Library (1,000 books, 65 current periodicals)

SWINTON
Manchester

See under **MANCHESTER** *for*
ECCLES AND DISTRICT HISTORY SOCIETY
(no. 1747)
SWINTON AND PENDLEBURY PUBLIC LIBRARIES
(no. 1786)

TAMWORTH
Staffs

2205

TAMWORTH COLLEGE OF FURTHER
    EDUCATION
Croft Street
Tamworth
Staffordshire

Tel.: Tamworth 2344 and 5355

Enquiries: To Principal

Scope: Adventure, art, biographies, biology, chemistry, commerce, building, cookery, dressmaking, engineering (mechanical, motor and electrical), English literature and language, fiction, flower arranging, general science, geography, history, hobbies, mathematics, mining, music, physics, radio, theatre, television, travel, works management

Stock: 10,000 books; 50 current periodicals; British Standards. Stock not available on loan

TAMWORTH
Staffs

2206

TAMWORTH PUBLIC LIBRARIES
Central Library
Corporation Street
Tamworth
Staffordshire

Tel.: Tamworth 3561

Enquiries: To Librarian

Scope: Tamworth Local History Collection: a collection of books, pamphlets, newscuttings, photographs and maps, dealing with the history of Tamworth. The collection extends to include material on the history of Staffordshire and Warwickshire but the treatment here tends to be broader and confined to books

Stock: 1,000 books; large collection of pamphlets (available on loan only in special circumstances)

TAPLOW
Maidenhead
Berks

See under **MAIDENHEAD** *for*
JOHN WYETH & BROTHER LTD (no. 1729)

TAUNTON
Somerset

2207

SOMERSET COLLEGE OF ART
Corporation Street
Taunton
Somerset

Tel.: Taunton 3451 ext. 565

Enquiries: To Librarian
Scope: Fine art; graphic design; printing
Secondary: Dress and fashion
Stock: 5,000 books and pamphlets; 70 current periodicals

TAUNTON
Somerset

2208

SOMERSET POSTGRADUATE CENTRE
Musgrove Park Hospital
Taunton
Somerset

Medical advice for all doctors in the area

Tel.: Taunton 3444 ext. 144

Enquiries: To Librarian
Scope: Medical textbooks and periodicals
Stock: 522 books; 50 pamphlets; 65 current periodicals. Stock available on loan to Doctors but not to other libraries

---

TAUNTON
Somerset

2209

SOMERSET RURAL COMMUNITY COUNCIL
St Margaret's
Hamilton Road
Taunton
Somerset

Tel.: Taunton 81222

Enquiries: To Secretary
Scope: Village halls, playing fields, music and drama (with large library of plays and some music), Old People's Welfare work (with clubs), rural industries
Stock: Plays and music scores (chiefly orchestral)
Publications: The Music Maker (quarterly)
Spotlight (annually, drama)

TAUNTON
Somerset

2210

TAUNTON PUBLIC LIBRARY
Corporation Street
Taunton
Somerset

Tel.: Taunton 84077 and 5342

Enquiries: To Librarian
Scope: Subject specialization: Furniture; decorating; flower arrangement; Islam. Taunton and Somerset local collections
Stock: 2,000 books; 5 current periodicals in these subjects

TELFORD Salop 2211	IRONBRIDGE GORGE MUSEUM TRUST LIMITED Southside Church Hill Ironbridge Telford Shropshire	*Tel.:* Ironbridge 3522

Preservation of the industrial monuments in the area and reconstruction of local life and industry of the past

Enquiries: To Manager

Scope: Visits to the Trust's museums and individual monuments in its care
Secondary: Origins of the Shropshire coal, iron and clay industries

No library

TENBURY WELLS
Worcs

2212

ST MICHAEL'S COLLEGE
Tenbury Wells
Worcestershire

Enquiries: To Hon. Librarian, by letter only

Scope: Antiquarian music, both printed and manuscript, and early books on music. No general library service, but scholars working on original material are welcome by appointment only

Stock: 1,500 music manuscripts

TILBURY
Essex

2213

THURROCK LOCAL HISTORY MUSEUM   *Tel.:* Tilbury 2612
Civic Square
Tilbury
Essex

Enquiries: To Chief Librarian and Curator

Scope: The museum includes collections of fossils; palaeolithic, neolithic and Bronze Age implements; Iron Age and pagan Saxon pottery; also pottery, glassware and coins of the Roman period, all found locally. In addition there are displays on various aspects of the social and industrial life in the district, together with many prints, pictures and maps

TOLWORTH
Surbiton
Surrey

See under **SURBITON** for
MINISTRY OF AGRICULTURE, FISHERIES AND
 FOOD, ANIMAL HEALTH DIVISION (no. 2190)
SURREY PRODUCTION CENTRE R.E., MAP
 RESEARCH AND LIBRARY GROUP (no. 2192)

TORBAY
Devon

See **TORQUAY**, Devon

TORQUAY
Devon

2214

TORBAY LIBRARY SERVICE   *Tel.:* (0803) 25211
Central Library   *Telex:* 42929
Lymington Road
Torquay
Devon

Enquiries: To Librarian

Scope: Moyse collection of 8,000 books on linguistics and literature. S.W.R.L.S. subject specialization: comparative and general linguistics. Devon and Cornwall Collection, with special emphasis on material relating to South Devon

TORQUAY, TORBAY LIBRARY SERVICE, *cont.*

Publications: The Hundred of Haytor, 1967
Supplement, including newspaper holdings, 1968. (A detailed checklist of material relating to South Devon and Torbay)

TOTNES
Devon

2215

TOTNES MUSEUM (THE ELIZABETHAN HOUSE)
70 Fore Street
Totnes
Devon

Museum of local history and crafts

Enquiries: To Secretary, by letter or in person

Scope: History of Totnes and surrounding area; old Totnes families. The Rutter library (reference books on Devon and general history). Mechanics Institute Library (1850)

Stock: 700 books; 200 pamphlets; 2 current periodicals; several boxes reports; old photographs, prints, voters' lists, posters

Publications: Leaflet about the house
Duplicated sheets on subjects of local interest

TROWBRIDGE
Wilts

2216

WILTSHIRE COUNTY LIBRARY
Cradle Bridge
Mortimer Street
Trowbridge
Wiltshire

Tel.: Trowbridge 4481
Telex: 44297

Enquiries: To County Librarian

Scope: Special collection of British Parliamentary Papers complete from January 1967, and good selection of non-Parliamentary publications

TRURO
Cornwall

2217

BISHOP PHILLPOTTS LIBRARY
Truro
Cornwall

Library for students of theology

Enquiries: To Librarian, by letter only

Scope: Ancient texts of Scripture (some 15th century) and Fathers
Secondary: Reformation and modern theology

Stock: 20,000 books; 4 current periodicals. Stock not available on loan

TRURO
Cornwall

2218

CITY OF TRURO PUBLIC LIBRARY
Pydar Street
Truro
Cornwall

Tel.: Truro 4555 ext. 23

Enquiries: To Librarian

Scope: National subject specialization: History of religion
S.W.R.L.S. subject specialization: Books about English literature; home care of children, sick, infirm, aged
Secondary: Cornish Collection (local history)

Stock: Cornish Collection: 1,000 books and pamphlets. Current periodicals taken include: Cornish Archaeology; Cornish Magazine; Old Cornwall; Cornish Link (published by the Cornish Amateur Radio Club); Cavalcade (published by the Cornwall Vintage Vehicle Society)

Local co-operation scheme on inter-library loans and Cornish bibliography
Cornwall Technical Co-operation Scheme (Union lists of Periodicals, Bibliographies, Reference books)

TRURO
Cornwall

2219

CORNWALL COUNTY LIBRARY   *Tel.:* Truro 4282
Old County Hall
Truro
Cornwall

Enquiries: To Librarian

Scope: Sociology; philosophy; local history (including Ashley Rowe Collection); geography and history of Russia and America

Stock: 10,000 books; 1,000 pamphlets

Publications: Union Lists published in conjunction with Cornwall Technical Co-operation Scheme
Subject lists issued irregularly

TRURO
Cornwall

2220

CORNWALL COUNTY RECORD OFFICE   *Tel.:* Truro 3698
County Hall
Truro
Cornwall

Enquiries: To County Archivist

Scope: Family and estate, parish and diocesan, probate and various records (not all family records, nor the records of all parishes. Diocesan records for the most part are at Exeter. Probate records (1600–1927) are for the former Archdeaconry of Cornwall, coterminous with the county, but do not include peculiars of the Bishop and Dean and Chapter of Exeter)
Reference books relating to history of Cornwall and Records

Stock: Several thousand books; several hundred pamphlets; 2 current periodicals. Stock not available on loan

Plans of the Mining Record Office of the Ministry of Power may be consulted

TRURO
Cornwall

2221

THE ROYAL INSTITUTION OF CORNWALL   *Tel.:* Truro 2205
The County Museum
River Street
Truro
Cornwall

Library in support of the Museum

Enquiries: To Curator, by letter only

Scope: Local genealogy. All aspects of the County of Cornwall. Fine arts

TRURO
Cornwall

2222

TRURO CATHEDRAL LIBRARY
Truro
Cornwall

Enquiries: To the Canon Librarian

Scope: 19th and early 20th century theology and ecclesiastical biography, and some material relating to Truro Diocese. The Doble Library: Books in English and French concerning early Celtic ecclesiastical history and legend on the saints and missionaries who, in the Dark Ages, travelled to and fro between Cornwall, Brittany, Ireland and Wales

TUNBRIDGE WELLS Kent 2223	KENT AND SUSSEX HOSPITAL MEDICAL LIBRARY (P.G.M.C.) Mount Ephraim Tunbridge Wells Kent	*Tel.:* Tunbridge Wells 20201

Medical library service for qualified hospital staff, general practitioners and the Postgraduate Medical Centre

Enquiries: To Medical Librarian, by letter only

Scope: General medicine, surgery, orthopaedics and ophthalmology, geriatrics

Stock: 260 books; 40 current periodicals. Stock not normally available on loan

TUNBRIDGE WELLS Kent 2224	PEMBURY HOSPITAL LIBRARY (Branch of Kent County Library) Pembury Tunbridge Wells Kent	*Tel.:* Pembury 2131

Enquiries: To Librarian, by letter only

Scope: General medicine
Secondary: Radiotherapy, gynaecology and obstetrics

Stock: 37 current periodicals. Stock not available on loan

TUNBRIDGE WELLS Kent 2225	TUNBRIDGE WELLS PUBLIC LIBRARY Mount Pleasant Tunbridge Wells Kent	*Tel.:* Tunbridge Wells 26121

Enquiries: To Librarian

Scope: Local collection on Tunbridge Wells and neighbourhood, mainly history and topography. Subject specialization includes: Arts and crafts in industry

Stock: 250 books and pamphlets in local collection; 72 in arts and crafts. Local collection stock not available on loan

Publications: Local History Catalogue. 1966

TUNBRIDGE WELLS Kent 2226	THE WORLD EDUCATION FELLOWSHIP 55 Upper Stone Street Tunbridge Wells Kent	*Tel.:* Tunbridge Wells 21770

Research and development of the theories and practices of progressive education

Enquiries: To General Secretary

Scope: Original records of the World Education Fellowship (formerly New Education Fellowship) are available and *bona fide* research workers on the history or development of progressive education are allowed to consult these if special permission is obtained

Publications: The New Era in Home and School (Yew Tree Cottage, Roundabouts, Five Ashes, Mayfield, Sussex)

TURTON Bolton Lancs	*See under* **BOLTON** for ST ANNE'S CHURCH TURTON (no. 180)

TWICKENHAM
Middx
 	
2227
	FEDERATION HALTEROPHILE INTERNATIONALE *Tel.*: 01-892 7019
	   (INTERNATIONAL WEIGHTLIFTING
	   FEDERATION)
	4 Godfrey Avenue
	Twickenham
	Middlesex	

The organization, control and development of weightlifting throughout the world

Enquiries: To Secretary
Scope: Weightlifting
No library
Publications: Rule book (in English and French)
Bulletin
Films of annual world championships

TWICKENHAM Middx 2228	MARIA GREY COLLEGE *Tel.*: 01-892 0031 300 St Margarets Road Twickenham Middlesex College of Education	

Enquiries: To Librarian
Scope: Any subjects relevant to education, particularly primary education. History of education. Collection of Victorian children's books
Stock: 35,000 books; 2,000 pamphlets; 200 current periodicals

TWICKENHAM Middx 2229	THE RUGBY FOOTBALL UNION Twickenham Middlesex

The promotion and furtherance of the playing of Rugby Union football in England

Enquiries: To Secretary, by letter only
Scope: Rugby Union football
No library
Publications: Illustrated History of the Rugby Football Union
Rugby Football Union Handbook
Laws of the Game with instructions to Referees and notes for guidance of Players
Why the Whistle Went   History of the Laws of Rugby Football
Rugger—How to Play the Game   The Art of Refereeing
A Guide for Coaches   Coaching Rugby Footballers
A Guide for Players   Training for Rugby Football

TWICKENHAM Middx 2230	ST MARY'S COLLEGE OF EDUCATION *Tel.*: 01-892 0051 ext. 52 Strawberry Hill Twickenham Middlesex	

Enquiries: To Librarian
Scope: Education; Childrens literature
Stock: 8,000 books; 2,000 pamphlets; 200 reports; 200 current periodicals (total stock). Stock not available on loan

TWICKENHAM Middx 2231	E. R. SQUIBB & SONS LTD Regal House Twickenham Middlesex	*Tel.:* 01-892 0164 *Telex:* 261537

Pharmaceutical manufacturing chemists

Enquiries: To Technical Services Manager

Scope: Limited to information on Squibb preparations and related subjects

TWICKENHAM Middx 2232	TWICKENHAM COLLEGE OF TECHNOLOGY Egerton Road Twickenham Middlesex	*Tel.:* 01-892 6656

Enquiries: To Librarian

Scope: Main coverage of stock is in engineering (electrical, electronic and control; automation, mechanical, and production; constructional and civil); building; printing, photography, and graphic design (including art and architecture), and in business and management (including cybernetics and economics). There are also collections in education (particularly further education), general studies, mathematics, the sciences (including geology), literature (including fiction), geography, history, and biography

Stock: 27,000 books; 1,000 pamphlets and reports; 400 current periodicals; illustrations; slides (Humanities and social sciences only: 12,000 books; 500 pamphlets and reports; 100 current periodicals; illustrations; slides)

Publications: Periodicals holdings list
List of new additions

UXBRIDGE Middx 2233	BRUNEL UNIVERSITY LIBRARY Kingston Lane Uxbridge Middlesex	*Tel.:* Uxbridge 37188

Enquiries: To University Librarian

Scope: Engineering, physics, chemistry, mathematics, education, computer science, biology, psychology, economics, social studies, cybernetics, production technology and metallurgy

Stock: 45,000 books; 1,000 pamphlets; 1,200 current periodicals

WAKEFIELD Yorkshire 2234	BRETTON HALL West Bretton Wakefield Yorkshire College of Education	*Tel.:* Bretton 261

Enquiries: To Librarian

Scope: Education, psychology, music, art, drama, sciences, English, religious education

Stock: 30,000 books and pamphlets; 200 current periodicals

Publications: Subject bibliographies (mainly for internal use)
Recent accessions lists

WAKEFIELD Yorkshire **2235**	BRITISH CHILDREN'S THEATRE ASSOCIATION County Education Offices Bond Street Wakefield Yorkshire	*Tel.:* Wakefield 75234

Aims to further education for children through drama and the arts of the theatre, to undertake and publish the results of research into methods of educating children through drama and the art of the theatre and to promote its aspects in schools, colleges, universities and Theatre Companies

Enquiries: To General Secretary, by letter only

Publications: Newsletters
Bibliography of Plays
Directory of Childrens' Theatres

WAKEFIELD Yorkshire **2236**	H.M. PRISON SERVICE STAFF COLLEGE Love Lane Wakefield Yorkshire	*Tel.:* Wakefield 71291

Lending and reference library for members of the prison service

Enquiries: To Librarian

Scope: Criminology; prison history; sociology; management; psychology; psychiatry; social welfare
Secondary: Education, physical education

Stock: 7,000 books and pamphlets; 73 current periodicals

Publications: Library Bulletin (monthly)

WAKEFIELD Yorkshire **2237**	WAKEFIELD CITY LIBRARY Central Library Drury Lane Wakefield Yorkshire	*Tel.:* Wakefield 75157

Enquiries: To Librarian

Scope: Local collection: history of Wakefield and Yorkshire
Gissing collection: works, criticism and other material on George Gissing
Green collection: art, architecture and local history
Regional subject specialization: Labour economics

Stock: 137,980 books (total stock including Local collection 2,100, Gissing collection 75, Green collection 500); 110 current periodicals

Houses the library of the Wakefield Historical Society

WAKEFIELD Yorkshire **2238**	WAKEFIELD TECHNICAL AND ART COLLEGE Margaret Street Wakefield Yorkshire	*Tel.:* Wakefield 74231

Enquiries: To Tutor Librarian

Scope: Social science, engineering, domestic science, fine arts

Stock: 9,000 books; 1,000 pamphlets; 250 current periodicals

WAKEFIELD Yorkshire 2239	WEST RIDING COUNTY LIBRARY County Library Headquarters Balne Lane Wakefield Yorkshire	*Tel.:* Wakefield 71231 *Telex:* 557330

Enquiries: To Librarian

Scope: Extensive stock of British and American books in all subjects. *Special collections:* Yorkshire collection of books, maps and other material

The County Library, in collaboration with the Doncaster Hospital Management Committee, operates the medical library at Doncaster Royal Infirmary. This serves the Doncaster Group of hospitals and general practitioners in the area (Stock: 1,000 books; 121 current periodicals) Subject specialization includes: Statistics; economics; law of contracts

Stock: 2,900,000 books; 750 current periodicals, including 40 indexes and abstracts journals (total stock)

WALLASEY Cheshire 2240	WALLASEY PUBLIC LIBRARIES Central Library Earlston Road Wallasey Cheshire	*Tel.:* 051-639 2334

Enquiries: To Librarian, by letter only

Scope: Regional subject specialization: Gynaecology; poetry, English: texts; poetry, American: texts; ethics

Stock: Gynaecology (113 books); poetry (4,460 books); ethics (350 books)

Publications: A bibliography of finely printed books of public and private presses, in stock at the Reference Library. 1969

WALLINGTON Surrey 2241	LONDON BOROUGH OF SUTTON PUBLIC LIBRARIES WALLINGTON PUBLIC LIBRARY Shotfield Wallington Surrey	*Tel.:* 01-647 4458

See no. 2196

WALLSEND Northumberland 2242	SOUTH EAST NORTHUMBERLAND TECHNICAL COLLEGE Embleton Avenue Willington Square Wallsend Northumberland	*Tel.:* Wallsend 624081

Enquiries: To Librarian

Scope: Electrical and mechanical engineering (mainly workshop practice). Small collection of British Standards in this field. Science, general commercial and secretarial subjects, economics, education, social sciences, history, geography, fine art, literature, management. Most stock is at an elementary level

Stock: 11,000 books; 98 current periodicals

WALLSEND
Northumberland

2243

WALLSEND PUBLIC LIBRARY
Central Library
Ferndale Avenue
Wallsend
Northumberland

Tel.: Wallsend 623438

Enquiries: To Librarian

Scope: General stock including reasonable coverage in social sciences, not at an advanced level

WALSALL
Staffs

2244

SOUTH STAFFORDSHIRE ARCHAEOLOGICAL
  AND HISTORICAL SOCIETY
307 Erdington Road
Aldridge
Walsall
Staffordshire

Tel.: Aldridge 52097

Enquiries: To Hon. Secretary, by letter only

Scope: Excavations and historical research in Staffordshire

Publications: Annual Volume of Transactions

WALSALL
Staffs

2245

WEST MIDLANDS COLLEGE OF EDUCATION
Gorway
Walsall
Staffordshire

Tel.: 0922 29141 ext. 15

Enquiries: To Librarian

Scope: Education and all aspects of teacher training. All subjects (except applied technology) to B.Ed. degree level. *Special collection* of children's literature (strongest on primary books) *Secondary:* Non-book materials—slides, records, teaching aids

Stock: 43,000 books and pamphlets including photocopies of educational articles; 275 current periodicals

WALTHAM CROSS
Herts

2246

CHESHUNT PUBLIC LIBRARY
Turners Hill
Cheshunt
Waltham Cross
Hertfordshire

Tel.: Waltham Cross 23582

Enquiries: To Librarian

Scope: Local collection including Cheshunt Urban District; Hertfordshire; Waltham Cross and Waltham Abbey

Stock: 1,100 books; 400 pamphlets; 5 current periodicals; 1,500 pictures

WARE
Herts

2247

ALL NATIONS MISSIONARY COLLEGE
Easneye
Ware
Hertfordshire

See no. 2063

WARE
Herts

2248

ALLEN AND HANBURYS LTD
Ware
Hertfordshire
Research and manufacturers of ethical pharmaceuticals

Tel.: Hertford 4567 and
        Ware 3232
Telex: 81144

WARE, ALLEN AND HANBURYS LTD, *cont.*

Enquiries: To Librarian

Scope: Chemistry; biochemistry; pharmacy; pharmacology; medicine; veterinary medicine; bacteriology; and toxicology

Stock: 7,500 books; 10,000 pamphlets; 275 current periodicals

Publications: Accessions list

WARE WARE COLLEGE *Tel.:* Ware 4941 ext. 23
Herts Scott's Road
 Ware
2249 Hertfordshire

Enquiries: To Librarian

Scope: Specialized collections of books and pamphlets supporting the courses run by College Departments. These are vocational courses (hairdressing, display, catering, child care, retailing, secretarial) and GCE 'O' and 'A' level courses in science and humanities subjects. There are also craft courses (bookbinding and printing for example)

Stock: 11,000 books; 500 pamphlets; 160 current periodicals: microfilm of *The Times* for 1785, 1789, 1815, 1846, 1848, 1857, 1870, 1910–1911, 1914–1918, 1931, 1938–1945

WARRINGTON PADGATE COLLEGE OF EDUCATION *Tel.:* Warrington 33571
Lancs Fearnhead
 Warrington
2250 Lancashire

Enquiries: To Librarian

Scope: The College Library provides a comprehensive selection of books to support courses in education and 16 main academic subjects up to General Degree level. It also provides a considerable range of general reference works

Stock: 50,000 books; 2,000 pamphlets; 360 current periodicals

Publications: Padgate College Studies in Education

WARRINGTON REGIMENTAL MUSEUM THE LANCASHIRE *Tel.:* Warrington 33563
Lancs   REGIMENT (P.W.V.)
 Peninsula Barracks
2251 Warrington
 Lancashire

Enquiries: To Regimental Secretary

Scope: History and Records of The Lancashire Regiment (P.W.V.), The East Lancashire Regiment and The South Lancashire Regiment (P.W.V.)

Stock: Extensive library; numerous photographs from 1860 onwards

WARRINGTON WARRINGTON PUBLIC LIBRARY *Tel.:* Warrington 31873
Lancs Museum Street
 Warrington
2252 Lancashire

Enquiries: To Librarian

Scope: N.W.R.L.S. subject specialization includes: Medical professions; study and teaching of medicine; nursing profession; medical museums and exhibits; examinations for physicians and surgeons; medical appliances; history of medicine. Antiquities and archaeology. Ancient history. The Local History Library contains an extensive collection of material on Warrington (12,000 items). Broadbent Collection of 232 early children's books

Stock: 94,000 books; 10,000 pamphlets; 300 current periodicals (total non-fiction stock)

WARWICK WARWICK COUNTY RECORD OFFICE *Tel.:* Warwick 43431 ext.
    Shire Hall   333 and 325
2253 Warwick

Enquiries: To County Archivist

Scope: *Warwickshire Manuscripts:* Quarter Sessions Records from 1625. Deposited Records, official and unofficial; Birmingham and Coventry Diocesan Records, mostly Parish Registers
Printed Works: Books: Warwickshire—General topology and Records, Particular Localities, Special Topics. General Reference—Other counties, topography, modern periodicals. Printed Maps of Warwickshire. Prints and drawings

Stock: 5,000 books; 2,000 pamphlets; 6 current periodicals

Publications: Warwick County Records. Vols. 1–9. Hearth Tax Returns, Vol. 1
The Printed Maps of Warwickshire 1576–1900. 1959
Sir William Dugdale, 1605–1686: A List of his Printed Works and of his Portraits, with Notes on his Life and the Manuscript Sources. M. D. Styles and A. Wood

WARWICK WARWICKSHIRE COUNTY LIBRARY *Tel.:* Warwick 43431
    The Butts
2254 Warwick

Enquiries: To Librarian

Scope: General stock strong in the fields of education and most art forms. Good collection on furniture and antiques. Local history collection; local government collection

Stock: 620,000 books and pamphlets; 230 current periodicals (total stock)

WATFORD BRITISH TEMPERANCE SOCIETY *Tel.:* Garston 72251
Herts Stanborough Park
    Watford
2255 Hertfordshire

Enquiries: To Secretary

Scope: Prevention of addiction to narcotics, alcohol and tobacco

Publications: Listen (monthly)
Alert (quarterly)
Many films

WATFORD CASSIO COLLEGE *Tel.:* Watford 24362
Herts Langley Road
    Watford
2256 Hertfordshire
    College of Further Education

Enquiries: To Librarian

Scope: Food industries; retailing; domestic studies; business studies; modern languages

Stock: Main Library: 14,000 books; Annexe Library: 4,500 books; 200 current periodicals

WATFORD Herts **2257**	WALL HALL COLLEGE OF EDUCATION Aldenham Watford Hertfordshire	*Tel.:* Radlett 4961 ext. 14

Local Education Authority college, and a constituent college of the Cambridge Institute of Education

Enquiries: To Librarian

Scope: Chief emphasis on developmental psychology, educational methods and philosophy, history of education, including government reports and studies, and other pamphlet material

Stock: 20,000 books (of which about 6,000 on educational/psychological subject fields); 200 reports; 100 current periodicals (of which about 50 are educational)

WATFORD Herts **2258**	WATFORD PUBLIC LIBRARIES Hempstead Road Watford Hertfordshire	*Tel.:* Watford 26239 and 26230

Enquiries: To Librarian

Scope: General stock; Local collection

Stock: 110,000 books and pamphlets; 240 current periodicals (total stock)

WEDNESBURY Staffs **2259**	WEST BROMWICH COLLEGE OF COMMERCE AND TECHNOLOGY Management Services Division Wood Green Wednesbury Staffordshire	*Tel.:* 021-569 4635

Enquiries: To Librarian

Scope: Accountancy, business law, management techniques and cases. Industrial psychology, office management and techniques, economics, economic and industrial history
Secondary: General and social history, economic geography. Foreign language literature

Stock: 18,000 books; 5,000 pamphlets; 229 current periodicals

WELLING- BOROUGH Northants **2260**	COLLET'S HOLDINGS LTD Denington Estate Wellingborough Northamptonshire	*Tel.:* Wellingborough 09333-4351

Importers and suppliers of specialized books and periodicals from the U.S.S.R. and Eastern Europe. General library suppliers and scientific publishers. Exporters of British and United States books and periodicals

Enquiries: To Import Department

Scope: No library but can provide bibliographical information on books and periodicals from Eastern Europe

WELLS Somerset **2261**	THE DEAN AND CHAPTER OF WELLS LIBRARY 8 The Liberty Wells Somerset BA5 2SU

Enquiries: To The Revd Chancellor, by letter only

Scope: The muniments and records of the Dean and Chapter, the great registers, the charters, the chapter act books, communar's accounts, and many other items of domestic importance. One special collection of interest is the collection of pamphlets in about 90 volumes, with index, made by Dean Burgon of Chichester, containing much important 19th century material
Secondary: Several thousand volumes of theology, canon and civil law, history, and the like almost all published before 1800; also works of scientific and literary interest, some of them rare and valuable

Stock not available on loan

WELLS
Somerset

2262

WELLS MUSEUM AND PLATTEN BEQUEST LIBRARY
Wells Museum
Wells
Somerset

Tel.: Wells 3477

Enquiries: To Hon. Curator, by letter only

Scope: All aspects of speleology; general and regional geology; Church history, particularly of Wells Cathedral and Diocese; archaeology and anthropology
Secondary: Natural history and botany

Stock: 2,000 books; 200 pamphlets; numerous speleological and geological periodicals; complete sets of Somerset Records Society volumes, Notes and Queries (Somerset and Dorset edition), Archaeologia, and Somerset Archaeological Society volumes

Publications: Mendip Nature Research Committee (quarterly report)
Wells Natural History and Archaeological Society Report

WELLS
Somerset

2263

WELLS THEOLOGICAL COLLEGE
Wells
Somerset BA5 2UP
Training for the Anglican Ministry

Tel.: Wells 3209

Enquiries: To Librarian, by letter only

Scope: Most fields of theology, both academic and pastoral

Stock: 11,000 books; 24 current periodicals. Stock not available on loan

WELWYN GARDEN CITY
Herts

2264

QUEEN ELIZABETH II HOSPITAL
Howlands
Welwyn Garden City
Hertfordshire

Tel.: Welwyn Garden 28111 ext. 295

Enquiries: To Librarian

Scope: Medical and professional library serving all hospital staff, medical, nursing, technical and administrative and General Practitioners and Health Department Staff in the area. Literature searches undertaken

Stock: 2,000 books; 64 current periodicals
Affiliated to Hertfordshire County Library (no. 709)

WELWYN GARDEN CITY
Herts

2265

ROCHE PRODUCTS LTD
Broadwater Road
Welwyn Garden City
Hertfordshire
Manufacturing chemists

Tel.: Welwyn Garden 28128

WELWYN GARDEN CITY, ROCHE PRODUCTS LTD, *cont.*

Enquiries: To Director of Research (technical enquiries) or Librarian, by letter only

Scope: Organic and physical chemistry, biochemistry, pharmacology, medicine, veterinary medicine

Stock: 5,200 books; 280 current periodicals

Publications: *Occasional booklets*, for example:
Aspects of Alcoholism
Pathophysiology of the Emotions
Neurophysiological and Pharmacological Aspects of Mental Illness
List of journal holdings
Chemical Aspects of Mental Illness
Famous People and their Illnesses

Member of HERTIS

WELWYN GARDEN CITY Herts

2266

SMITH KLINE & FRENCH LABORATORIES LTD
Mundells
Welwyn Garden City
Hertfordshire

Tel.: Welwyn Garden 25111
Telex: 261347

The research and development of pharmaceutical and veterinary products and medical instruments

Enquiries: To Librarian

Scope: Chemistry, particularly organic and analytical; biochemistry; medicine, with emphasis on drug literature; pharmacology and therapeutics; veterinary medicine

Stock: 3,750 books; 600 pamphlets; 400 current periodicals

Member of HASL

WEMBLEY Middx

2267

HOTEL AND CATERING INDUSTRY TRAINING BOARD
Ramsey House
Central Square
Wembley
Middlesex

Tel.: 01-902 8865

To help the industry to provide the right quality of training; ensure sufficient trained staff at all levels; to spread the cost of training more evenly among employers

Enquiries: To Librarian

Scope: Training, catering

Small library at present

WEMBLEY Middx

2268

ROUSSEL LABORATORIES LTD
Columbus House
Wembley Park
Middlesex

Tel.: 01-902 9701
Telex: 23126

Pharmaceutical manufacturers

Enquiries: To Medical Advisers

Scope: Antibiotics, hormones, hypnotics, steroids
Medical enquiries not accepted from laymen

Stock: 200 books; 86,000 reprints; 110 current periodicals

WEST BRETTON Wakefield Yorkshire

See under **WAKEFIELD** for BRETTON HALL (no. 2234)

WEST BROMWICH
Staffs

2269

WEST BROMWICH PUBLIC LIBRARIES
Central Library
High Street
West Bromwich
Staffordshire

Tel.: 021-569 2416
Telex: 338392

Enquiries: To Librarian
Scope: All aspects of commerce, the social sciences, the humanities and the sciences, pure and applied and includes directories, yearbooks, telephone directories, British maps, town guides, newspapers and periodicals
Stock: 250,000 books and pamphlets; 270 current periodicals (total stock)
Publications: Monthly list of additions
Member of WESLIB

WEST CALDER
Midlothian

2270

SCOTTISH NATIONAL PARTY
Publications and Research Departments
100 Main Street
West Calder
Midlothian

See no. 623

WEST DRAYTON
Middx

2271

LONDON BOROUGH OF HILLINGDON
Library Headquarters
Drayton Hall
West Drayton
Middlesex

Tel.: West Drayton 2275

Enquiries: To Librarian
Scope: All subjects at all levels
Stock: 320,000 books and pamphlets; 250 current periodicals

WEST WICKHAM
Kent

2272

COLOMA COLLEGE OF EDUCATION
Wickham Court
West Wickham
Kent

Tel.: 01-777 8321

Roman Catholic training college for women
Enquiries: To Principal, by letter only
Scope: Education, history and methods. Teaching methods and textbooks in most school subjects. Academic subjects, with special section on Roman Catholic religion. General coverage of most subjects in social sciences and humanities (not medicine) but with special emphasis on education (particularly primary school education), sociology and psychology
Stock: 20,000 books; 101 current periodicals. Stock not available on loan

WESTCLIFF-ON-SEA
Essex

2273

THE SIR THOMAS BEECHAM SOCIETY
46 Wellington Avenue
Westcliff-on-Sea
Essex

Aims to honour and preserve the name and work of Sir Thomas Beecham
Enquiries: To Hon. Chairman

WESTCLIFF-ON-SEA, THE SIR THOMAS BEECHAM SOCIETY, *cont.*

Scope: Library of books, programmes and photographs available on loan to members and interested parties

Publications: Le Grand Baton (quarterly)
Newsletter (bi-monthly)

WESTON-SUPER-MARE
Somerset

2274

WESTON-SUPER-MARE PUBLIC LIBRARY AND MUSEUM
Boulevard
Weston-super-Mare
Somerset

Tel.: Weston-super-Mare 24133

Enquiries: To Librarian

Scope: National subject specialization: Parish work; general Church history
S.W.R.L.S. subject specialization: Welfare services to special classes; education of special classes. Local history: Extensive collection of books, pamphlets, cuttings, photographs and tape recordings

Stock: 45,000 books (total non-fiction stock); many pamphlets on local topics; current periodicals include local parish magazines

WEYBRIDGE
Surrey

2275

COMMONWEALTH BUREAU OF ANIMAL HEALTH
Central Veterinary Laboratory
New Haw
Weybridge
Surrey

Tel.: Byfleet 42826

Collection and dissemination of information on animal diseases, with particular reference to research

Enquiries: To Director

Joint library with Central Veterinary Laboratory, Ministry of Agriculture, Fisheries and Food (no. 2276)

Publications: Veterinary Bulletin (monthly abstracting journal)
Index Veterinarius (quarterly list of titles)
Review series
Technical Communications

WEYBRIDGE
Surrey

2276

MINISTRY OF AGRICULTURE, FISHERIES AND FOOD
Central Veterinary Laboratory
New Haw
Weybridge
Surrey

Tel.: Byfleet 41111
Telex: 262318

Investigation and control of diseases of farm animals

Enquiries: To Librarian

Scope: Diseases of farm animals

Stock: 35,000 books, pamphlets, reports and bound volumes of periodicals; 570 current periodicals
This library is a joint library of the Central Veterinary Laboratory and the Commonwealth Bureau of Animal Health (no. 2275). There are branch libraries at Lasswade (no. 791) and the Cattle Breeding Centre, Shinfield, Reading, Berkshire

WEYBRIDGE Surrey 2277	WEYBRIDGE MUSEUM Church Street Weybridge Surrey	*Tel.:* Weybridge 43573

To collect, conserve, and present to the public the local archaeology and history of the Walton and Weybridge District of North-West Surrey

Enquiries: To Curator

Scope: The museum covers the Walton and Weybridge district of North-West Surrey and holds local archaeological and historical specimens and a fairly comprehensive collection of local water-colours and oil paintings. Only a selection of the collection is on display at any time but reserve material can be seen by researchers. Copies of historical maps can be seen on request

Secondary: Files of information are held on local houses, estates, and notable people. Much of this information has been gathered from the Public and County Record Offices and from other institutions. No original documents held

Publications: Various booklets on local history:
Oatlands Palace   Walton Bridge
Weybridge & The Locke Kings   A Dictionary of Local History

The Museum is willing to help school children and students with research projects in any subject covered by the local history of the district

WEYMOUTH Dorset 2278	WEYMOUTH AND MELCOMBE REGIS PUBLIC LIBRARY SERVICE Central Public Library Westway Road Weymouth Dorset	*Tel.:* Weymouth 6498

Enquiries: To Librarian

Scope: S.W.R.L.S. subject specialization includes: Ecclesiology, symbolism, religious art; sacred furniture, vestments, vessels, ornaments. Geography and history of Iceland, Faroe Islands, Netherlands, Belgium, Luxemburg, Switzerland, Byzantine Empire, Modern Greece, Turkey in Europe, Balkan States, Yugoslavia, Serbia, Bulgaria, Rumania, Greek Islands
Special collection on Dorset (all aspects)

Stock: Dorset Collection: 1,700 books; 1,300 pamphlets

WEYMOUTH Dorset 2279	WEYMOUTH COLLEGE OF EDUCATION Dorchester Road Weymouth Dorset	*Tel.:* Weymouth 2131

Enquiries: To Tutor Librarian

Scope: Education (philosophy, sociology, psychology, history, curriculum of primary and secondary schools)
Secondary: Sociology, philosophy, linguistics, English, French and Ameaican literature, divinity, history (including archaeology). Children's books

Stock: 24,000 books and pamphlets; 162 current periodicals

WHEATHAMP- **STEAD** St Albans Herts	See under **ST ALBANS** for ABORTION LAW REFORM ASSOCIATION (no. 2064(

WHITEHAVEN Cumberland 2280	WEST CUMBERLAND COLLEGE OF SCIENCE AND TECHNOLOGY WHITEHAVEN DIVISION Platt Walks Whitehaven Cumberland	*Tel.:* Whitehaven 2261

    Enquiries: To Tutor Librarian
        Scope: Dressmaking, embroidery, cooking and catering, nursing, sociology, art and careers
        Stock: 1,000 books; 500 pamphlets; 20 current periodicals

WHITEHAVEN Cumberland 2281	WHITEHAVEN PUBLIC LIBRARY Catherine Street Whitehaven Cumberland	*Tel.:* 0946-2664

    Enquiries: To Librarian
        Scope: General stock. Local collection relating to Cumberland and Westmorland
        Stock: 70,000 books; 500 pamphlets; 50 current periodicals (total stock). 2,200 books in local collection. File of local newspapers commencing 1774
   Publications: Whitehaven, a short history. D. Hay. 1968

WHITHORN Newton Stewart Wigtownshire	*See under* **NEWTON STEWART** for THE INDIVIDUAL POSTAL TUITION SERVICE (no. 1862)

WHITLEY BAY Northumberland 2282	BOROUGH OF WHITLEY BAY CENTRAL LIBRARY Park Road Whitley Bay Northumberland	*Tel.:* Whitley Bay 25209

    Enquiries: To Librarian
        Scope: Enquiries of a local character answered from local reference collection, and maintains a file of local organizations and a diary of events
        Stock: 2,000 books

WHITSTABLE Kent 2283	INDEPENDENT SCHOOLS ASSOCIATION INCORPORATED 49 Gordon Road Whitstable Kent	*Tel.:* Whitstable 4713

    Enquiries: To Secretary, by letter only
        Scope: Information about independent schools
   Publications: The Independent Schools Association Magazine (termly)
                 The I.S.A.I. Schools Year-Book

WIDNES Lancs 2284	WIDNES PUBLIC LIBRARY Victoria Road Widnes Lancashire	*Tel.:* 051-424 2061 (051-424 4482 after office hours and on Saturdays)

    Enquiries: To Librarian

Scope: Subject specialization: Human physiology—reproduction
Stock: 300 books and pamphlets

WIGAN ASHTON-IN-MAKERFIELD PUBLIC LIBRARY *Tel.:* Ashton-in-Makerfield
Lancs Wigan Road 77119
  Ashton-in-Makerfield
2285 Wigan
  Lancashire
Enquiries: To Librarian
Scope: N.W.R.L.S. subject specialization includes: Massage; travel and history of Spain and Portugal
Stock: Small collection of books

WIGAN WIGAN PUBLIC LIBRARIES *Tel.:* Wigan 41387
Lancs Central Library
  Rodney Street
2286 Wigan
  Lancashire
Enquiries: To Librarian or Director
Scope: Stock includes: Fine Arts; Lancashire and Wigan Collection; Edward Hall Diary Collection (in Record Office, part of Central Library)
Stock: 198,341 books; pamphlets; 355 current periodicals (total stock)

WILMSLOW CARPET INDUSTRY TRAINING BOARD *Tel.:* Wilmslow 27118
Cheshire Evelyn House
  32 Alderley Road
2287 Wilmslow
  Cheshire
Enquiries: To Secretary
Scope: Training in the carpet industry
Publications: Training Recommendations Operatives
  Guide to Grant Scheme
  Guide to Induction Training
  Basic Handbook for Instructors
  Half Day Course on Safety for Juveniles
  Guide to Recruitment and Selection for Manual Jobs
  Training Recommendations Managers and Supervisors
  Training Recommendations Clerical and Commercial Occupations
  Training Recommendations for Professional, Commercial and Administrative Trainees
  Guide to Group Training Schemes
  Report of Working Conference on Industrial Safety. April 1969

WIMBORNE CANFORD SCHOOL *Tel.:* Wimborne 2411
Dorset Wimborne
  Dorset
2288 *Enquiries:* To Headmaster, by letter or in person
  Scope: General academic library including the former special library of the Guest family, with a section on local history of Dorset

WIMBORNE, CANFORD SCHOOL, *cont.*

Stock: 10,000 books; 12 current periodicals (current affairs, art and architecture). Stock not available on loan

Publications: The Canfordian (school magazine, literary and information)

WINCHESTER Hants **2289**	HAMPSHIRE COUNTY LIBRARY 81 North Walls Winchester Hampshire	*Tel.:* Winchester 3301

Enquiries: To Librarian

Scope: Subject specialization: Law; public administration (central and local government); devotional; the Bible; history and geography of Germany; history of world wars; town planning; public health
Special collection of organ music

Stock: 533,000 books (total non-fiction stock); 440 current periodicals

Publications: Bibliography relating to organ music

The collection of organ music originated with the donation, by Sir Humphrey Prideaux Brune, of the entire collection which he had acquired over the years. It is now housed at County Library Headquarters

WINCHESTER Hants **2290**	KING ALFRED'S COLLEGE Sparkford Road Winchester Hampshire College of Education	*Tel.:* Winchester 62281

Enquiries: To Tutor Librarian

Scope: Education; educational psychology; general psychology; sociology; welfare services for children; teacher training
Secondary: Main subjects of academic courses: English, history, geography, music, art and craft, handicraft, physics, chemistry, biology, divinity, French, physical education, drama, mathematics. *Special collections:* History of education; local history

Stock: 50,000 books; 2,000 pamphlets; 240 current periodicals

WINCHESTER Hants **2291**	THOROLD AND LYTTELTON LIBRARY The Basement 11 The Close Winchester Hampshire Library for incumbents in the Dioceses of Winchester, Guildford and Portsmouth

Enquiries: To Librarian, by letter only

Scope: Theology
Secondary: Classical studies, history

Stock: 10,000 books; various theological periodicals. Stock not normally available on loan

WINCHESTER Hants **2292**	WINCHESTER CITY LIBRARY Jewry Street Winchester Hampshire	*Tel.:* Winchester 3909

Enquiries: To Librarian

Scope: Local history
Subject specialization: Geography and history of Great Britain

Stock: 80,000 books; 100 current periodicals; 2,000 photographs; Local press-cuttings (total stock)

WINCHESTER WINCHESTER CITY MUSEUMS *Tel.:* Winchester 3361
Hants The City Museum
  The Square
2293 Winchester
  Hampshire

Administration of the City Museum and the Westgate Museum, Winchester. The Museums specialize in the archaeology, history and geology of Winchester and central Hampshire. The library of the City Museum is for the use of the staff, and it is not open to the general public

Enquiries: To Curator, by letter only

Scope: The scope of the City Museum Library is as follows: Archaeology (mainly British), Hampshire (including Hampshire archaeology). Publications of other museums and museum organizations. Catalogues of other museums. Numismatics. Periodicals (including publications of national societies concerned with archaeology). Botany; geology; zoology; City of Winchester

Stock: 1,500 books; 16 current periodicals

WINDLESHAM LILLY RESEARCH CENTRE LIMITED *Tel.:* Bagshot 3631
Surrey Erl Wood Manor *Telex:* 85177
  Windlesham
2294 Surrey

Enquiries: To Librarian, by letter only

Scope: Organic, analytical and pharmaceutical chemistry. Biology, parasitology, pharmacology, bacteriology and chemotherapy

Library stock not available on loan

WINDSOR ETON COLLEGE *Tel.:* Windsor 66438 and
Berks The Provost & Fellows Library 68635
  Windsor
2295 Berkshire

Enquiries: To Keeper of College Library and Collections, Penzance, Eton College, by letter only

Scope: General, for a working College Library of 18th century. Subsequent additions mainly in bibliography, history, literature and theology
Special collections: Western and Oriental manuscripts; incunabula; Aldines; Elzeviers; 17th century pamphlets; pre-Restoration plays; fine bindings; modern presses; fore-edge paintings

Stock: 25,000 books; manuscripts and archives

The collections include also pictures and silver

WINDSOR HOUSEHOLD CAVALRY MUSEUM *Tel.:* Windsor 61391 ext. 30
Berks Combermere Barracks
  Windsor
2296 Berkshire

Enquiries: To Curator

Scope: Displays relics of Household Cavalry History (1660 to present day). Officers Service details 1st Life Guards, 2nd Life Guards and Royal Horse Guards (1780–1945). Orders; War Diaries;

WINDSOR, HOUSEHOLD CAVALRY MUSEUM, *cont.*

Regimental records of the Life Guards (1780 to 1945). Fragmentary records of The Royal Dragoons (1st Dragoons)

Stock: 1,000 manuscript and 1,000 printed books. Stock not available on loan but may be used on written application

WIRRAL
Cheshire

2297

BEBINGTON PUBLIC LIBRARIES
Mayer Public Library
Bebington
Wirral L63 7PN
Cheshire

Tel.: 051-645 3089 and 2080

Enquiries: To Librarian

Scope: Special collections include: Local history; floriculture; landscape art

Stock: 1,400 books; 250 pamphlets; 11 current periodicals

WIRRAL
Cheshire

2298

ELLESMERE PORT CORPORATION
CENTRAL LIBRARY
Civic Way
Ellesmere Port
Wirral
Cheshire

Tel.: 051-355 1332

Enquiries: To Librarian

Scope: Local history of Merseyside and Cheshire, particularly the borough of Ellesmere Port

Stock: 2,000 books; 500 pamphlets; 700 photographs; 14 current periodicals

WIRRAL
Cheshire

2299

HOYLAKE HISTORICAL SOCIETY
66 Manor Road
Hoylake
Wirral L47 3DF
Cheshire

Tel.: 051-632 4490

Enquiries: To Hon. Secretary

Scope: Local history of the Hoylake area

Stock: Several hundreds of volumes

Small permanent exhibition at Sandlea House, West Kirby

WIRRAL
Cheshire

2300

WEST CHESHIRE CENTRAL COLLEGE OF
 FURTHER EDUCATION
Carlett Park
Eastham
Wirral
Cheshire

Tel.: Eastham 1253

Enquiries: To Tutor Librarian

Scope: Only in management, economics and geography are stocks likely to be more comprehensive than those available in the local public libraries

Stock: 4,000 books; 500 pamphlets; 90 current periodicals (in subjects covered by this volume of the Directory)

WOKING Surrey 2301	ANIMAL VIRUS RESEARCH INSTITUTE Pirbright Woking Surrey	*Tel.:* Worplesdon 2441

      Enquiries: To Director

          Scope: Virology, particularly foot and mouth disease
                Secondary: Biochemistry, bacteriology

          Stock: 800 books; 50 reports; 90 current periodicals

Publications: Lists of reprints

WOKING Surrey 2302	THE DALCROZE SOCIETY (INCORPORATED) Redcourt Blackdown Avenue Pyrford Woking Surrey	

      Enquiries: To Secretary, 16 Heathcroft, Hampstead Way, London N.W.11 (*Tel.:* 01-455 1268)

          Scope: Dalcroze eurhythmics
                Secondary: Music and movement

            No library

Publications: Rhythm Music and Education. E. Jaques-Dalcroze
                      Eurhythmics Art and Education. E. Jaques-Dalcroze
                      Pathway to Eurhythmics. E. Driver
                      Dalcroze Eurhythmics—What is Eurhythmics? F. Martin

WOLVER- HAMPTON Staffs 2303	THE 'EXPRESS & STAR' LIBRARY 51/53 Queen Street Wolverhampton Staffordshire	*Tel.:* Wolverhampton 22351

      Enquiries: To Librarian

          Scope: Files of the *Wolverhampton Chronicle* from 1789 and of the *Express and Star* from 1884. Cuttings library set up in 1934 covers most subjects in the circulation areas of the papers, which is roughly that of the Black Country
                Secondary: Local history; municipal and industrial pamphlets

          Stock: 9,000 books and pamphlets; 500,000 cuttings; standard reference books
              Library open to the public on Saturday mornings only. Stock not available on loan

WOLVER- HAMPTON Staffs 2304	WOLVERHAMPTON PUBLIC LIBRARIES Central Library Snow Hill Wolverhampton Staffordshire	*Tel.:* Wolverhampton 20109 and 26988

      Enquiries: To Chief Librarian

          Scope: General stock including music, gramophone record collection. Local history collection, including cuttings. Books in Hindi, Punjabi, and Urdu

          Stock: 218 current periodicals

WOLVER-HAMPTON Staffs 2305	WOLVERHAMPTON TEACHERS' COLLEGE FOR DAY STUDENTS Walsall Street Wolverhampton Staffordshire College of Education for mature day students	*Tel.:* Wolverhampton 24420

Enquiries: To Principal

Scope: Education, particularly at the primary level. Educational psychology, sociology, history. Children's literature (embryonic collection of Victorian children's literature)
Secondary: General, for example, geography, mathematics, history

Stock: 27,000 books and pamphlets; 110 current periodicals

Publications: Bibliographies and booklists with particular reference to teaching, for example: Teaching of English to immigrant children, History of Education; and Historical fiction for juniors

WOLVER-HAMPTON Staffs 2306	WOLVERHAMPTON TECHNICAL TEACHERS COLLEGE Compton Road West Wolverhampton Staffordshire	*Tel.:* Wolverhampton 24286

Enquiries: To Librarian, by letter or appointment only

Scope: Education (theory and method); educational technology; industrial training; psychology; sociology
Secondary: Agriculture, business studies, engineering, general studies, horticulture, mathematics, science. The emphasis is on Teaching Method in the subsidiary subjects. Collection of reports from agricultural and horticultural research stations, dating from 1963

Stock: 10,000 books; 7,000 pamphlets; 50 reports; 200 current periodicals

WOLVER-HAMPTON Staffs 2307	WULFRUN COLLEGE OF FURTHER EDUCATION Paget Road Wolverhampton Staffordshire	*Tel.:* Wolverhampton 26512 ext. 16

Enquiries: To Tutor Librarian

Scope: Central and local governments, law, politics, nursing, economic history, Shakespeare, modern literature, educational topics, pharmacy, history, geography, business studies, management

Stock: 18,000 books; 1,000 pamphlets; 150 current periodicals; All England Law Reports

WOLVERTON Bucks 2308	WOLVERTON COLLEGE OF FURTHER EDUCATION Stratford Road Wolverton Buckinghamshire *and*	*Tel.:* Wolverton 3339
	WOLVERTON COLLEGE OF FURTHER EDUCATION BUSINESS STUDIES DEPARTMENT Westfield Road Bletchley Buckinghamshire	*Tel.:* Bletchley 2199

Enquiries: To Librarian, by letter only

Scope: At Wolverton: Mechanics, engineering science and electrical engineering to ONC level with restricted coverage to HNC level. Limited stock on automobile engineering and carpentry
At Business Studies Department at Bletchley: Commerce, social sciences, economics, business management and related subjects to OND level. Limited stock in history and geography to GCE 'O' level

Stock: 12,000 books; 500 pamphlets; 90 current periodicals

WORCESTER	ELGAR BIRTHPLACE MUSEUM Broadheath	*Tel.:* Cotheridge 224
2309	Worcester	

See no. 1124

WORCESTER	KING'S SCHOOL
	Worcester
2310	

Enquiries: To Librarian, by letter only
Scope: Library includes some fairly rare books on the topography of Worcester
Stock: 7,000 books (total stock)
Publications: The Vigornian

WORCESTER	WORCESTER CITY LIBRARY Foregate Street	*Tel.:* Worcester 22154
2311	Worcester	

Enquiries: To Librarian
Scope: Worcestershire Local Collection
Grainger: Stuart Collection (covers reigns of Stuart monarchs)
J. W. Willis Bond Collection (archaeology)
Stock: 104,500 books and pamphlets; 157 current periodicals (total stock)
Local collection items available on loan only if duplicate copies are held
Publications: Worcestershire Archaeological Newsletter
Periodicals Index (annually)

WORCESTER	WORCESTER COLLEGE OF EDUCATION Henwick Grove	*Tel.:* Worcester 25731 ext. 34
2312	Worcester	

Enquiries: To Librarian, by letter only
Scope: Social sciences, mainly education and sociology
Humanities, mainly English literature, art and history
Secondary: Small collection of works by Worcester and Worcestershire writers
Stock: 42,000 books, including teaching practice books (10,000 on subjects above); 5,000 pamphlets (300 on subjects above); 360 current periodicals (80 on subjects above)

WORCESTER	WORCESTERSHIRE COUNTY LIBRARY Loves Grove	*Tel.:* Worcester 23400 (23108 Saturdays only)
2313	Castle Street Worcester	

Enquiries: To Librarian
Scope: Special collections: Books relating to all aspects of Worcestershire. Collection of sets of plays. Orchestral library (sets). Choral library (sets)

WORCESTER, WORCESTERSHIRE COUNTY LIBRARY, *cont.*

Publications: Choral Library Catalogue
Orchestral Library Catalogue

WORCESTER　　WORCESTERSHIRE RECORD OFFICE　　*Tel.:* 090-5 23400
　　　　　　　　Shirehall
2314　　　　 Worcester

Enquiries: To County Archivist

Scope: Worcestershire history, as revealed by original archives and records, backed up by a fairly extensive library of reference books
Palaeography and archive administration are main topics, subordinate to Worcestershire
Secondary: General library. Short enquiries are dealt with; long and protracted searches must be done personally

Stock: 20,000 books and pamphlets; 5 current periodicals

WORCESTER　　THE WORCESTERSHIRE REGIMENTAL MUSEUM　　*Tel.:* Worcester 24301
　　　　　　　　Norton Barracks
2315　　　　 Worcester

Enquiries: To Lieut. Colonel J. D. Ricketts, by letter only

Scope: Uniforms, equipment and medals of members of The Worcestershire Regiment. History of the 29th Foot, 36th Foot, later The Worcestershire Regiment

Stock: 200 books; 100 pamphlets. Stock not available on loan

Publications: Firm (The Worcestershire Regimental Magazine)

WORKINGTON　　WEST CUMBERLAND COLLEGE OF SCIENCE　　*Tel.:* Workington 3527
Cumberland　　　　AND TECHNOLOGY
　　　　　　　　WORKINGTON DIVISION
2316　　　　 Park Lane
　　　　　　　　Workington
　　　　　　　　Cumberland

Enquiries: To Tutor Librarian

Scope: Law, business, management studies, education, catering
Special collection: All England Law Reports

Stock: 2,300 books; 300 pamphlets; 50 current periodicals

Publications: Scope (careers and college information magazine distributed free each term to 2,000 local school-leavers)

WORKINGTON　　WORKINGTON PUBLIC LIBRARY　　*Tel.:* Workington 3744
Cumberland　　　　Finkle Street
　　　　　　　　Workington
2317　　　　 Cumberland

Enquiries: To Librarian

Scope: Local history collection

WORKSOP　　NORTH NOTTS COLLEGE OF FURTHER　　*Tel.:* Worksop 3561
Notts　　　　　　EDUCATION
　　　　　　　　Carlton Road
2318　　　　 Worksop
　　　　　　　　Nottinghamshire

Enquiries: To Librarian

Scope: Books covering complete subject range
Special interests: Education, including further education and adult education; industrial training
Stock: 15,000 books and pamphlets; 150 current periodicals
Publications: Monthly Index of Articles in Education Periodicals
The Metric and Decimal Systems: bibliography (revised twice yearly)

WORKSOP   WORKSOP PUBLIC LIBRARY AND MUSEUM   *Tel.:* Worksop 2408
Notts   Memorial Avenue
     Worksop
2319   Nottinghamshire

Enquiries: To Librarian
Scope: General stock. Local history collection, relating to Worksop and Nottinghamshire
Stock: 66,000 books; 70 current periodicals (total stock)

A small museum concentrates on local archaeology and history, and on local natural history

WORTHING   BEECHAM RESEARCH LABORATORIES   *Tel.:* Worthing 39900
Sussex   Clarendon Road   *Telex:* 87418
     Worthing
2320   Sussex

Manufacturing pharmaceutical chemists

Enquiries: To Information Officer
Scope: Pharmaceutical chemistry; microbiology; chemistry; medicine
Stock: 2,000 books; 180 current periodicals

WORTHING   WORTHING COLLEGE OF FURTHER EDUCATION   *Tel.:* Worthing 31445
Sussex   Broadwater Road
     Worthing
2321   Sussex

Enquiries: To Librarian
Scope: Commerce (including economics, law, politics, business administration, accountancy, office practice), economic geography, modern languages, English literature, science (mathematics, physics, chemistry and biology), engineering (mechanical and electrical), liberal studies
Secondary: History, economic history; biography; fiction; building; education
Stock: 14,000 books; 200 pamphlets; 250 current periodicals
Publications: Periodicals Bulletin
Recent Additions Bulletin
Human Rights: a Booklist

WORTHING   WORTHING MUSEUM AND ART GALLERY   *Tel.:* Worthing 39189
Sussex   Chapel Road
     Worthing
2322   Sussex

Material relating to the geology, archaeology, history and crafts of Sussex, English costume (18th–20th centuries), English toys and dolls, English painting (18th–20th centuries), especially watercolours and paintings by Sussex artists, English pottery, porcelain and glass

Enquiries: To Curator

WORTHING, WORTHING MUSEUM AND ART GALLERY, *cont.*
- *Scope:* The archaeology of West Sussex; the history of Worthing and district
- *Secondary:* English costume, toys and dolls (18th–20th centuries)
- *Publications:* Guide to the Anglo-Saxon Collection (material from the Highdown Hill cemetery). A. E. Wilson
  - A Guide to the Bronze Age Collection. A. E. Wilson
  - Worthing—a Brief Account of the History of the Town from Neolithic times to the Present Day. L. M. Bickerton, ed.
  - Catalogue of the Costume Collection: Part I, 18th Century. Compiled by Daphne Bullard
  - Catalogue of the Costume Collection: Part II, 1800–30
  - Illustrated Guide to the Collections. L. M. Bickerton
  - Dolls in the Worthing Museum
  - Several offprints

WORTHING
Sussex

2323

WORTHING PUBLIC LIBRARY
Chapel Road
Worthing
Sussex

Tel.: Worthing 39189 and 34928

- *Enquiries:* To Librarian
- *Scope:* Regional subject specialization: Hunting and fishing industries; history of Art. Large local collection on Worthing and Sussex
- *Stock:* Subject specialization: 2,600 books; 300 pamphlets. Local collection: 5,000 books; 1,000 pamphlets; 2,000 photographs. 10 current periodicals. Local collection stock not available on loan
- *Publications:* Worthing in Manuscript (a list of manuscripts in local collection relating to Worthing)
  - Worthing: a Brief Account of the History of the Town. L. M. Bickerton

WOTTON-UNDER-EDGE
Glos

2324

FELINE ADVISORY BUREAU
The Barn Cottage
Tytherington
Wotton-Under-Edge
Gloucestershire

Tel.: Thornbury 2022

Advisory Service based on the up-to-date surveying of appropriate scientific literature, supplemented by reference to appropriate scientific, medical and veterinary experts. Sponsored research projects under the Central Fund for Feline Research

- *Enquiries:* To Hon. Secretary as above;
  - Librarian, 92 Church Road, Horley, Surrey; or
  - Cattery Information Service, The Wing, Orcheston House, Orcheston, Salisbury, Wiltshire
- *Scope:* Veterinary and genetic lending library for members. Will co-operate with other Libraries for exchange of information and indexing papers
- Stock not available on loan
- *Publications:* Bulletin (quarterly)
  - Nutrition Papers
  - General Papers
  - Conference Papers 1964, 1965, 1966, 1967, 1968 and 1969. Feline veterinary, breeding and cattery subjects
  - Feline Reproductive Failure and Neonatal Disease

WYE Ashford Kent	*See under* **ASHFORD** for WYE COLLEGE AGRICULTURAL MUSEUM (no. 31)	

YEOVIL
Somerset

2325

FLEET AIR ARM MUSEUM   *Tel.:* Ilchester 551 ext. 181
RNAS Yeovilton
Ilchester
Yeovil
Somerset

Maintains for public display aircraft, documents and exhibits of historical interest concerning the Royal Naval Air Service and the Fleet Air Arm

Enquiries: To Curator, by letter only

Scope: Small reference library available to visitors by arrangement with the Curator. Information covers the history of naval aircraft, squadrons, aircraft carriers and naval operations

Stock: 50 books. Stock not available on loan

YEOVIL
Somerset

2326

YEOVIL PUBLIC LIBRARY   *Tel.:* Yeovil 3144
King George Street
Yeovil
Somerset

Enquiries: To Librarian

Scope: Local (Somerset and Dorset) history and topography (The Charles Tite Collection)
Secondary: Regional subject specialization includes: Non-Christian religions

Stock: 50,000 books and pamphlets; 60 current periodicals (total stock)

YORK

2327

ASSOCIATION OF TEACHERS OF RUSSIAN   *Tel.:* York 22529
5 Albemarle Road
York

Enquiries: To Secretary

Scope: Any enquiries connected with the teaching of Russian
No library

Publications: Journal of Russian Studies (A.T.R. Journal)

YORK

2328

BRITISH RAILWAYS BOARD   *Tel.:* York 53022 ext. 2364
Railway Museum
York YO1 1HT

Exhibition of railway relics, prints, pictures, particularly North Eastern Area of England

Enquiries: To Curator

Scope: Information service is limited, but genuine enquiries concerning the exhibits in the museum, various aspects of railway relics and history will be dealt with as far as possible

Publications: Booklets:
The Railway Museum, York—A General Description of the Museum and Some of the Collection. L. T. C. Rolt
G.W.R. Museum, Swindon. L. T. C. Rolt
Transport Preserved (Clapham Museum of British Transport). B. Morgan
Steam Locomotive. A Retrospect of the Work of Eight Great Locomotive Engineers. O. S. Nock
Popular Carriage—Two Centuries of Carriage Design for Road and Rail. C. Hamilton Ellis

YORK, BRITISH RAILWAYS BOARD, *cont.*

        Royal Journey—A Retrospect of Royal Trains in the British Isles. C. Hamilton Ellis
        The Horse Bus as a Vehicle. C. E. Lee
        The Early Motor Bus. C. E. Lee
        London on Wheels—Public Transport in London in the Nineteenth Century
        Postcards
        Transparencies

YORK   CASTLE MUSEUM   *Tel.:* York 53611
        York

2329   The Folk Museum of Yorkshire life covering the past four centuries

    Enquiries: To Curator

    Scope: Fields covered by displays include domestic bygones, militaria, toys, costumes, craft workshops and musical instruments

YORK   ST JOHN'S COLLEGE OF EDUCATION   *Tel.:* York 56771
        Lord Mayor's Walk
2330   York

    Enquiries: To Librarian

    Scope: An index to current material on education, psychology and sociology is kept. There is a *special collection* of 3,000 19th century children's books

    Stock: 42,000 books and pamphlets; 300 current periodicals

    Publications: Selections from the index on current material in education are published for the use of the College and area schools every two months

YORK   UNIVERSITY OF YORK   *Tel.:* York 59861 ext. 274
        THE BORTHWICK INSTITUTE OF HISTORICAL
2331   RESEARCH
        St Anthony's Hall
        Peasholme Green
        York YO1 2PW

    The Institute is a record office specializing in ecclesiastical archives, especially those of the diocese and province of York. Its main aim is to list and calendar the archives so that they can be used by scholars for historical research

    Enquiries: To Archivist

    Scope: Ecclesiastical history of the northern province; ecclesiastical administration and law; palaeography; archive administration
        Secondary: Local history; family history

    Stock: 4,500 books; 1,000 pamphlets; 40 reports; 30 current periodicals. Stock not available on loan

    Publications: Borthwick Papers (published by St Anthony's Press)
        Summary Lists on certain classes of archives

    Chief work is on and with the various archival collections. The Library is only to provide the background material and sources necessary for the study of the records

YORK   UNIVERSITY OF YORK   *Tel.:* York 24919 or 59861
        INSTITUTE OF ADVANCED ARCHITECTURAL   ext. 832
2332   STUDIES
        King's Manor
        York YO1 2EP

    Enquiries: To Librarian

    Scope: Architectural design and practice. History of architecture. Town and country planning
    Secondary: Building construction
   Stock: 6,500 books; 200 current periodicals

YORK

2333

UNIVERSITY OF YORK   *Tel.:* 0904 59861
J. B. MORRELL LIBRARY   *Telex:* 57933
Heslington
York YO1 5DD

 Enquiries: To Librarian
   Scope: Within the interests of the present University teaching departments: Biology, Chemistry, Education, English and Related Literatures, History, Language, Music, Philosophy, Physics, Economics, Politics, Sociology, Social Administration and Social Work
   Secondary: Psychology; medieval art. Collections incorporated into the University Library include: English Language (library of the late Prof. G. N. Garmonsway); English Literature (17th and 18th century collection of Hugo Dyson Esq); Economics and Economic History (collections from the libraries of Lord Beveridge and Professor Henry Carter Adams); Social studies (collections from the library of Seebohm Rowntree)
   Stock: 130,000 books and pamphlets; 1,500 current periodicals

YORK

2334

UNIVERSITY OF YORK   *Tel.:* 0904 27844
SCHOOLS COUNCIL MODERN LANGUAGES
 PROJECT
Micklegate House
Micklegate
York YO1 1JZ

The Project, which was established as the Nuffield Foreign Language Teaching Materials Project in September 1963, has now entered its continuation phase under the auspices of the Schools Council and comprises the following sections: Headquarters, Publications, Evaluation, French, Spanish, Russian and German. In addition it operates a Language Teaching Information Centre and Tape Unit in collaboration with the City of Leeds (no. 800). The Nuffield Child Language Survey is continuing its work under the sponsorship of CRDML

 Enquiries: To the Director
    Scope: Teaching materials for French (age range 8–16), Spanish, German and Russian (11–16)
 Publications: Languages courses:
    Nuffield introductory French, German, Spanish and Russian Courses
    Child Language Survey: three series of transcripts of the speech of eight, nine and ten-year-old children, recorded in English Primary Schools
    Two series of transcripts of the speech of eleven and twelve-year-old children, recorded in English Secondary Schools
    The Written Language of Nine and Ten-year-old Children
    The Written Language of Eleven and Twelve-year-old Children
    Grammatical Analysis Code. R. Hasan
    Topics of Conversation and Centres of Interest of Eleven- and Twelve-year-old Children. R. J. Handscombe
    The First Thousand Clauses: a preliminary analysis. R. J. Handscombe
    Enquête sur le Langage de l'Enfant Français
    An analysis of 'Enquête sur le Langage de l'Enfant Français'
    Language Teaching Publications:
    An Introduction to the Language Laboratory. S. Moore and A. L. Antrobus
    A Puppet Theatre for Language Teaching. D. G. Rowlands

YORK, UNIVERSITY OF YORK, SCHOOLS COUNCIL MODERN LANGUAGES PROJECT, *cont.*
    Audio-visual French Courses for Primary Schools: an annotated bibliography
    French Readers for Primary Schools: an annotated bibliography. J. W. Naylor
    A Bibliography of Russian Teaching Materials. B. P. Pockney and N. Sollohub
    A Bibliography of Spanish Teaching Materials. H. Sharples
    A Survey of Russian Teaching in Schools in Great Britain. N. Sollohub
    16 mm films for Foreign Language Teaching. A. L. Antrobus
    Books and Materials for Language Teachers: catalogue with supplement 1
    Ancillary Teaching Aids:
    Puppet Films in French and Spanish
    Tape Recording of the Plays

YORK
2335
YORK CENTRAL COLLEGE OF FURTHER EDUCATION   *Tel.:* York 67161
Dringhouses
York

Enquiries: To Librarian
Scope: Building, engineering, science; commerce, social sciences and humanities
Stock: 14,000 books; 6,000 pamphlets and reports; 200 current periodicals

YORK
2336
YORK CITY ART GALLERY   *Tel.:* York 23839
Exhibition Square
York

Enquiries: To Curator
Scope: Information on artists, works of art and the Gallery
    No lending library
Publications: Preview (quarterly gallery bulletin)   Guide sheets
    Catalogues of Permanent Collection   Reproductions

YORK
2337
YORK CITY LIBRARIES   *Tel.:* York 55631
Museum Street
York YO1 2DS

Enquiries: To Librarian
Scope: Reference Library contains:
    York History Room—4,500 books and pamphlets about York and Yorkshire
    Sir John Marriott Memorial Library—4,500 books and pamphlets about modern European history
    National subject specialization: Public finance (500 books and pamphlets since 1959)

YORK
2338
YORKSHIRE PHILOSOPHICAL SOCIETY   *Tel.:* York 56713
The Lodge
Museum Gardens
York YO1 2DR

Enquiries: To Hon. Secretary
Scope: The geology, archaeology and natural history of Yorkshire
Publications: A History of Acomb. H. Richardson
    Hornport Lane and the Horners of York. L. P. Wenham
    The La Tene Cultures of Eastern Yorkshire. I. M. Stead
    A Catalogue of English Country Pottery in the Yorkshire Museum. P. Brears
    Clifton and its people in the Nineteenth Century. B. Hutton

NATIONAL, REGIONAL AND LOCAL SCHEMES OF LIBRARY CO-OPERATION

Even the most specialized libraries and information services nowadays find it impossible to provide an efficient service for their readers and enquirers solely from their own resources. To combat this situation there have grown up, over the years, various co-operative schemes, originally on a national basis, then on a regional one, and, more recently, on a much more local basis.

The list of organizations given below includes more than seventy schemes which supplement the bibliographical resources of single library systems. Many of these schemes are nationally well-known, and operate through formally administered services. Others are of more local significance, have been activated merely by a desire to be of mutual assistance and are run informally.

The collection of these schemes together in one list must not be taken to imply, however, that co-operation between information sources does not exist outside them. Very many of the organizations noted in the main section of this Directory are willing to co-operate with one another, and with other organizations, on an *ad hoc* basis. There are also of course, many examples of co-operative efforts on one particular aspect or another of library work. For example, in addition to the formal arrangement for co-operative acquisition of publications from African countries (SCOLMA, entry no. 2345 below), informal groups have been set up for the co-operative acquisition of materials from Japan, South East Asia, the Middle East, China and South Asia. The members of these groups include both librarians and the principal users of the material involved. Another field of considerable informal co-operation is in the preparation of Union Catalogues of periodicals within geographical areas, groups of organizations and subject fields.

NATIONAL SCHEMES

The major co-operative library schemes for England and Wales, Scotland, Ireland and the Metropolitan area are listed in this section. The three 'Central' libraries are formally administered organizations and act as international as well as national centres for library co-operation. Other 'national' libraries must also be considered when looking at co-operation in the United Kingdom. These are:

The British Museum (entry no. 996)
The National Lending Library for Science and Technology (entry no. 188)
The National Reference Library of Science and Invention (entry no. 1432–1434)
The Science Museum Library (entry no. 1578)

Details of some national co-operative schemes which link a number of organizations of the same type (for example, Libraries of Institutes and Schools of Education) are also given in this section.

NATIONAL CENTRAL LIBRARY

2339

Address: The Librarian
National Central Library
Store Street
London W.C.1

Tel.: 01-636 0755
Telex: 25816

The National Central Library is the centre of the national interlending system. It acts as a clearing house for loan requests, and by its agency loans are made between libraries of all types, including municipal and county libraries, all university libraries, and most specialized libraries, libraries of government departments and industrial firms. It is also the recognized centre for loans between British and overseas libraries

Services: Applications are accepted for books, periodicals, reports and theses in all subjects. Requests may be fulfilled by microform, photocopy or loan of the original material from the library's own stock or from that of any co-operating library
National Union Catalogue of Non-Fiction Books compiled from the stocks of co-operating libraries

NATIONAL CENTRAL LIBRARY, *cont.*

Special libraries lending regularly are termed Outlier libraries; these and other co-operating special libraries may borrow direct from N.C.L. Non-outlier libraries are however normally expected to borrow recent British material (post-1960) from a Regional Library System
British National Book Centre, a part of the Acquisitions Division of N.C.L., concerns itself with the redistribution of duplicates and surplus bookstock to libraries in the U.K. and abroad
Loans are made of collections of books to adult education classes organized by University Extra Mural Departments, the W.E.A. and the Department of Education and Science
Bibliographical enquiry service
Loans searches extended abroad if unfulfilled in the United Kingdom
Loans for foreign libraries obtained from British libraries
The following material is not available for loan: books in print costing 25s. or less; books in the applicant's own library; fiction; textbooks. Applications are not accepted from the Regional Library Systems for books listed in the British National Bibliography from January 1959
The National Central Library purchases currently all American scholarly books in the humanities and social sciences, and all British Government publications. The stock of about 500,000 volumes includes also many books in foreign languages and older British books

SCOTTISH CENTRAL LIBRARY

2340

Address: The Librarian
Scottish Central Library
Lawnmarket
Edinburgh EH1 2PJ

Tel.: 031-225 5321
Telex: 72279 SCOTCENLIB
EDIN

Services: Interlending from own stock as well as acting as Headquarters for library co-operation in Scotland
Bibliographical services
Number of special collections, for example Scottish material and library catalogues

Publications: Annual Report, 1952–
Scottish Newspapers
Scottish Family Histories
Out of print books and manuscripts on microfilm held in the Scottish Central Library

IRISH CENTRAL LIBRARY FOR STUDENTS

2341

Address: The Librarian
Irish Central Library for Students
53/54 Upper Mount Street
Dublin 2
Irish Republic

Tel.: Dublin 61167 and 61963

Services: Interlending
National Headquarters for co-operation
Bibliographical services
International loans, in co-operation with the National Central Library (no. 2339)

METROPOLITAN SPECIAL COLLECTIONS SCHEME

2342

Address: Application may be made to the local librarian at any Metropolitan Public Library

Aims: The Metropolitan Libraries, by agreement, collect all books, however specialized, published in Great Britain since 1948, and such foreign publications as are within their means
These collections are intended to meet the primary requirements of workers in most fields
The scheme supplements the national scheme of interlending in the Metropolitan area
Selective provision of periodicals in addition to books
Photocopying service

Other Metropolitan Co-operative Schemes:

Joint Fiction Reserve—a scheme for the preservation of out of print copies of novels (which normally are required to have been published twenty years or more previously). This scheme has operated since 1946

Sets of Plays—sets for play-reading groups consist of one copy per character plus one

Foreign fiction—collections of novels in fifteen foreign languages throughout London libraries, in addition to those in French, German, Italian and Spanish of which all London libraries are required to maintain a selection

LIBRARIES OF THE INSTITUTES AND SCHOOLS OF EDUCATION (LISE)

2343

Address: (Union Catalogue of Books)
The Secretary
School of Education Library
The University of Birmingham
PO Box 363
Birmingham 15

(Union Catalogue of Periodicals)
The Librarian
University of Newcastle Institute of Education
St Thomas' Street
Newcastle NE1 7RU

Services: Interlending between members
Union catalogue of books in all Institute libraries, regarded as an outlier of the National Central Library (no. 2339), and maintained at Birmingham
Union list of periodicals (revised annually)
Union lists of special material
Co-operative storage of obsolescent textbooks
Participation in Universities' 'Background materials scheme'
Co-operative storage of periodicals
Co-operative purchase of material of education overseas

Publications: Union lists of periodicals
Union lists of special material
Quinquennial surveys
Co-operative Projects: a descriptive pamphlet

STANDING CONFERENCE OF NATIONAL AND UNIVERSITY LIBRARIES (SCONUL)

2344

Address: The Hon. Secretary
SCONUL
The Library
University College
PO Box 78
Cardiff CF1 1XL

Membership: By invitation

Services: Graduate trainee placing scheme
Exhibitions of foreign book production
Courses on, for example, bibliography, binding, manuscripts, new media
'Exchange of Experience' seminars on library techniques and procedures
Sub-committees on Buildings, Documentary Reproduction, Education and Training, Interlending, Manuscripts, Shared Cataloguing and Automation, Latin-American, Oriental and Slavonic Materials

STANDING CONFERENCE OF NATIONAL AND UNIVERSITY LIBRARIES, *cont.*

Publications: Solanus: Bulletin of the Sub-Committee on Slavonic and East European materials ...
Career Opportunities in University Libraries. Revised edition 1969
Proceedings of Critical Visits to New University Library Buildings
Proceedings of York Conference on University Library Buildings. 1966
Directory of Libraries and Special Collections on Asia and North Africa
Sponsorship of an academic reprints scheme

STANDING CONFERENCE ON LIBRARY MATERIALS ON AFRICA (SCOLMA)

2345

Address: c/o the Library
School of Oriental and African Studies
Malet Street
London W.C.1

Aims: SCOLMA was established in 1962 to improve the coverage and provision of publications needed for African studies, by co-ordinating their acquisition and facilitating their use through bibliographic and other projects. The Conference has pursued an active programme of meetings, seminars and co-operation with other bodies interested in Africa and African bibliography in other countries

Membership: Full membership is intended for institutions in the United Kingdom actively acquiring materials on Africa, but supporting membership is open to other bodies interested in the aims of the organization. Membership at present consists of 114 institutions: 55 in the United Kingdom, 26 in Africa, 15 in the United States of America, 9 in Europe and 5 in Canada

Publications: Library Materials on Africa (newsletter, three times each year, with quinquennial index)
U.K. Publications and Theses on Africa (an annual bibliography of writings on Africa, published by Heffer, Cambridge. It lists books, pamphlets, periodical articles, theses and references in Hansard)
The SCOLMA Directory of Libraries and Special Collections on Africa. R. L. Collison. London, Crosby Lockwood. 2nd edition 1967
Theses on Africa accepted by Universities in the United Kingdom and Ireland. Cambridge, Heffer, 1964 (covers the period 1920 to 1962; supplementary information and corrections included in U.K. Publications and Theses on Africa, noted above)
Conference on the acquisition of material from Africa, University of Birmingham, 25 April 1969. V. J. Bloomfield, ed.
Debates and proceedings of legislative and legislative/advisory bodies in Africa. Cambridge, Heffer. (A union list)

A major list of periodicals published in Africa recording all periodicals published in Africa which have been traced, with locations in the United Kingdom, is in preparation. Preliminary lists for various regions have been issued as supplements to Library Materials on Africa, noted above

STANDING CONFERENCE ON PHYSICAL EDUCATION LIBRARY COOPERATION

2346

Address: The Librarian
The Physical Education Association of Great Britain and Northern Ireland
Ling House
10 Nottingham Place
London W.1

Membership: Groups of librarians representing most of the Colleges of Education with specialist or wing courses in physical education

Services: Interlending between members, or supply of photocopies
Union catalogue of periodicals held by members

Future Plans: Union catalogue of early books on physical education
Subject bibliographies
Indexing of periodicals

REGIONAL SCHEMES

There are eight regional systems of co-operation in England and Wales, the Scottish Central Library (no. 2340) acting also as the regional scheme for Scotland. The basis of each of these systems is a Union Catalogue of the books held by the major libraries in the area covered, and an interlending agreement which makes the bookstocks of these libraries widely available. In many of the entries for individual libraries in the main section of the text of this Directory specialized collections under regional schemes have been noted.

In the entries listed below, details are given of the areas covered by each scheme, and of any additional services offered.

EAST MIDLANDS REGIONAL LIBRARY SYSTEM

2347

Address: The Editor
E.M.R.L.S.
Reference Library
Bishop Street
Leicester

Tel.: Leicester 20644 ext. 15
Telex: 34643

Area covered: The counties of Cambridgeshire, Derbyshire, Huntingdonshire, Leicestershire, Lincolnshire, Norfolk, Northamptonshire, Nottinghamshire, Rutland and Suffolk

Additional services: Foreign fiction in non-European languages
Directory of Collections of Foreign Fiction

LONDON & SOUTH EASTERN LIBRARY REGION

2348

Address: The Executive Officer
London & South Eastern Library Region (L.A.S.E.R.)
c/o National Central Library
Store Street
London W.C.1

Tel.: 01-636 9383, 4684
and 9537
Telex: via 25816

Area covered: Greater London; the counties of Bedfordshire, Berkshire, Buckinghamshire, Essex, Hertfordshire, Kent, Surrey and Sussex; and the county boroughs of Brighton, Canterbury, Eastbourne, Hastings, Luton, Reading and Southend-on-Sea

NORTH WESTERN REGIONAL LIBRARY SYSTEM

2349

Address: The Editor
N.W.R.L.S.
Central Library
Manchester M2 5PD

Tel.: 061-236 7401
Telex: 66149

Area covered: The counties of Cheshire, Lancashire and the Isle of Man

Additional services: Sets of vocal scores (light opera). Requests are not handled by the System's office, but lists of titles, with locations, are given to each member library so that direct application may be made
Gramophone records. This scheme is limited to records not currently available, and to available records costing more than thirty shillings. Requests are forwarded on normal application forms to the regional office. Thirteen Public Libraries are willing to lend from their record collections.
R.L.S. Drama scheme. Play sets available from either Lancashire or Cheshire County Library services or Manchester Public Libraries
In addition to the union catalogue of books, the Bureau maintains the Union List of Periodicals held in 150 libraries in the North West. New edition of over 17,800 entries published in 1967. Master cards kept up to date at Bureau

NORTHERN REGIONAL LIBRARY SYSTEM

2350
Address: The Editor
N.R.L.S.
Central Library
Newcastle upon Tyne NE99 1MC

Tel.: Newcastle upon Tyne 610691
Telex: via 53373

Area covered: Northumberland, Co. Durham, Cumberland, Westmorland and Teesside

SOUTH WESTERN REGIONAL LIBRARY SYSTEM

2351
Address: The Librarian-in-Charge
S.W.R.L.S.
Central Library
College Green
Bristol BS1 5TL

Tel.: Bristol 23962
Telex: via 44200

Area covered: The counties of Cornwall, Devon, Dorset, Gloucestershire, Hampshire, the Isle of Wight, Oxfordshire, Somerset and Wiltshire

WELSH REGIONAL LIBRARY SYSTEM

2352
Addresses: The Hon. Secretary
W.R.L.S.
Aberystwyth Bureau
National Library of Wales
Aberystwyth

Tel.: Aberystwyth 3816
Telex: 35165

The Hon. Secretary
W.R.L.S.
Cardiff Bureau
Central Library
Cardiff

Tel.: Cardiff 22116

WEST MIDLANDS REGIONAL LIBRARY SYSTEM

2353
Address: The Editor
W.M.R.L.S.
Reference Library
Birmingham 1

Tel.: 021-643 2948 ext. 12
Telex: 33455 LIBRARY BHAM

Area covered: The counties of Herefordshire, Shropshire, Staffordshire, Warwickshire and Worcestershire

YORKSHIRE REGIONAL LIBRARY SYSTEM

2354
Address: The Hon. Secretary
Y.R.L.S.
Central Library
Sheffield 1

Tel.: Sheffield 78771
Telex: via 54243

Area covered: Yorkshire except for the Cleveland district

LOCAL SCHEMES

The success of the local co-operation schemes which form the subject of this section is essentially due to the degree of decentralization which these schemes possess, when viewed nationally or even regionally.

The need for these schemes may be questioned, when so many agencies already exist for the dissemination of printed materials and information. The short answer is that more information and interlending units are needed to meet rising demands. The regional and national interlending services created in the 1930s concerned themselves, as they still do for a large proportion of their work, with books. Current needs demand not only books, but also periodical literature, technical reports and serial publications, photocopies and microforms of material in restricted access and, particularly, information. An important requirement is that the enquirer and the supplier of information should remain in contact with each other.

The varied circumstances which brought the local co-operation schemes into existence make definition difficult. Essentially such a service consists of a number of interdependent organizations, not all of which necessarily possess established libraries, pooling literature resources to provide an interlending facility varying in its comprehensiveness and bibliographical support, and an information or enquiry service.

No ideal scheme for local co-operation can be laid down. However, there are factors which, if used creatively and formatively, will enable a scheme to be workable and efficient.

The first, implicit in any nascent local co-operation scheme, is a close study of user requirements. Should this study disclose participants' needs to be sufficiently numerous and complex, the creation of an administrative centre in a unit adequately equipped with bibliographical resources and personnel is reasonable and economic.

Secondly, the growth of the scheme needs close supervision at all stages of development. The constitution and regulations governing use must show a realization of this need. Instances occur where the success of a particular scheme has proved a limiting factor, as shown in the CICRIS (no. 2409) boundary limitations since 1964.

Economic evaluation of the clerical methods used and techniques employed in locating, receiving and disseminating material and information are closely associated with these factors. There is little evidence concerning the costing of the machinery of co-operation in the literature. Here the very informality can prove a danger and good personal relations between borrower and lending library can result in attempts to satisfy an enquiry becoming grossly uneconomic.

The fourth factor required to ensure that a scheme is workable and efficient is adequate and varied publicity.

A fifth factor is the range of services offered. The backbone of most schemes has been the production of a union list of periodicals. Interlending services may be subject to local restrictions. Further services may include:

Union catalogues of books available for interlending
Photocopying and photography services
Training schemes for new staff of member libraries
Production of bibliographies and reading lists
Exhibitions and displays in factories
Short courses in specific library subjects
Conferences and courses of lectures

Mention must be made also of current awareness services. Some schemes have a more dynamic conception than others of their responsibility for actively disseminating information on new products, processes and developments in subject fields of known interest to members, but the importance of this aspect of information work hardly requires emphasis here.

Early in 1964 representatives of thirteen library co-operative schemes met at Nottingham to discuss mutual problems of technical information co-operative schemes. At this meeting it was resolved that the groups represented should form the 'Standing Conference of Co-operative Commercial and Technical Library Services'. Various items have been discussed by the Conference, including a mutual scheme for indexing the Daily List of New Companies, in which about a dozen libraries are co-operating.

The Conference now meets annually, and early in 1969 was put on to a more formal footing under the new name of the Standing Conference of Co-operative Library Information Services (SCOCLIS).

Another subject discussed by SCOCLIS has been the role of the Ministry of Technology Industrial Liaison Officers (see Volume I, pages 725 to 733) in the orbit of the local co-operative group. The ILO, appointed for example as a member of the academic staff of a College of Technology, seeks to assist local industry in the solution of production and administrative problems. Many of the solutions can be found from books, periodicals and report literature, and other printed sources. No duplication of effort between the ILO and the local co-operative scheme is intended or indeed possible, and the one service complements the other.

In some of the entries for individual libraries and organizations in the main section of the text of this Directory, membership of one of the following local co-operative schemes has been noted.

ABERDEEN AND NORTH OF SCOTLAND LIBRARY AND INFORMATION CO-OPERATIVE SERVICE (ANSLICS)

2355 *Headquarters:* Robert Gordon's Institute of Technology
Schoolhill
Aberdeen AB9 1FR

A proposed scheme to extend and improve the existing informal co-operative arrangements between libraries in Aberdeen and the North of Scotland

ACHILLES SCHEME

2356 *Membership:* Public Libraries of Arnold, Carlton, Hucknall, Ilkeston, Long Eaton and Sutton-in-Ashfield
Aims: Co-operative interloan scheme

BATH AND DISTRICT ASSOCIATION OF LIBRARIES AND INFORMATION SERVICES (BADALIS)

2357 *Headquarters:* Central Reference Library
18 Queen Square
Bath BA1 2HP

Membership: Bath Municipal Libraries, College and University Libraries in the district, Institutions and firms in the area of Bath. No specific geographical limits

Services: Provides a forum for discussion on methods and a channel for the exchange of information pertaining to the day to day activities of the member bodies, including access to national and regional inter-lending facilities
Co-operative consideration of the provision of periodical, annual and special material and its retention, withdrawal and/or re-location

BATH UNIVERSITY, COLLEGE AND MUNICIPAL LIBRARIES

2358 *Headquarters:* No formal headquarters. Correspondence may be addressed to the Central Library, 18 Queen Square, Bath BA1 2HP or the University Library, Claverton Down, Bath BA2 7AY

Membership: Bath Municipal Libraries; Bath University of Technology; Bath College of Education (Home Economics); Newton Park College of Education; Bath Technical College; Bath Academy of Art

Services: Interlending of material; staff meetings; combined staff training sessions; informal discussion on methods and techniques

BERKSHIRE LIBRARIES GROUP

2359 *Headquarters:* (Hon. Secretary)
The Librarian
The Administrative Staff College
Greenlands
Henley-on-Thames
Oxon RG9 3AU

Membership: Public Libraries, College and Firms' libraries and other institutions. No set standards, but membership must be approved by the management committee

Services: Interlending of books and periodicals

Publications: Directory of Resources. 1967; amended 1968

BIRMINGHAM AND DISTRICT TECHNICAL PERIODICALS INTERCHANGE SCHEME

2360 *Headquarters:* Science and Technology Library
Birmingham 1

Membership: Libraries of firms and other organizations agreeing to lend freely to other members periodicals not in use
Extends to a radius of 10-15 miles of Birmingham city centre
(April 1969: 37 libraries)

Services: Union list of periodicals (at Headquarters)
(April 1969: 4,200 titles)
Interlending of periodicals
Bibliographical service

BIRMINGHAM WORKS LIBRARIES LOAN SCHEME

2361

Headquarters: Science and Technology Library, Central Library
Birmingham 1

Membership: Firms and other organizations maintaining a 'Properly constituted works library, under the charge of a Works Librarian or other responsible officer'. Membership is limited to Works, Institution, College and University libraries, situated within the Birmingham city boundaries.
(April 1969: 55 firms and institutions, 11 colleges, 2 universities)

Services: Loans of books and periodicals from the Science and Technology Library and the Reference Library to be used in Works Libraries
Technical enquiry service. Photocopying, Microfilm/fiche/card equipment. Telex
Scheme operated with Union list of technical periodicals (see Periodicals Interchange Scheme no. 2360 above). The period of loan is normally one week, renewable. Frequently used reference material is excluded

Publications: List of members

BRADFORD SCIENTIFIC, TECHNICAL AND COMMERCIAL SERVICE (BRASTACS)

2362

Headquarters: Central Library
Prince's Way
Bradford 5
Yorkshire

Tel.: Bradford 33081
Telex: 51480

Membership: Establishments which aim to provide a minimum of twenty-five books and three periodicals. The libraries must be 'interested in general or special aspects of pure and applied science, or commerce, located in Bradford and district'. Currently nineteen member libraries

Services: Interlending of books and periodicals in member libraries
Brastacs union catalogue of books, maintained on cards at Bradford Central Library, and containing more than 15,000 items
Brastacs union list of periodical holdings, over 2,000 titles with locations from fifteen libraries
Enquiry service for members operated from the Central Library

Publications: Constitution and publicity items
Annual Reports

CANTERBURY CIRCLE OF LIBRARIANS

2363

Headquarters: c/o The City Librarian
Canterbury Public Library
High Street
Canterbury
Kent

Membership: Libraries of all types in and around the Canterbury district. Currently ten member libraries

Services: Interlending of periodicals
Copies of each member's periodical holdings sent to all other members
Co-operative library resources list held by each member

CORNWALL TECHNICAL INFORMATION SERVICE

2364

Headquarters: Cornwall Technical College
Trevenson Road
Redruth
Cornwall

Membership: Local Public, College and Industrial Libraries. No set standards, but membership must be approved by the Committee

Services: Loan of library material of all kinds
An information service based on the College Library in co-operation with local Industrial Liaison Officer and the member libraries

Aims: To encourage the best possible use of the existing technical information resources in Cornwall and to improve them where necessary

Publications: Union List of Periodicals. 1969
Union List of Reference books. 1969
Union List of Bibliographies. 1969

COVENTRY AND DISTRICT INFORMATION GROUP (CADIG)

2365

Headquarters: CADIG Liaison Centre
Reference Library
Bayley Lane
Coventry CV1 5RG
Warwickshire

Tel.: Coventry 25555, ext. 2115, 2116 and 2165
Telex: 31469

Membership: No restrictions. Formal constitution 1960. It is expected that from 1970 the subscription will be ten guineas a year. No geographical limitations—the Group has associate overseas members

Services: Twice yearly computer print-out of location of 3,500 titles of all members periodical holdings
Provision of Directory of Membership and Resources
Publication of quarterly newsletters keeping members up-dated on local and national information activities
Meetings of interest to librarians and information officers
Educational courses for staffs of member organizations
Direct liaison visits by Liaison Officer to discuss information problems
Channels information requests to the appropriate source
Through the Standing Conference of Co-operative Library Information Services (SCOCLIS), is able to co-operate with all other local technical co-operative services in the country
Each member is circularized with STL-Bulletin, a select annotated list of scientific and technical books added to the Coventry Scientific and Technical Library
Mutual transactions of unwanted periodical files and information material arranged
Bibliographies of current interests published, for example, fluidics, metrication, explosive forming

Publications: Publicity material and constitution
Quarterly Newsletter
Directory of Membership and Resources. 4th edition 1969
Bibliographies

DENBIGHSHIRE LIBRARIES GROUP

2366

Headquarters: Public Library
Wrexham
Denbighshire

Membership: Cartrefle Training College, Wrexham; Colwyn Bay Public Library; Denbighshire County

Library; Denbighshire Technical College, Wrexham; Llandrillo Technical College, Colwyn Bay; Llysfasi Farm Institute; Monsanto Chemicals Ltd, Ruabon; Wrexham Public Library

Services: Inter-lending of books and periodicals
Co-operative purchase of books listed in the B.N.B. costing more than 63s.
Joint list of periodicals
Joint list of basic reference material
Photocopying service
Quarterly meetings for discussion of professional topics of mutual interest

DORSET COOPERATIVE SCHEME

2367

Headquarters: Dorset County Library Headquarters
Dorchester
Dorset

Membership: Co-operative scheme between Dorset County Library, Weymouth Public Library, South Dorset Technical College, Weymouth College of Education, Dorset College of Agriculture and local research libraries

Services: Interlending of books and other library material

ESSEX TECHNICAL AND COMMERCIAL LIBRARY SERVICE

2368

Headquarters: County Library Headquarters
Goldlay Gardens
Chelmsford
Essex

Tel.: Chelmsford 51141
Telex: 99223

Membership: No qualifications for membership. Co-operators number over sixty firms with libraries, plus all technical colleges and hospitals in the County. Small firms also make wide use of the service

Services: Loans of all types of material
Production of bibliographies as requested
List of abstracts journals
Photocopying service
Telex
Microfilm Readers available on loan
Large store of periodicals on a co-operative basis
Co-operation with Industrial Liaison Officers within the County
Extensive collection of commercial directories and statistical publications
Special emphasis on information for market research workers
T.I.M. Service available

Publications: Annual Report (included in County Library Annual Report)
List of Abstracts available
Select bibliographies

FLEETWOOD COOPERATIVE SCHEME

2369

Headquarters: Public Library
Fleetwood
Lancashire FY7 6AQ

Membership: Fifty-eight firms

Services: Interlending of library material
Central storage at the Public Library of unwanted periodicals
Union list of periodicals

Publications: Publicity brochure

GLOUCESTERSHIRE TECHNICAL INFORMATION SERVICE (GTIS)

2370

Headquarters: 205 Gloucester Road
Cheltenham
Gloucestershire

Membership: Open to industry, education and the general public throughout the County area

Services: Loan of comprehensive range of scientific and technical literature of all types
Current awareness service to industry by regular bulletins on all aspects of Engineering and Management
Bibliographies produced on request
Exhibitions of technical books indicating the Service's resources shown throughout the County
Science teachers in schools receive selected journals in the physical and biological sciences
Union list of serials
Subject specialization in Technical College Libraries
Co-operation with Industrial Liaison Officers based within the County

Publications: Union List of Serials. 1969
Annual Report and publicity material
Select bibliographies
Regular bulletins for current awareness scheme
Booklists to accompany exhibitions

HALIFAX AND DISTRICT INFORMATION SERVICE FOR BUSINESS AND INDUSTRY (HALDIS)

2371

Headquarters: Percival Whitley College of Further Education Library
Francis Street
Halifax
Yorkshire

Membership: Forty-three, including firms, the industrial liaison centre and other local bodies, 3 public libraries and the college library
Subscription: One or two guineas per annum according to size of organization

Aims: 'To promote the better accessibility and use of commercial, management and technical literature and information, within and on behalf of local industry and other organisations specially concerned' in co-operation with the Huddersfield industrial liaison centre

Services: Interlending of library material
Access by small firms to the N.L.L.
Technical/Management film shows and meetings
Translating and interpreting service
Books 'on approval' service

Publications: Bi-monthly current awareness and information bulletin
Register of senior and specialist staff in member organizations
Survey of test equipment held by members and other bodies, including guide to local information resources
Book lists
Quarterly industrial and management training bulletin

HAMPSHIRE TECHNICAL RESEARCH INDUSTRIAL COMMERCIAL SERVICE (HATRICS)

2372

Headquarters: Central Library
Civic Centre
Southampton

Membership: Major commercial and industrial undertakings with academic institutions, research organizations and public libraries in Hampshire and adjoining areas. Subscription three pounds per annum. The area served covers the central south coast

Services: Helping HATRICS members to help one another. The Headquarters is the link in the information network
Southampton Central Library acts as a clearing house for all enquiries
Computer compiled directory of resources
Courses held on sources of information and other subjects
News Bulletin circulated to members
Co-operation with local Industrial Liaison Officers
Abstracting and indexing services held by HATRICS members

Publications: Hatrics: a Directory of Resources. 3rd edition 1968
News Bulletin
A Bibliography of Critical Path Methods. 2nd edition 1969
Abstracting and Indexing Services. 1968
Containerization: a Bibliography. 2nd edition 1969
Marketing in the Sixties. 1968

HERTFORDSHIRE ASSOCIATION OF SPECIAL LIBRARIES (HASL)

2373

Addresses: Chairman, Dr H. H. Neville   *Tel.:* Garston 74040
Building Research Station
Garston
Watford WD2 7JR

Secretary, Mrs G. Scott   *Tel.:* Stevenage 2422 ext. 13
British Aircraft Corporation Limited
6 Hills Way
Stevenage
Hertfordshire

There is no other fixed headquarters address

Membership: This is open to all libraries in Hertfordshire and adjacent areas interested in special library work

Aims and Activities: Encouragement of co-operation, exchange of information and interlending between members. The arrangement of meetings and visits of interest to special librarians

Publications: List of members

HERTFORDSHIRE COUNTY COUNCIL TECHNICAL LIBRARY AND INFORMATION SERVICE (HERTIS)

2374

Headquarters: The Hatfield Polytechnic
Hatfield
Hertfordshire

Membership: Any industrial or commercial undertaking, local government department or individual capable of benefiting from the scheme. Subscription rates from £5 per annum upwards depending on the size and nature of the organization

Services: Union catalogue of stock in the Polytechnic and two College of Technology libraries in the County
Union catalogue of periodical holdings of fifteen Colleges
Enquiry and information service. Specialists on Polytechnic staff are prepared to assist in information problems
Interlending facilities
Weekly card service to industry principally within the County, of current information on

HERTFORDSHIRE COUNTY COUNCIL TECHNICAL LIBRARY AND INFORMATION SERVICE, *cont.*

nominated subjects from periodical articles and report literature. A small charge for each subject is made to cover postal costs

Extensive photocopying facilities

Chief Information and Industrial Liaison Officer to maintain contact with and between members, to ensure mutual co-operation

Tutor Librarians in the various college libraries to train future technologists, technicians and other personnel in the techniques of searching, evaluating and applying factual information from literature sources

Short courses

Publications: Range of bibliographies on specific subjects (printed list available)
Reading guides in many subjects   HERTIS Diary of Forthcoming Events
List of Periodical Holdings   News from the Industrial Liaison Office

HUDDERSFIELD AND DISTRICT INFORMATION SERVICE (HADIS)

2375

Headquarters: Public Library
Ramsden Street
Huddersfield
Yorkshire

Membership: Industrial firms in the Huddersfield area, including those outside the boundary which look towards Huddersfield as their natural centre. Public libraries and higher and further education institutions are also members

Services: Interlending service of technical and commercial literature
Technical enquiries service
Technical film shows and lectures
Co-operation with local Industrial Liaison Officers

Publications: Union List of Periodicals
List of Translators 1960–
Union list of books on management

HULL TECHNICAL INTERLOAN SCHEME (HULTIS)

2376

Headquarters: Library of Science, Technology and Commerce
Central Library
Hull HU1 3TF
Yorkshire

Membership: Intending members must possess three periodicals and at least twenty-five books and be willing and able to lend this material. The scheme is confined to Hull and the East Riding of Yorkshire

Services: Interlending of material, with the possible exception of current periodicals
Union Catalogue of Books
Union List of periodicals
Enquiry Service
List of Translators maintained
Instruction in library work given to the unqualified staff of member libraries at the Headquarters library
Advice in setting up a library service

Publications: Annual Report
Regulations Governing the Scheme

Hull Commercial and Technical Bulletin
Check List of Members' Periodicals, up-dated monthly
Occasional Bibliographies

INFORMATION EXCHANGE SCHEME KINGSTON AREA (INESKA)

2377
Headquarters: An informal organization without Headquarters

Membership: There are about 40 members who simply agree to make their library resources available to each other through direct contact. The members cover the same area as that covered by the Ministry of Technology Industrial Liaison Office in the area

LAMBETH INFORMATION NETWORK (LINK)

2378
Headquarters: London Borough of Lambeth Public Libraries
Reference Library
Tate Central Library
Brixton Oval
London S.W.2

Membership: Lambeth Public Libraries, manufacturing and business firms, educational and professional institutions, associations, offices and individuals in Lambeth. No subscription is charged. Present membership 99

Aims: To provide through its members a scientific, technical and commercial information and loans service of mutual benefit

Services: Enquiry and information services
Interlending service for scientific, technical and commercial materials
Compilation of reading lists and select bibliographies
Lectures and meetings
Photocopying and microform reading facilities
Reference Library acts as clearing house for all enquiries

Publications: Quarterly LINK Newsletter
Directory of LINK members
Booklists

LEEDS COOPERATIVE SCHEME

2379
Headquarters: Library of Commerce, Science and Technology
City Libraries
Leeds LS1 3AB

Membership: No regional or area limitations. Material is lent on the production of written authorization from responsible persons in the borrowing organization

Services: Loans of library materials   Photocopying
Technical enquiry service   British and foreign patent service

LEICESTERSHIRE TECHNICAL INFORMATION SERVICE (LETIS)

2380
Headquarters: Library
University of Technology
Loughborough
Leicestershire

Membership: The Service is subsidized by the education and library authorities within the administrative county of Leicestershire. Subscription rates for firms (no geographical limitations) range from £5 to £40 per annum depending on the size of the organization

LEICESTERSHIRE TECHNICAL INFORMATION SERVICE, *cont.*

    Services: Information and literature-searching service, backed up by the assistance of experts on the University academic staff
Photocopying service
Microfilm reading/printing facilities
Co-operation with Industrial Liaison Centre at Leicester
Short courses

    Publications: Publicity brochure

LEIGHTON INTER-LIBRARY SCHEME

2381

    Headquarters: Central Library
Swinton
Manchester

    Membership: Altrincham, Bury, Eccles, Hale, Heywood, Radcliffe, Sale, Salford, Stretford, and Swinton and Pendlebury Public Libraries

    Aims: To provide a means of co-operation among member libraries
To provide an inter-lending medium supplementary to the Regional and other systems

    Services: Direct interlending
Interavailability of readers' tickets
Lists of selective holdings of member libraries
Quarterly meetings to consider matters of mutual interest

    Publications: Annual reports

LIBRARIES OF NORTH STAFFORDSHIRE IN COOPERATION (LINOSCO)

2382

    Headquarters: Horace Barks Reference Library
Hanley
Stoke-on-Trent
Staffordshire

    Membership: Firms and institutions, who are required to have a librarian in charge of their libraries. The scheme is limited to libraries in North Staffordshire and South Cheshire only, and at present has twenty-seven member libraries

    Services: Interlending of books and periodicals
Union list of periodicals
Directory of members
Staff exchange schemes, on a limited basis
In-service training scheme for junior staff

    Publications: Union List of Periodicals. 4th edition
Directory of Members

LIBRARY INFORMATION SERVICE FOR TEESSIDE (LIST)

2383

    Headquarters: Teesside Public Libraries
Technical and Commercial Department
Central Library
Middlesbrough
Teesside

    Membership: Public Libraries, Technical Colleges, firms, organizations and academic institutions in the area. Participating organizations must take a minimum of five technical periodicals, and have a library of at least twenty-five books

Aims: 'To promote co-operation and mutual assistance between the various public, academic and industrial libraries in the area by co-ordinating library facilities available in Teesside. To make information readily available to industry and commerce. To assist smaller firms who do not have their own libraries.

To put at the service of industry the specialized knowledge and experience of librarians in identifying, locating and retrieving information in every subject field through books in their own libraries and in many other specialized libraries'

LIBRARY INFORMATION SERVICE TO INDUSTRY AND COMMERCE (LISIC)

2384

Headquarters: Gravesend Public Library *Tel.:* Gravesend 2758
Windmill Street
Gravesend
Kent

Membership: Open to any firm in the Gravesend area. At present 18 members

Aims: To assist firms with their information needs by a current awareness service using the British National Bibliography and British Technology Index; and by acting as a centre for loans. The service is intended primarily for small firms without their own resources

Publications: Select Bibliography of Business and Commerce

LIVERPOOL AND DISTRICT SCIENTIFIC, INDUSTRIAL AND RESEARCH LIBRARY ADVISORY COUNCIL (LADSIRLAC)

2385

Headquarters: Brown Library *Tel.:* 051-207 2147
William Brown Street *Telex:* 62500
Liverpool L3 8EW

Membership: Industrial firms in Liverpool, and, on special application, from other areas, particularly Merseyside and Western Lancashire, but no actual geographical limitation. There are two classes of membership; ordinary members (minimum subscription 3 guineas per annum) and members of the Industrial Liaison Committee at 100 guineas per annum. LADSIRLAC was formed in 1955

Services: Production enquiry field service
Literature searches
Ladsirlac Information Bulletins
Postal loans service
Translations advisory service
Exhibitions and lectures

Publications: Publicity leaflets
Annual Reports
Ladsirlac Technical Bulletin (monthly)
Ladsirlac Commercial Bulletin (monthly)

See also no. 866

LUTON AND DISTRICT INFORMATION SERVICE

2386

Headquarters: Central Library
Luton
Bedfordshire

Membership: No qualifications required

LUTON AND DISTRICT INFORMATION SERVICE, *cont.*

Services: (L or R indicates whether the Lending Library or the Reference Library is responsible for the service)

Union list of Technical Periodicals (holdings of 21 libraries)	L
Interlending of books and periodicals	L & R
Technical/commercial enquiry service	R
Co-operative redistribution of unwanted books and periodicals	R
List of translators in local area	R

Publications:

Union List of Technical Periodicals, available in the Luton area. 5th edition July 1968	L
Business and Technical Bulletin (every 2 months)	R
Technical Bulletins, listing additions to stock (irregular)	L

MANCHESTER SERVICE TO INDUSTRY

2387

Headquarters: Central Library
St Peters Square
Manchester 2

Membership: No regional or area limitations. Each firm or organization nominates a responsible officer for liaison with the service

Services: Loans of library material
Technical enquiry service
Staff exchange scheme in the United Kingdom and abroad
Panel of translators maintained
Photocopying and photographic services

Publications: Publicity material
Range of bibliographies and reading lists on specific subjects

MID STAFFORDSHIRE LIBRARIES IN COOPERATION (MISLIC)

2388

Headquarters: Staffordshire County Library Headquarters
Stafford

Membership: Forty-seven libraries, firms and local government departments in the mid and South Staffordshire area

Services: Interlending of periodicals, books and other forms of co-operation
One-Day Courses
Meetings to consider matters of interest

Publications: Union List of Periodicals, 2nd edition and supplements
Directory of Resources

NORFOLK INFORMATION EXCHANGE SCHEME (NINES)

2389

Headquarters: The Library
Norwich City College
Ipswich Road
Norwich NOR 67D
(This library acts as co-ordinator for an informal scheme)

Membership: Thirty libraries and firms within the region covered by the Norfolk Industrial Liaison Centre

Services: Members deal directly with each other in interlending and the provision of information

Publications: List of members 1969

NORTH EAST LANCASHIRE LIBRARIES

2390

Headquarters: Hon. Secretary
Central Library
Bacup
Lancashire

Membership: Accrington, Bacup, Blackburn, Burnley, Darwen, Haslingden, Nelson, Rawtenstall and Rochdale Public Libraries; Accrington College of Further Education; Blackburn College of Technology and Design; Burnley Municipal College; Nelson College of Further Education; and Rossendale College of Further Education

Aims: To encourage close co-operation between the libraries of North East Lancashire
To examine the British National Bibliography each month and co-operate in the purchase of items costing 40s. or more
To consider any matter of mutual interest to the library service in the area, and to co-operate in any way conducive to the efficiency and improvement of the library service

NORTH WALES URBAN LIBRARIES GROUP

2391

Headquarters: Public Library
Llandudno
Caernarvonshire

Membership: Bangor, Caernarvon, Colwyn Bay, Conway, Flint, Llandudno, Rhyl and Wrexham Public Libraries

Services: Loans of books
Catalogues of selective holdings of member libraries

NORTHERN CIRCLE OF COLLEGE LIBRARIANS

2392

Headquarters: Northumberland County Technical College *Tel.:* Ashington 3248 ext. 10
College Road
Ashington
Northumberland

Membership: Informal association of College Librarians, formed in 1963. Membership is open to staff of any Technical College (including Polytechnics, Colleges of Technology, and Colleges of Further Education), Colleges of Art, and Colleges of Education (including two University Institutes of Education) in the Northern region. No subscription

Services: Meetings two or three times a year

Aims: To promote co-operation among its members

Publications: Directory of Northern Libraries. 5th edition 1969

NOTTINGHAM AND NOTTINGHAMSHIRE TECHNICAL INFORMATION SERVICE (NANTIS)

2393

Headquarters: Commercial and Technical Library *Tel.:* Nottingham 43591
Central Library *Telex:* 37662
South Sherwood Street
Nottingham NG1 4DA

Membership: Any library, information service, research organization, industrial or commercial firm in the City of Nottingham and the County. Associate membership to any similar organization in industrial areas surrounding Nottinghamshire

Services: Interlending facilities, with the usual restrictions
Enquiry Service
Training courses in library and information work
Periodicals exchange scheme
Co-operation with local Industrial Liaison Officer

NOTTINGHAM AND NOTTINGHAMSHIRE TECHNICAL INFORMATION SERVICE, *cont.*

Publications: Publicity material
Handbook and Directory of Resources. 4th edition 1969
Technical Periodicals Review (monthly):
  Part 1: Technical and Engineering Topics
  Part 2: Management and Business Methods
Nantis News Bulletin (quarterly)
Constitution and Membership
Traffic Engineering Literature Review (monthly)
Panel of Translators. 1st edition 1968

PAISLEY AND DISTRICT TECHNICAL INFORMATION GROUP

2394

Headquarters: Paisley Public Library
High Street
Paisley
Renfrewshire

Membership: Public, College and industrial libraries in the area

Services: Compilation of union list of technical periodicals. Apparent gaps in coverage will be discussed, and there will be an attempt to add material in these subject fields
List of foreign language bilingual and multilingual directories
Regular meetings to be held to arrange future co-operation and to discuss matters of mutual interest

PORT TALBOT TECHNICAL INFORMATION SERVICE (PORTIS)

2395

Headquarters: Central Library
Commercial Road
Taibach
Port Talbot
Glamorgan

Membership: Any industrial firm or organization in the Borough is eligible for membership

Aims: Chiefly to act as a co-ordinating body for the exploitation of all information sources in the Borough, and to help, in particular, those firms and organizations with a small or non-existent library service by providing both material and advice on the establishment of such a service

Publications: Periodicals—a select list of periodicals of technical and commercial interest received at the Central Reference Library
Directories and Data Books—a select list of technical and commercial sources currently available in Port Talbot Central Reference Library
Register of Translators

PRESTON AND DISTRICT COMMERCIAL AND TECHNICAL INFORMATION SERVICES

2396

Headquarters: Harris Public Library
Preston
Lancashire

Membership: Twenty-five firms and libraries

Services: Interlending of periodicals

Publications: Periodicals List. 6th edition 1969

SHEFFIELD INTERCHANGE ORGANISATION (SINTO)

2397

Headquarters: Libraries of Commerce, Science and Technology
Central Library
Surrey Street
Sheffield S1 1XZ

Membership: Membership is limited, with certain exceptions, to the area of Sheffield and its immediate neighbourhood, and is open to any commercial, technical or scientific library with a minimum of fifty books and ten current periodicals

Services: Interlending of printed material (except confidential documents) using Telex and photo-copying facilities
Steel Specifications Index
One-day specialist training courses
Active sponsorship of anything concerned with obtaining technical information
Twelve hours a day telephone information service, six days a week
Staff exchanges with special libraries

Publications: Union List of Periodicals, 1st edition 1967
Cumulative Supplements, 1968–
Union List of Periodicals, 2nd edition (in preparation)
Annual Reports
SINTO News, 1965–
Publicity material

SOMERSET LIBRARIES

2398

Headquarters: c/o Central Reference Library
18 Queen Square
Bath BA1 2HP
(But no formal headquarters as such)

Membership: Bath, Bridgwater, Taunton, Weston-super-Mare, Yeovil Municipal Libraries, Somerset County Library

Services: Co-operative consideration in the purchase of the more expensive significant books and their location within the co-operation area
Direct interlending of all books in the stocks of the various libraries, and their exploitation by the joint publication of reading lists, both general and special, for the area as a whole
Co-ordination of intake and withdrawal of periodicals and annuals, and co-operative book-storage
Discussion of common problems and research into methods with a view to standardization
Exchanges of staffs, and senior staff meetings, for training purposes; co-operation in any service which will be advantageous to the readers in all the libraries

SOUTH EAST AREA LIBRARIES INFORMATION SERVICE (SEAL)

2399

Headquarters: No headquarters—service is run through the principal public reference libraries of the area

Membership: Open to public libraries, further educational institutions, industrial, commercial and research organizations. The area covered by the scheme is at present the area of responsibility of the Industrial Liaison Centre, Woolwich Polytechnic, and includes the Boroughs of Bexley, Dartford and Greenwich

Services: Commercial Technical Information service

Publications: Introductory leaflet
Union List of Periodicals
Metrication Bibliography
Directory of Translators (in preparation)

SOUTH EAST AREA LIBRARIES INFORMATION SERVICE, *cont.*

Aims: To provide a reference and information service for industrial and commercial organizations within the area

To promote the rapid exchange of both written and verbal information, and to ensure that all members are aware of the facilities available within the area

To broaden and strengthen the reference and information library facilities in the area by means of collaboration and co-operation between existing library services

SOUTH STAFFORDSHIRE COLLEGE LIBRARIANS (SOSCOL)

2400

Headquarters: No formal headquarters. Enquiries should be addressed to the Chairman, SOSCOL, Wolverhampton Polytechnic, Wolverhampton, Staffordshire

Membership: Technical College Librarians in the South Staffordshire area

Aims: To promote active co-operation in all forms of library service; to encourage the economic use of resources; and to provide a forum for the discussion and resolution of problems of mutual interest. The Group meets informally three times a year

Publications: Union List of Periodicals

Informal and private survey of member libraries

SOUTH WEST MIDLANDS CO-OPERATIVE SCHEME

2401

Headquarters: Worcester City Library
Foregate Street
Worcester

Membership: 31 libraries, covering Public Libraries, Technical Colleges, firms and academic institutions in the area of South Worcestershire, North Gloucestershire and Herefordshire

Services: Interlending of periodicals
Union List of Periodicals
Quarterly meetings to consider further areas for co-operation

SURREY AND SUSSEX LIBRARIES IN COOPERATION (SASLIC)

2402

Headquarters: No formal headquarters. Membership enquiries addressed to the Hon. Secretary, SASLIC, West Sussex County Library Headquarters, Tower Street, Chichester, Sussex

Membership: Any organization may make application for membership, provided that it is willing to participate in a co-operative scheme for the exchange and provision of information (other than confidential) and scientific, technical and commercial literature. Subscription £5 p.a.

Services: Interloans or photocopies of books, periodicals, reports and all types of non-confidential literature
Production of bibliographies, directories and reading lists
Co-operative purchase of reference, bibliographical and special material to ensure full coverage in meeting area needs
Training courses in the use of scientific and technical literature
Meetings and exhibitions to advance the aims of the scheme

Publications: SASLIC Directory of Member Organizations
SASLIC Co-operative List of Abstracts

SURREY REFERENCE AND INFORMATION GROUP (SRIG)

2403

Headquarters: Correspondence to: The Secretary, SRIG, Chertsey Library, Guildford Street, Chertsey, Surrey

Membership: Reference Librarians from Public, College, University and Special Libraries within the geographical area of the pre-1965 county of Surrey

Services: Discussion and business meetings
Catalogue of local authors and artists
Surrey Union List of Periodicals (at Chertsey Library, at present confined to North Surrey)
Survey of illustration files
Publications: North Surrey Union List of Periodicals

SWINDON AREA ASSOCIATION OF LIBRARIES OF INDUSTRY AND COMMERCE (SAALIC)

2404
Headquarters: Central Library
Swindon
Wiltshire
Membership: Swindon Public Library, Royal Military College of Science, Shrivenham, The College, Swindon and other libraries in the area
Services: Interlending of books and periodicals
Information requests
Co-operative filing of periodicals
Publications: Periodicals: a Preliminary Union List. 1968

TAMWORTH SCHEME

2405
Membership: Public Libraries of Burton-upon-Trent, Hinckley, Ilkeston, Lichfield, Long Eaton, Loughborough, Nuneaton, Sutton Coldfield and Tamworth
Aims: Co-operative interloan scheme

TYNESIDE ASSOCIATION OF LIBRARIES FOR INDUSTRY AND COMMERCE (TALIC)

2406
Headquarters: Central Library
Newcastle upon Tyne NE99 1MC
Membership: Open to all libraries in the Tyneside area
Services: Interlending of printed material including use of telex and photocopying facilities
Enquiry service
Headquarters link up with other Information Services through membership of the Standing Conference of Co-operative Library Information Services (SCOCLIS)
Union catalogue of periodicals maintained at TALIC Headquarters
Publications: Report of Progress (in Newcastle upon Tyne Libraries Annual Report)
Publicity given in *Industrial Tyneside* (published by the Tyneside Chamber of Commerce)

WANDSWORTH PUBLIC, EDUCATIONAL TECHNICAL LIBRARY SERVICE (WANDPETLS)

2407
Headquarters: Battersea Public Library
Lavender Hill
London S.W.11
Membership: Wandsworth Public Libraries, colleges, institutes of higher education, research associations and firms in the area
Services: Interlending of books and periodicals
Information requests
Union list of Periodicals

WESSEX LIBRARY GROUP

2408
Headquarters: Public Library
Aldershot
Hampshire
Membership: Aldershot, Andover, Salisbury and Winchester Public Libraries

WESSEX LIBRARY GROUP, *cont.*
    Services: Direct interlending
                Interavailability of readers' tickets
                Co-operative purchase of selected books costing more than 30s.
                Joint specific subject lists and list of periodicals and bibliographies
    Publications: Annual Reports

WEST LONDON COMMERCIAL AND TECHNICAL LIBRARY SERVICE (CICRIS) (formerly CO-OPERATIVE INDUSTRIAL AND COMMERCIAL REFERENCE AND INFORMATION SERVICE)

2409
    Headquarters: Acton District Library (London Borough of Ealing)   *Tel.:* 01-992 3295
                High Street
                London W.3
                (This library acts as co-ordinator. Each of the Public Libraries listed below is reponsible for all the members in its area)
    Membership: Intending members should possess a library or collection of material, be willing to lend, and in general take an active role in the organization. The current annual subscription is one guinea. The boundaries of the scheme are the London Boroughs of Barnet, Brent, Ealing, Hammersmith, Harrow, Hillingdon, Hounslow and Richmond upon Thames
    Services: Union catalogue of periodicals
                Loan facilities for all types of material
                Information service
                Photocopying services and telex
                Union lists including: periodicals; dictionaries (technical and translating); proceedings of conferences, congresses and symposia
                Exchange service between members for surplus technical and commercial publications
    Publications: Directory and Guide to Resources. 1968

WEST MIDLANDS COUNTY BOROUGHS LIBRARIANS' STANDING COMMITTEE (WESLIB)

2410
    Headquarters: Each Borough Librarian, in rotation, acts as Secretary
    Membership: Dudley, Walsall, Warley, West Bromwich and Wolverhampton Public Libraries
    Services: Inter-library loans
    Aims: To encourage close co-operation between the five library systems in every way likely to improve their efficiency

WEST SUSSEX REFERENCE AND TECHNICAL LIBRARY SERVICE

2411
    Headquarters: West Sussex County Library
                Chichester
                Sussex
    Membership: Seven regional branch libraries, three colleges of further education, and a mailing list to seventy industrial firms
    Services: Union catalogue of books and periodicals for Colleges of Further Education and County Library Branches
                Loans of books and periodicals
    Publications: Local Government Periodicals Bulletin

WILTSHIRE ASSOCIATION OF LIBRARIES OF INDUSTRY AND COMMERCE (WALIC)

2412

Headquarters: Wiltshire County Library Headquarters
Cradle Bridge
Mortimer Street
Trowbridge
Wiltshire

Membership: Wiltshire County Library, Colleges of Further Education and local firms

Services: Interlending of library material
Telex facility at County Headquarters
Co-operative book purchase scheme
Subject specialization scheme
Union catalogue
County Headquarters maintain most of the Association's holding of abstracts

Publications: Union List of Periodicals. 1962
WALIC publicity leaflets

WORCESTERSHIRE ASSOCIATION OF TECHNICAL LIBRARIES

2413

Headquarters: Industrial Liaison Centre
Worcester Technical College
Deansway
Worcester

Membership: Informal association of college and industrial libraries in Worcestershire and Herefordshire. No membership fee

Services: Informal agreement that a member will attempt to meet any reasonable request for published information from another member, subject to commercial interests
Meetings of College Librarians once each term
Annual meeting of all members

Publications: Union List of Periodicals
Register of Local Translators

YORKSHIRE COBOOK GROUP OF LIBRARIES

2414

Headquarters: Public Library
Batley
Yorkshire

Membership: Airborough, Batley, Bingley, Brighouse, Castleford, Elland, Harrogate, Horsforth, Ilkley, Morley, Normanton, Ossett, Pontefract, Rothwell, Shipley, Skipton, Sowerby Bridge, Spenborough and Wakefield Public Libraries

Services: Interlending of library material
Co-operative book purchase of expensive books listed in the British National Bibliography and in Aslib Booklist

NAME INDEX

This index includes the names of all the organizations, institutions, societies, Companies, libraries and special collections listed and noted in the entries. The numbers refer to entries, and *not* to pages.

A

Abbot Hall Art Gallery, 764
Aberdare Central Public Library, 2
Aberdeen and North of Scotland Library and Information Co-operative Service, 9, 2355
Aberdeen College of Education, 3
Aberdeen County Library, 4
Aberdeen Public Library, 5
Aberdeen School of Domestic Science, 9
Aberdeen University
   Centre for Social Studies, 12
   Library, 13
   Scottish Institute of Missionary Studies, 14
Abortion Law Reform Association, 2064
Abraham Wallace Collection, 1783
Accrington Public Library, 20
ACE, 273
Achilles Scheme, 2356
Acton Collection, 314
Acworth Collection, 67
Additional Curates Society, 675
Administrative Staff College, 700
Admiral Blake Museum, 213
Admiralty Library, 1425
Adverse Drug Reaction Bulletin Editorial Office, 415
Advertising Association, 884
Advisory Centre for Education (ACE) Ltd, 273
Advisory Council for the Church's Ministry, 885
Aeromedical International, 393
Africa Bureau, 886
African Studies Association of the United Kingdom, 126
Agent-General for Victoria, 887
Agnes and Norman Lupton Bequest, 801
Agricultural Research Council
   Institute for Research on Animal Diseases, 1828
   Institute of Animal Physiology, 274
Airdrie Public Library, 21
Aireborough Public Libraries, 749
Albanian Society, 743
Albany Trust, 888, 1207
Alderney Library, 22
Alderney Society and Museum 22
Aldershot Public Library, 23
Alfred Kitson Collection, 1783

All Nations Missionary College, 2063, 2247
All Saints' College, Leeds, 812
All Souls College, Oxford, 1921
Allen and Hanburys Ltd, 2248
Alma Tadema Collection, 154
Almonry Museum, 582
Alpine Club, 889
Altnagelvin Hospital, 1708
A.M.A., 1224
Amalgamated Association of Operative Cotton Spinners and Twiners, 1737
Amalgamated Union of Engineering and Foundry Workers (Foundry Section), 1738
Amateur Basket Ball Association, 795
Amateur Rowing Association, 890
Amateur Swimming Association, 891
Ambassador College, 2065
American Embassy, 892, 1648
American Memorial Library, 1882
American Museum In Britain, 69
An Comunn Gaidhealach, 751
Ancient Monuments Society, 893
Anderson Collection (National Maritime Museum), 1425
Anderson Collection (University of Strathclyde), 631
Andersonian Library, 631
Andrew Carnegie Collection, 478
Anerley Branch Library, 252
Anglesey County Library, 883
Anglo-Chilean Society, 894
Anglo-Danish Students' Bureau, 895
Anglo-Japanese Economic Institute, 896
Anglo-Jewish Archives, 897, 1383
Anglo-Mongolian Society, 2019
Anglo-Norse Society in London, 898
Angus and Kincardine County Library, 1815
Angus Library, 1944
Animal Diseases Research Association, 502
Animal Virus Research Institute, 2301
ANSLICS, 9, 2355
Anti-Common Market League, 899
Apostolic Delegation, 900
Archaeological and Architectural Society of Durham and Northumberland, 480
Archbishop Harsnett's Library, 408
Archbishop Wm. Sancroft Library, 284

Archdiocese of Glasgow, Catholic Youth Council, 601
Architectural Association, 901
Archive of British Music, 317
Archives of the Moravian Church, 229, 902
Argyll County Library, 479
Arlington Mill Museum, 404
Armagh County Museum, 29
Armour Pharmaceutical Company Limited, 495
Armouries, 903
Arms and Armour Society, 904
Army Branch Library
    Shorncliffe, 594, 906
    Thiepval Barracks, 856
Army Cadet Force Association, 905
Army Central Library, 906
Army Library Service, 81, 594, 856, 906, 1242
Army School of Education, 81
Arnold Bennett House Museum, 2170
Art Exhibitions Bureau, 1146
Arthritis & Rheumatism Council for Research in Gt Britain and the Commonwealth, 907
Arthur Findlay College, 1783, 2159
Arthurian Collection (Flintshire County Library), 1813
Arthurian Collection (National Library of Wales), 16
Artists of Chelsea, 1146
Arts Council of Great Britain, 908
Arts Council Poetry Library, 908
Ashley Collection, 1379
Ashley Rowe Collection, 2219
Ashmolean Museum Library, 1952
Ashridge Collection, 1688
Ashridge Management College, 114
Ashton-in-Makerfield Public Library, 2285
Ashton-under-Lyne College of Further Education, 33
Ashton-under-Lyne Public Libraries, 34
Aslib, 127, 909
Associated News Service, 910
Associates of the Late Dr Bray, 911, 1592
Association for Jewish Youth, 912
Association for Liberal Education, 275
Association for Programmed Learning and Educational Technology, 913
Association for Science Education, 686
Association for the Reform of Latin Teaching, 1070
Association for the Study of Medical Education, Television Section, 914
Association of British Correspondence Colleges, 915
Association of British Dental Surgery Assistants Ltd, 166
Association of British Theatre Technicians, 916
Association of Commonwealth Universities, 917
Association of Cricket Umpires, 768
Association of Dispensing Opticians, 918
Association of Optical Practitioners, 919
Association of Principals of Women's Colleges of Physical Education, 86
Association of Public Analysts, 920
Association of Public Health Inspectors, 921

Association of Scottish Climbing Clubs, 468
Association of Ski Schools in Gt Britain, 780
Association of Teachers in Colleges and Departments of Education, 922
Association of Teachers in Technical Institutions, 923
Association of Teachers of Russian, 2327
Association of University Teachers (Scotland), 602
Association of Voluntary Aided Secondary Schools, 83
Association of Workers for Maladjusted Children, 924
Astley Cheetham Public Library & Art Gallery (Stalybridge M.B.), 2156
Asthma Research Council, 925
Aston University
    Library, 152
    Social Sciences Library, 153
Astorga Collection, 529
Athenaeum, Liverpool, 857
Athenaeum, London, 926
Atherton Public Library, 1739
Atlantic Education Trust, 927
Atlantic Information Centre for Teachers, 927
ATV Network Ltd, 184
Austin Dobson Collection, 1326
Australian High Commission, 928
Australian News and Information Bureau, 928
Australian Reference Library, 928
Austrian Embassy, 1125
Austrian Institute, 929
Automobile Association, 930
Avery Hill College of Education, 931
Avery Historical Museum, 128
Aylesbury College of Further Education, 35
Ayr Carnegie Library, 41
Ayr County Library, 42
Ayrshire Archaeological and Natural History Society, 43

B

BACIE, 958
Bacup Public Library, 45
BADALIS, 2357
Bagshaw Museum, 78
Bagshawe Collection, 90
Baillie Library, 569
Baillie's Library, 603
Baker & McKenzie, 932
Balfour Library, 1969
Bamburgh Library, 492
Banbury Borough Library, 50
Banbury Historical Society, 50
Banffshire County Library, 763
Bangor City Library, 51
Bangor University Library, 51, 52, 54
Baptist Historical Society, 933
Baptist Missionary Society, 148, 934
Baptist Union of Great Britain and Ireland, 935
Baptist Union of Scotland, 604

Barber Fine Art Library, 154
Barking Public Libraries, 436
Barking Regional College of Technology, 435
　Business Management Studies Department, 435, 2048
Barnes Medical Library, 154
Barnet & District Local History Society, 2008
Barnet College of Further Education, 56, 275
Barnet Public Libraries, 1322
Barnsley Public Library, 57
Baron Collection, 1499
Baron de Ferrieres Gallery, 376
Barry Public Library, 60
Basic Ideology Research Unit, 936
Basingstoke Technical College, 63
Baskerville Collection, 133
Bateman Collection, 2113
Bath and District Association of Libraries and Information Services, 2357
Bath College of Education (Home Economics), 70
Bath Municipal Libraries and Victoria Art Gallery, 71
Bath Philatelic Society, 71
Bath Technical College, 73
Bath University, College and Municipal Libraries, 2358
Bath University of Technology, 72
Batley Art Gallery, 78
Batley Museums and Art Gallery, 78
Batley Public Library, 79
Battersea College of Education, 937
Bax Society, 938
BBC Television Enterprises, 208
Bebington Public Libraries, 2297
Beckenham Branch Library, 252
Beddington, C. E., Collection, 312
Bedford College, 1650
Bedford College of Physical Education, 87
Bedford Medical Institute, 88
Bedford Public Library, 89
Bedfordshire County Library, 90
Beecham Group Research and Development Product Laboratories, 207
Beecham Products U.K., 207
Beecham Research Laboratories, Betchworth, 117
Beecham Research Laboratories, Worthing, 2320
Beecroft Art Gallery, 2149
Beit Library, 315
Belfast City Libraries, 92
Belfast College of Domestic Science, 93
Belfast Transport Museum, 94
Bell Collection, 16
Bengeworth Parish Library, 154
Berkshire College of Art, 1727
Berkshire College of Education, 2020
Berkshire County Library, 2021
Berkshire Libraries Group, 2359
Bermondsey District Library, 1338
Bernard Wallis Collection, 579
Berwick-upon-Tweed Art Gallery, 115

Berwick-upon-Tweed Museum, 115
Berwick-upon-Tweed Public Library, Museum and Art Gallery, 115
Beth Din and Beth Hammidrash Library, 939
Bethlem Royal Hospital and the Maudsley Hospital, 1266
Bethnal Green Area Library, 1339
Bevan-Naish Collection, 158
Beveridge Collection, 2073
Bexley Libraries and Museums Department, 119
Bibliographical Society, 940
Bideford School of Art, 59
Bigger, F. J., Collection, 92
Bilston College of Further Education, 122
Biological Engineering Society, 941
Biomedical Information Project, 2108
Birkbeck College (University of London), 942
Birkenhead Public Libraries, 124
Birmingham Accident Hospital, 144
Birmingham and District Technical Periodicals Interchange Scheme, 2360
Birmingham Art Gallery, 138
Birmingham College of Art & Design, 129
Birmingham College of Education, 137
Birmingham Hebrew Congregation, 130
Birmingham Jewish Reference Library, 130
Birmingham Law Library, 131
Birmingham Law Society, 131
Birmingham Library, 132
Birmingham Medical Institute Library, 154
Birmingham Museum and Art Gallery, 138
Birmingham Public Libraries, 133
Birmingham Regional Hospital Board, 134
Birmingham University
　Centre for Child Study, 154
　Centre for Russian and East European Studies, 154
　Centre for Urban and Regional Studies, 154
　Centre of West African Studies, 154
　Institute for the Study of Worship and Religious Architecture, 154
　Institute of Child Health, 154
　Institute of Judicial Administration, 154
　Institute of Local Government Studies, 154
　Library, 154
　National Centre for Programmed Learning, 154, 155
　School of Education, 154, 156
　Shakespeare Institute, 154
Birmingham Works Libraries Loan Scheme, 2361
Bishop Auckland Technical College, 159
Bishop Edmund Gibson's Pamphlet Collection, 1585
Bishop Grosseteste College, 842
Bishop Lonsdale College of Education, 449
Bishop Phillpotts Library, 2217
Bishop Low Collection, 2073
Bishop, W. C., Liturgical Collection, 284
Bishopsgate Institute Library, 943
Black Watch (R.H.R.) Museum, 1986
Blackburn Art Gallery, 164

Blackburn College of Technology and Design, 161
Blackburn Law Association, 162
Blackburn Museum and Art Gallery, 164
Blackburn Public Libraries, 162
Blackpool and District Law Society Library, 167
Blackpool Central Public Library, 167
Blackpool College of Technology and Art, 168
Bladon Society of Arts and Crafts, 28
Blanche Leigh Collection, 813
Bloom Collection, 2179
Blumenthal Collection, 1783
B.M.A., 995
    South Wales and Monmouthshire Branch, 334
Board for Information and National Tests in Youth and Community Service, 503
Board for Social Responsibility of the Church of England, 944
Board of Deputies of British Jews, 945
Board of Dutch Studies, University of London, 1650
Board of Inland Revenue Library, 946
Board of Management for the County and City of Perth General Hospitals, 1987
Board of Trade, 947, 1425
    Statistics and Market Intelligence Library, 948
Bodleian Library, 1953, 1970
Bodmin Borough Museum, 171
Bodmin Medical Library, 172
Boehringer Ingelheim Limited, 757
Bognor Regis College of Education, 173
Bolling Hall Museum, 197
Bolt Collection, 1339
Bolton Art Gallery, 177
Bolton College of Education (Technical), 174
Bolton Institute of Technology, 175
Bolton Medical Institute Library, 176
Bolton Medical Society, 176
Bolton Museum and Art Gallery, 177
Bolton Public Libraries, 178
Bonnell Collection, 760
Book Development Council, 949
Book Information Bureau, 1404
Books Across the Sea of English Speaking Union, 950
Booth Hall Children's Hospital, 1740
Bootle Art Gallery, 183
Bootle College of Further Education, 182
Bootle Libraries, 183
Bootle Museum, 183
Boots Pure Drug Co. Ltd, 1886
Boreham Wood College of Further Education, 185
Borough of Colwyn Bay Public Library, 413
Borough of Port Talbot Public Libraries, 2001
Borough of Royal Leamington Spa Public Library, Art Gallery and Museum, 792
Borough of Whitley Bay Central Library, 2282
Borough Polytechnic, 951
Borough Road College, 758
Boston Parish Library, 186

Boston Public Library, 187
Bosworth Harcourt Bequest, 1882
Botswana High Commission, 952
Bournemouth & Poole College of Art, 189
Bournemouth and Poole Medical Society, 190
Bournemouth College of Technology, 191
Bournemouth Municipal Libraries, 192
Bowen Collection, 1425
Box Library, 1303
Brace Collection, 597
Bradford Central Public Library, 198
Bradford City Art Gallery and Museums, 199
Bradford Museums, 199
Bradford Scientific, Technical and Commercial Service, 2362
Bradford Technical College, 200
Bradford University Library, 201
Bradshaw Irish Collection, 314
Brasenose College, Oxford, 1918
BRASTACS, 2362
Brazenose Library, 2158
Brechin Diocesan Library, 474
Brecknock County Museum, 204
Breconshire County Library, 205
Brent Libraries Department, 1323
Brentwood College of Education, 210
Bretton Hall, 2234
Bridge of Earn Hospital, 1987
Bridgwater Public Library, 214
Bridgwater Technical College, 215
Bridlington Public Library, 218
Brierley Hill Branch Library, 219, 465
Brigg Manuscripts, 761
Briggs Collection, 1902
Brighton and Hove Natural History Society Library, 223
Brighton College of Art, 220
Brighton College of Education, 221
Brighton College of Technology, 222
Brighton Public Libraries, 223
Bristol and Gloucester Archaeological Society, 634
Bristol City Museum, 228
Bristol Moravian Church, 229
Bristol Polytechnic, 230
    Faculty of Art and Design, 231
Bristol Record Society, 232
Bristol Reference Library, 233
Bristol University
    Dental School, 237
    Wills Memorial Library, 246
Britannia Royal Naval College, 444
British Academy, 953
British Agricultural History Society, 2022
British Allergy Society, 954
British Amateur Press Association, 955
British Amateur Wrestling Association, 956
British and Foreign School Society, 758

British Antarctic Survey, 957
British Association for Commercial and Industrial Education, 958
British Association of Manipulative Medicine, 959
British Association of Sport and Medicine, 2130
British Association of the Hard of Hearing, 759
British Broadcasting Corporation
  Bristol, 234
  Music Library, 960
  Reference Library, 961
  TV Film Library, 208
British Cancer Council, 962
British Canoe Union, 963
British Caribbean Association, 964
British Centre of the International Theatre Institute, 965
British Children's Theatre Association, 2235
British Churches Housing Trust, 975
British College of Accordionists, 821
British Committee for Standards in Haematology, 966
British Council, 967
  Drama Library, 968
  English-Speaking Information Centre, The Language Teaching Library, 969, 1042, 1307
  Home Library, 970
  Language Teaching Library, 969, 1042, 1307
  Medical Library, 971
  Music Library, 972
  Periodicals Specimen Library, 973
British Council for Rehabilitation of the Disabled, 974
British Council of Churches, 975
British Council of the European Movement, 976
British Cycling Federation, 977
British Dental Association, 978
British Diabetic Association, 979
British Dietetic Association, 980
British Drama League, 981
British Epilepsy Association, 982
British Esperanto Association Incorporated, 983
British Film Academy, 1603
British Film Institute, 984, 1603
British Geriatrics Society, 985
British Homoeopathic Association, 986
British Horse Society, 767
British Hospitals Contributory Schemes Association (1948), 858
British Housewives League Ltd, 987
British Hungarian Friendship Society, 988
British Industrial and Scientific Film Association, 989
British Institute of Radiology, 990
British Institute of Recorded Sound, 991
British Judo Association, 992
British Legion Scotland, 504
British Leprosy Relief Association (LEPRA), 993
British Library of Political and Economic Science, 994
British Medical Association, 995
  South Wales and Monmouthshire Branch, 334
British Migraine Association, 193

British Museum
  Department of Printed Books, 996
  National Reference Library of Science and Invention, 1432–1434
  Newspaper Library, 997
British Music Hall Society, 998
British Music Information Centre, 999
British National Film Catalogue, 1000
British National Temperance League, 2105
British Neuropathological Society, 605
British Occupational Hygiene Society, 1831
British Optical Association, 1001
British Orienteering Federation, 505, 2013
British Piano Museum, 209
British Polio Fellowship, 1002
British Postal Chess Federation, 135
British Psychoanalytical Society, 1267
British Psychological Society, 1003, 1662
British Railways Board, 2328
British School of Osteopathy Ltd, 1004
British Science Fiction Association Limited, 2097
British Society for International Health Education, 1005
British Society for Research on Ageing, 796
British Society for the Study of Orthodontics, 1006
British Society of Dowsers, 2058
British Society of Master Glass Painters, 1007
British Society of Medical and Dental Hypnosis, 1008
British Soviet Friendship Society, 1009
British Speleological Association, 2102
British Surgical Export Group, 1010
British Temperance Society, 2255
British Theatre Museum Association, 1011
British Thoracic and Tuberculosis Association, 1012
British UNIMA, 1641
British Volunteer Programme, 1013, 1283
British Water Ski Federation, 573
British Youth Council, 1014
Britten Memorial Library, 1783
Brixton School of Building, 1015
Broadbent Collection, 2252
Bromhead Collection, 1662
Bromley College of Technology, 251
Bromley Public Libraries, 252
Bromsgrove College of Further Education, 255
Brontë Society, 760
Brook Hospital, 1697
Brooke Collection, 1924
Brotherton Collection, 813
Brotherton Library, 813
Brown Collection, 1538
Brownlee Collection, 1344
Brunel University Library, 2233
Brunner Public Library, 1872
Brynmor Jones Library, 739
Buck Bequest, 1882
Buckinghamshire County Library, 36
Buckinghamshire County Museum, 37

Bucklers' Hard Maritime Museum, 249
Bucks Archaeological Society, 38
Budgerigar Society, 136
Bullock Collection, 1791
Bunting Collection, 107
Bunyan Museum Library, 91
Bureau of Hygiene and Tropical Diseases, 1016
Burma Office, 1230
Burnley Grammar School Library, 258
Burnley Public Libraries, 258
Burrell Collection, 115
Burton-on-Trent and District Post Graduate Medical Centre, Medical Library, 259
Burton-Upon-Trent Public Library, 260
Burton-Upon-Trent Technical College, 261
Bury Public Library, 262
Bury St Edmunds Public Library, 263
Business Archives Council, 1017
Business Statistics Office, 2060
Bute Collection, 529
Bute County Library, 2055
Bute Museum, 2057
Butler Clarke Collection, 1972
Buxton Divisional Library and Museum, 266
Buxton Museum, 266
Buxton Water-Colours of Old Mansfield, 1795

C

Cabinet Office Library, 1199
CADIG, 418, 2365
Caerleon College of Education, 1854
Caernarvon Public Library, 267
Caernarvonshire and Anglesey Management Committee Medical Library, 52
Caernarvonshire County Library, 268
Calder, F. L., College of Education for Domestic Science, 864
Callendar Park College of Education, 590
Camberwell School of Art and Crafts, 1018
Camborne Public Library, 272
Camborne-Redruth Public Libraries, 272, 2033
Cambridge and County Folk Museum, 276
Cambridge Antiquarian Library, 310
Cambridge City Libraries, 277
Cambridge Institute of Education, 278
Cambridge Philosophical Society, 320
Cambridge University
   African Studies Centre, 298
   Appointments Board, 279
   Centre of Latin American Studies, 299
   Centre of South Asian Studies, 300
   Classical Faculty Library, 301
   Corpus Christi College, 282
   Department of Applied Economics, 302
   Department of Geography, 303
   Department of Medicine Library, 304
   Department of Pathology, 305
   Department of Pharmacology, 306
   Department of Radiotherapeutics, 307
   Department of Slavonic Studies, 311
   Department of Surgery, 308
   Divinity School, 309
   Dunn Nutritional Laboratory, 323
   Emmanuel College, 284
   Faculty of Archaeology and Anthropology, 310
   Faculty of Modern and Medieval Studies, 311
   Fitzwilliam Museum Library, 312
   Haddon Library, 310
   Institute of Criminology, 313
   Institute of Education, 278
   King's College, 288
   Library, 314
   Modern Languages Faculty Library, 315
   Museum of Archaeology and Ethnology, 310
   Museum of Classical Archaeology, 316
   Pembroke College, 291
   Pendlebury Library of Music, 317
   Postgraduate Medical School Library, 318
   Queen's College, 292
   St John's College, 294
   School of Veterinary Medicine, 319
   Scientific Periodicals Library, 320
   Selwyn College, 296
   Slavonic Library, 311
   Tyndale House, 297
   University Archives, 321
   Whipple Science Museum and Library, 322
Cambridge University Appointments Board, 279
Cambridgeshire and Isle of Ely County Library, 1796
Camden Public Libraries, 1324, 1325
Camden School for Girls, 1019
Campaign for Nuclear Disarmament, 1020
Canford School, 2288
Cannock Chase Technical College, 324
Canterbury Cathedral Chapter Library, 325
Canterbury Circle of Librarians, 2363
Canterbury College of Art, 326
Canterbury Public Library, 327
Canterbury Technical College, 328
Caravan Club, 1021
Cardiff College of Education, 331
Cardiff Medical Society, 334
Cardiff Naturalists Society's Library, 337
Cardiff Public Libraries, 332
Cardiff Royal Infirmary, 338, 344
Cardiganshire Antiquarian Society, 1
Careers Research and Advisory Centre, 280
Carlisle and Moorhouse Quaker Libraries, 354
Carlisle Cathedral Library, 346
Carlisle City Art Gallery, 347
Carlisle City Museum, 348
Carlisle College of Art and Design, 349
Carlisle Law Library, 354

Carlisle Public Libraries, 350
Carlisle Record Office, 354
Carlton Public Library, 1887
Carmarthenshire County Museum, 355
Carmarthenshire County Record Office, 356
Carnegie Dunfermline Trust, 475
Carnegie Hero Fund Trust, 476
Carnegie Historical Collection, 797
Carpet Industry Training Board, 2287
Carshalton College of Further Education, 359
Carshalton Postgraduate Medical Centre, 362
Carshalton Public Library, 360, 2196
Cassio College, 2256
Castle Library, Colchester, 408
Castle Society Subscription Library, 408
Castleford Public Libraries, 363
Cathedrals Advisory Committee, 1093
Catholic Central Library, 1022
Catholic Education Council, 1023
Catholic Marriage Advisory Council, 1024
Catholic Record Society, 1025
Catholic Teachers Federation, 1026
Catholic Youth Service Council, 1027
Cattery Information Service, 2087, 2324
C.B.D. Research Ltd, 84
Central Asian Research Centre, 1028
Central Bureau for Educational Visits and Exchanges, 1029
Central College of Commerce and Distribution, 606
Central Council for the Disabled, 1030
Central Council of Physical Recreation, 1031
Central Jewish Lecture Committee of the Board of Deputies of British Jews, 1032
Central Middlesex Hospital Medical Library, 1033
Central Midwives Board, 1034
Central Office of Information, 1035
  Photographs Library, 1036
Central Public Health Laboratory, 1037
Central Register of Charities, 1038, 1044
Central School of Art and Design, 1039
Central Statistical Office, 1040
Central Youth Employment Executive, 1041
Centre for Contemporary European Studies, 225
Centre for East Anglian Studies, 1885
Centre for Esperantist Documentation, 983
Centre for Information on Language Teaching, 1042, 1307
Centre for Information on the Teaching of English, 506
Centre for Insurance Studies, 225
Centre for Military Archives, 1303
Centre for Research in Collective Psychopathology, 225
Centre of South Asian Studies, 300
Centre for South East Asian Studies, 739
Ceramics Glass and Mineral Products Industry Training Board, 678
Chadderton Public Library, 1908
Chandler Collection, 1941
Charing Cross Hospital Medical School, 1043
Charities Information Service, 1143

Charity Commission, 1044
Charles Keene College of Further Education, 822
Charles Ower Collection, 472
Charles Tite Collection, 2326
Chartered Institute of Secretaries (Liverpool and District Branch) Library, 868
Chartered Insurance Institute, 1045
Chartered Society of Physiotherapy, 1046
Chatham Public Library, 366
Chelmsford and Essex Museum, 368
Chelmsford Cathedral Library, 369
Chelmsford Public Library, 370
Chelsea College of Physical Education, 496
Chelsea School of Art, 1047
Chelsea School of Chiropody, 1048
Cheltenham Art Gallery and Museum, 376
Cheltenham Museum, 376
Cheltenham Public Library, 377
Chertsey Library, 381
Cheshire College of Education, 425
Cheshire County Council Library & Museum Services, 382
Cheshire Record Office, 383
Cheshire Regiment Museum, 384
Cheshunt Public Library, 2246
Chest and Heart Association, 1049
Chester Archaeological Society, 385
Chester Beatty Research Institute, 1050, 1245
Chester College of Further Education, 386
Chester Public Library, 387
Chester Record Office, 385
Chesterfield College of Technology, 390
Chesterfield Public Library and Information Bureau, 391
Chetham's Library, 1741
Chichester Cathedral Library, 394
Chichester City Museum, 395
Chichester Postgraduate Medical Library, 396
Chichester Theological College, 397
Chick Collection, 323
Chief Rabbinate of Great Britain, 1458
Chigwell School, 400
Children's Writers Group, 1600
Chilean Iodine Educational Bureau, 1051
China Association, 1052
Chiswick Polytechnic, 1053
Cholmondeley (Houghton) MSS, 314
Chorley College of Education, 403
  Blackburn Division, 163
Christ Church College, Canterbury, 329
Christ Church, Oxford, 1919
Christchurch Mansion, Ipswich, 756
Christian Economic and Social Research Foundation, 1054
Christian Education Fellowship, 1284
Christian Medical Fellowship, 1284
Christian Science Committee on Publications for Great Britain and Ireland, 1055
Christian Science Monitor, 1056

Christian Socialist Movement, 1057
Christie Collection, 1791
Christie Hospital, 1742
Christ's College of Education, 859
Church in Wales Information Office, 1979
Church Missionary Society, 1058
Church of England Children's Society, 1059
Church of England Youth Council, 1060
Churches' Fellowship for Psychical and Spiritual Studies, 1061
Churchill Gardens Museum, 701
Churchill Hospital Medical Library, 1920
Church's Ministry Among the Jews, 1062
CIBA Foundation, 1063
CICRIS, 2409
City of Bath Technical College, 73
City of Birmingham Art Gallery, 138
City of Birmingham College of Education, 137
City of Birmingham Museum and Art Gallery, 138
City of Cardiff Public Libraries, 332
City of Coventry College of Art and Design, 417
City of Leeds and Carnegie College, 797
City of Leicester College of Education, 823
City of Leicester Polytechnic, 824
City of Liverpool Museums, 860
City of Liverpool Public Relations Office, 861
City of London College, 1064
City of Norwich Museums, 1873
City of Portsmouth College of Education, 2002
City of Stoke-on-Trent Art Gallery, 2170
City of Stoke-on-Trent Museum & Art Gallery, 2170
City of Truro Public Library, 2218
City of Westminster College, 1065
City of Westminster Libraries, 1688
City University, 1066
Civic Trust, 1067
Civic Trust for the North-East, 481, 1067
Civic Trust for the North-West, 1067, 1743
Civic Trust for Wales, 333, 1067
Civil and Public Services Association, 1068
Clapham Antiquarian Society, 1069
Clarendon Press, 1467
Clark Collection, 314
Clarke Collection (Cambridge), 303
Clarke Collection (Oxford), 1975
Clarke Papers, 1975
Classical Association, 1070
Cleveland Scientific Institution, 1806
Clifton College, 235
Clyde Yacht Clubs Association, 607
Clydebank Public Libraries, 405
Clyne Castle Collection, 2199
Coatbridge Technical College, 406
Cobden's Library, 223
Cockburn Association, 507
Codrington Library, 1921
Colchester and Essex Museum, 407

Colchester Public Library, 408
Cole, G. D. H., Collection, 1326, 1932
Cole Library, 2027
Coleg Harlech, 671
Coleg y Fro, 61
Colgate-Palmolive Ltd, 2082
College of All Saints, 1071
College of Arms, 1072
College of Craft Education, 732
College of Estate Management, 1073
College of Fashion and Clothing Technology, 1074
College of Librarianship, Wales, 15
College of Pathologists, 1075
College of Preachers, 1076
College of S. Mark & S. John, 1077, 1992
College of St Matthias, 236
College of Sarum St Michael, 2088
College of Special Education, 1078
College of the Venerable Bede, 482, 488
Colles Library, 433
Collet's Holdings Ltd, 2260
Colman and Rye Libraries, 1882
Colne Public Library, 412
Coloma College of Education, 2272
Colwyn Bay Public Library, 413
Combined Cadet Force Association, 1079
Comité International Tzigane, 1192
Commission on Industrial Relations, 1080
Commonwealth Association of Architects, 1081
Commonwealth Bureau of Agricultural Economics, 1922
Commonwealth Bureau of Animal Health, 2275
Commonwealth Bureau of Helminthology, 2066
Commonwealth Institute, 1082
    Scotland, 508, 1082
Commonwealth Society of Artists, 1146
Community Council for Cambridgeshire and Isle of Ely, Huntingdon and Peterborough, 281
Community Council of Lancashire, 1744
Community of the Resurrection, 1811
Community Relations Commission, 1497
Community Service Volunteers, 1083
Concourse Library, 2171
Confederate Historical Society, 833
Confederation of British Industry, 1084
Conference of Missionary Societies in Gt Britain and Ireland, 1085
Congregational Council for World Mission, 148, 1086
Constantine College of Technology, 1807
Construction Technology Building and Architecture in Scotland, 509
Consulate General of Monaco, 1087
Consumer's Association, 1088
Co-operative College, 1711
Cooperative Industrial and Commercial Reference and Information Service, 2409
Co-operative Union Ltd, 1711, 1745
Cope Collection, 2145

Cornwall County Language Laboratory Association Collection, 2034
Cornwall County Library, 2219
Cornwall County Record Office, 2220
Cornwall Technical College, 2034
Cornwall Technical Information Service, 2034, 2364
Corporation of London Records Office, 1089
Corpus Christi College, Cambridge, 282
Cosin's (the Episcopal) Library, 492
CoSIRA, 1092
Cotesworth Manuscripts, 599
Cottonian Collection, 1993
Council for Education in World Citizenship, 1090
Council for National Academic Awards, 1091
Council for Small Industries in Rural Areas, Advisory Services Division (CoSIRA), 1092
Council for the Care of Churches, 1093
Council for the Protection of Rural Wales, 1803
Council of Europe's Information Centre for Nature Conservation, 1096
Council of Industrial Design, 1094
Council of the British National Bibliography Ltd, 1095
County Borough of Blackburn Art Gallery, 164
County Borough of Blackburn Museum and Art Gallery, 164
County Borough of Bootle Art Gallery, 183
County Borough of Bootle Libraries, Museum and Art Gallery, 183
County Borough of Bootle Museum, 183
County Borough of Eastbourne Public Libraries, 497
County Seely Library, 1851
Countryside Commission, 1096
Courtauld Institute of Art, 1652
Coventry and District Information Group, 418, 2365
Coventry College of Art and Design, 417
Coventry Patmore Collection, 1902
Coventry Reference Library, 418
Coventry Technical College, 419
Cowper and Newton Museum, 1912
CPRW, 1803
Crabb Robinson Manuscripts and Transcripts, 1114
Craigie College of Education, 44
Crawley College of Further Education, 423
Crewe Public Library, 426
Critics' Circle Collection, 1688
Crompton Public Library, 1909
Crone, J. S., Collection, 92
Crosby Public Libraries, 862
Croydon College of Art, 430
Croydon Natural History and Scientific Society Limited, 429
Croydon Public Libraries, 431
Croydon Technical College, 430
CRUSE, 2037
Culham College of Education, 18
Cullum Collection, 263

Cumberland and Westmorland Antiquarian and Archaeological Society, 351
Cumberland Council of Social Service, 352
Cumberland County Library, 353
Cumberland County Record Office, 346, 354
Cuming Museum, 1097
Cuninghame Collection, 2092
Curnow Collection, 1783
Cymdeithas Diogelu Hardwdwch Cymru, 1803

D

Dacorum College of Further Education, 697
Daily Mirror Library, 1098
Daily Mirror Newspapers Ltd, 1098
Dalcroze Society (Incorporated), 1099, 2302
Danish Tourist Board, 1100
Dante Collection, 1972
Darlington Art Gallery, 439
Darlington College of Technology, 438
Darlington Museum, 439
Darlington Public Library, 439
Dartford and District Historical Society Library, 443
Dartford Borough Museum, 441
Dartford Hospital Management Committee, Medical Library, 442
Dartford Public Libraries, 443
Dartmoor Pony Society, 1861
Darwen Public Library, 445
David Davies Memorial Institute of International Studies, 1101
David Halstead Local History Collection, 2051
David Murray Collection, 630
Davy Faraday Research Laboratory, 1543
Dawkins Collection, 1972
Day Library of Natural History, 377
Dean and Chapter of Wells Library, 2261
Denbighshire County Library, 2062
Denbighshire Libraries Group, 2366
Department of Agriculture and Fisheries for Scotland, 553
Department of Education and Science, 1102
 Architect's and Building Branch, 1103
Department of Employment and Productivity Library, 1104
 Training Department (TD4), 1105
Department of Health and Social Security, 1106
 Social Security Library, 1107
Derby and District Colleges of Art and Technology, 450
Derby Borough Library, 451
Derby Cathedral Library, 452
Derbyshire County Library, 1799
 Matlock Branch Library, 1800
Design and Art Directors Association, 1108
Design & Industries Association, 1108
Deva Hospital Medical Library, 388
Development Documentation Centre, 1791
Devon County Library, 583

Devonshire Association, 58
Dialect Survey, 981
Dickens Fellowship, 1109
Dickens House, 1109
Didsbury College of Education, 1746
DIG, 638
Digby Stuart College of Education, 1110
Directorate General of Medical Services (R.A.F.), 1111
Directorate of Army Education, 1112
Disabled Living Activities Group of the Central Council for the Disabled, 1113
Disablement Income Group (DIG), 638
Disraeli Museum, 713
Dixon Collection, 67
Doble Library, 2222
Donald Newman Library, 2070
Donaldson Collection, 2073
Doncaster Hospital Management Committee, 2239
Doncaster Royal Infirmary, 2239
Donne Collection, 1379
Dorset Cooperative Scheme, 2367
Dorset County Library, 459
Dorset Natural History and Archaeological Society, 460
Doughty Museum, 649
Dover Public Library, 463
Dowlais Iron Company, 334
Down County Library, 48
Downey, W. & D., Collection, 1499
Downham Library, 1334
Doyle Collection, 92
Dr Barnardo's, 744
Dr Gordon Bottomley Bequest, 347
Dr Gordon Ward Notebooks, 2104
Dr Shepherd's Library, 2015
Dr William Goode's Pamphlet Collection, 1585
Dr William's Trust, 1114
Dryburn Hospital, 484
Dryden Collection, 1865
Duchy of Cornwall Office, 1115
Dudley Art Gallery, 465
Dudley College of Education, 464
Dudley Museum, 465
Dudley Public Libraries, Museum and Art Gallery, 465
  Brierley Hill Branch Library, 219
Dugdale Society, 2178
Duke of Edinburgh's Award Scheme, 1116
Dulwich District Library, 1338
Dumfries Burgh Museum, 466
Dumfries Technical College, 467
Duncan of Jordanstone College of Art, 469
Dundee College of Education, 470
Dundee College of Technology, 471
Dundee Public Libraries, 472
Dundee University Library, 474
Dunfermline College of Physical Education, 510
Dunfermline Museum, 477
Dunfermline Public Library, 478

Dunn Nutritional Laboratory, 323
Durham and Northumberland Coal Owners Association, 1843
Durham City Branch Library, Durham County Library, 483
Durham County Library, 483
Durham Postgraduate Medical Centre, 484
Durham Technical College, 485
Durham University
  College of the Venerable Bede, 482
  Department of Geography, 490
  Institute of Education, 491
  Library, 492
  Lowe Memorial Library, 486
  Neville's Cross College, 487
  St Hild's College, 488
  St John's College, 489
  University College, 486
  Ushaw College, 493
Durning H. Lawrence Collection, 1662

E

Ealing Public Libraries, 1326, 1327, 2137
Ealing Technical College, 1117
Earl of Dudley's Collection, 465
Early English Text Society Collection, 260
East Anglia University Library, 1885
East Anglian Regional Advisory Council for Further Education, 1874
East Anglian Regional Hospital Board, 283
East Berks College of Further Education, 1728
East Ham Technical College, 1118
East India Company, 1230
East Lancashire Regiment, 2251
East Lothian County Library, 664
East Midlands Economic Planning Council, 1888
East Midlands Regional Library System, 825, 2347
East Riding County Library, 118
East Suffolk County Library, 753
East Sussex County Library, 836
East Warwickshire College of Further Education, 2059
Eastbourne College of Education, 498
Eastbourne Public Libraries, 497
Eastern Counties Newspapers Ltd, 1875
Eastern Regional Hospital Board, 473
Eastgate House Museum, 2045
Eastlake Library, 1416
Eastleigh Technical College, 499
Eaton Hall College of Education, 2035
Eccles and District History Society, 1747
Eccles Public Library, 1748
Economics Association, 2193
Economist Intelligence Unit Limited, 1119
Economist Newspaper Ltd, 1120
Edge Hill College of Education, 1913
Edgehill Theological College, 95

Edinburgh Civic Trust, 507
Edinburgh College of Commerce, 511
Edinburgh Foot Clinic and School of Chiropody, 512
Edinburgh Public Libraries, 513
Edinburgh School of Chiropody, 512
Edinburgh University
   Central Medical Library, 565
   Centre of African Studies, 568
   Centre of European Governmental Studies, 566
   Law Library, 567
   Library, 568
   New College Library, 569
   Reid Music Library, 570
   Royal (Dick) School of Veterinary Studies, 571
   School of Scottish Studies, 572
Educational Foundation for Visual Aids, 1407
Educational Puppetry Association, 1121
Educational Writers Group, 1600
Edward Carpenter's Library, 2112
Edward Clark Collection, 527
Edward Grubb Collection, 158
Edward Hall Diary Collection, 2286
Edward Pease Public Library, Museum and Art Gallery, 439
Edward Stocks Massey Music Library, 258
EEG Society, 1122
Elder Park Library, 610
Electricity Supply Industry Training Board, 1123
Elgar Birthplace Museum, 1124, 2309
Elgar Birthplace Trust, 1124
Eli Lilly and Company Limited, 64
Elizabethan House, Totnes, 2215
Ellesmere Port Corporation Central Library, 2298
Elliot Collection, 223
Ellison Manuscripts, 599
Elms Technical College, 2171
Emanuel Green Collection, 233
Embassy of Austria, 1125
Embassy of Ireland, 1126
Embassy of Japan, 1289
Embassy of the Republic of Vietnam, 1127
Embroiderers' Guild, 1128
Emmanuel College, Cambridge, 284
E.M.R.L.S., 825, 2347
Endsleigh College of Education, 730
Enfield College of Technology, 576
English Art and Crafts Movement, 1692
English Association, 1129
English Cross Country Union, 285
English Goethe Society, 1658
English Lacrosse Union, 120
English New Education Fellowship, 1825
English Place-Name Society, 1130
English-Teaching Information Centre, 969, 1307
ENIT, 1287
Enk Library, 1303
Epilepsy Research Fund, 982

Epsom and Ewell Public Libraries, 578
Epsom College, 579
Enterprise Youth, 514
Ergonomics Information Analysis Centre, 139
Ergonomics Research Society, 1131
Esperanto Teachers Association, 211
Essex Archaeological Society, 407
Essex County Library, 371
Essex Record Office, 372
Essex Technical and Commercial Library Service, 2368
Essex University Library, 409
Eton College, Provost & Fellows Library, 2295
Ethicon Library, 520
Ethicon Limited, 515
Euclid Collection, 16
Eugenics Society, 1132
Euing Music Library, 630
Euratom, 1133
European Coal and Steel Community, 1133
European Commission, 1133
European Communities Press and Information Office, 1133
European Economic Community, 1133
Euthanasia Society, 1134
Evangelical Alliance, 1135
Evangelical Library, 1136
   Merseyside Branch, 1914
Evans Medical Ltd, 863
Evening Standard, 1137
Exeter Cathedral Library, 584, 586
Exeter College of Art, 585
Exeter College, Oxford, 1923
Exeter Medical Library, 586
Exeter Technical College, 587
Exeter University
   Institute of Education Library, 588
   Library, 589
'Express & Star' Library, 2303

F

Fabian Society, 1138
   Archives, 1932
Faculty of Actuaries, 516
Faculty of Advocates Library, 529
Faculty of Anaesthetists, 1139
Faculty of Architects and Surveyors, 1140
Faculty of Royal Designers for Industry, 1141
Faculty of Teachers in Commerce Limited, 2080
Failsworth Public Library, 1749
Fairbank Collection, 2112
Falmouth School of Art, 591
Family Planning Association, 1142
Family Welfare Association, 1143, 1418, 1662
Fanshawe Portraits and Collection, 436
Farnaby-Austen Manuscripts, 2104
Farnborough Hospital, 1915
Farnworth Public Library, 179

Federal Trust for Education and Research, 1144
Fédération Dentaire Internationale, 1145
Fédération Haltérophile Internationale, 2227
Federation of British Artists, 1146
Federation of Playgoer's Societies, 654
Federation of Specialised Film Associations, 1147
Federer Collection, 198
Feilden and Mawson, 1876
Feline Advisory Bureau, 730, 2324
Fellowship of Faith for the Muslims, 2063
Fellowship of Postgraduate Medicine, 1148
Fellowship of St Alban and St Sergius, 1149
Ferguson Collection, 630
Field Marshal Lord Wolseley and Viscountess Wolseley Collection, 724
Field Studies Council, 1150
Fielden Collection, 1538
Fiedler Collection, 1972
Fife County Library, 781
Film Centre (International) Ltd, 1151
Film Centre Production Library, 1152
Film Production Association of Great Britain, 1153
Financial Times, 1154
Finch Collection, 1972
Finnish Embassy, 1155
Finnish Tourist Board, United Kingdom Office, 1156
Finsbury Library, 1332
Fircroft College, 140
Fisons Pharmaceuticals Limited, Research & Development Laboratories, 1712
Fitzgerald Collection, 2045
Fleet Air Arm Museum, 2325
Fleetwood Cooperative Scheme, 2369
Flint Public Libraries, 593
Flintshire College of Technology, 446
Flintshire County Library, 1813
Flintshire Record Office, 447
Folkestone Public Library, 595
Folklore Society, 1157
Food and Agriculture Organization, 1646
Food Education Society, 1158
Forbes Collection, 2073
Ford Collection, 2145
Ford Green Hall Museum, 2170
Fordham Collection, 1538
Foreign Affairs Circle, 2038
Foreign and Commonwealth Office
   India Office Library, 1229
   India Office Records, 1230
   Library and Records Department, 1159
Forest Medical Society, 1160
Foresterhill College, 6
Forfar Public Library, 596
Forty Hall Museum and Art Gallery, 577
Fowler Collection (Bedford), 90
Fowler Collection (Leamington Spa), 792
Francis Thompson Collection, 2015

Free Church Federal Council, 1161
Free Church of Scotland College, 517
Freedom From Hunger Campaign, 1162
Freemasons' Hall, 1643
French Institute, 1163
French Protestant Hospital 'La Providence', 1219
Frere Manuscripts, 1878
Friends Historical Society, 1164
Frimley Sanatorium, 1254
Froebel Institute College of Education, 1165
Fulham Hospital Library, 1043, 1166
Fuller Collection, 1662
Fuller Maitland Music Collection, 787
Furzedown College of Education, 1167

G

Gainsborough Public Library, 597
Gallery of English Costume, 1750
Gallup Poll, 1168
Galpin Society, 518, 1169
Gamble Institute, 2076, 2077
Gardiner Institute Library, 608
Garnett College, 1170
Garretts Green Technical College, 141
Garside Collection, 639
Gas Industry Training Board, 1171
Gascoigne Collection, 802
Gaster Archives, 1383
Gateshead Public Libraries, 599
Geffrye Museum, 1172
Geldart Library, 1946
General and Municipal Workers' Union, 580
General Conference of the New Church, 1173
General Dental Council, 1174
General Dental Practitioners Association, 1751
General Register Office, 1175
General Register Office for Scotland, 519
General Register Office, Northern Ireland, 96
General Studies Association, 420
Geographical Association, 2106
George Hay Forbes Collection, 2073
George Howell Library, 943
George Jacob Holyoake Collection, 943
George MacDonald Collection, 4
George Reid Collection, 478
George Stephenson Collection, 391
German Embassy, 1176
German Institute, 1177
Gertrude Bell Collection, 1850
Gibb Collection, 314
Gillingham Public Library, 600
Gillow Archives, 1688
Gillow Collection, 1025
Gilstrap Public Library, 1826
Gipsy Hill College, 776
Girl Guides Association, 1178

681

Gissing Collection, 2237
Gladstone Library, 1423
Gladstone Memorial Library, 448
Glamorgan College of Education, 62
Glamorgan County Library, 212
Glamorgan County Record Office, 334
Glasgow Archaeological Society, 609
Glasgow Corporation Public Libraries, 610
Glasgow Museum of Transport, 611
Glasgow University
   Building Services Research Unit, 628
   Hunterian Museum, 629
   Library, 630
Glastonbury Antiquarian Society, 633
Glastonbury Branch Library, 633
Glaxo Laboratories Ltd, 648
Glaxo Research Ltd (Greenford), 648
Glaxo Research Ltd (Slough), 2131
Glenesk Folk Museum, 203
Gloucester City Libraries, 635
Gloucestershire College of Art and Design, 378
Gloucestershire College of Education, 636
Gloucestershire Record Office, 637
Gloucestershire Society for Industrial Archaeology, 2181
Gloucestershire Technical Information Service, 2370
Glyn, Mills & Co, 1179
Glynn Vivian Art Gallery, 2199
Goethe Collection, 1658
Goethe Institut, 1177
Goldsmith's College, 1653
Goldsmiths' Library, 1662
Goole Public Library, 639
Gorbals District Library, 610
Gordon Anthony Collection, 1499
Gordon Highlanders, 7
Gosforth Public Library, 1832
Gosport Public Libraries, 640
Gott Bequest, 802
Goulding Collection, 851
Government Information Service, Northern Ireland, 97
Government Social Survey Department, 1180
Grace Darling Museum, 49
Graduates Fellowship, 1284
Grainger Collection, 92
Grainger Stuart Collection, 2311
Granada Television Film Library, 1752
Granada Television Limited, 1753
Grand National Archery Society, 373
Grantham Museum, 641
Grantham Public Library & Museum, 641
Graves Art Gallery, 2111
Gravesend Central Library, 644
Gray's School of Art, 9
Great North of Scotland Railway Association, 8
Great Yarmouth Public Libraries, 647

Greater London Council
   (Member's) Library, 1181
   Public Information Branch Information Centre, 1182
Greater London Record Office, 1181, 1183
   (Middlesex Section), 1184
Greek Embassy Press and Information Office, 1539
Green Collection, 2237
Green Howards Museum, 2041
Greenwich Library, 1328
Greeynol, Private T., Collection, 671
Gregory Collection, 13
Grenfell and Hunt Papyrological Library, 1952
Grice Collection, 2111
Griffith Egyptological Library, 1952
Grimsby College of Technology, 650
Grimsby Public Library, 651
Grosvenor Museum, 389
GTIS, 2370
Guardian, 1754
Guild of Public Pharmacists, 1185
Guild of Teachers of Backward Children, 2151
Guild of Television Producers and Directors, 1603
Guildford County Technical College, 655
Guildford Museum and Muniment Room, 656
Guildford Public Library, 657
Guildhall Art Gallery, 1186
Guildhall Library, 1187
Guildhall Museum, 1188
Guildhall School of Music and Drama, 1189
Gundolph Collection, 1658
Gunnersbury Park Museum, 1190
Guttman-Maclay Collection, 1266
Guy's Hospital, 1191, 1430
Gypsy Council, 1192

H

Hackney Central Library, 1329
Hackney Hospital Medical Library, 1193
Haddon Collection, 310
Haddon Library, 310
HADIS, 2375
HALDIS, 667, 2371
Halesowen College of Further Education, 665
Halifax and District Information Service for Business and Industry, 667, 2371
Halifax Medical Library, 668
Halifax Public Library, 666
Hallé Concerts Society, 1755
Hallé Orchestra, 1755
Hambly and Rowe Collection, 2033
Hamilton College of Education, 669
Hamilton Jenkin Collection, 2033
Hamilton Museum, 670
Hamilton of Dalziel Collection, 1819
Hamilton Public Libraries and Museum, 670
Hamilton-Harty Collection, 107

682

Hammersmith College of Art & Building, 1194
Hammersmith Public Libraries, 1330
Hampshire County Library, 2289
Hampshire Technical Research Industrial Commercial Service, 2372
Hampstead Central Library, 1324
Hanbury Library, 1472
Handsworth and Erdington Technical College, 142
Hansard Society for Parliamentary Government, 1195
Harding Law Library, 154
Haringey Libraries, Museum and Arts Department, 1331
Harlech College, 671
Harlow Industrial Health Service, 672
Harlow Technical College, 673
Harlow Wood Orthopaedic Hospital, 1793
Harold Cohen Library, 878
Harperbury Hospital, 2067
Harris College, 2014
Harris Public Library, 2015
Harrogate College of Further Education, 676
Harrogate Public Library, 677
Harrow College of Technology and Art, 679
Harrow Public Libraries, 680
Harry Price Collection, 1662
Hart Collection, 163
Hartland Collection (Aberystwyth), 16
Hartland Collection (Manchester), 1791
Hartlebury Castle, 772
Hartlepool Public Libraries, 682
Hartley Victoria College, 1756
HASL, 2373
Haslingden Public Library, 2051
Hastings Art Gallery, 684
Hastings College of Further Education, 2079
Hastings Public Library, 683
Hastings Public Museum and Art Gallery, 684
Hatfield Polytechnic, 687, 707
HATRICS, 2372
Haverfield Library of Ancient History, 1952
Havering Public Libraries, 2050
Havering Technical College, 721
Hawick Archaeological Society, 692
Hawick Public Library, 692, 693
Haworth Parsonage Museum, 760
Health Education Council, 1196
Heath Branch Library, 1324
Heberden Coin Room Library, 1952
Heckmondwike Public Library, 695
Heffer, W., and Sons Ltd, 286
Helen Cruickshank's Library, 2166
Hely Hutchinson Collection, 154
Hendon College of Technology, 1197
Henley Parish Library, 2027
Henry Collection, 107
Henry George School of Social Science, 1198
Henry Watson Music Library, 1757
Hereford Cathedral Library, 702

Hereford City Library, 703
Hereford College of Education, 704
Herefordshire County Record Office, 705
Heriot-Watt University Library, 520
Hertford Museum, 708
Hertfordshire Association of Special Libraries, 2373
Hertfordshire County Council Technical Library and Information Service, 2374
Hertfordshire County Library, 709, 2264
HERTIS, 2374
Heythrop College, 401
Heywood Public Libraries, 712
High Commission for Ceylon in Britain, 1200
High Commission for Malaysia, 1201
High Commission of India, 1228
High Royds Hospital, 749
High Wycombe Public Library, 714
Highbury Technical College, 2003
Higher Education Research Unit, 1202
Highland Light Infantry, 613
Hillingdon Library Headquarters, 2271
Hinckley Public Libraries, 716
Hine Collection, 718
Historic Society of Lancashire and Cheshire, 125
Historical Association, 1203
Historical Manuscripts Commission, 1204
Historical Society of the Church in Wales, 357
Hitchin Art Gallery, 718
Hitchin College, 717
Hitchin Museum and Art Gallery, 718
H.M. Prison Service Staff College, 2236
H.M. Tower of London, 903
H.M. Treasury and Cabinet Office Library, 1199
Hobill Collection, 1756
Hockerill College of Education, 160
Hockey Association, 1205
Holborn Central Library, 1325
Hollymoor Hospital, 143
Holt Radium Institute, 1742
Home Office, 1206
Homerton Branch Library, 1329
Homosexual Law Reform Society, 1207
Hong Kong Government Office, 1208
Honourable Society of Lincolns Inn, 1209
Honourable Society of the Inner Temple, 1210
Honywood (Wren) Library, 844
Hopkinson-Berlioz Collection, 529
Horace Barks Reference Library, 2176
Hornby Library, 866
Horner Collection, 92
Horniman Museum and Library, 1211
Horserace Totalisator Board, 1212
Horsfall Turner Collection, 666
Horsforth Urban District Council Public Library, 798
Hospital Centre (King's Fund), 1113, 1213
Hospital Physicists' Association, 1214
Hotel and Catering Industry Training Board, 2267

Hounslow Library Services, 722
House of Commons Library, 1215
House of Lords Library, 1216
Household Cavalry Museum, 2296
Housing Centre Trust, 1217
Hove Public Library, 724
Howard League for Penal Reform, 1218
   Library, 422
Howard Lloyd & Co Limited, 80
Hoylake Historical Society, 2299
Huddersfield and District Information Service, 2375
Huddersfield College of Education (Technical), 725
Huddersfield College of Technology, 726
Huddersfield Public Libraries, 727
Hudson Memorial Library, 2068
Hugh Marwick Collection, 782
Hughenden Manor, 713
Hugo Dyson Collection, 2333
Huguenot Library, 1219
Huguenot Society of London, 1219
Hull City Libraries, 733
Hull College of Education, 734
Hull Museums, 735
Hull Nautical College, 736
Hull Regional College of Art, 731
Hull Technical Interloan Scheme, 2376
Hull University, Brynmer Jones Library, 739
HULTIS, 2376
Hunter Coin Cabinet Collection, 629
Hunterian Books and Manuscripts Collection, 630
Hunterian Museum, 1533
Huntingdon Technical College, 740
Huntingdonshire County Record Office, 741
Huyton-With-Roby Historic Society, 865
Hyde Public Library, 742

I

Icelandic Embassy, 1220
Ileostomy Association of Gt Britain & Ireland, 65
Ilkeston Public Library, 747
Ilkley College of Education, 750
Imperial Cancer Research Fund, 1221
Imperial Chemical Industries Ltd
   Industrial Hygiene Research Laboratories, 1723
   Pharmaceuticals Division, 1724
Imperial College
   Department of Biochemistry Library, 1222, 1366
Imperial Cricket Memorial Gallery, 1356
Imperial War Museum, Libraries and Archives, 1223
Incorporated Association of Assistant Masters in Secondary Schools (The A.M.A.), 1224
Incorporated Association of Preparatory Schools, 1225
Incorporated Society of Musicians, 1226
Independent Schools Association Incorporated, 2283
Independent Television Authority, 1227
India House Library, 1228

India Office Library, 1229
India Office Records, 1230
Individual Postal Tuition Service, 1862
Industrial Christian Fellowship, 1231
Industrial Co-Partnership Association, 1232
Industrial Health & Safety Centre, 1233
Industrial Training Research Unit, 287
Industrial Training Research Unit Library, 1441
INESKA, 2377
Information and Advisory Centres on Alcoholism, 876
Information Exchange Scheme Kingston Area, 2377
Ingatestone Hall, 372
Inner London Education Authority Library, 1234
Inner Temple, 1210
Innerpeffray Library, 428
Inns of Court School of Law, 1235
Institut Francais, 1163, 1688
Institute for Research into Mental Retardation Ltd, 1236
Institute for Strategic Studies, 1237
Institute for the Study and Treatment of Delinquency, 1238
Institute for the Study of Drug Dependence, 1239
Institute of Accident Surgery, 144
Institute of Actuaries, 1240
Institute of Advanced Motorists, 1241
Institute of Army Education, 81, 906, 1242
Institute of Bankers
   Collection of Paper Money, 1243
   Library, 1243
Institute of Basic Medical Sciences, 1532
Institute of British Geographers, 1244
Institute of Cancer Research, 1245
Institute of Cardiology, 1246
Institute of Child Psychology, 1247
Institute of Choreology, 1248
Institute of Civil Defence, 1249
Institute of Classical Studies, 1250
Institute of Clinical Science, Belfast, 108
Institute of Contemporary Art, 1108
Institute of Contemporary History and Wiener Library, 1251
Institute of Craft Education, 732
Institute of Dermatology, 1252
Institute of Development Studies, 224
Institute of Directors, 1253
Institute of Diseases of the Chest, 1254
Institute of Health Education, 2107
Institute of Hospital Administrators, 1255
Institute of Information Scientists, 1256
Institute of Jewish Affairs, 1257
Institute of Landscape Architects, 1108
Institute of Laryngology and Otology, 1258
Institute of Linguists, 1259
Institute of Manpower Studies, 225
Institute of Medical Laboratory Technology, 1260
Institute of Neurology, 1261
Institute of Occupational Medicine, 521
Institute of Operating Theatre Technicians, 1262

Institute of Ophthalmology, 1263
Institute of Orthopaedics, 1264
Institute of Practising Designers, 1265
Institute of Professional Designers, 1265
Institute of Psychiatry, 1266
Institute of Psycho-Analysis, 1267
Institute of Race Relations, 1497
Institute of Registered Architects, 1268
Institute of Shops Acts Administration, Shops and Other Acts Department, 1269
Institute of Sports Medicine, 1270
Institute of Urology, 1271
Institute of Professional Civil Servants, 1272
Institution of Training Officers, 82
Intake Trust Medical Library, 1794
International African Institute, 1273
International Amateur Radio Union Region I Division, 2049
International Association of M.M.M. Ltd, 1274
International Bureau for Epilepsy, 1275
International Commission on Radiological Protection, 2194
International Committee for Standardization in Haematology, 966
International Co-operative Alliance, 1276
International Federation of Library Associations, 2103
International Institute for Conservation of Historic and Artistic Works, 1277
International League against Epilepsy, 1275
International Leprosy Association, 2195
International Life-Boat Conference, 1546
International Medical Society of Paraplegia, 39
International Phonetic Association, 1278
International Planned Parenthood Federation, 1279
International Society for Clinical and Experimental Hypnosis, British National Division, 1280
International Society for the Protection of Animals (ISPA), 1281
International Transport Workers' Federation, 1282
International Vegetarian Union, 26
International Voluntary Service, 1283
International Weightlifting Federation, 2227
International Working Mens Association Minutes, 943
Inter-Varsity Fellowship of Evangelical Unions, 1284 Library, 297
Inter-Varsity Press, 1284
Intestinal Absorption Information Centre, 2108
Inverness Burgh Museum, 752
Ipswich and East Suffolk Hospital, 755
Ipswich Art Galleries, 756
Ipswich Civic College, 754
Ipswich Medical Library, 755
Ipswich Museums and Art Galleries, 756
Irish Central Library for Students, 2341
Irish Embassy, 1126
Ironbridge Gorge Museum Trust Limited, 2211
Islamic Cultural Centre, 1285

Isle of Wight Natural History and Archaeological Society, 1851
Isle of Wight Postgraduate Medical Centre, 1852
Isle of Wight Technical College, 1853
Islington Central Library, 1332
ISPA, 1281
Italian Embassy, 1286
Italian State Tourist Department (ENIT), 1287
Iveagh Bequest, Kenwood, 1288

J

Jackson Library, 350
James Dunn Collection, 164
James Graham College of Education, 799
James Munce Partnership, 98
Japan Information Centre, 1289
Japanese Embassy, 1289
Jeffries Jones, T. J., Youth Memorial Library, 671
Jesuit Library, 1025, 1290
Jewish Historical Society of England, 897, 1291, 1383
Jew's College, 1292
Johann Strauss Society of Great Britain, 216
John B. M. Camm Music Library, 192
John Bradshaw Collection, 584
John Bunyan Library, 89
John Burns Collection, 1181
John Clare Collection, 1865
John Conolly Hospital, 143
John Dalton College of Technology, 1758
John Horner Collection, 113
John H. Smith Collection, 846
John Keble Library, 1924
John Rylands Library, 1759
John Wilhelm Rowntree Collection, 158
John Wyeth & Brother Ltd, 1729
Johnson Birthplace Museum, 837, 840
Johnson Society, Lichfield, 837
Joint Archives Committee for Cumberland, Westmorland and Carlisle, 354, 765
Joint Association of Classical Teachers, 1070, 1293
Joint Executive Committee of the Associations of Head Masters, Head Mistresses, Assistant Masters and Assistant Mistresses, 1294
Joint Four, 1294
Joint Library of the Hellenic and Roman Studies, 1250, 1295
Joint Museum of Antiquities, 1849
Jordan Embassy, 1296
Joseph Cowen Collection, 1836
Joseph Livesey Library, 2105
Josephine Butler Educational Trust, 1297
Joyce Green Hospital, 442

K

Kay Sons & Daughter Ltd, 1298
Keats Memorial House, 1299

Keats Memorial Library, 1324
Keats-Shelley Memorial Association, 1300
Keble College, Oxford, 1924
Keele University Library, 1830
Keep Britain Tidy Group, 1301
Keighley and Craven Law Society Law Library, 761
Keighley Public Library, 761
Keighley Technical College, 762
Kelmscott Manor, 794, 1598
Kelmscott Press, 1692
Kennedy, J. F., Collection, 32
Kennington College, 1302
Kensington and Chelsea Public Libraries, 1522
Kent and Sussex Hospital Medical Library (P.G.M.C.), 2223
Kent County Library, 1731, 2224
Kent Sim Collection, 67
Kent University Library, 330
Ker, W. P., Collection, 1972
Kesteven College of Education, 642
Kesteven County Library, 2128
Keswick Hall, 1877
Kettering Art Gallery, 769
Kettering Museum, 769
Kettering Public Library, 769
Kettering Technical College, 770
Keynes Library, 288
Kidderminster and District Archaeological Society, 771
Kidderminster Art Gallery, 771
Kidderminster Museum, 771
Kidderminster Public Library Art Gallery and Museum, 771
Kidson Collection, 610
Kildare S. Meager Bequest, 2199
Kilmarnock Technical College, 773
Kilner Library of Plastic Surgery, 1925
King Alfred's College, 2290
King, G. A., Collection, 1878
King's College, Cambridge, 288
King's College, London, 1303
King's Lynn Art Gallery, 774
King's Lynn Museum and Art Gallery, 774
King's Lynn Public Library, 775
Kings Norton Parish Library, 133
King's Own Regiment Museum, 784
King's Own Royal Lancaster Regiment, 784
King's Own Scottish Borderers Regimental Museum, 116
King's School, Worcester, 2310
Kingston College of Art, 777
Kingston College of Technology, 778
Kingston Upon Hull City Libraries, 733
Kingston Upon Hull College of Education, 734
Kingston Upon Hull Museums, 735
Kingston Upon Hull Nautical College, 736
Kingston Upon Thames Public Libraries, 779
Kitson Collection, 802
Knightbridge Collection, 369

Korean Embassy, 1304
K.O.S.B. Regimental Museum, 116

L

La Sainte Union College of Education, 2138
Labour Party Library, 1305
LADSIRLAC, 866, 2385
Lady Mabel College of Education, 2052
Lakeland Dialect Society Library, 353
Lamb, A. C., Collection, 472
Lambeth Information Network, 2378
Lambeth Palace Library, 1306
Lambeth Public Libraries, 1333
Lancashire and Cheshire Antiquarian Society, 1760
Lancashire County Library, 2016
Lancashire Parish Register Society, 1761
Lancashire Record Office, 2017
Lancashire Regiment (P.W.V.), 2251
Lancaster & Morecambe College of Further Education, 785
Lancaster City Museum, 786
Lancaster Public Libraries, 787
Lancaster Royal Grammar School Memorial Library, 788
Lancaster University Library, 790
Lanchester College of Technology, 421
Lanchester, F. W., Collection, 421
Lanckoronski Collection, 1480
Lang Collection, 474
Langton Collection, 67
Language Teaching Information Centre, 800
Language-Teaching Library, 969, 1042, 1307
Language Tuition Centre, 1308
Laporte Industries Ltd, 745
L.A.S.E.R., 2348
Latimer House, Oxford, 1926
Law Commission, 1309
Law Society, 1310
Leadbitter Law Library, 493
League of Safe Drivers, 1311
Leamington Spa Art Gallery, 792
Leamington Spa Public Library, 792
Leamington Spa Museum, 792
Learning Resources Centre, 174
Leeds and Carnegie College, 797
Leeds City Art Galleries, 801
Leeds City Libraries, 802
  Archives Department, 803
Leeds Cooperative Scheme, 2379
Leeds (Old) Library, 804
Leeds Philatelic Society Library, 802
Leeds Polytechnic, 805
Leeds University
  Brotherton Library, 123, 813
  Dental Library, 814
  Department of Dialectology and Folk-lore, 123
  Department of English, 123
  Institute of Education Library, 815

Leeds University—*cont.*
  Law Library, 816
  Medical Library, 817
  Museum of the History of Education, 818
Leek Public Library, 820
Leicester City Information Centre, 825
Leicester City Libraries & Publicity Department, 825
Leicester City Publicity Department, 825
Leicester College of Education, 823
Leicester Polytechnic, 824
Leicester University
  Department of Museum Studies, 831
  Department of the History of Art, 831
  Library, 831
  Victorian Studies Centre, 831
Leicestershire County Library, 826
Leicestershire Rural Community Council, 827
Leicestershire Technical Information Service, 1714, 2380
Leigh Library, 1934
Leighton Inter-Library Scheme, 2381
LEPRA, 993
Leprosy Mission, 1312
Letchworth College of Technology, 834
Letchworth Public Library, 835
LETIS, 1714, 2380
Lewis Collection, 223
Lewis, H. K., & Co. Ltd, 1313
Lewis, T. B., Collection, 164
Lewisham Library Service, 1334, 1335
Lewisham Hospital Group, 1335
Liberal Party Organisation, 1314
Libraries of North Staffordshire in Cooperation, 2382
Libraries of the Institutes and Schools of Education, 2343
Library Association, 1315
  Northern Ireland Branch Library, 92
Library for Deaf Education, 1791
Library Information Service for Teeside, 1810, 2383
Library Information Service to Industry and Commerce, 2384
Library of the Grand Priory in the British Realm of the Most Venerable Order of the Hospital of St John of Jerusalem, 1316
Lichfield Cathedral Library, 838
Lichfield Joint Record Office, 839, 840, 2155
Lichfield Public Library, 839, 840
Life Guards, 2296
Lilly Research Centre Limited, 2294
Limehouse Area Library, 1339
Lincoln Archaeological Research Committee, 843
Lincoln Cathedral Library, 844
Lincoln Cathedral Treasury, 845
Lincoln City and County Museum, 843, 846
Lincoln City Libraries, 843, 847, 848, 854
Lincoln Medical Library, 847, 848
Lincoln No. 1 Hospital Group, 848
Lincoln Theological College, 849
Lincoln's Inn, 1209

Lincolnshire Architectural and Archaeological Society, 850
Lincolnshire Archives Office, 850
Lincolnshire Association, 852
Lincolnshire Local History Society, 850
Lincolnshire Naturalists' Union Collection, 846
Lindsey and Holland County Library, 851
LINK, 2378
LINOSCO, 2382
LISE, 2343
LISIC, 2384
LIST, 1810, 2383
Lister Collection, 1199
Lister Institute of Preventive Medicine, 1317
Lithuanian Association in Great Britain, 1318
Liverpool and District Scientific, Industrial and Research Library Advisory Council, 2385
Liverpool Central Libraries, 866
Liverpool College of Building, 867
Liverpool College of Commerce, 868
Liverpool Corporation Archives, 866
Liverpool Council of Social Service, 869
Liverpool Medical Institution, 870
Liverpool Museums, 860
Liverpool Public Libraries, 866
Liverpool Public Relations Office, 861
Liverpool Queen Victoria District Nursing Association, 881
Liverpool Regional College of Art and Design, 871
Liverpool Regional College of Technology, 872
Liverpool School of Tropical Medicine, 873
Liverpool University
  Harold Cohen Library, 878
  School of Education Library, 879
Llandaff Technical College, 335
Llandinam Library, 17
Llandrillo Technical College, 414
Llanelli Public Library, 882
Local Government Information Office, 1319
Local Government Operational Research Unit, 2023
Location of Offices Bureau, 1320
London & South Eastern Library Region, 2348
London Association for the Blind, 1321
London Borough of Barking Public Libraries, 436
London Borough of Barnet Public Libraries, 1322
London Borough of Bexley, Libraries and Museums Department, 119
London Borough of Brent Libraries Department, 1323
London Borough of Bromley Public Libraries, 252
  Anerley Branch Library, 252
  Beckenham Branch Library, 252
  Orpington Branch Library, 252
  Orpington Medical Library, 1915
London Borough of Camden
  Hampstead Central Library, 1324
  Heath Branch Library, 1324
  Holborn Central Library, 1325
  Keats Memorial Library, 1324
London Borough of Croydon Public Libraries, 431

London Borough of Ealing
   Acton District Library, 1327
   Central Library, 1326
   Southall District Library, 2137
London Borough of Greenwich
   Greenwich Library, 1328
   Local History Centre, 1328
   Plumstead Library, 1328
London Borough of Hackney Central Library, 1329
   Homerton Branch library, 1329
   Shoreditch District Library, 1329
   Stoke Newington District Library, 1329
London Borough of Hammersmith Public Libraries, 1330
London Borough of Haringey Libraries, Museum & Arts Department, 1331
London Borough of Harrow Public Libraries, 680
London Borough of Havering Public Libraries, 2050
London Borough of Hillingdon Library Headquarters, 2271
London Borough of Hounslow Library Services, 722
London Borough of Islington Libraries, 1332
   Finsbury Library, 1332
London Borough of Lambeth, 1333
   Minet Library, 1333
   North Lambeth Library, 1333
   Tate Central Library, 1333
London Borough of Lewisham Library Service, 1334
   Downham Library, 1334
   Medical and Patients Libraries, 1335
London Borough of Merton Public Libraries, 1336
   Mitcham Library, 1336
   Morden Library, 1336
   Wimbledon Library, 1336
London Borough of Newham
   Passmore Edwards Museum, 1470
London Borough of Newham Public Libraries, 1337
   Stratford Reference Library, 1337
London Borough of Redbridge Public Libraries, 746
London Borough of Richmond Upon Thames Central Reference Library, 2039
London Borough of Southwark
   Bermondsey District Library, 1338
   Dulwich District Library, 1338
   Newington District Library, 1338
London Borough of Sutton Public Libraries, 2196
   Carshalton Public Library, 2196
   Wallington Public Library, 2196
London Borough of Tower Hamlets Libraries Department, 1339
   Bethnal Green Area Library, 1339
   Limehouse Area Library, 1339
   Poplar Area Library, 1339
   Whitechapel Area Library, 1339
London Borough of Waltham Forest Public Libraries, 1340
London Borough of Wandsworth Public Library, 1341
London Clinic of Psychoanalysis, 1267
London Hospital Medical College Library, 1342
London Library, 1343

London Missionary Society, 148
London Natural History Society's Library, 1326
London Record Society, 828
London Records Office, 1089
London School of Economics, 994
London School of Hygiene and Tropical Medicine, 1016, 1344
London Topographical Society, 1345
London Tourist Board, 1346
London University
   Bedford College, 1650
   Birkbeck College, 942
   Board of Dutch Studies, 1650
   Chelsea College of Science and Technology Library, 1651
   Courtauld Institute of Art, 1652
   Goldsmiths' College, 1653
   Institute of Advanced Legal Studies, 1654
   Institute of Archaeology, 1655
   Institute of Basic Medical Sciences, 1532, 1656
   Institute of Classical Studies, 1250
   Institute of Education Library, 1657
   Institute of Germanic Studies, 1658
   Institute of Historical Research, 1659
   Institute of Latin American Studies, 1660
   Institute of United States Studies, 1661
   Joint Library of the Hellenic and Roman Studies, 1250, 1295
   Library, 1662
   Library Depository, 1303, 1662
   London Hospital Medical College Library, 1342
   London School of Economics and Political Science, 994
   London School of Hygiene and Tropical Medicine, 1344
   New College, London, 1663
   Queen Elizabeth College Library, 1664
   Queen Mary College Library, 1665
   Royal Holloway College, 574
   Royal Postgraduate Medical School, Wellcome Library, 1551
   Royal Veterinary College, 1561
   School of Oriental and African Studies, 1666
   School of Pharmacy, 1667
   School of Slavonic and East European Studies, 1668
   Sir John Cass College Library, 1586
   Westfield College, 1686
   Wye College Agricultural Museum, 31
Londonderry County Library, 410
Londonderry Post Graduate Medical Centre, 1708
Londonderry Public Libraries, 1709
Long Collection, 223
Long, D. F., & Co (Translations) Ltd, 1347
Long Eaton Public Library, 1889
Lord Beveridge Library, 2333
Lord Iveagh's Irish History Library, 1288
Lord's Day Observance Society Incorporated, 1348
Lotherton Hall, 801
Loughborough College of Art, 1713

Loughborough University of Technology, 1714
Louth Naturalists', Antiquarian and Literary Society, 1716
Lowe Memorial Library, 486
Lowestoft College of Further Education, 1717
Luton and District Information Service, 1721, 2386
Luton and Dunstable Hospital Medical Centre Library, 1718, 1721
Luton Art Gallery, 1720
Luton College of Technology, 1719
Luton Museum and Art Gallery, 1720
Luton Public Libraries, 1721
Luxembourg Embassy, 1349
Luxembourg National Tourist Office, 1350
Lyttleton Letters, 1686

M

Mabel Fletcher Technical College, 874
Macbean Collection (Aberdeen), 13
Macbean Collection (Nairn), 1821
Macclesfield Public Library, 1725
Maccoll Collection, 314
Mackay Collection, 2073
Mackintosh Library, 569
Macpherson, A. G. H., Collection, 1425
Madeley College of Education, 427
Magee University College, 1710
Magistrates' Association, 1351
Maidstone Art Gallery, 1733
Maidstone College of Art, 1732
Maidstone Museums and Art Gallery, 1733
Maitland/Sara Collection, 422
Malcolm Morley Collection, 1662
Maltby Collection, 492
Malvern Public Library, 1735
Manchester Arts Library, 1762
Manchester Cathedral, 1763
Manchester Central Board of Hebrew Education, 2083
Manchester City Art Galleries, 1750, 1764
Manchester College of Art and Design, 1765
Manchester College of Commerce, 1766
Manchester College, Oxford, 1927
Manchester Education Committee Library, 1767
Manchester Language and Literature Library, 1768
Manchester Literary and Philosophical Society, 1769
Manchester Literary Club, 1670
Manchester Local History Library, 1771
Manchester Medical Society Library, 1791
Manchester Museum Library, 1791
Manchester Service to Industry, 2387
Manchester Social Sciences Library, 1772
Manchester University
   Library, 1791
   Whitworth Art Gallery, 1792
Mankind Quarterly, 522
Mann Library, 493
Manners Collection, 1795

Mansfield and District General Hospital, 1794
Mansfield College, Oxford, 1928
Mansfield Local History Museum, 1795
Mansfield Public Library, 1795
Manx Museum Library, 462
Mappin Art Gallery, 2111
Marcus Paterson Collection, 1254
Margaret Morris Movement, 1274
Maria Assumpta College of Education, 1352
Maria Grey College, 2228
Marie Stopes Memorial Centre, 1353
Marist Fathers' House of Studies, 1976
Marlborough College, 1798
Marlowe Society, 1354
Marsden Collection, 1303
Martin Collection, 1972
Marylebone Cricket Club, 1356
Marx Memorial Library, 1355
Master Music Printers' and Engravers' Association, 27
Master Photographers Association of Great Britain, 1357
Masters' of Foxhounds Association, 402
Mathematical Association Library, 831
Mather College, 1773
Matlock College of Education, 1801
Matthew Boulton Technical College, 145
Matthews Collection, 223
May & Baker Ltd, 437
May Lamberton Becker Library, 1404
Mayer Public Library, 2297
Mayer-Gross Collection, 1266
McClean Bequest, 312
McDouall Collection, 107
McGillivray Collection, 2073
McLachlan Library, 1789
Mearns Hymnological Collection, 628
Medical Acupuncture Society, 1358
Medical Council on Alcoholism, 1359
Medical Officers of Schools Association, 1360
Medical Recording Service, 374
Medical Research Council
   Air Pollution Research Unit, 1361
   Applied Psychology Unit, 289
   Brain Metabolism Unit, 523
   Carshalton Laboratories, 361
   Clinical Genetics Unit, 1362
   Clinical Research Centre Library, 681
   Computer Unit (London), 1363
   Dental Unit, 237
   Developmental Psychology Unit, 1364
   Dunn Nutritional Laboratory, 323
   Environmental Radiation Unit, 806
   Epidemiology Unit, 336
   Experimental Pathology of Skin Unit, 146
   Experimental Radiopathology Unit, 1365
   Immunochemistry Unit, 1929
   Laboratory Animals Centre, 361
   Library, 1367

Medical Research Council—*cont.*
  Metabolic Reactions Research Unit, 1366
  Microbial Systematics Unit, 829
  Mineral Metabolism Unit, 807
  National Institute for Medical Research, 1367
  Neuroendocrinology Unit, 1930
  Neuropharmacology Unit, 147
  Neuropsychiatry Unit, 361
  Pneumoconiosis Research Unit, 1980
  Population Genetics Unit, 1931
  Project FAIR, Division of Biomedical Engineering, 1368
  Radiobiology Unit, 455
  Social Medicine Unit, 1369
  Social Psychiatry Research Unit, 1370
  Speech and Communication Unit, 524
  Toxicology Unit, 361
  Trachoma Unit, 1371
  Unit for Metabolic Studies in Psychiatry, 2109
  Unit for the Study of Environmental Factors in Mental and Physical illness, 1372
  Unit on Drug Sensitivity in Tuberculosis, 1373
Medical Society of London Library, 1678
MEDLARS, 188, 878, 1555
Medway and Maidstone College of Technology, 367, 1734
Medway College of Art, 2046
Medway School of Art and Crafts, 2046
Mellish Collection, 1902
Merchant Navy College, 1586
Merseyside Cancer Education Committee, 875
Merseyside Council on Alcoholism, 876
Merthyr Tydfil Public Libraries, 1804
Merton Public Libraries, 1336
Methodist Church Archives Centre, 1374, 1375
Methodist Church (Conference Office), 1375
Methodist Missionary Society, 1376
Metropolitan Police Office, 1377
Metropolitan Special Collections Scheme, 2342
Mexborough Schofeild Technical College, 1805
Mexican Embassy, 1378
Mid Essex Technical College and School of Art, 375
Mid Staffordshire Libraries in Cooperation, 2388
Mid-Warwickshire College of Further Education, 793
Middle Temple Library, 1379
Middlesex Hospital Medical School, 1380
Middleton Public Libraries, 1774
Middleton St George College of Education, 440
Midlothian County Library, 1820
Milton's Cottage, 365
Mimram Books, 710
Minet Library, 1333
Mingana Collection, 149
Ministry of Agriculture, Fisheries and Food
  Animal Health Division, 2190
  Central Veterinary Laboratory, 2276
  Tangley Place Laboratory, 658
  Veterinary Laboratory, Lasswade, 791

Ministry of Agriculture, Northern Ireland, Veterinary Research Laboratories, 99
Ministry of Defence (Army), Directorate of Army Education, 1112
Ministry of Defence, Directorate General of Medical Services (R.A.F.), 1111
Ministry of Housing and Local Government, 1381
Ministry of Overseas Development, 1159, 1382
Ministry of Power Mining Record Office, 2220
MISLIC, 2388
Mitcham Library, 1336
Mitchell Library, 610
Mocatta Library, 897, 1383
Mocatta Museum, 1383
Monaco Consulate-General, 1087
Monkwearmouth College of Further Education, 2182
Monmouth County Library, 1855
Monmouthshire Record Office, 1856
Monmouthshire Regiment Regimental Museum, 206
Montagu Motor Museum, 250
Montessori Society in England, 1384
Montrose Public Library, 1816
Moody Manners Collection, 610
Moore Collection, 92
Moravian Church Archives, 902
Moray and Nairn Library Headquarters, 575
Moray House College of Education, 525
Morden Library, 1336
Moredun Institute, 502
Morfill Collection, 1972
Morley College, 1385
Morley Public Library, 808
Morning Star, 1386
Morrell, J. B., Library, 2333
Morrison Library, 1404
Mothers' Union, 1387
Motherwell and Wishaw Public Libraries, 1819
Mott, C. F., College of Education, 2011
Mott Harrison Collection, 89
Mount Saint Bernard Abbey, 830
Mount Wise Naval History Library, 1996
Moyse Collection, 2214
Murison Burns Collection, 478
Murray Collection, 568
Muscular Dystrophy Group of Great Britain, 1388
Museum of Artillery, 1389
Museum of Banking History, 1179
Museum of British Transport, Clapham, 1390
Museum of Childhood, 526
Museum of Costume, Bath, 74
Museum of Isle of Wight Geology, 2093
Museum of Lakeland Life and Industry, 766
Museum of Leathercraft, 1391
Museum of Lincolnshire Life, 852
Museum of Postal History, 1331
Museum of the History of Education, 818
Museums Association, 1392

Musgrove Park Hospital, 2208
Music Advisers' National Association, 1890
Music Users Council, 1393
Musical Education of the Under-Twelves Association, 55

N

Nairn Literary Institute, 1821
NANTIS, 2393
Napier College of Science and Technology, 527
Napier Pamphlets, 1956
Narrow Gauge Railway Society, 728
National Anti-Vaccination League, 432
National Antivivisection Society Ltd, 1394
National Army Museum, 269
National Association for the Care and Resettlement of Offenders, 1395
National Association of Boys' Clubs, 1396
National Association of Leagues of Hospital Friends, 1397
National Association of Parish Councils, 1398
National Association of Probation Officers, 1399
National Association of State Enrolled Nurses, 1400
National Association of Tenants and Residents, 1401
National Association of Youth Orchestras, 652
National Audio-Visual Aids Centre, 1402, 1407
National Audio-Visual Aids Library, 1403, 1407
National Baseball League (U.K.), 737
National Book League, 1404
National Bureau for Co-operation in Child Care, 1405
National Central Library, 2339
National Centre for the International Occupational Safety and Health Information Service, 1508
National Citizen's Advice Bureaux Council, 1406
National College for the Training of Youth Leaders, 832
National Committee for Audio-Visual Aids in Education, 1407
National Council for Civic Theatres, 2183
National Council for Educational Technology, 1408
National Council of Social Service (Incorporated), 1409
National Council of Y.M.C.A.'s, 1410
National Council on Alcoholism, 1411
National Equestrian Centre, 767
National Farmers' Union, 1412
National Federation of Consumer Groups, 1413
National Federation of Gramophone Societies, 1916
National Federation of Old Age Pensions Associations, 165
National Federation of Professional Workers, 698
National Federation of Spiritual Healers, 659
National Foundation for Educational Research in England and Wales, 2132
National Froebel Foundation, 1414
National Gallery, 1415
  Scientific Department, 1416
National Gallery of Scotland, 528
National Greyhound Racing Society, 1417
National Hospital, 1261
National Institute for Medical Research, 1367
National Institute for Social Work Training, 1418
National Institute of Adult Education (England and Wales), 1419
National Institute of Economic and Social Research, 1420
National Institute of Industrial Psychology, 1421
National Institute of Medical Herbalists, 1422, 2110
National Lending Library for Science and Technology, 188
National Liberal Club, 1423
National Library for the Blind, 1424, 1775
National Library of Australia, Canberra, 928
National Library of Scotland, 529
National Library of Wales, 16
National Maritime Museum, 1425
National Monuments Record, 1426, 1535
National Museum of Antiquities of Scotland, 530
National Museum of the Theatre, 1011
National Museum of Wales, 337
National Nursery Examination Board, 1427
National Old People's Welfare Council, 1428
National Pharmaceutical Union, 1429
National Poisons Information Service, Belfast, 100
National Poisons Reference and Information Service, 1191, 1430
National Postal Museum, 1431
National Reference Library of Science and Invention, 996, 1432–1434
  Bayswater Division, 1433
  Holborn Division, 1434
National Reprographic Centre for documentation, 687
National Roller Hockey Association of Gt Britain, 1435
National Savings Committee, 1436
National Secular Society, 1437
National Society, 1146
National Society for Art Education, 688
National Society for Autistic Children, 1438
National Society for Clean Air, 1439
National Society for the Prevention of Cruelty to Children, 1440
National Unemployed Workers Association, 1441
National Union of Seamen, 1442
National Union of Teachers, 1443
National Union of Vehicle Builders, 1776
Natural History Society, Bacup, 46
Nautical College, 1586
Neath Public Library, 1822
Neath Technical College, 1823
Nelson Museum, 1814
Nelson Public Library, 1824
Netherlands Embassy, 1548
Netherne and Fairdene Hospitals, 416
Nevill Forbes Collection, 1972
Neville's Cross College, Durham, 487
New Church, 1173, 1622
New Education Fellowship, 2226
New English Art Club, 1146
New Freedom Group, 1444
New South Wales Government Offices, 1445

New University of Ulster Library, 411
New Zealand Film Library, 1446
New Zealand High Commission, 1447
Newark on Trent Art Gallery, 1827
Newark on Trent Museum & Art Gallery, 1826, 1827
Newburn Urban District Council Library, 1834
Newcastle Chronicle & Journal Ltd, 1835
Newcastle General Hospital, Post-graduate Medical Library, 1836, 1840
Newcastle-Under-Lyme Public Libraries, 1829
Newcastle Upon Tyne City Libraries, 1836
Newcastle Upon Tyne College of Education, 1837
Newcastle Upon Tyne College of Further Education, 1838
Newcastle Upon Tyne Literary and Philosophical Society, 1833
Newcastle Upon Tyne Polytechnic Library, 1839
Newcastle Upon Tyne Postgraduate Medical Library, 1840
Newcastle Upon Tyne University Library, 1850
Newham Public Libraries, 1337
Newington District Library, 1338
Newport and Monmouthshire College of Technology, 1857
Newport Art Gallery, 1859
Newport College of Art and Design, 1858
Newport Museum and Art Gallery, 1859
Newton Park College of Education, 75
Nichol Smith Collection, 529
Nicholas Research Institute, 2133
Nicoll Collection, 474
Nigeria High Commission, 1448
NINES, 2389
Norfolk and Norwich Archaeological Society, 1878
Norfolk and Norwich Incorporated Law Society Library, 1882
Norfolk and Norwich Library, 1879
Norfolk and Norwich Record Office, 1878
Norfolk County Library, 1880
Norfolk Information Exchange Scheme, 2389
Normal College of Education, Bangor, 53
Norman Baynes Byzantine Collection, 1114
Norman Stewart Institute, 2056
Normanby Hall, 2099
North Ayrshire Museum, 2092
North Berkshire College of Further Education, 19
North Bucks College of Education, 169
North Devon Athenaeum, 58
North Devon Technical College and College of Further Education, 59
North East Development Council, 1841
North East Lancashire Libraries, 2390
North Lambeth Library, 1333
North Lindsey Technical College, 2098
North London Blood Transfusion Centre, 501
North Notts College of Further Education, 2318
North of England Industrial Health Service, 1842
North of England Institute of Mining and Mechanical Engineers, 1843

North Riding County Library, 1863
North Riding Record Office, 1864
North Staffordshire Medical Institute, 2172
North Staffordshire Polytechnic, 2173
    School of Fine Art, 2174
    School of Printing and Graphic Design, 2174
North Staffordshire Society of Architects, 1797
North Wales Urban Libraries Group, 2391
North-Western Polytechnic, 1451
North Western Regional Library System, 2349
Northampton Central Public Library, 1865
Northampton College of Technology, 1866
Northampton School of Art, 1866
Northamptonshire County Library, 1867
Northamptonshire Record Office, 1868
Northamptonshire Record Society, 1869
Northern Arts Association, 1844
Northern Arts Poetry Library, 1844
Northern Circle of College Libraries, 2392
Northern Counties College of Education, 1845
Northern Ireland
    General Register Office, 96
    Government Information Service, 97
    Ministry of Agriculture, Veterinary Research Laboratories, 99
    Public Record Office, 106
Northern Ireland Association of Youth Clubs, 101
Northern Ireland Council of Social Service, 102
Northern Ireland Government Office, 1449
Northern Ireland Hospitals Authority, 103
Northern Ireland Tourist Board, 104
Northern Polytechnic, 1450
Northern Reform Union, 1836
Northern Regional Library System, 2350
Northern School of Music, 1777
Northumberland College of Education (Ponteland), 1846
Northumberland County Library, 1818
Northumberland County Record Office, 1843, 1849
Northumberland County Technical College, 32
Northumberland Local History Society, 1847
Northumberland Rural Community Council, 1848
Norwegian Embassy, 1452
Norwich Castle Museum, 1873
Norwich City College, 1881
Norwich Public Libraries, 1882
Norwich Museums, 1873
Norwich School of Art, 1883
Norwood Technical College, 1453
Notre Dame College of Education, Glasgow, 612
Notre Dame College of Education, Liverpool, 877
Nottingham and Derbyshire Regiment, 1900
Nottingham and Nottinghamshire Technical Information Service, 2393
Nottingham College of Art and Design, 1892
Nottingham College of Education, 1893
Nottingham City Library, 1891
Nottingham Industrial Museum, 1894

Nottingham Regional College of Technology, 1895
Nottingham University Library, 1902
Nottinghamshire County Library, 1896
Nottinghamshire Rural Community Council, 1897
N.R.L.S., 2350
N.R.L.S.I., 1432–1434
Nuffield Child Language Survey, 2334
Nuffield Collection, 1380
Nuffield College, Oxford, 1932
Nuffield Foreign Language Teaching Materials Project, 2334
Nuffield Library, 995
Nuffield Orthopaedic Centre, 1967
Nuneaton Art Gallery, 1904
Nuneaton Library, 1903
Nuneaton Museum and Art Gallery, 1904
Nuneaton School of Art, 1905
Nuneaton Technical College and School of Art, 1905
N.W.R.L.S., 2349

O

Oakwell Hall, 78
Oaten Collection, 1783
Observer, 1454
O'Dell Collection, 13
Office of Health Economics, 1455
Office of the Agent General for Quebec, 1456
Office of the Agent General for Tasmania, 1457
Office of the Chief Rabbi, 1458
Office of the High Commissioner for Singapore in the United Kingdom 1459
Office of the High Commissioner for Uganda, 1460
Old Bedford Library, 89
Old Water Colour Society's Club, 1461
Oldham College of Further Education, 1910
Oldham Public Library, 1911
Open Door Council, 1462
Open Door International British Branch, 1462
Ophthalmic Hospital in Jerusalem, 1316
Optical Information Council, 1463
Orbilean Society, 1070
Order of Friars-Servants of Mary, 1933
Organon Laboratories Ltd, 1817
Oriel College, Oxford, 1934
Orkney County Library, 782
Ornamental Pottery Association, 2175
Orpington Branch Library, 252
Orpington Medical Library, 1915
Oswestry College of Further Education, 1917
Ove Arup and Partners, Consulting Engineers, 1464
Oversea Visual Aid Centre, 1465
Overseas Development Institute, 1466
Overstone Library, 2027
Oxford City Libraries, 1935
Oxford Mail & Times (Westminster Press) Ltd, 1936
Oxford Polytechnic, 1937

Oxford Regional Hospital Board, 1938
Oxford University
    All Souls College, 1921
    Ashmolean Museum of Art and Archaeology, 1952
    Balfour Library, 1969
    Bodleian Library, 1953, 1970
    Brasenose College, 1918
    Christ Church, 1919
    Codrington Library, 1921
    Department of Educational Studies Library, 1954
    Department of Pharmacology, 1935
    English Faculty Library, 1956
    Exeter College, 1923
    Faculty of Music Library, 1957
    Faculty of Social Studies, Social Studies Library, 1958
    Grenfell and Hunt Papyrological Library, 1952
    Griffith Egyptological Library, 1952
    Haverfield Library of Ancient History, 1952
    Heberden Coin Room Library, 1952
    History Faculty Library, 1959
    Institute of Agricultural Economics, 1960
    Institute of Commonwealth Studies, 1961
    Institute of Economics and Statistics, 1962
    Institute of Psychiatry, 1963
    Institute of Social Anthropology, 1964
    Keble College, 1924
    Latimer House, 1926
    Law Library, 1953
    Library of Classical Archaeology, 1952
    Library of Classical Literature, 1952
    Library of Medieval Archaeology, 1952
    Library of the Department of Antiquities, 1952
    Library of the Department of Eastern Art, 1952
    Library of the Department of Western Art, 1952
    Library of the Griffith Institute, 1952
    Manchester College, 1927
    Mansfield College, 1928
    Modern Languages Faculty Library, 1965
    Museum of the History of Science, 1966
    Nuffield College, 1932
    Nuffield Department of Orthopaedic Surgery, 1967
    Oriel College, 1934
    Oriental Institute Library, 1968
    Pembroke College, 1941
    Pitt Rivers Museum, 1969
    Pusey House, 1942
    Queen's College, 1943
    Radcliffe Science Library, 1953, 1970
    Regent's Park College, 1944
    Rhodes House Library, 1953
    Ripon Hall, 1945
    St Anne's College, 1946
    St Antony's College, 1947
    St Edmund Hall, 1948
    St Hilda's College, 1949
    St Hugh's College, 1950
    School of Geography, 1971

Oxford University—*cont.*
  Taylor Institution, 1965, 1972
    Wadham College, 1973
    Worcester College, 1975
Oxford University Press, 1467
Oxfordshire County Library, 1939
Oxfordshire Rural Community Council, 1940

P

Paddington Technical College, 1468
Padgate College of Education, 2250
Paisley and District Technical Information Group, 2394
Paisley College of Technology, 1977
Paisley Public Libraries, 1978
Pali Text Society, 1469
Papworth Hospital, Medical Library, 290
Park Prewett Hospital, 66
Parke, Davis & Company, 723
Parker Collection, 133
Parkes Library, 2139, 2145
Passfield Collection, 994
Passmore Edwards Museum, 1470
Pastel Society, 1146
Patients' Association, 1471
Pavlova Memorial Library, 1688
P.D.S.A., 461
Peal Collection, 1326
Peck Collection, 2158
Pembroke College, Cambridge, 291
Pembroke College, Oxford, 1941
Pembrokeshire Community Council, 689
Pembrokeshire County Library, 690
Pembrokeshire Record Office, 691
Pembury Hospital Library, 2224
Penarth Public Library, 1981
Pendlebury Library of Music, 317
Penzance Natural History and Antiquarian Museum, 1984
Penzance Public Library, 1984, 1985
People's College of Further Education, 1898
People's Dispensary for Sick Animals, 461
Percival Library, 235
Percival Whitley College of Further Education, 667
Percy Collection, 107
Perkins Agricultural Library, 2145
Perth and Kinross County Library, 1988
Perth Royal Infirmary, 1987
Peterborough City Libraries, 1989
Peterborough Technical College, 1990
Petyt Library, 2127
Pfizer Limited, 2094
Pharmaceutical Society of Great Britain, 1472
  Scottish Department, 531
Philip Gosse Pirate Library, 1425
Philippa Fawcett College, 1473
Phillip Found Shorthand Collection, 327
Philological Society, 1474

Physical Education Association of Great Britain and Northern Ireland, 1270, 1475
Picton Reference Library, 866
Pilkington Glass Museum, 2075
Pilley Collection, 703
Pitt Collection, 2143
Platt Hall, 1750
Platten Bequest Library, 2262
Plumstead Library, 1328
Plunkett Foundation for Co-operative Studies, 1476
Plunkett Letters, 1476
Plymouth City Art Gallery, 1993
Plymouth College of Technology, 1994
Plymouth General Hospital Medical Library, 1995
Plymouth Medical Society, 1995
Plymouth Public Libraries, 1996
Poetry Society, 1477
Poisons Index, Bristol, 245
Poisons Information Service, Cardiff, 338
Police College, 67
Polish Cultural Institute, 1478
Polish Institute, 1479
Polish Library, 1480
Political Studies Association of the United Kingdom, 1481
Polytechnic of Central London (Designate), 1482
Ponsbourne College, 711
Pontefract Public Library, 1997
Pontypridd Public Libraries, 1998
Poole Museums, 1999
Poole Public Libraries and Museums, 1999
Poole Technical College, 2000
Poplar Area Library, 1339
Port Royal Library, 1585
Port Royale Collection, 1924
Port Talbot Public Libraries, 2001
Port Talbot Technical Information Service, 2395
Portens Collection, 1662
Porter Collection, 1902
Portico Library & Newsroom, 1778
PORTIS, 2395
Porton Collection, 802
Portsmouth City Libraries, 2004
Portsmouth College of Art and Design, 2005
Portsmouth College of Education, 2002
Portsmouth Medical Society, 2006
Post Office, 1483
Post Office Engineering Union, 1484
Postgate Collection, 730
Powicke, F. J., Collection, 158
Pre Retirement Association, 1485
Prehistoric Society, 1486
Presbyterian Church in Ireland, 105
Presbyterian Church of England Offices, 1487
Presbyterian Church of England Overseas Committee, 148
Presbyterian Historical Society of England, 1488
Prescot College of Further Education, 2012

Preston and District Commercial and Technical Information Services, 2396
Preston 'Blake' Library, 1688
Preston Collection, 813
Priaulx Library, 653
Priebsch-Closs Collection, 1658
Priestley Collection, 133
Prince Consort's Library, 24
Prince of Wales and St Ann's Medical Libraries, 1489
Princess Margaret Hospital Medical Library, 2204
Print Collectors' Club, 1490
Printing Historical Society, 1491
Prittlewell Priory and Museum, 2149
Private Libraries Association, 1991
Prof. G. N. Garmonsway Library, 2333
Prof. Henry Carter Adams Library, 2333
Professional Classes Aid Council (Inc), 1492
Public Health Inspectors Education Board, 1493
Public Record Office, 1494
Public Record Office, Northern Ireland, 106
Pulteney College, 1495
Pusey House, Oxford, 1942
Putteridge Bury College of Education, 1722
Pybus Collection, 1850

Q

Quaker Library, 158
Quakers, 1164, 1502
Queen Alexandra Hospital, 2006
Queen Elizabeth II Hospital, Welwyn Garden City, 709, 2264
Queen Victoria Hospital Medical Library, 494
Queen's College, Cambridge, 292
Queen's College, Oxford, 1943
Queen's Institute of District Nursing, 1496
Queen's Own Cameron Highlanders, 752
Queen's Own Highlanders (Seaforth and Camerons), 752
Queen's University, Belfast
   Faculty of Agriculture, 99
   Library, 99, 107
   Medical Library, 108
   Science Library
     Architectural and Planning Information Service, 109
Quick Collection, 1662

R

Race Relations Board, 1497
Rachel McMillan College of Education, 1498
Radbrook College, 2121
Radcliffe Meteorological Library, 1971
Radcliffe Public Library, 1779
Radcliffe Technical College, 1780
Radio Times Hulton Picture Library, 1499
R.A.F. Staff College, 195

Rathbone papers, 878
Rationalist Press Association Ltd, 1500
Ravensbourne College of Art and Design, 253
Reading College of Technology, 2024
Reading Pathological Society, 2025
Reading University
   Library, 2027
   Museum of English Rural Life, 2028
   Museum of Greek Archaeology, 2029
Reckitt and Colman Ltd, 738
Redbridge Public Libraries, 746
Redditch College of Further Education, 2030
Redditch Development Corporation, 2031
Redditch Public Library, 2032
Redland College of Education, 238
Redruth Public Library, 2033
Reece Collection, 1344
Reform Club, 1501
Regent's Park College, 1944
Regimental Museum K.O.S.B., 116
Regimental Museum of Seaforth Highlanders, the Queen's Own Cameron Highlanders and Queen's Own Highlanders (Seaforth and Camerons), 752
Regimental Museum the Lancashire Regiment (P.W.V.), 2251
Reginald M. Phillips Collection, 1431
Regional Advisory Council for the Organisation of Further Education in the East Midlands, 1899
Regional Council for Further Education for the South West, 239
Regional Transfusion and Immuno-Haematology Centre, Cambridge, 293
Register of Business Archives, 1017
Reid School of Music, 1169
Religious Education Centre, Penarth, 1979
Religious Society of Friends, 1164, 1502
Remploy Limited, 1503
Rendel Harris Collection, 149
Research Institute for Consumer Affairs, 1504
Reuters Ltd, 1505
Rev. Dr. A. Cohen Collection, 130
Rev. J. Russell's Pamphlet Collection, 1585
Rev. W. Scott's Pamphlet Collection, 1585
Reynolds Polar Library, 1425
Rhondda Borough Council Central Library, 1983
Rhyl Post-Graduate Medical Centre, 2036
Ribble Archaeological Society, 2018
Ribchester Museum of Roman Antiquities, 2018
Richard III Society, 1506
Richmond District Library, 2039
Richmond upon Thames Central Reference Library, 2039
Riddell Collection, 92
Rikker Laboratories, 1715
Ripon Cathedral Library, 2042
Ripon College of Education, 2043
Ripon Hall, Oxford, 1945
Rischgitz Collection, 1499

R.N.L.I., 1546
River Thames Society, 2040
Road Time Trials Council, 1507
Robert Gordon's Institute of Technology, 9
Robert Owen Collection, 16
Robert Sidlow Library, 1749
Robert White Collection, 1850
Rochdale Public Libraries & Arts Services, 2044
Roche Products Ltd, 2265
Rochester Public Libraries, 2047
Rockefeller Medical Library, 1261
Roman Baths and Museum, Bath, 76
Ronald Knox Collection, 1352
Rosenzweig Collection, 107
RoSPA, 1508
Ross and Cromarty County Library, 456
Ross Collection, 107
Ross Institute of Tropical Hygiene, 1344, 1509
Rotary International in Great Britain and Ireland, 1510
Roth Collection, 813
Rotherham Art Gallery, 2053
Rotherham Municipal Museum and Art Gallery, 2053
Rotherham Public Library, 2054
Rotherham School of Art and Crafts, 2055
Rotunda, The, 1389
Rothwell Public Library, 809
Roussel Laboratories Ltd, 2268
Routh Collection, 492
Rowe Music Library, 288
Royal Academy of Arts, 1511
Royal Academy of Dramatic Art, 1512
Royal Academy of Music, 1513, 1549
Royal African Society, 1514
Royal Air Force College, 2129
Royal Air Force Medical Services, 1111
Royal Air Force Museum, 1515
Royal Alexandra Hospital, 2036
Royal Anthropological Institute of Great Britain and Ireland, 1516
Royal Army Chaplains' Department Centre, 47
Royal Artillery Regimental Museum, 1517
Royal Asiatic Society of Great Britain and Ireland, 1518
Royal Association in Aid of the Deaf and Dumb, 1519
Royal Automobile Club, 1520
Royal Ballet Organization, 1521
Royal Ballet School, 1521
Royal Berkshire Hospital, 2025
Royal Borough of Kensington and Chelsea Public Libraries, 1522
Royal British Colonial Society of Artists, 1146
Royal Caledonian Curling Club, 532
Royal Cancer Hospital, 1245
Royal Cartographic Society Library, 513
Royal Central Asian Society, 1523, 2019
Royal College of Art, 1524
Royal College of General Practitioners, 1525
Royal College of Midwives, 1526

Royal College of Music, 1527
Royal College of Nursing and National Council of Nurse of the United Kingdom, 1528
  Scottish Board, 533
Royal College of Obstetricians and Gynaecologists, 1529
Royal College of Organists, 1530
Royal College of Physicians of Edinburgh, 534
Royal College of Physicians of London, 1531
Royal College of Surgeons of Edinburgh, 535
Royal College of Surgeons of England, 1532, 1656
  Hunterian Museum, 1533
Royal College of Veterinary Surgeons Wellcome Library, 1534
Royal Commission on Historical Monuments (England), 1535
Royal Danish Embassy, 1536
Royal Devon & Exeter Hospital, 586
Royal Dragoons, 2296
Royal Drawing Society, 1146
Royal Free Hospital School of Medicine, 1537
Royal Geographical Society, 1538
Royal Grammar School, Lancaster, Memorial Library, 788
Royal Greek Embassy Press and Information Office, 1539
Royal Halifax Infirmary, 668
Royal Highland Fusiliers Regimental Headquarters and Museum, 613
Royal Horse Guards, 2296
Royal Infirmary of Edinburgh, 554
Royal Institute of British Architects, 1540
Royal Institute of International Affairs, 1541
Royal Institute of Oil Painters, 1146
Royal Institute of Painters in Watercolour, 1146
Royal Institute of Public Administration, 1542
Royal Institution of Cornwall, 2221
Royal Institution of Great Britain, 1543
Royal Irish Fusiliers Regimental Museum, 30
Royal Leamington Spa Public Library, Art Gallery and Museum, 792
Royal Lincolnshire Regiment Museum, 853
Royal Manchester College of Music, 1781
Royal Marsden Hospital, 1245
Royal Medical Society, 536
Royal Military Academy Sandhurst, 270
Royal National Institute for the Blind, 1544
Royal National Institute for the Deaf, 1545
Royal National Life-Boat Institution, 49, 1546
Royal National Orthopaedic Hospital, 1264
Royal Naval College, 1425, 1547
Royal Netherlands Embassy, 1548
Royal Norfolk Regiment Museum, 1884
Royal Norwegian Embassy, 898
Royal Philharmonic Society, 1549
Royal Photographic Society, 1550
Royal Pioneer Corps Museum, 1870
Royal Portsmouth Hospital, 2006
Royal Postgraduate Medical School, Wellcome Library, 1551

Royal School of Church Music, 433
Royal Scots Fusiliers, 613
Royal Scottish Academy of Music and Drama, 614
Royal Scottish Geographical Society, 537
Royal Scottish Society for Prevention of Cruelty to Children, 538
Royal Shakespeare Theatre, 2179
    Library, 2179
Royal Society for the Prevention of Accidents, 1508
Royal Society for the Prevention of Cruelty to Animals, 1552
Royal Society of Arts, 1141, 1553
Royal Society of British Artists, 1146
Royal Society of British Sculptors, 1554
Royal Society of Edinburgh, 539
Royal Society of Marine Artists, 1146
Royal Society of Medicine, 1555
Royal Society of Miniature Painters, Sculptors and Gravers, 1146
Royal Society of Musicians of Great Britain, 1556
Royal Society of Painter-Etchers and Engravers, 1557
Royal Society of Painters in Water Colours, 1558
Royal Society of Portrait Painters, 1146
Royal Sussex Regiment Museum, 398
Royal Swedish Embassy, 1559
Royal United Service Institution, 1560
Royal Veterinary College, 1561
Royal Victoria Infirmary, Newcastle, Nurses Library, 1836
Roxburghshire County Library, 2074
R.S.P.C.A., 1552
Rubery Hill Hospital, 143
Rudler Collection, 1972
Rugby Fives Association, 1562
Rugby Football League, 810
Rugby Football Union, 2229
Runcorn Public Library, 2061
Runnymede Trust, 1497
Rural Music Schools Association, 719
Russell-Cotes Art Gallery and Museum, 194
Rutherglen Public Library, 615
Rutland County Library, 826, 1906
Rutland County Museum, 1907
Rutter Library, 2215

S

SAALIC, 2204, 2404
Sadler Collection, 1190
St Albans City Library, 2069
St Albans College of Further Education, 2070
St Albans Teachers Centre, 2070
St Andrew's Ambulance Association, 616
St Andrew's Hall, Birmingham, 148
St Andrew's University Library, 2073
St Anne's Church Turton, 180
St Anne's College, Oxford, 1946
St Antony's College, Oxford, 1947

St Bartholomew's Hospital Medical College, 1563
St Bride Institute, 1491
St Crispin Hospital, 1871
St David's University College Library, 783
St Deiniols Library, 448, 1423
St Dunstan's, 1564
St Edmund Hall, Oxford, 1948
St George's Hospital Medical School, 1565
St Helier Hospital, Carshalton, 362
St Helens Art Gallery, 2077
St Helens Central Public Library, 2076
St Helens Museum and Art Gallery, 2077
St Hilda's College, Oxford, 1949
St Hild's College, Durham, 488
St Hugh's College, Oxford, 1950
St Ives Public Library, 2078
Saint James' Hospital, 2006
St John Ambulance Association, 1316
St John Ambulance Brigade, 1316
St John's College, Cambridge, 294
St John's College, Durham, 489
St John's College of Education, 2330
St John's Hospital for Diseases of the Skin, 1252
St John's Hospital, Stone, 40
St Joseph's College of Education, 110
St Lawrence's Hospital, Bodmin, 172
St Lawrence's Hospital, Caterham, 364
St Margaret's Library Collection, 775
St Martin's College of Education, 789
St Martin's School of Art, 1566
St Mary's College of Education, Cheltenham, 379
St Mary's College of Education, Twickenham, 2230
Saint Mary's General Hospital, Portsmouth, Postgraduate Medical Centre, 2006
St Mary's Hospital Medical School, 1567
St Mary's Warwick Parish Library, 154
St Michael's College, Tenbury Wells, 2212
St Nicholas' Library Collection, 775
Saint Paul's Cathedral Library, 1568
St Paul's College of Education, 380
St Peter Hungate Church Museum, 1873
St Philip's Priory, 1933
St Richards Hospital, Chichester, 396
St Thomas's Hospital Medical School Library, 1569
St Wulstan's Hospital, 1736
Sale Public Library, 2081
Salford Art Gallery, 2085
Salford Central Library, 2084
Salford Museums and Art Gallery, 2085
Salford University Library, 2086
Salisbury and South Wiltshire Museum, 2089
Salisbury City Library, 2090
Salmon Collection, 758
Salop Record Office, 2122
Sandown–Shanklin Public Libraries, 2093
Salvation Army, 1570
    International Training College, 1571

Samaritans, 2134
Samuel Butler Collection, 294
Samuel Simms Collection, 108
Sanderson Collection, 802
Sandoz Products Ltd, 1572
Sasha London Theatre Collection, 1499
SASLIC, 2402
Saudi Arabian Embassy, 1573
Saunders Collection, 2179
Save the Children Fund, 1574
Savory Collection, 107
Scarborough Museum, 2095
Scarborough Public Libraries, 2096
Scawsby College of Education, 457
Schering Chemicals Ltd, 257
School Broadcasting Council for the United Kingdom, 1575
School Broadcasting Council for Wales, 339
School of Meditation, 1576
Schools Council for Curriculum and Examinations, 1577
Schools Music Association, 254
Science Museum Library, 1578
Science Research Council Library, 1589
SCOCLIS, page 651
SCOLMA, 2345
SCONUL, 2344
Scott Polar Research Institute, 295
Scott Sutherland School of Architecture, 9
Scottish Anglers' Association, 540
Scottish Anti-Vivisection Society, 617
Scottish Arts Council, 541
Scottish Association for National Certificates and Diplomas, 618
Scottish Association of Boys Clubs, 542
Scottish Association of Occupational Therapists, 543
Scottish Association of Voluntary Child Care Organisations, 544
Scottish Canoe Association, 10
Scottish Central Library, 2340
Scottish Civic Trust, 619, 1067
Scottish College Library, 631
Scottish College of Textiles, 598
Scottish Congregational College, 545
Scottish Conservative Central Office, 546
Scottish Council for Research in Education, 547
Scottish Council for the Unmarried Mother and Her Child, 548
Scottish Daily Record and Sunday Mail Ltd, 620
Scottish Development Department, 553
Scottish Education Department, 553
Scottish Epilepsy Association, 621
Scottish Genealogy Society, 549
Scottish History Society, 2164
Scottish Home and Health Department, 553
Scottish Hospital Centre, 550
Scottish Institute of Missionary Studies, 14
Scottish Library Association, 622

Scottish National Gallery of Modern Art, 551
Scottish National Party, 623
   Publications and Research Departments, 2270
Scottish National Portrait Gallery, 552
Scottish National Ski Council, 624
Scottish Office Library, 553
Scottish Orienteering Association, 434
Scottish Poisons Information Bureau, 554
Scottish Police College, 25
Scottish Record Society, 2164
Scottish Schoolmasters Association, 555
Scottish Society for Prevention of Cruelty to Animals, 556
Scottish Society for the Prevention of Vivisection, 557
Scottish Squash Rackets Association, 558
Scottish Tartans Society, 2161
Scottish Text Society, 2164
Scottish Tourist Board, 559
Scottish Trades Union Congress, 625
Scottish Women's Rural Institutes, 560
Scottish Youth and Community Service Information Centre, 503
Scottish Youth Hostels Association, 2162
Scout Association, 1579
Scunthorpe Art Gallery, 2099
Scunthorpe Museum and Art Gallery, 2099
Scunthorpe Public Library, 2100
Seafarers Education Service, 1580
Seaford College of Education, 2101
Seaforth Highlanders, 752
SEAL, 2399
Searle, G. D., and Co. Ltd, 715
Sedgley Park College of Education, 1782
Seebohm Rowntree Library, 2333
Seelig Collection, 1603
Selborne Society's Library, 1326
Selden Society, 1581
Selly Oak Colleges, 148, 149
   Library, 149
Selwyn College, Cambridge, 296
Senefelder Group, 1146
Service Civil International, 1283
Servites, 1933
Sevenoaks Public Library, 2104
Seymour Bell Collection, 1836
Shakespeare Library, 133
Shakespeare Birthplace Trust, 2179
   Library, 2179
Shakespeare Collection, 2179
Shakespeare Memorial Library, 2179
Shakespeare's Birthplace, 2179
Shaw Library, 994
Shaw Society, 1582
Sheepscar Branch Library, 803
Sheffield City Art Galleries, 2111
Sheffield City Libraries, 2112
Sheffield City Museums, 2113
Sheffield Collection, 2112

Sheffield Interchange Organization, 2397
Sheffield National Centre for Radiotherapy, 2114
Sheffield Polytechnic, 2115
    School of Art and Design, 2116
Sheffield Regional Hospital Board, 2117
Sheffield Society of Architects, 2118
Sheffield University Library, 2119
Sheldon Parish Library, 133
Shenstone College, 256
Sherlock Holmes Collection, 1688
Sherlock Holmes Society of London, 1583
Sherwood Foresters, 1900
Shipdham Parish Library, 1882
Shoreditch District Library, 1329
Shotley Bridge Hospital, 415
Shrewsbury Public Library, 2123
Shrewsbury School, 2124
Shropshire Archaeological Society, 2125
Shropshire County Library, 2126
Shropshire Law Society Library, 2126
Shuttleworth Collection, 121
Sidney D. Kitson Bequest, 801
Sidney Webb College of Education, 1584
Signet Library, 561
Sikorski Museum, 1479
Simms Collection, 107
Simplified Spelling Society, 248
Sino-British Trade Council, 1052
SINTO, 2397
Sion College, 1585
Sir Basil Henriques Library, 912
Sir Benjamin Stone Collection, 133
Sir John Cass College Library, 1586
Sir John Hammond Collection, 319
Sir John Marriot Memorial Library, 2337
Sir John Fenn Manuscripts, 1878
Sir F. Mott Collection, 143
Sir James Caird's Collection, 1425
Sir John Priestman Library, 2187
Sir John Soane Library, 1587
Sir John Soane's Museum, 1587
Sir Horace Plunkett's Diaries, 1476
Sir Humphrey Prideaux Brune Collection, 2289
Sir Leslie Joseph Collection, 2199
Sir Richard Burton Collection, 2039
Sir Richard Burton Library, 1516
Sir Thomas Beecham Society, 2273
Sir Thomas More Collection, 1187
Ski Club of Great Britain, 1588
Skinners' Library, 1066
Skipton Public Library, 2127
Slough College of Technology, 2135
Smith and Nephew Associated Companies, 674
Smith & Nephew Research Ltd, 674
Smith Art Gallery and Museum, 2163
Smith Kline & French Laboratories Ltd, 2266
Smith, W. F., Collection, 294

Snowden Collection, 761
Social Science Research Council, 1589
Socialist Educational Association, 1590
Society for African Church History, 11
Society for Comparative Physiology, 2140
Society for Cultural Relations with U.S.S.R., 1591
Society for Folk Life Studies, 562
Society for Promoting Christian Knowledge, 911, 1592
Society for Research into Higher Education Ltd, 1593
Society for the Aid of Thalidomide Children (Limited), 699
Society for the Protection of Unborn Children, 1594
Society for the Study of Addiction to Alcohol and Other Drugs, 1595
    Library, 1678
Society for Theatre Research, 1596
Society of Analytical Psychology Ltd, 1597
Society of Antiquaries of London, 1598
Society of Antiquaries of Newcastle Upon Tyne, 1849
Society of Antiquaries of Scotland, 530
Society of Archer-Antiquaries, 1599
Society of Authors, 1600, 1638
Society of Aviation Artists, 1146
Society of Cardiological Technicians Limited, 1601
Society of Chiropodists, 1602
Society of Film and Television Arts, Ltd, 1603
Society of Genealogists, 1604
Society of Graphic Artists, 1146
Society of Herbalists, 1605
Society of Indexers, 1606
Society of Industrial Artists and Designers, 1108, 1607
Society of Jesus, 401
Society of Lithograph Artists, Designers, Engravers and Process Workers, 1608
Society of Medical Officers of Health, Dental Group, 1609
Society of Metaphysicians Ltd, 685
Society of Miniaturists, 1610
Society of Mural Painters, 1146
Society of Occupational Medicine, 1611
Society of Ornamental Turners, 2009
Society of Portrait Sculptors, 1146
Society of Professional Musicians in Ulster Library, 92
Society of St Vincent de Paul, 1612
Society of Solicitors in the Supreme Courts of Scotland, 563
Society of Wildlife Artists, 1146
Society of Writers to Her Majesty's Signet, 561
Somerset College of Art, 2207
Somerset County Library, 217
    Glastonbury Branch, 633
Somerset Libraries, 2398
Somerset Postgraduate Centre, 2208
Somerset Rural Community Council, 2209
Somerville Collection, 107
SOSCOL, 2400
Souldern Lawrence Law Library, 294
Soundwell Technical College, 240
South African Embassy, 1613

South Birmingham Technical College, 150
South East Area Libraries Information Service, 2399
South East Berks College of Further Education, 196
South East Derbyshire College of Further Education (Ilkeston Branch), 748
South East Northumberland Technical College, 2242
South Lancashire Regiment (P.W.V.), 2251
South London Art Gallery, 1614
South London Regional Blood Transfusion Centre, 2197
South Shields Marine and Technical College, 2136
South Staffordshire Archaeological and Historical Society, 2244
South Staffordshire College Librarians, 2400
South Vietnamese Embassy, 1127
South Wales & Monmouthshire Branch of the British Medical Association, 334
South Wales Borderers Regimental Museum, 206
South-West London College, 1617
South West Midlands Co-operative Scheme, 2401
South Western Blood Transfusion Service, 241
South Western Laryngological Association, 242
South Western Regional Hospital Board, 243
South Western Regional Library System, 2351
South Yorkshire Industrial Museum, 458
Southall District Library, 2137
Southampton College of Art, 2141
Southampton College of Technology, 2142
Southampton General Hospital, 2147
Southampton Public Libraries, 2143
Southampton Technical College, 2144
Southampton University
  Library, 2145
  School of Education, 2146
Southend-on-Sea Historical Society, 2148
Southend-on-Sea Public Libraries, 2149
Southern Regional Council for Further Education, 2026
Southgate Technical College, 1615
Southlands College of Education, 1616
Southmead Hospital Medical Library, 244
Southport Public Libraries, 2150
Southwark Public Libraries, 1338
Southwell Minster Library, 2152
Sowerby Bridge Public Library, 2153
Sowter and Clerical Library, 2091
Spalding Club, 2164
S.P.C.K., 1592
Spencer Collection, 2015
Spiritualists National Union Ltd, 1783
Sports Council, 1031
Spotlight, 1618
Squibb, E. R., & Sons Ltd, 2231
SRIG, 2403
Staff College, 271
Staff College Collection, 271
Staffordshire County Library, 2154
Staffordshire Record Office, 2155
Staffordshire Regiment Regimental Museum, 841

Stamford Public Library, 2157
Stamford School, 2158
Standing Conference for Amateur Music, 1619
Standing Conference of Co-operative Commercial and Technical Library Services, page 651
Standing Conference of Co-operative Library Information Services, page 651
Standing Conference of National and University Libraries, 2344
Standing Conference of National Voluntary Youth Organisations, 1620
Standing Conference of Youth Organisations in N. Ireland, 111
Standing Conference on Library Materials on Africa, 2345
Standing Conference on Physical Education Library Co-operation, 2346
Stanley Library Collection, 775
Steers Collection, 303
Stephen Austin & Sons Ltd, 710
Sterling Collection, 1662
Sterling-Winthrop Group Limited, 2191
Stevenage College of Further Education, 2160
Stirling Public Library, 2164
Stirling-Maxwell Collection, 630
Stirling University Library, 2166
Stirlingshire County Library, 2165
Stockport College of Technology, 2167
Stockport Public Libraries, 2168
Stoke Mandeville Hospital, 39
Stoke Newington District Library, 1329
Stoke-on-Trent Art Gallery, 2170
Stoke-on-Trent City Libraries, 2176
Stoke-on-Trent College of Building and Commerce, 2171
Stoke-on-Trent Museum and Art Gallery, 2170
Stornoway Public Library, 2177
  Lewis District Library, 456
Stow College of Engineering, 626
Stranmillis College, 112
Stratford Reference Library, 1337
Stratford-Upon-Avon Public Library, 2180
Strathclyde University Library, 631
Stretford Public Libraries, 1784
Stretford Technical College, 1785
Stroud Civic Society, 2181
Stroud Museum, 2181
Stuckley Lean Collection, 233
Student Humanist Federation, 1621
Studio Lisa Royal Portraits, 1499
Sturrock Collection, 472
Styring Collection, 1425
Suffolk Regiment Museum, 264
Sully Hospital, 344
Sunderland Art Gallery, 2186
Sunderland Central Library, 2184
Sunderland College of Education, 2185
Sunderland General Hospital, 2189
Sunderland Museum and Art Gallery, 2186

Sunderland Polytechnic, 2187
   School of Art and Design, 2188
Sunderland Postgraduate Medical Centre, 2189
Surgical Dressings Manufacturers' Association, 392
Surrey and Sussex Libraries in Cooperation, 2402
Surrey Archaeological Society, 660
Surrey County Library, 581
Surrey Production Centre R.E., Map Research and Library Group, 2192
Surrey Reference and Information Group, 2403
Surrey University Library, 661
Sussex University
   Institute for the Study of International Organization, 225
   Library, 225
   School of African and Asian Studies, 225
   School of Cultural and Community Studies, 225
   School of Education Library, 226
   School of English and American Studies, 225
   School of European Studies, 225
   School of Social Sciences, 225
   Science Policy Research Unit, 227
Sutton Coldfield College of Further Education, 2198
Sutton Public Libraries, 2196
Swallow Library, 400
Swansea Memorial College, 2200
Swansea Public Library, 2201
Swedenborg Society, 1622
Swedish Embassy, 1559
Swedish Institute, 1623
Swimming Teachers' Association of Great Britain and the Commonwealth, 151
Swindon Area Association of Libraries for Industry and Commerce, 2204, 2404
Swindon College, 2203
Swindon Public Libraries, 2204
Swinton and Pendlebury Public Libraries, 1786
Swiss Bank Corporation, 1624
S.W.R.L.S., 2351
Syntex Pharmaceuticals, 1730

T

Tail-Waggers' Club (G.B.) Limited, 1625
TALIC, 2406
Tamworth College of Further Education, 2205
Tamworth Public Libraries, 2206
Tamworth Scheme, 2405
Taphouse Collection, 802
Tate Central Library, 1333
Tate Gallery, 1626
Taunton Public Library, 2210
Tavistock Clinic, 1627
Tavistock Institute of Human Relations and the Tavistock Clinic, 1627
Tavistock Joint Library, 1627
Taylor Collection, 13
Taylor Institution, 1972

Technical College of Monmouthshire, 1860
Teesside College of Art Library, 1808
Teesside College of Education, 1809
Teesside Public Libraries, 1810
Temple Newsam House, 801
Tennyson Research Centre, 847, 854
Tennyson Society, 854
Tennyson Trust, 854
Tenovus Laboratories, 341
Teulon-Porter, N., Collection, 2170
Textile Council
   Design and Export Centre, 1628
   Economics and Statistics Department, 1787
Thames Conservancy, 1629
Thames Television Limited, 1630
Thane Library of Medical Sciences, 1631
Theatres' Advisory Council, 1632
Theosophical Society in Scotland, 564
Thomas Bevill Peacock Collection, 1254
Thomas Bewick Collection, 1836
Thomas Hodgkin Collection, 158
Thomas Paine Collection, 1880
Thomlinson Collection, 1836
Thomson Collection, 2164
Thomson-Walker Collection, 568
Thomson Withy Grove Ltd, 1788
Thoresby Society, 811
Thornton & Ross Ltd, 729
Thorold and Lyttelton Library, 2291
Thoroton Society of Nottinghamshire, 1901
Thorpe Smith Collection, 2149
Thos. Wigan Library, 154
Thurrock Local History Museum, 2213
Thurrock Public Libraries, 645
Thurrock Technical College, 646
Thurstan Holland Collection, 1245
Tickenhill Collection, 772
Tillotsons Newspapers Ltd, 181
Tobacco Research Council, 1633
Tobacco Workers' Union, 1634
TOC H, 1635
Tomlin Collection, 337
Torbay Library Service, 2214
Totnes Museum, 2215
Tower Hamlets Libraries Department, 1339
Town Planning Institute, 1636
Townhead Library, 610
Training Council for Teachers of the Mentally Handicapped, 1637
Tramway Museum Society, 1802
Translators Association, 1638
Translators Guild, 1259
Treasury Library, 1199
Trent Polytechnic, 1895
Trinity and All Saints Colleges, Leeds, 812
Trinity College, Carmarthen, 358
Trinity College, Glasgow, 627

Truro Cathedral Library, 2222
Truro Public Library, 2218
T.U.C. Centenary Institute of Occupational Health, 1344, 1639
Tunbridge Wells Public Library, 2225
Turner Collection, 2027
Twickenham College of Technology, 2232
Twyford Pharmaceutical Services Ltd, 68
Tyndale House, Cambridge, 297, 1284
Tyndale Press, 1284
Tyneside Association of Libraries for Industry and Commerce, 2406
Tyrwhitt-Drake Museum, 1733

U

UFAW, 2010
U.K. Committee for the World Health Organization, 1640
Ulster Medical Society, 108
Ulster Museum, 113
Ulster Office, 97
U.N. Educational, Scientific & Cultural Organization, 1646
Union International De La Marionnette (British Section), 1641
Union of Post Office Workers, 1642
Unitarian College, 1789
Unitarian Historical Society, 1790
United Bristol Hospitals, Hospital Libraries, 245
United Grand Lodge of England Library and Museum, 1643
United Hebrew Congregations of the British Commonwealth, 1458
United Kingdom Alliance, 1644
United Kingdom Reading Association, 2169
United Lodge of Theosophists, 1645
United Nations Information Centre, 1646
United Society for the Propagation of the Gospel, 1647
United Society of Artists, 1146
United States Information Service Reference Library, 1648
Universities Council for Adult Education, 1951
Universities Federation for Animal Welfare, 2010
University College, Durham, 486
University College Hospital Medical School, 1649
University College, London, 897, 940, 1157, 1219, 1383
   Thane Library of Medical Sciences, 1631
University College of North Wales Library, 51, 52, 54
University College of Swansea Library, 2202
University College of Wales Library, 17
University of Aberdeen
   Centre for Social Studies, 12
   Library, 13
   Scottish Institute of Missionary Studies, 14
University of Aston in Birmingham
   Library, 152
   Social Sciences Library, 153
University of Birmingham
   Centre for Child Study, 154

Centre for Russian and East European Studies, 154
Centre for Urban and Regional Studies, 154
Centre of West Africa Studies, 154
Institute for the Study of Worship and Religious Architecture, 154
Institute of Child Health, 154
Institute of Judicial Administration, 154
Institute of Local Government Studies, 154
Library, 154
National Centre for Programmed Learning, 154, 155
School of Education, 154, 156
Shakespeare Institute, 154
University of Bradford Library, 201
University of Bristol
   Dental School, 237
   Wills Memorial Library, 246
University of Cambridge
   African Studies Centre, 298
   Appointments Board, 279
   Centre of Latin American Studies, 299
   Centre of South Asian Studies, 300
   Classical Faculty Library, 301
   Corpus Christi College, 282
   Department of Applied Economics, 302
   Department of Geography, 303
   Department of Medicine Library, 304
   Department of Pathology, 305
   Department of Pharmacology, 306
   Department of Radiotherapeutics, 307
   Department of Slavonic Studies, 311
   Department of Surgery, 308
   Divinity School, 309
   Dunn Nutritional Laboratory, 323
   Emmanuel College, 284
   Faculty of Archaeology and Anthropology, 310
   Faculty of Modern and Medieval Languages, 311
   Fitzwilliam Museum Library, 312
   Haddon Library, 310
   Institute of Criminology, 313
   Institute of Education, 278
   King's College, 288
   Library, 314
   Modern Languages Faculty Library, 315
   Museum of Archaeology and Ethnology, 310
   Museum of Classical Archaeology, 316
   Pembroke College, 291
   Pendlebury Library of Music, 317
   Postgraduate Medical School Library, 318
   Queen's College, 292
   St John's College, 294
   School of Veterinary Medicine, 319
   Scientific Periodicals Library, 320
   Selwyn College, 296
   Slavonic Library, 311
   Tyndale House, 297
   University Archives, 321
   Whipple Science Museum and Library, 322

University of Durham
  College of the Venerable Bede, 482
  Department of Geography, 490
  Institute of Education, 491
  Library, 492
  Lowe Memorial Library, 486
  Neville's Cross College, 487
  St Hild's College, 488
  St John's College, 409
  University College, 486
  Ushaw College, 493
University of East Anglia Library, 1885
University of Edinburgh
  Central Medical Library, 565
  Centre of African Studies, 568
  Centre of European Governmental Studies, 566
  Law Library, 567
  Library, 568
  New College Library, 569
  Reid Music Library, 570
  Royal (Dick) School of Veterinary Studies, 571
  School of Scottish Studies, 572
University of Essex Library, 409
University of Exeter
  Institute of Education Library, 588
  Library, 589
University of Glasgow
  Building Services Research Unit, 628
  Hunterian Museum, 629
  Library, 630
University of Hull, Brynmor Jones Library, 739
University of Keele Library, 1830
University of Kent at Canterbury Library, 330
University of Lancaster Library, 790
University of Leeds
  Brotherton Library, 813
  Dental Library, 814
  Department of Dialectology and Folk-Lore, 123
  Department of English, 123
  Institute of Education Library, 815
  Law Library, 816
  Medical Library, 817
  Museum of the History of Education, 818
University of Leicester
  Department of Museum Studies, 831
  Department of the History of Art, 831
  Library, 831
  Victorian Studies Centre, 831
University of Liverpool
  Harold Cohen Library, 878
  School of Education Library, 879
University of London
  Bedford College, 1650
  Birkbeck College, 942
  Board of Dutch Studies, 1650
  Chelsea College of Science and Technology Library, 1651
  Courtauld Institute of Art, 1652
  Goldsmiths' College, 1653
  Institute of Advanced Legal Studies, 1654
  Institute of Archaeology, 1655
  Institute of Basic Medical Sciences, 1532, 1656
  Institute of Education Library, 1657
  Institute of Classical Studies, 1250
  Institute of Germanic Studies, 1658
  Institute of Historical Research, 1659
  Institute of Latin American Studies, 1660
  Institute of United States Studies, 1661
  Joint Library of the Hellenic and Roman Studies, 1250, 1295
  Library, 1662
  Library Depository, 1303, 1662
  London Hospital Medical College Library, 1342
  London School of Economics and Political Science, 994
  London School of Hygiene and Tropical Medicine, 1344
  New College, London, 1663
  Queen Elizabeth College Library, 1664
  Queen Mary College Library, 1665
  Royal Holloway College, 574
  Royal Postgraduate Medical School, Wellcome Library, 1551
  Royal Veterinary College, 1561
  School of Oriental and African Studies, 1666
  School of Pharmacy, 1667
  School of Slavonic and East European Studies, 1668
  Sir John Cass College Library, 1586
  Westfield College, 1686
  Wye College Agricultural Museum, 31
University of Manchester
  Library, 1791
  Whitworth Art Gallery, 1792
University of Newcastle Upon Tyne Library, 1850
University of Nottingham Library, 1902
University of Oxford
  All Souls College, 1921
  Ashmolean Museum of Art and Archaeology, 1952
  Balfour Library, 1969
  Bodleian Library, 1953, 1970
  Brasenose College, 1918
  Christ Church, 1919
  Codrington Library, 1921
  Department of Educational Studies Library, 1954
  Department of Pharmacology, 1955
  English Faculty Library, 1956
  Exeter College, 1923
  Faculty of Music Library, 1957
  Faculty of Social Studies, Social Studies Library, 1958
  Grenfell and Hunt Papyrological Library, 1952
  Griffith Egyptological Library, 1952
  Haverfield Library of Ancient History, 1952
  Heberden Coin Room Library, 1952
  History Faculty Library, 1959
  Institute of Agricultural Economics, 1960
  Institute of Commonwealth Studies, 1961

University of Oxford—*continued*
  Institute of Economics and Statistics, 1962
  Institute of Psychiatry, 1963
  Institute of Social Anthropology, 1964
  Keble College, 1924
  Latimer House, 1926
  Law Library, 1953
  Library of Classical Archaeology, 1952
  Library of Classical Literature, 1952
  Library of Medieval Archaeology, 1952
  Library of the Department of Antiquities, 1952
  Library of the Department of Eastern Art, 1952
  Library of the Department of Western Art, 1952
  Library of the Griffith Institute, 1952
  Manchester College, 1927
  Mansfield College, 1928
  Modern Languages Faculty Library, 1965
  Museum of the History of Science, 1966
  Nuffield College, 1932
  Nuffield Department of Orthopaedic Surgery, 1967
  Oriel College, 1934
  Oriental Institute Library, 1968
  Pembroke College, 1941
  Pitt Rivers Museum, 1969
  Pusey House, 1942
  Queen's College, 1943
  Radcliffe Science Library, 1953, 1970
  Regent's Park College, 1944
  Rhodes House Library, 1953
  Ripon Hall, 1945
  St Anne's College, 1946
  St Antony's College, 1947
  St Edmund Hall, 1948
  St Hilda's College, 1949
  St Hugh's College, 1950
  School of Geography, 1971
  Taylor Institution, 1965, 1972
  Wadham College, 1973
  Worcester College, 1975
University of Reading
  Library, 2027
  Museum of English Rural Life, 2028
  Museum of Greek Archaeology, 2029
University of St Andrews Library, 2073
University of Salford Library, 2086
University of Sheffield Library, 2119
University of Southampton
  Library, 2145
  School of Education, 2146
University of Stirling Library, 2166
University of Strathclyde Library, 631
University of Surrey Library, 661
University of Sussex
  Institute for the Study of International Organization, 225
  Library, 225
  School of African and Asian Studies, 225
  School of Cultural and Community Studies, 225
  School of Education Library, 226
  School of English and American Studies, 225
  School of European Studies, 225
  School of Social Sciences, 225
  Science Policy Research Unit, 227
University of Wales Institute of Science and Technology, 340
University of Warwick Library, 422
University of York
  Borthwick Institute of Historical Research, 2331
  Institute of Advanced Architectural Studies, 2332
  Library, 2333
  Schools Council Modern Languages Project, 2334
Upper Norwood Public Library, 1669
Ushaw College, Durham, 493
Usher Collection, 855
Usher Gallery, 847, 854, 855
U.S.P.G., 1647

V

Vale of Evesham Historical Society, 582
Valence House, 436
Vegetarian Nutritional Research Centre, 26
Vegetarian Society of the United Kingdom Ltd, 26, 1670
Velindre Memorial Centre for Cancer Research, 341
VENISS, 1407
Venn Collection, 314
Verulamium Museum, 2071
Vestry House Museum, 1675
Veteran Car Club of Great Britain, 1671
Vicar's Library, Marlborough, 1798
Victoria Art Gallery, Bath, 71
Victorian Society, 1672
Victory Museum, 2007
Violet Hughes Library, 341
Viscount Furness's Collection, 2019
Visual Education National Information Service for Schools, 1407
Von Hugel Collection, 2073

W

Wade Collection, 314
Wadham College, Oxford, 1973
Wagner Collection, 1219
Wakefield City Library, 2237
Wakefield Historical Society, 2237
Wakefield Technical and Art College, 2238
WALIC, 2412
Walker Art Gallery, 880
Wall Hall College of Education, 2257
Wallace Collection, 1673
Wallasey Public Libraries, 2240
Wallington Public Library, 2196
Wallsend Public Library, 2243
Walter Raleigh Memorial Fund, 1956

Waltham Forest Public Libraries, 1340
Waltham Forest School of Art, 1674
Waltham Forest Technical College and School of Art, 1674
Walthamstow Antiquarian Society, 1675
WANDPETLS, 2407
Wandsworth Public, Educational Technical Library Service, 2407
Wandsworth Public Libraries, 1341
Wandsworth Technical College, 1676
Ware College, 2249
Warrington Public Library, 2252
Warwick County Record Office, 2253
Warwick University Library, 422
Warwickshire County Library, 2254
Watford Public Libraries, 2258
Watts Gallery, 662
Weaver Smith Collection, 1630
Wedgwood Collection, 154
Wedgwood Society, 1677
Wellcome Institute of the History of Medicine, 1678
Wellcome Museum of Medical Science, 1679
Wellcome Research Laboratories, 85
Wellington Museum, 1680
Wells Museum and Platten Bequest Library, 2262
Wells Theological College, 2263
Welsh Folk Museum, 342
Welsh Hockey Association, 343
Welsh National School of Medicine, 344
    Dental School, 345
Welsh Regional Library System, 2352
Welsh Secondary Schools Association, 1982
Wesley College, Bristol, 247
Wesley Historical Society, 696
WESLIB, 2410
Wessex Library Group, 2408
Wessex Medical Library, 2145, 2147
Wessex Regional Hospital Board, Regional Library and Information Service, 2145, 2147
West Bromwich College of Commerce and Technology, Management Services Division, 2259
West Bromwich Public Libraries, 2269
West Cheshire Central College of Further Education, 2300
West Cumberland College of Science and Technology
    Whitehaven Division, 2280
    Workington Division, 2316
West End Stage Management Association, 1681
West Ham College of Technology, 1682
West Highland Museum, Fort William, 752
West Hill District Library, 1341
West India Committee, 1683
West Kent Medico-Chirurgical Society, 1684
West London Commercial and Technical Library Service, 2409
West London Hospital Library, 1043, 1685
West Lothian County Library, 77
West Midlands College of Education, 2245

West Midlands County Boroughs Librarians' Standing Committee, 2410
West Midlands Regional Library System, 2353
West Park Museum and Art Gallery, 1726
West Riding County Library, 2234
West Suffolk County Library, 265
West Sussex County Library, 399
West Sussex Reference and Technical Library Service, 2411
Western Infirmary, Glasgow, 608
Western Regional Hospital Board (Scotland), 632
Westfield College (University of London), 1686
Westgate Museum, Winchester, 2293
Westhill College of Education, 157
Westminster Abbey, 1687
Westminster City Libraries, 1688
Westminster College of Education, 1974
Westminster Medical School, 1689
Westmorland County Record Office, 354, 765
Weston-Super-Mare Museum, 2274
Weston-Super-Mare Public Library and Museum, 2274
Weybridge Museum, 2277
Weymouth and Melcombe Regis Public Library Service, 2278
Weymouth College of Education, 2279
Wheeler, W. H., Collection, 187
Wheler Collection, 2179
Whipple Science Museum and Library, 322
Whipps Cross Hospital, 1160
Whitaker Collection, 813
Whitechapel Area Library, 1339
Whitehaven Public Library, 2281
Whitelands College of Education, 1690
Whitley Bay Central Library, 2282
Whitworth Art Gallery, 1792
Wickham Library, 844
Widnes Public Library, 2284
Wiener Library, 1251, 1691
Wigan Public Libraries, 2286
Wighton Music Collection, 472
Wiglesworth Ornithological Library, 246
William Charles Braithwaite Collection, 158
William Cobbett Manuscripts Collection, 1932
William Kelly Collection, 1810
William Littleboy Collection, 158
William Milner Collection, 666
William Morris Collections, 1340, 1674
William Morris Gallery, 1692
William R. Warner & Co. Ltd, 500
William Rathbone Staff College, 881
William Salt Library, 2155
Williamson Collection, 348
Willis Bond, J. W., Collection, 2311
Willmer House Museum, 592
Willoughby Gardner Collection, 337
Willoughby Memorial Art Gallery and Library, 643
Willoughby Memorial Trust, 643

Wills Memorial Library, 246
Wilmot Horton Collection, 451
Wilton Lodge Museum, 692, 694
Wiltshire Archaeological and Natural History Society, 453
Wiltshire Association of Libraries of Industry and Commerce, 2412
Wiltshire County Library, 2216
Wiltshire Regiment Museum, 454
Wimbledon Library, 1336
Wimbledon School of Art, 1693
Winchester City Library, 2292
Winchester City Museums, 2293
Winterbottom Collection, 492
Winterbottom Production Library, 1404
W.M.R.L.S., 2353
Wolverhampton Public Libraries, 2304
Wolverhampton Teachers' College for Day Students, 2305
Wolverhampton Technical Teachers College, 2306
Wolverton College of Further Education, 2308
  Business Studies Department, 170, 2308
Women's Employment Federation, 1694
Women's Group on Public Welfare, 1695
Women's International League for Peace and Freedom (British Section), 1696
Women's Royal Army Corps Regimental Museum, 663
Wood, G. H., Collection, 726
Woolbrooke College, 158
Wool, Jute and Flax Industry Training Board, 202
Woodhope Naturalists' Field Club, 706
  Library, 703
Woolwich Hospital Group, Postgraduate Medical Library, 1697
Woolwich Polytechnic, 1698
Worcester City Library, 2311
Worcester College, Oxford, 1975
Worcester College of Education, 2312
Worcestershire Association of Technical Libraries, 2413
Worcestershire County Library, 2313
Worcestershire County Museum, 772
Worcestershire Record Office, 2314
Worcestershire Regimental Museum, 2315
Workers' Educational Association, 1699
Working Men's College, 1700
Workington Public Library, 2317
Worksop Museum, 2319
Worksop Public Library & Museum, 2319
World Association for Christian Communication, 1701
World Confederation for Physical Therapy, 1702
World Congress of Faiths, 1703
World Education Fellowship, 1825, 2226
World Health Organization, 1640, 1646
World Jewish Congress, 1257
World's Woman's Christian Temperance Union, 1704
World Youth Symphony Orchestra, 652
Worley, J. J., Memorial Library, 1711
Worth Abbey, 424
Worthing Art Gallery, 2322
Worthing College of Further Education, 2321
Worthing Museum and Art Gallery, 2322
Worthing Public Library, 2323
Writers' Guild of Great Britain, 1705
W.R.L.S., 2352
Wulfrun College of Further Education, 2307
Wye College Agricultural Museum, 31

Y

Yeovil Public Library, 2326
Y.M.C.A., 1410
  Training College, 61
York and Lancaster Regt. Regimental Headquarters, 2120
York Castle Museum, 2329
York Central College of Further Education, 2335
York City Art Gallery, 2336
York City Libraries, 2337
York-Powell Collection, 1956
York Railway Museum, 2328
York University
  Borthwick Institute of Historical Research, 2331
  Institute of Advanced Architectural Studies, 2332
  Library, 2333
  Schools Council Modern Languages Project, 2334
Yorkshire Cobook Group of Libraries, 2414
Yorkshire Dialect Society, 123
Yorkshire Philosophical Society, 2338
Yorkshire Post Newspapers Ltd, 819
Yorkshire Ramblers' Club Library, 802
Yorkshire Regional Library System, 2354
Young Collection, 631
Young Men's Christian Association, 1410
  Training College, 61
Youth Hostels Association (England and Wales), 2072
Youth Service Association, 1706
Youth Service Information Centre, 832
Y.R.L.S., 2354
Yule Collection, 294

Z

Zambia High Commission, 1707

SUBJECT INDEX

The numbers refer to entries, and *not* to pages

A

Abbey of Port Royal	1585 (London EC4)		423 (Crawley)
Abdominal cavity	124 (Birkenhead)		511 (Edinburgh)
Aberdeen, local history	5 (Aberdeen)		1881 (Norwich)
Aberdeenshire, local history	4 (Aberdeen)		2173 (Stoke-on-Trent)
Abortion	1132, 1279 (London SW1)	*See also* Accountancy, Accounts	
law	2064 (St Albans)	Accounts	1302 (London SE11)
reform	1594 (London SW1)	*See also* Accountancy, Accounting	
Abyssinia		Acoustics	1791 (Manchester)
geography	1749 (Manchester)	*See also* Volume I	
history	1749 (Manchester)	Ackerman fine illustrations	223 (Brighton)
Academic awards	1091 (London W1N 2BA)	Actors, Actresses	1618 (London WC2)
Accident law	1322 (London NW4)	Acts of the Apostles	217 (Bridgwater)
Accident prevention	1508 (London SW1)	Actuarial Science	516 (Edinburgh)
Accident surgery	144 (Birmingham)		1240 (London WC1)
Accidents, of natural origin	36 (Aylesbury)	*See also* Volume I	
Accordion playing	821 (Leicester)	Acupuncture	1358 (London W1N 1PB)
Accountancy		Addiction	

(Volume I of this Directory includes accountancy, but it has also been indexed in this volume for organizations which do not appear in Volume I)

		alcohol	2255 (Watford)
		See also Alcoholism	
	145 (Birmingham)	narcotics	2255 (Watford)
	230 (Bristol)	tobacco	2255 (Watford)
	435 (Dagenham)	Administration	
	520 (Edinburgh)		
	606 (Glasgow)		
	687 (Hatfield)		
	717 (Hitchin)		

(Volume I of this Directory includes administration, but it has also been indexed in this Volume for organizations which do not appear in Volume I)

	868 (Liverpool)		153 (Birmingham)
	1243 (London EC3)		631 (Glasgow)
	1711 (Loughborough)		1421 (London W1M 8DR)
	1734 (Maidstone)		1483 (London EC1)
	1839 (Newcastle upon Tyne)		1860 (Newport, Mon)
	1895 (Nottingham)	archives	2314 (Worcester)
	2171 (Stoke-on-Trent)		2331 (York)
	2182 (Sunderland)	arts	1102 (London W1)
	2259 (Wednesbury)	business	994 (London WC2)
	2321 (Worthing)		1766 (Manchester)
See also Accounting, Accounts			2321 (Worthing)
Accounting		charity	744 (Ilford)
		civil	1330 (London W6)
		ecclesiastical	2331 (York)
		education	645 (Grays)

(Volume I of this Directory includes accounting, but it has also been indexed in this volume for organizations which do not appear in Volume I)

			1102 (London W1)
			1202 (London WC2)
	154 (Birmingham)	government	1418 (London WC1)
	330 (Canterbury)	health services	1938 (Oxford)
		hospital	533, 550 (Edinburgh)

Administration, hospital *(contd)*	881 (Liverpool)	Aerosols	1715 (Loughborough)
	1065 (London SW1)	Aeschylus	288 (Cambridge)
	1255 (London W1N 4AN)	Aesthetics	1727 (Maidenhead)
	2117 (Sheffield)		1808 (Middlesbrough)
industrial	1839 (Newcastle upon Tyne)	Africa	126 (Birmingham)
justice	154 (Birmingham)		225 (Brighton)
	313 (Cambridge)		270 (Camberley)
	1351 (London W1P 6DD)		298 (Cambridge)
laboratory	1260 (London W1)		568 (Edinburgh)
local government	154 (Birmingham)		886 (London WC2)
office	1065 (London SW1)		1028 (London SW3)
	1617 (London SW17)		1273 (London EC4)
police	25 (Alloa)		1791 (Manchester)
public	201 (Bradford)		2345
	421 (Coventry)	agriculture	298 (Cambridge)
	587 (Exeter)	anthropology	298 (Cambridge)
	700 (Henley-on-Thames)		1647 (London SW1)
	994 (London WC2)	bibliography	2345
	1053 (London W4)	biography	1647 (London SW1)
	1065, 1104 (London SW1)	Central	252 (Bromley)
	1309 (London WC1)		459 (Dorchester)
	1542 (London W1)	missions	934 (London W1H 4AA)
	2021 (Reading)	Christian history	11 (Aberdeen)
	2187 (Sunderland)	Christianity	14 (Aberdeen)
	2289 (Winchester)	church history	11 (Aberdeen)
Scotland	553 (Edinburgh)	culture	1273 (London EC4)
social	411 (Coleraine)	demography	298 (Cambridge)
	2145 (Southampton)	economics	298 (Cambridge)
	2333 (York)		1961, 1962 (Oxford)
theatres	2183 (Sunderland)	education	298 (Cambridge)
Adolescence	503 (Edinburgh)		967 (London W1Y 2AA)
	832 (Leicester)	ethnography	1273 (London EC4)
	912 (London E1)	European West	1749 (Manchester)
problems	388 (Chester)	geography	298 (Cambridge)
psychology	725 (Huddersfield)		1329 (London N16)
Adoption	1059 (London SE11)	history	298 (Cambridge)
	1405 (London W1)		644 (Gravesend)
Adult education	140 (Birmingham)		866 (Liverpool)
	671 (Harlech)		1273 (London EC4)
	722 (Hounslow)		1329 (London N16)
	906 (London N7)		1968 (Oxford)
	1102, 1419 (London W1)	humanities	1666 (London WC1)
	1699 (London W1H 8BY)	languages	710 (Hertford)
	1951 (Oxford)		1273 (London EC4)
	2198 (Sutton Coldfield)		1968 (Oxford)
	2318 (Worksop)	law	298 (Cambridge)
Adventure playgrounds	2205 (Tamworth)	linguistics	1273 (London EC4)
	503 (Edinburgh)	literature	866 (Liverpool)
Advertisements, historical			1968 (Oxford)
	884 (London WC2)	missions	934 (London W1H 4AA)
Advertising	884 (London WC2)		1085, 1086 (London SW1)
	1253 (London SW1)	North	490 (Durham)
	1839 (Newcastle upon Tyne)	North Central	1749 (Manchester)
art	253 (Bromley)	political science	298 (Cambridge)
careers	884 (London WC2)	politics	1961 (Oxford)
See also Volume I		problems	1514 (London WC2)
Aegean Islands	408 (Colchester)	religion	1968 (Oxford)

Africa (contd)
   social sciences   1273 (London EC4)
                                   1666 (London WC1)
   sociology   298 (Cambridge)
                                   1273 (London EC4)
                                   1961 (Oxford)
   South   1613 (London WC2)
     geography   1911 (Oldham)
     history   1911 (Oldham)
     law   1654 (London WC1)
     Methodist missions   1376 (London NW1)
   South East
     geography   1911 (Oldham)
     history   1911 (Oldham)
   Southern   459 (Dorchester)
     history   252 (Bromley)
   topography   866 (Liverpool)
   travel   492 (Durham)
                                   644 (Gravesend)
                                 1647 (London SW1)
   West   154 (Birmingham)
     missions   934 (London W1H 4AA)
Afrikaans literature   1972 (Oxford)
Aged, home care   2218 (Truro)
Ageing research   796 (Leeds)
Agriculture
   (Volume I of this Directory includes agriculture, but it has also been included in this volume for organizations which do not appear in Volume I)
                                 99 (Belfast)
                                 118 (Beverley)
                                 353 (Carlisle)
                                 437 (Dagenham)
                                 571 (Edinburgh)
                                 781 (Kirkcaldy)
                                 1534 (London SW1)
                                 1886 (Nottingham)
                                 2043 (Ripon)
                                 2306 (Wolverhampton)
   Africa   298 (Cambridge)
   chemicals, toxicology   1723 (Macclesfield)
   co-operation   1476 (London WC1)
   development   1162 (London WC2)
   economics   17 (Aberystwyth)
                                 836 (Lewes)
                                 1731 (Maidstone)
                                 1922, 1960 (Oxford)
   economists, biography 1731 (Maidstone)
   Farnham   592 (Farnham)
   history   530 (Edinburgh)
                                 703, 705 (Hereford)
                                 1115 (London SW1)
                                 1553 (London WC2)
                                 1960 (Oxford)
                                 2022, 2028 (Reading)
                                 2145 (Southampton)
   Bedfordshire, South   1720 (Luton)

Rutland   1907 (Oakham)
implements   31 (Ashford)
iodine   1051 (London EC2)
products   1412 (London SW1)
safety   1508 (London SW1)
Scotland   553 (Edinburgh)
Air conditioning, hospitals   628 (Glasgow)
Air forces   2074 (St Boswells)
Air pollution   1361 (London EC1)
                             1439 (London EC4)
See also Volume I
Air power   2129 (Sleaford)
Air warfare   2129 (Sleaford)
Aircraft
   history   2129 (Sleaford)
                             2325 (Yeovil)
   industry, Scotland   611 (Glasgow)
See also Volume I
Aircraft carriers, history   2325 (Yeovil)
A'Kempis, Thomas   294 (Cambridge)
Albania   408 (Colchester)
                             743 (Ilford)
   literature   1972 (Oxford)
Alcohol   1704 (London SW16)
Alcoholics   388 (Chester)
Alcoholism   876 (Liverpool)
                             1054 (London SW1)
                             1359 (London WC1)
                             1411 (London SW1)
                             1595 (London SW17)
                             2255 (Watford)
   education   876 (Liverpool)
   history   1595 (London SW17)
Alderney
   geology   22 (Alderney)
   history   22 (Alderney)
   natural history   22 (Alderney)
Aldershot, local history   23 (Aldershot)
Aldines   2295 (Windsor)
Aldosterone antagonists   715 (High Wycombe)
Alexander Kilham   1756 (Manchester)
Alexander Pope   2039 (Richmond)
Alexandre Dumas   1333 (London SW2)
Alfred Lord Tennyson   854, 855 (Lincoln)
Alfred Stevens   460 (Dorchester)
Algeria
   geography   1749 (Manchester)
   history   1749 (Manchester)
Alkali works   1381 (London SW1)
Allergy   117 (Betchworth)
                             954 (London SW3)
                             1337 (London E15)
Amenity
   Edinburgh   507 (Edinburgh)
   Monmouthshire   1803 (Meifod)
   Wales   1803 (Meifod)
America   225 (Brighton)

America *(contd)*	1253 (London SW1)	Anaesthesia	978 (London W1M 8AL)
	1661 (London WC1)		1139, 1532 (London WC2)
	1678 (London NW1)	Anaesthetics	154 (Birmingham)
	1746 (Manchester)		176 (Bolton)
	2145 (Southampton)		426 (Crewe)
arts	69 (Bath)		681 (Harrow)
Central, Christianity	14 (Aberdeen)		1033 (London NW10)
civil war	583 (Exeter)		1139, 1532 (London WC2)
	833 (Leigh on Sea)		1246 (London W1)
drama	581 (Esher)	Anatomical atlases	2025 (Reading)
fiction		Anatomy	87 (Bedford)
criticism	497 (Eastbourne)		154 (Birmingham)
history	497 (Eastbourne)		435 (Dagenham)
geography	1329 (London E9)		476 (Dumfries)
	1786 (Manchester)		773 (Kilmarnock)
	2219 (Truro)		836 (Lewes)
history	17 (Aberystwyth)		874 (Liverpool)
	69 (Bath)		1236 (London W1P 3LD)
	154 (Birmingham)		1261 (London WC1)
	583 (Exeter)		1475 (London W1M 4AX)
	1329 (London E9)		1532, 1533 (London WC2)
	1786 (Manchester)		1537 (London WC1)
	1822 (Neath)		1601 (London EC2)
	1953 (Oxford)		1631 (London WC1)
	2185 (Sunderland)		1656 (London WC2)
	2219 (Truro)		1805 (Mexborough)
letters	252 (Bromley)		1828 (Newbury)
literary criticism	1786 (Manchester)		1904 (Nuneaton)
literature	17 (Aberystwyth)	animal	773 (Kilmarnock)
	179 (Bolton)	ear	1791 (Manchester)
	583 (Exeter)	feet	1048 (London NW8)
	1326 (London W5)	morbid	681 (Harrow)
	1339 (London E1)		1075 (London W1)
	1850 (London NW1)	upper extremities	124 (Birkenhead)
	1855 (Newport, Mon)	Ancient monuments	893 (London W8)
	2011 (Prescot)	legislation	893 (London W8)
	2279 (Weymouth)	Anderson, John	631 (Glasgow)
criticism	2021 (Reading)	Andrew Carnegie	475, 476, 478 (Dunfermline)
history	2021 (Reading)	Andrew Marvell	733 (Hull)
North		Anglesey, local history	883 (Llangefni)
government	409 (Colchester)	Anglican churches	1322 (London NW4)
history	409 (Colchester)	history	1585 (London EC4)
literature	409 (Colchester)	Anglican missions	1647 (London SW1)
poetry	252 (Bromley)	Angling clubs, Scotland	540 (Edinburgh)
	1477 (London SW5)	Angling waters, Scotland	540 (Edinburgh)
	2240 (Wallasey)	Anglo-Egyptian relations	724 (Hove)
South	1824 (Nelson)	Anglo-Jewish archives	897 (London WC1)
Christianity	14 (Aberdeen)	Anglo-Jewish history	1383 (London WC1)
geography	2149 (Sunderland)	Anglo-Jewry	1458 (London WC1)
history	2149 (Sunderland)	Anglo-Saxon	
See also Latin America,		language	2128 (Sleaford)
United States of America		literature	282 (Cambridge)
Amines, biochemistry	2109 (Sheffield)		2021 (Reading)
Ammunition	1389 (London SE18)		2128 (Sleaford)
Amusements, indoor	1935 (Oxford)	Animals	
See also Games, Sports		anatomy	773 (Kilmarnock)
Anabolic steroids	1730 (Maidenhead)	disease	1828 (Newbury)

Animals, disease (contd)	2275 (Weybridge)	Lincoln	846 (Lincoln)
health	2275 (Weybridge)	Lincolnshire	846 (Lincoln)
husbandry	319 (Cambridge)	Northumberland	1849 (Newcastle upon Tyne)
	1828 (Newbury)	Nottinghamshire	1901 (Nottingham)
nursing	145 (Birmingham)	Roman	1250 (London WC1)
nutrition	1534 (London SW1)		2018 (Preston)
technology	1468 (London W2)		2053 (Rotherham)
treatments	1168 (London W1A 3AU)	Scotland	530 (Edinburgh)
welfare	461 (Dorking)	North East	13 (Aberdeen)
	556, 564 (Edinburgh)	Surrey	660 (Guildford)
	617 (Glasgow)	Westmorland	348, 351 (Carlisle)
	1281, 1552 (London SW1)	Anti-semitism	1062 (London WC2)
	2010 (Potters Bar)		1251 (London W1N 2BH)
Antarctic	295 (Cambridge)		1257, 1292 (London W1)
	957 (London SW1)		2139 (Southampton)
	1340 (London E17)	history	2145 (Southampton)
Anthropology	16 (Aberystwyth)	Anti-slavery movement	1502 (London NW1)
	266 (Buxton)	Anti-vaccination	432 (Croydon)
	320 (Cambridge)	Anti-vivisection	557 (Edinburgh)
	330 (Canterbury)		617 (Glasgow)
	522, 564 (Edinburgh)		1394 (London W1)
	942, 1157 (London WC1)	history	1394 (London W1)
	1132 (London SW1)	Apocalypse	192 (Bournemouth)
	1211 (London SE23)	Apocryphal books	192 (Bournemouth)
	1236 (London W1P 3LD)	Apologetics	517 (Edinburgh)
	1267 (London W1)		612 (Glasgow)
	1337 (London E15)	Aquatic arts	151 (Birmingham)
	1516 (London WC1)	Arab-Jewish relations	1257 (London W1)
	1627 (London NW3)	Arabia	640 (Gosport)
	1650 (London NW1)	geography	258 (Burnley)
	1808 (Middlesbrough)	history	258 (Burnley)
	1904 (Nuneaton)	Arabic	813 (Leeds)
	2173 (Stoke-on-Trent)	language	1285 (London NW8)
	2262 (Wells)	literature	81 (Beaconsfield)
Africa	298 (Cambridge)		1285 (London NW8)
	1647 (London SW1)		1791 (Manchester)
Latin America	299 (Cambridge)	Archaeological drawings	1865 (Northampton)
physical	310 (Cambridge)	Archaeological societies	1598 (London W1V 0HS)
social	311 (Cambridge)	Archaeology	17 (Aberystwyth)
	522 (Edinburgh)		76 (Bath)
	1964 (Oxford)		154 (Birmingham)
Antibiotics	117 (Betchworth)		177 (Bolton)
	648 (Greenford)		266 (Buxton)
	2268 (Wembley)		301, 310 (Cambridge)
Antiques	2077 (St Helens)		327 (Canterbury)
	2254 (Warwick)		371 (Chelmsford)
Antiquities	706 (Hereford)		385, 387, 389 (Chester)
	1338 (London SE22)		462 (Douglas)
	1850 (Newcastle upon Tyne)		466 (Dumfries)
	1952 (Oxford)		492 (Durham)
	2089 (Salisbury)		564 (Edinburgh)
	2186 (Sunderland)		609, 629 (Glasgow)
	2252 (Warrington)		660 (Guildford)
Cardiganshire	1 (Aberaeron)		692 (Hawick)
Cornwall	591 (Falmouth)		706 (Hereford)
Lake District	348 (Carlisle)		735 (Hull)
Lancashire, North	348, 351 (Carlisle)		756 (Ipswich)

Archaeology (contd)	860(Liverpool)	Western	530(Edinburgh)
	1157(London WC1)	Farnham	592(Farnham)
	1211(London SE23)	Glastonbury	633(Glastonbury)
	1337(London E15)	Gloucester	634(Gloucester)
	1341(London SW18)	Greek	316(Cambridge)
	1343(London SW1)		1250(London WC1)
	1416(London WC2)		2029(Reading)
	1426(London SW1)	Hampshire	2293(Winchester)
	1486(London WC1)	Herefordshire	706(Hereford)
	1598(London W1V 0HS)	industrial	417(Coventry)
	1662(London WC1)		1720(Luton)
	1760(Manchester)		2099(Scunthorpe)
	1849(Newcastle upon Tyne)		2181(Stroud)
	1878(Norwich)	Ireland	92, 113(Belfast)
	1946, 1969(Oxford)	Isle of Man	462(Douglas)
	2008(Potters Bar)	Isle of Wight	1851(Newport, Isle of Wight)
	2042(Ripon)		
	2068, 2071(St Albans)	Kent	1328(London SE10)
	2089(Salisbury)	North West	429(Croydon)
	2145(Southampton)	Kidderminster	771(Kidderminster)
	2163(Stirling)	King's Lynn	774(King's Lynn)
	2187(Sunderland)	Lancashire	1760(Manchester)
	2252(Warrington)	North	351(Carlisle)
	2262(Wells)	Latin America	1655(London WC1)
	2279(Weymouth)	Lincoln	843(Lincoln)
	2293(Winchester)	Lincolnshire	843, 846, 850(Lincoln)
	2311(Worcester)	London	1097(London SE17)
Ayrshire	43(Ayr)	medieval	1952(Oxford)
Bath	76(Bath)	Middle East	1850(Newcastle upon Tyne)
Battersea	1069(London SW12)	Monmouthshire	1859(Newport, Mon)
Bradford	199(Bradford)	Near East	1655(London WC1)
Breconshire	204(Brecon)		1952(Oxford)
Bridgwater	213(Bridgwater)	Newark	1827 (Newark)
Bristol	228(Bristol)	Nuneaton	1904(Nuneaton)
	634(Gloucester)	Norfolk	1875, 1878(Norwich)
British	113(Belfast)	photographs	154(Birmingham)
Buckinghamshire	37, 38(Aylesbury)	Roman	316(Cambridge)
Bute	2057(Rothesay)		1250(London WC1)
Carmarthenshire	355(Carmarthen)	Rutland	1907(Oakham)
Cheshire	385, 387, 389(Chester)	Scarborough	2095(Scarborough)
	1760(Manchester)	Scotland	530, 572(Edinburgh)
Chester	385, 387, 389(Chester)	Shropshire	2125(Shrewsbury)
Chichester	395(Chichester)	Somerset	633(Glastonbury)
City of London	1188(London EC2)	Staffordshire	2244(Walsall)
Clapham	1069(London SW12)	Stamford	2157(Stamford)
Classical	1952, 1975(Oxford)	Stroud	2181(Stroud)
Croydon	429(Croydon)	Surrey	656, 660(Guildford)
Cumberland	351(Carlisle)	North East	656(Guildford)
Darent Valley	441(Dartford)	West	656(Guildford)
Dartford	441(Dartford)	Sussex	2322(Worthing)
Devon, North	58(Barnstaple)	West	395(Chichester)
Dorset	460(Dorchester)		2322(Worthing)
Dumfries	466(Dumfries)	Wales	51(Bangor)
England, North East	480(Durham)		337(Cardiff)
Essex	1470(London E15)	North	385, 387, 389(Chester)
Europe	1341(London SW18)	Walton	2277(Weybridge)
	1655(London WC1)	Warwickshire	1904(Nuneaton)

Archaeology (contd)
    Westmorland   351(Carlisle)
    Weybridge   2277(Weybridge)
    Winchester   2293(Winchester)
    Worksop   2319(Worksop)
    Yorkshire   2338(York)
Archbishop Green of Wales   448(Deeside)
Archery   373(Chelmsford)
    1599(London SW13)
    clubs   373(Chelmsford)
Architects   1081(London W1N 4AD)
    1140(London W1H 3HL)
    1268(London W1)
    2118(Sheffield)
Architectural design   2081(Sale)
    2332(York)
Architectural drawings   1587(London WC2)
    1975(Oxford)
Architectural practice   1268(London W1)
    1540(London W1N 4AD)
Architecture   9(Aberdeen)
    72(Bath)
    92, 109(Belfast)
    129, 150(Birmingham)
    184(Boreham Wood)
    189(Bournemouth)
    201(Bradford)
    220(Brighton)
    235(Bristol)
    253(Bromley)
    326(Canterbury)
    340(Cardiff)
    349(Carlisle)
    378(Cheltenham)
    417(Coventry)
    450(Derby)
    469, 472(Dundee)
    585(Exeter)
    706(Hereford)
    726(Huddersfield)
    731(Hull)
    777(Kingston upon Thames)
    805(Leeds)
    824(Leicester)
    866, 867, 871(Liverpool)
    901(London WC1)
    1015(London SW4)
    1140(London W1H 3HL)
    1181(London SE1)
    1194(London W12)
    1265, 1288(London NW3)
    1341(London SW18)
    1377(London SW1)
    1425(London SE10)
    1450(London N7)
    1464(London W1)
    1482(London W1R 8AL)
    1540(London W1N 4AD)
    1587(London WC2)
    1727(Maidenhead)
    1765(Manchester)
    1797(Market Drayton)
    1806, 1808(Middlesbrough)
    1850(Newcastle upon Tyne)
    1858(Newport, Mon)
    1876(Norwich)
    1902(Nottingham)
    1937, 1975(Oxford)
    1990(Peterborough)
    2116, 2119(Sheffield)
    2141(Southampton)
    2187(Sunderland)
    2232(Twickenham)
    2237(Wakefield)
    Cheshire   385, 387(Chester)
    Chester   385, 387(Chester)
    Church   178(Bolton)
        579(Epsom)
    Cornwall   591(Falmouth)
    Denmark   895(London W1X 6HJ)
    descriptive   1748(Manchester)
    domestic   1779(Manchester)
    ecclesiastical   2152(Southwell)
    educational   178(Bolton)
    England   1426(London SW1)
        North East   480(Durham)
    French   223(Brighton)
    German   223(Brighton)
    history   109(Belfast)
        326(Canterbury)
        1093(London EC2)
        1748(Manchester)
        2332(York)
    Italian   223(Brighton)
    landscape   109(Belfast)
        378(Cheltenham)
        805(Leeds)
        1693(London SW19)
    Lincolnshire   850(Lincoln)
    naval   1425(London SE10)
    Norfolk   1873(Norwich)
    photographs   184(Boreham Wood)
    public buildings   178(Bolton)
    religions   154(Birmingham)
    Russia   1591(London SW9)
    scientific buildings   178,(Bolton)
    Scotland   509, 530(Edinburgh)
    stage   968(London W1Y 4HQ)
    training   1081(London W1N 4AD)
    tropical   901(London WC1)
    Wales   342(Cardiff)
        North   385, 387(Chester)
Archives
    administration   2314(Worcester)

Archives, administration (contd)
                          2331 (York)
  national   1494 (London WC2)
  United Kingdom   1494 (London WC2)
  University of Cambridge 321 (Cambridge)
  (Local collections of archives will be found under the town or county, usually under the sub-heading 'local history')
Arctic   295 (Cambridge)
                          1340 (London E17)
                          1904 (Nuneaton)
  economic development   295 (Cambridge)
Areas of Outstanding
  Natural Beauty   1096 (London NW1)
Argyll, local history   479 (Dunoon)
Aristotelia   1941 (Oxford)
Armagh see County Armagh
Armaments   1020 (London WC1)
See also Volume I
Armour   846 (Lincoln)
                         903 (London EC3)
                         904 (London WC1)
                        1673 (London W1)
                        1688 (London WC2)
  oriental   903 (London EC3)
Arms   846 (Lincoln)
                         903 (London EC3)
                         904 (London WC1)
                        1673 (London W1)
                        1688 (London WC2)
  oriental   903 (London EC3)
  small   1389 (London SE18)
Army   384 (Chester)
                        1986 (Perth)
  British   269 (Camberley)
  history   24 (Aldershot)
Army Cadet Force   905 (London SW1)
Army education   1112 (London SW1)
                        1242 (London SE9)
Army Lists   841 (Lichfield)
Arnold Bax   938 (London W3)
Arnold Bennett   2170 (Stoke-on-Trent)
Art   9 (Aberdeen)
                        32 (Ashington)
                        33 (Ashton-under-Lyne)
                        56 (Barnet)
                        59 (Barnstaple)
                        63 (Basingstoke)
                        75 (Bath)
                        93, 113 (Belfast)
                        138 (Birmingham)
                        168 (Blackpool)
                        182 (Bootle)
                        184 (Boreham Wood)
                        189 (Bournemouth)
                        198 (Bradford)
                        220 (Brighton)

235 (Bristol)
329 (Canterbury)
386 (Chester)
403 (Chorley)
409 (Colchester)
417 (Coventry)
427 (Crewe)
435 (Dagenham)
449, 450 (Derby)
457 (Doncaster)
470 (Dundee)
485 (Durham)
496, 498 (Eastbourne)
513 (Edinburgh)
574 (Egham)
578 (Epsom)
585, 587 (Exeter)
598 (Galashiels)
612, 630 (Glasgow)
646 (Grays)
653 (Guernsey)
673 (Harlow)
676 (Harrogate)
679 (Harrow)
704 (Hereford)
727 (Huddersfield)
750 (Ilkley)
754 (Ipswich)
801, 802, 805, 812 (Leeds)
866, 872, 877 (Liverpool)
1117 (London W5)
1118 (London E6)
1146 (London SW1)
1165 (London SW15)
1167 (London SW17)
1194 (London W12)
1211 (London SE23)
1288 (London NW3)
1302 (London SE11)
1339 (London E1)
1385 (London SE1)
1415 (London WC2)
1498 (London SE8)
1586 (London E1)
1587 (London WC2)
1614 (London SE5)
1615 (London N14)
1653 (London SE14)
1719, 1722 (Luton)
1746, 1765, 1782 (Manchester)
1801 (Matlock)
1808 (Middlesbrough)
1811 (Mirfield)
1837, 1845, 1846 (Newcastle upon Tyne)
1858 (Newport, Mon)

Art (*contd*)

	1866(Northampton)		199(Bradford)
	1893(Nottingham)		220(Brighton)
	1905(Nuneaton)		231(Bristol)
	1918, 1937, 1946(Oxford)		349(Carlisle)
	1990(Peterborough)		378(Cheltenham)
	1992(Plymouth)		422(Coventry)
	2000(Poole)		667(Halifax)
	2020(Reading)		734(Hull)
	2035(Retford)		777(Kingston upon Thames)
	2043(Ripon)		871(Liverpool)
	2050(Rotherham)		1018(London SE5)
	2070(St. Albans)		1713(Loughborough)
	2078(St Ives)		1839(Newcastle upon Tyne)
	2085(Salford)		1883(Norwich)
	2115(Sheffield)		1892(Nottingham)
	2135(Slough)		2111(Sheffield)
	2141(Southampton)		2188(Sunderland)
	2160(Stevenage)		2207(Taunton)
	2163(Stirling)		2242(Wallsend)
	2167(Stockport)	*See also* arts, fine	
	2187(Sunderland)	French	223(Brighton)
	2203(Swindon)		1163(London SW7)
	2205(Tamworth)		2111(Sheffield)
	2232(Twickenham)	galleries	2044(Rochdale)
	2234, 2237(Wakefield)	German	223(Brighton)
	2254(Warwick)		1177(London SW7)
	2280(Whitehaven)	graphic	871(Liverpool)
	2290(Winchester)		1165(London SW15)
	2312(Worcester)		1339(London E1)
	2336 (York)	Greek	1250(London WC1)
aesthetics	591(Falmouth)	glass	465(Dudley)
applied	177(Bolton)	history	129(Birmingham)
	231(Bristol)		189(Bournemouth)
	564(Edinburgh)		253(Bromley)
	734(Hull)		430(Croydon)
	860(Liverpool)		731(Hull)
Austria	929(London SW7)		787(Lancaster)
British	1626(London SW1)		793(Leamington Spa)
	2111(Sheffield)		831(Leicester)
ceramic	581(Esher)		880(Liverpool)
Chinese	2111(Sheffield)		942, 1039(London WC1)
cinema	984(London W1)		1302(London SE11)
commercial	667(Halifax)		1686 (London NW3)
	1339(London E1)		1692(London E17)
	1719(Luton)		1693(London SW19)
decorative	214(Bridgwater)		1713(Loughborough)
Derbyshire, North	2113(Sheffield)		1732(Maidstone)
Dutch	2111(Sheffield)		1808(Middlesbrough)
Eastern	1952(Oxford)		2116(Sheffield)
education	129(Birmingham)		2188(Sunderland)
	220(Brighton)		2323(Worthing)
	688(Havant)	English	1093(London EC2)
environment	189(Bournemouth)	Indian	2111(Sheffield)
European	2005(Portsmouth)	industrial	1253(London SW1)
history	1652(London W1H 0BE)		1339(London E1)
fine	17(Aberystwyth)	Islamic	2111(Sheffield)
	177(Bolton)	Italian	223(Brighton)

715

Art, Italian (contd)	2111 (Sheffield)		1665 (London E1)
Japanese	1733 (Maidstone)		1762, 1770, 1771
	2111 (Sheffield)		(Manchester)
landscape	1693 (London SW19)		1850 (Newcastle upon Tyne)
	2297 (Wirral)		1902 (Nottingham)
low countries	1883 (Norwich)		1927 (Oxford)
medieval	2333 (York)		2055 (Rotherham)
Mediterranean	2111 (Sheffield)		2059 (Rugby)
metalwork	252 (Bromley)		2073 (St Andrews)
	724 (Hove)		2119 (Sheffield)
	2141 (Southampton)		2123 (Shrewsbury)
movement	1165 (London SW15)		2145 (Southampton)
needlework	485 (Durham)	administration	1102 (London W1)
occult	564 (Edinburgh)	American	69 (Bath)
psychopathological	1266 (London SE5)	applied	78 (Batley)
religious	2278 (Weymouth)		231 (Bristol)
Roman	1250 (London WC1)		726 (Huddersfield)
Scottish	551 (Edinburgh)		1553 (London WC2)
teacher training	824 (Leicester)	Asia	1518 (London W1M 9LA)
theory	591 (Falmouth)	Commonwealth	1082 (Edinburgh)
Welsh	337 (Cardiff)		1082 (London W8)
Western	1952 (Oxford)	fine	35 (Aylesbury)
World Wars	1223 (London SE1)		71 (Bath)
Yorkshire, South	2111, 2113 (Sheffield)		78 (Batley)
See also Arts			92 (Belfast)
Arthritis	907 (London WC2)		129, 132, 142, 154, 157
Artillery equipment	1389 (London SE18)		(Birmingham)
Artistic works			160 (Bishop's Stortford)
conservation	1277 (London SW5)		161 (Blackburn)
restoration	1277 (London SW5)		167 (Blackpool)
Artists	1146 (London SW1)		201 (Bradford)
	2336 (York)		222 (Brighton)
British	1792 (Manchester)		253 (Bromley)
Dorset	460 (Dorchester)		291 (Cambridge)
organization	28 (Andover)		330 (Canterbury)
Scottish	527, 551 (Edinburgh)		430 (Croydon)
Societies	28 (Andover)		446 (Deeside)
Sussex	2322 (Worthing)		469, 474 (Dundee)
Wales, South	2199 (Swansea)		629 (Glasgow)
Arts	154 (Birmingham)		748 (Ilkeston)
	175 (Bolton)		762 (Keighley)
	246 (Bristol)		771 (Kidderminster)
	430 (Croydon)		778 (Kingston upon Thames)
	589 (Exeter)		793 (Leamington Spa)
	599 (Gateshead)		855 (Lincoln)
	631 (Glasgow)		926 (London SW1)
	636 (Gloucester)		1039 (London WC1)
	665 (Halesowen)		1074 (London W1)
	739 (Hull)		1110 (London SW15)
	740 (Huntingdon)		1387 (London SW1)
	804 (Leeds)		1473 (London SW16)
	831 (Leicester)		1511 (London W1V 0DS)
	878 (Liverpool)		1553 (London WC2)
	908 (London W1V 0AU)		1674 (London E17)
	1303 (London WC2)		1680 (London W1)
	1334 (London SE13)		1688 (London SW1)
	1343 (London SW1)		1891, 1902 (Nottingham)

Arts, fine (contd)	1993 (Plymouth)	religion	1523 (London W1N 1LN)
	2002 (Portsmouth)		1968 (Oxford)
	2011 (Prescot)	science	1961 (Oxford)
	2014 (Preston)	sociology	1961 (Oxford)
	2099 (Scunthorpe)	South	1229 (London SE1)
	2174 (Stoke-on-Trent)	economics	300 (Cambridge)
	2198 (Sutton Coalfield)	history	300 (Cambridge)
	2199 (Swansea)	social studies	300 (Cambridge)
	2221 (Truro)	South East	739 (Hull)
	2238 (Wakefield)	geography	258 (Burnley)
	2286 (Wigan)	Methodist missions	1376 (London NW1)
East European	1668 (London WC1)	travel	492 (Durham)
history	312 (Cambridge)	Asia Minor	
Japan	1289 (London W1X 9LB)	geography	2150 (Southport)
Slavonic	1668 (London WC1)	history	2150 (Southport)
See also Art, fine		Aspirin	745 (Ilford)
history	326 (Canterbury)	Aspirin salicylates	2133 (Slough)
Hungary	988 (London SW1)	Assyriological studies	1952 (Oxford)
industry	2225 (Tunbridge Wells)	Asthma	925 (London W2)
Russia	1591 (London SW9)	Astrology	564 (Edinburgh)
Scotland	541 (Edinburgh)	Astronomy	860 (Liverpool)
Sweden	1623 (London W1R 2DN)	nautical	1425 (London SE10)
theatre	154 (Birmingham)	See also Volume I	
United States of America	69 (Bath)	Athletics	154 (Birmingham)
useful	1387 (London SW1)		1475 (London W1M 4AX)
Arts and Crafts Movement	1692 (London E17)	Atlases (major collections	
Ascetic theology	830 (Leicester)	only)	492 (Durham)
Ascetical literature	401 (Chipping Norton)		813 (Leeds)
Ashbee, C. R.	288 (Cambridge)		1425 (London SE10)
Ashton-under-Lyne,			1538 (London SW7)
local history	34 (Ashton-under-Lyne)	anatomical	2025 (Reading)
Asia	225 (Brighton)	Wales	16 (Aberystwyth)
	270 (Camberley)	See also maps	
	412 (Colne)	Atmospheric pollution	521 (Edinburgh)
	1028 (London SW3)	See also Volume I	
arts	1518 (London W1M 9LA)	A.T.S.	663 (Guildford)
bibliography	1523 (London W1N 1LN)	Audio-lingual materials	800 (Leeds)
biography	1523 (London W1N 1LN)	Audiology	145 (Birmingham)
Central		units	1545 (London WC1)
geography	779 (Kingston upon Thames)	Audio-visual aids	155 (Birmingham)
history	779 (Kingston upon Thames)		174 (Bolton)
	1725 (Macclesfield)		1407 (London W1M 0AL)
travel	1725 (Macclesfield)	Audio-visual communication	1151 (London W1)
Christianity	14 (Aberdeen)	Audio-visual education	2003 (Portsmouth)
description	1999 (Poole)	Audio-visual materials	226 (Brighton)
economics	1961 (Oxford)		550 (Edinburgh)
education	967 (London W1Y 2AA)		590 (Falkirk)
geography	1999 (Poole)		800 (Leeds)
history	1230 (London SE1)		1465 (London WC1)
	1968 (Oxford)	overseas development	1465 (London WC1)
	1999 (Poole)	Audio-visual techniques	1898 (Nottingham)
languages	1523 (London W1N 1LN)	Austen Chamberlain	154 (Birmingham)
	1968 (Oxford)	Austin Dobson	1326 (London W5)
literature	1518 (London W1M 9LA)	Australasia	179 (Bolton)
	1968 (Oxford)	geography	431 (Croydon)
missions	1085 (London SW1)	history	431 (Croydon)
politics	1961 (Oxford)	topography	431 (Croydon)

717

Australia	928(London WC2)		681(Harrow)
culture	928(London WC2)		738(Hull)
history	866(Liverpool)		1075, 1260(London W1)
	928(London WC2)		1344(London WC1)
literature	866(Liverpool)		1828(Newbury)
	928(London WC2)		1886(Nottingham)
	950(London W1)		2248(Ware)
social sciences	928(London WC2)		2294(Windlesham)
topography	866(Liverpool)		2301(Woking)
Austria	929(London SW7)	medical	1468(London W2)
	1125(London SW1)	tuberculosis	1373(London W12)
art	929(London SW7)	See also Volume I	
folklore	929(London SW7)	Bacup	
history	436(Dagenham)	local history	45(Bacup)
	929(London SW7)	natural history	46(Bacup)
literature	929(London SW7)	Badges, police	67(Basingstoke)
music	929(London SW7)	Bahamas, Methodist	
theatre	929(London SW7)	missions	1376(London NW1)
topography	436(Dagenham)	Bakery	33(Ashton-under-Lyne)
Authors	1600(London SW10)		1823(Neath)
Greek, biography	1731(Maidstone)		1838(Newcastle upon Tyne)
Latin, biography	1731(Maidstone)		
Wiltshire	453(Devizes)		2182(Sunderland)
Authorship, history	1404(London W1X 4BB)	See also Volume I	
Autistic children		Balkan States	
education	1438(London NW11)	geography	2278(Weymouth)
welfare	1438(London NW11)	history	2278(Weymouth)
Aviation	195(Bracknell)	Ballads, Welsh	783(Lampeter)
	1042(London EC2)	Ballantyne, R. M.	513(Edinburgh)
behavioural problems	393(Chichester)	Ballet	968(London W1Y 4HQ)
civil	947(London SW1)		1248(London W6)
history	121(Biggleswade)		1322(London NW4)
psychology	393(Chichester)		1521(London W14)
See also Volume I			1688(London WC2)
Ayrshire			1872(Northwich)
archaeology	43(Ayr)	history	1521(London W14)
history	43(Ayr)	Banbury	
industrial archaeology	43(Ayr)	archaeology	50(Banbury)
local history	41(Ayr)	history	50(Banbury)
	2092(Saltcoats)	local history	50(Banbury)
natural history	43(Ayr)	Banffshire	
		local history	763(Keith)
B		Banking	

(Volume I of this Directory includes banking, but it has also been indexed in this volume for organizations which do not appear in Volume I)

Babylonian studies	1952(Oxford)		145(Birmingham)
Bacon	1662(London WC1)		511(Edinburgh)
Bacon–Shakespeare	1902(Nottingham)		606(Glasgow)
controversy	1333(London SW2)		676(Harrogate)
Bacteria, systematics	829(Leicester)		700(Henley-on-Thames)
Bacterial blood diseases	1323(London NW10)		1243(London EC3)
Bacteriology	6(Aberdeen)		1711(Loughborough)
	85(Beckenham)		1853(Newport, Isle of Wight)
	99(Belfast)		
	154(Birmingham)	history	1179, 1243(London EC3)
	305(Cambridge)	Banks, history	1243(London EC3)
	344(Cardiff)		
	502, 531(Edinburgh)		

Baptist Church	933, 935, 1161 (London WC1)	Benjamin Disraeli	713 (High Wycombe)
		Bennett, Arnold	2170 (Stoke-on-Trent)
history	1944 (Oxford)	Berlioz	529 (Edinburgh)
Baptist Union of Scotland, history	604 (Glasgow)	Berwick-upon-Tweed, local history	115 (Berwick-upon-Tweed)
Barber, John	1904 (Nuneaton)	Betjeman, John	1798 (Marlborough)
Barking, local history	436 (Dagenham)	Bexley, local history	119 (Bexley)
Barnes, William	459, 460 (Dorchester)	Bible	95 (Belfast)
Barnet, local history	2008 (Potters Bar)		158 (Birmingham)
Barnsley, local history	57 (Barnsley)		369 (Chelmsford)
Barnstaple, local history	58, 59 (Barnstaple)		397 (Chichester)
Bartok	988 (London SW1)		428 (Crieff)
Baseball	737 (Hull)		545, 569 (Edinburgh)
Basil Henriques	912 (London E1)		1292 (London W1)
Baskerville books	154 (Birmingham)		1334 (London SE13)
Basketball	795 (Leeds)		1571 (London SE5)
Basque literature	1972 (Oxford)		1789 (Manchester)
Bath, local history	71 (Bath)		2083 (Salford)
Batley, local history	78 (Batley)		2289 (Winchester)
Battersea		Acts of the Apostles	217 (Bridgwater)
archaeology	1069 (London SW12)	Apocalypse	192 (Bournemouth)
genealogy	1069 (London SW12)	Apocryphal Books	192 (Bournemouth)
local history	1069 (London SW12)	commentaries	119 (Bexley)
topography	1069 (London SW12)		584 (Exeter)
Battle of Sedgemoor	213, 214 (Bridgwater)		1076 (London SW7)
Bax, Arnold	938 (London W3)		1914 (Ormskirk)
Baxter, Richard	158 (Birmingham)		2042 (Ripon)
	771 (Kidderminster)		2124 (Shrewsbury)
	1190 (London W3)	criticism	1500 (London N1)
BBC Television	208 (Brentford)	Epistles	192 (Bournemouth)
Beaulieu River	249 (Brockenhurst)	exegesis	119 (Bexley)
Beauty culture	33 (Ashton-under-Lyne)		1076 (London SW7)
	1074 (London W1)	Gospels	217 (Bridgwater)
	2055 (Rotherham)	Hebrew	711 (Hertford)
See also Volume I		history	119 (Bexley)
Bebington, local history	2297 (Wirral)		612 (Glasgow)
Bede, Cuthbert	771 (Kidderminster)	languages	517 (Edinburgh)
Bedfordshire		literature	401 (Chipping Norton)
local history	90 (Bedford)	Old Testament	23 (Aldershot)
	1722 (Luton)	research	1284 (London WC1)
	2068 (St Albans)	studies	296, 297, 309 (Cambridge)
South			424 (Crawley)
agricultural history	1720 (Luton)		569 (Edinburgh)
industrial history	1720 (Luton)		1292 (London W1)
Bee Culture	2073 (St Andrews)		1927 (Oxford)
See also Volume I		Bibles (collections)	584 (Exeter)
Beecham, Sir Thomas	2273 (Westcliff-on-Sea)		1303 (London WC2)
Behavioural problems, aviation	393 (Chichester)		1791 (Manchester)
			1810 (Middlesbrough)
Behavioural sciences	1005 (London SE1)		2124 (Shrewsbury)
Beighton, Henry	1904 (Nuneaton)	Welsh	783 (Lampeter)
Belfast newspapers	92 (Belfast)	Bibliographies	84 (Beckenham)
Belgium	408 (Colchester)		583 (Exeter)
geography	2278 (Weymouth)		1578 (London SW7)
history	2278 (Weymouth)		1688 (London WC2)
Belloc, Hilaire	413 (Colwyn Bay)	English literature	286 (Cambridge)
Benjamin Brodie	1565 (London SW1)	history	286 (Cambridge)

Bibliography	71 (Bath)		1955 (Oxford)
	223 (Brighton)		2067 (St Albans)
	492 (Durham)		2094 (Sandwich)
	569 (Edinburgh)		2131 (Slough)
	630 (Glasgow)		2140 (Southampton)
	813 (Leeds)		2301 (Woking)
	940 (London W1V 0NS)	amines	2109 (Sheffield)
	1096 (London W1P 2AL)	brain	1366 (London SW7)
	1117 (London W5)	human	2081 (Sale)
	1338 (London SE22)	intestinal	1366 (London SW7)
	1662 (London WC1)	steroids	2109 (Sheffield)
	1956 (Oxford)	See also Volume I	
	2295 (Windsor)	Bio-engineering	550 (Edinburgh)
Africa	2345		631 (Glasgow)
Asia	1523 (London W1N 1LN)		681 (Harrow)
Cornwall	2218 (Truro)		941 (London NW7)
Eastern Europe	2260 (Wellingborough)		1551 (London W12)
history	940 (London W1V 0NS)		
historical	1315 (London WC1)	See also Biomedical	
John Bunyan	91 (Bedford)	engineering; and Volume I	
Kent	2046 (Rochester)	Biography	95 (Belfast)
legal	1210 (London EC4)		235 (Bristol)
Scotland	622 (Glasgow)		394 (Chichester)
subject	1315 (London WC1)		413 (Colwyn Bay)
Bicycles, history	121 (Biggleswade)		435 (Dagenham)
Bioassays	715 (High Wycombe)		438 (Darlington)
vasopressin	2109 (Sheffield)		653 (Guernsey)
Biochemistry	85 (Beckenham)		700 (Henley-on-Thames)
	99 (Belfast)		746 (Ilford)
	117 (Betchworth)		836 (Lewes)
	147, 154 (Birmingham)		844 (Lincoln)
	207 (Brentford)		961 (London W1A 1AA)
	257 (Burgess Hill)		1098 (London EC1)
	274, 306 (Cambridge)		1132 (London SW1)
	335, 341 (Cardiff)		1210 (London EC4)
	361 (Carshalton)		1219 (London WC1)
	437 (Dagenham)		1253, 1298, 1305 (London SW1)
	455 (Didcot)		1322 (London NW4)
	502, 1520 (Edinburgh)		1326 (London W5)
	674 (Harlow)		1522 (London W8)
	951 (London SE1)		1566 (London WC2)
	1063 (London W1N 4BN)		1578 (London SW7)
	1252 (London WC2)		1615 (London N14)
	1261 (London WC1)		1780 (Manchester)
	1266 (London SE5)		1811 (Mirfield)
	1366 (London SW7)		1819 (Motherwell)
	1367 (London NW7)		2091 (Salisbury)
	1433, 1532 (London WC2)		2205 (Tamworth)
	1537 (London WC1)		2232 (Twickenham)
	1551 (London W12)		2321 (Worthing)
	1631 (London WC1)	Africa	1647 (London SW1)
	1656 (London WC2)	agricultural economists	1731 (Maidstone)
	1664 (London W8)	America	1326 (London W5)
	1712 (Loughborough)	Asia	1523 (London W1N 1LN)
	1723, 1724 (Macclesfield)	Brahman	1935 (Oxford)
	1823 (Neath)	Charles Dickens	2047 (Rochester)
	1886 (Nottingham)	children	436 (Dagenham)

Biography (contd)
  co-operativists   2143 (Southampton)
  disabled   1030 (London SW1)
  doctors   1731 (Maidstone)
  dramatic   968 (London W1Y 4HQ)
  dreamers   1731 (Maidstone)
  early   223 (Brighton)
  ecclesiastical   2222 (Truro)
  economists   2143 (Southampton)
  English theatre   2179 (Stratford-upon-Avon)
  farmers   1731 (Maidstone)
  French literature   381 (Chertsey)
  Greek authors   1731 (Maidstone)
  Hindu   1935 (Oxford)
  Hugeonots   1219 (London WC1)
  John Bunyan   91 (Bedford)
  Kentish men and women 1731 (Maidstone)
  linguists   1731 (Maidstone)
  Marxists   2143 (Southampton)
  medical   978 (London W1M 8AL)
                              1063 (London W1N 4BN)
                              1531 (London NW1)
                              1563 (London EC1)
                              1731 (Maidstone)
  merchants   2143 (Southampton)
  military   24 (Aldershot)
  missionaries   2063 (Saffron Walden)
  musical instrument
    makers   1731 (Maidstone)
  musicians   999 (London W1)
                              1731 (Maidstone)
  Norwich   1875 (Norwich)
  novelists
    American   497 (Eastbourne)
    English   497 (Eastbourne)
  philologists   1731 (Maidstone)
  political   24 (Aldershot)
  road safety   381 (Chertsey)
  Salvation Army   1571 (London SE5)
  scientific   1543 (London W1)
  Services   24 (Aldershot)
  socialists   2143 (Southampton)
  somnambulists   1731 (Maidstone)
  statesmen   1199 (London SW1)
  temperance   2105 (Sheffield)
  trade unionists   2143 (Southampton)
  United States of
    America   950 (London W1)
  women   2149 (Southend-on-Sea)
Biological engineering
  See Bioengineering
Biological sciences
  See Biology
Biological warfare   1020 (London WC1)
Biology   6 (Aberdeen)
                              32 (Ashington)
                              58 (Barnstaple)
                              117 (Betchworth)
                              152 (Birmingham)
                              207 (Brentwood)
                              375 (Chelmsford)
                              403 (Chorley)
                              427 (Crewe)
                              435, 437 (Dagenham)
                              449 (Derby)
                              457 (Doncaster)
                              496 (Eastbourne)
                              510, 531 (Edinburgh)
                              579 (Epsom)
                              612 (Glasgow)
                              648 (Greenford)
                              734 (Hull)
                              750 (Ilkley)
                              812 (Leeds)
                              1132 (London SW1)
                              1165 (London SW15)
                              1236 (London W1P 3LD)
                              1302 (London SE11)
                              1317 (London SW1)
                              1341 (London E1)
                              1367 (London NW1)
                              1380 (London W1P 7PN)
                              1434 (London W2)
                              1495 (London W1)
                              1537 (London WC1)
                              1724 (Macclesfield)
                              1730 (Maidenhead)
                              1809 (Middlesbrough)
                              1837 (Newcastle upon Tyne)
                              1893, 1895 (Nottingham)
                              1948 (Oxford)
                              2020 (Reading)
                              2043 (Ripon)
                              2052 (Rotherham)
                              2205 (Tamworth)
                              2290 (Winchester)
                              2294 (Windlesham)
                              2321 (Worthing)
                              2333 (York)
  applied   335, 340 (Cardiff)
  Essex   1470 (London E15)
  experimental   1828 (Newbury)
  human   141 (Birmingham)
                              163 (Blackburn)
                              403 (Chorley)
                              748 (Ilkeston)
                              1651 (London SW3)
  low temperature   681 (Harrow)
  medical   1679 (London NW1)
  textbooks   815 (Leeds)
See also Volume I
Biomedical engineering   1368 (London NW3)
                              2173 (Stoke-on-Trent)
See also Bioengineering

Biophysics	455 (Didcot)		312 (Cambridge)
	1367 (London NW1)		332 (Cardiff)
	1433 (London WC2)		666 (Halifax)
	1551 (London W12)		724 (Hove)
	1631 (London WC1)		866 (Liverpool)
Birds	399 (Chichester)		2124 (Shrewsbury)
	1902 (Nottingham)		2295 (Windsor)
	2190 (Surbiton)	Bookkeeping	1495 (London W1)
Birmingham, local history	133 (Birmingham)	Bookplates	866 (Liverpool)
Birth control	1142 (London W1N 8BQ)		1480 (London SW7)
	1353 (London W1)	Books	949 (London NW10)
Black Country			950 (London W1)
industrial history	465 (Dudley)		1404 (London W1X 4BB)
local history	465 (Dudley)	Australian	950 (London W1)
	2303 (Wolverhampton)	Canadian	950 (London W1)
Black Watch (R.H.R.),		collecting	940 (London W1V 0NS)
history	1986 (Perth)		1991 (Pinner)
Blackpool, local history	167 (Blackpool)	illustrations	408 (Colchester)
Blacksmith's craft	592 (Farnham)	illustrators	2014 (Preston)
Blake, Robert	213, 214 (Bridgwater)	manufacture	1404 (London W1X 4BB)
Blake, William	1333 (London SW2)	New Zealand	950 (London W1)
	1688 (London WC2)	production	527 (Edinburgh)
Blind		Books of hours	783 (Lampeter)
employment	1321 (London SE15)	Bookselling	1315 (London WC1)
libraries	1424 (London SW1)	history	934 (London W1V 0NS)
rehabilitation	1424, 1775 (Manchester)		1404 (London W1X 4BB)
	1564 (London NW1)	Bootle, local history	183 (Bootle)
training	1321 (London SE15)	Border History	1850 (Newcastle upon Tyne)
welfare	645 (Grays)	Botany	435 (Dagenham)
	1321 (London SE15)		860, 874 (Liverpool)
	1544 (London W1)		1302 (London SE11)
	1564 (London NW1)		1472 (London WC1)
Blood diseases	1730 (Maidenhead)		1586 (London EC3)
bacterial	1323 (London NW10)		1605 (London W1)
Blood Groups			1809 (Middlesbrough)
genetics	501 (Edgware)		1858 (Newport, Mon)
serology	501 (Edgware)		2131 (Slough)
Blood products	241 (Bristol)		2262 (Wells)
Blood transfusion	241 (Bristol)		2293 (Winchester)
	293 (Cambridge)	Derbyshire, North	2113 (Sheffield)
	501 (Edgware)	history	1472 (London WC1)
	2197 (Sutton)	medical	1605 (London W1)
'Bloomsbury' group	288 (Cambridge)	Wales	373 (Cardiff)
Board of control, India	1230 (London SE1)	Yorkshire, South	2113 (Sheffield)
Boat races	890 (London W1N 5TB)	*See also* Volume I	
Boating, River Thames	2040 (Richmond)	Boston, local history	187 (Boston)
Bodmin, local history	171 (Bodmin)	Boston Dock	187 (Boston)
Body, hygiene	2044 (Rochdale)	Botswana	952 (London SW1)
Body fluid abnormalities	1909 (Oldham)	Bourne, Hugh	1756 (Manchester)
Bolton, local history	181 (Bolton)	Boys' clubs	542 (Edinburgh)
Bone	807 (Leeds)		1396 (London WC1)
Bookbinding	430 (Croydon)	Bradford	
	1018 (London SE5)	archaeology	199 (Bradford)
	2141 (Southampton)	geology	199 (Bradford)
	2249 (Ware)	history	197 (Bradford)
history	940 (London W1V 0NS)	industry	199 (Bradford)
Bookbindings	162 (Blackburn)	local history	197, 198, 199 (Bradford

Bradford (contd)	
natural history	199 (Bradford)
Bradlaugh, Charles	1865 (Northampton)
Bradshaw, John	584 (Exeter)
Brahman biography	1935 (Oxford)
Brahmanism	1935 (Oxford)
Brain biochemistry	1366 (London SW7)
'Brain drain'	227 (Brighton)
Brangwyn, Frank	771 (Kidderminster)
	1692 (London E17)
Brass rubbings	1598 (London W1V 0HS)
Brassey, Earl	683 (Hastings)
Brazil, missions	934 (London W1H 4AA)
Brechin, local history	203 (Brechin)
Breconshire	
archaeology	204 (Brecon)
history	204 (Brecon)
local history	204, 205 (Brecon)
natural history	204 (Brecon)
Bridgwater	
archaeology	213 (Bridgwater)
history	213, 214 (Bridgwater)
local history	213, 214 (Bridgwater)
Bridlington, local history	218 (Bridlington)
Brighton	
local history	724 (Hove)
natural history	233 (Brighton)
Bristol	
archaeology	228 (Bristol)
	634 (Gloucester)
folk life	228 (Bristol)
history	232, 233 (Bristol)
industrial history	228 (Bristol)
local history	232, 233 (Bristol)
	634 (Gloucester)
natural history	228 (Bristol)
Britain	270 (Camberley)
British and Foreign School Society	758 (Isleworth)
British archaeology	113 (Belfast)
British armed services, history	1560 (London SW1)
British army	269 (Camberley)
British art, history	1732 (Maidstone)
British artists	1792 (Manchester)
British aviation, history	1515 (London NW9)
British civilization	970 (London WC1)
British Commonwealth	
history	866 (Liverpool)
literature	13 (Aberdeen)
	866 (Liverpool)
topography	866 (Liverpool)
British constitution	711 (Hertford)
	1302 (London SE11)
	1495 (London W1)
	1881 (Norwich)
	2144 (Southampton)
British Dominions law	1654 (London WC1)
British geography	1334 (London SE13)
British history	160 (Bishop's Stortford)
	1334 (London SE13)
	1881 (Norwich)
British industry	1253 (London SW1)
British institutions	970 (London WC1)
British Isles law	1654 (London WC1)
British poetry	1477 (London SW5)
British seamen	1442 (London SW4)
British shipping industry	1442 (London SW4)
British-Soviet relations	1009 (London EC1)
British theatre history	1596 (London W2)
British topography	1604 (London SW7)
Broadcasting	234 (Bristol)
	961 (London W1A 1AA)
	1253 (London SW1)
history	961 (London W1A 1AA)
	1483 (London EC1)
schools	339 (Cardiff)
	1575 (London W1A 1AA)
statistics	961 (London W1A 1AA)
surveys	961 (London W1A 1AA)
Broadsides	1598 (London W1V 0HS)
Brockenhurst, local history	249 (Brockenhurst)
Brodie, Benjamin	1565 (London SW1)
Bronchitis	1168 (London W1A 3AU)
chronic	1361 (London E11)
Brontë family	760, 761 (Keighley)
	1746, 1768 (Manchester)
Brontëana	760 (Keighley)
Bronze Age pottery	641 (Grantham)
Brooke, Rupert	288 (Cambridge)
Browning, Oscar	683 (Hastings)
Buckinghamshire	
archaeology	37, 38 (Aylesbury)
costume	37 (Aylesbury)
folk life	37 (Aylesbury)
geology	37 (Aylesbury)
history	37, 38 (Aylesbury)
local history	36, 37, 38 (Aylesbury)
	1722 (Luton)
natural history	37 (Aylesbury)
paintings	37 (Aylesbury)
prints	37 (Aylesbury)
records	38 (Aylesbury)
Bucklers' Hard	249 (Brockenhurst)
Buddhism	1469 (London W2)
Buddhist texts	1469 (London W2)
Budgerigars	136 (Birmingham)
Building	
(Volume I of this Directory includes building, but it has been indexed in this Volume as well, particularly as architecture is included in Volume II)	
	9 (Aberdeen)
	32 (Ashington)
	33 (Ashton-under-Lyne)

Building (contd)	59 (Barnstaple)	See also Architecture	
	63 (Basingstoke)	Buildings	1535 (London SW1)
	72 (Bath)	educational	1103 (London W1)
	109 (Belfast)	Norfolk	1876 (Norfolk)
	150, 152 (Birmingham)	preservation	893 (London W8)
	168 (Blackpool)	types	1540 (London W1N 4AD)
	191 (Bournemouth)	Bulgaria	408 (Colchester)
	200 (Bradford)	folklore	311 (Cambridge)
	326, 328 (Canterbury)	geography	2278 (Weymouth)
	340 (Cardiff)	history	311 (Cambridge)
	386 (Chester)		2278 (Weymouth)
	406 (Coatbridge)	language	311 (Cambridge)
	419, 421 (Coventry)	literature	311 (Cambridge)
	430 (Croydon)	philosophy	311 (Cambridge)
	450 (Derby)	religion	311 (Cambridge)
	469, 471 (Dundee)	Bulwer Lytton	1190 (London W3)
	485 (Durham)	Bunyan, John	89, 91 (Bedford)
	527 (Edinburgh)	Bureaucracy	1441 (London W1)
	587 (Exeter)	Burke, Edmund	2112 (Sheffield)
	726 (Huddersfield)	Burma	
	731 (Hull)	missions	934 (London W1H 4AA)
	785 (Lancaster)	Methodist	1376 (London NW1)
	824 (Leicester)	Burma Office	1230 (London SE1)
	867 (Liverpool)	Burns, Robert	41 (Ayr)
	901 (London WC1)		478 (Dunfermline)
	1015 (London SW4)		610 (Glasgow)
	1073 (London W8)	Bury St Edmunds, local	
	1118 (London E6)	history	256 (Bury St Edmunds)
	1194 (London W12)	Burton	1956 (Oxford)
	1341 (London SW18)	Burton, Richard	2039 (Richmond)
	1377 (London SW1)	Burton, Robert	1903 (Nuneaton)
	1450 (London N7)	Business	
	1464 (London W1)	(Volume I of this Directory includes business, but it has	
	1540 (London W1N 4AD)	also been indexed in this volume for organizations which	
	1719 (Luton)	do not appear in Volume I)	
	1807 (Middlesbrough)		423 (Crawley)
	1823 (Neath)		587 (Exeter)
	1876 (Norwich)		631 (Glasgow)
	1905 (Nuneaton)		667 (Halifax)
	1910 (Oldham)		726 (Huddersfield)
	1937 (Oxford)		1772 (Manchester)
	1990 (Peterborough)		2316 (Workington)
	2000 (Poole)	administration	994 (London WC2)
	2003 (Portsmouth)		1766 (Manchester)
	2024 (Reading)		2321 (Worthing)
	2034 (Redruth)	cycles	695 (Heckmondwike)
	2098 (Scunthorpe)	history	246 (Bristol)
	2115 (Sheffield)		1017 (London EC4)
	2167 (Stockport)	law	1065 (London SW1)
	2171 (Stoke-on-Trent)		2259 (Wednesbury)
	2203 (Swindon)	management	9 (Aberdeen)
	2205 (Tamworth)		153 (Birmingham)
	2232 (Twickenham)		230 (Bristol)
	2321 (Worthing)		435 (Dagenham)
	2332, 2335 (York)		438 (Darlington)
Scotland	509 (Edinburgh)		868 (Liverpool)
tropical	901 (London WC1)		1715 (Loughborough)

Business, management (*contd*)	1839 (Newcastle upon Tyne)	Cambridge University	314 (Cambridge)
	1881 (Norwich)	history	321 (Cambridge)
	2309 (Bletchley)	Cambridgeshire	277 (Cambridge)
statistics	2060 (Ruislip)	folk life	276 (Cambridge)
studies	154 (Birmingham)	history	276 (Cambridge)
	340 (Cardiff)	local history	276, 310 (Cambridge)
	422 (Coventry)		1796 (March)
	485 (Durham)	photographs	276 (Cambridge)
	511 (Edinburgh)	social welfare services	281 (Cambridge)
	665 (Halesowen)	voluntary organizations	281 (Cambridge)
	676 (Harrogate)	Camping	1328 (London SE10)
	679 (Harrow)	Canada	
	717 (Hitchin)	books	950 (London W1)
	790 (Lancaster)	food legislation	920 (London SE1)
	822 (Leicester)	food standards	920 (London SE1)
	1053 (London W4)	history	866 (Liverpool)
	1065 (London SW1)	literature	866 (Liverpool)
	1117 (London W5)	Methodist missions	1376 (London NW1)
	1118 (London E6)	topography	866 (Liverpool)
	1170 (London SW15)	Cancer	344 (Cardiff)
	1451 (London NW5)		870, 875 (Liverpool)
	1698 (London SE18)		962 (London W1N 1AA)
	1719 (Luton)		1168 (London W1A 3AU)
	1728 (Maidenhead)		1245 (London SW3)
	2182 (Sunderland)		1337 (London E15)
	2306, 2307 (Wolverhampton)		1730 (Maidenhead)
training	866 (Liverpool)		1742 (Manchester)
Bute			2114 (Sheffield)
archaeology	2057 (Rothesay)	education	875 (Liverpool)
local history	2056 (Rothesay)		962 (London W1N 1AA)
natural history	2057 (Rothesay)	lung	1361 (London EC1)
Butler, Samuel	294 (Cambridge)		1633 (London SW1)
Buxton, local history	266 (Buxton)	research	341 (Cardiff)
Byron	133 (Birmingham)		1221 (London WC2)
	1299 (London NW3)		1245 (London SW3)
	1300 (London SW14)	treatment	307 (Cambridge)
	1891 (Nottingham)		1245 (London SW3)
Byzantine Empire		Canoeing	963 (London W1N 4DT)
geography	2278 (Weymouth)	Scotland	10 (Aberdeen)
history	2278 (Weymouth)	Canon law	401 (Chipping Norton)
literature	1972 (Oxford)		492 (Durham)
			1568 (London EC4)
C			1976 (Paignton)
			2261 (Wells)
Cabinet making	450 (Derby)	Canterbury	
	2141 (Southampton)	local history	327 (Canterbury)
See also Carpentry; and Volume I		topography	327 (Canterbury)
		Caravan touring	1021 (London W1Y 2AB)
Caernarvon	267 (Caernarvon)	Caravanning	1021 (London W1Y 2AB)
Camborne, local history	272 (Camborne)	Cardiac metabolism	1366 (London SW7)
Cambridge	277 (Cambridge)	Cardiganshire	355 (Carmarthen)
folk life	276 (Cambridge)	antiquities	1 (Aberaeron)
history	276 (Cambridge)	folklore	1 (Aberaeron)
local history	276, 310 (Cambridge)	history	1 (Aberaeron)
music, history	317 (Cambridge)	local history	1 (Aberaeron)
photographs	276 (Cambridge)	Cardiology	681 (Harrow)
Cambridge Platonists	158 (Birmingham)		1246 (London W1)

Cardiology (contd)	1601 (London EC2)	Catechisms, Welsh	783 (Lampeter)
Cardiovascular diseases	178 (Bolton)	Catering	
	1246 (London W1)	(Volume I of this Directory includes catering, but it has also been indexed where it occurs in Volume II)	
Cardiovascular surgery	1246 (London W1)		
Cardiovascular system	178 (Bolton)		33 (Ashton-under-Lyne)
Careers	227 (Brighton)		59 (Barnstaple)
	279, 280 (Cambridge)		93 (Belfast)
	647 (Great Yarmouth)		122 (Bilston)
	882 (Llanelli)		191 (Bournemouth)
	1041 (London W1P 0ER)		414 (Colwyn Bay)
	1334 (London SE13)		450 (Derby)
	1982 (Penarth)		527 (Edinburgh)
	2280 (Whitehaven)		665 (Halesowen)
advertising	884 (London WC2)		726 (Huddersfield)
chiropody	512 (Edinburgh)		785 (Lancaster)
	1602 (London W1M 8BX)		874 (Liverpool)
dentistry	1174 (London W1M 8DQ)		1117 (London W5)
film technicians	1603 (London W1N 6JJ)		1170 (London SW15)
linguists	1259 (London SE1)		1197 (London NW4)
nursery nursing	1427 (London SW1)		1823 (Neath)
osteopathy	1004 (London SW1)		1838 (Newcastle upon Tyne)
psychology	1003 (London W1X 4DN)		2003 (Portsmouth)
television technicians	1603 (London W1N 6JJ)		2024 (Reading)
Caribbean	964 (London EC4)		2034 (Redruth)
	1683 (London WC2)		2121 (Shrewsbury)
Methodist missions	1376 (London NW1)		2135 (Slough)
travel	1683 (London WC2)		2182 (Sunderland)
voyages	1683 (London WC2)		2249 (Ware)
Carlisle			2280 (Whitehaven)
history	354 (Carlisle)		2316 (Workington)
local history	346, 353 (Carlisle)	industry, training	2267 (Wembley)
Carlton, local history	1887 (Nottingham)	management	661 (Guildford)
Carmarthenshire		Cats	2324 (Wotton-under-Edge)
archaeology	355 (Carmarthen)	Caving	233 (Bristol)
history	356 (Carmarthen)	C.C.T.V.	812 (Leeds)
local history	355 (Carmarthen)	Cell biology	455 (Didcot)
Carnegie, Andrew	475, 476, 478 (Dunfermline)		1712 (Loughborough)
Carnegie Dunfermline Trust	475 (Dunfermline)	Cell pathology	681 (Harrow)
Carnegie Hero Fund trust	476 (Dunfermline)	Celtic	
Carpenter, Edward	2112 (Sheffield)	history	2073 (St Andrews)
Carpentry	2308 (Wolverton)	literature	13 (Aberdeen)
See also Cabinet making; and Volume I			16 (Aberystwyth)
			1972 (Oxford)
Carpet industry, training	2287 (Wilmslow)		2073 (St Andrews)
Carpets	1688 (London WC2)	Cemeteries	746 (Ilford)
Cartography	513, 537 (Edinburgh)	planning	45 (Bacup)
	942 (London WC1)		377 (Cheltenham)
	1425 (London SE10)	Censorship	936 (London W1)
	1538 (London SW7)		1315 (London WC1)
Cartoons	408 (Colchester)	Censuses	1175 (London WC2)
Cartularies	2042 (Ripon)	distribution	2060 (Ruislip)
Carvings	1873 (Norwich)	production	2060 (Ruislip)
Catalan		Century Guild	1692 (London E17)
language	315 (Cambridge)	Ceramics	129, 138 (Birmingham)
literature	315 (Cambridge)		189 (Bournemouth)
Catechetics	612 (Glasgow)		197, 199 (Bradford)
	1022 (London SW1)		349 (Carlisle)

Ceramics (contd)	430 (Croydon)	Charles Bradlaugh	1865 (Northampton)
	450 (Derby)	Charles Dickens	366 (Chatham)
	577 (Enfield)		1109 (London WC1)
	591 (Falmouth)		2045, 2047 (Rochester)
	724 (Hove)	biography	2047 (Rochester)
	860 (Liverpool)	criticism	2047 (Rochester)
	1018 (London SE5)	first editions	497 (Eastbourne)
	1039 (London WC1)	Charles Lamb	1299 (London NW3)
	1165 (London SW15)	Chartist movement	943 (London EC2)
	1524 (London SW7)	Chatham, local history	600 (Gillingham)
	1673 (London W1)		2047 (Rochester)
	1678 (London NW1)	Chelmsford, local history	368, 370 (Chelmsford)
	1688 (London WC2)	Cheltenham, local history	376, 377 (Cheltenham)
	1713 (Loughborough)	Chemical pathology	1075, 1260 (London W1)
	1727 (Maidenhead)	Chemical warfare	1020 (London WC1)
	1764 (Manchester)	Chemistry	
	1804 (Merthyr Tydfil)	(Volume I of this Directory includes chemistry, but it has also been indexed in this volume for organizations which do not appear in Volume I, and where it occurs in conjunction with, for example, medicine)	
	1806, 1808 (Middlesbrough)		
	1873 (Norwich)		
	2077 (St Helens)		
	2085 (Salford)		340 (Cardiff)
	2089 (Salisbury)		361 (Carshalton)
	2116 (Sheffield)		403 (Chorley)
	2141 (Southampton)		437 (Dagenham)
	2154 (Stafford)		457 (Doncaster)
	2170, 2174, 2176 (Stoke-on-Trent)		500 (Eastleigh)
			531 (Edinburgh)
art	581 (Esher)		579 (Epsom)
history	312 (Cambridge)		612, 630 (Glasgow)
industry	581 (Esher)		648 (Greenford)
Irish	113 (Belfast)		723 (Hounslow)
See also Volume I			812 (Leeds)
Cervantes	133 (Birmingham)		863, 874 (Liverpool)
Ceylon	1200 (London W2)		1317 (London SW1)
missions	934 (London W1H 4AA)		1367 (London NW1)
Methodist	1376 (London NW1)		1380 (London W1P 7PN)
Chalfont St Giles, local history	365 (Chalfont St Giles)		1472 (London WC1)
			1495 (London W1)
Chamberlain, Austen	154 (Birmingham)		1537 (London WC1)
Chamberlain, Joseph	154 (Birmingham)		1586 (London EC3)
Chancery proceedings	1604 (London SW7)		1601 (London EC2)
Channel Islands			1715 (Loughborough)
genealogy	653 (Guernsey)		1724 (Macclesfield)
local history	653 (Guernsey)		1828 (Newbury)
See also individual islands			1837, 1839 (Newcastle upon Tyne)
Chaplains, military	47 (Bagshot)		
Character analysis	36 (Aylesbury)		1886, 1893 (Nottingham)
Charities	1044 (London SW1)		1948 (Oxford)
	1662 (London WC1)		2290 (Winchester)
	1851 (Newport, Isle of Wight)		2320, 2321 (Worthing)
			2333 (York)
	1940 (Oxford)	analytical	674 (Harlow)
	2021 (Reading)		729 (Huddersfield)
administration	744 (Ilford)		2294 (Windlesham)
history	1044 (London SW1)	applied	1724 (Macclesfield)
information service	1143 (London SW1)	clinical	681 (Harrow)
Charity schools	1592 (London NW1)		1468 (London W2)

Chemistry (contd)		local history	389(Chester)
hair	2109(Sheffield)	national history	389(Chester)
history	246(Bristol)	photographic survey	387, 389(Chester)
	630, 631(Glasgow)	Chesterfield, local history	391(Chesterfield)
medicinal	738(Hull)	Chichester	
organic	437(Dagenham)	archaeology	395(Chichester)
	674(Harlow)	folk life	395(Chichester)
	1712(Loughborough)	history	395(Chichester)
	1724(Macclesfield)	local history	394, 395(Chichester)
	1729(Maidenhead)	pastimes	395(Chichester)
	2294(Windlesham)	trade	395(Chichester)
pharmaceutical	531(Edinburgh)	Child care	255(Bromsgrove)
	1667(London WC1)		544(Edinburgh)
	2294(Windlesham)		587(Exeter)
photographic	437(Dagenham)		744(Ilford)
physical	207(Brentford)		793(Leamington Spa)
Chemotherapy	85(Beckenham)		874(Liverpool)
	307(Cambridge)		1059(London SE11)
	341(Cardiff)		1405(London W1)
	674(Harlow)		1451(London NW5)
	2294(Windlesham)		1574(London SW1)
tuberculosis	1373(London W12)		1853(Newport, Isle of Wight)
Chertsey	381(Chertsey)		
Cheshire	34(Ashton-under-Lyne)		1994(Plymouth)
	2156(Stalybridge)		2160(Stevenage)
archaeology	385, 387, 389(Chester)		2249(Ware)
	1760(Manchester)	services	2014(Preston)
architecture	385, 387(Chester)	Child development	12(Aberdeen)
customs	1760(Manchester)		238(Bristol)
genealogy	1760(Manchester)		931(London SE9)
history	125(Birkenhead)		1236(London W1P 3LD)
	383, 385, 387, 389(Chester)		1722(Luton)
	1760(Manchester)	Child health	154(Birmingham)
local history	125(Birkenhead)		1102(London W1)
	389(Chester)		1142(London W1N 8BQ)
	742(Hyde)		1360(London W1)
	839(Lichfield)	Child morbidity	1360(London W1)
	866(Liverpool)	Child psychiatry	1871(Northampton)
	1760(Manchester)	Child psychology	169(Bletchley)
	2168(Stockport)		252(Bromley)
	2298(Wirral)		329(Canterbury)
natural history	389(Chester)		331(Cardiff)
topography	382, 389(Chester)		789(Lancaster)
traditions	1760(Manchester)		797(Leeds)
Cheshire Regiment, history	384(Chester)		1247(London W11)
Cheshunt, local history	2246(Waltham Cross)		1443(London WC1)
Chess	135(Birmingham)		1597(London W1)
Chest diseases	290(Cambridge)		1616(London SW19)
	1033(London NW10)		1767(Manchester)
	1049(London WC1)		1837(Newcastle upon Tyne)
Chest medicine	1012(London W1)		1855(Newport, Mon)
	1254(London SW3)		1871(Northampton)
Chest surgery	1254(London SW3)		2011(Prescot)
Chester	387, 389(Chester)		2020(Reading)
archaeology	385, 387, 389(Chester)		2035(Retford)
architecture	385, 387(Chester)		2146(Southampton)
history	385, 387(Chester)		2168(Stockport)

Child study	154(Birmingham)		2252(Warrington)
	823(Leicester)		2330(York)
	931(London SE9)	United States of America	950(London W1)
	1102(London W1)	Children's literature	62(Barry)
	1234(London SE1)		92(Belfast)
	1717(Lowestoft)		137(Birmingham)
Child welfare	744(Ilford)		612(Glasgow)
	1440(London W1)		1809(Middlesbrough)
	2168(Stockport)		1837(Newcastle upon Tyne)
services	789(Lancaster)		
	1695(London WC1)		2020(Reading)
	2290(Winchester)		2035(Retford)
Childhood, history	526(Edinburgh)		2185(Sunderland)
Children			2230(Twickenham)
biography	436(Dagenham)		2245(Walsall)
education	1405(London W1)		2305(Wolverhampton)
gifted	1405(London W1)	Victorian	2305(Wolverhampton)
handicapped	1305(London W1)	Children's poetry	1477(London SW5)
home care	2218(Truro)	Children's theatre	2235(Wakefield)
maladjusted	924(London W14)	Chile	
psychology	1405(London W1)	history	894(London W1)
sociology	1405(London W1)	language	894(London W1)
Children's books		literature	894(London W1)
(collections)	44(Ayr)	China	217(Bridgwater)
	112(Belfast)		813(Leeds)
	133(Birmingham)		1253(London SW1)
	210(Brentwood)	art	2111(Sheffield)
	223(Brighton)	economics	1052(London EC2)
	329(Canterbury)	geography	2076(St Helens)
	331(Cardiff)	history	581(Esher)
	425(Crewe)		1968(Oxford)
	449(Derby)		2038(Richmond)
	498(Eastbourne)		2076(St Helens)
	590(Falkirk)	language	492(Durham)
	669(Hamilton)		1117(London W5)
	704(Hereford)		1968(Oxford)
	724(Hove)	literature	1052(London EC2)
	842(Lincoln)		1968(Oxford)
	859, 877, 879(Liverpool)	missions	1086(London SW1)
	1341(London SW18)	Methodist	1376(London NW1)
	1352(London W8)	North, missions	934(London W1H 4AA)
	1387(London SW1)	politics	1052(London EC2)
	1746, 1758, 1773 (Manchester)	religion	1968(Oxford)
		science	227(Brighton)
	1845(Newcastle upon Tyne)	topography	581(Esher)
	1854(Newport, Mon)	trade	1052(London EC1)
	2002(Portsmouth)	Chiropody	145(Birmingham)
	2034(Redruth)		335(Cardiff)
	2043(Ripon)		512(Edinburgh)
	2228(Twickenham)		835(Letchworth)
	2279(Weymouth)		1048(London NW8)
early	71(Bath)		1602(London W1M 8BX)
	217(Bridgwater)	careers	512(Edinburgh)
	636(Gloucester)		1602(London W1M 8BX)
	1690(London SW15)	history	1048(London NW8)
	1891, 1902(Nottingham)		1602(London W1M 8BX)
	2015(Preston)	Choreographic scores	1248(London W6)

Choreology	1248(London W6)			2274(Weston super Mare)
Christian Aid	975(London SW1)	Africa		11(Aberdeen)
Christian Church	1322(London NW4)	law		1322(London NW4)
Christian communication	1701(London SW1)	music		433(Croydon)
Christian education	1387(London SW1)	plate		845(Lincoln)
Christian ethics	569(Edinburgh)	Lincoln		845(Lincoln)
Christian history	1927(Oxford)	Lincolnshire		845(Lincoln)
Africa	11(Aberdeen)	services		675(Harpenden)
Christian missions	14(Aberdeen)	State		1322(London NW4)
	149(Birmingham)	Church in Wales, history		357(Carmarthen)
	934(London W1H 4AA)			1979(Penarth)
	1085(London SW1)	Church of England		1763(Manchester)
Christian sacraments	377(Cheltenham)	social work		944(London SW1)
Christian science	1055(London WC2)	Churches		675(Harpenden)
Christian socialism	1057(London WC2)			2152(Southwell)
Christian Socialists	1700(London NW1)	architecture		178(Bolton)
Christian sociology	1999(Poole)	industrial work		1231(London EC3)
Christian traditions	1149(London W11)	Methodist		1376(London NW1)
Christianity	158(Birmingham)	Oriental		119(Bexley)
	1062(London WC2)	preservation		1093(London EC2)
	1330(London W6)	primitive		119(Bexley)
	1387(London SW1)	Protestant		459(Dorchester)
	1998(Pontypridd)	Cinema		235(Bristol)
Africa	14(Aberdeen)			417(Coventry)
America, Central	14(Aberdeen)			734(Hull)
America, South	14(Aberdeen)			1566, 1688(London WC2)
Asia	14(Aberdeen)			1858(Newport, Mon)
evangelical	1135(London WC1)			2024(Reading)
history	1571(London SE5)			2039(Richmond)
Christopher Marlowe	1354(London SE19)			2174(Stoke-on-Trent)
Church		art		984(London W1)
Anglican	1322(London NW4)	history		984(London W1)
architecture	579(Epsom)	Russia		1591(London SW9)
buildings, law	1093(London EC2)	Cine-photography		189(Bournemouth)
Christian	1322(London NW4)			1676(London SW18)
communication	1701(London SW1)	Ciphers		327(Canterbury)
denominations	47(Bagshot)	Circulatory systems		20(Accrington)
furnishings	1093(London EC2)	Cistercian history		830(Leicester)
history	95(Belfast)	Citizens' Advice Bureaux		1143(London SW1)
	119(Bexley)			1406(London WC1)
	309(Cambridge)	City of London,		
	394, 397(Chichester)	archaeology		1188(London EC2)
	401(Chipping Norton)	City of Westminster,		
	424(Crawley)	local history		1688(London SW1)
	517, 545, 569(Edinburgh)	Civic theatres		2183(Sunderland)
	627(Glasgow)	Civic Trusts		1067(London SW1)
	1022(London SW1)	Civil administration		1330(London W6)
	1585(London EC4)	Civil aviation		947(London SW1)
	1647(London SW1)	Civil defence		1249(London SW1)
	1914(Ormskirk)	Civil law		2261(Wells)
	1942(Oxford)	Civil liberties		1437(London SE1)
	2042(Ripon)	Civil Service		1272(London WC2)
	2065(St Albans)	history		1272(London WC2)
	2073(St Andrews)	staff		1272(London WC2)
	2143(Southampton)	Civil war		133(Birmingham)
	2200(Swansea)			1826(Newark)
	2261, 2262(Wells)			1975(Oxford)

Civil War *(contd)*		Clowes, William	1756 (Manchester)
tracts	733 (Hull)	Clyde, shipbuilding	611 (Glasgow)
Clans	2161 (Stirling)	Clydebank, local history	405 (Clydebank)
Clapham		Co. Durham	
archaeology	1069 (London SW12)	history	2184 (Sunderland)
genealogy	1069 (London SW12)	topography	2184 (Sunderland)
local history	1069 (London SW12)	Coal mining	363 (Castleford)
topography	1069 (London SW12)		391 (Chesterfield)
Clare, John	1865 (Northampton)	*See also* Volume I	
Clarendon Press	1467 (London W1X 4AH)	Coalbrookdale	2126 (Shrewsbury)
Classical dancing	1322 (London NW4)	Cobbett, William	1911 (Oldham)
Classical grammars	2124 (Shrewsbury)	Cobden, Richard	1932 (Oxford)
Classical literature	492 (Durham)		223 (Brighton)
	1918, 1946 (Oxford)	Codes	327 (Canterbury)
	2124 (Shrewsbury)	Co-determination	1232 (London SW1)
Classical studies	1070, 1250 (London WC1)	Cohort studies	1372 (London WC2)
	2291 (Winchester)	Coins	138 (Birmingham)
Classics	17 (Aberystwyth)		629 (Glasgow)
	223 (Brighton)		1688 (London WC2)
	235 (Bristol)		1783 (Norwich)
	291, 292, 301 (Cambridge)		1904 (Nuneaton)
	330 (Canterbury)		1952 (Oxford)
	492 (Durham)		2186 (Sunderland)
	574 (Egham)		2213 (Tilbury)
	783 (Lampeter)	Colchester	
	788 (Lancaster)	history	407, 408 (Colchester)
	813 (Leeds)	local history	407, 408 (Colchester)
	942 (London WC1)	natural history	407 (Colchester)
	1303 (London WC2)	Cole, G. D. H.	1326 (London W5)
	1665 (London E1)		1932 (Oxford)
	1686 (London NW3)	College of S Mark and	
	1789 (Manchester)	S John, history	1077 (London SW10)
	1924 (Oxford)	Colonial history	1659 (London WC1)
	2073 (St Andrews)	Colonies	327 (Canterbury)
	2145 (Southampton)	Combined Cadet Force	
criticism	788 (Lancaster)	Commerce	
teaching	1293 (London WC1)	(Volume I of this Directory includes commerce, but it	
textbooks	815 (Leeds)	has also been indexed in this Volume)	
Clayton, P. B.	1635 (London EC3)		32 (Ashton-under-Lyne)
Clean air	1381 (London SW1)		324 (Cannock)
	1439 (London EC4)		406 (Coatbridge)
Clergy, pay	675 (Harpenden)		419 (Coventry)
Clifton College, history	235 (Bristol)		520 (Edinburgh)
Climbing clubs	468 (Dunblane)		606 (Glasgow)
Clock-making	342 (Cardiff)		676 (Harrogate)
Cloth pattern designs	2167 (Stockport)		721 (Hornchurch)
Clothing	835 (Letchworth)		734 (Hull)
	1170 (London SW15)		866, 868 (Liverpool)
design	1074 (London W1)		994 (London WC2)
history	1074 (London W1)		1064 (London EC2)
manufacture	1074 (London W1)		1302 (London SE11)
	2141 (Southampton)		1711 (Loughborough)
	2182 (Sunderland)		1724 (Macclesfield)
technology	2182 (Sunderland)		1838, 1839 (Newcastle upon Tyne)
trades	835 (Letchworth)		
See also Volume I			2187 (Sunderland)
Clotting disorders	501 (Edgware)		2269 (West Bromwich)

Commerce (contd)	2309(Bletchley)	Community nursing	1496(London SW1)
	2321(Worthing)	Community organization,	
	2335(York)	Northern Ireland	102(Belfast)
Commercial art	667(Halifax)	Community service	1083(London E1)
	726(Huddersfield)	Community studies	225(Brighton)
	1339(London E1)	Community work	503(Edinburgh)
	1719(Luton)	Company histories	1253(London SW1)
Commercial education	414(Colwyn Bay)	Company law	516(Edinburgh)
	958(London W1N 4AP)		1253(London SW1)
	2080(Sale)		2187(Sunderland)
Commercial fishing, history	1425(London SE10)	Comparative education	725(Huddersfield)
Commercial law	252(Bromley)		2011(Prescot)
	2142(Southampton)	Comparative law	1309, 1654(London WC1)
Commercial vehicles,		Comparative linguistics	522(Edinburgh)
history	1337(London E15)	Comparative medicine	1534(London SW1)
Common law	1309(London WC1)	Comparative physiology	2140(Southampton)
Common Market	899(London W8)	Comparative religion	95(Belfast)
law	1210(London EC4)		149(Birmingham)
Commonwealth	508, 1082(Edinburgh)		309(Cambridge)
	1035(London SE1)		564(Edinburgh)
	1082(London W8)		1211(London SE23)
	1159, 1253(London SW1)		1331(London N17)
arts	1082(Edinburgh)		1597(London W1)
	1082(London W8)		1645(London WC2)
economics	1082(Edinburgh)		1789(Manchester)
	1082(London W8)	Compensatory education	1746(Manchester)
	1159(London SW1)	Computer manuals	2023(Reading)
geography	1082(Edinburgh)	Computer programs,	
	1082(London W8)	numerical taxonomy	829(Leicester)
history	1082(Edinburgh)	Computer programming	527(Edinburgh)
	1082(London W8)		587(Exeter)
	1953(Oxford)	Computer science	341(Cardiff)
illustrations	1035(London SE1)		1886(Nottingham)
laws	1082(Edinburgh)		2233(Uxbridge)
	1082(London W8)	Computer studies	446(Deeside)
	1159(London SW1)	Computer technology	1724(Macclesfield)
	1210, 1379(London EC4)	Computer theory	2023(Reading)
	1654(London WC1)	Computers	685(Hastings)
literature	1082(Edinburgh)	medicine	550(Edinburgh)
	1082(London W8)		1363(London N1)
period	89(Bedford)	Computing	1651(London SW3)
politics	1082(Edinburgh)	See also Volume I	
	1082(London W8)	Confectionery industry	1997(Pontefract)
religions	1082(Edinburgh)	Confederate history	833(Leigh-on-Sea)
	1082(London W8)	Congregational Church	1161(London WC1)
statistics	1159(London SW1)	Connective tissue disorders	1730(Maidenhead)
Universities	917(London WC1)	Conrad, Joseph	1480(London SW7)
Communicable diseases	1731(Maidstone)	Conradiana	1480(London SW7)
Communication disorders	1545(London WC1)	Conservation	109(Belfast)
Communications	812(Leeds)		860(Liverpool)
	2187(Sunderland)		1281(London SW1)
industry	1104(London SW1)		2040(Richmond)
media, Christianity	1701(London SW1)	artistic works	1277(London SW5)
visual	2188(Sunderland)	churches	1093(London EC2)
Communism	1386(London EC1)	paintings	1416(London WC2)
	2038(Richmond)	Constitution	119(Bexley)
Community development	1664(London W8)		1195(London SW1)

732

Consular service	722 (Hounslow)			2221 (Truro)
Consumer affairs	1276 (London W1X 9PA)	antiquities		591 (Falmouth)
	1504 (London WC2)	architecture		591 (Falmouth)
Consumer behaviour	1088 (London WC2)	bibliography		2218 (Truro)
Consumer education	467 (Dumfries)	folklore		591 (Falmouth)
Consumer goods, testing	1088 (London WC2)	genealogy		2221 (Truro)
Consumer groups	1413 (London WC2)	history		1115 (London SW1)
Consumer information	1088, 1504 (London WC2)	local history		591 (Falmouth)
Consumer legislation	1413 (London WC2)			2218, 2219, 2220 (Truro)
Consumer periodicals	1088 (London WC2)	personages		591 (Falmouth)
Consumer protection	1088, 1413, 1504 (London WC2)	shipping		591 (Falmouth)
		Correspondence Colleges		915 (London EC1)
Consumer surveys	1413 (London WC2)	Corticosteroids		648 (Greenford)
Containerization	2143 (Southampton)	Cosmetics		207 (Brentford)
Contraception	1279 (London SW1)			674 (Harlow)
	1730 (Maidenhead)			729 (Huddersfield)
oral	715 (High Wycombe)			1605 (London W1)
Contract law	1322 (London NW4)			1712 (Loughborough)
	2239 (Wakefield)			2082 (Salford)
Convalescent homes	858 (Liverpool)	See also Volume I		
Cookery	70 (Bath)	Cosmographies		186 (Boston)
	93 (Belfast)	Cosmology		2149 (Southend-on-Sea)
	485 (Durham)	Costume		74 (Bath)
	750 (Ilkley)			92 (Belfast)
	874 (Liverpool)			197 (Bradford)
	1302 (London SE11)			772 (Kidderminster)
	2098 (Scunthorpe)			866 (Liverpool)
	2101 (Seaford)			903 (London EC3)
	2205 (Tamworth)			968 (London W1Y 4HQ)
	2280 (Whitehaven)			1688 (London WC2)
herb	1605 (London W1)			1693 (London SW19)
history	813 (Leeds)			1762, 1764 (Manchester)
vegetarian	26 (Altrincham)			1858 (Newport, Mon)
See also Volume I				1873 (Norwich)
Co-operation	1276 (London W1X 9PA)			1939 (Oxford)
	1476 (London WC1)			1981 (Penarth)
	1711 (Loughborough)			2043 (Ripon)
	1745 (Manchester)			2116 (Sheffield)
	2044 (Rochdale)			2187 (Sunderland)
	2104 (Sevenoaks)			2329 (York)
agricultural	1476 (London WC1)	British		113 (Belfast)
economic	2143 (Southampton)	Buckinghamshire		37 (Aylesbury)
history	1745 (Manchester)	clothing manufacture		874 (Liverpool)
Co-operative library schemes	2339–2414	English		592 (Farnham)
				701 (Hereford)
Co-operative movements	1276 (London W1X 9PA)			2322 (Worthing)
	1745 (Manchester)	history		74 (Bath)
Co-operative Retail Societies, history	1711 (Loughborough)			142 (Birmingham)
				378 (Cheltenham)
Co-operativists, biography	2143 (Southampton)			1750 (Manchester)
Co-partnership, industrial	1232 (London SW1)	Irish		113 (Belfast)
Copyright	909 (London SW1)	Victorian		404 (Cirencester)
	1315 (London WC1)	Welsh		342 (Cardiff)
music	1393 (London SW1)	See also Volume I		
Copywriting	844 (London WC2)	Cotswolds, local history		376, 377 (Cheltenham)
Cornwall	1984, 1985 (Penzance)	Cotton industry		1737 (Manchester)
	2214 (Torquay)	Counter-intelligence		2038 (Richmond)

Countryside	1096(London NW1)	Criminology	25(Alloa)
	1381(London SW1)		35(Aylesbury)
organizations	1096(London NW1)		60(Barry)
County Armagh			67(Basingstoke)
history	29(Armagh)		183(Bootle)
natural history	29(Armagh)		313(Cambridge)
pre-history	29(Armagh)		714(High Wycombe)
County Down, local history	48(Ballynahinch)		781(Kirkcaldy)
Coventry	418(Coventry)		1218(London SE11)
Coventry Patmore	1902(Nottingham)		1238(London W1)
Cowper, William	1912(Olney)		1309(London WC1)
Crafts	33(Ashton-under-Lyne)		1958(Oxford)
	427(Crewe)		2145(Southampton)
	449(Derby)		2236(Wakefield)
	457(Doncaster)	history	313(Cambridge)
	1586(London E1)	Critical path methods	2143(Southampton)
	1893(Nottingham)	Criticism	235(Bristol)
	1992(Plymouth)	American	497(Eastbourne)
	2035(Retford)	drama	683(Hastings)
	2043(Ripon)	literature	1786(Manchester)
	2059(Rugby)		2021(Reading)
	2070(St Albans)	arts	1524(London SW7)
	2249(Ware)	biblical	1500(London N1)
	2290(Winchester)	Charles Dickens	2047(Rochester)
education	732(Hull)	classical literature	788(Lancaster)
industry	2225(Tunbridge Wells)	drama	154(Birmingham)
judging	560(Edinburgh)		968(London W1Y 4HQ)
Norfolk	1873(Norwich)	Elizabethan	1354(London SE19)
Norwich	1873(Norwich)	English	497(Eastbourne)
Welsh	342(Cardiff)		529(Edinburgh)
Worcestershire	772(Kidderminster)	drama	683(Hastings)
workshops	2329(York)	fiction	377(Cheltenham)
Craftsmen	28(Andover)		1748(Manchester)
C. R. Ashbee	288(Cambridge)	literature	451(Derby)
Crawley, local history	424(Crawley)		2021(Reading)
Creative arts	812(Leeds)	French	529(Edinburgh)
Creative dance	1274(London SE22)	literature	788(Lancaster)
Crete	408(Colchester)		1911(Oldham)
Cricket	768(Kenley)	Greek literature	1731(Maidstone)
	1336(London SW19)	Italian literature	1322(London NW4)
	1336(Mitcham)	Latin literature	1731(London NW4)
	1356(London NW8)	literary history	612(Glasgow)
laws	768(Kenley)	literature	1731(Maidstone)
history	768(Kenley)		2150(Southport)
umpiring	768(Kenley)	Portuguese literature	1322(London NW4)
Crime prevention	1218(London SE11)	Rumanian literature	1322(London NW4)
	1351(London W1P 6DD)	Spanish literature	788(Lancaster)
	1395(London SE11)		1322(London NW4)
Criminal behaviour	313(Cambridge)	Teutonic literature	443(Dartford)
Criminal investigation	25(Alloa)	theological	1500(London N1)
Criminal law	25(Alloa)	Croydon	
	313(Cambridge)	archaeology	429(Croydon)
	1218(London SE11)	geography	429(Croydon)
	1238(London W1)	geology	429(Croydon)
Scotland	25(Alloa)	history	429(Croydon)
Criminal statistics	1218(London SE11)	industrial archaeology	429(Croydon)
Criminal trials	561(Edinburgh)	industry	429(Croydon)

Croydon (contd)		Dalbon	994 (London WC2)
local history	429 (Croydon)	Dalcroze eurhythmics	2302 (Woking)
natural history	429 (Croydon)	Dance	87 (Bedford)
planning	429 (Croydon)		403 (Chorley)
topography	429 (Croydon)		427 (Crewe)
Cross country running	285 (Cambridge)		496 (Eastbourne)
Cruising, River Thames	2040 (Richmond)		510 (Edinburgh)
Cryobiology	305 (Cambridge)		1274 (London SE22)
Crystal Palace	252 (Bromley)		1475 (London W1M 4AX)
	1669 (London SE19)		1688 (London WC2)
Cultural relations	967 (London W1Y 2AA)		1808 (Middlesbrough)
	970 (London WC1)		1846 (Newcastle upon Tyne)
Cultural studies	225 (Brighton)		2052 (Rotherham)
Culture		Dancing	1328 (London SE10)
Africa	1273 (London EC4)	classical	1322 (London NW4)
Germany	1176 (London SW1)	folk	1322 (London NW4)
Cumberland	350 (Carlisle)	Daniel Defoe	1662 (London WC1)
	787 (Lancaster)	Daniel Gardner	764 (Kendal)
antiquities	348, 351 (Carlisle)	Dante	1338 (London SE22)
archaeology	351 (Carlisle)		1902 (Nottingham)
geology	348 (Carlisle)		1972 (Oxford)
history	351, 354 (Carlisle)		2145 (Southampton)
local history	353 (Carlisle)	Darent Valley	
	2281 (Whitehaven)	archaeology	441 (Dartford)
natural history	348 (Carlisle)	geology	441 (Dartford)
social service	352 (Carlisle)	history	441 (Dartford)
social welfare	352 (Carlisle)	local history	441 (Dartford)
Curling	532 (Edinburgh)	natural history	441 (Dartford)
Current affairs	2198 (Sutton Coldfield)	Darling, Grace	49 (Bamburgh)
Curriculum development	226 (Brighton)	Darlington, local history	439 (Darlington)
Customs	1760 (Manchester)	Dartford	
	1939 (Oxford)	archaeology	441 (Dartford)
Cheshire	1760 (Manchester)	geology	441 (Dartford)
Lancashire	1760 (Manchester)	history	441, 443 (Dartford)
Cuthbert Bede	771 (Kidderminster)	local history	441, 443 (Dartford)
Cybernetics	1253 (London SW1)	natural history	441 (Dartford)
	2023 (Reading)	Dartmoor ponies	1861 (Newton Abbot)
	2233 (Uxbridge)	Data processing	511 (Edinburgh)
Cycling	977 (London W1)		1065 (London SW1)
time trials	1507 (London N17)	*See also* Volume I	
Cytogenetics	455 (Didcot)	Davy	1543 (London W1)
Czechoslovakia		de la Mare, Walter	252 (Bromley)
folklore	311 (Cambridge)	de Wint	855 (Lincoln)
history	311 (Cambridge)	Deaf	
	436 (Dagenham)	clinics	1545 (London WC1)
	1251 (London W1N 2BH)	education	1791 (Manchester)
language	311 (Cambridge)	visually handicapped	1519 (London W3)
literature	311 (Cambridge)	welfare	759 (Iver)
philosophy	311 (Cambridge)		1519 (London W3)
religion	311 (Cambridge)		1545 (London WC1)
topography	436 (Dagenham)	welfare services	645 (Grays)
		Deafness	759 (Iver)
D			1545 (London WC1)
		Decentralization, offices	1320 (London WC2)
Dagenham, local history	436 (Dagenham)	Decimal currency	560 (Edinburgh)
Dahomey, Methodist		Decision theory	2023 (Reading)
missions	1376 (London NW1)	Decorating	220 (Brighton)

Decorating *(contd)*	726 (Huddersfield)	Dental surgery	1532 (London WC2)
	871 (Liverpool)		2006 (Portsmouth)
	1719 (Luton)	assistants	166 (Blackpool)
	2055 (Rotherham)	Dental technology	1453 (London SE1)
	2141 (Southampton)	Dental undergraduate	
	2210 (Taunton)	education	1174 (London W1M 8DQ)
See also Volume I		Dentistry	145, 154 (Birmingham)
Decorative arts	214 (Bridgwater)		344, 345 (Cardiff)
	1540 (London W1N 4AD)		396 (Chichester)
Decorative glass	1007 (London WC1)		565, 568 (Edinburgh)
Defector reports	2038 (Richmond)		630 (Glasgow)
Defence	195 (Bracknell)		814 (Leeds)
	1560 (London SW1)		878 (Liverpool)
	2038 (Richmond)		978 (London W1M 8AL)
Defoe, Daniel	1662 (London WC1)		1145 (London W1)
Demography	516 (Edinburgh)		1342 (London E1)
	1142 (London W1N 8BQ)		1433 (London WC2)
	1175 (London WC2)		1649 (London WC1)
	1240 (London WC1)		1688 (London NW1)
	1279 (London SW1)		1751 (Manchester)
	2145 (Southampton)		1850 (Newcastle upon Tyne)
Africa	298 (Cambridge)		2039 (Richmond)
Northumberland	1848 (Newcastle upon Tyne)		2082 (Salford)
See also Volume I			2172 (Stoke-on-Trent)
Denbighshire		careers	1174 (London W1M 8DQ)
local history	2062 (Ruthin)	children's	1609 (London WC1)
maps	2062 (Ruthin)	conservative	154 (Birmingham)
Denmark	895 (London W1X 6HJ)	history	474 (Dundee)
architecture	895 (London W1X 6HJ)		978 (London W1M 8AL)
humanities	1536 (London SW1)	preventive	1609 (London WC1)
language	315 (Cambridge)	Dentists	1174 (London W1M 8DQ)
	651 (Grimsby)	Derby, local history	451 (Derby)
literature	315 (Cambridge)	Derbyshire	34 (Ashton-under-Lyne)
	651 (Grimsby)	history	1800 (Matlock)
medicine	1536 (London SW1)	industries	391 (Chesterfield)
social sciences	1536 (London SW1)	local history	391 (Chesterfield)
sociology	895 (London W1X 6HJ)		451 (Derby)
tourism	1100 (London W1R 8PY)		742 (Hyde)
Dental auxiliaries	1174 (London W1M 8DQ)		839 (Lichfield)
Dental caries, pathology	237 (Bristol)	maps	451 (Derby)
Dental education	1145 (London W1)	North	
Dental ethics	1174 (London W1M 8DQ)	art	2113 (Sheffield)
Dental health	154 (Birmingham)	botany	2113 (Sheffield)
education	1174 (London W1M 8DQ)	geology	2113 (Sheffield)
Dental hygienists	1174 (London W1M 8DQ)	history	2113 (Sheffield)
Dental hypnosis	1008 (London W1)	zoology	2113 (Sheffield)
Dental laboratory		Dermatology	257 (Burgess Hill)
technology	335 (Cardiff)		1252 (London WC2)
Dental manpower	1145 (London W1)	Design	75 (Bath)
Dental-political publications	1751 (Manchester)		184 (Boreham Wood)
Dental postgraduate			231 (Bristol)
education	1174 (London W1M 8DQ)		253 (Bromley)
Dental prosthetics	154 (Birmingham)		349 (Carlisle)
Dental research	1145 (London W1)		380 (Cheltenham)
Dental science	207 (Brentford)		403 (Chorley)
	1532 (London WC2)		417 (Coventry)
	978 (London W1M 8AL)		450 (Derby)

Design (contd)
  581 (Esher)
  598 (Galashiels)
  726 (Huddersfield)
  731 (Hull)
  805, 812 (Leeds)
  860, 866 (Liverpool)
  884 (London WC2)
  1047 (London SW3)
  1108 (London SW1)
  1141 (London WC2)
  1265 (London NW3)
  1727 (Maidenhead)
  1732 (Maidstone)
  1746, 1765, 1782 (Manchester)
  1808 (Middlesbrough)
  2014 (Preston)
  2115 (Sheffield)
  2150 (Southport)
 applied 2141 (Southampton)
 architectural 1540 (London W1N 4AD)
  2081 (Sale)
 decorative 214 (Bridgwater)
 dress 1566 (London WC2)
 engineering 417 (Coventry)
 furniture 253 (Bromley)
 graphic 253 (Bromley)
  349 (Carlisle)
  417 (Coventry)
  430 (Croydon)
  450 (Derby)
  469 (Dundee)
  824 (Leicester)
  1018 (London SE5)
  1039 (London WC1)
  1047 (London SW3)
  1566 (London WC2)
  1732 (Maidstone)
  1883 (Norwich)
  2024 (Reading)
  2055 (Rotherham)
  2141 (Southampton)
  2207 (Taunton)
  2232 (Twickenham)
 history 326 (Canterbury)
  1553 (London WC2)
  1808 (Middlesbrough)
 hospital pharmacies 1185 (London WC1)
 hospitals 550 (Edinburgh)
  2147 (Southampton)
 Index 1096 (London SW1)
 industrial 253 (Bromley)
  349 (Carlisle)
  527 (Edinburgh)
  824 (Leicester)
  1039 (London WC1)
  1094, 1108 (London SW1)
  1141 (London WC2)
  1265 (London NW3)
  1524 (London SW7)
  1607 (London SW1)
  1719 (Luton)
  2116 (Sheffield)
  2174 (Stoke-on-Trent)
 interior 349 (Carlisle)
  469 (Dundee)
  1094 (London SW1)
  1265 (London NW3)
  1524 (London SW7)
  1540 (London W1N 4AD)
  1688 (London WC2)
  1808 (Middlesbrough)
  1858 (Newport, Mon)
  2116 (Sheffield)
  2141 (Southampton)
 jewellery 1039 (London WC1)
 package 253 (Bromley)
 product 1094 (London SW1)
 shoe 824 (Leicester)
 stage 968 (London W1Y 4HQ)
  1693 (London SW19)
 textile 771 (Kidderminster)
  1039 (London WC1)
 theatre 430 (Croydon)
  1039 (London WC1)
 three-dimensional 777 (Kingston upon Thames)
 typographic 1018 (London SE5)
 See also Volume I
Detergents 729 (Huddersfield)
  2082 (Salford)
 See also Volume I
Developing countries 1159 (London SW1)
  1791 (Manchester)
  1961, 1962 (Oxford)
 education 967 (London W1Y 2AA)
Development plans 1636 (London W1)
Development studies 224 (Brighton)
Developmental psychology 1364 (London WC1)
  2201 (Swansea)
  2214 (Torquay)
  2215 (Totnes)
  2257 (Watford)
Devon
 history 583 (Exeter)
  1115 (London SW1)
 local history 1992 (Plymouth)
 North 58 (Barnstaple)
  archaeology 58 (Barnstaple)
  local history 58 (Barnstaple)
  maps 58 (Barnstaple)
 South 2214 (Torquay)
Devotional literature 401 (Chipping Norton)
  2289 (Winchester)
Devotions 1998 (Pontypridd)

D. H. Lawrence	747 (Ilkeston) 1891, 1896, 1902 (Nottingham)	resettlement social welfare Disarmament	974 (London WC1) 638 (Godalming) 1020 (London WC1)
Diabetes	979 (London WC1)	nuclear	1020 (London WC1)
Dialects	123 (Bingley) 1774 (Manchester)	Diseases	119 (Bexley) 1731 (Maidstone) 2156 (Stalybridge)
Lake District	353 (Carlisle)		
Lincolnshire	850 (Lincoln)	animal	2275, 2276 (Weybridge)
Northumberland	1847 (Newcastle upon Tyne)	bacterial blood blood	1323 (London NW10) 1730 (Maidenhead)
survey	981 (London W1P 6AE)	cardiovascular system	178 (Bolton)
Welsh	342 (Cardiff)	climatic	1337 (London E15)
Dickens, Charles	366 (Chatham) 1109 (London WC1) 2045, 2047 (Rochester)	communicable ear	681 (Harrow) 1731 (Maidstone) 1774, 1791 (Manchester)
biography	2047 (Rochester)	farm animals	502 (Edinburgh)
criticism	2047 (Rochester)		791 (Lasswade)
first editions	497 (Eastbourne)		1828 (Newbury)
Dictionaries (large collections only)			2275, 2276 (Weybridge)
	947 (London SW1)	gastro-intestinal tract	715 (High Wycombe)
	1259, 1347 (London SE1)	genito-urinary system	443 (Dartford)
	1433, 1688 (London WC2)		715 (High Wycombe)
	1774 (Manchester)	glandular system	162 (Blackburn)
	1972 (Oxford)	infections	746 (Ilford)
	2187 (Sunderland)	musculoskeletal system	742 (Hyde)
biographical	1688 (London WC2)	nervous system	2076 (St Helens)
Dutch	1658 (London WC1)	neuro muscular	1388 (London SE1)
English	16 (Aberystwyth)	poultry	791 (Lasswade)
German dialect	1658 (London WC1)	skin	1323 (London NW10)
medical	1784 (Manchester)	special development periods	399 (Chichester)
Scandinavian	1658 (London WC1)		
Diet	1168 (London W1A 3AU)	tropical	1016 (London WC1)
Dietary foods	1712 (Loughborough)	venereal	1323 (London NW10)
Dietetics	9 (Aberdeen)	Disinfectants	729 (Huddersfield)
	497 (Eastbourne)		738 (Hull)
	681 (Harrow)	Disinfection	746 (Ilford)
	980 (London SW3)		1037 (London NW9)
	1450 (London N7)	Display	33 (Ashton-under-Lyne)
	2044 (Rochdale)		2249 (Ware)
Dietitians	980 (London SW3)	Disposal, dead	746 (Ilford)
Digestion	20 (Accrington)	Disraeli, Benjamin	713 (High Wycombe)
Digestive systems, medicine	167 (Blackpool)	Dissenting history	1663 (London NW3) 1789 (Manchester)
Diplomacy	722 (Hounslow)	Distribution	1253 (London SW1)
Directories (large collections only)		censuses	2060 (Ruislip)
	84 (Beckenham)	District nursing	1496 (London SW1)
	1187 (London EC2)	Liverpool, history	881 (Liverpool)
trade	680 (Harrow)	Diving	151 (Birmingham)
Directors	1253 (London SW1)	Divinity	13 (Aberdeen)
Disabled	974 (London WC1)		329 (Canterbury)
	1113 (London SW1)		449 (Derby)
biographies	1030 (London SW1)		569 (Edinburgh)
education	1030 (London SW1)		630 (Glasgow)
employment	1503 (London NW2)		812 (Leeds)
further education	974 (London WC1)		859, 877 (Liverpool)
physically	1030 (London SW1)		1165 (London SW15)
rehabilitation	1030 (London SW1)		1167 (London SW17)

Divinity (contd) 1498 (London SE8)
1616 (London SW19)
1663 (London NW3)
1801 (Matlock)
1846 (Newcastle upon Tyne)
1893 (Nottingham)
2035 (Retford)
2073 (St Andrews)
2279 (Weymouth)
2290 (Winchester)

See also Theology

Dobson, Austin 1326 (London W5)
Doctors
 biography 1731 (Maidstone)
 portraits 568 (Edinburgh)
Doctrine 397 (Chichester)
 Salvation Army 1571 (London SE5)
Doctrinal theology 233 (Bristol)
583 (Exeter)
Document reproduction 909 (London SW1)
Documentation 909 (London SW1)
1315 (London WC1)
Doddridge, Philip 1663 (London NW3)
1885 (Northampton)
Dogmatics 517, 569 (Edinburgh)
Dogs 21 (Airdrie)
1625 (London WC1)
Dolls, English 2322 (Worthing)
Domestic affairs, political
 aspects 987 (London E1)
Domestic architecture 1779 (Manchester)
Domestic history 1172 (London E2)
 Rutland 1907 (Oakham)
Domestic implements,
 Welsh 342 (Cardiff)
Domestic life 1720 (Luton)
Domestic science
(Volume I of this Directory includes domestic science, but it has been indexed in this volume for organizations not appearing in Volume I)
9 (Aberdeen)
32 (Ashington)
93 (Belfast)
122 (Bilston)
167 (Blackpool)
255 (Bromsgrove)
414 (Colwyn Bay)
446 (Deeside)
450 (Derby)
485 (Durham)
587 (Exeter)
646 (Grays)
673 (Harlow)
864 (Liverpool)
1695 (London WC1)
1990 (Peterborough)
2000 (Poole)
2003 (Portsmouth)
2101 (Seaford)
2238 (Wakefield)
 history 813 (Leeds)
Domestic studies 2167 (Stockport)
2256 (Watford)
Domestic subjects 191 (Bournemouth)
430 (Croydon)
667 (Halifax)
Domestic trade 2143 (Southampton)
Dorset 2278 (Weymouth)
 archaeology 460 (Dorchester)
 artists 460 (Dorchester)
 bygones 460 (Dorchester)
 geology 460 (Dorchester)
 history 459 (Dorchester)
 literature 459 (Dorchester)
 local history 460 (Dorchester)
2288 (Wimborne)
2326 (Yeovil)
 natural history 460 (Dorchester)
 photographs 460 (Dorchester)
 rural life 460 (Dorchester)
 topography 459 (Dorchester)
2326 (Yeovil)
Dowsers 2058 (Rugby)
Dowsing 2058 (Rugby)
Drama 154 (Birmingham)
163 (Blackburn)
353 (Carlisle)
403 (Chorley)
427 (Crewe)
457 (Doncaster)
470 (Dundee)
485 (Durham)
496 (Eastbourne)
561 (Edinburgh)
581 (Esher)
612, 614 (Glasgow)
704 (Hereford)
709 (Hertford)
734 (Hull)
750 (Ilkley)
812 (Leeds)
859 (Liverpool)
906 (London N7)
961 (London W1A 1AA)
968 (London W1Y 4HQ)
981 (London W1P 6AE)
1165 (London SW15)
1189 (London EC4)
1248 (London W6)
1339 (London E1)
1512 (London WC1)
1615 (London N14)
1692 (London SW19)
1746, 1782 (Manchester)

Drama (contd)	1818 (Morpeth)		450 (Derby)
	1844 (Newcastle upon Tyne)		750 (Ilkley)
	1863 (Northallerton)		1053 (London W4)
	1896 (Nottingham)		2046 (Rochester)
	1993, 1996 (Plymouth)		2207 (Taunton)
	2016 (Preston)	design	70 (Bath)
	2052 (Rotherham)		129 (Birmingham)
	2126 (Shrewsbury)		189 (Bournemouth)
	2209 (Taunton)		1566 (London WC2)
	2234 (Wakefield)	Dumfries	466 (Dumfries)
	2290 (Winchester)	military	903 (London EC3)
American	581 (Esher)	Dressmaking	122 (Bilston)
criticism	683 (Hastings)		874 (Liverpool)
history	683 (Hastings)		1074 (London W1)
biography	968 (London W1Y 4HQ)		1302 (London SE11)
criticism	154 (Birmingham)		1858 (Newport, Mon)
	968 (London W1Y 4HQ)		2141 (Southampton)
Elizabethan	647 (Great Yarmouth)		2205 (Tamworth)
English	124 (Birkenhead)		2280 (Whitehaven)
	538 (Exeter)	Drink	207 (Brentford)
	581 (Esher)	Driver training	1520 (London SW1)
	1975 (Oxford)	Driving standards	1241 (London W4)
	2179 (Stratford-upon-Avon)		1311 (London N12)
criticism	124 (Birkenhead)	Drugs	1704 (London SW16)
	683 (Hastings)		2266 (Welwyn Garden City)
history	124 (Birkenhead)		
	683 (Hastings)	addiction	388 (Chester)
literature	1512 (London WC1)		1706 (London N17)
Dramatists, French	1972 (Oxford)	clinical trials	1730 (Maidenhead)
Drawing	253 (Bromley)	control	45 (Bacup)
	258 (Burnley)	dependence	1239 (London W1M 0BR)
	408 (Colchester)		1595 (London SW17)
	469 (Dundee)	history	1595 (London SW17)
	805 (Leeds)	evaluation	757 (Isleworth)
	866 (Liverpool)	manufacture	1433 (London WC2)
	1339 (London E1)	reactions, adverse	415 (Consett)
	1688 (London WC2)	sensitivity, tuberculosis	1373 (London W12)
	1693 (London SW19)	Dudley, local history	465 (Dudley)
	1774 (Manchester)	Duke of Edinburgh's Award Scheme	1116 (London SW1)
	1858 (Newport, Mon)		
	2055 (Rotherham)	Duke of Wellington	1680 (London W1)
history	253 (Bromley)	Dulcimers	209 (Brentford)
technical	2160 (Stevenage)	Dumas, Alexandre	1333 (London SW2)
Drawings	880 (Liverpool)	Dumb welfare	1519 (London W3)
	1511 (London W1V 0DS)	Dumfries	
	2141 (Southampton)	archaeology	466 (Dumfries)
European	1792 (Manchester)	bygones	466 (Dumfries)
history	312 (Cambridge)	dress	466 (Dumfries)
Scottish	528 (Edinburgh)	folk life	466 (Dumfries)
Watts	662 (Guildford)	history	466 (Dumfries)
Drayton, Michael	1903 (Nuneaton)	local history	466 (Dumfries)
Dreamers, biography	1731 (Maidstone)	natural history	466 (Dumfries)
Dreams	1731 (Maidstone)	Dunbartonshire, local history	405 (Clydebank)
Dress	93 (Belfast)	Dundee, history	472 (Dundee)
	220 (Brighton)	Dunfermline	
	349 (Carlisle)	local history	477, 478 (Dunfermline)
	430 (Croydon)	natural history	477 (Dunfermline)

Durham
  antiquities   1849(Newcastle upon Tyne)
  industrial archaeology   1849(Newcastle upon Tyne)
  local history   486, 488(Durham)
    1833, 1849(Newcastle upon Tyne)
Dust hazards   521(Edinburgh)
  sampling and control   1980(Penarth)
Dutch *See* Holland
Dylan Thomas   2201(Swansea)

E

Ealing
  history   1190(London W3)
  topography   1190(London W3)
Ear
  anatomy   1791(Manchester)
  diseases   1774, 1791(Manchester)
Ear, nose and throat
  medicine   755(Ipswich)
    1336(London SW19)
Earl Brassey   683(Hastings)
Earl of Strafford   2112(Sheffield)
Early English literature   107(Belfast)
Early English Text Society   260(Burton-on-Trent)
    1882(Norwich)
Earthenware, Leeds   801, 804(Leeds)
East Anglia   1885(Norwich)
  library resources   1885(Norwich)
  local history   1879(Norwich)
East Ham, local history   1337(London E15)
East India Company, history   1230(London SE1)
East Lancashire Regiment,
  history   2251(Warrington)
East Lothian, local history   664(Haddington)
East Midlands Region
  further education   1899(Nottingham)
  planning   1888(Nottingham)
East–West relations   1659(London WC1)
    2038(Richmond)
Eastbourne, local history   497(Eastbourne)
Eccles, history   1747(Manchester)
  local history   1748(Manchester)
Ecclesiastical administration   2331(York)
Ecclesiastical architecture   2152(Southwell)
Ecclesiastical biography   2222(Truro)
Ecclesiastical history   569(Edinburgh)
    702(Hereford)
    1114(London WC1)
    1210(London EC4)
    1303(London W2)
    1306(London SE1)
    1945, 1946(Oxford)
  Celtic   2222(Truro)
  Yorkshire   2331(York)
Ecclesiastical law   1210(London EC4)

Ecclesiastical polity   583(Exeter)
Ecclesiology   2278(Weymouth)
  Lincolnshire   850(Lincoln)
Econometrics   154(Birmingham)
    1420(London SW1)
    2145(Southampton)
Economic affairs   947(London SW1)
  overseas   947(London SW1)
Economic co-operation   2143(Southampton)
Economic development   1090(London SE1)
    1119(London SW1)
  Arctic   295(Cambridge)
  North East England   1841(Newcastle upon Tyne)
Economic geography   520(Edinburgh)
    1117(London W5)
    2259(Wednesbury)
    2321(Worthing)
Economic history   19(Abingdon)
    142, 154(Birmingham)
    328, 330(Canterbury)
    587(Exeter)
    606(Glasgow)
    671(Harlech)
    748(Ilkeston)
    762(Keighley)
    994(London WC2)
    1064(London EC2)
    1302(London SE11)
    1495(London W1)
    1711(Loughborough)
    1808(Middlesbrough)
    1917(Oswestry)
    1990(Peterborough)
    2024(Reading)
    2143(Southampton)
    2171(Stoke-on-Trent)
    2259(Wednesbury)
    2307(Wolverhampton)
    2321(Worthing)
    2333(York)
  Wiltshire   453(Devizes)
Economic integration   1144(London W1R 9PL)
Economic organization   60(Barry)
Economic planning   79(Batley)
Economic statistics   422(Coventry)
  British   948(London EC4)
  foreign   948(London EC4)
Economic theory   431(Croydon)
Economics   17(Aberystwyth)
    19(Abingdon)
    35(Aylesbury)
    72(Bath)
    140, 142, 150, 153, 154, 157 (Birmingham)
    161(Blackburn)
    168(Blackpool)
    191(Bournemouth)

Economics (contd)
195 (Bracknell)
198, 201 (Bradford)
215 (Bridgwater)
223 (Brighton)
240 (Bristol)
261 (Burton-on-Trent)
270 (Camberley)
291, 302 (Cambridge)
330 (Canterbury)
359 (Carshalton)
390 (Chesterfield)
403 (Chorley)
406 (Coatbridge)
409 (Colchester)
411 (Coleraine)
413 (Colwyn Bay)
421, 422 (Coventry)
423 (Crawley)
427 (Crewe)
435 (Dagenham)
438 (Darlington)
446 (Deeside)
450 (Derby)
469, 471 (Dundee)
485, 488 (Durham)
499 (Eastleigh)
511, 516, 520 (Edinburgh)
576 (Enfield)
580 (Esher)
587 (Exeter)
598 (Galashiels)
606 (Glasgow)
646 (Grays)
665 (Guildford)
667 (Halifax)
671 (Harlech)
687 (Hatfield)
700 (Henley-on-Thames)
717 (Hitchin)
725 (Huddersfield)
734 (Hull)
748 (Ilkeston)
754 (Ipswich)
762 (Keighley)
773 (Kilmarnock)
778 (Kingston upon Thames)
788 (Lancaster)
793 (Leamington Spa)
805, 812, 813 (Leeds)
868, 872 (Liverpool)
884 (London WC2)
943 (London EC2)
946 (London WC2)
947 (London SW1)
994 (London WC2)
1015 (London SW4)
1042, 1064 (London EC2)
1073 (London W8)
1084 (London SW1)
1117 (London W5)
1119 (London SW1)
1154 (London EC4)
1180 (London EC1)
1197 (London NW4)
1198, 1199 (London SW1)
1240 (London WC1)
1243 (London EC3)
1302 (London SE11)
1305, 1420 (London SW1)
1473 (London SW16)
1482 (London W1R 8AL)
1484 (London W5)
1495 (London W1)
1501, 1617 (London SW1)
1650 (London NW1)
1662 (London WC1)
1665 (London E1)
1676 (London SW18)
1698 (London SE18)
1711, 1714 (Loughborough)
1724 (Macclesfield)
1728 (Maidenhead)
1754, 1766, 1786, 1791 (Manchester)
1806, 1807 (Middlesbrough)
1823 (Neath)
1839, 1850 (Newcastle upon Tyne)
1853 (Newport, Isle of Wight)
1860 (Newport, Mon)
1881 (Norwich)
1891, 1895 (Nottingham)
1918, 1921, 1937, 1947, 1948, 1958, 1962 (Oxford)
1990 (Peterborough)
2011, 2012 (Prescot)
2023, 2024, 2027 (Reading)
2030 (Redditch)
2059 (Rugby)
2086 (Salford)
2098 (Scunthorpe)
2115, 2119 (Sheffield)
2129 (Sleaford)
2142, 2144, 2145 (Southampton)
2166 (Stirling)
2173 (Stoke-on-Trent)
2198 (Sutton Coldfield)
2201, 2202 (Swansea)
2232 (Twickenham)
2233 (Uxbridge)
2239 (Wakefield)

Economics (contd) 2242 (Wallsend)
2259 (Wednesbury)
2300 (Wirral)
2309 (Bletchley)
2321 (Worthing)
2333 (York)
   Africa 298 (Cambridge)
1961, 1962 (Oxford)
   agriculture 17 (Aberystwyth)
836 (Lewes)
1412 (London SW1)
1922, 1960 (Oxford)
   Asia 1961 (Oxford)
      South 300 (Cambridge)
   China 1052 (London EC2)
   Commonwealth 1082 (London W8)
1082 (Edinburgh)
1159 (London SW1)
   defence 2129 (Sleaford)
   development 1466 (London W1V 0JS)
   education 1202 (London WC2)
2193 (Sutton)
   Europe 566 (Edinburgh)
      East 1668 (London WC1)
   food manufacture 836 (Lewes)
   foreign 1159 (London SW1)
   government 2014 (Preston)
   health 1455 (London W1)
   historical 762 (Huddersfield)
1662 (London WC1)
   home 185 (Boreham Wood)
750 (Ilkley)
   horticulture 1412 (London SW1)
   housing 1381 (London SW1)
   Hungary 988 (London SW1)
   industrial 118 (Beverley)
154 (Birmingham)
   international 661 (Guildford)
1541 (London SW1)
   Japan 896 (London WC2)
   labour 1962 (Oxford)
2039 (Richmond)
2142 (Southampton)
2237 (Wakefield)
   land 1960 (Oxford)
      Scotland 1977 (Paisley)
   Latin America 299 (Cambridge)
1961, 1962 (Oxford)
   manufacturing industries 183 (Bootle)
   mathematical 154 (Birmingham)
   medical care 1455 (London W1)
   pharmaceutical industry 1724 (Macclesfield)
   Poland 1479 (London SW1)
   production 118 (Beverley)
   science 227 (Brighton)
   Scotland 546 (Edinburgh)
623 (Glasgow)
   secondary manufacturing industries 808 (Leeds)
   shipping 2142 (Southampton)
   Slavonic 1668 (London WC1)
   social 1302 (London SE11)
   statistical 51 (Aberdeen)
   textbooks 647 (Great Yarmouth)
   textiles 1787 (Manchester)
   West Indies 1961 (Oxford)
See also Volume I
Economists, biography 2143 (Southampton)
Ecumenism 369 (Chelmsford)
975, 1022 (London SW1)
1058 (London SE1)
1060, 1085 (London SW1)
1149 (London W11)
Eddy, Mary Baker 1055 (London WC2)
Edinburgh 513 (Edinburgh)
   amenity 507 (Edinburgh)
Editing 909 (London SW1)
Edmund Burke 2112 (Sheffield)
Education 3, 4 (Aberdeen)
15, 17 (Aberystwyth)
18 (Abingdon)
33 (Ashton-under-Lyne)
42, 44 (Ayr)
53 (Bangor)
62 (Barry)
70, 72, 73, 75 (Bath)
107, 110, 112 (Belfast)
137, 140, 142, 152, 154, 156, 157, 158 (Birmingham)
160 (Bishop's Stortford)
161, 163 (Blackburn)
169 (Bletchley)
173 (Bognor Regis)
174 (Bolton)
198, 201 (Bradford)
210 (Brentwood)
217 (Bridgwater)
221, 225, 226, 227 (Brighton)
236, 238, 240 (Bristol)
256 (Bromsgrove)
261 (Burton-on-Trent)
273, 278, 298 (Cambridge)
324 (Cannock)
328, 329 (Canterbury)
331 (Cardiff)
353 (Carlisle)
358 (Carmarthen)
379, 380 (Cheltenham)
390 (Chesterfield)
403 (Chorley)
411 (Coleraine)
425, 427 (Crewe)
435 (Dagenham)

Education (contd)
  438, 440 (Darlington)
  446 (Deeside)
  449 (Derby)
  457 (Doncaster)
  464 (Dudley)
  467 (Dumfries)
  470 (Dundee)
  485, 487, 488, 491 (Durham)
  496, 498 (Eastbourne)
  503, 506, 510, 525, 533 (Edinburgh)
  576 (Enfield)
  587, 588 (Exeter)
  590 (Falkirk)
  612 (Glasgow)
  636 (Gloucester)
  642 (Grantham)
  646 (Grays)
  655 (Guildford)
  664 (Haddington)
  669 (Hamilton)
  700 (Henley-on-Thames)
  704 (Hereford)
  725 (Huddersfield)
  730, 734 (Hull)
  740 (Huntingdon)
  748 (Ilkeston)
  750 (Ilkley)
  754 (Ipswich)
  758 (Isleworth)
  762 (Keighley)
  776 (Kingston upon Thames)
  789 (Lancaster)
  793 (Leamington Spa)
  797, 799, 805, 812, 815 (Leeds)
  822, 823, 831 (Leicester)
  834 (Letchworth)
  842 (Lincoln)
  859, 864, 877, 878, 879 (Liverpool)
  906 (London N7)
  922 (London WC1)
  931 (London SE9)
  937 (London SW4)
  937 (London SW15)
  975 (London SW1)
  1015 (London SW4)
  1041 (London W1P 0ER)
  1053 (London W4)
  1071 (London N17)
  1102 (London W1)
  1110 (London SW15)
  1144 (London W1R 9PL)
  1165 (London SW15)
  1167 (London SW17)
  1170 (London SW5)
  1181 (London SE1)
  1202 (London WC2)
  1234 (London SE1)
  1236 (London W1P 3LD)
  1238 (London W1)
  1276 (London W1X 9PA)
  1303 (London WC2)
  1307 (London WC1)
  1334 (London SE13)
  1341 (London SW18)
  1352 (London W8)
  1387 (London SW1)
  1408 (London W1N 5TB)
  1443 (London WC1)
  1466 (London W1V 0JS)
  1473 (London SW16)
  1498 (London SE8)
  1584 (London W1M 6DE)
  1590 (London SW1)
  1616 (London SW19)
  1653 (London SE14)
  1657 (London WC1)
  1688 (London W9)
  1690 (London SW15)
  1714 (Loughborough)
  1717 (Lowestoft)
  1721, 1722 (Luton)
  1746, 1758, 1767, 1773, 1782, 1791 (Manchester)
  1801 (Matlock)
  1805 (Mexborough)
  1809 (Middlesbrough)
  1823 (Neath)
  1825 (New Malden)
  1837, 1845, 1846, 1850 (Newcastle upon Tyne)
  1854, 1855, 1857 (Newport, Mon)
  1877 (Norwich)
  1893, 1895, 1902 (Nottingham)
  1913 (Ormskirk)
  1948, 1954, 1974 (Oxford)
  1978 (Paisley)
  1982 (Penarth)
  1990 (Peterborough)
  1992 (Plymouth)
  2002, 2003 (Portsmouth)
  2011 (Prescot)
  2014 (Preston)
  2020, 2021, 2023, 2027 (Reading)
  2030 (Redditch)
  2034 (Redruth)
  2035 (Retford)
  2043 (Ripon)

Education (contd)
    2052(Rotherham)
    2067, 2070(St Albans)
    2073(St Andrews)
    2088(Salisbury)
    2101 (Seaford)
    2121, 2126(Shrewsbury)
    2135(Slough)
    2138, 2144, 2146(Southampton)
    2160(Stevenage)
    2166(Stirling)
    2185, 2187(Sunderland)
    2198(Sutton Coldfield)
    2204(Swindon)
    2228, 2230, 2232(Twickenham)
    2233(Uxbridge)
    2234, 2236(Wakefield)
    2242(Wallsend)
    2245(Walsall)
    2250(Warrington)
    2254(Warwick)
    2257(Watford)
    2272(West Wickham)
    2274(Weston super Mare)
    2279(Weymouth)
    2290(Winchester)
    2305, 2306, 2307(Wolverhampton)
    2312(Worcester)
    2316(Workington)
    2318(Worksop)
    2321(Worthing)
    2330, 2333(York)
 adult 140(Birmingham)
    671(Harlech)
    722(Hounslow)
    906(London N7)
    1102, 1419(London W1)
    1688(London W1H 8BY)
    1951(Oxford)
    2198(Sutton Coldfield)
    2318(Worksop)
 African 298(Cambridge)
    967(London W1Y 2AA)
 alcoholism 876(Liverpool)
 Army 1112(London SW1)
    1242(London SE9)
 art 129(Birmingham)
    220(Brighton)
    688(Havant)
 Asia 967(London W1Y 2AA)
 autistic children 1438(London NW11)
 cancer 875(Liverpool)
    962(London W1N 1AA)
 children 1242(London SE9)
    1405(London W1)

 Christian 1387(London SW1)
 commercial 958(London W1N 4AP)
    2080(Sale)
 comparative 75(Bath)
    725(Huddersfield)
    2011(Prescot)
 compensatory 1746(Manchester)
 consumer 1088(London WC2)
 craft 732(Hull)
 curriculum 645(Grays)
 deaf 1791(Manchester)
 dental 1145(London W1)
  postgraduate 1174(London W1M 8DQ)
  undergraduate 1174(London W1M 8DQ)
 dental health 1174(London W1M 8DQ)
 dental surgery assistants 166(Blackpool)
 developing countries 967(London W1Y 2AA)
 disabled 1030(London SW1)
 economics 1202(London WC2)
    2193(Sutton)
 English, history 1077(London SW10)
 epilepsy 982(London WC1)
 E.S.N. children 1854(Newport, Mon)
 film 2020(Reading)
 food 587(Exeter)
    1159(London W1)
 foot health 512(Edinburgh)
 Froebel 1414(London W1M 5RF)
 further 174(Bolton)
    185(Boreham Wood)
    280(Cambridge)
    555(Edinburgh)
    667(Halifax)
    923(London WC1)
    958(London W1N 4AP)
    1060(London SW1)
    1170(London SW15)
    1202(London WC2)
    1874(Norwich)
    2070(St Albans)
    2142(Southampton)
    2198(Sutton Coldfield)
    2232(Twickenham)
    2318(Worksop)
  disabled 974(London WC1)
  East Midlands Region 1899(Nottingham)
  South West England 239(Bristol)
  Southern Region 2026(Reading)
 general studies 420(Coventry)
 handicapped 498(Eastbourne)
  children 1767(Manchester)
 health 374(Chelmsford)
    612(Glasgow)
    1005(London SE1)
    1049(London WC1)
    1142(London W1N 8BQ)
    1165(London SW15)

Education, health (contd)	1196(London WC1)	nursery	1498(London SE8)
	1475(London W1M 4AY)	nursing	174(Bolton)
	1574(London SW1)		533(Edinburgh)
	1846(Newcastle upon Tyne)		1528(London W1M 0AB)
		offenders	1218(London SE11)
	2107(Sheffield)	pharmacists	1472(London WC1)
higher	280(Cambridge)	physical	86, 87(Bedford)
	722(Hounslow)		157(Birmingham)
	923(London WC1)		163(Blackburn)
	958(London W1N 4AP)		329(Canterbury)
	1102(London W1)		331(Cardiff)
	1202(London WC2)		380(Cheltenham)
	1593(London WC1)		403(Chorley)
	2011(Prescot)		427(Crewe)
history	75(Bath)		449(Derby)
	210(Brentwood)		457(Doncaster)
	491(Durham)		470(Dundee)
	636(Gloucester)		488(Durham)
	778(Kingston upon Thames)		496(Eastbourne)
			510(Edinburgh)
	818(Leeds)		612(Glasgow)
	823(Leicester)		734(Hull)
	1165(London SW15)		773(Kilmarnock)
	1473(London SW16)		797, 812(Leeds)
	1616(London SW19)		824(Leicester)
	1662(London WC1)		1167(London SW17)
	1767(Manchester)		1272(London SE22)
	1954(Oxford)		1475(London W1M 4AX)
	2011(Prescot)		1615(London N14)
	2121(Shrewsbury)		1746(Manchester)
	2138(Southampton)		1801(Matlock)
	2187(Sunderland)		1846(Newcastle upon Tyne)
	2204(Swindon)		1893(Nottingham)
	2228(Twickenham)		2011(Prescot)
	2257(Watford)		2020(Reading)
	2272(West Wickham)		2043(Ripon)
	2279(Weymouth)		2052(Rotherham)
	2290(Winchester)		2135(Slough)
	2305(Wolverhampton)		2187(Sunderland)
Hungary	988(London SW1)		2236(Wakefield)
industrial	958(London W1N 4AP)		2290(Winchester)
infant	1809(Middlesbrough)		2346
Japan	1289(London W1X 9LB)	history	797(Leeds)
Jewish	1292(London W1)	primary	44(Ayr)
	2083(Salford)		555(Edinburgh)
junior	1809(Middlesbrough)		645(Grays)
law	1235(London WC1)		937(London SW15)
liberal	275(Cambridge)		1443(London WC1)
librarianship	1315(London WC1)		1820(Musselburgh)
management	1253(London SW1)		2011(Prescot)
medical	1574(London SW1)		2070(St Albans)
use of television	914(London SE6)		2228(Twickenham)
Merchant Navy	1580(London SE17)		2272(West Wickham)
Montessori	1384(London WC1)		2279(Weymouth)
movement	87(Bedford)		2305(Wolverhampton)
musical	1890(Nottingham)	progressive	1825(New Malden)
nautical	736(Hull)		2226(Tunbridge Wells)

Education (contd)		Educational filmstrips	1407(London W1M 0AL)
religious	403(Chorley)	Educational finance	1202(London WC2)
	1387(London SW1)	Educational philosophy	1102(London W1)
	1979(Penarth)		2011(Prescot)
	2020(Reading)		2257(Watford)
	2234(Wakefield)		2279(Weymouth)
remedial	112(London SW1)	Educational planning	1202(London WC2)
Roman Catholic	1023, 1026(London SW7)	Educational policy	1294(London WC1)
	2138(Southampton)	Educational psychology	44(Ayr)
Russia	1591(London SW9)		75(Bath)
science	1651(London SW3)		93(Belfast)
Scotland	553, 555(Edinburgh)		174(Bolton)
secondary	555(Edinburgh)		210(Brentwood)
	645(Grays)		506, 547(Edinburgh)
	1443(London WC1)		590(Falkirk)
	2011(Prescot)		645(Grays)
	2070(St Albans)		725(Huddersfield)
	2279(Weymouth)		823(Leicester)
secular	1500(London N1)		906(London N7)
service children	1112(London SW1)		1102(London W1)
sex	1142(London W1N 8BQ)		1170(London SW15)
	1279(London SW1)		1877(Norwich)
Singapore	1459(London SW1)		1992(Plymouth)
social	503(Edinburgh)		2020(Reading)
social work	1418(London WC1)		2035(Retford)
socialist	1138, 1590(London SW1)		2121(Shrewsbury)
special	18(Abingdon)		2138(Southampton)
	1078(London W1P 3LD)		2187(Sunderland)
	1992(Plymouth)		2279(Weymouth)
	2014(Preston)		2290(Winchester)
E.S.N.	18(Abingdon)		2305(Wolverhampton)
S.S.N.	18(Abingdon)	Educational puppetry	1121(London WC1)
State	77(Bathgate)	Educational research	527(Edinburgh)
subnormal	1236(London W1P 3LD)		1202(London WC2)
Sweden	1623(London W1R 2DN)		2132(Slough)
technical	35(Aylesbury)	Scotland	547(Edinburgh)
	185(Boreham Wood)	Educational retardation	2151(Southport)
	335(Cardiff)	Educational sociology	75(Bath)
	470(Dundee)		506(Edinburgh)
	834(Letchworth)		1170(London SW15)
	923(London WC1)		1992(Plymouth)
	2059(Rugby)		2279(Weymouth)
	2136(South Shields)		2305(Wolverhampton)
television	2020(Reading)	Educational subnormality	2151(Southport)
temperance	1704(London SW16)	Educational system	1202(London WC2)
University	1102(London W1)	Scotland	503(Edinburgh)
visual	1407(London W1M 0AL)	Educational technology	174(Bolton)
visual aids	1676(London SW18)		403(Chorley)
vocational	725(Huddersfield)		913(London WC1)
	923(London WC1)		1408(London W1N 5TB)
welfare	667(Halifax)		2306(Wolverhampton)
white-collar workers	698(Hemel Hempstead)	Educational tests	2132(Slough)
women, history	1019(London SW5)	Educational travel	1029(London SW1)
Educational administration	1102(London W1)	Educational visits	1029(London SW1)
	1202(London WC2)	Edward Carpenter	2112(Sheffield)
Educational buildings	1103(London W1)	Edward Jenner	1565(London SW1)
Educational films	1407(London W1M 0AL)	Edward Hall	2286(Wigan)

Edward Wilson	376 (Cheltenham)	foreign	92 (Belfast)
Egypt	399 (Chichester)	medical	1784 (Manchester)
antiquities	1726 (Macclesfield)	Endocrine glands	1930 (Oxford)
Egyptology	177 (Bolton)	Endocrinology	257 (Burgess Hill)
	492 (Durham)		681 (Harrow)
	1952 (Oxford)		1063 (London W1N 4BN)
E. H. W. Meyerstein	1956 (Oxford)		1367 (London NW7)
Ekistics	1636 (London W1)		1817 (Morden)
Elderly, welfare	1106 (London SE1)		1828 (Newbury)
	1428 (London WC1)	Enfield, antiquities	577 (Enfield)
Eleanor Farjeon	1324 (London NW3)	Engineering	
Elections	119 (Bexley)	(Engineering and its special branches are covered thoroughly in Volume I of the Directory, and have not been indexed in this Volume except in the following few cases which relate more closely to the general subject matter)	
first secret ballot	1997 (Pontefract)		
Electrical services, hospitals	628 (Glasgow)		
Electricity supply industry, training	1123 (London SW1)		
Electrocardiography	1601 (London EC2)	biological	550 (Edinburgh)
Electroencephalography	1122 (London SE18)		631 (Glasgow)
	2109 (Sheffield)		681 (Harrow)
Electron microscopy	681 (Harrow)		941 (London NW7)
	1260 (London W1)		1551 (London W12)
	1828 (Newbury)	biomedical	1368 (London NW3)
Electrophysiology	393 (Chichester)		2173 (Stoke-on-Trent)
Elgar	1124 (London SW1)	design	417 (Coventry)
Elgin, local history	575 (Elgin)	history	246 (Bristol)
Eliot, George	418 (Coventry)	military	23 (Aldershot)
	1903, 1904 (Nuneaton)	England	
Eliot, T. S.	288 (Cambridge)	architecture	1426 (London SW1)
Elizabethan criticism	1354 (London SE19)	history	2155 (Stafford)
Elizabethan drama	647 (Great Yarmouth)	local history	831 (Leicester)
Elizabethan history	1354 (London SE19)	North East	
Elizabethan literature	1354 (London SE19)	archaeology	480 (Durham)
Ellesmere Port, local history	2298 (Wirral)	architecture	480 (Durham)
Elzeviers	2295 (Windsor)	Civic Trust	480 (Durham)
Emanuel Swedenborg	1173, 1622 (London WC1)	economic development	1841 (Newcastle upon Tyne)
Emblem books	1662 (London WC1)	North West	
Emblem literature	630 (Glasgow)	history	1741 (Manchester)
Embroidery	129 (Birmingham)	topography	1741 (Manchester)
	793 (Leamington Spa)	place-names	1130 (London WC1)
	1074 (London W1)	South East	429 (Croydon)
	1128 (London W1M 8AX)	topography	1187 (London EC2)
	1878 (Norwich)	English	
	2055 (Rotherham)	(See also English language and English literature. An index entry has been included under 'English' where this was not qualified in any way in the relevant entry)	
	2141 (Southampton)		
	2280 (Whitehaven)		
See also Volume I			93 (Belfast)
Emigrants, Scottish	549 (Edinburgh)		163 (Blackburn)
Employee-shareholding	1232 (London SW1)		225 (Brighton)
Employment	742 (Hyde)		329, 330 (Canterbury)
	1104 (London SW1)		340 (Cardiff)
	2044 (Rochdale)		403 (Chorley)
blind	1321 (London SE15)		427 (Crewe)
disabled	1503 (London NW2)		449 (Derby)
girls	1694 (London SW3)		470 (Dundee)
State Enrolled Nurses	1400 (London W1M 9HQ)		487 (Durham)
women	1694 (London SW3)		498 (Eastbourne)
Encyclopaedias	1688 (London WC2)		574 (Egham)

English (contd) 704(Hereford)
750(Ilkley)
783(Lampeter)
788(Lancaster)
813(Leeds)
884(London WC2)
942(London WC1)
1112(London SW1)
1197(London NW4)
1451(London NW5)
1498(London SE8)
1665(London E1)
1746(Manchester)
1801(Matlock)
1809(Middlesbrough)
1838, 1846(Newcastle upon Tyne)
1853(Newport, Isle of Wight)
1893(Nottingham)
1992(Plymouth)
2052(Rotherham)
2145(Southampton)
2166(Stirling)
2234(Wakefield)
2290(Winchester)

English Art and Crafts Movement 1692(London E17)
English countryside, history 2028(Reading)
English costume 592(Farnham)
701(Hereford)
  history 1750(Manchester)
English criticism 529(Edinburgh)
English dialects 123(Bingley)
English dictionaries 16(Aberystwyth)
English dissent, history 1927(Oxford)
English drama 124(Birkenhead)
529(Edinburgh)
581(Esher)
583(Exeter)
  criticism 124(Birkenhead)
  history 124(Birkenhead)
English education, history 1077(London SW10)
English fiction
  criticism 497(Eastbourne)
  history 497(Eastbourne)
English glass 2199(Swansea)
  paper weights 592(Farnham)
English grammars 16(Aberystwyth)
English history 71(Bath)
492(Durham)
1210(London EC4)
1869(Northampton)
1946(Oxford)
  medieval 90(Bedford)
English language 75(Bath)
123(Bingley)
141, 154(Birmingham)
457(Doncaster)
486(Durham)
640(Gosport)
667(Halifax)
778(Kingston upon Thames)
812(Leeds)
1129(London SW7)
1302(London SE11)
1307(London WC1)
1336(London SW19)
1495(London W1)
1653(London SE14)
1774(Manchester)
1837, 1839, 1845(Newcastle upon Tyne)
1862(Newton Stewart)
1895(Nottingham)
1946, 1956(Oxford)
2144(Southampton)
2182(Sunderland)
2205(Tamworth)
2333(York)
  teaching 506(Edinburgh)
967(London W1Y 2AA)
English law 816(Leeds)
1302(London SE11)
1309(London WC1)
1928(Oxford)
  history 1581(London E1)
English letters 252(Bromley)
English literature 17(Aberystwyth)
71, 73, 75(Bath)
140, 141, 154(Birmingham)
160(Bishop's Stortford)
222(Brighton)
235(Bristol)
291(Cambridge)
422(Coventry)
435(Dagenham)
457(Doncaster)
485, 486, 492(Durham)
529(Edinburgh)
576(Enfield)
579(Epsom)
636(Gloucester)
667(Halifax)
671(Harlech)
734(Hull)
754(Ipswich)
778(Kingston upon Thames)
813(Leeds)
1129(London SW7)
1165(London SW15)
1210(London EC4)
1302(London SE11)
1326(London W5)

English literature (contd)	1495(London W1)	E.N.T. medicine	681(Harrow)
	1650(London NW1)		755(Ipswich)
	1653(London SE14)		1336(London SW9)
	1662(London WC1)	Entertainment	1688(London WC2)
	1688(London SW1)	industry	1618(London WC2)
	1782, 1789(Manchester)	Entomology	873(Liverpool)
	1837, 1839, 1845,	Environment	163(Blackburn)
	1850(Newcastle upon		1067(London SW1)
	Tyne)		1540(London W1N 4AD)
	1854, 1855, 1860(Newport,		1636(London W1)
	Mon)		1846(Newcastle upon Tyne)
	1862(Newton Stewart)	Environmental art	189(Bournemouth)
	1895(Nottingham)	Environmental conservation	1101(London SW1)
	1917(Oswestry)	Environmental design	109(Belfast)
	1918, 1946, 1948,		189(Bournemouth)
	1956(Oxford)	Environmental health	6(Aberdeen)
	2011(Prescot)		921, 1381(London SW1)
	2020(Reading)	Environmental hygiene	45(Bacup)
	2035(Retford)	Environmental medicine	1361(London EC1)
	2043(Ripon)	Environmental radiation	
	2129(Sleaford)	effects	806(Leeds)
	2144(Southampton)	Enzymes	495(Eastbourne)
	2205(Tamworth)	Epidemiology	336(Cardiff)
	2218(Truro)		681(Harrow)
	2279(Weymouth)		1344(London WC1)
	2312(Worcester)	Epigraphy	
	2321(Worthing)	Greek	1250(London WC1)
	2333(York)	Roman	1250(London WC1)
bibliographies	286(Cambridge)	Epilepsy	621(Glasgow)
criticism	451(Derby)		982(London WC1)
	612(Glasgow)	education	982(London WC1)
	2021(Reading)	social aspects	1275(London WC1)
French translations	813(Leeds)	Epileptics	621(Glasgow)
history	612(Glasgow)	Epistles	192(Bournemouth)
	2021(Reading)	Epping Forest, local history	1675(London E17)
teaching	506(Edinburgh)	Epsom, local history	578(Epsom)
textbooks	647(Great Yarmouth)	Equestrian sports	1328(London SE10)
English novels			767(Kenilworth)
criticism	1748(Manchester)		1328(London SE10)
history	1748(Manchester)	Ergonomics	139(Birmingham)
English poetry	583(Exeter)		521, 527(Edinburgh)
	1799(Matlock)		1253(London SW1)
	2240(Wallasey)		1131(London SW16)
English pottery	183(Bootle)		1714(Loughborough)
	2322(Worthing)	Ernest Jones	943(London EC2)
English speech	1129(London SW7)	E.S.N. education	18(Abingdon)
English watercolours	801, 802(Leeds)	children	1854(Newport, Mon)
English writing	1129(London SW7)	Esoteric associations and	
Engraving	162(Blackburn)	societies	836(Lewes)
	1557(London W1)	Esotericism	685(Hastings)
	1804(Merthyr Tydfil)	Esperanto	211(Brentwood)
	1836(Newcastle upon Tyne)		983(London W11)
	2044(Rochdale)		1786(Manchester)
Engravings	1511(London W1V 0DS)	Espionage subversion	2038(Richmond)
	1630(London WC2)	Essex	
	2186(Sunderland)	archaeology	1470(London E15)
history	312(Cambridge)	biology	1470(London E15)

Essex (contd)
  genealogy   372(Chelmsford)
  geology   1470(London E15)
  history   372(Chelmsford)
    407, 408(Colchester)
    1470(London E15)
  local history   368, 370(Chelmsford)
    407, 408(Colchester)
    436(Dagenham)
    645(Grays)
    1337, 1470(London E15)
    2050(Romford)
  natural history   407(Colchester)
  South East, topography   2148(Southend-on-Sea)
  topography   372(Chelmsford)
Estate duty   1253(London SW1)
Estate management   868(Liverpool)
    1073(London W8)
    1450(London N7)
    1839(Newcastle upon Tyne)
See also Volume I
Estonian
  language   651(Grimsby)
  literature   651(Grimsby)
Etching   1804(Merthyr Tydfil)
Ethics   397(Chichester)
    459(Dorchester)
    1500(London N1)
    2240(Wallasey)
  Christian   569(Edinburgh)
  Jewish   2139(Southampton)
  nursing   533(Edinburgh)
  national   1437(London SE1)
  sexual   443(Dartford)
Ethiopia
  geography   1749(Manchester)
  history   1749(Manchester)
Ethno-genetics   522(Edinburgh)
Ethnography   629(Glasgow)
    1121(London SE23)
    1904(Nuneaton)
  Africa   1273(London EC4)
Ethnology   16(Aberystwyth)
    522(Edinburgh)
    756(Ipswich)
    860(Liverpool)
    1627(London NW3)
    1969(Oxford)
    2163(Stirling)
  photographs   310(Cambridge)
  Wales   342(Cardiff)
Ethno-psychology   522(Edinburgh)
Etiquette   1323(London NW10)
Euclid   16(Aberystwyth)
Eugenics   1132(London SW1)
Euratom   1133(London SW1)
Eurhythmics   2302(Woking)

Europe   72(Bath)
    225(Brighton)
    1746(Manchester)
  archaeology   1341(London SW18)
    1655(London WC1)
  art, history   1652(London W1N 0BE)
  drawings   1792(Manchester)
  Eastern   154(Birmingham)
    411(Coleraine)
    1647(Oxford)
    1668(London WC1)
    bibliography   2260(Wellingborough)
    States, history   2038(Richmond)
  economics   566(Edinburgh)
  geography   1341(London SW18)
    2196(Sutton)
  history   445(Darwen)
    1251(London W1N 2BH)
    1341(London SW18)
    1659(London WC1)
    1855(Newport, Mon)
    1946(Oxford)
    2337(York)
  integration   976(London SW1)
  Jewry, history   1251(London W1N 2BH)
  languages   270(Camberley)
    486, 492(Durham)
    1965, 1972(Oxford)
  law   566(Edinburgh)
    1654(London WC1)
  literature   291(Cambridge)
    486, 492(Durham)
    1965, 1972(Oxford)
  Methodist missions   1376(London NW1)
  politics   566(Edinburgh)
  travel   1341(London SW18)
  Western   1947(Oxford)
    archaeology   530(Edinburgh)
European Coal and Steel
  Community   1133(London SW1)
European Commission   1133(London SW1)
European Communities   566(Edinburgh)
    1133(London SW1)
  law   1654(London WC1)
European Economic
  Community   976, 1133, 1253(London SW1)
European Free Trade Area   1253(London SW1)
Euthanasia   1134(London W8)
Evangelical Christianity   1135(London WC1)
Evangelical hymnology   1136(London WC1)
Evangelical literature   1136(London W1M 2HB)
Evangelical movement,
  history   1135(London WC1)
Evangelism   1284(London WL1)
    1570(London EC4)
    1571(London SE5)
    1647(London SW1)

Evangelism *(contd)*	1779 (Manchester)		2276 (Weybridge)
	1811 (Mirfield)	Farmers, biography	1731 (Maidstone)
	1914 (Ormskirk)	Farming tools	1907 (Oakham)
Everett, James	1756 (Manchester)	Farnham	
Evesham Abbey	582 (Evesham)	agriculture	592 (Farnham)
Evesham, local history	582 (Evesham)	architecture	592 (Farnham)
Evolution	581 (Esher)	arts	592 (Farnham)
	734 (Hull)	crafts	592 (Farnham)
	1132 (London SW1)	local history	592 (Farnham)
	1500 (London N1)	transport	592 (Farnham)
	1739 (Manchester)	Faroe Islands	
human	522 (Edinburgh)	geography	2278 (Weymouth)
Ewell, local history	578 (Epsom)	history	2278 (Weymouth)
Examinations	1577 (London W1N 6LL)	Fascism, history	1251 (London W1N 2BH)
medical	2252 (Warrington)	Fashion	33 (Ashton-under-Lyne)
Scotland	618 (Glasgow)		253 (Bromley)
Exegetics	517 (Edinburgh)		349 (Carlisle)
Exeter, local history	584 (Exeter)		378 (Cheltenham)
Exhibition catalogues	1858 (Newport, Mon)		450 (Derby)
	2114 (Sheffield)		777 (Kingston upon Thames)
			824 (Leicester)
Expedition files, Polar regions	295 (Cambridge)		871 (Liverpool)
Exploration	1425 (London SE10)		1053 (London W4)
	1538 (London SW7)		1524 (London SW7)
Exports	1253 (London SW1)		1713 (Loughborough)
Extra-sensory perception	1061 (London SW1)		1719 (Luton)
Eye care	919 (London W1Y 2DT)		1727 (Maidenhead)
	1463 (London WC2)		1750, 1765 (Manchester)
Eye diseases	581 (Esher)		1892 (Nottingham)
Eye surgery	581 (Esher)		2055 (Rotherham)
			2135 (Slough)
			2207 (Taunton)
F		history	2141 (Southampton)
		plates	802 (Leeds)
Fabian publications	1138 (London SW1)	*See also* Volume I	
Fabian Society	1932 (Oxford)	Fathers, the	1568 (London EC4)
Factories Act and Regulations	1233 (London SW1)		2217 (Truro)
Factory and shops inspection	1104 (London SW1)	Feet	
Family allowances	1107 (London WC2)	anatomy	1048 (London NW8)
	1387 (London SW1)	pathology	1048 (London NW8)
Family history	1935 (Oxford)	physiology	1048 (London NW8)
Family law	779 (Kingston upon Thames)	*See also* chiropody	
Family planning	1142 (London W1N 8BQ)	Feline advice	2324 (Wotton-under-Edge)
	1279 (London SW1)	Fens	187 (Boston)
Family prayers	2143 (Southampton)	drainage	187 (Boston)
Family welfare	1143, 1387 (London SW1)	local history	1796 (March)
	1418, 1662 (London WC1)		1989 (Peterborough)
Family services	459 (Dorchester)	maps	187 (Boston)
Fanshawe portraits	436 (Dagenham)	Fertility	1279 (London SW1)
F.A.O.	1646 (London W1)		1817 (Morden)
Far East	1947 (Oxford)	differential	1132 (London SW1)
Far Eastern Islands	217 (Bridgwater)	Festschriften	1658 (London WC1)
Faraday	1543 (London W1)	Fevers	1909 (Oldham)
Farjeon, Eleanor	1324 (London NW3)	Fiction	
Farm animals, diseases	502 (Edinburgh)	American	847 (Lincoln)
	791 (Lasswade)	criticism	497 (Eastbourne)
	1828 (Newbury)	history	497 (Eastbourne)

Fiction (contd)
- English
  - criticism 497(Eastbourne)
  - history 497(Eastbourne)
- foreign 2342
- history 451(Derby)
- out of print 2342
- rare 804(Leeds)

Field studies 1150(London WC2)
Fife, West, local history 478(Dunfermline)
Film 427(Crewe)
585(Exeter)
961(London W1A 1AA)
1152(London W1)
1524(London SW7)
1752(Manchester)
1844(Newcastle upon Tyne)
2116(Sheffield)
2141(Southampton)
- distribution 1151(London W1)
- education 2020(Reading)
- festivals 1147(London W1)
- making 1151, 1152(London W1)
1153(London W1Y 3AD)
- personalities 984(London W1)
- production 989(London W1)
1151, 1152(London W1)
1153(London W1Y 3AD)
- programmes 989(London W1)
- research 989(London W1)
- scripts 1705(London W2)
- technicians 1603(London W1N 6JJ)
  - careers 1603(London W1N 6JJ)
- writing 1705(London W2)

Filming 734(Hull)
Films 984, 989, 1000(London W1)
1603(London W1N 6JJ)
- awards 1603(London W1N 6JJ)
- educational 1407(London W1M 0AL)
- World War 1223(London SE1)
See also Volume I

Filmstrips, educational 1407(London W1M 0AL)
Finance 423(Crawley)
520(Edinburgh)
1045(London EC2)
1144(London W1R 9PL)
1154(London EC4)
1199(London SW1)
1243(London EC3)
1711(Loughborough)
- public 2337(York)
See also Volume I

Financial aid, professional
people 1492(London W1M 6HY)
Financial law 516(Edinburgh)
Financial statistics 946(London WC2)
Fine art 17(Aberystwyth)

Fine arts
199(Bradford)
220(Brighton)
349(Carlisle)
378(Cheltenham)
417, 422(Coventry)
629(Glasgow)
667(Halifax)
734(Hull)
777(Kingston upon Thames)
824(Leicester)
871(Liverpool)
1018(London SE5)
1713(Loughborough)
1839(Newcastle upon Tyne)
1883(Norwich)
1892, 1902(Nottingham)
35(Aylesbury)
71(Bath)
78(Batley)
92(Belfast)
129, 132, 142, 154, 157 (Birmingham)
160(Bishop's Stortford)
161(Blackburn)
167(Blackpool)
201(Bradford)
222(Brighton)
231(Bristol)
253(Bromley)
291(Cambridge)
330(Canterbury)
430(Croydon)
446(Deeside)
469, 474(Dundee)
748(Ilkeston)
762(Keighley)
771(Kidderminster)
778(Kingston upon Thames)
793(Leamington Spa)
802(Leeds)
855(Lincoln)
926(London SW1)
1039(London WC1)
1074(London W1)
1110(London SW15)
1387(London SW1)
1473(London SW16)
1511(London W1V 0DS)
1553(London WC2)
1674(London E17)
1680(London W1)
1688(London WC2)
1688(London SW1)
1891(Nottingham)
1993(Plymouth)
2002(Portsmouth)
2011(Prescot)

Fine arts *(contd)*	2014 (Preston)	Folk life	462 (Douglas)
	2099 (Scunthorpe)		562 (Edinburgh)
	2111 (Sheffield)		2099 (Scunthorpe)
	2174 (Stoke-on-Trent)	Bristol	228 (Bristol)
	2188 (Sunderland)	Buckinghamshire	37 (Aylesbury)
	2198 (Sutton Coldfield)	Cambridge	276 (Cambridge)
	2199 (Swansea)	Cambridgeshire	276 (Cambridge)
	2207 (Taunton)	Chichester	395 (Chichester)
	2221 (Truro)	Dumfries	466 (Dumfries)
	2238 (Wakefield)	Isle of Man	462 (Douglas)
	2242 (Wallsend)	Scotland	572 (Edinburgh)
	2286 (Wigan)	Sussex, West	395 (Chichester)
East European	1668 (London WC1)	Wales	337, 342 (Cardiff)
history	312 (Cambridge)	Folk lore	16 (Aberystwyth)
Japan	1289 (London W1C 9LB)		233 (Bristol)
Slavonic	1668 (London WC1)		310 (Cambridge)
Fine press books	878 (Liverpool)		342 (Cardiff)
Finland	1155 (London SW1)		591 (Falmouth)
literature	1338 (London SE22)		1157 (London WC1)
tourism	1156 (London SW1)		1323 (London NW10)
travel	1156 (London SW1)		1808 (Middlesbrough)
Fire hazards, industrial	1045 (London EC2)		1939 (Oxford)
Fire protection	463 (Dover)	Austria	929 (London SW7)
Fire services, Scotland	553 (Edinburgh)	Bulgaria	311 (Cambridge)
Firearms	903 (London EC3)	Cambridge	276 (Cambridge)
First aid	36 (Aylesbury)	Cambridgeshire	276 (Cambridge)
	616 (Glasgow)	Cardiganshire	1 (Aberaeron)
	672 (Harlow)	Cornwall	591 (Falmouth)
First secret ballot election	1997 (Pontefract)	Czechoslovakia	311 (Cambridge)
Fish culture	2051 (Rossendale)	Germany	1177 (London SW7)
Fishes	377 (Cheltenham)	Gypsy	878 (Liverpool)
Fisheries	1425 (London SE10)	Isle of Man	462 (Douglas)
helminthology	2066 (St Albans)	Poland	311 (Cambridge)
Fishing	214 (Bridgwater)	Russia	311 (Cambridge)
	1328 (London SE10)	Scotland	572 (Edinburgh)
	2323 (Worthing)	Yorkshire	123 (Bingley)
history	649 (Grimsby)	Yugoslavia	311 (Cambridge)
Fitness	1270 (London W1M 4AX)	Folk music	
Flags	1425 (London SE10)	Hungary	988 (London SW1)
Fleet Air Arm, history	2325 (Yeovil)	Wales	342 (Cardiff)
Flint, local history	593 (Flint)	Folkestone, local history	595 (Folkestone)
Flintshire		Folksong, Gaelic	572 (Edinburgh)
history	447 (Deeside)	Food	207 (Brentford)
local history	593 (Flint)		414 (Colwyn Bay)
	1813 (Mold)		1605 (London W1)
photographs	447 (Deeside)		1664 (London W8)
Florence Nightingale	881 (Liverpool)		1719 (Luton)
Floriculture	2297 (Wirral)	additives legislation	45 (Bacup)
Flower arrangement	2205 (Tamworth)		1723 (Macclesfield)
	2210 (Taunton)	adulteration	746 (Ilford)
Fluoridation	1145 (London W1)	education	587 (Exeter)
	1168 (London W1A 3AU)		1158 (London W1)
Focal sepsis	143 (Birmingham)	hygiene	1106 (London SE1)
Folk art, Hungary	988 (London SW1)	industries	2256 (Watford)
Folk dancing	1248 (London W6)	legislation	
	1322 (London NW4)	Canada	920 (London SE1)
Wales	342 (Cardiff)	United Kingdom	920 (London SE1)

Food, legislation (contd)		travel	1851(Newport, Isle of Wight)
United States of America	920(London SE1)	Francis Brett Young	154(Birmingham)
manufacture, economics	836(Lewes)	Francis Thompson	2015(Preston)
reform	1670(London W8)		771(Kidderminster)
science	93(Belfast)	Frank Brangwyn	1692(London E17)
	1886(Nottingham)	Frederic Ozanam	1612(London SW1)
standards		Free Churches	1161(London WC1)
Canada	920(London SE1)	history	787(Lancaster)
United Kingdom	920(London SE1)	Freemasonry, history	1643(London WC2)
United States of America	920(London SE1)	Freethought	1437(London SE1)
technology	168(Blackpool)		1500(London N1)
	200(Bradford)	French	
	1453(London SE1)	(See also French language and French literature. An index entry has been included under 'French' where this was not qualified in any way in the relevant entry)	
	2182(Sunderland)		
trades	430(Croydon)		141, 152(Birmingham)
values	323(Cambridge)		163(Blackburn)
Food and Agriculture Organization	1646(London W1)		330(Canterbury)
			403(Chorley)
Foot and mouth disease	2301(Woking)		427(Crewe)
Foot disabilities	512(Edinburgh)		449(Derby)
Foot disorders	1048(London NW8)		487(Durham)
Foot health	1602(London W1M 8BX)		498(Eastbourne)
education	512(Edinburgh)		574(Egham)
Forced labour	2038(Richmond)		576(Enfield)
Fore-edge paintings	2295(Windsor)		783(Lampeter)
Foreign affairs	1020(London WC1)		813(Leeds)
	1159(London SE1)		942(London WC1)
	2038(Richmond)		1167(London SW17)
Foreign aid	1466(London W1V 0JS)		1302(London SE11)
Foreign countries	1159(London SW1)		1451(London NW5)
Foreign exchange rates	1624(London EC2)		1495(London W1)
Foreign law	1210(London EC4)		1650(London NW1)
Foreign literature	2259(Wednesbury)		1665(London E1)
Foreign poetry	1477(London SW5)		1782(Manchester)
Foreign policy	1863(Northallerton)		1853(Newport, Isle of Wight)
	2038(Richmond)		1893(Nottingham)
Foreign relations	722(Hounslow)		1928, 1948(Oxford)
Foreign trade	1466(London W1V 0JS)		2145(Southampton)
	2143(Southampton)		2166(Stirling)
Forensic medicine	1191(London SE1)		2290(Winchester)
Fortification	903(London EC3)	French architecture	223(Brighton)
Fossils	2213(Tilbury)	French art	223(Brighton)
Fostercare	1059(London SE11)		2111(Sheffield)
	1405(London W1)	French criticism	529(Edinburgh)
Foxhunting	402(Chipping Norton)		788(Lancaster)
Fra Giarni	1933(Oxford)	French dramatists	1972(Oxford)
Fra Paolo Sarpi	1933(Oxford)	French glass paper weights	592(Farnham)
France	1947(Oxford)	French history	1210(London EC4)
art	1163(London SW7)		1219(London WC1)
history	1163(London SW7)	French humanists	1791(Manchester)
	1251(London W1N 3BH)	French language	154(Birmingham)
law	1851(Newport, Isle of Wight)		160(Bishop's Stortford)
	1309(London WC1)		201(Bradford)
life	1163(London SW7)		315(Cambridge)

755

French language (contd)	435 (Dagenham)	education	1165 (London SW15)
	485 (Durham)		1414 (London W1M 5RF)
	520 (Edinburgh)	Fry, Roger	288 (Cambridge)
	778 (Kingston upon Thames)	Funnels	1425 (London SE10)
		Furnishings	1340 (London E17)
	800, 812 (Leeds)		1748 (Manchester)
	1117 (London W5)	church	1093 (London EC2)
	1165 (London SW15)	soft	2055 (Rotherham)
	1307 (London WC1)	See also Volume I	
	1326 (London W5)	Furniture	197 (Bradford)
	1653 (London SE14)		450 (Derby)
	1686 (London NW3)		577 (Enfield)
	1839, 1846 (Newcastle upon Tyne)		724 (Hove)
			1039 (London WC1)
	2011 (Prescot)		1288 (London NW3)
	2020 (Reading)		1329 (London N1)
	2086 (Salford)		1340 (London E17)
	2144 (Southampton)		1524 (London SW7)
	2187 (Sunderland)		1688 (London WC2)
	2334 (York)		1713 (Loughborough)
French literature	154 (Birmingham)		1748, 1764 (Manchester)
	201 (Bradford)		2116 (Sheffield)
	315 (Cambridge)		2141 (Southampton)
	381 (Chorley)		2210 (Taunton)
	422 (Coventry)		2254 (Warwick)
	435 (Dagenham)	artistic	1340 (London E17)
	485 (Durham)	British	113 (Belfast)
	529 (Edinburgh)	design	129 (Birmingham)
	778 (Kingston upon Thames)		253 (Bromley)
		French	1673 (London WC1)
	788 (Lancaster)	Gillow	764 (Kendal)
	805 (Leeds)	Irish	113 (Belfast)
	1163 (London SW7)	sacred	2278 (Weymouth)
	1165 (London SW15)	Victorian	404 (Cirencester)
	1210 (London EC4)	See also Volume I	
	1653 (London SE14)	Furriery	1074 (London W1)
	1839, 1846 (Newcastle upon Tyne)	Further education	174 (Bolton)
			185 (Boreham Wood)
	1851 (Newport, Isle of Wight)		280 (Cambridge)
			555 (Edinburgh)
	1895 (Nottingham)		667 (Halifax)
	1911 (Oldham)		923 (London WC1)
	1918, 1946, 1965, 1972 (Oxford)		958 (London W1N 4AP)
			1060 (London SW1)
	2011 (Prescot)		1170 (London SW15)
	2100 (Scunthorpe)		1202 (London WC2)
	2279 (Weymouth)		1874 (Norwich)
French memoirs	831 (Leicester)		2070 (St Albans)
French Protestant history	1219 (London WC1)		2142 (Southampton)
French revolution	17 (Aberystwyth)		2198 (Sutton Coldfield)
	1902 (Nottingham)		2232 (Twickenham)
	2027 (Reading)		2318 (Worksop)
newspapers	71 (Bath)	disabled	974 (London WC1)
Freud	1267 (London W1)	East Midlands Region	1899 (Nottingham)
Friedrich Gundolph	1658 (London WC1)	South West England	239 (Bristol)
Frimley Sanatorium, history	1254 (London SW3)	Southern Region	2026 (Reading)
Froebel	1165 (London SW15)	F. W. Lanchester	421 (Coventry)

G

Gaelic	456 (Dingwall)
folksong	572 (Edinburgh)
folktale	572 (Edinburgh)
geneaology	751 (Inverness)
history	751 (Inverness)
language	751 (Inverness)
literature	513, 517, 572 (Edinburgh)
Gainsborough, local history	597 (Gainsborough)
Galsworthy, John	154 (Birmingham)
Gambia, Methodist missions	1376 (London NW1)
Games	87 (Bedford)
indoor	1328 (London SE10)
	1475 (London W1M 4AX)
	1935 (Oxford)
outdoor	1328 (London SE10)
	1475 (London W1M 4AX)
Garden City Movement	835 (Letchworth)
Gardening	802 (Leeds)
Gardner, Daniel	764 (Kendal)
Garibaldi's British Legion	943 (London EC2)
Gas industry, training	1171 (London SW1)
Gaskell	1768 (Manchester)
Gastro-intestinal tract, diseases	715 (High Wycombe)
Gateshead, local history	599 (Gateshead)
G. B. Shaw	1891 (Nottingham)
G. D. H. Cole	1326 (London W5)
	1932 (Oxford)
Genealogy	263 (Bury St Edmunds)
	522 (Edinburgh)
	1072, 1210, 1379 (London EC4)
	1598 (London W1V 0HS)
	1604 (London SW7)
	1760 (Manchester)
	1813 (Mold)
	1891 (Nottingham)
	1935 (Oxford)
	2004 (Portsmouth)
	2196 (Sutton)
Battersea	1069 (London SW12)
Channel Islands	653 (Guernsey)
Cheshire	1760 (Manchester)
Clapham	1069 (London SW12)
Cornwall	2221 (Truro)
Essex	372 (Chelmsford)
Gaelic	751 (Inverness)
Gloucestershire	635, 637 (Gloucester)
Guernsey	653 (Guernsey)
Lancashire	1760 (Manchester)
Lichfield	839 (Lichfield)
Manchester	1772 (Manchester)
Scotland	519, 549, 561 (Edinburgh)
	610 (Glasgow)
Staffordshire	639 (Lichfield)
Stratford-upon-Avon	2179 (Stratford-upon-Avon)
Truro	2221 (Truro)
Wales, West	690 (Haverfordwest)
Warwickshire	2179 (Stratford-upon-Avon)
Wiltshire	453 (Devizes)
General and Municipal Workers' Union	580 (Esher)
General election addresses	1423 (London SW1)
Genetic psychology	581 (Esher)
	1739 (Manchester)
Genetics	293 (Cambridge)
	455 (Didcot)
	522 (Edinburgh)
	681 (Harrow)
	1132, 1279 (London SW1)
	1367 (London NW7)
	1828 (Newbury)
	2067 (St Albans)
clinical	1362 (London WC1)
Genito-urinary system, diseases	443 (Dartford)
	715 (High Wycombe)
Genito-urinary tract, diseases	715 (High Wycombe)
Geographical statistics	2153 (Sowerby Bridge)
Geography	17 (Aberystwyth)
	35 (Aylesbury)
	58 (Barnstaple)
	75 (Bath)
	141, 142, 154, 157 (Birmingham)
	161 (Blackburn)
	195 (Bracknell)
	198, 201 (Bradford)
	212 (Bridgend)
	261 (Burton-on-Trent)
	270 (Camberley)
	303, 320 (Cambridge)
	329 (Canterbury)
	359 (Carshalton)
	390 (Chesterfield)
	403 (Chorley)
	411 (Coleraine)
	421 (Coventry)
	427 (Crewe)
	435 (Dagenham)
	438 (Darlington)
	446 (Deeside)
	449 (Derby)
	457 (Doncaster)
	470 (Dundee)
	485, 486, 487, 490, 492 (Durham)
	498 (Eastbourne)
	511, 520, 537, 539, 568 (Edinburgh)
	576 (Enfield)

Geography (contd)
587 (Exeter)
612 (Glasgow)
636 (Gloucester)
646 (Grays)
655 (Guildford)
667 (Halifax)
704 (Hereford)
726 (Huddersfield)
734 (Hull)
748 (Ilkeston)
750 (Ilkley)
754 (Ipswich)
762 (Keighley)
778 (Kingston upon Thames)
783 (Lampeter)
788 (Lancaster)
793 (Leamington Spa)
812, 813 (Leeds)
927 (London SW1)
942 (London WC1)
1110, 1165 (London SW15)
1167 (London SW17)
1197 (London NW4)
1244 (London SW7)
1302 (London SE11)
1331 (London N17)
1341 (London SW18)
1387 (London SW1)
1451 (London NW5)
1473 (London SW16)
1495 (London W1)
1498 (London SE8)
1538, 1578 (London SW7)
1586 (London EC3)
1615 (London N14)
1617 (London SW17)
1650 (London NW1)
1665 (London E1)
1676 (London SW18)
1719, 1722 (Luton)
1746, 1782 (Manchester)
1801 (Matlock)
1809 (Middlesbrough)
1823 (Neath)
1837, 1839, 1845, 1846 (Newcastle upon Tyne)
1853 (Newport, Isle of Wight)
1891, 1893, 1895 (Nottingham)
1918, 1928, 1946, 1948, 1971 (Oxford)
1990 (Peterborough)
1992 (Plymouth)
2002, 2003 (Portsmouth)
2011, 2012 (Prescot)
2014 (Preston)

Abyssinia
Africa
    European West
    North Central
    South
    South East
Algeria
America

    South
Arabia
Asia
    Central
    South East
Asia Minor
Australasia
Balkan States
Belgium
British
Bulgaria
Byzantine Empire
China
Commonwealth

Croydon
economic

Ethiopia
European

Faroe Islands
Germany

2020 (Reading)
2034 (Redruth)
2035 (Retford)
2043 (Ripon)
2086 (Salford)
2106 (Sheffield)
2124 (Shrewsbury)
2129 (Sleaford)
2144, 2145, 2146 (Southampton)
2173 (Stoke-on-Trent)
2187 (Sunderland)
2198 (Sutton Coldfield)
2205 (Tamworth)
2219 (Truro)
2232 (Twickenham)
2242 (Wallsend)
2290 (Winchester)
2300 (Wirral)
2305, 2307 (Wolverhampton)
2309 (Bletchley)
1749 (Manchester)
298 (Cambridge)
1329 (London N16)
1749 (Manchester)
1749 (Manchester)
1911 (Oldham)
1911 (Oldham)
1749 (Manchester)
1329 (London E1)
1786 (Manchester)
2219 (Truro)
2149 (Southend-on-Sea)
258 (Burnley)
1999 (Poole)
779 (Kingston upon Thames)
258 (Burnley)
2150 (Southport)
431 (Croydon)
2278 (Weymouth)
2278 (Weymouth)
1334 (London SE13)
2278 (Weymouth)
2278 (Weymouth)
2076 (St Helens)
1082 (Edinburgh)
1082 (London W8)
429 (Croydon)
1117 (London W5)
2259 (Wednesbury)
2321 (Worthing)
1749 (Manchester)
1341 (London SW18)
2196 (Sutton)
2278 (Weymouth)
2289 (Winchester)

758

Geography (contd)
  Great Britain   162 (Blackburn)
                    2292 (Winchester)
  Greece   2278 (Weymouth)
  Greek Islands   2278 (Weymouth)
  Herefordshire   706 (Hereford)
  historical   942 (London WC1)
                    2106 (Sheffield)
  human   330 (Canterbury)
                    490 (Durham)
                    522 (Edinburgh)
  Hungary   988 (London SW1)
  Iceland   2278 (Weymouth)
  Iran   2150 (Southport)
  Iraq   2150 (Southport)
  Isle of Man   462 (Douglas)
  Japan   2076 (St Helens)
  Kent, North West   429 (Croydon)
  Luxembourg   2278 (Weymouth)
  Morocco   1749 (Manchester)
  Near East   779 (Kingston upon Thames)
  Netherlands   2278 (Weymouth)
  physical   490 (Durham)
  Polar regions   1329 (London E9)
  regional   490 (Durham)
  River Thames   2040 (Richmond)
  Rumania   2278 (Weymouth)
  Russia   1591 (London SW9)
                    2219 (Truro)
  Scotland   2150 (Southport)
                    2161 (Stirling)
  Serbia   2278 (Weymouth)
  Siberia   779 (Kingston upon Thames)
  Surrey, North East   429 (Croydon)
  Switzerland   2278 (Weymouth)
  teaching   2106 (Sheffield)
  textbooks   647 (Great Yarmouth)
  Turkey   2278 (Weymouth)
  United States of America   431 (Croydon)
  Yugoslavia   2278 (Weymouth)
Geology   17 (Aberystwyth)
              58 (Barnstaple)
              435 (Dagenham)
              485 (Durham)
              568 (Edinburgh)
              630 (Glasgow)
              710 (Hertford)
              756 (Ipswich)
              860 (Liverpool)
              1586 (London EC3)
              1948 (Oxford)
              2163 (Stirling)
              2262 (Wells)
              2293 (Winchester)
  Alderney   22 (Alderney)
  Bradford   199 (Bradford)
  Buckinghamshire   37 (Aylesbury)
  Croydon   429 (Croydon)
  Cumberland   348 (Carlisle)
  Darent Valley   441 (Dartford)
  Dartford   441 (Dartford)
  Derbyshire, North   2113 (Sheffield)
  Dorset   460 (Dorchester)
  Essex   1470 (London E15)
  Hampshire   2293 (Winchester)
  Isle of Wight   2093 (Sandown)
  Kent, North West   429 (Croydon)
  King's Lynn   774 (King's Lynn)
  Lake District   348 (Carlisle)
  Lancashire   348 (Carlisle)
  Monmouthshire   1859 (Newport, Mon)
  Norfolk   1873 (Norwich)
  Nuneaton   1904 (Nuneaton)
  Stroud   2181 (Stroud)
  Surrey, North East   429 (Croydon)
  Sussex   2322 (Worthing)
  Wales   337 (Cardiff)
  Warwickshire   1904 (Nuneaton)
  Westmorland   348 (Carlisle)
  Winchester   2293 (Winchester)
  Yorkshire   2338 (York)
    South   2113 (Sheffield)
See also Volume I
Geophysics   295 (Cambridge)
Geo-politics   271 (Camberley)
George Bernard Shaw   1582 (London N8)
George Eliot   418 (Coventry)
              1903, 1904 (Nuneaton)
George Frederic Watts   662 (Guildford)
George Gissing   2237 (Wakefield)
George, Henry   1198 (London SW1)
George Howell   943 (London EC2)
George Jacob Holyoake   943 (London EC2)
              1745 (Manchester)
George MacDonald   4 (Aberdeen)
George Romney   764 (Kendal)
George Stephenson   391 (Chesterfield)
George Vancouver   2039 (Richmond)
Geriatrics   176 (Bolton)
              416 (Coulsdon)
              681 (Harrow)
              985 (London SW7)
              2223 (Tunbridge Wells)
German
  (*See also* German language and German literature. The index entry 'German' has been used where the term was not qualified in any way in the relevant entry)
              141, 152 (Birmingham)
              330 (Canterbury)
              427 (Crewe)
              574 (Egham)
              576 (Enfield)
              783 (Lancaster)
              813 (Leeds)

German (contd)	942(London WC1)		1339(London E2)
	1302(London SE11)		1653(London SE14)
	1451(London NW5)		1658(London WC1)
	1495(London W1)		1891, 1895(Nottingham)
	1650(London NW1)		1918, 1965, 1972(Oxford)
	1853(Newport, Isle of Wight)		1839(Newcastle upon Tyne)
			2011(Prescot)
	1928, 1948(Oxford)		2100(Scunthorpe)
	2145(Southampton)	German philology	1972(Oxford)
	2166(Stirling)	Germanic languages	847(Lincoln)
German architecture	223(Brighton)	Germanic literatures	847(Lincoln)
German art	223(Brighton)	Germanic philology	1956(Oxford)
	1177(London SW7)	Germany	1176(London SW1)
German books	1177(London SW7)		1947(Oxford)
German culture	1177(London SW7)	culture	1176(London SW1)
German dialect dictionaries	1658(London WC1)	geography	2289(Winchester)
German folklore	1177(London SW7)	history	436(Dagenham)
German history	1177(London SW7)		1251(London W1N 2BH)
	1665(London E1)		2289(Winchester)
	1972(Oxford)	law	1309(London WC1)
German Jewry, history	1251(London W1N 2BH)	life	1176(London SW1)
German language	154(Birmingham)	science	1176(London SW1)
	160(Bishop's Stortford)	topography	436(Dagenham)
	201(Bradford)	Ghana, Methodist missions	1376(London NW1)
	315(Cambridge)	Gifted children	1405(London W1)
	435(Dagenham)	Gillingham, local history	600(Gillingham)
	485(Durham)		2047(Rochester)
	520(Edinburgh)	Gillow furniture	764(Kendal)
	778(Kingston upon Thames)	Girl Guide movement	1178(London SW1)
	800(Leeds)	Girls	
	1117(London W5)	employment	1694(London SW3)
	1177(London SW7)	training	1694(London SW3)
	1307(London WC1)	Gissing, George	2237(Wakefield)
	1326(London W5)	Glaciology	295(Cambridge)
	1653(London SE14)	Gladstone	448(Deeside)
	1658(London WC1)	Glamorgan	
	1686(London NW3)	history	334(Cardiff)
	1839(Newcastle upon Tyne)	local history	2001(Port Talbot)
		Glandular systems	20(Accrington)
	1895(Nottingham)	diseases	162(Blackburn)
	1946, 1965(Oxford)	Glasgow	612(Glasgow)
	1989(Peterborough)	local history	603, 610, 630(Glasgow)
	2011(Prescot)	public transport	611(Glasgow)
	2020(Reading)	transport, history	611(Glasgow)
	2086(Salford)	Glass	465(Dudley)
	2144(Southampton)		577(Enfield)
	2187(Sunderland)		657(Guildford)
	2334(York)		724(Hove)
German literature	143(Birmingham)		1524(London SW7)
	201(Bradford)		1764(Manchester)
	315(Cambridge)		2112(Sheffield)
	422(Coventry)		2182, 2186(Sunderland)
	435(Dagenham)		2322(Worthing)
	485(Durham)	containers	2077(St Helens)
	778(Kingston upon Thames)	decorative	1007(London WC1)
	805(Leeds)	English	2199(Swansea)
	1177(London SW7)	making	465(Dudley)

Glass making (contd)
- history 2075(St Helens)
- painters 1007(London WC1)
- stained 657(Guildford)

See also Volume I

Glassware 113(Belfast)
377(Cheltenham)
1688(London WC2)
2213(Tilbury)

Glastonbury
- archaeology 633(Glastonbury)
- history 633(Glastonbury)
- local history 633(Glastonbury)

Glossaries (collections) 1347(London SE1)
1433(London WC2)

Gloucester
- archaeology 634(Gloucester)
- local history 634(Gloucester)

Gloucestershire
- genealogy 635, 637(Gloucester)
- local history 635, 636, 637(Gloucester)

Glucagon 1366(London SW7)
God 214(Bridgwater)
Goethe 1658(London WC1)
1972(Oxford)
Goitre 1051(London EC2)
Goldsmiths' work 1688(London WC2)
Gonadotrophins 715(High Wycombe)
Goole
- local history 639(Goole)
- photographs 639(Goole)

Gordon Highlanders, history 7(Aberdeen)
Gosforth, local history 1832(Newcastle upon Tyne)
Gospels 217(Bridgwater)
Government 140, 145(Birmingham)
201(Bradford)
370(Chelmsford)
390(Chesterfield)
409(Colchester)
423(Crawley)
438(Darlington)
761(Keighley)
763(Keith)
866(Liverpool)
947, 1195(London SW1)
1617(London SW17)
1711(Loughborough)
1853(Newport, Isle of Wight)
1990(Peterborough)
2086(Salford)
2144(Southampton)
2173(Stoke-on-Trent)
2198(Sutton Coldfield)
- administration 520(Edinburgh)
1418(London WC1)

America, Latin 409(Colchester)
America, North 409(Colchester)
British 1881(Norwich)
2173(Stoke-on-Trent)
Central 25(Alloa)
485(Durham)
2142(Southampton)
2289(Winchester)
2307(Wolverhampton)
economics 2014(Preston)
local *See* local government
publications 994(London WC2)
Russia 409(Colchester)
Scotland 546(Edinburgh)
Grace Darling 49(Banbury)
Grammar 1774(Manchester)
Grammars (collections) 1972(Oxford)
2187(Sunderland)
- classical 2124(Shrewsbury)
- English 16(Aberystwyth)
- Greek 186(Boston)
- Hebrew 186(Boston)
2124(Shrewsbury)
- Latin 186(Boston)
Gramophone record catalogues 651(Grimsby)
Gramophone Societies 1916(Orpington)
Grand Duchy of Luxembourg 1349(London SW1)
Grantham, local history 641, 643(Grantham)
Graphic art 591(Falmouth)
871(Liverpool)
1165(London SW15)
Graphic arts 1339(London E1)
1858(Newport, Mon)
Graphic design 33(Ashton-under-Lyne)
129(Birmingham)
168(Blackpool)
184(Boreham Wood)
189(Bournemouth)
220(Brighton)
253(Bromley)
349(Carlisle)
417(Coventry)
430(Croydon)
450(Derby)
469(Dundee)
676(Harrogate)
777(Kingston upon Thames)
824(Leicester)
1018(London SE5)
1039(London WC1)
1047(London SW3)
1566(London WC2)
1732(Maidstone)
1883(Norwich)
2024(Reading)

Graphic design (contd)	2055 (Rotherham)	Greek language	154 (Birmingham)
	2141 (Southampton)		301 (Cambridge)
	2207 (Taunton)		486 (Durham)
	2232 (Twickenham)		1250 (London WC1)
Graphics	585 (Exeter)		1965 (Oxford)
	805 (Leeds)	Greek literature	154 (Birmingham)
	1094 (London SW1)		186 (Boston)
	1808 (Middlesbrough)		301 (Cambridge)
	2116 (Sheffield)		486 (Durham)
	2174 (Stoke-on-Trent)		1250 (London WC1)
Great Britain	1035 (London SE1)		1338 (London SE22)
geography	162 (Blackburn)		1731 (Maidstone)
	2292 (Winchester)		1972 (Oxford)
history	1659 (London WC1)	Greek New Testament	711 (Hertford)
	2292 (Winchester)	Greek papyrology	1250 (London WC1)
illustrations	1035 (London SE1)	Greek philosophy	1250 (London WC1)
law	1379 (London EC4)	Green Howards	
maritime history	1425 (London SE10)	history	2041 (Richmond, Yorkshire)
photographs	1035 (London SE1)	uniform	2041 (Richmond, Yorkshire)
Universities	917 (London WC1)	Greenaway, Kate	1324 (London NW3)
Great North of Scotland		Greyhound racing	1417 (London W1)
Railway	8 (Aberdeen)	Grimsby, local history	651 (Grimsby)
Great Yarmouth, local		Group therapy	416 (Coulsdon)
history	647 (Great Yarmouth)		1218 (London SE11)
Greater London	1181, 1182 (London SE1)	Growth	399 (Chichester)
history	1181 (London SE1)	Guernsey	
topography	1181 (London SE1)	genealogy	653 (Guernsey)
Greater London Council	1181, 1182 (London SE1)	local history	653 (Guernsey)
Greece	408 (Colchester)	Guerilla warfare	2038 (Richmond)
	2051 (Rossendale)	Gundolph, Friedrich	1658 (London WC1)
geography	2278 (Weymouth)	Gunnersbury	
history	1539 (London W1)	history	1190 (London W3)
	2278 (Weymouth)	topography	1190 (London W3)
humanities	1539 (London W1)	Guyana, Methodist missions	1376 (London NW1)
literature	1539 (London W1)	Gymnastics	1475 (London W1M 4AX)
politics	1539 (London W1)	medical	797 (Leeds)
social sciences	1539 (London W1)		1475 (London W1M 4AX)
statistics	1539 (London W1)	Gynaecology	154 (Birmingham)
Greek			176 (Bolton)
(*See also* Greek language			399 (Chichester)
and Greek literature)			681 (Harrow)
	223 (Brighton)		1033 (London NW10)
	1293 (London WC1)		1279 (London SW1)
	1303 (London WC2)		1529 (London NW1)
	1451 (London NW5)		1817 (Morden)
	1650 (London NW1)		1911 (Oldham)
	1686 (London NW3)		2224 (Tunbridge Wells)
Greek antiquities	1250 (London WC1)		2240 (Wallasey)
Greek archaeology	316 (Cambridge)	Gypsies	1192 (London N3)
	1250 (London WC1)		1323 (London NW10)
Greek art	1250 (London WC1)	folklore	878 (Liverpool)
Greek epigraphy	1250 (London WC1)	literature	878 (Liverpool)
Greek grammars	186 (Boston)		
Greek history	1250 (London WC1)	**H**	
Greek Islands			
geography	2278 (Weymouth)	Habitation	2044 (Rochdale)
history	2278 (Weymouth)	Haematology	293, 304, 305 (Cambridge)

Haematology (contd)	344 (Cardiff)	Harrogate, local history	677 (Harrogate)
	681 (Harrow)	Hartlepool, local history	682 (Hartlepool)
	966 (London W12)	Haslingden, local history	2051 (Rossendale)
	1075, 1260 (London W1)	Hastings, local history	683, 684 (Hastings)
	1468 (London W2)	Havering, local history	2050 (Romford)
	1828 (Newbury)	Health	661 (Guildford)
Hagiography	1093 (London EC2)		1053 (London W4)
Hagiology	1022 (London SW1)		1633 (London SW1)
Hair, chemistry	2109 (Sheffield)		1704 (London SW16)
Hairdressing	33 (Ashton-under-Lyne)		2043 (Ripon)
	122 (Bilston)	economics	1455 (London W1)
	200 (Bradford)	education	374 (Chelmsford)
	255 (Bromsgrove)		612 (Glasgow)
	414 (Colwyn Bay)		1005 (London SE1)
	500 (Eastleigh)		1049 (London WC1)
	667 (Halifax)		1142 (London W1N 8BQ)
	721 (Hornchurch)		1165 (London SW15)
	785 (Lancaster)		1196 (London WC1)
	1053 (London W4)		1475 (London W1M 4AX)
	1074 (London W1)		1574 (London SW1)
	1719 (Luton)		1846 (Newcastle-upon-Tyne)
	1838 (Newcastle upon Tyne)		2107 (Sheffield)
	2003 (Portsmouth)	industrial	1233 (London SW1)
	2055 (Rotherham)	international	1106 (London SE1)
	2135 (Slough)	mental	393 (Chichester)
	2160 (Stevenage)	screening	715 (High Wycombe)
	2249 (Ware)	services	1471 (London WC1)
		administration	283 (Cambridge)
See also Volume I			1255 (London W1N 4AN)
Halesowen, local history	665 (Halesowen)		1938 (Oxford)
Halifax			
literature	666 (Halifax)	organization	1213 (London W1H 6AN)
local history	2153 (Sowerby Bridge)	planning	1213 (London W1H 6AN)
Hall, Edward	2286 (Wigan)	visiting	222 (Brighton)
Hallé concerts society,			435 (Dagenham)
history	1755 (Manchester)		461 (Dundee)
Hallé orchestra, history	1755 (Manchester)	visitors	951 (London SE1)
Hamilton, history	670 (Hamilton)		1994 (Plymouth)
Hamilton of Dalziel	1819 (Motherwell)	Hearing aids	759 (Iver)
Hampshire	2145 (Southampton)	Hearing disorders	1545 (London WC1)
archaeology	2293 (Winchester)	Hearing loss	759 (Iver)
geology	2293 (Winchester)	Heart diseases	1033 (London NW10)
history	2293 (Winchester)		1049 (London WC1)
local history	2002, 2009 (Portsmouth)		1633 (London SW1)
Hampstead, local history	1324 (London NW3)	Heating, hospitals	628 (Glasgow)
Handel	288 (Cambridge)	Hebraica	130 (Birmingham)
Handicapped children	699 (Hemel Hempstead)	Hebrew	107 (Belfast)
	1102, 1405 (London W1)		1303 (London WC2)
education	498 (Eastbourne)		1339 (London E1)
	1767 (Manchester)		1968 (Oxford)
welfare	1106 (London SE1)		2083 (Salford)
	1544 (London W1)	Biblical	711 (Hertford)
Handicrafts	470 (Dundee)	grammars	186 (Boston)
	560 (Edinburgh)		2124 (Shrewsbury)
	2290 (Winchester)	literature	186 (Boston)
Hardy, Thomas	459, 460 (Dorchester)		1383 (London WC1)
	1327 (London W3)	Helminthology	873 (Liverpool)
Haringey, local history	1331 (London N17)		2066 (St Albans)

763

Helminthology (contd)		Histochemistry	1260(London W1)
animal	2066(St Albans)	Histology	305(Cambridge)
fisheries	2066(St Albans)		1828(Newbury)
medical	2066(St Albans)	Histopathology	1260(London W1)
veterinary	2066(St Albans)		1468(London W2)
Henriques, Sir Basil	912(London E1)	Historic buildings	893(London W8)
Henry Beighton	1904(Nuneaton)	Historical bibliography	1315(London WC1)
Henry George	1198(London SW1)	Historical geography	942(London WC1)
Henry Irving	194(Bournemouth)	North Riding	1864(Northallerton)
Heraldry	92(Belfast)	Historical manuscripts	1204(London WC2)
	522(Edinburgh)	Historical Manuscripts	
	1072, 1210,	Commission	2020(Reading)
	1379(London EC4)	Histories	1819(Motherwell)
	1598(London W1V 0HS)	architectural	1093(London EC2)
	1935(Oxford)	business	1017(London EC4)
	2116(Sheffield)	Regimental	2161(Stirling)
	2141(Southampton)	See also individua	
	2161(Stirling)	Regiments	
	2196(Sutton)	History	17(Aberystwyth)
Herb cookery	1605(London W1)		35(Aylesbury)
Herbal medicine	186(Boston)		73, 75(Bath)
	2110(Sheffield)		95(Belfast)
Herbals	1472(London WC1)		132, 140, 141, 142, 152, 154,
	1605(London W1)		157(Birmingham)
Herbs	1605(London W1)		161(Blackburn)
Heredity	581(Esher)		195(Bracknell)
Hereford, local history	703(Hereford)		198, 201(Bradford)
Herefordshire			222(Brighton)
archaeology	706(Hereford)		235, 247(Bristol)
geography	706(Hereford)		261(Burton-on-Trent)
history	706(Hereford)		268(Caernarvon)
local history	705(Hereford)		270(Canterbury)
natural history	706(Hereford)		291, 301, 315(Cambridge)
Hertford, local history	708(Hertford)		325, 330(Canterbury)
Hertfordshire, local history	708(Hertford)		359(Carshalton)
	718(Hitchin)		390(Chesterfield)
	1722(Luton)		401(Chipping Norton)
	2068, 2069(St Albans)		403(Chorley)
	2246(Waltham Cross)		411(Coleraine)
Heywood, local history	712(Heywood)		417, 422(Coventry)
H. G. Wells	252(Bromley)		427(Crewe)
Hibernica	107(Belfast)		438(Darlington)
Higher education	280(Cambridge)		446, 448(Deeside)
	722(Hounslow)		449(Derby)
	923(London WC1)		457(Doncaster)
	958(London W1N 4AP)		470(Dundee)
	1102(London W1)		486, 487, 488, 492 (Durham)
	1202(London WC2)		498(Eastbourne)
	1593(London WC1)		522(Edinburgh)
	2011(Prescot)		576(Enfield)
Highland dress	2161(Stirling)		584, 587(Exeter)
Highland Light Infantry	613(Glasgow)		612(Glasgow)
Hilaire Belloc	413(Colwyn Bay)		633(Glastonbury)
Hill, Sir Rowland	771(Kidderminster)		636(Gloucester)
Hindi literature	2304(Wolverhampton)		641(Grantham)
Hindu biography	1935(Oxford)		653(Guernsey)
Hine, Reginald L.	718(Hitchin)		655(Guildford)

History (*contd*)
667 (Halifax)
700 (Henley-on-Thames)
704 (Hereford)
726 (Huddersfield)
734 (Hull)
754 (Ipswich)
773 (Kilmarnock)
783 (Lampeter)
788 (Lancaster)
793 (Leamington Spa)
812, 813 (Leeds)
837 (Lichfield)
844 (Lincoln)
866, 877 (Liverpool)
906 (London N7)
926, 927 (London SW1)
942 (London WC1)
953 (London W1)
994, 1062 (London WC2)
1110, 1165 (London SW15)
1167 (London SW17)
1203 (London SE11)
1215 (London SW1)
1293 (London WC1)
1302 (London SE11)
1305 (London SW1)
1334 (London SE13)
1336 (London SW19)
1336 (Morden)
1338 (London SE22)
1341 (London SW18)
1343 (London SW1)
1379 (London EC4)
1387, 1423 (London SW1)
1451 (London NW5)
1473 (London SW16)
1486 (London WC1)
1495 (London W1)
1498 (London SE8)
1585 (London EC4)
1598 (London W1V 0HS)
1615 (London N14)
1617 (London SW17)
1650 (London NW1)
1653 (London SE14)
1659, 1662 (London WC1)
1686 (London NW3)
1693 (London SW19)
1711 (Loughborough)
1722 (Luton)
1741, 1746, 1760, 1772, 1782 (Manchester)
1801 (Matlock)
1809 (Middlesbrough)
1811 (Mirfield)
1823 (Neath)
1837, 1839, 1845,

1846 (Newcastle upon Tyne)
1858 (Newport, Mon)
1882 (Norwich)
1891, 1893, 1895 (Nottingham)
1905 (Nuneaton)
1910, 1911 (Oldham)
1918, 1921, 1928, 1945, 1946, 1947, 1948, 1952, 1958, 1959, 1975 (Oxford)
2002, 2003 (Portsmouth)
2008 (Potters Bar)
2011, 2012 (Prescot)
2014 (Preston)
2020, 2027 (Reading)
2034 (Redruth)
2035 (Retford)
2043 (Ripon)
2065, 2068 (St Albans)
2079 (St Leonards-on-Sea)
2091 (Salisbury)
2099 (Scunthorpe)
2113, 2124 (Shrewsbury)
2127 (Skipton)
2129 (Sleaford)
2144, 2145, 2146 (Southampton)
2152 (Southwell)
2163, 2166 (Stirling)
2187 (Sunderland)
2198 (Sutton Coldfield)
2205 (Tamworth)
2215 (Totnes)
2232 (Twickenham)
2242 (Wallsend)
2252 (Warrington)
2261 (Wells)
2279 (Weymouth)
2290, 2291 (Winchester)
2295 (Windsor)
2305, 2307 (Wolverhampton)
2309 (Bletchley)
2312 (Worcester)
2321 (Worthing)
2333 (York)
1749 (Manchester)

Abyssinia 884 (London WC2)
advertisements
Africa 298 (Cambridge)
644 (Gravesend)
816 (Liverpool)
1273 (London EC4)
1329 (London N16)
1968 (Oxford)
Central 252 (Bromley)
European West 1749 (Manchester)
North Central 1749 (Manchester)

765

History, Africa (contd)			831 (Leicester)
South	252 (Bromley)		880 (Liverpool)
	1911 (Oldham)		942, 1039 (London WC1)
South East	1911 (Oldham)		1302 (London SE11)
agriculture	530 (Edinburgh)		1566 (London WC2)
	703, 705 (Hereford)		1686 (London NW3)
	1115, 1412 (London SW1)		1692 (London E17)
	1553 (London WC2)		1693 (London SW19)
	1960 (Oxford)		1713 (Loughborough)
	2022, 2028 (Reading)		1732 (Maidstone)
	2145 (Southampton)		1808 (Middlesbrough)
Bedfordshire South	1720 (Luton)		2116 (Sheffield)
implements	31 (Ashford)		2188 (Sunderland)
machinery	31 (Ashford)		2323 (Worthing)
Rutland	1907 (Oakham)	English	1093 (London EC2)
aircraft	2129 (Sleaford)	European	1652 (London W1H 0BE)
	2325 (Yeovil)	arts	1524 (London SW7)
naval	2325 (Yeovil)	Asia	1230 (London SE1)
aircraft carriers	2325 (Yeovil)		1968 (Oxford)
alcoholism	1595 (London SW17)		1909 (Poole)
Alderney	22 (Alderney)	Central	779 (Kingston upon Thames)
Algeria	1749 (Manchester)		1725 (Macclesfield)
America	17 (Aberystwyth)	South	300 (Cambridge)
	69 (Bath)	Asia Minor	2150 (Southport)
	154 (Birmingham)	A.T.S.	663 (Guildford)
	583 (Exeter)	Australasia	431 (Croydon)
	1329 (London E9)	Australia	866 (Liverpool)
	1786 (Manchester)		928 (London WC2)
	1953 (Oxford)	Austria	436 (Dagenham)
	2185 (Sunderland)		929 (London SW7)
	2219 (Truro)	authorship	1404 (London W1X 4BB)
drama	683 (Hastings)	aviation	121 (Biggleswade)
fiction	497 (Eastbourne)	Ayrshire	43 (Ayr)
Latin	1659 (London WC1)	Balkan States	2278 (Weymouth)
	299 (Cambridge)	ballet	1521 (London W14)
	409 (Colchester)	banking	1179 (London EC3)
literature	2021 (Reading)	banks	1243 (London EC3)
North	409 (Colchester)	Baptist Church	933, 935 (London WC1)
South	2149 (Southend-on-Sea)		1944 (Oxford)
anatomy	1532 (London NW1)	Baptist Union of Scotland	604 (Glasgow)
Anglican Church	1585 (London EC4)	Belgium	2278 (Weymouth)
Anglo-Jewish	1383 (London WC1)	Bible	119 (Bexley)
Anti-Semitism	2145 (Southampton)		612 (Glasgow)
Anti-vivisection	1394 (London W1)	bibliographies	286 (Cambridge)
Arabic	258 (Bromley)	bibliography	940 (London W1V 0NS)
	1285 (London NW8)	bicycles	121 (Biggleswade)
architecture	109 (Belfast)	Black Watch (R.H.R.)	1986 (Perth)
	326 (Canterbury)	book trade	994 (London WC2)
	2332 (York)	bookbinding	940 (London W1V 0NS)
art	129 (Birmingham)	bookcollecting	940 (London W1V 0NS)
	189 (Bournemouth)	bookselling	940 (London W1V 0NS)
	253 (Bromley)		1404 (London W1X 4BB)
	326 (Canterbury)	Borders	1850 (Newcastle upon Tyne)
	430 (Croydon)	botany	1472 (London WC1)
	731 (Hull)	Bradford	197 (Bradford)
	787 (Lancaster)	Breconshire	204 (Brecon)
	793 (Leamington Spa)	Bridgwater	213, 214 (Bridgwater)

History (contd)
  Bristol 232, 233 (Bristol)
  British 160 (Bishop's Stortford)
    1334 (London SE13)
    1882 (Norwich)
    armed forces 1560 (London SW1)
    art 1732 (Maidenhead)
    aviation 1515 (London NW9)
    theatre 1596 (London W2)
  broadcasting 961 (London W1A 1AA)
    1483 (London EC1)
  Buckinghamshire 37, 38 (Aylesbury)
  Bulgaria 311 (Cambridge)
    2278 (Weymouth)
  business 246 (Bristol)
    1017 (London EC4)
  Byzantine Empire 2278 (Weymouth)
  Cambridge 276 (Cambridge)
  Cambridgeshire 276 (Cambridge)
  Canada 866 (Liverpool)
  Cardiganshire 1 (Aberaeron)
  Carlisle 354 (Carlisle)
  Carmarthenshire 356 (Carmarthen)
  Celtic 2073 (St Andrews)
  ceramics 312 (Cambridge)
  charities 1044 (London SW1)
  chemistry 246 (Bristol)
    630, 631 (Glasgow)
  Cheshire 125 (Birkenhead)
    383, 385, 387, 389 (Chester)
    1760 (Manchester)
  chest medicine 1254 (London SW3)
  chest surgery 1254 (London SW3)
  Chester 385, 387, 389 (Chester)
  Chester Regiment 384 (Chester)
  Chichester 395 (Chichester)
  childhood 526 (Edinburgh)
  Chile 894 (London W1)
  china 2076 (St Helens)
  China 581 (Esher)
    1968 (Oxford)
    2038 (Richmond)
  chiropody 1048 (London NW8)
    1602 (London W1M 8BX)
  Christianity 1571 (London SE5)
    1927 (Oxford)
  Church 95 (Belfast)
    119 (Bexley)
    309 (Cambridge)
    394, 397 (Chichester)
    401 (Chipping Norton)
    424 (Crawley)
    517, 545, 569 (Edinburgh)
    584 (Exeter)
    627 (Glasgow)
    1022 (London)
    1585 (London EC4)
    1647 (London SW1)
    1914 (Ormskirk)
    1942 (Oxford)
    2042 (Ripon)
    2065 (St Albans)
    2073 (St Andrews)
    2143 (Southampton)
    2200 (Swansea)
    2261, 2262 (Wells)
    2274 (Weston-super-Mare)
  Church in Wales 357 (Carmarthen)
    1979 (Penarth)
  cinema 984 (London W1)
  Cistercians 830 (Leicester)
  City of London 1188 (London EC2)
  Civil Service 1272 (London WC2)
  Clifton College 235 (Bristol)
  clothing 1074 (London W1)
  Co Durham 2184 (Sunderland)
  Colchester 407, 408 (Colchester)
  College of S Mark &
    S John 1077 (London SW10)
  Colonial 1659 (London WC1)
  commercial fishing 1425 (London SE10)
  Commonwealth 866 (Liverpool)
    1082 (Edinburgh)
    1082 (London W8)
    1953 (Oxford)
  companies 1253 (London SW1)
  Confederate 833 (Leigh-on-Sea)
  Congregationalism,
    Scotland 545 (Edinburgh)
  cookery 813 (Leeds)
  co-operative 1745 (Manchester)
    retail societies 1711 (Loughborough)
  Cornwall 1115 (London SW1)
  costume 142 (Birmingham)
    378 (Cheltenham)
    1750 (Manchester)
  country 1210 (London EC4)
  County Armagh 29 (Armagh)
  cricket law 768 (Kenley)
  criminology 313 (Cambridge)
  Croydon 429 (Croydon)
  Cumberland 351, 354 (Carlisle)
  Czechoslovakia 311 (Cambridge)
    436 (Dagenham)
    1251 (London W1N 2BH)
  Darent Valley 441 (Dartford)
  Dartford 441, 443 (Dartford)
  dentistry 474 (Dundee)
    978 (London W1M 8AL)
  Derbyshire 1800 (Matlock)
    North 2113 (Sheffield)
  design 326 (Canterbury)
    1553 (London WC2)
    1808 (Middlesbrough)

History (contd)
   Devon   583 (Exeter)
                                            1115 (London SW1)
   Dissenting   1663 (London NW3)
                                            1789 (Manchester)
   district nursing,
     Liverpool   881 (Liverpool)
   domestic   1172 (London E2)
     management   813 (Leeds)
     Rutland   1907 (Oakham)
   Dorset   459 (Dorchester)
   drawing   253 (Bromley)
   drawings   312 (Cambridge)
   drug dependence   1595 (London SW17)
   Dumfries   466 (Dumfries)
   Dundee   472 (Dundee)
   Ealing   1190 (London W3)
   East Europe   1668 (London WC1)
                                            2038 (Richmond)
   East India Company   1230 (London SE1)
   East Lancashire Regiment 2251 (Warrington)
   Eccles   1747 (Manchester)
   ecclesiastical   492 (Durham)
                                            569 (Edinburgh)
                                           702 (Hereford)
                                        1114 (London WC1)
                                        1210 (London EC4)
                                        1303 (London WC2)
                                        1306 (London SE1)
                                        1945, 1946 (Oxford)
   Celtic   2222 (Truro)
   economic   19 (Abingdon)
                                        142, 154 (Birmingham)
                                        328, 330 (Canterbury)
                                        587 (Exeter)
                                        606 (Glasgow)
                                        671 (Harlech)
                                        726 (Huddersfield)
                                        748 (Ilkeston)
                                        762 (Keighley)
                                        994 (London WC2)
                                        1064 (London EC2)
                                        1302 (London SE11)
                                        1495 (London W1)
                                        1662 (London WC1)
                                        1711 (Loughborough)
                                        1808 (Middlesbrough)
                                        1917 (Oswestry)
                                        1990 (Peterborough)
                                        2024 (Reading)
                                        2143 (Southampton)
                                        2171 (Stoke-on-Trent)
                                        2259 (Wednesbury)
                                        2307 (Wolverhampton)
                                        2321 (Worthing)
                                        2333 (York)
   education   75 (Bath)
                                           491 (Durham)
                                           636 (Gloucester)
                                         778 (Kingston upon Thames)
                                         818 (Leeds)
                                         823 (Leicester)
                                        1165 (London SW15)
                                        1473 (London SW16)
                                        1616 (London SW19)
                                        1662 (London WC1)
                                        1767 (Manchester)
                                        1954 (Oxford)
                                        2011 (Prescot)
                                        2138 (Southampton)
                                        2187 (Sunderland)
                                        2204 (Swindon)
                                        2228 (Twickenham)
                                        2257 (Watford)
                                        2272 (West Wickham)
                                        2279 (Weymouth)
                                        2290 (Winchester)
                                        2305 (Wolverhampton)
   English   1077 (London SW10)
     women   1019 (London NW5)
     Elizabethan   1354 (London SE19)
     engineers   246 (Bristol)
   England   71 (Bath)
                                         492 (Durham)
                                         831 (Leicester)
                                        1210 (London EC4)
                                        1750 (Manchester)
                                        1869 (Northampton)
                                        1946 (Oxford)
                                        2155 (Stafford)
     medieval   90 (Bedford)
     North West   1741 (Manchester)
     English countryside   2028 (Reading)
     English Dissent   1927 (Oxford)
     English drama   683 (Hastings)
     English fiction   497 (Eastbourne)
     English law   1581 (London E1)
     English literature   2021 (Reading)
     English novel   1748 (Manchester)
     English theatre   2179 (Stratford-upon-Avon)
     engravings   312 (Cambridge)
     Essex   372 (Chelmsford)
                                         407, 408 (Colchester)
                                        1470 (London E15)
     South East   2148 (Southend-on-Sea)
     Ethiopia   1749 (Manchester)
     Europe   445 (Darwen)
                                         492 (Durham)
                                        1251 (London W1N 2BH)
                                        1341 (London SW18)
                                        1659 (London WC1)
                                        1855 (Newport, Mon)
                                        1946 (Oxford)
                                        2196 (Sutton)

History, Europe (contd)	2337 (York)	Iceland	1220 (London SW1)
painting	1047 (London SW3)		2278 (Weymouth)
sculpture	1047 (London SW3)	illuminated manuscripts	312 (Cambridge)
evangelical movement	1135 (London WC1)	Imperial	1303 (London WC2)
family	1935 (Oxford)		1659 (London WC1)
Faroe Islands	2278 (Weymouth)	India	866 (Liverpool)
Fascism	1251 (London W1N 2BH)		1230 (London SE1)
fashion	2141 (Southampton)		1872 (Northwich)
Fenland	1796 (March)		1968 (Oxford)
fiction	451 (Derby)	South	1592 (London NW1)
fine arts	312 (Cambridge)	industry	667 (Halifax)
fishing industry	649 (Grimsby)		1711 (Loughborough)
Fleet Air Arm	2325 (Yeovil)		2259 (Wednesbury)
Flintshire	447 (Deeside)	Bedfordshire, South	1720 (Luton)
France	1163 (London SW7)	iron	705 (Hereford)
	1210 (London EC4)	mines	2102 (Settle)
	1219 (London WC1)	Ulster	113 (Belfast)
	1251 (London W1N 2BH)	international	994 (London WC2)
	1851 (Newport, Isle of Wight)	Iran	2150 (Southport)
		Iraq	2150 (Southport)
	1946 (Oxford)	Ireland	92, 113 (Belfast)
literature	1911 (Oldham)		866 (Liverpool)
Free Church	787 (Lancaster)		1288 (London NW3)
Freemasonry	1643 (London WC2)	Islamic	1285 (London NW8)
Frimley Sanatorium	1254 (London SW3)	Isle of Man	462 (Douglas)
Gaelic	751 (Inverness)	Isle of Wight	2093 (Sandown)
geography	2106 (Sheffield)	Italy	1251 (London W1N 2BH)
Germany	436 (Dagenham)	Japan	581 (Esher)
	1177 (London SW7)		1289 (London W1X 9LB)
	1665 (London E1)		1968 (Oxford)
	1972 (Oxford)		2076 (St Helens)
Glamorgan	334 (Cardiff)	Jewish	912, 1339 (London E1)
glassmaking	2075 (St Helens)		1383 (London WC1)
Glastonbury	633 (Glastonbury)		2184 (Sunderland)
Great Britain	1659 (London WC1)	Jews	2139 (Southampton)
	2292 (Winchester)	Commonwealth	1291 (London W1)
Greater London	1181 (London SE1)	judo	992 (London W1)
Greece	1539 (London W1)	Kent	1731, 1732, 1733 (Maidstone)
	2278 (Weymouth)	North West	429 (Croydon)
Greek	1250 (London WC1)	King's Lynn	774 (King's Lynn)
Greek Islands	2278 (Weymouth)	King's Own Royal	
Green Howards	2041 (Richmond, Yorkshire)	Lancaster Regiment	784 (Lancaster)
Guernsey	1251 (London W1N 2BH)	K.O.S.B.	116 (Berwick-upon-Tweed)
	2289 (Winchester)		
Gunnersbury	1190 (London W3)	labour	422 (Coventry)
Hallé Concerts Society	1755 (Manchester)		739 (Hull)
Hallé Orchestra	1755 (Manchester)		943 (London EC2)
Hamilton	670 (Hamilton)		1355 (London EC1)
Herefordshire	706 (Hereford)	Lancashire	125 (Birkenhead)
horology	1187 (London EC2)		1744, 1760, 1761 (Manchester)
horticulture	1412 (London SW1)		
Hounslow	1190 (London W3)	North	351 (Carlisle)
Household Cavalry	2296 (Windsor)	language	1474 (London WC1)
Humberside, South	2099 (Scunthorpe)	law	131 (Birmingham)
Hungary	436 (Dagenham)		493 (Durham)
	988 (London SW1)		1210 (London EC4)
Huyton-with-Roby	865 (Liverpool)	leather use	1391 (London SE1)

769

History (contd)
 Leeds 811(Leeds)
 libraries 15(Aberystwyth)
 Lichfield 837, 839(Lichfield)
 Life Guards 2296(Windsor)
 Lincolnshire 651(Grimsby)
   850(Lincoln)
  North 2099(Scunthorpe)
 linen industry, Ulster 113(Belfast)
 liquorice growing
  industry 1997(Pontefract)
 literature 847(Lincoln)
   1731(Maidstone)
   2150(Southport)
  English 612(Glasgow)
  Italian 1322(London NW4)
  Portuguese 1322(London NW4)
  Rumanian 1322(London NW4)
  Spanish 1322(London NW4)
 local *See* Local history and subdivisions
 London 828(Leicester)
   943, 1089 (London EC2)
   1181(London SE1)
   1184(London SW1)
 Luxembourg 2278(Weymouth)
 Manchester 1771(Manchester)
 maritime 1425(London SE10)
 mathematics 246(Bristol)
 medicine 13(Aberdeen)
   108(Belfast)
   245, 246(Bristol)
   474(Dundee)
   531, 533, 534, 536, 568(Edinburgh)
   630(Glasgow)
   755(Ipswich)
   870(Liverpool)
   978(London W1M 8AL)
   1043(London WC2)
   1254(London SW3)
   1342(London E1)
   1531(London NW1)
   1563(London EC1)
   1631(London WC1)
   1678(London NW1)
   1684(London SE6)
   1791(Manchester)
   1850(Newcastle upon Tyne)
   1943(Oxford)
   2006(Portsmouth)
   2025, 2027(Reading)
   2122(Shrewsbury)
   2172(Stoke-on-Trent)
   2252(Warrington)
   90(Bedford)
 medieval 493(Durham)

   1924(Oxford)
Merchant Navy 1580(London SW17)
merchant shipping 1425(London SE10)
Methodism 95(Belfast)
   247(Bristol)
   696(Helston)
   1375, 1376(London SW1)
   1756(Manchester)
   1974(Oxford)
Methodist Church 1375, 1376(London SW1)
Middle East 1251(London W1N 2BH)
   2139(Southampton)
Middlesex 1184(London SW1)
 West 1190(London W3)
military 24(Aldershot)
   71(Bath)
   81(Beaconsfield)
   270, 271(Camberley)
   802(Leeds)
   856(Lisburn)
   903(London EC3)
   906(London N7)
   1303(London WC2)
   1560(London SW1)
   1659(London WC1)
   1688(London W9)
   2129(Sleaford)
   2185(Sunderland)
 British 724(Hove)
mining industry 1843(Newcastle upon Tyne)
missions 1058(London SE1)
monastic 424(Crawley)
Monmouthshire 1859(Newport, Mon)
Morocco 1749(Manchester)
motor cycles 121(Biggleswade)
motor transport 121(Biggleswade)
   250(Brockenhurst)
mountaineering 889(London W1)
music 724(Hove)
   802(Leeds)
   866(Liverpool)
   972(London W1)
 Cambridge 317(Cambridge)
 printing 27(Amersham)
Muslim 1285(London NW8)
National Union of
 Seamen 1442(London SW4)
National Union of
 Vehicle Builders 1776(Manchester)
natural *See* Natural history
nautical sciences 736(Hull)
naval 71(Bath)
   444(Dartford)
   583(Exeter)
   802(Leeds)
   1425(London SE10)
   1659(London WC1)

History, naval (contd)	1688 (London W9)	Presbyterian Church of	
	1996 (Plymouth)	England	1487, 1488 (London WC1)
	2004, 2007 (Portsmouth)	printing	871 (Liverpool)
	2165 (Stirling)		940 (London W1V 0NS)
Navy	366 (Chatham)		1491 (London EC4)
Near East	779 (Kingston upon Thames)	prisons	2236 (Wakefield)
needle-making	2032 (Redditch)	probation officers	1399 (London WC1)
Netherlands	2278 (Weymouth)	Protestant	1219 (London WC1)
neurology	1261 (London WC1)	psychiatry	1266 (London SE5)
New Church	1173 (London WC1)	publishing	940 (London W1V 0NS)
Nonconformist	1114 (London WC1)		1404 (London W1X 4BB)
Norfolk	1873 (Norwich)	Puritan	1663 (London NW3)
Norway	782 (Kirkwall)	Q.M.A.A.C.	663 (Guildford)
	2073 (St Andrews)	Quakers	1164, 1502 (London NW1)
Nottingham and Derbyshire Regiment	1900 (Nottingham)	Queen's Own Cameron Highlanders	752 (Inverness)
Nottinghamshire	1896, 1901 (Nottingham)	Queen's Own Highlanders (Seaforth and	
numismatics	312 (Cambridge)	Camerons)	752 (Inverness)
Nuneaton	1904 (Nuneaton)	Queen's Own Royal West	
nursing	533 (Edinburgh)	Kent Regiment	1733 (Maidstone)
	1528 (London W1M 0AB)	railways	391 (Chesterfield)
Order of Friar-Servites	1933 (Oxford)		439 (Darlington)
organizations	700 (Henley-on-Thames)		2328 (York)
painting	253 (Bromley)	Ireland	94 (Belfast)
	312 (Cambridge)	London	1390 (London SW4)
	1866 (Northampton)	recreation	1328 (London SE10)
paintings	1614 (London SE5)	recusant	401 (Chipping Norton)
Palestine	595 (Folkestone)		730 (Hull)
Papal	493 (Durham)	Reform Club	1501 (London SW1)
pathology	1075 (London W1)	Regimental	24 (Aldershot)
Pendlebury	1747 (Manchester)		1560 (London SW1)
Persia	1968 (Oxford)	*See also* individual	
pharmacy	531 (Edinburgh)	Regiments	
	1472 (London WC1)	religion	2218 (Truro)
philosophy	212 (Bridgend)	research	2331 (York)
photographs	1550 (London W1)	road transport, London	1390 (London SW4)
photography	1550 (London W1)	Rochford Hundred	2148 (Southend-on-Sea)
physical education	154 (Birmingham)	Roman	1250 (London WC1)
	797 (Leeds)	Roman Catholic	612 (Glasgow)
Poland	311 (Cambridge)		1025 (London W1)
	436 (Dagenham)	Romani communities	1192 (London N3)
	1479 (London SW1)	Rotherham	2053 (Rotherham)
	1479, 1480 (London SW7)	rowing	890 (London W1)
Polar Regions	1329 (London E9)	Royal Academy	1511 (London W1V 0DS)
police	1377 (London SW1)	Royal Air Force	24 (Aldershot)
political	748 (Ilkeston)		1515 (London NW9)
	761 (Keighley)		2129 (Sleaford)
	994 (London WC2)	Royal Artillery	1517 (London SE18)
England	1506 (London SW9)	Royal Dragoons	2296 (Windsor)
Portugal	2285 (Wigan)	Royal Flying Corps	1515 (London NW9)
Post Office	1642 (London SW4)	Royal Highland Fusiliers	613 (Glasgow)
trades union	1642 (London SW4)	Royal Horse Guards	2296 (Windsor)
postal	1331 (London N17)	Royal Irish Fusiliers	30 (Armagh)
	1431, 1483 (London EC1)	Royal Lincolnshire	
Presbyterian	105 (Belfast)	Regiment	853 (Lincoln)
	1487, 1488 (London WC1)	Royal Naval Air Service	1515 (London NW9)

History, Royal Naval Air Service *(contd)*	2325 (Yeovil)	Sherwood Foresters	1900 (Nottingham)
		Shropshire	2113 (Shrewsbury)
Royal Naval Lifeboat Institution	1546 (London SW1)	Siberia	779 (Kingston upon Thames)
Royal Navy	24 (Aldershot)		1725 (Macclesfield)
Royal Norfolk Regiment	1884 (Norwich)	Slavonic	1668 (London WC1)
Royal Philharmonic Society	1549 (London SW7)	social	1972 (Oxford)
			154 (Birmingham)
Royal Pioneer Corps	1870 (Northampton)		748 (Ilkeston)
Royal Society for the Prevention of Cruelty to Animals	1552 (London SW1)		761 (Keighley)
			872 (Liverpool)
			994, 1566 (London WC2)
Royal Society of Arts	1553 (London WC2)		1700 (London NW1)
Royal Sussex Regiment	398 (Chichester)		1808 (Middlesbrough)
Rumania	2278 (Weymouth)		1917 (Oswestry)
Russia	167 (Blackpool)		2259 (Wednesbury)
	311 (Cambridge)	England	1506 (London SW9)
	409 (Colchester)	Scotland	596 (Forfar)
	1340 (London E17)	social science	2122 (Shrewsbury)
	1591 (London SW9)	socialist movements	994 (London WC2)
	2219 (Truro)	Society of St Vincent de Paul	1612 (London SW1)
sailing	1425 (London SE10)		
St David's University College	783 (Lampeter)	sociology	726 (Huddersfield)
		Somerset	633 (Glastonbury)
Salford	2084 (Salford)	South Lancashire Regiment	2251 (Warrington)
Salvation Army	1571 (London SE5)		
Scandinavia	262 (Bury)	Soviet	1591 (London SW9)
science	13 (Aberdeen)	Spain	1972 (Oxford)
	227 (Brighton)		2285 (Wigan)
	322 (Cambridge)	Staffordshire	2206 (Tamworth)
	568 (Edinburgh)		2244 (Walsall)
	631 (Glasgow)	Staffordshire Regiment	841 (Lichfield)
	951 (London SE1)	Suffolk Regiment	264 (Bury St Edmunds)
	1543 (London W1)	Sunderland	2184 (Sunderland)
	1553 (London WC2)	surgery	1532 (London NW1)
	1578 (London SW7)		1533 (London WC2)
	1651 (London SW3)	Surrey	656 (Guildford)
	1698 (London SE18)	North East	429 (Croydon)
	1741 (Manchester)	West	656 (Guildford)
	1966 (Oxford)	Sussex	2322 (Worthing)
	2073 (St Andrews)	West	395 (Chichester)
	2143 (Southampton)	swimming	891 (London EC4)
	2187 (Sunderland)	Swinton	1747 (Manchester)
scientific instruments	322 (Cambridge)	Switzerland	2278 (Weymouth)
	1966 (Oxford)	teaching methods	464 (Dudley)
Scotland	21 (Airdrie)		1203 (London SE4)
	530, 561 (Edinburgh)	technology	20 (Accrington)
	603, 610, 612 (Glasgow)		1187 (London EC4)
	866 (Liverpool)		1578 (London SW7)
	2150 (Southport)		1698 (London SE18)
	2161, 2164 (Stirling)		1741 (Manchester)
North East	13 (Aberdeen)	telecommunications	1483 (London EC1)
sculpture	253 (Bromley)	temperance movement	1644 (London SW1)
	312 (Cambridge)		1704 (London SW16)
Seaforth Highlanders	752 (Inverness)		2105 (Sheffield)
Serbia	2278 (Weymouth)	Teutonic literature	443 (Dartford)
Servites	1933 (Oxford)	textbooks	647 (Great Yarmouth)

History, textbooks (*contd*)	1203(London SE11)	York and Lancaster	
textiles	312(Cambridge)	Regiment	2120(Sheffield)
theatre	194(Bournemouth)	Yorkshire	2329(York)
	968(London W1Y 4MA)	South	2113(Sheffield)
	981(London W1P 6AE)	Young Men's Christian	
	1688(London WC2)	Association	61(Barry)
British	1011(London W14)	Yugoslavia	311(Cambridge)
trade unionism	943(London EC2)		2278(Weymouth)
	1737(Manchester)	Hitchin, local history	718(Hitchin)
transport	831(Leicester)	H.M.S. Victory	2007(Portsmouth)
Ireland	94(Belfast)	Hobbies	2205(Tamworth)
transport technology	611(Glasgow)	Hockey	343(Cardiff)
tuberculosis	1254(London SW3)		1205(London W1)
Tunbridge Wells	2225(Tunbridge Wells)	Holborn, local history	1325(London WC1)
Turkey	1968(Oxford)	Holidays	1168(London W1A 3AU)
	2278(Weymouth)	Scotland	559(Edinburgh)
Ulster	113(Belfast)	Holland	1650(London NW1)
Unitarian	1789, 1790(Manchester)	art	2111(Sheffield)
United Kingdom	866(Liverpool)	books	847(Lincoln)
United States of America	69(Bath)	dictionaries	1658(London WC1)
	431(Croydon)	history	2278(Weymouth)
	866(Liverpool)	language	315(Cambridge)
	950(London W1)		2086(Salford)
	1659(London WC1)	literature	315(Cambridge)
	1791(Manchester)		1658(London WC1)
	1882(Norwich)	Holtby, Winifred	218(Bridlington)
University of Cambridge	321(Cambridge)		733(Hull)
U.S.S.R.	1251(London W1N 2BH)	Holy See	900(London SW19)
	2038(Richmond)	Holyoake, George Jacob	943(London EC2)
W.A.A.C.	663(Guildford)		1745(Manchester)
Wales	51, 54(Bangor)	Home care	2218(Truro)
	866(Liverpool)	aged	2218(Truro)
North	385, 387, 389(Chester)	children	2218(Truro)
wars	195(Bracknell)	infirm	2218(Truro)
Warwickshire	1904(Nuneaton)	sick	2218(Truro)
	2178(Stratford-upon-Avon)	Home economics	70(Bath)
			185(Boreham Wood)
	2206(Tamworth)		427(Crewe)
weighing	128(Birmingham)		467(Dumfries)
West Indies	1683(London WC2)		470(Dundee)
Westminster Abbey	1687(London SW1)		750(Ilkley)
Westmorland	351, 354(Carlisle)		805, 812(Leeds)
Whitehall	1199(London SW1)		836(Lewes)
Wiltshire	453(Devizes)		937(London SW4)
Wiltshire Regiment	454(Devizes)		1071(London N17)
Women personalities	1696(London WC1)		1110(London SW15)
Women's Royal Army			1450(London N7)
Corps	663(Guildford)		1584(London W1M 6DE)
Worcestershire Regiment	2315(Worcester)		1772(Manchester)
Worksop	2319(Worksop)		1845 (Newcastle upon Tyne)
World War II	581(Esher)		2024(Reading)
	1199(London SW1)		2121(Shrewsbury)
World Wars	2289(Winchester)		2135(Slough)
Worsley	1747(Manchester)		2182(Sunderland)
Worthing	2322(Worthing)	Home nursing	616(Glasgow)
W.R.A.C.	663(Guildford)	Home safety	1508(London SW1)
Y.M.C.A.	61(Barry)	Homecrafts	419(Coventry)

Homecrafts (*contd*)	560(Edinburgh)		550(Edinburgh)
See also Housecraft, Household arts			628(Glasgow)
			2147(Southampton)
Homiletics	95(Belfast)	electrical services	628(Glasgow)
	517, 569(Edinburgh)	equipment	1213(London W1H 6AN)
	2042(Ripon)	heating	628(Glasgow)
Jewish	1292(London W1)	libraries	550(Edinburgh)
Homoeopathic medicine	986(London W1N 1RJ)	management	6(Aberdeen)
Homoeopathy	986(London W1N 1RJ)		134(Birmingham)
	1605(London W1)		632(Glasgow)
Homosexual behaviour, law	1207(London W1V 8EP)		2147(Southampton)
Homosexuality	888(London W1V 8EP)		2172(Stoke-on-Trent)
	1207(London W1V 8EP)	mental	119(Bexley)
Honduras, Methodist missions	1376(London NW1)	Northern Ireland	103(Belfast)
		organization	1213(London W1H 6AN)
Hong Kong	1208(London SW1)		1255(London W1N 4AN)
Methodist missions	1376(London NW1)	pharmacies	
Hop production	31(Ashford, Kent)	design	1185(London WC1)
Horace Plunkett	1476(London WC1)	equipment	1185(London WC1)
Hormones	495(Eastbourne)	planning	1185(London WC1)
	2268(Warmsley)	physics	1214(London SW1)
Horology, historical	1187(London EC2)	piped services	628(Glasgow)
Horse-drawn carriages	1733(Maidstone)	planning	533, 550(Edinburgh)
Horse racing	1212(London EC4)		632(Glasgow)
Horses	767(Kenilworth)		1213(London W1H 6AN)
Horticulture	437(Dagenham)	Scotland	553(Edinburgh)
	1412(London SW1)	services	681(Harrow)
	1886(Nottingham)		2137(Southall)
	2306(Wolverhampton)	administration	2117(Sheffield)
economics	1412(London SW1)	Scotland	473(Dundee)
history	1412(London SW1)	ventilation	628(Glasgow)
marketing	1412(London SW1)	waste disposal	628(Glasgow)
policies	1412(London SW1)	Hotels	2034(Redruth)
politics	1412(London SW1)	management	168(Blackpool)
Scotland	553(Edinburgh)		191(Bournemouth)
See also Volume I			414(Colwyn Bay)
Hosiery industry	747(Ilkeston)		661(Guildford)
Hospitals	134(Birmingham)		1117(London W5)
	762(Keighley)		1197(London NW4)
	1106(London SE1)		2003(Portsmouth)
	1213(London W1H 6AN)	See also Volume I	
	1236(London W1P 3LD)	Hounslow	
	1851(Newport, Isle of Wight)	history	1190(London W3)
		topography	1190(London W3)
	1938(Oxford)	Housecraft	32(Ashington)
administration	6(Aberdeen)		2101(Sleaford)
	243, 245(Bristol)	See also Homecrafts, Household arts	
	533, 550(Edinburgh)	Household arts	2203(Swindon)
	868(Liverpool)	Household Cavalry, history	2296(Windsor)
	1065(London SW1)	Household management	93(Belfast)
	1255(London W1N 4AN)	Household utilities	836(Lewes)
	1335(London SE13)	Housekeeping	836(Lewes)
air conditioning	628(Glasgow)	Housewives, welfare	987(London E1)
architects' plans	550(Edinburgh)	Housing	975, 1217, 1381 (London SW1)
catering advisory service	1213(London W1H 6AN)		
contributory schemes	858(Liverpool)		2023(Reading)
design	98(Belfast)	design	1381(London SW1)

Housing (contd)			792 (Leamington Spa)
economics	1381 (London SW1)		813 (Leeds)
Russia	1591 (London SW9)		826 (Leicester)
Hove			866, 872, 878 (Liverpool)
local history	724 (Hove)		926 (London SW1)
natural history	223 (Brighton)		951 (London SE1)
Howell, George	943 (London EC2)		970, 996, 1114 (London WC1)
Hoylake, local history	2299 (Wirral)		
Huddersfield, local history	727 (Huddersfield)		1323 (London W3)
Hugh Bourne	1756 (Manchester)		1326 (London W5)
Huguenots	107 (Belfast)		1332 (London N7)
	1219 (London WC1)		1333 (London SW2)
biographies	1219 (London WC1)		1334 (London SE13)
Hull, local history	733, 734, 735 (Hull)		1343, 1501 (London SW1)
Human biology	141 (Birmingham)		1585 (London EC4)
	163 (Blackburn)		1650 (London NW1)
	403 (Chorley)		1674 (London E17)
	748 (Ilkeston)		1688 (London WC2)
	770 (Kettering)		1698 (London SE18)
	773 (Kilmarnock)		1710 (Londonderry)
	1132 (London SW1)		1759 (Manchester)
Human evolution	522 (Edinburgh)		1833 (Newcastle upon Tyne)
Human geography	330 (Canterbury)		1885 (Norwich)
	522 (Edinburgh)		1950 (Oxford)
Human locomotion	512 (Edinburgh)		1988 (Perth)
Human movement	812 (Leeds)		2004 (Portsmouth)
Human relations	375 (Chelmsford)		2027 (Reading)
industry	1232 (London SW1)		2137 (Southall)
Humanism	1437 (London SE1)		2184 (Sunderland)
	1500 (London N1)		2201, 2202 (Swansea)
	1621 (London W8)		2232 (Twickenham)
Humanists			2249 (Ware)
French	1791 (Manchester)		2269 (West Bromwich)
Italian	1791 (Manchester)		2272 (West Wickham)
Humanities	3, 5 (Aberdeen)		2312 (Worcester)
	92, 107 (Belfast)		2335 (York)
	152 (Birmingham)		2339
	159 (Bishop Auckland)	African	1666 (London WC1)
	175 (Bolton)	Denmark	1536 (London SW1)
	186 (Boston)	East European	1668 (London WC1)
	330 (Canterbury)	Greece	1539 (London W1)
	366 (Chatham)	Oriental	1666 (London WC1)
	400 (Chigwell)	Slavonic	1668 (London WC1)
	413 (Colwyn Bay)	Humberside, South, history	2099 (Scunthorpe)
	418 (Coventry)		
	474 (Dundee)	Humour	1999 (Poole)
	483 (Durham)	English	2081 (Sale)
	520, 529 (Edinburgh)	Hungary	988 (London SW1)
	650 (Grimsby)	arts	988 (London SW1)
	661 (Guildford)	economics	988 (London SW1)
	671 (Harlech)	education	988 (London SW1)
	683 (Hastings)	folk art	988 (London SW1)
	721 (Hornchurch)	folk music	988 (London SW1)
	746 (Ilford)	geography	988 (London SW1)
	758 (Isleworth)	history	436 (Dagenham)
	773 (Kilmarnock)		988 (London SW1)
	779 (Kingston upon Thames)	language	315 (Cambridge)

Hungary, language (*contd*)	651(Grimsby)			2278(Weymouth)
literature	315(Cambridge)	language		315(Cambridge)
	651(Grimsby)			651(Grimsby)
	1330(London W6)			813(Leeds)
music	988(London SW1)	law		1220(London SW1)
theatre	988(London SW1)	literature		315(Cambridge)
topography	436(Dagenham)			651(Grimsby)
Hunt, Leigh	1299(London NW3)			1972(Oxford)
	1300(London SW14)	philology		1972(Oxford)
Hunter, John	1533(London WC2)	saga		782(Kirkwall)
	1565(London SW1)	Ileostomy		65(Basingstoke)
Hunting	214(Bridgwater)	Ilkeston		
	1328(London SE10)	industries		747(Ilkeston)
	2051(Rossendale)	local history		747(Ilkeston)
	2323(Worthing)	Illuminated manuscripts		
Huntingdon		history		312(Cambridge)
social welfare services	281(Cambridge)	medieval		630(Glasgow)
voluntary organizations	281(Cambridge)	Illumination		581(Esher)
Huntingdonshire, local		Illustration		469(Dundee)
history	741(Huntingdon)			2141(Southampton)
Husbandry	1534(London SW1)	Illustrations		961(London W1A 1AA)
Huyton-with-Roby				2141(Southampton)
history	865(Liverpool)	ships		1339(London E1)
local history	865(Liverpool)	Immunochemistry		1929(Oxford)
Hyde, local history	742(Hyde)	Immunoglobulins		1929(Oxford)
Hygiene	467(Dumfries)	Immunology		85(Beckenham)
	1016(London WC1)			241(Bristol)
	1037(London NW9)			274, 293, 305, 306(Cambridge)
	1196(London WC1)			
	1805(Mexborough)			502(Edinburgh)
	2121(Shrewsbury)			681(Harrow)
	2172(Stoke-on-Trent)			746(Ilford)
body	2044(Rochdale)			863(Liverpool)
mental	119(Bexley)			1252(London WC2)
nervous system	119(Bexley)			1317(London SW1)
personal	217(Bridgwater)			1367(London NW7)
recreation	2051(Rossendale)			1468(London W2)
tropical	873(Liverpool)			1828(Newbury)
	1344(London WC1)	trachoma		1371(London SW1)
Hymnals	433(Croydon)	Imperial history		1303(London WC2)
Welsh	783(Lampeter)			1659(London WC1)
Hymnology	569(Edinburgh)	Income		1040, 1420(London SW1)
	627(Glasgow)	Income and wealth		727(Huddersfield)
Methodist	95(Belfast)	Incunabula		16(Aberystwyth)
Hypnosis	1280(London W1)			71(Bath)
	2268(Worthing)			133, 149(Birmingham)
dental	1008(London W1)			162(Blackburn)
medical	1008(London W1)			223(Brighton)
				288, 312(Cambridge)
I				702(Hereford)
				775(King's Lynn)
Ibbetson, Julius Caesar	764(Kendal)			783(Lampeter)
Ice	295(Cambridge)			866(Liverpool)
Iceland	408(Colchester)			1882(Norwich)
	1220(London SW1)			2042(Ripon)
geography	2278(Weymouth)			2295(Windsor)
history	1220(London SW1)	Independent schools		2283(Whitstable)

776

Indexing	1606 (London SW1)		2174 (Stoke-on-Trent)
India	36 (Aylesbury)	Industrial development,	
	1228 (London WC2)	Northumberland	1848 (Newcastle upon Tyne)
	1229 (London SE1)	Industrial disease	1191 (London SE1)
	1560 (London SW1)	Industrial economics	118 (Beverley)
	1939 (Oxford)		154 (Birmingham)
art	2111 (Sheffield)	Industrial education	958 (London W1N 4AP)
history	866 (Ilford)	Industrial enterprise	695 (Heckmondwike)
	1230 (London SE1)	Industrial hazards	648 (Greenford)
	1968 (Oxford)		672 (Harlow)
	1872 (Northwich)	Industrial health	672 (Harlow)
languages	1968 (Oxford)		1233 (London SW1)
literature	866 (Liverpool)		1738 (Manchester)
	1968 (Oxford)		1842 (Newcastle upon Tyne)
Methodist missions	1376 (London NW1)	Industrial history	1711 (Loughborough)
missions	934 (London W1H 4AA)		2259 (Wednesbury)
	1086 (London SW1)	Bedfordshire, South	1720 (Luton)
religion	1968 (Oxford)	Black Country	465 (Dudley)
South, history	1592 (London NW1)	Bristol	228 (Bristol)
topography	866 (Liverpool)	mines	2102 (Settle)
	1872 (Northwich)	Northumberland	1847 (Newcastle upon Tyne)
India Office	1230 (London SE1)	Ulster	113 (Belfast)
Indo-European	107 (Belfast)	Industrial hygiene	521 (Edinburgh)
Indoor games	1328 (London SE10)		1723 (Macclesfield)
	1935 (Oxford)		2039 (Richmond)
Industrial administration	520 (Edinburgh)	Industrial injury pensions	1107 (London WC2)
	1839 (Newcastle upon Tyne)	Industrial legislation	1084 (London SW1)
Industrial archaeology	417 (Coventry)	Industrial living conditions	809 (Leeds)
	1720 (Luton)	Industrial medicine	1980 (Penarth)
	2181 (Stroud)		2172 (Stoke-on-Trent)
Ayrshire	43 (Ayr)	Industrial products, design	1108 (London SW1)
Croydon	429 (Croydon)	Industrial psychology	114 (Berkhamsted)
Durham	1848 (Newcastle upon Tyne)		1117 (London W5)
Kent, North West	429 (Croydon)		2259 (Wednesbury)
Northumberland	1848 (Newcastle upon Tyne)	Industrial radiology	990 (London W1M 7PG)
Surrey, North East	429 (Croydon)	Industrial relations	114 (Berkhamsted)
Wiltshire	453 (Devizes)		215 (Bridgwater)
Industrial art	1253 (London SW1)		335 (Cardiff)
	1339 (London E1)		580 (Esher)
Industrial chemicals,			687 (Hatfield)
toxicology	1723 (Macclesfield)		700 (Henley-on-Thames)
Industrial commercial law	153 (Birmingham)		1068 (London SW17)
Industrial co-partnership	1232 (London SW1)		1080 (London WC2)
Industrial democracy	1232 (London SW1)		1084, 1104 (London SW1)
Industrial design	129 (Birmingham)		1282 (London SW4)
	253 (Bromley)		1617 (London SW17)
	349 (Carlisle)		1642 (London SW4)
	527 (Edinburgh)		1699 (London W1H 8BY)
	824 (Leicester)		1719 (Luton)
	1039 (London WC1)		2039 (Richmond)
	1094 (London SW1)	Industrial safety	175 (Bolton)
	1141 (London WC2)		1233, 1508 (London SW1)
	1265 (London NW3)		2039 (Richmond)
	1524 (London SW7)	Industrial science	2166 (Stirling)
	1607 (London SW1)	Industrial toxicology	1723 (Macclesfield)
	1719 (Luton)	Industrial training	82 (Beaconsfield)
	2116 (Sheffield)		174 (Bolton)

Industrial training (contd)	202 (Bradford)	Information systems	
	287 (Cambridge)	planning	909 (London SW1)
	363 (Castleford)	Information work, training	1256 (London EC2)
	390 (Chesterfield)	Inheritance	779 (Kingston upon Thames)
	527, 542 (Edinburgh)	Inner London Education	
	580 (Esher)	Authority	1181 (London SE1)
	678 (Harrow)	Inns of Court	1209, 1210 (London WC2)
	725 (Huddersfield)	Inoculation, dangers	432 (Croydon)
	740 (Huntingdon)	Insect control	2190 (Surbiton)
	1080 (London WC2)	Institutions, mental	119 (Bexley)
	1105 (London W1)	Instructional media	812 (Leeds)
	1421 (London W1M 8DR)	Instructional technology	1112 (London SW1)
	2306 (Wolverhampton)	Instrumentation	1857 (Newport, Mon)
	2318 (Worksop)	Insulin	1366 (London SW7)
gas industry	1171 (London SW1)	Insurance	225 (Brighton)
wool, jute and flax			511 (Edinburgh)
industry	202 (Bradford)		868 (Liverpool)
Industrial work, Churches	1231 (London EC3)		1045 (London EC2)
Industrial working			1520 (London SW1)
conditions	809 (Leeds)		1806 (Middlesbrough)
Industrialized building	1381 (London SW1)		2136 (South Shields)
Industries		See also Volume I	
Derbyshire	391 (Chesterfield)	Intelligence measurement	1132 (London SW1)
Norfolk	1873 (Norwich)	Interior decoration	1340 (London E17)
Norwich	1873 (Norwich)		1450 (London N7)
rural	1092 (London SW19)		1748 (Manchester)
Shropshire	2211 (Telford)		2055 (Rotherham)
Wales	337 (Cardiff)	Interior design	129 (Birmingham)
Yorkshire			189 (Bournemouth)
South	458 (Doncaster)		220 (Brighton)
West Riding	458 (Doncaster)		349 (Carlisle)
Industry	1084 (London SW1)		469 (Dundee)
	1154 (London EC4)		1094 (London SW1)
	1199, 1305 (London SW1)		1265 (London NW3)
	2173 (Stoke-on-Trent)		1524 (London SW7)
arts	2225 (Tunbridge Wells)		1540 (London W1N 4AD)
Bradford	199 (Bradford)		1688 (London WC2)
British	1253 (London SW1)		1808 (Middlesbrough)
crafts	2225 (Tunbridge Wells)		1858 (Newport, Mon)
Croydon	429 (Croydon)		2116 (Sheffield)
history	667 (Halifax)		2141 (Southampton)
human relations	1232 (London SW1)	International affairs	140 (Birmingham)
iodine	1051 (London EC2)		271 (Camberley)
Kent, North West	429 (Croydon)		975, 1159, 1541 (London SW1)
Surrey, North East	429 (Croydon)		1547 (London SE10)
See also Volume I			1560 (London SW1)
Infant education	1809 (Middlesbrough)		1947 (Oxford)
Infertility	715 (High Wycombe)		2038 (Richmond)
	1132 (London SW1)	International disputes	1101 (London SW1)
Infirm		International economics	1541 (London SW1)
care	497 (Eastbourne)	International health	1106 (London SE1)
home care	2218 (Truro)	International history	994 (London WC2)
Information science	909 (London SW1)	International jurisprudence	1541 (London SW1)
	1839 (Newcastle upon Tyne)	International language movement	983 (London W11)
Information scientists	1256 (London EC2)	International law	436 (Dagenham)
Information sources	909 (London SW1)		

International law (contd)	816(Leeds)	population census	96(Belfast)
	994(London WC2)	topography	866(Liverpool)
	1159(London SW1)	transport history	94(Belfast)
	1210(London EC4)	Iron founding	747(Ilkeston)
	1309, 1654(London WC1)	Iron industry, history	705(Hereford)
	1939(Oxford)	Ironbridge	2211(Telford)
International organization	225(Brighton)	Irving, Sir Henry	194(Bournemouth)
	1144(London W1R 9PL)	Islam	34(Ashton-under-Lyne)
International organizations	722(Hounslow)		149(Birmingham)
International phonetic alphabet	1278(London WC1)	literature	2210(Taunton) 1285(London NW8)
International politics	17(Aberystwyth)	teaching	1285(London NW8)
International relations	158(Birmingham)	Islands, South Indian Ocean	459(Dorchester)
	403(Chorley)	Isle of Ely	
	421(Coventry)	local history	1796(March)
	927(London SW1)	social welfare services	281(Cambridge)
	1144(London W1R 9PL)	voluntary organizations	281(Cambridge)
	1939(Oxford)	Isle of Man	462(Douglas)
International studies	2145(Southampton)	archaeology	462(Douglas)
International Working Men's Association	943(London EC2)	folk lore geography	462(Douglas) 462(Douglas)
International treaties	722(Hounslow)	history	462(Douglas)
Interpreters	1259(London SE1)	language	462(Douglas)
Intestinal absorption	2108(Sheffield)	natural history	462(Douglas)
Intestinal biochemistry	1366(London SW7)	Isle of Wight	1851(Newport, Isle of Wight)
Intestinal physiology	1366(London SW7)		
Invalids' care	497(Eastbourne)		2145(Southampton)
Investiture Ceremony	1911(Caernarvon)	archaeology	1851(Newport, Isle of Wight)
	267(Coventry)		
Investment	1168(London W1A 3AU)	geology	2093(Sandown)
Iodine, applications	1051(London EC2)	history	2093(Sandown)
Ionizing radiation, effects	806(Leeds)	local history	2002(Portsmouth)
Ipswich, local history	753(Ipswich)	natural history	1851(Newport, Isle of Wight)
Iran			
geography	2150(Southport)	Isotopes	681(Harrow)
history	2150(Southport)	Israel	1292(London W1)
Iraq			2083(Salford)
geography	2150(Southport)		2139(Southampton)
history	2150(Southport)	history	1251(London W1N 2BH)
Ireland	92(Belfast)	Italian	
	314(Cambridge)	(See also Italian language and Italian literature)	330(Canterbury)
	1126(London SW1)		574(Egham)
	1710(Londonderry)		813(Leeds)
antiquities	92(Belfast)		942(London WC1)
archaeology	92, 113(Belfast)		1650(London NW1)
books	410(Coleraine)		1853(Newport, Isle of Wight)
ceramics	113(Belfast)		
history	92, 113(Belfast)		1958(Oxford)
	866(Liverpool)	books	1791(Manchester)
	1288(London NW3)	humanists	1791(Manchester)
literature	92(Belfast)	language	154(Birmingham)
	866(Liverpool)		277, 315(Cambridge)
local history	92(Belfast)		1117(London W5)
maps	92(Belfast)		1307(London WC1)
music	92, 107(Belfast)		1326(London W5)
newspapers	92(Belfast)		1686(London NW3)
readership	1168(London W1A 3AU)		1946, 1965(Oxford)

Italian, language (*contd*)	2086 (Salford)	Jewish ethics	2139 (Southampton)
	2187 (Sunderland)	Jewish history	912 (London E1)
literature	154 (Birmingham)		1292 (London W1)
	277, 315 (Cambridge)		1339 (London E1)
	422 (Coventry)		1383 (London WC1)
	805 (Leeds)		2139 (Southampton)
	1918, 1965 (Oxford)		2184 (Sunderland)
	2100 (Scunthorpe)	Jewish homiletics	1292 (London W1)
criticism	1322 (London NW4)	Jewish jurisprudence	939 (London WC1)
history	1322 (London NW4)	Jewish language	1292 (London W1)
Italy	1286 (London W1)	Jewish life	1032 (London WC1)
	1947 (Oxford)	Jewish literature	1292 (London W1)
architecture	223 (Brighton)		1339 (London E1)
art	223 (Brighton)	Jewish liturgy	912 (London E1)
	2111 (Sheffield)	Jewish music	1292 (London W1)
history	1251 (London W1N 2BH)	Jewish religion	1339 (London E1)
tourism	1287 (London W1)		1458 (London W11)
Ivory Coast, Methodist			2139 (Southampton)
missions	1376 (London NW1)	*See also* Judaism	
		Jewish religious law	939 (London WC1)
J		Jewish religious observance	912 (London E1)
		Jewish social life	1339 (London E1)
Jacobites	13 (Aberdeen)	Jewish society	2139 (Southampton)
James Everett	1756 (Manchester)	Jewish sociology	912 (London E1)
James Nasmyth	1748 (Manchester)		1383 (London WC1)
Jansenist literature	1924 (Oxford)	Jewish subjects	130 (Birmingham)
Japan	217 (Bridgwater)	Jewish Youth clubs	912 (London E1)
	896 (London WC2)	Jewry	
	1289 (London W1X 9LB)	European, history	1251 (London W1N 2BH)
art	1733 (Maidstone)	German, history	1251 (London W1N 2BH)
	2111 (Sheffield)	Jews	327 (Canterbury)
economics	896 (London WC2)		1257 (London W1)
education	1289 (London W1X 9LB)	Commonwealth, history	1291 (London W1)
fine arts	1289 (London W1X 9LB)	education	1292 (London W1)
geography	2076 (St Helens)	sociology	1257 (London W1)
history	581 (Esher)	J. F. Kennedy	32 (Ashington)
	1289 (London W1X 9LB)	J. F. Powys	459 (Dorchester)
	1968 (Oxford)	John Anderson	631 (Glasgow)
	2076 (St Helens)	John Barber	1904 (Nuneaton)
languages	1968 (Oxford)	John Betjeman	1798 (Marlborough)
	1289 (London W1X 9LB)	John Bradshaw	584 (Exeter)
literature	1968 (Oxford)	John Bunyan	89, 91 (Bedford)
prints	164 (Blackburn)	John Clare	1865 (Northampton)
topography	581 (Esher)	John Galsworthy	154 (Birmingham)
J. C. Powys	459 (Dorchester)	John Hunter	1533 (London WC2)
Jenner, Edward	1565 (London SW1)		1565 (London SW1)
Jewellery	129 (Birmingham)	John Keats	1299 (London NW3)
	1524 (London SW7)		1300 (London SW14)
	1688 (London WC2)		1324 (London NW3)
	2055 (Rotherham)	John Keble	1924 (Oxford)
	2116 (Sheffield)	John Milton	133 (Birmingham)
	2141 (Southampton)		365 (Chalfont St Giles)
design	1039 (London WC1)		1956 (Oxford)
See also Volume I		John Moore	906 (London N1)
Jewish affairs	1257 (London W1)	John Newton	1912 (Olney)
Jewish community	945 (London WC1)	John Ruskin	764 (Kendal)
Jewish education	2083 (Salford)		1690 (London SW15)

John Wesley	2100 (Scunthorpe)	bibliography	2046 (Rochester)
Johnson, Samuel	133 (Birmingham)	East	
	837, 840 (Lichfield)	local history	327 (Canterbury)
	1941 (Oxford)	topography	327 (Canterbury)
Joint consultation	1232 (London SW1)	history	1731, 1733 (Maidstone)
Jonathan Swift	113 (Belfast)	local history	119 (Bexley)
Jones, Ernest	943 (London EC2)		595 (Folkestone)
Jordan	1296 (London W8)		600 (Gillingham)
Joseph Chamberlain	154 (Birmingham)		683 (Hastings)
Joseph Conrad	1480 (London SW7)		1328 (London SE10)
Joseph Lancaster	758 (Isleworth)	natural history	1733 (Maidstone)
Journalism	438 (Darlington)	North West	
	673 (Harlow)	archaeology	429 (Croydon)
	1331 (London N17)	geography	429 (Croydon)
	1338 (London SE22)	geology	429 (Croydon)
Judaica	130 (Birmingham)	history	429 (Croydon)
	802, 813 (Leeds)	industrial	
	1339 (London E1)	archaeology	429 (Croydon)
Judaism	192 (Bournemouth)	industry	429 (Croydon)
	912 (London E1)	local history	429 (Croydon)
	1032 (London WC1)	natural history	429 (Croydon)
	1062 (London WC2)	planning	429 (Croydon)
	1257 (London W1)	topography	429 (Croydon)
	1789 (Manchester)		1328 (London SE10)
Judiciary	57 (Barnsley)		1731 (Maidstone)
	683 (Hastings)	Kentish men and women,	
	1210 (London EC4)	biography	1731 (Maidstone)
Judo	992 (London W1)	Kenya, Methodist missions	1376 (London NW1)
history	992 (London W1)	Kesteven, local history	2128 (Sleaford)
Julius Caesar Ibbetson	764 (Kendal)	Kettering, local history	769 (Kettering)
Junior education	1809 (Middlesbrough)	Kidderminster	
Jurisprudence	816 (Leeds)	archaeology	771 (Kidderminster)
	1541 (London SW1)	local history	771 (Kidderminster)
Jewish	939 (London WC1)	Kilham, Alexander	1756 (Manchester)
Justice, administration	154 (Birmingham)	Kinesiology	87 (Bedford)
	313 (Cambridge)		445 (Darwen)
	1351 (London W1P 6DD)		1248 (London W6)
Jute	471 (Dundee)	King Arthur	16 (Aberystwyth)
Juvenile delinquency	252 (Bromley)		1813 (Mold)
	459 (Dorchester)	King's Lynn	
	1238 (London W1)	archaeology	774 (King's Lynn)
	1369 (London WC1)	geology	774 (King's Lynn)
		history	774 (King's Lynn)
		local history	774, 775 (King's Lynn)
K		natural history	775 (King's Lynn)
		topography	775 (King's Lynn)
Kabala	564 (Edinburgh)	King's Own Royal Lancaster	
Kate Greenaway	1324 (London NW3)	Regiment, history	784 (Lancaster)
Keats, John	1299 (London NW3)	Kingston upon Hull *See* Hull	
	1300 (London SW14)	Kinross-shire, local history	1988 (Perth)
	1324 (London NW3)	Kippington estate	2104 (Sevenoaks)
Keble, John	1924 (Oxford)	Kirkwall, local history	782 (Kirkwall)
Keighley, local history	761 (Keighley)	Kodaly	988 (London SW1)
Kelmscott Press	1692 (London E17)	Korea	1304 (London SW1)
Kennedy, J. F.	32 (Ashington)	K.O.S.B. Regimental	
Kennels	1625 (London WC1)	history	116 (Berwick-upon-
Kent	429 (Croydon)		Tweed)
archaeology	1328 (London SE10)		

781

L

Laboratory administration	1260(London W1)
Laboratory animal breeding	455(Didcot)
Laboratory animal science	361(Carshalton)
Laboratory animals	147(Birmingham)
	502(Edinburgh)
	681(Harrow)
Laboratory hazards	648(Greenford)
Laboratory management	1260(London W1)
Laboratory techniques	874(Liverpool)
Labour	742(Hyde)
	1442(London SW4)
disputes	363(Castleford)
economics	1962(Oxford)
	2039(Richmond)
	2237(Wakefield)
history	422(Coventry)
	739(Hull)
	1355(London EC1)
medicine	412(Colne)
movement, history	943(London EC2)
wastage, shipping industry	1169(London W1A 3AU)
Lace	1889, 1892(Nottingham)
machine	1894(Nottingham)
Lacrosse	120(Bexleyheath)
Lake District	350(Carlisle)
antiquities	348(Carlisle)
dialects	353(Carlisle)
geology	348(Carlisle)
local history	764, 766(Kendal)
maps	350(Carlisle)
natural history	348(Carlisle)
Lamb, Charles	1299(London NW3)
Lambeth, local history	1333(London SE5)
Lanarkshire, North, local history	21(Airdrie)
Lancashire	34(Ashton-under-Lyne)
archaeology	1760(Manchester)
customs	1760(Manchester)
genealogy	1760(Manchester)
history	125(Birkenhead)
	1744, 1760, 1761(Manchester)
local history	125(Birkenhead)
	742(Hyde)
	866(Liverpool)
	1760(Manchester)
	2017(Preston)
	2286(Wigan)
North	787(Lancaster)
antiquities	348, 351(Carlisle)
archaeology	351(Carlisle)
geology	348(Carlisle)
history	351(Carlisle)
natural history	348(Carlisle)
South	
local history	839(Lichfield)
traditions	1760(Manchester)
voluntary organizations	1744(Manchester)
Lancashire Regiment, history	2251(Warrington)
Lancaster, Joseph	758(Isleworth)
Lancaster, local history	786, 787(Lancaster)
Lanchester, F. W.	421(Coventry)
Land	1340(London E17)
economics	1960(Oxford)
Scotland	1977(Paisley)
surveying	1674(London E17)
taxation	1198(London SW1)
use	109(Belfast)
	1198, 1381, 1412(London SW1)
	1340(London E17)
Landscape	469(Dundee)
	1540(London W1N 4AD)
architecture	109(Belfast)
	129(Birmingham)
	373(Cheltenham)
	805(Leeds)
	1693(London SW19)
art	1693(London SW19)
	2297(Wirral)
reserves	377(Cheltenham)
Landscaping	1265(London NW3)
Language	142(Birmingham)
	168(Blackpool)
	198(Bradford)
	390(Chesterfield)
	511(Edinburgh)
	587(Exeter)
	716(Hinckley)
	813(Leeds)
	1768, 1774(Manchester)
	1910(Oldham)
	1918(Oxford)
	2333(York)
behaviour	524(Edinburgh)
history	1474(London WC1)
method	1167(London SW17)
records	1339(London E1)
teachers	1259(London SE1)
teaching	185(Boreham Wood)
	800(Leeds)
	1042(London WC1)
	1307(London WC1)
	1308(London W1A 4DY)
	2034(Redruth)
	2334(York)
training	1112(London SW1)
Languages	17(Aberystwyth)
	63(Basingstoke)
	72(Bath)

Languages (contd)
                   122 (Bilston)
                   152 (Birmingham)
                   161 (Blackburn)
                   191 (Bournemouth)
                   196 (Bracknell)
                   200 (Bradford)
                   230, 235 (Bristol)
                   315 (Cambridge)
                   421 (Coventry)
                   430 (Croydon)
                   435 (Dagenham)
                   470 (Dundee)
                   606, 612 (Glasgow)
                   646 (Grays)
                   673 (Harlow)
                   676 (Harrogate)
                   726 (Huddersfield)
                   805, 812 (Leeds)
                   822 (Leicester)
                   866, 868 (Liverpool)
                   906 (London N7)
                   1064 (London E2)
                   1065 (London SW1)
                   1117 (London W5)
                   1118 (London E6)
                   1385 (London SE1)
                   1482 (London W1R 8AL)
                   1615 (London N14)
                   1688 (London W1)
                   1698 (London SE18)
                   1768 (Manchester)
                   1891 (Nottingham)
                   1905 (Nuneaton)
                   1937 (Oxford)
                   2059 (Rugby)
                   2098 (Scunthorpe)
                   2129 (Sleaford)
                   2135 (Slough)
                   2150 (Southport)
                   2160 (Stevenage)
                   2182 (Sunderland)
                   2198 (Sutton Coldfield)
                   2203 (Swindon)
                   2256 (Watford)
                   2321 (Worthing)
African   710 (Hertford)
                   1273 (London EC4)
                   1968 (Oxford)
Arabic   1285 (London NW8)
Asia   1523 (London W1N 1LN)
                   1968 (Oxford)
Biblical   517 (Edinburgh)
Bulgaria   311 (Cambridge)
Catalan   315 (Cambridge)
Chile   894 (London W1)
China   1117 (London W5)
                   1968 (Oxford)

Czechoslovakia   311 (Cambridge)
Danish   315 (Cambridge)
                   651 (Grimsby)
Dutch   315 (Cambridge)
                   2086 (Salford)
East European   1668 (London WC1)
English   154 (Birmingham)
                   457 (Doncaster)
                   486 (Durham)
                   640 (Gosport)
                   667 (Halifax)
                   778 (Kingston upon Thames)
                   812 (Leeds)
                   1129 (London SW7)
                   1302 (London SE11)
                   1307 (London WC1)
                   1336 (London SW19)
                   1495 (London W1)
                   1653 (London SE14)
                   1686 (London NW3)
                   1774 (Manchester)
                   1837, 1839, 1845 (Newcastle upon Tyne)
                   1862 (Newton Stewart)
                   1895 (Nottingham)
                   1956 (Oxford)
                   2144 (Southampton)
                   2182 (Sunderland)
                   2205 (Tamworth)
                   2333 (York)
Estonian   651 (Grimsby)
European   270 (Camberley)
                   486, 492 (Durham)
                   667 (Halifax)
                   1965, 1972 (Oxford)
French   154 (Birmingham)
                   315 (Cambridge)
                   435 (Dagenham)
                   485 (Durham)
                   520 (Edinburgh)
                   778 (Kingston upon Thames)
                   800, 812 (Leeds)
                   1117 (London W5)
                   1307 (London WC1)
                   1653 (London SE14)
                   1686 (London NW3)
                   1839, 1846 (Newcastle upon Tyne)
                   1895 (Nottingham)
                   1946, 1965 (Oxford)
                   2011 (Prescot)
                   2020 (Reading)
                   2086 (Salford)
                   2144 (Southampton)
                   2187 (Sunderland)
                   2334 (York)
Gaelic   751 (Inverness)

Languages (contd)
German 154(Birmingham)
315(Cambridge)
435(Dagenham)
485(Durham)
520(Edinburgh)
778(Kingston upon Thames)
800(Leeds)
1117(London W5)
1177(London SW7)
1307(London WC1)
1653(London SE14)
1658(London WC1)
1686(London NW3)
1839(Newcastle upon Tyne)
1895(Nottingham)
1946, 1965(Oxford)
1989(Peterborough)
2011(Prescot)
2020(Reading)
2086(Salford)
2144(Southampton)
2187(Sunderland)
2334(York)
Germanic 847(Lincoln)
Greek 154(Birmingham)
301(Cambridge)
486(Durham)
1250(London WC1)
1965(Oxford)
Hungarian 315(Cambridge)
651(Grimsby)
Icelandic 315(Cambridge)
651(Grimsby)
Indian 1968(Oxford)
international 983(London W11)
See also Esperanto
Italian 154(Birmingham)
277, 315(Cambridge)
1117(London W5)
1307(London WC1)
1686(London NW3)
1946, 1965(Oxford)
2086(Salford)
2187(Sunderland)
Japan 1968(Oxford)
Jewish 1292(London W1)
Lapp 651(Grimsby)
Latin 154(Birmingham)
301(Cambridge)
486(Durham)
medieval 315(Cambridge)
Latin American 1965(Oxford)
Lettish 651(Grimsby)
Manx 462(Douglas)
Norwegian 315(Cambridge)
651(Grimsby)

898(London SW1)
1946(Oxford)
Persian 1968(Oxford)
Polish 311(Cambridge)
2086(Salford)
Portuguese 154(Birmingham)
315(Cambridge)
1686(London NW3)
1965(Oxford)
2086(Salford)
Roman 1250(London WC1)
Romance 1851(Newport, Isle of Wight)
Rumanian 315(Cambridge)
1686(London NW3)
1965(Oxford)
Russian 311(Cambridge)
520(Edinburgh)
778(Kingston upon Thames)
800(Leeds)
1117(London W5)
1307(London WC1)
1839(Newcastle upon Tyne)
1946(Oxford)
2086(Salford)
2187(Sunderland)
2334(York)
Slavonic 311(Cambridge)
1668(London WC1)
1965, 1972(Oxford)
Spanish 154(Birmingham)
315(Cambridge)
520(Edinburgh)
788(Kingston upon Thames)
800, 812(Leeds)
1117(London W5)
1307(London WC1)
1686(London NW3)
1799(Matlock)
1946, 1972(Oxford)
2086(Salford)
2187(Sunderland)
2334(York)
Swedish 651(Grimsby)
2086(Salford)
Teutonic 1851(Newport, Isle of Wight)
Turkey 1968(Oxford)
Yugoslavia 311(Cambridge)
Lapp
language 651(Grimsby)
literature 651(Grimsby)
Laryngology 176(Bolton)
242(Bristol)
1258(London WC1)
Lathes 2009(Potters Bar)
Latin 223(Brighton)

Latin (contd)	1293 (London WC1)	212 (Bridgend)
	1302 (London SE11)	240, 246 (Bristol)
	1451 (London NW5)	291, 292, 294 (Cambridge)
	1650 (London NW1)	324 (Cannock)
	1686 (London NW3)	328, 330 (Canterbury)
grammars	186 (Boston)	354 (Carlisle)
language	301 (Cambridge)	359 (Carshalton)
	486 (Durham)	375 (Chelmsford)
literature	154 (Birmingham)	418, 421, 422 (Coventry)
	186 (Boston)	435 (Dagenham)
	301 (Cambridge)	438 (Darlington)
	486 (Durham)	446 (Deeside)
	1338 (London SE22)	474 (Dundee)
	1731 (Maidstone)	485, 492 (Durham)
	1799 (Matlock)	499 (Eastleigh)
medieval		511, 520, 561, 563,
language	315 (Cambridge)	567 (Edinburgh)
literature	315 (Cambridge)	584, 587, 589 (Exeter)
Latin America	630 (Glasgow)	599 (Gateshead)
	1660 (London WC1)	630, 631 (Glasgow)
	1947 (Oxford)	655 (Guildford)
	2145 (Southampton)	665 (Harlesowen)
anthropology	299 (Cambridge)	676 (Harrogate)
archaeology	1655 (London WC1)	687 (Hatfield)
economics	299 (Cambridge)	700 (Henley-on-Thames)
	1961, 1962 (Oxford)	725, 727 (Huddersfield)
government	409 (Colchester)	739 (Hull)
history	299 (Cambridge)	748 (Ilkeston)
	409 (Colchester)	761, 762 (Keighley)
	1659 (London WC1)	788 (Kingston upon Thames)
language	1965 (Oxford)	793 (Leamington Spa)
law	1654 (London WC1)	805, 816 (Leeds)
literature	409 (Colchester)	866, 868, 878 (Liverpool)
	1303 (London WC2)	884, 932, 946, 994 (London WC2)
	1965 (Oxford)	
missions	1085 (London SW1)	1015 (London SW4)
politics	299 (Cambridge)	1045, 1064 (London EC2)
	1961 (Oxford)	1117 (London W5)
social sciences	290 (Cambridge)	1144 (London W1P 9PL)
sociology	299 (Cambridge)	1168 (London W1A 3AU)
	1961 (Oxford)	1206 (London SW1)
Laundering	836 (Lewes)	1209, 1210 (London WC2)
	2082 (Salford)	1243 (London EC3)
Welsh	342 (Cardiff)	1303 (London WC2)
Law	13 (Aberdeen)	1309 (London WC1)
	17 (Aberystwyth)	1310 (London WC2)
	25 (Alloa)	1330 (London W6)
	35 (Aylesbury)	1351 (London W1P 6DD)
	67 (Basingstoke)	1473 (London SW16)
	92, 107 (Belfast)	1482 (London W1R 8AL)
	119 (Bexley)	1617 (London SW17)
	131, 142, 145, 150, 152, 154 (Birmingham)	1665 (London E1)
		1711 (Loughborough)
	161, 162 (Blackburn)	1728 (Maidenhead)
	167, 168 (Blackpool)	1734 (Maidstone)
	191 (Bournemouth)	1766, 1791 (Manchester)
	201 (Bradford)	1806 (Middlesbrough)

Law (contd)	1823(Neath)	Company	516(Edinburgh)
	1839, 1850(Newcastle upon Tyne)		932(London WC2)
			1253(London SW1)
	1860(Newport, Mon)		2187(Sunderland)
	1882(Norwich)	comparative	399(Chichester)
	1891, 1895, 1902(Nottingham)		1309, 1654(London WC1)
		constitutional	802(Leeds)
	1918, 1921, 1946, 1948, 1953(Oxford)	contracts	1322(London NW4)
			2239(Wakefield)
	1994(Plymouth)	criminal	25(Alloa)
	2012(Prescot)		313(Cambridge)
	2014(Preston)		1218(London SE11)
	2021(Reading)		1238(London W1)
	2030(Redditch)	East European	1668(London WC1)
	2059(Rugby)	ecclesiastical	1210(London EC4)
	2112, 2119(Sheffield)	education	1235(London WC1)
	2124, 2126(Shrewsbury)	English	816(Leeds)
	2135(Slough)		1210(London EC4)
	2142, 2145(Southampton)		1302(London SE11)
	2171, 2173(Stoke-on-Trent)		1309(London WC1)
	2198(Sutton Coldfield)		1928(Oxford)
	2289(Winchester)	history	1581(London E1)
	2307(Wolverhampton)	Europe	566(Edinburgh)
	2316(Workington)		1654(London WC1)
	2321(Worthing)	European Communities	1654(London WC1)
	2331(York)	family	779(Kingston upon Thames)
abortion	2064(St Albans)		2112(Sheffield)
reform	1594(London SW1)	financial	516(Edinburgh)
accident	1322(London NW4)	food additives	1723(Macclesfield)
Africa	298(Cambridge)	foreign	1159(London SW1)
ancient monuments	893(London W8)		1210(London EC4)
Arabic	1285(London NW8)	forestry	1073(London W8)
bibliography	1210(London EC4)	France	1309(London WC1)
British	2054(Rotherham)	Germany	1309(London WC1)
British Dominions	1654(London WC1)	Great Britain	1379(London EC4)
British Isles	1654(London WC1)	historical	399(Chichester)
business	1065(London SW1)	history	131(Birmingham)
	2259(Wednesbury)		493(Durham)
canon	492(Durham)		1210(London EC4)
	1568(London EC4)	homosexual behaviour	1207(London W1V 8EP)
	1976(Paignton)	Iceland	1220(London SW1)
	2261(Wells)	industrial	153(Birmingham)
child welfare	538(Edinburgh)		1084(London SW1)
church	1322(London NW4)	inheritance	779(Kingston upon Thames)
buildings	1093(London EC2)		2112(Sheffield)
civil	2261(Wells)	international	436(Dagenham)
commercial	153(Birmingham)		802, 816(Leeds)
	252(Bromley)		994(London WC2)
	2112(Sheffield)		1159(London SW1)
	2142(Southampton)		1210(London EC4)
common	1309(London WC1)		1309, 1654(London WC1)
Common Market	1210(London EC4)		1939(Oxford)
Commonwealth	1082(Edinburgh)	Islamic	1285(London NW8)
	1082(London W8)	Latin America	1654(London WC1)
	1159(London SW1)	marine	2136(South Shields)
	1210, 1379(London EC4)	maritime	872(Liverpool)
	1654(London WC1)		2112(Sheffield)

Law (contd)
  martial 387(Chester)
   581(Esher)
  motoring 1520(London SW1)
  Muslim 1285(London NW8)
  nobiliary 522(Edinburgh)
  persons 459(Dorchester)
  pharmacy 531(Edinburgh)
  Poland 1479(London SW1)
  property 459(Dorchester)
   779(Kingston upon Thames)
   2054(Rotherham)
  real estate 1073(London W8)
  reform 1309(London WC1)
  religions, Jewish 939(London WC1)
  Scandinavian 1309(London WC1)
  Scotland 553, 561(Edinburgh)
  shops 1269(London EC2)
  Slavonic 1668(London WC1)
  South Africa 1654(London WC1)
  taxation 946(London WC2)
  town planning 893, 1073(London W8)
  trade union 580(Esher)
   698(Hemel Hempstead)
  United States of America 1379(London EC4)
   1654(London WC1)
  West Indies 1683(London WC2)
Lawrence, D. H. 747(Ilkeston)
   1891, 1896, 1902(Nottingham)
Lawrence, T. E. 459(Dorchester)
   2129(Sleaford)
Leadership 2129(Sleaford)
Lead-mining 391(Chesterfield)
Leagues of Hospital Friends 1397(London SW1)
Leamington Spa, local history 792(Leamington Spa)
Learning psychology 725(Huddersfield)
Leather
  technology 1866(Northampton)
  use, history 1391(London SE1)
Leeds
  earthenware 801, 802(Leeds)
  history 811(Leeds)
  local history 802, 803, 811(Leeds)
Leek, local history 820(Leek)
Legends 564(Edinburgh)
Legislation See Law
Legislatures 1997(Pontefract)
Leicester, local history 825(Leicester)
Leicestershire, local history 825, 826, 827(Leicester)
Leigh Hunt 1299(London NW3)
   1300(London SW14)
Leisure 503(Edinburgh)
   1475(London W1M 4AX)
Leprosy 262(Bury)
   746(Ilford)
   993(London W1)
   1312(London W1N 3DG)
   2195(Sutton)
  mission 1312(London W1N 3DG)
  workers 1312(London W1N 3DG)
Lettering 450(Derby)
   581(Esher)
   1858(Newport, Mon)
   2141(Southampton)
Letterpress printing 349(Carlisle)
Letters
  American 252(Bromley)
  English 252(Bromley)
Lettish
  language 651(Grimsby)
  literature 651(Grimsby)
Leukemia 304(Cambridge)
Libel 1323(London NW10)
Liberal education 275(Cambridge)
Liberal Party 1314(London WC2)
Liberal politics 1423(London SW1)
Librarians' Associations 2103(Sevenoaks)
Librarianship 9(Aberdeen)
   15(Aberystwyth)
   92(Belfast)
   152(Birmingham)
   222(Brighton)
   868(Liverpool)
   970(London WC1)
   1117(London W5)
   1315(London WC1)
   1326(London W5)
   1338(London SE22)
   1451(London NW5)
   1766(Manchester)
   1839(Newcastle upon Tyne)
   2142(Southampton)
   2187(Sunderland)
  school 2035(Retford)
  Scotland 622(Glasgow)
Libraries 949(London NW10)
   2103(Sevenoaks)
  blind 1424(London SW1)
   1424, 1775(Manchester)
  East Anglia 1885(Norwich)
  equipment 909(London SW1)
   1315(London WC1)
  furnishing 909(London SW1)
  history 15(Aberystwyth)
   1592(London NW1)
  hospital 550(Edinburgh)
  planning 909(London SW1)
  school 1102(London W1)
Library associations 2103(Sevenoaks)
Library catalogues 2340
Library education 1315(London WC1)
Library mechanization 909(London SW1)

787

Library science	909(London SW1)		2279(Weymouth)
Library techniques	2103(Sevenoaks)	Africa	1273(London EC4)
Library of Thorkelin	529(Edinburgh)	comparative	123(Bingley)
Lichfield			522(Edinburgh)
genealogy	839(Lichfield)	Linguists	1259(London SE1)
history	837, 839(Lichfield)	biography	1731(Maidstone)
local history	837, 839, 840(Lichfield)	careers	1259(London SE1)
Life assurance	1240(London WC1)	training	1259(London SE1)
Lifeboat problems	1546(London SW1)	Lip reading tuition	759(Iver)
Life Guards, history	2296(Windsor)	Liquorice growing, history	1997(Pontefract)
Lighting, Welsh	342(Cardiff)	Literary composition	277(Cambridge)
Lincoln		Literary methods	90(Bedford)
antiquities	846(Lincoln)	Literary theory	315(Cambridge)
archaeology	846(Lincoln)	Literature	32(Ashington)
Church Plate	845(Lincoln)		35(Aylesbury)
local history	846, 847(Lincoln)		132, 142, 154,
natural history	846(Lincoln)		157(Birmingham)
pictures	855(Lincoln)		161(Blackburn)
topography	844(Lincoln)		191(Bournemouth)
Lincolnshire	2100(Scunthorpe)		198(Bradford)
antiquities	846(Lincoln)		261(Burton-on-Trent)
archaeology	843, 846, 850(Lincoln)		315(Cambridge)
architecture	850(Lincoln)		328(Canterbury)
Church Plate	845(Lincoln)		359(Carshalton)
dialect	850(Lincoln)		390(Chesterfield)
ecclesiology	850(Lincoln)		406(Coatbridge)
history	651(Grimsby)		409(Colchester)
	850(Lincoln)		411(Coleraine)
literature	651(Grimsby)		417(Coventry)
local history	597(Gainsborough)		448(Deeside)
	651(Grimsby)		493(Durham)
	846, 847, 850, 851, 852(Lincoln)		584, 585, 587(Exeter)
			606, 612(Glasgow)
natural history	846(Lincoln)		655(Guildford)
North	2099(Scunthorpe)		665(Halesowen)
pictures	855(Lincoln)		671(Harlech)
topography	844, 850(Lincoln)		673(Harlow)
Lindisfarne gospels	2042(Ripon)		748(Ilkeston)
Linen industry, history, Ulster	113(Belfast)		762(Keighley)
			813(Leeds)
Linguistic Atlas	123(Bingley)		866, 872, 877(Liverpool)
Linguistics	154(Birmingham)		926(London SW1)
	301, 310, 315(Cambridge)		1110(London SW15)
	330(Canterbury)		1167(London SW17)
	403(Chorley)		1334(London SE13)
	506(Edinburgh)		1339(London E1)
	612(Glasgow)		1343(London SW1)
	661(Guildford)		1379(London EC4)
	800, 812, 813(Leeds)		1387(London SW1)
	994(London WC2)		1473(London SW16)
	1117(London W5)		1587(London WC2)
	1307, 1474(London WC1)		1615(London N14)
	1650(London NW1)		1693(London SW19)
	1662(London WC1)		1732(Maidstone)
	2014(Preston)		1768, 1770,
	2035(Retford)		1778(Manchester)
	2214(Torquay)		1808(Middlesbrough)

Literature (contd)	1811 (Mirfield)	Catalan	315 (Cambridge)
	1819 (Motherwell)	Celtic	1972 (Oxford)
	1823 (Neath)	Chile	894 (London W1)
	1844 (Newcastle upon Tyne)	Chinese	1052 (London EC2)
	1858 (Newport, Mon)		1968 (Oxford)
	1882 (Norwich)	classical	58 (Barnstaple)
	1891 (Nottingham)		492 (Durham)
	1910, 1911 (Oldham)		788 (Lancaster)
	1918, 1975 (Oxford)		1918, 1946, 1952 (Oxford)
	1993 (Plymouth)		2124 (Shrewsbury)
	1998 (Pontypridd)	Commonwealth	1082 (Edinburgh)
	1999 (Poole)		1082 (London W8)
	2002 (Portsmouth)	criticism	2150 (Southport)
	2012 (Prescot)	Czechoslovakia	311 (Cambridge)
	2027 (Reading)	Danish	315 (Cambridge)
	2030 (Redditch)		651 (Grimsby)
	2073 (St Andrews)	devotional	401 (Chipping Norton)
	2098 (Scunthorpe)	Dorset	459 (Dorchester)
	2135 (Slough)	dramatic	1512 (London WC1)
	2198 (Sutton Coldfield)	Early English	107 (Belfast)
	2214 (Torquay)	East European	1668 (London WC1)
	2232 (Twickenham)	emblem	630 (Glasgow)
	2242 (Wallsend)	English	17 (Aberystwyth)
	2295 (Windsor)		71, 73, 75 (Bath)
	2307 (Wolverhampton)		141, 154 (Birmingham)
Africa	866 (Liverpool)		160 (Bishop's Stortford)
	1968 (Oxford)		222 (Brighton)
Afrikaans	1972 (Oxford)		235 (Bristol)
Albania	1972 (Oxford)		291 (Cambridge)
American	17 (Aberystwyth)		422 (Coventry)
	179 (Bolton)		435 (Dagenham)
	583 (Exeter)		457 (Doncaster)
	1326 (London W5)		485, 486, 492 (Durham)
	1339 (London E1)		529 (Edinburgh)
	1650 (London NW1)		576 (Enfield)
	1855 (Newport, Mon)		579 (Epsom)
	2011 (Prescot)		636 (Gloucester)
	2279 (Weymouth)		647 (Great Yarmouth)
criticism	2021 (Reading)		667 (Halifax)
history	2021 (Reading)		671 (Harlech)
Anglo-Saxon	2021 (Reading)		734 (Hull)
Arabic	81 (Beaconsfield)		754 (Ipswich)
	1285 (London NW8)		778 (Kingston upon Thames)
ascetical	401 (Chipping Norton)		813 (Leeds)
Asia	1518 (London W1M 9LA)		837 (Lichfield)
	1968 (Oxford)		1129 (London SW7)
Australia	866 (Liverpool)		1165 (London SW15)
	928 (London WC2)		1210 (London EC4)
Austria	929 (London SW7)		1302 (London SE11)
Basque	1972 (Oxford)		1326 (London W5)
Biblical	401 (Chipping Norton)		1495 (London W1)
Braille	610 (Glasgow)		1650 (London NW1)
British Commonwealth	13 (Aberdeen)		1653 (London SE14)
	866 (Liverpool)		1688 (London SW1)
Bulgaria	311 (Cambridge)		1782, 1789 (Manchester)
Byzantine	1972 (Oxford)		1837, 1839, 1845, 1850
Canada	866 (Liverpool)		(Newcastle upon Tyne)

Literature, English (contd)	1854, 1855, 1860(Newport, Mon)		2011(Prescot)
	1862(Newton Stewart)		2100(Scunthorpe)
	1895(Nottingham)	translation	2279(Weymouth)
	1918, 1946, 1948,	Gaelic	813(Leeds)
	1956(Oxford)	German	513, 517, 572(Edinburgh)
	2011(Prescot)		154(Birmingham)
	2020(Reading)		201(Bradford)
	2035(Retford)		315(Cambridge)
	2043(Ripon)		422(Coventry)
	2129(Sleaford)		435(Dagenham)
	2144(Southampton)		485(Durham)
	2205(Tamworth)		778(Kingston upon Thames)
	2218(Truro)		805(Leeds)
	2279(Weymouth)		1177(London SW7)
	2312(Worcester)		1339(London E1)
	2321(Worthing)		1653(London SE14)
	2333(York)		1658(London WC1)
bibliographies	286(Cambridge)		1839(Newcastle upon Tyne)
criticism	2021(Reading)		1891, 1895(Nottingham)
Elizabethan	1354(London SE19)		1918, 1965, 1972(Oxford)
history	612(Glasgow)		2011(Prescot)
	2021(Reading)		2100(Scunthorpe)
Estonian	651(Grimsby)	Germanic	847(Lincoln)
European	291(Cambridge)	Greek	154(Birmingham)
	486, 492(Durham)		186(Boston)
	667(Halifax)		301(Cambridge)
	1965, 1972(Oxford)		486(Durham)
evangelical	1136(London W1M 2HB)		1250(London W1)
Finnish	1338(London SE22)		1338(London SE22)
foreign	222(Brighton)		1539(London W1)
	610(Glasgow)		1731(Maidstone)
	2259(Wednesbury)	Gypsy	1965, 1972(Oxford)
French	154(Birmingham)	Halifax	878(Liverpool)
	201(Bradford)	Hebrew	666(Halifax)
	315(Cambridge)		186(Boston)
	381(Chertsey)	Hindi	1383(London WC1)
	422(Coventry)	history	2304(Wolverhampton)
	435(Dagenham)		140(Birmingham)
	485(Durham)		847(Lincoln)
	529(Edinburgh)	Holland	2150(Southport)
	778(Kingston upon Thames)		315(Cambridge)
	788(Lancaster)	Hungarian	1658(London WC1)
	805(Leeds)		315(Cambridge)
	1163(London SW7)		651(Grimsby)
	1165(London SW15)	Icelandic	1330(London W6)
	1210(London EC4)		315(Cambridge)
	1339(London E1)	Indian	651(Grimsby)
	1653(London SE14)		1972(Oxford)
	1839, 1946(Newcastle upon Tyne)	Irish	866(Liverpool)
	1851(Newport, Isle of Wight)		1968(Oxford)
			92, 107(Belfast)
		Islamic	866(Liverpool)
	1895(Nottingham)	Italian	1285(London NW8)
	1911(Oldham)		154(Birmingham)
	1918, 1965, 1972(Oxford)		277, 315(Cambridge)
			422(Coventry)
			805(Leeds)

Literature, Italian (contd)	1322(London NW4)		1591(London SW9)
	1918, 1965(Oxford)		1839(Newcastle upon Tyne)
	2100(Scunthorpe)		2100(Scunthorpe)
Japan	1289(London W1X 9LB)	Scandinavian	1658(London WC1)
	1968(Oxford)		1972(Oxford)
Jewish	1292(London W1)	Scottish	603, 610(Glasgow)
	1339(London E1)		866(Liverpool)
Lapp	651(Grimsby)		2166(Stirling)
Latin	154(Birmingham)	Serbian	1330(London W6)
	186(Boston)	Slavonic	1668(London WC1)
	301(Cambridge)		1965, 1972(Oxford)
	486(Durham)	Socialist	422(Coventry)
	1338(London SE22)	Soviet	1591(London SW9)
	1731(Maidstone)	Spanish	154(Birmingham)
	1800(Matlock)		201(Bradford)
medieval	315(Cambridge)		315(Cambridge)
Latin America	409(Colchester)		778(Kingston upon Thames)
	1303(London WC2)		788(Lancaster)
	1965(Oxford)		805(Leeds)
Lettish	651(Grimsby)		1918, 1972(Oxford)
Lincolnshire	651(Grimsby)		2100(Scunthorpe)
modern	233(Bristol)	Swedish	315(Cambridge)
musical	192(Bournemouth)		651(Grimsby)
Muslim	1285(London NW8)	Talmudic	1292(London W1)
North American	409(Colchester)	Teutonic	1851(Newport, Isle of Wight)
Norwegian	315(Cambridge)		
	651(Grimsby)	criticism	443(Dartford)
	1338(London SE22)	history	443(Dartford)
	2073(St Andrews)	tractarian	397(Chichester)
Oriental	291(Cambridge)	Turkey	1968(Oxford)
Patristic	1942(Oxford)	United Kingdom	866(Liverpool)
Persian	1968(Oxford)	United States of America	866(Liverpool)
Polish	311(Carlisle)		950(London W1)
	1333(London SW2)		1791(Manchester)
	1479(London SW1)	Urdu	2304(Wolverhampton)
	1480(London SW7)	Welsh	17(Aberystwyth)
	2100(Scunthorpe)		54(Bangor)
Portuguese	154(Birmingham)		866(Liverpool)
	315(Cambridge)	Worcester	2312(Worcester)
	1322(London NW4)	Yorkshire	666(Halifax)
	1339(London E1)	Yugoslavian	311(Cambridge)
	1965, 1972(Oxford)	Lithography	162(Blackburn)
Punjabi	2304(Wolverhampton)		349(Carlisle)
Puritan	1136(London W1M 2HB)		1608(London WC1)
Rabbinic	1292(London W1)	Lithuania	1318(London N11)
Roman	1250(London WC1)	Litter	1301(London WC2)
Romance	107(Belfast)	disposal	1301(London WC2)
Rumanian	315(Cambridge)	Liturgical revision	1979(Penarth)
	1322(London NW4)	Liturgiology	95(Belfast)
	1965(Oxford)		569(Edinburgh)
Russian	81(Beaconsfield)	Liturgy	284, 296(Cambridge)
	201(Bradford)		397(Chichester)
	311(Cambridge)		401(Chipping Norton)
	409(Colchester)		424(Crawley)
	778(Kingston upon Thames)		433(Croydon)
	805(Leeds)		492(Durham)
	1330(London W6)		584(Exeter)

Liturgy (contd)	1022 (London SW1)	Barnstaple	58, 59 (Barnstaple)
	1093 (London EC2)	Bath	71 (Bath)
	1647 (London SW1)	Batley	78 (Batley)
	1851 (Newport, Isle of Wight)	Battersea	1069 (London SW12)
		Bebington	2297 (Wirral)
	1924, 1942 (Oxford)	Bedfordshire	90 (Bedford)
	2042 (Ripon)		1722 (Luton)
	2073 (St Andrews)		2068 (St Albans)
Jewish	912 (London E1)	Bexley	119 (Bexley)
Protestant	1219 (London WC1)	Berwick-upon-Tweed	115 (Berwick-upon-Tweed)
Liverpool	861 (Liverpool)	Black Country	415 (Dudley)
district nursing, history	881 (Liverpool)		2303 (Wolverhampton)
local history	857, 859, 866 (Liverpool)	Blackpool	167 (Blackpool)
social service	869 (Liverpool)	Bodmin	171 (Bodmin)
voluntary organizations	869 (Liverpool)	Bolton	181 (Bolton)
Ll. Powys	459 (Dorchester)	Bootle	183 (Bootle)
Llanelli pottery	2199 (Swansea)	Boston	187 (Boston)
Local co-operative schemes	2355–2414	Bradford	197, 198, 199 (Bradford)
Local government	25 (Alloa)	Brechin	203 (Brechin)
	370 (Chelmsford)	Breconshire	204, 205 (Brecon)
	485 (Durham)	Bridgwater	213, 214 (Bridgwater)
	667 (Halifax)	Bridlington	218 (Bridlington)
	676 (Harrogate)	Brighton	724 (Hove)
	1181 (London SE1)	Bristol	232, 233 (Bristol)
	1319, 1381 (London SW1)		634 (Gloucester)
	1398 (London WC1)	Brockenhurst	249 (Brockenhurst)
	1711 (Loughborough)	Buckinghamshire	36, 37, 38 (Aylesbury)
	1829 (Newcastle)		1722 (Luton)
	1853 (Newport, Isle of Wight)	Bury St Edmunds	265 (Bury St Edmunds)
		Bute County	2056 (Rothesay)
	2021 (Reading)	Buxton	266 (Buxton)
	2126 (Shrewsbury)	Camborne	272 (Camborne)
	2142 (Southampton)	Cambridge	276, 310 (Cambridge)
	2254 (Warwick)	Cambridgeshire	276, 310 (Cambridge)
	2289 (Winchester)		1796 (March)
	2307 (Wolverhampton)	Canterbury	327 (Canterbury)
administration	154 (Birmingham)	Cardiganshire	1 (Aberaeron)
Scotland	553 (Edinburgh)	Carlisle	346, 353 (Carlisle)
statistics	2023 (Reading)	Carlton	1887 (Nottingham)
Local history	61 (Barry)	Carmarthenshire	355 (Carmarthen)
	133 (Birmingham)	Chalfont St Giles	365 (Chalfont St Giles)
	479 (Dunoon)	Channel Islands	653 (Guernsey)
	560 (Edinburgh)	Chatham	600 (Gillingham)
	831 (Leicester)		2047 (Rochester)
Aberdeen	5 (Aberdeen)	Chelmsford	368, 370 (Chelmsford)
Aberdeenshire	4 (Aberdeen)	Cheltenham	376, 377 (Cheltenham)
Aldershot	23 (Aldershot)	Cheshire	125 (Birkenhead)
Anglesey	833 (Llangefni)		389 (Chester)
Ashton-under-Lyne	34 (Ashton-under-Lyne)		742 (Hyde)
Ayrshire	41 (Ayr)		840 (Lichfield)
	2092 (Saltcoats)		866 (Liverpool)
Bacup	45 (Bacup)		1760 (Manchester)
Banbury	50 (Banbury)		2168 (Stockport)
Banffshire	763 (Keith)		2298 (Wirral)
Barking	436 (Dagenham)	Cheshunt	2246 (Waltham Cross)
Barnet	2008 (Potters Bar)	Chester	389 (Chester)
Barnsley	57 (Barnsley)	Chesterfield	391 (Chesterfield)

Local history (contd)
- Chichester — 394, 395 (Chichester)
- City of Westminster — 1688 (London SW1)
- Clapham — 1069 (London SW12)
- Clydebank — 405 (Clydebank)
- Colchester — 407, 408 (Colchester)
- Cornwall — 591 (Falmouth)
  2218, 2219, 2220 (Truro)
- Cotswolds — 376, 377 (Cheltenham)
- County Down — 48 (Ballynahinch)
- Coventry — 418 (Coventry)
- Crawley — 424 (Crawley)
- Croydon — 429 (Croydon)
- Cumberland — 353 (Carlisle)
  2281 (Whitehaven)
- Dagenham — 436 (Dagenham)
- Darent Valley — 441 (Dartford)
- Darlington — 439 (Darlington)
- Dartford — 441, 443 (Dartford)
- Denbighshire — 2062 (Ruthin)
- Derby — 451 (Derby)
- Derbyshire — 391 (Chesterfield)
  451 (Derby)
  742 (Hyde)
  840 (Lichfield)
- Devon — 1992 (Plymouth)
  North — 58 (Barnstaple)
- Dorset — 460 (Dorchester)
  2288 (Wimborne)
  2326 (Yeovil)
- Dudley — 465 (Dudley)
- Dumfries — 466 (Dumfries)
- Dunbartonshire — 405 (Clydebank)
- Dunfermline — 477, 478 (Dunfermline)
- Durham — 486 (Durham)
  1833, 1849 (Newcastle upon Tyne)
- East Anglia — 1879 (Norwich)
- East Ham — 1337 (London E15)
- East Lothian — 664 (Haddington)
- Eastbourne — 497 (Eastbourne)
- Eccles — 1748 (Manchester)
- Elgin — 575 (Elgin)
- Ellesmere Port — 2298 (Wirral)
- Epping Forest — 1675 (London E17)
- Epsom — 578 (Epsom)
- Essex — 368, 370 (Chelmsford)
  407, 408 (Colchester)
  436 (Dagenham)
  645 (Grays)
  1337, 1470 (London E15)
  2050 (Romford)
- Evesham — 582 (Evesham)
- Ewell — 578 (Epsom)
- Exeter — 584 (Exeter)
- Farnham — 592 (Farnham)
- Fens — 1796 (March)

- 1989 (Peterborough)
- Fife, West — 478 (Dunfermline)
- Flint — 593 (Flint)
- Flintshire — 593 (Flint)
  1813 (Mold)
- Folkestone — 595 (Folkestone)
- Gainsborough — 597 (Gainsborough)
- Gateshead — 599 (Gateshead)
- Gillingham — 600 (Gillingham)
  2047 (Rochester)
- Glamorgan — 2001 (Port Talbot)
- Glasgow — 603, 610, 630 (Glasgow)
- Glastonbury — 633 (Glastonbury)
- Gloucestershire — 634, 635, 636, 637 (Gloucester)
- Goole — 636 (Goole)
- Gosforth — 1832 (Newcastle upon Tyne)
- Grantham — 641, 643 (Grantham)
- Great Yarmouth — 647 (Great Yarmouth)
- Guernsey — 653 (Guernsey)
- Halesowen — 665 (Halesowen)
- Halifax — 2153 (Sowerby Bridge)
- Hampshire — 2002, 2004 (Portsmouth)
- Hampstead — 1324 (London NW3)
- Haringey — 1331 (London N17)
- Harrogate — 677 (Harrogate)
- Hartlepool — 681 (Hartlepool)
- Haslingden — 2051 (Rossendale)
- Hastings — 683 (Hastings)
- Havering — 2050 (Romford)
- Hereford — 703 (Hereford)
- Herefordshire — 705 (Hereford)
- Hertford — 708 (Hertford)
- Hertfordshire — 709 (Hertford)
  718 (Hitchin)
  1722 (Luton)
  2068, 2069 (St Albans)
  2246 (Waltham Cross)
- Heywood — 712 (Heywood)
- Hitchin — 718 (Hitchin)
- Holborn — 1325 (London WC1)
- Hoylake — 2299 (Wirral)
- Huddersfield — 727 (Huddersfield)
- Hull — 733, 734, 735 (Hull)
- Huntingdonshire — 741 (Huntingdon)
- Huyton-with-Roby — 865 (Liverpool)
- Hyde — 742 (Hyde)
- Ilkeston — 747 (Ilkeston)
- Ipswich — 753 (Ipswich)
- Ireland — 92 (Belfast)
- Isle of Ely — 1796 (March)
- Isle of Wight — 2002 (Portsmouth)
- Keighley — 761 (Keighley)
- Kent — 119 (Bexley)
  595 (Folkestone)
  600 (Gillingham)
  683 (Hastings)

Local history, Kent (contd)	1328 (London SE10)		1821 (Nairn)
East	327 (Canterbury)	Nelson	1824 (Nelson)
North West	429 (Croydon)	Newark	1826, 1827 (Newark)
Kesteven	2128 (Sleaford)	Newburn	1834 (Newcastle upon Tyne)
Kettering	769 (Kettering)	Newcastle	1829 (Newcastle)
Kidderminster	771 (Kidderminster)	Newcastle upon Tyne	1833, 1834 (Newcastle upon Tyne)
King's Lynn	774, 775 (King's Lynn)	Norfolk	775 (King's Lynn)
Kinross-shire	1988 (Perth)		1878, 1879, 1882 (Norwich)
Kirkwall	782 (Kirkwall)	Northampton	1865, 1866 (Northampton)
Lake District	764, 766 (Kendal)	Northamptonshire	769 (Kettering)
Lambeth	1333 (London SE5)		1866, 1868, 1869 (Northampton)
Lanarkshire, North	21 (Airdrie)	Northumberland	1818 (Morpeth)
Lancashire	125 (Birkenhead)		1833, 1836, 1847, 1849 (Newcastle upon Tyne)
	742 (Hyde)		
	866 (Liverpool)		
	1760 (Manchester)		
	2017 (Preston)		
	2286 (Wigan)	Norwich	1875, 1882 (Norwich)
South	840 (Lichfield)	Nottingham	1891 (Nottingham)
Lancaster	786, 787 (Lancaster)	Nottinghamshire	1891 (Nottingham)
Leamington Spa	792 (Leamington Spa)		1902 (Nottingham)
Leeds	802, 803, 811 (Leeds)		2319 (Worksop)
Leek	820 (Leek)	Nuneaton	1903 (Nuneaton)
Leicester	825 (Leicester)	Oldham	1911 (Oldham)
Leicestershire	825, 826, 827 (Leicester)	Orkney	782 (Kirkwall)
Lichfield	837, 839, 840 (Lichfield)	Oswestry	2126 (Shrewsbury)
Lincoln	846, 847 (Lincoln)	Oxford	1935, 1936 (Oxford)
Lincolnshire	597 (Gainsborough)	Oxfordshire	1940 (Oxford)
	651 (Grimsby)	Paddington	1688 (London NW1)
	846, 847, 850, 851, 852 (Lincoln)	Paisley	1978 (Paisley)
		Pembrokeshire	690, 691 (Haverfordwest)
North	2099 (Scunthorpe)	Pendlebury	1786 (Manchester)
Liverpool	857, 859, 866 (Liverpool)	Perthshire	428 (Crieff)
London	1337 (London E15)		1988 (Perth)
Londonderry	1709 (Londonderry)	Peterborough	1989 (Peterborough)
Louth	851 (Lincoln)	Plymouth	1992, 1996 (Plymouth)
	1716 (Louth)	Poole	1999 (Poole)
Lowestoft	753 (Ipswich)	Port Talbot	2001 (Port Talbot)
Ludlow	2126 (Shrewsbury)	Portslade	724 (Hove)
Luton	1721 (Luton)	Portsmouth	2002, 2004 (Portsmouth)
Macclesfield	1725 (Macclesfield)	Potters Bar	2008 (Potters Bar)
Madeley	2126 (Shrewsbury)	Radcliffe	1779 (Manchester)
Malvern	1735 (Malvern)	Redruth	2033 (Redruth)
Manchester	1771 (Manchester)	Rhondda	1983 (Pentre)
Mansfield	1795 (Mansfield)	Richmond	2039 (Richmond)
Medway Towns	600 (Gillingham)	Ripon	2042 (Ripon)
	2047 (Rochester)	Rochester	600 (Gillingham)
Merseyside	183 (Bootle)		2047 (Rochester)
	2298 (Wirral)	Rossendale	45 (Bacup)
Middlesex	1184 (London SW1)		2051 (Rossendale)
Midlothian	1820 (Musselburgh)	Rotherham	2054 (Rotherham)
Monmouth	1814 (Monmouth)	Roxburghshire	692, 693, 694 (Hawick)
Monmouthshire	1855, 1856 (Newport, Mon)	Runcorn	2061 (Runcorn)
Montrose	1815, 1816 (Montrose)	Rutherglen	615 (Glasgow)
Morayshire	575 (Elgin)	Rutland	1906 (Oakham)
Morpeth	1818 (Morpeth)	St Albans	2068, 2069 (St Albans)
Nairn	575 (Elgin)	St Helens	2077 (St Helens)

Local history (contd)
  St Ives   2078 (St Ives)
  St Leonards   683 (Hastings)
  St Marylebone   1688 (London NW1)
  St Pancras   1324 (London NW3)
  Salford   2084, 2085 (Salford)
  Salisbury   2090, 2091 (Salisbury)
  Saltcoats   2092 (Saltcoats)
  Scarborough   2095, 2096 (Scarborough)
  Scottish Border   692, 693, 694 (Hawick)
  Scotland   530, 572 (Edinburgh)
  Sevenoaks   2104 (Sevenoaks)
  Sheffield   2112 (Sheffield)
  Shropshire   2124, 2125,
                                             2126 (Shrewsbury)
  Sleaford   2128 (Sleaford)
  Soke of Peterborough   1868 (Northampton)
  Somerset   633 (Glastonbury)
                                           2210 (Taunton)
                                           2326 (Yeovil)
  Southampton   2143 (Southampton)
  Southport   2150 (Southport)
  Southwell   2152 (Southwell)
  Staffordshire   839, 840 (Lichfield)
                                           2155 (Stafford)
  Stamford   2157, 2158 (Stamford)
  Stirling   2161, 2164, 2165 (Stirling)
  Stockport   2168 (Stockport)
  Stoke-on-Trent   2176 (Stoke-on-Trent)
  Stratford-upon-Avon   2179, 2180 (Stratford-upon-Avon)
  Suffolk   1879 (Norwich)
    East   753 (Ipswich)
  Sunderland   2186 (Sunderland)
  Surrey   581 (Esher)
                                           1333 (London SE5)
    North East   429 (Croydon)
  Sussex   497 (Eastbourne)
                                           683 (Hastings)
                                           2323 (Worthing)
    East   399 (Chichester)
    West   395, 399 (Chichester)
  Swansea   2201 (Swansea)
  Swindon   2204 (Swindon)
  Swinton   1786 (Manchester)
  Tamworth   2206 (Tamworth)
  Taunton   2210 (Taunton)
  Thurrock   645 (Grays)
                                           2213 (Tilbury)
  Tilbury   2213 (Tilbury)
  Totnes   2215 (Totnes)
  Tottenham   1331 (London N17)
  Tower Hamlets   1339 (London E1)
  Truro   2219 (Truro)
  Tunbridge Wells   2225 (Tunbridge Wells)
  Wakefield   2237 (Wakefield)
  Wales, North   389 (Chester)
  Waltham Abbey   2246 (Waltham Cross)
  Waltham Cross   2246 (Waltham Cross)
  Walthamstow   1675 (London E17)
  Walton   2277 (Weybridge)
  Warrington   2252 (Warrington)
  Warwick   2253, 2254 (Warwick)
  Warwickshire   418 (Coventry)
                                           792 (Leamington Spa)
                                           840 (Lichfield)
                                           1903 (Nuneaton)
                                           2178, 2179 (Stratford-upon-Avon)
                                           2254 (Warwick)
  Watford   2258 (Watford)
  West Ham   1337 (London E15)
  West Lothian   77 (Bathgate)
  Westminster   1688 (London SW1)
  Westmorland   2281 (Whitehaven)
  Weston super Mare   2274 (Weston super Mare)
  Weybridge   2277 (Weybridge)
  Whitchurch   2126 (Shrewsbury)
  Whitley Bay   2282 (Whitley Bay)
  Wigan   2286 (Wigan)
  Wiltshire   453 (Devizes)
                                           2090, 2091 (Salisbury)
    North   2204 (Swindon)
  Winchester   2290, 2292 (Winchester)
  Wolverhampton   2303 (Wolverhampton)
  Worcestershire   771 (Kidderminster)
                                           2311, 2314 (Worcester)
  Workington   2317 (Workington)
  Worksop   2319 (Worksop)
  Worthing   2323 (Worthing)
  York   2337 (York)
  Yorkshire   677 (Harrogate)
                                           742 (Hyde)
                                           819 (Leeds)
                                           2237 (Wakefield)
                                           2331, 2337 (York)
    East Riding   218 (Bridlington)
    North Riding   1863, 1864 (Northallerton)
  See also History
Location of offices   1320 (London WC2)
Locomotor medicine   959 (London W1M 7AE)
Logic   1939 (Oxford)
London   1181, 1182 (London SE1)
                                           1187 (London EC2)
                                           1586 (London EC3)
                                           1662 (London WC1)
                                           1674 (London E17)
  archaeology   1097 (London SE17)
  history   828 (Leicester)
                                           943, 1089 (London EC2)
                                           1181 (London SE1)
                                           1184 (London SW1)
  local history   1337 (London E15)
  maps   943 (London EC2)

London (*contd*)
   natural history   1326(London W5)
   paintings   1186(London EC2)
   pictures   1630(London WC2)
   railways, history   1390(London SW4)
   road transport, history   1390(London SW4)
   topography   943(London EC2)
       1181(London SE1)
       1210(London EC4)
       1332(London N7)
       1345(London SE5)
   tourism   1346(London W1V 9DD)
Londonderry, local history   1709(Londonderry)
Londonderry County   410(Coleraine)
   paintings   410(Coleraine)
Lord Tennyson   854, 855(Lincoln)
Lord's Day observance   1348(London EC4)
Louth, local history   851(Lincoln)
       1716(Louth)
Low countries   2051(Rossendale)
   art   1883(Norwich)
Low temperature work   455(Didcot)
Lowestoft, local history   753(Ipswich)
Lowestoft porcelain   1873(Norwich)
L. S. Lowry   2085(Salford)
Lucas, William   718(Hitchin)
Ludlow, local history   2126(Ludlow)
Lung
   cancer   1633(London SW1)
   physiology   1980(Penarth)
Lustre ware   1795(Mansfield)
Luther   1972(Oxford)
Luton, local history   1721(Luton)
Luxembourg   408(Colchester)
       1349(London SW1)
   geography   2278(Weymouth)
   history   2278(Weymouth)
   tourism   1350(London SW1)
Lyttelton   1686(London NW3)
Lytton, Bulwer   1190(London W3)

M

Macclesfield, local history   1725(Macclesfield)
MacDonald, George   4(Aberdeen)
MacDonald, Ramsay   994(London WC2)
MacNeice   1798(Marlborough)
Madeley, local history   2126(Madeley)
Magic   591(Falmouth)
       1662(London WC1)
Magna Carta   845(Lincoln)
Maladjusted children   924(London W14)
Malaysia   1201(London SW1)
Malta   1316(London EC1)
Malvern, local history   1735(Malvern)
Management   114(Berkhamsted)
       145(Birmingham)
       271(Camberley)
       375(Chelmsford)
       390(Chesterfield)
       423(Crawley)
       511(Edinburgh)
       587(Exeter)
       598(Galashiels)
       606(Glasgow)
       646(Grays)
       665(Halesowen)
       667(Halifax)
       700(Henley-on-Thames)
       726(Huddersfield)
       754(Ipswich)
       770(Kettering)
       778(Kingston upon Thames)
       872(Liverpool)
       942(London WC1)
       1042(London EC2)
       1074(London W1)
       1080(London WC2)
       1117(London W5)
       1199, 1253(London SW1)
       1276(London W1X 9PA)
       1421(London W1M 8DR)
       1451(London NW5)
       1482(London W1R 8AL)
       1560(London SW1)
       1664(London W8)
       1698(London SE18)
       1719(Luton)
       1724(Macclesfield)
       1728(Maidenhead)
       1734(Maidstone)
       1808(Middlesbrough)
       1886, 1895(Nottingham)
       2030(Redruth)
       2121(Shrewsbury)
       2171(Stoke-on-Trent)
       2236(Wakefield)
       2300(Wirral)
       2307(Wolverhampton)
       2316(Workington)
   business   1839(Newcastle upon Tyne)
   catering   661(Guildford)
   consultancy   1119(London SW1)
   domestic   1695(London WC1)
   economics   114(Berkhamsted)
   education   1253(London SW1)
   estate   1073(London W8)
   hospitals   881(Liverpool)
       2147(Southampton)
   hotel   661(Guildford)
   nursing   587(Exeter)
   office   700(Henley-on-Thames)
       2259(Wednesbury)

Management (contd)			872(Liverpool)
personnel	700(Henley-on-Thames)	Maritime signals	1425(London SE10)
	1719(Luton)	Maritime studies	340(Cardiff)
production	700(Henley-on-Thames)	Maritime subjects	883(Llangefni)
science	2129(Sleaford)	Market information, foreign	948(London EC4)
wage	1681(London W4)	Market research	1119(London SW1)
work	2205(Tamworth)	Marketing	145(Birmingham)
See also Volume I			511, 520(Edinburgh)
Managers	1253(London SW1)		606(Glasgow)
Manchester Diocese,			646(Grays)
Church of England	1763(Manchester)		700(Henley-on-Thames)
Manchester			717(Hitchin)
genealogy	1772(Manchester)		884(London WC2)
history	1771(Manchester)		1119, 1253(London SW1)
local history	1771(Manchester)		1617(London SW17)
medicine	1791(Manchester)		1839(Newcastle upon Tyne)
music	1755(Manchester)	agriculture	1412(London SW1)
Manipulative medicine	959(London W1M 7AE)	horticulture	1412(London SW1)
Manipulative treatment	959(London W1M 7AE)	See also Volume I	
Manor houses, Sussex	724(Hove)	Marlburian poets,	
Manpower	225, 227(Brighton)	prose-writers and Scholars	1798(Marlborough)
	1104(London SW1)	Marlowe	1354(London SE19)
Mansfield		Marquis of Rockingham	2112(Sheffield)
local history	1795(Mansfield)	Marriage	1132(London SW1)
water-colours	1795(Mansfield)		1142(London W1N 8BQ)
Manuscripts historical	1204(London WC2)		1387(London SW1)
Manx language	462(Douglas)	counselling	1024(London W11)
Maps (collections)	490(Durham)		1142(London W1N 8BQ)
	513, 537(Edinburgh)	problems	1353(London W1)
	996(London WC1)	Martial law	387(Chester)
	1159(London SE1)		581(Esher)
	1538(London SW7)	Martinware pottery	2137(Southall)
	1662(London WC1)	Martyrs	119(Bexley)
	1971(Oxford)	Marvell, Andrew	733(Hull)
	2100(Scunthorpe)	Marxism	
	2186(Sunderland)	books	1386(London EC1)
	2192(Surbiton)	ideology	2038(Richmond)
Denbighshire	2062(Ruthin)	theory	1355(London EC1)
Derbyshire	451(Derby)	Marxists, biography	2143(Southampton)
Devon, North	58(Barnstaple)	Mary Baker Eddy	1055(London WC2)
Ireland	92(Belfast)	Massage	2285(Wigan)
Lake District	350(Carlisle)	Materia medica	1472(London WC1)
London	943(London EC2)		1605(London W1)
Poland	1480(London SW7)		2150(Southport)
Surrey	660(Guildford)	Materials science	1839(Newcastle upon Tyne)
Wales	16(Aberystwyth)	Maternity services overseas	1526(London W1M 0BE)
Warwickshire	2253(Warwick)	Mathematical economics	154(Birmingham)
World Wars	1223(London SE1)	Mathematical statistics	2023(Reading)
Yorkshire	2239(Wakefield)	Mathematics	
Marie Antoinette	1949(Oxford)	(Volume I of the Directory includes mathematics, but it	
Marine law	2136(South Shields)	has also been indexed here for organizations which do not	
Maritime affairs	249(Brockenhurst)	appear in Volume I)	
Maritime books	2143(Southampton)		
Maritime countries,			75(Bath)
topography	1425(London SE10)		329(Canterbury)
Maritime history	1425(London SE10)		340(Cardiff)
Maritime law	736(Hull)		403(Chorley)
			406(Coatbridge)

Mathematics (contd)	419 (Coventry)	Medical dictionaries	1784 (Manchester)
	427 (Crewe)	Medical education	1574 (London SW1)
	435 (Dagenham)	use of television	914 (London SE6)
	446 (Deeside)	Medical encyclopaedias	1784 (Manchester)
	449 (Derby)	Medical examinations	2252 (Warrington)
	457 (Doncaster)	Medical gymnastics	797 (Leeds)
	470 (Dundee)		1475 (London W1M 4AX)
	487 (Durham)	Medical helminthology	2066 (St Albans)
	498 (Eastbourne)	Medical herbalism	2110 (Sheffield)
	516, 564 (Edinburgh)	Medical history	1531 (London NW1)
	574 (Egham)	Medical hypnosis	1008 (London W1)
	612 (Glasgow)	Medical instruments	1433 (London WC2)
	726 (Huddersfield)		2266 (Welwyn Garden City)
	734 (Hull)	Medical laboratory science	1453 (London SE1)
	788 (Lancaster)	Medical laboratory	
	812 (Leeds)	technology	145 (Birmingham)
	822 (Leicester)		335 (Cardiff)
	942 (London WC1)		770 (Kettering)
	994 (London WC2)		872 (Liverpool)
	1165 (London SW15)		1260 (London W1)
	1167 (London SW17)		1468 (London W2)
	1170 (London SW15)	Medical microbiology	1037 (London NW9)
	1175 (London WC2)	Medical missions	1570 (London EC4)
	1495 (London W1)	Medical museums	2252 (Warrington)
	1586 (London E1)	Medical mycology	1252 (London WC2)
	1722 (Luton)	Medical physics	341 (Cardiff)
	1746, 1782 (Manchester)		990 (London W1M 7PG)
	1801 (Matlock)		1214 (London SW1)
	1809 (Middlesbrough)		1245 (London SW3)
	1819 (Motherwell)	Medical portraiture	1531 (London NW1)
	1837, 1839,	Medical practice	1106 (London SE1)
	1846 (Newcastle upon	Medical professions	2242 (Warrington)
	Tyne)	Medical sciences	188 (Boston Spa)
	1853 (Newport, Isle of		1303 (London WC2)
	Wight)		1380 (London W1P 7PN)
	1893 (Nottingham)		1432 (London W2)
	1948 (Oxford)	history	1631 (London WC1)
	1992 (Plymouth)	Medical sociology	12 (Aberdeen)
	2020, 2023 (Reading)	Medical specialists,	
	2030 (Redditch)	biography	1731 (Maidstone)
	2043 (Ripon)	Medical theses	995 (London WC1)
	2129 (Sleaford)	Medicinal chemistry	738 (Hull)
	2173 (Stoke-on-Trent)	Medicinal plants	1605 (London W1)
	2232 (Twickenham)	Medicinal products	1605 (London W1)
	2290 (Winchester)	Medicine	6, 13 (Aberdeen)
	2305, 2306 (Wolverhampton)		52, 54 (Bangor)
	2321 (Worthing)		63, 64, 66, 68 (Basingstoke)
history	246 (Bristol)		80 (Batley)
McMillan, Rachel	1498 (London SE8)		88 (Bedford)
Meat hygiene	2190 (Surbiton)		99, 108 (Belfast)
Mechanics	2308 (Wolverton)		117 (Betchworth)
Medals	7 (Aberdeen)		152, 154 (Birmingham)
	1904 (Nuneaton)		159 (Bishop Auckland)
Medical appliances	2252 (Warrington)		176 (Bolton)
Medical biographies	1063 (London W1N 4BN)		188 (Boston Spa)
	1531 (London NW1)		190 (Bournemouth)
Medical biology	1679 (London NW1)		198, 201 (Bradford)

Medicine (contd)
207 (Brentford)
244, 245, 246 (Bristol)
257 (Burgess Hill)
258 (Burnley)
291, 292, 304, 305, 306, 318, 320 (Cambridge)
344 (Cardiff)
362 (Carshalton)
366 (Chatham)
371, 374 (Chelmsford)
396 (Chichester)
437 (Dagenham)
442 (Dartford)
474 (Dundee)
484 (Durham)
500 (Eastleigh)
510, 534, 536, 539, 565, 571 (Edinburgh)
584, 586 (Exeter)
608, 630 (Glasgow)
648 (Greenford)
668 (Halifax)
674 (Harlow)
681 (Harrow)
683 (Hastings)
723 (Hounslow)
733 (Hull)
746 (Ilford)
749 (Ilkley)
755 (Ipswich)
757 (Isleworth)
773 (Kilmarnock)
779 (Kingston upon Thames)
817 (Leeds)
848 (Lincoln)
863, 866, 870, 878, 881 (Liverpool)
882 (Llanelli)
971 (London W1Y 2AA)
978 (London W1M 8AL)
995 (London WC1)
1033 (London NW10)
1043 (London WC2)
1063 (London W1N 4BN)
1160 (London E11)
1193 (London E9)
1236 (London W1P 3LD)
1254 (London SW3)
1261 (London WC1)
1266 (London SE5)
1313 (London WC1)
1317 (London SW1)
1326 (London W5)
1327 (London W3)
1335 (London SE13)
1342 (London E1)
1379 (London EC4)
1429 (London N14)
1433 (London WC2)
1489 (London N15)
1528 (London W1M 0AB)
1532 (London WC2)
1534 (London SW1)
1537 (London WC1)
1551 (London W12)
1555 (London W1M 8AE)
1563 (London EC1)
1565 (London SW1)
1567 (London W2)
1569 (London SE1)
1572 (London W1N 8AE)
1649 (London WC1)
1688 (London NW1)
1689 (London SW1)
1697 (London SE18)
1708 (Londonderry)
1712, 1715 (Loughborough)
1721 (Luton)
1723, 1724 (Macclesfield)
1729 (Maidenhead)
1731 (Maidstone)
1791 (Manchester)
1794 (Mansfield)
1828 (Newbury)
1840, 1850 (Newcastle upon Tyne)
1852 (Newport, Isle of Wight)
1886, 1902 (Nottingham)
1905 (Nuneaton)
1915 (Orpington)
1918, 1920, 1946, 1948, 1950, 1970 (Oxford)
1987 (Perth)
1995 (Plymouth)
2006 (Portsmouth)
2011 (Prescot)
2025 (Reading)
2036 (Rhyl)
2073 (St Andrews)
2086 (Salford)
2094 (Sandwich)
2119 (Sheffield)
2124 (Shrewsbury)
2133 (Slough)
2137 (Southall)
2145, 2147 (Southampton)
2172 (Stoke-on-Trent)
2184, 2187, 2189 (Sunderland)
2191 (Surbiton)
2201 (Swansea)
2208 (Taunton)

Medicine (contd)	2223, 2224 (Tunbridge Wells)	occupational	521 (Edinburgh)
	2239 (Wakefield)		1611 (London NW1)
	2248 (Ware)	oral	344 (Cardiff)
	2252 (Warrington)	physical	1967 (Oxford)
	2264, 2265, 2266 (Welwyn Garden City)	postgraduate courses	1148 (London WC1)
		psychological	344 (Cardiff)
	2320 (Worthing)		1963 (Oxford)
biography	978 (London W1M 8AL)	psychosomatic	1267 (London W1)
	1563 (London EC1)	rehabilitation	974 (London WC1)
chest	1012 (London W1)	Royal Air Force	1111 (London WC1)
	1254 (London SW3)	social	154 (Birmingham)
history	1254 (London SW3)		344 (Cardiff)
comparative	1534 (London SW1)		565, 568 (Edinburgh)
computers	1363 (London E1)		1344, 1369 (London WC1)
Denmark	1536 (London SW1)	sociology	1650 (London NW1)
digestive system	167 (Blackpool)	sports	1270, 1475 (London W1M 4AX)
diseases at special developmental periods	34 (Ashton-under-Lyne)		2130 (Slough)
E.N.T.	1336 (London SW19)	tropical	85 (Beckenham)
environmental	1361 (London EC1)		873 (Liverpool)
forensic	1191 (London SE1)		1344 (London WC1)
general practice	1525 (London SW7)		1679 (London NW1)
herbal	186 (Boston)		1909 (Oldham)
history	13 (Aberdeen)	veterinary	291, 319 (Cambridge)
	108 (Belfast)		437 (Dagenham)
	245, 246 (Bristol)		539 (Edinburgh)
	474 (Dundee)		583 (Exeter)
	531, 533, 534, 536, 568 (Edinburgh)		630 (Glasgow)
			681 (Harrow)
	630 (Glasgow)		1433 (London WC2)
	755 (Ipswich)		1534 (London SW1)
	870 (Liverpool)		1730 (Maidenhead)
	978 (London W1M 8AL)		1886 (Nottingham)
	1043 (London WC2)		2248 (Ware)
	1254 (London SW3)		2265, 2266 (Welwyn Garden City)
	1563 (London EC1)		
	1678 (London NW1)	Medicines	1605 (London W1)
	1684 (London SE6)	Medico-psychology	1238 (London W1)
	1791 (Manchester)	Medieval history	493 (Durham)
	1850 (Newcastle upon Tyne)		1924 (Oxford)
	1943 (Oxford)	Meditation	564 (Edinburgh)
	2006 (Portsmouth)		1576 (London W1)
	2025, 2027 (Reading)	Mediterranean art	2111 (Sheffield)
	2122 (Shrewsbury)	MEDLARS	188 (Boston Spa)
	2172 (Stoke-on-Trent)		878 (Liverpool)
	2252 (Warrington)		1555 (London W1M 8AE)
homoeopathic	968 (London W1N 1RJ)	Medway Towns, local history	600 (Gillingham)
industrial	1980 (Penarth)		
	2172 (Stoke-on-Trent)		2047 (Rochester)
iodine	1051 (London EC2)	Mental derangements	119 (Bexley)
locomotor	959 (London W1M 7AE)	Mental health	393 (Chichester)
Manchester	1791 (Manchester)		1236 (London W1P 3LD)
manipulative	959 (London W1M 7AE)	Mental hospitals	119 (Bexley)
mechanical remedies	34 (Ashton-under-Lyne)	Mental hygiene	119 (Bexley)
nautical	736 (Hull)	Mental illness	1061 (London SW1)
nuclear	341 (Cardiff)		1372 (London WC2)
	990 (London W1M 7PG)		1871 (Northampton)

Mental illness (contd)			1974(Oxford)
treatment	119(Bexley)	hymnology	95(Belfast)
Mental institutions	119(Bexley)	theology	95(Belfast)
Mental pathology	119(Bexley)		247(Bristol)
Mental physiology	119(Bexley)	Methodist church	1161(London WC1)
Mental retardation	485(Durham)		1375, 1376(London SW1)
	1236(London W1P 3LD)	history	1375, 1376(London SW1)
Mental subnormality	154(Birmingham)	Methodists	1756(Manchester)
	364(Caterham)	Primitive	1756(Manchester)
	2151(Southport)	Methodology	1636(London W1)
Mentally handicapped	1647(London SE1)	Metrication	550(Edinburgh)
teaching	2014(Preston)	Mexico	1378(London SW1)
Mentally handicapped		Meyerstein, E. H. W.	1956(Oxford)
children	823(Leicester)	Michael Drayton	1903(Nuneaton)
teaching	1895(Nottingham)	Microbial systematics	829(Leicester)
Merchant navy	1580(London SW17)	Microbiology	207(Brentford)
education	1580(London SW17)		335(Cardiff)
history	1580(London SW17)		674(Harlow)
Merchant shipping	947(London SW1)		779(Kingston upon Thames)
history	1425(London SE10)		863(Liverpool)
Merchants, biography	2143(Southampton)		1367(London NW1)
Mergers	1253(London SW1)		1729(Maidenhead)
Merseyside			2131(Slough)
local history	183(Bootle)		2320(Worthing)
	2298(Wirral)	medical	1037(London NW9)
social service	869(Liverpool)	Microorganisms, systematics	829(Leicester)
Metabolic reactions	1366(London SW7)	Microscopy	1260(London W1)
Metabolic studies,		Middle East	270(Camberley)
psychiatry	2109(Sheffield)		490, 492(Durham)
Metabolism	344(Cardiff)		1947(Oxford)
	681(Harrow)		2145(Southampton)
brain	523(Edinburgh)	archaeology	1850(Newcastle upon Tyne)
calcium	807(Leeds)	history	1251(London W1N 2BH)
cardiac	1366(London SW7)		2139(Southampton)
mineral	807(Leeds)	Middlesex	
Metallurgy	406(Coatbridge)	history	1184(London SW1)
	1586(London E1)	local history	1184(London SW1)
	1948(Oxford)	West	
See also Volume I		history	1190(London W3)
Metalwork	33(Ashton-under-Lyne)	topography	1190(London W3)
	450(Derby)	Midlothian, local history	1820(Musselburgh)
	2055(Rotherham)	Midwifery	1526(London W1M 0BE)
artistic	162(Blackburn)	Midwives, training	1034(London SW7)
Metaphysics	685(Hastings)	Miéville family	724(Hove)
	882(Llanelli)	Migraine	193(Bournemouth)
Metapsychology	36(Aylesbury)	Migration	327(Canterbury)
Meteorology	295(Cambridge)		1132(London SW1)
	1902(Nottingham)	Military archives	1303(London WC2)
	1971(Oxford)	Military chaplains	47(Bagshot)
See also Volume I		Military dress	903(London EC3)
Methodism	1375, 1376(London SW1)	Military engineering	23(Aldershot)
	1974(Oxford)	Military fiction	1560(London SW1)
history	95(Belfast)	Military history	24(Aldershot)
	247(Bristol)		71(Bath)
	696(Helston)		81(Beaconsfield)
	1375, 1376(London SW1)		271(Camberley)
	1756(Manchester)		802(Leeds)

Military history (contd)	856 (Lisburn)	Latin America	1085 (London SW1)
	903 (London EC3)	leprosy	1312 (London W1N 3DG)
	906 (London N7)	medical	1570 (London EC4)
	1303 (London WC2)	Methodist	1376 (London NW1)
	1560 (London SW1)	Pacific	1085 (London SW1)
	1659 (London WC1)	Pakistan	934 (London W1H 4AA)
	1688 (London SW1)	Papua	1086 (London SW1)
	2129 (Sleaford)	South Seas	1086 (London SW1)
	2185 (Sunderland)	theology	1058 (London SE1)
Britain	724 (Hove)	West Indies	934 (London W1H 4AA)
Military organization	24 (Aldershot)	Molecular biology	306 (Cambridge)
Military science	23, 24 (Aldershot)		951 (London SE1)
	81 (Beaconsfield)	Molecular ecology	455 (Didcot)
	856 (Lisburn)	Molluscs	337 (Cardiff)
	905 (London N7)	Monaco	1087 (London W1)
	1688 (London SW1)	Monastic history	424 (Crawley)
Military strategy	1560 (London SW1)	Money	700 (Henley-on-Thames)
Millinery	874 (Liverpool)	Mongolia	2019 (Reading)
	1074 (London W1)	Mongolism	1236 (London W1P 3LD)
Milner, William	666 (Halifax)	Monmouth, local history	1814 (Monmouth)
Milton, John	133 (Birmingham)	Monmouth rebellion	213 (Bridgwater)
	365 (Chalfont St Giles)	Monmouthshire	
	1956 (Oxford)	amenities	1803 (Meifod)
Mineral waters	246 (Bristol)	archaeology	1859 (Newport, Mon)
	677 (Harrogate)	geology	1859 (Newport, Mon)
Mineral workings	1381 (London SW1)	history	1859 (Newport, Mon)
Mines, industrial history	2102 (Settle)	local history	1855, 1856 (Newport, Mon)
Miniatures	855 (Lincoln)	natural history	1859 (Newport, Mon)
	1610 (London W1)	Monopolies	798 (Leeds)
Mining industry, history	1843 (Newcastle upon Tyne)		1104, 1253 (London SW1)
Missionaries	1086 (London SW1)	Montessori education	1384 (London WC1)
	2222 (Truro)	Montrose, local history	1815, 1816 (Montrose)
biographies	2063 (Saffron Walden)	Monuments	1426, 1535 (London SW1)
Missionary work, training	148 (Birmingham)	Moore, Sir John	906 (London N7)
Missions	148 (Birmingham)	Moral conditions	1348 (London EC4)
	369 (Chelmsford)	Moral philosophy	520 (Edinburgh)
	517, 545, 569 (Edinburgh)	Moravian church	229 (Bristol)
	975 (London SW1)	Morayshire, local history	575 (Elgin)
	1058 (London SE1)	Morbid anatomy	681 (Harrow)
	1376 (London NW1)		1075 (London W1)
	1811 (Mirfield)	Morbidity, children	1360 (London W1)
Africa	1085, 1086 (London SW1)	Morbidity statistics	473 (Dundee)
Central	934 (London W1H 4AA)	More, Sir Thomas	1187 (London EC2)
West	934 (London W1H 4AA)	Morocco	1538 (London SW7)
Anglican	1647 (London SW1)	geography	1749 (Manchester)
Asia	1085 (London SW1)	history	1749 (Manchester)
Brazil	934 (London W1H 4AA)	Morpeth, local history	1818 (Morpeth)
Burma	934 (London W1H 4AA)	Morris, William	1336 (London SW19)
Ceylon	934 (London W1H 4AA)		1340 (London E17)
China	1086 (London SW1)		1598 (Lechlade)
North	934 (London W1H 4AA)		1674, 1692 (London E17)
Christian	14 (Aberdeen)	Motor-boating	1328 (London SE10)
	934 (London W1H 4AA)	Motor cars, history	121 (Biggleswade)
to Muslims	2063 (Saffron Walden)	Motor cycles, history	121 (Biggleswade)
history	1058 (London SE1)	Motor industry, Scotland	611 (Glasgow)
India	934 (London W1H 4AA)	Motor transport	250 (Brockenhurst)
	1086 (London SW1)	history	250 (Brockenhurst)

Motor vehicle engineering
   industry   740(Huntingdon)
Motoring   930(London WC2)
                            1328(London SE10)
                            1520(London SW1)
   law   1520(London SW1)
   sport   1520(London SW1)
Mountaineering   21(Airdrie)
                            468(Dunblane)
                            802(Leeds)
                            889(London W1)
                            1328(London SE10)
   history   889(London W1)
Movement   1274(London SE22)
                            1475(London W1M 4AX)
                            2302(Woking)
   education   87(Bedford)
Mrs Humphrey Ward   1942(Oxford)
Muscular dystrophy   1388(London SE1)
Musculoskeletal system,
   diseases   742(Hyde)
Museology   78(Batley)
                            466(Dumfries)
                            1392(London W1P 2BX)
                            1416(London WC2)
                            2099(Scunthorpe)
                            2293(Winchester)
Museums   831(Leicester)
                            1392(London W1P 2BX)
                            2044(Rochdale)
   education service   860(Liverpool)
   medical   2252(Warrington)
Music   17(Aberystwyth)
                            23(Aldershot)
                            32(Ashington)
                            75(Bath)
                            107(Belfast)
                            154(Birmingham)
                            160(Bishop's Stortford)
                            163(Blackburn)
                            167(Blackpool)
                            192(Bournemouth)
                            198(Bradford)
                            235(Bristol)
                            258(Burnley)
                            259, 260(Burton-on-Trent)
                            288, 291, 312, 317(Cambridge)
                            329, 330(Canterbury)
                            332(Cardiff)
                            353(Carlisle)
                            370(Chelmsford)
                            403(Chorley)
                            405(Clydebank)
                            408(Colchester)
                            417, 422(Coventry)

427(Crewe)
433(Croydon)
435(Dagenham)
449(Derby)
457(Doncaster)
470, 472(Dundee)
486(Durham)
498(Eastbourne)
513, 570(Edinburgh)
574(Egham)
581(Esher)
583(Exeter)
610, 612, 614, 630(Glasgow)
652(Grimsby)
666(Halifax)
673(Harlow)
677(Harrogate)
704(Hereford)
709, 724(Hove)
733, 734(Hull)
750(Ilkley)
787(Lancaster)
802, 812, 813(Leeds)
825, 826(Leicester)
866, 877(Liverpool)
938(London W3)
960(London W1)
961(London W1A 1AA)
972(London W1)
996(London WC1)
999(London W1)
1118(London E6)
1165(London SW15)
1167(London SW17)
1177(London SW7)
1187(London EC2)
1189(London EC4)
1302(London SE11)
1303(London WC2)
1339(London E1)
1385(London SE1)
1498(London SE8)
1513(London NW1)
1527, 1549(London SW7)
1566(London WC2)
1615(London N14)
1653(London SE14)
1662(London WC1)
1688(London SW1)
1669(London SE19)
1722(Luton)
1731(Maidstone)
1746, 1757, 1777, 1781, 1782, 1791(Manchester)
1801(Matlock)
1809(Middlesbrough)
1811(Mirfield)

Music (contd)	1833, 1837, 1844, 1845, 1846 (Newcastle upon Tyne)		999(London W1)
			1619(London WC1)
	1867, 1893, 1896,	Strauss family	216(Bridgwater)
	1902(Nottingham)	symphonic	1755(Manchester)
	1919, 1934, 1948,	therapy	1688(London NW1)
	1957(Oxford)	Viennese	216(Bridgwater)
	1983(Pentre)	Music Hall	998(London N16)
	1996(Plymouth)	Musical boxes	209(Brentford)
	2016(Preston)	Musical education	1890(Nottingham)
	2020, 2027(Reading)	Musical instruments	209(Brentford)
	2035(Retford)		1169(London SE21)
	2043(Ripon)		1211(London SE23)
	2052(Rotherham)		1527(London SW7)
	2100(Scunthorpe)		1781(Manchester)
	2112(Sheffield)		2329(York)
	2126(Shrewsbury)	makers, biography	1731(Maidstone)
	2135(Slough)	manufacture	1731(Maidstone)
	2145(Southampton)	Musical literature	192(Bournemouth)
	2187(Sunderland)	Musical profession	1226(London W1A 4LN)
	2205(Tamworth)	Musicians	972(London W1)
	2209(Taunton)		1226(London W1A 4LN)
	2212(Tenbury Wells)		1731(Maidstone)
	2234(Wakefield)	amateur	1688(London SW1)
	2290(Winchester)	biography	1731(Maidstone)
	2302(Woking)	British	972(London W1)
	2304(Wolverhampton)	welfare	1556(London W1)
	2313(Worcester)	Muslim religion	2063(Saffron Walden)
	2333(York)	Muslims	2063(Saffron Walden)
amateur	1619(London WC1)	Mycology, medical	1252(London WC2)
Austria	929(London SW7)	Mysticism	1022, 1061(London SW1)
biography	999(London W1)	Mythology	564(Edinburgh)
British	972(London W1)		
Cambridge, history	317(Cambridge)	**N**	
Church	433(Croydon)		
copyright	1393(London SW1)	Nairn, local history	575(Elgin)
history	724(Hove)		1821(Nairn)
	802(Leeds)	Nantgarw porcelain	2199(Swansea)
	866(Liverpool)	Napoleon	71(Bath)
	972(London W1)		733(Hull)
	1549(London SW7)	manuscripts	2166(Stirling)
Hungary	928(London SW1)	wars	2007(Portsmouth)
Ireland	92, 107(Belfast)	Narcotics addiction	2255(Watford)
Jewish	1292(London W1)	Nasmyth, James	1748(Manchester)
layout	27(Amersham)	National archives	1494(London WC2)
Manchester	1755(Manchester)	National defence	1237(London WC2)
medieval	2042(Ripon)	National expenditure	1962(Oxford)
notation	27(Amersham)	National Gallery	1415(London WC2)
organ	1530(London SW7)	National Health Service	196(Eastbourne)
	2289(Winchester)		550(Edinburgh)
pipe	2161(Stirling)		881(Liverpool)
Poland	1480(London SW7)		1542(London W1)
primary schools	55(Banstead)	National income	1962(Oxford)
printing, history	27(Amersham)	statistics	1040(London SW1)
recorded	1385(London SE1)	National insurance	1107(London WC2)
sacred	702(Hereford)	National libraries	2339–2341
schools	254(Bromley)	National Monuments	
	719(Hitchin)	Record	1535(London SW1)

National Parks	1096(London NW1)	North	389(Chester)
National Savings		Westmorland	348(Carlisle)
Movement	1436(London WC2)	Wiltshire	453(Devizes)
National Union Catalogue	2339	Worksop	2319(Worksop)
National Union of		Yorkshire	2338(York)
Seamen, history	1442(London SW4)	See also Volume I	
National Union of Vehicle		Natural resources	1340(London E17)
Builders, history	1776(Manchester)		1381(London SW1)
Nationalized industries	1253(London SW1)	Natural sciences	3(Aberdeen)
Natural history	377(Cheltenham)		492(Durham)
	643(Grantham)		643(Grantham)
	756(Ipswich)		788(Lancaster)
	1211(London SE23)		1165(London SW15)
	1326(London W5)		1303(London WC2)
	1808(Middlesbrough)		1928(Oxford)
	2077(St Helens)	See also Volume I	
	2099(Scunthorpe)	Nature conservation	1096(London NW1)
	2186(Sunderland)	Nautical astronomy	1425(London SE10)
	2262(Wells)	Nautical education	736(Hull)
Alderney	22(Alderney)	Nautical sciences, history	736(Hull)
Ayrshire	43(Ayr)	Nautical subjects	736(Hull)
Bacup	46(Bacup)		1170(London SW15)
Bradford	199(Bradford)	Naval aircraft, history	2325(Yeovil)
Breconshire	204(Brecon)	Naval architecture	1425(London SE10)
Brighton	223(Brighton)	Naval history	71(Bath)
Bristol	228(Bristol)		444(Dartford)
Bute	2057(Rothesay)		583(Exeter)
Cheshire	389(Chester)		802(Leeds)
Chester	389(Chester)		1425, 1547(London SE10)
Colchester	407(Colchester)		1659(London WC1)
County Armagh	29(Armagh)		1688(London W9)
Croydon	429(Croydon)		1996(Plymouth)
Cumberland	348(Carlisle)		2004, 2007(Portsmouth)
Darent Valley	441(Dartford)		2165(Stirling)
Dartford	441(Dartford)	Naval science	1688(London W9)
Dorset	460(Dorchester)	Navigation	1425(London SE10)
Dumfries	466(Dumfries)		1586(London EC3)
Dunfermline	477(Dunfermline)	Near East	492(Durham)
Essex	407(Colchester)	archaeology	1655(London WC1)
Herefordshire	706(Hereford)	geography	779(Kingston upon Thames)
Hove	223(Brighton)	history	779(Kingston upon Thames)
Isle of Man	462(Douglas)	Neath, local history	1822(Neath)
Isle of Wight	1851(Newport, Isle of Wight)	Needlecraft	93(Belfast)
			864(Liverpool)
Kent	1733(Maidstone)	needle-making	2032(Redditch)
North West	429(Croydon)	history	2032(Redditch)
King's Lynn	774(King's Lynn)	Needlework	70(Bath)
Lake District	348(Carlisle)		122(Bilston)
Lancashire	348(Carlisle)		450(Derby)
Lincoln	846(Lincoln)		470(Dundee)
Lincolnshire	846(Lincoln)		750(Ilkley)
London	1326(London W5)		2043(Ripon)
Monmouthshire	1859(Newport, Mon)	See also Embroidery	
Norfolk	1873(Norwich)	Nelson, local history	1824(Nelson)
River Thames	2040(Richmond)	Nelson, Lord	1336(London SW19)
Surrey, North East	429(Croydon)		1814(Monmouth)
Wales	337(Cardiff)		2007(Portsmouth)

Nematology, plant	2066 (St Albans)	Newcastle upon Tyne,	
Nervous physiology	119 (Bexley)	local history	1833, 1834 (Newcastle upon Tyne)
Nervous system			
diseases	2076 (St Helens)	News	910, 1505 (London EC4)
hygiene	119 (Bexley)	Newspapers	997 (London NW9)
physiology	1725 (Macclesfield)	Belfast	92 (Belfast)
Netherlands	408 (Colchester)	Ireland	92 (Belfast)
	1548 (London SW7)	Newton, John	1912 (Olney)
geography	2278 (Weymouth)	Nickelodeons	209 (Brentford)
history	2278 (Weymouth)	Nigeria	1448 (London WC2)
Neuroanatomy	147 (Birmingham)	Methodist missions	1376 (London NW1)
	1261 (London WC1)	Nightingale, Florence	881 (Liverpool)
	1266 (London SE5)	Nobiliary law	522 (Edinburgh)
Neurochemistry	274 (Cambridge)	Noise hazards	521 (Edinburgh)
	1266 (London SE5)	Non-Christian religions	413 (Colwyn Bay)
	1366 (London SW7)		581 (Esher)
Neuroendocrinology	1266 (London SE5)		1688 (London WC2)
	1930 (Oxford)		1688 (London NW1)
Neuroleptic drugs	715 (High Wycombe)	Nonconformist history	1114 (London WC1)
Neurology	143 (Birmingham)	Norfolk	
	172 (Bodmin)	archaeology	1873, 1878 (Norwich)
	416 (Coulsdon)	architecture	1873 (Norwich)
	681 (Harrow)	buildings	1876 (Norwich)
	1261 (London WC1)	craft	1873 (Norwich)
	1266 (London SE5)	geology	1873 (Norwich)
	1871 (Northampton)	history	1873 (Norwich)
	2067 (St Albans)	industries	1873 (Norwich)
history	1261 (London WC1)	local history	775 (King's Lynn)
research	1248 (London W6)		1878, 1879, 1882 (Norwich)
Neuromuscular diseases	1388 (London SE1)	natural history	1873 (Norwich)
Neuropathology	605 (Glasgow)	Norse See Norway	
Neuropharmacology	147 (Birmingham)	North Sea gasfields	1785 (Manchester)
Neurophysiology	1122 (London SE18)	Northampton, local history	1865, 1866 (Northampton)
	1261 (London WC1)	Northamptonshire	1865 (Northampton)
	1266 (London SE5)	history	50 (Banbury)
Neuropsychiatry	361 (Carshalton)	local history	769 (Kettering)
Neuropsychopharmacology	1266 (London SE5)		1866, 1868,
Neurosciences	1266 (London SE5)		1869 (Northampton)
Neurosurgery	154 (Birmingham)	Northern Ireland	97 (Belfast)
	1261 (London WC1)		1449 (London W1)
New Church	1173, 1622 (London WC1)	community organization	102 (Belfast)
history	1173 (London WC1)	hospitals	103 (Belfast)
New South Wales	1445 (London WC2)	records	106 (Belfast)
New Testament	217 (Bridgwater)	social service	102 (Belfast)
	545, 569 (Edinburgh)	tourism	104 (Belfast)
	1939 (Oxford)	vital statistics	96 (Belfast)
Greek	711 (Hertford)	Youth service	111 (Belfast)
New towns	1381 (London SW1)	See also Ulster	
	2031 (Redditch)	Northern Reform Union	1836 (Newcastle upon Tyne)
New Zealand	1447 (London SW1)	Northumberland	
books	950 (London W1)	antiquities	1849 (Newcastle upon Tyne)
films	1446 (London SW1)	demography	1848 (Newcastle upon Tyne)
Newark		dialect	1847 (Newcastle upon Tyne)
archaeology	1827 (Newark)	industrial archaeology	1849 (Newcastle upon Tyne)
local history	1826, 1827 (Newark)	industrial development	1848 (Newcastle upon Tyne)
Newburn, local history	1834 (Newcastle upon Tyne)	industrial history	1849 (Newcastle upon Tyne)
Newcastle, local history	1829 (Newcastle)	local history	1818 (Morpeth)

Northumberland, local history (*contd*)	1833, 1836, 1847, 1849 (Newcastle upon Tyne)	Nursery education	1498(London SE8)
		Nursery nursing	667(Halifax)
social and economic conditions	1848(Newcastle upon Tyne)		1427(London SW1)
			2182(Sunderland)
Norway	898, 1452(London SW1)	careers	1427(London SW1)
books	782(Kirkwall)	training	1427(London SW1)
history	782(Kirkwall)	Nursing	6(Aberdeen)
	2073(St Andrews)		161(Blackburn)
language	315(Cambridge)		240, 245(Bristol)
	651(Grimsby)		467(Dumfries)
	898(London SW1)		533(Edinburgh)
	1946(Oxford)		681(Harrow)
literature	651(Grimsby)		721(Hornchurch)
	1338(London SE22)		762(Keighley)
	2073(St Andrews)		874, 881(Liverpool)
philology	782(Kirkwall)		1106(London SE1)
Norwich			1193(London E9)
archaeology	1875(Norwich)		1236(London W1P 3LD)
biography	1875(Norwich)		1336(London SW19)
crafts	1873(Norwich)		1528(London W1M 0AB)
industries	1873(Norwich)		1688(London NW1)
local history	1875, 1882(Norwich)		1785(Manchester)
Norwich Cathedral	1876(Norwich)		1794(Mansfield)
Nottingham, local history	1891(Nottingham)		1839(Newcastle upon Tyne)
Nottingham and Derby-			1915(Orpington)
shire Regiment, history	1900(Nottingham)		2067(St Albans)
Nottinghamshire			2147(Southampton)
antiquities	1901(Nottingham)		2184(Sunderland)
history	1896, 1901(Nottingham)		2198(Sutton Coldfield)
local history	1891, 1902(Nottingham)		2264(Welwyn Garden City)
	2319(Worksop)		2280(Whitehaven)
rural life	1896(Nottinghamshire)		2307(Wolverhampton)
Nuclear disarmament	1020(London WC1)	animals	145(Birmingham)
Nuclear medicine	341(Cardiff)	community	1496(London SW1)
	990(London W1M 7PG)	district	1496(London SW1)
Nugent Wade	1942(Oxford)	education	174(Bolton)
Numerical taxonomy,			533(Edinburgh)
computer programs	829(Leicester)		1528(London W1M 0AB)
Numismatics	113(Belfast)	ethics	533(Edinburgh)
	162(Blackburn)	history	533(Edinburgh)
	197(Bradford)		1528(London W1M 0AB)
	301(Cambridge)	home	616(Glasgow)
	389(Chester)	management	587(Exeter)
	1598(London W1V 0HS)	nursery	667(Halifax)
	2089(Salisbury)		1427(London SW1)
	2099(Scunthorpe)		2182(Sunderland)
	2293(Winchester)	occupational health	672(Harlow)
British	113(Belfast)	pediatric	773(Kilmarnock)
history	312(Cambridge)	profession	2252(Warrington)
Irish	113(Belfast)	psychology	467(Dumfries)
Scotland	530(Edinburgh)	thoracic	1012(London W1)
See also Volume I		training	433(Edinburgh)
Nuneaton		Nutrition	6(Aberdeen)
archaeology	1904(Nuneaton)		70(Bath)
geology	1904(Nuneaton)		93(Belfast)
history	1904(Nuneaton)		319, 323(Cambridge)
local history	1903, 1904(Nuneaton)		648(Greenford)

Nutrition (contd)	681(Harrow)		2259(Wednesbury)
	864, 874(Liverpool)	Office practice	19(Abingdon)
	980(London SW3)		485(Durham)
	1158(London W1)		676(Harrogate)
	1302(London SE11)		2321(Worthing)
	1344, 1369(London WC1)	Offices, Shops and Railway Premises Act, 1963	
	1450(London N7)		1269(London EC2)
	1574(London SW1)	Oil paintings	124(Birkenhead)
	1664(London W8)	American	124(Birkenhead)
	1828(Newbury)	British	124(Birkenhead)
	2101(Seaford)		164(Blackburn)
	2121(Shrewsbury)	French	124(Birkenhead)
animal	1534(London SW1)	Old age pensions	165(Blackburn)
vegetarian	26(Altrincham)	Old Icelandic	1956(Oxford)
		Old Norse	813(Leeds)
O		Old people, welfare	1940(Oxford)
			2209(Taunton)
Obstetrics	154(Birmingham)	Old Sheffield plate and cutlery	
	176(Bolton)		2113(Sheffield)
	399(Chichester)	Old Testament	23(Aldershot)
	412(Colne)		545, 569(Edinburgh)
	681(Harrow)		1303(London WC2)
	1033(London NW10)	Oldham, local history	1911(Oldham)
	1193(London E9)	Ollard	1942(Oxford)
	1279(London SW1)	Operating theatre technicians, training	
	1526(London W1M 0BE)		1262(London WC1)
	1529(London NW1)	Operational research	700(Henley-on-Thames)
	2224(Tunbridge Wells)		790(Lancaster)
Occult	685(Hastings)		2023(Reading)
art	564(Edinburgh)		2135(Slough)
sciences	564(Edinburgh)	Ophthalmic instruments	918(London W1M 4AT)
	1341(London SW18)	Ophthalmic optical profession	
	2021(Reading)		919(London W1Y 2DT)
Occupational health	672(Harlow)	Ophthalmic optics	201(Bradford)
	1344(London WC1)		626(Glasgow)
	1611(London NW1)		1001(London W1Y 2DT)
	1723(Macclesfield)		1066(London EC1)
	1842(Newcastle upon Tyne)	Ophthalmic surgery	1532(London WC2)
nursing	672(Harlow)	Ophthalmology	176(Bolton)
Occupational hygiene	1831, 1842(Newcastle upon Tyne)		681(Harrow)
			755(Ipswich)
Occupational medicine	521(Edinburgh)		1001(London W1Y 2DT)
	1611(London NW1)		1263(London WC1)
Occupational psychology	942(London WC1)		1532(London WC2)
	1421(London W1M 8DR)		1688(London NW1)
Occupational therapy	543(Edinburgh)		2223(Tunbridge Wells)
Oceanography	295(Cambridge)	Optical dispensing	626(Glasgow)
	736(Hull)		918(London W1M 4AT)
See also Volume I		Optics	1001(London W1Y 2DT)
Offenders		physiological	1001(London W1Y 2DT)
after-care	1395(London SE11)	Oral contraception	715(High Wycombe)
education	1218(London SE11)	Oral health	2082(Salford)
treatment	1351(London W1P 6DD)	Oral medicine	344(Cardiff)
Office administration	1065(London SW1)	Oral pathology	154(Birmingham)
	1617(London SW17)	Oral surgery	494(East Grinstead)
Office management	230(Bristol)	Oralogy	176(Bolton)
	700(Henley-on-Thames)	Orchestras, youth	652(Grimsby)

Orchestrelles	209(Brentford)	Osteoporosis	807(Leeds)
Orchestrions	209(Brentford)	Oswestry, local history	2126(Oswestry)
Order of Friar-Servites, history	1933(Oxford)	Otology	176(Bolton) 1258(London WC1)
Order of St John	1316(London EC1)	Otorhinolaryngology	242(Bristol)
Orders of chivalry	522(Edinburgh)		1258(London WC1)
Ordination	711(Hertford)	Outdoor activities	87(Bedford)
	885(London SW1)	Outdoor games	1328(London SE10)
Organ music	1530(London SW7)	Overseas aid	1162(London WC2)
Organ transplantation	308(Cambridge)	Overseas development	1466(London W1V 0JS)
Organization	1276(London W1X 9PA)	audio-visual aids	1465(London WC1)
		Owen, Robert	16(Aberystwyth)
Organization and Methods	1065(London SW1)		1711(Loughborough) 1745(Manchester)
Organizational studies	1627(London NW3)	Oxford, local history	1935, 1936(Oxford)
Organizations		Oxford University	1467(London W1X 4AH)
history	700(Henley-on-Thames)	Oxford University Press	1467(London W1X 4AH)
international	722(Hounslow)	Oxfordshire, history	50(Banbury)
Organs	1530(London SW7)	Ozanam, Frederic	1612(London SW1)
reproducing	209(Brentford)		
street	209(Brentford)	**P**	
Oriental books	223(Brighton)		
Oriental churches	119(Bexley)	Pacific, missions	1085(London SW1)
Oriental humanities	1666(London WC1)	Package design	253(Bromley)
Oriental literature	291(Cambridge)	Packaging	500(Eastleigh)
Oriental manuscripts	149(Birmingham)		1715(Loughborough)
	2295(Windsor)		1724(Macclesfield)
Oriental philosophers	581(Esher)		2082(Salford)
Oriental philosophy	413(Colwyn Bay)	Paddington	
Oriental social sciences	1666(London WC1)	local history	1688(London NW1)
Orientalia	1678(London NW1)	topography	1688(London NW1)
Orienteering	434(Currie)	Paediatrics	36(Aylesbury)
	505(Edinburgh)		154(Birmingham)
	2013(Preston)		176(Bolton)
Orkney, local history	782(Kirkwall)		344(Cardiff)
Ornamental pottery	2175(Stoke-on-Trent)		681(Harrow)
Ornamental turning	2009(Potters Bar)		1526(London W1M 0BE)
Ornaments, sacred	2278(Weymouth)		1740(Manchester)
Ornithology	246(Bristol)		2168(Stockport)
	1534(London SW1)	nursing	773(Kilmarnock)
Orthodontics	1006(London W1)	Paine, Thomas	1880(Thetford)
Orthography	248(Broadstairs)	Painted glass	465(Dudley)
Orthopaedic surgery	755(Ipswich)	Painting	113(Belfast)
	1532(London WC2)		253(Bromley)
Orthopaedics	124(Birkenhead)		258(Burnley)
	176(Bolton)		349(Carlisle)
	870(Liverpool)		371(Chelmsford)
	1033(London NW10)		377, 378(Cheltenham)
	1264(London W1)		435(Dagenham)
	1793(Mansfield)		450(Derby)
	1967(Oxford)		469(Dundee)
	2223(Tunbridge Wells)		585(Exeter)
Oscar Browning	683(Hastings)		591(Falmouth)
Osteopaths	1004(London SW1)		676(Harrogate)
Osteopathy			724(Hove)
careers	1004(London SW1)		805(Leeds)
training	1004(London SW1)		866, 871(Liverpool)

Painting (contd)	1018(London SE5)	Papal addresses	900(London SW19)
	1047(London SW3)	Papal encyclicals	900(London SW19)
	1288(London NW3)	Papal history	493(Durham)
	1339(London E1)	Paper money	1243(London EC3)
	1524(London SW7)	Paper weights, glass	592(Farnham)
	1566(London WC2)	Papua, missions	1086(London SW1)
	1673(London W1)	Papyri	149(Birmingham)
	1688(London WC2)		1952(Oxford)
	1693(London SW19)	Papyrology	16(Aberystwyth)
	1719(Luton)	Greek	1250(London WC1)
	1727(Maidenhead)	Roman	1250(London WC1)
	1808(Middlesbrough)	Paranormal perception	1061(London SW1)
	1858(Newport, Mon)	Paraphysics	685(Hastings)
	2005(Portsmouth)	Paraplegia	39(Aylesbury)
	2015(Preston)	Parapsychology	685(Hastings)
	2055(Rotherham)	Parasitic diseases	1323(London NW10)
	2116(Sheffield)	Parasitology	99(Belfast)
	2141(Southampton)		873(Liverpool)
European, history	1047(London SW3)		1075, 1260(London W1)
history	253(Bromley)		1344(London WC1)
	312(Cambridge)		1367(London NW7)
materials	1416(London WC2)		1828(Newbury)
technique	581(Esher)		2066(St Albans)
	1191(Oldham)		2294(Windlesham)
	1416(London WC2)	veterinary	502(Edinburgh)
water colour	1461(London W1)	Parental responsibility	1387(London SW1)
Paintings	138(Birmingham)	Parish councils	1398(London WC1)
	347(Carlisle)	Parish work	1998(Pontypridd)
	880(Liverpool)		2274(Weston-super-Mare)
	1764(Manchester)	Parliamentary Papers	2145(Southampton)
	1873(Norwich)		2216(Trowbridge)
	2186(Sunderland)	Parliamentary procedure	1309(London WC1)
Buckinghamshire	37(Aylesbury)	Parliamentary publications	1215(London SW1)
conservation	1416(London WC2)	Parliaments	1195(London SW1)
Dutch	376(Cheltenham)		1997(Pontefract)
English	2322(Worthing)	Particle counting	521(Edinburgh)
European	162(Blackburn)	Pastoral theology	90(Bedford)
history	1614(London SE5)	Patents	227(Brighton)
London	1186(London EC2)	Pathology	154(Birmingham)
Londonderry County	410(Coleraine)		274, 305(Cambridge)
Scottish	528(Edinburgh)		344(Cardiff)
Watts	662(Guildford)		502(Edinburgh)
Paisley, local history	1978(Paisley)		738(Hull)
Pakistan, missions	934(London W1H 4AA)		1033(London NW10)
Palaeography	17(Aberystwyth)		1132(London SW1)
	1662(London WC1)		1160(London E11)
	1956(Oxford)		1191(London SE1)
	2314(Worcester)		1193(London E9)
	2331(York)		1533(London WC2)
Palestine	1292(London W1)		1551(London W12)
	2139(Southampton)		1656(London WC2)
history	595(Folkestone)		1723, 1724(Macclesfield)
travel	595(Folkestone)		1731(Maidstone)
Palestiniana	1383(London WC1)		1828(Newbury)
Pali	1469(London W2)	chemical	1075(London W1)
Palmistry	564(Edinburgh)	dental caries	237(Bristol)
Panama, Methodist missions	1376(London NW1)	experimental	455(Didcot)

Pathology (contd)			1719 (Luton)
feet	1048 (London NW8)	Perspective	1774 (Manchester)
history	1075 (London W1)	Perthshire, local history	428 (Crieff)
lung	1980 (Penarth)		1988 (Perth)
mental	119 (Bexley)	Pesticides	1724 (Macclesfield)
oral	154 (Birmingham)		2082 (Salford)
skin	146 (Birmingham)		2190 (Surbiton)
surgical	1532 (London WC2)	Pet care	461 (Dorking)
Patients	1471 (London WC1)	Peter de Wint	855 (Lincoln)
Patmore, Coventry	1902 (Nottingham)	Peterborough	
Patristic literature	1942 (Oxford)	local history	1989 (Peterborough)
Patristic theology	401 (Chipping Norton)	social welfare services	281 (Cambridge)
Patristics	296 (Cambridge)	voluntary organizations	281 (Cambridge)
	492 (Durham)	Pharmaceutical chemicals	745 (Ilford)
	569 (Edinburgh)	Pharmaceutical chemistry	531 (Edinburgh)
	2073 (St Andrews)		1667 (London WC1)
P. B. Clayton	1653 (London EC3)		2320 (Worthing)
Peace	1502 (London NW1)	Pharmaceutical engineering	
Peak District	266 (Buxton)	science	1667 (London WC1)
Pelvic cavity	124 (Birkenhead)	Pharmaceutical industry,	
Pembrokeshire	355 (Carmarthen)	economics	1724 (Macclesfield)
local history	690, 691 (Haverfordwest)	Pharmaceutical research	2133 (Slough)
Penal reform	422 (Coventry)	Pharmaceutical sciences	631 (Glasgow)
	1218 (London SE11)	Pharmaceuticals	64, 68 (Basingstoke)
Pendlebury			117 (Betchworth)
history	1747 (Manchester)		207 (Brentford)
local history	1786 (Manchester)		257 (Burgess Hill)
Penology	67 (Basingstoke)		437 (Dagenham)
	183 (Bootle)		500 (Eastleigh)
	1218 (London SE11)		648 (Greenford)
	1238 (London W1)		715 (High Wycombe)
Pension funds	1240 (London WC1)		723 (Hounslow)
Pensions	504 (Edinburgh)		729 (Huddersfield)
	1806 (Middlesbrough)		738 (Hull)
industrial injury	1107 (London WC2)		745 (Ilford)
old age	165 (Blackburn)		757 (Isleworth)
supplementary	1107 (London WC2)		863 (Liverpool)
war	1107 (London WC2)		1572 (London W1N 8AE)
Performing right	999 (London W1)		1712, 1715 (Loughborough)
Perfumery formularies	729 (Huddersfield)		1724 (Macclesfield)
Perfumes	1605 (London W1)		2082 (Salford)
analysis	2082 (Salford)		2094 (Sandwich)
See also Volume I			2191 (Surbiton)
Periodicals	997 (London NW9)		2231 (Twickenham)
British	973 (London WC1)		2248 (Ware)
Permafrost	295 (Cambridge)		2266 (Welwyn Garden City)
Persia			
books	1791 (Manchester)		2268 (Wembley)
history	1968 (Oxford)		2320 (Worthing)
languages	1968 (Oxford)	Pharmaceutics	531 (Edinburgh)
literature	1968 (Oxford)		1667 (London WC1)
religion	1968 (Oxford)	Pharmacies, hospital	
Personages, Cornwall	591 (Falmouth)	design	1185 (London WC1)
Personal hygiene	217 (Bridgwater)	equipment	1185 (London WC1)
effects of stimulation and		Pharmacists	1472 (London WC1)
narcotics	183 (Bootle)	education	1472 (London WC1)
Personnel management	700 (Henley-on-Thames)	training	531 (Edinburgh)

Pharmacognosy	1651(London SW3)		863, 872(Liverpool)
	1667(London WC1)		1429(London N14)
Pharmacology	64(Basingstoke)		1472(London WC1)
	80(Batley)		1572(London W1N 8AE)
	85(Beckenham)		
	117(Betchworth)		1651(London SW3)
	147, 154(Birmingham)		1667(London WC1)
	257(Burgess Hill)		1712, 1715(Loughborough)
	274, 306(Cambridge)		
	344(Cardiff)		1724(Macclesfield)
	435, 437(Dagenham)		1729(Maidenhead)
	531(Edinburgh)		1886(Nottingham)
	674(Harlow)		2015(Preston)
	681(Harrow)		2133(Slough)
	738(Hull)		2172(Stoke-on-Trent)
	757(Isleworth)		2187(Sunderland)
	1033(London NW10)		2248(Ware)
	1193(London E9)		2307(Wolverhampton)
	1337(London E15)	history	531(Edinburgh)
	1367(London NW7)		1472(London WC1)
	1433(London WC2)	law	531(Edinburgh)
	1472(London WC1)	Philately	71(Bath)
	1532(London WC2)		802(Leeds)
	1537, 1631(London WC1)		1431, 1483(London EC1)
	1651(London SW3)	*See also* Volume I	
	1656(London WC2)	Philip Doddridge	1663(London NW3)
	1667(London WC1)		1865(Northampton)
	1712, 1715(Loughborough)	Philologists, biography	1731(Maidstone)
	1723, 1724(Macclesfield)	Philology	154(Birmingham)
	1729, 1730(Maidenhead)		492(Durham)
	1828(Newbury)		953(London W1)
	1886(Nottingham)		1303(London WC2)
	1955(Oxford)		1474(London WC1)
	2094(Sandwich)		1956(Oxford)
	2133(Slough)		2014(Preston)
	2140(Southampton)	English	1956(Oxford)
	2191(Surbiton)	German	1956, 1972(Oxford)
	2248(Ware)	Icelandic	1972(Oxford)
	2265, 2266(Welwyn Garden City)	Norse	782(Kirkwall)
		Romance	315(Cambridge)
	2294(Windlesham)		1686(London NW3)
Pharmacopoeias	1472(London WC2)	Scandinavian	1972(Oxford)
European	2191(Surbiton)	Philosophers	
Pharmacy	9(Aberdeen)	ancient	217(Bridgwater)
	72(Bath)		581(Esher)
	80(Batley)	oriental	217(Bridgwater)
	117(Betchworth)		581(Esher)
	145, 152(Birmingham)	Philosophies	1645(London WC2)
	201(Bradford)	Philosophy	3(Aberdeen)
	207(Brentford)		17(Aberystwyth)
	222(Brighton)		140, 152, 154, 157(Birmingham)
	340(Cardiff)		
	437(Dagenham)		201(Bradford)
	500(Eastleigh)		235, 246, 247(Bristol)
	520, 531(Edinburgh)		291, 309, 315(Cambridge)
	674(Harlow)		330(Canterbury)
	824(Leicester)		397(Chichester)

Philosophy (contd)
　　401 (Chipping Norton)
　　403 (Chorley)
　　413 (Colwyn Bay)
　　417, 422 (Coventry)
　　424 (Crawley)
　　435 (Dagenham)
　　448 (Deeside)
　　449 (Derby)
　　486, 492 (Durham)
　　510, 564, 569 (Edinburgh)
　　576 (Enfield)
　　583 (Exeter)
　　591 (Falmouth)
　　612, 627 (Glasgow)
　　641 (Grantham)
　　671 (Harlech)
　　783 (Lampeter)
　　799, 813 (Leeds)
　　866 (Liverpool)
　　942 (London WC1)
　　953 (London W1)
　　994 (London WC2)
　　1022 (London SW1)
　　1114 (London WC1)
　　1177 (London SW7)
　　1198 (London SW1)
　　1324 (London NW3)
　　1334 (London SE13)
　　1451 (London NW5)
　　1500 (London N1)
　　1566 (London WC2)
　　1650 (London NW1)
　　1693 (London SW19)
　　1711 (Loughborough)
　　1772, 1789 (Manchester)
　　1808, 1809 (Middlesbrough)
　　1839, 1845 (Newcastle upon Tyne)
　　1858 (Newport, Mon)
　　1882 (Norwich)
　　1891 (Nottingham)
　　1918, 1921, 1927, 1942, 1945, 1946, 1947, 1948, 1958 (Oxford)
　　1976 (Paignton)
　　2027 (Reading)
　　2042 (Ripon)
　　2068 (St Albans)
　　2073 (St Andrews)
　　2104 (Sevenoaks)
　　2145 (Southampton)
　　2149 (Southend-on-Sea)
　　2166 (Stirling)
　　2173, 2174 (Stoke-on-Trent)
　　2188 (Sunderland)
　　2198 (Sutton Coldfield)
　　2200 (Swansea)
　　2219 (Truro)
　　2279 (Weymouth)
　　2333 (York)
　　ancient　　301 (Cambridge)
　　　　413 (Colwyn Bay)
　　Bulgaria　　311 (Cambridge)
　　Czechoslovakia　　311 (Cambridge)
　　East European　　1668 (London WC1)
　　education　　1102 (London W1)
　　　　2011 (Prescot)
　　　　2257 (Watford)
　　　　2279 (Weymouth)
　　Greek　　1250 (London WC1)
　　history　　212 (Bridgend)
　　moral　　520 (Edinburgh)
　　oriental　　413 (Colwyn Bay)
　　Poland　　311 (Cambridge)
　　religion　　95 (Belfast)
　　　　517 (Edinburgh)
　　Roman　　1250 (London WC1)
　　Russia　　311 (Cambridge)
　　science　　322 (Cambridge)
　　　　951 (London SE1)
　　　　1651 (London SW3)
　　　　2187 (Sunderland)
　　Scottish　　474 (Dundee)
　　Slavonic　　1668 (London WC1)
　　social　　520 (Edinburgh)
　　Yugoslavia　　311 (Cambridge)
Phonetics　　1278 (London WC1)
Phonographs　　209 (Brentford)
Photobiology　　1252 (London WC2)
Photographic chemistry　　437 (Dagenham)
Photographic science　　1550 (London W1)
Photographic technology　　1468 (London W2)
Photographs (major and local collections only)
　　　　1499 (London W1M 1AA)
　　　　1566 (London WC2)
　　Cambridge　　276 (Cambridge)
　　Cambridgeshire　　276 (Cambridge)
　　Chester　　387 (Chester)
　　Dorset　　460 (Dorchester)
　　ethnology　　310 (Cambridge)
　　Flintshire　　447 (Deeside)
　　Goole　　639 (Goole)
　　historical　　1550 (London W1)
　　ships　　1339 (London E1)
　　World Wars　　1223 (London SE1)
Photography　　2 (Aberdare)
　　　　33 (Ashton-under-Lyne)
　　　　129 (Birmingham)
　　　　168 (Blackpool)
　　　　189 (Bournemouth)
　　　　201 (Bradford)
　　　　435 (Dagenham)
　　　　450 (Derby)
　　　　527 (Edinburgh)

Photography (contd)	585 (Exeter)		2135 (Slough)
	591 (Falmouth)		2187 (Sunderland)
	679 (Harrow)		2236 (Wakefield)
	731 (Hull)		2290 (Winchester)
	746 (Ilford)		2346
	860, 866, 871 (Liverpool)	history	154 (Birmingham)
	1357 (London SW1)		797 (Leeds)
	1550 (London W1)	training	86 (Bedford)
	1566 (London WC2)	Physical medicine	1967 (Oxford)
	1578 (London SW7)	Physical recreation	1031 (London W1N 4AJ)
	1615 (London N14)	Physical therapy training	1702 (London WC2)
	1676 (London SW18)	Physically handicapped	
	1732 (Maidstone)	children	1113 (London SW1)
	1858 (Newport, Mon)		823 (Leicester)
	2024 (Reading)	Physics	
	2055 (Rotherham)	(Volume I of this Directory includes physics, but it has been indexed in this volume for organizations which do not appear in Volume I)	
	2116 (Sheffield)		
	2141 (Southampton)		
	2174 (Stoke-on-Trent)		403 (Chorley)
	2187, 2188 (Sunderland)		406 (Coatbridge)
	2232 (Twickenham)		435 (Dagenham)
history	1550 (London W1)		449 (Derby)
See also Volume I			457 (Doncaster)
Physical anthropology	310 (Cambridge)		531 (Edinburgh)
Physical chemistry	207 (Brentford)		579 (Epsom)
Physical education	87 (Bedford)		612 (Glasgow)
	154, 157 (Birmingham)		726 (Huddersfield)
	163 (Blackburn)		812 (Leeds)
	329 (Canterbury)		874 (Liverpool)
	331 (Cardiff)		1341 (London E1)
	380 (Cheltenham)		1380 (London W1P 7PN)
	403 (Chorley)		1495 (London W1)
	419 (Coventry)		1537 (London WC1)
	427 (Crewe)		1586 (London EC3)
	449 (Derby)		1601 (London EC2)
	457 (Doncaster)		1837, 1839 (Newcastle upon Tyne)
	470 (Dundee)		
	488 (Durham)		1855 (Newport, Mon)
	496 (Eastbourne)		1893 (Nottingham)
	510 (Edinburgh)		1948 (Oxford)
	602 (Glasgow)		2290 (Winchester)
	734 (Hull)		2321 (Worthing)
	773 (Kilmarnock)		2333 (York)
	797, 812 (Leeds)	applied	340 (Cardiff)
	824 (Leicester)	biology	1214 (London SW1)
	1167 (London SW17)	hospital	1214 (London SW1)
	1274 (London SE22)	medical	341 (Cardiff)
	1475 (London W1M 4AX)		990 (London W1M 7PG)
	1615 (London N14)		1214 (London SW1)
	1746 (Manchester)		1245 (London SW3)
	1801 (Matlock)	radiological	1742 (Manchester)
	1846 (Newcastle upon Tyne)		2114 (Sheffield)
	1893 (Nottingham)	Physiography	303 (Cambridge)
	2011 (Prescot)	Physiological optics	1001 (London W1Y 2DT)
	2020 (Reading)	Physiology	87 (Bedford)
	2043 (Ripon)		147, 152, 154 (Birmingham)
	2052 (Rotherham)		172 (Bodmin)

Physiology (contd)	217 (Bridgwater)	Place names	
	274, 306 (Cambridge)	English	1130 (London WC1)
	435, 437 (Dagenham)	Scotland	572 (Edinburgh)
	455 (Didcot)	Planning	109 (Belfast)
	467 (Dumfries)		1181 (London SE1)
	630 (Glasgow)		1198 (London SW1)
	681 (Harrow)		1540 (London W1N 4AD)
	738 (Hull)		1636 (London W1)
	773 (Kilmarnock)		1937 (Oxford)
	874 (Liverpool)		2031 (Redditch)
	1236 (London W1P 3LD)	Croydon	429 (Croydon)
	1261 (London WC1)	East Midlands Region	1888 (Nottingham)
	1367 (London NW7)	hospital	533, 550 (Edinburgh)
	1475 (London W1M 4AX)	Kent, North West	429 (Croydon)
	1533 (London WC2)	pharmacies	1185 (London WC1)
	1537 (London WC1)	Surrey, North East	429 (Croydon)
	1551 (London W12)	*See also* Town and country planning, Town planning	
	1601 (London EC2)	Plant breeding, Scotland	553 (Edinburgh)
	1631 (London WC1)	Plant diseases, Scotland	553 (Edinburgh)
	1651 (London SW3)	Plant nematology	2066 (St Albans)
	1656 (London WC2)	Plant pests	553 (Edinburgh)
	1664 (London W8)	Plant physiology	1605 (London W1)
	1723, 1724 (Macclesfield)	Plastic surgery	426 (Crewe)
	1748 (Manchester)		494 (East Grinstead)
	1805 (Mexborough)		978 (London W1M 8AL)
	1828 (Newbury)		1925 (Oxford)
	1955 (Oxford)	Plastics	674 (Harlow)
	2052 (Rotherham)		2182 (Sunderland)
applied	1532 (London WC2)	Playbills	733 (Hull)
comparative	2140 (Southampton)	Playgroups	1574 (London SW1)
feet	1048 (London NW8)	Playing fields	2209 (Taunton)
human	836 (Lewes)	Plays	550 (Edinburgh)
mental	119 (Bexley)		583 (Exeter)
nervous	119 (Bexley)		906 (London N7)
nervous system	1725 (Macclesfield)		981 (London W1P 6AE)
plant	1605 (London W1)		1692 (London SW19)
reproduction	1730 (Maidenhead)		1768 (Manchester)
respiration	1980 (Penarth)		1863 (Northallerton)
Physiotherapy	681 (Harrow)		1867 (Northampton)
	1046 (London WC1)		2100 (Scunthorpe)
	1248 (London W6)		2313 (Worcester)
	1475 (London W1M 4AX)		2342
		British	968 (London W1Y 4HQ)
Pianos		pre-Restoration	2295 (Windsor)
barrel	209 (Brentford)	Playwrights	1600 (London SW10)
reproducing	209 (Brentford)	Pleasure sailing, history	1425 (London SE10)
square	209 (Brentford)	Plunkett, Sir Horace	1476 (London WC1)
street	209 (Brentford)	Plymouth, local history	1992, 1996 (Plymouth)
Pictures	2295 (Windsor)	Pneumoconiosis	521 (Edinburgh)
Lincoln	855 (Lincoln)		1980 (Penarth)
Lincolnshire	855 (Lincoln)	Poetry	564 (Edinburgh)
London	1630 (London WC2)		585 (Exeter)
Pilgrim's Progress	91 (Bedford)		908 (London W1V 0AU)
Pipe and fiddle music, Scottish	572 (Edinburgh)		1768 (Manchester)
Pipe music	2161 (Stirling)		1844 (Newcastle upon Tyne)
Piped services, hospitals	628 (Glasgow)		2166 (Stirling)
Piracy	1425 (London SE10)	American	252 (Bromley)

Poetry, American (contd)	1477(London SW5)	Scotland	553(Edinburgh)
	2240(Wallasey)	training	25(Alloa)
anthologies	1477(London SW5)		67(Basingstoke)
British	1477(London SW5)	Poliomyelitis	1002(London NW1)
	1889(Nottingham)	Political economy	1355(London EC1)
children's	1477(London SW5)	Political history	748(Ilkeston)
criticism	1477(London SW5)		761(Keighley)
English	265(Bury St Edmunds)		994(London WC2)
	583(Exeter)		1506(London SW9)
	1731(Maidstone)	England	
	1799(Matlock)	Political integration	1144(London W1R 9PL)
	1975(Oxford)	Political parties	371(Chelmsford)
	2240(Wallasey)	Political science	17(Aberystwyth)
			154(Birmingham)
foreign	1477(London SW5)		270(Camberley)
Scotland	610(Glasgow)		438(Darlington)
Poisons	100(Belfast)		587(Exeter)
	245(Bristol)		666(Halifax)
	338(Cardiff)		671(Harlech)
	554(Edinburgh)		947(London SW1)
	1191, 1430(London SE1)		994(London WC2)
Poland	1478(London W1)		1195(London SW1)
	1479(London SW1)		1839(Newcastle upon Tyne)
	1479, 1480(London SW7)		
economics	1479, 1480(London SW1)		1918(Oxford)
	1479, 1480(London SW7)		2129(Sleaford)
folklore	311(Cambridge)		2201(Swansea)
history	311(Cambridge)	African	298(Cambridge)
	436(Dagenham)	Political theory	431(Croydon)
	1479, 1480(London SW1)		700(Henley-on-Thames)
	1479, 1480(London SW7)	Political warfare	2038(Richmond)
language	311(Cambridge)	Politics	140, 153(Birmingham)
	2086(Salford)		191(Bournemouth)
law	1479, 1480(London SW1)		195(Bracknell)
	1479, 1480(London SW7)		201(Bradford)
literature	311(Cambridge)		223(Brighton)
	1333(London SW2)		330(Canterbury)
	1479, 1480(London SW1)		390(Chesterfield)
	1479, 1480(London SW7)		421, 422(Coventry)
	2100(Scunthorpe)		485, 488, 492(Durham)
maps	1480(London SW7)		546(Edinburgh)
music	1480(London SW7)		580(Esher)
philosophy	311(Cambridge)		700(Henley-on-Thames)
religion	311(Cambridge)		778(Kingston upon Thames)
topography	436(Dagenham)		
Polar exploration	957(London SW1)		805, 813(Leeds)
Polar Regions	217(Bridgwater)		1098(London EC1)
	295(Cambridge)		1154(London EC4)
	1538(London SW7)		1215, 1253(London SW1)
expedition files	295(Cambridge)		1309(London WC1)
geography	1329(London E9)		1330(London W6)
history	1329(London E9)		1386(London EC1)
Police	25(Alloa)		1343(London SW1)
administration	25(Alloa)		1423, 1481(London WC2)
badges	67(Basingstoke)		1501(London SW1)
history	1377(London SW1)		1711, 1714(Loughborough)
science	25(Alloa)		1754(Manchester)
	67(Basingstoke)		1836(Newcastle upon Tyne)

Politics (contd)	1946, 1947, 1948, 1958 (Oxford)	Portraits	1036 (London SE1)
	2014 (Preston)	doctors	568 (Edinburgh)
	2038 (Richmond)	engineers	1578 (London SW7)
	2115 (Sheffield)	scientists	1578 (London SW7)
	2142, 2145 (Southampton)	Portraiture	
	2173, 2174 (Stoke-on-Trent)	medical	1531 (London NW1)
	2187 (Sunderland)	Scottish	552 (Edinburgh)
	2198 (Sutton Coldfield)	Portslade, local history	724 (Hove)
	2307 (Wolverhampton)	Portsmouth, local history	2002, 2004 (Portsmouth)
	2321 (Worthing)	Portugal	
	2333 (York)	history	2285 (Wigan)
Africa	1961 (Oxford)	language	154 (Birmingham)
agriculture	1412 (London SW1)		315 (Cambridge)
Asia	1961 (Oxford)		813 (Leeds)
China	1052 (London EC2)		1303 (London WC2)
Commonwealth	1082 (Edinburgh)		1686 (London NW3)
	1082 (London W8)		1965 (Oxford)
			2086 (Salford)
Europe	566 (Edinburgh)	literature	154 (Birmingham)
foreign	1159 (London SW1)		315 (Cambridge)
Greece	1539 (London W1)		1339 (London E2)
horticulture	1412 (London SW1)		1965, 1972 (Oxford)
international	17 (Aberystwyth)	criticism	1322 (London NW4)
	1541 (London SW1)	history	1322 (London NW4)
Latin America	299 (Cambridge)	Post Office	1483 (London E4)
	1961 (Oxford)	history	1642 (London SW4)
liberal	1423 (London SW1)	Post office trades union,	
Scotland	623 (Glasgow)	history	1642 (London SW4)
West Indies	1961 (Oxford)	Postal history	1331 (London N17)
Poll books	1187 (London EC2)		1431, 1483 (London EC1)
Pollen counts	925 (London W2)	Postal service	370 (Chelmsford)
Ponies	767 (Kenilworth)		1483 (London EC1)
Dartmoor	1861 (Newton Abbot)		1815 (Montrose)
Poole, local history	1999 (Poole)		1999 (Poole)
Poor laws	1106 (London SE1)	Postal tuition	915 (London EC1)
Pope, Alexander	2039 (Richmond)	Posters	1866 (Northampton)
Population	436 (Dagenham)	Postgraduate medical	
	1142 (London W1N 8BQ)	courses	1148 (London WC1)
	1279 (London SW1)	Pot-holing	233 (Bristol)
	1353 (London W1)	Potters Bar, local history	2008 (Potters Bar)
	1960 (Oxford)	Pottery	469 (Dundee)
census, Ireland	96 (Belfast)		801 (Leeds)
genetics research	1931 (Oxford)		1999 (Poole)
problems	1466 (London W1V 0JS)		2046 (Rochester)
Scotland	519 (Edinburgh)		2135 (Slough)
statistics	675 (Harpenden)		2154 (Stafford)
	948 (London EC4)		2199 (Swansea)
	1132 (London SW1)		2213 (Tilbury)
Porcelain	801 (Leeds)	Bronze Age	641 (Grantham)
	855 (Lincoln)	English	183 (Bootle)
	2199 (Swansea)		376 (Cheltenham)
	2322 (Worthing)		2322 (Worthing)
English	348 (Carlisle)	Greek	2029 (Reading)
	376 (Cheltenham)	Leeds	801 (Leeds)
Nantgarw	2199 (Swansea)	Llanelli	2199 (Swansea)
Swansea	2199 (Swansea)	Martinware	2137 (Southall)
Port Talbot, local history	2001 (Port Talbot)	medieval	1188 (London EC2)

Pottery (contd)			527 (Edinburgh)
ornamental	2175 (Stoke-on-Trent)		731 (Hull)
Staffordshire	404 (Cirencester)		868, 871 (Liverpool)
Sunderland	2186 (Sunderland)		1018 (London SE5)
Swansea	2199 (Swansea)		1117 (London W5)
Welsh	2199 (Swansea)		1165, 1170 (London SW15)
Poultry			1727 (Maidenhead)
diagnostic service	99 (Belfast)		1765 (Manchester)
diseases	791 (Lasswade)		1808 (Middlesbrough)
Poverty	1142 (London W1N 8BQ)		1858 (Newport, Mon)
Powys, J. F.	459 (Dorchester)		2024 (Reading)
Prayers, family	2143 (Southampton)		2141 (Southampton)
Preaching	1076 (London SW7)		2174 (Stoke-on-Trent)
	1998 (Pontypridd)		2207 (Taunton)
Pregnancy tests	1353 (London W1)		2232 (Twickenham)
Preparatory schools	1225 (London W8)		2249 (Ware)
Pre-Raphaelites	1692 (London E17)	fine	472 (Dundee)
Pre-retirement	1485 (London W1M 9FB)		724 (Hove)
Presbyterian Church	1161 (London WC1)	history	630 (Glasgow)
Presbyterian Church in			871 (Liverpool)
Ireland	105 (Belfast)		940 (London W1V 0NS)
Presbyterian Church of			1491 (London EC4)
England	1487 (London WC1)		1866 (Northampton)
history	1487, 1488 (London WC1)	See also Volume I	
Presbyterian churches	1487 (London WC1)	Printmakers	1490 (London W1)
Presbyterian history	105 (Belfast)	Printmaking	220 (Brighton)
	1487, 1488 (London WC1)		377 (Cheltenham)
Preservation	1797 (Market Drayton)		450 (Derby)
Pressure-sensitive			585 (Exeter)
adhesive tapes	674 (Harlow)		1614 (London SE5)
Prices	695 (Heckmondwike)		2141 (Southampton)
Prices and incomes	1104 (London SW1)	Prints	377 (Cheltenham)
policy	1962 (Oxford)		880 (Liverpool)
Primary education	44 (Ayr)		1490 (London W1)
	645 (Grays)		1614 (London SE5)
	937 (London SW15)		1808 (Middlesbrough)
	1443 (London WC1)		2186 (Sunderland)
	1820 (Musselburgh)	Buckinghamshire	37 (Aylesbury)
	2011 (Prescot)	Prisons	
	2070 (St Albans)	history	2236 (Wakefield)
	2228 (Twickenham)	Scotland	553 (Edinburgh)
	2272 (West Wickham)	Private presses	233 (Bristol)
	2279 (Weymouth)		1866 (Northampton)
	2305 (Wolverhampton)	books	332 (Cardiff)
Scotland	555 (Edinburgh)		472 (Dundee)
Primary school			1692 (London E17)
mathematics teaching	859 (Liverpool)		2015 (Preston)
music	55 (Banstead)		2112 (Sheffield)
Primitive churches	119 (Bexley)	illustrations	2141 (Southampton)
Primitive Methodism	1756 (Manchester)	printing	944 (London SW19)
Printing	129 (Birmingham)	Probation Officers	1399 (London WC1)
	189 (Bournemouth)	history	1399 (London WC1)
	220, 223 (Brighton)	Proclamations	1598 (London W1V 0HS)
	417 (Coventry)	Procreation	1142 (London W1N 8BQ)
	430 (Croydon)	Product design	1094 (London SW1)
	450 (Derby)	Production	
	469 (Dundee)	censuses	2060 (Ruislip)

Production (contd)
  economics   118(Beverley)
  management   700(Henley-on-Thames)
Productivity   1104(London SW1)
Professional people,
  financial aid   1492(London W1M 6HY)
Profit-sharing   1232(London SW1)
Progestational agents   715(High Wycombe)
Programmed instruction   576(Enfield)
Programmed learning   154, 155(Birmingham)
    174(Bolton)
    527(Edinburgh)
    725(Huddersfield)
    913(London WC1)
    1898(Nottingham)
Progressive education   1825(New Malden)
    2226(Tunbridge Wells)
Property law   779(Kingston upon Thames)
Property valuation   1073(London W8)
Prophets, minor   640(Gosport)
Proprietary medicines   207(Brentford)
    1472(London WC1)
Prosthetics   1433(London WC2)
Prostitution   1132(London SW1)
    1297(London SW1)
Protestant churches   459(Dorchester)
Protestant liturgies   1219(London WC1)
Protestant psalters   1219(London WC1)
Protozoology   873(Liverpool)
    1367(London NW1)
Proverbs   233(Bristol)
Psalmody   13(Aberdeen)
Psalters   433(Croydon)
  Protestant   1219(London WC1)
Psychiatric illness   1370(London SE5)
Psychiatric rehabilitation   1736(Malvern)
Psychiatry   6(Aberdeen)
    40(Aylesbury)
    66(Basingstoke)
    119(Bexley)
    143, 154(Birmingham)
    172(Bodmin)
    212(Bridgend)
    313(Cambridge)
    388(Chester)
    416(Coulsdon)
    565, 568(Edinburgh)
    681(Harrow)
    749(Ilkley)
    1193(London E9)
    1236(London W1P 3LD)
    1238(London W1)
    1261(London WC1)
    1266(London SE5)
    1267(London W1)
    1380(London W1P 7PN)
    1597(London W1)
    1627(London NW3)
    1871(Northampton)
    1963(Oxford)
    2067(St Albans)
    2236(Wakefield)
  child   1871(Northampton)
  history   1266(London SE5)
  metabolic studies   2109(Sheffield)
  social   416(Coulsdon)
    1370(London SE5)
Psychic research   1783(Manchester)
    2159(Stansted)
Psychic science   564(Edinburgh)
    1783(Manchester)
    2159(Stansted)
Psychical phenomena   1061(London SW1)
    1662(London WC1)
Psychics   685(Hastings)
Psychoanalysis   119(Bexley)
    1218(London SE11)
    1238(London W1)
    1266(London SE5)
    1267, 1597(London W1)
    1627(London NW3)
Psycholinguistics   506(Edinburgh)
Psychological health   888(London W1V 8EP)
Psychological medicine   344(Cardiff)
    1963(Oxford)
Psychological tests   2132(Slough)
Psychological warfare   2038(Richmond)
Psychologists   1003(London W1X 4DN)
Psychology   3, 6(Aberdeen)
    36, 40(Aylesbury)
    124(Birkenhead)
    140, 143, 147, 152, 153, 156,
      157(Birmingham)
    172(Bodmin)
    201(Bradford)
    247(Bristol)
    330(Canterbury)
    379, 380(Cheltenham)
    393(Chichester)
    403(Chorley)
    416(Coulsdon)
    417, 422(Coventry)
    435(Dagenham)
    449(Derby)
    457(Doncaster)
    470(Dundee)
    488, 491(Durham)
    510, 511, 520, 533, 564
      (Edinburgh)
    588(Exeter)
    591(Falmouth)
    612(Glasgow)
    669(Hamilton)
    700(Henley-on-Thames)

Psychology (contd)   725 (Huddersfield)
789 (Lancaster)
805, 812 (Leeds)
877 (Liverpool)
884 (London WC2)
912 (London E1)
931 (London SE9)
942 (London WC1)
994 (London WC2)
1003 (London W1X 4DN)
1132 (London SW1)
1165 (London SW15)
1167 (London SW17)
1180 (London EC1)
1218 (London SE11)
1234 (London SE1)
1236 (London W1P 3LD)
1247 (London W11)
1261 (London WC1)
1266 (London SE5)
1267 (London W1)
1324 (London NW3)
1418 (London WC1)
1421 (London W1M 8DR)
1498 (London SE8)
1528 (London W1M 0AB)
1566 (London WC2)
1627 (London NW3)
1650 (London NW1)
1653 (London SE14)
1662 (London WC1)
1682 (London E15)
1767, 1789, 1791 (Manchester)
1808 (Middlesbrough)
1813 (Mold)
1839, 1845, 1846 (Newcastle upon Tyne)
1871 (Northampton)
1895 (Nottingham)
1948, 1958 (Oxford)
2011 (Prescot)
2043 (Ripon)
2067, 2068 (St Albans)
2145 (Southampton)
2166 (Stirling)
2173 (Stoke-on-Trent)
2187, 2188 (Sunderland)
2198 (Sutton Coldfield)
2233 (Uxbridge)
2272 (West Wickham)
2234, 2236 (Wakefield)
2290 (Winchester)
2306 (Wolverhampton)
2330, 2333 (York)

abnormal   2201 (Swansea)
adolescence   725 (Huddersfield)
analytical   1597 (London W1)

applied   289 (Cambridge)
aviation   393 (Chichester)
careers   1003 (London W1X 4DN)
child   169 (Bletchley)
252 (Bromley)
329 (Canterbury)
331 (Cardiff)
789 (Lancaster)
797 (Leeds)
1247 (London W11)
1405 (London W1)
1443 (London WC1)
1597 (London W1)
1616 (London SW19)
1767 (Manchester)
1837 (Newcastle upon Tyne)
1855 (Newport, Mon)
2011 (Prescot)
2020 (Reading)
2035 (Retford)
2146 (Southampton)
2168 (Stockport)
clinical   393 (Chichester)
developmental   75 (Bath)
1364 (London WC1)
2257 (Watford)
education   823 (Leicester)
1102 (London W1)
1992 (Plymouth)
2035 (Retford)
2138 (Southampton)
2279 (Weymouth)
2290 (Winchester)
educational   75 (Bath)
174 (Bolton)
506 (Edinburgh)
590 (Falkirk)
906 (London N7)
1170 (London SW15)
1877 (Norwich)
2020 (Reading)
2121 (Shrewsbury)
experimental   320 (Cambridge)
genetic   581 (Esher)
1739 (Manchester)
groups   459 (Dorchester)
industrial   114 (Berkhamsted)
1117 (London W5)
2259 (Wednesbury)
Jung   1597 (London W1)
nursing   467 (Dumfries)
occupational   942 (London WC1)
1421 (London W1M 8DR)
religion   95 (Belfast)
social   369 (Chelmsford)
1266 (London SE5)
training   1003 (London W1X 4DN)

Psychometrics	1421(London W1M 8DR)	Public welfare	1695(London WC1)
Psychopathological art	1266(London SE5)	Publishing	1315(London WC1)
Psychopathology	225(Brighton)	history	934(London W1V 0NS)
	313(Cambridge)		1404(London W1X 4BB)
	1132(London SW1)	private press	955(London SW19)
Psychopharmacology	2109(Sheffield)	See also Volume I	
Psychosomatic medicine	1266(London SE5)	Punjabi literature	2304(Wolverhampton)
	1267(London W1)	Puppetry	1641(London WC1)
Psychotherapy	1247(London W11)	educational	1121(London WC1)
	1267(London W1)	Puritan history	1663(London NW3)
Public administration	25(Alloa)	Puritan literature	1136(London W1M 2HB)
	33(Ashton-under-Lyne)	Puritan works	1914(Ormskirk)
	201(Bradford)	Pusey	1942(Oxford)
	421(Coventry)		
	520(Edinburgh)	**Q**	
	587(Exeter)		
	700(Henley-on-Thames)	Q.M.A.A.C.	663(Guildford)
	994(London WC2)	Quakers	158(Birmingham)
	1053(London W4)		354(Carlisle)
	1065(London SW1)		439(Darlington)
	1104(London SW1)		718(Hitchin)
	1309(London WC1)		1502, 1164(London NW1)
	1542(London W1)	history	158(Birmingham)
	2021(Reading)		502, 1164(London NW1)
	2187(Sunderland)	Quantity surveying	1073(London W8)
	2289(Winchester)	Quebec Province	1456(London W1)
		Queen's Own Cameron	
See also Volume I		Highlanders, history	752(Inverness)
Public analysis	920(London SE1)	Queen's Own Highlanders	
Public cleansing	145(Birmingham)	(Seaforth and Camerons),	
Public dental health		history	752(Inverness)
services	1145(London W1)	Queen's Own Royal West	
	1609(London WC1)	Kent Regiment, history	1733(Maidstone)
Public education system	2132(Slough)	Quinine	745(Ilford)
Public finance	2337(York)		
Public health	746(Ilford)	**R**	
	817(Leeds)		
	921(London SW1)	Rabbinic literature	1292(London W1)
	971(London W1Y 2AA)	Rabbinica	1383(London WC1)
	1191(London SE1)	Rabbis, training	1292(London W1)
	1344, 1369(London WC1)	Rabelais	294(Cambridge)
	1377(London SW1)	Rabindranath Tagore	564(Edinburgh)
	1528(London W1M 0AB)	Race crossing	1132(London SW1)
	2003(Portsmouth)	Race relations	195(Bracknell)
	2121(Shrewsbury)		1058(London SE1)
	2172(Stoke-on-Trent)		1497(London SW1)
	2289(Winchester)		1502(London NW1)
engineering	867(Liverpool)	Rachel McMillan	1498(London SE8)
inspection	145(Birmingham)	Radcliffe, local history	1779(Manchester)
inspectors, training	1493(London SW1)	Radiation hazards	341(Cardiff)
Scotland	553(Edinburgh)		990(London W1M 7PG)
Public opinion surveys	1168(London W1A 3AU)	Radiation protection	341(Cardiff)
Public relations	700(Henley-on-Thames)		990(London W1M 7PG)
Public safety	1206(London SW1)		2194(Sutton)
	2039(Richmond)	Radio	33(Ashton-under-Lyne)
Public schools	235(Bristol)		2141(Southampton)
Public services	1253(London SW1)		2205(Tamworth)
Public transport, Glasgow	611(Glasgow)		

Radio (*contd*)			1762 (Manchester)
communications	2049 (Romford)		2198 (Sutton Coldfield)
writers	1600 (London SW10)	history	1328 (London SE10)
writing	1705 (London W2)	hygiene	2051 (Rossendale)
Radioactivity	341 (Cardiff)	Recruitment	287 (Cambridge)
effects	806 (Leeds)	staff	1168 (London W1A 3AU)
	1365 (London W12)	Recusant history	401 (Chipping Norton)
Radiobiology	341 (Cardiff)		730 (Hull)
	455 (Didcot)	Redruth, local history	2033 (Redruth)
	990 (London W1M 7PG)	Reform club, history	1501 (London SW1)
	2114 (Sheffield)	Reform league	943 (London EC2)
Radiochemistry	455 (Didcot)	Reformation	
Radiography	257 (Burgess Hill)	theology	2217 (Truro)
Radioisotopes	341 (Cardiff)	writings	282 (Cambridge)
Radiological physics	1742 (Manchester)	Reformed religion	1135 (London WC1)
	2114 (Sheffield)	Refugee experience	2038 (Richmond)
Radiological protection	2194 (Sutton)	Refuse disposal	1381 (London SW1)
Radiology	341, 344 (Cardiff)		2023 (Reading)
	681 (Harrow)	Regimental histories	24 (Aldershot)
	990 (London W1M 7PG)		1560 (London SW1)
	1245 (London SW3)		2161 (Stirling)
industrial	990 (London W1M 7PG)	*See also* individual Regiments	
medical	990 (London W1M 7PG)	Reginald L. Hine	718 (Hitchin)
Radiotherapy	307 (Cambridge)	Regional development	109 (Belfast)
	341 (Cardiff)	Regional Library Schemes	2347–2354
	1365 (London W12)	Regional planning	2020 (Reading)
	1742 (Manchester)	Regional studies	154 (Birmingham)
	2114 (Sheffield)		411 (Coleraine)
	2224 (Tunbridge Wells)		2115 (Sheffield)
Railways	13 (Aberdeen)	Regionalism	1841 (Newcastle upon Tyne)
	2204 (Swindon)	Registration	1175 (London WC2)
history	391 (Chesterfield)	Rehabilitation	416 (Coulsdon)
	439 (Darlington)	blind	1564 (London NW1)
	2328 (York)	disabled	1030 (London SW1)
Ireland	94 (Belfast)	medicine	974 (London WC1)
London	1390 (London SW4)	Religion	3 (Aberdeen)
narrow gauge	728 (Huddersfield)		75 (Bath)
relics	2328 (York)		160 (Bishop's Stortford)
Raleigh, Sir Walter	1956 (Oxford)		201 (Bradford)
Ramsay MacDonald	994 (London WC2)		235 (Bristol)
Rapid reading techniques	909 (London SW1)		310 (Cambridge)
Rathbone, William	881 (Liverpool)		379 (Cheltenham)
Rational ethics	1437 (London SE1)		413 (Colwyn Bay)
Rationalism	1500 (London N1)		427 (Crewe)
Rattles, police	67 (Basingstoke)		435 (Dagenham)
Reading	2169 (Stockport)		457 (Doncaster)
habits	1315 (London WC1)		470 (Dundee)
	1404 (London W1X 4BB)		498 (Eastbourne)
problems	2169 (Stockport)		522 (Edinburgh)
rapid	909 (London SW1)		641 (Grantham)
Reconstructive surgery	494 (East Grinstead)		671 (Harlech)
	1925 (Oxford)		702 (Hereford)
Recorded sound	991 (London SW7)		734 (Hull)
Records, Northern Ireland	106 (Belfast)		866 (Liverpool)
Recreation	866 (Liverpool)		1334 (London SE13)
	1328 (London SE10)		1500 (London N1)
	1475 (London W1M 4AX)		1693 (London SW19)

Religion (contd)	1746, 1756, 1772, 1782 (Manchester)		2234 (Wakefield)
		Religious knowledge	1302 (London SE11)
	1837, 1845 (Newcastle upon Tyne)	Religious life	1022 (London SW1)
		Religious observance, Jewish	912 (London E1)
	1882 (Norwich)	Religious philosophy	517 (Edinburgh)
	1891 (Nottingham)	Religious sociology	247 (Bristol)
	2043 (Ripon)		859 (Liverpool)
	2091 (Salisbury)	Rembrandt etchings	801, 802 (Leeds)
Africa	1968 (Oxford)	Remedial education	1112 (London SW1)
Arabic	1285 (London NW8)	Renal diseases	807, 862 (Liverpool)
Asia	1523 (London W1N 1LN)	Renewed Moravian Church	229 (Bristol)
	1968 (Oxford)	Repertory movement	965 (London SE1)
Bulgaria	311 (Cambridge)	Repertory theatre	654 (Guildford)
China	1968 (Oxford)	Reproduction, documents	884 (London WC2)
Commonwealth	1082 (Edinburgh)		909 (London SW1)
	1082 (London W8)	Reproduction, physiology	1730 (Maidenhead)
comparative	309 (Cambridge)		2284 (Widnes)
	564 (Edinburgh)	Reproductive system	443 (Dartford)
	1211 (London SE23)	Reprography	687 (Hatfield)
	1331 (London N17)	Republic of Vietnam	1127 (London W8)
	1597 (London W1)	Research	
	1645 (London WC2)	educational	527 (Edinburgh)
	1789 (Manchester)		1202 (London WC2)
Czechoslovakia	311 (Cambridge)		2132 (Slough)
East European	1668 (London WC1)	Scotland	547 (Edinburgh)
India	1968 (Oxford)	higher education	1593 (London WC1)
Islamic	1285 (London NW8)	pharmaceutical	2133 (Slough)
Japan	1968 (Oxford)	psychic	2159 (Stansted)
Jewish	1339 (London E1)	scientific and industrial	1253 (London SW1)
	1458 (London WC1)	Resettlement	
	2139 (Southampton)	disabled	974 (London WC1)
Muslim	1285 (London NW8)	soldiers	1112 (London SW1)
non-Christian	34 (Ashton-under-Lyne)	Residents' associations	1401 (London SE1)
	413 (Colwyn Bay)	Resolutions, Women's organizations	1695 (London WC1)
	581 (Esher)	Respiration	20 (Accrington)
	1688 (London NW1)		124 (Birkenhead)
	1688 (London WC2)		
	2326 (Yeovil)	diseases	1980 (Penarth)
Persia	1968 (Oxford)	physiology	1980 (Penarth)
Poland	311 (Carlisle)	Restoration, artistic works	1277 (London SW5)
primitive peoples	299 (Chichester)	Restoration period	89 (Bedford)
Roman Catholic	2272 (West Wickham)	Restorers, artistic works	1277 (London SW5)
Russia	311 (Cambridge)	Restrictive trade practices	798 (Leeds)
Slavonic	1668 (London WC1)		1253 (London SW1)
Turkey	1968 (Oxford)	Retail trades	606 (Glasgow)
Welsh	342 (Cardiff)		676 (Harrogate)
World	1703 (London W2)	distribution	717 (Hitchin)
Yugoslavia	311 (Cambridge)		874 (Liverpool)
Religious architecture	154 (Birmingham)	Reuters	1505 (London EC4)
Religious art	2278 (Weymouth)	Rh haemolytic disease	241 (Bristol)
Religious books	223 (Brighton)	Rheumatic disease	907 (London WC2)
Religious commentaries	428 (Crieff)	Rhodesia, Methodist missions	1376 (London NW1)
Religious controversy	492 (Durham)		
Religious education	403 (Chorley)	Rhondda, local history	1983 (Pentre)
	1387 (London SW1)	Ribchester	2018 (Preston)
	1979 (Penarth)	Richard Baxter	158 (Birmingham)
	2020 (Reading)		771 (Kidderminster)

Richard Baxter (contd)	1190(London W3)	education	1023, 1026(London SW7)
Richard Burton	2039(Richmond)		2138(Southampton)
Richard Cobden	223(Brighton)	history	612(Glasgow)
Richard III	1506(London SW9)		1025(London W1)
Richmond (Surrey), local history	2039(Richmond)	religion	2272(West Wickham)
		social doctrine	612(Glasgow)
Rickets	712(Heywood)	teaching	1026(London NW4)
	746(Ilford)	theology	424(Crawley)
Riding schools	767(Kenilworth)		612(Glasgow)
River Clyde	2056(Rothesay)		2138(Southampton)
River craft	2040(Richmond)	youth organizations	1027(London SW7)
River pollution	1381(London SW1)	Roman epigraphy	1250(London WC1)
	2040(Richmond)	Roman history	1250(London WC1)
River Thames	2040(Richmond)	Roman language	1250(London WC1)
boating	2040(Richmond)	Roman literature	1250(London WC1)
cruising	2040(Richmond)	Roman papyrology	1250(London WC1)
geography	2040(Richmond)	Roman philosophy	1250(London WC1)
natural history	2040(Richmond)	Roman Wall	1834, 1849(Newcastle upon Tyne)
R. L. Stevenson	513(Edinburgh)		
R. M. Ballantyne	513(Edinburgh)	Romance languages	1851(Newport, Isle of Wight)
Road accidents	381(Chertsey)		
Road books	1538(London SW7)	Romance literature	107(Belfast)
Road safety	25(Alloa)	Romance philology	315(Cambridge)
	381(Chertsey)		1686(London NW3)
	1508, 1520(London SW1)	Romani movement	1192(London N3)
Road signs	381(Chertsey)	communities, history	1192(London N3)
Road traffic	67(Basingstoke)	literature	813(Leeds)
control	25(Alloa)	Romney, George	764(Kendal)
Road transport, London, history	1390(London SW4)	Ronald Knox	1352(London W8)
		Rossendale, local history	45(Bacup)
Roads	2023(Reading)		2051(Rosendale)
system	1520(London SW1)	Rotarians, voluntary work	1510(London SW14)
Robert Blake	213, 214(Bridgwater)	Rotary clubs	1510(London SW14)
Robert Burns	41(Ayr)	Rotherham	
	478(Dunfermline)	history	2053(Rotherham)
	610(Glasgow)	local history	2054(Rotherham)
Robert Burton	1903(Nuneaton)	Rowing	890(London W1N 5TB)
Robert Owen	16(Aberystwyth)		1328(London SE10)
	1711(Loughborough)	history	890(London W1N 5TB)
	1745(Manchester)	Rowland Hill	771(Kidderminster)
Robin Hood	1891(Nottingham)	Roxburghshire, local history	692, 693, 694(Hawick)
Rochester (author)	288(Cambridge)	Royal Academy	1511(London W1V 0DS)
Rochester, local history	600(Gillingham)	history	1511(London W1V 0DS)
	2047(Rochester)	Royal Air Force	
Rochford Hundred, history	2148(Southend-on-Sea)	history	24(Aldershot)
Rockingham pottery	639(Goole)		1515(London NW9)
	2053, 2054(Rotherham)		2129(Sleaford)
Rodent control	2190(Surbiton)	medical aspects	1111(London WC1)
Roger Fry	288(Cambridge)	Royal Artillery, history	1517(London SE18)
Roller hockey	1435(London N8)	Royal Dragoons, history	2296(Windsor)
Roman antiquities	1250(London WC1)	Royal Flying Corps, history	1515(London NW9)
Roman archaeology	316(Cambridge)		
	1250(London WC1)	Royal Highland Fusiliers, history	613(Glasgow)
Roman art	1250(London WC1)		
Roman Bath	76(Bath)	Royal Horse Guards, history	2296(Windsor)
Roman Catholic Church	217(Bridgwater)		
	1352(London W8)	Royal House of Stuart	2161(Stirling)

Royal Irish Fusiliers, history	30 (Armagh)	Rural trades	1720 (Luton)
Royal Lincolnshire Regiment, history	853 (Lincoln)	Ruskin, John	764 (Kendal)
			1690 (London SW15)
Royal National Lifeboat Institution, history	1546 (London SW1)	Russia	154 (Birmingham)
			411 (Coleraine)
Royal Naval Air Service, history	1515 (London NW9)		813 (Leeds)
			1253 (London SW1)
	2325 (Yeovil)		1340 (London E17)
Royal Navy, history	24 (Aldershot)		1947 (Oxford)
	366 (Chatham)	architecture	1591 (London SW9)
	1425 (London SE10)	arts	1591 (London SW9)
Royal Norfolk Regiment, history	1884 (Norwich)	Asiatic	1523 (London W1N 1LN)
		books	1028 (London SW3)
Royal Philharmonic Society, history	1549 (London SW7)	cinema	1591 (London SW9)
		education	1591 (London SW9)
Royal Pioneer Corps, history	1870 (Northampton)	folklore	311 (Cambridge)
		geography	1591 (London SW9)
Royal Scots Fusiliers	613 (Glasgow)		2219 (Truro)
Royal Shakespeare Theatre	2179 (Stratford upon Avon)	government	409 (Colchester)
Royal Society for the Prevention of Cruelty to Animals, history	1552 (London SW1)	history	167 (Blackpool)
			311 (Cambridge)
			409 (Colchester)
Royal Society of Arts, history	1553 (London WC2)		1340 (London E17)
			1591 (London SW9)
Royal Sussex Regiment, history	398 (Chichester)		2219 (Truro)
		housing	1591 (London SW9)
Rugby fives	1562 (London SW7)	language	152 (Birmingham)
Rugby league football	810 (Leeds)		201 (Bradford)
Rugby union football	2229 (Twickenham)		311 (Cambridge)
Rumania	408 (Colchester)		330 (Canterbury)
	2051 (Rossendale)		520 (Edinburgh)
geography	2278 (Weymouth)		778 (Kingston upon Thames)
history	2278 (Weymouth)		800 (Leeds)
language	315 (Cambridge)		1117 (London W5)
	1686 (London NW3)		1307 (London WC1)
	1965 (Oxford)		1665 (London E1)
literature	315 (Cambridge)		1839 (Newcastle upon Tyne)
	1965 (Oxford)		1893 (Nottingham)
criticism	1322 (London NW4)		1946, 1948 (Oxford)
history	1322 (London NW4)		2086 (Salford)
Runcorn, local history	2061 (Runcorn)		2187 (Sunderland)
Rupert Brooke	288 (Cambridge)		2334 (York)
Rural crafts	643 (Grantham)	teaching	2327 (York)
	1720 (Luton)	literature	81 (Beaconsfield)
Rural development	1466 (London W1V 0JS)		201 (Bradford)
Rural economy	2022 (Reading)		311 (Cambridge)
Rural industries	1092 (London SW19)		409 (Colchester)
	2209 (Taunton)		778 (Kingston upon Thames)
Rural life	827 (Leicester)		805 (Leeds)
Dorset	460 (Dorchester)		1330 (London W6)
Nottinghamshire	1897 (Nottingham)		1591 (London SW9)
Rural science	17 (Aberystwyth)		1839 (Newcastle upon Tyne)
Rural sociology	1922, 1960 (Oxford)		2100 (Scunthorpe)
Rural studies	403 (Chorley)	philosophy	311 (Cambridge)
	1073 (London W8)	religion	311 (Cambridge)
	2020 (Reading)	science	1591 (London SW9)
	2035 (Retford)	sculpture	1591 (London SW9)

Russia (*contd*)				837, 840(Lichfield)
social science	1591(London SW9)			1941(Oxford)
technology	1591(London SW9)	Sanitary inspection		746(Ilford)
theatre	1591(London SW9)	Sanitation		45(Bacup)
travel	167(Blackpool)	Sanskrit		107(Belfast)
Rutherglen, local history	615(Glasgow)			1469(London W2)
Rutland		Sassoon		1798(Marlborough)
agricultural history	1907(Oakham)	Satire, English		2081(Sale)
domestic history	1907(Oakham)	Saudi Arabia		1573(London SW1)
local history	1906(Oakham)	Savings		1168(London W1A 3AU)
		banks		1168(London W1A 3AU)
S		Scandinavia		
		books		529(Edinburgh)
Sabbath	1322(London NW4)	dictionaries		1658(London WC1)
Sadler's Wells Theatre	1332(London EC1)	history		262(Bury)
Safety	521(Edinburgh)	law		1309(London WC1)
	1508(London SW1)	literature		1658(London WC1)
agricultural	1508(London SW1)			1972(Oxford)
engineering	672(Harlow)	philology		1972(Oxford)
home	1508(London SW1)	travel		262(Bury)
industrial	1233, 1508(London SW1)	Scarborough		
	2039(Richmond)	archaeology		2095(Scarborough)
public	2039(Richmond)	local history		2095, 2096(Scarborough)
road	1508(London SW1)			
sea	1425(London SE10)	Scholastic theology		401(Chipping Norton)
Sailing pilots	1425(London SE10)			830(Leicester)
St Albans, local history	2068, 2069(St Albans)	Schools		1060(London SW1)
St David's University				1202(London WC2)
College, history	783(Lampeter)	administration		645(Grays)
Saint-Évremond	288(Cambridge)	broadcasting		339(Cardiff)
St Helens, local history	2077(St Helens)			1575(London W1A 1AA)
St Ives, local history	2078(St Ives)	buildings		1102(London W1)
St Leonards, local history	683(Hastings)	curriculum		1577(London W1N 6LL)
St Marylebone		libraries		44(Ayr)
local history	1688(London NW1)			1102(London W1)
topography	1688(London NW1)	music		254(Bromley)
St Pancras, local history	1324(London NW3)			719(Hitchin)
Saints	119(Bexley)			999(London W1)
	2222(Truro)	organization		645(Grays)
Salaries, white-collar		preparatory		1225(London W8)
workers	698(Hemel Hempstead)	voluntary aided		
Sales catalogues	1673(London W1)	Secondary		83(Beaconsfield)
Salford		Science		
history	2084(Salford)	(All aspects of Science were included in Volume I of the Directory, but they have been indexed here for organizations which did not appear in Volume I)		
local history	2084, 2085(Salford)			
topography	2084(Salford)			
Salisbury, local history	2090, 2091(Salisbury)			329(Canterbury)
Saltcoats, local history	2092(Saltcoats)			380(Cheltenham)
Salvation Army	1570(London EC4)			414(Colwyn Bay)
	1571(London SE5)			417, 419(Coventry)
biographies	1571(London SE5)			427(Crewe)
doctrine	1571(London SE5)			444(Dartford)
history	1571(London SE5)			449(Derby)
Salzburger emigration	1592(London NW1)			470, 474(Dundee)
Samaritans	2134(Slough)			485, 487, 492(Durham)
Samuel Butler	294(Cambridge)			498(Eastbourne)
Samuel Johnson	133(Birmingham)			574(Egham)

Science (contd)	584, 589 (Exeter)		1560 (London SW1)
	630 (Glasgow)		1688 (London W9)
	646 (Grays)	naval	1688 (London W9)
	665 (Halesowen)	philosophy	322 (Cambridge)
	679 (Harrow)		951 (London SE1)
	740 (Huntingdon)		1651 (London SW3)
	812 (Leeds)		2187 (Sunderland)
	822 (Leicester)	police	25 (Alloa)
	942 (London WC1)	policy	227 (Brighton)
	1110, 1170 (London SW15)	psychic	2159 (Stansted)
		Russia	1591 (London SW9)
	1313 (London WC1)	sociology	227 (Brighton)
	1498 (London SE8)	statistics	227 (Brighton)
	1500 (London N1)	war	270 (Camberley)
	1650 (London NW1)	Scientific and industrial	
	1722 (Luton)	research	1253 (London SW1)
	1746, 1782 (Manchester)	Scientific instruments,	
	1808 (Middlesbrough)	history	322 (Cambridge)
	1833 (Newcastle upon Tyne)		1966 (Oxford)
		Scilly Islands	1592 (London NW1)
	2002 (Portsmouth)	Scotland	513, 529, 553 (Edinburgh)
	2043 (Ripon)		1326 (London W5)
	2124 (Shrewsbury)		1821 (Nairn)
	2129 (Sleaford)		1949 (Oxford)
	2182 (Sunderland)		1988 (Perth)
	2234 (Wakefield)		2340
	2269 (West Bromwich)	administration	553 (Edinburgh)
	2306 (Wolverhampton)	agriculture	553 (Edinburgh)
	2321 (Worthing)	aircraft industry	611 (Glasgow)
	2335 (York)	angling clubs	540 (Edinburgh)
Asia	1518 (London W1M 9LA)	angling waters	540 (Edinburgh)
biography	227 (Brighton)	archaeology	572 (Edinburgh)
economics	227 (Brighton)	architecture	509, 530 (Edinburgh)
education	686 (Hatfield)	art	551 (Edinburgh)
	1651 (London SW3)	artists	528, 551 (Edinburgh)
fiction	2097 (Scunthorpe)	arts	541 (Edinburgh)
Germany	1176 (London SW1)	bibliography	622 (Glasgow)
history	13 (Aberdeen)	building	509 (Edinburgh)
	227 (Brighton)	canoeing	10 (Aberdeen)
	322 (Cambridge)	Civic Trust	619 (Glasgow)
	568 (Edinburgh)	civil engineering	509 (Edinburgh)
	631 (Glasgow)	criminal law	25 (Alloa)
	951 (London SE1)	drawings	528 (Edinburgh)
	1543 (London W1)	economics	546 (Edinburgh)
	1553 (London WC2)		623 (Glasgow)
	1578 (London SW7)	education	503, 553, 555 (Edinburgh)
	1651 (London SW3)	emigrants	549 (Edinburgh)
	1698 (London SE18)	examinations	618 (Glasgow)
	1741 (Manchester)	family history	549 (Edinburgh)
	1966 (Oxford)	fire services	553 (Edinburgh)
	2073 (St Andrews)	folk-life	572 (Edinburgh)
	2143 (Southampton)	folklore	572 (Edinburgh)
	2187 (Sunderland)	genealogy	519, 549, 561 (Edinburgh)
laboratory technology	1468 (London W2)		610 (Glasgow)
military	23, 24 (Aldershot)	geography	2150 (Southport)
	81 (Beaconsfield)		2161 (Stirling)
	906 (London N7)	Government	546 (Edinburgh)

Scotland (contd)
  Highlands 13(Aberdeen)
    751(Inverness)
  history 21(Airdrie)
    530, 561(Edinburgh)
    603, 610, 612(Glasgow)
    866(Liverpool)
    2150(Southport)
    2161, 2164(Stirling)
  holidays 559(Edinburgh)
  horticulture 553(Edinburgh)
  hospital services 473(Dundee)
  land economics 1977(Paisley)
  law 553, 561(Edinburgh)
  librarianship 622(Glasgow)
  life 603(Glasgow)
  literature 603, 610(Glasgow)
    866(Liverpool)
    2166(Stirling)
  local government 553(Edinburgh)
  local history 530, 572(Edinburgh)
  motor industry 611(Glasgow)
  North East
    antiquities 13(Aberdeen)
    history 13(Aberdeen)
    topography 13(Aberdeen)
  numismatics 530(Edinburgh)
  orienteering 434(Currie)
  paintings 528(Edinburgh)
  philosophy 474(Dundee)
  pipe and fiddle music 572(Edinburgh)
  poetry 610(Glasgow)
  police 553(Edinburgh)
  politics 623(Glasgow)
  population statistics 519(Edinburgh)
  portraiture 552(Edinburgh)
  prisons 553(Edinburgh)
  public health 553(Edinburgh)
  social affairs 623(Glasgow)
  social history 596(Forfar)
  social services 553(Edinburgh)
  sociology 572(Edinburgh)
  songs 2161(Stirling)
  surveying 509(Edinburgh)
  teachers 555(Edinburgh)
  topography 537, 561(Edinburgh)
    866(Liverpool)
  tourism 559(Edinburgh)
  Town and country
    planning 553(Edinburgh)
  Universities 602(Glasgow)
  voluntary services 514(Edinburgh)
  welfare services 553(Edinburgh)
  West, transport, history 611(Glasgow)
  women's rural institutes 560(Edinburgh)
  Youth Hostels 2162(Stirling)
Scott, Sir Walter 513(Edinburgh)

Scottish Border
  local history 692, 693, 694(Hawick)
  natural history 694(Hawick)
Scout Association 1579(London SW1)
Scout movement 1579(London SW1)
Scripture 748(Ilkeston)
  830(Leicester)
  1022(London SW1)
  2217(Truro)
  commentaries 180(Bolton)
Scrofula 712(Heywood)
  746(Ilford)
Sculptors 1554(London SW1)
Sculpture 113(Belfast)
  189(Bournemouth)
  253(Bromley)
  349(Carlisle)
  378(Cheltenham)
  431(Croydon)
  435(Dagenham)
  450(Derby)
  469(Dundee)
  585(Exeter)
  591(Falmouth)
  676(Harrogate)
  805(Leeds)
  866, 871, 880(Liverpool)
  1018(London SE5)
  1047(London SW3)
  1165(London SW15)
  1339(London E1)
  1524(London SW7)
  1554(London SW1)
  1566(London WC2)
  1673(London W1)
  1688(London WC2)
  1693(London SW19)
  1727(Maidenhead)
  1808(Middlesbrough)
  1858(Newport, Mon)
  1908(Oldham)
  2005(Portsmouth)
  2055(Rotherham)
  2116(Sheffield)
  2141(Southampton)
  European, history 1047(London SW3)
  history 253(Bromley)
    312(Cambridge)
  Russia 1591(London SW9)
Seaforth Highlanders,
  history 752(Inverness)
Seal casts 1598(London W1V 0HS)
Seals 1662(London WC1)
Seamen, British 1442(London SW4)
Secondary education 555(Edinburgh)
  645(Grays)

Secondary education (contd)	1443 (London WC1)		860 (Liverpool)
	2011 (Prescot)		1042 (London EC2)
	2070 (St Albans)		1339 (London E1)
	2279 (Weymouth)	Company house flags	1339 (London E1)
Secretarial studies	33 (Ashton-under-Lyne)	Cornwall	591 (Falmouth)
	2182 (Sunderland)	economics	2143 (Southampton)
	2249 (Ware)	industry, British	1442 (London SW4)
		merchant	947 (London SW1)
See also Volume I		Ships	1425 (London SE10)
Secular education	1500 (London N1)	illustrations	1339 (London E1)
Secularism	1437 (London SE1)	photographs	1339 (London E1)
Securities	1624 (London EC2)	Shoe design	824 (Leicester)
Selection techniques	393 (Chichester)	Shooting	214 (Bridgwater)
Semitics	813 (Leeds)		1328 (London SE10)
	1968 (Oxford)	Shops	
Serbia		law	1269 (London EC2)
geography	2278 (Weymouth)	Shops Acts 1950–1965	1269 (London EC2)
history	2278 (Weymouth)	Shorthand	327 (Canterbury)
literature	1330 (London W6)		1495 (London W1)
Sermons	428 (Crieff)	Shrewsbury, local history	2124 (Shrewsbury)
	584 (Exeter)	Shropshire	
	1076 (London SW7)	history	2123 (Shrewsbury)
	1942 (Oxford)	industries	2211 (Telford)
Serology	241 (Bristol)	local history	839 (Lichfield)
	293 (Cambridge)		2124, 2125,
Service books	783 (Lampeter)		2126 (Shrewsbury)
Service clubs	836 (Lewes)		
Servite history	1933 (Oxford)	Siberia	
Settlement of Georgia	1592 (London NW1)	geography	779 (Kingston upon Thames)
Sevenoaks, local history	2104 (Sevenoaks)	history	779 (Kingston upon Thames)
Sewage disposal	1381 (London SW1)		1725 (Macclesfield)
Sex	443 (Dartford)	travel	1725 (Macclesfield)
	1132 (London SW1)	Sick, home care	2218 (Truro)
behaviour	936 (London W1)	Sickert, Walter Richard	1332 (London N7)
education	1142 (London W1N 8BQ)	Signal books	1425 (London SE10)
	1279 (London SW1)	Signals, maritime	1425 (London SE10)
ethics	443 (Dartford)	Silver	113 (Belfast)
problems	1142 (London W1N 8BQ)		855 (Lincoln)
restrictions	1462 (London SW19)		1764 (Manchester)
Shakespeare	133, 154 (Birmingham)		1873 (Norwich)
	1662 (London WC1)		2112, 2116 (Sheffield)
	1799 (Matlock)		2186 (Sunderland)
	2100 (Scunthorpe)		2295 (Windsor)
	2179 (Stratford-upon-Avon)	Silversmithing	129 (Birmingham)
	2307 (Wolverhampton)		1713 (Loughborough)
Shaw, G. B.	1891 (Nottingham)		2055 (Rotherham)
Sheep dogs	21 (Airdrie)	Silverware	1688 (London WC2)
Sheffield, local history	2112 (Sheffield)	Singapore	1459 (London SW1)
Shelley	1299 (London NW3)	education	1459 (London SW1)
	1300 (London SW14)	Sir Basil Henriques	912 (London E1)
Sherlock Holmes	1583 (London SW1)	Sir Frank Brangwyn	771 (Kidderminster)
	1688 (London NW1)	Sir Henry Irving	194 (Bournemouth)
Sherwood Foresters, history	1900 (Nottingham)	Sir Horace Plunkett	1476 (London WC1)
Ship models	649 (Grimsby)	Sir John Moore	906 (London N7)
Shipbuilding	249 (Brockenhurst)	Sir Richard Burton	2039 (Richmond)
Clyde	611 (Glasgow)	Sir Rowland Hill	771 (Kidderminster)
Shipping	646 (Grays)	Sir Thomas Beecham	2273 (Westcliff-on-Sea)
	735 (Hull)	Sir Thomas More	1187 (London EC2)

829

Sir Walter Raleigh	1956(Oxford)		1566(London WC2)
Sir Walter Scott	513(Edinburgh)		1700(London NW1)
	2166(Stirling)		1808(Middlesbrough)
Sitwelliana	1799(Matlock)		1917(Oswestry)
Ski-ing	624(Glasgow)		2259(Wednesbury)
	780(Kingussie)	England	1506(London SW9)
	1588(London SW1)	Hastings	683(Hastings)
Skin	1323(London NW10)	Scotland	596(Forfar)
	1824(Nelson)	West Riding	458(Doncaster)
diseases	1323(London NW10)	Yorkshire, South	458(Doncaster)
pathology	146(Birmingham)	Social issues	1500(London N1)
Slaughter-houses	2190(Surbiton)	Social legislation	744(Ilford)
Slavery	36(Aylesbury)	Social life, Jewish	1339(London E1)
	733, 735(Hull)	Social medicine	154(Birmingham)
	1683(London WC2)		344(Cardiff)
	1786(Manchester)		565, 568(Edinburgh)
Slavonic			1344, 1369(London WC1)
history	1972(Oxford)	Social organization	411(Coleraine)
languages	311(Cambridge)	Social philosophy	520(Edinburgh)
	1902(Nottingham)	Social problems	1695(London WC1)
	1965, 1972(Oxford)	Social psychiatry	416(Coulsdon)
literature	1965, 1972(Oxford)		1370(London SE5)
studies	311(Cambridge)	Social psychology	369(Chelmsford)
	813(Leeds)		725(Huddersfield)
	1668(London WC1)		1266(London SE5)
Sleaford, local history	2128(Sleaford)	Social responsibility	975(London SW1)
Sleep	1731(Maidstone)	Social sciences	3, 5(Aberdeen)
	2051(Rossendale)		72(Bath)
learning	1168(London W1A 3AU)		92, 107(Belfast)
Smoke	746(Ilford)		132, 133, 140, 142, 153, 154,
	1439(London EC4)		157(Birmingham)
Smoking	1633(London SW1)		159(Bishop Auckland)
Snow	295(Cambridge)		160(Bishop's Stortford)
Soaps	1605(London W1)		175(Bolton)
	2082(Salford)		188(Boston Spa)
Social administration	154(Birmingham)		198, 200(Bradford)
	411(Coleraine)		224, 225(Brighton)
	2145(Southampton)		230, 235, 246(Bristol)
	2333(York)		261(Burton-on-Trent)
Social affairs, Scotland	623(Glasgow)		270(Camberley)
Social and economic conditions, Northumberland	1848(Newcastle upon Tyne)		324(Cannock)
			330(Canterbury)
Social anthropology	149(Birmingham)		359(Carshalton)
	310(Cambridge)		366(Chatham)
	1964(Oxford)		421(Coventry)
	2173(Stoke-on-Trent)		435(Dagenham)
Social clubs	836(Lewes)		464(Dudley)
Social development	1090(London SE1)		474(Dundee)
	1119(London SW1)		483, 486(Durham)
Social deviance	313(Cambridge)		520, 539(Edinburgh)
Social economics	1302(London SE11)		587(Exeter)
Social education	503(Edinburgh)		626, 630(Glasgow)
Social history	154(Birmingham)		650(Grimsby)
	748(Ilkeston)		655, 661(Guildford)
	761, 762(Keighley)		665(Halesowen)
	872(Liverpool)		671(Harlech)
	994(London WC2)		683(Hastings)

Social sciences (contd)
687 (Hatfield)
700 (Henley-on-Thames)
721 (Hornchurch)
725 (Huddersfield)
739 (Hull)
746 (Ilford)
750 (Ilkley)
758 (Isleworth)
773 (Kilmarnock)
778 (Kingston upon Thames)
785 (Lancaster)
792, 793 (Leamington Spa)
812, 813 (Leeds)
831 (Leicester)
864, 866, 877, 878 (Liverpool)
926, 947 (London SW1)
970 (London WC1)
994 (London WC2)
996 (London WC1)
1004 (London SE1)
1066 (London EC1)
1206 (London SW1)
1175 (London WC2)
1215, 1305 (London SW1)
1309 (London WC1)
1322 (London NW4)
1326 (London W5)
1327 (London W3)
1332 (London N7)
1333 (London SW2)
1334 (London SE13)
1355 (London EC1)
1387 (London SW1)
1473 (London SW16)
1615 (London N14)
1650 (London NW1)
1653 (London SE14)
1688 (London WC2)
1699 (London W1H 8BY)
1772 (Manchester)
1833 (Newcastle upon Tyne)
1858 (Newport, Mon)
1885 (Norwich)
1891, 1902 (Nottingham)
1910 (Oldham)
1913 (Ormskirk)
1917 (Oswestry)
1918, 1932, 1937, 1950 (Oxford)
1977 (Paisley)
1988 (Perth)
2000 (Poole)
2004 (Portsmouth)
2012 (Prescot)
2027 (Reading)
2079 (St Leonards-on-Sea)
2137 (Southall)

Africa
Australia
Denmark
Greece
history
Latin America
Oriental
research
Russia
See also Sociology
Social security
Social service

Cumberland
Liverpool
Merseyside
Northern Ireland
Social services

Church of England
Scotland
Social statistics

Social studies

2145 (Southampton)
2173 (Stoke-on-Trent)
2184 (Sunderland)
2198 (Sutton Coldfield)
2201, 2202 (Swansea)
2232 (Twickenham)
2238 (Wakefield)
2242, 2243 (Wallsend)
2269 (West Bromwich)
2272 (West Wickham)
2309 (Bletchley)
2312 (Worcester)
2335 (York)
2339
1273 (London EC4)
1666 (London WC1)
928 (London WC2)
1536 (London SW1)
1539 (London W1)
2122 (Shrewsbury)
299 (Cambridge)
1666 (London WC1)
1589 (London WC1)
1591 (London SW9)

1107 (London WC2)
1283 (London NW10)
1409 (London WC1)
1570 (London EC4)
1571 (London SE5)
352 (Carlisle)
869 (Liverpool)
869 (Liverpool)
102 (Belfast)
201 (Bradford)
779 (Kingston upon Thames)
971 (London W1Y 2AA)
1199 (London SW1)
1418 (London WC1)
1526 (London W1M 0BE)
2021 (Reading)
944 (London SW1)
553 (Edinburgh)
163 (Blackburn)
1040 (London SW1)
1442 (London SW4)
70 (Bath)
158 (Birmingham)
222 (Brighton)
251 (Bromley)
340 (Cardiff)
406 (Coatbridge)
409 (Colchester)
430 (Croydon)
589 (Exeter)
631 (Glasgow)
805 (Leeds)

Social studies (*contd*)	1053 (London W4)		2143 (Southampton)
	1197 (London NW4)	Socialist education	1138, 1590 (London SW1)
	1664 (London W8)	Socialist literature	422 (Coventry)
	1791 (Manchester)	Socialist movements, history	994 (London WC2)
	1850 (Newcastle upon Tyne)	Socialists, biography	2143 (Southampton)
	1945 (Oxford)	Society for Promoting	
	2003 (Portsmouth)	Christian Knowledge	1592 (London NW1)
	2014 (Preston)	Society of Friends *See* Quakers	
	2115, 2119 (Sheffield)	Society of St Vincent	
	2146 (Southampton)	de Paul, history	1612 (London SW1)
	2198 (Sutton Coldfield)	Socio-economics	1276 (London W1X 9PA)
	2233 (Uxbridge)	Sociolinguistics	506 (Edinburgh)
	2333 (York)	Sociology	6 (Aberdeen)
Asia, South	300 (Cambridge)		63 (Basingstoke)
United States of America	950 (London W1)		72, 73 (Bath)
Social surveys	1636 (London W1)		93 (Belfast)
methods	1180 (London EC1)		140, 145, 149, 150, 153, 154,
Social welfare	145 (Birmingham)		156 (Birmingham)
	435 (Dagenham)		161, 163 (Blackburn)
	488 (Durham)		169 (Bletchley)
	550 (Edinburgh)		198, 201 (Bradford)
	869 (Liverpool)		268 (Caernarvon)
	882 (Llanelli)		330 (Canterbury)
	1107 (London WC2)		403 (Chorley)
	1819 (Motherwell)		409 (Colchester)
	1851 (Newport, Isle of		423 (Crawley)
	Wight)		438 (Darlington)
	1881 (Norwich)		449, 452 (Derby)
	1958 (Oxford)		457 (Doncaster)
	2187 (Sunderland)		469 (Dundee)
	2198 (Sutton Coldfield)		485, 488, 491 (Durham)
	2236 (Wakefield)		510, 511, 520, 533,
Cambridgeshire	281 (Cambridge)		564 (Edinburgh)
Cumberland	352 (Carlisle)		576 (Enfield)
disabled	638 (Godalming)		580 (Esher)
Huntingdon	281 (Cambridge)		588 (Exeter)
Isle of Ely	281 (Cambridge)		636 (Gloucester)
Peterborough	281 (Cambridge)		641 (Grantham)
voluntary	1409 (London WC1)		646 (Grays)
Social work	12 (Aberdeen)		667 (Halifax)
	149 (Birmingham)		673 (Harlow)
	503 (Edinburgh)		687 (Hatfield)
	754 (Ipswich)		697 (Hemel Hempstead)
	1083 (London E1)		700 (Henley-on-Thames)
	1143 (London SW1)		711 (Hertford)
	1418 (London WC1)		734 (Hull)
	1451 (London NW5)		748 (Ilkeston)
	1662 (London WC1)		754 (Ipswich)
	1734 (Maidstone)		762 (Keighley)
	1871, 1895 (Nottingham)		778 (Kingston upon Thames)
	1994 (Plymouth)		789 (Lancaster)
	2333 (York)		812, 813 (Leeds)
Church of England	944 (London SW1)		859, 868 (Liverpool)
education	1418 (London WC1)		912 (London E1)
training	1418 (London WC1)		942 (London WC1)
Social workers	1717 (Lowestoft)		951 (London SE1)
Socialism	1305 (London SW1)		1015 (London SW4)

Sociology (contd)
- 1022(London SW1)
- 1098(London EC1)
- 1110(London SW15)
- 1132(London SW1)
- 1157(London WC1)
- 1167(London SW17)
- 1177(London SW7)
- 1180(London EC1)
- 1218(London SE11)
- 1236(London W1P 3LD)
- 1238(London W1)
- 1266(London SE5)
- 1302(London SE11)
- 1330(London W6)
- 1418, 1443(London WC1)
- 1451(London NW5)
- 1482(London W1R 8AL)
- 1528(London W1M 0AB)
- 1627(London NW3)
- 1650(London NW1)
- 1676(London SW18)
- 1682(London E15)
- 1711(Loughborough)
- 1717(Lowestoft)
- 1746, 1766(Manchester)
- 1805(Mexborough)
- 1807, 1808(Middlesbrough)
- 1809(Middlesbrough)
- 1839, 1845, 1846(Newcastle upon Tyne)
- 1927, 1946, 1958 (Oxford)
- 2002(Portsmouth)
- 2014(Preston)
- 2020, 2023(Reading)
- 2030(Redditch)
- 2035(Retford)
- 2067, 2068(St Albans)
- 2086(Salford)
- 2098(Scunthorpe)
- 2121(Shrewsbury)
- 2142, 2144, 2145(Southampton)
- 2160(Stevenage)
- 2166(Stirling)
- 2173(Stoke-on-Trent)
- 2182, 2187, 2188(Sunderland)
- 2203(Swindon)
- 2219(Truro)
- 2236(Wakefield)
- 2272(West Wickham)
- 2279(Weymouth)
- 2280(Whitehaven)
- 2290(Winchester)
- 2306(Wolverhampton)

Africa
Asia
children
Christian
Denmark
education

history
Jewish

Jews
Latin America

medicine
nautical
religion

rural
science
Scotland
West Indies
See also Social sciences
Soke of Peterborough, local history
Soldiers, resettlement
Somerset
   archaeology
   history
   local history

   topography
Somnambulism
Somnambulists, biography
South Lancashire Regiment, history
South Seas, missions
South Wales Borders and Monmouthshire Regiment, history
Southampton, local history
Southern Region, further education
Southport, local history
Southwell, local history
Soviet Central Asia
Soviet history
Soviet institutions

- 2312(Worcester)
- 2330, 2333(York)
- 298(Cambridge)
- 1273(London EC4)
- 1961(Oxford)
- 1961(Oxford)
- 1405(London W1)
- 1999(Poole)
- 895(London W1X 6HJ)
- 506(Edinburgh)
- 1170(London SW15)
- 1992(Plymouth)
- 2279(Weymouth)
- 2305(Wolverhampton)
- 726(Huddersfield)
- 912(London E1)
- 1383(London WC1)
- 1257(London W1)
- 299(Cambridge)
- 1961(Oxford)
- 12(Aberdeen)
- 1650(London NW1)
- 736(Hull)
- 247(Bristol)
- 859(Liverpool)
- 1922, 1960(Oxford)
- 227(Brighton)
- 572(Edinburgh)
- 1961(Oxford)

- 1868(Northampton)
- 1112(London SW1)
- 217(Bridgwater)
- 233(Bristol)
- 633(Glastonbury)
- 633(Glastonbury)
- 633(Glastonbury)
- 2210(Taunton)
- 2326(Yeovil)
- 2326(Yeovil)
- 1731(Maidstone)
- 1731(Maidstone)

- 2251(Warrington)
- 1086(London SW1)

- 206(Brecon)
- 2143(Southampton)

- 2026(Reading)
- 2150(Southport)
- 2152(Southwell)
- 1028(London SW3)
- 1591(London SW9)
- 630(Glasgow)

Soviet literature	1591 (London SW9)	Spelling	248 (Broadstairs)
Soviet Union *See* U.S.S.R.		Spinal cord injuries	39 (Aylesbury)
Spain	529 (Edinburgh)	Spinal cord lesions	39 (Aylesbury)
history	2285 (Wigan)	Spinning	2161 (Stirling)
travel	2285 (Wigan)	Spiritual conditions	1348 (London EC4)
Spanish		Spiritual healing	659 (Guildford)
(*See also* Spanish language and Spanish literature. The index entry 'Spanish' has been used where this was unqualified in any way in the relevant entry)			2159 (Stansted)
		Spiritual science	685 (Hastings)
	813 (Leeds)	Spiritualism	1783 (Manchester)
	942 (London WC1)		1998 (Pontypridd)
	1302 (London SE11)		2159 (Stansted)
	1303 (London WC2)	Sports	270 (Camberley)
	1451 (London NW5)		435 (Dagenham)
	1948 (Oxford)		496 (Eastbourne)
	2145 (Southampton)		510 (Edinburgh)
Spanish history	1972 (Oxford)		1031 (London W1N 4AJ)
Spanish language	154 (Birmingham)		1248 (London W6)
	201 (Bradford)		1356 (London NW8)
	315 (Cambridge)		1475 (London W1M 4AX)
	520 (Edinburgh)		2198 (Sutton Coldfield)
	778 (Kingston upon Thames)	indoor	1328 (London SE10)
	800, 812 (Leeds)		1475 (London W1M 4AX)
	1117 (London W5)	injuries	1270 (London W1M 4AX)
	1307 (London WC1)	medicine	1270 (London W1M 4AX)
	1326 (London W5)		1475 (London W1M 4AX)
	1686 (London NW3)		2130 (Slough)
	1799 (Matlock)	outdoor	1328 (London SE10)
	1946, 1965, 1972 (Oxford)		1475 (London W1M 4AX)
	2086 (Salford)	Squash rackets	558 (Edinburgh)
	2187 (Sunderland)	S.S.N. education	18 (Abingdon)
	2334 (York)	S.S. 'Forfarshire'	49 (Bamburgh)
Spanish literature	154 (Birmingham)	Staff associations	1272 (London WC2)
	201 (Bradford)	Staff college	271 (Camberley)
	315 (Cambridge)	Staffordshire	2154 (Stafford)
	778 (Kingston upon Thames)	archaeology	2244 (Walsall)
	788 (Lancaster)	genealogy	839 (Lichfield)
	805 (Leeds)	history	2206 (Tamworth)
	1918, 1965, 1972, 1973 (Oxford)		2244 (Walsall)
		local history	133 (Birmingham)
	2100 (Scunthorpe)		839 (Lichfield)
criticism	788 (Lancaster)		2155 (Stafford)
	1322 (London NW4)	pottery	404 (Cirencester)
history	1322 (London NW4)	Staffordshire Regiment, history	841 (Lichfield)
Spas	246 (Bristol)	Stage architecture	968 (London W1Y 4HQ)
Special education	18 (Abingdon)	Stage design	968 (London W1Y 4HQ)
	1078 (London W1P 3LD)		1693 (London SW19)
	1972 (Plymouth)	Stage management	1681 (London W4)
	2014 (Preston)	Stained glass	465 (Dudley)
Spectacles	1463 (London WC2)		1878 (Norwich)
Speech	470 (Dundee)	Stamford	
	612 (Glasgow)	archaeology	2157 (Stamford)
disorders	1545 (London WC1)	local history	2157, 2158 (Stamford)
therapy	1688 (London NW1)	Ware	2157 (Stamford)
Speleology	802 (Leeds)	Standards	1088 (London WC2)
	2102 (Settle)	State education	77 (Bathgate)
	2262 (Wells)	State enrolled nurses	1400 (London W1M 9HQ)

State papers	1326(London W5)		1817(Morden)
Statesman, biographies	1199(London SW1)	Sterilization	1132(London SW1)
Statistics	153(Birmingham)	Steroid hormones	1730(Maidenhead)
	330(Canterbury)	Steroids	1730(Maidenhead)
	371(Chelmsford)		2268(Wembley)
	455(Didcot)	anabolic	1730(Maidenhead)
	485(Durham)	biochemistry	2109(Sheffield)
	511(Edinburgh)	Stevens, Alfred	460(Dorchester)
	574(Egham)	Stevenson, R. L.	513(Edinburgh)
	598(Galashiels)	Stirling, local history	2161, 2164, 2165 (Stirling)
	681(Harrow)	Stock Exchange	1253(London SW1)
	700(Henley-on-Thames)	Stockport, local history	2168(Stockport)
	948(London EC4)	Stoke-on-Trent, local	
	994(London WC2)	history	2176(Stoke-on-Trent)
	1040(London SW1)	Strategic planning	1237(London WC2)
	1175(London WC2)	Strategic studies	195(Bracknell)
	1199(London SW1)		1237(London WC2)
	1240(London WC1)		2145(Southampton)
	1330(London W6)	Strategy	271(Camberley)
	1369(London WC1)	military	1560(London SW1)
	1420(London SW1)	Stratford on Avon	
	1617(London SW17)	genealogy	2179(Stratford on Avon)
	1682(London E15)	local history	2179, 2180(Stratford on Avon)
	1724(Macclesfield)		
	1960, 1962(Oxford)	topography	2179(Stratford on Avon)
	2060(Ruislip)	Strathspey	1168(London W1A 3AU)
	2239(Wakefield)	Strauss family	216(Bridgwater)
broadcasting	961(London W1A 1AA)	Street maps	1721(Luton)
Commonwealth	1159(London SW1)	Strikes	742(Hyde)
criminal	1218(London SE11)	Stroud	
economic	422(Coventry)	archaeology	2181(Stroud)
	948(London EC4)	geology	2181(Stroud)
	2145(Southampton)	Stuart monarchs	2311(Worcester)
financial	946(London WC2)	Student power	1168(London W1A 3AU)
geographical	2153(Sowerby Bridge)	Student protests	1020(London WC1)
Greece	1539(London W1)	Subfertility	1142(London W1N 8BQ)
local government	2023(Reading)	Subject bibliography	1315(London WC1)
mathematical	2023(Reading)	Subnormality	2067(St Albans)
morbidity	473(Dundee)		2109(Sheffield)
national income	1040(London SW1)		2151(Southport)
population	948(London EC4)	education	1236(London W1P 3LD)
	1132(London SW1)	Suffolk	
science	227(Brighton)	East, local history	753(Ipswich)
social	163(Blackburn)	local history	1879(Norwich)
	1040(London SW1)	Suffolk Regiment, history	264(Bury St Edmunds)
	1442(London SW4)	Suffrage	119(Bexley)
	2145(Southampton)	women	1696(London WC1)
textiles	1787(Manchester)	Sugar	1683(London WC2)
trade	948(London EC4)	Suicide prevention	2134(Slough)
vital	436(Dagenham)	Suicide research	2134(Slough)
	1132(London SW1)	Sunderland	
	1175(London WC2)	history	2184(Sunderland)
	1344(London WC1)	local history	2186(Sunderland)
See also Volume I		pottery	2186(Sunderland)
Stephenson, George	391(Chesterfield)	topography	2184(Sunderland)
Sterility	1142(London W1N 8BQ)	Superannuation	1240(London WC1)
	1279(London SW1)	Supplementary pensions	1107(London WC2)

Surgeons	1533 (London WC2)	antiquities	660 (Guildford)
Surgery	6 (Aberdeen)	archaeology	656, 660 (Guildford)
	154 (Birmingham)	history	656 (Guildford)
	176 (Bolton)	local history	581 (Esher)
	244, 245 (Bristol)		1333 (London SE5)
	305, 318 (Cambridge)	maps	660 (Guildford)
	344 (Cardiff)	North East	
	426 (Crewe)	archaeology	429 (Croydon)
	535 (Edinburgh)	geography	429 (Croydon)
	586 (Exeter)	geology	429 (Croydon)
	608 (Glasgow)	history	429 (Croydon)
	681 (Harrow)	industrial archaeology	429 (Croydon)
	755 (Ipswich)	industry	429 (Croydon)
	870 (Liverpool)	local history	429 (Croydon)
	978 (London W1M 8AL)	natural history	429 (Croydon)
	1033 (London NW10)	planning	429 (Croydon)
	1160 (London E11)	topography	429 (Croydon)
	1313 (London WC1)	West	
	1342 (London E1)	archaeology	656 (Guildford)
	1532 (London WC2)	history	656 (Guildford)
	1569 (London SE1)	Surveying	485 (Durham)
	1689 (London SW1)		1140 (London W1H 3HL)
	1697 (London SE18)		1194 (London W12)
	1828 (Newbury)		1377 (London SW1)
	2006 (Portsmouth)		1450 (London N7)
	2025 (Reading)		1538 (London SW7)
	2172 (Stoke-on-Trent)		1839 (Newcastle upon Tyne)
	2223 (Tunbridge Wells)		2003 (Portsmouth)
accident	144 (Birmingham)	Scotland	509 (Edinburgh)
cardiovascular	1246 (London W1)	See also Volume I	
chest	1254 (London SW3)	Surveyors	1140 (London W1H 3HL)
history	1254 (London SW3)	Surveys	
dental	2006 (Portsmouth)	broadcasting	961 (London W1A 1AA)
eye	581 (Esher)	consumers	1413 (London WC2)
history	1533 (London WC2)	Sussex	223 (Brighton)
oral	494 (East Grinstead)	archaeology	2322 (Worthing)
organ transplantation	308 (Cambridge)	artists	2322 (Worthing)
	1246 (London W1)	crafts	2322 (Worthing)
orthopaedic	755 (Ipswich)	East, local history	399 (Chichester)
plastic	426 (Crewe)	geology	2322 (Worthing)
	494 (East Grinstead)	history	2322 (Worthing)
	978 (London W1M 8AL)	local history	497 (Eastbourne)
	1925 (Oxford)		683 (Hastings)
reconstructive	494 (East Grinstead)		2323 (Worthing)
	1925 (Oxford)	manor houses	724 (Hove)
thoracic	1246 (London W1)	photographic survey	223 (Brighton)
transplant	308 (Cambridge)	villages	724 (Hove)
	1246 (London W1)	West	
Surgical dressings	392 (Chesterfield)	archaeology	395 (Chichester)
	674 (Harlow)		2322 (Worthing)
Surgical instruments	1010 (London SW1)	folk life	395 (Chichester)
Surgical ligatures	515 (Edinburgh)	history	395 (Chichester)
Surgical operations	124 (Birkenhead)	local history	395, 399 (Chichester)
Surgical pathology	1532 (London WC2)	pastimes	395 (Chichester)
Surgical sutures	495 (Eastbourne)	trade	395 (Chichester)
	515 (Edinburgh)	Swansea porcelain	2199 (Swansea)
Surrey	429 (Croydon)	Swansea pottery	2199 (Swansea)

Sweden	1559 (London W1)		922 (London WC1)
	1623 (London W1R 2DN)		951 (London SE1)
arts	1623 (London W1R 2DN)		1451 (London NW5)
education	1623 (London W1R 2DN)		2290 (Winchester)
language	315 (Cambridge)	*See also* Education, Teaching	
	651 (Grimsby)	Teachers	1202 (London WC2)
	2086 (Salford)		1224 (London WC1)
literature	315 (Cambridge)	salaries	923 (London WC1)
	651 (Grimsby)	Scotland	555 (Edinburgh)
Swedenborg, Emanuel	1173, 1622 (London WC1)	Teaching	645 (Grays)
Swedenborgiana	1173 (London WC1)		1616 (London SW19)
Swift, Jonathan	113 (Belfast)	classics	1293 (London WC1)
Swimming	151 (Birmingham)	English language	506 (Edinburgh)
	891 (London EC4)	English literature	506 (Edinburgh)
	1475 (London W1M 4AX)	geography	2106 (Sheffield)
history	891 (London EC4)	history	1203 (London SE11)
underwater	151 (Birmingham)	materials	2334 (York)
Swindon, local history	2204 (Swindon)	mentally handicapped	1637 (London SE1)
Swinton			2014 (Preston)
history	1747 (Manchester)	children	1895 (Nottingham)
local history	1786 (Manchester)	methods	329 (Canterbury)
Switzerland	408 (Colchester)		331 (Cardiff)
	1624 (London EC2)		464 (Dudley)
	2051 (Rossendale)		725 (Huddersfield)
geography	2278 (Weymouth)		823 (Leicester)
history	2278 (Weymouth)		931 (London SE9)
Swords	67 (Basingstoke)		2011 (Prescot)
Symbolism	564 (Edinburgh)		2035 (Retford)
	2278 (Weymouth)	history	464 (Dudley)
Symphony orchestras	1755 (Manchester)	Roman Catholic	1026 (London NW4)
Synagogue ritual-ware	1383 (London WC1)	Russian	2327 (York)
		Technical colleges	2198 (Sutton Coldfield)
T		Technical courses	2026 (Reading)
		Technical drawing	587 (Exeter)
Tailoring	1074 (London W1)		2160 (Stevenage)
ladies	874 (Liverpool)	Technical education	35 (Aylesbury)
Talmudic literature	1292 (London W1)		185 (Boreham Wood)
Tamworth, local history	2206 (Tamworth)		335 (Cardiff)
Tapestries	1340 (London E17)		470 (Dundee)
	1748 (Manchester)		834 (Letchworth)
Tapestry	1688 (London WC2)		923 (London WC1)
Tartans	2161 (Stirling)		2059 (Rugby)
Tasmania	1457 (London WC2)		2136 (South Shields)
films	1457 (London WC2)	Technical illustration	2046 (Rochester)
Tate Gallery	1626 (London SW1)	Technical training	1102 (London W1)
Taunton, local history	2210 (Taunton)	Technology	
Taxation	606 (Glasgow)	(Volume I of this Directory includes technology, but it has also been indexed in this Volume for organizations which do not appear in Volume I)	
	744 (Ilford)		
	932 (London WC2)		
	1253 (London SW1)		417 (Coventry)
	1711 (Loughborough)		1313 (London WC1)
company	932 (London WC2)		1808 (Middlesbrough)
direct	946 (London WC2)	chemical	1839 (Newcastle upon Tyne)
European	932 (London WC2)	history	20 (Accrington)
land	1198 (London SW1)		1187 (London EC2)
law	946 (London WC2)		1578 (London SW7)
Teacher training	226 (Brighton)		1698 (London SE18)

Technology, history (contd)	1741(Manchester)		450(Derby)
Russia	1591(London SW9)		471(Dundee)
T. E. Lawrence	459(Dorchester)		591(Falmouth)
	2129(Sleaford)		674(Harlow)
Telecommunications	734(Hull)		731(Hull)
	1483(London EC1)		824(Leicester)
history	1483(London EC1)		864, 871, 874(Liverpool)
industry	1484(London W5)		1018(London SE5)
Television	33(Ashton-under-Lyne)		1165(London SW15)
	184(Boreham Wood)		1524(London SW7)
	984(London W1)		1566(London WC2)
	1253(London SW1)		1713(Loughborough)
	1603(London W1N 6JJ)		1765(Manchester)
	2205(Tamworth)		1808(Middlesbrough)
awards	1603(London W1N 6JJ)		1892(Nottingham)
BBC	208(Brentford)		1910(Oldham)
education	2020(Reading)		1978(Paisley)
film programmes	1151, 1152(London W1)		2055(Rotherham)
	1153(London W1Y 3FD)		2082(Salford)
medical education	914(London SE6)		2141(Southampton)
production	1676(London SW18)	design	129(Birmingham)
services	1227(London SW3)		771(Kidderminster)
technicians	1603(London W1N 6JJ)		1039(London WC1)
careers	1603(London W1N 6JJ)	economics	1787(Manchester)
writing	1705(London W2)	history	312(Cambridge)
Temperance	2105(Sheffield)		1792(Manchester)
	2255(Watford)	industries	726(Huddersfield)
biographies	2105(Sheffield)	statistics	1787(Manchester)
education	1704(London SW16)	See also Volume I	
history	1704(London SW16)	Thalidomide	699(Hemel Hempstead)
movement	1644(London SW1)	Thames Conservancy	1629(London WC2)
	2105(Sheffield)	Thames Valley, tourism	2040(Richmond)
history	1644(London SW1)	Theatre	2(Aberdare)
	2105(Sheffield)		184(Boreham Wood)
Temple of Mithras	1188(London EC2)		235(Bristol)
Templeborough	2053(Rotherham)		417(Coventry)
Tenants' associations	1401(London SE1)		595(Folkestone)
Tennis	1336(London SW19)		614(Glasgow)
Tennyson, Alfred Lord	854, 855(Lincoln)		792(Leamington Spa)
Testing			866(Liverpool)
consumer goods	1088(London WC2)		981(London W1P 6AE)
psychology	725(Huddersfield)		1566(London WC2)
Teutonic languages	1851(Newport, Isle of Wight)		1662(London WC1)
			1688(London WC2)
Teutonic literature	1851(Newport, Isle of Wight)		1762(Manchester)
			1808(Middlesbrough)
criticism	443(Dartford)		1845(Newcastle upon Tyne)
history	443(Dartford)		2141(Southampton)
Textbooks (major collections only)			2187(Sunderland)
	815(Leeds)		2205(Tamworth)
	1954(Oxford)	administration	2183(Sunderland)
	2146(Southampton)	arts	154(Birmingham)
history	1203(London SE11)	Austria	929(London SW7)
Textiles	220(Brighton)	biography	2179(Stratford on Avon)
	253(Bromley)	British	965(London SE1)
	349(Carlisle)	history	1011(London W14)
	430(Croydon)	building	2183(Sunderland)

Theatre (contd)
    buildings 1632(London W1P 6AE)
    children 2235(Wakefield)
    civic 2183(Sunderland)
    design 129(Birmingham)
        1039(London WC1)
        430(Croydon)
    history 194(Bournemouth)
        968(London W1Y 4HQ)
        981(London W1P 6AE)
        1596(London W2)
        1688(London WC2)
        2179(Stratford on Avon)
    Hungary 988(London SW1)
    programmes 154(Birmingham)
    repertory 654(Guildford)
    Russia 1591(London SW9)
    technical aspects 916(London W1P 6AE)
Theology 47(Bagshot)
    95(Belfast)
    132, 149, 154, 157(Birmingham)
    160(Bishop's Stortford)
    198(Bradford)
    247(Bristol)
    291, 292, 296, 297, 309 (Cambridge)
    325, 330(Canterbury)
    369(Chelmsford)
    394, 397(Chichester)
    401(Chipping Norton)
    408(Colchester)
    448(Deeside)
    452(Derby)
    486, 488, 489, 492, 493 (Durham)
    517, 545, 569(Edinburgh)
    584(Exeter)
    604, 612, 627(Glasgow)
    711(Hertford)
    783(Lampeter)
    813(Leeds)
    844, 849(Lincoln)
    926, 1022(London SW1)
    1062(London WC2)
    1076(London SW7)
    1110(London SW15)
    1114(London WC1)
    1149(London W11)
    1219, 1284(London WC1)
    1303(London WC2)
    1334(London SE13)
    1343(London SW1)
    1473(London SW16)
    1568(London EC4)
    1571(London SE5)
    1585(London EC4)
    1647(London SW1)
    1663(London NW3)
    1756, 1789, 1791 (Manchester)
    1810(Middlesbrough)
    1811(Mirfield)
    1882(Norwich)
    1914(Ormskirk)
    1918, 1919, 1924, 1926, 1927, 1928, 1942, 1944, 1945, 1946, 1948, 1973(Oxford)
    1976(Paignton)
    2002(Portsmouth)
    2011(Prescot)
    2021(Reading)
    2042(Ripon)
    2068(St Albans)
    2073(St Andrews)
    2124(Shrewsbury)
    2127(Skipton)
    2145(Southampton)
    2152(Southwell)
    2164(Stirling)
    2198(Sutton Coldfield)
    2200(Swansea)
    2217, 2222(Truro)
    2261, 2263(Wells)
    2291(Winchester)
    2295(Windsor)
    ascetic 830(Leicester)
    Catholic 612(Glasgow)
    criticism 1500(London N1)
    doctrinal 233(Bristol)
        583(Exeter)
    Methodist 95(Belfast)
        247(Bristol)
    missions 1058(London SE1)
    natural 1330(London W6)
    pastoral 90(Bedford)
    patristic 401(Chipping Norton)
    Reformation 492(Durham)
        2217(Truro)
    Roman Catholic 424(Crawley)
        2138(Southampton)
    scholastic 401(Chipping Norton)
        830(Leicester)
    Scriptural 492(Durham)
    Tridentine 492(Durham)
Theosophy 564(Edinburgh)
    1645(London WC2)
Therapeutics 258(Burnley)
    306(Cambridge)
    1337(London E15)
    2015(Preston)
    2150(Southport)
    2266(Welwyn Garden City)
Thomas A'Kempis 294(Cambridge)

Thomas Beecham	2273 (Westcliff-on-Sea)	Essex	372 (Chelmsford)
Thomas, Dylan	2201 (Swansea)	South East	2148 (Southend-on-Sea)
Thomas Hardy	459, 460 (Dorchester)	Germany	436 (Dagenham)
	1327 (London W3)	Greater London	1181 (London SE1)
Thomas More	1187 (London EC2)	Gunnersbury	1190 (London W3)
Thomas Paine	1880 (Thetford)	Hounslow	1190 (London W3)
Thompson, Francis	2015 (Preston)	Hungary	436 (Dagenham)
Thoracic nursing	1012 (London W1)	India	866 (Liverpool)
Thoracic surgery	1246 (London W1)		1872 (Northwich)
Thorax	124 (Birkenhead)	Ireland	866 (Liverpool)
Thurrock, local history	645 (Grays)	Japan	581 (Esher)
	2213 (Tilbury)	Kent	1328 (London SE10)
Thyroid gland	1051 (London EC2)		1731 (Maidstone)
Tilbury, local history	2213 (Tilbury)	East	327 (Canterbury)
Tipstaves	67 (Basingstoke)	North West	429 (Croydon)
Tissue transplantation	455 (Didcot)	King's Lynn	774 (King's Lynn)
Tobacco		Lincoln	844 (Lincoln)
addiction	2255 (Watford)	Lincolnshire	850 (Lincoln)
industry	1634 (London N1)	London	943 (London EC2)
Toc H	1635 (London EC3)		1181 (London SE1)
Togo, Methodist missions	1376 (London NW1)		1210 (London EC4)
Toiletries	207 (Brentford)		1332 (London N7)
	738 (Hull)		1345 (London SE5)
	1712 (Loughborough)	maritime countries	1425 (London SE10)
See also Volume I		Middlesex, West	1190 (London W3)
Topographical art		Paddington	1688 (London NW1)
Cheshire	389 (Chester)	Poland	436 (Dagenham)
Chester	389 (Chester)	Ripon	2042 (Ripon)
Wales, North	389 (Chester)	St Marylebone	1688 (London NW1)
Topography	58 (Barnstaple)	Salford	2084 (Salford)
	223 (Brighton)	Scotland	537, 561 (Edinburgh)
	263 (Bury St Edmunds)		866 (Liverpool)
	492 (Durham)	North East	13 (Aberdeen)
	866 (Liverpool)	Somerset	2326 (Yeovil)
	1741 (Manchester)	Stratford on Avon	2179 (Stratford on Avon)
	2027 (Reading)	Sunderland	2184 (Sunderland)
Africa	866 (Liverpool)	Surrey, North East	429 (Croydon)
Australia	866 (Liverpool)	Tunbridge Wells	2225 (Tunbridge Wells)
Australasia	431 (Croydon)	United Kingdom	866 (Liverpool)
Austria	436 (Dagenham)	United States of America	431 (Croydon)
Battersea	1069 (London SW12)	Wales	866 (Liverpool)
British	1604 (London SW7)	Warwickshire	2179 (Stratford on Avon)
British Commonwealth	866 (Liverpool)		2253 (Warwick)
Canada	866 (Liverpool)	Wiltshire	453 (Devizes)
Canterbury	327 (Canterbury)	Worcester	2310 (Worcester)
Cheshire	382, 389 (Chester)	Yorkshire, North Riding	1863 (Northallerton)
China	581 (Esher)	Tort	1322 (London NW4)
churches	1093 (London EC2)		2112 (Sheffield)
Clapham	1069 (London SW12)	Totalisator	1212 (London EC4)
Co Durham	2184 (Sunderland)	Totnes, local history	2215 (Totnes)
Croydon	429 (Croydon)	Tottenham, local history	1331 (London N17)
Czechoslovakia	436 (Dagenham)	Touring, Great Britain	1520 (London SW1)
Dorset	459 (Dorchester)	Tourism	191 (Bournemouth)
	2326 (Yeovil)	Denmark	1100 (London W1R 8PY)
Ealing	1190 (London W3)	Finland	1156 (London SW1)
England	1187 (London EC2)	Italy	1287 (London W1)
North West	1741 (Manchester)	London	1346 (London W1V 9DD)

Tourism (contd)		Tractarian literature	397 (Chichester)
Luxembourg	1350 (London SW1)	Tracts	783 (Lampeter)
Northern Ireland	104 (Belfast)	Trade	153 (Birmingham)
Scotland	559 (Edinburgh)		423 (Crawley)
Thames Valley	2040 (Richmond)		947 (London SW1)
Uganda	1460 (London WC2)		1144 (London W1R 9PL)
Tower Hamlets, local			1199 (London SW1)
history	1339 (London E1)		2173 (Stoke-on-Trent)
Tower of London	903 (London EC3)	agricultural products	1412 (London SW1)
Town and country		Chichester	395 (Chichester)
planning	129 (Birmingham)	China	1052 (London EC2)
	201 (Bradford)	domestic	2143 (Southampton)
Scotland	553 (Edinburgh)	foreign	2143 (Southampton)
	867 (Liverpool)	statistics	948 (London EC4)
	1217, 1381 (London SW1)	Sussex, West	395 (Chichester)
	2332 (York)	See also Volume I	
legislation	893 (London W8)	Trade union activities	1444 (London W1)
See also Town planning		Trade union agreements,	
Town guides	1721 (Luton)	vehicle building industry	1776 (Manchester)
Town planning	340 (Cardiff)	Trade union history	1737 (Manchester)
	378 (Cheltenham)	Trade union law	580 (Esher)
	421 (Coventry)	Trade union movement	1634 (London N1)
	469 (Dundee)	Trade union reform	1444 (London W1)
	805 (Leeds)	Trade union training	1080 (London WC2)
	835 (Letchworth)	Trade unionism	215 (Bridgwater)
	1015 (London SW4)		625 (Glasgow)
	1073 (London W8)		1282 (London SW4)
	1340 (London E17)	history	943 (London EC2)
	1341 (London SW18)	transport industry	1282 (London SW4)
	1450 (London N7)	Trade unionists, biography	2143 (Southampton)
	1727 (Maidenhead)	Trade unions	363 (Castleford)
	1797 (Market Drayton)		742 (Hyde)
	1892 (Nottingham)		1253 (London SW1)
	2142 (Southampton)		1705 (London W2)
	2187 (Sunderland)		1932 (Oxford)
	2289 (Winchester)	legislation	698 (Hemel Hempstead)
See also Town and country		Trade warfare	2038 (Richmond)
planning, Urban planning		Trades Union Congresses	943 (London EC2)
Toxicity	338 (Cardiff)	Training	1408 (London W1N 5TB)
Toxicology	344 (Cardiff)		1617 (London SW17)
	361 (Carshalton)	architecture	1081 (London W1N 4AD)
	437 (Dagenham)	blind	1321 (London SE15)
	1191 (London SE1)	carpet industry	2287 (Wilmslow)
	1472 (London WC1)	catering industry	2267 (Wembley)
	1712 (Loughborough)	courses	678 (Harrow)
	1729, 1730 (Maidenhead)	dental surgery assistants	166 (Blackpool)
	1828 (Newbury)	drivers	1520 (London SW1)
	2082 (Salford)	electricity supply industry	1123 (London SW1)
	2248 (Ware)	girls	1694 (London SW3)
agricultural chemicals	1723 (Macclesfield)	industrial	174 (Bolton)
drugs	757 (Isleworth)		202 (Bradford)
industrial chemicals	1723 (Macclesfield)		287 (Cambridge)
Toys	1873 (Norwich)		363 (Castleford)
	2329 (York)		390 (Chesterfield)
English	2322 (Worthing)		1080 (London WC2)
Trachoma	1371 (London SW1)		1421 (London W1M 8DR)
immunology	1371 (London SW1)		2306 (Wolverhampton)

Training, industrial (contd)	2318 (Worksop)	Yorkshire, South	458 (Doncaster)
information work	1256 (London EC2)	See also Volume I	
linguists	1259 (London SE1)	Transportation	1636 (London W1)
midwives	1034 (London SW7)		2187 (Sunderland)
nursery nursing	1427 (London SW1)	Trapping	2051 (Rossendale)
nursing	533 (Edinburgh)	Travel	58 (Barnstaple)
operating theatre			212 (Bridgend)
technicians	1262 (London WC1)		270 (Camberley)
osteopathy	1004 (London SW1)		492 (Durham)
pharmacists	531 (Edinburgh)		584 (Exeter)
physical education	86 (Bedford)		930 (London WC2)
psychology	1003 (London W1X 4DN)		1211 (London SE23)
public health inspectors	1493 (London SW1)		1303 (London WC2)
Rabbis	1292 (London W1)		1341 (London SW18)
social work	1418 (London WC1)		1538 (London SW7)
State Enrolled Nurses	1400 (London W1M 9HQ)		1566 (London WC2)
teachers See Teacher			1588 (London SW1)
training, Education			1975 (Oxford)
technical	1102 (London W1)		2124 (Shrewsbury)
trade union	1080 (London WC2)		2205 (Tamworth)
vocational	923 (London WC1)	Africa	492 (Durham)
	1102 (London W1)		644 (Gravesend)
white-collar workers	698 (Hemel Hempstead)		1647 (London SW1)
women	1694 (London SW3)	Asia	492 (Durham)
youth leaders	1060 (London SW1)	Central	1725 (Macclesfield)
youth work	912 (London E1)	Caribbean	1683 (London WC2)
Trams	1802 (Matlock)	educational	1029 (London SW1)
Tramways	1802 (Matlock)	European	1341 (London SW18)
Transcaucasia	1523 (London W1N 1LN)	Finland	1156 (London SW1)
		France	1851 (Newport, Isle of Wight)
Transfer pictures	581 (Esher)		
Translation	1638 (London SW10)	Palestine	595 (Folkestone)
Translations	866 (Liverpool)	Portugal	2285 (Wigan)
Translators	1600 (London SW10)	Russia	167 (Blackpool)
	1259, 1347 (London SE1)	Scandinavia	262 (Bury)
	1638 (London SW10)	Siberia	1725 (Macclesfield)
Transplant surgery	1246 (London W1)	Spain	2285 (Wigan)
Transport	2 (Aberdare)	World	1341 (London SW18)
	511 (Edinburgh)	Treaties, international	722 (Hounslow)
	735 (Hull)	Treaty of Rome	899 (London W8)
	868 (Liverpool)	Tropical architecture	901 (London WC1)
	994 (London WC2)	building	901 (London WC1)
	1064 (London EC2)	Tropical diseases	1016 (London WC1)
	1181 (London SE1)	Tropical hygiene	873 (Liverpool)
	1451 (London NW5)		1344 (London WC1)
	1858 (Newport, Mon)	Tropical medicine	85 (Beckenham)
Farnham	592 (Farnham)		873 (Liverpool)
history	831 (Leicester)		1344 (London WC1)
Glasgow	611 (Glasgow)		1679 (London NW1)
Ireland	94 (Belfast)		1909 (Oldham)
industry	1282 (London SW4)	Truncheons	67 (Basingstoke)
motor	250 (Brockenhurst)	Truro	
history	250 (Brockenhurst)	genealogy	2221 (Truro)
Scotland, West	611 (Glasgow)	local history	2219 (Truro)
technology, history	611 (Glasgow)	T. S. Eliot	288 (Cambridge)
trade unionism	1282 (London SW4)	Tuberculosis	344 (Cardiff)
West Riding	458 (Doncaster)		712 (Heywood)

Tuberculosis (contd)	746 (Ilford)	United Nations	
	1012 (London W1)	Organization	722 (Hounslow)
	1254 (London SW3)	United States of America	892 (London W1A 1AE)
bacteriology	1373 (London W12)		1648 (London W1)
chemotherapy	1373 (London W12)		166, 1662 (London WC1)
drug sensitivity	1373 (London W12)		1882 (Norwich)
history	1254 (London SW3)	biography	950 (London W1)
Tumours	1337 (London E15)	books	950 (London W1)
Tunbridge Wells		children's	950 (London W1)
history	2225 (Tunbridge Wells)	food legislation	920 (London SE1)
local history	2225 (Tunbridge Wells)	food standards	920 (London SE1)
topography	2225 (Tunbridge Wells)	geography	431 (Croydon)
Turkey		history	69 (Bath)
geography	2278 (Weymouth)		431 (Croydon)
history	1968 (Oxford)		866 (Liverpool)
	2278 (Weymouth)		950 (London W1)
languages	1968 (Oxford)		1659 (London WC1)
literature	1968 (Oxford)		1791 (Manchester)
religion	1968 (Oxford)		1882 (Norwich)
Tyndall	1543 (London W1)	law	1379 (London EC4)
Typewriting	1495 (London W1)		1654 (London WC1)
Typographic design	1018 (London SE5)	literature	866 (Liverpool)
Typography	223 (Brighton)		950 (London W1)
	349 (Carlisle)		1791 (Manchester)
	726 (Huddersfield)	Methodist missions	1376 (London NW1)
	824 (Leicester)	social studies	950 (London W1)
	1524 (London SW7)	topography	431 (Croydon)
			866 (Liverpool)
		Universities	1202 (London WC2)
U			1951 (Oxford)
Uganda	1460 (London WC2)	Commonwealth	917 (London WC1)
tourism	1460 (London WC2)	Great Britain	917 (London WC1)
Ulster	97 (Belfast)	Scotland	602 (Glasgow)
	1449 (London W1)	University education	1102 (London W1)
history	113 (Belfast)	University of Cambridge	314 (Cambridge)
industrial history	113 (Belfast)	archives	321 (Cambridge)
linen industry, history	113 (Belfast)	history	321 (Cambridge)
See also Northern Ireland		Unmarried mothers	548 (Edinburgh)
Unemployed, senior		Urban and Regional	
executives	1441 (London NW3)	planning	901 (London WC1)
Unemployment	1104 (London SW1)	Urban development	1381 (London SW1)
	1441 (London NW3)		1636 (London W1)
U.N.E.S.C.O.	1646 (London W1)	Urban planning	2020 (Reading)
Unitarian history	1789, 1790 (Manchester)	See also Town planning,	
United Kingdom		Town and country	
archives	1494 (London WC2)	planning	
food legislation	920 (London SE1)	Urban sociology	109 (Belfast)
food standards	920 (London SE1)	Urban studies	154 (Birmingham)
history	866 (Liverpool)		2115 (Sheffield)
literature	866 (Liverpool)	Urdu literature	2100 (Scunthorpe)
topography	866 (Liverpool)		2304 (Wolverhampton)
United Nations	1090 (London SE1)	Urology	862 (Liverpool)
	1646 (London W1)		1271 (London WC2)
forces	1101 (London SW1)	U.S.S.R.	1009 (London EC1)
United Nations Educational,			1591 (London SW9)
Scientific and Cultural		history	1251 (London W1N 2BH)
Organization	1646 (London W1)		2038 (Richmond)

V

Vaccination	1344 (London WC1)
dangers	432 (Croydon)
Vaccines	863 (Liverpool)
Valuation, property	1073 (London W8)
Vancouver, George	2039 (Richmond)
Vasopressin, assays	2109 (Sheffield)
Vatican city	900 (London SW1)
Vegetarianism	26 (Altrincham)
	1670 (London W8)
Vehicle building industry, trade union agreements	1776 (Manchester)
Venereal diseases	1323 (London NW10)
Ventilating, hospitals	628 (Glasgow)
Verulamium	2071 (St Albans)
Vessels, sacred	2278 (Weymouth)
Vestments	2278 (Weymouth)
Veteran cars	1671 (London W1)
Veterinary helminthology	2066 (St Albans)
Veterinary medicine	68 (Basingstoke)
	99 (Belfast)
	291, 319 (Cambridge)
	437 (Dagenham)
	539 (Edinburgh)
	583 (Exeter)
	630 (Glasgow)
	681 (Harrow)
	1433 (London WC2)
	1534 (London SW1)
	1724 (Macclesfield)
	1730 (Maidenhead)
	1828 (Newbury)
	1886 (Nottingham)
	2248 (Ware)
	2265, 2266 (Welwyn Garden City)
iodine	1051 (London EC2)
Veterinary parasitology	502 (Edinburgh)
Veterinary pathology	99 (Belfast)
Veterinary science	85 (Beckenham)
	99 (Belfast)
	274 (Cambridge)
	396 (Chichester)
	437 (Dagenham)
	571 (Edinburgh)
	648 (Greenford)
	773 (Kilmarnock)
	791 (Lasswade)
	863, 878 (Liverpool)
	1317 (London SW1)
	1367 (London NW1)
	1434 (London W2)
	1534 (London SW1)
	1561 (London NW1)
	1817 (Morden)
	2047 (Rochester)
	2172 (Stoke-on-Trent)
	2190 (Surbiton)
Veterinary supplies	863 (Liverpool)
Victoria	887 (London WC2)
Victorian buildings	1672 (London W4)
Victorian fiction	2201 (Swansea)
Victorian furniture	404 (Cirencester)
Victorian literature, children	2305 (Wolverhampton)
Victorian period	1672 (London W4)
Victorian studies	831 (Leicester)
Vietnam, South	1127 (London W8)
Vietnam war	1020 (London WC1)
Village halls	2209 (Taunton)
Violins, automatic	209 (Brentford)
Virology	85 (Beckenham)
	99 (Belfast)
	305 (Cambridge)
	502 (Edinburgh)
	863 (Liverpool)
	1075, 1260 (London W1)
	1828 (Newbury)
	2131 (Slough)
	2301 (Woking)
Visual aids	4 (Aberdeen)
	133 (Birmingham)
	989 (London W1)
education	1676 (London SW18)
Visual arts	
criticism	1524 (London SW7)
history	1524 (London SW7)
Visual education	1407 (London W1M 0AL)
Visual perception	1808 (Middlesbrough)
Visually handicapped deaf, welfare	1519 (London W3)
Vital statistics	436 (Dagenham)
	1132 (London SW1)
	1175 (London WC2)
	1344 (London WC1)
Northern Ireland	96 (Belfast)
Scotland	519 (Edinburgh)
Vitamins	323 (Cambridge)
Vocational education	725 (Huddersfield)
	923 (London WC1)
Vocational guidance	725 (Huddersfield)
	1041 (London W1P 0ER)
	1421 (London W1M 8DR)
Vocational training	667 (Halifax)
	958 (London W1N 4AP)
	1102 (London W1)
Voluntary Aided Secondary Schools	83 (Beckenham)
Voluntary organizations	
Cambridgeshire	281 (Cambridge)
Huntingdon	281 (Cambridge)
Isle of Ely	281 (Cambridge)
Lancashire	1744 (Manchester)

Voluntary organizations (*contd*)		lighting	342 (Cardiff)
Liverpool	869 (Liverpool)	literature	17 (Aberystwyth)
Peterborough	281 (Cambridge)		54 (Bangor)
Voluntary service			671 (Harlech)
Scotland	514 (Edinburgh)		866 (Liverpool)
Voluntary service overseas	1013 (London WC1)	manuscripts	16 (Aberystwyth)
Voluntary social welfare	1409 (London WC1)	maps	16 (Aberystwyth)
Voyages, Caribbean	1683 (London WC2)	natural history	227 (Cardiff)
Vulgate	1919 (Oxford)	North	
		archaeology	385, 387, 389 (Chester)
W		architecture	385, 387 (Chester)
		history	385, 387 (Chester)
W.A.A.C.	663 (Guildford)	local history	389 (Chester)
Wade, Nugent	1942 (Oxford)	natural history	389 (Chester)
Wages	2039 (Richmond)	periodicals	783 (Lampeter)
Waiting	874 (Liverpool)	portraits	2199 (Swansea)
Wakefield, local history	2237 (Wakefield)	potteries	2199 (Swansea)
Wales	205 (Brecon)	prints	16 (Aberystwyth)
	267 (Caernarvon)	records	16 (Aberystwyth)
	332, 337 (Cardiff)	religion	342 (Cardiff)
	413 (Colwyn Bay)	South, artists	2199 (Swansea)
	593 (Flint)	topography	866 (Liverpool)
	2201 (Swansea)	West, genealogy	690 (Haverfordwest)
agriculture	342 (Cardiff)	zoology	337 (Cardiff)
amenities	1803 (Meifod)	Wallace collection	1673 (London W1)
archaeology	51 (Bangor)	Walter de la Mare	252 (Bromley)
	337 (Cardiff)	Walter Raleigh	1956 (Oxford)
architecture	342 (Cardiff)	Walter Richard Sickert	1332 (London N7)
arts	337 (Cardiff)	Walter Scott	513 (Edinburgh)
atlases	16 (Aberystwyth)		2166 (Stirling)
ballads	783 (Lampeter)	Waltham Abbey, local	
bibles	783 (Lampeter)	history	2246 (Waltham Cross)
books	15 (Aberystwyth)	Waltham Cross, local	
	205 (Brecon)	history	2246 (Waltham Cross)
	1813 (Mold)	Walthamstow, local history	1675 (London E17)
	1854 (Newport, Mon)	Walton	
botany	337 (Cardiff)	archaeology	2277 (Weybridge)
catechisms	783 (Lampeter)	local history	2277 (Weybridge)
Civic Trust	333 (Cardiff)	War	271 (Camberley)
costume	342 (Cardiff)	customs	1323 (London NW10)
crafts	342 (Cardiff)	disablement pensions	504 (Edinburgh)
dialect	342 (Cardiff)		1107 (London WC2)
domestic implements	342 (Cardiff)	histories	195 (Bracknell)
drawings	16 (Aberystwyth)	studies	1303 (London WC2)
ethnology	342 (Cardiff)	Ward administration	467 (Dumfries)
folk dancing	342 (Cardiff)	Warfare	
folk life	342, 347 (Cardiff)	air	2129 (Sleaford)
folk tales	342, 347 (Cardiff)	biological	1020 (London WC1)
geology	337 (Cardiff)	chemical	1020 (London WC1)
history	51, 54 (Bangor)	guerilla	2038 (Richmond)
	866 (Liverpool)	political	2038 (Richmond)
hymnals	783 (Lampeter)	psychological	2038 (Richmond)
industries	337 (Cardiff)	trade	2038 (Richmond)
language	17 (Aberystwyth)	Warrington, local history	2252 (Warrington)
	783 (Lampeter)	Warwick, local history	2254 (Warwick)
laundering	342 (Cardiff)	Warwickshire	418 (Coventry)
life	51 (Bangor)	archaeology	1904 (Nuneaton)

Warwickshire (contd)			2168 (Stockport)
genealogy	2179 (Stratford on Avon)		2290 (Winchester)
geology	1904 (Nuneaton)	law	538 (Edinburgh)
history	50 (Banbury)	deaf	645 (Grays)
	1904 (Nuneaton)		759 (Iver)
	2178 (Stratford on Avon)		1519 (London W3)
	2206 (Tamworth)		1545 (London WC1)
local history	133 (Birmingham)	disabled	1030 (London SW1)
	792 (Leamington Spa)	dumb	1519 (London W3)
	839 (Lichfield)	ex-service	504 (Edinburgh)
	1903, 1904 (Nuneaton)	family	1387 (London SW1)
	2178, 2179 (Stratford on Avon)		1662 (London WC1)
		handicapped	1106 (London SE1)
	2253, 2254 (Warwick)		1544 (London W1)
maps	2253 (Warwick)	housewives	987 (London E1)
topography	2179 (Stratford on Avon)	musicians	1556 (London W1)
	2253 (Warwick)	old people	689 (Haverfordwest)
Warwickshire Photographic			1106 (London SE1)
Survey	133 (Birmingham)		1427 (London WC1)
Waste disposal, hospitals	628 (Glasgow)		1940 (Oxford)
Watches	855 (Lincoln)		2209 (Taunton)
Water colour painting	1461 (London W1)	paupers	370 (Chelmsford)
Water colours	1558 (London W1)	public	1695 (London WC1)
English	164 (Blackburn)	unmarried mothers	548 (Edinburgh)
	801, 802 (Leeds)	Wellington	1680 (London W1)
Mansfield	1795 (Mansfield)	Wells Cathedral	2262 (Wells)
Water ions, absorption	2108 (Sheffield)	Wells, H. G.	252 (Bromley)
Water ski-ing	573 (Egham)	Welsh Marches, local history	2126 (Oswestry)
Water supply	1381 (London SW1)	Wesley, John	696 (Helston)
Waterways	2040 (Richmond)		2100 (Scunthorpe)
Watford, local history	2258 (Watford)	Wesleys	247 (Bristol)
Watts, George Frederic	662 (Guildford)	West Ham, local history	1337 (London E15)
Wealth	1420 (London SW1)	West Indies	964 (London EC4)
Weapon development	1237 (London WC2)	economics	1961 (Oxford)
Webbs	994 (London WC2)	history	1683 (London WC2)
Weaving	2161 (Stirling)	law	1683 (London WC2)
Wedgwood	1677 (London N7)	missions	934 (London W1H 4AA)
Weighing, history	128 (Birmingham)	politics	1961 (Oxford)
Weightlifting	2227 (Twickenham)	sociology	1961 (Oxford)
Welfare	6 (Aberdeen)	West Lothian, local history	77 (Bathgate)
	153 (Birmingham)	Western manuscripts	2295 (Windsor)
	252 (Bromley)	Westminster Abbey, history	1687 (London SW1)
	553 (Edinburgh)	Westminster, local history	1688 (London SW1)
	1106 (London SE1)	Westmorland	350 (Carlisle)
	1823 (Neath)		787 (Lancaster)
	2137 (Southall)	antiquities	348, 351 (Carlisle)
	2274 (Weston-super-Mare)	archaeology	351 (Carlisle)
		geology	348 (Carlisle)
aged	370 (Chelmsford)	history	351, 354 (Carlisle)
associations	2021 (Reading)	local history	2281 (Whitehaven)
autistic children	1438 (London NW11)	natural history	348 (Carlisle)
blind	645 (Grays)	Weston-super-Mare,	
	1321 (London SE15)	local history	2274 (Weston-super-Mare)
	1544 (London W1)	Weybridge	
	1564 (London NW1)	archaeology	2277 (Weybridge)
child	538 (Edinburgh)	local history	2277 (Weybridge)
	789 (Lancaster)	Whaling	733, 735 (Hull)

Wheelwrights' craft	592 (Farnham)	Women	
Whitchurch, local history	2126 (Whitchurch)	biographies	2149 (Southend-on-Sea)
White-collar workers		education, history	1019 (London NW5)
education	698 (Hemel Hempstead)	employment	1694 (London SW3)
salaries	698 (Hemel Hempstead)	personalities, history	1696 (London WC1)
training	698 (Hemel Hempstead)	public welfare	1695 (London WC1)
Whitehall, history	1199 (London SW1)	organizations	1695 (London WC1)
Whitley Bay, local history	2282 (Whitley Bay)	resolutions	1695 (London WC1)
Whitleyism	1272 (London WC2)	rights	1297 (London W1)
Whitman	178 (Bolton)	suffrage	1696 (London WC1)
W.H.O.	1640 (London WC1)	training	1694 (London SW3)
	1646 (London W1)	Women's Royal Army	
Widows, advisory service	2037 (Richmond)	Corps, history	663 (Guildford)
Wigan, local history	2286 (Wigan)	Woodcarving	431 (Croydon)
Wilberforce, William	733 (Hull)	Worcester	
Wildlife	2190 (Surbiton)	topography	2310 (Worcester)
William Barnes	459, 460 (Dorchester)	writers	2312 (Worcester)
William Blake	1333 (London SW2)	Worcestershire	2313 (Worcester)
	1688 (London WC2)	books	772 (Kidderminster)
William Clowes	1756 (Manchester)	costume	772 (Kidderminster)
William Cobbett	1911 (Oldham)	crafts	772 (Kidderminster)
	1932 (Oxford)	local history	133 (Birmingham)
William Cowper	1912 (Olney)		771 (Kidderminster)
William Lucas	718 (Hitchin)		2311 (Worcester)
William Milner	666 (Halifax)		2314 (Worcester)
William Morris	1336 (London SW19)	writers	2312 (Worcester)
	1340 (London E17)	Worcestershire Regiment,	
	1598 (Lechlade)	history	2315 (Worcester)
	1674, 1692 (London E17)	Wordsworth	350 (Carlisle)
William Rathbone	881 (Liverpool)	Work study	1248 (London W6)
William Shakespeare See Shakespeare			1806 (Middlesbrough)
			2003 (Portsmouth)
William Wilberforce	733 (Hull)	Workington, local history	2317 (Workington)
Wilson, Edward	376 (Cheltenham)	Works management	2205 (Tamworth)
Wiltshire		Workshop motor manuals	1669 (London SE19)
archaeology	453 (Devizes)	Worksop	
economic history	453 (Devizes)	archaeology	2319 (Worksop)
genealogy	453 (Devizes)	history	2319 (Worksop)
history	453 (Devizes)	local history	2319 (Worksop)
industrial archaeology	453 (Devizes)	natural history	2319 (Worksop)
local history	453 (Devizes)	World food resources	1132 (London SW1)
	2090, 2091 (Salisbury)	World Health Organization	1640 (London WC1)
natural history	453 (Devizes)		1646 (London W1)
North, local history	2204 (Swindon)	World War I	20 (Accrington)
topography	453 (Devizes)		2020 (Reading)
Wiltshire Regiment, history	454 (Devizes)	poetry	133 (Birmingham)
Winchester		World War II	1251 (London W1N 2BA)
archaeology	2293 (Winchester)	history	581 (Esher)
geology	2293 (Winchester)		1199 (London SW1)
history	2293 (Winchester)	World Wars	1223 (London SE1)
local history	2290, 2292 (Winchester)	art	1223 (London SE1)
Window display	2141 (Southampton)	exhibits	1223 (London SE1)
Winifred Holtby	218 (Bridlington)	films	1223 (London SE1)
	733 (Hull)	history	2289 (Winchester)
Wolseley family	724 (Hove)	maps	1223 (London SE1)
Wolverhampton, local history	2303, 2304 (Wolverhampton)	photographs	1223 (London SE1)
		Worship	154 (Birmingham)

Worsley, history	1747(Manchester)	Potteries	2053, 2054(Rotherham)
Worthing		social history	458(Doncaster)
history	2322(Worthing)	transport	458(Doncaster)
local history	2323(Worthing)	zoology	2113(Sheffield)
W.R.A.C.	663(Guildford)	West Riding	
Wrestling	956(London N5)	industries	458(Doncaster)
Writers		social history	458(Doncaster)
Worcester	2312(Worcester)	transport	458(Doncaster)
Worcestershire	2312(Worcester)	Young, Francis Brett	154(Birmingham)
Writing	909(London SW1)	Young Men's Christian	
	1705(London W2)	Association	61(Barry)
			1410(London WC1)
Y		history	1410(Leeds WC1)
		Youth	975(London SW1)
Yacht racing	607(Glasgow)	Associations	836(Lewes)
Yachting	607(Glasgow)	Employment Service	1041(London W1P 0ER)
	1328(London SE10)	hostelling	2072(St Albans)
	1425(London SE10)	Hostels	2162(Stirling)
Yiddish	1339(London E1)	Scotland	2162(Stirling)
Y.M.C.A.	61(Barry)	leaders	832(Leicester)
	1410(London WC1)		1014(London NW1)
history	61(Barry)	statistics	1706(London N17)
Yoga	564(Edinburgh)	training	1060(London SW1)
York, local history	2337(York)	leadership	61(Barry)
York and Lancaster			87(Bedford)
Regiment, history	2120(Sheffield)		503(Edinburgh)
York Minster	1876(Norwich)	orchestras	652(Grimsby)
Yorkshire	34(Ashton-under-Lyne)	organizations	601(Glasgow)
	57(Barnsley)		1620(London WC1)
	363(Castleford)		1748(Manchester)
	2239(Wakefield)	Roman Catholic	1027(London SW7)
archaeology	2338(York)	service	503(Edinburgh)
books	198(Bradford)		832(Leicester)
dialects	123(Bingley)		1060(London SW1)
East Riding, local history	218(Bridlington)		1102(London W1)
ecclesiastical history	2331(York)		
folk lore	123(Bingley)	Northern Ireland	111(Belfast)
geology	2338(York)	societies	836(Lewes)
history	2329(York)	visits	1029(London SW1)
life	2329(York)	work	101(Belfast)
literature	666(Halifax)		503(Edinburgh)
local history	677(Harrogate)		671(Harlech)
	742(Hyde)		832(Leicester)
	819(Leeds)		912(London E1)
	2237(Wakefield)		1014(London NW1)
	2331, 2337(York)		1027(London SW7)
			1706(London N17)
natural history	2338(York)	training	912(London E1)
North Riding		workers	1014(London NW1)
historical geography	1864(Northallerton)	Yugoslavia	408(Colchester)
local history	1863, 1864(Northallerton)	folklore	311(Cambridge)
topography	1863(Northallerton)	geography	2278(Weymouth)
South		history	311(Cambridge)
art	2111, 2113(Sheffield)		2278(Weymouth)
botany	2113(Sheffield)	language	311(Cambridge)
geology	2113(Sheffield)	literature	311(Cambridge)
history	2113(Sheffield)	philosophy	311(Cambridge)
industries	458(Doncaster)	religion	311(Cambridge)

Z

Zambia	1707 (London W1)		1586 (London EC3)
Methodist mission	1376 (London NW1)		1828 (Newbury)
Zionism	2139 (Southampton)		1858 (Newport, Mon)
Zoological stock shot film	1752 (Manchester)	Derbyshire, North	2293 (Winchester)
Zoology	295 (Cambridge)	invertebrate	2113 (Sheffield)
	435 (Dagenham)	vertebrate	860 (Liverpool)
	568 (Edinburgh)	Yorkshire, South	860 (Liverpool)
	874 (Liverpool)	Wales	2113 (Liverpool)
	1211 (London SE23)	*See also* Volume I	337 (Cardiff)

Z
791
A1 A8
v.2